Tolley's Tax Guide 2017–18

by

Claire Hayes

Ruth Newman

Consultant Editor:

Chris Jones

Members of the LexisNexis Group worldwide

United Kingdom	RELX (UK) Limited trading as LexisNexis, 1–3 Strand, London WC2N 5JR and 9-10 St Andrew Square, Edinburgh EH2 2AF
Australia	Reed International Books Australia Pty Ltd trading as LexisNexis, Chatswood, New South Wales
Austria	LexisNexis Verlag ARD Orac GmbH & Co KG, Vienna
Benelux	LexisNexis Benelux, Amsterdam
Canada	LexisNexis Canada, Markham, Ontario
China	LexisNexis China, Beijing and Shanghai
France	LexisNexis SA, Paris
Germany	LexisNexis GmbH, Dusseldorf
Hong Kong	LexisNexis Hong Kong, Hong Kong
India	LexisNexis India, New Delhi
Italy	Giuffrè Editore, Milan
Japan	LexisNexis Japan, Tokyo
Malaysia	Malayan Law Journal Sdn Bhd, Kuala Lumpur
New Zealand	LexisNexis NZ Ltd, Wellington
Singapore	LexisNexis Singapore, Singapore
South Africa	LexisNexis Butterworths, Durban
USA	LexisNexis, Dayton, Ohio

© 2017 RELX (UK) Limited.

Published by LexisNexis
This is a Tolley title

ISBN: 9780754553908
A CIP Catalogue record for this book is available from the British Library.

Printed and bound in Great Britain by CPI Group (UK) Ltd, Croydon, CR0 4YY

Visit LexisNexis at www.lexisnexis.co.uk

About this book

This is the thirty-sixth edition of Tolley's Tax Guide, which is one of the range of Tolley annuals on all aspects of taxation.

The Guide is updated annually to incorporate the changes in law and practice that occur each year. This year, due to the disruption caused by the snap general election, we have had two Finance Acts. The Guide is published in October 2017, after the passing of Finance Act 2017, and shortly before F(No 2)A 2017 receives Royal Assent. After publication any in-year changes (via secondary legislation etc) will be published online on a weekly basis to ensure the commentary provided by Tolley's Tax Guide is as comprehensive and up to date as possible.

The aim of the book is to provide clear and concise guidance on all aspects of taxation that are likely to be encountered day-to-day by tax advisers and personal and business taxpayers. It deals with income tax and capital gains tax, corporation tax, inheritance tax, value added tax and stamp taxes. There are also chapters on council tax and business rates, national insurance contributions and statutory sick pay, statutory maternity pay, adoption and paternity pay, and shared parental pay. There are numerous examples to demonstrate how the provisions work in practice.

Tax planning opportunities in the various areas are highlighted as 'tax points' at the end of most chapters.

This edition gives the position for the tax year 2017–18 and covers all legislation, HMRC's published guidance and other relevant sources of information including the provisions of Finance Act 2017 and the September 2017 Finance Bill. Where appropriate the position for earlier years is also explained.

All chapters have been revised to incorporate the many changes that have taken place since the previous edition, and there is a useful summary of the main changes at page xxix.

The general law, as opposed to tax law, is not always the same in Scotland and in Northern Ireland as in England and Wales. Except where otherwise stated, this book is concerned with the law in England and Wales. Readers in Scotland and Northern Ireland should take advice if in any doubt. With regard to tax law, there is commentary on the Scottish rate of income tax and on land and buildings transaction tax which applies in Scotland in place of stamp duty land tax.

Any comments on this publication will, as always, be welcomed by the publishers.

LexisNexis

Contents

Contents

MISCELLANEOUS

Abbreviations

CAA 2001	Capital Allowances Act 2001
CFC	Controlled foreign company
CGT	Capital gains tax
CTA 2009	Corporation Tax Act 2009
CTA 2010	Corporation Tax Act 2010
CTFA 2004	Child Trust Funds Act 2004
EEA	European Economic Area
EIS	Enterprise Investment Scheme
ESC	Extra-statutory concession
FA	Finance Act
FYA	First-year allowance
F(No 2)A	Finance (No 2) Act
HMRC	Her Majesty's Revenue and Customs
IHT	Inheritance tax
IHTA 1984	Inheritance Tax Act 1984
ISA	Individual Savings Account
ITA 2007	Income Tax Act 2007
ITEPA 2003	Income Tax (Earnings and Pensions) Act 2003
ITTOIA 2005	Income Tax (Trading and Other Income) Act 2005
ITPA 2014	Inheritance and Trustees' Powers Act 2014
LBTT(S)A 2013	Land and Buildings Transaction Tax (Scotland) Act 2013
MIRAS	Mortgage interest relief at source
NIC	National insurance contributions
NICA 2014	National Insurance Contributions Act 2014
NICA 2015	National Insurance Contributions Act 2015
PAYE	Pay As You Earn
reg	Regulation
RSTPA 2014	Revenue Scotland and Tax Powers Act 2014

s	Section
SA 1891	Stamp Act 1891
SAYE	Save As You Earn
Sch	Schedule
SDLTA 2015	Stamp Duty Land Tax Act 2015
SEIS	Seed Enterprise Investment Scheme
SI	Statutory instrument
SITR	Social Investment Tax Relief
SP	HMRC Statement of Practice
SSCBA 1992	Social Security Contributions and Benefits Act 1992
TA 1988	Income and Corporation Taxes Act 1988
TCA 2002	Tax Credits Act 2002
TCGA 1992	Taxation of Chargeable Gains Act 1992
TIOPA 2010	Taxation (International and Other Provisions) Act 2010
TMA 1970	Taxes Management Act 1970
VAT	Value added tax
VATA 1994	Value Added Tax Act 1994
VCT	Venture Capital Trust

Table of rates and allowances

[TRA]

(Correct to 13 September 2017)

INCOME AND CORPORATION TAX

Personal reliefs (see chapter 2)

	2016–17 £	2017–18 £
Personal allowance		
Basic personal allowance	11,000	11,500
personal allowance income limit	100,000	100,000
Married couple's allowance		
either partner born before 6 April 1935	8,355*	8,445*
age allowance income limit	27,700	28,000
minimum where income exceeds limit	3,220*	3,260*
Transferable tax allowance	1,100	1,150
Blind person's allowance	2,290	2,320
Dividend allowance	5,000	5,000
Savings allowance		
basic rate taxpayer	1,000	1,000
higher rate taxpayer	500	500

*These allowances attract tax relief at only 10%.

Income tax rates on taxable income (see chapter 2)

Rate	2016–17		2017–18	
	Band	Tax	Band	Tax
	£	£	£	£
Starting for savings income 0%*	0–5,000		0–5,000	
Basic 20%	0–32,000	6,400	0–33,500**	6,700
Higher 40%	32,001–150,000	47,200	33,501–150,000	46,600
Additional 45%	Over 150,000		Over 150,000	

*The starting rate for savings income applies only if non-savings income is within certain limits (see **2.5**). See **2.26** and **2.27** for full details of the rates of tax on savings and dividend income.

£31,500 for Scottish taxpayers on non-savings income (see **2.5).

Company cars – private use benefit (see chapter 10)

The taxable benefit is the appropriate percentage of the list price of the car plus certain accessories. The percentage for cars registered after 31 December 1997 which have an approved carbon dioxide (CO_2) emissions figure can be found using the table below.

2016–17 g/km	% of price taxable		2017–18 g/km	% of price taxable	
0	7		0	9	
50	7	*	50	9	*
75	11	*	75	13	*
94	15	*	94	17	*
95	16	*	95	18	*
100	17	*	100	19	*
105	18	*	105	20	*
110	19	*	110	21	*
115	20	*	115	22	*
120	21	*	120	23	*
125	22	*	125	24	*
130	23	*	130	25	*
135	24	*	135	26	*

2016–17 g/km	% of price taxable		2017–18 g/km	% of price taxable	
140	25	*	140	27	*
145	26	*	145	28	*
150	27	*	150	29	*
155	28	*	155	30	*
160	29	*	160	31	*
165	30	*	165	32	*
170	31	*	170	33	*
175	32	*	175	34	*
180	33	*	180	35	**
185	34	*	185	36	***
190	35	**	190	37	****
195	36	***			
200	37	****			

*Add 3% if car runs solely on diesel.

**Add 2% if car runs solely on diesel.

***Add 1% if car runs solely on diesel.

****No diesel supplement.

See **10.38** regarding company car tax in general.

Cars first registered before 1 January 1998, and cars which have no approved CO_2 emissions figure, are taxed as follows.

Engine size	% of price taxable	
	Pre-1.1.98 cars	Post-31.12.97 cars with no emissions figure
0–1,400 cc	18	18*
1,401–2,000 cc	29	29*
2,001 cc and over	37	37

*Plus 3% supplement for diesel cars.

Company cars – car fuel benefit (see chapter 10)

The fuel benefit is calculated by reference to CO_2 emissions, where the car was new on or after 1 January 1998 and has an approved CO_2 emissions figure.

The same percentage as for car benefit (ranging from 9% to 37% depending on CO_2 emissions) is applied to the fixed sum of £22,600 (£22,200 for 2016–17).

Where the car has no approved CO_2 emissions figure, the same percentage figure used to calculate company car benefit is used.

Company cars – advisory fuel rates from 1 September 2017 (see chapter 10)

	Petrol	Diesel	LPG
1400cc or less	11p	—	7p
1600cc or less	—	9p	—
1401cc to 2000cc	13p	—	8p
1601cc to 2000cc	—	11p	—
Over 2000cc	21p	12p	13p

Company vans – benefit (see chapter 10)

The taxable benefit is as follows:

	Vans which emit CO_2 when driven	Vans which do not emit CO_2 when driven
2017–18	£3,230	£646
2016–17	£3,170	£634

Company vans – fuel benefit (see chapter 10)

2017–18	£610
2016–17	£598

Use of own transport – authorised mileage rates applying from 6 April 2011 (see chapter 10)

Cars

	First 10,000 business miles	Additional business miles
All cars	45p	25p
Each passenger making same business trip	5p	5p

Cycles

The authorised mileage rate for cycles is 20p per mile for all business miles.

Motorcycles

The authorised mileage rate for motor cycles is 24p per mile for all business miles.

Official rate of interest: cheap loans (see chapter 10)

From 6 April 2017	2.50% p.a.
6 April 2015–5 April 2017	3.00% p.a.

Interest on unpaid tax (see chapter 9)

From 23 August 2016	2.75% p.a.
29 September 2009–22 August 2016	3.00% p.a.

Interest on overpaid tax (see chapter 9)

From 29 September 2009	0.50% p.a.

The rates of interest on unpaid and overpaid tax outlined above apply, where appropriate, to most taxes and duties including corporation tax (other than unpaid instalments) (see CHAPTER 3), income tax (see CHAPTER 2) and capital gains tax (see CHAPTER 4), inheritance tax (see CHAPTER 5), national insurance contributions (see CHAPTERS 13 and 24), stamp duty, stamp duty land tax and stamp duty reserve tax (see CHAPTER 6), and diverted profits tax (see 3.32). Note that the same rates of interest apply to land and buildings transaction tax (see CHAPTER 6) from 1 April 2015 but the interest is payable to Revenue Scotland, not HMRC. For further details see 9.55 and 9.56.

Interest on unpaid instalment payments for 'large companies' (see chapter 3)

From 15 August 2016	1.25% p.a.
16 March 2009–14 August 2016	1.50% p.a.

Interest on overpaid instalment payments for 'large companies' and on early payments by other companies (see chapter 3)

From 21 September 2009	0.50% p.a.

Corporation tax rates (see chapter 3)

Year beginning	1 April 2016	1 April 2017
Main rate	20%	19%

Capital gains are generally included in profits and therefore chargeable at the applicable corporation tax rate, subject to the charge to capital gains tax on disposal of high value properties (see **3.1**). From 6 April 2015, certain non-UK resident companies may be liable to capital gains tax on the disposal of UK residential property; see **41.46**.

CAPITAL GAINS TAX (see chapter 4)

Capital gains remaining after deduction of the annual exemption will be taxed at the rates outlined in **4.2**. The annual exempt amount for individuals, personal representatives and trustees for disabled people is:

2017–18	£11,300
2016–17	£11,100

See **4.44** and **4.45** regarding personal representatives and trustees.

Retail prices index (for indexation allowance)

	1982	1983	1984	1985	1986	1987	1988	1989	1990
January		82.61	86.84	91.20	96.25	100.0	103.3	111.0	119.5
February		82.97	87.20	91.94	96.60	100.4	103.7	111.8	120.2
March	79.44	83.12	87.48	92.80	96.73	100.6	104.1	112.3	121.4
April	81.04	84.28	88.64	94.78	97.67	101.8	105.8	114.3	125.1
May	81.62	84.64	88.97	95.21	97.85	101.9	106.2	115.0	126.2
June	81.85	84.84	89.20	95.41	97.79	101.9	106.6	115.4	126.7
July	81.88	85.30	89.10	95.23	97.52	101.8	106.7	115.5	126.8
August	81.90	85.68	89.94	95.49	97.82	102.1	107.9	115.8	128.1
September	81.85	86.06	90.11	95.44	98.30	102.4	108.4	116.6	129.3
October	82.26	86.36	90.67	95.59	98.45	102.9	109.5	117.5	130.3
November	82.66	86.67	90.95	95.92	99.29	103.4	110.0	118.5	130.0
December	82.51	86.89	90.87	96.05	99.62	103.3	110.3	118.8	129.9

	1991	1992	1993	1994	1995	1996	1997	1998	1999
January	130.2	135.6	137.9	141.3	146.0	150.2	154.4	159.5	163.4
February	130.9	136.3	138.8	142.1	146.9	150.9	155.0	160.3	163.7
March	131.4	136.7	139.3	142.5	147.5	151.5	155.4	160.8	164.1
April	133.1	138.8	140.6	144.2	149.0	152.6	156.3	162.6	165.2
May	133.5	139.3	141.1	144.7	149.6	152.9	156.9	163.5	165.6
June	134.1	139.3	141.0	144.7	149.8	153.0	157.5	163.4	165.6
July	133.8	138.8	140.7	144.0	149.1	152.4	157.5	163.0	165.1
August	134.1	138.9	141.3	144.7	149.9	153.1	158.5	163.7	165.5
September	134.6	139.4	141.9	145.0	150.6	153.8	159.3	164.4	166.2
October	135.1	139.9	141.8	145.2	149.8	153.8	159.5	164.5	166.5
November	135.6	139.7	141.6	145.3	149.8	153.9	159.6	164.4	166.7
December	135.7	139.2	141.9	146.0	150.7	154.4	160.0	164.4	167.3

	2000	2001	2002	2003	2004	2005	2006	2007	2008
January	166.6	171.1	173.3	178.4	183.1	188.9	193.4	201.6	209.8
February	167.5	172.0	173.8	179.3	183.8	189.6	194.2	203.1	211.4
March	168.4	172.2	174.5	179.9	184.6	190.5	195.0	204.4	212.1
April	170.1	173.1	175.7	181.2	185.7	191.6	196.5	205.4	214.0
May	170.7	174.2	176.2	181.5	186.5	192.0	197.7	206.2	215.1
June	171.1	174.4	176.2	181.3	186.8	192.2	198.5	207.3	216.8
July	170.5	173.3	175.9	181.3	186.8	192.2	198.5	206.1	216.5
August	170.5	174.0	176.4	181.6	187.4	192.6	199.2	207.3	217.2
September	171.7	174.6	177.6	182.5	188.1	193.1	200.1	208.0	218.4
October	171.6	174.3	177.9	182.6	188.6	193.3	200.4	208.9	217.7
November	172.1	173.6	178.2	182.7	189.0	193.6	201.1	209.7	216.0
December	172.2	173.4	178.5	183.5	189.9	194.1	202.7	210.9	212.9

	2009	2010	2011	2012	2013	2014	2015	2016	2017
January	210.1	217.9	229.0	238.0	245.8	252.6	255.4	258.8	265.5
February	211.4	219.2	231.3	239.9	247.6	254.2	256.7	260.0	268.4
March	211.3	220.7	232.5	240.8	248.7	254.8	257.1	261.1	269.3
April	211.5	222.8	234.4	242.5	249.5	255.7	258.0	261.4	270.6

	2009	2010	2011	2012	2013	2014	2015	2016	2017
May	212.8	223.6	235.2	242.4	250.0	255.9	258.5	262.1	271.7
June	213.4	224.1	235.2	241.8	249.7	256.3	258.9	263.1	272.3
July	213.4	223.6	234.7	242.1	249.7	256.0	258.6	263.4	272.9
August	214.4	224.5	236.1	243.0	251.0	257.0	259.8	264.4	274.7
September	215.3	225.3	237.9	244.2	251.9	257.6	259.6	264.9	
October	216.0	225.8	238.0	245.6	251.9	257.7	259.5	264.8	
November	216.6	226.8	238.5	245.6	252.1	257.1	259.8	265.5	
December	218.0	228.4	239.4	246.8	253.4	257.5	260.6	267.1	

The post-April 1998 figures are relevant only for calculating capital gains of companies. The index was re-referenced in January 1987 from 394.5 to 100.

NATIONAL INSURANCE CONTRIBUTIONS

Employers and employees: Class 1 NICs (see chapter 13)

	2016–17	2017–18
Weekly lower earnings limit (LEL)	£112	£113
Weekly upper earnings limit (UEL)	£827	£866
Weekly upper secondary threshold (UST/AUST)*	£827	£866
Weekly primary threshold	£155	£157
Weekly secondary threshold	£156	£157

*Upper secondary threshold applies to employers' NIC only for employees under age 21 and apprentices under age 25 (see **13.9**)

Rates: 2016–17 and 2017–18

Not contracted out

Band of weekly earnings	2016–17	2017–18
Employee		
£0 to primary threshold	—	—
Primary threshold to UEL	12%	12%
Over UEL	2%	2%
Employer		
£0 to secondary threshold	—	—
Over secondary threshold*	13.8%	13.8%

*For employees aged under 21 and apprentices aged under 25 the rate of 13.8% applies to earnings over *upper* secondary threshold.

Reduced rate for certain married women and widows

	2016–17	2017–18
Payable on earnings in the band from the primary threshold to UEL	5.85%	5.85%
Over UEL	2%	2%

Employers: Class 1A NICs on benefits in kind (see chapter 13)

13.8% of the taxable benefit

Self-employed: Class 2 and Class 4 NICs (see chapter 24)

	2016–17	2017–18
Class 2 contributions per week	£2.80	£2.85
Small profits threshold	£5,965	£6,025
Class 4 contributions rate	9%	9%
on profits between	£8,060 and £43,000	£8,164 and £45,000
Class 4 contributions rate	2%	2%
on profits over	£43,000	£45,000

Voluntary: Class 3 NICs (see chapters 13 and 24)

	2016–17	2017–18
Class 3 contributions per week	£14.10	£14.25

Statutory sick pay from 6 April 2017 (see chapter 14)

Average weekly earnings	£113 and over
SSP flat weekly rate	£89.35

Statutory maternity pay and statutory adoption pay from 6 April 2017 (see chapter 14)

Amount payable during first six weeks:

90% of average weekly earnings.

Amount payable after first six weeks:

The lower of £140.98 and 90% of average weekly earnings.

Statutory paternity pay from 6 April 2017 (see chapter 14)

Amount payable during two qualifying weeks:

The lower of £140.98 and 90% of average weekly earnings.

Shared parental pay from 6 April 2017 (see chapter 14)

Amount payable during qualifying weeks (in place of statutory maternity/ adoption pay):

The lower of £140.98 and 90% of average weekly earnings.

MAIN STATE BENEFITS (see chapter 10)

	2016–17 £	2017–18 £
Taxable (weekly rates[5])		
Retirement pension — retired after 5 April 2016	155.65	159.55
Retirement pension — retired before 6 April 2016		
—single[1]	119.30	122.30
—non-contributory[1] (higher amount)	71.50	73.30
—adult dependency increase[3]	65.70	66.35
Bereavement benefits — deaths before 6 April 2017[9]		
—widowed parent's allowance	up to 112.55	up to 113.70
—bereavement allowance (standard rate)	up to 112.55	up to 113.70
Employment and support allowance (contribution-based)[2, 4]		
—assessment phase rate (under 25)	57.90	57.90
—assessment phase rate (25 or over)	73.10	73.10
—main phase rate (work-related)	up to 102.15	up to 73.10
—main phase rate (support group)	up to 109.30	up to 109.65
Carer's allowance		
—single	62.10	62.70
Jobseekers allowance[4] (taxable maximum) Single		

—under 25	57.90	57.90
—25 or over	73.10	73.10
Couple		
—both 18 or over	114.85	114.85

Non-taxable (weekly rates)
(excluding income-related benefits)
Child benefit

—eldest child	20.70	20.70
—other children	13.70	13.70
Maternity allowance		
—standard rate	139.58	140.98

Disability living allowance[6]
care component

—higher rate	82.30	83.10
—middle rate	55.10	55.65
—lower rate	21.80	22.00
mobility component		
—higher rate	57.45	58.00
—lower rate	21.80	22.00

Personal independence payment[6]
daily living component

—enhanced rate	82.30	83.10
—standard rate	55.10	55.65
mobility component		
—enhanced rate	57.45	58.00
—standard rate	21.80	22.00

Severe disablement allowance[8]

—single (standard rate)	74.65	75.40

Non-taxable (amount payable per assessment period)
Universal credit (standard allowance)[4]
Single

—under 25	251.77	251.77
—25 or over	317.82	317.82
Couple		
—both under 25	395.20	395.20
—either 25 or over	498.89	498.89

1   A taxable age addition of 25p per week is payable to persons aged 80 or over with these benefits.

2   Employment and support allowance replaced incapacity benefit and income support, paid because of illness or disability, for new claims from 27 October 2008. See www.gov.uk/employment-support-allowance/overview. The main phase rate starts from week 14 of the claim if the Work Capability Assessment shows that the claimant's illness or disability does restrict the ability to work. Claimants entitled to the income-related allowance may receive more than the contribution-based amounts and the rates vary.

3   Not available to new retirees from April 2010. To be withdrawn completely on 5 April 2020.

4   Universal credit is being phased in from April 2013 to replace various benefits (see **10.6**) including income-based jobseeker's allowance and income-related employment and support allowance.

5   A cap applies to the total amount of benefit that most people aged between 16 and 64 can receive (see **10.6**).

6   Personal independence payment started to replace disability living allowance (DLA) for new claims in 2013–14. It will be phased in over a number of years for existing DLA claimants.

7   An assessment period is a calendar month from effective date of claim.

8   Severe disablement allowance has been replaced with employment and support allowance except for those who reached retirement age before 6 April 2014.

9   For deaths after 5 April 2017 non-taxable bereavement support payments replace bereavement benefits. Those with children under 20 in full-time education will receive a first payment of £3,500 and up to 18 monthly payments of £350. Otherwise the first payment is £2,500 and monthly payments are £100.

TAX CREDITS (see chapter 2)

	2016–17 £ p.a.	2017–18 £ p.a.
Working tax credit[1]		
— basic	1,960	1,960
— additional couple's and lone parent element	2,010	2,010
— 30 hour	810	810
— disabled worker	2,970	3,000
— addition for severe disablement	1,275	1,290
— childcare: maximum eligible cost	300 p.w.	300 p.w.
— childcare: maximum eligible cost (one child)	175 p.w.	175 p.w.
— percent of eligible costs recovered	70%	70%
Child tax credit[1]		
— family (only one family element per family)	545	545
— child	2,780	2,780
— disabled child addition	3,140	3,175
— severely disabled child addition	1,275	1,290
For both working credit and child credit		

— first income threshold	6,420	6,420
— first withdrawal rate	41%	41%
— first threshold (those entitled to child credit only)	16,105	16,105
— income rise disregard	2,500	2,500
— income fall disregard	2,500	2,500

[1] Universal credit is being phased in from April 2013 to replace various benefits (see **10.6**) including working tax credit and child tax credit.

VALUE ADDED TAX (see chapter 7)

Standard rate	From 4 Jan 2011	20%

	From 1 April 2016	From 1 April 2017
Registration threshold taxable supplies		
—in last 12 months	More than £83,000	More than £85,000
—in next 30 days	More than £83,000	More than £85,000
unless taxable supplies in next year not expected to exceed	£81,000	£83,000
Deregistration		
taxable supplies in next year	£81,000 or less	£83,000 or less

VAT—private motoring—road fuel scale charges from 1 May 2017

CO_2 emissions, g/km	Annual returns £	Quarterly returns £	Monthly returns £
120 or less	563	140	46
125	842	211	70
130	901	224	74
135	955	238	79
140	1,013	252	84
145	1,068	267	88
150	1,126	281	93
155	1,180	295	98
160	1,239	309	102
165	1,293	323	107
170	1,351	337	111

CO_2 emissions, g/km	Annual returns £	Quarterly returns £	Monthly returns £
175	1,405	351	116
180	1,464	365	121
185	1,518	379	125
190	1,577	393	131
195	1,631	408	136
200	1,689	422	140
205	1,743	436	145
210	1,802	449	149
215	1,856	463	154
220	1,914	478	159
225 or more	1,969	492	163

Interest payable on VAT (default interest)

From 23 August 2016	2.75% p.a.
29 September 2009–22 August 2016	3.00% p.a.

Repayment supplement

Repayment supplement of 5% of the tax due (or £50 if greater) is paid on overpaid VAT if the return was made by the due date, the return did not overstate the amount repayable by more than the greater of £250 and 5% of the amount due, and directions for repayment are not issued by HMRC within 30 days from the day following the return due date, or the date the return was received if *later*.

Statutory interest payable by HMRC on overpaid VAT in cases of official error

From 29 September 2009   0.50% p.a.

INHERITANCE TAX (see chapter 5)

Rate of tax

A rate of inheritance tax of 40% (20% for lifetime transfers), applies to the excess of gross cumulative chargeable transfers over the 'nil rate' threshold shown below. However a reduced rate of 36% applies for deaths on or after

6 April 2012 where 10% or more of the deceased's net estate is left to charity or registered community amateur sports club.

Transfers between 6 April 2009 and 5 April 2021   £325,000

In 2017–18 an additional residence nil-rate band of £100,000 applies when a home is passed on death to direct descendants of the deceased on or after 6 April 2017, though there is a tapered withdrawal for estates valued at over £2 million. It also applies where an individual downsizes from a higher value residence to a lower value one or ceases to own a home on or after 8 July 2015 and assets of equivalent value are passed on death to direct descendants.

For interest on unpaid and overpaid inheritance tax see under income and corporation tax.

Main Tax Changes

The main changes that have been enacted by Finance Act 2017 and various statutory instruments in the previous 12 months, and thought likely to be of relevance to most readers, are outlined below. Proposals from the September 2017 Finance Bill are also mentioned throughout the book where appropriate.

Income tax (chapters 2, 36 and 37)

The basic rate of income tax remains at 20%. Dividends within the basic rate band are chargeable at 7.5%. The rates for income above the basic rate limit (£33,500) and up to the higher rate limit (£150,000) remain unchanged at 40% for non-dividend income and 32.5% for dividend income. The rates above the higher rate limit are 45% for non-dividend income and 38.1% for dividend income. Note, however, that the Scottish basic rate limit for non-savings income only is £31,500, though the Scottish rate of income tax is the same as the rest of the UK. The starting rate for savings remains at 0% on a band of income of £5,000. The dividend allowance of £5,000 for all individuals, and the savings allowance of £1,000 for basic rate taxpayers and £500 for higher rate taxpayers, still all apply. Income within the dividend and savings allowance is taxed at 0%. From 6 April 2017 tax is not deducted at source from interest distributions from open-ended investment companies, authorised unit trusts and investment trust companies and from interest on peer-to-peer loans.

For 2017–18 the personal allowance is £11,500. The transferable tax allowance is £1,150. The married couple's allowance of £8,445 is restricted to the extent that income exceeds £28,000, but will not fall below £3,260. If an individual's income exceeds £100,000 the personal allowance is restricted for all individuals regardless of age and can be reduced to zero.

Corporation tax (chapters 3, 20, 26, 29 and 43)

From 1 April 2017 the 'main rate' of corporation tax is 19%, although a 'small ring-fence profits' rate continues to apply for ring fence profits from oil activities. The main rate will be reduced to 17% from 1 April 2020. There are new rules for the carry forward of post-1 April 2017 corporate losses, and from 1 April 2017 there is also a new corporate interest restriction for companies with net interest expense in excess of £2 million.

Capital gains tax (chapters 4, 29, 30, 39 and 41)

The annual exemption for individuals and personal representatives remains at £11,300, with corresponding exemptions for trustees. The capital gains tax rates are unchanged. Those applying to gains up to the basic rate limit for individuals are 10% or 18% (depending on the type of gains), and all gains above that limit are taxed at 20% or 28%, subject to any reliefs applying. Gains arising to trustees and personal representatives are taxed at 20% or 28% (depending on the type of gains).

Inheritance tax (chapters 5, 35 and 42)

The inheritance tax nil threshold remains at £325,000. From 6 April 2017 non-domiciled individuals are chargeable to inheritance tax in respect of UK residential property held indirectly by them.

Value added tax (chapter 7)

The VAT registration limit was increased to £85,000 and the deregistration limit to £83,000, with effect from 1 April 2017.

Employments and pensions (chapters 10, 11, 13, 14, 15 and 16)

The official rate of interest which applies to some benefits in kind is reduced to 2.5% for 2017–18. From 6 April 2017 employers may use the HMRC online service to payroll vouchers and credit tokens. From April 2017 there are limits to the income tax and NICs advantages of providing benefits under optional remuneration arrangements. The date by which an employee must 'make good' certain benefits has been aligned to 6 July following the tax year from 2017–18.

The Government plans to bring in a digital PAYE settlement agreement process from April 2018.

The pension money purchase annual allowance is reduced to £4,000 from 6 April 2017.

From 2018–19 changes are made to the termination payments regime to make the existing rules fairer and remove the incentives for employers to try and manipulate the rules.

Business and property taxes (chapters 20, 24 and 32)

A £1,000 allowance has been introduced for both property income and trading income with effect from 2017–18. The treatment of expenditure under the cash basis for small businesses has been simplified. A cash basis has been introduced for unincorporated property businesses from 2017–18. Trading losses cannot be created from capital losses arising in respect of appropriations of trading stock made after 7 March 2017. Anti-avoidance provisions prevent trading profits disguised as other receipts escaping the charge to tax from 6 April 2017. Class 2 NICs are proposed to be abolished from 6 April 2018.

Capital allowances (chapter 22)

A first year allowance is available on electric charge-point equipment.

Administration (chapter 9 and Table of rates and allowances)

The Government has confirmed that the 'making tax digital' initiative will be rolled out from April 2019. From this date digital reporting and record keeping will only be compulsory for VAT records/accounts for businesses with a turnover above the VAT registration threshold.

Overseas issues (chapter 41)

Changes have been made to the domicile rules for income tax, capital gains tax and inheritance tax to broadly align the rules for all three purposes.

Part I

Introduction

1

Introduction

[1.1] Tolley's Tax Guide first appeared 35 years ago. The tax world has changed out of all recognition over the last three decades and the pace of change has also increased dramatically over recent years, with the annual Finance Act being supplemented by rafts of secondary legislation and HMRC announcements etc throughout the year.

To ensure that Tax Guide commentary is as accurate and up to date as possible, new developments affecting the current published commentary are now added on a weekly basis to our online service on *Tolley Library*. Please contact Customer Services on 0845 370 1234 for subscription queries.

The volume of legislation has been considerably increased over recent years because of the recent project to rewrite tax law in simpler language. Making it simpler has, unfortunately, resulted in using a lot more words. The legislative rewrite process is now completed, but the simplification process continues on a more piecemeal process. Legislation has been introduced (to take effect from a date to be appointed) to put the Office of Tax Simplification (OTS) onto a permanent basis and be given a wider remit. We can therefore expect more efforts to simplify the tax system over the next few years — see for example, the recent recommendation by the OTS for a further review on the closer alignment of income tax and NICs; **13.1**.

[1.2] UK tax law applies throughout the UK, but there are sometimes specific provisions that recognise the different legal systems in Scotland and, to a lesser extent, in Northern Ireland. These differences are generally not dealt with in this book, although the devolved taxes are discussed in context where necessary. The current state of play on the devolved taxes is as follows:

(a) Scotland: From 1 April 2015 certain taxes (namely land and buildings transactions tax (**6.18**) and Scottish landfill tax) are fully devolved to the Scottish Parliament. In addition, the Scotland Act 2012 and Scotland Act 2016 give revised tax powers to the Scottish Parliament to set a Scottish rate of income tax for Scottish taxpayers which applies from April 2016. This is not a devolved tax, but forms part of the UK income tax system and HMRC will continue to administer and collect it; see **2.4**.

(b) Wales: From April 2018 stamp duty land tax is to be replaced by a new Welsh land transaction tax (**6.9**). The Wales Act 2014 also provides for the devolution of landfill tax from 2018–19 and the creation of Welsh rates of income tax from 2019–20. The Tax Collection and Management (Wales) Act 2016 puts in place the legal framework necessary for the future collection and management of devolved taxes in Wales.

(c)   Northern Ireland: The Northern Ireland Executive has the power to set
        the rate of corporation tax on certain trading profits from 1 April 2018.
        It is expected the rate will be set at 12.5%. This will require companies
        separately to identify profits arising in Northern Ireland from profits
        arising elsewhere in the UK. The devolved rate will apply to trading
        profits only and primarily to micro, small or medium-sized enterprises
        for whom at least 75% of their staff time and costs relate to work in
        Northern Ireland. It will apply to large companies and corporate
        partners to the extent that profits are attributable to a Northern Ireland
        trading presence. HMRC and the NI Department of Finance and
        Personnel have signed a Memorandum of Understanding setting out
        arrangements for the devolved corporation tax rate in Northern
        Ireland. The Government has indicated it will not legislate to implement
        the devolved tax until the Northern Ireland Executive's finances are on
        a 'sustainable footing'.

[1.3] UK tax law must comply with the regulations and directives of the
European Commission. EU member states must allow members of other EU
states freedom of establishment and not tax them at higher rates than their
own nationals. One EU state may require another state to take proceedings to
recover both direct and indirect taxes owed in the first state, and an EU state
may ask the UK tax authorities to deliver documents to a UK taxpayer on their
behalf in relation to a tax liability in that EU state. UK tax law must also be
compatible with the European Convention on Human Rights and the Human
Rights Act 1998.

Some tax legislation applies not only to EU members but is extended to include
members of the European Economic Area (EEA). The EEA consists of the
members of the EU plus Iceland, Liechtenstein and Norway.

[1.4] The work of HMRC was done by the Inland Revenue and HM Customs
and Excise until those departments merged in 2005. The merger was followed
by the establishment of an independent authority, the Revenue and Customs
Prosecutions Office (RCPO), to deal with prosecution work. In January 2010 RCPO merged with the Crown Prosecution Service (CPS) to become
a specialist Revenue and Customs Division within the Central Fraud Group of
the CPS. It merged with the Fraud Prosecution Division of the CPS in April
2010 to form the Central Fraud Group (CFG) and was subsequently renamed
as the Specialist Fraud Division (SFD). The SFD divides its work into two
broad categories: fiscal and non-fiscal.

HMRC are allowed to disclose information to the police in the UK and abroad
in connection with criminal investigations and also to the intelligence services.
Information is also available to government departments as a result of the
money laundering regulations (see CHAPTER 9).

[1.5] Knowing how the UK system works, what taxes can be charged and
what deductions and allowances are available, as well as the tax effect of
alternative courses of action, will help a taxpayer cope with his responsibilities
and make sure that all relevant tax reliefs and allowances are obtained.

The first part of this book contains a brief outline of all the various taxes covered, including council tax. The following sections go on to deal with specific subject areas such as employment, pensions, trades, land, tax and the family, and choosing investments. Tax saving opportunities and possible problems are highlighted in the form of 'tax points' at the end of each chapter.

Statutory references will help to track down the relevant legislation if a topic needs to be researched in more depth. The main Acts dealing with taxation are the Inheritance Tax Act 1984, the Taxation of Chargeable Gains Act 1992, the Value Added Tax Act 1994, the Capital Allowances Act 2001, the Income Tax (Earnings and Pensions) Act 2003, the Income Tax (Trading and Other Income) Act 2005, the Income Tax Act 2007, the Corporation Tax Act 2009, the Corporation Tax Act 2010 and the Taxation (International and Other Provisions) Act 2010. In addition there are annual Finance Acts which alter some of the existing provisions and bring in new ones.

Statutory instruments are increasingly being used to provide detailed regulations on various aspects of the main Acts but also to make changes to the provisions of the Acts, partly because legislation is often introduced in haste and without the benefit of detailed consultation and/or parliamentary scrutiny. In the June 2010 Budget, the Government announced that it intends to impose 'sunset clauses' on regulations, under which they will cease to be law after seven years unless Parliament has confirmed that they are still necessary and proportionate, or they were explicitly set to have a longer timeframe.

Published statements of practice and extra-statutory concessions set out HMRC's views on particular aspects and sometimes allow matters to be treated more sympathetically than the strict letter of the law allows. No new concessions are being introduced following doubts expressed in the courts about HMRC's legal power to make such concessions. There is an ongoing programme of reviewing existing concessions: some concessions are now being written into legislation, while others are being withdrawn.

Much of the published material is posted on the HMRC website well in advance of the paper versions. Indeed some publications, including the self-assessment Help Sheets and Revenue and Customs Briefs, are only available online. It is the Government's declared aim to increase the use of electronic communication with taxpayers. Indeed regulations came into force on 27 March 2014 which provide for a wider range of taxpayer communications in connection with self-assessment which HMRC may, with the taxpayer's consent, conduct online. This will include communications regarding notices to file a return, enquiries, determinations, assessments, penalties and other reminders. HMRC's long term aim is to digitise as much of the administration and operation of the tax system as possible and over the next few years it is likely that most interactions between HMRC and taxpayers will be via digital means. The Making Tax Digital (MTD) process is still very much on the agenda, albeit that the pace of implementation has slowed (**9.2**).

[1.6] Despite the vast array of tax statutes and supplementary material, it is not always clear what the law means. Alternatively, the meaning of the law may not be in doubt, but the facts of the case may be unclear. It is therefore possible to take a different view from the tax authorities either on the interpretation of the law, or on the facts, or a mixture of the two.

As far as income tax, capital gains tax and corporation tax are concerned, since they are self-assessed it is up to the taxpayer to calculate how much tax is owed based on their view of the law (unless HMRC has issued a simple assessment notice (**9.8**)). If there are areas of doubt, these should be drawn to the attention of HMRC. If a self-assessment tax return is completed, HMRC will initially deal with points of difference by raising an enquiry into the return, at the end of which they have the right to make amendments if they disagree with the taxpayer's figures. They also have the right to issue assessments themselves in cases of careless or deliberate actions of the taxpayer or if inadequate information is provided. The power of HMRC to raise these 'discovery' assessments is a highly complex area of the law and taxpayers faced with such assessments should consider taking professional advice.

Appeals may be made to an independent appeals tribunal in cases of disagreement with an HMRC assessment etc. The distinction between questions of law and fact is important, because what an appeal tribunal decides on questions of fact is generally binding on both the taxpayer and HMRC. A tribunal's decision on points of law, however, can be referred by the losing party to the courts. It is important, however, to think very carefully before taking an appeal on a question of law to the appeal tribunal, because it may take a very long time before it is settled, it may well be costly, and at the end of the day the case may still be lost. In addition, a taxpayer's victory may be short-lived if the Government decide to change the law to reverse the effect of the court's decision.

[1.7] The appeals system comprises a First-tier Tribunal and an Upper Tribunal (with a separate First-tier and Upper Tribunal for Scotland). In the event of an appeal from the Upper Tribunal, the appeal will go to the Court of Appeal rather than the High Court. Where leave is granted, further appeal may be made to the Supreme Court. There is the further possibility of going to the European Court on the grounds that UK law is not in accordance with European Union rules. Most referrals to the European Court relate to VAT, but some relate to direct taxes. There is also the possibility of appealing to the European Court of Human Rights if it is felt that rights under the European Human Rights Convention have been breached.

Taxpayers and their advisers wishing to undertake tax planning need to bear in mind that HMRC have a good deal of 'anti-avoidance' legislation at their disposal coupled with the fact that disclosure is required by promoters (and in some cases, taxpayers) where certain tax schemes are used. HMRC may also be able to challenge a series of transactions with a tax avoidance motive so that only the end result of the series is taken into account. In addition the general anti-abuse rule, or 'GAAR' (for all taxes) empowers HMRC to make adjustments to counter tax advantages arising from arrangements that are abusive; see **45.5**. As yet the GAAR has not been invoked against any tax arrangements, but the threat of counteraction has undoubtedly had a deterrent effect and has significantly reduced the market for aggressive avoidance schemes.

[1.8] Most people do not want to be involved in disputes with the tax authorities, and merely wish to make sure that they comply with their obligations without paying more than is legally due. It is necessary, however, to understand the difference between tax avoidance and tax evasion. Tax avoidance means using the tax rules to best advantage, whereas tax evasion means illegally reducing tax bills, for example by understating income, over claiming expenses or deliberately disguising the true nature of transactions. It seems reasonable to distinguish tax avoidance from more straightforward tax planning or mitigation, with some avoidance being regarded as unacceptable by HMRC — some 'structured avoidance' schemes might be regarded, for example, as setting out to defeat the purpose of the legislation — and planning or mitigation being regarded as acceptable. However, there are no firm definitions in this area and increasingly HMRC and the Government are looking at ways to defeat aggressive tax planning as well as out and out avoidance.

Some ministers and HMRC officials have been accused of blurring the distinction between evasion and avoidance in an effort to highlight what they have regarded as unethical practice on the part of some taxpayers and professional advisers engaged in 'aggressive' or 'artificial' avoidance schemes.

Where tax has been illegally evaded, it can result in criminal prosecution as well as payment of the relevant tax plus interest and penalties. The tax authorities collect billions of pounds from their investigation, audit and review work, and undertake a number of major criminal prosecutions.

The UK also has wide-ranging international arrangements to help combat tax evasion, and information is exchanged with countries with whom the UK has double taxation agreements or tax information exchange agreements. A country with which the UK has a double taxation or tax information exchange agreement may also ask HMRC to require a UK taxpayer to provide information relating to tax liabilities with the overseas country. Over the next few years we are likely to see exchanges of information between tax authorities become routine and automatic.

The sensible course for taxpayers to follow is to try to understand what their liabilities are and to seek professional advice on non-straightforward matters. It is important to consider all the risks including any chance of retrospective legislation. This book aims to explain the basic rules on how tax liabilities are calculated and how they can be managed without falling foul of the law.

Part II

Outline of UK tax system

2

Income tax and tax credits: general principles

Basis of income tax charge (ITA 2007, Pts 1 and 2)

[2.1] In order to establish an individual's income tax position it is necessary to understand what 'income' is. Tax law classifies amounts received under various headings, and an item must come within one of these headings to be charged as income. The main income headings are set out in 2.7.

Capital receipts are dealt with under the capital gains tax rules (see CHAPTER 4). Sometimes tax law requires capital items to be treated as income. For example, when a landlord charges a tenant a premium in return for the grant of a short-term lease, part of the lump sum is taxed as income (see **32.21**). See also **20.11** and **32.6** regarding the treatment of certain capital receipts under the cash basis. Generally, however, an amount cannot be charged to income tax unless it has the quality of income. Usually commissions, cashbacks and discounts received by ordinary retail customers are not taxable, but such amounts may be taxable when received by employees or traders. See **37.3** for the tax treatment of cash received on building society mergers, takeovers etc.

Tax credits (see **2.34** to **2.41**) and universal credit (see **10.6**) are welfare benefits and do not enter into the calculation of taxable income, but they are dealt with by HMRC and are means-tested by reference to a claimant's annual income.

Exempt income

[2.2] Certain types of income are specifically exempt from tax, notably the following, most of which are dealt with in other chapters as indicated:

	Chapter
Income within individual savings accounts (ISAs and junior ISAs)	36, 38
Income and gains of a child trust fund	33
Increase in value of national savings certificates	36
Premium bond prizes	36
Other prizes and betting winnings	4
Bonuses and profits on life assurance policies (subject to detailed anti-avoidance rules)	40
The capital element in amounts received from a purchased life annuity	34
Financial support received by adopters and guardians (and certain qualifying carers) from local authorities and adoption agencies	20
Local authority home improvement grants	
Some social security benefits (but others are taxable)	10
Benefits payable under health and employment insurance policies	10
Damages and compensation for personal injury (whether received as a lump sum or by periodic payments), including payments from the Thalidomide Children's Trust	
Save As You Earn account bonuses	11
Shares and share options allocated by an employer under certain tax-advantaged schemes	11
Educational grants and scholarships	
Statutory redundancy pay and certain amounts received from an employer on termination of employment	15
Maintenance payments following divorce or separation	33
Certain payments to members of the Armed Forces	
Compensation paid by UK or foreign banks and building societies on frozen accounts of Holocaust victims	
Profits from commercial occupation of woodland	31
First £7,500 rent per year from a lodger in only or family home — £3,750 if split jointly	30
Interest that the Pensions Regulator may require an employer to pay on late paid pension contributions	16
Qualifying bonus payments of up to £3,600 made to employees, and qualifying former employees, of certain qualifying employee-owned companies	10

Generally no tax is due on the compensation element of payments received due to mis-sold payment protection insurance (PPI), although any additional interest paid on it is taxable.

A special rule provides a tax exemption for low-income employees meeting certain conditions, for example migrant workers who are employed in seasonal work in the agricultural or service sectors in both the UK and in other countries in the same tax year, whose overseas income is taxed where it is earned. The provision removes the requirement to file a self-assessment return in most cases where there would be little or no UK tax liability.

Paragraph **41.42** explains that basic rate tax may be deducted by the payer from certain UK earnings of non-resident entertainers, sportsmen and sportswomen. However, special provisions exempted some participants in various sporting events held in the UK such as the Olympic Games and Champions League Finals. The Treasury may now make regulations providing for exemption from income tax and corporation tax in relation to such major sporting events, removing the need to legislate in a Finance Bill. In 2017 an exemption applies to the Champions League Final and the World Athletics and Paralympics Championships.

Earnings paid by certain overseas governments to members of forces (including civilians employed by, or attached to, such forces) from other countries who are serving in the UK are exempt from tax, provided they are not British citizens.

Persons chargeable

[2.3] Each individual, whether man, woman or child, is chargeable to tax on his/her own income. The income of a child under 18 may be treated as the parent's income if it, or the capital which produces it, comes from the parent (see **33.10**). Personal representatives and trustees pay income tax on estate and trust income (see CHAPTER **42**). Companies generally pay corporation tax instead of income tax (see CHAPTER **3**).

Income tax is charged broadly on the income of UK residents, whether it arises in the UK or abroad, subject to special rules for individuals who are not domiciled in the UK. Non-residents are liable to income tax only on income that arises in the UK. Double tax relief is available where income is taxed both in the UK and abroad. A statutory residence test was introduced from 2013–14 to clarify the rules regarding whether or not individuals are resident in the UK for tax purposes (see **41.5**). Overseas aspects are discussed in CHAPTER **41**.

Rates of tax payable by individuals (ITA 2007, ss 6–21; FA 2017, ss 1–4, 11 and Sch 5; Scotland Act 1998, s 80C; Scotland Act 2016, ss 12, 13)

[2.4] The rates of tax payable depend on the type of income, which for this purpose is divided into three classes, namely dividends, other savings income and non-savings income.

From 2016–17 the Scottish Parliament has had the power to set a Scottish rate of income tax for Scottish taxpayers. It is not a devolved tax, but forms part of the UK income tax system and HMRC will continue to administer and collect it. The definition of a Scottish taxpayer is based on the location of an individual's main place of residence. The rate is charged on non-savings income only (see **2.23**). For 2016–17 the rate was calculated by reducing the basic, higher and additional rates of income tax levied by the UK Government by 10 pence in the pound and adding the Scottish rate of 10% which meant no change from the UK rates. From 2017–18 the Scottish Parliament can set its own income tax rates and bands and for 2017–18 the rates remain unchanged from the UK rates (though the basic rate band to be set against non-savings income is different — see **2.5**). A Scottish taxpayer's non-savings income is subject to the Scottish rates first, savings income is then subject to the appropriate UK main rate(s) and dividend income is subject to the appropriate UK dividend rate(s).

The tax will remain covered by existing UK double taxation agreements. Trusts retain their current UK or non-UK residence status and are taxed at UK rates where appropriate, although trust or estate income of an individual Scottish beneficiary is chargeable to the Scottish rate. For further details regarding the application of the tax see www.gov.uk/scottish-rate-income-tax.

Tax rates — 2017–18

[2.5] For 2017–18 the UK (i.e. non-Scottish) rates of income tax on non-savings income are:

- the basic rate of 20% on the first £33,500;
- the higher rate of 40% on income above the 'basic rate limit' of £33,500 and up to the 'higher rate limit' of £150,000; and
- the additional rate of 45% on income above the 'higher rate limit' of £150,000.

For 2017–18 the Scottish rates of income tax on non-savings income are:

- the basic rate of 20% on the first £31,500;
- the higher rate of 40% on income above the 'basic rate limit' of £31,500 and up to the 'higher rate limit' of £150,000; and
- the additional rate of 45% on income above the 'higher rate limit' of £150,000.

The UK basic rate band of £33,500 still applies to Scottish taxpayers' savings and dividend income, and also to determine the capital gains tax rates (see **4.2**). So it is possible for a Scottish taxpayer to be liable at 40% on their non-savings income where this exceeds £43,000 (personal allowance of £11,500 plus Scottish basic rate band of £31,500) but at only 20% on savings income.

> *Example 1*
>
> In 2017–18 a Scottish taxpayer has a salary of £43,500 and £2,000 savings income. Their tax payable is as follows:
>
> | | £ |
> |---|---|
> | Salary | 43,500 |
> | Savings income | 2,000 |
> | | 45,500 |

Personal allowance				(11,500)
Taxable income				34,000
Tax payable:	Salary	31,500	@ 20%	6,300
		500	@ 40%	200
	Savings income	500	@ 0%	
		1,000	@ 20%	200
		500	@ 40%	200
		34,000		6,900

The Scottish basic rate band applied to the salary is £31,500 leaving £500 taxable at 40%. The taxpayer is a higher rate taxpayer when taking into account the UK basic rate band so he is entitled to a savings allowance of £500 (see below). After taking account of the salary and savings allowance there is £1,000 remaining of the UK basic rate band of £33,500 to allocate to the savings income.

There is a 0% 'starting rate for savings', which applies to savings income other than dividends. It applies to so much of income, up to a 'starting rate limit' of £5,000, as is savings income. However, for this purpose savings income is treated as the highest part of total income, except where an individual has dividend income, in which case the dividend income is treated as the highest part. There are also exceptions in relation to tax payable on certain lump sum termination payments and benefits (see **15.6**) and on a chargeable event gain on a life policy (see **40.5**). This means that this 0% rate will apply only if the £5,000 band is not already used against non-savings income such as earnings and pensions.

From 2016–17 a 'savings nil rate' applies to an individual's savings income which is within their 'savings allowance' (referred to by HMRC as the personal savings allowance, see www.gov.uk/government/publications/personal-savings-allowance-factsheet/personal-savings-allowance). The savings allowance is not a deduction in arriving at total income or taxable income so is perhaps better thought of as a savings nil rate band. It is £1,000 per year for basic rate taxpayers and £500 for higher rate taxpayers. It is not available to additional rate taxpayers. Note that if dividend income is chargeable at 'the dividend nil rate' (see below) but would otherwise have been chargeable at the dividend upper or additional rate, it is treated as if it had been chargeable at that upper or additional rate in order to determine the amount (if any) of the savings allowance. Where applicable, the savings nil rate applies to savings income not already covered by other allowances, such as the personal allowance (see **2.15**) or the 0% starting rate for savings.

Example 2 illustrates the interaction between the 0% starting rate for savings and the savings nil rate. See also Examples 4 and 5 in **2.27** which include the dividend allowance.

Example 2

In 2017–18 tax will be charged at the rates shown below where the taxable income is £6,500 (the non-savings income having been reduced by the personal allowance) and it includes savings income of (a) £1,500 and (b) £2,000.

	(a) £		(b) £	
Non-savings income	5,000	@ 20%	4,500	@ 20%
Savings income in the 'starting rate for savings' band			500	@ 0%
Savings income covered by the savings allowance	1,000	@ 0%	1,000	@ 0%
Balance of taxable savings income	500	@ 20%	500	@ 20%
Taxable income	6,500		6,500	

In short, the 0% starting rate for savings is not available where non-savings income exceeds the amount of the personal allowances plus £5,000. However, the savings allowance is still available to basic rate and higher rate taxpayers.

As a consequence of the introduction of the savings allowance and the savings nil rate, from 6 April 2016 there is no longer a requirement for banks, building societies and some other institutions to deduct tax from the interest and other returns they make on certain savings income (see **2.9**). This interest is therefore paid gross to all savers. In addition from 6 April 2017 the requirement to deduct tax from interest distributions from open-ended investment companies, authorised unit trusts and investment trust companies and from interest on peer-to-peer loans has been removed. Tax is still deducted from certain payments of interest made to individuals by companies (see **3.23**).

Savings income not within the savings nil rate is taxed at the appropriate rate depending on which band of income it falls in — 20%, 40% or 45%.

Also from 2016–17 a 'dividend nil rate' applies to dividends within the 'dividend allowance', which is £5,000 per year for basic, higher and additional rate taxpayers. The dividend allowance is not a deduction in arriving at total income or taxable income so is perhaps better thought of as a dividend nil rate band. Where dividends exceed the dividend allowance the rates applying are 7.5% (called the dividend ordinary rate) on income up to the basic rate limit, 32.5% (the dividend upper rate) on income above the basic rate limit up to the higher rate limit, and 38.1% (the dividend additional rate) on income above the higher rate limit — see **2.22** to **2.26**. Dividends received by pension funds that are exempt from tax (see **16.10**), and dividends received on shares held in an ISA (see **36.16**) continue to be tax-free.

September 2017 Finance Bill which is expected to receive Royal Assent in November 2017 includes legislation to reduce the dividend nil rate to £2,000 from 2018–19 onwards.

Tax rates — earlier years

[2.6] For 2016–17 the rates of income tax on non-savings income were:

- the basic rate of 20% on the first £32,000;
- the higher rate of 40% on income above the 'basic rate limit' of £32,000 and up to the 'higher rate limit' of £150,000; and
- the additional rate of 45% on income above the 'higher rate limit' of £150,000.

The starting rate for savings was 0% up to the limit of £5,000 and the savings nil rate and dividend nil rate applied. The dividend ordinary rate (see **2.5**) was 7.5%, the dividend upper rate was 32.5% and the dividend additional rate was 38.1%.

Calculating taxable income (ITA 2007 ss 22–32)

[2.7] The tax year runs from 6 April in one year to 5 April in the next, the current year from 6 April 2017 to 5 April 2018 being known as 2017–18.

Taxable income is broadly worked out by adding together the amounts under the headings listed below to arrive at 'total income', then deducting certain reliefs (for example for trade losses or interest payments, see **2.13** and **2.14**) to arrive at 'net income', then deducting the personal allowance (and blind person's allowance if relevant) to arrive at the income on which tax is calculated at the rates indicated in **2.5**.

There is then an entitlement to deduct from the calculated amount certain 'tax reductions' which save a specified amount of tax. Tax reductions include married couple's allowance (see **2.19**) and transferable tax allowance (see **2.17**), and double tax relief (see **41.20**), which is deducted after all other tax reductions. The resulting amount is the income tax liability for the year, unless there is a liability to pay additional tax under a specific provision, such as where the amount of tax treated as deducted from gift aid donations made exceeds the tax liability for the year (see **43.18**), or the high income child benefit charge applies (see **10.7**). In that event the appropriate amount is added to arrive at the final income tax liability.

Unless there is a specific provision to the contrary, reliefs, allowances and tax reductions are deducted in the way which results in the lowest tax bill, as illustrated later in this chapter.

The main headings under which income is charged are as follows:

- Employment income, pensions and some social security benefits (see CHAPTERS **10** to **17**).
- Trading income, including profits from trades, professions or vocations (see CHAPTERS **18** to **29**).
- Property income (see CHAPTERS **30** to **32**).
- Savings and investment income (see CHAPTERS **36** to **40**).
- Miscellaneous income (see **19.1**).

The amount chargeable is sometimes affected by the taxpayer's residence and domicile. The meaning of these terms and their effect on UK tax liability is dealt with in CHAPTER **41**.

How is tax collected?

[2.8] Tax is collected from most individuals without the need for any direct contact with HMRC. The most common sources of income are earnings from employment, savings interest and dividends on shares. Tax on earnings, and on occupational and personal pensions, is collected through the Pay As You Earn (PAYE) system (see CHAPTER 10). Tax on some small items of other income received in full (such as interest from National Savings income bonds) may be collected through an adjustment in the PAYE code.

Deduction of tax from savings income

[2.9] As explained in 2.5 there is no longer a requirement for deduction of tax at source from most savings income, though tax is still deducted from certain payments of interest made to individuals by companies. Tax is not deducted from interest on any security issued by a company that is listed on a stock exchange (including building society permanent interest-bearing shares), nor from most interest on gilt-edged securities — see **36.8**, **37.4** and **38.4**.

[2.10] There are various finance arrangements, in particular those designed to meet the requirements of Islamic law, that do not involve paying or receiving interest but have a similar effect. Special rules equate the tax treatment of such payments and receipts with the treatment of interest.

[2.11] A dividend allowance of £5,000 (proposed to be reduced to £2,000 from 2018–19) is available to set against dividends received and any balance is taxable at the dividend rates outlined in **2.5**.

Companies sometimes give shareholders the opportunity of taking shares instead of dividends (i.e. scrip dividends). The shareholders are treated as receiving dividends.

Paying tax directly to HMRC

[2.12] A minority of employees and pensioners, and all self-employed people, are required to fill in tax returns (see **9.2**) and pay some or all of their income tax directly to HMRC. Taxpayers liable to the high income child benefit charge are also required to make a return (see **10.7**), as are those with capital gains above the annual exempt amount (see **4.29**), who must pay the tax directly. Tax that is due to be paid direct to HMRC is normally collected by means of two half-yearly payments on account, payable on 31 January in the tax year and the next 31 July, based on the total income tax payable directly for the previous tax year. A balancing payment, plus the first payment on account for the following tax year, is payable on the next 31 January. Any capital gains tax due is included in the balancing payment. This is dealt with in more detail at **9.4**. See also **2.32**.

From 2016–17 a simple assessment system applies for certain taxpayers. This is part of the Government's commitment to abolish tax returns for millions of individuals and small businesses by the introduction of digital tax accounts. For full details see **9.2**.

Deductions (TA 1988, ss 365, 369; ITA 2007, Pts 2, 5, 5B, 6, 7, 8; FA 2004, ss 188–195A)

[2.13] Certain payments made are allowable as reliefs in arriving at 'net income' (see 2.7), saving tax at the top rate, subject to a cap for various reliefs for 2013–14 onwards. The deductible reliefs are listed in ITA 2007, s 24 and include items such as trade losses and allowable interest payments (but not personal and blind person's allowances, which are deducted from net income (see 2.15)).

The allowable interest payments dealt with in 2.14 (other than home income plan interest, see below) are made in full (i.e. without deduction of tax), and relief is given by having the PAYE tax code adjusted or in working out the self-assessment or simple assessment (see 9.2).

An individual is entitled to tax relief on pension contributions paid under an occupational or personal pension scheme, subject to a contributions limit of the higher of 100% of 'relevant earnings' and £3,600 gross, and overriding annual and lifetime allowances. For further details see CHAPTERS 16 and 17.

Pension contributions are not usually deducted as 'reliefs' in calculating net income. If an employee is in an occupational pension scheme, his contributions will reduce his taxable pay (but not his pay for NICs). As far as personal pension scheme contributions are concerned, employees pay the contributions net of basic rate tax, and any relief at higher rates to which they are entitled is given by means of a PAYE coding adjustment. Self-employed people and those without earned income also obtain basic rate relief by deducting it from their contributions, and relief at higher rates where relevant is given in their self-assessment or simple assessment.

Premiums on pre-1 July 1988 pension contracts (retirement annuity policies) may still be paid gross, in which case they reduce the taxpayer's taxable earnings, relief being given in the self-assessment or simple assessment, or by coding adjustment.

An individual can also save tax at the top rate if he gives quoted shares or securities, land and buildings, or certain other investments to charity (see 43.22). The amount of the net benefit to the charity, which is normally the market value of the investment, is deducted in arriving at net income.

Relief is also available at the top tax rate on all 'gift aid' cash donations to charities and registered community amateur sports clubs. The cash amount donated is treated as being paid net of basic rate tax and the individual normally retains the tax deducted as the tax relief. If he is taxable at higher rates (either on income or on capital gains), he will get the extra relief to which he is entitled by an adjustment in his coding, self-assessment or simple assessment. If the individual does not pay enough tax to allow him to retain all the tax relief on his charitable payments, he may have to account to HMRC for the shortfall — see 43.18.

Income tax relief applies from 6 April 2015 on irrecoverable peer to peer (P2P) loans. Relief is available where a person has made a P2P loan via a regulated P2P platform, and any outstanding amount of the principal of that loan has, on or after 6 April 2015, become irrecoverable. The amount of relief available is the amount originally lent, less any repayments of the loan principal already received. Where the original lender has assigned the right to recover the loan principal to another person in exchange for payment, the right to relief passes to the assignee, though the latter's claim is limited to the amount paid for the right to recover the loan principal, less any of the principal already recovered.

For loans that became irrecoverable between 6 April 2015 and 5 April 2016 a claim for relief against P2P income must be made (under the general time limit for claims, see **9.15**). However, for loans that become irrecoverable on or after 6 April 2016 relief is firstly given *automatically* against interest from other qualifying P2P loans held through the same platform. If any balance remains relief may be *claimed* against interest received from loans made through a different P2P platform. Finally, any unused relief may be claimed against interest received from loans made through P2P platforms in the four tax years following the year in which the amount became irrecoverable, earliest year first. Relief cannot be claimed against any other form of income. If no claim is made for loans that became irrecoverable before 6 April 2016 capital loss relief may be available (see **4.3**). From 6 April 2016 the income tax relief takes priority over capital loss relief. If any of the loan principal is subsequently recovered, it is treated as P2P interest received at the time of the recovery.

An individual is entitled to tax relief at a specified rate (a 'tax reduction' — see **2.7**) on certain other payments, the main ones being as follows:

Interest on the first £30,000 of a pre-9 March 1999 loan to a borrower aged 65 or over to buy a life annuity, the loan being secured on the borrower's home (home income plans — see **34.10**)	23%
Up to £3,260 of qualifying maintenance payments to former or separated spouse or civil partner where either spouse/partner was born before 6 April 1935 (see **34.4**)	10%
Venture Capital Trust (VCT) subscriptions up to £200,000 (see **29.49**)	30%
Enterprise Investment Scheme (EIS) subscriptions up to £1 million (see **29.30**)	30%
Seed Enterprise Investment Scheme (SEIS) subscriptions up to £100,000 (see **29.37**)	50%
Social Investment Tax Relief (SITR) investments of up to £1 million (see **29.55**)	30%
Amounts invested in Community Development Finance Institutions (CDFIs — see **29.54**), relief being 25% of the investment spread over five years, giving an annual relief of	5%
Married couple's allowance (see **2.19**)	10%
Transferable tax allowance (see **2.17**)	20%

The limited tax relief for the over 65s on interest paid on pre-March 1999 home income plans is usually given by deduction of tax before the payment is made. Maintenance payments, VCT, EIS, and SEIS subscriptions and SITR and

CDFI investments are paid in full and the tax saving is given by an adjustment in the coding, or self-assessment or simple assessment. The tax saved on such payments cannot exceed the tax payable on income.

There is a cap on certain income tax reliefs which an individual may deduct in their income tax calculation for 2013–14 onwards. The limit is the greater of £50,000 or 25% of the individual's adjusted total income for the tax year. Adjusted total income is the total income for the year, increased by any payroll giving deductions previously allowed (see **43.23**), but reduced by the gross amount of any pension contributions paid under deduction of tax at source, by the excess pension contributions where they qualify for excess relief under the net pay arrangements, and by the amount of the pension contributions where they qualify for relief on making a claim (see **16.14**).

The following income tax reliefs, taken together, will be limited to the extent that they can be relieved by individuals against general income:

(a) Trade loss relief against general income (see **25.6**);
(b) Early trade losses relief (see **25.8**);
(c) Post-cessation trade relief (see **21.10**);
(d) Property loss relief against general income (see **31.13** and **32.9**);
(e) Post-cessation property relief (see **32.10**);
(f) Employment loss relief (see **10.15**);
(g) Former employees deduction for liabilities (see **10.15**);
(h) Share loss relief on non-Enterprise Investment Schemes / Seed Enterprise Investment Schemes shares (see **38.23**);
(i) Losses on deeply discounted securities (see **38.35**);
(j) Qualifying loan interest (see **2.14**).

Example 3

A has adjusted total income in 2017–18 of £300,000 and his relief limit is £75,000 (25% of £300,000, being greater than £50,000). His payments and losses available for relief are as follows:

– Qualifying loan interest £40,000
– Property losses £45,000
– Trade losses £20,000

He decides to claim relief in 2017–18 for all the qualifying loan interest as he cannot use this relief in another year. He makes up the remainder of his limit by claiming £35,000 property losses in 2017–18, carrying forward the balance of £10,000 against 2018–19 total income. The trade loss is carried forward against future income of the same trade.

For losses, the year of loss must be considered when deciding whether the cap applies. The cap does apply where loss relief is claimed for a tax year before 2013–14 in relation to losses made in 2013–14 or later. However, it does not apply to property loss relief against general income arising from a loss made in 2012–13 where the loss is claimed against general income in 2013–14. The cap does not apply where the deduction is made from profits of the trade or business to which the relief relates (see Example 3 in **25.6**). Nor does it affect relief for losses attributable to overlap relief in the final tax year or on a change of accounting date (see **21.6**), or attributable to business premises renovation allowances (see **32.19**).

HMRC guidance can be found in Helpsheet HS204.

Allowable interest (TA 1988, ss 365, 369; ITA 2007, ss 24A, 383–412)

[2.14] See **2.13** regarding the cap that applies from 2013–14 on certain income tax reliefs, one of which is qualifying loan interest. The cap does not apply where the interest is deducted from the profits of the trade or business.

Interest relating to let property is usually deductible from rental income, saving tax at the top rate but from April 2017 this is restricted to the basic rate of tax on residential properties, although the restriction will be phased in over a four-year period so that the full restriction does not apply until 2020–21 (see **32.8**). Interest paid on business borrowings is usually deductible from business income (see **20.17**), saving tax at the top rate, but subject to a restriction where profits are calculated on the cash basis for small businesses (see **20.4**). Relief at the top tax rate may also be allowed (subject to the cap mentioned in **2.13**), the payments being deducted in arriving at the taxable income, for interest paid on a loan to:

(a) buy a partnership share, to introduce capital to a partnership or to lend money to it, providing that the individual is not a limited partner or a partner in an 'investment' limited liability partnership (i.e. one whose business consists wholly or mainly of making investments) and providing he is still a partner when the interest is paid. This relief is also available to salaried partners in certain circumstances (see **20.17** and **23.15**). Where profits of the partnership are calculated under the cash basis, either for small businesses (see **20.4**) or for property businesses (see **32.6**), relief is only available if the loan is used to buy a partnership share.

(b) buy shares in or lend money to a trading company controlled either by its directors or by five or fewer people (known as a close company), so long as, at the time the interest is paid, either the individual owns more than 5% of the issued ordinary share capital or he owns any part of the ordinary share capital, however small, and works for the greater part of his time in the management or conduct of the company or an associated company. If he or his spouse or civil partner has claimed income tax relief or capital gains deferral relief in respect of shares acquired under the Enterprise Investment Scheme (see CHAPTER **29**), he cannot also claim interest relief on a loan to buy the shares. From 2014–15 this relief is extended to interest paid by qualifying individuals investing in companies which are resident in the EEA (see **1.3**) other than the UK that would be close companies if they were resident in the UK.

See **32.8** regarding the restriction of interest from April 2017 on loans to invest in partnerships carrying on a property business where income is generated from a dwelling.

(c)   buy plant or machinery on which capital allowances are available for use in the individual's partnership (see **23.15**) or employment (see **10.15**). Where profits of the partnership are calculated under the cash basis, either for small businesses (see **20.4**) or for property businesses (see **32.6**), this relief is not available.

(d)   personal representatives of a deceased person to pay inheritance tax (see **42.4**).

(e)   acquire shares in an employee-controlled trading company. From 2014–15 this relief is extended to interest paid by qualifying individuals investing in such companies which are resident in the EEA (see **1.3**) other than the UK.

(f)   acquire one or more shares in, or to lend money to, a co-operative.

Relief under (a), (b), (e) and (f) is restricted if the shares are sold or the partnership, company or co-operative repays all or part of the loan, without the borrowing being reduced by an equivalent amount. Interest is allowable on loans which replace existing qualifying loans. Relief is only available as the interest is paid. It is not spread over the period of accrual and will not be allowed if it is never paid.

Bank overdraft interest is never allowed as a deduction from *total* income. Relief is only available where the overdraft is part of the funding of a trade or property letting and therefore allowable as an expense in arriving at trading or rental profits.

As indicated in **2.13**, relief is available for pre-9 March 1999 home income plan loans to the over 65s, interest on the first £30,000 of such loans qualifying for tax relief at 23% (not the basic rate of 20%). Relief for such interest continues if the individual moves home, or remortgages, or goes into a nursing home (see **34.10**).

There are provisions to block the artificial creation of allowable interest and to prevent tax relief being obtained on interest that would not otherwise qualify for tax relief by means of various devices such as converting the interest into an annuity.

See **2.10** for the treatment of special finance arrangements such as those designed to meet the requirements of Islamic law.

Personal reliefs (ITA 2007, Pt 3)

[2.15] In addition to claiming a deduction for particular payments etc. as indicated above, an individual may reduce his taxable income, or the amount of tax payable as the case may be, by certain personal reliefs, as detailed below. The amounts stated relate to the tax year 2017–18. For the rates of allowance for 2016–17, see the TABLE OF RATES AND ALLOWANCES (**TRA**) under 'Personal Reliefs'. Personal reliefs are available only to UK residents and specified categories of non-resident (see **41.36**).

The personal allowance and blind person's allowance are deducted from 'net income' (see **2.13**) and save tax at the top rate. This is subject to the restriction in the value of the personal allowance for individuals with income over £100,000 (see **2.16**). The married couple's allowance, which applies both to married couples and civil partners where certain conditions are satisfied, saves tax at only 10% and is given by reducing the amount of tax payable (but it cannot create a repayment) (see **2.19**). The transferable tax allowance (see **2.17**) also reduces the amount of tax payable. For the way in which relief is given under PAYE, see **10.61**.

An individual is not entitled to personal reliefs for any tax year for which he claims the remittance basis (see **41.16**).

Personal allowances (ITA 2007, ss 35–37, 55A–55D, 58)

[2.16] From 2016–17 there is one level of personal allowance for all individuals and for 2017–18 it is £11,500. In future, once the allowance reaches £12,500 the original intention is that it will be linked to the annual equivalent of 30 hours per week on the national minimum wage adult rate, though it is proposed to change this to being indexed by reference to the Consumer Price Index.

The amount of the personal allowance otherwise available is reduced where 'adjusted net income' (see **2.20**) exceeds £100,000. The reduction is one half of the excess until the allowance is reduced to nil. Therefore in 2017–18 where adjusted net income is £123,000 or above, no personal allowance will be due. See www.gov.uk/guidance/adjusted-net-income for HMRC examples of the calculations.

[2.17] An individual who is not liable to income tax above the basic rate is able to transfer £1,150 (£1,100 for 2016–17) of their personal allowance to their spouse or civil partner, provided the transferee is also not liable to income tax above the basic rate. Only the set amount can be transferred. If the election is made the transferor's personal allowance is reduced by the transferable amount and the transferee is entitled to a tax reduction of 20% (i.e. the basic rate) of the transferable amount (see **2.13**). If the transferee dies in the tax year the reduction still applies but the transferor's allowance is not reduced. Married couples or civil partnerships entitled to claim the married couple's allowance will not be entitled to make a transfer.

The election must be made by the transferor spouse or civil partner no later than four years after the end of the tax year to which it relates. If the conditions continue to be met, it will have effect for subsequent tax years until it is withdrawn, unless it was made after the end of the tax year to which it relates, in which case it only has effect for that year. A transferor can only withdraw the election with effect from the tax year following the one in which the withdrawal is made, unless the marriage or civil partnership comes to an end during the tax year of withdrawal. In that case the withdrawal has effect for the tax year in which it is made. The election ceases to have effect if the transferee spouse or civil partner does not obtain a tax reduction in a tax year, and the cessation applies from the following tax year. An individual cannot have more than one such tax reduction or election in a tax year, regardless of whether they are a party to more than one marriage or civil partnership.

Blind person's allowance (ITA 2007, ss 38–40)

[2.18] An allowance of £2,320 for 2017–18 is available to a person who is registered blind (in England and Wales) or is ordinarily resident in Scotland or Northern Ireland and unable because of blindness to do any work for which eyesight is essential. The allowance saves tax at the individual's top tax rate. A married couple or registered civil partners who are both blind may each claim the allowance. A married blind person or blind civil partner may transfer unused blind person's allowance to the spouse/partner (whether or not the spouse/partner is blind).

Married couple's allowance (ITA 2007, ss 42–55, 1011)

[2.19] Married couple's allowance is available to married couples and to civil partners, providing at least one spouse or partner was born before 6 April 1935 (i.e. was 65 before the start of tax year 2000–01) and they are living together in the tax year. The allowance for 2017–18 is £8,445 (but see 'income limit' in **2.20**) and it saves tax at 10%, not at the individual's top rate of tax.

A couple is treated as living together unless they are separated under a court order or by deed of separation, or they are separated in such circumstances that the separation is likely to be permanent. The married couple's allowance is given in full in the year of separation or death of either spouse/partner. If a separated couple become reconciled in a later tax year, the full married couple's allowance is available in the year of reconciliation (unless they had divorced or dissolved the civil partnership). If the reconciliation takes place in the same tax year as the separation, they will usually be taxed as if they had not been separated. When a spouse/partner dies, the surviving spouse/partner will get the benefit of any part of the allowance that has not been used by the deceased spouse/partner (see **33.13**).

Where a married couple has been entitled to the allowance since before 5 December 2005, the allowance is given to the husband (subject to any claim by his wife — see below). For marriages or civil partnership registrations taking place on or after that date, the allowance is based on the income of, and given to, the spouse or partner with the higher income (subject to a claim by the other spouse or partner).

A couple who were married before 5 December 2005 may elect for the new rules to apply to them instead of the old rules. However, where a wife has the higher income, the effect of the election may be a reduction in the tax saved.

The allowance is restricted if income exceeds a certain limit (see **2.20**) but it will not be reduced below a specified minimum amount (£3,260 for 2017–18).

A married woman (for pre-5 December 2005 marriages) or lower income spouse/partner (for marriages or civil partnership registrations on or after 5 December 2005) is entitled as of right to claim one half of a specified amount of the married couple's allowance (half of £3,260, i.e. £1,630 for 2017–18). The claim for the allowance must be made *before* the tax year in which it is first to apply (except in the year of marriage or registration when the claim may be made within that year). A claim in respect of 2018–19 must therefore be made by 5 April 2018. Claims must be made on Form 18, available on the GOV.UK website. The allowance will then be allocated in the chosen way until the claim is withdrawn. Alternatively the couple may jointly claim for an allowance equal to the whole of the specified amount, i.e. £3,260 to be given to the wife or lower income spouse/partner as the case may be. In either case the allowance available to the other spouse/civil partner is reduced accordingly.

Spouses and civil partners can use the transferred allowance to reduce any of their tax for the year, even if the tax relates to income arising before the marriage/civil partnership or after the date of separation or of the death of the other spouse or partner (see **33.13**).

If either spouse or civil partner pays insufficient tax to use the married couple's allowance, he/she may notify HMRC (not later than four years after the end of the relevant tax year) that the unused amount is to be transferred to the other spouse/partner. The unused amount is *not* transferred automatically. Provision for transferring surplus allowances is made in tax returns and notice of the transfer is given on Form 575, which is also available on the GOV.UK website.

The allowance starts in the year of marriage or registration as civil partners, but in that year the available allowance (after taking into account the income restriction where appropriate) is reduced by one-twelfth for each complete tax month (ending on the 5th) before the date of marriage/registration.

Since the allowance is given as a fixed amount of tax saving, transferring all or half of the specified amount from one to the other does not save tax overall unless one has insufficient income to pay tax. A transfer from one to the other may, however, improve cash flow if, say, one spouse or partner would get the reduction in the tax on self-employed profits that is paid half-yearly as part of the provisional and balancing payments under self-assessment or simple assessment whereas the other is an employee who would pay reduced PAYE tax from the beginning of the tax year.

Couples entitled to claim the married couple's allowance are not entitled to elect for the transferable tax allowance (see **2.17**).

Income limit

[2.20] As outlined in **2.16** the basic personal allowance is reduced by £1 for every £2 by which 'adjusted net income' exceeds £100,000. 'Adjusted net income' is 'net income' less the gross amount of charitable donations and pension contributions but disallowing any deductions for contributions to trade unions and police organisations. 'Net income' is total income less certain allowable reliefs as outlined in **2.13**. See www.gov.uk/guidance/adjusted-net-income.

The married couple's allowance is similarly reduced by half of the excess of income over £28,000, but it cannot fall below a specified minimum amount, which is £3,260 for 2017–18. For those who have been entitled to the allowance since before 5 December 2005 the amount available depends on the husband's income only. The wife's income is not taken into account, even if the allowance is given because of her date of birth rather than the husband's, or if the tax saving is transferred to the wife because the husband's income is too low to use it. This treatment does not apply to those marrying or registering as civil partners on or after 5 December 2005. The main person claiming the allowance will be the partner with the higher income, and it will be that person's income that will be taken into account to calculate any reduction in the married couple's allowance.

For detailed information on the tax treatment of senior citizens, see CHAPTER 34.

Pre-eminent gifts relief (FA 2012, s 49 and Sch 14; SI 2013/587)

[2.21] Tax relief is available for qualifying gifts to the nation of objects which are of pre-eminent national, scientific, historic, artistic, architectural or scenic interest. Following the gift via the relevant government minister, the objects may then be loaned or given by the minister to appropriate institutions, including certain charities and accredited museums, for safe-keeping and to provide public access. In return, donors will receive a reduction in their UK tax liability based on a percentage of the value of the object they are donating. The tax relief is available to individuals other than personal representatives and trustees, and to companies and the provisions apply in relation to liabilities for tax years and accounting periods beginning on or after 1 April 2012.

Although the taxpayer may make the offer of a gift, there is no guarantee that it will be accepted. To be a qualifying gift the taxpayer must be legally and beneficially entitled to the property which must not be held jointly or in common with others, the offer must be made, registered and accepted in accordance with the rules of the scheme, and the gift made accordingly. In determining whether the object offered will be accepted, the scheme rules are similar to those applying to the inheritance tax 'acceptance in lieu scheme' (see 5.53). Full details of the scheme, known as the 'cultural gift scheme' can be found at www.gov.uk/government/publications/guidance-on-the-cultural-gifts -scheme.

A potential donor will offer to give a pre-eminent object (or collection of objects) to the nation with a self-assessed valuation of the object. A panel of experts will consider the offer and, if it considers the object is pre-eminent and should be accepted, the panel will agree the value of the object with the donor. If the donor decides to proceed based on that valuation they will receive a tax reduction, which for individuals can be against income tax and/or capital gains tax, and for companies is against corporation tax, as a fixed percentage of the object's agreed value — 30% for individuals and 20% for companies. Individuals, but not companies, will be able to spread the tax reduction forward across a period of up to five years starting with the tax year in which the object is offered.

Gifts under the scheme are exempt from inheritance tax and capital gains tax.

Tax reductions under this scheme, and taxes offset under the existing inheritance tax acceptance in lieu scheme (5.53) are subject to a total annual limit of £30 million.

Calculating tax on taxable income (ITA 2007, Pt 2; ITTOIA 2005, ss 397, 863I; FA 2017, ss 1–4; Scotland Act 1998, s 80C; Scotland Act 2016, ss 12, 13)

[2.22] As indicated in 2.4, there are different rates of tax payable depending on whether the income is dividend income, other savings income or non-savings income. The main types of income within each of these three categories are as follows.

Non-savings income

[2.23] The possible rates for 2017–18: basic rate/ Scottish basic rate 20%, higher rate/ Scottish higher rate 40%, additional rate/ Scottish additional rate 45%.

Non-savings income:

- Income from employment and self-employment;
- Pensions from the state and from occupational and personal pension schemes;
- Taxable social security benefits (see **10.6**);
- Property income.

[2.24] The income chargeable at the 'non-savings income' rates includes both interest and dividends from abroad taxable on the 'remittance basis' which is applicable to someone who is resident but not domiciled in the UK. Such individuals are not taxed on such foreign income unless it is brought into the UK (see **41.16**).

From 2014–15 certain partnership profits relating to alternative investment fund managers are automatically charged at the additional rate (see **23.5**).

Savings income other than dividends

[2.25] The possible rates for 2017–18: starting rate for savings 0%, savings nil rate 0%, basic rate 20%, higher rate 40%, additional rate 45%.

Savings income other than dividends:

- Interest arising on bank and building society accounts, gilt-edged securities, private loans etc., both in the UK and abroad (other than that charged on the remittance basis as indicated above);
- The income element of a purchased life annuity (see **34.7**);
- Profits from deeply discounted securities (see **38.35**);
- Accrued income charges on the sale/purchase of interest-bearing securities (see **36.11**);

- Chargeable event gains on life policies on which an individual or personal representatives of a deceased individual are liable to income tax (see **40.5**).

Dividend income

[2.26] The possible rates for 2017–18: dividend nil rate 0%, dividend ordinary rate 7.5%, dividend upper rate 32.5% and dividend additional rate 38.1%.

UK and foreign dividends (other than that charged on the remittance basis as indicated above).

Taxable income, deductions and allowances

[2.27] The legislation treats savings income as the top slice of the taxable income apart from dividend income (subject to the exceptions mentioned below). An illustration of how this works is in Example 4.

Example 4

In 2017–18 tax will be charged at the rates shown below where a taxpayer's taxable income is as indicated. The savings allowance and dividend allowance apply (see **2.5**), the non-savings income has been reduced by the personal allowance and the additional rate does not apply as the income does not exceed £150,000.

	(a) £			(b) £			(c) £		
Non-savings income	1,000		@ 20%	17,000		@ 20%	24,500		@ 20%
Non-dividend savings income	4,000	*	@ 0%						
	1,000	**	@ 0%	1,000	**	@ 0%	500	**	@ 0%
	10,000		@ 20%	4,000		@ 20%	7,500		
	16,000			22,000			32,500		
Dividends	3,000	***	@ 0%	3,500	***	@ 0%	1,000	***	@ 0%
							33,500		
							4,000	***	@ 0%
Dividends (balance)							2,000		@ 32.5%
Taxable income	19,000			25,500			39,500		

* In (a) the non-dividend savings income is £15,000 and there is £4,000 of the 0% 'starting rate for savings' band of £5,000 (see **2.5**) available to be allocated against that income.

** The savings allowance (see 2.5) is £1,000 in (a) and (b) because it is a basic rate taxpayer, and £500 in (c) because it is a higher rate taxpayer. Savings income within the allowance is subject to the savings nil rate.

*** Total dividends in (a) and (b) are within the dividend allowance (see 2.5) and therefore subject to the dividend nil rate. Total dividends in (c) are £7,000, of which £5,000 are covered by the dividend allowance. The balance of £2,000 is taxable at the dividend upper rate of 32.5% because they all fall into the higher rate band.

There are two instances where savings income is not treated as the top slice of income, namely the receipt of a lump sum taxed under the 'golden handshake' rules (see **15.6**) and a chargeable event gain on a life policy (see **40.5**).

Before applying the different tax rates to income in the order shown in Example 4, however, it is necessary to decide which sources of income have been reduced by deductions and allowances and to what extent. Deductions and allowances can be set against income in the order that saves most tax, which normally means setting them against non-savings income first, then savings income other than dividends, then dividends. However, following the introduction of the savings allowance and dividend allowance it may be more beneficial to allocate some of the personal allowance to dividends, as illustrated in Example 5.

Example 5

In 2017–18 a taxpayer has a salary of £9,500, savings income of £7,200 and dividend income of £8,000. The personal allowance is allocated first to the salary and then to the savings income.

	£	£	£	Tax payable
	9,500	7,200	8,000	
Less personal allowance	(9,500)	(2,000)		
		5,200		
Income within the 0% starting rate for savings band		—	(5,000)	
Income within the savings allowance / dividend allowance		(200)	(5,000)	
		—	3,000 @7.5%	£225

If only sufficient of the remaining personal allowance after allocation to salary is allocated to the savings income to allow the full savings allowance to be utilised the tax payable is reduced by £60 as follows.

	£	£	£	Tax payable
	9,500	7,200	8,000	
Less personal allowance	(9,500)	(1,200)	(800)	

	6,000	7,200		
Income within the 0% starting rate for savings band	—	(5,000)		
Income within the savings allowance / dividend allowance	(1,000)	(5,000)		
	—	2,200	@7.5%	£165

Effect of rate charging structure on marginal tax rates

[2.28] The complex rate charging structure means that although the higher rate of tax is 40%, the marginal rate of tax payable if taxable income increases may be higher than that, as illustrated in Example 6.

Example 6

An individual non-Scottish taxpayer has taxable income in 2017–18 of £33,500 (i.e. equal to the basic rate limit) as follows:

		£
Salary		39,000
Dividends		6,000
		45,000
Personal allowance		(11,500)
Taxable income		33,500

Tax payable:	Salary	27,500	@ 20%	5,500
	Dividends covered by dividend allowance	5,000	@ 0%	—
	Dividends balance	1,000	@ 7.5%	75
		33,500		£5,575

If his dividends increase by £100, these will fall into the dividend upper rate and an extra £32.50 tax will be payable. If, however, the *salary* increases by £100, the extra salary will be taxed at 20% but £100 of the dividends will again fall into the dividend upper rate and be taxed at 32.5% instead of 7.5%, so that the total tax on the extra £100 will be the £20 on salary plus the net £25 on dividends — £45, giving a marginal tax rate of 45%.

If the taxable salary had already been above the basic rate limit, extra salary would cost extra tax of 40% and extra dividends would cost extra tax of 32.5%.

Looked at from the opposite point of view, the marginal rates of tax illustrated in Example 6 will be *saved* by making a payment qualifying for tax relief (such as a personal pension contribution or a gift aid donation to charity) so that taxable income moves from a point above the basic rate limit to a point below it. Where the taxpayer is entitled to tax credits (see **2.34** onwards) the payment would also reduce income for tax credits purposes, possibly saving a further 41% (see Example 9 in **2.41**).

Losses from miscellaneous transactions (ITA 2007, ss 152–155, 1016)

[2.29] An individual, or a partnership of which he is a member, may make a claim for loss relief if a loss is sustained in a miscellaneous transaction (i.e. one which falls within ITA 2007, s 1016). The relief is denied where the loss arises as a result of relevant tax avoidance arrangements on or after 3 December 2014. In addition, from 6 April 2015 the relief may only be given against 'relevant miscellaneous income', i.e. miscellaneous income that is chargeable to income tax in the same tax year under, or by virtue of, the same provision as that under which the loss would have been chargeable had it been profits or other income instead of a loss. Any unrelieved loss is carried forward against any relevant miscellaneous income in future years.

Relief must be claimed within four years of the end of the tax year of loss, but a separate claim may be made within the time limit in relation to the question of whether, and if so how much, loss relief should be given. The relief does not arise from offshore life insurance policies.

Payment of tax, interest and penalties on tax paid late and interest on tax overpaid (TMA 1970, Pts VA and IX, and Sch 3ZA; TA 1988, s 824; FA 2009, ss 101, 102 and Schs 53, 54, 56)

[2.30] As indicated in **2.8**, much of the tax due on income is deducted before the income is received, under the PAYE system for employees and those receiving occupational and personal pensions.

Tax that is not deducted at source in this way is payable to HMRC separately (see **9.2**). Interest and penalties (see **9.56** and **9.71**) are charged on tax paid late, and HMRC pays interest on tax overpaid. The interest rates are adjusted in line with commercial interest rates — for details of recent rates see the TABLE OF RATES AND ALLOWANCES (**TRA**). Interest on unpaid tax is not deductible in calculating the tax liability, and tax is not due on any interest received on overpaid tax.

A claim that results in tax relief being given in relation to an earlier tax year (e.g. because of a claim to carry back a trading loss in a new business — see **25.8**) takes effect by means of an adjustment to the tax liability for the year of claim, so that interest is payable only by reference to the balancing payment date (see **2.12**) for the claim year. For example, where a claim is made in 2017–18 affecting the tax liability of 2014–15, the repayment would be calculated according to the 2014–15 tax position, but interest would be payable only from 31 January 2019. Carry-back claims also have an anomalous effect in relation to payments on account (see **9.16**).

[2.31] If an individual is required to fill in a self-assessment tax return he is also required to work out his tax liability. However, HMRC will do the calculation if a paper return is filed by 31 October after the end of the tax year. If the return is filed online, the calculation is done automatically.

HMRC are able to 'determine' the tax owed if a return is not submitted, but their tax figure will be replaced by the self-assessment when it is received. If HMRC enquire into a return, the taxpayer has the right to appeal against any amendments they make to the figures, and also to apply to postpone payment of any disputed amount until the appeal is settled.

In some circumstances claims are made separately from returns and there is a right to appeal against HMRC amendments to such claims, although not to postpone payment of the tax. From 2016–17 onwards a simple assessment regime applies — see **9.2**. There are some other limited circumstances where HMRC still issue assessments outside the self-assessment system and tax on such assessments is payable 30 days after the issue of the assessment. Interest on such assessments, however, runs from 31 January following the tax year to which the assessment relates, regardless of when the assessment was issued. Apart from such exceptions, HMRC will not make assessments themselves unless they discover that tax has been underpaid through a taxpayer's omission brought about carelessly or deliberately, or because of inadequate disclosure of information (see **9.46**). See CHAPTER 9 for detailed information on appeal and postponement procedures, claims made outside returns and HMRC enquiries.

[2.32] Payments on account are payable for the current tax year on 31 January in the tax year and 31 July following the tax year, each payment equal to half the total net income tax and self-employed Class 4 NICs (see **24.6**) payable for the previous tax year *unless* the amount due is less than the limits stated below. The balance of tax due, including capital gains tax and from 2015–16 Class 2 NICs (see below) if any, should then be paid on the following 31 January, or a refund claimed if tax has been overpaid. At any time before that 31 January date a claim may be made to reduce the payments on account (or get a refund) if the taxpayer thinks the current year's tax will be lower (subject to penalties if the claim has a careless or deliberate inaccuracy). Interest is charged on underpaid payments on account and balancing payments from the due dates, and HMRC pay interest on tax overpaid from the date of the overpayment to the date of repayment.

If a claim is made to reduce payments on account, under the harmonised interest regime (see **9.56**), late payment interest will be charged from the due dates on any shortfall compared with the lesser of (i) the total of each reduced payment on account and 50% of the balancing payment (excluding capital gains tax and student loan repayments), and (ii) the amount of tax that would have been payable as a payment on account if the claim to reduce their payments on account had not been made. If the final income tax bill is less than the payments on account (net of any repayments already claimed), HMRC will pay interest on half of the difference from the date each payment on account was made.

Example 7

Assume payments on account are made on the due dates. Total income tax payable directly to HMRC for 2016–17 is £15,000, so that the payments on account for 2017–18 should be £7,500 on each of 31 January 2018 and 31 July 2018. The due date for the final payment/repayment is 31 January 2019.

Scenario (a)
If no claim is made to adjust payments on account, no interest will be charged on them if final tax exceeds £15,000; if final tax is less than £15,000, repayment interest will be paid on half of the difference from each of the 31 January 2018 and 31 July 2018 payment dates.

Scenario (b)
The taxpayer made a claim to reduce the payments on account to £6,000 each. The final tax liability for 2017–18 is £16,000 and the taxpayer makes the final balancing payment of £4,000 on the due date of 31 January 2019.

Each payment on account that the taxpayer should have made is equal to the lesser of (i) the amount of the payment on account, plus half of the balancing payment (£8,000), and (ii) the amount of tax which would have been payable as a payment on account if the claim to reduce the payments on account had not been made (£7,500). Therefore, the taxpayer should have made two payments on account of £7,500, and late payment interest is calculated on the difference between this amount and the amount actually paid in each case of £6,000. Thus late payment interest is charged on £1,500 from the due date in each case (31 January 2018 or 31 July 2018) until the date the balancing payment is paid (31 January 2019).

A taxpayer does not have to make payments on account if the previous year's income tax bill (excluding tax deducted at source) was below £1,000, or if more than 80% of the tax due was collected at source.

Where there is a repayment of tax deducted at source (including over-deductions under PAYE), repayment interest is payable from 31 January following the relevant tax year.

From 2015–16 Class 2 NICs are also due through the self-assessment system no later than 31 January following the tax year, though some self-employed earners do not pay through self-assessment and will be sent a bill by HMRC (see **24.2**).

HMRC have a statutory power to withdraw a notice to file a self-assessment for individuals, partnerships and trustees (see **9.13**). Where a further notice to file is issued after the withdrawal of a notice, it is treated as if it were the original notice to file for the purposes of the payment dates for income tax and capital gains tax, so the payment dates are unchanged.

The Government proposes that from April 2019 a payment on account of any capital gains tax due on the disposal of residential property will be required to be made within 30 days of the completion of the disposal.

Repayment claims

[2.33] People often overpay tax because, for example, tax has been deducted at source from much of their income and they have not received the full benefit of their personal allowances and/or lower rates of tax, or because they have incurred losses in a business that can be set against income on which tax has been paid. They are entitled to claim repayment of the overpaid amount, although many of those entitled do not put in claims. From 6 April 2016 some of the need for repayment claims has been removed because tax is no longer deducted at source from most savings income (see **2.5**).

Example 8

A taxpayer has income in 2017–18 comprising an occupational pension of £19,900 from which £2,000 has been deducted under PAYE, and bank interest of £1,200. Tax can be reclaimed as follows:

			Tax paid
		£	£
Pensions		19,900	2,000
Bank interest	1,200		
Less savings allowance (see **2.5**)	(1,000)	200	
		20,100	
Less personal allowance		(11,500)	
Taxable income		8,600	
Tax thereon @ 20%			1,720
Repayment due			£280

If the repayment is made after 31 January 2019, HMRC would pay repayment interest from that date.

If a taxpayer does not receive a tax return, he may use form R40 to claim repayment. The general time limit for making a repayment claim (i.e. where no specific time limit applies) is four years from the end of the tax year. For claims by expatriates see **41.36**. See also www.gov.uk/claim-tax-refund for further advice.

Vouchers or certificates of tax deducted where applicable do not need to be sent with a claim, but must be kept for a specified period (see **9.32**).

Tax credits (TCA 2002)

[2.34] The main legislation relating to child tax credits and working tax credit is contained in the Tax Credits Act 2002, but most of the detail is contained in statutory instruments. Although tax credits are welfare benefits, they are administered by HMRC and guidance is available at www.gov.uk/b rowse/benefits/tax-credits. The Welfare Reform Act 2012 introduced universal credit which is a new benefit to replace the current complex system of working-age benefits and tax credits (see **10.6**). The process of moving claimants on to universal credit will be gradual and should be completed by 2021.

To qualify for tax credits, the individual must be aged 16 or over and must normally live in the UK (although some non-residents qualify, and from 1 July 2014 there is a three-month residency qualification for child tax credit). For married couples, civil partners, couples living together as husband and wife and co-habiting same-sex couples, a joint claim must be made. Claims must be made via the GOV.UK website. Whether a person can make a new tax credit claim depends on the status of universal credit in their area, and they may have to claim the latter instead.

Tax credits are means-tested, so they are progressively withdrawn from claimants with incomes above a stipulated income threshold. The rate of withdrawal where income exceeds the threshold is 41%.

Generally payments of tax credit are not backdated for more than one month, except in certain cases of disability or for those seeking asylum, so claims for 2017–18 should have been made by 5 May 2017.

The amount of the tax credit for a tax year is initially based on the previous year's income. After the end of the tax year, the claim is finalised on the basis of either the previous year's income or the current year's income (i.e. the income for the year of the claim) depending on changes in income levels. There is an income rise disregard of £2,500 and an income fall disregard of £2,500.

After the end of the tax year HMRC send claimants a renewal notice. For claimants entitled to only the family element of child tax credit (see **2.40**), the award will be automatically renewed and they only have to respond to the renewal notice if their income and/or personal circumstances have changed. Other claimants must confirm or amend the information in the notice by 31 July following the tax year, or the payment of tax credits may stop. As far as income is concerned, where final figures are not available at that date, an estimate must be given, with the final figures being notified by the following 31 January at the latest (i.e. by 31 January 2018 for 2016–17). A penalty may be charged if the declaration is not submitted (see **2.38**). For HMRC guidance which explains how the tax credit annual review process works and advises the action which should be taken at various times, see www.gov.uk/renewing-yo ur-tax-credits-claim.

Definition of income

[2.35] Income for tax credit purposes equates fairly closely with taxable income, but there are many differences both in the income and the deductions that may be made. Where there are joint claimants, joint income is taken into account.

The first £300 of the total income (or the joint total income for joint claimants) that falls within one or more of five categories is ignored. Those categories are pension income, investment income (which includes chargeable event gains on life policies), property income, foreign income and notional income.

Notional income covers amounts that are specifically included in taxable income, such as premiums on let property and scrip dividends, and also income someone has deliberately deprived himself or herself of, or failed to apply for, or could have received for services he or she provided (other than for voluntary or charitable bodies) cheaply or without charge.

If a trading loss is incurred in the year, it is deducted from the total income of the claimant (or the combined total income where there are joint claimants) for that year. Any balance of loss not relieved against the total income of the current year is carried forward to set against the *trading* income in future years. (Note that losses may be treated differently for income tax, and different rules apply for Class 4 NICs (see CHAPTER 25).)

Notification of changes in income

[2.36] A claimant is not *required* to notify changes in income levels during the tax year. He is, however, required to notify certain other changes in circumstances (see **2.38**). If he does not notify changes in income, then when he sends in his renewal notice showing the actual amount his entitlement for the year will be revised subject to certain disregards of changes in income level.

Any overpayment is normally recovered from future tax credits or, if that is not possible, by direct payment to HMRC (see HMRC's Code of Practice booklet COP 26). An overpayment may be collected by a deduction from benefit or by direct earnings attachment. In future HMRC will be able to recover overpayments of working tax credit from child tax credit payments and vice versa.

For self-employed people, the current income (based normally on the profits of the accounting year ended in the tax year — see **21.2**) will not be known early enough to decide whether credits will be available, and as indicated in **2.34**, awards are not backdated for more than one month. The self-employed should therefore make claims at the appropriate time, even though their previous year's income would not give them any entitlement. HMRC will then issue a nil award, which will be adjusted after the end of the tax year in the light of actual income and any other change in circumstances. HMRC are obliged to permit such 'protective claims'.

Calculation of entitlement

[2.37] HMRC provide an online calculator to calculate roughly how much tax credit an individual might be entitled to, see www.gov.uk/tax-credits-calculator. Where entitlement starts or ends part way through the year, or circumstances change during the year, the year will be split into 'relevant periods', with the maximum available credits for each period being calculated according to the daily amounts for the credits available in the period multiplied by the number of days in each period.

Income is calculated over the whole year and then apportioned on a time basis to each of the relevant periods. The relevant income thresholds for withdrawing credits are similarly reduced according to the days in each relevant period. The credits due for each period are then added together to give the total credit award for the year. For simplicity, annual figures are used in the rest of this section.

Changes in circumstances, interest and penalties

[2.38] Certain changes in circumstances may be notified in advance, such as where someone expects to start work within seven days, or where a child nearing age 16 is going to continue in non-advanced full-time education (see 2.40).

The following changes in circumstances *must* be notified via the GOV.UK website within one month after the date of the change, or within one month after becoming aware of the change (except for changes under (f), where this later date does not apply):

(a)   A claimant no longer counts as a single claimant, or is no longer part of a claimant couple.

(b)   One member of a claimant couple goes abroad either permanently or for longer than a specified period.

(c)   Approved childcare costs either cease or decrease by £10 or more a week for more than four consecutive weeks, or there are certain changes involving the childcare provider in particular with regard to their registration or approval.

(d)   A claimant's working hours fall to less than 16 or 30 hours a week (or 24 hours a week jointly for a couple) as the case may be (see **2.39**).

(e)   A claimant ceases to be responsible for one or more children.

(f)   A child ceases to be a qualifying child (other than by reaching age 20).

(g)   A child dies. Child tax credit continues for eight weeks following the child's death, or until the date the child would have reached age 20 if earlier.

Registration of a same-sex couple as a civil partnership, or entering into an unregistered same-sex partnership, comes within heading (a).

Other changes in circumstances need not be notified immediately, but if they increase the tax credits payable the increase will not be backdated for more than one month and if they decrease the credits they take effect from the date of the change.

A penalty of up to £300 may be imposed for failure to notify within the time limit. A penalty of up to £300 may also be imposed for failing to provide information or evidence relating to a claim, including failing to submit the year-end renewal notice. If the failure continues, a further penalty of up to £60 a day may be charged. A penalty of up to £3,000 may be charged for fraudulent or negligent claims. Interest is chargeable on any unpaid penalties and also on any tax credit overpaid through the claimant's fraud or neglect.

Working tax credit

[2.39] Working tax credit (WTC) is available to employees and the self-employed who usually do 16 hours or more paid work a week, and who are aged 16 or over and are either responsible for one or more children or are disabled, or are aged 25 or over and usually work at least 30 hours a week. Subject to certain exceptions, a couple with children must jointly work for at least 24 hours weekly and one of them must work at least 16 hours weekly. If only one of them works that person must work at least 24 hours weekly. If both members of a couple satisfy the conditions, there is only one credit and they may decide which of them will receive it. Individuals aged 60 or over qualify for WTC if they work at least 16 hours per week, regardless of whether they have dependent children.

WTC is calculated by adding together the following amounts (from 6 April 2017):

	Maximum annual amount
	£
Basic element	1,960
Addition for couple or single parent	2,010
Additional element for those working 30 or more hours a week	810
Additional element for disability*	3,000
Additional element for severe disability*	1,290

* Two elements are payable if both claimant and partner satisfy conditions.

The WTC may be increased by a childcare element for working claimants who pay for childcare, subject to detailed conditions. The claimant must work at least 16 hours a week (or for joint claimants each must work 16 hours a week unless one is incapacitated). The childcare element amounts to 70% of eligible costs up to £175 per week for one child, or up to £300 per week for two or more children. It is not available after 1 September following the child's 15th birthday (or 16th birthday if the child is blind or disabled). See **10.52** for the interaction of the childcare element of WTC with childcare vouchers provided by the employer.

The WTC is reduced by 41p for every £1 of income above an annual income threshold of £6,420 (for both single and joint claims). The non-childcare element of WTC is withdrawn before the childcare element. For those entitled to both WTC and child tax credit (CTC, see **2.40**), the same income threshold of £6,420 applies to the child element (but not the family element) of child tax credit and the WTC is withdrawn first.

WTC for both employees and the self-employed is paid directly by HMRC (into a bank, building society, NS&I or post office card account), except for the childcare element, which is paid direct to the main carer along with CTC.

Child tax credit

[2.40] Child tax credit (CTC) replaced all the previous child elements within social security payments, except child benefit, which continues to be available to anyone with eligible children regardless of income (although see **10.7** regarding the high income child benefit charge). An individual qualifies for CTC if they are responsible for at least one child under 16 or under 20 if still in full-time non-advanced education (or undergoing unpaid work based training). For children not in full-time non-advanced education or unpaid training CTC ends on their 16th birthday unless they have ceased full-time education and registered for work or training with the Careers Service, in which case CTC will continue for up to 20 weeks.

CTC comprises a family element and a child element. The family element is paid to any family responsible for one or more children but is not payable to those starting a family after 5 April 2017. The child element is payable for each qualifying child, higher rates applying for children with a disability. If a child dies, the entitlement for that child ends eight weeks after death, or the date when the child would have reached age 20 if earlier. CTC is payable direct to the main carer.

The maximum amounts of CTC from 6 April 2017 are as follows:

		Maximum annual amount £
Family element (one only):		
Standard amount		545
Child element (per child):		
Either	Standard amount	2,780
Or	Amount for disabled child	5,955
Or	Amount for severely disabled child	7,245

CTC is withdrawn progressively from claimants on higher incomes. As indicated in **2.39**, for those entitled to both WTC and CTC, the annual income threshold for both WTC and the child element of CTC is £6,420, and WTC is withdrawn first. For those entitled to CTC only, the income threshold is £16,105. The withdrawal is at the rate of 41p for each £1 of excess income over the threshold, and the child element is withdrawn first.

From April 2016 the child element is no longer awarded for third and subsequent children born after 6 April 2017, unless there is a multiple birth. This will not affect payment of the amount for a disabled or severely disabled child.

Conclusion

[2.41] The above is just a summary of the tax credits provisions, which are complex. Example 9 below gives a very basic illustration of some of the principles. Example 10 illustrates the possible combined tax/tax credit effect of making payments, such as pension contributions or gift aid payments, that reduce taxable income.

Example 9

Married couple are both full-time employees and have two children aged 2 and 4. They make childcare payments of £340 a week. Their final entitlement to tax credits for 2017–18 will be as follows, given joint income for 2017–18 (after excluding £300 of their investment income) at the following levels:

(a) £36,000   (b) £56,000

Tax credits maximum amount (worked on annual basis for simplicity):

	£
WTC:	
Basic	1,960
Couple addition	2,010
30 hour element	810
	4,780
Childcare element (max. 70% × £300 × 52)	10,920
	15,700
CTC:	
Child element (2 × £2,780)	5,560
Family element	545
Maximum amount	21,805

	(a) £	(b) £
Maximum credits excluding CTC family element	21,260	21,260
Restrict according to income:		
(36,000 − 6,420 =) 29,580 × 41%	(12,128)	
(56,000 − 6,420 =) 49,580 × 41%		(20,328)
	9,132	932
CTC family element	545	545
Tax credits payable to main carer	9,677	1,477

Note — The income threshold for the CTC family element in this example is £58,274, i.e. the lowest amount of income that would result in the tax credits other than the CTC family element being reduced to nil.

Example 10

The couple in part (b) of Example 9, who had income of £56,000 in 2017–18, lost £20,328 of the maximum tax credits available, i.e. 41% of £49,580. If, say, the husband had paid a personal pension contribution in the year of £2,000 gross, the tax credit entitlement would have increased by 41% of

£2,000, i.e. £820. The payment would also reduce his tax bill by 40% if he were a higher rate taxpayer (or possibly more depending on the mix of his income — see Example 6), so that the 'net of tax' cost of the pension contribution would be around £380 (£2,000 x 60% – £820).

3

Corporation tax: general principles

Basis of charge (CTA 2009, ss 2–8, 931A–931W; TCGA 1992, ss 2C, 2D)

[3.1] Companies are generally charged to corporation tax although gains on certain high value properties held by companies are charged to capital gains tax (see **4.7**). In addition, companies that own such property are liable to an annual charge on the property (see **32.48**). The liability of non-UK resident companies is discussed in CHAPTER **41**.

Corporation tax

Corporation tax is charged on the profits of companies and of unincorporated bodies that are not partnerships, for example members' clubs (see **3.35**). The term profits includes all sources of income and capital gains, other than those gains that are specifically charged to capital gains tax — see below. It also includes dividends (UK and overseas), although most will not be taxable (see **3.20**).

Corporation tax is charged on the worldwide profits of UK-resident companies. Non-resident companies carrying on a trade in the UK through a 'permanent establishment' are charged on the income arising from the permanent establishment and on capital gains on the disposal of assets in the UK used for the purposes of the trade or otherwise for the permanent establishment. Double taxation relief is available where profits are taxed twice. Non-resident companies that deal in or develop land in the UK are liable to corporation tax on the profits of that trade; see **41.65**.

Capital gains tax

Gains realised on the disposal of high value residential properties that fall within the annual tax on enveloped dwellings (ATED) regime are charged to capital gains tax; see **4.8**. This charge is in addition to the annual charge on such properties (see **32.48**). The ATED regime applies to all UK and non-UK resident 'non-natural persons'. Broadly, this consists of companies and certain collective investment schemes. Companies that are within the charge to UK corporation tax will be liable to a capital gains tax charge in respect of such disposals rather than corporation tax. Also, certain non-UK resident companies may be liable to capital gains tax on the disposal of UK residential property; see **41.50**.

Notification of liability (FA 2004, s 55)

[3.2] A company must give written notice to HMRC when it first comes within the charge to corporation tax (which can be done using HMRC's online services). The notice must be given not later than three months after the beginning of the accounting period. Similar notice must be given of the beginning of any accounting period that does not immediately follow the end of a previous accounting period. A penalty may be imposed if the notice is not given as required, unless the company had a reasonable excuse for not doing so and complied without reasonable delay after the excuse ceased. The penalties regime is discussed in CHAPTER 9.

Self-assessment (TMA 1970, ss 59D, 59E; FA 1998, s 117 and Sch 18)

[3.3] The corporation tax provisions are broadly the same as those that apply for income tax self-assessment, subject to the following exceptions. Companies are required to self-assess their corporation tax (they do not have the option of asking HMRC to work out the tax (see **9.21**)) and they must pay the amount due within nine months and one day after the end of the accounting period, except for certain large companies which are required to pay their tax by instalments (see **3.25**). They must file a statutory return (CT 600) with supporting accounts and computations within 12 months after the end of the accounting period. Automatic penalties apply for late returns. Company tax returns must be filed online and accounts and computations must be filed in a set format — Inline eXtensible Business Reporting Language (iXBRL).

The detailed provisions on returns, assessments and penalties are in CHAPTER 9. The payment provisions are dealt with at **3.24** and interest on underpaid or overpaid tax is discussed at **3.27**.

The Office of Tax Simplification (OTS) has published a report on simplification of the corporation tax computation. Recommendations include aligning the computation more closely with the company accounts and replacing capital allowances with a tax deduction for accounts depreciation.

Calculation of profits (CTA 2009, Pts 2–10; TCGA 1992, ss 8, 16A)

[3.4] Business profits are calculated in accordance with generally accepted accounting practice (see CHAPTER 20). A company's taxable income is computed using the rules applying to each source of income. The main sources are as follows:

(a)   Trading income (see **20.2**)
(b)   Property income (see CHAPTER **32**)
(c)   Non-trading profits from loan relationships, and relationships treated as loan relationships (see **3.6**)
(d)   Profits from derivative contracts (see **3.8**)
(e)   Non-trading gains on intangible fixed assets (see **20.36**)
(f)   Intellectual property: Disposals of know-how and sales of patent rights
(g)   Miscellaneous income including estate income of corporate beneficiaries; income from holding an office, distributions from unauthorised unit trusts, sale of foreign dividend coupons, and annual payments and other income not otherwise charged to tax.

Different rules from those for income tax apply to interest paid and received by companies. Interest on underpaid corporation tax is allowable as a deduction from profits and interest on overpaid corporation tax is taxable, and is taken into account under the 'loan relationships' rules (see **3.6**).

Dividends paid by a UK resident company do not reduce the company's taxable profits, because they represent a distribution of profit. Most dividends *received* by a company from both UK resident and non-UK resident companies are in practice exempt from corporation tax (unless they are trade receipts of a company other than a general insurance company). The tax treatment of dividends paid and received is dealt with at **3.19**. Special rules apply to certain dividends from authorised investment funds (see **38.29**).

In computing the company's trading profits, capital allowances are deducted as trading expenses, and balancing charges treated as trading income (see CHAPTER **22**). Expenditure of a revenue nature (see **20.11**) incurred not more than seven years before the trade started is treated as incurred on the first day of trading (see **21.8**).

A company's chargeable gains are broadly computed using capital gains tax principles (see CHAPTER **4**) but there is no annual exemption. Most gains are charged to corporation tax. The following gains are, however, charged to capital gains tax:

(a)   gains on property that is within the ATED regime; see **4.8**; and
(b)   gains by certain non-UK resident companies on the disposal of UK residential property; see **41.50**.

Furthermore, profits and losses on a company's capital transactions relating to loans, certain derivative contracts and foreign exchange are brought into account in calculating income rather than chargeable gains (see **3.6** and **3.8**). Profits and losses on intangible assets created or acquired on or after 1 April 2002, such as goodwill and intellectual property, are also brought into account in calculating income (see **20.35** to **20.41**). A special 'substantial shareholdings exemption' applies where companies dispose of holdings of 10% or more in other trading companies (see **3.34**). In arriving at chargeable gains, allowable capital losses of the current period and unrelieved losses from earlier periods are deducted.

There are a number of anti-avoidance provisions relating to company losses, particularly for companies that are members of a group (see **3.31, 26.25, 45.15** and **45.17**). In particular, companies are denied relief for a loss that arises as a result of arrangements made to secure a tax advantage. This restriction also applies to individuals, trustees and personal representatives.

Corporate debt

[3.5] The taxation of corporate debt in the UK is complex. There are several different sets of rules governing the amount and timing of tax deductions available for interest and other amounts relating to corporate debt. In particular, special rules apply to loan relationships (**3.6**) and derivative contracts (**3.8**). The deductibility of these amounts may, from 1 April 2017, also be affected by the corporate interest restriction (**3.9**).

Loan relationships (CTA 2009, Pts 5 and 6)

[3.6] Special rules apply to a company's 'loan relationships', which cover all loans made both by and to the company, excluding trading transactions for goods and services. Loans to the company include bank overdrafts and loans by the company include holdings of gilt-edged securities and corporate bonds. Gains and losses on building society permanent interest-bearing shares (PIBS, dealt with in **37.4**) are included within the loan relationships rules.

Subject to special provisions concerning particular types of security, all UK and foreign interest paid and received by companies is brought into account in calculating profits, normally on an accruals basis (i.e. taking into account amounts in arrears and advance). The accrued income scheme (see **36.11**) does not apply to companies. Most net expenses of loan relationships will be caught by the corporate interest restriction where the £2 million de minimus threshold is exceeded (see **3.9**).

Profits or losses made on loans (whether as borrower or lender) are treated as income or expenses. The amounts are arrived at using 'generally accepted accounting practice' (see **20.2**). Special rules apply where a connected creditor company is resident in, or managed in, a 'non-qualifying' territory. Foreign exchange differences on loan relationships and other monetary debts are dealt with under the loan relationships rules. For brief notes on foreign exchange aspects see **41.81**.

Amounts that relate to the trade are taken into account in arriving at the trading profit or loss. Interest receivable and profits/losses on loans will not normally relate to the trade, except for financial businesses.

Amounts that do not relate to the trade (e.g interest on underpaid and overpaid corporation tax) are aggregated and merged with any non-trading debits and credits (see **3.8**). An overall profit is chargeable to corporation tax. If there is an overall loss (a 'non-trading deficit'), relief is available similar to that available for trading losses. For the treatment of company losses in relation to money borrowed or lent, see **26.8**.

Income tax is not deducted from most interest paid and received by companies. Where tax is deducted, it is at the basic rate of 20% (see **3.23**).

There are numerous provisions designed to counter avoidance transactions in relation to the loan relationship rules. These provisions are complex, the detail of which is outside the scope of this book.

Alternative finance arrangements (CTA 2009, ss 501–521)

[3.7] There are various finance arrangements, in particular those designed to meet the requirements of Islamic law, that do not involve paying or receiving interest but have a similar effect. Current legislation equates the tax treatment of such payments and receipts with the treatment of interest, so that they are brought into account for companies under the loan relationships rules. The range of alternative finance arrangements covered by the legislation has been extended by several Finance Acts and further amendments may be made by Treasury Order.

Derivative contracts (CTA 2009, Pt 7)

[3.8] There are separate provisions to deal with profits and losses on 'derivative contracts' (i.e. options and futures). This area is extremely complex and highly technical. It covers a wide range of instruments used by companies for managing interest rate and currency risk. The rules are closely aligned with the loan relationships rules dealt with in **3.6**. Foreign exchange gains and losses on currency contracts are included within the provisions. Profits are charged (and losses allowed) in calculating income, being brought into account either as trading debits and credits or non-trading debits and credits as the case may be. Non-trading debits and credits are brought into account as if they related to loan relationships of the company (see **3.6**). They are accordingly treated as part of an overall non-trading deficit on loan relationships where appropriate (see **26.8**). Some derivative contract debits may be caught by the corporate interest restriction where the £2 million de minimus threshold is exceeded (see **3.9**).

Again, as for loan relationships, there are detailed anti-avoidance provisions which are outside the scope of this book.

Corporate interest restriction (TIOPA 2010, Pt 10 (ss 372–498), Sch 7A)

[3.9] The September 2017 Finance Bill, which is expected to receive Royal Assent in November 2017, introduced a radical change to the long standing principle that corporate trading interest expenses could be deducted in full.

The Bill introduced, from 1 April 2017, a 'corporate interest restriction' that applies to companies that have a net interest expense in excess of £2 million. This means that the vast majority of small and medium sized companies will, in practice, be unaffected by this measure. The rules are complex in drafting and application and this paragraph provides no more than a brief summary of the new regime.

Broadly, the corporate interest restriction places a limit on the amount of interest expenses and certain other financing costs that large businesses can deduct when calculating the profits subject to corporation tax. The rules operate in relation to a worldwide group (which can, by definition, include just a standalone UK company) and apply from 1 April 2017. Where an accounting period straddles this date the period is split into two notional periods with profits and losses being allocated on a just and reasonable basis.

The corporate interest restriction rules repeal and replace the worldwide debt cap regime (**3.31**) and apply as follows, where a group's interest costs are greater than £2 million:

(a)   The default 'fixed ratio' calculation provides that a deduction for net interest expense is restricted to the lower of:
    (i)   30% of the group's UK earnings before interest, taxes, depreciation and amortisation (EBITDA). Depreciation, in this case is essentially capital allowances; and
    (ii)   adjusted net group interest expense (ANGIE), calculated in accordance with detailed and complex provisions contained in the legislation; or

(b)   Where a group elects, an alternative 'group ratio' calculation can be used which will allow a deduction restricted to the lower of:
    (i)   a group ratio percentage of the qualifying net group interest expense (QNGIE) relative to the EBITDA for the worldwide group. So if, for example, the net group interest expense is £3,000,000 and the group EBITDA comes to £8,000,000, the group ratio percentage is 37.5%; and
    (ii)   group ratio debt cap — this is the QNGIE, which is calculated in accordance with detailed and complex provisions contained in the legislation.

It is generally beneficial for an election to be made for option (b) above where the calculation results in a group ratio percentage larger than 30%.

Any unrelieved interest can be carried forward indefinitely and claimed as a deduction in a later period, provided there is sufficient capacity.

The corporate interest restriction applies after other potential restrictions on interest deductibility such as the transfer pricing regime (**3.32**). However the proposed loss restriction rules (**26.2**) are intended to be applied after the corporate interest restriction.

Qualifying charitable donations (ITA 2007, Pt 15; CTA 2010, Pt 6)

[3.10] Having arrived at the company's total profits (both income and capital), qualifying charitable donations are deducted to arrive at the profits chargeable to corporation tax. For details of what constitutes a qualifying charitable donation see CHAPTER **43**. The amount deducted from profits is the amount of the qualifying charitable donations paid in the accounting period.

If the qualifying charitable donations exceed profits, no relief is available unless the company is one of a group of companies, in which case group relief may be available (see **26.17**).

Grassroots sport contributions (CTA 2010, Pt 6A (ss 217A–217D)

[3.11] The September 2017 Finance Bill, which is expected to receive Royal Assent in November 2017, provides for a corporation tax deduction for contributions to grassroots sports for expenditure incurred on or after 1 April 2017. If the payment is made directly to 'grassroots sports' the maximum deduction is £2,500 (proportionally reduced for accounting periods of less than 12 months). If the payment is to a 'qualifying sport body' the deduction is unlimited.

To qualify, the expenditure must be charitable in nature, facilitate participation in amateur sport and no deduction must otherwise be available. This prevents a deduction for an expense that would already qualify as an expense of a trade, or as a charitable donation.

The deduction is from the company's total profits (both income and capital), after any other reliefs other than qualifying charitable donations relief, group relief and group relief for carried forward losses.

If the qualifying contributions exceed profits, no relief is available unless the company is one of a group of companies, in which case group relief may be available (see **26.17**).

Periods of account and chargeable accounting periods (CTA 2009, ss 9–12, 52)

[3.12] A company's taxable profits are computed for a chargeable accounting period, which normally means the period for which the company's accounts are made up, no matter how short it is. If, however, a company makes up an account for a period greater than 12 months, it is split into one or more chargeable accounting periods of 12 months plus a chargeable accounting period covering the remainder of the period of account.

In arriving at the split of profits for an account exceeding 12 months, the trading profit is usually split on a time basis. Capital allowances (see CHAPTER **22**) are calculated for each chargeable accounting period.

Example 1

Assume an account was made up for the 15 months from 1 July 2016 to 30 September 2017 and plant was bought in August 2017, the first writing down allowance for the new plant would be given against the profit of the three months to 30 September 2017.

Interest received or paid that relates to the trade is taken into account in arriving at the trading profit of the period of account, and is normally time apportioned in the same way as the trading profit. Non-trading interest is also time apportioned. Rental income is calculated in the same way as trading profits, so that it is split on a time basis (see CHAPTER 32 and also CHAPTER 41 for overseas aspects of rental income). If there are any other sources of income they are allocated to the chargeable accounting period in which they arise. Chargeable gains are similarly allocated to the chargeable accounting period in which the disposal occurs, and qualifying charitable donations (see 3.10) to the chargeable accounting period in which they are paid.

If a company ceases to trade, the date of cessation marks the end of a chargeable accounting period even if the period of account continues to the normal accounting date. The commencement of winding-up also marks the end of a chargeable accounting period with subsequent accounting periods then running for successive periods of 12 months until the winding-up is completed. These rules are varied in some circumstances for companies in administration. If a company enters administration, an accounting period will end immediately before that date. An accounting period will also end when the period of administration ends. If immediately before a company enters administration it is in the course of being wound up, the normal rule about accounting periods running for successive 12-month periods during the winding-up will not apply. See 3.28.

Losses (CTA 2010 ss 37–47; CTA 2009, ss 456–463)

[3.13] When a company incurs a trading loss, it may set the loss against any other profits of the same accounting period, both income and capital, and then, if it wishes, carry any balance back against the total profits of the previous 12 months so long as the trade was carried on in that year. However, the carry back period is extended to the previous three years if the loss occurs in the last 12 months of trading. The carry back loss set-off is proportionately restricted to exclude profits of an accounting period falling partly outside the one year or three year carry-back period.

Any balance of loss remaining (or the whole loss if the company does not wish to claim the current set-off and carry-back) is carried forward to set against later profits (see 26.6). These loss reliefs are not available for trades carried on *wholly* abroad.

Where a non-trading deficit arises under the loan relationships rules (see 3.6), the relief available is similar to that for trading losses.

Capital losses are set against capital gains of the same chargeable accounting period (or in certain circumstances relieved intra-group, see 4.43), any excess being carried forward to set against future gains. Capital losses cannot be carried back.

For detailed notes on trading losses and non-trading deficits, including transferring loss reliefs within groups, see CHAPTER 26. The treatment of losses on rented property and furnished holiday lettings is dealt with in CHAPTER 32. For foreign property letting businesses and losses on trades carried on wholly abroad see CHAPTER 41. Capital losses are dealt with in CHAPTER 4 and in context in other chapters.

Rates of tax (CTA 2009, ss 7, 8)

[**3.14**] Corporation tax rates are fixed for financial years ending 31 March. Financial years are identified by the calendar year in which they commence, so the financial year 2017 is the year to 31 March 2018. Where the tax rate changes during a company's chargeable accounting period, the total profits are apportioned on a time basis (in days) and charged at the respective rates in calculating the corporation tax payable for the period. For details of the corporation tax rates in recent years, see the TABLE OF RATES AND ALLOWANCES (TRA).

Main rate (F(No 2)A 2015, s 7; FA 2017, s 5)

[**3.15**] For the current 2017 financial year the main rate of corporation tax is set at 19%. This rate has also been set for financial years 2018 and 2019, dropping to 17% for the financial year 2020.

For companies with 'ring fence' profits the main rate of corporation tax is 30%, although this falls to 19% for such companies with 'small ring-fence profits' (**3.16**).

Small ring-fence profits rate (CTA 2010, ss 279A–279H)

[**3.16**] From 1 April 2015 tax is charged at two rates on ring-fence profits (i.e. profits from oil extraction and oil rights in the UK and the UK Continental Shelf). The 'main ring-fence profits rate' is fixed at 30% and applies to companies with profits over £1,500,000. The small ring-fence profits rate is 19% and applies to companies with profits below £300,000.

There is a special definition of profits for the small ring-fence profits rate. It is defined as the profits that would have been chargeable to corporation tax on the assumption that the provisions charging certain gains to capital gains tax do not apply; see **3.1** (and instead the gains are deemed to be charged to corporation tax). It also includes dividends received from other UK resident and non-UK resident companies. This dividend income is received gross and is referred to as 'exempt ABGH distribution' income.

The inclusion of exempt ABGH distribution income in the calculations means that it is not possible for a company with a large amount of income in that form to obtain the benefit of the small profits rate on only a small amount of profits chargeable to corporation tax.

Marginal relief

Where a company's profits fall between £300,000 and £1,500,000, marginal relief ensures that the corporation tax rate on the profits is gradually increased to the full level.

The marginal relief is given by calculating tax on the profits chargeable to corporation tax at the full corporation tax rate and reducing it by an amount arrived at by the following formula:

$$R \times (U - A) \times \frac{N}{A}$$

where R = Marginal relief fraction (i.e. 11/400)
       U = Upper limit
       A = Income and gains chargeable to corporation tax plus exempt ABGH distributions
       N = Taxable total profits, i.e. income and gains chargeable to corporation tax

The £300,000 and £1,500,000 limits are annual limits and they are scaled down proportionately if an accounting period is less than 12 months. They are also scaled down where, for any part of a chargeable accounting period, a company has related 51% group companies. A company is a related 51% group company if it is a 51% subsidiary of another company, even if this is for different parts of the accounting period. Specifically excluded are non-trading companies.

If, for example, there are five related 51% group companies, the present limits for each company are £60,000 and £300,000. If four companies have profits of £70,000 and one £20,000 the small profits rate will only apply to the last one, and the others will have profits subject to the marginal relief. On the other hand if, say, there were two related 51% group companies and one's profits were £1,800,000 and the other's £150,000, the company with £150,000 profits would qualify for the small profits rate even though the combined profits greatly exceeded the upper maximum.

Patent box rate (CTA 2010, Pt 8A (ss 357A–357GE))

[3.17] Companies can elect to apply a 10% rate of corporation tax to all profits attributable to qualifying patents, whether paid separately as royalties or embedded in the sales price of products. The stated aim of this 'patent box' rate is to strengthen the incentives to invest in innovative industries. The patent box rate is not given as reduced rate of tax on eligible profits, instead a deduction is given from trading profits of an amount that has the same effect as reducing the main rate of corporation tax on eligible profits to the special patent box rate.

Although the rules applied from 1 April 2013, they were phased in over five years from FY 2013 to FY 2017.

The regime also applies to other qualifying intellectual property rights such as regulatory data protection (also called 'data exclusivity'), supplementary protection certificates (SPCs) and plant variety rights. Other non-qualifying profits in these companies continue to be taxed at the main rate.

An election for the patent box rate must be made in writing, specifying the first accounting period to which the rules apply and must be made within 12 months of the fixed filing date of the return for the first accounting period for which the company wishes to elect in to the regime. An election will apply equally to all trades of the company and for all subsequent accounting periods until it is revoked by notice in writing. Once an election has been revoked, a fresh election will have no effect for any accounting period which begins less than five years after the last day of the accounting period specified in the revocation notice. This is to prevent companies dipping in and out of the regime for purposes which would amount to an abuse of the regime, for example to exclude periods when a company would be required to register a set-off amount that would affect the relief available to other group companies. This rule is overridden however to allow a company which had elected out of the regime for a period ending on or before 30 June 2016 to elect back in because from that date the method of calculation of the patent box profit was amended to reflect the amount of research and development activity on the qualifying assets.

HMRC have provide detailed guidance on the patent box regime including many useful examples as to how they anticipate the rules applying. See also w ww.gov.uk/guidance/corporation-tax-the-patent-box for further HMRC guidance, explaining who can elect for the patent box rate, which patents are eligible, and how and when to claim.

Bank levy (FA 2011, s 73 and Sch 19; FA 2014, ss 285–288; F(No 2)A 2015, s 16 and Sch 2)

[**3.18**] A levy based on banks' balance sheets applies for periods of account ending on or after 1 January 2011. It essentially imposes a charge on specified liabilities reported in banks' balance sheets (although the charge is not imposed on the first £20 billion of chargeable liabilities). Its stated intention is 'to encourage banks to move to less risky funding profiles'.

Further, for all banking companies, there is a surcharge of 8% on taxable profits (excluding the first £25 million) arising on or after 1 January 2016.

The rates for years 2017–2020 have been set as follows:

(i)   from 1 April 2017: 0.170% (short term) and 0.085% (long term);
(ii) from 1 April 2018: 0.160% (short term) and 0.080% (long term);
(iii) from 1 April 2019: 0.150% (short term) and 0.075% (long term);
(iv) from 1 April 2020: 0.140% (short term) and 0.070% (long term).

The levy is not deductible for corporation tax purposes and can be paid through the existing corporation tax self assessment system. A single group member within the charge to corporation tax is responsible for both returning the liability and payment of the bank levy on behalf of the relevant group.

A code of practice on taxation for banks applies, to which many of the major banks have signed up to. From 2015, HMRC must publish a report on the operation of this code and if they conclude that a group or entity has breached the code during a reporting period they may name the group or entity. The first annual report will be for the period 5 December 2013 to 31 March 2015. After that, each year beginning with 1 April is a 'reporting period'.

The bank levy charge provides a framework for double tax relief with respect to the bank levy and similar levies that may be imposed by foreign territories. Double tax relief can be provided either bilaterally or unilaterally and, where it is claimed, credit can be claimed for the foreign equivalent tax, but not so much as to reduce the UK bank levy to nil.

Dividends and other distributions (FA 1998, ss 31, 32)

[3.19] From 1973 to 5 April 1999, companies had to pay some of their corporation tax in advance when they paid dividends. Advance corporation tax (ACT) was abolished with effect from 6 April 1999, but companies with profits above the upper limit (£1,500,000) are now required to pay their corporation tax by quarterly instalments (see **3.24**).

Many companies were not able to offset all the ACT they had paid against their tax bills, giving rise to surplus (unrelieved) ACT at 5 April 1999. They still have the right to offset any remaining surplus ACT even though ACT has been abolished, but only under the provisions of a shadow ACT system, which will still leave many companies with large unrecovered amounts. The detailed provisions of the shadow ACT system are dealt with in earlier editions of this book.

Where a company supplies goods or services to a shareholder for more than cost but at a price concession, this is not treated as a distribution because there is no cost to the company, as distinct from a reduction in profit margins, so that no part of the company profits has been distributed.

Corporate recipients (CTA 2009, ss 931A–931W)

[3.20] Distributions paid by a UK or overseas company are chargeable to corporation tax on the recipient unless the distribution is exempt. Although the detail of the provisions are complex, in practice most distributions will fall to be exempt.

Dividend income is received gross and is referred to as 'exempt ABGH' income.

Exempt ABGH income is taken into account when calculating the corporation tax liability of the company for marginal relief purposes, where applicable (**3.16**).

Non-corporate recipients (ITTOIA 2005, ss 383–385, 397–397C; ITA 2007, s 8; FA 2015, s 1)

[3.21] Dividends are received gross and a dividend allowance of £5,000 is available. Any balance is taxable at 7.5% on income up to the basic rate limit, 32.5% on income above the basic rate limit up to the higher rate limit, and 38.1% on income above the higher rate limit. Note that the September 2017 Finance Bill, which is expected to receive Royal Assent in November 2017, reduces the dividend allowance to £2,000 from 2018–19 onwards. See further 2.5.

Bonus share issues (CTA 2010, ss 1100, 1101; ITTOIA 2005, ss 399–401)

[3.22] Where a distribution is made that, broadly, confers a future rather than a current claim on the company's assets, such as a bonus issue of redeemable shares, certain additional rules apply, such as:

(a)   when the shares are redeemed, the redemption is a distribution, but any tax paid by the shareholder on the initial distribution may be set against any tax due from him on the later distribution;

(b)   the company is required to notify HMRC within 14 days after the end of the quarter in which the initial distribution is made.

Deduction of income tax from patent royalties, interest, etc (ITA 2007, Pt 15)

[3.23] Companies do not have to deduct tax from interest or patent royalties (or from annuities or other annual payments, although such payments are rare) if they reasonably believe that the recipient is a company liable to corporation tax on the amount received, a local authority, or a body exempt from tax (such as a charity, pension fund or an ISA fund manager). These provisions enabling payments to be made gross also apply (subject to various conditions) to payments of interest, patent royalties etc to companies of another EU state, or a permanent establishment in an EU state of such a company. Anti-avoidance provisions apply which impose a withholding tax where a payment of a royalty is made to a non-resident connected person as part of arrangements the purpose of which is to obtain a tax advantage by virtue of a provision of a double tax agreement.

If it turns out that tax should have been deducted, the payer is liable to pay the tax plus interest, but no penalty will be charged unless it should have been clear to the payer that it should have deducted tax. Tax must still be deducted from payments of interest, patent royalties etc by companies and local authorities that do not come within the above provisions, unless covered by a specific exception.

As far as payments to individuals are concerned, the general rule is that tax at 20% is deducted from annual interest paid to individuals, and from patent royalty payments paid to individuals. Interest that is payable in respect of compensation is treated as a payment of annual interest. Consequently, the person paying the interest will be required to deduct income tax at source from it. However, tax is not deducted from interest on 'quoted Eurobonds', which are interest-bearing securities issued by a company (or unincorporated association such as a building society) and listed on a recognised stock exchange. Nor is tax deducted from bank and building society interest paid to individuals (**36.5**). Where a company *receives* patent royalties from an individual, they will be received net of 20% tax. Interest received from individuals will usually be received gross.

Where companies are required to deduct income tax from payments made, they have to account to HMRC for the tax deducted. Any income tax deducted from a company's income may be offset against the tax deducted on the company's payments if any. Where income tax suffered on a company's income is not recovered in this way, it will be set against the company's corporation tax liability, or if that is insufficient it will be repaid.

Tax payable is accounted for at the appropriate rate on form CT 61. Returns are made to 31 March, 30 June, 30 September and 31 December, the tax being due within 14 days after the quarter ends. Where a company's accounting year does not end on one of the four calendar quarter days the company has five return periods, the first running from the first day of the account to the next calendar quarter day and the last ending at the end of the accounting period.

Date of payment of corporation tax (TMA 1970, ss 59D, 59DA and 59E, 98; SI 1998/3175)

General rule

[3.24] Companies are required to self-assess their corporation tax, as indicated in **3.3**. Companies with profits at or above the upper limit (i.e. £1.5 million, reduced pro rata where there are 51% group companies and for accounting periods of less than 12 months; see **3.16**), are required to pay their corporation tax by equal quarterly instalments (see **3.25**). Companies not required to pay by instalments are due to pay their corporation tax nine months and one day after the end of the accounting period. They must, however, account on a quarterly basis for any income tax they have deducted from interest payments etc as indicated in **3.23**.

Example 2

A company pays interest to and receives interest from other companies and pays patent royalties to an individual. The company's results for the year to 31 March 2018 are:

	£
Trading profits, net of allowable expenses other than interest and patent royalties	311,000
Rental income, net of allowable expenses	14,000

Interest received:	June 2017	15,000
	December 2017	15,000
Chargeable gains		104,000
Patent royalties paid (gross amount):	May 2017	20,000
	November 2017	28,000
Loan interest relating to the trade, paid February 2018		10,000

Interest received and interest receivable are the same amounts. The interest payable for the year exceeds the interest paid during the year by £3,000. Patent royalties paid in the year exceed patent royalties payable by £2,000.

The company paid a dividend of £100,000 in December 2017.

There were no amounts brought forward from earlier years.

Corporation tax computation for year to 31 March 2018	£
Trading profits, net of £13,000 interest and £46,000 patent royalties payable	252,000
Interest received	30,000
Rental income	14,000
Chargeable gains	104,000
Profits chargeable to corporation tax	400,000
Corporation tax on £400,000 @ 19% payable 1 January 2018	76,000

Income tax is accounted for as follows:

CT 61 return for quarter to 30 June 2017

Income tax deducted from patent royalties paid May 2017: 20,000 @ 20%	4,000
Income tax payable by 14 July 2017	4,000

CT 61 return for quarter to 31 December 2017

Income tax deducted from patent royalties paid November 2017: 28,000 @ 20%	5,600
Payable by 14 January 2018	5,600

No tax was deducted from the interest paid to and received from other companies. There were no taxed payments or taxed income in the quarters to 30 September 2017 and 31 March 2018, so CT 61 returns were not required for those quarters. The payment of the dividend does not affect the computation.

At any time before the corporation tax liability is finally determined, companies may claim repayments if they consider they have overpaid tax, but interest will be charged from the normal due date on any tax finally found to be due (or allowed on overpayments); see **3.27**.

Instalment payments

[3.25] The instalment paying provisions for companies with profits above the upper limit affect only a small proportion of corporation tax-paying companies. The detailed provisions are in regulations, and companies are liable to penalties if they fail to provide, or provide incorrect, information, records, etc.

The first instalment is due 14 days after the end of the sixth month of the accounting period and the remaining three instalments at quarterly intervals thereafter. The instalments are based on the company's estimated corporation tax liability for the accounting period (including, where appropriate, amounts payable under the provisions relating to loans to directors (see **12.13** to **12.15**) and under the controlled foreign companies rules (see **45.25**)). Companies can recover quarterly payments if they decide they should not have been paid.

If a company's profits are below the upper limit in one year, they will not have to make quarterly payments in the following year if their profits in that year do not exceed £10 million (reduced pro rata where there are 51% group companies (**3.16**)). If a company's corporation tax liability does not exceed £10,000 in an accounting period, it is not required to make quarterly payments, even though its profits exceed the marginal relief limits because of the number of its 51% group companies or because of its dividend income.

Groups of companies may pay their corporation tax on a group-wide basis (referred to as 'group payment arrangements'), without needing to allocate instalments paid to particular companies until the respective liabilities are formalised. See www.gov.uk/guidance/corporation-tax-group-payment-arrangements#7.

It has been announced that, for accounting periods commencing on or after 1 April 2019, the instalment payment dates will be brought forward for UK companies with profits over £20 million and will instead be due in the third, sixth, ninth and twelfth months of the accounting period. For groups, the £20 million profits threshold will be divided by the number of companies in the group. Draft legislation will be published in due course.

Pre-eminent gifts relief (FA 2012, s 49 and Sch 14)

[3.26] A tax relief is available (to companies and individuals) for qualifying gifts to the nation of objects which are of pre-eminent national, scientific, historic, artistic, architectural or scenic interest. For further details see **2.21**.

Companies that choose to claim the relief are entitled to a deduction equal to 20% of the value of the object donated. The company may choose to accept a lower percentage if it wishes, for example where the value of the gift is very high or the company's tax liability for that particular accounting period will not be sufficient to use the full amount of the tax deduction. The deduction is applied to the accounting period in which the offer is registered and has the effect of settling part (or all) of the corporation tax due for that period.

Interest on overdue and overpaid tax (TMA 1970, ss 87A, 90; TA 1988, ss 826, 826A; FA 1989, s 178)

[3.27] Interest is charged on overdue corporation tax and allowed on overpaid corporation tax. The latest rates of interest are shown in the TABLE OF RATES AND ALLOWANCES (**TRA**). The interest is brought into account as non-trading interest under the 'loan relationships' provisions (see **3.6**) in computing profits chargeable to corporation tax, subject to what is said at **3.28** concerning companies in liquidation or administration. The fact that interest is taken into account in calculating profits is reflected in the formula for determining interest rates. For companies required to make quarterly payments, however, a different formula is used in order to reduce the differential between the two rates during the period from the first instalment date (14 days after the end of the sixth month of the accounting period) to the date nine months and one day after the end of the accounting period, after which the normal rates apply. This is intended to avoid penalising companies who make mistakes in their estimates.

Although different interest rates apply depending upon whether the company is paying tax by instalments of not, interest on overdue/overpaid tax, runs as follows:

(a)   on overdue tax, interest runs from the normal due date to the date of payment. If a company is late paying the income tax due under the CT 61 quarterly accounting procedure (see **3.23**), interest is charged from the due date for the quarterly return until the payment date. If any of the tax becomes repayable in a subsequent return period, some of the interest already charged is repaid, but only from the date the later return is due or, if earlier, from the date the later return is actually filed;

(b)   on overpaid tax, interest runs from the later of the normal due date and the payment date to the date of repayment. If a company makes quarterly payments in the mistaken belief that its profits will exceed the upper limit, it will be entitled to interest on the overpayment from the payment date. Where a company is entitled to a refund of income tax suffered on its taxed income (see **3.23**), interest will be paid on the refund from the day after the end of the accounting period.

Companies that pay tax before the normal due date are entitled to credit interest from HMRC. Such interest is payable from the later of the date on which the tax was paid, and the date on which, if the company had been a large company, the first instalment of tax for the accounting period would have been due, to the normal due date.

A company that pays its instalments late may be liable to a penalty not exceeding twice the amount of interest payable, but this penalty is unlikely to be imposed other than in exceptional circumstances.

Liquidation and administration (CTA 2010, ss 626–633; CTA 2009, ss 9–12)

[3.28] A company liquidation is usually preceded by a cessation of trade. The cessation of trade triggers the end of a chargeable accounting period, and a chargeable accounting period also ends at the commencement of winding-up (and at 12-monthly intervals until the winding-up is completed, subject to what is said below about companies in administration). Self-assessment returns must be completed accordingly. To help liquidators who want to finalise matters before formal completion of the winding-up, HMRC will accept an informal return, such as a letter, and will also, where appropriate, provide a clearance that they will not open an enquiry into the return. See also tax point at **28.13** regarding the use of the 'defunct company' procedure as an alternative to a formal liquidation.

The above rules are varied if a company goes into administration. An accounting period will end immediately before the commencement of the administration and also at the date the company comes out of administration. Unlike the rule for companies in liquidation (see above), there is no requirement for accounting periods to run for 12 months during the administration period and the normal accounting date may be retained. Under the insolvency procedures, certain creditors or the liquidator of a company that is in the process of winding-up may apply to the court for an administration order instead. If the order is granted the winding-up order will be discharged and the rule that accounting periods must end at 12-monthly intervals until the winding-up is completed will cease to apply.

Under self-assessment, interest on underpaid and overpaid tax is taken into account in calculating taxable profits (see **3.27**). If interest on overpaid tax is received or receivable by a company in liquidation in its final accounting period, however, the interest will not be included in taxable profits if it does not exceed £2,000. The same provisions apply in respect of the final accounting period where a company is in administration if the company moves from administration to dissolution.

Problems can arise when a company that has been making trading losses realises chargeable gains on the sale of its assets, because if the gains are realised after the trade ceases there will be no current trading losses to offset them, but it is not possible to part with the assets until the trade has ceased. This problem can be avoided if an unconditional contract for sale of the assets takes place before ceasing to trade, with completion taking place subsequently. The contract date is the relevant disposal date for capital gains purposes, and any trading losses occurring in the accounting period in which the trade ceases will then be available to reduce the gains. The gains cannot, however, be reduced by trading losses brought forward (see CHAPTER 26 for the detailed provisions on company losses).

Close companies (CTA 2010, ss 34, 438–465)

[3.29] A close company is a company under the control of five or fewer participators (which broadly means shareholders, although it is defined more widely), or under the control of its directors. In considering what rights an individual has in a company, the rights of his 'associates' are included, which covers close family, spouses, civil partners, business partners and the trustees of any family settlements.

As well as being subject to the normal corporation tax rules, close companies are subject to additional requirements.

Benefits in kind to participators are treated as distributions (except where already treated as earnings under the benefits rules, see CHAPTER 10). In addition there is a tax charge imposed if a close company makes a loan to a participator or a close company is party to arrangements under which benefit is conferred on a participator in the close company. These provisions are dealt with in CHAPTER 12.

Groups of companies (CTA 2010, ss 97–188, 973–980; TCGA 1992, ss 170–175, 179–181, 190 and Schs 7A, 7AA, 7AB; FA 1998, Sch 18 paras 66–77A; CTA 2009, ss 457, 1305A; TIOPA 2010, ss 260–353)

[3.30] The Taxes Acts do not treat a group of companies as one taxable entity. The corporation tax position of each company in the group is computed independently (small profits rate (where applicable) and various other limits being scaled down according to the number of 51% group companies. There are, however, various provisions as indicated below that recognise the group structure and give special treatment in the appropriate circumstances. It is also provided under the self-assessment regime that if group companies are required to pay their tax in instalments, the tax may be paid on a group-wide basis (see **3.25**). See **6.23** for stamp taxes provisions relating to groups.

The group provisions are not restricted to UK resident companies. Groups and consortia may be established through non-resident companies, enabling the benefit of the provisions to be claimed providing the companies concerned are within the charge to UK corporation tax. As a corollary, tax payable by a non-resident company may be recovered from another group company. See **41.76** for special provisions applicable when companies operating in different European Union member states merge to form 'European Companies' (SEs) or 'European Cooperative Societies' (SCEs).

Members of a group or consortium are determined by reference not only to ordinary share capital held, but also to beneficial entitlement to profits available for distribution to equity holders and assets available for distribution to equity holders in a winding-up. An equity holder includes ordinary shareholders and loan creditors in relation to loans that are not normal commercial loans. Loans made on or after 21 March 2012 that carry a right to conversion into the shares or securities of a wholly unconnected listed company fall within the definition of normal commercial loans and the holders of the loans are not treated as equity holders.

Parent company and its 75% subsidiaries

[3.31] The following issues are important when considering the tax treatment of a company and its 75% subsidiaries:

(a) Trading losses (and UK property business losses and qualifying charitable donations in excess of other profits) can be surrendered to other group members for use against total profits (including capital gains) of the corresponding accounting period. The same applies to an excess of non-trading losses/payments on loans over non-trading income on loans. (Trading interest paid and losses on trade loans are treated as trading expenses and thus form part of a trading loss.) These 'group relief' provisions are dealt with in CHAPTER **26**.

(b) For capital gains purposes, assets (other than those that fall within the annual tax on enveloped dwellings (ATED) regime, **4.8**) transferred from one group company to another are treated as transferred on a no gain/no loss basis. Where a chargeable gain or allowable loss accrues to one group company it can elect to transfer part or all of that gain or loss to another group member. Companies within a group that are non-UK resident can elect to pool all NRCGT gains and losses (**41.50**).

(c) A chargeable gain made by one group company on a business asset qualifying for rollover relief may be rolled over or held over against an acquisition by another group company (see **29.16**).

(d) Where a company leaves a group within six years of acquiring an asset intra-group on a no gain/no loss basis, a deemed gain arises (known as the degrouping charge), unless the transaction falls within one of the statutory exceptions. Where a company leaves a group as a result of the disposal of its shares, any degrouping charge is treated as additional consideration for the disposal. This ensures that shareholder reliefs such as the substantial shareholding exemption (**3.34**) will also apply to the degrouping charge. Claims can be made to reduce the amount of the degrouping charge where tax is charged on the same economic gain both through the degrouping charge and through a chargeable gain on the shares. Where a company leaves a group, an election can be made for a degrouping charge to be transferred to another group company. This election (which must be made by both companies concerned) can only be made at a time when both companies are members of the same group, and a disposal of the asset between them would otherwise be on a no gain/no loss basis. Special rules apply where the transferee company is an insurance company. Degrouping charges also apply under the intangible fixed assets regime (see **20.40**).

(e) The tax deduction for finance expenses (such as payments of interest), of groups of companies with either a UK or foreign parent may be restricted under the corporate interest restriction regime from 1 April 2017 (**3.9**). Prior to 1 April 2017, there was another restriction (the 'worldwide debt cap') which applied to UK companies of 'large worldwide groups' where the UK net debt of the group exceeded 75% of the worldwide gross debt of the group (referred to as the 'gateway test'). Where the restriction applied the aggregate UK tax deduction for the UK members of a group of companies that had net finance expenses was limited to the consolidated gross finance expense of that group. The corporate interest restriction rules repeal and replace the worldwide debt cap regime. They were introduced by the September 2017 Finance Bill, which is expected to receive Royal Assent in November 2017, but apply from 1 April 2017.

The group provisions have frequently been manipulated in order to make tax savings over and above that intended by the legislation, and there are numerous anti-avoidance provisions. These include provisions denying group relief for losses where there are 'arrangements' under which some or all of a company's shares could be disposed of to another party (see **26.25**) and provisions preventing groups reducing their capital gains liability by acquiring companies with capital losses or by bringing companies with capital gains into a group that has unrelieved capital losses (see **45.17**). Also no deduction is permitted where arrangements are entered into between two companies, who are members of the same group, to transfer profits between them for tax avoidance reasons. In such situations the company profits are computed as if the transfer had not taken place. The definition of a group is widely drawn for these purposes so that it will allow joint venture entities and smaller groups that might not be required to be fully consolidated in group accounts under the Companies Act to fall within the definition.

Transfer pricing (TIOPA 2010, ss 146–230)

[3.32] To prevent groups reducing their taxable profits by having a high level of debt to equity, the transfer pricing provisions require non-arm's length interest payments between connected companies to be treated as distributions and therefore not deductible in arriving at profits. Similarly, the transfer pricing rules require prices between non-arm's length companies to be adjusted to an arm's length price. The rules apply not only to transactions between UK and overseas companies but also between UK companies. There are exemptions for most small and medium-sized companies. The provisions are covered briefly in **45.30**.

Diverted profits tax (FA 2015, ss 77–114 and Sch 16)

[3.33] The diverted profits tax (DPT) applies for accounting periods beginning on or after 1 April 2015; if a company's accounting period straddles this date it is split into two notional periods, with income/expenses etc apportioned to the two periods on a just and reasonable basis. The stated objective of the tax is to counteract contrived arrangements used by large groups (typically multinational enterprises) that result in the erosion of the UK tax base. The DPT is complex in its operation, but as it does not apply to small and medium sized companies, it is only mentioned briefly in this book.

The main features of the tax are as follows:

(a)   tax (at 25%; 55% for ring fence profits) is charged on taxable diverted profits of a company for an accounting period if:

    (i)   a company (other than a SME), which is taxable in the UK creates a tax advantage by involving entities or transactions which lack 'economic substance'; or

    (ii)   a foreign company (other than those where UK sales revenues do not exceed £10 million, or UK related expenses do not exceed £1 million) structures its affairs so as to avoid a UK taxable presence;

(b)   a company within the charge to DPT must notify HMRC within three months of the end of the accounting period (six months for periods ending on or before 31 March 2016). There is, however, no duty to self-assess. The tax is imposed by HMRC issuing a charging notice to the company;

(c)   the DPT must be paid within 30 days after the date on which the charging notice is issued. Following the issue of the charging notice there is then a one-year review period in which HMRC must review the notice at least once. If the company has paid the tax, HMRC may issue one or more amending notices reducing the amount charged. If HMRC consider that the charge is insufficient they may issue one supplementary charging notice imposing an additional charge. The review period starts immediately after the date on which the tax is due and payable and can be brought to an early end by agreement between HMRC and the company or by the company alone following the issuing of a supplementary charging notice. After the end of the review period the company has 30 days to appeal against the charging notice and any supplementary charging notice.

Although in many cases the arrangements put in place to divert profits will involve non-UK companies, DPT may also apply in circumstances where wholly domestic structures are used.

HMRC guidance can be found at www.gov.uk/government/publications/diverted-profits-tax-guidance.

Disposals of substantial shareholdings (TCGA 1992, s 192A and Sch 7AC)

[3.34] The September 2017 Finance Bill, which is expected to receive Royal Assent in November 2017, simplified the substantial shareholding exemption for disposals on or after 1 April 2017. Broadly the exemption (both before and after 1 April 2017) provides that, where certain conditions are met, gains and losses realised by a company on a disposal of a shareholding in another company are exempt from tax.

For the exemption to apply the following key conditions must be met:

(a)   Disposals on or after 1 April 2017. The investing company must have held a 'substantial shareholding' in the target company throughout a continuous 12-month period beginning not more than six years before the date of disposal (the 'qualifying period'). There is no requirement that the investing company be a trading company. The investee company has to be a trading company or a holding company in a trading group before the sale (but not after, except if the sale is to a connected party).

(b) Disposals prior to 1 April 2017. The investing company must have held a 'substantial shareholding' in the target company throughout a continuous 12-month period beginning not more than two years before the date of disposal (the 'qualifying period'). The investing company had to be a trading company throughout the qualifying period and after the sale. The investee company also had to be a trading company or a holding company in a trading group before and after the sale.

Substantial' means the company disposing of the shares must have owned 10% or more of the ordinary shares in the other company (and be entitled to 10% or more of the company's profits available for distribution and of its assets on a winding-up). The 'look back' period of six years (two years prior to 1 April 2017) means that where a shareholding is sold in tranches it may still qualify for relief.

> *Example 3*
>
> Lee Ltd has owned 15% of Denise Ltd since 2002. On 1 June 2017, Lee Ltd sold a 10% stake in the company at a profit. The gain on this disposal clearly qualifies for the substantial shareholding exemption. However, some months later the directors of Lee Ltd are considering the possibility of selling the remaining 5% shareholding. Even though the shares in Denise Ltd no longer constitute a substantial shareholding, the exemption is still available for disposals in the 5 years following 1 June 2017.

There are provisions to aggregate the shares held by companies and their 51% subsidiaries. The exemption applies to qualifying holdings in overseas companies as well as UK companies.

HMRC gave detailed comments on their understanding of the meaning of 'trading company' and 'trading group' in their December 2002 Tax Bulletin and HMRC Brief 29/2011. The exemption is subject to anti-avoidance provisions, and HMRC issued Statement of Practice SP 5/02 in this connection. Detailed guidance is provided in HMRC's Capital Gains Manual at CG53100.

Members' clubs

[3.35] As stated at **3.1**, the profits of members' clubs are chargeable to corporation tax. This does not apply to clubs that are registered as community amateur sports clubs, which are treated in a similar way to charities. For further details see **43.33**.

The corporation tax charge on clubs applies only to profits from transactions other than between the club members themselves, so it covers such items as interest received on deposits of the club's funds, and any trading profits on transactions with non-members, no matter how small such income may be.

The fact that clubs are within the definition of companies for corporation tax means that banks and building societies are able to pay interest to them without deducting tax, so the clubs are due to account for tax on the full amount of the interest at the appropriate rate of corporation tax under the self-assessment system. By concession, HMRC will normally treat a club as dormant if its annual corporation tax liability is not expected to exceed £100, and the club is run exclusively for the benefit of its members. This is subject to various conditions, which are set out at HMRC COTAX Manual COM23110. Where dormant status has been granted, clubs will not normally need to complete corporation tax returns, although HMRC will review the situation at least every five years. If a club is not already treated as dormant but considers it meets the conditions, it should contact its tax office. Clubs must notify HMRC within 12 months after the end of the relevant accounting period if their circumstances change.

HMRC operate a special simplified scheme for investment clubs (i.e. people who join together to invest on the Stock Exchange), allowing them to submit less detailed calculations of members' gains and income than are strictly required by law if the club satisfies certain criteria.

Encouraging business investment, enterprise and efficiency

[3.36] Various measures are available to enable companies to operate in a tax-efficient manner and to stimulate investment in new and expanding ventures, including:

- Capital gains tax entrepreneurs' relief
- Rollover relief on replacement of business assets
- Corporate venturing
- Venture capital trusts
- Demergers

These are dealt with separately in CHAPTER 29.

4

Capital gains tax: general principles

Introduction

[4.1] Capital gains tax is a tax on the chargeable gains of individuals, personal representatives and trustees and, in some cases, companies and certain non-natural persons (see **4.7**).

The main capital gains tax rates were reduced for most types of gains accruing on or after 6 April 2016, so that most gains realised by individuals are taxed at 10% (rising to 20% in certain circumstances, see **4.2**). However a rate of 18% (rising to 28%) still applies to some gains. In computing gains realised by individuals there is no entitlement to any indexation allowance, although there is entrepreneurs' relief available which allows up to £10 million of gains on qualifying business disposals to be taxed at 10% (see **29.2**). In addition a new investors' relief will allow up to £10 million of gains on disposals after 5 April 2019 of qualifying shares in an unlisted trading company to be taxed at 10% (see **29.12**).

The capital gains tax position of personal representatives and trustees is dealt with at **4.44** and **4.45**.

For companies, their gains are computed broadly on the same basis as for individuals etc, but there are some important differences (e.g. availability of indexation allowance, computation of gains on the disposal of stocks and shares). A company's gains are usually charged to corporation tax, not capital gains tax, although for disposals on or after 6 April 2013 gains on certain high value properties held by companies are charged to capital gains tax (see **4.7**). From 6 April 2015 capital gains tax may also be charged on gains realised on disposals of UK residential property by non-resident companies (see **41.50**).

Basis of charge for individuals, personal representatives and trustees (TCGA 1992, Pts 1 and 2 (ss 1–57); ITTOIA 2005, s 25A; SI 2017/377)

Rate of tax

[4.2] Capital gains tax applies to a disposal (see **4.17**) of chargeable assets. The first £11,300 of an individual's net chargeable gains in 2017–18 (£11,100 in 2016–17) are exempt. Any gains in excess of that amount are taxed as follows:

(a) for individuals:
  (i) 10% (or 20% for gains that exceed the basic rate income tax band, currently £33,500) for gains on all chargeable assets excluding residential property interests and certain profit-related sums paid to investment managers (carried interest, see **20.31**);
  (ii) 18% (or 28% for gains that exceed the basic rate band) for gains on residential property interests (where not exempt, see **30.3**) and carried interest — referred to in the legislation as 'upper rate gains';
(b) for personal representatives and trustees:
  (i) 20% for gains on all chargeable assets excluding residential property interests and carried interest;
  (ii) 28% for gains on residential property interests and carried interest.

Note that for calculating the rate at which Scottish taxpayers pay capital gains tax, it is the UK basic rate band of £33,500 which is applied, not the Scottish basic rate band of £31,500 (see **2.5**).

A residential property interest is one used or intended to be used as a dwelling (excluding certain types of residential property such as care or nursing homes, purpose built student accommodation, hospitals, hospices, military accommodation, prisons etc).

For these purposes from 6 April 2016 the unused part of the basic rate band is first reduced by any gains chargeable to tax at the entrepreneurs' relief or investors' relief rate (see **4.1**). The annual exempt amount and losses can be applied in a way that produces the lowest possible tax charge, subject to any existing legislation that limits the way in which certain losses may be set off. Also from 6 April 2016 where an individual has upper rate gains and some unused basic rate band he may choose which upper rate gains and which other gains are subject to the lower capital gains rates (10% or 18%). This means the unused basic rate band can be used in the most beneficial way.

Example 1

In 2017–18, X's taxable income, after all allowable deductions and the personal allowance, is £26,500. The upper limit of the income tax basic rate band is £33,500. X sells a plot of land in May 2017 and realises a chargeable gain of £17,000. In November 2017 X sells another plot of land, realising a chargeable gain of £25,300. X has no allowable losses to set against these gains, and the annual exempt amount for 2017–18 is £11,300. The plots of land are not residential property interests and he has no gains qualifying for entrepreneurs' relief.

X's total taxable gains realised in 2017–18 are £42,300. The annual exempt amount of £11,300 is offset against this, leaving £31,000 liable to tax. As X's taxable income is £7,000 less than the upper limit of the basic rate band (£33,500–£26,500), the first £7,000 of the £31,000 is taxed at 10% and the remaining £24,000 is taxed at 20%.

If the two assets sold had been residential property interests, the first £7,000 of the £31,000 would be taxed at 18% and the remaining £24,000 would be taxed at 28%.

See **4.44** and **4.45** for the capital gains position of personal representatives and trustees.

Chargeable gain

[4.3] Gains and losses are calculated separately for each asset. In general, the cost of an asset acquired before 31 March 1982 is taken to be its value on 31 March 1982. If allowable losses exceed chargeable gains, the excess loss is carried forward to be used against later gains. Excess losses cannot be carried back other than on death (see **4.44**). Losses are not allowable losses if they arise through arrangements to secure a tax advantage.

The gains and losses arising on all disposals of chargeable assets during a tax year are aggregated to give the net chargeable gains or allowable losses for the year. Broadly, if losses exceed gains, the losses are carried forward without time limit, to set against later gains to the extent that those gains are not covered by the annual exempt amount (see **4.29**).

Relief for losses is usually claimed in tax returns, with an overall time limit to make the claim of four years from the end of the tax year in which the loss occurred (but this has no effect on the time for which losses may be carried forward). Where brought-forward losses are used to reduce gains, losses in years from 1996–97 onwards are regarded as set off before pre-1996–97 losses. This could delay, or at worst prevent, a pre-1996–97 loss on a transaction with a connected person being set off against later gains on transactions with that person (see **4.11**), since any post-1996–97 losses would have to be set off first.

Where profits are being or have been calculated on the cash basis either for a trade or a property business (see **20.4** and **32.6**), disposals of assets other than land will not give rise to a chargeable gain or loss (because the proceeds are liable to income tax).

Trading losses

[4.4] Sole traders and partners may set off unrelieved trading losses against their capital gains in certain circumstances (see **25.7**).

Residence and domicile (TCGA 1992, ss 2, 10–12)

[4.5] The liability to capital gains tax depends essentially on the residence status of the individual.

UK resident

Individuals who are resident in the UK are liable to capital gains tax on all gains wherever they arise if they are also UK domiciled (see **41.10**). Non-domiciled individuals or 'non-domiciles', i.e. those who do not have a UK domicile, are liable on gains arising in the UK, but their liability on foreign gains is limited to gains brought into the UK if the remittance basis applies (see **41.16**).

Personal representatives essentially are treated as having the deceased's residence and domicile and their liability will follow accordingly. Trustees are liable to capital gains tax if they are, as a body, treated as resident in the UK during any part of the year in question. Details of CGT liabilities arising to personal representatives and trustees are in CHAPTER **42**.

Non-UK resident

Non-resident individuals are liable to capital gains tax if they are carrying on a trade in the UK; the liability being in respect of gains arising on the disposal of business assets in the UK.

From 6 April 2015, non-resident individuals, personal representatives, trustees (plus certain companies or funds) are liable to capital gains tax on gains made on the disposal of UK residential property. The liability also applies to individuals who are non-resident in the overseas part of a split year. This non-resident capital gains charge (NRCGT) rule takes precedence over the temporary non-residence rule, meaning that the temporary non-residence rules only apply to gains which are not UK residential property. For details of the NRCGT charge see **41.50**.

Temporary non-UK resident

Individuals who become non-resident may escape capital gains tax unless they are deemed to be temporarily non-resident (**41.49**). In that event they will be liable to tax on gains arising during their absence. The NRGCT rules in **41.50** take precedence over the temporary non-residence rules.

Overseas aspects generally are dealt with in CHAPTER **41**.

Spouses and civil partners (TCGA 1992, ss 2, 58)

[4.6] The gains of spouses or civil partners living together are calculated and charged separately, each being entitled to the annual exempt amount (£11,300 for 2017–18). Losses of one may not be set against the other's gains. Disposals between husband and wife or civil partners in a tax year when they are living together are, however, treated as made on a no gain/no loss basis (see **4.43**), and it should be possible through advance planning and transfers of assets between spouses/partners to ensure that one is not left with unrelieved losses while the other has gains in excess of the annual exempt amount.

The above treatment of assets acquired from the other spouse or civil partner has no relevance to assets acquired on a spouse's or civil partner's death. Any such assets are treated for capital gains tax as acquired at market value at the date of death. See **33.14** for the capital gains tax treatment on breakdown of the marriage or civil partnership.

Basis of charge for companies (TCGA 1992, ss 2B–2F, 8, 14B–14H, 16A, 184G–184I; CTA 2009, s 4)

Rate of tax

[4.7] The capital gains of companies are usually charged to corporation tax at the company's applicable rate for the accounting period (see **3.14**). However gains that are realised by non-natural persons (i.e. companies and certain collective investment schemes) on a disposal of a high value property that falls within the annual tax on enveloped dwellings (ATED) regime (**32.48**) are charged to capital gains tax at 28%; see **4.8**.

From 6 April 2015, there are special rules to charge gains realised by certain non-resident companies (essentially those that are closely controlled) on the disposal of UK residential property to capital gains tax at 20%; see **41.50**.

Chargeable gain

[4.8] The capital gains of companies are broadly computed on capital gains tax principles, although different rules apply depending upon whether the gain is realised on property that falls within the annual tax on enveloped dwellings (ATED) regime, or not.

Gains not within the ATED regime

The gains for an accounting period are reduced by current and brought forward allowable capital losses. Companies are not entitled to an annual exempt amount although they are entitled to indexation allowance (see **4.22**). Companies are also treated differently in relation to gains on stocks and shares (see CHAPTER 38). From 6 April 2015, certain non-UK resident companies may be liable to capital gains tax on the disposal of UK residential property; see **41.50**.

Gains within the ATED regime

Gains realised by UK and non-UK resident 'non-natural persons' (i.e. companies and certain collective investment schemes) on a disposal of a high value property that falls within the ATED regime are chargeable to capital gains tax at 28%. Property is high value where its disposal consideration is, from 1 April 2016, in excess of £500,000, although where the disposal is of the whole of a person's fractional share the threshold amount is reduced proportionately by reference to that share. Increases (and decreases) in the value of property before 6 April 2013 are outside the capital gains tax charge but remain subject to the existing corporation tax rules on capital gains.

Individuals, trustees and personal representatives are excluded from this charge if they hold property directly, are a member of a partnership and the gain accrues on a disposal of a partnership asset, or if they are a participant in a 'relevant collective investment scheme' and the gain accrues on property held for the purposes of the scheme.

The chargeable amount is the lower of (a) the full ATED-related gain, and (b) 5/3 times the difference between the consideration for the disposal and the threshold amount for that disposal. This restriction does not, however, affect the amount of an allowable loss accruing on the disposal of an asset, or the amount of any loss (whether it is an ATED-related loss or not).

Example 2

A property that falls within the ATED regime was purchased on 30 April 2017. It was sold on 1 March 2018 for £1.1m, realising a gain of £1.2m. The threshold amount is £500,000. 5/3 of the difference between the consideration for the disposal and the threshold amount is £1m.

Assume the whole of the gain on the disposal is ATED-related

The chargeable gain is the lower of:

(a) the full ATED-related gain — £1,200,000; and
(b) 5/3 of the difference between the consideration for the disposal and the threshold amount — £1,000,000

So the chargeable gain is capped at £1,000,000.

Assume part of the gain on the disposal is ATED-related

If only part of the gain is ATED-related, say 4/10, the ATED-related gain chargeable to CGT is capped at 4/10 × £1,000,000 = £400,000. The gain that is not ATED-related is unaffected.

See **5.2** regarding the inheritance tax charge from April 2017 for non-domiciled individuals on UK residential property held indirectly by them. The Government states that the change may incentivise some non-domiciles to transfer their UK residential properties from overseas vehicles into simpler structures outside the scope of ATED charges.

Capital losses

[4.9] Capital losses on disposals made on or after 5 December 2005 are not allowable if they arise through arrangements to secure a tax advantage. Specific anti-avoidance provisions counter arrangements to secure a tax advantage by converting an income receipt into a capital receipt in order to secure a deduction for capital losses (provided HMRC have given the company notice in relation to the arrangements). Similarly arrangements aimed at using capital losses to reduce a chargeable gain, can be countered where the transaction that produced the gain resulted in expenditure that reduced income profits (again provided HMRC have given the company notice in relation to the arrangements).

Losses arising on disposals of high value property that falls within the ATED regime are 'ring-fenced' and can only be set against ATED-related chargeable gains in the same tax year or, when the losses exceed the gains for the year, the unused losses are carried forward and set off against ATED-related chargeable gains in later years. For the treatment of losses arising to certain non-UK resident companies on the disposal of UK residential property; see **41.50**.

Reliefs

[4.10] A 'substantial shareholdings exemption' applies to trading companies disposing of holdings of 10% or more in other trading companies — see **3.34** for brief details. There are also separate 'intangible fixed assets' rules for companies under which gains and losses on such assets (notably goodwill) are dealt with in computing income profits and losses rather than capital gains and losses — see **20.35** to **20.41**. Other differences in the capital gains provisions for companies are mentioned in context as they occur. See **3.31** in relation to the capital gains of groups of companies.

Transactions with connected persons (TCGA 1992, ss 18–20, 286)

[4.11] All transactions made between connected persons, or made not at arm's length, are regarded as made for a consideration equal to open market value (subject again to the special treatment for transfers between spouses or civil partners living together). Broadly, a person is connected with his spouse or civil partner; his or his spouse's or civil partner's close relatives (see below) and their spouses or civil partners; business partners and their spouses or civil partners and relatives (except in relation to normal commercial transactions). The relatives that are taken into account are brothers and sisters, ancestors (i.e. parents, grandparents, etc.), and lineal descendants (i.e. children, grandchildren, etc.). Companies under the same control are connected with each other and with the persons controlling them. The trustee of a settlement is connected with the settlor (if an individual) and with any person connected with the settlor.

Where an asset is disposed of to a connected person (other than the individual's spouse or civil partner) and a loss arises, the loss may not be set against general gains but only against a later gain on a transaction with the same connected person. See **4.2** for the possible adverse effect of the set-off order for brought forward losses. Where someone disposes of assets (for example, unquoted shares) on different occasions within a period of six years to one or more persons connected with him, and their value taken together is higher than their separate values, then the disposal value for each of the transactions is a proportionate part of the aggregate value, and all necessary adjustments will be made to earlier tax charges.

Chargeable assets and exempt assets (TCGA 1992, ss 21–27, 251–253; FA 2017, s 13)

[4.12] All forms of property are chargeable unless specifically exempt. A disposal of a chargeable asset may give rise to a chargeable gain or allowable loss. A chargeable gain or allowable loss may also arise when a capital sum is realised without any disposal taking place (for example if compensation is received for damage to an asset, although if the compensation is used to restore the asset no gain arises).

Where an asset is exempt, no chargeable gain or allowable loss can normally arise, although there are some special rules about losses on chattels (see the table below). As indicated in **4.10**, there is a special exemption for the disposal by trading companies of substantial shareholdings in other companies.

Exempt assets		
	Statutory reference	*See further*
Cars: Private motor cars, including veteran and vintage cars	TCGA 1992, s 263	CHAPTER 39
Chattels: Non-wasting and business chattels where disposal proceeds do not exceed £6,000	TCGA 1992, s 262	CHAPTER 39
Chattels: Wasting assets, unless used in a business and capital allowances have been, or could have been, claimed; or unless used as plant in a business by a third party	TCGA 1992, s 45	CHAPTER 39
Compensation: For personal or professional wrong or injury and certain compensation from the UK or a foreign government for property lost or confiscated	TCGA 1992, ss 51, 268B	
Compensation: Rights to receive compensation from UK or foreign banks and building societies on frozen accounts of Holocaust victims	TCGA 1992, s 268A	
Compensation: Rights to take court action to recover compensation or damages. From 27 January 2014, where compensation is not linked to an underlying asset (for example where a professional adviser gives misleading advice, or fails to claim a tax relief in time) there is a maximum limit of £500,000 which will be exempt. Where compensation is linked to an asset chargeable to capital gains tax, the exemption is unlimited	ESC D33	

Decorations for valour: If disposed of by the original holder or legatees but not by a purchaser	TCGA 1992, s 268	
Exempt property: Sale of property that is 'exempt property' under the remittance basis, where certain conditions are met	ITA 2007, ss 809YA–809YD	41.16
Foreign currency bank accounts	TCGA 1992, ss 251, 252, 252A, Sch 8A	4.14
Gifts: To charities and certain amateur sports clubs	TCGA 1992, s 257	CHAPTER 43
Inheritance tax conditional exemption relief: Disposal of certain assets that have or could qualify for the relief	TCGA 1992, s 258(2)	4.15
Life assurance policies: In the hands of the original owner or beneficiaries	TCGA 1992, s 210	CHAPTER 40
Pre-eminent gift relief: Disposal of assets that qualify for this relief	TCGA 1992, s 258(1A)	2.21
Prizes and betting winnings	TCGA 1992, s 51	4.13
Residence: An individual's only or main residence — all or part of the gain may be exempt.	TCGA 1992, ss 222, 223	CHAPTER 30
SAYE contracts, savings certificates and premium bonds	TCGA 1992, s 121	CHAPTER 11, CHAPTER 36
Securities: Employee shareholder shares acquired under an employee shareholder agreement entered into before 1 December 2016 (or 2 December 2016 in cases where the employee received professional advice in relation to the share offer on 23 November 2016 before 1.30pm) worth up to £50,000, subject to lifetime limit on gains	TCGA 1992, ss 236B–236G	11.36
Securities: Government securities and qualifying company loan stock	TCGA 1992, s 115	CHAPTER 38
Sterling currency, and foreign currency for an individual's own spending and maintenance of assets abroad	TCGA 1992, ss 21, 269	CHAPTER 39

Prizes and betting winnings

[4.13] If a lottery prize is won, it is exempt from capital gains tax. If playing as a member of a group, the group should draw up an agreement setting out how the group will operate, who will buy tickets and claim prizes, and how any prize money is to be shared, otherwise a group claimant passing on shares of prize money to other group members could be regarded as making gifts for inheritance tax purposes (see CHAPTER 5). The same would apply to similar group arrangements, such as for football pools. There would not, however, be any inheritance tax to pay unless the person who passed on the shares of prize money died within seven years, and even then there may be exemptions available to cover the gifts.

Foreign currency bank accounts

[4.14] No chargeable gain or allowable loss accrues on deposits or withdrawals to or from foreign currency bank accounts where the account stands to the credit of an individual, trustee or personal representative.

Assets that qualify for IHT conditional exemption

[4.15] If the requirements for inheritance tax conditional exemption (5.16) have or could be satisfied in relation to particular assets, a corresponding relief from capital gains tax is available if a disposal is:

(a)   a gift or sale to any of the bodies listed in IHTA 1984, Sch 3 (for example, the National Gallery, the National Trust and any UK university); or

(b)   to HMRC as acceptance of the property in lieu of inheritance tax (5.53).

Treatment of loans

[4.16] For companies, capital transactions relating to loans are brought into account for income purposes (see **3.4**). For individuals, trustees and personal representatives, a debt is not within the capital gains provisions unless it is a 'debt on a security' (which broadly means marketable loan stock). Even then, most loan stock is within the definition of a 'qualifying corporate bond' (see **38.6**), and is exempt from capital gains tax. The effect is that if capital gains or losses arise on simple debts, or on qualifying corporate bonds, no relief is available for the losses (subject to some special rules for loans to UK traders — see **4.37** and **38.40**), and gains are exempt.

For the treatment of loan stock that is outside the definition of qualifying corporate bonds see **38.6**. Where a simple debt has been assigned other than to someone with whom the creditor is 'connected' (see **4.11**), the debt is a chargeable asset for the assignee, thus giving rise to a chargeable gain or allowable loss on a disposal by the assignee.

Computation of gains and losses (TCGA 1992, ss 2, 15–17, 35–57 and Schs A1, 2–4, 4ZZA)

Meaning of disposal (TCGA 1992, ss 1, 26, 26A, 62)

[4.17] Capital gains tax is chargeable on chargeable gains accruing on the disposal of an asset. No definition of 'disposal' is given in TCGA 1992, so the word takes its normal meaning. A disposal occurs when an asset is sold, exchanged or gifted and includes a part disposal. Certain transactions are however specifically treated as involving no disposal, for example:

(a)   where an asset is transferred by way of security;

(b)   on the issue of shares by a company and the satisfaction of a liability, such as the repayment of a debt;

(c)   on a transfer of funds in a dormant account to an authorised reclaim fund. See **37.1** for the treatment of interest credited to such accounts;

(d)   on death (there is no disposal of the assets comprised in the estate of the deceased individual, see **4.44**).

Calculation of initial gain

[4.18] Gains and losses on individual assets are worked out by deducting from the sale proceeds or, in some instances, from the market value at the time of disposal (see, for example, **4.11** and **4.31**) the following amounts:

(a)   original cost and incidental costs of acquisition;
(b)   expenditure that has increased the value of the asset;
(c)   incidental costs of disposal.

For companies, providing the gain is not an ATED-related gain (see **4.8**), an indexation allowance (see **4.22**) may then be given to reduce or eliminate a gain, but the allowance cannot create or increase a loss. For individuals, personal representatives and trustees no indexation allowance is available and entrepreneurs' relief (or from 2019–20 investors' relief) may be available (see **4.30**). The Government announced its intention to introduce a digital calculator for CGT from October 2016.

Gains within the ATED regime

[4.19] ATED-related gains (see **4.8**) are calculated using the usual capital gains tax principles, although no indexation allowance is available. Where the chargeable interest disposed of was acquired before 6 April 2013 and disposed of after that date, the gain is calculated by computing a 'notional post-April 2013' gain on the assumption that the interest was acquired at its market value on 5 April 2013. It is possible for an election to be made to disapply this rule in which case the gain is calculated as if the ATED regime were in force throughout the period of ownership. Such an election is irrevocable and must be made in a capital gains tax return for the tax year in which the interest is disposed of.

The computational steps are essentially the same for losses, but no notional indexation allowance is available to increase any non-ATED related loss (because indexation allowance under the normal rules cannot create or increase a loss).

Effect of capital allowances (TCGA 1992, s 41)

[4.20] A taxpayer's business or rental income may be reduced by capital allowances (see CHAPTER **22**). Capital gains on some assets that qualify for capital allowances are exempt from capital gains tax, such as gains on items of movable plant and machinery sold for less than £6,000 (see **39.4**). Where an asset is not exempt, capital allowances are not deducted from the cost in computing a capital gain (though they will be recovered by way of a balancing charge in the capital allowances pool, see **22.19**). This means that there will be a gain only if the asset is sold for more than its original cost. Capital allowances are, however, taken into account in computing a capital loss. Capital allowances (that have not been recovered by way of a balancing charge) are deducted from the original acquisition cost. This means in practice that capital losses on such disposals do not normally arise since the capital allowance system has usually covered any drop in value. For an example, see **22.46**. 'Capital allowance' for these purposes includes any deduction of capital expenditure in calculating the profits on the cash basis either for small businesses or property businesses (see **20.4** and **32.6**).

Indexation allowance (TCGA 1992, ss 53, 54)

Individuals, trustees and personal representatives

[4.21] The indexation allowance (see **4.18**) was abolished for individuals, trustees and personal representatives with effect for disposals after 5 April 2008.

Companies

[4.22] Indexation remains available to companies (although not for ATED-related gains; see **4.8**). The allowance is calculated by applying to each item of expenditure the increase in the retail prices index between the month when the expenditure was incurred, or March 1982 if later, and the month of disposal of the asset. That increase is expressed as a decimal and rounded (up or down) to three decimal places. The movement in the index is published monthly and the figure for each month since March 1982 is in the TABLE OF RATES AND ALLOWANCES (**TRA**) under 'Retail prices index'. The formula for working out the increase is:

$$\frac{RD - RI}{RI} \quad \text{or put more simply} \quad \frac{RD}{RI} - 1$$

RD is the index for the month of disposal and RI the index for the month in which the expenditure was incurred. For example, using the figures in the 'Retail prices index' table in the TABLE OF RATES AND ALLOWANCES (**TRA**), the increase from November 1992 to April 2017 is:

$$\frac{270.6}{139.7} - 1 = .937 \text{ (or as a percentage, 93.7\%)}$$

The indexation allowance can only reduce or eliminate a gain and cannot create or increase a loss.

Where the expenditure was incurred before 31 March 1982, the indexation calculation is made by reference to the value of the asset at 31 March 1982 if the taxpayer has elected to be treated as if he had acquired all the assets he owned on 31 March 1982 at their market value on that day (see **4.23**). If the election has not been made, the 31 March 1982 value is still used to calculate the indexation allowance unless using original cost would give a higher figure, in which case that higher figure is taken.

Assets held on 31 March 1982 (TCGA 1992, ss 35, 36 and Schs 3, 4)

[4.23] Originally, capital gains tax applied to gains or losses made on or after 6 April 1965, and there were special rules relating to assets already owned on that date to ensure that pre-6 April 1965 gains and losses on such assets were excluded. Since 6 April 1988, broadly speaking, only gains or losses arising since 31 March 1982 have been taken into account.

Individuals, trustees and personal representatives

[4.24] For individuals, trustees and personal representatives there is an automatic 'rebasing' of allowable expenditure to 31 March 1982. This means that all assets owned on 31 March 1982 are automatically treated as having been acquired at their market value on 31 March 1982.

Companies

[4.25] Companies, however, have the option to make an irrevocable 'rebasing' election for all assets owned on 31 March 1982 (except plant and machinery on which capital allowances have been, or could have been, claimed) to be treated as having been acquired at their market value on that day.

The time limit for making the rebasing election dates from the *first disposal after 5 April 1988*, and must be made no later than two years after the end of the accounting period of disposal. Most disposals that normally result in no chargeable gain or allowable loss are not, however, treated as triggering the time limit (see HMRC Statement of Practice SP 4/92).

If the rebasing election is not made, the 31 March 1982 value is still used to calculate gains and losses, unless using original cost would show a lower gain or lower loss, in which case the lower figure is taken. If one method shows a gain and the other a loss the result is neither a gain nor a loss. In making these calculations indexation allowance is always based on the higher of cost and 31 March 1982 value (see **4.22**).

For many assets it may be costly to find out their value at 31 March 1982, but this has to be done whether the election to use 31 March 1982 value is made or not.

Example 3

A chargeable asset was bought for £20,000 in 1980 and was worth £24,000 on 31 March 1982. It was sold in February 2017. The company had made no other disposals since 5 April 1988, so it can make a rebasing election, which will then apply to all subsequent disposals of chargeable assets owned on 31 March 1982.

Assume indexation gives an indexation allowance of £57,000 (based on the 31 March 1982 value, since it is higher than cost).

The position is as follows.

If general rebasing election is not made

	(a)	(b)	(c)
	£	£	£
Sale proceeds, say	90,000	19,000	22,000
31.3.82 value (giving lower gain)	(24,000)		
Cost (giving lower loss)		(20,000)	
Unindexed gain (loss)	66,000	(1,000)	
Indexation allowance	(57,000)	—	No gain,
Chargeable gain (allowable loss)	9,000	(1,000)	no loss

If general rebasing election is made

	(a)	(b)	(c)
	£	£	£
Sale proceeds as above	90,000	19,000	22,000
31.3.82 value	(24,000)	(24,000)	(24,000)
Unindexed gain (loss)	66,000	(5,000)	(2,000)
Indexation allowance	(57,000)	—	—
Chargeable gain (allowable loss)	9,000	(5,000)	(2,000)

Rebasing election is either neutral or favourable in relation to this asset, depending on sale proceeds.

Example 4

Using the same figures as in Example 3, but assuming that cost price was £24,000 and 31.3.82 value was £20,000, i.e. figures are reversed, the position is as follows.

If general rebasing election is not made

The outcome will be the same as in Example 3, since the lower gain or loss is always taken, and there is no gain or loss where one computation shows a gain and the other a loss.

If general rebasing election is made

Cost of £24,000 becomes irrelevant. Assume the indexation allowance on 31.3.82 value of £20,000 is £47,000.

	(a)	(b)	(c)
	£	£	£
Sale proceeds as above	80,000	19,000	22,000

31.3.82 value	(20,000)	(20,000)	(20,000)
Unindexed gain (loss)	60,000	(1,000)	2,000
Indexation allowance	(47,000)	—	(2,000)
Chargeable gain (allowable loss)	13,000	(1,000)	—

Rebasing election is unfavourable or neutral in relation to this asset, depending on sale proceeds.

Where the right to make a rebasing election is still available, it is not possible to be selective. If it is made at all, it applies to all chargeable assets owned on 31 March 1982 (except plant and machinery) and it cannot be revoked. The election does simplify the calculations and it makes it unnecessary to maintain pre-31 March 1982 records.

Various reliefs allow gains to be deferred to a later time, either by treating the gains as reducing other expenditure, or by treating them as arising at a later time. Where gains were deferred before 31 March 1982, the effect of using 31 March 1982 value to calculate later gains is that these deferred gains will escape tax altogether, since the cost from which the deferred gain was deducted is no longer used.

Where an asset acquired after 31 March 1982 but before 6 April 1988 has been disposed of after 5 April 1988, and the gain related wholly or partly, directly or indirectly, to an asset acquired before 31 March 1982 (in other words, where a claim for deferral was made between 31 March 1982 and 5 April 1988 that related to an asset acquired before 31 March 1982), the taxpayer is able to make a claim for one-half of the gain to be exempt from tax. The purpose of this 'halving relief' is to compensate the taxpayer for the fact that part of the gain charged on his disposal related to gains accruing in the period up to 31 March 1982.

Assets held on 6 April 1965 (TCGA 1992, s 35 and Sch 2)

[4.26] Assets already owned on 6 April 1965, the original start date for capital gains tax, are treated as acquired at market value on 31 March 1982 if either the rebasing election is made or automatic rebasing applies on a post-5 April 2008 disposal by an individual, trustee or personal representative (see 4.24).

Where rebasing does not apply the position is more complicated. The old rules for calculating the position on assets owned on 6 April 1965 contained separate provisions for land with development value, for quoted securities and for all other assets.

The gain or loss on land with development value was calculated by comparing the proceeds either with the original cost or with the value at 6 April 1965, whichever showed the lower gain or loss. If one method showed a gain and the other a loss, there was neither a gain nor loss. The same rules applied to quoted securities, except that it was possible to elect for quoted securities to be treated as having been acquired on 6 April 1965 at their value on that date and pooled with later acquisitions of shares of the same class in the same company. The detailed provisions for shares are in CHAPTER 38.

Where an asset other than quoted securities or land with development value was acquired before 6 April 1965, only the time proportion of the gain falling after 6 April 1965 was chargeable, although the earliest date that could be used in a time apportionment calculation was 6 April 1945. It was possible to elect to work out the gain by using the 6 April 1965 value as the cost instead of using time apportionment, but once made this election was irrevocable, even if it resulted in more tax being payable.

Following the 1988 changes (see **4.23**), in the absence of a rebasing election (where available) the above rules are modified to bring the 31 March 1982 value into the calculation. The calculation is first made using the old rules for assets owned on 6 April 1965 but with indexation allowance based on 31 March 1982 value if higher. When making the time apportionment calculation for assets other than quoted securities and land with development value, indexation allowance is deducted before the gain is time apportioned. The resulting gain or loss is compared with the result using 31 March 1982 value. The lower gain or loss is then taken and if one calculation shows a gain and the other a loss, the result is neither a gain nor loss. If, however, the old 6 April 1965 rules have already resulted in a no gain/no loss result, that position is not disturbed.

Example 5

A company has owned a chargeable asset since 6 April 1964, which it sells on 6 April 2017. The gain will be calculated as follows:

Cost of antique 6.4.64	£4,250
Value at 6.4.65	£4,500
Value at 31.3.82	£10,000
Sale proceeds 6.4.17	£54,700

If no election is made to use 31.3.82 value for all assets

Calculation using 6 April 1965 rules:

	£	£
Sale proceeds	54,700	54,700
Cost	(4,250)	
6.4.65 value		(4,500)
Indexation allowance on 31.3.82 value of £10,000 (say)	(25,700)	(25,700)
Overall gain	£24,750	

Time proportion since 6.4.65

$$\frac{52}{53} \times 24,750 = \underline{\qquad 24,283 \qquad} \qquad \underline{\qquad\qquad}$$

$$\text{Gain} \quad \underline{£24,283} \quad \text{or} \quad \underline{£24,500}$$

Therefore no election would be made to use 6.4.65 value and gain under 6 April 1965 rules is £24,283.

	£
Calculation using March 1982 rules:	
Sale proceeds	54,700
31.3.82 value	(10,000)
Indexation allowance (say)	(25,700)
Gain under March 1982 rules	£19,000

Chargeable gain is the lower of £24,283 and £19,000, i.e. £19,000.

If election made to use 31.3.82 value for all assets

Chargeable gain is not affected, since the 31 March 1982 value is used in any event.

Part disposals (TCGA 1992, ss 42, 242)

[4.27] Where part only of an asset is disposed of, the cost of the part disposed of is worked out by taking the proportion of the overall cost that the sale proceeds bear to the sum of the sale proceeds plus the market value of what remains unsold. Any indexation allowance is calculated on the apportioned part of the cost and not on the total.

Where part of a holding of land is sold for £20,000 or less, and the proceeds represent not more than 20% of the value of the whole holding, the taxpayer may claim not to be treated as having made a disposal, but the amount received reduces the allowable cost of the remaining land for a future disposal. Any available indexation allowance on a subsequent disposal is calculated on the full cost in the usual way, but is then reduced to take account of the previous part disposal. This claim may not be made if other disposals of land are made in the same year, and the total proceeds for all disposals of land exceed £20,000.

Leases (TCGA 1992, s 240 and Sch 8)

[4.28] The grant of a lease at a premium gives rise to a capital gains tax liability, and if the term is 50 years or less there is also an income tax liability. The calculation of the income and capital elements is shown in **32.23**. Where a tenant assigns a lease at a premium to another tenant, the premium is charged to capital gains tax in the normal way if the lease has more than 50 years to run at the time of the assignment. If, however, it has 50 years or less to run, it is a wasting asset and the cost has to be depreciated over those 50 years according to a table in TCGA 1992, Sch 8 which ensures that the cost is depreciated more slowly during the early part of the 50-year period than during the later years.

Annual exempt amount (TCGA 1992, s 3 and Sch 1; SI 2017/377)

[4.29] The capital gains tax annual exempt amount is £11,300 for 2017–18 (£11,100 for 2016–17), available to each individual, whether single, married or a civil partner. If an individual's gains for a tax year are below this amount, no capital gains tax is payable. Any unused exemption cannot be carried forward and set against future gains.

The annual exempt amount is not available to companies. For the annual exempt amount available to personal representatives and trustees, see **4.44** and **4.45**.

Reliefs

[4.30] Specific reliefs, which either reduce the capital gains tax liability or defer it, are available. The following current reliefs relating to businesses are examined in CHAPTER **29**:

(a)   entrepreneurs' relief for qualifying business disposals after 5 April 2008;

(b)   investors' relief on disposals of qualifying shares in an unlisted trading company after 5 April 2019;

(c)   rollover relief on the replacement of business assets;

(d)   reliefs under the enterprise investment scheme, the seed enterprise investment scheme and the venture capital trusts scheme;

(e)   social investment tax relief.

Incorporation relief on the transfer of a business to a company is examined in **27.9**. Disincorporation relief, when a company transfers its business to some or all of the shareholders of the company, is detailed at **27.18**. Private residence relief and chattel relief are discussed in CHAPTER **30** and CHAPTER **39** respectively. The remainder of this chapter includes a brief description of:

(i)   holdover relief for gifts of certain assets (**4.32**);

(ii)   relief for assets of negligible value (**4.36**);

(iii)   relief for losses on certain loans (**4.37**);

(iv)   relief on gains accruing on the disposal of shares in a trading company (or in a holding company of a trading group) to a special trust which operates for the benefit of all employees (**4.38**).

In addition anti-avoidance provisions apply to prevent taxpayers escaping tax by abusing a concession which permits a deferral of capital gains tax (**4.39**).

Gifts (TCGA 1992, ss 17, 67, 165–169G, 258–261, 281 and Sch 7)

[4.31] For capital gains tax purposes a gift of a chargeable asset is regarded as a disposal at open market value (except for transfers between spouses or civil partners living together, see **4.6**), and the chargeable gain or allowable loss is computed in the usual way, unless gift relief (see below) is available.

Gift relief (TCGA 1992, ss 165–169G, 260, 281 and Sch 7)

[4.32] Where a gain arises on the gift of an asset by an individual or trustees, a claim may be made to defer the gain if the asset qualifies for gift relief (subject to various anti-avoidance provisions mentioned below). Gift relief is also available where assets are not given outright but are disposed of for less than their value.

Gift relief used to be available on virtually any asset, but the gifts that now qualify for relief are as shown below (although note that relief for gifts of shares or securities under (c) is not available if the gift is to a company):

(a)   gifts of assets used in a trade or profession carried on by:
        (i)   the donor or his personal 'trading company' (i.e. one in which he owns at least 5% of the voting rights);
        (ii)   a company in a 'trading group' of which the 'holding company' is the donor's personal trading company; or
        (iii)   (in the case of a transfer by trustees) the trustees themselves or a beneficiary who has an interest in possession in the trust property (see **42.19**);
(b)   gifts of farm land and buildings that would qualify for inheritance tax agricultural property relief (see **5.48**); note that this enables relief to be claimed on agricultural land held as an investment, providing the appropriate conditions are satisfied;
(c)   gifts of shares or securities in trading companies or holding companies of trading groups where:
        (i)   the shares or securities are unlisted;
        (ii)   if the transferor is an individual, the company is his personal company; or
        (iii)   if the transferor is a trustee the trustees held at least 25% of the voting rights at the time of the disposal (see **42.19**);
(d)   gifts that:
        (i)   are *immediately* chargeable to inheritance tax (or would be immediately chargeable if they were not covered by the inheritance tax annual exemption); or
        (ii)   fall within certain specified inheritance tax exemptions (i.e. gifts of heritage property (works of art, historic buildings, etc.), gifts to funds for the maintenance of heritage property (see **5.17**) or gifts to political parties).

A 'trading company' is a company carrying on trading activities whose activities do not include 'to a substantial extent' activities other than trading activities. A 'holding company' is a company with one or more 51% subsidiaries. A group of companies (i.e. a company and its '51% subsidiaries') is a 'trading group' if one or more of its members carries on trading activities and the activities of all members taken together do not include to a substantial extent activities other than trading activities.

[4.33] Where gift relief is claimed, the donor is not charged to tax on the gain and the value at which the donee is treated as having acquired the asset is reduced by the gain, so that the donee will make a correspondingly larger gain (or smaller loss) when he disposes of the asset. HMRC have stated that in most circumstances it will not be necessary to agree market values at the time of the gift relief claim. Establishing the market value at the date of the gift can normally be deferred until the donee disposes of the asset (HMRC Statement of Practice SP 8/92).

[4.34] Claims for gift relief to apply must be made by the donor and donee jointly except where the donees are trustees, in which case only the donor need make the claim. Under self-assessment, claims will usually be sent in with tax returns. There is a form for making the claim in HMRC helpsheet HS295. The overall time limit for claims is four years from the end of the relevant year of assessment.

Where a gift on which the gift holdover relief is claimed attracts inheritance tax, either immediately or as a result of the donor's death within seven years, the donee's base cost for capital gains tax is increased by the inheritance tax (but not so as to create a loss on future disposal). If, however, a lifetime gift does not qualify for holdover relief and capital gains tax is paid, there is no direct inheritance tax relief for the capital gains tax paid if the gift becomes chargeable for inheritance tax because of the donor's death within seven years (although the capital gains tax paid has reduced the wealth of the donor and therefore the amount liable to inheritance tax on his death).

Where tax remains payable after gift relief, it may be paid by ten annual instalments if the gift was one of land, a controlling shareholding in a company, or minority holding of unquoted shares or securities in a company. Interest is, however, charged on the full amount outstanding and not just on any instalment which is paid late.

Residence

[4.35] The general rule is that gift relief is not available if the donee is not resident in the UK. However, from 1 April 2015, gift relief is available where business assets (in the form of UK residential property) are disposed of as a gift from a UK resident to a non-UK resident, if the asset would otherwise be chargeable to NRCGT (see **41.50**) in the hands of the donee. The full amount of the held-over gain accrues as a chargeable NRCGT gain for the donee on a subsequent disposal, in addition to any gain that actually accrues.

To prevent abuse of the general rule it is provided that if the donee is an individual resident in the UK at the time of the gift, but becomes non-resident before disposing of the asset and within six years after the end of the tax year in which the gift was made, the gain is then charged to tax. This charge will not apply if the asset has previously been disposed of, the donee is leaving the UK to take up an overseas employment or the donee resumes UK residence within three years of the initial change of residence. In addition, no gain or loss will accrue at the time of becoming non-resident (if the donee so elects), if the gain at that time would be a chargeable NRCGT gain on the donee. On a subsequent disposal, the 'held-over' NRCGT charge accrues to the donee in addition to any subsequent gain/loss and the whole amount is charged to tax as a NRCGT.

Note, the above provisions do not apply to trustees, because separate rules impose a tax charge on all trust assets when a trust becomes non-resident — see **41.86**. Gift relief is not available on disposals to trusts in which the settlor has an interest (see **42.14**), although this is relaxed for gifts to maintenance funds for historic buildings (see **5.17**) where the trustees have (or could have) made an election that the income of the fund or the expenditure on maintenance shall be treated as income of the trust, rather than the settlor. There are also provisions to prevent the exploitation of the interaction between gift relief and the private residence exemption dealt with in CHAPTER 30 (see **30.11**).

Assets of negligible value (TCGA 1992, s 24)

[4.36] If an asset is lost, destroyed or extinguished, it is treated as disposed of at that time, even if no compensation is received. This means, for example, that shareholders of a company that goes into liquidation, will be regarded as disposing of the shares when the liquidation is completed, and relief may be claimed for the loss.

It is, however, possible to get relief before an asset is lost or destroyed if its value has sunk to a negligible level. (HMRC maintain a list of quoted shares which are accepted as being of negligible value. A claim is automatically accepted for any shares on this list). A claim can be made for the asset to be treated as sold and reacquired at that negligible value, establishing an allowable loss accordingly. The disposal will be deemed to take place either on the date of the claim or on an earlier date indicated in the claim. The earlier date must fall within the two years before the tax year or accounting period in which the claim is made, and the asset must have been of negligible value on that earlier date (whether or not it was of negligible value before then). There is no requirement to make a negligible value claim so that, for example, a claim should not be made if it would mean wasting the annual exempt amount.

Relief for losses on loans (TCGA 1992, ss 251–253)

[4.37] Relief is available to the lender or guarantor for losses on loans or guarantees if the borrower is UK resident and uses the money lent wholly for the purposes of a trade carried on by him. Upon an appropriate claim by the lender or guarantor, an irrecoverable loan or payment under guarantee gives rise to an allowable loss for capital gains tax, provided that the debt or the rights acquired by the guarantor following the guarantee payment are not assigned. If any amount is subsequently recovered (whether from the borrower or from any co-guarantor) it will be treated as a capital gain. The loss under these provisions is treated as a loss at the date of the claim, unless the claim stipulates an earlier time falling not more than two years before the beginning of the tax year of the claim, and providing the amount was irrecoverable at the earlier date.

This relief is not available if the loss arises because of something the lender, or guarantor, has done or failed to do, or where the amount has become irrecoverable in consequence of the terms of the loan, nor is it available where the claimant and borrower are spouses or civil partners.

For the treatment of loans generally see **4.16**.

Disposals to employee-ownership trusts (TCGA 1992, ss 236H–236S)

[4.38] For disposals made on or after 6 April 2014, by a person other than a company, there is relief from capital gains tax on disposals of shares in a trading company or in the parent company of a trading group. This relief is designed to support employee ownership, and if the qualifying conditions are met and a claim is made, the consideration received on the disposal is deemed to be an amount which results in no gain and no loss.

A claim for relief can be made if the following conditions are met:

(a) the shares disposed of are shares of a trading company (or parent company of a trading group) from the time of the disposal to the end of the tax year in which the disposal takes place;

(b) the trust is for the benefit of all eligible employees of the company (or, as the case may be, the group headed by the company) on the same terms from the time of the disposal to the end of the tax year in which the disposal takes place. (For disposals from 6 April 2014 to 25 June 2014 the settlement just had to meet the all-employee benefit requirement at the time of disposal). Trustees can, however, breach this requirement in certain situations, without jeopardising this qualifying condition (e.g. they can pay benefits for up to 12 months to a spouse etc of a former employee; apply the money for a charitable purpose; comply with an employee's written request not to receive the benefit of the settlement etc, etc). Transitional provisions apply if a trust was created before 10 December 2013 and it is not able to satisfy the all employee benefit. It may still qualify if it meets the inheritance tax definition of employee trust (see **42.49**) and the trustees held a significant interest in the company which they would later control;

(c) the trustees begin to control the company during the tax year of disposal and continue to control it up to and including the end of the tax year. (For disposals from 6 April 2014 to 25 June 2014 the trustees had to begin to control the company during the tax year and control it at the end of the tax year). Trustees will have control if they hold a majority of the company's shares, are entitled to the majority of profits available for distribution and are entitled to a majority of profits available for distribution on a winding up;

(d) neither the claimant nor anyone connected with him has received relief under this provision in an earlier year in relation to ordinary share capital of the same company or of a company in the same group; and

(e) at no time during the 12 months ending immediately after the disposal is the claimant a participator in the company and the 'participator fraction' exceeds 2/5. Furthermore, for disposals on or after 26 June 2014, the participator fraction must not exceed 2/5 at any time in the period beginning with the disposal and ending at the end of the tax year in which the disposal occurs. The participator fraction is the ratio of people who are both employees and participators (plus those who are both employees and connected with those who are both employees and participators) over the total number of employees. There is a 'grace period' of up to six months during which the participator fraction may exceed 2/5 if it is as a result of events beyond the reasonable control of the trustees.

For disposals on or after 26 June 2014, no relief is available if any of the relief requirements cease to be met in the tax year following the tax year in which the disposal occurs, and any claim already made will be revoked with adjustments being made by assessment where necessary. If at any time later any of the relief requirements cease to be met, the trustees are deemed to dispose of and reacquire the shares at market value immediately before the disqualifying event, with any gain being charged accordingly.

Shares acquired by trustees of a qualifying employee-ownership trust where this capital gains tax exemption applies are pooled separately from other shares and the share identification rules (see **38.18**) apply separately to these shares.

Abuse of concessions (TCGA 1992, s 284A)

[4.39] Where someone defers a gain under the capital gains provisions under a concession first published before 9 March 1999, or a later replacement concession with substantially the same effect, then if the deferred gain becomes chargeable (e.g. on the disposal of the asset) and the person on whom the gain arises seeks to avoid bringing it into charge, he is treated as having made a chargeable gain equal to the deferred gain in the tax year or company accounting period in which the deferred gain should have been brought back into charge. The person on whom the charge arises could be the same taxpayer or another taxpayer to whom the asset had been transferred with the benefit of capital gains deferral.

An example of the sort of abuse these measures counter is where a trader makes a gain on the sale of a business asset and incurs enhancement expenditure on an existing asset rather than buying another asset. Rollover relief to defer the gain (see **29.16** onwards) is not strictly available in these circumstances, but concession D22 enables the enhancement expenditure to be treated as the acquisition of a qualifying asset. Since the gain is deferred only by concession, the trader could not, without this provision, be compelled to bring it into account on the disposal of the asset on which the enhancement expenditure was incurred.

Returns, due date of payment, interest on overdue tax and repayment supplement (TCGA 1992, ss 3A, 283; TMA 1970, ss 59B, 86)

[4.40] Under the self-assessment system, the annual tax return contains details of capital gains, although in some instances the capital gains pages of the return do not have to be completed. The same payment date and interest rules apply for both income tax and capital gains tax (see **2.30**), except that capital gains tax is not included in payments on account and is payable in full on 31 January following the end of the tax year. Interest on underpaid tax is charged from the due date and repayment supplement is paid on overpaid tax from the date of overpayment to the date the repayment is made. For the latest interest rates see the Table of Rates and Allowances (**TRA**).

The Government proposes that from April 2019 a payment on account of any capital gains tax due on the disposal of residential property will be required to be made within 30 days of the completion of the disposal.

For companies, capital gains (other than ATED-related gains (see **4.8**) and gains subject to the NRCGT charge (see **41.50**)) are charged to corporation tax.

Payment by instalments (TCGA 1992, s 280)

[4.41] Capital gains tax may, at the taxpayer's option, be paid by instalments where the proceeds are being received by instalments over 18 months or more. The instalments run over eight years, or until the last instalment of the price is received if sooner, with relief for bad debts being available if part of the amount due proves irrecoverable. Interest is charged on any instalments paid late (but only on the instalment and not on the full amount outstanding).

Capital gains tax may also be paid by instalments on certain gifts, but interest is then payable on the full amount outstanding, not just on overdue instalments.

Quoted and unquoted shares and securities

[4.42] Special rules apply to the capital gains tax treatment of both quoted and unquoted shares and securities, which are detailed at chapter **38**.

No gain/no loss disposals

[4.43] Special provisions apply to certain disposals, the main ones being:

(a)   Transfers on company reconstructions (TCGA 1992, s 139).

(b)   Transfers within a 75% group of companies (TCGA 1992, s 171). Companies in a 75% group may make a joint election under TCGA 1992, s 171A to set one group company's loss against another group company's gain without actually transferring assets intra-group under TCGA 1992, s 171 (see **3.31**).

(c)   Most transfers between spouses and civil partners living together (TCGA 1992, s 58).

(d)   Certain disposals to employee ownership trusts (TCGA 1992, ss 236H–236S); see **4.38**.

The disposal is effectively treated as giving rise to neither a gain nor a loss, and the transferee's acquisition cost is the original cost plus any available indexation allowance. (Any indexation allowance added to cost cannot, however, create or increase a loss on ultimate disposal but this rule does not apply to indexation allowance that had been added to cost up to the time of the last no gain/no loss transfer made before 30 November 1993).

A wide-ranging anti-avoidance provision applies from 6 December 2006 (5 December 2005 for companies) to deny relief for losses arising from arrangements made to secure a tax advantage. The Government has stated that taking advantage of a statutory relief, such as that in (*c*) above for spouses and civil partners, does not come within this anti-avoidance provision.

Death (TCGA 1992, ss 3(7), 4, 62 and Sch 1)

[4.44] No capital gains tax charge arises on increases in value of assets up to the point of death. If losses arise in the year of death these may be carried back and set against gains chargeable to tax in the three previous tax years (see **42.3**), latest first (with the set-off being made only against any gains not covered by the annual exempt amount in those years). Tax will be refunded accordingly, with repayment interest where appropriate running from the payment date for the tax year of death (see **9.55**).

The personal representatives or legatees are treated as acquiring the assets at the market value at the date of death. When personal representatives dispose of assets at values in excess of the values at death, gains arising will be charged to tax (and exemptions the deceased could have claimed may not be available, for example on a private residence) but they may claim the annual exempt amount, currently £11,300, in respect of disposals by them in the tax year of death and in each of the following two tax years. Any remaining gains in excess of the annual exempt amount are taxed at either 20% or 28% for gains accruing on or after 6 April 2016 depending on the type of gain (see **4.2**).

Where within two years after a death the persons entitled to the estate vary the way in which it is distributed, they may specify in the variation that it is to apply for capital gains tax. The variation is then not regarded as a disposal by those originally entitled but as having been made by the deceased at the date of death so that no capital gains tax charge arises on any increase in value since death — see **35.15** to **35.17**.

For further details regarding personal representatives see **42.2** to **42.6**.

Trusts (TCGA 1992, ss 3, 4, 68–98 and Schs 1, 5)

[4.45] Trustees are chargeable persons for capital gains tax. Trustees are entitled to an annual exempt amount of £5,650 for 2017–18 (£5,550 in 2016–17) unless the trust is for the disabled, in which case the exempt amount is £11,300 (£11,100 in 2016–17). The exemption is divided where there are several trusts created by the same settlor, but with each trust getting a minimum exemption of £1,130 (£1,110 in 2016–17). Any remaining gains in excess of the annual exempt amount are taxed at either 20% or 28% for gains accruing on or after 6 April 2016 depending on the type of gain (see **4.2**).

The detailed capital gains tax provisions for trusts are dealt with in CHAPTER **42**, with the overseas element being dealt with in CHAPTER **41**.

Options (TCGA 1992, ss 114, 143–148)

[4.46] The grant of an option is treated as a disposal of an asset (i.e. the option). It is not a part disposal of the underlying asset. Therefore the full amount of the consideration for the grant of the option is chargeable as a gain (less any costs associated with the grant).

Options with a life of 50 years or less are treated as wasting assets, so that their cost wastes away over their life, restricting loss relief accordingly if they lapse or become valueless. If such options are abandoned, no allowable loss can arise. The forfeiture of a deposit is treated as the abandonment of an option.

The following options however are not treated as wasting assets:

(a) quoted options to subscribe for new shares (usually called share warrants);
(b) traded options to buy or sell shares or other financial instruments quoted on a recognised stock exchange or futures exchange and 'over the counter' financial options; and
(c) options to acquire assets for use by the option holder in his business.

This means that when they are disposed of or abandoned, an allowable loss or chargeable gain may arise.

On the exercise of the option the price paid for the option is incorporated with that of the asset to form a single transaction both as regards the seller and the buyer. In the case of a put option, the cost of the option is netted off against both the grantor's cost of acquiring the asset and the grantee's disposal proceeds. Where a call option is exercised and settled in cash, rather than by delivery of the asset, the grantor of the option is treated as having disposal proceeds equal to the price paid by the grantee for the option, less the cash payment made by the grantor, and the grantee is treated as having disposal proceeds equal to the cash received less the cost of the option. An exercise of an option to acquire an asset on non-arm's length terms is treated as if it were a sale of the underlying asset at market value. The exercise price and any consideration given for the option will be ignored.

For individuals, the disposal of an option to buy or sell gilt-edged securities or qualifying corporate bonds is exempt. For companies, such options are taken into account in calculating profits under the 'loan relationships' rules (as to which see **3.6**).

There are special rules concerning options connected with employment (see CHAPTER **11**). For companies, options in connection with financial instruments, such as currency options and interest rate options, are taken into account in calculating income (see **3.8**) and are not subject to the capital gains tax provisions outlined above. Transactions in futures and options can produce a guaranteed return which is treated as disguised interest for tax purposes. A comprehensive income tax charge was introduced from 2013–14 for all forms of disguised interest; see **36.3**.

Deferred consideration

[4.47] Transactions are sometimes structured such that only part of the consideration is received at the time of the sale, with further amounts depending upon later events, for example profit performance in the case of the sale of a family company. This aspect is dealt with briefly in CHAPTER **28**.

5

Inheritance tax: general principles

Introduction

[5.1] Inheritance tax is charged on transfers of capital by individuals. It may be payable on certain lifetime gifts, on wealth at death, on certain transfers into and out of trusts and on certain transfers made by close companies. The law is contained in the Inheritance Tax Act 1984 (abbreviated in this book to IHTA 1984). The tax was introduced in 1975 to replace estate duty, and was called capital transfer tax until 1986.

Persons liable (IHTA 1984, ss 1–6, 267, 267ZA, 267ZB, Sch A1)

[5.2] UK domiciled individuals are chargeable to inheritance tax in respect of property anywhere in the world. Non-UK domiciled individuals are chargeable in respect of UK property that is held directly by them. From 6 April 2017, non-domiciled individuals are also chargeable to inheritance tax in respect of UK residential property held indirectly by them, e.g. through an offshore company or partnership. This extension is legislated for in the September 2017 Finance Bill, and is expected to receive Royal Assent in November 2017.

Spouses and civil partners are chargeable separately, so that any available exemptions apply to each of them and each can make transfers free of tax up to the nil rate threshold (see **5.24**).

For transfers made on or after 6 April 2013, individuals can elect to be treated as domiciled in the UK for the purposes of inheritance tax if they are domiciled outside the UK and at any time on or after 6 April 2013 and during the seven years before the election is made, they have/had a UK-domiciled spouse or civil partner. In certain circumstances personal representatives can also make this election. Such an election, once made, is irrevocable but will cease to have effect if the person is not UK resident for the purposes of income tax for a period of four successive tax years at any time after the election is made. In such situations the election ceases to have effect at the end of the four year period. The election does not apply for the purposes of certain types of savings or when applying double tax agreements which determine the domicile of an individual.

Domicile is a legal term that is not easy to define but essentially it means the country an individual regards as 'home'. It is extended in certain circumstances so that, for example, a person will be domiciled if he was resident in the UK for at least 15 out of the past 20 tax years immediately preceding the relevant year *and* at least one of the four tax years ending with the relevant year. For more details see **41.10**.

Note, the extended definition of domicile is ignored in determining whether or not a person is qualified to make an election to be treated as domiciled in the UK (for transfers made on or after 6 April 2013).

Double taxation relief is given where the transfer of assets attracts foreign tax as well as UK tax.

HMRC have confirmed in guidance (HMRC Brief 34/2010) that only where there is a significant risk of loss of UK tax will they consider opening an enquiry into the domicile of a person.

Exempt transfers etc

[5.3] Certain transfers are not taken into account for inheritance tax. These include the following:

Transfers 'not intended to confer gratuitous benefit' (IHTA 1984, s 10)

[5.4] Such a transfer is not taken into account providing it was either an arm's length transaction between unconnected persons or it was on terms similar to those that would be expected in an arm's length transaction.

Capital transfers for family maintenance (IHTA 1984, s 11)

[5.5] It may sometimes be necessary to make transfers of capital in order to provide for family, for example, following divorce or dissolution of a civil partnership, when the usual exemption for transfers between spouses or civil partners (see **5.11**) no longer applies, or to make reasonable provision for a dependent relative. Such transfers do not attract inheritance tax. 'Dependent relative' is defined as a relative of either spouse or civil partner who is incapacitated by old age or infirmity, or the parents of either spouse or civil partner.

Waivers of remuneration and dividends (IHTA 1984, ss 14, 15)

[5.6] A waiver or repayment of remuneration that would have been employment income for income tax does not attract inheritance tax. Nor does a waiver of dividends made within 12 months before any right to the dividend arises.

Small gifts to same person (IHTA 1984, s 20)

[5.7] Any outright lifetime gifts to any one person in any one tax year are exempt if the total gifts to that person do not exceed £250 in that year.

Gifts in consideration of marriage or civil partnership (IHTA 1984, s 22)

[5.8] Gifts of up to £5,000 by a parent, £2,500 by a grandparent, £2,500 by one party to the marriage or civil partnership to the other, or £1,000 by anyone else are exempt.

Normal expenditure out of income (IHTA 1984, s 21)

[5.9] To obtain this exemption the gift must be part of the donor's normal expenditure. It must, taking one year with another, be made out of the donor's income and must not reduce his available net income (after all other transfers) below that required to maintain his usual standard of living. The exemption will often apply to life insurance policy premiums paid for the benefit of someone else. HMRC require details of income and expenditure for the seven years before death in support of a claim to this exemption (see 9.26).

Where a loan is made free of interest, there is no transfer of capital and it is usually possible to regard the interest forgone as being normal expenditure out of income and thus exempt. If, however, a loan is made for a fixed period, or is not repayable on demand, it may be treated as a transfer of value equal to the difference between the amount lent and the present value of the future right to repayment.

Annual transfers not exceeding £3,000 (IHTA 1984, s 19)

[5.10] The first £3,000 of lifetime transfers in any tax year are exempt. Any unused portion of the exemption may be carried forward for one year only for use in the following tax year after the exemption for that following tax year has been used.

Transfers between spouses or civil partners (IHTA 1984, ss 18, 144; F(No 2)A 2015, s 14)

[5.11] Transfers between spouses or civil partners are exempt. Where a spouse or civil partner domiciled in the UK makes a transfer to a foreign domiciled spouse or civil partner, the exemption is limited to £325,000 — the current nil rate band — less the amount of any previous transfers covered by the same exemption. The future level of this cap will be linked to any changes in the nil rate band (5.24).

An appointment made from a trust within three months of the date of death in favour of the deceased's surviving spouse or civil partner, is exempt as if it were a transfer between spouses (i.e. it can be 'read back' into the will).

Gifts to charities etc (IHTA 1984, s 23)

[5.12] Gifts to charities, either outright or to be held on trust for charitable purposes, and gifts to registered community amateur sports clubs, are exempt. Proof must also be provided to show that the charity has received the goods being given to it.

Gifts to political parties (IHTA 1984, s 24)

[5.13] Gifts to political parties that qualify by having either at least two MPs in the House of Commons, or one MP and at least 150,000 votes in their candidates' favour at the last general election, are exempt. It was announced at Autumn Statement 2016 that legislation will be introduced to extend this exemption for political donations to parties with representatives in the devolved legislatures of Scotland, Wales and Northern Ireland. In addition parties whose representatives are elected at by-elections (as well as general elections) will qualify.

Gifts of land to registered housing associations (IHTA 1984, s 24A)

[5.14] Gifts of land in the UK to registered social landlords or registered housing associations are exempt.

Gifts for national purposes (IHTA 1984, s 25 and Sch 3)

[5.15] Gifts to any of the bodies listed in IHTA 1984, Sch 3 (for example, the National Gallery, the National Trust and any UK university) are exempt. In addition gifts to the nation of objects which qualify for pre-eminent gifts relief (2.21) are also exempt.

Conditional exemption for heritage property (IHTA 1984, ss 30–35A, 78–79A)

[5.16] Providing various undertakings are given, for example in relation to public access, a conditional exemption applies to the transfer of property which is designated by the Treasury as of pre-eminent national, scientific, historic, artistic, architectural or scenic interest (e.g. works of art and historic buildings). A claim for such designation must be made not later than two years after the date of the transfer, or where a potentially exempt transfer (see 5.26) becomes chargeable, the date of the donor's death or in either case within such longer period as HMRC may allow. If there is any breach of an undertaking, inheritance tax becomes payable by the donee.

A disposal of property that either qualifies for conditional exemption to a Sch 3 body (5.15) or is by way of acceptance in lieu of inheritance tax (5.53), turns the conditional exemption of that property into absolute exemption.

For property that is settled in a heritage trust there is an exemption from the ten-yearly charge, provided the trustees make a claim and obtain a heritage property designation. The claim can be made within two years of the date of the ten-yearly charge (or such longer period as HMRC may allow).

Maintenance funds for heritage property (IHTA 1984, s 27 and Sch 4)

[5.17] A transfer into a settlement established for the maintenance, repair or preservation of heritage property is exempt providing a Treasury direction is in effect, or is given after the time of the transfer. A claim for a direction must be made not later than two years (or such longer period as HMRC may allow) after the date of the transfer.

Employee trusts (IHTA 1984, ss 13, 13A, 28, 28A)

[5.18] Where an individual transfers shares or securities of a company to which he is beneficially entitled, to a trust the transfer is exempt provided:

(a) the transfer is on or after 6 April 2014, the company is a trading company, the settlement meets the all-employee benefit requirement and the trustees hold more than half of the share capital and have a majority voting power (this type of trust is known as an employee-ownership trust); for details see 4.38; or

(b) the trust is an employee trust (i.e. a trust that meets the inheritance tax definition of an employee trust contained within IHTA 1984, s 86 (see 42.49)) and the trust property is to be applied for the benefit of all or most of people employed by the company.

[5.19] Similar provisions apply to transfers by close companies. Where a close company transfers property to an employee trust (i.e. a trust that meet the inheritance tax definition of an employee trust contained within IHTA 1984, s 86 (see 42.49) the transfer is deemed not to be a transfer of value provided:

(a) the transfer is on or after 6 April 2014, the close company is a trading company, the settlement meets the all-employee benefit requirement and the trustees hold more than half of the share capital and have a majority voting power (this type of trust is known as an employee-ownership trust); for details see 4.38; or

(b) the trust property is to be applied for the benefit of all or most of people employed by the company or a subsidiary.

Armed forces, emergency personnel, police constables (IHTA 1984, ss 153A, 154, 155A)

[5.20] Estates of the following individuals are exempt from IHT:

(a)   police constables and service personnel (i.e. members of the armed forces or civilians subject to service discipline) that die on or after 19 March 2014, as a result of being targeted because of their status;

(b)   emergency service personnel and humanitarian aid workers that die on or after 19 March 2014 when responding to emergency circumstances;

(c)   members of any of the armed forces of the Crown that die from a wound, disease etc inflicted at a time when on active service or, for deaths on or after 19 March 2014, when responding to emergency circumstances etc.

For the exemptions for deaths on or after 19 March 2014, it is specifically stated that they apply not only to the estate but also to any additional IHT due on death for previous lifetime transfers and potentially exempt transfers.

Late compensation for World War II claims (IHTA 1984, s 153ZA)

[5.21] Payments under various schemes established to provide compensation for wrongs suffered during the World War II era, made either to the victim or the surviving spouse, are excluded from inheritance tax. For deaths on or after 1 January 2015, this provision is put on a statutory footing; previously the treatment was concessionary (ESC F20).

Mutual transfers (FA 1986, s 104)

[5.22] Where a potentially exempt transfer (see 5.26) or a chargeable transfer is made and the donee then makes a gift back to the donor, there are provisions to avoid a double charge to tax if the donor dies within seven years.

Excluded property (IHTA 1984, ss 3, 5, 6, 48, 74A, 74B)

[5.23] Inheritance tax is not chargeable on lifetime transfers of excluded property, nor is such property taken into account in valuing an estate at death. Excluded property includes:

(a)   property situated overseas where the person beneficially entitled to it is not domiciled in the UK;

(b)   a reversionary interest in trust funds (i.e. the right to the capital when the rights to the income come to an end). Anti-avoidance provisions ensure that property will cease to be excluded property (and a charge to inheritance tax will arise) where a UK domiciled individual acquires an interest in settled excluded property which, as a result of arrangements concerned with that acquisition, results in a reduction in the value of that individual's estate;

(c)   certain government securities if the beneficial owner is not resident (nor, for securities issued before 29 April 1996, not domiciled) in the UK;

(d)   savings owned by persons domiciled in the Isle of Man or the Channel Islands;

(e)   decorations and medals (awarded in the UK or overseas) that are designed to be worn to denote membership of an Order, awarded to the armed services/emergency responders, or made by the Crown for achievements and service in public life, provided they do not consist of money and have never been sold. If they have been sold at any time, the exclusion does not apply.

In limited circumstances, excluded property may need to be taken into account in valuing lifetime transfers of other property, but in general excluded property is treated in the same way as property that is exempt.

Basis of charge (IHTA 1984, ss 1–8FE and Schs 1, 1A; F(No 2)A 2015, ss 9, 10)

[5.24] A running total is kept of chargeable lifetime transfers and no tax is payable either on the lifetime gifts or on wealth at death until a threshold (the 'nil rate band') is reached. The threshold, from 6 April 2009, has been fixed at £325,000 until 2020–21. In addition, for deaths on or after 6 April 2017 a 'residence nil rate band' (RNRB) applies which is not available against lifetime charges. The RNRB means that there will be an additional IHT nil rate band which will be available when the value of a residence is passed, on death, to one or more direct descendants, such as children or grandchildren. The RNRB will be applied to the entire taxable value of the death estate before the application of the nil rate band.

The RNRB will initially be £100,000, increasing to £175,000 by 2020–21. There will be a tapered withdrawal of the band for estates valued at more than £2 million. In certain circumstances the RNRB will be available where an individual has downsized or has ceased to own a residence on or after 8 July 2015 and other assets are passed on death to direct descendants. For HMRC guidance see www.gov.uk/guidance/inheritance-tax-residence-nil-rate-band and www.gov.uk/guidance/how-downsizing-selling-or-gifting-a-home-affects-t he-additional-inheritance-tax-threshold.

Any annual increases in the nil rate band do not enable tax paid on earlier transfers to be recovered. The consumer prices index is used as the default indexation increase assumption unless Parliament decides otherwise.

Where a surviving spouse or civil partner dies after 8 October 2007 a claim may be made for any part of the nil rate band unused on the death of the first spouse or civil partner to die to be added to the survivor's own nil rate band on his or her death. Similarly, unused RNRB can be transferred between spouses/civil partners (see **35.4**).

The full rate of tax on transfers above the threshold is 40%. A reduced rate applies (36%) where 10% or more of a deceased's net estate (after deducting inheritance tax exemptions, reliefs and the nil rate band) is left to a charity or registered community amateur sports club (**5.30**). Chargeable lifetime transfers above the nil rate threshold are charged at only 20% (but see **5.31**). The rates and thresholds for earlier years are shown in the TABLE OF RATES AND ALLOWANCES (**TRA**). Transfers are excluded from the running total seven years after they are made.

Lifetime transfers

[5.25] Most of the transfers a person is likely to make in a lifetime will be wholly exempt from tax (see **5.3** to **5.22**). Transfers that do not fall within those categories will either be potentially exempt (**5.26**) or a chargeable lifetime transfer (**5.27**).

Potentially exempt transfers (IHTA 1984, s 3A)

[5.26] Potentially exempt transfers are only chargeable to tax if the donor dies within seven years of making them (subject to what is said at **5.41** about retaining a benefit). Even then, there will be no tax to pay on a potentially exempt transfer unless, when added to reckonable chargeable transfers in the seven years before it (see **5.27**), it exceeds the nil rate threshold at death. Potentially exempt transfers that become chargeable will, however, be taken into account to establish how much, if any, of the nil rate band is available to set against the value of an estate at death. Clearly, a very wealthy individual who had made no chargeable transfers could make a series of annual gifts, each of which (after exemptions) equaled the threshold at that time. If he survived the last of the series by seven years, a substantial amount would have been given away with no inheritance tax consequences. If, however, he died, say, within eight years after the first gift, an extremely large inheritance tax bill would arise in respect of the lifetime gifts before considering the estate at death (although tapering relief would apply on gifts made more than three years before death (see **5.32**)).

Example 1

The only lifetime transfer made by a widower is a gift of £100,000 on 10 June 2015 to his sister towards the cost of buying a house. He dies in May 2017, leaving an estate at death of £300,000.

After deducting two years' annual exemptions totalling £6,000 (see **5.10**), there is a potentially exempt transfer of £94,000 on 10 June 2015, which becomes chargeable because of the widower's death within seven years. No tax is payable on that transfer because it falls within the £325,000 nil rate threshold applying at the date of death. There is then, however, only £231,000 of the nil rate threshold remaining, so that £69,000 of the death estate of £300,000 is chargeable to tax at 40%.

If the widower had survived until 10 June 2022 the lifetime gift would have been completely exempt, and tax would only have been payable if the estate at death had exceeded the nil rate threshold at that time.

A potentially exempt transfer which becomes chargeable on death within seven years of the original transfer is brought into account at the value of the gift when it was originally made. Tax is calculated, taking into account any chargeable transfers (including potentially exempt transfers that have become chargeable) within the seven years before that transfer. The nil rate threshold and rate of tax used are, however, those in force at the date of death.

It is therefore possible to fix the value of the transfer by giving in lifetime and this may be particularly useful where there are appreciating assets, since any later growth in value is in the hands of the donee. The capital gains tax effect must also be considered, however, because a lifetime gift of a chargeable asset will be liable to capital gains tax unless the gain can be deferred (see CHAPTER 4), whereas if the asset is held until death the increase in value up to that time escapes capital gains tax. Any capital gains tax paid on a gift that is a potentially exempt transfer cannot be offset in calculating any inheritance tax that becomes payable, but the wealth of the donor will have been depleted by the capital gains tax paid, thus reducing the inheritance tax liability.

If capital gains tax gift relief *is* available, and the potentially exempt transfer becomes liable to inheritance tax, that tax will be payable by the donee and will be deducted in computing the donee's capital gain (but cannot create a loss) when he eventually disposes of the asset.

See **5.31** for the treatment of a gift that has fallen in value by the time of the donor's death. See CHAPTER 42 for specific transfers into interest in possession trusts that are treated as potentially exempt.

Chargeable lifetime transfers (IHTA 1984, ss 2, 3, 5)

[5.27] The value of a chargeable lifetime transfer is the difference between the value of the donor's estate before and after the transfer, reduced by any available exemptions (see **5.3** to **5.22**) and ignoring disposals of excluded property (see **5.23**). This is referred to as the 'loss to the donor' principle. In many cases the value of the transfer will be the same as the market value of the asset transferred, but this is not always the case, particularly when unquoted shares are disposed of. In some instances other 'related property' also has to be taken into account (see **5.36**).

From 22 March 2006 the main category of transfers which are immediately chargeable in lifetime are those to all lifetime trusts except disabled trusts (see CHAPTER 42 for details). Prior to 22 March 2006, the main category were those to discretionary trusts (i.e. trusts in which no-one has a right to the income, and it is up to the trustees how much of the income is distributed).

The annual exemption and the nil rate threshold of £325,000 (**5.24**) are available providing they have not already been used against earlier chargeable transfers. As with potentially exempt transfers, chargeable lifetime transfers are taken into account in the running total at death if the donor dies within seven years after making them. Tax is recalculated on them at the full rate, taking into account any chargeable transfers (including potentially exempt transfers that have become chargeable) within the seven years before the transfer.

If the gifted asset was a chargeable asset for capital gains tax, and the gain had been deferred under the capital gains gift relief provisions (see **4.32** to **4.34**), any inheritance tax paid, immediately or on the donor's death within seven years, is deducted in computing the donee's capital gain when he eventually disposes of the asset.

The inheritance tax on a chargeable lifetime gift is usually paid by the recipient, but it may be paid by the donor. In that event, the amount chargeable to tax is found by grossing up the amount of the gift to allow for the tax which the donor has to pay.

Example 2

Donor makes a chargeable lifetime transfer of £8,000 when the nil rate threshold had already been used, so that the rate of tax is 20%. He pays the tax.

The value for inheritance tax is £8,000 × 100/80 = £10,000.

Being:	The chargeable transfer	10,000
	Tax payable @ 20%	2,000
	Leaving for the donee	£8,000

If the donor fails to pay the capital gains tax on a gift, it may be collected from the recipient, and in that event it is deducted from the value of the gift in calculating the value for inheritance tax.

Transfers on death (IHTA 1984, s 4)

[5.28] On death, the individual is treated as making a final transfer of the whole of his estate. The tax charged depends on the value of the estate (**5.29**), the amount donated to charity (**5.30**) plus the total of chargeable lifetime transfers and potentially exempt transfers within the previous seven years (**5.31**). No account is taken of 'excluded property' (see **5.23**).

Value of estate (IHTA 1984, ss 157, 162–162C; 175–175A)

[5.29] In arriving at the value of an estate, any liabilities at the date of death are deducted (unless they are excluded under anti-avoidance provisions such as those that prevent a deduction for a liability which is not repaid after death), and also reasonable funeral expenses, mourning expenses and the cost of a headstone. Balances on UK bank accounts denominated in a foreign currency held by an individual who is not domiciled and not resident in the UK immediately before death are not taken into account in determining the value of that person's estate. Any liability incurred to finance the foreign currency bank account is only deductible to the extent that it exceeds the balance of the foreign currency account.

The estate is the total of all the property to which the individual was beneficially entitled (with the exclusion of any powers over trust property (see **42.8**)). The estate also includes:

(a)   any interests held as a joint tenant. Such an interest is automatically transferred to the other joint tenant(s) on death, but it still forms part of the estate for tax purposes (this differs from a share as a tenant in common, where each person has a separate share which he may dispose of as he wishes, and which therefore counts as his own property for all purposes); and

(b)   the capital value of a trust fund where the individual was entitled to the trust income (called an interest in possession or a life interest) if the interest in the trust arose before 22 March 2006, or arose on or after that date and comes within certain limited categories.

The inclusion of the capital value in a trust fund in an estate ((b) above) means that, on death, the beneficiary is treated as making a chargeable transfer of the capital in the fund, although the tax on that amount is paid by the trustees.

On the other hand, if, because of the beneficiary's entitlement to the income, the capital is treated for inheritance tax purposes as part of his estate already, there is no charge to tax if, in his lifetime, he was allocated part of the capital which supports his life interest.

Where assets in the estate at death are left to a spouse or civil partner, no tax is payable (unless the spouse or civil partner is not domiciled in the UK, in which case the exempt amount is limited to £325,000; see **5.11**). The other exempt transfers listed at **5.3** to **5.22** are also left out of account. For more detailed points relating to the death estate, see CHAPTER 35.

Donations to charity (IHTA 1984, Sch 1A)

[5.30] If 10% or more of the net value of a person's estate is left to a qualifying charity (i.e. one recognised as such by HMRC) the tax due may be paid at a reduced rate of 36% (as opposed to 40%). The net value of an estate is the sum of all the assets after deducting any debts, liabilities, reliefs, exemptions and the nil rate band.

To establish whether the reduced rate applies it is necessary to split a persons estate into three 'components' — assets owned jointly, assets owned in trust and assets owned outright. If a person only has assets falling into one component, then the split is not necessary.

For each component, add up the assets then deduct any debts, liabilities, reliefs and exemptions that apply to each component, apportion the nil rate band and then add back in the value of the donation to charity — the resultant figure is known as the 'baseline amount' for each component. If the charitable donation is 10% or more than this amount, the reduced rate applies.

As a consequence of dividing the estate into components, it is possible that one part of an estate may pay 36% inheritance tax and another pay 40%, although one or more components can be merged to gain the maximum benefit from the reduced rate.

> **Example 3**
>
> Mr A died on 17 June 2017 leaving an estate to his brother valued at £750,000 after the deduction of liabilities. He left, in his will, £50,000 to a national charity. The applicable rate of tax for his estate is calculated as follows:

On his death the IHT is calculated as follows:

(i)   Deduct the £50,000 charitable donation from £750,000 (the net estate). This gives a figure of £700,000.

(ii)   Deduct £325,000 (the nil rate band) from £700,000. This gives a figure of £375,000.

(iii)   Add the £50,000 charitable donation back to £375,000. This gives a figure of £425,000 — the 'baseline amount'.

(iv)   Calculate 10% of the baseline amount. This is £42,500.

This estate qualifies for the reduced rate of IHT because the charitable donation of £50,000 is more than 10% of the 'baseline amount'. The IHT payable on the chargeable estate of £375,000 will be £135,000 compared to £150,000 if IHT was paid at the full rate.

Example 4

An estate at death in December 2017 amounted to £950,000. There were bequests of £50,000 to registered charities and £400,000 to the surviving spouse. The rest of the estate (the residue) was left to the nephews of the deceased. The costs of administration were £10,000.

The estate would be divided as follows:

	£	£	£
Estate at death		950,000	
Exempt legacies:			
Charities	50,000		
Spouse	400,000	(450,000)	
		500,000	500,000
Threshold for IHT		(325,000)	
Chargeable to IHT		175,000	
IHT at 36%**		63,000	(63,000)
Costs of administration			(10,000)
Residuary legatees (nephews)			427,000

**IHT calculated as follows:

(i)   Deduct the exempt legacies (gift to charity and spouse) from £950,000. This gives a figure of £500,000.

(ii)   Deduct £325,000 (the nil rate band) from £500,000. This gives a figure of £175,000.

(iii)   Add the £50,000 charitable donation back to £175,000. This gives a figure of £225,000 — the 'baseline amount'.

(iv)   Calculate 10% of the baseline amount. This is £22,500.

This estate qualifies for the reduced rate of IHT because the charitable donation of £50,000 is more than 10% of the 'baseline amount'.

Transfers made within the seven years before death (IHTA 1984, s 7)

[5.31] Where a chargeable lifetime transfer has been made, all or part of which has been charged at the 20% rate, and the donor dies within seven years of making it, additional tax may be payable. This is because the tax is recomputed at the full scale rate applicable at the date of death, taking into account other chargeable transfers (including potentially exempt transfers that have become chargeable) within the seven years before the transfer and using the nil rate threshold applicable at the date of death. The donee has to pay the amount by which the tax at the appropriate percentage of the full-scale rate exceeds any tax paid on the gift in lifetime. If, however, the lifetime tax exceeds the death tax, no repayment is available.

If any potentially exempt transfers have been made in the seven years before death, they become chargeable and are taken into account in the running total, along with any chargeable lifetime transfers, according to the date each transfer was made. The re-allocation of the nil rate threshold may mean that some or all of it is no longer available against a chargeable lifetime transfer, causing tax, or more tax, to be payable.

Example 5

Donor who died on 25 May 2017 made the following gifts in lifetime (after taking annual and other exemptions into account):

9 April 2010	To brother	£40,000
26 July 2010	To son	£70,000
15 September 2011	To daughter	£75,000
10 April 2015	To discretionary trust (tax paid by trustees)	£335,000
30 June 2016	To sister	£20,000

The only chargeable lifetime gift was the gift to the discretionary trust on 10 April 2015, on which, using the nil rate band at that date, the tax was:

(£335,000 – £325,000 nil rate band) = £10,000 @ 20%	£2,000

On death on 25 May 2017:

The gift on 9 April 2010 to brother is not taken into account, since it was more than seven years before donor's death. Gifts to son, daughter and sister become chargeable, but no tax is payable on gifts to son and daughter, since those two gifts together are below the nil rate threshold. The threshold remaining is, however, (£325,000 – £145,000) = £180,000.

	£
Tax on gift to trust	
(£335,000 – £180,000) = £155,000 @ 40%	62,000
Less paid in lifetime	(2,000)

Tax payable by trustees		£60,000
Tax payable by sister on gift to her	£20,000 @ 40%	£8,000

Tax @ 40% will also be paid on the estate at death.

Where a charitable donation is made (5.30) it is necessary to include any lifetime transfers made in the previous seven years in the normal manner before calculating which rate applies to the estate.

Example 6

Mr D died on 17 July 2017 leaving an estate valued at £750,000 (after deducting liabilities). He had sold his only residence in March 2014 and moved to his daughters. In his will he left £50,000 to a national charity. In his lifetime he had made a gift to his daughter of £150,000 in April 2014 (less than seven years before his death).

On his death on 17 July 2017, the IHT is calculated as follows:

(i) Deduct the £50,000 charitable donation from £750,000 (the net estate). This gives a figure of £700,000.
(ii) Deduct the £150,000 gift to his daughter from £325,000 (the nil rate band). This gives a figure of £175,000.
(iii) Deduct the figure obtained in (ii) from the figure obtained in (i) — £700,000 – £175,000. This gives a figure of £525,000.
(iv) Add the £50,000 charitable donation back to £525,000. This gives a figure of £575,000 — the 'baseline amount'.
(v) Calculate 10% of the baseline amount. This is £57,500.

This estate doesn't qualify for the reduced rate of IHT because the charitable donation of £50,000 is less than 10% of the baseline amount. The beneficiaries of this estate could choose to increase the charitable donation by another £7,500 by making an instrument of variation so that the 10% test is passed. This would mean IHT on the chargeable estate of £525,000 could be paid at the reduced rate of £189,000 rather than £210,000. This is a tax saving of £21,000, which will cover the additional payment to charity.

If the value of a gifted asset that is not a 'wasting asset' has fallen between the time of the gift and death, the lower value may be used to calculate the tax. If the donee had sold the asset before the donor's death in an arm's length, freely negotiated sale, to an unconnected person, the sale proceeds may be used instead if they are lower than the value when the gift was made.

Tapering relief

[5.32] When working out the tax, or additional tax, payable on gifts within the seven years before death, the tax is reduced if the donor survives the gift by more than three years. The percentage of the full scale rate payable following the reduction is as follows:

Time between chargeable gift and death	% payable
Up to 3 years	100
More than 3 but not more than 4 years	80
More than 4 but not more than 5 years	60
More than 5 but not more than 6 years	40
More than 6 but not more than 7 years	20

Example 7

The only chargeable transfer made by a taxpayer in lifetime is a transfer to a discretionary trust of £375,000 (after exemptions) on 30 September 2015. The tax payable by the trustees is (£375,000 – £325,000 nil rate band = £50,000 @ 20%), i.e. £10,000.

Assuming that the tax rate and threshold remained unchanged, so that £20,000 was in fact the amount of tax at the full rate of 40%, the effect of the tapering relief would be as follows:

If taxpayer died in	Time between gift and death	% of £20,000 payable	Amounting to
			£
October 2016	Less than 3 yrs	100	20,000
December 2018	3 to 4 yrs	80	16,000
January 2021	5 to 6 yrs	40	8,000
Therefore:			

Extra tax payable if death had occurred in October 2016 would be £10,000.

Extra tax payable if death had occurred in December 2018 would be £6,000.

No extra tax would be due if death occurred in January 2021 because the reduced tax of £8,000 would be less than the tax already paid of £10,000. No tax would, however, be repayable.

If the lifetime gift had been to an individual it would have been potentially exempt, and no tax would have been paid on it in lifetime, but the calculation of the tax at death would be as shown above.

Valuation of property (IHTA 1984, ss 160–198)

[5.33] The value of property for inheritance tax is the amount it might reasonably be expected to fetch if sold in the open market. The price is not, however, to be reduced on the grounds that the whole property is placed on the market at one time.

If the asset to be transferred will give rise to a capital gains tax liability, and the donee agrees to pay that tax, then the value transferred is reduced by the capital gains tax paid. However, capital gains tax may sometimes not arise on gifts because of the availability of gift holdover relief. See **4.32** to **4.34**.

Valuation on death

[5.34] The way in which the death estate is valued, and the reliefs which are available, are dealt with below. The various exemptions that may be available are dealt with at **5.3** onwards.

Transfers of 'excluded property' are ignored in valuing the death estate (see **5.23**).

Apart from life insurance policies (see **5.37**), the value of property to be included in the estate at death is that immediately before death. Changes in the value of the estate as a result of the death are taken into account, for example the increased value of life insurance policies and the reduction in the value of goodwill which depends upon the personal qualities of the deceased. Allowance is made for reasonable funeral expenses, mourning expenses and the cost of a headstone. In the case of overseas property, allowance is also made for additional expenses incurred because of its situation, subject to a limit of 5% of the value of the property.

Quoted securities and land transferred on death

[5.35] Where an estate on death includes quoted securities, and they are sold by the personal representatives within 12 months after death for less than their value at death, then the total sales proceeds before expenses may be substituted for the death value. A revised value may also be included for quoted securities that are cancelled, or in which dealings are suspended, within the 12 months after death. In claiming this relief, *all* sales in the 12-month period, including those at a profit, must be taken into account in the total proceeds figure. The relief is restricted if any purchase of quoted securities takes place in the period from the date of death to the end of two months after the last sale within the 12 months after death.

HMRC have provided guidance on valuing entitlements arising from takeovers, mergers and flotations of building societies/other mutual organisations and the valuation of compensation rights received on a failure of a bank or building society (see HMRC Inheritance Tax Manual IHTM10072 onwards).

If the estate includes land which is sold by the personal representatives within four years after death, a claim may be made (on form IHT38), subject to certain restrictions, to substitute the total sale proceeds before expenses for the value at death.

Related property

[5.36] If an individual owns part of an asset (and part is owned by a spouse or civil partner), or an individual has made an exempt transfer of part of an asset to a charity, political party or national heritage body and it is still owned by that body or has been so owned at any time within the previous five years, the related property provisions apply. These provisions are mainly relevant to valuing transfers of unquoted shares and where freehold or leasehold property is owned jointly.

The value of a part of related property is taken as an appropriate portion of the total value of all the property if it produces a higher value than its unrelated value.

Example 8

The shareholders of Related Ltd, an unquoted company, are Mr R 40%, Mrs R 25%, others 35%. Shareholdings are valued as follows:

65% holding	£117,000
40% holding	£48,000
25% holding	£30,000

Inheritance tax values are:

Mr R 40/65 × £117,000	£72,000 (being greater than £48,000)
Mrs R 25/65 × £117,000	£45,000 (being greater than £30,000)

Business property relief may be available (see **5.45**).

If related property is sold within three years after death to an unconnected person, a claim may be made for the tax at death to be recomputed using its unrelated value (not its sale value).

Life insurance policies

[5.37] The valuation of life insurance policies depends on whether the transfer is during the lifetime or on the death of the donor. Policies transferred in lifetime are valued at the greater of the surrender value and the premiums paid. Sometimes it is the policy premiums, rather than the policy itself, which are transfers of value (e.g. where a policy is written in trust for another person and the premiums are paid by the person whose life is assured). In such cases, depending on the policy arrangements and conditions, each premium payment may be a potentially exempt transfer unless it is already exempt as a gift out of income or as a small gift or because of the annual exemption.

On death, the maturity value of a policy taken out by a person on his own life will be included in his estate unless it has been assigned to someone else in lifetime (when it will be reckoned as a lifetime transfer), or it has been written in trust for the benefit of someone else.

Survivorship clauses (IHTA 1984, s 92)

[5.38] Although the tax on successive transfers may be reduced by quick succession relief (**5.50**) where death occurs within five years after the first transfer, this is not so beneficial as the value not being included at all. It is possible to include a survivorship clause in a will stipulating that assets do not pass to the intended beneficiary unless he/she survives the deceased by a prescribed period, limited to a maximum of six months (see **35.14**). This avoids the double charge to tax.

Varying the distribution of the estate (IHTA 1984, ss 17, 142, 218A)

[5.39] The way in which the estate liable to inheritance tax at death is distributed may be varied by those entitled to it, and legacies may be disclaimed wholly or in part. Where this happens within two years after the death, the variation or disclaimer takes effect for inheritance tax purposes as if it had applied at the date of death. The variation or disclaimer must not be for consideration. For variations (but not disclaimers) this is subject to the proviso that those making it (and the personal representatives if additional inheritance tax is payable) state in the variation that they intend it to have this effect. Where additional tax is payable, then within six months after the date of the variation the personal representatives must notify HMRC of the amount of extra tax and send a copy of the variation. Following the variation/disclaimer, inheritance tax will be payable as if the revised distribution had operated at death. Similar provisions apply for capital gains tax (see **4.44**). For further details, see CHAPTER **35**.

Anti-avoidance provisions

[5.40] Anti-avoidance provisions have been introduced to prevent exploitation of potentially exempt transfers, in particular where taxpayers give property away in a series of connected operations (known as associated operations), or where property is gifted but the donor retains a benefit. The main anti-avoidance provisions are discussed below.

Gifts with reservation of benefit (FA 1986, ss 102–102C and Sch 20)

[5.41] Property that is given away is treated as still belonging to the donor if he continues to enjoy any benefit from it (or the donee does not assume possession and enjoyment of it). This rule does not apply if the gift qualifies for one of the exemptions listed at **5.7**, **5.8**, **5.11** to **5.15** or **5.17** and **5.19**.

Where the property given is an interest in land, the donor will be regarded as having retained a benefit if there is some interest, right or arrangement which enables or entitles him to occupy the land to a material degree without paying full consideration, and the gift is made within seven years after the interest, right or arrangement is created or entered into. If the donor still retains a benefit at the time of his death, the property is treated as remaining in his estate and is taxed accordingly.

Example 9

A donor gives away his house but continues to live in it rent free. His continued occupation is a reservation of benefit. He will be treated as making a second gift at the time when he ceases to occupy the house or starts to pay a proper rent for his occupation, so that inheritance tax may be payable if he does not then survive for a further seven years.

The donor will not be treated as retaining an interest if an unconditional gift of a *share* in the home is made and both donor and donee continue to live there and each pays a *full* share of the outgoings.

The gifts with reservation rules were extended to apply to certain life interests in trusts that come to an end on or after 22 March 2006, where the former holder of the interest continues to enjoy a benefit from the trust assets.

The rules about retaining a benefit can result in a double inheritance tax charge and there are special rules to eliminate any double charges that occur.

This is a complex aspect of inheritance tax. Detailed guidance is available from HMRC at HMRC Inheritance Tax Manual IHTM14301 onwards.

Various schemes have been devised to circumvent the gifts with reservation rules. An *income tax* 'pre-owned assets' charge is made where someone has disposed of assets since *18 March 1986* but retains a benefit. The charge is based on the annual value of the use of the assets. If the total annual value amounts to £5,000 or less, however, no income tax charge will arise (see **5.42**).

Pre-owned assets (FA 2004, s 84 and Sch 15; SI 2005/724; SI 2005/3441)

[5.42] An income tax charge is imposed where a taxpayer has the benefit of free or low-cost use of an asset that he has previously owned. The provisions apply to land, chattels and gifts into trusts of intangible assets (which include cash). The charge for land is based on the rental value and the charge for other assets is calculated by applying the official rate of interest to the value of the asset, reduced in the case of chattels by any payments made for use of the asset and reduced in the case of intangible assets by any income tax or capital gains tax payable in respect of the assets. Land and chattels are valued at 6 April 2005 (or when the asset first becomes chargeable) for the purpose of arriving at the first and subsequent annual charges and revaluations will be made at 6 April every five years. There is no charge if the value of the benefit is £5,000 per annum or less.

The provisions do not apply to property:

(a)   that ceased to be owned before 18 March 1986;
(b)   sold for an arm's length price;
(c)   given outright to the former owner's spouse or civil partner (or former spouse or civil partner, under a court order);
(d)   that was a cash gift towards the purchase of land or chattels, made at least seven years before the individual occupied the land or had use of the chattels (excluding outright cash gifts made before 6 April 1998);

(e)   where the transfer is within the inheritance tax annual or small gifts exemptions (see **5.7, 5.10**) or the 'gifts for family maintenance' exemption (see **5.5**);

(f)   that is still included in the estate of the taxpayer or his/her spouse or civil partner for inheritance tax, for example because the property has been transferred to a trust in which the transferor has an interest in possession which is reckoned for inheritance tax at his death, or because of the gifts with reservation rules (as to which see **5.41**). This exemption does not apply where a taxpayer has disposed of an asset and continues to benefit from it through an interest in possession which escapes inheritance tax on his death because the asset then reverts to the settlor;

(g)   previously owned only by virtue of a will or intestacy which has subsequently been varied by agreement between the beneficiaries.

The provisions do not affect bona fide equity release schemes made at arm's length, or in some instances otherwise than at arm's length (see **34.9** onwards). Life policies put into trust before 22 March 2006 (see **40.11**) are not within the provisions, nor are nil rate band trusts created by will (see **35.5**).

The provisions do not apply to those who are not resident in the UK, nor to overseas property in relation to someone who is UK resident but domiciled abroad.

There are basically three ways of dealing with the pre-owned assets provisions:

(a)   Leave the provisions in place and pay the annual income tax charge (or a market rent). This means that the asset will not form part of the estate for inheritance tax (providing the taxpayer survives the gift by seven years).

(b)   Leave the provisions in place but notify HMRC on or before the filing date for the self-assessment return that the gift is to be treated as within the gifts with reservation rules (see **5.41**). From 21 March 2007 HMRC may accept elections made after the filing date, even if the filing date was before 21 March 2007. The notification is made on form IHT500. This avoids the income tax charge but for inheritance tax the asset is then still treated as part of the estate at death. Furthermore, for capital gains tax the donee will have acquired the asset at the market value at the date of the gift, so may face a large capital gains tax bill when it is sold.

(c)   Unravel the scheme. This may be quite complicated, and the costs involved may be significant. There is relief for double charges where the value is included for inheritance tax under more than one provision.

Associated operations (IHTA 1984, s 268)

[5.43] There are rules to enable HMRC to treat a series of connected operations as a single transfer of assets made at the time of the last of them.

Reliefs

[5.44] There are a number of reliefs available either to reduce the amount chargeable to inheritance tax or to reduce the amount of tax due. The main reliefs are discussed below.

Business property relief (IHTA 1984, ss 103–114)

[5.45] Business property relief is available on the value of transfers of business property (in the UK or elsewhere), providing certain conditions as to the length of ownership and type of business are satisfied. The relief is given at the following rates:

A business or interest in a business (including a partnership share)	100%
Transfers out of a holding of unquoted shares	100%
Transfers out of a holding of unquoted *securities* in a company which, together with any unquoted *shares* in the company (including in both cases 'related property' holdings), gave the holder control of the company	100%
Transfers out of a controlling shareholding in a quoted company (including control through 'related property' holdings)	50%
Land or buildings, machinery or plant used for a business carried on by a company of which the donor had control; or a partnership in which he or she was a partner; or the donor, where the property was settled property in which he or she had an interest in possession	50%

Shares on the Alternative Investment Market (AIM), OFEX market, EU junior market or NASDAQ Europe market are treated as unquoted shares for the purposes of this relief.

The property transferred must normally have been owned by the donor throughout the previous two years. Business property relief is not available where the business consists of dealing in stocks and shares (except market makers on the Stock Exchange and discount houses), dealing in land and buildings or holding investments (including land which is let).

The relief is applied automatically without a claim and is given after agricultural property relief (see below) but before available exemptions.

Binding contract for sale (IHTA 1984, ss 113, 124)

[5.46] Property does not qualify for business or agricultural relief (5.48) if it is subject to a binding contract for sale (except a contract relating to the conversion of an unincorporated business to a company, or a company reconstruction). A 'buy and sell' agreement made by partners or company directors to take effect on their death is considered by HMRC to constitute such a contract, but not a double option agreement whereby the deceased's personal representatives have an *option* to sell and the surviving partners or directors an *option* to buy.

Calculation of tax on lifetime transfers following death within seven years (IHTA 1984, ss 113A, 113B, 124A, 124B)

[5.47] In computing the tax payable as a result of death, business and agricultural property relief is applicable so long as:

(a)   the original property (or qualifying property which has replaced it) was owned by the donee throughout the period beginning with the date of the transfer and ending with the death of the donor; this condition will be regarded as satisfied if there is a period of up to three years between the sale of one qualifying property and the acquisition of another; and

(b)   immediately before the death of the donor, the property (or any replacement property) is qualifying business or agricultural property (this may not apply because, for example, there might have been a change of use, or at the time of death there might be a binding contract for sale). In order for unquoted shares to be qualifying business property they must still be unquoted when the donor dies.

If the donee died before the donor, the periods at (a) and (b) are from the date of the gift to the date of death of the donee.

Proportionate relief is available where only part of the property continues to qualify, for example, where part of the property has been sold.

Since any increase in the value of assets up to the date of death is also exempt from capital gains tax (see **4.44**), the availability of the 100% business or agricultural property relief is an important influence in estate planning, because where it applies there will be no tax benefit from making potentially exempt transfers in lifetime. On the other hand, it cannot be certain that the tax regime will remain as favourable as it is now.

Agricultural property relief (IHTA 1984, ss 115–124C)

[5.48] Agricultural property relief is available on the transfer of agricultural property situated in the UK, Channel Islands, Isle of Man or (from 22 April 2009) in any country that is a member of the European Economic Area, so long as various conditions are met. The extension to EEA countries also applies to any earlier chargeable occasion where inheritance tax in respect of that occasion was due or paid on or after 23 April 2003.

Agricultural property is agricultural land or pasture (including short rotation coppice land and farmland dedicated to wildlife habitats under Government Habitat Schemes), woodland and buildings used for rearing livestock or fish where the occupation of the woodland and buildings is ancillary to that of the agricultural land, and cottages, farm buildings and farmhouses occupied with the agricultural land. The relief only applies to the agricultural value of the property, and in arriving at that value any loan secured on the agricultural property must be deducted.

The agricultural property must at the time of the transfer have been either occupied by the donor for agriculture throughout the two years ending with the date of transfer or owned by the donor throughout the previous seven years and occupied for agriculture by him or someone else throughout that period.

This enables relief to be given on agricultural investment property. In certain circumstances these rules are modified if the property transferred was acquired as a replacement for other agricultural property.

Relief is available both on the transfer of agricultural property itself, and on the transfer of shares out of a controlling holding in a farming company to the extent of the underlying agricultural value.

The rates of relief are:

(a)   100% where the donor had the right to vacant possession immediately before the transfer, or the right to obtain vacant possession within the next 12 months. By HMRC concession F17, the 100% rate is given on tenanted agricultural property where vacant possession is obtainable within 24 months, or where the property is valued broadly at vacant possession value despite the tenancy.
(b)   100% for other tenanted agricultural property where the letting commenced on or after 1 September 1995 (including successions to tenancies following the death of the previous tenant on or after that date).
(c)   50% for transfers of property let before 1 September 1995.
(d)   100% on tenanted agricultural property where the donor had been beneficially entitled to his interest in the property since before 10 March 1981 and would have been entitled to the higher rate of relief (then 50%) under the provisions for agricultural relief which operated before that date.

Where agricultural property satisfies the conditions for business property relief, agricultural property relief is given first and business property relief is given on the non-agricultural value. As with business property relief, agricultural property relief is given without the need for a claim.

The provisions discussed at **5.46** and **5.47** apply equally to agricultural property relief.

Growing timber (IHTA 1984, ss 125–130)

[5.49] Where an estate on death includes growing timber, an election may be made to leave the timber (but not the land on which it stands) out of account in valuing the estate at death. The relief is dealt with in **31.25**.

Quick succession relief (IHTA 1984, s 141)

[5.50] Where a donee dies after receiving a chargeable transfer, the transfer will have increased his estate at death and therefore attracts tax in his estate as well as tax possibly having arisen on the earlier transfer. Relief is given where the death occurs within five years after the earlier transfer. There is no requirement to retain the actual asset obtained by that transfer.

The total tax on the chargeable estate is calculated in the normal way and reduced by the quick succession relief. The relief is arrived at by first making the following calculation:

Previous transfer net of tax/Previous gross transfer x Tax paid on previous transfer

The relief is the following percentage of the calculated amount:

Years between transfer and death	Percentage relief
Up to 1 year	100%
More than 1 but not more than 2	80%
More than 2 but not more than 3	60%
More than 3 but not more than 4	40%
More than 4 but not more than 5	20%

Example 10

Thomas, who died on 28 June 2017 leaving an estate of £400,000, had received a gift of £50,000 from his father on 30 October 2014, on which he had paid tax of £20,000 following his father's death on 26 May 2016.

Tax on Thomas's estate will be reduced by quick succession relief as follows (Thomas having died more than two years but not more than three years after gift):

Net transfer (30,000)/Gross transfer (50,000) x Tax (20,000) x 60% = £7,200

Quick succession relief is also available where there are successive charges within five years on trust property which has been reckoned for inheritance tax by reference to the death of the person entitled to the income. The rates of relief are the same as those quoted above, with the percentage relief depending on the period between the successive charges.

It may be that at the time the donee dies, the transfer to him is still classed as a potentially exempt transfer because the donor is still alive, but the donor may then die, after the donee but within the seven-year period, so that the potentially exempt transfer becomes chargeable by reference to the donor's estate, with the personal representatives of the donee being liable to pay any tax. Quick succession relief will then be available in the donee's estate by reference to that tax.

Administration

[5.51] Inheritance tax is administered by the Inheritance Tax Offices. Unlike other taxes, inheritance tax is not based on an annual process. Instead the tax will only arise when a transfer of value is made either during the lifetime of an individual or on his death.

HMRC have introduced a new Inheritance Tax online service, which will enable people to proceed with their application for probate and submit Inheritance Tax accounts online. To date regulations and subsequent directions have been introduced which provide the framework for the inheritance tax online service; the regulations came into force on 6 July 2015. The service itself is now being introduced in phases.

The main payment provisions are discussed below.

Date of payment; interest on overdue or overpaid inheritance tax (IHTA 1984, ss 226–236; FA 2014, Sch 25)

[5.52] The normal due dates of payment are as follows:

(a)　chargeable lifetime transfers between 6 April and 30 September — 30 April in following year;

(b)　chargeable lifetime transfers between 1 October and 5 April — 6 months after end of month in which transfer was made;

(c)　death (including additional tax on chargeable lifetime transfers and tax on potentially exempt transfers which become chargeable) — 6 months after end of month in which death occurs;

(d)　trustees' tax on periodic and exit charges — 6 months after end of month in which the chargeable transfer is made;

(e)　conditionally exempt transfer (**5.16**) becoming chargeable — 6 months after the end of the month in which the chargeable transfer is made (e.g. breach of an undertaking in respect of heritage property);

(f)　maintenance fund for heritage property (**5.17**) becoming chargeable — 6 months after the end of the month in which the chargeable transfer is made (e.g. property ceases to be subject to the maintenance fund and none of the exemptions apply).

The personal representatives of a deceased's estate must, however, pay any tax for which they are liable, and which may not be paid by instalments, at the time they apply for probate, even if this is before the due date as shown above. If the personal representatives take out a loan to pay the inheritance tax, relief for the interest paid on the loan is given in calculating the tax payable on the income of the estate (see **42.4**).

If there are funds on bank or building society accounts belonging to the deceased, the personal representatives may arrange for a direct transfer to HMRC before probate is granted rather than taking out a loan to pay the inheritance tax (see **42.2**).

Interest is payable on overdue tax (or repayable on overpaid tax). For recent rates see the TABLE OF RATES AND ALLOWANCES (**TRA**). Interest on overdue tax is not deductible in arriving at income tax payable by the personal representatives and interest on overpaid tax is tax-free. Overpayments carry interest from the date of payment.

From 1 April 2016, fees apply to payments made to HMRC by credit card. The fees vary depending on whether the credit card is a personal or corporate credit card and the type of card used.

For further details see **9.55** onwards.

[5.53] On the application of any person liable to pay inheritance tax, certain property can be accepted in lieu of inheritance tax. The property that can be accepted includes:

(a)   any picture, print, book, manuscript, work of art, scientific object or other item which the Secretary of State is satisfied is pre-eminent for its national, scientific, historic or artistic interest;

(b)   any land (if an appropriate recipient for it can be found and it is capable of being used for the public benefit); and

(c)   certain objects which are or have been kept in a particular building where the Secretary of State considers it desirable for such objects to remain associated with the building.

The acceptance of property in satisfaction of tax is generally on the basis of its value on the date it is offered, rather than the date it is accepted and interest will cease to run on the outstanding inheritance tax from the offer date. Taxpayers may, however, opt for an acceptance date basis of valuation, with interest running until that date (see HMRC Statement of Practice SP 6/87).

Tax offset under this scheme, and tax reductions under the pre-eminent gifts relief scheme (**2.21**), are subject to a total annual limit of £30 million.

Payment by instalments

[5.54] Inheritance tax may be paid by equal yearly instalments over ten years on qualifying assets. This applies where the assets are transferred on death, and also to chargeable lifetime transfers if the *donee* pays the tax. The option to pay by instalments also applies to a potentially exempt transfer of qualifying property which becomes a chargeable transfer on the death of the donor within seven years after the gift, so long as the donee still owns the gifted property (or, for transfers of property qualifying for business or agricultural relief, replacement property) at the time of the donor's death. The first instalment is due on chargeable lifetime transfers on the normal due date and in the case of tax payable in consequence of death, six months after the end of the month in which the death occurred.

The instalment option applies to land wherever situated, to a business or interest in a business, to timber when it becomes chargeable after being left out of account on a previous death, to controlling shareholdings, and to unquoted shares if certain conditions are met. For unquoted shares, the instalment option is not available for tax payable as a result of the donor's death, unless the shares are still unquoted when the donor dies (or, if earlier, when the donee dies).

Interest normally runs only from the date the instalment falls due and not on the full amount of the deferred tax. This does not apply in the case of land, other than land included in a business or partnership interest and agricultural land, nor in the case of shares in an investment company. Interest in those two cases is charged on the total amount remaining unpaid after the normal due date, the interest being added to each instalment as it falls due.

If the asset is sold, the outstanding tax becomes payable immediately.

Liability for tax (IHTA 1984, ss 199–214, 237)

[5.55] On lifetime transfers of property which are immediately chargeable (other than transfers of property in a trust fund), primary liability for payment rests with the donor. The donor and donee may, however, agree between them who is to pay, the transfer having to be grossed up if the donor pays (see the example at 5.27).

In the case of lifetime chargeable transfers of property which is within a trust, the primary liability is that of the trustees.

On death, the personal representatives are liable to pay the tax on the assets coming into their hands, while the liability for tax on trust property which becomes chargeable at death rests with the trustees. See the example at **42.23**.

Where, as a result of the death of the donor within seven years, additional tax becomes payable on a lifetime transfer, or a potentially exempt transfer becomes liable to tax, the primary responsibility for paying the tax is that of the donee. The personal representatives are only liable if the tax remains unpaid 12 months after the end of the month in which the donor died, or to the extent that the tax payable exceeds the value of the gifted property held by the donee.

In addition to the persons mentioned above, certain other people may be liable to pay inheritance tax, but usually only where tax remains unpaid after the due date. Where tax is unpaid HMRC are usually able to take a legal charge on the property concerned.

The person who is liable to pay inheritance tax is not necessarily the person who ultimately bears the tax. The trustees of a settlement are liable to pay any tax arising on trust funds, but those next enjoying the income or receiving the capital bear the tax because the trust funds are correspondingly lower. Personal representatives are liable to pay the tax on the assets of the deceased at death, but the residuary legatees (those who receive the balance of the estate after all other legacies) will suffer the tax by a reduction in the amount available for them, the other legatees receiving their legacies in full unless the will specifies that any particular legacy should bear its own tax.

Personal representatives, trustees and others liable to pay inheritance tax have to deliver an account to HMRC Inheritance Tax. For details see **9.25** onwards.

Use of insurance

[5.56] There are many instances in the inheritance tax provisions where the potential liability to tax is not known at the time of the transfer, notably when potentially exempt transfers are made, but also when chargeable transfers are made, because if the donor dies within seven years additional tax may be payable. Temporary insurance cover may be taken out by the donee on the life of the donor to provide for the possible tax liability, with the policies being tailored to take account of the reduction in potential liability once the donor has survived the gift by three years. See also CHAPTER **40**.

6

Stamp taxes

Background

[6.1] Stamp duty is a fixed or ad valorem charge on documents and duty is not payable if there is no document. A separate charge — stamp duty reserve tax — was introduced in 1986 to cover share transactions that escaped stamp duty (see **6.6**). The Electronic Communications Act 2000 made it possible to remove the legal requirement for transactions to be evidenced by paper documents, and the electronic transfer of land and buildings was facilitated by the introduction of a separate tax — stamp duty land tax. Following the introduction of stamp duty land tax, stamp duty applies only to stock and marketable securities and certain transfers of interests in partnerships (see **6.21**).

Stamp duties and taxes are administered by HMRC Stamp Taxes. The Scottish equivalent (land and buildings transaction tax; LBTT) tax is administered by Revenue Scotland. HMRC guidance can be found in their stamp taxes on shares manual (STSM), covering the application of stamp duty on shares and stamp duty reserve tax (SDRT). It includes sections on exemptions and reliefs, bearer instruments, derivatives and pension schemes. Revenue Scotland's guidance on LBTT can be found at www.revenue.scot/land-buildings-transaction-tax/guidance.

Stamp duty is dealt with in **6.2** to **6.5**, stamp duty reserve tax in **6.6** and **6.7**, stamp duty land tax in **6.8** to **6.17** and LBTT in **6.18** to **6.20**. Paragraphs **6.21** to **6.24** deal with topics relevant to stamp duty, stamp duty land tax and LBTT (although the LBTT provisions are legislated for by the relevant Scottish legislation, and there are minor necessary modifications to terminology etc).

Stamp duty

Instruments chargeable and rates (FA 1986, s 67; FA 1999, ss 112, 113 and Schs 13–16; SI 2011/2205)

[6.2] Stamp duty applies in the following situations:

(a)   to transfers of stock and marketable securities (executed in the UK or relating to UK property, wherever executed) excluding securities admitted to trading on a recognised growth market (e.g. AIM and the High Growth Segment of the main market). Also included are certain transfers of interests in partnerships (**6.21**). The rate of stamp duty is 0.5%;

(b)   to bearer instruments issued in the UK or by a UK company. The rate of stamp duty is 1.5%;

(c)   to deposit certificates in non-UK companies or bearer instruments issued by non-UK companies. The rate of stamp duty is 0.2%;

(d)   to the issue of depository receipts or shares put into a duty free clearance system (other than between corporate nominees or between a depositary receipt system and a clearance service (or vice versa)). The rate of stamp duty is 1.5%.

Stamp duty is not chargeable where the amount or value of the consideration is less than £1,000. No duty arises on transactions carried out orally. No duty is payable in connection with gifts to charities (**43.11**) gilt-edged securities, including gilt warrants, nor on a conveyance, transfer or lease to the Crown.

There are special exemptions from duty for financial intermediaries trading in UK securities, and in connection with stock borrowing and sale and repurchase arrangements. Furthermore there is relief from stamp duty (and SDRT) where, under a stock lending or sale and repurchase arrangement, securities are not returned to the originator because of the insolvency of one of the parties. Where the lender or seller buys securities to replace those lost the purchase is relieved from stamp duty and SDRT. HMRC have confirmed that any person who has paid stamp duty in such circumstances, is entitled to a repayment.

Shares which are traded over-the-counter will involve a number of transfers between a central counterparty to clear and settle the transactions. Regulations ensure that multiple charges to stamp duty or SDRT will not arise in such circumstances.

Generally, documents should be stamped before they take effect, although in practice stamping is permitted within 30 days without any penalty being charged.

Duty is either fixed or based on value depending on the heading under which the transaction falls. Ad valorem duties are rounded up to the nearest multiple of £5.

Adjudication and valuation (SA 1891, ss 12–13B)

[6.3] Adjudication is the assessment by a Stamp Office of how much duty, if any, is payable on a document and also the amount of any penalty payable for late stamping (as to which see **6.4**). Additionally, if after adjudication an unstamped or insufficiently stamped document is not duly stamped within 30 days, a penalty of up to £300 may be charged. Adjudication may be voluntary or compulsory. Anyone may ask a Stamp Office to state whether a document is chargeable, and if so, how much duty is payable. Sometimes, adjudication is compulsory, for example where exemption from duty is claimed on a company reconstruction without change in ownership.

Having considered the document the Stamp Office will either stamp it 'adjudged not chargeable with any stamp duty' or they will assess the duty and when it is paid, they will stamp the document 'adjudged duly stamped'. An adjudication stamp is normally conclusive evidence of due stamping.

An appeal may be made against an adjudication. Such an appeal must be made within 30 days and the duty plus any interest or penalty must be paid first. Appeals relating to late stamping penalties go first to the First-tier Tribunal and other appeals to the High Court.

Interest and penalties (SA 1891, ss 15–15B; FA 1989, s 178)

[6.4] Where documents are submitted late for stamping, interest and penalties may be charged, as follows.

Interest is chargeable on all documents liable to ad valorem duty that are not stamped within 30 days of execution, but rounded down to a multiple of £5 and not charging amounts of £25 or less. Interest is also chargeable on stamp duty penalties (other than late stamping penalties).

Interest will be paid on repayments of overpaid duty from 30 days after execution or from the date of payment if later (except for repayments of less than £25).

The rates of interest are the same as for income tax.

If documents are submitted for stamping more than 30 days after execution a (mitigable) penalty may be charged as follows:

(a) documents late by up to 12 months — 10% of the duty, capped at £300;
(b) documents late by 12 to 24 months — 20% of the duty;
(c) documents late by more than 24 months — 30% of the duty.

For delays of 12 months or more, the penalty rate may be higher if there is evidence that the failure to submit documents for stamping was deliberate. The more serious the reason, the greater the penalty can be, calculated as a percentage of the duty unpaid.

The above provisions are modified slightly in relation to bearer instruments, depository receipts and clearance systems.

Anti-avoidance provisions (FA 1986, s 67; FA 2000, ss 117–122 and Sch 33)

[6.5] The sharply increasing rates of stamp duty over recent years have led to an increase in devices to avoid stamp duty. Finance Act 2000 introduced a general provision that regulations may be issued to block such devices as they arise, where they relate to any extent to land, stock or marketable securities. Such regulations will cease to be valid after 18 months unless they have been included in a Finance Act. These anti-avoidance provisions are relevant only to stock and marketable securities and certain partnership transactions from 1 December 2003 following the introduction of stamp duty land tax.

Duty is charged at the shares rate where:

(a)   marketable securities are transferred in exchange for property that is exempt from stamp duty reserve tax;

(b)   the consideration for a sale is the right to a future issue of securities.

Also, anti-avoidance provisions apply where securities are transferred to a depository receipt issuer or clearance service (**6.2**) as the result of an exercise of an option and the option was entered into on or after 25 November 2015 and exercised on or after 23 March 2016. In these situations stamp duty is charged on the higher of the consideration for the exercise of the option or the market value of the securities. These rules were introduced to target arrangements where parties were agreeing a low price for the options (and therefore paying stamp duty on a lower value) and the seller was then receiving a large part of the consideration in the form of a high premium for the option, which was not subject to stamp duty.

Stamp duty reserve tax (FA 1986, ss 86–99; FA 1990, ss 110, 111; FA 1997, ss 100, 101; FA 1999, s 122 and Sch 19; FA 2001, s 94; SI 1986/1711; SI 1997/1156; SI 2001/964)

[6.6] Stamp duty reserve tax is dealt with mainly by Stock Exchange brokers and financial intermediaries. The following is a brief outline of the tax.

Stamp duty reserve tax (SDRT) at the rate of 0.5% applies to:

(a)   share transactions which escape stamp duty, for example, sales of renounceable letters of allotment and transactions within the same Stock Exchange account. Specifically excluded though are securities admitted to trading on a recognised growth market (e.g. AIM and the High Growth Segment of the main market). Following the introduction of the CREST system of paperless share dealing on the Stock Exchange, CREST transactions that would have attracted stamp duty now attract SDRT instead;

(b)   transfers of foreign currency bearer shares and of sterling or foreign currency bearer loan stock that is convertible or equity related. This charge does not apply if the securities are listed on a recognised stock exchange and the transfer is not made as part of a takeover.

SDRT also applies to shares converted into depositary receipts or put into a duty free clearing system. The rate of tax on these transactions is 1.5%. This higher rate acts as a 'season ticket' with subsequent transfers within the 1.5% system being exempt from the ordinary 0.5% charges. Where securities that have been subject to a 1.5% entry charge are subsequently transferred to another 1.5% regime, relief is available to ensure that there is no double charge. Anti-avoidance provisions apply where securities are transferred to a depository receipt issuer or clearance service as the result of an exercise of an option and the option was entered into on or after 25 November 2015 and exercised on or after 23 March 2016. In these situations SDRT is charged on the higher of the consideration for the exercise of the option or the market value of the securities. This was introduced to target arrangements where parties were agreeing a low price for the options (and therefore paying SDRT on a lower value) and the seller was then receiving a large part of the consideration in the form of a high premium for the option, which was not subject to SDRT.

There are several exceptions to this charge (e.g. it does not apply to transfers between certain corporate nominees, it does not apply on the issue or transfer of UK bearer instruments (unless they are renounceable letters of allotment and the rights are renounceable within six months of issue or they are foreign currency instruments which do not raise new consideration) etc.).

Clearing systems are able to elect to pay stamp duty or SDRT in the normal way on their transactions, and in that event, the 1.5% charge does not apply when chargeable securities are put into the system. Regulations (see **6.2**) ensure that multiple charges to SDRT will not arise when transactions involve a number of transfers between a central counterparty to clear and settle the transaction.

SDRT does not apply to gilt-edged stocks, traded options and futures, non-convertible loan stocks, foreign securities not on a UK register, depositary interests in foreign securities, transfers of units in foreign unit trusts, the issue of new securities and purchases by a charity. There are also special exemptions for financial intermediaries. Furthermore there is relief from SDRT (and stamp duty) where, under a stock lending or sale and repurchase arrangement, securities are not returned to the originator because of the insolvency of one of the parties. Where the lender or seller buys securities to replace those lost the purchase is relieved from stamp duty and SDRT. HMRC have confirmed that any person who has paid stamp duty in such circumstances (and where the relevant insolvency occurred on or after 1 September 2008), is entitled to a repayment.

Liability to SDRT arises at the date of the agreement (or if the agreement is conditional, at the date the condition is satisfied). For transactions via an exchange (in particular CREST transactions), the tax is payable on a date agreed with HMRC (or if there is no agreed date, the fourteenth day after the transaction). For other transactions the due date is the seventh day of the month following the month in which the transaction occurred and the person liable to pay the tax (i.e. the broker, dealer or purchaser) must give notice of the charge to HMRC on or before that date.

SDRT is only payable to the extent that it exceeds any ad valorem stamp duty on the transaction, and where the ad valorem duty exceeds the amount of SDRT, no SDRT is payable. If duty is paid after SDRT has been paid, the SDRT is refunded (plus income tax free interest on refunds over £25).

HMRC guidance on SDRT is available at www.gov.uk/stamp-duty-reserve-tax-the-basics.

Interest and penalties (SI 1986/1711 reg 20 and Sch)

[6.7] Interest is charged on overdue SDRT (or paid on SDRT repayments) from 14 days after the transaction date for exchange transactions and otherwise from seven days after the end of the month of the transaction, and there are various penalties for defaults, including a mitigable penalty of £100, plus £60 a day following a declaration by HMRC, where the appropriate notice of liability has not been given and the tax has not been paid.

The rates of interest are the same as for income tax.

Stamp duty land tax (FA 2003, ss 42–124 and Schs 3–19)

[6.8] Stamp duty land tax (SDLT) charges tax on transactions relating to UK land whether or not any party to the transaction is present or resident in the UK and whether or not a document is used. This tax does not apply to land and buildings situated in Scotland — instead land and buildings transaction tax (LBTT) applies; see **6.18**. Note also that the Wales Act 2014 has devolved stamp duty land tax to the Welsh Assembly from April 2018.

If a document is used, SDLT is charged whether or not it is executed in the UK. If a contract for a land transaction is 'substantially performed' (broadly when most of the consideration is paid or possession is taken of the property) before being formally completed, SDLT arises at that time. Otherwise it arises at the time of completion.

Where the purchaser of an interest in land, before completing that purchase, transfers the rights/interest in the land to another person there is only one charge to SDLT. Specifically excluded from this relief is a grant or assignment of an option; such a grant or assignment does not fall within the definition of a transfer of rights for these purposes. Anti-avoidance provisions address particular schemes that attempt to abuse this relief; for example schemes involving sub-sales or other transfer or rights which are not to be completed for a number of years do not qualify for this relief.

The consideration for an SDLT transaction is the amount payable in money or moneys' worth. Where consideration is contingent, tax is payable on the assumption that the consideration will be payable. Where consideration is uncertain, a reasonable estimate must be made. Where all or part of contingent or uncertain consideration is payable more than 18 months after the effective date of the transaction, an application may be made to defer the appropriate amount of tax. Provision is made for the tax to be adjusted upwards or downwards when the contingency occurs (or it is clear it will not occur), or when uncertain consideration is ascertained. Where a company purchases land from a connected person, the purchase price is deemed to be not less than the market value.

Certain transactions are exempt from SDLT, as indicated in **6.13** and **6.22**. For stamp taxes and charities see **43.11**. HMRC guidance on SDLT is available at www.gov.uk/stamp-duty-land-tax.

Rates of tax (FA 2003, ss 55, 55A, 57AA and Sch 4A)

[6.9] The rates of SDLT are set out below, based on the value of the consideration paid for the property.

SDLT does not apply to property transactions in Scotland as land and buildings transactions tax (LBTT) applies instead; see **6.18**. From April 2018, SDLT will also not apply in Wales. It will be replaced by a new Welsh land transaction tax. The proposed rates and bands will be announced by October 2017 but it has been confirmed that the higher, 3% rate of SDLT for additional residential properties, in force from 1 April 2016, will continue to be levied in Wales when SDLT is replaced by the land transaction tax.

Special rules apply to equate the SDLT payable in relation to Sharia-compliant mortgages with the tax payable in relation to conventional mortgages.

Residential property: natural persons

Consideration	Standard rate	Additional residential property rate
Up to £40,000	Nil	Nil
Over £40,000 and up to £125,000	Nil	3%
Over £125,000 and up to £250,000	2%	5%
Over £250,000 and up to £925,000	5%	8%
Over £925,001 and up to £1,500,000	10%	13%
Over £1,500,000	12%	15%

The tax operates on a progressive basis, similar to income tax with the higher rates applying to the amount of consideration that falls within the respective bands. If, for example, property was sold for £300,000 the 2% rate would apply to the consideration falling over £125,000 and up to £250,000 and the 5% rate would apply to the remaining £50,000.

The 'additional residential property rate' applies to transactions completed on or after 1 April 2016 on purchases of additional residential properties, such as buy to let properties and second homes. The higher rates are 3% above the current SDLT rates, but they do not apply to:

(a)   purchases of property where exchange of contracts was before 26 November 2015 and completion was after 1 April 2016;

(b)   purchases of property below £40,000;

(c)   purchases of caravans, mobile homes or houseboats;

(d)   purchases of leasehold interests originally granted for a period of less than seven years; or

(e)   purchases of freehold or leasehold interests that are reversionary on leases with more than 21 years remaining at the date of purchase.

If a person's first residence hasn't been sold on the day of completion of the new purchase, the higher rates apply, but it may be possible to get a refund if the first residence is sold within 36 months. For HMRC guidance see www.gov.uk/guidance/stamp-duty-land-tax-buying-an-additional-residential-property.

Residential property: non-natural persons

The SDLT rate is increased to 15% for residential property transactions entered into by certain non-natural persons (broadly companies, collective investment schemes and partnerships with a member who is a company or a collective investment scheme) where the chargeable consideration exceeds £500,000. This increased charge does not apply (and instead the standard rates for natural persons will apply) if:

(a)   the purchaser is a company acting in its capacity as trustee of a settlement;

(b)   the purchaser is a company carrying out a business of letting, trading in or redeveloping properties;

(c)   the purchaser acquires the interest with the intention of exploiting the dwelling to generate income by providing access to a significant part of the interior;

(d)   the purchaser is a financial institution carrying on a business that involves the lending of money and the property is bought with the intention of resale in the course of its business;

(e)   the purchaser carries on a trade and buys the dwelling to house employees or partners with a limited interest in the company;

(f)   the property is (or is to be) a farmhouse occupied for the purposes of that trade by a qualifying farm worker;

(g)   (for transactions on or after 1 April 2016) the purchaser acquires the property for use as business premises or to convert/demolish and subsequently use as business premises;

(h)   (for transactions on or after 1 April 2016) the purchaser is an authorised plan provider and acquires the whole or part of the dwelling exclusively for the purposes of entering into an equity release scheme; specifically a home reversion plan;

(i)   (for transactions on or after 1 April 2016) the purchaser is a tenant management company, buying the property for a resident caretaker; or

(j)   (for transactions on or after 1 April 2016) the property is purchased in order to provide accommodation to an employee of a property rental business.

Relief will only apply if the property continues to satisfy the relevant qualifying conditions throughout the three years following purchase. In addition, for relief under (h) the property must be sold without delay when the last individual living in the property either dies or goes into long term care. Otherwise, additional SDLT will become payable and the purchaser must deliver a further return within 30 days after the relevant date on which the condition was breached.

This increased charge (to 15%) aims to disincentivise the ownership of high value residential property in complex structures that might otherwise allow the indirect ownership of such property to be transferred in a way that would not be chargeable to SDLT. This provision, combined with the annual charge on such property owned by the same sorts of non-natural persons (**32.48**), is intended to result in a reduction in the number of high value properties owned in such structures.

Non-residential or mixed use property: completion on or after 17 March 2016

Consideration	Rate
Up to £150,000	Nil
Over £150,000 and up to £250,000	2%
Over £250,000	5%

For transactions completing on or after 17 March 2016 (subject to transitional rules, see below), the tax operates on a progressive basis, similar to income tax with the higher rates applying to the amount of consideration that falls within the respective bands. If, for example, property was sold for £300,000 the nil rate would apply to the consideration falling up to £150,000 and the 1% rate would apply to the remaining £50,000.

Transitional relief applies so that where contracts were exchanged before 17 March 2016 but the contract is completed on or after that date, purchasers can choose not to apply the new rules and so pay SDLT under the old rules. To choose the old rates, the purchaser just has to enter the appropriate amount of SDLT in the land transaction return.

Non-residential or mixed use property: completion before 17 March 2016

Consideration	Rate
Up to £150,000	Nil
Over £150,000 and up to £250,000	1%
Over £250,000 and up to £500,000	3%
Over £500,000	4%

For transactions that take place before 17 March 2016 (subject to transitional rules, see above) the tax operated on the so called 'slab' system with a single tax rate being applied to the whole amount of the consideration; so if, for example property was sold for £300,000 the 3% rate was applied to the full £300,000.

Leases of land and buildings (FA 2003, ss 55, 56, 77, 120 and Schs 5, 17A)

[6.10] SDLT applies both to lease premiums and to the rental element of a lease.

Lease premiums

Lease premiums are charged at the same rates as for freehold transfers (see 6.9).

Rental element

The SDLT payable on the rental element of leases is 1% of the excess of the net present value (NPV) of the rental payments over the thresholds of £125,000 for residential property or £150,000 for non-residential property. In addition, from 17 March 2016, there is a 2% rate for rent paid under a lease of non-residential property where the NPV of the rent is above £5 million.

Transitional relief applies so that where contracts were exchanged before 17 March 2016 but the contract is completed on or after that date, purchasers can choose not to apply the new rules and so pay SDLT under the old rules. To choose the old rates, the purchaser just has to enter the appropriate amount of SDLT in the land transaction return.

Example 1

The calculation of the SDLT due on the rental element of a lease granted on 20 March 2017, where the NPV of the rent is £6 million is as follows:

	Rate	£
First £150,000	Nil	—
Over £150,000 up to £5 million	1%	48,500
Over £5 million	2%	20,000
Total		68,500

All variations of a lease in the first five years that increase the rent (other than to reflect changes in the retail prices index) are treated as the grant of a new lease. SDLT applies to a capital payment by a landlord where the term of a lease is reduced, and to a capital payment by a tenant to commute all or part of the rent. After the first five years of a lease, any rent increases are ignored in calculating NPV and the rent value used for later periods is the highest rent in any 12 months in the first five years. Where rent is uncertain (e.g. related to turnover), the NPV is originally based on a reasonable estimate. If the rent is still uncertain after five years, a single additional land transaction return is required in which the NPV will be based on the actual rent in the first five years and the highest rent in any 12 months during those years, as above, for the remaining years of the lease. If the rent becomes certain within the five years the single additional return will be required at that time.

Where a lease is surrendered, SDLT is payable on any consideration paid by the landlord as for a sale. If a reverse premium is paid by the tenant, SDLT is not chargeable. Where a lease is surrendered in return for a new lease, the grant of the new lease does not count as chargeable consideration for the surrender, and the surrender does not count as chargeable consideration for the new lease. Furthermore, credit is given in computing the SDLT on the new lease for the amount of rent due for the surrendered years.

The grant of a lease for less than seven years or the assignment of such a lease only has to be notified to the Stamp Office if there is tax to pay or a relief to be claimed. Other grants/assignments of leases up to seven years may be self-certified.

Where a lease of land in Scotland is granted before 1 April 2015 and in accordance with these rules tax becomes due on or after that date, the lease remains subject to SDLT.

Multiple purchase relief

[6.11] Relief is available for purchasers of more than one dwelling from the same vendor. In such situations, instead of the rate of SDLT being based on the total consideration, it is based on the mean consideration, i.e. by the aggregate consideration divided by the number of dwellings (subject to a minimum rate of 1%). This relief includes purchases of superior interests in dwellings subject to a long lease, where the transaction is the lease element of a 'lease and leaseback' funding arrangement entered into by a housing association or other qualifying body.

If, for transactions on or after 1 April 2015, the properties are situated in Scotland and elsewhere in the UK the relief is calculated according to the number of dwellings which are subject to SDLT (i.e. excluding the properties in Scotland). For dwellings situated in Scotland, multiple dwellings relief is available under the separate Scottish provisions.

Part exchanges, sale and leaseback and other reliefs (FA 2003, ss 57A, 58A and Sch 6A)

[6.12] Relief is available, subject to various conditions, where a builder takes a home in part exchange, or where someone buying a new home from a builder sells their old home to a property trader, or where a property trader buys a home from someone whose sale of the property has fallen through to enable that person to proceed with the purchase of another property. Where the conditions are satisfied, the acquisition by the builder or property trader is exempt from SDLT.

Sale and leaseback transactions involve a buyer agreeing to purchase land or buildings from a seller, then that same buyer leasing the land or buildings, or part of them, back to the seller who then becomes the tenant. Relief for sale and leaseback transactions is available for both commercial property and residential property. The effect of the relief is that the 'leaseback' element of the transaction is exempt from SDLT.

Transfers and leases of land and buildings by and to Registered Social Landlords (FA 2003, ss 49, 71 and Sch 3)

[6.13] Land transactions under which property is acquired by Registered Social Landlords (RSLs) or registered providers of social housing (e.g. Housing Associations) are, in specified circumstances, exempt from SDLT.

Leases by RSLs or registered providers of social housing are also exempt from SDLT if the lease is for an indefinite term or terminable by notice of a month or less and it is provided under contracts with local authorities to house the homeless (the RSL itself having obtained the property on a lease of five years or less).

Relief for public bodies (FA 2003, s 67A; SI 2016/558)

[6.14] Where a land transaction occurs as the result of a statutory reorganisation, and both the buyer and the seller are public bodies, the buyer may claim relief from SDLT. A 'public body' includes:

(a)   a minister of the Crown;
(b)   a county or district council;
(c)   the National Health Service Commissioning Board;
(d)   a clinical commissioning group established under the National Health Service Act 2006 s 14D;
(e)   an NHS foundation trust;
(f)   a Local Health Board established under the National Health Service (Wales) Act 2006 s 11;
(g)   a National Health Service trust established under the National Health Service Act s 18;
(h)   a Health and Social Services trust established under the Health and Personal Social Services (Northern Ireland) Order 1991.

Any transfers of land affected under the Housing and Regeneration Act 2008 will qualify for relief from SDLT, where either the purchaser or vendor is a public body.

Value Added Tax (HMRC Brief 08/2013)

[6.15] The value on which SDLT is charged on sales and leases of land and buildings includes any value added tax on the transaction. Where, however, a landlord has the option to charge VAT, but has not chosen to do so by the date of the transaction, VAT will be excluded from the chargeable consideration for the lease.

HMRC have stated that if VAT was charged on the grant of an interest in land when in fact the transaction qualified as a transfer of a going concern (7.52), and no VAT should have been charged, a business may make a claim for overpayment relief because the SDLT would have been assessed on a VAT-inclusive value rather than a VAT-exclusive one. Claims must be made within four years of the date of transaction.

For further details on the VAT position on property, see CHAPTER 32.

Returns etc (FA 2003, ss 76–78, 81, 82A, Schs 10, 11A)

[6.16] Purchasers (or agents on their behalf) must send the Stamp Office a return notifying a land transaction within 30 days after the effective date of the transaction. With limited exceptions this applies even if no tax is payable.

A return is not, however, required in certain circumstances (for example there is a notification threshold of £40,000 for most freehold and leasehold transactions). In such cases a self-certificate must be submitted stating that no land transaction return is required. Where tax is payable, the land transaction return must include a self-assessment and payment must be made on or before the filing date for the return (i.e. 30 days after the effective date of the transaction).

A further return will be required within 30 days after any event causing SDLT relief to be withdrawn under, for example, the groups or charities provisions, accompanied by the tax due.

It is now possible in most circumstances to complete SDLT returns online via www.gov.uk/sdlt-online and in that event the tax will normally be automatically calculated. If the online service is used, the return *must* be filed online, and a paper printout should not be submitted. SDLT returns, online or paper, will only be accepted if lead purchasers use the new style forms and supply the unique identifiers on the return. Individual lead purchasers can use their National Insurance Number and date of birth. Companies should use their company UTR or VAT registration number, whilst partnerships should use their UTR or VAT registration number. A unique transaction reference number (UTRN) will be provided when the return is filed. HMRC strongly recommend electronic payment for returns filed online, but other payment methods are acceptable. HMRC guidance is at www.gov.uk/guidance/sdlt-co mpleting-the-paper-return.

There are provisions similar to the income tax self-assessment rules providing for separate claims to be made where they cannot be made in an SDLT return or amended return, requiring records to be kept and providing for HMRC enquiries into returns, HMRC determinations and assessments, and appeals against HMRC decisions. (HMRC have produced a booklet SD8 explaining how settlements are negotiated at the end of an enquiry under SDLT). There are also similar penalties for failing to deliver a return, failing to preserve records etc. Penalties may also be imposed for carelessly or deliberately delivering an incorrect return or for failing to comply with notices to provide documents or information, assisting in incorrect returns etc. Criminal proceedings may be taken for fraudulent evasion of SDLT. Interest is payable on overdue SDLT and on overdue penalties, and interest is payable to taxpayers on overpaid tax. The rates of interest are the same as for income tax. For details see CHAPTER 9.

When registering land transactions with the Chief Land Registrar, purchasers must produce either an HMRC certificate that a land transaction return has been delivered or a self-certificate that no land transaction return is required. There are provisions requiring records to be kept and there are related penalty provisions.

Anti-avoidance provisions (FA 2000, ss 117–122, 128 and Sch 33; FA 2002, ss 111–115 and Schs 34–36; FA 2003, ss 62, 75A–75C, 104, 109, 120 and Schs 7, 15, 17A)

[6.17] There is a general anti-avoidance provision in relation to stamp duty land tax (SDLT) at Finance Act 2003, s 75A. In addition, disclosure requirements were introduced from 1 August 2005 relating to certain SDLT schemes and arrangements, see 45.2 and a general anti-abuse rule or GAAR applies to all taxes (including SDLT) for any tax arrangements entered into on or after 17 July 2013, see 45.5.

There are also various specific provisions to counter SDLT avoidance schemes in relation to group relief, leases and partnerships. In addition HMRC have power to issue regulations to counter stamp duty and SDLT avoidance devices as they arise. Specific provisions treat a series of linked transactions as a notional land transaction, and amend the SDLT rules for partnerships. Finance Act 2008 contained SDLT measures to counter avoidance by groups of companies; to counter 'misuse' of rules designed to encourage use of alternative finance structures; and to amend some of the Finance Act 2007 provisions retrospectively. Finance Act 2011 introduced further anti-avoidance rules to ensure or put beyond doubt that certain SDLT avoidance schemes are ineffective.

Land and buildings transaction tax (LBTT(S)A 2013)

Scope

[6.18] Land and buildings transaction tax (LBTT) is a tax on transactions in land situated in Scotland. LBTT applies to standard house purchases and to other types of land transaction, for example leases where the effective date (completion or grant of a lease etc) is on or after 1 April 2015. If a land transaction has an effective date before 1 April 2015, the SDLT regime will still apply (see 6.8).

There are several exempt transactions/interests. Transactions that fall within these categories will not be chargeable to LBTT and no return is required to be made:

(a)   the acquisition of a security interest such as the creditor's interest in a standard security;

(b)   land or buildings that are gifted to another person for no 'chargeable consideration'. Note that where a land transaction involves the buyer both being gifted property and assuming existing debt (such as assuming the liability of a mortgage), then the debt assumed is chargeable consideration for LBTT purposes;

(c)   acquisitions by the Crown;

(d)   the grant of a short duration residential lease where the main subject matter consists entirely of an interest in land that is residential property;

(e)   transactions in connection with a divorce/dissolution of a civil partnership;

(f)   appropriations by personal representations; and

(g)   variation of testamentary dispositions etc.

Where a transaction falls within the LBTT regime, there are several reliefs that may apply, which are legislated for in LBTT(S)A 2013 but broadly follow the reliefs available under the SDLT regime as follows. The available reliefs include:

(i)   multiple purchases relief (**6.11**);

(ii)   part exchanges, sale and leaseback (**6.12**);

(iii)   transfers and leases of land and buildings by and to Registered Social Landlords (**6.13**); and

(iv)   relief for public bodies (**6.14**).

The provisions discussed at **6.21–6.24** broadly apply, with necessary modifications to terminology etc, to transactions within the LBTT regime. The Scottish GAAR applies to LBTT (**45.6**).

This is necessarily only a very brief overview of the regime; detailed guidance can be found at www.revenue.scot/land-buildings-transaction-tax/guidance/lbtt-legislation-guidance.

Rates of tax

[6.19] The rates of LBTT are set out below. As for SDLT, the rate of tax is determined by reference to amounts of the chargeable consideration falling within the relevant bands (i.e. on a progressive basis).

Residential land

Chargeable consideration	Rate
Up to £145,000	Nil
Above £145,000 to £250,000	2%
Above £250,000 to £325,000	5%
Above £325,000 to £750,000	10%
Over £750,000	12%

In a similar vein to SDLT there is, from 1 April 2016, an additional dwelling supplement of 3% applied to the purchase price of additional residential properties in Scotland (such as buy-to-let properties and second homes) of £40,000 or more.

Generally, leases of residential property are exempt from LBTT.

Non-residential or mixed use property

LBTT is charged on the purchase of non-residential etc property, based on the amount of chargeable consideration for the purchase at the following rates.

Chargeable consideration	Rate
Up to £150,000	Nil
Above £150,000 to £350,000	3%
Above £350,000	4.5%

Where non-residential property is leased, any premium paid on the grant of the lease is subject to LBTT at the above rates, based on the amount of the premium. Any rent is also chargeable to LBTT at the following rates, based on the net present value (NPV) of the rent payable under the lease.

NPV of rent payable	Rate
Up to £150,000	Nil
Above £150,000	1%

Where six or more separate homes are the subject of a single transaction or a grant of a lease over them, then those homes are treated as non-residential property (subject to multiple dwellings relief (**6.11**).

Returns etc

[6.20] LBTT is a self-assessed tax and it is the responsibility of the taxpayer to complete and submit an accurate LBTT return, where required, to Revenue Scotland and pay any tax due. The tax is charged regardless of whether there is a document setting out the terms of the transaction, whether any document was executed in Scotland and whether any party to the transaction was present or resident in Scotland at the effective date of the transaction.

All land transactions need to be notified to Revenue Scotland by means of an LBTT return although there are exceptions that apply, for example, to exempt transactions (**6.18**) or where the chargeable consideration is less than £40,000. Where tax is payable, it must be made at the same time as the LBTT return filing date (i.e. 30 days after the effective date of the transaction). A further return may be required within 30 days after any event in consequence of a later linked transaction, when a contingency ceases or where a relief is withdrawn accompanied by the tax due.

A purchaser that is required to make an LBTT return is also required to keep and preserve certain records. A purchaser in a land transaction which is not notifiable is also required in some instances to keep and preserve certain records, mostly to evidence that the transaction was not notifiable. Penalties are payable for non-compliance. Interest is payable on overdue LBTT and on overdue penalties, and interest is payable to taxpayers on overpaid tax. Penalties are levied for inaccurate documentation (9.59), late returns (9.63) and late payment (9.72).

Transfers of interests in partnerships (FA 2003, Sch 15, Pt 3)

[6.21] SDLT applies to partnership transactions in the following circumstances:

(a)　where there are land transfers to or from an unconnected third party by the partnership; SDLT applies in the usual way, including any applicable reliefs;

(b)　where land is transferred to a partnership by a partner (or a person who becomes a partner in return for the land or the land is transferred by a person connected with either person); the amount chargeable is the proportion of the market value of the land that has been transferred;

(c)　where there is a transfer of a partnership interest in a property investment partnership, but not in any other form of partnership, when the partnership property includes land (whether any consideration is given). The chargeable consideration is based on the market value of the relevant partnership property, although the precise calculation differs depending upon whether there is consideration or not for the transfer. A property investment partnership is a partnership whose sole or main activity is investing in or dealing in land whether that involves carrying out construction operations on land or not.

Stamp duty continues to apply to instruments effecting transfers of partnership interests, but only on the amount of consideration equal to the value of any stock or marketable securities included in the transfer.

Distribution of a deceased's estate; transfers of property on break-up of marriage or civil partnership (FA 1985, ss 83, 84; FA 2003, ss 49, 58A and Schs 3, 6A)

[6.22] All qualifying variations of the distribution of a deceased's estate (see CHAPTER 35) and deeds conveying property under an order on divorce or dissolution of a civil partnership, or on separation, are exempt from stamp duty and SDLT where the property concerned is an interest in land and buildings.

No charge to SDLT arises when property passes to a beneficiary under a will or intestacy, nor when personal representatives dispose of a deceased's home to a property trader.

Intra-group transfers and company reconstructions etc. (FA 1930, s 42; FA 1967, s 27; FA 1986, ss 75–77A; FA 2002, ss 111, 113 and Schs 34, 35; FA 2003, s 62 and Sch 7)

[6.23] Stamp duty is not chargeable on transfers of property between companies within a 75% group, on company reconstructions without a change of ownership or on share-for share exchanges (**28.8**). These provisions are subject to stringent anti-avoidance provisions (for example, the relief for share-for share exchanges is not available in relation to any instrument executed on or after 29 June 2016, where arrangements are in place at the time of the share-for-share exchange for a change of control of the acquiring company).

A 'company' for these group relief purposes is defined as a body corporate which includes a Limited Liability Partnership (LLP) incorporated under the Limited Liability Partnership Act 2000. This inclusion of LLPs means that an LLP can be the parent in a group structure. However, as an LLP does not itself have issued ordinary share capital it cannot be the subsidiary of other companies. For further details see www.gov.uk/government/publications/group-relief-for-stamp-duty-land-tax-and-stamp-duty-partnerships.

For transfers of shares and securities not within these provisions (takeovers etc.), stamp duty is charged at 0.5%.

Similar reliefs and restrictions apply in respect of stamp duty land tax. There are also specific anti-avoidance provisions to prevent transactions avoiding the clawback of group relief.

Foreign exchange currency rules (SA 1891, s 6; FA 2003, Sch 4 para 9)

[6.24] All foreign currency amounts on which duty is payable are converted to sterling at the rate applying on the date of the document. For stamp duty land tax, foreign currency amounts are converted to sterling at the London closing exchange rate on the effective date of the transaction, unless the parties have used a different rate.

7

Value added tax: general principles

Basis of charge (VATA 1994, ss 1, 2, 4, 41A)

[7.1] Value added tax (VAT) is charged on the supply of goods and services in the UK and on the import of goods into the UK from outside the European Union. The principal legislation is contained in Value Added Tax Act 1994 (VATA 1994), but many of the detailed rules are in regulations. European Union law on VAT, including Directive 2006/112/EC, takes precedence over UK law in the event of any inconsistency.

VAT is charged either at the standard rate of 20%, the reduced rate of 5% or the zero-rate (see **7.22**). Certain supplies are specifically exempt from VAT (see **7.26**).

VAT applies to taxable supplies made in the course of a business by a taxable person, i.e. an individual, firm or company registered, or liable to be registered, for VAT (see **7.8**). It is specifically provided that public bodies are not to be treated as taxable persons unless their exemption would lead to distortion of competition or they carry out certain activities (listed in Annex 1 of Directive 2006/112/EC) on a more than negligible basis.

Special rules apply to transactions within the European Union (see **7.37**). See **32.40** for VAT on transactions relating to land and buildings.

How the VAT system works (VATA 1994, Pt 1, s 51B, Schs 6 and 10A)

[7.2] VAT is an indirect tax on the supply of goods and services. Each person in the chain between the first supplier and the final consumer is charged VAT (input tax) on taxable supplies to him and charges VAT (output tax) on taxable supplies made by him. The excess of output tax over input tax is paid over to HMRC. If input tax exceeds output tax, a refund is made by HMRC. The broad effect of the scheme is that businesses are not affected by VAT except in so far as they are required to administer it, and the burden of the tax falls on the final consumer.

However, VAT does represent a cost to any business that cannot set off or recover all of its input tax. Non-VAT registered businesses cannot recover any VAT at all, partially exempt businesses (i.e. those making taxable and exempt supplies, see 7.27) cannot recover all their VAT, and VAT on certain items cannot be recovered at all (see 7.4).

For income tax and corporation tax purposes, input tax that cannot be recovered forms part of the related expenditure, which may be allowed as a deduction in calculating profits or may qualify for capital allowances.

VAT repayments are likely to arise where most supplies are zero-rated, since input tax is likely to exceed output tax.

Output tax

[7.3] Output tax must be charged on all taxable supplies, including, for example, sales of fixed assets like plant and machinery. In most situations, this is a fairly straightforward calculation, however some transactions are less clear cut, as detailed below.

If a discount is offered for prompt payment, VAT is charged only on the discounted amount whether or not the discount is taken. This is subject to exceptions in relation to payment by instalments and contingent discounts. See HMRC Brief 49/2014.

The treatment of face value vouchers (such as gift vouchers and 'phone' cards) is broadly as follows, but those issuing vouchers need to study the detailed rules carefully:

(a)   retailers issuing single purpose face value vouchers which they will exchange for goods or services must account for VAT at the time of issue. This is because, as the voucher can only be redeemed for a single type of good or service, the VAT treatment is known at the time that the voucher is sold and there is therefore sufficient information to determine the liability of the supply for VAT purposes;

(b)   retailers issuing vouchers that are not single purpose which they will exchange for goods or services do not have to account for VAT until the vouchers are redeemed. Intermediate suppliers who sell vouchers are, however, liable to account for VAT when the vouchers are sold, subject to the normal rules concerning recovery of input tax. Sales of postage stamps at or below face value are disregarded for VAT purposes.

Where a manufacturer gives 'cashbacks' to his customers, he is entitled to reduce his output tax providing he charged VAT on the original supply. The cashback reduces the taxable value of the supply to the customer, who must reduce his input tax accordingly.

Where business cars on which no input tax was recovered are sold, VAT is not normally chargeable. Where business cars on which any input tax was recovered are sold, VAT is payable on the full selling price. In most cases, VAT-registered businesses can't reclaim the VAT when they buy a car. However they may be able to reclaim the VAT when they buy a commercial vehicle, motorcycle or motor home; see www.gov.uk/reclaim-vat/cars for HMRC guidance.

There is a supply of services where business goods are used privately. The value of the supply for VAT purposes, where there is no actual consideration, is normally the cost of the goods to the business.

A gift of business assets is a supply of goods unless the total value of gifts given to the same person in the same year does not exceed £50 or one of a number of other exemptions applies. There is not usually a VAT liability on a gift of services. HMRC guidance on business gifts and samples is available in VAT Notice 700/35 and HMRC Brief 51/2010.

Particular care is needed with licensing and franchise arrangements, and even if someone is regarded as self-employed, they may be treated as the agent of the licensor/franchisor, so that the VAT liability depends on the licensor's/franchisor's VAT status. VAT tribunals have often come to conflicting decisions about people doing similar work, particularly in cases relating to driving instructors and hairdressers, some of whom have been held to be self-employed principals and some to be acting as agents. Even if regarded as a principal, a hairdresser will usually be treated as paying for composite supplies chargeable at the standard rate of VAT rather than merely renting space.

Input tax

[7.4] Subject to the restrictions for partially exempt businesses, input tax can be recovered on goods purchased for resale and on business expenses and capital expenditure. Where there is mixed business and non-business use, an adjustment needs to be made (see **20.25** onwards).

Even when VAT incurred is attributable to a fully taxable supply, it is not possible to recover input tax in respect of certain business entertaining (see **20.15**), most cars and related supplies (see **20.26**). Special rules apply in relation to input tax recovery for business vehicle fuel bills (see **7.5**). Companies cannot recover input tax on repairs, refurbishments and other expenses relating to domestic accommodation provided for directors or their families.

A late claim to recover input tax can only be made within four years after the due date for the return (see **7.41**) in which the claim should have been made.

Business vehicle fuel bills (VATA 1994, ss 56, 57, Sch 6)

Fuel bought by the business: no charge for private use

[7.5] When a business's road fuel is used in private journeys for no consideration the business may opt for all such supplies made to be taxed on a flat rate basis, i.e. by the application of the scale charge. Details of the scale charge, together with rules and notes setting out the application of the charge, are set out in SI 2013/2911. Otherwise the supply of fuel is treated as a deemed supply of goods in the course of the business and VAT is accounted for in the usual manner on essentially an open market value.

By concession:

(i)   input tax may be recovered on the basis of detailed mileage records which separate business and private motoring costs (VAT Notice 700/64);

(ii)   a person is not required to account for output tax on fuel for private use if he disclaims the right to input tax and so avoids the scale charge; and

(iii)   where input tax on fuel is apportioned for partial exemption then the scale charge can be apportioned at the same rate.

Fuel bought by the business: charge for private use

[7.6] Where employers provide fuel to an employee for their private use and make a real charge to the employee (albeit at less than cost price), VAT is accounted for on the basis of the amount charged, although where the charge is artificially low, VAT must be accounted on the open market value of the supply.

Fuel bought by employees

[7.7] Where employees buy fuel for their employers and are reimbursed, either on an actual cost or mileage allowance basis, the employers can recover the VAT on the fuel so long as the employee has provided them with a VAT invoice and the fuel is used in making taxable supplies. Other acceptable ways for employees to purchase fuel for the employer are by use of an employer's credit or debit card, or by charging the fuel to an employer's account at the garage.

Input tax on repair and maintenance costs paid by the business is fully recoverable, and no private use adjustment is required, except that input tax cannot be reclaimed if a proprietor uses a vehicle solely for private purposes.

Registration (VATA 1994, Schs 1–3A; SI 1995/2518 Pt II)

Compulsory registration

[7.8] The compulsory registration rules apply differently depending on whether a person is UK-established or not, as detailed below. This ensures that the UK law is in line with the judgment of the Court of Justice of the European Union in Schmelz C-97/09.

UK-established person

[7.9] Only UK-established persons can benefit from the compulsory registration thresholds. These thresholds mean that UK-established persons who are in business and make or intend to make taxable supplies are liable to be registered for VAT at the end of *any month* if the taxable supplies of all business activities in the year ended on the last day of that month exceed £85,000 (£83,000 prior to 1 April 2017), unless they can satisfy HMRC that the taxable supplies in the next 12 months will not exceed £83,000 (£81,000 prior to 1 April 2017). A person is UK-established if essential management decisions and central administration functions are carried out in the UK and/or the business has a permanent physical presence with the human and technical resources to make or receive taxable supplies in the UK.

HMRC must be notified within 30 days of the end of the month in which the yearly limit is exceeded, and registration is compulsory from the beginning of the next month or such earlier date as is agreed with HMRC.

Example 1

Turnover for the 12 months ended 31 October 2017 is £86,000, having been below the yearly limit at the end of previous months. HMRC must be notified by 30 November 2017 and registration must be from 1 December 2017 (or from an earlier date agreed with HMRC) unless it can be shown that turnover in the year to 31 October 2018 will not exceed £83,000.

Liability to register also arises at any time if taxable supplies in the next 30 days are expected to exceed £85,000. HMRC must be notified within 30 days after the day on which liability arose and registration is compulsory from the day on which liability arose.

Example 2

On 16 September 2017 trading commences and it is expected that the first month's turnover will be £86,000. Liability to register must be notified by 15 October 2017 and the business will be registered from 16 September 2017.

Non UK-established person

Non UK-established businesses (essentially overseas traders) cannot benefit from the UK VAT registration threshold limits. Consequently any such business is liable to register for VAT when:

(a)   it can be reasonably anticipated that it will make taxable supplies in the UK within the next 30 days; or

(b)   it does in fact make such supplies.

Where liability arises under (a), the business must notify liability to register before the end of the relevant period and HMRC must register that business from the beginning of that period. Where liability arises under (b), the business must notify liability to register within 30 days of the liability arising and HMRC must register that business from the date when the liability arose.

Where there is a liability to register for VAT, the business can either register directly or appoint an agent or VAT representative to act on his behalf. The key difference between an agent and a VAT representative is that an agent does not have joint and several liability for the VAT debts of his principal, whereas a VAT representative does. A VAT representative does not have to be registered in the UK but must be established in the UK. HMRC can refuse to register a VAT representative appointed by a non-EU trader if they do not consider the VAT representative to be a fit and proper person to act in that capacity.

Other compulsory registration

[7.10] Registration may also be required in relation to acquisitions from other countries in the European Union (see **7.37**). Farmers are able to avoid VAT registration if they opt to become 'flat rate farmers' (see **31.12**). Small businesses may join an optional flat-rate scheme, but they will still be required to be registered for VAT (see **7.31**). See also **7.12** and **7.52** below as regards voluntary registration and selling a business as a going concern.

Administration

[7.11] An application for registration is made on form VAT 1 and HMRC will issue a certificate of registration VAT 4 showing the VAT registration number. Application for registration may be made online via www.hmrc.gov.uk/vat. Groups of companies may register as a single taxable person (see **7.51**).

HMRC have discretion to exempt a business from registration if they are satisfied that only zero-rated supplies (see **7.24**) are made. In such cases HMRC must be notified within 30 days of a material change in the nature of supplies made, or within 30 days after the end of the quarter in which the change occurred if the day of the change is not identifiable.

A business registering for VAT is able to recover tax incurred on goods and services before their effective date of registration as long as they are used by the taxable person to make taxable supplies once registered. Services must have been received less than sixmonths before the effective date of registration for VAT to be deductible. Goods have a four-year time limit for deductibility providing the assets are still in use by the business at the effective date of registration; see HMRC Brief 16/2016.

There are provisions to prevent the splitting of businesses in order to stay below the VAT registration threshold. HMRC have the power to direct that where two or more persons are carrying on separate business activities which are effectively parts of the same business, they are to be treated for VAT purposes as the same business, e.g. where one spouse is a publican and the other runs the catering within the public house. Such a direction only affects future supplies and is not retrospective.

There are anti-avoidance provisions requiring non-UK registered overseas businesses to register in the UK if they sell goods in the UK on which they have claimed a refund of UK VAT under the EU or export/import provisions.

Voluntary registration

[7.12] HMRC allow a person to register voluntarily if the business makes taxable supplies even though its turnover is below the statutory limits. Once a business is registered, it charges VAT on its supplies and recovers input tax suffered. This may be beneficial if its customers are mainly taxable persons, but not where they are the general public. Registration brings an administrative burden so it may not be considered worthwhile in some cases, even though a price advantage may arise.

Example 3

A person is in business as a handyman and incurs input tax of £1,000 on business expenses in the quarter to 30 September 2017. Turnover is £30,000, of which £1,000 covers the input tax that cannot be recovered because he is not registered for VAT.

If he registers voluntarily for VAT, he need only charge £29,000 (VAT exclusive) for the same supplies and turnover will then be:

£29,000 + VAT at 20% (£5,800) = £34,800.

HMRC will be paid £5,800 less £1,000 = £4,800, leaving the business with £30,000 (including £1,000 to cover the VAT suffered) as before. If the customers are the general public, prices to them will be higher, but if they are VAT registered persons they will recover the VAT. The services provided by the handyman will thus be more expensive to the general public but less expensive to the business community.

Intending trader registration

[7.13] If a business is not currently making taxable supplies, but intends to do so in the future, it may apply for registration and HMRC are required to register it. This enables such businesses to recover any input tax suffered even though no taxable supplies are being made. Evidence of the intention to trade may be required.

Variation of registration

[7.14] If there is a change in the name, constitution or ownership of a business or any other change in circumstances that may require registration to be varied, HMRC must be notified within 30 days of the change.

De-registration

UK-established person

[7.15] A UK-established person is no longer liable to be registered if taxable supplies in the next 12 months will be £83,000 (£81,000 prior to 1 April 2017) or less, unless the reason for taxable supplies not exceeding that amount is that the person will cease making taxable supplies in that year, or will suspend making them for 30 days or more. It is, however, possible to remain voluntarily registered (see **7.12**) so long as the trade continues. A person is UK-established if essential management decisions and central administration functions are carried out in the UK and/or the business has a permanent physical presence with the human and technical resources to make or receive taxable supplies in the UK.

Within 30 days of ceasing to make taxable supplies HMRC must be notified. If HMRC are satisfied that registration is no longer required (and a request is made by the relevant person) the registration will be cancelled. Cancellation will be effective from the date of notification or a later date agreed with HMRC. VAT will be payable on a deemed supply of goods (with certain exceptions) forming part of the business assets, at their value at the time of deregistration. This charge does not apply if the business is transferred as a going concern (see **7.52**) or the VAT would not exceed £1,000. Goods on which no input tax was recovered (see **7.4**) are excluded if they were not acquired on the transfer of a going concern.

Non UK-established person

[7.16] A person liable to be registered as a non UK-established person ceases to be so liable if it ceases to make taxable supplies or it forms an establishment in the UK (and therefore becomes a UK-established person).

Within 30 days of ceasing to make taxable supplies HMRC must be notified and any registration can be cancelled on the same basis as detailed at **7.15**, unless the person is required to be registered under another VATA 1994 provision. VAT will also be due on deemed supplies as for UK-established persons.

Time of supply (tax point) (VATA 1994, s 6; SI 1995/2518 Pt XI)

[7.17] The basic tax point is normally when goods are made available or services are performed, unless they are invoiced and/or paid for earlier, in which case the earlier date is the tax point. Where goods or services are invoiced within 14 days after supply, the later date is the tax point and if a business invoices monthly it can adopt a monthly tax point. In any case the tax point will still be the date payment is received if earlier. Where payment is made online by credit or debit card when the goods are ordered, the tax point is the payment date, even though the customer has the right under the distance selling regulations to cancel the contract. For certain continuous supplies (including electricity, gas or any form of power, heat, refrigeration or other cooling or ventilation) the tax point is normally the date of invoice or the payment date if earlier. To combat exploitation of these rules by connected businesses, some of which cannot recover all their input tax, annual tax points apply in certain circumstances for connected persons and groups of companies to ensure that VAT payments are not indefinitely or excessively delayed.

Place of supply (VATA 1994, ss 5, 7–9A and Sch 3BA, 4A)

[7.18] VAT applies to supplies 'made in the UK' with separate rules applying to supplies of services (**7.19**) and supplies of goods (**7.20**).

Services

[7.19] For supplies of services, the general rule is that business-to-business supplies are taxed at the place where the customer belongs and business-to-consumer supplies are taxed at the place where the supplier belongs. There are exceptions however in relation to certain supplies such as passenger transport, cultural, educational and entertainment services, restaurant and catering services, short-term hire of means of transport and the provision of telecommunication and broadcasting services.

In particular the place of supply for business-to-consumer supplies of broadcasting, telecommunications and e-services (digital services) are determined by the location of the consumer, i.e. they are taxed where the customer belongs. For details see www.gov.uk/guidance/register-and-use-the-vat-mini-one-stop-s hop.

The main outcome of these place of supply rules is that many services between EU customers are dealt with under the 'reverse charge' system (see **7.36**). HMRC provide guidance in VAT Notice 741A.

Goods

[7.20] Goods are normally supplied where they are physically located when they are allocated to a customer's order.

Taxable supplies (VATA 1994, Sch 4)

[7.21] All supplies in the UK of goods and services to UK or overseas customers (including goods taken for own use) are taxable supplies, apart from items which are specifically exempt (see **7.26**). Special 'place of supply' rules to determine whether a supply is made 'in the UK' (see **7.18**).

Rates of VAT (VATA 1994, s 2)

[7.22] There are three rates of VAT:

(a)   a standard rate of 20%;
(b)   a reduced rate of 5% (see **7.23**); and
(c)   the zero rate (see **7.24**).

The distinction between exempt supplies (**7.26**) and zero-rated supplies is important. Those who make exempt supplies do not charge VAT, and can only recover any VAT suffered on expenses and purchases (input tax, see **7.2**) by adjusting their selling prices. Those making zero-rated supplies are charging VAT, albeit at a nil rate, and can recover the related input tax.

The VAT fraction used in calculating the VAT element in tax-inclusive supplies at the 20% rate is 1/6 and at the 5% reduced rate it is 1/21.

Reduced rate (VATA 1994, s 29A and Sch 7A; HMRC Brief 43/2011)

[7.23] The items charged at the reduced rate of 5% are:

(a)   Supplies of domestic fuel or power. (This includes the first connection to the gas or electricity mains supply if the supply of the connection and provision of the utility is made by the same person. If not, the connection charge is standard rated).
(b)   Installation of energy-saving materials in residential accommodation.
(c)   Grant-funded installation of heating equipment or security goods or connection of gas supply. (This includes connection or reconnection to a mains gas supply if the residence is a person's sole or main residence).
(d)   Women's sanitary products (although these are to be zero-rated from a date to be appointed).
(e)   Children's car seats.
(f)   Certain residential conversions, renovations and alterations (see **32.41**).
(g)   Contraceptive products.
(h)   Welfare advice or information.
(i)   Installation of mobility aids for the elderly.
(j)   Smoking cessation products.
(k)   Caravans which exceed the limits of size of a trailer permitted to be towed on roads by a motor vehicle and with a maximum weight of 3,500 kg.
(l)   Small, cable-suspended transport systems carrying not more than nine passengers. The reduced rate applies to the transport of passengers only and not where systems are located in areas such as theme parks which make an overall charge for admission.

Note that in June 2015, the European Court held that the UK had implemented the reduced rate for the installation of energy saving materials in a way that was not in accordance with EU law. In essence, the court found that the UK had applied the reduced rate too widely. The Government intends to legislate to ensure compliance with EU law, with any changes to apply from later in 2016. Until then, all supplies of the installation of energy savings materials will continue to be reduced rated; any changes will only apply to future supplies. See HMRC Brief 13/2015.

Zero rate (VATA 1994, s 30 and Sch 8)

[7.24] The following supplies are zero-rated items, as follows (see also CHAPTER 43 re charities):

(a) Food (note this does not include takeaway food intended to be served hot or food that is kept hot for sale; such supplies are liable to VAT at the full rate. Hot takeaway food that is not kept warm in a special cabinet prior to sale (i.e. is left to cool after cooking) remains zero-rated).

(b) Sewerage services and water. First time connection charges made by the same person who is supplying the water to the same customer will follow the treatment of the utility and be zero-rated providing the supplier of the water and connection are made by the same taxable person to the same customer.

(c) Books etc (although supplies of printed matter connected with a supply of services made by a different supplier are specifically excluded from zero-rating).

(d) Talking books for the blind and handicapped and wireless sets for the blind.

(e) Construction/conversion of buildings for use as a dwelling/dwellings or for a relevant residential or a relevant charitable purpose (see **43.10**). HMRC have recently confirmed that this includes the first time connection to gas or electricity mains supply. Also, they have confirmed that extra care accommodation (i.e. self-contained flats, houses, bungalows etc that are sold or let with the option for the occupant to purchase varying degrees of care to suit his or her needs as and when they arise) falls within this group, but accommodation where the occupant needs care or supervision of a type typically provided by an institution does not. HMRC now accept that a person acquiring a completed residential or charitable building as part of a transfer of a going concern (**7.52**) inherits 'person constructing' status and is capable of making a zero-rated supply (see HMRC Brief 27/2014).

(f) Protected buildings — zero rating applies to the first sale or long lease of a substantially reconstructed protected building.

(g) International services.

(h) Transport.

(i) Caravans (which exceed the limits of size of a trailer permitted to be towed on roads by a motor vehicle and with a maximum weight of 3,500 kg and are manufactured to a residential park home standard (BS 3632:2005 or BS 3632:2015)) and houseboats.

(j) Gold.

(k) Bank notes.

(l) Drugs, medicines, aids for the handicapped etc. (This includes motor vehicles supplied to a disabled wheelchair user provided they are adapted before being supplied to the disabled person and boats designed or substantially and permanently adapted for the domestic or personal use of disabled persons).

(m) Imports, exports etc (but see **7.37** re the European Union).

(n) Charities etc.

(o) Clothing and footwear.

(p)   The supply of goods or services to an ERIC (i.e. a body set up as a European Research Infrastructure Consortium).

(q)   Women's sanitary products (from a date to be appointed).

These are only broad categories. There are very detailed rules setting out which heading an item falls under. Many disputes between HMRC and the taxpayer have been settled by VAT tribunals or the courts.

Mixed and composite supplies

[7.25] Supplies may sometimes be a mixture of various elements. There is a distinction between supplies treated as mixed or multiple supplies, i.e. a combination of two separate supplies each taxable at its own rate, and composite supplies, which are held to be a single supply, with any ancillary elements being taxed at the same rate as the main supply. Disputes as to the appropriate treatment have led to a large number of court cases, and the European Court has laid down various tests that need to be considered.

Exempt supplies (VATA 1994, s 31 and Sch 9)

[7.26] Supplies under the following headings (i.e. Groups 1–16 in Sch 9) are exempt, detailed rules applying as to what comes under each heading:

(a)   Land (excluding self-storage facilities). For HMRC's view on the supply of land by commercially operated sports leagues see HMRC Brief 04/2011.

(b)   Insurance. This includes certain supplies of insurance introductory services provided via the internet (HMRC Brief 31/2010). From 1 April 2013, supplies to insurers of certain mis-selling review services and helpline services are no longer exempt from VAT and instead are standard-rated. This does not change HMRC's treatment of PPI mis-selling review services. Such supplies have always been and continue to be standard rated (HMRC Brief 33/2012).

(c)   Postal services that are public postal services provided by Royal Mail. Other postal services (such as those provided by Parcelforce) are standard rated.

(d)   Betting, gaming and lotteries. For HMRC's treatment of electronic lottery machines and bingo machines see HMRC Brief 01/2011.

(e)   Finance.

(f)   Education. This does not include commercial providers of higher education and further education.

(g)   Health and welfare.

(h)   Burial and cremation.

(i)   Subscriptions to trade unions, professional and other public interest bodies.

(j)   Sport, sports competitions and physical education. This includes supplies of sporting services to both members and non-members of non-profit making sports clubs.

(k)   Works of art etc.

(l)   Fund-raising events by charities and other qualifying bodies.

(m)   Cultural services etc.

(n)   Supplies of goods where input tax cannot be recovered.

(o)   Investment gold.

(p)   Supplies of services by groups involving cost sharing provided that the members of the group are each engaged in exempt or non-taxable activities, the supply is made for and is directly necessary for those activities, only exact reimbursement is claimed and the relief is not likely to cause distortion of competition. For HMRC guidance see VAT Information Sheet 07/12 and the online HMRC Cost Sharing Exemption Manual (www.gov.uk/hmrc-internal-manuals/vat-cost-sharing-exemption-manual).

Partial exemption (SI 1995/2518 Pt XIV)

[7.27] If only exempt supplies are made VAT is not charged. This means however that input tax cannot be recovered, so any prices on onward supplies must include an element to recover the VAT suffered. Some businesses make both taxable and exempt supplies and are thus partially exempt.

If a business is partially exempt it can still recover all input tax suffered despite the exempt supplies if the following de minimis threshold is not exceeded:

(a)   main test: the input tax on exempt supplies does not exceed £625 a month on average and does not exceed 50% of total input tax; or

(b)   simplified tests: (test 1) its total input tax is no more than £625 per month on average and the value of exempt supplies is no more than 50% of the value of all supplies, or (test 2) its total input tax less input tax directly attributable to taxable supplies is no more than £625 per month on average and the value of exempt supplies is no more than 50% of the value of all supplies.

If the de minimis limits are exceeded, there are rules to determine how much input tax can be recovered. Only the input tax directly attributable to taxable supplies plus a proportion the input tax that relates to overheads can be recovered.

Under the standard method this proportion is calculated on the amount that taxable supplies bear to total supplies. It is expressed as a percentage, rounded up to the nearest whole number, or to two decimal places if the relevant input tax exceeds £400,000 per month on average. The standard method covers input tax on all supplies except for input tax incurred in relation to investment gold and supplies made by foreign branches (HMRC Brief 22/2015). Input tax which relates to supplies of certain financial instruments are included in the standard method, but instead of using the values-based calculation, input tax incurred on these supplies must be attributed using a method based on use.

The proportion of input tax a business may claim for each VAT period is an estimated figure. At the end of the VAT year the position must be recalculated for the whole of that VAT year and an annual adjustment made.

Businesses using the standard method must adjust their deductible input tax if the method produces an amount which does not properly reflect the extent to which the goods and services are used to make taxable supplies, and the difference is 'substantial', defined as (i) more than £50,000 or (ii) more than 50% of the residual input tax and not less than £25,000. This does not apply where the *total* residual input tax does not exceed £50,000 (£25,000 for a company that is part of a group that is not a VAT group (see **7.51**)).

When setting the partial exemption recovery rate:

(a)   a business may use the previous year's recovery percentage to fix a provisional recovery rate for each VAT return, and make an annual adjustment;

(b)   a business may bring forward its annual adjustment calculation to the last VAT return of its tax year;

(c)   a new partly exempt business may recover input tax on the basis of the use or intended use of 'input tax bearing costs' in making taxable supplies.

Detailed guidance is provided in HMRC's VAT Information Sheet 4/09.

Alternatively, a 'special method' can be agreed in writing with HMRC. Certain exempt supplies can be ignored in these calculations, for example where they are supplies of capital goods used for the business or are 'incidental' to the business activities. There is a right of appeal against the decision of HMRC on the proportion of input tax which is recoverable. Businesses may be able to agree a single special input tax recovery method to take account not only of exempt use but also of non-business use. A business wishing to use a special method must submit a declaration that its proposed special method is fair and reasonable before gaining approval from HMRC. Businesses that make overseas supplies may be able to apply for a 'combined method' enabling them to recover the input tax on those supplies.

Where businesses use a special method, and the method does not fairly and reasonably reflect the proportion of VAT relevant to taxable supplies, an override notice may be served either by HMRC or by the business to correct the results of the special method until a replacement method is implemented. This will apply only where it is considered that a new method would not be agreed quickly and either HMRC or the business would lose out.

Capital goods scheme (SI 1995/2518 Pt XV)

[7.28] Input tax recovery on certain capital items does not depend just on the initial use of the asset but must be adjusted over a longer period where use changes between exempt supplies/non-business use and taxable supplies.

The assets concerned are ships, aircraft, computers, or computer equipment with a tax-exclusive value of £50,000 or more per item, and land and buildings (including refurbishment costs to existing buildings), or civil engineering works, with a tax-exclusive value of £250,000 or more. The adjustment period is ten years except for computers and leases for less than ten years, where the adjustment period is five years. The adjustments are reflected in the business capital allowances computations for the calculation of tax on profits (see **22.21**).

Lost goods (VATA 1994, s 73) and bad debts (VATA 1994, ss 26A, 36)

[7.29] If goods are lost or destroyed before being sold, output tax is not chargeable. But once a supply has been made, VAT is generally chargeable.

If a customer fails to pay, VAT may be reclaimed on any debt which is more than six months old and has been written off in the accounts. VAT must be accounted for on any part of the debt that is later recovered. If the debt has been assigned to someone else, payments received by the assignee are not taken into account unless the assignor and assignee are connected. If the debtor is declared insolvent, the claim in the insolvency will be the VAT-inclusive amount, because VAT will have to be accounted for on any debt recoveries.

Debtors must repay to HMRC the input tax they have reclaimed on supplies if they fail to pay the supplier within six months after the date of invoice (or after the date on which payment was due, if later), regardless of whether the supplier claims bad debt relief.

Where the goods were supplied on credit, the credit element is exempt from VAT, so that appropriate adjustments need to be made on the basis of the commercial method used by the supplier to allocate payments between the goods and the credit element. Guidance on bad debt relief is provided in HMRC's VAT Notice 700/18.

Alternative accounting methods/schemes

Second-hand goods (VATA 1994, s 50A)

[7.30] Many second-hand goods sold in the course of business have been obtained from the general public rather than from VAT registered traders, and if there were no special rules, the dealer buying the second-hand goods would have to charge VAT on the selling price without having any input tax to recover. EU countries operate a margin scheme which may be used for the sale of all second-hand goods, works of art, antiques and collectors' items except precious metals, investment gold and gemstones, unless VAT was charged on the invoice under which the goods were acquired. Where goods are sold under the margin scheme, VAT is charged on each item only on the excess of the selling price over cost (i.e. the dealer's margin). VAT must not be shown separately on the invoice, and no input tax is recoverable by the purchaser. Where individual items cost £500 or less and are purchased in bulk, businesses may also adopt 'global accounting', under which they work out the margin on the difference between total purchases and sales rather than item by item. Global accounting cannot be used for aircraft, boats and outboard motors, caravans, horses and ponies and motor vehicles, including motor cycles. The margin scheme does not have to be used for all second-hand sales, so that VAT may be charged in full under a normal VAT invoice on sales to VAT-registered businesses.

Anti-avoidance provisions prevent the scheme being abused where goods that would not otherwise have been eligible are transferred under the provisions for transfers of going concerns (see **7.52**) and where goods have been acquired through the assignment of rights under hire purchase or conditional sale agreements. Goods acquired under such transfers are not eligible unless they would have been eligible in the hands of the transferor.

EU margin scheme sales are charged to VAT in the country of origin rather than the country of destination. This means that UK margin scheme sales to someone from a country within the EU are taxed only in the UK (exports outside the EU are zero-rated). Acquisitions from countries in the EU are dealt with in the same way as purchases in the UK. VAT is not charged on acquisitions from private EU individuals, and the margin scheme may be used when the goods are sold in the UK. Acquisitions from EU VAT registered businesses may either be made through the scheme (so that the scheme may be used on resale), or outside the scheme, in which case VAT will be recoverable but the scheme cannot be used for the resale.

Imports of second-hand goods from outside the EU are subject to import VAT in the normal way (see **7.35**), except that imports of certain works of art, antiques and collectors' items are charged at an effective import VAT rate of 5%.

Optional flat-rate scheme (VATA 1994, s 26B; SI 1995/2518 Pt VIIA)

[7.31] Under the flat-rate scheme the business continues to charge VAT on its taxable supplies but, instead of paying over to HMRC the output tax (less recoverable input tax) in the normal way, the business pays an amount equal to the appropriate flat-rate percentage of turnover (as listed in VAT Notice 733). For details of the relevant flat rate percentages see www.hmrc.gov.uk/v at/start/schemes/flat-rate.htm.

A business may apply to use the scheme if there are reasonable grounds for believing that taxable supplies (excluding VAT) in the next year will not exceed £150,000. Those using the scheme cannot also use the cash accounting scheme (**7.33**), margin scheme (**7.30**) or retail scheme (**7.32**). They can, however use the annual accounting scheme (**7.34**) at the same time.

A business may opt to leave the flat-rate scheme at any time. It is required to leave the scheme if, on any anniversary of the date on which it was authorised to use the scheme, total income (including VAT) in the previous year exceeded £230,000 or there are reasonable grounds to believe that income for the next 30 days (excluding sales of capital assets) will exceed that amount. The business may be allowed to continue in the scheme, however, if HMRC are satisfied that income in the next year will not exceed £191,500.

Where a business includes two or more trade sectors (e.g. a pub that also supplies food), the percentage for the trade sector with the higher turnover is taken. Businesses who register for VAT and join the flat-rate scheme will pay 1% less than the flat-rate percentage for their trade sector for the first year from the date of their VAT registration.

When invoicing supplies to their customers, flat-rate scheme traders add VAT in the normal way showing the normal VAT rate. The trader retains any VAT charged to his VAT registered customers but does not normally make a separate claim for input tax which is covered by the flat-rate percentage. If, however, the trader has acquired capital goods in the period with a tax-inclusive value of more than £2,000, he may recover the input tax on them. If such goods are subsequently sold, VAT must be accounted for at the full rate rather than the flat-rate.

See **20.28** for the way flat-rate scheme traders deal with VAT in their business accounts.

Special schemes for retailers

[7.32] The normal VAT procedure requires records to be kept of every separate transaction. Some retailers would find it virtually impossible to keep such detailed records, so there are special schemes which enable retailers to calculate output tax in a way that suits their particular circumstances. Such schemes are restricted to businesses that cannot be expected to account for VAT in the normal way. There are three types of published retail schemes, namely point of sale, apportionment and direct calculation (see VAT Notice 727). Any retailer with annual turnover in excess of £130 million is, however, required to arrange a bespoke scheme with HMRC (see VAT Notice 727/2). Businesses using one of the retail schemes can use the annual accounting scheme (see **7.34**) at the same time.

Cash accounting (VATA 1994, s 25; SI 1995/2518 Pt VIII)

[7.33] Businesses with a tax-exclusive turnover of not more than £1.35 million may use the cash accounting system providing they are up-to-date with their VAT returns and have either paid over all VAT due or have arranged to pay any overdue amount by instalments. HMRC guidance is contained in VAT Notice 731. Businesses using cash accounting can use the annual accounting scheme (see **7.34**) at the same time.

Tax invoices still have to be issued but output tax does not have to be accounted for until the cash is received. On the other hand, input tax is not recoverable until suppliers are paid. Businesses that have many bad debts may find the scheme particularly useful. Certain transactions are excluded from the scheme, including hire purchase and similar transactions, supplies of goods and services invoiced in advance, and supplies for which payment is not due in full within six months after the invoice date. HMRC can refuse entry to the scheme, or withdraw the scheme, if they think it necessary to protect tax revenue.

A business can leave the scheme voluntarily at the end of any tax period. A business is required to stop using the scheme in specified circumstances, including where taxable supplies have exceeded £1.6 million in a period of one year. HMRC may be prepared to allow the business to remain in the scheme in the event of a large 'one-off' increase in sales arising from genuine commercial activity.

A business that leaves the cash accounting scheme in a VAT period may either account for all outstanding VAT due in the return for that period or opt to account for it over a period of six months.

Annual accounting (SI 1995/2518 Pt VII)

[7.34] Businesses with an annual tax-exclusive turnover of not more than £1.35 million may apply (on form VAT 600) to join the annual accounting scheme under which they are required to make payments on account of their VAT liability during the year. New businesses may join the scheme as soon as they are registered. The annual return and balancing payment have to be made within two months after the end of the year. Once in the scheme, a business may remain in it unless annual turnover reaches £1.6 million. HMRC guidance is provided in VAT Notice 732.

Transactions outside the EU (VATA 1994, ss 30, 37)

Goods

[7.35] When goods are imported from outside the European Union (see 7.37 for special rules relating to the EU), the UK importer normally has to pay VAT on the goods at that time. VAT is charged at the rate that would apply had the goods been supplied in the UK (subject to the various reliefs that are available). Subject to any restriction for partial exemption etc., the importer gets a credit for the input tax on his next return, thus cancelling or reducing the VAT cost to him. If the goods are for resale, output tax will be accounted for in the normal way when they are sold. There is a deferment scheme enabling importers to pay both Customs duty and VAT monthly on paying an amount as security. No VAT is payable on goods temporarily imported for repair, processing or modification, then re-exported. Goods which have been temporarily exported and are re-imported by the same person after repair, process, or modification bear VAT only on the value of the repair, etc. plus freight and insurance.

Exports outside the EU are generally zero-rated provided the exporter complies with several conditions (in relation to, for example, record keeping requirements, use of goods prior to export etc.).

Services

[7.36] The liability of overseas services depends upon the place of supply rules (see 7.18). If the place of supply is outside the UK the services are outside the scope of UK VAT.

If the place of supply is in the UK a 'reverse charge' procedure applies for services from abroad that are:

(a)   treated as supplied in the UK (and in relation to certain services (such as passenger transport, cultural, educational and entertainment services, restaurant and catering services and short-term hire of means of transport) the recipient is registered for VAT in the UK);
(b)   received by a business person that belongs in the UK; and
(c)   supplied by a person who belongs in a country other than the UK.

The reverse charge procedure requires the UK business to account for VAT on the supplies, with a corresponding deduction for input tax on the same return. In essence the UK recipient is treated as if he himself has supplied the services in the UK in the course or furtherance of his business. Consequently the services must be included in the value of his taxable supplies for the purpose of determining his liability to registration (see 7.8).

Transactions within the EU (VATA 1994, Sch 2)

Goods

[7.37] Supplies of goods between EU countries are not referred to as imports and exports, but as 'acquisitions' and 'supplies'.

Acquisitions

[7.38] If a non-VAT registered person in the UK makes acquisitions of goods from an EU supplier, the supplier will be liable to register in the UK if:

(a)   he is required to register as a non-UK established person; or
(b)   his supplies (known as 'distance sales') to such non-registered persons exceed £70,000 in a calendar year. The supplier must register in the UK within 30 days of exceeding this limit, registration taking effect from the date the limit is exceeded.

The supplies will then be subject to UK VAT. The supplier may opt to register in the UK even if he does not fall within (a) or (b). If, however, he is neither required to register in the UK nor wishes to register in the UK, he must charge VAT at the rate applicable in the country where he is registered.

If the non-registered person's acquisitions exceed the registration thresholds (see 7.8) he will become liable to register in his own right. The cumulative turnover limit for such acquisitions relates to the calendar year, i.e. to acquisitions from 1 January to the end of the relevant month. Goods subject to excise duty and new means of transport are not taken into account because they are subject to separate rules.

When a UK VAT registered person makes acquisitions from a supplier who is registered for VAT in another EU country, the supplier does not pay UK VAT. Output tax must be accounted for on the UK registered person's next VAT return, but with an equivalent amount being deducted as input tax in the same return (subject to any partial exemption or other restriction).

Supplies

[7.39] Where there is a supply of goods by a VAT registered UK business to a VAT registered EU customer the supplier does not pay UK VAT. VAT is accounted for on the acquisition of those goods by the customer at his country's VAT rate, i.e. the country of destination. Special rules apply to new motor vehicles, motor cycles, boats and aircraft, under which VAT is charged at the rate applicable in the purchaser's country. Supplies to non-VAT registered EU customers are at the rate applicable in the UK, although if sales to an EU country exceed that country's stipulated limit the distance selling rules apply and the seller must register for VAT in that country or he may appoint a tax representative to act for him; that country will then become the place of supply. Again, the seller may opt to register in the country of the customer if the limit is not exceeded.

There are special rules where there is an intermediate supplier between the original supplier and the customer.

For supplies to VAT registered EU customers, a UK seller must state both his own and the customer's VAT number on VAT invoices. In addition to making his normal VAT returns, he also has to submit a return of all supplies to VAT registered customers in the EU for each calendar quarter (known as EU sales statements).

Larger businesses (acquisitions above £1,500,000 or supplies above £250,000) are required to complete supplementary declarations under the Intrastat system (HMRC Brief 38/2013 and 44/2011). See 7.30 for the EU treatment of second-hand goods and 7.46 for EU provisions relating to invoicing. HMRC guidance on the single market and Instrastat is provided in VAT Notices 725 and 60.

Services

[7.40] The provisions at 7.36 apply equally to intra-EU supplies of services. Business-to-business supplies of services are generally taxed at the place where the customer is established (see 7.19). Consequently the supplies of such services are subject to a reverse charge in the customer's member state.

Business-to-consumer supplies are generally determined by the location of the supplier. However business-to-consumer supplies of digital services are determined by the location of the consumer, which means that the supplier is responsible for accounting for VAT at the VAT rate applicable in the consumer's EU member state. A UK supplier of digital services to the EU can register for the VAT Mini One Stop Shop (VAT MOSS) scheme which means that they won't have to register for VAT in every EU member state where they make digital service supplies to consumers. Instead they will need to submit a single VAT MOSS return and payment to HMRC each calendar quarter. HMRC will then forward the relevant parts of the return and payment to the tax authorities in the member state(s) where the consumers are located. Micro businesses registering for MOSS need to apply for UK VAT registration and complete a quarterly VAT return. Any VAT refund or expenses claims must be directly attributable to cross-border EU sales activities (see HMRC Brief 46/2014).

Administration

Tax periods, VAT account and tax returns (VATA 1994, ss 59, 79; SI 1995/2518 Pt V)

[7.41] A tax period is normally three months, but if VAT repayments are regularly claimed (for example because mainly zero-rated supplies are made) it is possible to have a one-month period. The advantage of earlier repayments in those circumstances must be weighed against the disadvantage of having to complete 12 returns annually.

Quarterly return dates are staggered over the year depending on the business classification. The dates can be changed to coincide with the businesses accounting period.

The transactions for each tax period must be summarised in a VAT account. Returns are made to HMRC on form VAT 100 for each tax period, showing the VAT payable or repayable and certain statistical information (including specific entries for European Union sales and purchases).

All VAT returns now have to be made online and VAT paid electronically, although VAT registered persons can decide as to whether they communicate with HMRC electronically or not for certain other specified communications, including:

(a)   registration and group applications;
(b)   transfer of a going concern applications;
(c)   annual accounting scheme applications and notifications;
(d)   flat rate scheme notifications.

For HMRC guidance see the online HMRC VAT Accounting Manual (www .hmrc.gov.uk/manuals/vatacmanual/index.htm).

Submission and payment deadlines: general

[7.42] For online filing the submission and payment deadline is one month and seven days after the end of the tax period. These rules do not apply for businesses in the annual accounting and payments on account schemes (see 7.34, 7.43).

Submission and payment deadlines: large VAT payers (VATA 1994, s 28; SI 1993/2001; SI 1995/2518 Pt VI)

[7.43] Traders who make quarterly VAT returns and pay VAT of more than £2.3 million have to make payments on account at the end of the second and third months of each VAT quarter. A balancing payment is made with the quarterly VAT return.

HMRC calculate the payments on account. Each payment is fixed by dividing by 24 the annual VAT liability in the 12-month period in which the business exceeded the threshold. Future payments on account are determined by reference to an annual cycle and a reference year.

Payments on account must be made by electronic transfer and there is no seven-day period of grace. Traders may elect to make monthly VAT returns, or to make monthly payments of VAT based on the actual liability for the preceding month without making a monthly VAT return. One of these options may be preferable where there are seasonal variations in turnover. HMRC guidance is provided in VAT Notice 700/60.

Penalties

[7.44] For details of the penalty regime for late filing of returns and late payment of taxes (see **9.68** and **9.71**). The provisions for imposing penalties for errors in relation to VAT documentation are detailed at **9.58** onwards.

Records and returns (VATA 1994, Sch 11)

[7.45] VAT registered businesses must supply tax invoices in respect of taxable supplies, keep a VAT account showing the calculations of the VAT liability for each tax period, keep all invoices received and copies of all VAT invoices issued, retain all business and accounting records, and make returns to HMRC showing the VAT payable or repayable (see **7.41**).

For HMRC guidance see the online VAT Traders' Records Manual (http://www.hmrc.gov.uk/manuals/vatrecmanual/index.htm).

VAT invoices (SI 1995/2518 Pt III)

[7.46] Where a taxable supply is made to another taxable person a VAT invoice must be provided showing the following details:

(a) A sequential number that uniquely identifies the document
(b) Time of supply, or tax point (see **7.17**)
(c) Date of issue of the invoice
(d) Trader's name, address and VAT registration number
(e) Customer's name and address
(f) Description of goods or services supplied, and for each description the quantity or extent, the rate of VAT and the VAT-exclusive amount payable
(g) Total amount payable excluding VAT and, for countable goods or services, the unit price (for example, in the case of services, the hourly rate)
(h) Rate of any cash discount offered
(i) Where a margin scheme is applied (see **7.30**) the reference 'margin scheme: works of art', 'margin scheme: antiques or collectors' items', 'margin scheme: second-hand goods', or 'margin scheme: tour operators' as appropriate
(j) Where a VAT invoice relates in whole or part to a supply where the person supplied is liable to pay the tax, the reference 'reverse charge'
(k) Total VAT chargeable

There are special rules for supplies to persons in other EU member states. Where the consideration for a supply does not exceed £250, less detailed invoices may be provided, omitting the customer's name and address and the amount (but not the rate) of VAT. Copies of these less detailed invoices need not be kept.

Provision is made for customers to self-bill their suppliers, subject to specified conditions. Provision is also made for electronic invoicing (see HMRC guidance in VAT Notice 700/63).

Assessments (VATA 1994, ss 73, 76, 77)

[7.47] If a taxpayer fails to make returns, or HMRC consider returns are incomplete or incorrect, they may issue assessments of the amount of VAT due. Assessments cannot be made later than four years after the end of the return period, except in cases involving loss of VAT brought about deliberately or resulting from failure to comply with certain obligations, when the period is increased to 20 years. Where the taxpayer has died, no assessment can be made later than four years after the death. For details see 9.46.

Interest, repayment supplement and statutory interest (VATA 1994, ss 78–81; FA 1996, s 197; CTA 2009, s 1286; ITTOIA 2005, ss 54, 869)

[7.48] Interest is charged on overdue tax etc. from the date the amount of tax etc. became due, and repayment supplement is payable from the payment dates on tax etc. overpaid. For details see 9.55 onwards.

Repayment supplement

[7.49] A repayment supplement of 5% of the tax due (or £50 if greater) is paid on overpaid VAT if the return was made by the due date, the return did not overstate the amount repayable by more than the greater of £250 and 5% of the amount due, and repayment has been unnecessarily delayed by HMRC. Unnecessary delay is defined as more than 30 days from the day following the end of return period, or the date the return was received if later. This supplement is not chargeable to income tax or corporation tax.

Statutory interest

[7.50] Where overpaid VAT has not been recovered through the normal accounting procedures, a claim may be made for a refund, which is increased by statutory interest where the overpayment is a result of error by HMRC. Unlike the repayment supplement, statutory interest is chargeable to direct tax, i.e. income tax or corporation tax. A claim to interest under this heading must be made within four years after the end of the 'applicable period'. (See also HMRC Brief 14/2009).

For the latest rates of interest see 'Statutory interest payable by HMRC in cases of official error' in the TABLE OF RATES AND ALLOWANCES (TRA).

Groups of companies (VATA 1994, ss 43, 43A–43D, 44 and Sch 9A; SI 2004/1931)

[7.51] Two or more companies that are established or have a fixed establishment in the UK may apply to be treated as a VAT group if one of them controls each of the others, or if an individual, partnership or company controls all of them. Only one VAT return is then required and supplies between group members are disregarded for VAT purposes. HMRC may remove companies from VAT groups if they are no longer eligible or if their membership poses a threat to tax revenue. Where a taxpayer is deregistered under their existing VAT registration number on joining a VAT group, the representative member of that group is not liable for liabilities incurred before the taxpayer joined the group, only future VAT due.

There are provisions to ensure that unfair advantages are not obtained by group treatment, and HMRC have powers to counter VAT avoidance involving group transactions. There are additional eligibility rules for groups with turnover exceeding £10 million, and a company cannot be a member of more than one VAT group at the same time. Supplies made by one member of a VAT group to another are disregarded, therefore no VAT is chargeable when, for example, supplies from outside the UK are brought into a UK VAT group by a member belonging overseas. Anti-avoidance provisions apply to prevent the reverse charge (see 7.36) being avoided in this manner where services are ultimately consumed in the UK.

Where there is no group registration, VAT has to be added to charges for supplies from one company to the other, such as management charges, and care must be taken to ensure that this is not overlooked.

Basic activities of holding companies, such as holding shares and acquiring subsidiaries, are not regarded under EU law as business activities and any associated input tax cannot be recovered. This only applies, however, to holding companies that neither trade themselves, nor have active trading subsidiaries making taxable supplies outside the VAT group, nor provide genuine management services to separate trading subsidiaries.

Where a business is transferred as a going concern to a partially exempt group, the transfer is treated as a supply to and by the group. The group therefore has to account for output tax, and is only able to recover its allowable proportion of input tax according to the partial exemption rules (see 7.27). This does not apply if the person who transferred the assets to the group acquired them more than three years previously. Nor does it apply to items covered by the capital goods scheme (see 7.28).

The group provisions are intended to reduce administrative burdens on businesses, but they also enable groups to improve the overall VAT position by including or excluding companies from the group registration. Where an application is made for a company to leave a VAT group, HMRC may delay the removal of the company from the VAT group registration if VAT avoidance is involved. HMRC guidance on group registration is provided in VAT Notice 700/2.

Transferring a business as a going concern (SI 1995/1268; HMRC Brief 30/2012; HMRC Brief 27/2014)

[7.52] If a VAT registered trader sells all or part of a business as a going concern, the seller does not normally have to account for VAT on the sale consideration, and the purchaser does not have any input tax to reclaim where the purchaser is a taxable person or becomes a taxable person immediately after the sale. HMRC have also stated that a transaction can still be treated as a TOGC if the transferor of the business retains a small reversionary interest in the property transferred (provided the interest retained is small enough not to disturb the substance of the transaction and the other usual conditions are satisfied). They initially stated this applied to property rental businesses only but now state that it applies to all businesses, for example where a retailer disposes of the retail business but transfers the premises by granting a lease. For details see **27.12**. The transfer of a business to a company in a VAT group can constitute a TOGC if that company intends to continue to use the transferred assets to operate the same kind of business in providing services to other group members, and those other group members use the services to make supplies outside of the group (HMRC Brief 11/2016).

The general TOGC rule does not apply to the transfer of land and buildings on which the option to charge VAT has been exercised or to commercial buildings and civil engineering works that are unfinished or less than three years old unless the purchaser has also opted to charge VAT and has so notified HMRC by the date of the transfer. The purchaser must also notify the seller that his option to tax will not be disapplied. (For details of the option to charge VAT, see **32.42**). If the purchaser is not already registered, the rules for deciding whether he is liable are the same as those outlined at **7.8** to **7.10**, except that the seller's supplies in the previous 12 months are treated as made by the purchaser. The purchaser must notify his liability within 30 days after the transfer, and will be registered from the date of the transfer. If the seller was not, and was not required to be, VAT registered, his turnover would not have to be taken into account by the purchaser in deciding when registration was necessary. As a general rule sellers are normally required to retain the business records, unless it is essential for VAT compliance purposes for the records to be passed to the purchaser.

The above rules do not apply on a sale of assets, rather than an identifiable part of the business which is capable of separate operation and which the purchaser intends to continue. The sale of a family company is dealt with in CHAPTER 28.

HMRC guidance is provided in VAT Notice 700/9. Anti-avoidance rules apply to transfers to partially exempt groups (see **7.51**), and further rules prevent these going concern provisions being used to enable businesses to give goods away without accounting for VAT.

Anti-avoidance

Combating VAT evasion and money laundering (VATA 1994, ss 26AB, 55A, 69B, 77A–77D and Sch 11; SI 2003/3075; SI 2010/2239; SI 2010/2240; SI 2013/701; SI 2014/1458; SI 2016/12)

[7.53] HMRC have extensive powers to combat VAT evasion, including the power to require security to be provided by traders reclaiming input tax if the traders deal with businesses in a VAT supply chain that are considered to be involved in tax evasion. In addition there are special rules to counter 'missing trader intra-community' (MTIC) fraud. Under the rules the customer becomes the person liable to register for VAT (if not already registered) and account for and pay the VAT on the supply of specified goods or services which are commonly used to perpetrate the fraud. This 'reverse charge' procedure applies, with some exclusions, to:

(a)   supplies of mobile phones and computer chips that are made by one VAT-registered business to another (valued at £5,000 and over);
(b)   emissions allowances;
(c)   certain wholesale supplies of gas and electricity; and
(d)   wholesale supplies of electronic communications services, including calls and data over landlines, mobile networks and internet.

The powers of HMRC to inspect goods have been strengthened, and they are able to require businesses to keep records about goods on which they believe VAT may not be paid, subject to a penalty for failure to do so.

Businesses that deal in goods and accept the equivalent of €15,000 or more in *cash* for a single transaction (referred to as High Value Dealers — HVDs) are required to register with HMRC and put anti-money laundering systems in place. The registration is renewable annually and an annual fee based on the number of premises from which high value transactions are made. HMRC guidance is available at www.hmrc.gov.uk/mlr. Any breach of the regulations may lead to a financial penalty or criminal proceedings.

A notification system applies for arrivals of new or used road vehicles into the UK for permanent use on UK roads. The details of the system are set out in regulations, but the principle requirement is that HMRC have to be notified within 14 days of the arrival of the road vehicle in the UK. The notification may be made either in paper form or electronically. A paper notification must be made on form VAT NOVA 1 and an electronic notification is made by enrolling in the NOVA online service. In the case of an acquisition of a new road vehicle from within the EU, private individuals and non-VAT registered businesses will be required to pay any VAT due at the time of notification. VAT registered customers will continue to make payment via their VAT returns. In the case of a road vehicle imported from outside the EU, VAT will continue to be collected under existing arrangements. There are exceptions from this, for example, UK diplomats or members of the UK forces bringing vehicles permanently into the UK from outside the EU, bringing a vehicle into the UK which has remained registered for road use in the UK during the time it was outside the country, etc.

As part of a package of measures aimed at non-UK businesses that sell goods in the UK using an online marketplace without accounting for UK VAT, HMRC have the power to make the operator of the online marketplace jointly and severally liable for the VAT debts of such businesses.

VAT avoidance schemes

[7.54] There are special disclosure rules for VAT avoidance schemes (see 45.3).

8

Council tax and business rates

Introduction

[8.1] This chapter gives an outline of council tax and business rates. Additional points of detail relating to specific areas are dealt with in the appropriate chapters, in particular let property in CHAPTER 32.

Council tax was introduced from 1 April 1993 in England, Wales and Scotland. Domestic rates are payable in Northern Ireland. There are some differences in the system in Wales and Scotland and this chapter deals mainly with the system for England.

Council tax in England is based at present on property values in 1991. There are powers for a future revaluation date to be set by the Secretary of State, but at the time of writing it is unclear when the next revaluation in England will take place. A revaluation did take place in Wales (see **8.2**).

Businesses pay business rates at a uniform level fixed by central Government. The uniform business rate, or multiplier, is applied to the rateable value of the property. There are some differences in the business rates provisions for Scotland and Wales, and this chapter briefly summarises the position in England. See **8.10** onwards.

Council tax — the general rules

[8.2] Council tax is payable on a 'dwelling', i.e. a separate unit of living accommodation along with any garden, yard, garage or outbuildings attached to it. Broadly, a self-contained unit within a dwelling (an annexe) is counted as a separate dwelling, but where an elderly dependent relative occupies an annexe as his or her main residence then he or she may be exempt from payment. Any part of a property that is wholly used for business purposes is subject to the business rate, with the council tax applying to the 'dwelling' part. Some dwellings are exempt (see **8.3**). Guidance is available at www.gov .uk/council-tax.

Council tax bills may be reduced by one or more of the following:

(a)   Discounts where there is only one occupier (see **8.5**).
(b)   Reduction for disabilities (see **8.6**).
(c)   Council tax support schemes (see **8.7**).
(d)   Discounts where an annexe is in use by a resident of the property or occupied by a relative of the person who pays the property's council tax (see **8.8**).

Councils have some flexibility over setting discounts and exemptions, to allow them to reflect local circumstances. This includes giving councils power to reduce discounts for second homes and long-term unfurnished empty properties and most councils have taken the opportunity to reduce such discounts (see **8.3**).

The amount of the bill before any available deductions depends, for properties in England and Scotland, on the estimated value of the property at 1 April 1991 but taking into account any significant alteration to the property before 1 April 1993. Newly built property is similarly valued back to what it would have been worth at 1 April 1991. Properties in Wales were revalued by reference to values at 1 April 2003.

The bill is calculated according to which of the following valuation bands the property falls in:

Band	England	Scotland	Wales
A	Up to £40,000	Up to £27,000	Up to £44,000
B	£40,001–£52,000	£27,001–£35,000	£44,001–£65,000
C	£52,001–£68,000	£35,001–£45,000	£65,001–£91,000
D	£68,001–£88,000	£45,001–£58,000	£91,001–£123,000
E	£88,001–£120,000	£58,001–£80,000	£123,001–£162,000
F	£120,001–£160,000	£80,001–£106,000	£162,001–£223,000
G	£160,001–£320,000	£106,001–£212,000	£223,001–£324,000
H	Over £320,000	Over £212,000	£324,001–£424,000
I			Over £424,000

The council tax bills for the various bands vary according to proportions laid down by law. The full bill for a band H dwelling is twice that for a band D dwelling and three times that for a band A dwelling. Slightly different calculations apply for properties in Scotland (www.gov.scot/Topics/Governm ent/local-government/17999/counciltax).

Properties will normally only be re-valued for banding purposes when they are sold or let on lease for seven years or more, even if they have been substantially improved or extended. Although note that properties cannot be revalued for banding purposes simply because the owner of the property has entered into a lease under the rent-a-roof or similar scheme for the installation of solar panels or other microgeneration plants (SI 2013/467).

Generally a revaluation takes effect from the date the transaction is completed. There is, however, provision for adjusting values downwards at any time if there is a major change in the area, such as a new sewerage treatment plant being opened nearby, or if part of the property is demolished, or if the property is adapted for someone who is disabled.

It is possible to appeal against a valuation in certain circumstances (see **8.9**). If, because of inaccuracies in the original list, a valuation is wrong, it can be corrected. If the effect of the correction is to *increase* the valuation, the revaluation takes effect only from the day the valuation list is altered. Decreases take effect from the date the valuation list was compiled.

Council tax is calculated on a daily basis and is adjusted appropriately when a change of circumstances affects the bill, such as the property becoming or ceasing to be eligible for exemption or discount. This means that householders need to notify their councils of changes affecting their liability.

Council tax is normally paid by ten monthly instalments, but other payment methods may be offered. If payment is not made on time the right to pay by instalments may be lost and action may be taken for recovery. Collection may then be enforced in various ways, including an attachment of earnings order requiring an employer to deduct the outstanding tax from salary and account for it to the council. If payment is not made at all, the defaulter may be sent to prison.

Exempt dwellings

[8.3] Exemption may be claimed in the following circumstances. The council must be notified if the exemption ceases to apply, otherwise penalties may be imposed:

(a)   Unoccupied property that needs structural alteration/major repair work, or is undergoing such work, or has undergone such work and less than six months have elapsed since the work was substantially completed, but the exemption is limited to a maximum period of 12 months.

(b)   Empty property owned and last used by a charity, exemption applying for up to six months.

(c)   Empty, unfurnished property, for up to six months (ignoring any period of reoccupation for less than six weeks), although some councils may charge up to 50% extra council tax if a home has been empty for two years or more.

(d)   Property left empty by someone in prison (other than for not paying fines or council tax).

(e)   Property left empty by someone now living in hospital or in residential care.

(f)   Property empty following the occupier's death, for up to six months after granting of probate or administration.

(g)   An empty property in which occupation is prohibited by law, e.g. pending compulsory purchase.

(h)   Property left vacant for a minister of religion.

(i)   Property that is empty because the occupier is now living elsewhere to receive care because of old age, disablement, illness, alcohol/drug dependence or mental disorder.

(j)   Property empty because the occupier is resident elsewhere to look after someone needing care as indicated in (i) above.

(k)   Empty property last occupied by a student whose main residence it was but who now lives elsewhere to be near to his place of education.

(l)   Unoccupied mortgaged property that has been repossessed by the lender.

(m)   Students' halls of residence.

(n)   Property wholly occupied by students as their full-time or term-time residence.

(o)   Properties used as accommodation for members of the Armed Forces.

(p)   Properties occupied by Visiting Forces.

(q)   Unoccupied property for which someone is liable only as a Trustee in Bankruptcy.

(r)   A vacant caravan pitch or boat mooring.

(s)   Properties occupied only by people under 18 years of age.

(t)   An annex that cannot be let separately from the main dwelling without breaching planning conditions.

(u)   Properties occupied only by severely mentally impaired people who would otherwise be liable to pay the council tax.

(v)   Properties occupied by diplomats or members of certain international organisations.

(w)   Self-contained annexes and 'granny flats' occupied by dependent relatives aged 65 years or over, or severely disabled. Where this full exemption does not apply (because, for example, younger adult family members live together), the national annexe discount may apply instead — this is intended to help support extended families (8.8).

Who is liable to pay?

[8.4] Each dwelling has only one council tax bill. The person liable is the person who comes first on the following list.

(a)   An owner-occupier, i.e. a resident freeholder.

(b)   A resident leaseholder (including assured tenants under the Housing Act 1988).

(c)   A resident statutory or secure tenant.

(d)   A resident who has a contractual licence to occupy the property, such as someone living in a tied cottage.

(e)   A resident with no legal interest in the property, such as a squatter or someone who has permission to stay.

(f)   The owner (where the dwelling has no residents).

A resident is someone over 18 who lives in the property as his only or main home.

Generally, joint owners or joint tenants are jointly liable for the tax, and couples living together are jointly liable even if only one member of the couple owns or leases the property.

Where there are no residents, the owner is liable. The owner is also liable instead of the residents in the case of the following dwellings:

(i)   Multi-occupied properties such as bedsits where rent is paid separately for different parts of the property.

(ii)   Residential care homes, nursing homes, and some hostels providing a high level of care.

(iii) Dwellings occasionally occupied by the owner whose domestic staff are resident there.

(iv)   Monasteries, convents, and dwellings occupied by ministers of religion.

(v)   Property occupied by asylum seekers under statutory arrangements.

Discounts

[8.5] The full amount of council tax is payable if two or more adults live in the dwelling. The bill is reduced by 25% if a person lives alone.

Councils may offer a second homes' discount of between 10% and 50% for second homes, holiday homes and job-related accommodation, and they may offer an empty homes discount of up to 50% for dwellings that have been empty and unfurnished for more than six months. Although where a property has been empty for two years or more, councils can charge up to 50% extra council tax. Guidance is usually provided on the relevant local authority's website.

Certain people are not counted in deciding how many residents there are, providing certain conditions are met. These include:

(a)   full-time students, student nurses, apprentices or young people in training;

(b)   severely mentally impaired people;

(c)   hospital patients, or those being looked after in care homes;

(d)   low-paid care workers;

(e)   people with diplomatic privileges or immunities;

(f)   members of visiting forces;

(g)   members of religious communities;.

(h)   people aged 18–19 and either in full time education or between school and further or higher education;

(i)   people staying in certain hostels or night shelters;

(j)   people caring for someone with a disability who is not a spouse, partner or child under 18.

Not being counted as a resident does not alter a person's responsibility for payment. But where, after ignoring those who are not counted, the dwelling is no one's main home, the person liable to pay the tax would get a 50% discount, possibly reduced to 10% as indicated above.

The council must be notified if a discount is no longer applicable (or a smaller discount should apply). Penalties apply if notification is not made.

Reduction for disabilities

[8.6] Homes that provide one of the following special features for a substantially and permanently disabled adult or child who lives in the property qualify for a one-band reduction in the bill if they are in bands B to H. Band A properties qualify for a reduction equal to one ninth of the band D charge. Any discounts and benefits then apply to the reduced amount. The special features are:

(a)   a room other than a bathroom, kitchen or toilet, that is mainly for the use of the disabled person (such as a ground floor bedroom in a two-storey property);
(b)   an extra bathroom or kitchen for the disabled person's use;
(c)   extra floor space for a wheelchair.

To qualify for the reduction, the additional feature need not be specially built, but it must be shown that the disabled person would be severely adversely affected if the feature was not available. A claim should be made each year to the council, who may require additional evidence that the conditions for the reduction are satisfied.

Council tax support scheme

[8.7] All councils in the country must have in place their own 'Council Tax Support Scheme'. This means that every council will have its own local scheme to help its residents on low incomes with their council tax payments depending on their age, income and savings.

Annexes (SI 2013/2977)

[8.8] Annexes which are used by the occupier of the main house as part of the main home, or annexes which are occupied by a relative of the person living in the main house are entitled to a 50% reduction in the council tax payable on the annexe.

This 50% reduction is on top of any other discount. For example, if the owner's adult son is living in the annexe on his own, he will be liable for council tax and be entitled to a 25% single occupier discount and a 50% annexe discount.

The criteria for the annexe discount is:

(a) the annexe must form part of a single property which includes at least one other property: i.e. the annexe must be within the grounds of the main house (not necessarily attached) and must be included in the title deeds of the main house and not registered separately;

(b) the annexe is used by the resident of the main house, as part of their main home, or the annexe is lived in by a relative of the person who lives in the main house. For this purpose a relative is defined as a partner, parent, child, step child, grandparent, grandchild, brother, sister, uncle, aunt, nephew and niece (also includes great grandparent, great grandchild etc and great great grandparent etc).

Appeals

[8.9] It is possible to appeal against a council tax banding. Appeals are made initially to the local valuation office. The taxpayer then has the option of referring the case to a valuation tribunal once the valuation office has reviewed the banding. Guidance is provided at www.gov.uk/council-tax-appeals.

In limited circumstances it is possible to challenge a council tax valuation list entry, e.g. where part of the property has been demolished.

Appeals may also be made on the grounds that:

(a) a home should not be liable to tax;

(b) liability is disputed, either because a person does not consider himself to be the liable person, or because of the calculation of available reductions;

(c) a penalty imposed is disputed; or

(d) a completion notice is disputed identifying the date from which a new building becomes a dwelling, or when structural alterations are completed.

Appeal procedures differ depending on the nature of the appeal.

Business rates

[8.10] Businesses pay a uniform business rate (also called the non-domestic rate) on the rateable value of business premises. Business rates and reliefs are similar for properties in Scotland, Wales and Northern Ireland but there are differences. Guidance on the different regimes is provided at www.gov.uk/introduction-to-business-rates.

Business rates are calculated using the rateable value and the multiplier set by the Government. In England the standard multiplier for 2017–18 is 47.9 pence; therefore a business with a rateable value of £10,000 will pay business rates of £4,790 (excluding any discounts or reductions that may be available). In Scotland. Wales and Northern Ireland the standard multiplier is 46.6 pence, 49.9 pence and 32.92 pence respectively. Businesses are able to pay their bill in 12 monthly instalments (SI 2014/479).

The business rate is collected by individual local councils but it is paid into a national pool and is then distributed on a formula basis to county and district councils.

Revaluation

[8.11] Rateable values are updated every five years or so, the latest revaluation for England, Scotland and Wales was made on 1 April 2017. In Northern Ireland the last revaluation was 2015, the previous one having taken place in 2001. The revaluation is intended to reflect changes in the property market and redistribute the total tax liability for business rates. This means that some rates bills will rise but others will fall, and transitional relief will be available (see 8.12).

A rise in rateable value at a revaluation does not lead to a rise in overall revenue from business rates. The multiplier is adjusted to ensure that the overall yield from rates remains the same. To ensure overall revenue neutrality, the multiplier was adjusted in 2017–18. In England, the standard multiplier fell from 49.4 pence to 47.9 pence. Conversely, total rateable value in Wales fell at the 2017 revaluation, so the multiplier rose from 48.6 pence to 49.9 pence.

Transitional arrangements

[8.12] The revaluation at 1 April 2017 increased many rateable values, but decreased others. Transitional arrangements apply in England only for the years up to and including 2021–22 which essentially cap the increases and decreases for these years by a set percentage. Transitional relief limits how much a bill can change each year. It stops when a bill reaches the full amount set by a revaluation.

The caps are as follows if a bill is increasing:

Rateable value	2017/18	2018/19	2019/20	2020/21	2021/22
Up to £20,000 (£28,000 in London)	5%	7.5%	10%	15%	15%
20,001 (28,001 in London) to £99,999	12.5%	17.5%	20%	25%	25%
Over £100,000	42%	32%	49%	16%	6%

The caps are as follows if a bill is decreasing:

Rateable value	2017/18	2018/19	2019/20	2020/21	2021/22
Up to £20,000 (£28,000 in London)	20%	30%	35%	55%	55%
20,001 (28,001 in London) to £99,999	10%	15%	20%	25%	25%
Over £100,000	4.1%	4.6%	5.9%	5.8%	4.8%

Business rate reliefs

[8.13] A number of reliefs from business rates are available. A relief does not change the rateable value of a property — it is a discount from the payment owed by the liable business. If the occupier of the property changes, the business rates liability may also change. Separately, certain types of property are exempt from business rates.

Councils have power to give business rates relief on hardship grounds.

The reliefs available include:

(a)   small business relief (**8.14**);
(b)   charitable reliefs (**8.15**);
(c)   rural rate relief (**8.16**);
(d)   enterprise zone relief (**29.62**).

In addition, there are a few measures, aimed at encouraging retail / commercial occupation as follows:

(a)   for each of the years 2014–15 and 2015–16 all occupied retail properties with a rateable value of £50,000 or less will receive a business rates discount. The discount is £1,500 for 2015–16 and £1,000 for 2014–15;

(b)   businesses moving into previously empty retail premises between 1 April 2014 and 31 March 2016 are entitled to a 50% business rates discount for 18 months;

(c)   newly built commercial property that was completed between 1 October 2013 and 30 September 2016 is exempt from business rates for the first 18 months after the property was completed. Where this extended exemption doesn't apply there is a three months exemption for empty property (six months for warehouses and industrial property), and rates are payable after the period of exemption has elapsed.

Small business rate relief (SI 2017/102)

[8.14] The small business rate relief (SBRR) is available to all businesses, depending on the rateable value of the property. In England the relief applies as follows:

(a)   Post 1 April 2017:
      (i)   if the rateable value is £12,000 or less the rates are reduced by 100%;
      (ii)   if the rateable value is between £12,001 to £15,000 the relief tapers down from 0% to 100%, on the basis of 1% relief for every £30 of rateable value;
      (iii)   if the rateable value is between £15,001 to £50,999 the rates are calculated using the small business multiplier
(b)   Pre 31 March 2017:
      (i)   if the rateable value is £6,000 or less the rates are reduced by 100%;
      (ii)   if the rateable value is between £6,000 and £12,000 the relief tapers down from 100% to 0%;
      (iii)   if the rateable value is more than £12,000 and below £18,000 (£25,500 in London), the rates are calculated using the small business multiplier.

The SBRR is available in Scotland, Wales and Northern Ireland also, but different rules and calculations apply.

Where businesses take on an additional property which would normally have meant the loss of small business rate relief, they are able to keep the relief for a period of 12 months. After that period of grace, businesses with more than one property are only eligible for SBRR if their additional property or properties all have rateable values of under £2,900, and the total rateable value of all their properties does not exceed £19,999 (£27,999 in London).

Charitable relief

[8.15] Properties which are occupied by charities and wholly or mainly used for charitable purposes are entitled to relief from business rates, as are community amateur sports clubs (CASCs). 'Charitable purposes' includes shops used for the sale of goods donated to the charity.

The mandatory relief is 80% and discretionary relief can increase this to 100%, so that no rates are payable. Discretionary relief up to 100% may be awarded by local authorities to various non-profit-making organisations such as schools and colleges, societies concerned with literature and the arts, and recreational clubs and societies.

Rural rate relief

[8.16] Public houses or petrol stations which are the only such business in a rural settlement, and which have a rateable value of less than £12,500, are entitled to 50% mandatory Rural Rate Relief. Sole shops, general stores or post offices with a rateable value of less than £8,500 are also entitled to this relief. This relief takes precedence over small business rate relief. See also **31.27**.

Miscellaneous points

[8.17] Agricultural land and buildings are generally exempt from business rates, although riding stables, farm shops and self-catering holiday cottages which are available for short-term letting for 140 days or more in a year are all subject to business rates

If bed and breakfast accommodation is offered, a person will not be liable to business rates if they intend to offer such accommodation for not more than six people, live in the property at the same time and the property's main use is still as their home.

People in mixed business and private accommodation pay the business rate on the non-domestic part and council tax on the private part (see **8.2**).

9

Administration

Structure

[9.1] UK taxes are administered by the Commissioners for Her Majesty's Revenue and Customs (HMRC), operating through their appointed officers.

In addition to being responsible for income tax, corporation tax, capital gains tax, inheritance tax, VAT and stamp taxes, HMRC deal with national insurance contributions, statutory sick pay, other statutory payments and child benefit. Welfare tax credits are also dealt with by HMRC, although these are being phased out and replaced with a universal credit (see **10.6**) which is administered by the Department for Work and Pensions, although dependent on information provided by HMRC.

HMRC have published a charter setting out the standards of behaviour and values to which they aspire in dealing with people in the exercise of their functions. This can be found at www.gov.uk/government/publications/your-charter. HMRC have also published details of their strategy to become a 'more digital' organisation, setting out their aims for the near and longer term, including plans for the automation of most taxpayer interactions with HMRC.

In keeping with the Open Government initiative, HMRC's non-statutory clearance service is available to all business and non-business taxpayers and their advisers who need clarification on either guidance or legislation. The object is to help taxpayers understand their rights and obligations so that they can pay the right amount of tax at the right time. Guidance can be found in HMRCs 'Other Non-Statutory Clearance Guidance Manual'.

The Revenue Scotland and Tax Powers Act, which came into effect on 1 April 2015 establishes Revenue Scotland as the authority responsible for collecting and managing the taxes devolved to the Scottish Government. Currently there are two devolved taxes, the Land and Buildings Transactions Tax (**6.18**) and the Scottish Landfill tax.

Income and capital gains tax assessment

[9.2] This section deals with an individual's tax liability to income and capital gains. The UK operates a self-assessment system and, for 2016–17 onwards, a simple assessment system for certain taxpayers.

Under self-assessment, individuals are required to 'self-assess' their tax liability in a tax return. The return must detail the total amount payable for the tax year (i.e. income tax and capital gains tax, national insurance contributions and, where relevant, student loan repayments).

Under simple assessment, HMRC are able to issue an assessment to individuals with straightforward tax affairs where they already hold all the information needed to calculate the individual's tax position. There is no need for the individual to self-assess or complete a tax return. This assessment procedure is part of the Government's commitment to abolish the tax return which was announced in the March 2015 Budget.

For details of the simple assessment regime see **9.8–9.11**. Details of the self-assessment regime are at **9.12–9.20**. See CHAPTER **23** regarding partnership returns and **9.21** for corporate returns.

In addition to the introduction of simple assessment (and as part of the Government's commitment to abolish tax returns for millions of individuals and small businesses) the Government is rolling out digital tax accounts (known as 'making tax digital'). This will require businesses and individuals to keep records and returns digitally. It will not be compulsory until April 2019 and even then only for VAT records/accounts for businesses with a turnover above the VAT registration threshold; see www.gov.uk/government/publicatio ns/making-tax-digital/overview-of-making-tax-digital.

Notification of liability (TMA 1970, s 7)

[9.3] A person must notify HMRC of chargeability if he is liable to make a return and:

(a)   he has not received a notice to file a return from HMRC — notification must be made within six months of the end of the tax year; or

(b)   a notice to file a return has been withdrawn — notification must be made within the later of six months of the end of the tax year or 30 days after the notification of withdrawal was made.

Where the taxpayer has been notified of a simple assessment (**9.8**) there is no requirement for the taxpayer to notify HMRC separately of chargeability in respect of the income or gains included in the simple assessment.

See **10.7** regarding the requirement to notify liability to the high income child benefit charge.

Payments on account

[9.4] Payments on account need only be made if the amount of income tax etc. due directly to HMRC (i.e. not deducted at source) for the previous year was (a) at least £1,000, and (b) at least 20% of the total tax etc. liability for that year.

Two equal payments on account (calculated as indicated below) should be made; one on 31 January in the tax year and another on 31 July following the end of the tax year, with the balance payable or repayable (taking into account any capital gains tax due) on the following 31 January. Payment may be made by post to the Accounts Office, by bank Giro, by cheque or cash at post offices, by electronic funds transfer through BACS or CHAPS, or via online banking or telephone banking. HMRC recommend that payment is made electronically. If paying by cheque it is essential that either the personal payslip is used or the payer's tax reference number, name and address are given, and it would be sensible to keep a copy of the cheque. If payment is made by credit card, transaction fees will be levied.

[9.5] Each payment on account for a tax year will normally be equal to half of the net *income tax* etc. liability (capital gains tax is ignored) of the previous tax year (see Example 6 in **2.32**). Where income has fallen, it is possible to make a claim on form SA 303 at any time before the 31 January after the end of the tax year to reduce or eliminate the payments on account. If one or more of the payments has already been paid, the appropriate amount will be refunded with interest from the payment date. On the other hand, if payments are reduced below what they should have been, interest will have to be paid on the shortfall from each payment date and possibly a penalty may be imposed.

HMRC operate a 'time to pay' policy, if a taxpayer is unable to pay a tax debt that is due. Under this policy taxpayers may be given the opportunity of clearing tax arrears by instalments (paid by direct debit), rather than recovery proceedings being instituted for the full amount. This will be particularly likely for those who have not previously been late with their payments. Interest will, however, still be charged on the late payments, although no additional penalties will be imposed. Additional support is also available from the Business Payment Support Service Unit for taxpayers wanting to negotiate a time to pay arrangement with HMRC.

Where a viable business is due to pay tax on the previous year's business profits and is likely to make a trading loss in the current year, those losses could be taken into account when agreeing the level of payments to be made.

HMRC are able to secure payment of tax and tax credit debts directly from debtors' bank/building society accounts and cash ISAs where the tax debt is over £1,000. This is known as the Direct Recovery of Debts (DRD). This power is subject to robust safeguards in that only debtors who have received a face-to-face visit, have not been identified as vulnerable, have sufficient money in their accounts and have still refused to settle their debts will be considered for debt recovery through DRD. Debtors affected by this policy have 30 days to object before any money is transferred to HMRC and HMRC must always leave a minimum of £5,000 across a debtor's accounts above the amount that has been held. If debtors do not agree with HMRC's decision, they are able to appeal against this to a county court on specified grounds, including hardship and third party rights. For HMRC guidance see www.go v.uk/government/publications/direct-recovery-of-debts-and-vulnerable-custom ers.

Form 64-8

[9.6] Form 64-8 is a form that authorises HMRC to communicate with an accountant, tax agent or adviser acting on behalf of the taxpayer. It provides authorisation for individual tax affairs (including partnerships and trusts) and business taxes (VAT, PAYE for employers and corporation tax). A personal representative can also use form 64-8 to authorise an agent to deal with some individual tax affairs for the estate of a deceased person. The National Insurance number or unique tax reference of the deceased person should be included in the boxes on the right. If an agent is needed to act on behalf of a person in relation to the high income child benefit charge (**10.7**), a form CH995 will need to be completed.

Agents who have registered to use the internet for self-assessment (**9.12**) are able to send clients' returns online providing HMRC hold the agent's authorisation form 64-8 for the client. If the form is not held, the client may register with HMRC and provide the appropriate authorisation. Agents must retain a signed hard copy (or electronically signed copy) of completed returns. The online filing system allows attachments to be sent with a return, but it cannot cope with aspects of some returns and it may therefore be necessary to supplement the return with paper information. For HMRC guidance see www.gov.uk/guidance/client-authorisation-an-overview.

HMRC rulings

[9.7] HMRC have a system of 'post-transaction rulings', under which it may be possible to obtain a ruling if the tax treatment of a transaction is in doubt because, for example, it was unusual or was entered into in unusual circumstances. It is also possible to ask for any valuations made for capital gains tax to be checked before sending in the return etc.

A non-statutory clearance service enables businesses to obtain written confirmation of HMRC's view of the tax consequences of a transaction or event, either before or after the event, providing that there is 'material uncertainty' and that the issue is 'commercially significant'.

Simple assessment regime

[9.8] As announced in the March 2015 Budget, the Government is committed to abolishing the tax return as far as possible. As part of this initiative, Finance Act 2016 gave HMRC the power to issue a simple assessment notice to individuals and trustees, setting out their tax liability without the need for the taxpayer to submit a self-assessment tax return.

Issue of simple assessment notice (TMA 1970, ss 28H–28J)

[9.9] A simple assessment notice must be based on information held by HMRC that has been provided by the taxpayer themselves or third parties.

The simple assessment will detail:

(a)   the amounts which are chargeable to income tax and capital gains tax, taking into account any relief or allowance that is applicable;
(b)   how much tax is due and the information HMRC used when calculating this;
(c)   how the amount due may be paid and the date it is due.

A simple assessment notice is a legally enforceable demand for payment. HMRC can issue more than one simple assessment in a tax year for the same person. They also have the power to withdraw a simple assessment notice by giving notice to the person concerned. Once withdrawn the notice no longer has effect.

If a taxpayer has other income or gains that are not included in the simple assessment notice there is a requirement to notify HMRC of any chargeability to tax in relation to these (**9.3**).

Payment of tax (TMA 1970, s 59BA)

[9.10] Where a simple assessment has been issued, the amount of tax assessed (less any payments on account made for the tax year concerned; see **9.4**) is generally due on or before 31 January after the end of the tax year concerned. However, if the simple assessment notice is issued after 31 October following the end of the tax year concerned, payment is due three months after the date on which the notice is given.

The late payment penalties regime (**9.71**) will apply to amounts payable under simple assessment but these will be made effective in due course by statutory instrument. So there may be a period of grace while the system settles in.

Right of appeal (TMA 1970, s 31AA)

[9.11] There is no right of appeal (**9.43**) against a simple assessment until the person concerned has raised a query about the simple assessment and been given a final response by HMRC. The right to query is exercisable within a 60 day period after the date on which the simple assessment notice was issued (or such longer time as HMRC may allow). If HMRC decide that they need time to consider the query, they have a power to postpone the notice, in whole or in part. Whilst a simple assessment is postponed there is no obligation to pay any tax that has been postponed. After the query has been considered by HMRC, they must confirm, amend or withdraw the simple assessment and notify the person concerned, in writing.

Self-assessment regime

[9.12] Taxpayers that are not within the simple assessment regime, may be required to 'self-assess' their liability by reporting all income, gains etc in a tax return; see **9.13**.

Sending in the tax return (TMA 1970, ss 8–9C, 28C)

[9.13] Every person sent a notice to file a tax return by HMRC is required to complete and file a return with HMRC. HMRC have a statutory power to withdraw a notice to file a self-assessment for individuals, partnerships and trustees. Where a further notice to file is issued after the withdrawal of a notice, it is treated as if it were the original notice to file for the purposes of the payment dates for income tax and capital gains tax, so the payment dates are unchanged.

The normal filing date for a paper return is 31 October after the end of the tax year. The normal filing date for a return filed online is 31 January after the end of the tax year. There are penalties for late returns, though HMRC will accept reasonable excuses at face value and 'want to move away from sending out penalty notices as a mechanical reaction to a single missed deadline'.

Self-assessment tax returns (forms SA 100), or notices for those who file online, are normally sent out from April. If tax is paid under PAYE, coding notices (**10.61**) will show the amounts of any underpayments dealt with by coding adjustment.

The tax is calculated automatically for returns filed online. Where a paper return is filed, individuals may calculate their own liability but HMRC will do the calculation so long as the return is filed on time, i.e. by 31 October.

If tax is paid under PAYE and a return (paper or online) is filed by 30 December following the end of the tax year, HMRC will try to adjust the PAYE code to collect an underpayment of up to £3,000 unless it is indicated in the return that the taxpayer prefers to pay the outstanding tax by the 31 January following the end of the tax year. HMRC may also collect outstanding Class 2 by an adjustment in PAYE codes. See **10.61** regarding the maximum amount of tax debt that may be collected via a coding adjustment. Taxpayers can claim repayments of tax, overpaid through the PAYE system, via the online refund service. The overpaid tax will be returned directly to taxpayers' bank accounts 'within 3–5 days'. For details see www.gov.uk/gov ernment/news/faster-easier-tax-repayments-at-the-heart-of-the-personal-tax-a ccount.

If pence are included in the return they will not be taken into account. Instead, income and gains should be rounded down and tax paid should be rounded up, to the nearest pound. A return containing entries such as 'to be agreed', is incomplete. If the correct figure cannot be established in time a 'best estimate' should be included and it should be clearly marked that a provisional figure has been used. The correct figure should then be notified as soon as possible. It is important to remember that interest is charged on tax paid late. A penalty may be imposed if HMRC consider that there was insufficient reason to use a provisional figure or they believe an 'unreasonable' one was used. The use of estimated figures may prompt HMRC to open an enquiry into the return.

If a return is not sent in by the due date, HMRC have the power to 'determine' the tax etc. that is owed. There is no right of appeal but their figure will be replaced by the self-assessment figure when it is received.

Corrections, amendments and enquiries (TMA 1970, ss 9ZA–9ZB)

[9.14] HMRC normally have nine months from the date they receive a return to correct obvious errors or omissions, but the taxpayer has the right to reject such a correction within 30 days. The taxpayer will normally have a year from 31 January following the end of the tax year to make amendments to the return, whether it was filed on paper or electronically. For returns issued after 31 October following the end of the tax year the 12-month period runs, broadly, from three months after the date the return was issued.

HMRC may handle minor queries on a return by telephone contact with the taxpayer or his agent. They may open a formal enquiry into the return providing they give the appropriate notice, normally within 12 months from the date the return is filed.

Claims for reliefs, allowances, etc. (TMA 1970, ss 42–43C and Sch 1A)

[9.15] Where a claim is made for capital allowances (see **22.13** onwards), the claim must normally be in the return or an amended return, so the time limits indicated above for the return and amendments apply. Most other claims for reliefs and allowances are made in the same way. For claims that are not included in a return or amended return, a separate claims procedure is laid down, under which HMRC have the same nine-month period after the claim to correct obvious errors and the taxpayer has 12 months from the date of the claim to amend it. Unless another time limit is stipulated in the legislation, the time limit for separate claims is four years after the end of the tax year to which it relates. Where capital losses are incurred, relief may be claimed against capital gains so long as the losses are notified to HMRC within the time limit for claims. There is, however, no time limit during which carried forward capital losses have to be used (see **4.2**).

In certain situations, HMRC may accept a late claim for reliefs, allowances etc. if the delay results from events clearly outside the taxpayer's control or any other reasonable cause.

It is possible to provide certain information and make claims by telephone where appropriate. This applies only to individuals (or authorised third parties) and not to partners, trustees or personal representatives. A wider range of services, including the ability to make certain changes to self-assessments, is available to individuals and their agents (HMRC Statement of Practice SP 1/05).

Backdated claims (TMA 1970, s 42 and Sch 1B)

[9.16] Where relief is claimed for a loss incurred or payment made in one tax year to be set against the income or gains of an earlier tax year, then although the tax saving from the claim is calculated by reference to the tax position of the earlier year, the claim is treated as relating to the later year and is given effect in relation to that later year. Repayment interest (see **9.55**) is therefore paid only from the balancing payment date for the later tax year (e.g. 31 January 2019 if the later year is 2017–18). This also applies to claims for averaging farming profits (see **31.6** and **31.7**) and carrying back post-cessation receipts (see **21.9**). In these latter two cases, the effect of the claim may be to *increase* the tax etc. payable for an earlier year. Interest on overdue tax etc. (see **9.55**) similarly runs from 31 January following the later tax year.

In calculating the revised tax position for the earlier year, the effect on claims and allowances that were made or could have been made is taken into account. For example, the effect of reducing income may be that age-related married couple's allowance becomes available, or that surplus married couple's allowance is available to transfer to a spouse, or following a loss carryback, the facility to pay personal pension contributions may be restricted, resulting in loss of tax relief on contributions already paid.

Payment of tax (TMA 1970, ss 59A, 59B, 59G, 59H, 70A and Sch 3ZA; SI 1996/1654; F(No 2)A 2015, s 51 and Sch 8)

[9.17] The tax due for a tax year is paid in three instalments, as payments on account (**9.4**), with the final payment being due by 31 January following the end of the tax year. Where a taxpayer is within self-assessment, HMRC will issue a self-assessment statement based on the tax return but taking account of any amounts owing from earlier years and any payments on account that are outstanding for the current year.

If an amendment is made to a return resulting in extra tax etc. payable, the additional amount is due 30 days after the amendment (although interest on overdue tax etc. runs from the original due date).

Self assessment timetable

[9.18] The key dates for the 2017–18 tax return are as follows:

31 January 2018	2016–17 online returns to be filed. Final payment/repayment for 2016–17, including CGT, plus 1st payment on account for 2017–18 (based on half 2016–17 tax etc. paid directly on all income).
April 2018	2017–18 returns issued.
31 July 2018	2nd payment on account due for 2017–18.
31 October 2018	2017–18 paper returns to be filed.
31 January 2019	2017–18 online returns to be filed. Final payment/repayment for 2017–18, plus 1st payment on account for 2018–19.

Form of self-assessment tax return

[9.19] The 'core return' contains the questions most likely to be relevant. Additional information pages are provided for the less common types of income and tax reliefs etc. Supplementary pages are to be completed for details of income from employment, self-employment, partnerships, property etc. and any capital gains.

HMRC sends a short tax return (four pages) to taxpayers with simple tax affairs including pensioners, some employees, and self-employed taxpayers with turnover below £85,000 (for 2017–18; the limit is £83,000 for 2016–17). Taxpayers that have self-employment income or have income from property below the £85,000 (or £83,000 for 2016–17) limit do not need to itemise business expenses or property expenses in their return.

Guidance notes and a tax calculation guide accompany the returns and supplementary pages. HMRC help sheets provide more detailed guidance on particular topics but these are available online only, at www.gov.uk/self-asses sment-forms-and-helpsheets.

To file online it is necessary to register with HMRC via www.gov.uk/log-in-f ile-self-assessment-tax-return. Not all of the supplementary pages can be filed using HMRC's own, free Self Assessment Online service. A wider range of supplementary pages is available using third party software products and HMRC provide a list of third party software companies who have products successfully tested to ensure that their forms and supplementary pages can be filed online. Partnerships and trustees, as well as individuals, may file returns online using third party software.

Additional information

[9.20] The self-assessment return is intended to be comprehensive and most taxpayers are not expected to need to submit accounts and other additional material. If, however, HMRC are not provided with full information and tax is consequently underpaid, they may make a 'discovery assessment'. Any additional material the taxpayer considers relevant may be sent in with the return, but swamping HMRC with information will not provide immunity from a discovery assessment unless the relevance of the additional material is pointed out.

The return requires details of income, claims for reliefs and allowances and, if relevant, capital gains details, for the year ended 5 April. It is sensible to keep a copy of the return in order to keep a full record of the information provided. Remember that even though supporting documentation is not necessarily required with the return, taxpayers may be charged a stiff penalty if they do not keep detailed records relating to their tax affairs for the specified period (see **9.32**). See **9.34** regarding an obligation to notify HMRC if tax is payable and a return form is not received.

Corporation tax assessment (TMA 1970, ss 59D, 59E; FA 1998, s 117 and Sch 18; FA 2007, ss 93–97; FA 2009, s 93 and Sch 46)

[9.21] Most of the self-assessment provisions follow those for income tax. The main differences are detailed below:

(a)   simple-assessment (**9.8**) does not apply to companies;

(b)   companies must file a statutory return (CT 600) with supporting accounts and computations within 12 months after the end of the accounting period (or three months after receiving the notice to deliver the return if later);

(c)   all companies must generally submit their tax returns online. There are however exceptions to this for companies subject to winding up orders, in administration, in administrative receivership, in a creditors' voluntary winding up, with a provisional liquidator appointed or with a voluntary arrangement or a compromise arrangement in place. There are also exceptions for a limited liability partnership being wound up and where the use of online filing is incompatible with religious beliefs. For HMRC guidance on their approach to mandatory online filing at the end of a company's life see www.gov.uk/government/publications/corporation-tax-mandatory-online-filing-and-the-end-of-a-companys-life;

(d)   companies must file accounts and computations in a set format — Inline eXtensible Business Reporting Language (iXBRL). HMRC provide guidance at www.gov.uk/prepare-file-annual-accounts-for-limited-company and www.gov.uk/file-an-annual-return-with-companies-house. A list of recognised commercial software that is compatible with the Corporation Tax Online service is provided at www.gov.uk/government/publications/corporation-tax-commercial-software-suppliers;

(e)   between three and seven weeks after the end of the accounting period the company will receive a notice to deliver a corporation tax return (form CT603). Where relevant, companies will need to send in supplementary pages, the main ones being loans to close company participators (CT600A), controlled foreign companies (CT600B), and group relief claims and surrenders (CT600C). Where a return is filed online, the supporting accounts and documentation must also be filed online as attachments. If the attachments are not sent, the filing obligation is not satisfied;

(f)   companies do not have the option of leaving the tax calculation to HMRC. In addition to self-assessing the tax on its profits, a company is also required to self-assess its liability for tax on close company loans (see **12.14**) and under the controlled foreign companies rules (see **45.25**);

(g)   the general rule is that the corporation tax payment date for companies is nine months and one day after the end of the accounting period. Companies with profits which exceed £1.5 million in an accounting period are required to pay their tax by instalments (see **3.24**);

(h)   payments of corporation tax, interest and any flat or fixed rate penalties must be paid electronically. If payment is made by credit card, transaction fees will be levied.

Senior accounting officers of certain companies are required to take steps to ensure that the company (and any subsidiaries) establishes and maintains 'appropriate' tax accounting arrangements to enable the company's tax liabilities to be calculated accurately. This measure affects companies and groups, broadly, with a turnover of more than £200 million or a balance sheet total of more than £2 billion.

Note that from April 2019 digital tax accounts are being introduced for VAT purposes only for businesses with a turnover above the VAT registration threshold. This means that from April 2019, affected businesses will have to keep digital VAT records and complete digital VAT returns. It is anticipated that the requirement to keep digital records etc for other taxes will not be implemented until 2020 at the earliest.

Corrections, amendments and enquiries

[9.22] HMRC are able to correct obvious errors in the return within nine months, and the company may notify amendments within 12 months after the filing date. For most companies, where the return is delivered by the filing date, HMRC have 12 months from the day on which the return was delivered in which to select the return for enquiry. However the 12-month period runs from the statutory filing date for groups of companies that are not 'small groups'. (A group is 'small' if it has aggregate turnover of not more than £6.5 million net, aggregate balance sheet total of not more than £3.26 million net and aggregate employees of not more than 50). The enquiry 'window' is extended broadly as for income tax for returns delivered late and amended returns, see **9.41**.

A company may notify amendments to its return within the time limit stated above even when HMRC are enquiring into the return, but the amendments will not take effect until the enquiry is completed. The company and HMRC may jointly refer questions arising during the enquiry to the tribunal. If the return is not selected for enquiry, the self-assessment will stand unless an underpayment of tax is subsequently discovered that arises because the company gave inadequate information or because of its careless or deliberate actions. See **3.28** for returns for companies in liquidation.

Companies may ask HMRC (on form CG34) to check the valuations used to compute their capital gains before sending in their returns. The form and relevant information must be received by HMRC at least two months before the relevant filing deadline in order for the valuation to be checked and processed on time. Companies involved in non-arm's length sales (see **45.30**) are required to include any necessary transfer pricing adjustments in their returns.

Claims

[9.23] Claims for capital allowances and group relief must be made in the return or an amended return. If HMRC enquire into the return, the time limit for claims is extended to 30 days after the enquiry is completed (see **22.14** to **22.18** and **26.23**). The procedure for making other claims is the same as for income tax (see **9.15**). Such claims are subject to a time limit of four years from the end of the accounting period, unless some other time limit is specified. Where a return is amended following a discovery assessment, provision is made for the company to make additional or amended claims (see **9.46**). See CHAPTER **26** for further details on loss claims and group relief.

Company law

[9.24] A company's tax return must be accompanied by copies of accounts as prepared in accordance with the Companies Acts (including directors' and auditors' reports). Company law requires companies to file accounts with Companies House not later than six months after the end of the accounting period for a public company, or nine months for a private company. There are automatic penalties for late filing, as set out in guidance note GP5 available at www.gov.uk/government/publications/late-filing-penalt ies. Companies House accept company accounts in iXBRL which is the format used for all company tax returns from April 2011.

Micro-businesses are able to prepare simplified accounts and also have the option to file these simplified accounts with HMRC. To qualify as a micro-business a company must meet the definition of a small company and also meet two of the following three conditions:

(a)   the gross assets do not exceed £316,000;
(b)   the annual turnover does not exceed £632,000;
(c)   there are 10 or fewer employees on average.

There are some types of company which are ineligible, such as financial institutions, charities and LLPs, and there are special rules relating to group companies.

In general, companies do not have to have their accounts audited provided they meet two of the following three conditions:

(i)   the gross assets do not exceed £5.1 million;
(ii)   the annual turnover does not exceed £10.2 million;
(iii)   there are 50 or fewer employees on average.

See www.gov.uk/audit-exemptions-for-private-limited-companies for exceptions to the exemption.

Inheritance tax assessment (IHTA 1984, ss 216–225A, 245–248; SI 2008/605)

Lifetime transfers

[9.25] Most lifetime transfers are 'potentially exempt' from inheritance tax but an account of a lifetime transfer on form IHT 100 is required when there is a chargeable event, e.g. a chargeable transfer is made by an individual, or a transferor dies within seven years of making a potentially exempt transfer. This requirement is subject to various exceptions.

A lifetime transfer made by an individual on or after 6 April 2007 is excepted if it meets either of the following conditions:

(a)   the value transferred is attributable to cash or quoted stocks and securities, and that value together with the value of chargeable transfers made in the previous seven years does not exceed the inheritance tax threshold; or

(b)   the value transferred, together with the value of chargeable transfers made in the previous seven years, does not exceed 80% of the inheritance tax nil rate threshold *and* the value of the value transferred by the current transfer does not exceed the 'net inheritance tax threshold' (i.e. the amount of the threshold less the value of chargeable transfers made in the previous seven years).

Returns are strictly not required until 12 months after the end of the month in which the transfer takes place, but interest on overdue tax runs from earlier dates, so returns should be lodged accordingly (see CHAPTER 5).

Transfers on death

[9.26] In the case of death, the return is made in conjunction with the application for a grant of probate (where there is a will) or of administration (where there is no will or where the named executors cannot or will not act).

Guidance on completion of form IHT 400 and the various schedules, and guidance on application for probate, is available at www.hmrc.gov.uk/inherit ancetax.

Form IHT 403 is required where the deceased made lifetime transfers. This form requires an annual breakdown of income and expenditure for the seven years before death where the 'normal expenditure out of income' exemption is claimed. It may be prudent for taxpayers makings gifts that may qualify for this exemption to have a copy of form IHT 403 to complete each year, so that in the event of their death within seven years the appropriate evidence is available.

If a deceased's estate is varied (see **5.39**, **35.15** and **35.16**) and the variation results in extra tax being payable, a copy of the variation, together with the additional tax, must be sent to HMRC within six months after the variation.

Anyone liable to pay tax on a potentially exempt transfer that becomes chargeable as a result of the donor's death is required to submit an account. Personal representatives are required to include in their account details of earlier transfers, whether chargeable or potentially exempt at the time, which are required for the calculation of the tax payable at death (see CHAPTER 5). It is therefore essential that full records of lifetime gifts are kept.

Excepted estates

[9.27] Personal representatives need not submit an account if the estate is an 'excepted estate'. This means that where the deceased died domiciled in the UK, no account need be delivered where:

(a) the gross value of the estate does not exceed the inheritance tax nil rate band *or* it is an 'exempt estate';

(b) if the estate includes any assets in trust, they are held in a single trust and the gross value does not exceed £150,000;

(c) if the estate includes foreign assets, their gross value does not exceed £100,000;

(d) if there are any specified transfers their chargeable value does not exceed £150,000. (Specified transfers are chargeable lifetime transfers made in the seven years prior to death, which do not fall within the gift with reservation of benefit rules (**5.41**)).

An estate is an exempt estate where the gross value of the estate does not exceed £1 million and there is no tax to pay because the assets passing under the estate are exempt from inheritance tax by virtue of passing either to a surviving spouse/civil partner, or to charity. If, in the seven years prior to death, a person has transferred over £3,000 that is considered to be exempt as part of normal expenditure out of income, the amount transferred will nevertheless be included in the value of that person's estate for the purpose of determining whether the personal representatives are excused from the requirement to deliver an inheritance tax account to HMRC, even though the transfer itself may qualify for the exemption.

HMRC will only consider the values of the assets in a person's estate when IHT is due. Where an estate is returned to HMRC as an excepted estate and no IHT is due, HMRC have not considered the value of any asset within the estate at the date of death. They will not therefore amend the value of the property previously reported to them for a subsequent sale price.

This is a very brief summary. Detailed guidance is provided in IHT 400 Notes: Guide to completing your Inheritance Tax account.

Where the excepted estates provisions do not apply but certain other conditions are met, a reduced account may be submitted where, because of exemptions, most of the estate is free from inheritance tax.

Personal representatives of estates covered by the procedures for excepted estates may provide the relevant details to a probate registry, such information being treated as provided direct to HMRC. Probate applications in respect of excepted estates must be accompanied by a form IHT 205 (return of estate information) or IHT 207 if the deceased lived abroad.

Trusts (IHTA 1984, Pt III, Ch III)

[9.28] Trustees of settlements on which tax is chargeable under the main-stream inheritance tax regime (**42.31**), must deliver an inheritance tax account six months after the end of the month in which a chargeable event occurs.

HMRC 'determinations'

[9.29] HMRC have the power to issue a notice of determination in connection with various inheritance tax matters (for example the value of unquoted shares), against which there is a right of appeal. HMRC also have the power, with the consent of the tribunal, to give notice requiring someone to provide information, documents etc. relevant for inheritance tax purposes. There is no appeal against such a notice. Similar notice (but without the need for the tribunal's consent) may be given to those who are required to deliver an account, against which there is a right of appeal.

Other assessments

Annual tax on enveloped dwellings (FA 2013, s 159A)

[9.30] The returns and payments under the annual tax on enveloped dwellings (ATED) regime (**32.48**) are due by 30 April at the beginning of the ATED return period each year. A return must be made for each dwelling where any ATED liability is due. An ATED return period begins on 1 April, so for the ATED period beginning 1 April 2017, the return and the payment will be generally due by 30 April 2017. When dwellings are acquired, the return and payment will be due within 30 days. If the dwelling is newly built, the return and payment must be made within 90 days. It is possible to register and submit the annual ATED return online.

Aside from an interim relief claim, there may be an adjustment of the chargeable amount for the period where the total of daily amounts for all days on which tax is chargeable differs from the initial charged amount. Where the adjusted chargeable amount is less than the initial amount charged, a claim for relief must be made in a return or amended return by the end of the chargeable period following the one to which the claim relates. Where the adjusted chargeable amount exceeds the initial amount charged, a further return must usually be submitted, and the further tax paid, within 30 days of the end of the chargeable period.

Where a relief is claimed in relation to a dwelling that reduces the ATED liability to nil, it is possible to use a simplified 'Relief Declaration Return'. The normal filing dates apply for this form.

There are specific provisions regarding ATED returns, the duty to keep records, enquiries into returns, HMRC determinations and assessments, relief for overpaid tax and reviews and appeals, and a number of them are similar in many ways to the stamp duty land tax self-assessment regime. However, the existing information and inspection powers, and penalty provisions for errors in returns, late returns and late tax payments will apply (see **9.37**, **9.58**, **9.61** and **9.71**).

Non-resident capital gains tax charge (TMA 1970, ss 12ZA–12ZN, 28G, 29A)

[9.31] All persons making a non resident capital gains tax (NRCGT) disposal (**41.50**) have 30 days from the conveyance of the property (not the date of exchange) to submit a NRCGT return to HMRC. A NRCGT return is not required if:

(a)   the UK residential property is transferred within companies in a NRCGT group;

(b)   the disposal is on a no gain/no loss basis; or

(c)   there is an arm's length lease granted to a person unconnected with the grantor, for no premium (such that there is therefore no chargeable gain on the disposal).

If there is any uncertainty around whether the person is, in fact, non-resident, a NRCGT return should be filed and can later be treated as not having been made if the person is found to be UK resident. Normally a separate NRCGT return is required for each NRCGT disposal, but if more than one disposal occurs on the same day then all those disposals can be recorded on the same return.

The NRCGT return must include a calculation of the chargeable gain or allowable loss and the amount of UK CGT due unless the person has already been issued with a self assessment tax return (**9.13**) or an ATED return (**9.30**) has been filed instead. It is possible to file a provisional calculation using a reasonable estimate and amend the return once the final UK taxable income figure is available. If the person has been issued a notice to complete a self assessment return, a NRCGT return is still required but the calculation of the chargeable gain/loss is not.

If the person is required to include the calculation of the chargeable gain/loss within the NRCGT return, the tax due must be paid within 30 days of conveyance (i.e. the same deadline as the return). Therefore those persons who have been issued a notice to complete a self assessment tax return do not need to pay the tax within 30 days. The normal due date for payment of the tax applies. For individuals, trustees and personal representatives the tax must be paid by 31 January after the end of the tax year (i.e. 31 January 2019 for disposals in the 2017–18 tax year).

The compliance regime is modelled on the existing rules, meaning that, for example:

(a)   the return can be amended by the taxpayer at any point following the filing of the return until the anniversary of 31 January following the end of the tax year in which the disposal took place;

(b)   the return can be corrected by HMRC within nine months of it being filed;

(c)   HMRC have the usual time limits to enquire into the return (**9.14**) and the taxpayer can amend the return during the enquiry;

(d)   HMRC have the power to issue a determination of the tax due if the return has not been filed by the due date;

(e)   HMRC are able to make a discovery assessment for tax not self-assessed on an NRCGT return as long as certain conditions are met;

(f)   the information and inspection powers are extended to allow HMRC to issue taxpayer information notices in respect of the return.

Tax-geared penalties can be charged for the submission of an inaccurate NRCGT return under the harmonised penalty regime (**9.58**). Penalties can also be imposed for late filing of a return (**9.61**).

Record keeping requirements

Individuals etc (TMA 1970, s 12B)

[9.32] It is not usually necessary to send accounts and supporting documents with the return (see **9.20**) but all records relevant to the return must be kept for a specified period. The period is normally 22 months from the end of the tax year, unless the taxpayer is in business or lets property, in which case the records must be kept for 5 years and 10 months from the end of the tax year (or such shorter period as specified by HMRC). If HMRC have commenced a formal enquiry into a return before the expiry of the time limit, the records must be kept until the enquiry is completed.

Where a claim is made other than in a return (see **9.15**), records relating to the claim must be kept until the day on which any HMRC enquiry into the claim (or amendment to a claim) is completed, or, if there is no such enquiry, until HMRC are no longer able to open such an enquiry (see **9.41**). As far as claims for relief for capital losses are concerned (see **9.15**) this means that the time limit for retaining the records relating to the losses may have expired before the time when the losses are used to reduce a gain.

Records may be kept on computerised systems providing they can be produced in legible form if required.

A penalty of up to £3,000 may be imposed if these records are not kept.

For details of the record keeping requirements of VAT registered persons see 7.45 onwards.

Companies (FA 1998, s 117 and Sch 18; FA 2013, s 162 and Sch 33; FA 2016, s 161 and Sch 19)

[9.33] Companies must keep records relating to information in their returns for six years from the end of the relevant accounting period, or sometimes longer in enquiry cases and where returns are late. Normally the record keeping requirement will be satisfied by the same records that satisfy Companies Act requirements, except for transfer pricing purposes. Records may be kept on computerised systems providing they can be produced in legible form if required. A penalty of up to £3,000 may be imposed if these records are not kept.

Large companies, groups, partnerships and UK permanent establishments are required to publish their tax strategy online as it relates to or affects UK taxation. This only affects very large businesses with, broadly, a turnover of more than £200 million and/or a balance sheet total of more than £2 billion. Non-publication or incomplete content may lead to appealable penalties of up to £7,500. There is provision for further monthly penalty of £7,500 per month for failures continuing after six months. See **45.9**.

For details of the record keeping requirements of VAT registered persons see **7.45** onwards.

Provision of information to HMRC

Notification of liability

Individuals (TMA 1970, s 7)

[9.34] If a taxpayer does not receive a return or a simple-assessment notice (**9.8**), but has taxable income or gains on which tax has not been paid and of which HMRC are unaware, the onus is on the taxpayer to tell HMRC. There are penalties for non-compliance (see **9.60**). The time limit for notification of chargeability is 5 October following the end of the tax year, e.g. by 5 October 2018 for 2017–18 income and gains.

There is no obligation to notify income where the tax liability has been met by deduction of tax at source. Employees who have a copy P11D from their employers may assume that HMRC know about its contents unless they have reason to believe otherwise, and they are not obliged to notify so long as they are satisfied that the P11D information is correct.

Companies (FA 1998, s 117 and Sch 18)

[9.35] A company coming within the charge to corporation tax is required to notify HMRC of the date when its first accounting period begins. Notice must be given not later than three months after the beginning of that period. If a company with taxable profits does not receive a return, it must notify HMRC within 12 months after the end of the accounting period that it is chargeable to tax.

Employers

[9.36] For details of the reporting requirements for various employee share schemes see CHAPTER 11.

HMRC information and inspection powers (FA 2008, s 113 and Sch 36; FA 2009, s 97 and Sch 49; FA 2011, ss 86, 87 and Schs 23, 25; SI 2015/974)

[9.37] HMRC's investigatory powers are wide ranging. For the purpose of criminal investigations, certain powers under the Police and Criminal Evidence Act 1984 are available to HMRC officers dealing with direct taxes. Additionally HMRC officers undertaking criminal investigations into direct tax or tax credit offences can seize suspected criminal cash under the Proceeds of Crime Act 2002 (POCA) and exercise POCA search and seizure warrants. HMRC also have a common set of information and inspection powers which, broadly, give an HMRC officer the power to:

(a)   obtain information and documents by means of a taxpayer (first-party) notice provided it is reasonably required for the purpose of checking that person's tax position. A similar power may be used to obtain information from a third party to check the tax position of another person. That other person must be named in the notice, except where the First-tier Tribunal has approved the notice and disapplied this requirement. Additionally HMRC are empowered to obtain, from a third party, information about a taxpayer whose identity is not known (where a serious loss of tax is suspected). HMRC are also empowered to obtain 'identifying' information about a taxpayer (name, address, date of birth) from a third party provided HMRC are satisfied the third party has obtained such information in the course of business;

(b)   enter a person's 'business premises' and inspect the premises and any business assets and business documents (as defined) on the premises if the inspection is reasonably required for the purpose of checking that person's tax position. He may not enter or inspect any part of the premises that is used solely as a dwelling.

The information powers are able to be used to obtain information in relation to relevant foreign tax of a territory outside the UK. HMRC also have the power to issue notices requiring third parties to provide (for example) contact details for people in debt to HMRC and any other relevant data. The September 2017 Finance Bill (which is expected to receive Royal Assent in November 2017) contains provisions to extend HMRC's bulk data-gathering powers to include customer data held by money service businesses. The intention being that this will assist HMRC identify those hiding undeclared income.

HMRC guidance is available in the department's Compliance Handbook.

Tax agents – dishonest conduct (FA 2012, s 223 and Sch 38)

[9.38] HMRC have extensive powers to take action against those tax agents they determine as having engaged in dishonest conduct. Under these powers, HMRC can issue a dishonest conduct notice, require access to all the working papers of an agent to whom such a notice has been issued and impose a civil penalty of up to £50,000. Interest is charged on penalties paid late (**9.56**). These powers apply across all taxes and HMRC are able to publish details on their website of dishonest tax agents who are penalised and fail to fully disclose their dishonesty.

Employment intermediaries (ITEPA 2003, s 716B; TMA 1970, s 98; SI 2003/2682)

[9.39] Regulations provide for certain employment intermediaries to keep specified information, records or documents and provide them to HMRC. Strictly, failure to provide such information will result in penalties of £3,000 per failure and a £600 per day penalty for each day of continued failure after the £3,000 penalty. However HMRC appear to have decided not to charge the maximum permissible and instead has set out a sliding scale according to the number of offences in any 12-month period of £250 (first offence), £500 (second offence) and £1,000 (third and subsequent offences).

Money laundering

[9.40] The definition of money laundering includes any process of concealing or disguising the proceeds of *any* criminal offence, including tax evasion.

Accountants and tax advisers, among others, need to have a money laundering reporting officer within their organisation, and to have appropriate systems and staff training programmes. Failing to report to the National Crime Agency (NCA) knowledge or suspicion of money laundering is an offence punishable by imprisonment or an unlimited fine, and HMRC has powers to impose civil penalties for failure to comply with certain requirements set out in the regulations.

A particularly difficult problem is that it is an offence to warn the person concerned that a report is going to be made. Professional legal advisers and accountants, auditors and tax advisers who are members of appropriate professional bodies are, however, exempt from reporting the knowledge or suspicion of money laundering acquired in 'privileged' circumstances. Tax advisers should consider carefully in each case whether the 'privileged reporting exemption' applies.

Accountancy service providers who are not supervised by a designated professional body are required to be registered with HMRC. Guidance is provided at www.gov.uk/money-laundering-regulations-introduction.

Enquiries, assessments and appeals (TMA 1970, ss 9A–9C, 19A, 28ZA–36, 43A–43C; FA 1998, s 117 and Sch 18; IHTA 1984, s 222; FA 2014, ss 199–207, 217, 219–225, 227–229 and Sch 32)

HMRC enquiries

[9.41] HMRC normally have a period of 12 months after the day on which a return is delivered to notify their intention to enquire into the return. If the return is filed late, or an amendment is made to it, this enquiry 'window' extends to the quarter day (31 January, 30 April, 31 July or 31 October) after the first anniversary of the day on which the return or the amendment was filed.

A return may be amended while an enquiry is in progress, although amendments to the amount of tax payable will not take effect until the enquiry is completed. Even then they may be rejected by HMRC or be incorporated in their amendments rather than being dealt with separately. During the enquiry, questions arising may be referred to the tribunal by joint notice from the taxpayer and HMRC. The taxpayer may apply for a direction requiring an HMRC officer to close the enquiry within a specified period.

On completion of the enquiry, HMRC will issue a closure notice and make any necessary amendments and the taxpayer has 30 days in which to lodge any appeal. HMRC have similar powers to enquire into claims made separately from the return.

The September 2017 Finance Bill (which is expected to receive Royal Assent in November 2017) introduces a new power, enabling HMRC to achieve early resolution and closure of one or more aspects of a tax enquiry whilst leaving other aspects open.

[9.42] HMRC have the power to require the production of relevant documents in connection with an enquiry, and a penalty may be imposed for failure to do so. For details of HMRC information and inspection powers see **9.37**.

Dealing with an HMRC enquiry will almost certainly involve extra costs, particularly accountancy expenses, which would not normally be allowable in calculating taxable profits (see **20.9**). If the enquiry results in no addition to profits, or an adjustment to profits for the year of review only without a charge to interest or penalties, the additional expenses will be allowed (see HMRC Statement of Practice SP 16/91).

Appeals

Procedure

[9.43] Appeals must normally be made within 30 days after the date of issue of an assessment (or HMRC amendment to a self-assessment). An appeal must state the grounds on which it is made. Late appeals may be allowed if HMRC are satisfied that there was a good reason for the delay. Certain appeals to the tax tribunal can now be made online. This allows taxpayers to lodge their appeal and receive an acknowledgement with a reference number in a one-step process.

If an appeal is not settled between the taxpayer and HMRC it may be referred to an independent tribunal. There is no right of appeal against a simple assessment (**9.8**) until the person concerned has raised a query about the simple assessment and been given a final response by HMRC (**9.11**).

Most appeals will be heard by the First-tier Tribunal in the first instance, and the Upper Tribunal will hear appeals against decisions of the First-tier Tribunal on a point of law. If either HMRC or the taxpayer is dissatisfied with a tribunal decision on a point of law, further appeal is possible to the High Court, the Court of Appeal and, where leave is granted, the Supreme Court.

However a decision to take an appeal to the tribunal on a point of law must be weighed very carefully because of the likely heavy costs involved, particularly if the taxpayer should be successful at the earlier stages and lose before a higher court.

Alternative dispute resolution

[9.44] There is an alternative dispute resolution (ADR) process for small and medium enterprises (SME), individual customers and large/complex cases. The aim of ADR is to provide such customers with a quick and fair way of resolving tax disputes in compliance checks. ADR involves an independent person from HMRC (called a 'facilitator'), who has not been involved in the dispute before. For large and complex cases this may be an external mediator, due to the potential complexity of issues involved. The facilitator/mediator will work with both the customer and the HMRC case owner to try to broker an agreement between them. ADR is available where a tax issue is in dispute, whether or not an appealable tax decision or assessment has been made by HMRC. ADR covers both VAT and direct taxes disputes, and entering into the ADR process will not affect the customer's existing review and appeal rights. ADR cannot guarantee resolution of the dispute but by the end of the process there will be clarity on the outstanding issues and what happens next.

Postponement of payment of tax

[9.45] Tax etc. still has to be paid on the normal due dates even though an appeal has been lodged, except that in relation to income tax, corporation tax, capital gains tax and stamp duty land tax an application may be made to postpone payment of all or part of the tax etc. The postponement application is separate from the appeal itself and must state the amount of tax etc. which it is considered has been overcharged and the grounds for that belief. The amount to be postponed will then be agreed with the inspector or decided by the tribunal. Any tax etc. not postponed will be due 30 days after the date of the decision as to how much tax etc. may be postponed, or on the normal due date if later.

The appeal itself may be settled by negotiation with the inspector or, failing that, by following the appeal procedure to the tribunal and then if necessary to the courts. Once the appeal has been finally settled, any underpaid tax etc. will be payable within 30 days after the inspector issues a notice of the amount payable. Any overpaid tax etc. will be repaid. Although a postponement application may successfully delay payment of tax, it will not stop interest being charged against the taxpayer on any postponed tax etc. which later proves to be payable (see the due date and interest provisions in CHAPTERS 2 to 4).

HMRC determinations etc

Determinations/additional assessments

[9.46] HMRC may issue a determination of the amount of tax they believe to be payable if a company fails to file its corporation tax return by the filing date, or if this date cannot be established by the later of:

(a)   18 months from the end of the period specified in the return notice; or
(b)   3 months from the date of issue of the return notice.

The determination is HMRC's best estimate of the company's tax liability based on the information available to them at that time. The determination has effect as though it was the company's self-assessment of its liability, which means HMRC have the ability to charge interest and penalties, and to enforce payment of the liability. A company can supersede a determination by filing a self-assessment by the later of 12 months from the date of issue and three years from the date the determination could first have been made.

HMRC are able to issue an additional assessment for a year within the normal time limits of four years after 31 January following the end of the tax year concerned (for individuals) and four years after the end of the accounting period concerned (for companies) without alleging that the taxpayer is at fault.

Discovery

[9.47] If HMRC do not start an enquiry within the time limit, the tax etc. as calculated will normally stand. However, HMRC may make a 'discovery' assessment in the circumstances set out in TMA 1970, s 29, e.g. where there has been inadequate disclosure or loss of tax due to the taxpayer's careless or deliberate actions. Although the implication is that the innocent taxpayer may regard the year as closed after the 12-month period in **9.41**, this does not sit easily with the fact that in most cases HMRC will not require business accounts and other documents to be sent to them. In order to be sure of finality, it seems that taxpayers will need to make sure that HMRC are given all relevant information relating to their tax affairs, including accounts if appropriate, and draw their attention to any contentious points (see **9.20**).

Under the self-assessment provisions for companies HMRC may also make 'discovery determinations', to which the same provisions apply as to discovery assessments. They may 'discover' that an assessment is inadequate through considering facts already in their hands, such as by comparing gross profit rates from year to year, or through new facts, or even because they change their minds on how something should be interpreted. They have, however, stated that they will not normally reopen an assessment they later believe to be incorrect if they had been given full and accurate information and either the point was specifically agreed or the view implicit in the computation submitted was a tenable one.

The taxpayer is protected from further assessment after the HMRC period of enquiry expires (see **9.14** and **9.22**) unless there has been a loss of tax etc. due to the taxpayer's careless or deliberate actions, or HMRC have not been supplied with full and accurate information. The protection given to the taxpayer by this provision was seriously undermined by a Court of Appeal case concerning a property valuation relating to a director's benefit in kind. The Court held that a discovery assessment outside the normal enquiry period was possible unless HMRC had been clearly alerted by the taxpayer or his representatives to the insufficiency of the taxpayer's self-assessment. Following that case HMRC issued guidance on their ability to raise discovery assessments and what information should be included in tax returns (Statement of Practice SP 1/06). Where a discovery assessment is made, other than one arising from the taxpayer's careless or deliberate actions, provision is made for claims, elections, notices etc. to be made, revoked or varied within one year after the end of the tax year or company accounting period in which the assessment is made.

To reopen years outside the normal time limit, HMRC have to show careless or deliberate actions of the taxpayer. In that event, assessments may be made at any time up to six years (for careless actions) or 20 years (for deliberate actions) after the tax year/company accounting period concerned.

Follower notices

[9.48] HMRC are able to issue a 'follower notice' to a person in relation to a particular return/claim if a tax enquiry is in progress in relation to the return/claim or there is an open appeal in a relation to a tax advantage arising from a particular fact pattern and HMRC are of the opinion that there is a judicial ruling relevant to the person's return/claim or appeal.

The follower notice requires the person to amend his return if the return is still under enquiry. If a closure notice or tax assessment is under appeal the taxpayer is required to enter into an agreement with HMRC to settle the dispute. The taxpayer must also give HMRC a notice stating that he has taken the necessary corrective action and the amount of additional tax which has become payable as a result. He has 90 days in which to comply.

A judicial ruling is relevant if it is a final ruling and relates to tax arrangements that would, if applied to the current arrangements, deny the advantage claimed or part of it. A follower notice can only be issued within 12 months of the day of the relevant judicial ruling or the day the return/claim was received by HMRC or the appeal was made, whichever is the later. If however a judicial ruling is made before 17 July 2014 the time limit is extended to 24 months from 17 July 2014 or 12 months of the return/claim or appeal, whichever is the later.

It is possible to object (but not appeal) against a follower notice; such an objection must be made within 90 days of receipt of the follower notice. HMRC must then determine whether the follower notice still applies and notify the person accordingly who must take corrective action in relation to the denied tax advantage.

Follower notices apply to income tax, capital gains tax, corporation tax, inheritance tax, stamp duty land tax, the annual tax on enveloped dwellings and, from 12 February 2015, national insurance contributions. Penalties will apply if the necessary corrective action is not taken (see **9.77**).

Accelerated payment notices

[9.49] HMRC are able to issue an 'accelerated payment notice' to a person in relation to a particular return/claim, which requires the taxpayer to pay the disputed tax upfront. Where a company has losses from the arrangements it is not required to pay over any amounts at that point because it may have no actual tax to pay when the dispute is resolved. However, to prevent abuse, it is specifically provided that any 'loss' amounts that are in dispute are not able to be surrendered to other group companies while the dispute is in progress.

Accelerated payment notices can be used if a tax enquiry is in progress in relation to the return/claim or there is an open appeal in a relation to a tax advantage and:

(a)   the return/claim or appeal is made on the basis that a particular tax advantage results from the arrangements;

(b)   either HMRC have issued a follower notice or a GAAR counteraction notice in relation to the arrangements or the arrangements are certain DOTAS arrangements.

It is possible to object against an accelerated payment notice; such an objection must be made within 90 days of receipt of the original notice. HMRC must then determine whether the notice still applies and notify the person accordingly if it is to be upheld, amended or withdrawn. Once a notice is determined, payment must be made to HMRC of the relevant amount within 90 days of the original notice (or 30 days after determination if an objection was made, if later).

Where an accelerated payment notice is issued in relation to an amount that is the subject of an enquiry, a payment is treated as a payment on account of the tax in dispute. When the final liability is agreed, this payment will be set against it, and any interest payable on that final liability will be adjusted so that no interest will be charged on the amount of the accelerated payment from the date that it was paid. If the final liability is lower than the accelerated payment any excess will be repaid with interest. Where an accelerated payment notice is issued in relation to an amount under appeal any tax that is the subject of the notice cannot be postponed.

Accelerated payment notices apply to income tax, capital gains tax, corporation tax, inheritance tax, stamp duty land tax, the annual tax on enveloped dwellings and, from 12 February 2015, national insurance contributions. Penalties will apply for late payments of accelerated payments (see **9.78**).

Cases of suspected fraud

[9.50] Criminal investigation of fraud is reserved for a minority of cases where HMRC need to send a strong deterrent message and/or where the conduct involved is such that only a criminal sanction is appropriate. Investigations are undertaken by the Specialist Fraud Division (SFD). The SFD divides its work into two broad categories: fiscal and non-fiscal.

In the vast majority of cases, investigations are undertaken using civil procedures. The investigation will be handled by HMRC's Special Civil Investigations Office under their code of practice COP 9. HMRC are not able to give an absolute guarantee at the outset of an investigation under COP 9 that a taxpayer will not be investigated criminally, with a view to prosecution for the suspected tax fraud. Such a guarantee is only given if the taxpayer enters into a contractual arrangement to disclose, and makes an outline disclosure under that arrangement. The guarantee is also restricted so that it only covers the tax frauds disclosed on the outline disclosure form, under the terms of the contract. The taxpayer has 60 days to respond to HMRC and accept the standard terms of the CDF in writing. Otherwise HMRC reserve the right to commence their own investigation, which could also include a criminal investigation.

The outline disclosure must be submitted to HMRC within the same 60-day time limit and should set out as clearly as possible the specific tax frauds together with a formal admission of deliberately bringing about a loss of tax. In most cases a disclosure report will need to be prepared before the taxpayer will be in a position to proceed to the disclosure. The taxpayer will need to agree what he owes, arrange payment and certify that he has disclosed all irregularities. Provided a valid outline disclosure is made, HMRC will look to conclude the investigation without unnecessary delay. Failure to submit a disclosure or submission of an invalid disclosure could lead to either civil or criminal investigation.

Where tax fraud is not suspected, HMRC will usually invite the taxpayer to co-operate in establishing the understated income or gains. Where co-operation is provided, they will then not normally have to resort to their statutory powers to call for documents and to enter and search premises. See 9.40 regarding problems caused for tax advisers in investigation cases as a result of the money laundering provisions.

Establishing the tax etc. lost

[9.51] In relation to direct taxes, an HMRC investigation will include some or all of the following for the appropriate period:

(a)   A full review of the business accounts, often including verification of transactions by third parties such as suppliers.

(b)   A detailed reconstruction of the private affairs, establishing whether increases in private wealth can be substantiated; or a less time-consuming review ensuring that lodgements into non-business bank and building society accounts can be explained.

(c)   A business model based on a sample period, adapted for changing circumstances and compared with the results shown by the business accounts.

(d)   A living expenses review and comparison with available funds to establish the extent to which personal and private expenditure could not have been met out of disclosed income and gains.

At the conclusion of the review, if the need for a revision of profits, income or gains has been established, the calculation of tax underpaid follows automatically.

Where irregularities include an underpayment of VAT, any additional VAT payable will be reflected in the revised profits for income tax or corporation tax.

National insurance contributions (SI 2001/1004 regs 87A–87G)

[9.52] Class 4 contributions payable by the self-employed and Class 2 contributions are collected along with income tax through the self-assessment system and are subject to the same provisions in relation to interest on overdue and overpaid amounts, penalties and appeal procedures.

Where employers or employees have a disagreement with HMRC about a national insurance matter that cannot be resolved informally, HMRC will make a formal decision and notify the employer/employee accordingly. An appeal against the decision may be made within 30 days and the appeal will be dealt with under the same procedures as an income tax appeal (as to which see **9.43**). The disputed national insurance liability and interest thereon need not be paid until the appeal is settled, but if the appeal fails the amount payable will attract interest from 14 days after the end of the tax year in which it became due.

Criminal proceedings may be taken for fraudulent evasion of NICs.

Death of taxpayer (TMA 1970, s 40)

[9.53] Death of a taxpayer restricts HMRC's right to raise new or additional assessments for tax which arose before the taxpayer's death to the four years from the end of the tax year in which the death occurs, whatever the reason for the unpaid tax.

Companies and company directors

[9.54] While the liabilities of a company and its directors are entirely separate, their financial affairs will be looked at together if they are suspected of being at fault. Unexplained wealth increases or funding of living expenses will generally be regarded as extractions from the company, and, under his duty to preserve the company's assets, the director must account to the company for the extracted funds. The director does not have to pay income tax on the extracted funds, but is required to account to the company for the extractions, the company's accounts having to be rewritten accordingly and the extractions being subject to tax at corporation tax rates where they represent additional company profits. The company is also accountable for tax at 32.5% of the extractions unless they are repaid, covered by an amount already standing to the credit of the director or written off (see **12.14**). The tax liability attracts interest and is reckoned in the tax due to HMRC when calculating penalties. The extractions may also affect the income tax payable by the director on the calculated benefit which he has enjoyed from the interest-free use of the company's money.

Interest and penalty regime

Interest (TMA 1970, ss 86–92, 106A; TA 1988, s 824; FA 1998, s 117 and Sch 18; SI 2014/1017; SI 2014/992)

[9.55] Interest is charged on overdue tax etc. from the date the amount of tax etc. became due, and repayment interest is payable from the payment dates on tax etc. overpaid (subject to what is said at **9.16**). For further details and an illustration see **2.30** to **2.33**. For repayment supplement in relation to VAT see **7.49**.

Where an amendment is made to a return, interest is due on any additional tax etc. payable from the original due date, even though the tax itself is payable 30 days after the amendment.

In addition to the payment of tax etc. and interest, HMRC have statutory powers to impose penalties when it has been established that tax etc. has been lost through a taxpayer's careless or deliberate actions. For details see **9.57**.

HMRC have the power to reduce penalties. They will usually accept a smaller penalty where a settlement is reached with a taxpayer without formal proceedings being taken.

Harmonised interest regime (FA 2009, ss 101, 102 and Schs 53, 54; SI 2010/1878; SI 2010/1879; SI 2011/701; SI 2013/280; SI 2013/2472; SI 2014/1017; SI 2014/992; SI 2014/3269; SSCBA 1992, s 11A; SI 2015/974)

[9.56] Finance Act 2009 created a harmonised interest regime for all taxes and duties administered by HMRC. Implementation of interest harmonisation was staged over a number of years and now applies to virtually all taxes with the notable exception of corporation tax, inheritance tax and VAT.

The harmonised interest regime applies a consistent interest charge to late payments and a consistent repayment interest to overpayments across all taxes and duties. Where a person owes any sum to HMRC which arises from taxes, duties etc. imposed by statute, HMRC may charge interest from the date that the sum should have been paid to the date it was actually paid (or satisfied by set-off). Any interest charged will be simple interest and will not generally be deductible in computing profits or income. Repayment interest is payable from the payment dates on tax etc. overpaid to the date repayment is made (subject to what is said at **9.16**).

For annual payments such as Class 1A and Class 1B NIC, HMRC continue to charge interest/pay repayment interest on any amount which remains unpaid after the due date.

Until the Finance Act 2009 regime is fully implemented, the current interest rate setting regulations have been amended (from 12 August 2009) to harmonise the existing regime along the same lines.

Interest is levied on Scottish LBTT (**6.18**) at the same rates as apply under the harmonised interest regime but the interest setting provisions are legislated for by The Revenue Scotland and Tax Powers Act 2014. The interest is payable to Revenue Scotland, not HMRC.

Penalties

[9.57] Over the last few years a unified penalty regime has been introduced (although parts are still to be phased in over the next few years) that essentially applies across all taxes. There will be higher penalties for prolonged and repeated delays, but penalties will not be charged where a time to pay arrangement has been agreed.

HMRC are able to publish information, including names, relating to deliberate tax defaulters, i.e. people who have been penalised for inaccuracies, failure to notify etc., where the tax lost exceeds £25,000.

Penalties for inaccurate documents (FA 2007, s 97 and Sch 24)

[9.58] There is a cross-taxes regime for charging penalties for errors and inaccuracies contained in specified documents including:

(a)   returns of income and capital gains (including construction industry returns), allowances claims, PAYE returns;
(b)   ATED returns, NRCGT returns, apprenticeship levy returns;
(c)   partnership statements and accounts, corporation tax returns, statements and accounts;
(d)   VAT returns and statements; inheritance tax returns; stamp duty land tax and stamp duty reserve tax returns; and
(e)   for all the above taxes, any document HMRC are likely to rely on without further enquiry to decide a taxpayer's liability and payments or repayments due.

The regime also applies for an inaccuracy in any Full Payment Submissions (FPS), including in-year returns, submitted as part of the RTI reporting (see **10.58**). It is based on the potential lost revenue for the FPS that was incorrect. HMRC may issue one penalty notice for multiple inaccuracy penalties in a year.

Penalties are imposed when a person provides a specified document which contains an inaccuracy that leads to an understatement of tax payable, or a false or inflated statement of a loss, or a false or inflated repayment claim. The penalty regime also applies where HMRC have issued an assessment and the person assessed did not take reasonable steps to notify them within 30 days that the assessment understated their liability. A penalty under these provisions is not reduced by the amount of any penalty charged under the follower notices/accelerated payment notices regime (see **9.77**, **9.78**).

The penalties are based on the amount of tax lost and are stepped according to the degree of culpability as follows:

Type of behaviour	Statutory maximum penalty
Careless	30% of tax lost
Deliberate but not concealed	70% of tax lost
Deliberate and concealed	100% of tax lost

An inaccuracy in a document is careless if the taxpayer failed to take reasonable care, deliberate but not concealed if the taxpayer did not make arrangements to conceal a deliberate inaccuracy, or deliberate and concealed if the taxpayer made arrangements to conceal a deliberate inaccuracy. An inaccuracy (that was neither careless nor deliberate at the time the documents were originally submitted) that is discovered after the documents are sent to HMRC will be treated as careless if the taxpayer found out about it later and did not tell HMRC.

The penalties will be reduced if the taxpayer discloses the inaccuracies and cooperates in the investigation of the amount of tax lost. HMRC will also be able to suspend a penalty for a careless inaccuracy for up to two years, subject to specified conditions. They can only do so if this would help the taxpayer to avoid further such penalties. Providing the taxpayer complies with the conditions, the penalty or part of it may be cancelled at the end of the stipulated period. For HMRC guidance on penalties charged for an inaccuracy on a return that would have been automatically reversed in a subsequent return, see HMRC Brief 15/2011.

The level of penalties charged under these provisions can be increased significantly where an income or capital gains tax liability arises on certain undeclared offshore assets. For HMRC guidance see HMRC Brief 14/2011. From 1 April 2016 this offshore penalty regime was extended to apply to inheritance tax. It also applies from 6 April 2016 where the proceeds of non-compliance are hidden offshore. See also **45.28** for civil penalties that apply from 1 January 2017 for deliberate enablers of offshore tax evasion where a person has become liable to a penalty under these provisions.

Penalties in relation to LBTT (RSTPA 2014, ss 182, 183)

[9.59] Where a document in relation to LBTT (**6.18**) contains an inaccuracy which leads to an understatement of tax liability or an inflated claim for relief etc then the following penalties may be levied:

Type of behaviour	Statutory maximum penalty
Careless	30% of tax lost
Deliberate inaccuracy	100% of tax lost

Penalties for failure to notify chargeability (FA 2008, s 123 and Sch 41)

[9.60] Specific provisions apply a penalty regime for failing to notify charge-ability to tax, liability to register for tax etc, aligned across all relevant taxes and duties. The penalties are based on the amount of tax lost and are stepped according to the degree of culpability, as detailed at **9.58**.

A penalty under these provisions is not reduced by the amount of any penalty charged under the follower notices/accelerated payment notices regime (see **9.77**, **9.78**).

The level of penalties charged under these provisions can be increased significantly where an income or capital gains tax liability arises on certain undeclared offshore assets. For HMRC guidance see HMRC Brief 14/2011. From 6 April 2016 this offshore penalty regime was extended to apply where the proceeds of non-compliance are hidden offshore. See also **45.28** for civil penalties that apply from 1 January 2017 for deliberate enablers of offshore tax evasion where a person has become liable to a penalty under these provisions.

Penalties for failure to make returns

Unified penalty regime for failure to make returns (FA 2009, s 106 and Sch 55; SI 2011/702; SI 2011/2391; SI 2014/3269)

[9.61] A unified penalty regime applies for failure to make or deliver returns or documents on or before the statutory filing date for the particular return in question, which applies to essentially all taxes and duties for which HMRC are responsible. Whilst broadly aligned across all the taxes, the rules are modified for CIS returns (see **9.64**) and for Real Time Information (RTI) returns (**9.65**). A separate penalty regime applies to P11D returns and (prior to 2016–17) P9D returns (**9.66**). The unified regime does not yet apply to corporation tax (**9.67**), VAT (**9.68**) or inheritance tax (**9.68**) returns.

A penalty under these provisions is not reduced by the amount of any penalty charged under the follower notices/accelerated payment notices regime (see **9.77**, **9.78**).

The level of penalties charged under these provisions can be increased significantly where an income or capital gains tax liability arises on certain undeclared offshore assets. For HMRC guidance see HMRC Brief 14/2011. From 6 April 2016 this offshore penalty regime was extended to apply where the proceeds of non-compliance are hidden offshore. See also **45.28** for civil penalties that apply from 1 January 2017 for deliberate enablers of offshore tax evasion where a person has become liable to a penalty under these provisions.

With the introduction of Real Time Information (RTI, see **10.58**) there could be an increase in the number of inaccurate returns submitted by employers. When an inaccuracy is made on a RTI or CIS return and is repeated in subsequent returns, HMRC are able to notify the penalties together rather than individually.

HMRC may cancel the liability to a late filing penalty where they have agreed to the withdrawal of the notice to file a tax return for individuals, trustees or partnerships (9.13).

Penalties: harmonised rules

[9.62] The penalties for late filing of a tax return start with a fixed penalty of £100, due immediately after the filing date. If the failure continues for over three months, the penalty level escalates by a fixed £10 per day up to a maximum of 90 days. Following representations, HMRC confirmed in June 2017 that they would no longer issue daily penalties for late filing of NRCGT returns (9.31) and any past daily penalties issued would be withdrawn.

For more serious non-compliance where the failure is prolonged beyond six or twelve months, there are further penalties of either £300 or 5% of the tax liability on the return (whichever is the greater). Penalties of up to 100% of the tax will be charged where the failure is intended deliberately to withhold information to prevent HMRC correctly assessing the tax. HMRC will accept reasonable excuses for late filing of returns at face value because they 'want to move away from sending out penalty notices as a mechanical reaction to a single missed deadline' and concentrate on investigating major tax avoidance, see www.gov.uk/government/news/self-assessment-penalties.

Penalties in relation to LBTT (RSTPA 2014, ss 160–163)

[9.63] For failure to make an LBTT return (6.18) the same penalty amounts apply, but are legislated for under The Revenue Scotland and Tax Powers Act 2014 (RSTPA 2014).

Penalties: CIS regime

[9.64] From 6 October 2011, the penalties for late filing of a CIS return starts with a fixed penalty of £100, due immediately after the filing date. If the failure continues for more than two months after the penalty date, there is a further fixed penalty of £200. If the failure continues for more than six months after the penalty date there is a further fixed penalty equal to the greater of £300 or 5% of the liability that would have been shown in the return. If the failure continues after 12 months a further penalty (of the greater of £300 or 5% of the tax liability) is imposed. Penalties of up to 100% of the tax will be charged where the failure is intended deliberately to withhold information to prevent HMRC correctly assessing the tax. Special rules apply to the first returns made on registration for CIS to cap the first and second fixed penalties. Fixed penalties replace the tax-geared penalties for returns relating to persons registered for gross payment only. From 16 June 2015, late filing penalties may be appealed using HMRC's Online Penalty Appeal Service.

Penalties: RTI regime

[9.65] From 6 October 2014 onwards a separate penalty regime applies to RTI returns which are not made on time for employers that employ 50 or more employees. For employers that employ fewer than 50 employees and those that become new real time information employers after 6 October 2014, the regime applies from 6 March 2015.

Where an RTI return is not filed by the due date (**10.59**) in any tax month, the employer is liable to a penalty, although no penalty is chargeable:

(a)   for the first failure in any tax year — so a maximum of 11 fixed penalties can be charged for late filing in a tax year;

(b)   for a 'new employer' if their first FPS is received within 30 days of making the first payment to their employee(s) (the 'initial period'). After this period, normal penalty rules will apply if there is a failure to file on time;

(c)   for 'short delays' of up to three days when filing an FPS (this applies from 6 March 2015 to 5 April 2018) although employers who persistently file after the payment date but within three days may be contacted or considered for a penalty.

HMRC have stated that they will only charge one penalty for each tax month that there is a failure to file on time but penalties will apply separately to each PAYE scheme. So, for example, if a weekly filer makes two (or more) returns late within a tax month, they will only charge one penalty. The penalty is a fixed amount based on the number of employees (monthly penalty of £100 for 1–9 employees, £200 for 10–49 employees, £300 for 50–249 employees, £400 for 250 or more employees).

A further penalty applies where a return is outstanding for three months (classed as an 'extended failure'). This penalty is not automatic, but will be imposed, at the rate of 5% of the amount that would have been shown on the missing return, where HMRC decide that such a penalty should be paid. The penalty may be imposed for each extended failure in the tax year, which may be charged separately or together. In these circumstances, HMRC will issue a written notice specifying the date from which the penalty is payable. The payment date may be earlier than the date of the notice, but may not be earlier than the period of three months beginning with the day after the filing date.

Penalties will be charged quarterly, subject to the usual reasonable excuse and appeal provisions. Penalties must be paid within 30 days of the notice, or interest will be charged.

Rather than issue late filing penalties automatically when a deadline is missed, HMRC have confirmed that they will take a more proportionate approach and concentrate on the more serious defaults on a risk-assessed basis (see www.g ov.uk/government/news/pay-as-you-earn-paye-late-filing-penalties).

P11D and P9D returns (TMA 1970, s 98)

[9.66] Penalties are charged for late filing of forms P11D and, prior to 2016–17, P9D (see **10.67**). For *each form*, there is an initial penalty of up to £300 plus up to £60 a day if the failure continues. The penalty for late filing of form P11D(b) is £100 for every 50 employees (or part of 50) for each month or part month the return is late. If the failure continues beyond 12 months there is an additional penalty not exceeding the amount of the Class 1A NICs paid late.

Corporation tax returns (FA 1998, s 117 and Sch 18)

[9.67] Until the unified penalty regime (see **9.61**) is applied to corporation tax, the following penalties are charged for late corporation tax returns:

(a)   £100 if the return is up to three months late (£500 for third consecutive late return), £200 if the return is over three months late (£1,000 for third consecutive late return); plus

(b)   10% of tax unpaid 18 months after the end of the accounting period (if the return is submitted 18 to 24 months after the end of the accounting period), 20% of tax unpaid if the return is submitted more than 24 months after the end of the accounting period.

Where, because of exceptional circumstances, a company cannot produce final figures within the time limit, 'best estimates' may be used without attracting late filing penalties, but the figures must be adjusted as soon as the company is aware that they no longer represent the best estimate, and any late payment of tax will attract interest.

VAT returns (VATA 1994, s 59; SI 1995/2518 Pt V; VAT Notice 700/50)

[9.68] Until the unified penalty regime (see **9.61**) is applied to VAT, a 'default surcharge' is payable if two or more returns within a year are not made on time. When a return is late, a 'surcharge liability notice' is issued. The notice remains in force for a period of one year, unless a further return is made late, in which case the surcharge liability period is extended for a year from the last day of the period covered by that return and so on. The surcharge is 2% of the tax due for the first late return in the surcharge liability period, then 5%, 10% and a maximum 15% for subsequent late returns. The 2% and 5% surcharges will not be collected if they are less than £400. The minimum surcharge at 10% or 15% is £30. If no VAT is due, or the VAT is paid on time even though the return is late, then although the late return affects the surcharge liability period, the surcharge does not apply and the rate for subsequent late returns is not increased. If HMRC accept that a business has a reasonable excuse for late payment no default will be recorded.

Inheritance tax returns

[9.69] Until the unified penalty regime (see **9.61**) is applied to inheritance tax, if an account is not submitted by the due date, HMRC may impose an initial penalty of £100 plus a further penalty (on a direction by the tribunal) of up to £60 a day until the account is delivered. If an account is delivered late more than six months later but before HMRC have taken proceedings before the tribunal, the penalty is increased to £200. If an account is delivered more than 12 months late, a penalty of up to £3,000 may be charged. The same applies if notification of a variation of a deceased's estate is made more than 12 months late. Fixed penalties (but not daily penalties) cannot exceed the tax chargeable and penalties will not be charged if there is a reasonable excuse for the delay.

Employee share schemes

[9.70] For details of the penalties for late filing of returns for various employee share schemes see CHAPTER 11.

Penalties for late payment: unified regime (FA 2009, s 107 and Sch 56; SI 2010/466; SI 2011/702; SI 2014/472; SI 2014/992; SI 2014/3269)

[9.71] As for late filing, a unified regime applies in relation to the imposition of penalties for essentially all taxes and duties for which HMRC are responsible, including (from a date to be appointed) amounts payable under simple assessments (**9.10**). The unified regime is applied in a modified format to corporation tax (see **9.73**) and some payments under PAYE or the CIS regulations (see **9.74**).

The unified regime imposes escalating penalties which are chargeable at a fixed rate based on the amount of tax unpaid, or still unpaid, at any of the three statutory dates:

(i)   where tax is not paid in full by the 'penalty date' (which varies depending upon which type of tax is involved; the relevant dates being listed in FA 2009, Sch 56), a penalty of 5% is charged on the unpaid amount;

(ii)   where tax is still unpaid five months after the penalty date, an additional penalty of 5% is charged on that unpaid tax; and

(iii)   if the non-payment continues after 11 months from the penalty date, a further penalty of 5% is charged on the unpaid amount.

All penalties are due for payment 30 days following the date of the penalty notice. Penalties not paid by this time will attract interest.

A 'payment tolerance' of £100 applies for the CIS and PAYE late payment penalties, meaning that, where an employer or contractor pays over a sum that is within £100 of the total sum due to HMRC for the tax period in question, no late payment penalty will be due. The tolerance will not apply where the payment relates to a correcting return submitted after 19 April following the tax year end. Additionally, HMRC announced that, rather than be issued automatically, the late payment penalties will continue to be reviewed on a risk-assessed basis rather than be issued automatically (see www.gov.uk/gove rnment/news/hmrc-will-not-impose-paye-filing-penalties-for-short-delays-fro m-march-2015).

Penalties in relation to LBTT (RSTPA 2014, ss 169)

[9.72] For late payment of LBTT (**6.18**) the same penalty amounts apply, but are legislated for under The Revenue Scotland and Tax Powers Act 2014 (RSTPA 2014).

Corporation tax payments

[9.73] From a date to be appointed, the unified late payment penalty regime will apply, in a slightly modified form, for corporation tax. These separate provisions are required as the penalty dates are different; the first penalty date being the date after the filing date, rather than the date after the due date for the tax, which is usually three months earlier. The penalty structure is as follows:

(a)   where tax is not paid in full by the 'penalty date', a penalty of 5% is charged on the unpaid amount;

(b) where tax is still unpaid three months after the penalty date, an additional penalty of 5% is charged on that unpaid tax; and

(c) if the non-payment continues after nine months from the penalty date, a further penalty of 5% is charged on the unpaid amount.

CIS payments and PAYE payments

[9.74] The penalty structure is applied a little differently to payments of tax under PAYE and the CIS regulations which relate to a period of six months or less. The penalty is determined by reference to the number of 'defaults' in relation to the tax year, and is payable even if the default is remedied before the end of the year. The penalties structure is as follows:

(a) the first failure during the tax year does not count as a default;

(b) if the taxpayer defaults:

    (i) up to three times during the tax year, the penalty is 1% of the total of those defaults;

    (ii) between four and six times during the tax year, the penalty is 2% of the total of those defaults;

    (iii) between seven and nine times during the tax year, the penalty is 3% of the total of those defaults; and

    (iv) ten or more times during the tax year, the penalty is 4% of the total of those defaults;

(c) where tax is still unpaid at the end of the period of six months beginning with the penalty date, a further penalty is charged of 5% of any tax remaining unpaid at that date;

(d) where tax is still unpaid at the end of the period of 12 months beginning with the penalty date, a further penalty is charged (in addition to any incurred at the six-month stage) of 5% of any tax remaining unpaid at that date.

HMRC provide guidance at www.gov.uk/what-happens-if-you-dont-pay-paye -and-national-insurance-on-time. They currently use a risk-based approach to identify employers who are not complying with their payment obligations and who therefore might be liable to late payment penalties.

In-year RTI payments

[9.75] The penalties outlined in **9.74** are charged in-year where RTI payments are made late, rather than at the end of the tax year. Each penalty is ring-fenced so that if further defaults arise earlier penalties do not have to be recalculated and a penalty will be able to be amended once it has been issued, rather than it having to be withdrawn and reissued.

Other penalties for late payment

Corporation tax payments (SI 1998/3175)

[9.76] Until the unified regime is implemented for corporation tax (**9.73**), penalties for late payment of corporation tax are not generally charged although the company will be liable to pay interest on overdue tax. However large companies, that are liable to make quarterly instalment payments, are potentially subject to penalties if the company has deliberately or recklessly failed to make the payment. The penalty imposed can be up to an amount not exceeding twice the amount of the interest charge. A similar penalty is imposed where a fraudulent or negligent claim is made for repayment of an instalment payment.

Follower notice penalties (FA 2014, ss 208–216, Schs 30, 31)

[9.77] If the recipient of a follower notice (9.48) takes no corrective action he is liable to a penalty equal to 50% of the 'denied advantage' (i.e. the additional amount of tax due or payable resulting from the advantage being counteracted). This is reduced to 20% for relevant partners. This penalty may be reduced if he co-operates with HMRC but only up to a maximum of 10% of the denied advantage. Any follower notice penalty must be paid within 30 days from notification. There is a limit on the total penalty that can be imposed where penalties may apply under this provision and one or more of the other penalty provisions. This limit ranges from the greater of 100% to 200% of the amount of tax at stake; and a flat £300, depending upon the nature of the other penalty.

It is possible to appeal against a penalty imposed under a follower notice; such an appeal must be made within 30 days of receiving notification of the penalty.

Accelerated payment notice penalties (FA 2014, s 226)

[9.78] If the recipient of an accelerated payment notice (9.49) pays the tax late, a late payment penalty is imposed in respect of the accelerated payment. The rates and structure are based on the provisions in 9.71.

Inheritance tax penalties

[9.79] In addition to the specific penalties mentioned at 9.58 and 9.69, someone required to deliver a return in connection with a settlement by a UK-domiciled settlor with non-resident trustees is liable to a penalty of up to £300 plus a daily penalty of up to £60 once the failure has been declared by a court or the tribunal.

Offshore asset move penalties (FA 2015, s 121 and Sch 21)

[9.80] An 'additional' penalty can be imposed for income tax, capital gains tax and inheritance tax where assets are moved from a 'specified territory' to a 'non-specified territory' and the main, or one of the main purposes, of the movement is to prevent the discovery of a loss of revenue by HMRC. The penalty will apply where:

(a) a person is liable for an earlier penalty for a failure to comply with certain income tax, capital gains tax or inheritance tax obligations; and

(b) there is a related transfer or change in ownership of an asset situated or held outside the UK to prevent or delay the discovery of that original failure.

The additional penalty is 50% of the amount of the original penalty payable in respect of the first failure. This penalty can be appealed in the usual manner.

See also **45.28** for civil penalties that apply from 1 January 2017 for deliberate enablers of offshore tax evasion where a person has become liable to a penalty under these provisions.

Penalty for failure to disclose offshore interests

[9.81] The September 2017 Finance Bill, which is expected to receive Royal Assent in November 2017, provides that a penalty can be imposed on individuals and businesses with undeclared UK tax liabilities in respect of offshore interests. The penalty can be imposed if they have not corrected the situation by disclosing the relevant information to HMRC within the 'requirement to correct' (RTC) period which runs from 6 April 2017 to 30 September 2018. The end of this period coincides with the date on which all signatory countries to the Common Reporting Standard will begin to exchange data (and which will enable HMRC more easily to pursue those who have not complied).

These provisions do not distinguish between careless and deliberate behaviour, but no penalty may be charged where the person has a reasonable excuse.

The penalty is 200% of the potential lost revenue that has not been corrected within the RTC period.

Overpayment relief (TMA 1970, ss 30–33 and Sch 1AB; FA 1998, s 117 and Sch 18)

[9.82] If income tax, corporation tax or capital gains tax has been paid and the taxpayer believes that the payment was excessive it is possible may make a claim for overpayment relief if no other statutory steps are available and the taxpayer has used any available rights of appeal. This claim must be made four years after the end of the relevant tax year or accounting period. HMRC are required to give such relief as is 'reasonable and just'. No relief is given if the return was made in accordance with practice generally prevailing at the time it was made provided the tax charged was not imposed contrary to EU law.

Official error (TMA 1970, s 43; FA 1998, s 117 and Sch 18; Concessions A19, B41)

[9.83] Unless a specific time limit is stated, the normal time limit for individuals to claim reliefs is four years after the end of the tax year. For companies the time limit is four years after the end of the relevant accounting period. Repayments will, however, be made on claims made outside the time limit where the overpayment was caused by an error by HMRC or another government department, providing the facts are not in dispute.

Where HMRC discover that they have undercharged income tax or capital gains tax, although they have been given full information at the proper time either by the taxpayer, or by his employer, or (in relation to pensions) by the Department for Works and Pensions, they may not collect the underpayment. This will apply only if the taxpayer could reasonably have believed his affairs to be in order.

Special relief (TMA 1970, Sch 1AB para 3A; FA 1998, Sch 18 para 51BA)

[9.84] The time limits for appealing against assessments, and for substituting a taxpayer's own self-assessment for an HMRC determination or simple assessment, are indicated at **9.43** and **9.46** respectively. If action is not taken within the time limits, the tax assessed or determined becomes payable. Where income tax (including tax due from employers under PAYE) or capital gains tax that has legally become due is higher than it would have been if all the relevant information had been submitted at the proper time, there is a statutory, 'special relief' available, which allows a claim for relief to be made for overpaid tax where the usual time limits for such relief have expired. Relief is only available if it would be unconscionable for HMRC to seek to recover the amount or to refuse to repay it, the claimant's tax affairs are otherwise up to date and the claimant has not previously claimed special relief. For HMRC guidance see HMRC Brief 17/2011.

Right of set-off (FA 2008, ss 130–133)

[9.85] HMRC have a statutory power to set-off any tax credit owed to a taxpayer against any tax owed by that taxpayer (except in an insolvency situation). Consequently if, for example, a taxpayer has a VAT credit but owes unpaid corporation tax then it will be offset.

Certificates of tax deposit

[9.86] Certificates of tax deposit may be purchased by individuals, partnerships, personal representatives, trustees or companies, subject to an initial deposit of £500, with minimum additions of £250. The certificates may be used to pay any tax except PAYE, VAT, tax deducted from payments to subcontractors and corporation tax, but may be used to pay Class 4 NICs. Interest accrues daily for a maximum of six years, and provision is made for varying interest rates during the term of the deposit. A lower rate of interest applies if the deposit is withdrawn for cash rather than used to settle tax liabilities. The interest accrued at the time the deposit is used or cashed is charged to tax. Tax deposit certificates are a way of ensuring that liquid resources are earmarked for the payment of tax when due. They also prevent the risk of interest charges when tax is in dispute, because when they are used to pay tax, interest on overdue tax will not be payable unless and to the extent that the deposit was made after the date the tax was due for payment. HMRC guidance and details of interest rates are provided at www.gov.uk/guidance/certificate-of-tax-deposit-scheme.

Disclosure opportunities

HMRC current campaigns

[9.87] HMRC regularly run specific campaigns targeted at particular groups of people, providing them with opportunities to voluntarily put their tax affairs in order in return for reduced penalties. Each campaign has time limits for making notifications, disclosures and payment and once the time limits have expired HMRC clamp down on those who have failed to respond.

Future campaigns are announced by HMRC. If a person thinks they may be affected by forthcoming campaigns they can come forward in advance of the official start date.

Participants are invited to settle their tax liabilities by agreement, without the need for litigation. Where people decline the settlement opportunity, HMRC has stated that it will increase the pace of investigations and accelerate disputes into litigation.

Disclosures of previously undeclared UK tax liabilities relating to offshore interests can be made through the Worldwide Disclosure Facility and via the online Digital Disclosure Service.

UK-Swiss agreement (FA 2012, Sch 36)

[9.88] In 2013 Switzerland introduced a new withholding tax on interest, dividends and gains. Also, for accounts held at 31 December 2010 which remained open on 31 May 2013, funds held by UK taxpayers in Swiss banks were subjected to a one-off deduction of between 21% and 41% to settle past tax liabilities (which was handed to the UK authorities). Thereafter ongoing withholding tax is applied.

Account holders can avoid these charges by declaring income and gains from a Swiss asset to HMRC and by consenting to the disclosure of their details by the bank to HMRC. Certain transfers made under this agreement do not give rise to a taxable remittance where they are made by a person who is taxed on the remittance basis (see **41.16**).

US FATCA (FA 2013, s 222; SI 2013/1962)

[9.89] Regulations implement the US Foreign Account Tax Compliance Act (FATCA) provisions. The FATCA provisions are US legislation aimed at reducing tax evasion by US citizens. They require financial institutions outside the US to pass information about the accounts of US persons to the US tax administration. Any institution that fails to comply with this is liable to a 30% withholding tax on any US source income. In the UK, certain financial institutions are required to provide HMRC with the necessary information. HMRC will then forward that information to the US tax authorities.

The US has agreed to provide the UK with reciprocal data on the US accounts of UK persons.

Other international tax compliance agreements (SI 2014/520)

[9.90] Regulations came into force on 31 March 2014 and implement the FATCA-style agreements on international tax compliance between the UK and Isle of Man, Guernsey, Jersey and Gibraltar.

Tax points

[9.91] Note the following:

- Self-assessment is a difficult exercise even for those with straightforward tax affairs. Remember that individuals *do not have to calculate their own tax*, but a paper return must be submitted by 31 October to avoid a late filing penalty and it would be sensible to ensure that HMRC will calculate the tax in time for tax payments to be made on the due dates.
- Companies must pay their tax and file their tax returns promptly. If they fail to meet the deadlines, they incur automatic interest and penalties. Companies should also be aware of the company law penalties for late filing of accounts.
- It is essential to retain records relating to tax affairs for a stipulated period (see 9.32). HMRC guidance is available at www.gov.uk/keeping-your-pay-tax-records.
- Where a claim is made to backdate a loss incurred or payment made to an earlier year, the resulting tax etc. adjustment is made for the tax year of loss or payment, so there is no extra benefit in terms of interest on tax overpaid.
- If starting a new business, HMRC will probably need extra information, and they may only be able to get this by making an enquiry into a return. It may therefore be advisable to submit full accounts and explanatory notes (for example the source of monies introduced to start the business) with the tax return (see 9.41 to 9.42).
- The self-employed, with a turnover of less than £85,000 a year (£83,000 for 2016–17), need only show turnover, allowable expenses and net profit on their tax return. They must still have detailed records in case HMRC want to see them.
- If a taxpayer is aware of irregularities in his tax affairs, a full disclosure to HMRC before they make a challenge will ensure the maximum penalty reduction when an offer in settlement is eventually made. Furthermore, a payment on account of the tax eventually to be accounted for will reduce the interest charge and also possibly any penalty.

- Whilst HMRC will usually settle for a cash sum comprising tax, interest and penalties, they may also take criminal proceedings in cases which they believe amount to provable fraud. They may still seek a civil money penalty on those aspects not brought before the court or where the taxpayer has been acquitted of fraud and they feel able to prove negligence (HMRC codes of practice COP 8 and COP 9).
- HMRC have substantial powers to require banks, lawyers, accountants etc. to provide information and documents that may be relevant in establishing tax liabilities, including cross-border agreements with other countries.
- If business accounts or taxation affairs generally are under investigation, HMRC will issue appropriate leaflets and their Code of Practice. These are no substitute for appropriate professional representation but they do explain taxpayer's rights and are helpful in explaining HMRC procedures.

Part III

Employment

10

Employments: taxable income and allowable deductions

Introduction

[10.1] The tax law relating to employment income is contained in the Income Tax (Earnings and Pensions) Act 2003 (ITEPA 2003), as amended by later Finance Acts. ITEPA 2003 deals with employment income (Pts 2–8), pension income (Pt 9) and social security benefits (Pt 10). This chapter discusses employment income and taxable social security benefits. Pensions are dealt with in CHAPTERS 16 and 17.

Basis of charge (ITEPA 2003, ss 1–13, 44–47, 682–686)

[10.2] The legislation covers the employment earnings of employees and directors. Tax on such earnings is normally collected by employers through the Pay As You Earn (PAYE) scheme, which also deals with the collection of national insurance contributions (NICs). Class 1 NICs are payable by employees and employers and accounted for by employers along with the tax on the earnings, and Class 1A NICs on employee benefits are payable by employers only and accounted for at the tax year end (see **10.66**). Employees' and employers' NICs are also discussed in CHAPTER 13.

It is often hard to decide whether someone is employed or self-employed — see CHAPTER 19. If an employer wrongly treats an employee as self-employed, he is liable for the PAYE and NICs that should have applied, with only limited rights of recovery from the employee of his share. The worker who is classed as employed rather than self-employed will find significant differences in his allowable expenses, the timing of tax payments and the liability for NICs.

Some members of limited liability partnerships are treated as employed, see **23.33**.

Most agency workers are required to be treated as employees and there are rules to prevent the avoidance of employment taxes and obligations by disguising employment as self-employment. The agency is usually responsible for the operation of PAYE but the client is responsible if he pays the worker direct. For the rules which ensure that the correct amount of tax and NICs is paid when UK and UK Continental Shelf workers are employed by offshore companies or engaged by or through offshore employment intermediaries, see **41.22**.

Agencies are normally required to deduct PAYE tax and NICs from payments to construction workers supplied by them — see CHAPTER **44** for further guidance on construction workers.

Anti-avoidance

IR35 rules (ITEPA 2003, ss 48–61; FA 2017, s 6 and Sch 1)

[10.3] Special rules known as the IR35 rules prevent the avoidance of tax and NICs by operating through a personal service company rather than being employed directly (see **19.4** to **19.12**). Further rules relate to 'managed service companies', which are subject to separate rules rather than the IR35 rules. Payments to those working for such companies are treated as employment income if they would not otherwise be so treated, and various other special provisions apply. From 2017–18 reforms have been made to the treatment of public sector engagements. See **19.14** to **19.18**.

Sale of income from personal occupation (ITA 2007, ss 773–789)

[10.4] This prevents those with high personal earning potential, such as entertainers, avoiding tax by means of contracting their services to a company in which they hold the shares and thereby turning income into capital by later selling the shares at a price reflecting the personal earnings.

Employment income provided through third parties (ITEPA 2003, Pt 7A; SI 2016/1250)

[10.5] There is anti-avoidance legislation aimed at employees, directors and employers who use arrangements involving trusts and other vehicles to avoid, reduce or defer income tax liabilities on rewards of employment, or to avoid restrictions on pensions tax relief. The legislation applies in certain circumstances where employees and their employers enter into arrangements which result in a payment of money or the provision of an asset by a third party rather than the employer. The legislation creates a tax charge applying to—

(a)   certain loans of money or assets to the employee by the third party;

(b)   the earmarking of money or assets for the employee by the third party, and in very limited circumstances by the employer; and

(c)   the outright payments of money or transfer of assets to the employee by the third party (including, from 6 April 2017, the transfer or release of loans, although certain employment-related loans which do not exceed £10,000 are excluded);

where these would not otherwise be taxed as earnings from employment (see, in particular **10.29** and **10.67**). This is commonly known as the charge on disguised remuneration.

Third party intermediary arrangements are often used in addition to registered pension schemes to remunerate individuals above the annual and lifetime allowances (for example employer-financed retirement benefit schemes — see **16.50**), and this legislation applies to those arrangements. However, third party arrangements which are not tax avoidance are not included.

Broadly, a charge to tax (and NIC) is made if—

(i)   a person (A) is a present, former or prospective employee of another person (B);

(ii)   there is an arrangement to which A is a party or which relates to A;

(iii)   it is reasonable to suppose that the arrangement is a means of providing rewards or recognition or loans in connection with A's employment with B;

(iv)   a 'relevant step' is taken by a third party; and

(v)   it is reasonable to suppose that the relevant step is taken in pursuance of the relevant arrangement or there is some other connection between the relevant step and the arrangement.

A relevant step is one of the methods of reward outlined in (a) to (c) above and such a step still occurs where the underlying transaction is void or in breach of trust. The tax and NIC charge is based on the sum of money made available, or on the higher of cost or market value of the asset provided or transferred. The amount concerned is treated as a payment of employment income and subject to PAYE and NIC.

Where A is temporarily non-resident (see **41.49**) certain relevant steps which relate to the payment of lump sums under a relevant scheme are treated as if they were taken in the period of return. A relevant scheme is either a employer-financed retirement benefit scheme or a superannuation fund administered in the UK to provide pensions for employees working wholly overseas in an overseas trade.

These provisions do not apply to sporting testimonial payments made under the rules outlined in **10.12**.

September 2017 Finance Bill which is expected to receive Royal Assent in November 2017 introduces a tax charge on loans or equivalent arrangements from disguised remuneration schemes which were made after 5 April 1999 and are outstanding at 5 April 2019. Certain loans, such as those made on commercial terms, are excluded from the charge.

For HMRC's views on the application of the legislation see HMRC Employment Income Manual EIM45000 onwards.

Social security benefits (ITEPA 2003, ss 660–677; Pensions Act 2014, ss 30–32, Sch 16)

[10.6] The tax treatment of social security benefits is complex and the detailed rules are outside the scope of this book. The list below shows which of the main social security benefits are taxable and which are exempt. See the TABLE OF RATES AND ALLOWANCES (**TRA**) for the current amounts payable. A list of taxable and non-taxable social security benefits can be found at HMRC Employment Income Manual EIM76100 to EIM76101.

TAXABLE:

— Bereavement allowance and widowed parent's allowance*
— Carer's allowance*
— Incapacity benefit* (after first 28 weeks)
— Employment and support allowance (if contribution-based)
— Industrial death benefit paid as pension
— Jobseeker's allowance (up to the 'taxable maximum')
— State pension
— Statutory maternity pay, statutory paternity pay and statutory adoption pay
— Statutory sick pay

*Excluding any addition for dependent children

EXEMPT:

— Attendance allowance
— Back to work bonus
— Bereavement payment, and bereavement support payment
— Child benefit* and child's special allowance
— Christmas bonus and winter fuel payment for pensioners
— Cold weather payments
— Disability living allowance
— Employment and support allowance (if income-related)
— Guardian's allowance
— Housing benefit
— Incapacity benefit (for first 28 weeks of entitlement)
— Incapacity benefit to those receiving the former invalidity benefit at 12 April 1995 for the same incapacity
— Income support (except where the claimant is involved in a trade dispute and is claiming in respect of a partner)
— Industrial injuries benefit
— Maternity allowance
— Pension credit
— Personal independence payment
— Severe disablement allowance
— Tax credits (see **2.34**)
— Universal credit
— War widow's pension

*But see **10.7** regarding the high income child benefit charge

The Welfare Reform Act 2012 introduced universal credit in Great Britain to replace the complex system of working-age benefits and tax credits. The process of moving claimants on to universal credit will be gradual and should be completed by 2021. Universal credit is exempt from income tax. The following social security benefits will be abolished when universal credit is fully phased in—

(a)   Income support;
(b)   Income-based jobseeker's allowance;
(c)   Income-related employment and support allowance;
(d)   Housing benefit;
(e)   Child tax credit and working tax credit.

Budgeting loans and crisis loan alignment payments are being replaced by payments on account (an advance of universal credit) in cases of need. Council tax benefit, crisis loans for other needs and community care grants have also been abolished. Responsibility for an equivalent has been passed to local authorities or devolved governments. Council tax benefit was replaced by council tax reduction.

All other benefits will remain, including—

(i)   Contribution-based jobseeker's allowance;
(ii)   Contributory employment and support allowance;
(iii)   Child benefit;
(iv)   Carer's allowance;
(v)   Bereavement payment, bereavement allowance, widowed parent's allowance, and bereavement support payment;
(vi)   Maternity allowance;
(vii)   Industrial injuries disablement allowance;
(viii)   Statutory maternity, paternity and adoption pay;
(ix)   Statutory sick pay; and
(x)   Maternity grants, funeral payments and cold weather payments.

Disability living allowance for adults of working age is gradually being replaced by personal independence payment (PIP). Bereavement support payment has replaced bereavement allowance, bereavement payment and widowed parent's allowance for persons whose spouse or civil partner dies on or after 6 April 2017, and is exempt from tax.

A cap has been placed on the total amount of benefit that most people aged 16 to 64 can receive. The cap applies to the total amount that the people in a household receive from certain benefits. From 7 November 2016 the cap is £384.61 a week (or £442.30 in Greater London) for couples (with or without children living with them) and single parents whose children live with them, and £257.69 (or £296.34 in Greater London) a week for single adults who don't have children, or whose children don't live with them. See www.gov.uk/benefit-cap.

High income child benefit charge (SSAA 1992, s 13A; ITEPA 2003, ss 681B–681H)

[10.7] An income tax charge applies to a taxpayer who is entitled to child benefit (or whose partner is entitled to child benefit) and whose adjusted net income (see **2.20**) exceeds £50,000 in a tax year. Where both partners have income exceeding the limit the charge applies to the partner with the higher income.

The charge is equal to 1% of the amount of child benefit for every £100 of net income above £50,000, and will be on the full amount of child benefit where net income exceeds £60,000. It only applies to weeks in which there is entitlement to child benefit or, in cases where the charge arises because the taxpayer's partner is in receipt of child benefit, to weeks throughout which they are partners. Partners are a married couple or those in a civil partnership who are not separated under a court order or in circumstances likely to become permanent, and a couple who are not married or in a civil partnership but who are living together as if they were so.

> **Example 1**
>
> A taxpayer has net adjusted income of £58,000 and receives child benefit for two children of £1,789 for a complete tax year. The percentage charge is calculated as follows:
> $$£58,000 - £50,000 = 8,000/100 = 80\%.$$
> Thus the charge equals 80% of £1,789 — i.e. £1,431.

Where the child does not live with the child benefit claimant, but with another individual or individuals who have net income over £50,000 and who receive the value of the child benefit directly or indirectly from the child benefit claimant, the charge falls on the individual with the highest income with whom the child is living. The exception to this is where the claimant had previously claimed child benefit on the basis that they were living with the child and after a period of less than 52 weeks they resume the claim on the same basis.

There are provisions to ensure that the charge does not arise on any child benefit payment made after the death of a child, and that no double charge arises in the case of polygamous marriages.

Taxpayers must notify their liability to the charge and are required to complete a self-assessment return. The charge can be avoided if the person entitled to child benefit elects not to receive it. The election can be revoked at a later date to restore payment of child benefit, and where the election was made in the erroneous belief that the charge would arise, it may be revoked within two years from the end of the tax year in order for child benefit for that period to be paid.

The charge is collected via a PAYE coding adjustment where possible, unless the taxpayer objects.

Health and employment insurance payments (ITEPA 2003, s 325A; ITTOIA 2005, ss 735–743)

[10.8] Benefits payable under an insurance policy taken out to cover periods of sickness or unemployment are exempt from tax. Such policies include mortgage protection policies, permanent health insurance and insurance to meet domestic bills etc. Various conditions must be satisfied, in particular no deduction must have been received for the premiums in calculating taxable income.

Persons liable (ITEPA 2003, Pt 2)

[10.9] Liability to tax on earnings depends on the individual's country of residence and domicile. From 2013–14 a statutory residence test applies. Broadly, domicile is the country regarded as the individual's permanent home (subject to further caveats that apply from 6 April 2017; see **41.10**). See **41.7** to **41.14** regarding residence and domicile.

Currently, an individual who is resident and domiciled in the UK is normally charged to tax on world-wide earnings. Non-residents are liable to tax on their UK earnings.

Personal reliefs are available only to UK residents and specified categories of non-resident (see **41.36**). An individual is not entitled to personal reliefs for any tax year for which he claims the remittance basis (see **41.16**). Liability to UK and overseas tax may be varied by double taxation agreements. See **41.22** regarding UK residents working abroad and **41.39** regarding a non-resident's UK earnings.

Taxable earnings (ITEPA 2003, ss 9–13, 226E, 306B, 312A–312I)

[10.10] Pay for income tax purposes includes wages, salaries, commissions, bonuses, tips and certain benefits in kind. To count as pay, earnings must be 'in the nature of a reward for services rendered, past, present or future'. See CHAPTER 15 for lump sum payments received on taking up or ceasing employment.

Pay for the purpose of Class 1 NICs is broadly the same as pay for income tax. There are, however, still some instances where the treatment differs, and it is essential to study carefully the employers' guides provided by HMRC, in particular CWG2, the appendix of which provides a list of other useful HMRC forms and guidance. It can be accessed online at www.gov.uk/government/pu blications/cwg2-further-guide-to-paye-and-national-insurance-contributions.

Employers' Class 1A NICs are payable on virtually all benefits in kind (see **10.49**), except where the benefits are included in a PAYE settlement agreement and contributions are paid under Class 1B (see **10.69**).

Pay for Class 1 NICs is not reduced by charitable payments under the payroll deduction scheme (see **43.23**), nor by the employee's occupational or personal pension contributions. Employer contributions to registered company pension schemes, or to certain other employer-finance schemes, or an employee's registered pension plan, do not count as earnings for either tax or NICs but only where paid in respect of the employee — see CHAPTERS 16 and 17.

The treatment of tips and service charges depends on how they are paid. PAYE and NIC does not apply if the customer gives a cash tip directly to the employee and the employee keeps it without the involvement of the employer. However the employee should notify HMRC of any tips received and tax will usually be deducted by an adjustment to the employee's PAYE tax code. Both PAYE and NIC should be deducted by the employer from compulsory service charges added to customers' bills. If the distribution of tips and voluntary service charges is decided by the employer then PAYE and NIC should be deducted. If the distribution is decided by someone else such as a troncmaster but the payment is by the employer, PAYE but not NIC should be deducted. Where a troncmaster is responsible for distributing tips and voluntary service charges the employer must notify HMRC of the arrangements as soon as he is aware. The troncmaster will have to operate a computerised payroll and deduct PAYE when paying employees. Where this is the case and someone other than the employer decides the distribution, then again NIC is not due. However if the employer is directly or indirectly involved in the distribution of the money, then the employer must pay the NIC through his own PAYE scheme. See www.gov.uk/government/publications/e24-tips-gratuities-service-charges-and-troncs.

If an employer pays a bill that the employee has incurred and is legally liable to pay, this counts as the equivalent of a payment of salary. The employee is charged Class 1 NICs, but not income tax, at the time the employer pays the bill. The employer will show the payment on the year-end form P11D (see 10.67), and the tax on it will be included in the amount of tax the employee owes for the year. Details of the NIC and P11D treatment of various common benefits can be found in HMRC booklet CWG5 Appendix 1, see www.gov.uk/government/publications/cwg5-class-1a-national-insurance-contributions-on-benefits-in-kind.

Employers must deduct and account for tax and Class 1 NICs under PAYE when they provide pay in certain non-cash forms — see 10.31.

Tax is charged on the earnings received in the tax year if an employee is resident and domiciled in the UK, no matter what period the earnings relate to. Certain expenses incurred may be deducted in arriving at the taxable earnings — see 10.14 and 10.15.

See 11.36 regarding the income tax and capital gains tax provisions relating to employee shareholder status, under which employees give up certain employment rights in return for shares in their employer's company.

[10.11] An exemption from income tax applies on qualifying bonus payments of up to £3,600 made to employees (and former employees where the payment is made within 12 months of their employment ceasing), of certain qualifying employee-owned companies (other than certain service companies). The £3,600 limit applies separately where an employee receives such a payment from more than one employer, other than where the employers are in the same group. A qualifying bonus payment is an amount other than regular salary that is paid to all employees of the company (or group of which it is a member) on equal terms, although the bonus can be set by reference to a percentage of salary, or length of service, or hours worked.

The company must be a trading company, or be a member of a trading group, and must be controlled (or the principal company of the group must be controlled in the case of a group company) by a trust which is broadly for the benefit of all eligible employees on the same terms (see **4.38** for details of how the trustees can breach this requirement in certain circumstances). The number of directors or office-holders (or company employees connected with them) must not exceed 2/5 of the total number of employees both on the date of payment and throughout the 12 months preceding payment with the exception of 90 days. The trustees will have control if they hold a majority of the company's shares, are entitled to the majority of profits available for distribution and are entitled to a majority of assets available for distribution on a winding up.

Note that there is no NICs exemption for such bonus payments, either for the employer or the employee.

For related capital gains tax exemptions see **4.38**. For IHT provisions see **5.18**, **5.19** and **42.49**.

[10.12] Where the right to a sporting testimonial is written into a sportsperson's contract, or where their club always grants a testimonial after a set qualifying period of service, the proceeds are taxable as earnings and NIC is payable. Where this is not the case, HMRC's practice has been to treat the proceeds as exempt. For sporting testimonial events held on or after 6 April 2017 where the testimonial has been awarded on or after 25 November 2015, income arising from a non-contractual or non-customary sporting testimonial for an employed sportsperson is liable to income tax and NIC as employment income although it will be subject to an exemption for the first £100,000. The exemption is available for 12 months beginning with the date the first testimonial event is held. For HMRC guidance see www.gov.uk/guidance/sporting-testimonials-income-tax-and-national-insurance-payments. The disguised remuneration provisions (see **10.5**) do not apply to the making of a sporting testimonial payment.

Reporting benefits and expenses (ITEPA 2003, s 684; SI 2016/1137)

[10.13] The rules outlined below in **10.14** to **10.56** apply to the reporting of benefits and expenses and any benefits which are liable to tax and NIC at the time they are paid must be included on the Full Payment Submission (FPS). See www.gov.uk/employer-reporting-expenses-benefits.

A statutory framework for voluntary payrolling of benefits in kind applies and employers are able to opt to payroll all benefits other than living accommodation and beneficial loans (vouchers and credit tokens having been added from 6 April 2017). Where they do so, they do not have to make a return on form P11D for these benefits, but can instead report the value of the benefits through Real Time Information (RTI, see **10.58**). The cash equivalent of the benefit (see **10.29**) is pro-rated over the number of pay days in the tax year for each employee, and the resulting amount is the amount on which PAYE must be operated on each pay day.

HMRC opened a 'payrolling benefits-in-kind' online service and employers must register well before the start of the tax year in which they wish to use it. Once an employer starts payrolling benefits, they must continue to do so for the full tax year unless either there is insufficient income to cover the tax on the benefit or they stop paying the benefit to the employee. If the employer stops payrolling benefits for other reasons penalties for incorrect returns will apply.

Class 1A NICs must still be reported and paid separately (see **10.49**). Employers will be required to provide an annual statement to their employees of the total taxable amount of the benefits on which PAYE has been operated.

For HMRC guidance see www.gov.uk/guidance/payrolling-tax-employees-ben efits-and-expenses-through-your-payroll.

From 6 April 2016 exempt expenses paid to an employee are no longer required to be entered on a form P11D (see **10.16**). However, if an employer pays non-allowable expenses, or a scale rate that is not an approved scale rate, or they do not operate a suitable checking system, or they pay expenses through a salary sacrifice (or similar) arrangement (as to which, see **10.30**) they must operate PAYE on those payments. Legislation specifically provides that non-approved mileage allowance payments and non-approved passenger payments should be included on the P11D. There is also still a requirement for employers to make annual returns on form P11D where they pay an expense on behalf of their employee, or provide an employee with a non-cash benefit in kind (see **10.67**), but payrolled expenses and benefits need not be included.

Allowable expenses and deductions (ITEPA 2003, ss 316A, 333–360A, 555–564; ITA 2007, ss 24A, 128)

Travelling expenses paid by the employee

[10.14] In arriving at taxable pay, an employee can deduct expenses that he is obliged to incur and pay as holder of the employment and that are incurred wholly, exclusively and necessarily in the performance of the duties of that employment. Relatively few expenses satisfy this stringent rule. Others are specifically allowable by statute or by concession. HMRC provide guidance on various expenses and benefits at www.gov.uk/expenses-and-benefits-a-to-z.

An employee can deduct qualifying travelling expenses. He is entitled to relief for the full cost he is obliged to incur in travelling in the performance of his duties or travelling to or from a place he has to attend in the performance of his duties, as long as the journey is not ordinary commuting between his home and his permanent workplace or private travel (i.e. travel for a private rather than business purpose).

Site-based employees with no permanent workplace are allowed the cost of travelling to and from home (unless the job at the site is expected to last for more than 24 months, in which case the site counts as a permanent workplace). The 24-month rule does not allow home to work travelling expenses to be claimed by someone whose *employment*, as distinct from temporary place of work, is expected to last 24 months or less.

The full cost of meals and accommodation while travelling or staying away on business is allowable as part of the cost of travel. Business travel includes travelling on business from home where the nature of the job requires the employee to carry out his duties at home (but doing work at home for convenience rather than because of the nature of the job does not turn home into a workplace). Where a journey has both a business and a private purpose, the expense will be allowed if the journey is substantially for business purposes.

A deduction is allowed for certain travel expenses of directors for journeys between their workplace and that of a 'linked' employment with another company. An exemption from income tax also applies to the payment or reimbursement of certain employment-related travel expenses (such as from home to board meetings) of unpaid directors of not-for-profit companies.

In most cases the employer will reimburse allowable expenses, so that expenditure is balanced by the employer's payment. Where this is not the case, the employee needs to claim tax relief himself. See **10.26** regarding expenses paid or reimbursed by the employer.

Other expenses paid by the employee

[10.15] Flat rate expenses allowances are available for the upkeep of tools and special clothing in various occupations, although this does not stop an employee claiming relief for the actual cost if that is higher. The flat rate expenses currently allowable are listed in HMRC's Employment Income Manual at EIM32712. See also EIM50125 regarding the laundering of armed forces uniforms. The cost of normal clothing is not allowed even if it costs more than the employee would normally pay and he would not wear the clothes outside work.

If it is *necessary* for an employee to work at home, he may claim the appropriate proportion of the cost of light, heat, telephone calls, etc, but not council tax. Reasonable expenses payments by employers to cover additional household expenses where an employee regularly works at home under homeworking arrangements are exempt from tax. HMRC have stated that up to £4 a week, or £18 per month for monthly paid employees, may currently be paid without supporting evidence of actual costs. They will allow a similar deduction for expenses met by the employee himself. See HMRC's Employment Income Manual at EIM32760 to EIM32830 for their views on when relief for homeworking expenses is allowable. See also **10.29** regarding exempt benefits, some of which enable employers to provide those working at home with furniture, supplies etc, without a tax charge, where private use is insignificant. See also **30.24**.

The courts have decided that a deduction for training costs incurred by an employee should be allowed if the employee was employed on a training contract where training was an intrinsic contractual duty of the employment — see HMRC Employment Income Manual EIM32535. See **10.55** for the treatment of work-related training costs paid or reimbursed by the employer.

Other allowable expenses include contributions to a registered pension scheme (see CHAPTERS **16** and **17**), charitable donations under the payroll giving scheme (see **43.23**) and most professional subscriptions that are relevant to a job — see www.gov.uk/government/publications/professional-bodies-approved-for-tax-r elief-list-3. The cost of business entertaining is not allowed, but the disallowance may fall on the employee or on the employer depending on how payment is made. A deduction cannot be claimed for entertaining expenses paid out of salary or out of a round sum allowance. See **10.26** regarding expenses paid or reimbursed by the employer.

An employee can claim a deduction in calculating the tax on his earnings for:

(a) Capital allowances (see CHAPTER **22**) if he buys equipment that is necessarily provided for use in his job. The allowances are restricted by reference to any private use, and are not available for expenditure on a car, van, motor cycle or cycle, for which mileage allowances are available instead (see **10.17**).

(b) Interest on money borrowed to finance the purchase of such equipment (restricted by any private use proportion). Relief is not available for interest due and payable more than three years after the end of the period of account (for capital allowances purposes) in which the loan was made.

An employee who meets the cost of directors' liability insurance, professional indemnity insurance and work-related uninsured liabilities (provided the main purpose(s) of the payment is not the avoidance of tax) may treat it as an allowable expense. This treatment is extended to payments made by him at any time up to six years after the end of the tax year in which the employment ends, but is subject to the cap on certain reliefs from 2013–14 (see **2.13**). Any excess that cannot be set off against total income may be treated as a loss for capital gains tax purposes (see **25.7**). For payments by the employer see **10.26**.

Tax relief for a loss in employment may be available in limited circumstances. HMRC have previously stated that the loss must arise directly from the conditions of the employment and the employee must be contractually obliged to suffer a part of the employer's loss, for example a salesperson responsible for bad debts arising from orders taken by him. Where the relief is available it may be claimed against the total income of the year of loss or the previous year, or both, subject to restrictions for 2013–14 onwards as explained in **2.13**. Any unused loss may be treated as a loss for capital gains tax purposes (see **25.7**). Relief is denied for employment losses derived from arrangements, one of the main purposes of which is the avoidance of tax.

Expenses payments and reimbursed expenses

Exemption for paid or reimbursed expenses (ITEPA 2003, ss 289A–289E)

[10.16] The strict application of the rule for allowable expenses would require all expenses payments to employees to be treated as employment income, leaving the employee to claim relief for the allowable part. To avoid a lot of unnecessary work, certain paid or reimbursed expenses are exempted from 6 April 2016 provided the payment or reimbursement is not made as part of a salary sacrifice arrangement (as to which, see **10.30**). The exemption applies if an amount equal to or exceeding the payment or reimbursement, made by either the employer or a third party, would be a deductible expense. The exemption also applies if employees are paid a scale rate in respect of a qualifying expense provided there is a system in place for checking that the deductible expense is actually incurred, and neither the payer nor any other person operating the system knows or suspects that the employee is not incurring the deductible expense. The scale rate can either be a rate set by HMRC in secondary legislation, or a rate that has been agreed with HMRC. For HMRC guidance see www.gov.uk/employer-reporting-expenses-benefits/d ispensations.

See **10.13** regarding the reporting of expenses.

Travelling and subsistence expenses (ITEPA 2003, ss 229–249)

[10.17] There is a statutory system of tax-free approved mileage allowances for business journeys in an employee's own transport. He is taxable only on any excess over the approved rates and employers should operate PAYE on it (see **10.13**). The mileage rates are as follows:

Cars and vans:	First 10,000 miles in tax year	45p per mile
	Each additional mile	25p per mile
Motor cycles		24p per mile
Cycles		20p per mile

If the employer pays less than these amounts, the employee can claim tax relief for the unused balance of the approved amount.

From 6 April 2016 there is an exemption from income tax and NICs for qualifying payments made by a local authority in respect of travel expenses incurred by a member on a journey between home and permanent workplace, provided the member's home is in the area of the authority or within 20 miles of the boundary of the area. The exemption for mileage payments is limited to the authorised mileage rates above.

Payment by the employer of congestion charges in London (or elsewhere) will in the first instance count as an employee benefit where an employee uses his own car, and will be offset by an equivalent allowable expense if incurred on business travel.

[10.18] For NICs, the NICs-free rates for motor cycles and cycles are the same as for tax. For cars and vans, the NICs-free amounts are based on the 45p rate regardless of the number of business miles travelled. The *total* amount paid in the pay period (whether as a rate per mile or regular or one-off lump sum payment) is compared with the NICs-free amount for the number of business miles travelled and Class 1 contributions are payable on any excess. HMRC have argued that there must be a clear link between the payment made and the actual use of the vehicle for the payments to be NIC-free, but the Court of Appeal has held that the fact that payments were not directly linked to mileage did not prevent them from qualifying as relevant motoring expenditure. If an employee is paid less than the NICs-free amount there is no relief for the balance.

[10.19] If an employee carries fellow employees on business trips, either in his own car or van or an employer's car or van, and receives mileage allowance payments (see **10.17**), the employer may pay up to 5p per mile for each fellow employee free of tax and NICs. The employee cannot claim any relief if the employer does not pay an allowance.

[10.20] See **7.5** regarding VAT and fuel for business vehicles.

[10.21] An employee away from home overnight on business is exempt from tax and NICs on payment or reimbursement by his employer of incidental personal expenses such as newspapers and telephone calls so long as they do not exceed a VAT inclusive amount of £5 a night (£10 if outside the UK) and certain conditions are met.

HMRC publish annual scale rates which employers may use when paying accommodation and subsistence expenses to employees whose duties require them to travel abroad, without the need for the employees to produce expenses receipts. Employees will not be liable for tax or NICs on payments at or below the published rates and employers need not include them on forms P11D. If an employer decides to pay less than the published rates employees are not automatically entitled to tax relief for the shortfall. They can only obtain relief for their actual expenses, less any amounts paid by their employer. These tax/NIC-free amounts are in addition to the incidental overnight expenses that employers may reimburse. See further www.gov.uk/government/publications/scale-rate-expenses-payments-employee-travelling-outside-the-uk.

Removal and relocation expenses (ITEPA 2003, ss 271–289)

[10.22] When an employee moves home because of his job, qualifying removal expenses and benefits are exempt from income tax up to a maximum of £8,000 per move, providing they are incurred, broadly speaking, during the period from the date of the job change to the end of the next following tax year. In order for the expenses and benefits to qualify for relief various conditions must be satisfied. Allowable expenses include expenses of disposing of the old property and buying another, removal expenses, providing replacement domestic goods, travelling and subsistence, and bridging loan expenses (see **30.22**).

Employers do not have to operate PAYE on qualifying expenses payments and benefits, even if they exceed £8,000, but PAYE applies to non-qualifying expenses payments if reimbursed to the employee. Qualifying expenses payments and benefits in excess of £8,000, and non-qualifying expenses and benefits, other than those reimbursed to the employee and taxed under PAYE, must be reported on year-end form P11D.

Where an employer makes a payment to an employee to compensate him for a fall in value when he sells his home, the payment is fully taxable as earnings. It does not qualify for relief as a relocation expense. See **10.23** regarding selling the home to the employer or a relocation company and sharing in a later profit.

As far as NICs are concerned, Class 1 contributions are charged on all relocation expenses payments that are not eligible for tax relief, except where the contract is between the supplier and the employer, in which case Class 1A employer's contributions are payable (see **10.49**). No contributions are payable on qualifying removal expenses and benefits up to £8,000, but Class 1A contributions are payable on any excess over £8,000.

Sale of home to relocation company or to employer (TCGA 1992, s 225C)

[10.23] Where there is a guaranteed selling price scheme, the treatment depends on the precise details of the scheme. There will, however, be no taxable benefit where an employee sells his home to the employer or a relocation company at market value and pays his own selling expenses. HMRC guidance is available in the Employment Income Manual at EIM03130.

Where the employee has a right to share in any later profits when the home is sold, he will be exempt from capital gains tax on any additional amount paid to him to the same extent as he was exempt on the original sale (see CHAPTER 30), providing the later sale occurs within three years. Part of the original gain may have been chargeable because the home had not always been the main residence, or had been let, etc., in which case the same proportion of the later amount will be chargeable.

Mobile telephones, home telephones and internet access (ITEPA 2003, ss 316, 316A, 319)

[10.24] The provision to an employee of a single mobile phone, including line rental and private calls paid directly by an employer on that phone, is exempt.

Before 6 April 2006 this exemption covered the provision of phones both to an employee and to his family and household. Where such provision was made, the exemption continues to apply to those particular phones.

Provision of a mobile phone solely for business use is exempt under the general rule discussed at **10.29** (accommodation, supplies or services used in performing the duties of the employment) so long as any private use is not significant.

HMRC accept that smartphones (as understood and configured at the start of January 2012) qualify as mobile phones. Full details are given in HMRC Brief 02/2012.

If the employee contracts to pay the bills for the mobile phone, but the bills are paid by the employer, the amounts should be included on form P11D and Class 1 NICs paid. If the employer reimburses the employee, the employee is liable to tax and Class 1 NICs on the amount reimbursed. In both cases there may be an appropriate deduction for an amount that is wholly and exclusively attributable to business calls, but it will depend on the terms of the contract whether there is in fact a cost to the employee of business calls.

[10.25] If an employer pays an employee's home telephone bills, then unless private use is insignificant, the amounts should be included on form P11D and Class 1 NICs paid on the amounts paid for line rental and private calls. The employee may claim a tax deduction for business calls. If the employer reimburses the employee for the cost of the bills, the employee is liable to tax and Class 1 NICs (via the payroll) on the amount paid by the employer for the line rental and private calls.

If the employer is the subscriber rather than the employee then, unless any private use is insignificant, the full amount of rental and charges must be included on form P11D. The employee may claim a tax deduction for business calls. The employer is liable for Class 1A NICs on both the line rental and the calls, unless the employee has made good the cost of private calls. If on the other hand there is a clear business need for the telephone to be provided, and the employer has procedures to ensure that private calls are kept to a minimum, the employee may not be taxed either on the line rental or the calls if the cost of the calls is insignificant compared with the total cost. In this event Class 1A contributions would not be due either.

If an employer pays for broadband internet connection in an employee's home solely for work purposes, any private use being insignificant and no break-down being possible between work and private use, and the cost of the package is not affected by the private use, the cost of the connection will not be a taxable benefit. If the employee pays for the internet connection and is reimbursed by his employer, it will not usually be possible to identify a separate business element, so that the employee will be taxed on the reimbursement and will not be entitled to any expenses deduction. However, payments made by an employer to reimburse the employee for 'reasonable additional costs' incurred whilst working at home may be exempt from tax. HMRC guidance indicates that such costs would include a broadband subscription where an employee who does not have a broadband connection needs one in order to work from home, but payments to an employee who already subscribes for broadband would not be exempt.

Other expenses payments

[10.26] If an employee receives a specific entertaining allowance from his employer or he is specifically reimbursed for entertaining expenses, he is not taxed on the amount received, provided it is for business purposes, but no deduction for it can be claimed by the employer in calculating his taxable profit (see **10.67** for the PAYE treatment).

An employee does not have to pay either tax or NICs on any payment by his employer to meet the cost of directors' liability insurance, professional indemnity insurance and work-related uninsured liabilities provided the main purpose(s) of the payment is not the avoidance of tax. This treatment is extended to payments made by his employer at any time up to six years after the end of the tax year in which the employment ends. September 2017 Finance Bill, which is expected to receive Royal Assent in November 2017, includes provisions to extend this relief from 2017–18 to cover cases where no allegation is made against the employee, such as the requirement to give evidence before a public inquiry. The amended legislation will also ensure that payments made on behalf of individuals subject to a termination settlement or the personal representatives of those who have died are eligible for the relief.

Benefits in kind (ITEPA 2003, ss 62–191, 201–220, 237–249, 261–265, 290–290G, 306A, 316–325A, 326A)

[10.27] From 6 April 2016 all employees, other than 'lower-paid' ministers of religion (see **10.28**), are taxed on benefits in kind in the same way and are therefore subject to tax on the benefits listed in **10.31** to **10.48**.

[10.28] 'Lower-paid' ministers of religion (i.e. *not* earning at a rate of £8,500 a year or more or a director) are not normally taxed on benefits unless they could be turned into cash, and the amount treated as pay is the cash which could be obtained. For example, if they are given a suit which cost the employer £250 but which was valued second-hand at only £30, they are taxed only on £30. They are not taxed on the use of an employer's asset (see **10.37**) and they also escape tax on the benefit of use of a car, unless they have the choice of giving up the car for extra wages. In that event, the car could be turned into cash at any time by taking up the offer, so they would be treated as having the extra wages (although from 6 April 2017 the 'optional remuneration' arrangements may apply, see **10.30** and **10.40**). The rule in **10.45** does not apply to 'lower-paid' ministers of religion. There is also a specific exemption from the benefit arising on the provision of living accommodation for 'lower-paid' ministers of religion residing in a house owned by a charity or any ecclesiastical corporation.

[10.29] All employees, other than 'lower-paid' ministers of religion, are charged to tax on all expenses payments received (unless exempted, see **10.16**) and on the cash equivalent of virtually all benefits provided either direct to the employee or to his family or household, subject to replacement of the cash equivalent for a 'relevant amount' where benefits are provided under optional remuneration arrangements set up from 6 April 2017 (see **10.30**). The cash equivalent of a benefit is normally the extra cost to the employer of providing the benefit (including VAT where appropriate, whether recovered or not) less any contribution from the employee. See **10.37** for the calculation of the benefit of use of an asset provided by the employer. Benefits in the form of accommodation, supplies or services used in performing the duties of the employment either on the employer's premises or elsewhere are exempt despite some insignificant private use unless they are motor vehicles, boats, or aircraft, or they involve extension, conversion etc. of living accommodation. This exemption may cover the provision to homeworkers of furniture and equipment, stationery and supplies, providing any private use is insignificant.

Case law previously established that something which is a 'fair bargain', where the employer receives something in return and the arrangement matches arm's length terms, is not a benefit. However from 2016–17 the provision of living accommodation (see **10.32**), beneficial loans (see **10.48**) and cars, vans and related benefits (see **10.38** to **10.46**) is always treated as a benefit regardless of whether the terms on which they are made available are a fair bargain.

The provision of computer equipment is covered under the 'accommodation, supplies and services' exemption outlined above. The use of a computer provided under an arrangement entered into before 6 April 2006 with an annual benefit value up to £500 is exempt, with only an excess being chargeable. See **10.24** regarding telephones.

HMRC have the power to make regulations exempting minor benefits. They have used it, for example, to exempt private use of equipment, services or facilities provided to disabled people (e.g. wheelchairs) to enable them to do their work.

The charging rules include benefits provided by someone other than the employer, except for corporate hospitality (providing it is not arranged by the employer and is not in return for services rendered by the employee) and gifts costing not more than £250 in total from any one donor. See **10.67** for the year-end requirements for third parties providing benefits.

Optional remuneration arrangements (ITEPA 2003, ss 69A, 69B, 228A; FA 2017, s 7 and Sch 7)

[10.30] With effect for arrangements set up from 6 April 2017, provisions have been introduced to limit the income tax and NICs advantages of providing benefits under optional remuneration arrangements. They apply where a benefit is provided under one of two types of arrangement, i.e. either where an amount of earnings is given up in return for the benefit (often known as salary sacrifice) or where the employee agrees to be provided with a benefit rather than an amount of earnings (often known as flexible benefit). Where the provisions apply tax is charged on the higher of the cash equivalent, and the amount foregone (usually the amount of earnings given up) less certain deductions. For most benefits that are subject to an exemption, that exemption is disapplied if the benefit is provided in conjunction optional remuneration arrangements, although this is subject to a number of exceptions, in particular the provision of pensions, childcare, and cycles and cyclists safety equipment (see **10.50**). Any arrangements in place before 6 April 2017 can continue unaffected until 2018 (with a further extension until 2021 for existing longer term agreements covering cars and vans, living accommodation and school fees provided they are not renewed or varied). The rules relating to specific benefits are covered elsewhere in this chapter.

For HMRC guidance see HMRC Employment Income Manual EIM44010–44130 and www.gov.uk/guidance/salary-sacrifice-and-the-effects-on-paye.

Readily convertible assets

[**10.31**] Tax has to be accounted for under PAYE where pay is provided in the form of 'readily convertible assets', i.e. stocks and shares (see below), gold bullion, futures or commodities that may be sold on a recognised investment exchange such as the Stock Exchange; assets subject to a fiscal warehousing regime; assets that give rise to cash without any action being taken by the employee; assets in the form of debts owed to the employer that have been assigned to the employee, and assets for which trading arrangements exist or are likely to come into existence. All shares and other securities are within the definition of readily convertible assets unless the employer company is entitled to a deduction for them in calculating corporation tax payable (see **11.1** and **11.3**). The convertible assets provisions apply equally where vouchers and credit tokens are used to provide the assets, and they apply to agency workers and to those working for someone in the UK but employed and paid by someone overseas. Benefits chargeable under the convertible assets provisions are referred to as notional pay. They would have been taxable in any event, but charging tax under PAYE accelerates the payment date for the tax (see **10.62**). Pay in the form of convertible assets is similarly charged to Class 1 NICs.

PAYE also applies where pay is provided in the form of the enhancement of the value of an asset owned by the employee (such as paying premiums to increase the value of an employee-owned life policy).

See CHAPTER 11 for the detailed provisions dealing with share and securities options and incentives provided by the employer. Where an employee is taxable under ITEPA 2003 when a risk of forfeiture of shares or securities is lifted, or when shares or securities are converted into shares or securities of a different class, PAYE and Class 1 NICs must be applied if the shares or securities are readily convertible assets. PAYE and, for options granted on or after 6 April 1999, Class 1 NICs must also be charged on any gains realised when a share or securities option is exercised (other than under certain tax-advantaged schemes) or is assigned or released. Options which were not tax-advantaged and which were granted before 6 April 1999 were liable to Class 1 NICs when they were granted.

Living accommodation (ITEPA 2003, ss 97–113, 313–315, 364; FA 2017, s 7 and Sch 2; SI 2017/305)

[**10.32**] If the employer provides an employee or a member of the employee's family or household with living accommodation, other than under optional remuneration arrangements (see **10.30** and **10.35**), the employee is charged to tax on the amount by which its 'rental value' (see below), or the rent paid by the employer if higher, exceeds any any amount made good by the employee. For leases of ten years or less entered into on or after 22 April 2009 a lease premium paid is to be treated as if it were rent and spread over the period of the lease. There is no charge to tax if:

(a)   the employer is an individual and the accommodation is provided in the normal course of his domestic, family or personal relationships; or

(b)   the accommodation is provided by a local authority under its usual terms for non-employees; or

(c)   the employee is a representative occupier, for example, a caretaker; or

(d)   it is customary for employees (e.g. police officers, clergymen) to be provided with living accommodation for the better performance of their duties; or

(e)   the accommodation is provided for security reasons.

Where the accommodation provided by a company falls within (c) or (d) above, a director qualifies for exemption only if he does not have a material interest in the company and either (i) he works full-time for the company or (ii) the company is non-profit-making or established for charitable purposes only. A director has a material interest in the company if he owns or controls more than 5% of the ordinary share capital or, in the case of a close company (see **3.29**), he is entitled to more than 5% of the assets on a winding up.

A limited exemption applies for holiday homes outside the UK where the property is bought through the taxpayer's own company, for legal or other reasons, and the taxpayer is a director or other officer of the company who would otherwise be liable to tax because the property is available to him — see guidance in HMRC Employment Income Manual EIM11374.

The 'rental value' is the rent that would be payable if the property was let to the employee at an annual rent equal to the 'annual value', and the annual value is the rent that might be expected to be charged if the employee paid the council tax and other charges usually paid by a tenant, and the landlord paid for repairs and maintenance. HMRC practice for a UK property is to take the gross rateable value under the old system of rates. For a property outside the UK, HMRC take the amount of rent that could be obtained on the open market.

See **10.28** for the treatment of living accommodation for 'lower-paid' ministers of religion. From 6 April 2016 there is a specific exemption for board and/or lodging provided to certain home care workers.

Additional charge

[10.33] The charge for living accommodation is increased where the accommodation cost more than £75,000 except, broadly, in cases where the annual value is taken to be the open market value (such as non-UK properties). The extra charge over and above the rental value is calculated as follows:

((Cost less £75,000) × appropriate %) less the amount by which any rent the employee pays exceeds the rental value.

The cost is the purchase price of the property plus the cost of any improvements incurred before the start of the tax year, less any payment by the employee in reimbursement of the initial cost or improvements, or for the grant of the tenancy. The appropriate percentage is the official rate of interest chargeable on beneficial loans, as at the beginning of the tax year. This rate is 2.5% p.a. from 6 April 2017 (3% from 6 April 2015 to 5 April 2017).

If, throughout the period of six years up to the date the employee first occupied the accommodation, an interest in it was held by the employer, the person providing it, or another person (other than the employee) connected with either of them, cost is substituted by—

(i)   the market value of the property at the date it was first occupied by the employee; plus

(ii)   the cost of any improvements made between that date and the beginning of the tax year concerned; less

(iii) any payment by the employee in reimbursement of the initial cost or improvements, or for the grant of the tenancy.

Example 2

Employee A first occupied a house provided by his employer on 1 March 2009. His employer had acquired the house in 2002 at a cost of £100,000. Improvements were carried out in January 2008 at a cost to the employer of £2,000. Further improvements were carried out in May 2009 at a cost of £10,000, of which A contributed £4,000. The market value of the house on 1 March 2009 was £200,000.

The additional charge in 2017–18 is computed as follows—

Market value of property at 1 March 2009	£200,000
Add: Cost of improvements carried out between 1 March 2009 and 5 April 2016	10,000
	210,000
Deduct: A's contribution to cost of improvements	(4,000)
	206,000
Deduct:	(75,000)
Excess over £75,000	£131,000
£131,000 @ 2.5% (official rate at 6 April 2017)	£3,275

The basic and, where appropriate, additional charges are proportionately reduced if the property is provided for only part of the year, and also to the extent that any part of the property is used exclusively for business. Where the accommodation is provided for more than one employee at the same time, the total benefit charges are restricted to what would have been charged on a single employee.

Other benefits in connection with living accommodation

[10.34] If an employee is exempt under one of headings (c) to (e) in 10.32 above, he is also exempt from both tax and NICs on the payment of council tax and water charges by the employer. If he is not exempt, such items reimbursed by the employer count as pay for both tax and Class 1 NICs. Amounts paid by the employer directly to the council or utility company are entered on form P11D but are subject to Class 1 NICs.

Where other benefits are provided in connection with the accommodation, an employee is chargeable on their value whether or not he is chargeable on the rental value, but if he is exempt from the charge on letting value under headings (c) to (e) above the charge for other benefits cannot exceed 10% of his net earnings excluding those benefits. Net earnings means earnings after deducting allowable expenses including, where appropriate, contributions to registered pension schemes and capital allowances.

Living accommodation provided under optional remuneration arrangements

[10.35] Where the benefit of living accommodation is provided under optional remuneration arrangements set up from 6 April 2017 (see **10.30**), in certain cases the amount to be treated as earnings is the relevant amount rather than the cash equivalent as shown in **10.32** and **10.33**. The relevant amount is determined through a comparison of the modified cash equivalent of the benefit (see below) and the amount foregone under the arrangements. If the amount foregone is greater than the modified cash equivalent, the 'relevant amount' is charged to tax.

The 'modified cash equivalent' is the rental value as calculated in **10.32** and **10.33** but without deducting the amount made good by the employee or the amount by which any rent the employee pays exceeds the rental value. The modified cash equivalent is zero if the benefit would be exempt were it not provided under these arrangements. The relevant amount is the amount foregone less the deductible amount. Where the cost of the accommodation is £75,000 or less, the 'deductible amount' is any sum made good by the employee on or before 6 July in the following tax year. Where the cost is over £75,000 the 'deductible amount' is any sum made good by the employee on or before 6 July in the following tax year, but only up to the rental value, plus the amount of rent paid by the employee on or before 6 July in the following tax year that exceeds the rental value.

Any arrangements in place before 6 April 2017 can continue unaffected until 2021 provided they are not renewed or varied.

Vouchers (ITEPA 2003, ss 73–96A, 266–270B, 289D, 362, 363; FA 2017, s 7 and Sch 2)

[10.36] The vouchers rules generally apply to all employees and are wide-ranging. The taxable amount is usually the cash equivalent of the vouchers but differing rules apply to vouchers provided under optional remuneration arrangements set up from 6 April 2017 (see **10.30** and below).

Cash vouchers are treated as earnings and are taxable through the PAYE system at the time the voucher is provided, as are both cash vouchers and non-cash vouchers exchangeable for readily-convertible assets (see **10.31**).

Most other non-cash vouchers are taxable, although not through the PAYE scheme but from 6 April 2017 employers may voluntarily payroll them (see **10.13**). Any taxable sum may be reduced by a deduction which could have been claimed by the employee if he had incurred and paid the cost of the relevant goods or services. From 6 April 2016 vouchers for which an employe could have claimed such a deduction are exempt. Where HMRC use their power to exempt minor benefits from tax (see **10.29**), non-cash vouchers in connection with such benefits are also exempt. There is a general provision enabling regulations to be issued to exempt non-cash vouchers that are used to obtain specified exempt benefits.

The employer has to provide HMRC with details of the cost of providing non-exempt vouchers and the cost of goods or services obtained through the provision of employer's credit cards. Tax on the value of the vouchers is usually collected by a PAYE coding adjustment.

Exempt non-cash vouchers include vouchers in connection with a works bus service (see **10.50**), or to obtain a parking space for a car, van, motor cycle or bicycle at or near the workplace, or in connection with cycles or cyclists' safety equipment provided by the employer, vouchers provided by third parties for corporate hospitality, vouchers for incidental overnight expenses within the limits stated at **10.21**, vouchers used in connection with sporting or recreational facilities and childcare vouchers (see **10.51**).

No tax arises on free canteen meals that are provided to staff generally as long as they are not provided as part of a salary sacrifice or flexible benefit arrangement (as to which, see **10.30**), so the meal voucher rules discriminate against employers who are too small to have their own canteen.

Where vouchers are provided under optional remuneration arrangements set up from 6 April 2017 (see **10.30**), the amount treated as earnings for cash vouchers is the greater of the cash equivalent and the amount foregone. For non-cash vouchers the amount treated as earnings is the greater of the cost of provision, and the amount foregone less any amount made good by the employee by 6 July in the tax year following the tax year of receipt. Where the benefit would be exempt were it not provided under such arrangements the amount treated as earnings is the amount foregone (less any amount made good in the case of non-cash vouchers).

Any arrangements in place before 6 April 2017 can continue unaffected until 2018 provided they are not renewed or varied.

Class 1 NICs are payable on most non-cash vouchers, subject to various exceptions which mainly mirror income tax provisions such as those indicated above and the childcare voucher exemption dealt with in **10.51**. See further HMRC National Insurance Manual NIM02416. Non-cash vouchers are valued for NICs as for tax purposes.

Vouchers in connection with employer-provided cars and car fuel for such cars are not charged under Class 1 but Class 1A may apply (see **10.49**).

See **10.69** regarding accounting for tax and NICs on non-cash vouchers through the taxed award scheme.

Use of employer's assets (ITEPA 2003, ss 205–210; FA 2017, s 8)

[10.37] A tax charge normally arises each year if an employee is allowed private use of an asset that belongs to his employer, the amount of the charge usually being the private use proportion of 20% of the cost of the asset plus any expenses, such as a rent or hire charge incurred in connection with the provision of the benefit.

From 6 April 2017 the benefit is reduced by periods during which the asset is unavailable for private use by the employee or his family/household, or where the asset is shared by two or more employees. An asset is 'unavailable' in the period before the asset was given to the employee or after it was taken away by the employer, and during periods of more than 12 hours during which the asset is not fit for use, is undergoing repairs or could not be lawfully used.

Different benefit rules apply to living accommodation (see **10.32**) and cars and vans (see **10.38** to **10.46**). There is normally no tax charge on cycles and cyclists' safety equipment (see **10.50**). There is a specific exemption for private use of computers provided before 6 April 2006 (see **10.29**).

If an asset that has been used or has depreciated is given to the employee, then if it is a car, or a computer made available before 6 April 2006, cycle or cyclists' safety equipment provided as indicated in **10.50**, the employee is charged to tax on its market value. For any other asset, he is charged to tax on the higher of its market value at the date of the transfer to him and the original market value less the benefits already charged to tax (either on him or on others).

Example 3

A television set cost an employer £1,000. It is used by a director for two years, then given to him when the market value is £100.

Tax will be charged on the following amounts:

For use of asset, 20% × £1,000 =	£200	per year

On gift of asset, higher of
(i) £100
(ii) £1,000 − (2 × £200) = £600   £600

Motor cars (ITEPA 2003, ss 114–153, 167–172; FA 2017, s 7 and Sch 2; SI 2016/1174)

[10.38] The benefit of private use of a car made available by reason of employment is charged to tax according to the price of the car, certain accessories and the 'appropriate percentage' (see below) based on the car's CO_2 emissions figure. An additional charge is made in respect of car fuel provided for private use (see **10.42**). HMRC guidance is available at www.gov.uk/tax-company-benefits/tax-on-company-cars, which includes an online car benefit calculator and a service to allow taxpayers to update their company car details online. A car or van is not made available by reason of employment where the employer's normal business is the hire of cars or vans and the employee hires the vehicle on the same terms as a member of the public.

Where the car is provided under optional remuneration arrangements (see **10.30**) the benefit is calculated under the rules in **10.40** rather than the rules in this article and in **10.39**.

The price of the car for this purpose is normally the manufacturer's list price including VAT and delivery charges. There are detailed rules to determine when the cost of accessories is to be added to the price of the car. The cost of mobile phones and any equipment provided for use in the performance of the duties, or provided to enable a disabled person to use a car or to enable the car to run on road fuel gas, is excluded. From 6 April 2011 certain security enhancements provided to meet the threat to an employee's personal physical security arising from the nature of the employment are also excluded.

Where an employee pays towards the initial cost of a car or accessories, a contribution of up to £5,000 is deducted from the list price. The appropriate percentage is then applied to the net figure.

Classic cars valued at more than £15,000 and at least 15 years old at the end of the tax year are taxed according to their open market value if that is more than the price of the car.

Disabled drivers of automatic cars who hold a blue badge may use the list price of an equivalent manual car in computing their car benefit.

If a car is provided for only part of the year (for example, in the year when employment starts or ceases) the charge is proportionately reduced. It is also proportionately reduced if the car is incapable of being used for a period of 30 consecutive days or more. Where a car is replaced during the year, the appropriate proportion of each benefit figure is charged. Employers are required to notify HMRC of certain changes (see **10.65**).

Any contribution an employee makes to his employer for the use of the car is deducted from the car benefit charge, provided, from 2014–15 onwards, it is made before the end of the tax year, though September 2017 Finance Bill, which is expected to receive Royal Assent in November 2017, changes this date to 6 July following the end of the tax year. The car benefit charge covers the whole benefit obtained from the use of a car, except the expense of providing a driver, which is charged in addition but may be the subject of a claim for allowable expenses. For example, for employees driving company cars in London no additional taxable benefit arises where the employer pays the congestion charge. Employees using their own cars will, however, only be entitled to relief where the charge is incurred in the course of business travel (see **10.14**).

The charge arises even if an amount constitutes earnings in respect of the car benefit under another provision.

Calculation of benefit

[10.39] The amount calculated as set out in **10.38** is multiplied by the 'appropriate percentage' according to the level of the car's CO_2 to find the 'cash equivalent' of the benefit. The CO_2 emissions figure is recorded on the vehicle's registration certificate but it can also be found via the 'vehicle enquiry' link at www.gov.uk/get-vehicle-information-from-dvla.

For cars registered on or after 1 January 1998 the appropriate percentage for 2017–18 is:

- 9% for cars with CO_2 emissions of 50 grams per kilometre driven or less, including those which cannot in any circumstances emit CO_2 by being driven,
- 13% for cars with CO_2 emissions of more than 50 g/km but not more than 75g/km,

- 17% for cars with CO_2 emissions of more than 75 g/km but not more than 94 g/km, and
- 18% (the 'threshold percentage') for cars with CO_2 emissions of 95 g/km.

The threshold percentage is increased by 1% for every 5 g/km above the 95 g/km threshold, up to a maximum of 37%. If the car's CO_2 emissions figure is not a multiple of 5, it is rounded down accordingly.

The appropriate percentage is increased by 3% for diesel cars, subject to the overall maximum of 37%.

For 2018–19 the relevant threshold will remain at 95 g/km but the percentage applying at that threshold will be 20%. A 13% rate will apply for emissions of 50 g/km or less, including cars incapable of emitting CO_2 when driven. A 16% rate will apply for emissions from 51–75 g/km and a 19% rate for emissions from 76–94 g/km.

See the TABLE OF RATES AND ALLOWANCES (**TRA**) for the full list of appropriate percentages.

Example 4

Car benefit charges for 2017–18 for a car costing £15,000

		£
Petrol car with rounded emissions figure of 170 g/km	33%	4,950
Diesel car with rounded emissions figure of 185 g/km	37%*	5,550

* The diesel supplement is only 1%, to bring the charge up to the maximum 37%

The appropriate percentage for cars registered before 1 January 1998, and for cars registered after that date with no approved CO_2 emissions figures, is as follows:

Engine size	Pre–1.1.98 cars	Post-31.12.97 cars with no approved emissions figures
0–1400cc	18%[2]	18%[1,2]
1401–2000cc	29%[3]	29%[1,3]
2001cc and over	37%	37%

[1] plus 3% supplement for diesel cars
[2] 20% in 2018–19
[3] 31% in 2018–19

The appropriate percentage for cars with no cylinder capacity and no approved emissions figure is 9% for cars which cannot produce CO_2 emissions under any circumstances and 37% for other cars (whether or not registered before 1 January 1998). In 2018–19 these percentages will be 13% and 37% respectively.

Cars provided under optional remuneration arrangements

[**10.40**] Where the benefit of a car with CO_2 emissions greater than 75g/km is provided under optional remuneration arrangements set up from 6 April 2017 (see **10.30**), in certain cases the amount to be treated as earnings is the relevant amount rather than the cash equivalent as shown in **10.38** and **10.39**. The relevant amount is determined through a comparison of the modified cash equivalent of the benefit (see below) and the amount foregone under the arrangements. If the amount foregone is greater than the modified cash equivalent, the 'relevant amount' is charged to tax.

The 'modified cash equivalent' is calculated as in **10.38** and **10.39** but excluding any contribution the employee pays towards the initial cost of a car or accessories, and any contribution from the employee for the use of the car. The modified cash equivalent is zero if the benefit of the car would be exempt but for being provided under optional remuneration arrangements. The 'relevant amount' is the amount forgone less the appropriate percentage (see **10.39**) of any contributions (up to a maximum total of £5,000) the employee pays towards the cost, less any amount paid for use of the car.

Any arrangements in place before 6 April 2017 can continue unaffected until 2021 provided they are not renewed or varied.

Pool cars and shared private use

[**10.41**] It is possible to escape tax and Class 1A NICs on the benefit of use of a car if it is a pool car as defined, but the conditions are restrictive. A pool car is one where the private use is merely incidental to the business use, the car is not normally kept overnight at an employee's home, and the car is not ordinarily used by only one employee to the exclusion of other employees.

Where private use of a car is shared, the charge is calculated as if the employee had exclusive use and then reduced on a 'just and reasonable' basis.

Car fuel charge

[**10.42**] A further charge is made if, in addition to being provided with a car, an employee is provided with car fuel for private use.

The car fuel scale charge is based on a set figure, fixed at £22,600 for 2017–18 (£22,200 for 2016–17). This figure is multiplied by the 'appropriate percentage' (see **10.39**). The charge is proportionately reduced where an employee stops receiving fuel part way through the year, unless he again receives fuel in the same tax year, in which case the full scale will apply. See **10.43** for the charge where optional remuneration arrangements set up from 6 April 2017 apply.

There is no reduction in the car fuel charge for a contribution to the cost of fuel for private journeys. To escape the fuel charge an employee must reimburse the whole cost of private fuel to the employer, or pay for it himself in the first place. The reimbursement can be made after the end of the tax year provided there is not unreasonable delay, though September 2017 Finance Bill, which is expected to receive Royal Assent in November 2017, changes this date to

6 July following the end of the tax year. The employee should keep detailed records of both business and personal mileage to confirm that the amount reimbursed for private mileage is correct, remembering that travel between home and work is regarded as private mileage (see **10.46** relating to the contrasting position for vans).

HMRC publish advisory fuel rates which an employer may use to reimburse the cost of business mileage an employee has incurred or to recoup the cost of private mileage where the employer paid for the fuel. These rates will be accepted as not giving rise to taxable benefits or Class 1 NICs liability but higher rates may be acceptable where, for example, the employer can show that employees need a particular type of car to cover rough terrain.

The advisory fuel rates from 1 September 2017 are as follows:

	Petrol	Diesel	LPG
0–1400cc	11p	—	7p
0–1600cc	—	9p	—
1401–2000cc	13p	—	8p
1601–2000cc	—	11p	—
2001cc and over	21p	12p	13p

Hybrid cars are treated as petrol for this purpose.

Earlier rates are set out at www.gov.uk/government/publications/advisory-fuel-rates.

Car fuel provided under optional remuneration arrangements

[10.43] Where fuel is provided under optional remuneration arrangements for a car in respect of which the employee is chargeable (whether under optional remuneration arrangements or not) the amount to be treated as earnings is the amount foregone where this is greater than the cash equivalent. The cash equivalent is zero if the benefit of the provision of fuel would be exempt but for being provided under optional remuneration arrangements.

Any arrangements in place before 6 April 2017 can continue unaffected until 2021 provided they are not renewed or varied.

National insurance contributions and VAT

[10.44] The provision of a car for private use and of private fuel for the car also attracts Class 1A employers' (but not employees') NICs — see **10.49**. The amounts of the car and fuel benefits for tax purposes are used to determine the Class 1A amounts payable. Employers also have to account for VAT on private fuel provided to employees whether the car is provided by them or owned by the employee — see **7.5**. VAT does not apply to the provision of the car itself, even if the employee makes a payment for private use (unless the employer recovered all of the input VAT on the car, or leases it from a lessor who reclaimed the input VAT on it, in which case a payment by the employee would attract VAT).

Salary alternative

[10.45] The increasing cost of providing employees with cars and private fuel has led many employers to offer employees extra salary instead. The tax and NICs for an employee are based on what the employee actually gets, either salary or use of a car, although from 6 April 2017 this only applies to cars with CO_2 emissions not exceeding 75g/km. Otherwise the rules in 10.40 now apply.

Vans (ITEPA 2003, ss 114–119, 154–164, 168, 169A; SI 2016/1174)

[10.46] The benefit of private use of a van (i.e. a goods vehicle with a design weight not exceeding 3,500 kilograms) made available by reason of employment is charged to tax. A car or van is not made available by reason of employment where the employer's normal business is the hire of cars or vans and the employee hires the vehicle on the same terms as a member of the public. Unless the van is provided under optional remuneration arrangements (see 10.30 and 10.47) the 2017–18 cash equivalent of the benefit is £3,230 for conventionally fuelled vans (£3,170 for 2016–17). The cash equivalent where the van cannot in any circumstances emit CO_2 by being driven is £646, which is 20% of the amount for conventionally fuelled vans (£634 for 2016–17). For 2018–19 the benefit for vans not emitting CO_2 will be increased to 40% of the amount for conventionally fuelled vans, and the percentage will increase each year until the rates are equalised in 2022–23.

There is no charge where a van is provided mainly for business use, and private use is restricted to commuting, with any other private use being insignificant. HMRC say insignificant private use would include trips such as an occasional trip to the tip, or to the local shop, but not regular supermarket shopping. See 10.50 for exemption in relation to emergency vehicles.

The taxable benefit is reduced proportionately if the van is not provided for the whole year, or is unavailable for 30 consecutive days or more. The taxable amount is also reduced by any payment by the employee for private use, provided, from 2014–15 onwards, it is made before the end of the tax year, though September 2017 Finance Bill, which is expected to receive Royal Assent in November 2017, changes this date to 6 July following the end of the tax year.

Where there is shared use of a van, the charge is calculated as if the employee had exclusive use and then reduced on a 'just and reasonable' basis.

Where the employer provides fuel for private use in a van which does not satisfy the 'mainly for business use' requirements outlined above, or is not a zero emissions van, there is a separate fuel charge of £610 (£598 for 2016–17), reduced appropriately for shared vans. The provisions in 10.41 regarding pooled and shared cars apply equally to pooled and shared vans, and the salary alternative position in 10.45 applied equally to vans before 6 April 2017.

The charge arises even if an amount constitutes earnings in respect of the van benefit under another provision.

Vans provided under optional remuneration arrangements (ITEPA 2003, ss 154A–160A; FA 2017, s 7 and Sch 2)

[10.47] Where the benefit of a van and is provided under optional remuneration arrangements set up from 6 April 2017 (see **10.30**), in certain cases the amount to be treated as earnings is the relevant amount rather than the cash equivalent as shown in **10.46**. The relevant amount is determined through a comparison of the modified cash equivalent of the benefit (see below) and the amount foregone under the arrangements. If the amount foregone is greater than the modified cash equivalent, the 'relevant amount' is charged to tax.

The 'modified cash equivalent' is calculated as in **10.46** but excluding any contribution the employee pays for the private use of the van. The modified cash equivalent is zero if the benefit of the provision of van would be exempt but for being provided under optional remuneration arrangements. The 'relevant amount' is the amount forgone less any contribution the employee pays for the private use of the van provided such payment is required as a condition of use of the van and it is made by 6 July in the following tax year.

Where fuel is provided for a van under optional remuneration arrangements in respect of which the employee is chargeable (whether under optional remuneration arrangements or not) the amount to be treated as earnings is the amount foregone where this is greater than the cash equivalent. The cash equivalent is zero if the benefit of the provision of fuel would be exempt but for being provided under optional remuneration arrangements.

Any arrangements in place before 6 April 2017 can continue unaffected until 2021 provided they are not renewed or varied.

Cheap loans (ITEPA 2003, ss 173–191; FA 2017, s 7 and Sch 2; SI 2017/305)

[10.48] If an employer lends an employee money interest-free, or at a rate of interest below the official rate, and not under an optional remuneration arrangement set up from 6 April 2017 (see **10.30** and below), the employee is charged to tax on an amount equal to interest at the official rate (see below) less any interest paid.

This does not apply if the loan qualifies for tax relief either in calculating the employee's income (see **2.14**) or as a deduction from business profits or rental income, and the *whole* of the interest would qualify for tax relief. Such wholly qualifying loans are exempt from the charge. If part of the interest on the loan would not qualify for relief, tax is first calculated on the full amount of the loan at the official rate and then reduced by the appropriate tax saving on both the beneficial loan interest and any interest actually paid.

The official rate of interest is 2.5% p.a. from 6 April 2017 (3% from 6 April 2015 to 5 April 2017). The rate is varied by Treasury Order and is normally fixed in advance for the whole of the tax year, but may be changed during the year to reflect significant changes in interest rates. For a list of earlier rates see www.gov.uk/government/publications/rates-and-allowances-beneficial-loan-a rrangements-hmrc-official-rates.

Where the loan is provided under optional remuneration arrangements set up from 6 April 2017 (see **10.30**), in certain cases the amount to be treated as earnings is the relevant amount rather than the cash equivalent. The relevant amount is determined through a comparison of the modified cash equivalent of the benefit (see below) and the amount foregone under the arrangements. If the amount foregone is greater than the modified cash equivalent, the 'relevant amount' is charged to tax.

The 'modified cash equivalent' is still calculated as the amount of interest that would have been payable for the year on the loan at the official rate but excluding any interest paid by the employee. The modified cash equivalent is zero if the benefit of the provision of loan would be exempt but for being provided under optional remuneration arrangements. The 'relevant amount' is the amount forgone less any interest actually paid on the loan.

Any arrangements in place before 6 April 2017 can continue unaffected until 2018 provided they are not renewed or varied.

There is no tax charge on loans made to employees on commercial terms by employers who lend or supply goods or services on credit to the general public despite the interest paid being less than the official rate. Nor is there any charge if the total of all non-qualifying beneficial loans to an employee does not exceed £10,000 at any time in the tax year. Where a director or employee receives an advance for expenses necessarily incurred in performing his duties, or for incidental overnight expenses (see **10.21**), the advance is not treated as a loan provided that:

(a)   the maximum amount advanced at any one time does not exceed £1,000,
(b)   the advances are spent within six months, and
(c)   the director or employee accounts to the company at regular intervals for the expenditure.

If the loan is written off, the employee is charged to tax on the amount written off whether he is still employed or not, with Class 1 NICs also applying (but see **12.15** for controlling directors of close companies). Note that the charge on loans written off can apply to 'lower-paid' ministers of religion (see **10.28**) if the loan was made when he was not lower-paid.

The above provisions relating to cheap loans apply where on or after 22 March 2006 employers enter into low cost 'alternative finance arrangements' with their employees (such arrangements usually being made to comply with Islamic law prohibiting the payment of interest).

Class 1A NICs (SSCBA 1992, ss 10, 10ZA–10ZC and Sch 1; SI 2001/1004, Pt 3)

[10.49] Class 1A NICs at 13.8% are payable only by employers, not by employees. They are payable on virtually all taxable benefits in kind unless the benefits have already been charged to Class 1 contributions, or to Class 1B contributions under a PAYE settlement agreement (see **10.69**). See **10.66** for the way in which Class 1A contributions are accounted for.

The amounts liable to Class 1A are taken from forms P11D (see **10.67**), the relevant P11D boxes being colour coded and marked 1A. Any amounts made good by the employee are taken into account. The total on which contributions are payable is shown on form P11D(b) (see **10.66**) and is then multiplied by the relevant percentage to give the amount payable. Payment is due by 19 July following the end of the tax year (or 22 July if paid electronically).

Benefits which are exempted (see **10.13** and **10.16**) are not shown on forms P11D and are not liable to either tax or Class 1A contributions. If there is both business and private use of a benefit shown on form P11D, Class 1A contributions are payable on the full amount, even though for tax purposes the employee may claim a deduction for the business proportion in his tax return.

Where private fuel is provided for use in an employee's own car from an employer's own pump, or is provided by means of an employer's credit card, garage account or agency card and the garage is told that the fuel is being bought on behalf of the employer, Class 1 contributions are not due but Class 1A contributions are payable. Where private fuel is supplied in other circumstances, Class 1 contributions are payable. See **10.18** for the treatment where a mileage allowance is paid.

Where goods or services are obtained through a company credit card for the personal use of the employee, Class 1 contributions are payable. Where the goods or services are obtained on behalf of the employer, and the supplier is told that that is the case, contributions are not payable unless the goods or services are then transferred to the employee, in which case Class 1A contributions are payable.

For details of Class 1A contributions payable on benefits such as home telephones, company cars, vouchers and removal and relocation expenses, see under the individual benefit headings.

Non-taxable benefits

[10.50] From 6 April 2016 a statutory exemption from income tax and NICs applies for trivial benefits in kind provided to an employee or a member of their family or household where the cost of providing the benefit does not exceed £50. The benefit cannot be cash or a cash voucher, and must not be provided in connection with salary sacrifice arrangements (as to which, see **10.30**) or any other contractual obligation, or in recognition of particular services performed, or to be performed, by the employee in connection with their employment. The exemption is capped at £300 per year if the employer is a close company (see **3.29**) and the benefit is provided to a director or other office-holder, or an employee who is a member of the family or household of such.

The other main benefits that are not chargeable to tax are:

- Free or subsidised meals or light refreshments provided in a staff canteen by the employee's own or another employer, so long as the meals etc. are available to staff generally and are not provided as part of a salary sacrifice or flexible benefit arrangement (as to which, see **10.30**).

- Employer's contributions to a registered occupational or personal pension scheme in respect of the employee only and the provision of pension information and advice costing not more than £150 per year. September 2017 Finance Bill, which is expected to receive Royal Assent in November 2017, increases the limit to £500, and extends it to general financial and tax issues relating to pensions.
- Payments by employers in respect of independent advice provided to employees in relation to conversions and transfers of pension scheme benefits.
- Directors' liability or professional indemnity insurance etc., subject to anti-avoidance provisions (see **10.15**).
- Provision of parking facilities for cars, vans, cycles, or motor cycles at or near the workplace.
- Sporting and recreational facilities provided either by the employee's own or another employer.
- Counselling services to redundant employees and welfare counselling services available to employees generally.
- Provision for an employee of one health screening assessment and one medical check-up per tax year. The exemption does not extend to the employee's family or household, nor to a diagnosis or treatment for the employee (but see below).
- Provision of medical treatment or insurance that relates to treatment outside the UK when on a business trip. Payments for medical expenses abroad, and insurance against such expenses, also escape NICs.
- The provision of eye care tests and/or corrective glasses in connection with an employee's use of visual display units.
- Certain childcare provision (see **10.51**).
- Commissions, discounts and cashbacks available to employees on the same basis as to members of the general public (because such benefits do not arise from the employment). To escape tax, cashbacks must be provided under a contract separate from the employment contract and not be given gratuitously.
- Mobile telephones (see **10.24**).
- Employer-provided cycles and cyclist's safety equipment, providing they are available to staff generally and used mainly for journeys between home and work and for business journeys.
- Certain works bus services providing the services are used mainly for journeys between home and work, free or subsidised travel on local public stopping bus services used by employees for journeys between home and work, and employer support for other bus services used for such journeys providing employees do not obtain the services on more favourable terms than other passengers. The use of works buses on workdays for trips of up to 10 miles (20 miles return) to local shops or other amenities is also not taxable. See HMRC's Employment Income Manual at EIM21850 for guidance on when the exemption applies.
- The benefit of one or more annual staff parties and functions, providing the cost to the employer for each person attending is not more than £150 a year including VAT. If, say, there were three annual functions at £70 each per employee, the exemption would cover two of them and the employee would be taxed on £70.

- Long service awards for those with 20 or more years' service, providing no such award has been made within the previous 10 years. The value of the award must not exceed £50 for each year of service. Such awards may be tangible assets or shares in the employer company (or a group company). Cash payments and cash vouchers are excluded.
- The reimbursement or payment by an employer of an employee's fees for registering under the Protection of Vulnerable Groups Scheme.
- The reimbursement or payment by an employer of fees for the Disclosure and Barring Service on-line Update Service, and certain fees for Criminal Record Bureau checks required in connection with the Update Service.
- The provision of qualifying independent advice to individuals who are considering entering into an agreement to adopt the status of an employee shareholder (see **11.36**).

See also HMRC Helpsheet HS207 for further details.

No taxable benefit arises where benefits such as air miles, points to obtain gifts, etc. are obtained by employees in the same way as members of the public, even though the purchase relates to the business. If, however, employers distributed air miles, etc. under an incentive scheme tax would be charged.

There is no taxable benefit when emergency personnel working for the fire, ambulance and police services have to take their emergency vehicles home when on call.

Scholarships to employees' children are caught unless they are fortuitous awards paid from a trust fund or scheme open to the public at large under which not more than 25% of the total payments relate to employees.

From 1 January 2015 there is an exemption from income tax on any benefit in kind or payment of earnings, up to an annual cap of £500 per employee, when an employer meets the cost of 'recommended' medical treatment, provided it is not made via salary sacrifice or flexible remuneration arrangements (as to which, see **10.30**). Recommended treatment is that provided in accordance with a written recommendation by a healthcare professional as part of an occupational health service in order to help an employee return to work after a period of absence due to ill-health or injury. It applies where the employee has been assessed as unfit for work, or has been absent from work because of ill-health or injury, for at least 28 consecutive days. The benefit or payment is also exempt from NICs. See **14.12** regarding the abolition of the statutory sick pay recovery scheme which is linked to these provisions.

Special rules apply to share option and incentive schemes (see CHAPTER **11**), the use of cars and vans and the provision of cheap loans (see **10.38** to **10.45**, **10.46** and **10.48**).

Provision of childcare

Childcare (ITEPA 2003, ss 270A, 270B, 318–318D; Childcare Payments Act 2014; SI 2016/1017; SI 2016/1021; SI 2016/1078; SI 2016/1083; SI 2017/578)

[10.51] The benefit of a workplace nursery provided by an employer alone or with other employers, local authorities, etc., but with each employer being partly responsible for finance and management, is exempt from both tax and NICs. This exemption also applies to another employer's staff if they are allowed to use the nursery facility while working at the provider's premises. The exemption continues despite the introduction of tax-free childcare (see 10.52).

The provision of employer-contracted 'qualifying childcare' is also exempt from both tax and NICs to the extent of £55 a week per employee who joined the scheme before 6 April 2011, tax and NICs being charged on any excess over the exempt amount. Where an employee joins an employer-supported childcare scheme involving vouchers or contracted childcare on or after 6 April 2011 the employer is required to estimate the employee's likely annual earnings and for those whose expected level of earnings is between the basic and higher rate limits (see **2.5**) the exempt limit is £28 per week. For those with expected earnings exceeding the higher rate limit the exempt limit is £25 per week. The exempt limit for those with earnings below the basic rate limit remains at £55 per week. However, see **10.52** regarding the ending of relief for such schemes to new entrants from 21 April 2017. Qualifying childcare can be contracted for with a local childminder or nursery or provided by childcare vouchers, but there is no exemption if the employer provides cash to cover employees' own childcare expenses. In the case of vouchers, the voucher administration costs are also exempt.

There are very detailed conditions to be complied with for the limited exemption to apply, but the main requirements are that the scheme must be generally available to all employees other than those with earnings at or near the national minimum wage, the child must be the employee's child or a child who lives with the employee for whom the employee has parental responsibility, and the childcare must be registered or approved childcare. This does not include care by the employee's spouse or partner, or by a relative either in the child's home or in the relative's home unless the relative also looks after one or more unrelated children. A person is a 'child' until 1 September following his or her 15th birthday (or 16th birthday for a child who is certified severely sight impaired or blind, or is disabled).

[10.52] The effect of childcare provision on tax credit entitlement needs to be carefully considered because a reduction in the employee's own childcare costs through having the vouchers will affect the childcare element of working tax credit. HMRC provide a calculator, see www.gov.uk/childcare-vouchers-better-off-calculator.

[10.53] A new scheme for tax-free childcare is being phased in from 21 April 2017. The Government will make a top-up payment of 25% of payments into a childcare account up to a maximum of £8,000 per child per year, or £16,000 for a disabled child. The support will therefore be capped at a maximum of £2,000 per year per child, or £4,000 for a disabled child. A child is a qualifying child until the last day of the week containing the 1 September after the child's 11th birthday, or 16th birthday in the case of a disabled child. There will be no liability to income tax or NICs under the scheme.

A declaration of eligibility for the payments must be made and at that date various conditions must be met. Broadly the person declaring eligibility must be 16 or over, be in the UK, be responsible for the child, and they and any partner must both be in paid employment or self-employment with expected income, in the period of three months from the declaration of eligibility, in excess of an amount equal to 16 hours at the national minimum wage or national living wage (as appropriate) per week for all the weeks in that period. This is equivalent to an average of approximately £115 per week for the three-month period. Neither must have adjusted net income (see **2.20**) of more than £100,000 per year, be claiming universal credit, be in a relevant childcare scheme, nor receive other childcare support. This means that they cannot be in the current system of vouchers and directly contracted childcare outlined above, nor can they be receiving tax credits as this has an element of childcare support. The scheme is available to persons on paid sick leave and paid or unpaid statutory maternity, paternity and adoption leave. To support newly self-employed persons, a start-up period of 12 months will apply during which they will not have to earn the minimum income level.

Tax-free childcare accounts are run by HMRC in partnership with National Savings & Investments and anyone may pay into the account. If the money in the account is withdrawn other than to pay childcare costs, the Government will withdraw its corresponding contribution.

Tax relief on the system of vouchers and directly contracted childcare (see **10.51**) is now closed to new entrants and those who move employers after that date. However, employees may leave such schemes in order to qualify for tax-free childcare. Employers' workplace nurseries will not be affected.

Training and education

Scholarship and apprentice schemes

[10.54] Employees on full-time and sandwich courses at universities and colleges lasting one year or more may receive tax-free pay while they are on the course of up to £15,480 (HMRC Statement of Practice SP 4/86 revised in August 2007). This exemption also applies for NICs.

Work-related training courses (ITEPA 2003, ss 250–260)

[10.55] An employee is not taxed on the payment or reimbursement by his employer of the cost of work-related training, including not only directly job-related training but also training in health and safety and to develop leadership skills appropriate to the employee. As well as the direct costs, the exemption covers learning materials, examination fees and registration of qualifications. Travelling and subsistence expenses are allowed to the same extent as they would be for employment duties. HMRC consider that generally, training cannot be 'work-related' unless the trainee is employed by the employer when the training is undertaken, but they recognise that in some cases the link between the employment and the pre-commencement training will be strong enough that the reimbursement will qualify for exemption.

Retraining costs (ITEPA 2003, s 311)

[**10.56**] Where a retraining course in the UK for up to two years is made generally available to appropriate employees, the employee is not assessed on the course costs and any incidental travelling expenses paid for by the employer. The employee must have been employed full-time or part-time for at least two years, must leave the employment within two years after the end of the course, and must not be re-employed within two years after leaving.

Summary of main benefits provisions

[**10.57**] This is a summary of the calculation of the main benefits when not provided under optional remuneration arrangements from 6 April 2017 (see next page).

BENEFIT	AMOUNT CHARGEABLE TO TAX
Use of car	Charge based on % of list price according to the car's CO_2 emissions
Car fuel for private motoring	£22,600 × % used to calculate car benefit
Parking facilities	Not taxable
Use of van	Charge of £3,230 (£646 where no CO_2 emissions) if there is unrestricted private use, and £610 for private fuel if the use does not satisfy the 'mainly for business use' requirement. Proportionate charge for shared vans
Living accommodation	Letting value plus 2.5% of excess cost of property over £75,000 (unless accommodation is job-related)
Provision of services and use of furniture in living accommodation	Cost of services plus 20% p.a. of cost of furniture (but charge cannot exceed 10% of other reckonable earnings from the employment if exempt from living accommodation charge as indicated in **10.32**)
Use of other assets (excluding heavy commercial vehicles)	20% of cost
Vouchers other than childcare vouchers	Full value
Use of employers' credit cards	Cost of personal goods and services obtained
Medical insurance	Cost to employer
Beneficial loans	Interest at official rate (see **10.48**) less any interest paid, but no charge if non-qualifying loans total £10,000 or less.
Loans written off	Amount written off
Workplace nursery	Not taxable
Free or subsidised canteen meals	Not taxable if available to all employees (but see **10.50**)
Pension provision under approved schemes	Not taxable
* See **10.28** regarding benefits for 'lower-paid' ministers of religion.	

Example 5

An employee is paid a salary of £30,000 in 2017–18.

He is provided with a two-year old 1500 cc petrol driven company car with a list price of £15,000, and CO_2 of 150 g/km driven. The car is maintained by the employer, including the provision of private petrol and a mobile phone for business and private use.

The employee receives an overnight allowance amounting to £649, which HMRC have agreed is exempt (see 10.16).

He pays hotel and meal bills on business trips amounting to £1,540 and spends £500 on entertaining customers. These expenses are reimbursed by his employer. Home telephone bills amounting to £350 are paid by his employer, of which the business use proportion of the calls, as evidenced by the employee's records, amounts to £200.

He receives a round sum expenses allowance of £1,200 out of which allowable expenses of £200 are paid.

The taxable employment income is:

	£	£
Salary		30,000
Charge for use of car (£15,000 × 29%*)		4,350
Car fuel charge (£22,600 × 29%)		6,554
Mobile phone (exempt)		—
Overnight allowance (covered by dispensation)		—
Hotel and meal bills reimbursed		1,540
Entertaining expenses reimbursed		500
Home telephone account paid by employer		350
Round sum expenses allowance		1,200
		44,494
Less: Hotel and meal bills reimbursed	1,540	
Entertaining expenses reimbursed (disallowed in calculating tax on employer's profit)	500	
Proportion of telephone account relating to employment	200	
Other allowable expenses	200	(2,440)
Employment income		£42,054

National insurance. As well as the salary, pay for Class 1 NICs will include the round sum expenses allowance (except to the extent of any identified business expenses).

A private telephone use figure that is supported by the employee's records is accepted for NIC purposes, so that Class 1 contributions in this example will be due only on £150. If there are no such records, pay for Class 1 NICs includes payment of telephone bills, unless the telephone contract is in the employer's name, in which case the employer will be charged Class 1A contributions.

The employer will also pay Class 1A contributions at 13.8% on the car and fuel charges of (£4,350 + £6,554) = £10,904. Class 1A contributions are not payable on business expenses that are wholly offset by a matching expenses allowance for tax, so there is no liability on the reimbursed hotel and entertaining expenses.

There will be no NICs on the overnight allowance.

Value added tax. The employer will pay output VAT on the car fuel by reference to a scale rate of £281** per quarter, unless no input VAT is being claimed on fuel for any motor vehicle. The input VAT on the mobile phone will be restricted according to the private use proportion, unless the employee pays for the private use, in which case the employer must account for output VAT on the amount received from the employee (see 7.5).

* % charge for car with CO_2 emissions of 150 g/km – see 10.39

** VAT charge based on CO_2 emissions of 150 g/km — see 7.5

PAYE (ITEPA 2003, ss 222, 682–712; SI 2003/2682)

Operation of PAYE

[10.58] The object of the PAYE system is to require employers to collect and account for tax and NICs on employment income. Employers also have to collect student loan repayments.

From 6 April 2013 HMRC introduced Real Time Information (RTI), designed to improve the operation of PAYE and support the introduction of universal credit (see 10.6). Under the system an employer pays PAYE electronically and sends HMRC details of an employee's pay and deductions for tax, NICs, student loan deductions together with the payee's identity at the time that the employee is paid. The information to be submitted is produced from computerised payroll systems and is submitted automatically as part of the process for making payments to HMRC. As a result HMRC are now able to amend tax codes to reflect in-year changes in a timely fashion, and the process when an employee joins and leaves, and the tax year-end reporting requirements are simplified.

Care and support employers who submit their own returns, and employers with religious objections are exempt from filing online if a claim is made, and may continue to send paper returns quarterly.

There is extensive guidance on HMRC's website regarding the operation of PAYE, see www.gov.uk/paye-for-employers.

[10.59] Employers (and pension providers) report payroll information by submitting Full Payment Submissions (FPS) and Employer Payment Summaries (EPS). Almost all employers must report payroll information *on or before* the date of payment which can be the contractual date if the pay day falls on a non-banking day. All payments must be reported even if they are below the lower earnings limit (LEL, £113 per week). They may also have to report certain summary information about statutory payments recovered and other deductions each pay period, and report if they do not pay anyone in a pay period. They must report end of year information at the end of the tax year, and certain information if the PAYE scheme closes. They will have to report when they provide an employee with a car, or replace or withdraw one. They may also have to report expenses and benefits and there is an option for voluntarily payrolling certain benefits from 6 April 2016 (see **10.13**).

A summary of when to report is as follows. If employees are paid weekly, a weekly FPS must be submitted, or if paid monthly, a monthly FPS. If an employer has some weekly and some monthly paid employees, both weekly and monthly FPSs will need to be submitted. If employees are paid more than once in a week or month, an FPS must be submitted on each occasion. Each FPS only needs to contain information about the employees who are actually paid. An FPS can be sent to HMRC in advance, so if for example payroll staff are going on holiday for two weeks, they can make three separate weekly submissions immediately, one after the other, before they leave. If an employee is paid an additional amount between standard paydays another FPS must be sent on or before the employer makes that payment. The same applies if the employer recovers an amount from an employee, for example to correct an overpayment. If no one at all has been paid in the pay period, or the employer wants to recover statutory payments or Construction Industry Scheme (CIS) deductions suffered, then the employer must send an EPS instead of an FPS. An employer can report on an EPS up to 12 months in advance if there will be a period of inactivity.

If employees are paid annually in a single tax month, the employer can ask HMRC to treat the PAYE scheme as an annual scheme. The employer must first advise HMRC of the month they expect to pay employees. In this case an EPS would not be required for each month in which no one at all is paid.

There may be occasion when an employer is unable to report payroll information each time an employee is paid and HMRC have provided a table to show the situations where an FPS does not have to be submitted on or before a payment is made to an employee, and what employers must do instead, see www.gov.uk/running-payroll/fps-after-payday.

HMRC will automatically cancel PAYE schemes on which there has been no activity for at least 120 days, although schemes registered as annual schemes will not be closed by this process.

Operating the PAYE system and making payments to HMRC

[10.60] Employers can use HMRC's Basic PAYE Tools software which can be downloaded from the GOV.UK website and updated as necessary to calculate pay details. Alternatively employers may choose to use one of the commercial software packages available. Manual tax tables or an online PAYE calculator are provided by HMRC for the small number of employers who are exempt from filing online (see **10.59**).

Employers must make monthly payments (but see below regarding quarterly payments) of the total tax and student loan deductions due, and the total employees' and employer's Class 1 NICs, net of recoveries relating to statutory payments.

The payments to HMRC must be made within 14 days after the end of each income tax month ending on the 5th of the month, i.e. by the 19th of each month, or by the 22nd of the month for electronic payments. HMRC guidance is provided at www.gov.uk/pay-paye-tax. Large employers with 250 or more employees are required to make PAYE payments electronically. If the due date falls at the weekend payment must be made by the previous Friday. The few employers not filing online must notify HMRC by telephone or completed 'nil' payslip if there is no PAYE/NIC due for the month, quarter or previous year. This will prevent HMRC sending payment reminders. RTI online employers must still submit either an FPS or an EPS (see **10.58**).

Interest and penalties are charged on any unpaid PAYE amounts and penalties apply for non-compliance with filing and reporting requirements (see **10.68**). If during the tax year the cumulative tax paid by an employee exceeds the cumulative amount due, the excess is refunded to him by the employer, who then deducts it from the amount due to HMRC.

Employers who expect their average net monthly PAYE payment to be less than £1,500 may pay quarterly instead of monthly.

HMRC have the power to ask for a security from employers for PAYE and NIC that is seriously at risk. The required security will usually be either a cash deposit from the business or director which is held by HMRC or paid into a joint HMRC/taxpayer bank account, or a bond from an approved financial institution which is payable on demand. The measure introduces a criminal offence for non-payment of the security.

For details on NICs, see CHAPTER **13**. For details of statutory sick pay and statutory maternity etc. pay, see CHAPTER **14**.

Code numbers

[10.61] Employers calculate tax using code numbers notified by HMRC either on form P9 or via the PAYE online service, or by using the specified 'emergency' procedure where no code number is received. Once a code number is issued it remains in force from year to year until HMRC notify a change. A change in code number may result from a claim by the employee for further reliefs or allowances. From May 2017 tax codes are adjusted in-year using real time information.

A code represents the tax allowances an employee is entitled to, such as personal allowances and allowable expenses in employment, less any deduction to collect the tax due on other income such as the state pension, savings interest or employee benefits such as cars or loans, or to collect underpayments arising in earlier years. Allowances may be restricted in order to limit the tax relief given on certain allowances to tax at 10%, and any restriction will vary according to whether the employee is expected to pay basic, higher, or additional rate tax. Coding adjustments may also be made to give effect to reliefs such as losses (see **25.6**).

The code number is the amount of allowances less the last digit. For example, if allowances total £11,500 the code number is 1,150. The code effectively spreads the tax allowances evenly over the tax year. This means that if an employee earns some extra pay in a pay period there is no extra tax-free allowance to set against it, so that the whole of the extra suffers tax.

Most codes are three or four numbers followed by a suffix L, M, N, S or T. Code suffix L denotes the basic personal allowance of £11,500. Code M denotes an employee who can receive a transfer of some of their spouse or civil partner's personal allowance (see **2.17**), and code N denotes an employee who can transfer some of their personal allowance to their spouse or civil partner. Code S is for a taxpayer whose income or pension is taxed at the Scottish rate of income tax (see **2.4**). The code suffixes enable HMRC to implement changes in allowances by telling employers to increase relevant codes by a specified amount. Suffix T means that the code is only to be changed if a specific notification is received from the tax office. A code T may be requested by a taxpayer who does not want his status to be disclosed in this way to his employer. Code 0T means that all allowances have been used elsewhere and income is taxed at the employee's relevant tax rates. It must be used on employment income of a new employee who fails to complete a Starter Checklist (see **10.64**), on pension income of a person still in receipt of employment income from the employer paying the pension, and on payments to a person who has left an employment and the P45 (see **10.64**) has already been completed, including on payments in connection with employment related securities.

Some codes have a prefix K instead of a suffix. Prefix K enables tax to be collected during the year where the amount of an employee's taxable benefits or an employed pensioner's state pension exceeds available allowances. Other codes are BR, which means basic rate tax applies; NT, which means no tax is to be deducted; D0, which means that all pay is to be taxed at the higher rate because all allowances, and the basic rate band, are used against other income; and D1 which means all pay is to be taxed at the additional rate.

Employees can view their coding notices online if they are enrolled to file tax returns electronically, or by registering for the 'Check your income tax' service. HMRC may now issue a coding notice to an employee by electronic means, but are not required to notify them of their code where they are not liable to tax on any PAYE income.

The tax deducted under any code cannot exceed 50% of cash pay (but see **10.62** regarding notional pay).

HMRC normally collect an underpayment of less than £3,000 via a PAYE coding adjustment. The maximum amount of tax debts that HMRC can collect through an individual's code was increased from 6 April 2015, ranging from £3,000 up to a maximum of £17,000, based on a graduated scale of earnings between £30,000 and £90,000. The increase does not apply to PAYE underpayments or self-assessment balancing payments. However, HMRC can collect tax credit debts in this way.

Outstanding Class 2 NIC can also be collected via a PAYE coding adjustment (see **24.2**).

Payments in non-cash form (notional payments) (ITEPA 2003, ss 222, 687, 687A, 689, 693–700, 710)

[10.62] Where employers provide employees with certain assets that are readily convertible into cash (see **10.31**), PAYE and Class 1 NICs must be charged on the amount which, using the employer's best estimate, is likely to be chargeable as employment income, and accounted for in respect of the pay period in which the asset is provided, whether or not the employee has sufficient pay in that period to enable the tax and employee's NICs to be deducted. Any such tax and NIC that is not deducted from pay should be made good by the employee within 90 days of the end of the tax year in which the asset is provided. If the employee does not do so, the unrecovered amount must be shown as further pay on year-end form P11D. The 50% overriding limit on deduction of tax under all codes (see **10.61**) is ignored when dealing with the deductions for notional payments.

Tax tables and PAYE calculator

[10.63] For the very few employers still using tax tables (see **10.60**), Table A shows the cumulative free pay based on the tax code for each tax week or month, and it includes the adjustments needed to increase the tax collected from employees with K codes by increasing taxable pay. Table B shows the tax due on taxable pay to date at basic rate up to the basic rate limit, Table C1 shows the tax due at the higher rate and Table C2 shows tax due at the additional rate. Table D is non-cumulative, and is a higher and additional rate tax ready reckoner for use with Table C and for D codes. The PAYE calculator works out tax in the same way as tax tables.

Changing jobs or retiring

[10.64] When an employee leaves his job, then unless the employer will be paying a pension, the employer should complete form P45, which is in four parts. He gives the employee parts 1A, 2 and 3, parts 2 and 3 being for the new employer and part 1A for the employee to retain (he will need it if he has to fill in a tax return, and he needs to retain it in any event as part of his tax records — see **10.70**). The employer should not send part 1 to HMRC, but the leaving details from it should be included in an FPS. The P45 shows the total pay and tax to date in the tax year, the code number in use and whether student loan deductions are to be made. Passing the form to the new employer when the employee starts another job enables the employer to continue to deduct tax on the correct basis. An employer should still obtain a starter declaration (see below) for an employee who produces a P45. Statutory redundancy pay and certain other amounts received when the employee leaves are not normally treated as pay, but they may be subject to tax under special rules (see CHAPTER 15).

If an employee cannot produce form P45 his new employer needs to obtain certain information on a Starter Checklist which he should then keep for his own records, having extracted the information to send to HMRC on an FPS. The employee should be asked to declare whether (A) this is his first job since

6 April and he has not received certain benefits or a pension, or (B) this is now his only job but since 6 April he has had another job or received certain benefits, but he does not receive a state or occupational pension, or (C) he has another job or receives a pension. This procedure enables employers to deduct tax on a cumulative basis straight away for those who tick box A, so that they get the benefit of the personal allowance from the beginning of the tax year. If the employee ticks box B, he will be allocated a single person's allowance, code 1150L, on a non-cumulative basis (called week 1 or month 1 basis), which means he will get only one week's (or month's) proportion of the allowance against each week's (month's) pay. If he ticks box C he will pay tax at the basic rate. The employee must also indicate whether he has a student loan, other than one required to be repaid through his bank or building society account. HMRC will notify revised codes as appropriate after receiving the new employee information. If the employee does not provide a P45 or starter information before his first payment, the employer will deduct tax from his pay on a non-cumulative basis using code 0T (see **10.61**).

Employees seconded to work in the UK must provide further information and the employer may use the Expat Starter Checklist.

If the employee is retiring and the employer is not paying him pension, the employer must include leaving details on the FPS. If the employer will be paying a pension, no leaving details should be included in the FPS. The employer will deduct tax from the pension using the existing code on a week 1 or month 1 basis (see above) until HMRC tell him what code number to use. The employer should give the former employee a retirement statement showing their previous employment details up to the date of their retirement. Where the employee starts to receive pension payments in addition to employment payments the employer should set up a separate payroll record, use code 0T on a week 1 or month 1 basis on the employee's pension payment and continue to use the same code as before on the employment income.

If an employee or pensioner dies, the date of death is used as the date of leaving on the FPS. Other Government sources will inform HMRC of the death. No P45 is issued to the personal representatives.

Employers' records and returns

[10.65] Employers must keep payroll records for each employee including details of their monthly payments in respect of net income tax and net Class 1 NICs (see **10.60**). For the few employers exempt from filing online, the totals should be recorded monthly or quarterly either on the employer payment record or in the payslip booklet. For online filers the payroll software enables records to be kept. Employers are required to keep PAYE records for at least the current tax year and the previous three tax years. However, the self-assessment rules require businesses to retain records for longer than this (see for example **9.32**).

Employers should submit their final FPS and/or EPS for the final pay period as normal indicating that it is the 'Final submission for the tax year'. They must do this even if they have not made any deductions of PAYE tax or NICs from employees in that pay period. After that date an Earlier Year Update can be submitted by 19 May to avoid a late filing penalty. Forms P60 must be given to the employees who were in employment at the end of the tax year, showing the total pay (including any statutory sick pay and statutory maternity/paternity/adoption/shared parental pay), student loan deductions and tax and NICs deducted in the year. Forms P60 can be provided on paper or electronically and must be given by 31 May after the tax year. P60s relating to former employees are scrapped. Where necessary, employers may issue duplicate P60s (clearly marked as such).

A copy of form P11D (see **10.67**) must be given to employees as appropriate by 6 July. Copies for employees who left after 5 April may be sent to the last known address. Employers may consider it appropriate to provide copy P11Ds to employees who left *during* the tax year, but they are not *required* to do so unless the employee makes a written request (within three years after the end of that year).

National insurance contributions (SSCBA 1992, s 10; NICA 2014, ss 1–8, Sch 1)

[10.66] Employers' Class 1A NICs (see **10.49**) are calculated annually from the P11D entries, the boxes on the P11D relevant for Class 1A contributions being colour coded. The total of the amounts liable to Class 1A contributions is recorded on form P11D(b) and multiplied by the appropriate percentage (13.8%), and the payment is sent to HMRC Accounts Office using a special Class 1A payslip. The due date for payment is 19 July after the relevant tax year, i.e. by 19 July 2018 for 2017–18. For payments made electronically the payment date is 22 July. When a business ceases, Class 1A contributions are due within 14 days after the end of the income tax month in which the last payment of earnings is made. If a business changes hands, the employer before the change must similarly pay over Class 1A contributions for any employee not continuing with the new owner within 14 days after the end of the final month. The liability for payment of the Class 1A contributions for continuing employees falls on the successor.

For further details regarding employer's NICs see CHAPTER 13.

An employment allowance of £3,000 per year for businesses, charities and community amateur sports clubs can be offset against their employer Class 1 NICs. If a business runs multiple PAYE schemes, the allowance can only be claimed against one of them. The allowance is claimed as part of the normal payroll process through RTI. Employers exempt from filing online can use the paper Employer Payment Summary at the beginning of the tax year. Only one company or charity in a group can claim the allowance, and excluded employers include certain employers of domestic staff, public authorities and other employers who carry out functions of a public nature. The allowance is available to employers of care and support workers where the duties of employment relate to the employer's personal, family or household affairs but not to companies where the director is the sole employee. For guidance see www.gov.uk/claim-employment-allowance.

Forms P11D

[10.67] Employers are required to provide all current employees (and former employees if they so request) with copies of forms P11D (see **10.65**). The forms themselves, together with form P11D(b), which is a combined return for employers' Class 1A contributions and for declaring either that forms P11D are attached for all relevant employees or that no benefits have been provided, must be submitted to HMRC by 6 July after the end of the tax year. Penalties apply for late submission, see **10.68**. Forms P11D and P11D(b) may be filed online but if corrections are required paper versions must be submitted.

Forms P11D show the cash equivalents of benefits for all employees. HMRC provide optional working sheets for working out the cash equivalents for living accommodation, cars and fuel, vans, mileage allowance payments and passenger payments, beneficial loans and relocation expenses.

P11Ds do not have to show amounts covered by a PAYE settlement agreement (see **10.69**) or, from 2016–17, any exempt expenses (see **10.16**). Expenses paid by the employer on behalf of their employee must still be included. Non-exempt and non-allowable expense payments must be taxed through PAYE and the HMRC P11D guide indicates which ones should be included on form P11D. Legislation specifically provides that non-approved mileage allowance payments and non-approved passenger payments should be included on the P11D (see **10.13**).

An employer must include on P11Ds any benefits he has arranged for a third party to provide (for example, where another group company provides cars or medical insurance). The onus of providing the information falls on the third party rather than the employer if the employer has not arranged for the third party to provide the benefits, and the third party must provide the information to the employee by 6 July after the end of the tax year. The rules for benefits provided directly by third parties do not apply to gifts costing not more than £250 per year or to corporate hospitality. Third parties do not need to send details of the taxable benefits to HMRC unless they receive a return requiring them to do so. Class 1A contributions are payable on taxable third party benefits, including non-cash vouchers (see **10.49**). See **10.69** regarding the liability for paying the Class 1A contributions.

See **10.5** regarding anti-avoidance provisions relating to employment income provided through third parties.

See **10.13** regarding the voluntary payrolling of certain benefits from 6 April 2016.

Interest and penalties

[10.68] As stated at **10.60**, interest is charged if PAYE and NICs are paid late; see **9.55** and **9.56**.

Late payment penalties also apply to the monthly, quarterly and annual PAYE periods; see **9.74**.

Penalties are payable by employers who do not file year-end RTI returns by 19 May; see **9.65**.

Penalties for a careless or deliberate error in most PAYE returns apply. The penalties are based on a percentage of potential lost revenue, with reductions for disclosure; see **9.58**.

Penalties are also charged for late filing of forms P11D; see **9.66**.

PAYE settlement agreements and taxed award schemes

[10.69] Employers may enter into a PAYE settlement agreement (PSA) with HMRC, under which they make a single annual payment covering the tax and NICs on certain benefits and possibly expenses payments. Items covered by the PSA are not shown on year-end forms FPS and P11D and employees are not subject to tax or NICs on them. The scheme covers items which are either minor or occasional, or are made in circumstances when it would be impracticable to apply PAYE (e.g. on shared benefits). Details are in HMRC Statement of Practice SP 5/96. PAYE settlements frequently include payments for those who had been treated as self-employed and are reclassified as employees.

As far as NICs are concerned, employers pay a special class of contributions, Class 1B, at 13.8% on the benefits etc. taxed under the PSA plus the tax thereon, to the extent that there would have been an NICs liability under Class 1 or Class 1A. Both the tax payment under the PSA and the Class 1B contributions thereon are payable by 19 October after the end of the tax year to which the payment relates. For payments made electronically the payment date is 22 October. Interest is charged from the due date if the payment is made late.

September 2017 Finance Bill, which is expected to receive Royal Assent in November 2017, removes the need for PSAs to be agreed with HMRC. This will result in introduction of a digital PSA process, replacing the paper return with a digital return, from April 2018. Employers will be able to submit their PSA request at the tax year end, and to make ad hoc requests during the year.

Employers and third parties who operate formal incentive award schemes are able to enter into arrangements known as taxed award schemes (TAS), which work in a similar way to PSAs. Employers operating such schemes directly (but not third parties) may use a PSA instead if they wish. Employers have to account for Class 1 or Class 1A NICs as the case may be on non-cash vouchers or other benefits provided to employees, where the vouchers/benefits are provided directly or where the employers arranged for them to be provided by a third party. They also have to pay Class 1 contributions on the tax paid under a TAS. Where non-cash vouchers or other benefits are provided by a third party (whether under a TAS or not), Class 1A rather than Class 1 contributions are payable. Where the employer has not arranged for the awards to be provided, third parties must pay the Class 1A contributions on the award, and if they also pay the associated tax, they are liable for the Class 1A contributions on the tax payment. Third parties may use the TAS accounting arrangements to make payment. Guidance is provided in HMRC's Employment Income Manual at EIM11235. The taxed award scheme is outside the scope of RTI.

Employees' records and self-assessment

[10.70] All taxpayers are required to keep records relating to their tax liabilities (see **9.32**). Most employees will not need to fill in tax returns unless they are subject to the high income child benefit charge (see **10.7**), because their tax will usually be dealt with through the PAYE system (see **9.34**), but they should still keep records for the statutory period in case there is any query. Employees need to keep records for 22 months from the end of the tax year (or 15 months after the return was submitted if later), unless they are also self-employed or receive rental income, in which case the period is 5 years 10 months (or such earlier date as may be specified in writing by HMRC). In both cases, if HMRC are conducting an enquiry into the taxpayer's affairs (see **9.41**), the period is extended until the enquiry is completed.

The main records employees need to keep are year-end certificates P60 and forms P11D, details from the employer of any benefits voluntarily payrolled (see **10.13**), forms P45 when they change jobs, and records, receipts and vouchers to support expenses claims. They should also keep any other records that relate to their employment income, such as coding notices, information relating to employee share schemes, information relating to earnings abroad, and proof of any foreign tax deducted.

Apprenticeship levy (FA 2016, ss 98–121)

[10.71] The apprenticeship levy was introduced on 1 April 2017 and applies to UK employers. It is set at a rate of 0.5% of an employer's paybill and paid through PAYE. Each employer receives an allowance of £15,000 to offset against their levy payment. This means that the levy will only be paid on any paybill in excess of £3 million. The paybill is the total of employee earnings subject to Class secondary 1 NIC as if disregarding the secondary threshold (see **13.4**). Employers will be able to draw down on apprenticeship levy funds for the purpose of establishing apprenticeships. See www.gov.uk/government/publications/apprenticeship-levy-how-it-will-work/apprenticeship-levy-how-it-will-work.

Tax points

[10.72] Note the following:

- Employers' Class 1A NICs on taxable benefits in kind removes the main advantage of paying such benefits, though an employee's NICs saving for employees earning less than the upper earnings limit of £8,667 a week may be available. Even where there is no such saving, it may be possible to provide benefits for less than the employee would have paid himself, by use of in-house services, or staff discounts.
- Where tips are received, great care needs to be taken in relation to the PAYE and NICs treatment.

- The 'pecuniary liability' trap should be borne in mind. Payment by an employer of an *employee's* debt counts as pay for employees and must be reported on year-end forms P11D. Class 1 NICs are payable at the time of the payment.

- Travelling expenses from home to a permanent workplace are not deductible in calculating taxable earnings unless the nature of the employee's job requires him to carry out his duties at home. Area representatives and those holding part-time employments, such as consultants and tribunal members, should seek to establish that their place of employment is at their home or other workbase, making their travelling expenses from that base deductible.

- HMRC's compliance checks apply to PAYE. Factsheet CC/FS1a gives general guidance.

- HMRC test payroll software packages and award a payroll standard kitemark to those that meet the PAYE requirements.

- HMRC offer to help small businesses with PAYE problems in various ways, including offering online presentations, e-learning courses and access to tax information videos, see www.gov.uk/government/news/webinars-emails-and-videos-on-employing-people.

- Forms P11D are increasingly subject to close scrutiny and testing by HMRC as to their accuracy, for example through visits to business premises, knowledge of directors' personal circumstances and a close inspection of the position as regards loans to directors. Care should therefore be taken to ensure that all sections of the form are correctly completed.

- The total cost in tax, NICs and VAT of the provision of private car fuel to employees has risen dramatically and in many cases it will be cheaper, as well as far more straightforward in terms of reporting requirements, to pay the employee extra wages to compensate him for buying his own private fuel.

- An employee's contribution towards the cost of a car (maximum £5,000) and payments for the private use of a car both reduce the car benefit charge (see **10.38**), but payments by the employee for car fuel are not taken into account unless they cover the whole cost of private use.

- If a car is provided for a relative of an employee, the benefit will be charged on the car user rather than the employee if the car user is also an employee and the duties of the employment are such that the car is required in the performance of those duties (e.g. where the employee is a commercial traveller) and would be provided to any employee in equivalent circumstances.

- If an employee is required to use his own vehicle, motor cycle or bicycle in employment, mileage allowances based on HMRC approved mileage rates (see **10.17**) may be received from the employer free of both tax and NICs. If he pays his own running expenses, he can claim the approved rates for the business miles. If the employer pays him a mileage allowance below the approved rates he can claim an allowance for the shortfall for tax but not NIC purposes.

- There is no tax on an interest-free loan to an employee to buy a season ticket unless the total loans at a nil or beneficial interest rate that are outstanding in that tax year from the employee exceed £10,000.
- An employee is charged to tax on benefits arising from employment even though the employer is not the payer. The most common example is tips (but see **10.10**). Another example is where one of the employer's suppliers pays for the employee to have a foreign holiday as a sales achievement reward. Such a supplier may operate a 'taxed award scheme' under which he accounts for the tax. The employee must be provided with relevant details of all third party benefits to enable him to complete his tax return, but he is responsible for the entries on the return.
- Third party benefits to employees in the form of corporate hospitality, such as entrance to and entertainment at sporting and cultural events, and non-cash gifts to an employee from a third party costing not more than £250 in a tax year, are exempt providing the benefits and/or gifts are not procured by the employer and are not related to services performed or to be performed in the employment.
- HMRC frequently reviews the list of professional subscriptions which are allowable in computing the taxable pay of an employee. An employee should therefore check if his own subscription has not so far been allowed, see www.gov.uk/government/publications/professional-bodies-approved-for-tax-relief-list-3.
- If an employee *occasionally* works very late, he is not charged to tax if his employer pays for his transport home. Those who regularly work late get no such exemption, although exemption applies if the employer pays for the transport home because of a temporary breakdown in regular home to work car sharing arrangements.
- 'Payment' for PAYE purposes can be triggered much earlier than when money changes hands, especially as regards directors (see CHAPTER 12).
- Under self-assessment, an individual needs to keep records relating to his tax affairs — see **10.70**. HMRC provide guidance at www.gov.uk/keeping-your-pay-tax-records.

11

Employee share options and awards

Background

[11.1] Tax law provides various incentives to encourage employees and directors to participate in their employing companies. HMRC guidance recognises that studies have shown that 'when the interests of employees are aligned with those of their employer through shareholdings in the employer company, there is a correlation with increased company productivity'. Four long-standing statutory arrangements are designed to 'encourage employees to hold shares in their employer'. These are:

- SAYE linked share option schemes (SAYE, often known as 'sharesave') — see **11.10**
- Company share option plans (CSOPs) — see **11.12**
- Enterprise management incentive (EMI) share option schemes — see **11.13**
- Share incentive plans (SIPs) — see **11.20**

HMRC guidance is available at www.gov.uk/topic/business-tax/employment-r elated-securities and in HMRC's Employment Related Securities Manual and Employee Tax Advantaged Share Scheme User Manual.

The legislation applies to employment-related 'securities'. Employment-related means, broadly, acquired in connection with an employment. Securities include shares, debentures, loan stock and other securities issued by companies, and a wide range of other financial instruments including options, futures, contracts for differences and rights under contracts of insurance.

Some employees could previously adopt the employee shareholder status, under which they give up certain employment rights in return for shares in their employer's company but the income tax and capital gains tax reliefs in relation to employee shareholder shares have been abolished for arrangements entered into on or after 1 December 2016 (or 2 December 2016 in cases where the potential employee shareholder received professional advice in relation to the share offer on 23 November 2016 before 1.30pm). Whilst this scheme is not within the legislation relating to employment-related securities, commentary on it can be found at **11.36**.

Reporting requirements (ITEPA 2003, ss 421J–421L)

[11.2] There is a general requirement to report certain events relating to shares and securities obtained by reason of an employment. The 'responsible person' (broadly the employer or person from whom the securities were acquired) must file an annual return online (other than where HMRC have allowed another form of filing) no later than 6 July following the end of the tax year. Returns containing the information required by HMRC must be made for each tax year during a 'reportable event period' which starts when the first reportable event occurs for which that person is responsible, and ends when that person will no longer be responsible for reportable events. There are penalties for incorrect and late returns (unless there is a reasonable excuse for a late return). There is an initial penalty of £100 for late filing. If the failure to file continues for three months there is a further penalty of £300, followed by a further £300 penalty if the failure continues beyond six months. If the failure continues beyond nine months and HMRC give notice, a daily penalty of £10 applies. If the return or accompanying information is not filed in the form required by HMRC or has a material inaccuracy which is careless or deliberate, or it is not corrected after the error is discovered by the responsible person, a penalty up to a maximum of £5,000 applies.

The reportable events include:

- a person's acquisition or deemed acquisition of securities, or an interest in securities or a securities option, where the acquisition is pursuant to a right or opportunity available by reason of his employment or another person's employment;
- a 'chargeable event' in relation to restricted securities, restricted interests in securities, convertible securities or interests in convertible securities;
- the doing of anything that artificially enhances the market value of the securities and gives rise to a tax charge on 'non-commercial increases';
- an event which discharges a 'notional loan' that arose where, for example, securities were acquired for less than market value;
- a disposal of securities for more than market value in certain circumstances;
- the receipt of a benefit from securities or interest in securities giving rise to taxable employment income;
- the assignment or release of an employment-related securities option in certain circumstances; and

- the receipt of a benefit in money or money's worth in connection with an employment-related securities option.

There are, however, a large number of exceptions from the reporting requirements. These include transfers of shares in the normal course of family or personal relationships, share for share exchanges, and rights and bonus issues.

PAYE tax and NICs (ITEPA 2003, ss 696–702)

[11.3] Employers are required to operate PAYE, and account for tax and Class 1 NICs, when shares etc. that are 'readily convertible assets' (see **10.31**) are acquired by a person (not necessarily the employee) and the right or opportunity to make the acquisition is available by reason of an employment of that person or any other person outside the terms of a tax-advantaged scheme.

Shares etc. are readily convertible assets if they may be sold on the Stock Exchange or arrangements exist or are likely to exist for them to be traded. These provisions apply to shares etc. acquired directly and through the exercise of non-tax-advantaged options that were granted on or after 27 November 1996. They also apply where tax is charged when a share or securities option is assigned or released (see **11.7**), or a chargeable event occurs under the anti-avoidance provisions outlined in **11.6**.

Where shares etc. acquired in such circumstances are not readily convertible assets, neither Class 1 nor Class 1A NICs are payable, but tax is chargeable through the self-assessment system (see **11.35**). However, shares etc. that would not otherwise be readily convertible assets are automatically treated as such (except for the purposes of the share incentive plan rules at **11.28**) if no corporation tax deduction is available under the provisions at **11.33**. Where the chargeable event takes the form of a receipt of money, or of an asset which is a readily convertible asset, PAYE etc. applies regardless of whether or not the scheme shares are themselves readily convertible assets. Where the tax treatment of readily convertible assets is retrospectively amended (as it was in Finance Act 2006 in relation to securities options — see **11.7**), the deemed payment date for PAYE purposes will be the date the relevant Act is passed, except in relation to PAYE arising from the Finance Act 2006 provisions, for which the deemed payment date was 6 April 2007. Detailed and complex provisions apply as to the way in which the payments are treated, including re-allocating the payments to the appropriate tax year and providing revised PAYE forms.

In the case of share options granted on or after 6 April 1999 that relate to shares that are readily convertible assets, NICs are payable when the options are exercised. Because of the unpredictable timing and amount of a company's liability to pay employer's secondary contributions on non-tax-advantaged options, employees and employers may make formal joint elections to HMRC for the employees to pay the employers' secondary NICs when the option is exercised. Such elections need HMRC approval. Alternatively the employer and employee may make an agreement for the contributions to be paid by the employee. In this event the formal liability remains with the employer. In either case, any amount paid by the employee will reduce the amount chargeable as employment income in respect of the option for tax purposes (but not for NICs). It will not affect the corporation tax deduction allowable to the company (see **11.33**), nor the allowable cost of the shares for capital gains tax, but see **11.8**. The same provisions apply in relation to chargeable events in respect of restricted securities and convertible securities (see **11.6**).

Other provisions

[11.4] Subject to certain restrictions, employers can get tax relief for the costs of setting up tax-advantaged share option schemes and share incentive plans, and see the relief at **11.33** for the cost of providing shares for employee share schemes. For capital gains tax purposes, on the grant of an option under a tax-advantaged or non-tax-advantaged scheme, the employer is treated as receiving the amount, if any, paid by the employee for the option (rather than market value, which usually applies to non-arm's length transactions — see **4.31**), so no tax charge on chargeable gains arises.

Shares acquired under SAYE option schemes and share incentive plans may be transferred free of capital gains tax into an Individual Savings Account up to the annual limit for ISA investments (see **36.15**) even if they are unquoted. There is no similar provision in relation to enterprise management incentive share options, but favourable capital gains tax treatment applies to such options. Shares acquired under SAYE schemes or share incentive plans may be transferred into registered pension schemes and tax relief obtained thereon (see **17.6**).

Special rules apply where employees of universities and other research institutions acquire shares in 'spinout' companies formed to develop intellectual property (IP) that the employees helped to create. The value of the IP will not be taken into account at the time it is transferred to the spinout company, thus removing a potential tax and NICs charge at that time, and various other provisions in this chapter are disapplied.

Share awards outside tax-advantaged schemes

Issue of shares for less than market value (ITEPA 2003, ss 446Q–446W)

[11.5] If shares are issued at a price equal to the current market value, with the price being paid by agreed instalments, no charge will arise under the general charging provisions since full market value is being paid, and this will apply even though the market value has increased by the time the shares are paid for. Any growth in value of the shares is liable only to capital gains tax.

A director or an employee who acquires shares other than under the tax-advantaged schemes and does not pay the full price for shares immediately is, however, regarded as having received an interest-free loan equal to the deferred instalments, on which tax is charged at the beneficial loans interest rate (see TABLE OF RATES AND ALLOWANCES (**TRA**)) unless the total of all beneficial loans outstanding from that director or employee in the tax year, including the deferred instalments, does not exceed £10,000 (see **10.48**). The loan is regarded as being repaid as and when the instalments are paid. Any amount written off is taxed as employment income at that time; any amount so taxed is taken into account for capital gains tax purposes when the shares are disposed of.

The notional loan provisions do not apply if something affecting the shares has been done as part of a scheme to avoid tax and/or NICs. Instead the amount that would have been treated as a loan is treated as employment income in the tax year when the acquisition takes place.

Anti-avoidance rules

[11.6] There are wide ranging anti-avoidance provisions in relation to employment-related shares and securities. They do not apply in relation to shares that comply with the provisions of tax-advantaged schemes, but enterprise management incentive schemes (see **11.13**) are not regarded as tax-advantaged schemes for this purpose. The provisions apply to advantages gained not just by the employee but by 'associated persons'. 'Associated persons' include the person who acquired the shares (if not the employee), persons connected with the employee (or with the person who acquired the shares) and members of the same household as the employee (or person who acquired the shares). The definition of 'connected' is broadly the same as in **4.11**. There are exemptions from some of the provisions where the shares are acquired under a public offer, or are shares in an employee-controlled company or where the event in question affects all the company's shares of the same class and the majority of them are held by outside shareholders; these exceptions apply in respect of restricted shares, convertible shares and post-acquisition benefits.

The anti-avoidance provisions under which tax and NICs charges may arise fall under the following headings:

- Restricted securities (ITEPA 2003, ss 422–432)
- Convertible securities (ITEPA 2003, ss 435–444)
- Securities with artificially depressed market value (ITEPA 2003, ss 446A–446J)
- Securities with artificially enhanced market value (ITEPA 2003, ss 446K–446P)
- Securities acquired for less than market value (ITEPA 2003, ss 446Q–446W — see **11.5**)
- Securities disposed of for more than market value (ITEPA 2003, ss 446X–446Z)
- Post-acquisition benefits from securities (ITEPA 2003, ss 447–450)

A form of rollover relief from income tax applies for certain cases in which restricted securities are exchanged for other restricted securities, so that neither the disposal of the old securities nor the acquisition of the new securities will give rise to a tax liability.

If the securities concerned are readily convertible assets, the amounts chargeable will be liable to PAYE tax and Class 1 NICs (see **11.3**).

Under legislation applying before 6 April 2015 the provisions listed above (and those in **11.7** relating to non-tax-advantaged options) applied if the individual concerned was UK resident at the time of acquisition. This means that an exception to the provisions applied if, at the time of acquisition, the earnings from the employment in question were not earnings for a year when the employee was resident in the UK or were not, where the remittance basis applied (see **41.16**), broadly overseas earnings taxable because they were remitted to the UK. Therefore, any foreign securities income (broadly any securities income received from a foreign employer where employment duties are performed wholly outside the UK) was exempt except in certain circumstances where the main purpose was the avoidance of PAYE and NICs.

From 6 April 2015 there are simplified tax and NICs arrangements for employment-related securities (ERS) and ERS options awarded to internationally mobile employees which broadly preserve the above rules but also clarify the income which is to be subject to UK income tax either on a normal arising basis or the remittance basis where this applies. Any ERS income attributable to days when an individual is not in the UK social security system is disregarded and not subject to an NICs liability. For HMRC guidance see Employment-Related Securities Manual ERSM162000.

Exercise, assignment, release etc. of option (ITEPA 2003, ss 420, 471–484, TCGA 1992, ss 119A, 120, 144, 144ZA–144ZD)

[11.7] Where a director or employee is granted an option to acquire shares or securities (referred to as shares etc. in what follows) by reason of employment (whether his own or someone else's), there are various circumstances in which a tax charge can arise. However, favourable tax treatment is given for options under tax-advantaged schemes (see **11.10** to **11.19**). Securities options such as call options are excluded from the tax charging provisions unless they were acquired on or after 2 December 2004 for the purpose of avoiding tax or NICs.

Where the option is granted other than under a tax-advantaged scheme, an income tax charge arises when the option is *exercised* on the difference between the open market value at that time and the cost of the shares. If the shares are readily convertible assets, the tax will be collected through PAYE, and Class 1 NICs will also be payable, although the employee may agree to pay the employer's secondary Class 1 NICs (see **11.3**).

Legislation clarifies that from 6 April 2016 the acquisition or the exercise of an option is charged to tax under these provisions, rather than any provisions that deal with earnings.

For both tax-advantaged schemes and other options, where a right to acquire shares etc. is assigned or released, an income tax charge arises on the amount received. The same applies where the option holder realises a gain or benefit by allowing the option to lapse, or granting someone else an option over the shares etc. The same comments apply as above if the shares etc. are readily convertible assets.

These tax charges apply on the exercise, assignment or release of the option by any associated person and not just by the employee (i.e. the person by reason of whose employment the option was granted). 'Associated persons' include the person to whom the option was granted (if not the employee), persons connected with the employee (or with the grantee) and members of the same household as the employee (or grantee).

A tax charge also arises on the amount or market value of any benefit received, in money or money's worth, by the employee (or an associated person) in connection with the option, which might include, for example, sums received for varying the option or as compensation for its cancellation.

Whatever the reason for a tax charge, any amount paid for the option itself and expenses incurred in connection with the exercise, assignment, release or receipt of benefit are deductible in determining the taxable amount.

[11.8] For capital gains tax, the amount taxed as income on exercise of a non-tax-advantaged employee shares etc. option often counts as part of the cost of acquisition of the shares etc. (as does anything paid for the option itself). However, HMRC changed their view in relation to shares acquired on the exercise of an option before 10 April 2003. The acquisition cost of such shares is the market value of the shares at the time the option was exercised, and no deduction is allowed for any amount charged to income tax on the exercise. See HMRC Briefs 30/2009 and 60/2009 for full details.

Grant of option (ITEPA 2003, s 475)

[11.9] No income tax liability arises on the *grant* of an option, unless exceptionally the option is granted at a discount under a company share option plan scheme (see **11.12**). (The cost figure taken into account for capital gains tax is, however, subject to anti-avoidance provisions.) Where a discount is charged to tax on the grant of an option it is deducted from the amount chargeable when the option is exercised.

SAYE linked share option schemes (ITEPA 2003, ss 516–519, Sch 3; TCGA 1992, Sch 7D; ITTOIA 2005, Pt 6 Ch 4)

[11.10] These tax-advantaged schemes enable an employer company to grant to employees and directors an option to acquire shares in the company in the future at today's price, the shares eventually being paid for out of the proceeds of a linked Save As You Earn (SAYE) scheme. No income tax charge arises on the grant of the option, and there is no charge on the difference between cost and market value of the shares when the option is exercised. HMRC guidance is provided in the Employee Tax Advantaged Share Scheme User Manual at ETASSUM30100.

Contributions of between £5 and £500 per month are paid for up to five years, and are normally deducted from pay, under an SAYE contract with a bank or building society. The employee/director will normally be able to exercise the option after three years, five years or seven years, when the SAYE contract ends, although the 7-year savings period was withdrawn for new SAYE contracts from July 2013. The contributions will be of an amount that will secure as nearly as possible, when interest is added, the repayment of a sum equal to the exercise price. Interest and bonuses added to contributions are tax-free.

Various conditions must be met. In particular the scheme must be available to all full-time directors and all employees with a stipulated length of service which cannot be set at more than five years, and all members of the scheme must participate on similar terms. Part-time employees must be included, but part-time directors may be excluded.

A purpose test states that schemes must provide benefits for employees and directors in the form of share options, and must not provide benefits other than in accordance with the rules in ITEPA 2003, Sch 3. In particular the scheme must not provide cash as an alternative to shares or share options. For schemes which were approved before 6 April 2014, this test only applies if there is an alteration to a key feature on or after that date.

The shares to be acquired must be ordinary shares in the company that established the scheme or a company which controls it. If the employing company or the part of its business in which the employee works is sold or otherwise leaves the group operating the scheme, the scheme may provide for the employee to exercise the option within six months after that event, but if this results in the employee exercising the option within three years of joining the scheme, any gain arising is charged to income tax and NICs (see **11.3**).

An employee who has been transferred to an associated company which is not participating in the scheme may nonetheless be permitted by the scheme rules to exercise his option within six months after his savings contract matures. If an employee dies before completing the contract, the option may be exercised within 12 months after the date of death. If an employee leaves through injury, disability, redundancy, retirement, or certain company take-overs, the option may be exercised within the following six months. An option held by an employee leaving for any other reason must lapse, unless he had held it for at least three years, in which case he may be permitted to exercise it within six months after leaving.

Regardless of the treatment of the option, the SAYE contract itself may be continued by an employee after he leaves, by arrangement with the savings body, so that the benefit of receiving tax-free interest and bonuses at the end of the contract (see below) is retained. Contributions will then be paid direct to the savings body.

The price at which the option may be exercised must not normally be less than 80% of the market value of the shares at the time the option is granted, or such earlier time which may be determined in accordance with HMRC guidance. The employee does not get tax relief for the SAYE contributions but he gets the benefit of tax-free interest and bonuses at the end of the contract, and when the shares are taken up there is no income tax charge on the excess of the market value over the price paid. If the shares are not taken up, the employee retains the proceeds of the SAYE contract together with the tax-free interest and bonuses.

The scheme must not stipulate a minimum monthly contribution higher than £10 and it must not have features that discourage eligible employees from participating. Companies may require scheme shares to be sold if an employee or director leaves the company, thus helping family companies who wish to ensure that their control is not diluted, and scheme rights can be exchanged for equivalent rights in a company taking over the employer company.

There are rules regarding self-certification of schemes and online filing of returns. In order for the scheme to qualify for favourable tax treatment the scheme organiser must give notice to HMRC and make a declaration that it meets the relevant conditions no later than 6 July in the tax year following the one in which the first option is granted under the scheme, though for notices given on or after 6 April 2016 a reasonable excuse provision for late notification is introduced. Once notice has been given, scheme organisers must submit annual returns containing the information HMRC require no later than 6 July following the tax year end. The return must give details of any changes to key features of the scheme, and of any variations made to the terms of the SAYE options to take account of variations in share capital, together with a declaration that the changes have not prevented the scheme meeting the relevant conditions. Errors in returns must be corrected without delay and returns must be submitted for every tax year until such time as all share options granted have been exercised, or are no longer capable of being exercised, and no further options will be granted. The notice and returns must be submitted online, unless HMRC allow submission in another way. Existing schemes had to be registered by 6 July 2015 and companies had to self-certify that any tax-advantaged schemes met certain requirements to avoid losing those tax advantages. Schemes which were refused approval or had approval withdrawn before 6 April 2014 cannot be tax-advantaged schemes under these provisions.

There are penalties for incorrect and late returns which are the same as those outlined in 11.2 for other employee share schemes.

HMRC may make enquiries into the scheme in certain specified circumstances such as their believing that the relevant conditions have not been met. Subsequently they may decide that the scheme is not to be a qualifying scheme from a specified date, in which case the scheme organiser is liable to a penalty not exceeding twice the amount of income tax and NICs that HMRC estimate employees have not paid on options granted under the scheme before that date. If HMRC decide that the breach of conditions is insufficient to result in the scheme not being a qualifying scheme, the scheme organiser must correct any failure in a specified time and is liable to a penalty not exceeding £5,000. If the failure is not so corrected further penalties apply. There are provisions for the scheme organiser to appeal against HMRC decisions such as the decision that the scheme is not a qualifying scheme, and the imposition of penalties.

Capital gains tax

[11.11] The capital gains tax base cost of the shares is the price paid by the employee both for the option and the shares, so that when they are disposed of, the benefit of acquiring them at less than their market value is then partly lost, because the gain is charged to tax (except for the benefit of any unused capital gains tax annual exemption — see **4.29**). The employee has, however, had the benefit of the SAYE tax-free interest and bonuses. See **11.32** for the special capital gains tax rules for identifying share disposals with acquisitions. If the opportunity is taken to transfer the shares into an Individual Savings Account (ISA) within 90 days of exercise of the option and within the annual ISA limits (see **36.16**), the capital gain on the transfer to the ISA is tax-free.

Company Share Option Plan (CSOP) schemes (ITEPA 2003, ss 521–526, Sch 4; TCGA 1992, Sch 7D)

[11.12] Options under tax-advantaged company share option plans must not be granted at a discount (i.e. at an option price below the market value of the shares at the time the option is granted, or such earlier time which may be determined in accordance with HMRC guidance) and the total market value of shares that may be acquired under the option and any other tax-advantaged options held by the employee under the company share option plan must not exceed £30,000. Providing the scheme complies with these and other conditions, there is no tax charge when options are granted. If, exceptionally, an option *is* granted at a discount, the discount is taxed as employment income for the tax year in which the option is granted, though the amount taxed is deductible in computing any amount that falls to be taxed subsequently, for example on exercise of the option when the scheme no longer meets the qualifying conditions, or in determining the amount of any interest-free loan under **11.5**. HMRC guidance is provided in the Employee Tax Advantaged Share Scheme User Manual at ETASSUM40100.

There is no income tax charge when the option is exercised, providing it is exercised between three and ten years after it was granted. There is also no income tax charge if the option is exercised within three years after it was granted but within six months of the employment coming to an end because of injury, disability, redundancy, retirement, or certain company takeovers. Where the income tax exemption applies, tax (i.e. capital gains tax) is payable only at the time of disposal of the shares. The total amount paid for the shares, including any discount charged to income tax when the option was granted and any amount paid for the option itself, is deducted from the proceeds in calculating any capital gain. See **11.32** for the special capital gains tax rules for identifying share disposals with acquisitions. If options are exercised in breach of the stipulated time limits or at a time when the scheme no longer meets the qualifying conditions, they are taxable in the same way as non-tax-advantaged options, with PAYE tax and NICs applying if the shares are readily convertible assets (see 11.7). PAYE also applies if the option is exercised more than ten years after it was granted.

Both full-time and part-time employees may be included in a scheme, but only full-time directors are eligible. HMRC guidance indicates that 'full-time' is taken to mean a working week of at least 25 hours excluding meal breaks. In contrast to SAYE linked share option schemes at 11.10, there is no requirement that the scheme be made available to all directors and employees who are eligible.

An individual cannot participate if he has a material interest (or has had one at any time in the previous 12 months) in either a close company (see 3.29) whose shares may be acquired as a result of exercising the options or a close company controlling the company whose shares may be acquired. A material interest is defined, broadly, as owning or controlling (alone or together with certain associates) more than 30% of the ordinary share capital or rights to more than 30% of the assets in a winding up.

There is a purpose test which states that schemes must provide benefits for employees and directors in the form of share options, and must not provide benefits other than in accordance with the rules in ITEPA 2003, Sch 4. In particular the scheme must not provide cash as an alternative to shares or share options. For schemes which were approved before 6 April 2014, this test only applies if there is an alteration to a key feature on or after that date. In addition, for options granted on or after 6 April 2014, certain terms of the options must be stated at the time of grant. This includes the time and price at which the shares may be acquired by exercise of the option; the number and description of the shares which may be so acquired; the restrictions to which the shares may be subject; and the circumstances in which the option will lapse or be cancelled.

The shares to be acquired must be ordinary shares in the company that established the scheme or a company which controls it. Options granted on or after 24 March 2010 cannot be over shares in an unlisted company which is under the control of a listed company. There was a transitional period of six months during which the scheme rules could be amended in order to prevent withdrawal of HMRC approval of the scheme.

Schemes may provide that participants must exercise their options when their employment ends but may also provide for options to be exchanged for equivalent options in a company taking over the employer company. The scheme may provide for options to be exercised within one year after the employee's death.

There are rules regarding self-certification of schemes and online filing of returns. In order for the scheme to qualify for favourable tax treatment the scheme organiser must give notice to HMRC and make a declaration that it meets the relevant conditions no later than 6 July in the tax year following the one in which the first option is granted under the scheme, though for notices given on or after 6 April 2016 a reasonable excuse provision for late notification is introduced. Once notice has been given, scheme organisers must submit annual returns containing the information HMRC require no later than 6 July following the tax year end. The return must give details of any changes to key features of the scheme, and of any variations made to the terms of the options to take account of variations in share capital, together with a declaration that the changes have not prevented the scheme meeting the relevant conditions. Errors in returns must be corrected without delay and returns must be submitted for every tax year until such time as all share options granted have been exercised, or are no longer capable of being exercised, and no further options will be granted. The notice and returns must be submitted online, unless HMRC allow submission in another way. Existing schemes had to be registered by 6 July 2015 and companies had to self-certify that any tax-advantaged schemes met certain requirements to avoid losing those tax advantages. Schemes which were refused approval or had approval withdrawn before 6 April 2014 cannot be tax-advantaged schemes under these provisions.

There are penalties for incorrect and late returns which are the same as those outlined in **11.2** for other employee share schemes.

HMRC may make enquiries into the scheme in certain specified circumstances in the same way as outlined in **11.10** for SAYE schemes.

Enterprise management incentive share options (ITEPA 2003, ss 527–541, Sch 5; TCGA 1992, s 169I and Sch 7D)

[11.13] Small, higher-risk companies may offer their employees enterprise management incentive (EMI) share options, subject to a limit of £3 million on the total value of shares in respect of which there are unexercised share options. Providing the scheme rules are complied with, there will normally be no income tax or employers' and employees' NICs to pay on the exercise of the option. There is no requirement for the scheme to be registered, but notice must be given when options are granted (see **11.17**). HMRC guidance is provided in the Employee Tax Advantaged Share Scheme User Manual at ETASSUM50000. State aid approval has been granted until April 2018 and the Government plans to seek to extend this.

For an option to be a qualifying EMI option, the company must be a qualifying company (see **11.14**), the employee must be an eligible employee (**11.15**), and certain conditions must be satisfied in relation to the option itself (**11.16**).

Qualifying companies

[11.14] For a company to be a qualifying company, the following conditions must be satisfied. The company may be either quoted and unquoted:

(a)   The company must not be a 51% subsidiary, or otherwise controlled by another company and persons connected with that company. A company which is subject to an employee-ownership trust (see **42.49**) will not be excluded by this rule.

(b)   If the company has subsidiaries, they must be 51% owned, except for property managing subsidiaries, which must be 90% owned.

(c)   The company's (or if relevant, the group's) gross assets must not exceed £30 million.

(d)   For options granted by a 'single company' on or after 21 July 2008, the company must have fewer than 250 'full-time equivalent employees'. The number is calculated by taking the number of full-time employees and adding 'just and reasonable' fractions for other employees. Directors (but not employees on maternity or paternity leave, or parental leave, or students on vocational training) are counted as employees for this purpose. In the case of a parent company, employees of both the parent and its subsidiaries count towards the limit. HMRC regard 'full-time' for this purpose as a standard working week, excluding lunch breaks and overtime, of at least 35 hours.

(e)   Broadly, the company or group must carry on one or more qualifying trades on a commercial basis and with a view to profit, and, have a permanent establishment in the UK. Qualifying trades exclude:
dealing in land, commodities, futures, shares, securities or other financial instruments;
dealing in goods other than in an ordinary trade of wholesale or retail distribution;
banking, insurance, money-lending, debt-factoring, hire-purchase financing or other financial activities;
leasing or receiving royalties or licence fees (with certain exclusions);
legal and accountancy services;
property development;
farming or market gardening, woodlands, forestry activities and timber production;
hotels, nursing homes or residential care homes; and
shipbuilding, producing coal, or producing steel.

Eligible employees

[11.15] The employee must be employed by either the company whose shares are the subject of the option or that company's qualifying subsidiary. He must be required to work, on average, at least 25 hours a week or, if less, 75% of his working time (which includes time spent in both employment and self-employment). He and his associates must not have a 'material interest' in the company. A material interest is defined, broadly, as owning or controlling more than 30% of the ordinary share capital or, where the company is a close company, rights to more than 30% of the assets in a winding-up.

Qualifying options

[11.16] Various other requirements must be met in relation to the option itself. The principal additional requirements are:

(i)   The option must be granted for commercial reasons to recruit or retain an employee and not for tax avoidance purposes.

(ii)   An employee may not hold unexercised options (including any CSOP options — see **11.14**) in respect of shares with a total value of more than £250,000 at the time the options were granted. Any excess share options are not qualifying options. In addition, if an employee has been granted *EMI* options with a total value of £250,000, then whether or not the options have been exercised or released, any further options granted within three years after the date of the grant of the last qualifying EMI option are not qualifying options.

(iii)   The total value of shares in respect of which there are unexercised qualifying EMI options must not exceed £3 million.

(iv)   The shares that may be acquired under the option must be fully paid, irredeemable ordinary shares, and the option must be capable of being exercised within ten years from the date it is granted and must be non-transferable.

Returns and notifications

[11.17] The company must give notice of the option to HMRC within 92 days after it is granted, together with such supporting information as HMRC require which, for options granted on or after 6 April 2014, includes confirmation that a declaration has been made by the relevant employee that he meets the 'working time' requirement (see **11.15**), and that the declaration is held by the company. The company must give a copy of the declaration to the employee within seven days of it being made and produce it to HMRC if so requested within seven days of the request. The notice must be submitted online unless HMRC allow it to be submitted in another way, and HMRC have the right to correct obvious errors in the notice within nine months, and to enquire into an option within 12 months after the 92-day period. The enquiry may be made to the company or, in relation to whether the 'working time' requirement is met, to the relevant employee. If at the conclusion of an enquiry, HMRC decide that the qualifying option requirements have not been met, the company and the relevant employee have the right to appeal against the decision.

Companies whose shares are or have been the subject of an EMI option must file an annual return online (other than where HMRC have allowed another form of filing) no later than 6 July following the end of the tax year. Returns containing the information required by HMRC must be made for each tax year during a 'qualifying option period' which starts when the first qualifying option to which the company's shares are subject is granted and ends when the company's shares are no longer, and will no longer be, subject to qualifying options. The company must submit an amended return as soon as it becomes aware of an error. There are penalties for inaccurate and late returns which are the same as those outlined in **11.2** for other employee share schemes. A penalty of £500 applies if the company fails to give a copy of the declaration regarding the working time requirement to the employee or fails to produce the declaration to HMRC by the time they are required to do so. The company may appeal against the imposition or amount of a penalty.

Income tax and NICs

[11.18] There is no charge to tax or NICs when the option is granted. Providing the option is exercised within ten years after it was granted, there is also not normally a tax charge when it is exercised except to the extent that the market value when the option was granted (or when it was exercised if lower) exceeds the amount paid for the shares. There are, however, detailed provisions about disqualifying events. Where tax is charged on the exercise of the option, Class 1 NICs would be payable if the shares were readily convertible assets (see **11.3**). The anti-avoidance rules at **11.6** apply to shares acquired under qualifying options as they do to shares acquired under non-tax-advantaged schemes.

Capital gains tax

[11.19] The excess of any sale proceeds for the shares over the sum of the amount paid for them plus, in certain circumstances, any amount charged to income tax (see **11.18**) is charged to capital gains tax. However, HMRC changed their view in relation to shares acquired on the exercise of an option before 10 April 2003. The acquisition cost of such shares is the market value of the shares at the time the option was exercised, and no deduction is allowed for any amount charged to income tax on the exercise. See HMRC Briefs 30/2009 and 60/2009 for full details. Gains made on shares acquired through exercising EMI options on or after 6 April 2012 can qualify for entrepreneurs' relief (see **29.2**). See **11.32** for the special capital gains tax rules for identifying share disposals with acquisitions.

Share incentive plans (ITEPA 2003, ss 488–515, Sch 2; ITTOIA 2005, ss 392–396, 405–408, 770; TCGA 1992, Sch 7D)

[11.20] Companies may set up a share incentive plan or SIP under which employees may allocate part of their salary to acquire shares in their employer company (known as partnership shares) without paying tax or NICs, nor will employers' NICs be payable. Employers may also award free shares to employees, including extra free shares (matching shares) for employees who have partnership shares.

SIPs are operated through a trust and the trustees hold the shares for the employees until they are taken out of the plan or sold. A parent company may have a group SIP for itself and its subsidiaries. The legislation is lengthy and complex, and what follows is only an outline. HMRC guidance for employers and advisers is provided in the Employee Tax Advantaged Share Scheme User Manual at ETASSUM20000.

General rules

[11.21] The SIP must be available to all eligible employees and must not contain features which would discourage eligible employees from participating. Employees must be entitled to participate on the same terms (but taking into account remuneration, length of service and hours worked), and the SIP must not have features likely to have the effect of conferring benefits wholly or mainly on directors and employees on higher levels of remuneration. The SIP must not contain arrangements for loans to any of the employees. Shares must be withdrawn from a SIP when an employee leaves the employment. The SIP may provide for employees to lose their free or matching shares if they leave within three years, and for employees who leave to be required to sell their shares.

There is a purpose test which states that schemes must not provide benefits other than in accordance with the rules in ITEPA 2003, Sch 2, unless the benefits are the same as the employee would have received had the shares been acquired outside the SIP. In particular the scheme must not provide cash as an alternative to shares. For schemes which were approved before 6 April 2014, this test only applies if there is an alteration to a key feature on or after that date.

With effect from 15 September 2016 certain disqualifying events cause a SIP to cease to be tax-advantaged. They enforce the principle that preferential shares cannot be issued to select employees by providing that an alteration cannot be made to the company's share capital any of whose shares are subject to the SIP (or to the rights attaching thereto) which materially affects the value of the shares subject to the SIP, and that shares of a class subject to the SIP cannot receive different treatment (i.e. dividend payable) from the other shares of that class.

Eligible employees

[11.22] Eligible employees must be employees of the company or a group company and, if so provided by the SIP, must have been an employee throughout a qualifying period of (broadly) not more than 18 months. An employee within a group satisfies the qualifying period conditions even though he has worked for more than one group company during the period. An employee cannot participate *simultaneously* in two or more awards of shares under different SIPs established by the same company or a connected company. *Successive* participation in two or more awards in the same tax year is permitted but the limits on free shares, partnership shares and reinvested dividends (see **11.24**, **11.25** and **11.27**) apply as if all such SIPs were a single SIP.

Eligible shares

[11.23] There are detailed requirements for shares to be eligible shares, the main points being that the shares must be in a quoted company (or its subsidiary), or an unquoted company not controlled by another company, or from 1 October 2014 shares in a company which is subject to an employee-ownership trust (see **42.49**), and the SIP shares must be fully paid, non-redeemable ordinary shares. They may, however, be non-voting shares. Shares in a 'service company', i.e. one whose main business is the provision of its employees' services to a person or persons having control of the company, or to an associated company, are prohibited.

Free shares

[11.24] The company can award free shares in any tax year valued at up to £3,600 per employee at the time of the award. SIPs may provide for the awards to be linked to performance, statutory rules being laid down for such performance allowances. Details of the relevant performance targets must be provided to employees. Free shares must normally be kept in the SIP for a stipulated period, which may not be less than three years nor more than five years.

Partnership shares

[11.25] Employees may authorise employers to deduct part of their salary to acquire partnership shares, such deductions reducing the pay for tax and NICs (but not pension) purposes. The maximum permitted deduction is £1,800 in any tax year, or 10% of salary if less. The minimum stipulated deduction on any occasion cannot exceed £10. Earnings of a kind specified in the SIP, e.g. bonuses or overtime payments, may be excluded from 'salary' in applying the 10% rule. The amount deducted will be held by the SIP trustees until used to acquire partnership shares. The SIP may stipulate a maximum number of partnership shares that may be purchased. Employees may stop and restart deductions to the SIP on giving written notice to the company, or may give notice to withdraw from the SIP, in which case any money held will be refunded. Any money refunded will be liable to tax and NICs. Partnership shares may be withdrawn from the SIP at any time (but see **11.28** for the tax position).

Matching shares

[11.26] A SIP may provide for employees who acquire partnership shares to be awarded matching shares at the same time, on the basis of not more than two matching shares for one partnership share. The same holding period requirements apply as for other free shares.

Reinvestment of cash dividends and rights shares

[11.27] SIPs may either provide that dividends on SIP shares be reinvested in further SIP shares or that they be paid over to employees. Reinvested dividends are free of income tax providing that the shares acquired are held in the SIP for three years.

Trustees must normally act on an employee's instructions in relation to rights issues. This may include selling some of the rights shares in order to raise funds to acquire the remainder. No capital gains tax is payable on the proceeds of such rights sales. Rights shares acquired in this way are treated as having been acquired when the SIP shares were acquired. If rights shares are acquired using funds other than from such rights sales, they are not SIP shares.

Income tax and capital gains tax

[11.28] There is no charge to income tax or NICs at the time when SIP shares (including dividend shares) are awarded, nor will there be a charge on any free, partnership or matching shares held in a SIP for five years. If such shares are held for between three and five years, income tax (and Class 1 NICs if the shares are readily convertible assets — see **11.3**) will be charged on the initial value of the shares, or their value at the time of withdrawal if lower. If the tax charge is based on the initial value of the shares, it will be reduced by any tax charged on capital receipts (see below). Where the shares are held for less than three years, tax (and Class 1 NICs if the shares are readily convertible assets) will be payable on their value at the time when they cease to be held in the SIP. Where the shares are readily convertible assets, the tax and NICs will be collected from employers under PAYE. The employee's PAYE amount must be paid over to the employer either by the employee or the trustees (who are empowered to dispose of an employee's SIP shares for this purpose). Tax payable in respect of shares that are not readily convertible assets will be payable through the self-assessment system (see **11.35**).

If dividend shares are held in a SIP for less than three years, an amount equal to the reinvested dividends is chargeable to tax. Further tax will be due if the employee is a higher or additional rate taxpayer.

The charges on SIP shares do not apply if the employee leaves through injury, disability, redundancy, retirement, or certain company takeovers, nor on the employee's death.

PAYE tax and Class 1 NICs will be charged on capital receipts (sale of rights etc.) in relation to SIP shares acquired fewer than five years earlier (three years for dividend shares). This does not apply where the trustees sell some rights shares to raise funds to buy the remainder (see **11.27**).

If shares are kept in a SIP until they are sold, employees will not be liable to capital gains tax. If employees take them out of the SIP and sell later, there will be a chargeable gain equal to the increase in value after the shares were withdrawn from the SIP.

Shares withdrawn from a SIP may be transferred free of capital gains tax into an Individual Savings Account (ISA — see **36.15**) within 90 days from the date they cease to be SIP shares.

Returns and notification

[11.29] Rules apply regarding self-certification of schemes and online filing of returns. In order for the scheme to qualify for favourable tax treatment the company must give notice to HMRC and make a declaration that it meets the relevant conditions no later than 6 July in the tax year following the one in which the first award of shares is made under the scheme, though for notices given on or after 6 April 2016 a reasonable excuse provision for late notification is introduced. Once notice has been given, the company must submit annual returns containing the information HMRC require no later than 6 July following the tax year end. The return must give details of any alterations in key features of the share incentive plan or the plan trust, together with a declaration that the changes have not prevented the scheme meeting the relevant conditions. Errors in returns must be corrected without delay and returns must be submitted for every tax year until such time as a plan termination notice has ben issued and certain accompanying conditions have been satisfied. The notice and returns must be submitted online, unless HMRC allow submission in another way. Existing schemes had to be registered before 6 July 2015 and companies had to self-certify that any tax-advantaged schemes met certain requirements to avoid losing those tax advantages. Schemes which were refused approval or had approval withdrawn before 6 April 2014 cannot be tax-advantaged schemes under these provisions.

There are penalties for incorrect and late returns which are the same as those outlined in **11.2** for other employee share schemes.

HMRC may make enquiries into the scheme in certain specified circumstances in the same way as outlined in **11.10** for SAYE schemes.

Capital gains tax rollover relief (TCGA 1992, s 236A, Sch 7C)

[11.30] A special rollover relief is available in relation to unquoted companies, which is particularly relevant where family members and family trusts wish to transfer shares to employees. The relief applies where existing shareholders (other than companies) transfer ownership of shares they hold in the company to a tax-advantaged SIP that holds (either immediately or within 12 months after the transfer) 10% of the company's shares. Gains arising on the shares transferred may be treated as reducing the acquisition cost of replacement chargeable assets acquired within six months after the disposal (unless the replacement assets are shares on which enterprise investment scheme income tax relief is given (see **29.23**) and subject to some special provisions relating to dwelling houses).

Corporation tax (CTA 2009, ss 983–998)

[11.31] In computing its taxable profits, the company is entitled to deduct the costs of setting up and running the SIP. It is also entitled to deduct the market value of free or matching shares at the time they are acquired by the trustees, and the excess of the market value of partnership shares on acquisition by the trustees over the employees' contributions, such deductions being made in the accounting period in which the shares are awarded. Subject to the deduction for running expenses, no deduction is allowed for any expenses in providing dividend shares.

An earlier corporation tax deduction for the provision of SIP shares may be claimed where the company makes a contribution to the SIP trustees to enable them to acquire the company's shares, providing that the shares are not acquired from a company, and that at the end of 12 months from the date of purchasing shares with the money contributed, the trustees hold at least 10% of the company's total ordinary share capital. Where that condition is satisfied, the deduction is given in the accounting period in which the 12-month anniversary falls, and no deduction is then given when the shares are awarded to employees. There are further detailed conditions, including a requirement for at least 30% of the shares acquired with the contribution to be transferred to employees within five years, and all the shares to be transferred within ten years.

Anti-avoidance provisions prevent a corporation tax deduction if one of the main purposes of the company making the payment is to obtain the deduction.

Capital gains tax treatment of shares (TCGA 1992, Sch 7D para 4)

[11.32] Where a shareholder makes several acquisitions of shares of the same class in a company, special rules apply to a disposal to identify which shares were disposed of (see CHAPTER 38). The shares are pooled together and shares disposed of are matched with the shares comprised in the pool — subject to prior rules for shares bought and sold on the same day or within the following 30 days. SIP shares are treated as being of a separate class while they are retained by the trustees. This means that any disposals of shares owned by the employee outside the SIP are not matched with SIP shares.

Corporation tax relief for cost of shares provided (CTA 2009, Pt 12)

[11.33] A corporation tax deduction is given for the cost of providing shares for employee share schemes where the employees are taxable in respect of the shares they acquire or would be taxable if the scheme were not a tax-advantaged scheme. The deduction is normally based on the market value of the shares, at the time they are awarded or the share option is exercised (whichever is applicable), less any contribution made by the employee towards them. (Payment by the employee of the company's secondary NICs is not taken into account — see **11.3**.) The deductions allowed for shares provided under share incentive plans (see **11.31**) take priority over this relief. This relief relates only to the cost of providing shares; it does not displace reliefs for costs of setting up or administering schemes. The shares themselves must be fully-paid, non-redeemable, ordinary shares in a quoted company, a subsidiary of a quoted company or an unquoted company not under the control of another company.

The relief is generally given for the accounting period in which the employee acquires the shares, subject to special rules for restricted shares and convertible shares.

No such corporation tax deduction is available in relation to employee share options where the shares are not acquired by the employees pursuant to the option. Any other corporation tax deduction is also excluded where the statutory relief is available under CTA 2009, Part 12.

Subject to certain conditions this relief is available in relation to shares acquired within a 90-day period following the takeover of a company by an unlisted company. In addition, from 6 April 2015, relief is available where the conditions are met for shares acquired or share options obtained by an individual who is employed by a company not within the charge to corporation tax, and the individual either works for, but does not have employment with, a company within the charge to corporation tax (for example under a secondment), or takes up employment with such a company.

Employee share plans will often relate to a group of companies. HMRC provide guidance relating to the transfer pricing issues (including those relating to UK–UK transactions) that may arise on such group plans. The guidance is available at www.gov.uk/guidance/transfer-pricing-transactions-between-connected-companies.

Priority share allocations for employees (ITEPA 2003, ss 542–548)

[11.34] When shares are offered to the public, a priority allocation is often made to employees and directors. Where there is no price advantage, the general rule is that right to shares in priority to other persons is not a taxable benefit, so long as the shares that may be allocated do not exceed 10% of those being offered, all directors and employees entitled to an allocation are entitled on similar terms (albeit at different levels), and those entitled are not restricted wholly or mainly to persons who are directors or whose remuneration exceeds a particular level. This treatment still applies where the offer to employees is strictly not part of the public offer, as a result of the employees' offer being restricted to shares in one or more companies and the public offer being a package of shares in a wider range of companies.

Where employees get shares at a discount compared with the price paid by the public, the discount is chargeable to income tax. The employee's base cost for capital gains tax is the amount paid plus the amount of the discount.

Self-assessment — employees' responsibilities

[11.35] Employees who do not get tax returns must notify HMRC by 5 October after the end of the year if they have income or gains that have not been fully taxed (see 9.34).

HMRC provide detailed guidance, in the additional information notes to the self-assessment tax return, as to which items should be returned in respect of shares and options. These include amounts arising from both tax-advantaged and non-tax-advantaged schemes, and amounts that may have been taxed under PAYE.

Employers tick a box on forms P11D if there are taxable benefits relating to shares, but do not give details of taxable amounts, so the employee needs to obtain the relevant information himself. Since employers are required to report details to HMRC (see 11.2), they should be able to provide the appropriate figures.

Employee shareholder shares (ITEPA 2003, ss 226A–226D, TCGA 1992, ss 236B–236G, ITTOIA 2005, s 385A; FA 2017, ss 12–14)

[11.36] Under the employee shareholder status employees give up certain employment rights in return for shares in their employer's company. Income tax and capital gains tax reliefs are available from 1 September 2013 but these have been abolished for employee shareholder shares acquired under employee shareholder agreements entered into on or after 1 December 2016 (or 2 December 2016 in cases where the potential employee shareholder received professional advice in relation to the share offer on 23 November 2016 before 1.30pm). In addition, it is proposed that legislation be introduced to ensure the status itself is closed to new arrangements. The reliefs available for agreements entered into before these dates are outlined below.

For arrangements entered into before 1 December 2016 (or 2 December 2016 as applicable), and subject to certain conditions, gains on disposals of employee shareholder shares worth up to £50,000 on receipt are exempt from capital gains tax on disposal. However, there is a lifetime limit of £100,000 on exempt capital gains that an employee can make on the disposal of shares acquired under employee shareholder agreements entered into after 16 March 2016. The income tax and NICs due when employee shareholders acquire shares (other than employment-related securities) are reduced or eliminated by deeming that they have paid £2,000 for the shares. This ensures that the first £2,000 of share value received by employee shareholders is not subject to income tax or NICs.

Where the market value of the shares acquired exceeds £2,000 the market value is apportioned accordingly. Market value is broadly as defined for capital gains tax purposes (see **4.18**) but ignoring certain provisions regarding restricted or convertible shares. The £2,000 exemption only applies on the first occasion that an individual acquires employee shareholder shares, and does not apply where the employee shareholder, or a person connected with them, has a material interest in the employer company, or its parent company (or has had at any time in the previous 12 months). An individual has a material interest if at least 25% of the voting rights in the company are exercisable by that individual or persons connected with him (or the both together), or in the case of a close company 25% of the net assets are available for distribution to that individual or persons connected with him (or the both together).

There is no income tax charge if the employee sells the shares back to the employer company when he is no longer an employee. The capital gains tax rules will apply, but any gain may be exempt. A gain which accrues on the first disposal of an exempt employee shareholder share is not chargeable, subject to the lifetime limit on exempt gains if applicable (see above). An employee shareholder share is exempt broadly if, immediately after its acquisition, the total value of such shares acquired under an employee shareholder agreement relating to the employer company or an associated company does not exceed £50,000. Where the shares acquired take the total value of shares over the £50,000 limit, the excess are treated as acquired separately. The exemption does not apply where the employee shareholder, or a person connected with him, has a material interest (as defined above) in the employer company or its parent company. The normal share identification rules (see **38.18**) are disapplied, so that where a person holds both exempt and non-exempt employee shareholder shares of the same class in a company, he can specify how many exempt shares he has disposed of, up to the number held. The relinquishment of employee rights is not the disposal of an asset for capital gains purposes.

For HMRC guidance see www.gov.uk/guidance/employee-shareholders.

Tax points

[11.37] Note the following:

- There is no clearance procedure under any of the anti-avoidance rules at **11.6**. To the extent that charges to tax, and possibly NICs, arise under these rules other than on an acquisition or disposal, employment-related shares and securities are particularly vulnerable to uncertainty.
- In the case of unquoted companies, the value of shares has to be agreed when appropriate with HMRC's valuation division.
- Group employees may participate in schemes through their parent company.
- If an employee acquires shares under a tax-advantaged share option scheme and immediately disposes of them, the gain will be subject to capital gains tax (unless covered by reliefs or exemptions). Gains on shares acquired under SAYE linked options and under a tax-advantaged share incentive plan can be sheltered to the extent that shares valued at up to the annual limit are transferred into an ISA (see **36.15**).
- Employers face penalties if they fail to provide to HMRC the returns and information required under the provisions outlined in this chapter.
- A tax-advantaged SAYE share option scheme or share incentive plan cannot apply to a subsidiary company unless the parent is a non-close company listed on the Stock Exchange. For a company share option plan the subsidiary cannot be an unlisted company under the control of a listed company (see **11.12**).
- Unquoted companies may see disadvantages to tax-advantaged share incentive plans, because they cannot choose which employees may participate, there may not be a ready market for the shares if the employee wants to sell, an immediate market valuation is not available and the effect on existing shareholders must be considered. A condition can, however, be imposed that employees must sell their shares when the employment ends.
- Where an employee has a tax liability in connection with share schemes, he should make sure he includes the appropriate entries on his tax return (see **11.35**).

Directors of small and family companies

Directors and shareholders

[12.1] In family companies, directors and shareholders are usually the same people, and they can benefit from the company in various ways, e.g. the payment of remuneration, the provision of benefits or the distribution of profits through dividends.

The freedom to use company profits in the most tax-efficient manner has been challenged by HMRC in some circumstances under the 'settlements' legislation (see **12.10**). Special rules apply to personal service companies and managed service companies (see **19.4** and **19.14**), and the material in this chapter is not relevant for such companies that are caught by those rules.

When considering to what extent, and in what form, to withdraw profits, the treatment for tax and NICs is an important factor and companies need to be aware of the comparative tax and NIC cost of paying remuneration and dividends at different profit levels. There are other considerations, in particular the effect on pensions. Remuneration and benefits are earned income in the hands of the shareholder, whereas dividends are unearned income. Only earned income is taken into account in calculating the maximum tax relievable contributions to a registered pension scheme. Therefore, taking a low salary means that tax-efficient pension contributions are correspondingly restricted, although it is possible to contribute up to £3,600 a year to a personal pension scheme regardless of earnings level. See CHAPTERS **16** and **17**.

The national minimum wage (NMW) and the national living wage (NLW) also need to be taken into account. From 1 April 2017 the NLW of £7.50 per hour (£7.20 from 1 April 2016) must be paid to employees aged 25 and over. The Government intends that this will rise to over £9 per hour by 2020. The NMW is £7.05 per hour for those aged 21 to 24, £5.60 for those aged between 18 and

20, £4.05 for 16 and 17-year-olds, and £3.50 for apprentices under 19 or 19 or over and in the first year of their apprenticeship. The previous rates, in force from October 2016, were £6.95, £5.55, £4.00, and £3.40 respectively. Travelling and subsistence expenses which qualify for tax relief and which are paid to the employee do not count towards the NMW pay. This is to prevent businesses using certain schemes to try to circumvent the NMW regulations. HMRC guidance indicates that an exemption for work done by certain family members does not apply to a business carried on by a company.

HMRC enforce the NMW and NLW on behalf of the Department for Business, Energy and Industrial Strategy. Guidance on the NMW and directors in Tax Bulletin 50 (December 2000) indicated that a director who does not have an 'explicit' employment contract is highly unlikely to be subject to the NMW legislation. Where such a contract (which need not be in writing) exists, however, the legislation is likely to apply — even if the company is making losses — on the basis that a worker/employer relationship has been created. HMRC indicated that where there is no express employment contract it is not normally necessary to pay the NMW to directors of new businesses; loss-making family companies; group companies; dormant companies; trade associations; companies where the director works out of a sense of public duty rather than for payment; or flat management companies. The NLW will be treated in the same way.

Interns are usually entitled to the NMW or NLW if they are classed as a worker (as to which see www.gov.uk/employment-status/worker) unless they are students required to do an internship for less than one year as part of a UK-based further or higher education. HMRC may make checks where employers have advertised internships to ensure that they are paying all their workers the correct NMW/NLW rate.

HMRC guidance regarding government checks on the NMW and NLW can be found in NMW FS1 and NMW FS2.

Taking profits as pay

[12.2] For 2017–18, profit taken as pay costs the company 13.8% Class 1 NICs on pay in excess of £157 a week (unless the employee is aged under 21 or an apprentice aged under 25, see **13.4**), but the contributions are deducted in arriving at taxable profits for corporation tax purposes. Class 1 or Class 1A NICs are also payable on virtually all taxable benefits in kind (see Chapter 10). Employees do not have to pay NICs on the first £157 a week, but those earning £113 or more have their rights to state benefits protected. From 6 April 2017, the rate of employees' contributions on earnings between £157 and £866 per week is 12% and employees must also pay contributions at 2% on all earnings above £866 a week.

The additional cost of the employer's 13.8% NICs on pay above £157 per week for the year to 31 March 2018, after deducting tax relief at the 19% rate of corporation tax (see **3.15**) is 11.18%.

Taking profits as dividends

[12.3] When profits are taken as dividends, the dividends are not deducted in calculating taxable profits. From 2016–17 dividends within the dividend allowance of £5,000 per year are not taxable (proposed to be reduced to £2,000 from 6 April 2018, see **2.5**). Where dividends exceed the allowance the rates applying are 7.5% on income up to the basic rate limit, 32.5% on income above the basic rate limit up to the higher rate limit, and 38.1% on income above the higher rate limit.

In all cases it should be remembered that dividend income from shares jointly owned by spouses/civil partners is split according to the actual ownership (see **33.6**).

Comparative tax rates for pay and dividends

[12.4] For 2017–18, there are various factors to take into account when comparing tax rates for salary and dividends. Clearly the £5,000 dividend allowance means that once the personal allowance is exceeded there will be a tax saving on paying the next £5,000 profit extraction as dividends because they will be tax free. The following examples illustrate the effect of extraction of higher levels of profit.

Example 1

Company uses profits of £25,000 in the year to 31 March 2018 to make a payment to a director/shareholder who has no other income. Director does not have an explicit contract of employment so the national minimum wage/national living wage should not apply (see **12.1**). His personal allowance for 2017–18 is £11,500.

If profit is taken as	salary only	salary and divi- dend
	£	£
Company's tax position on the payment is:		
Profits	25,000	25,000
Salary	(22,958)	(11,500)
Employer's NICs	(2,042)	(460)
Taxable profits	—	13,040
Corporation tax at 19%		(2,478)
Director's dividend income		10,562
Director's tax position:		
Salary	22,958	11,500
Dividend, including tax credit	—	10,562
	22,958	22,062
Personal allowance	(11,500)	(11,500)

Taxable income	11,458	10,562
Tax payable (£11,458 @ 19%)	2,177	
(dividends £5,000 @ 0%; £5,562 @ 7.5%)		417
Disposable income:		
Salary	22,958	11,500
Employee's NICs	(1,775)	(400)
Dividend	—	10,562
Tax	(2,177)	(417)
	19,006	21,245
Saving through paying dividend		£2,239

The saving through paying the dividend is made up as follows:

Extra income available as dividend through saving in employer's NICs (2,042 – 460)	1,582	
Less 19% corporation tax thereon (i.e. reduced tax relief for employer's NICs)	(301)	1,281
On the balance of taxable profits, i.e. 13,040 – 1,582 = 11,458:		
Company pays corporation tax 11,458 @ 19%	2,177	
Director saves income tax 11,458 @ 19% on salary	(2,177)	(—)
Director pays income tax on dividends		(417)
Reduction in employee's NICs (1,775 – 400)		1,375
		£2,239

The salary in the second alternative has been fixed at the personal allowance of £11,500. Fixing the salary at the Class 1 NICs primary threshold of £8,164 would remove the liability to employers' and employees' NICs (even though rights to social security benefits would be protected because the salary was in excess of the lower earnings limit of £113 a week, see **13.4**). However, some personal allowances would be wasted.

Example 2

Director is liable to tax at 40% and already drawing salary such that he is paying maximum NICs at the 12% rate. In addition he has already received more than £5,000 in dividends so has no dividend allowance available. The effective tax rate on payment of an extra £100 of profit as either salary or a dividend is as follows.

(a) Salary payment

	£	£
Available profit		100.00
Employer's NIC on salary (13.8% of 87.88)		12.12
Gross salary*		87.88
Tax @ 40%	35.15	
Employee's NIC @ 2%	1.76	36.91
Net income		50.97
Effective tax rate on available profit		49.03%

(b) Dividend payment

	£
Available profit	100.00
Corporation tax @ 19%	19.00
Cash dividend payable to shareholder	81.00
Tax @ 32.5%	26.32
Net income	54.68
Effective tax rate	45.32%

* £100 profit is employers' NIC inclusive. Gross salary is £100 x 100/113.8.

Director is liable to tax at 45% and already drawing salary such that he is paying maximum NICs at the 12% rate. In addition he has already received more than £5,000 in dividends so has no dividend allowance available. The effective tax rate on payment of an extra £100 of profit as either salary or a dividend is as follows.

(a) Salary payment

	£	£
Available profit		100.00
Employer's NIC on salary (13.8% of 87.88)		12.12
Gross salary		87.88
Tax @ 45%	39.54	
Employee's NIC @ 2%	1.76	41.30
Net income		46.58
Effective tax rate on available profit		53.42%

(b) Dividend payment

Available profit	100.00
Corporation tax @ 19%	19.00
Cash dividend paid to shareholder	81.00
Tax @ 38.1%	30.86
Net income	50.14
Effective tax rate	49.86%

Dividends for the director/shareholders in the above Examples are therefore more tax-effective than salary, mainly because of the NICs cost of a salary. In previous years the tax savings by paying dividends were greater, however it was one of the stated aims of the changes to dividend taxation (see 2.5) to reduce the incentive to incorporate and then remunerate through dividends rather than through salary in order to reduce tax liabilities.

Retention of profits within the company or payment as remuneration or dividends

[12.5] Retaining profits within the company will increase the net assets and hence the value of the shares if a subsequent sale is based wholly or partly on the underlying assets. Having already suffered corporation tax, the retained profits will thus swell the value of the shares and the potential gain chargeable to capital gains tax.

Paying remuneration or dividends may, therefore, ultimately reduce the shareholders' chargeable gains, but this must be weighed against the immediate tax cost of drawing profits, the maximum rate of capital gains tax on shares of 20% depending upon the individual's tax circumstances (see 4.2) and the availability of entrepreneurs' relief (see 29.2) and other capital gains tax reliefs (see 4.30). Reducing taxable profit by means of a permissible contribution to a pension fund from which the director will benefit will sometimes be an attractive alternative (see 12.8).

Effect on earlier years (CTA 2010, ss 37–44)

[12.6] A decision on whether to pay remuneration or leave profits to be charged to corporation tax should not be taken by reference to the current year in isolation. The payment of remuneration may convert a trading profit into a trading loss, which, after being set against any non-trading profits of the current year, may be carried back against the profits of the previous year, both from the trade and from other sources. See CHAPTER 26.

Looking into the future

[**12.7**] If all current-year profits are used to pay remuneration, there will be nothing against which to carry back any future trading losses. Expected future performance, including any imminent capital expenditure which will attract capital allowances (see CHAPTER 22), should therefore be taken into account in considering whether to take steps to reduce or eliminate taxable profits for the current year.

Pensions

[**12.8**] The current pensions regime applies to both occupational and personal schemes. Tax relief is available on contributions when they are put into a scheme, subject to relevant earnings, and annual and lifetime allowance limits (see **16.14** and **16.9**).

The company may have its own pension scheme, either through an insurance company or self-administered. Provided that the possible benefits under the scheme are within the parameters laid down by the legislation, the company's contributions in respect of the director only (and therefore not those into a family member's scheme) are not taxable on the director. The contributions will be allowed in calculating the company's taxable profit providing they are *wholly and exclusively for the purposes of the trade*. In deciding whether this rule is breached in small and family companies, HMRC consider the overall remuneration package of directors and family members. HMRC guidance is available in the Business Income Manual at BIM46035.

A director may pay premiums himself under a personal pension plan but employees' pension contributions do not reduce earnings for employers' and employees' NICs. The company could itself contribute to the director's pension plan within the available limits, and neither tax nor NICs would be payable on the amount contributed by the company in respect of the director only. Again this is subject to the caveat that the company's contributions must satisfy the 'wholly and exclusively' rule.

Since the income and gains of both company and personal pension funds are usually exempt from tax, paying permissible pension contributions rather than taking salary and investing it privately will normally be a more tax-efficient method of saving for the future, although of course the pension benefits available will depend on the performance of the pension investments and on the changing legislation. For the detailed provisions on pensions, see CHAPTERS 16 and 17.

Limits on allowable remuneration and waiver of remuneration (IHTA 1984, s 14)

[**12.9**] Remuneration, like any other trading expense, must be incurred wholly and exclusively for the purposes of the trade (see CHAPTER 20). If it is regarded as excessive in relation to the duties, part may not be allowed as a deduction in calculating company profits. This should be borne in mind when considering payments of remuneration, either by way of cash or as benefits in kind, to members of a director's or shareholder's family. On the other hand, the national minimum wage/national living wage legislation may prevent wages being paid at too low a level (see **12.1**).

Employing a spouse or civil partner and children in the family company may be useful, particularly if they are not otherwise using their personal allowance, but the work done must be of sufficient quantity and quality to justify the amount paid. The quantum of remuneration must not be determined by the relationship. If children are under 16 the regulations as to permitted hours of work must also be complied with, which vary according to local bye-laws. Payments by a farmer to his very young children were held to be 'pocket money' and disallowed in calculating the taxable profits of the farm.

A higher rate taxpayer might consider (subject to the national minimum wage/national living wage legislation) waiving entitlement to remuneration to assist, for example, in a difficult period of trading. See **12.10**, however, regarding the possible application of the settlements rules and the possibility of legislation being enacted to counter 'income shifting'. No inheritance tax liability arises from such a waiver providing certain conditions are met. The waiver might enable the company to pay higher remuneration to other directors or family members (provided always that it is justifiable under the 'wholly and exclusively' rule) or to increase its profits available for dividends.

'Income shifting' and the settlements rules (ITTOIA 2005, ss 624–627)

[12.10] The rules relating to 'settlements' prevent someone gaining a tax advantage by arranging to divert his/her income to family or friends taxable at a lower or nil rate. An outright gift of income-producing property (such as shares in the case of a family company) is outside these provisions unless, for example, (a) the gift does not carry a right to the whole of the income, or (b) the property given is wholly or substantially a right to income.

HMRC increased their use of these rules to attack some tax planning arrangements in family companies and partnerships. They gave detailed guidance and illustrations setting out their interpretation of the rules, including how they affect family companies. The illustrations included a main earner drawing a low salary from a family company so that there were higher profits out of which to pay dividends to family or friends. Many professional advisers disagreed with HMRC's detailed guidance. In July 2007 the House of Lords decided the long-running 'Arctic Systems' case in favour of the taxpayers, on the basis that, while there was a settlement, an exemption for outright gifts between spouses applied.

Whilst the Government did not proceed with its subsequent intention to make changes to the legislation in order to counter 'income shifting', it reiterated that it firmly believes that 'it is unfair to allow a minority of individuals to benefit financially from shifting part of their income to someone else who is subject to a lower rate of tax'.

Recent cases have confirmed the view that dividend waivers made in favour of shareholders' wives were settlements. It is essential to look very carefully at any arrangements that are being considered, or are already in existence, and to take appropriate professional advice which should take account of HMRC's views as set out in their Trusts, Settlements and Estates Manual at TSEM4000. HMRC have recently confirmed that they will not give clearances or advice in respect of the application of the settlements legislation.

Employee benefits provided by the company

[12.11] Employees are charged to tax on the cash equivalent of benefits provided either for them or for their family or household. NICs are also payable on virtually all taxable benefits, either Class 1 contributions payable by both employer and employee or Class 1A contributions by the employer only depending on the benefit. In most cases, therefore, it will usually be equally tax/NICs efficient, and far more straightforward, to provide cash pay rather than benefits. See CHAPTER 10 for details.

Gifts of company assets (CTA 2010, s 1064; IHTA 1984, s 94)

[12.12] Gifts of company assets to directors and employees are covered by the benefits rules mentioned above and explained in detail in CHAPTER 10. If a close company (see 3.29) gives an asset to a shareholder who is not a director or employee, the cost is treated as a dividend and the total of the cost of the asset is included in the shareholder's taxable income.

If a close company makes a transfer of value for inheritance tax purposes (see CHAPTER 5) that value may be apportioned among the 'participators' (as defined, to include shareholders and others) according to their interests in the company and treated as a transfer made by them for inheritance tax purposes. There is no apportionment, however, of any amount that is treated as the participator's income.

Loans from the company (TMA 1970, s 109; CTA 2010, ss 455–459, 464A–464D; TA 1988, s 826(4); ITEPA 2003, ss 173–191, 223; ITTOIA 2005, ss 415–421)

[12.13] Employees who overdraw their current accounts with the company or who receive specific loans from the company, either interest-free or at a beneficial rate, are treated as having received remuneration equivalent to interest at the 'official rate' (see 10.48) on the amount overdrawn or lent, less any amount paid to the company towards the benefit they have received. This does not apply if the whole of the interest on the loans qualifies for tax relief, nor if the total non-qualifying loans outstanding in a tax year do not exceed £10,000. The loans provisions apply to loans made to a spouse, civil partner or relatives of the director or employee, as well as to the director/employee himself. Where a director or employee receives an advance for expenses necessarily incurred in performing his duties, or for incidental overnight expenses (see **10.21**), the advance is not treated as a loan provided that:

(a)   the maximum amount advanced at any one time does not exceed £1,000,

(b)   the advances are spent within six months, and

(c)   the director or employee accounts to the company at regular intervals for the expenditure.

Tax effect on company

[12.14] As well as the tax charge on the director or employee on interest-free or cheap loans, there are tax implications for the company if it is a close company in which the director or employee is a 'participator' or associate of a participator (see **3.29**), and these provisions do not depend on whether any interest is charged. 'Participators' are not confined to shareholders but the rest of this chapter refers to shareholders only.

Loans and advances to shareholders give rise to a tax liability on the company, unless the loan is made in the ordinary course of the company's trade, or the loan (together with any other outstanding loans to the borrower) does not exceed £15,000 and is made to a full-time working director or employee who does not own more than 5% of the ordinary share capital. Where a loan does not fall within the above exceptions, the company has to notify HMRC not later than 12 months after the end of the accounting period in which the loan is made, and must pay tax at the dividend upper rate (currently 32.5%, see **2.26**) applying for the tax year in which the loan is made on the amount of the loan or overdrawn account balance.

The due date for payment of the tax is nine months after the end of the accounting period in which the loan is made (i.e. the same as the due date for the corporation tax of that period). For companies required to pay tax by instalments under corporation tax self-assessment (see **3.24**) the tax on such a loan is to be taken into account in the instalment payments. Under corporation tax self-assessment, companies show the tax on loans as part of the total tax due, but may claim an offsetting deduction in certain circumstances (see below) if the loan has been repaid or if it has been released or written off.

Various anti-avoidance provisions take effect from 20 March 2013. From that date the tax charge can arise on the company where the loan or advance is made to trustees of a settlement in which at least one trustee, beneficiary or potential beneficiary is a participator, or is made to a Limited Liability Partnership (LLP, see **23.33**) or other partnership where at least one of the partners is both an individual and a participator. In addition, from that date, a tax charge (now 32.5% but at that time 25%) arises if the company is party to tax avoidance arrangements which confer a benefit on a participator or his associate which does not otherwise give rise to a tax charge on the company, the participator or the associate. A participator in a controlling company is treated as a participator in the controlled company for these purposes. Where a payment in respect of the benefit is made to the company, and no consideration is given for it, relief for the tax charge may be claimed, subject to the comments below.

Note, however, that the charge does not apply to a loan or advance made on or after 25 November 2015 to trustees of a charitable trust and applied for the purposes of that trust only.

From 20 March 2013 rules were also introduced to prevent the 'bed and breakfasting' of loans, where the loan is cleared and a further loan is made within a short time. Where, within a 30-day period, a company receives repayments totalling at least £5,000 which repay a chargeable payment (i.e. a loan, an advance or a conferral of benefit (as highlighted above) to a participator), and the company subsequently makes a further chargeable payment to the same person or associate in an accounting period which is later than the accounting period in which the original chargeable payment was made, then the repayments are matched as far as possible with the new chargeable payments — repayments are available to set off against the original chargeable payments only to the extent that the repayments are in excess of the new chargeable payments. Note that for these provisions to apply, the repayments and new chargeable payments may be in the same accounting period, but the new chargeable payments must be made in a later accounting period than the original chargeable payments. New chargeable payments which are repaid within the 30-day period under consideration are not taken into account.

Example 3

A Ltd lends a participator £30,000 which is still outstanding at the end of the accounting period. In the following accounting period before the tax becomes due for payment, the participator receives a further loan of £35,000 from the company. The original loan of £30,000 is repaid using £30,000 of the new loan. It is likely that the repayment of £30,000 would be treated as a repayment of £30,000 of the new £35,000 loan so the original loan would be treated as not repaid and the tax would be due for payment.

The same restrictions on set-off apply where the outstanding amounts owed to the company total at least £15,000, and, at the time the amount is repaid, arrangements had been made to replace some or all of the amount repaid, and broadly the payments then made under those arrangements to the person or their associate total £5,000 or more.

Example 4

B Ltd lends a participator £20,000 which is still outstanding at the end of the accounting period. Before the due date for payment of the tax, the full amount is repaid using a bank loan. The bank loan is repaid using a further loan of £20,000 from the company. HMRC would argue that there are clear arrangements here and so the original loan would be treated as not repaid and the tax would be due for payment unless a further repayment was made.

Where the loan is repaid after the tax falls due in circumstances which are not subject to any of the anti-avoidance provisions outlined above, any tax paid by the company may be reclaimed within four years of the end of the financial period in which the repayment is made. The tax repayment is due nine months after the end of the accounting period in which the loan is repaid, and will be increased by interest from that nine months date if relevant.

Example 5

A close company with an accounting year end of 31 December makes an interest-free loan of £20,000 to a director/shareholder on 10 January 2016. The company is not liable to pay its corporation tax by instalments. The director repays the loan on:

(a)   10 September 2017

Since this is before 1 October 2017, when the company is due to pay its corporation tax for the year to 31 December 2016, the company will not have to pay tax at 25% of the loan (being the rate applying for loans made before 6 April 2016), as the tax due is off set by the tax repayable.

(b)   10 October 2017

Since the loan has not been repaid by 1 October 2017 the company must pay tax on that date at 25%, i.e. £5,000, and cannot claim repayment of the tax until 30 September 2018.

The director/shareholder will in any event be taxed under the benefits rules on interest on the loan at the official rate from 10 January 2016 to the repayment date.

Loans written off or released

[12.15] If a loan or overdrawing is written off or released by the company, the tax treatment is different for loans made to shareholders by close companies and for other loans.

If a loan by a close company to a shareholder is written off, the amount written off is not an allowable expense in calculating corporation tax, although the company can recover the tax it paid when the loan was made provided the repayment is not subject to certain anti-avoidance provisions (see **12.14**). Loans written off by non-close companies are allowable in calculating corporation tax under the 'loan relationships' rules (see **26.8**), except for loans between companies where one controls the other or both are under common control.

The write-off of loans does not affect the shareholder unless he is liable to tax at a higher rate. Tax is chargeable on the amount written off at the excess of the dividend upper rate of 32.5% (or, where applicable, the dividend additional rate of 38.1% (see **2.26**)) over the dividend ordinary rate of 7.5% which is treated as having been paid.

Loans written off during a period of temporary non-residence (**41.49**) are treated as if they were written off in the period of return.

If the borrower is not a shareholder, but the loan was obtained by reason of his employment, whether or not it is at a rate of interest below the 'official rate', the borrower is treated as having received an equivalent amount of remuneration at the time of the write-off. This applies even after the employee has left, but not if the loan is written off on death. Class 1 NICs are due on the amount written off (see **12.14, 10.48**).

If the borrower is both a shareholder and an employee or director, the treatment of the amount written off as income on which the dividend ordinary rate of tax is treated as paid takes priority over the charge as remuneration.

Liabilities in connection with directors' remuneration

[12.16] Remuneration is regarded as paid not only when it forms part of the payroll but also when it is credited to the director's current account with the company, and the liability of the company to account for PAYE and NICs arises at that time. The credit to the current account should therefore be made net of employee's tax and NICs. Drawings from the account can be made without any further liability once PAYE and NICs have been accounted for to HMRC. If a company pays remuneration to a director and bears the PAYE itself, the amount that should have been borne by the director is treated as extra remuneration and charged to tax and NICs accordingly.

Where a director receives payments in advance or on account of future remuneration this has to be treated as pay for tax and NICs purposes at the time of the advance, unless the advances are covered by a credit balance on the director's loan account or are on account of expenses as indicated at **12.13**. An advance payment of remuneration is not the same as a loan. The income tax treatment of loans is stated at **12.13**.

Where a director's account becomes overdrawn, or there is an increase in the amount by which the account becomes overdrawn, and the director normally receives advance or anticipatory payments, Class 1 NICs are payable on the overdrawn amount if the withdrawal is made in anticipation of a payment of earnings (see HMRC Leaflet CA44), but not if it is made in anticipation of payments which are not earnings, such as dividends (although Class 1A NICs may be due if the payment is a benefit — see **10.49**). If the account becomes overdrawn, or there is an increase in the amount by which the account is overdrawn, and the director does not normally receive advance or anticipatory payments, the amount overdrawn is not earnings unless the company authorises payment of the amount overdrawn, either in writing or by the other directors agreeing verbally that they are aware of the situation. If the amounts overdrawn are properly authorised, Class 1 NICs are due on the amounts. If payment of a director's personal bills by his company is not covered by a credit balance on the director's account, and the debit to his account is made in anticipation of future earnings, Class 1 NICs are due on the amount paid. No liability to Class 1 NICs arises if the debit is made in anticipation of payments which are not earnings, such as dividends.

Directors' NICs cannot be reduced by paying remuneration at uneven rates and irregular intervals, because of the rules for calculating earnings limits. The detailed provisions are in CHAPTER **13**.

If employers fail to deduct and account for PAYE and NICs when due, they may incur interest and/or penalties (see **10.68**). Directors may also be personally liable to pay the tax on their remuneration if they knew of the failure to deduct or account for tax.

Tax points

[12.17] Note the following:

- The combined company/director/shareholder position should be looked at in considering the most appropriate way of dealing with available profits, and past years and the following year as well as the current year should also be considered.
- Effective use should be made of company or personal pension funds, which should grow faster than individual investments because of their available tax exemptions. In the case of company pension funds, in calculating corporation tax, relief is only given in the accounting period when the contribution is paid to the pension scheme, so that it is not possible to reduce taxable profits of one year by making a payment in the next year and relating it back. It is therefore essential to anticipate the profit level if a pension contribution is to be used as a way of reducing corporation tax for a particular accounting period.
- Dividend payments may affect the valuation of shareholdings.
- Dividend income on shares in family companies held jointly by spouses or civil partners in unequal proportions is split according to their actual ownership rather than being split equally (see **33.6**).
- In considering the payment of a dividend instead of remuneration, the national minimum wage/national living wage rules, which are enforced by HMRC, must be taken into account. The legislation does not regard family companies as a special case, although directors who do not have an explicit employment contract are unlikely to be covered by the rules.
- The existing 'settlements' rules may prevent a person from gaining a tax advantage by diverting income to others whose income is taxable at a lower rate. It must be borne in mind that specific rules may be introduced to counter 'income shifting' (see **12.10**).
- Tax or NICs are not charged on pension contributions paid by an employer to a registered company scheme or personal pension scheme in respect of the employee only. Employee contributions either to a company or private scheme reduce income for income tax purposes, but not for employees' NICs.
- Remuneration is regarded as paid when it is credited to an account with the company in the name of a director. The fact that it is not drawn by him but left to his credit in the company (in other words, available for drawing) does not prevent the appropriate tax and NICs being payable at the time the remuneration is credited. The director's account should be credited only with the net amount after tax and NICs. If the gross amount is credited, whether or not it is drawn out, and the company fails to account to HMRC for the tax and NICs, the director may be personally liable for the failure under the PAYE regulations.

- Interest and penalties are charged on late paid PAYE/NICs (see **10.68**).
- If the company has failed to pay over the PAYE tax and NICs on remuneration within 14 days (or 17 days for electronic payments) after the end of each pay period (month or quarter), HMRC may look to the individual for payment plus interest if they were aware of the company's failure to comply with the PAYE regulations. Additionally, they may be held personally liable as a director for *any* unpaid NICs due from the company if the non-payment is due to their fraud or negligence.
- If, before a director is credited with additional remuneration, his current account with the company is overdrawn, HMRC will invariably contend that the date on which the additional remuneration can be regarded as credited is that on which the accounts are signed (or the date when a clear entitlement to the remuneration was established — for example a properly evidenced directors'/shareholders' meeting) rather than the end of the accounting year for which the additional remuneration was paid. This can significantly affect the tax charge on the director in respect of beneficial loan interest (see **10.48**) and can also affect the liability of the company to pay tax under the provisions for loans to directors (see **12.14**).
- If it is intended to pay additional remuneration to a director after the end of the accounting period, a board minute to that effect should be in place before the end of the accounting period. Otherwise HMRC may argue that the remuneration cannot be charged in calculating the taxable profit of the accounting period to which the remuneration relates. If the minute is precise as to the amount, it may also enable the credit to a director's loan account to be made at an earlier date than the date of adoption of the accounts for the period (see previous bullet point).
- Where HMRC discover that a director's private expenses have been paid by a company and not shown as benefits on form P11D, they will usually seek to treat the payments as loans to the director. Such payments, including any VAT, must be reimbursed to the company by the director or charged against money owed by the company to the director. They are neither allowable as an expense in calculating the company taxable profit nor assessable as income on the director.
- Even though a director is taxable on his remuneration, the amount of the remuneration must be commensurate with the director's duties for it to be allowable in calculating the company's taxable profits.

13

National insurance contributions: employees and employers

Introduction

[13.1] A large part of the cost of the social security system is funded from national insurance contributions (NICs) based on the present day earnings of employed and self-employed workers. The main provisions are found in the Social Security Contributions and Benefits Act 1992 (SSCBA 1992) and statutory instruments. Great Britain excludes Northern Ireland, which has its own system of social security law, but arrangements provide effectively for a single system of social security in the UK so that, in general, references in this chapter to Great Britain may be read as references to the UK.

NICs for self-employed people are discussed in CHAPTER 24. See also **9.52**, and **9.55** onwards for interest, penalties and appeals relating to NICs. The General Anti-Abuse Rule (GAAR, see **45.5**) applies to NICs in relation to tax arrangements entered into on or after 13 March 2014. See CHAPTER **10** for employment aspects of NICs and collection of contributions through the PAYE system.

The amount of NICs payable and the rules for collecting it depend upon which 'class' of contribution is payable (see **13.4**), and the contribution rates are shown in the TABLE OF RATES AND ALLOWANCES (**TRA**). HMRC's National Insurance Contributions Office (NICO) deals with NICs but the Department for Work and Pensions is responsible for social security benefits.

The Office of Tax Simplification (OTS) has published a further review on the closer alignment of income tax and NICs. They have put forward a 5-year plan in which two main recommendations are to move to an annual, cumulative and aggregated assessment period for employees' NICs, similar to PAYE income tax, and to change employers' NICs to a payroll levy.

Persons liable to pay Class 1 contributions (SSCBA 1992, ss 2, 4AA, 6(1), 9, 9A, 9B, 120; NICA 2015, s 1)

[13.2] 'Employed earners' and their employers are required to pay Class 1 NICs unless they are exempt (see below). An 'employed earner' is a person who is gainfully employed in Great Britain (either under a contract of service or in an office) with earnings that are chargeable to tax as employment income (see CHAPTER 10). See **19.1** regarding the importance of distinguishing between employment and self-employment.

Certain people are specifically brought within the liability to pay Class 1 NICs, including office cleaners, some agency workers, a spouse or civil partner working in the other spouse's/partner's business (other than in a partnership), and ministers of religion paid chiefly by way of stipend or salary. Any entertainers treated for tax purposes as employees on basic principles, including those on Equity contracts, are liable to Class 1 NICs. With effect from 6 April 2014 entertainers engaged under a contract for services are classed as being self-employed and therefore subject to Class 2 and Class 4 NICs.

Some members of limited liability partnerships are treated as employed, see **23.33**.

An anti-avoidance rule ensures that workers employed through agencies who would be employees but for the imposition of artificially constructed intermediary arrangements are treated as employees for NICs purposes. Provisions also prevent avoidance of NICs by the use of offshore employment payroll intermediary companies (see **41.22**).

Certain employees are exempt from payment of Class 1 contributions as indicated below. The exemptions also apply to employers' contributions, except for employees in category (a) below who are over state pension age.

(a)   People aged under 16 or over pensionable age (see **16.2**).

(b)   People whose earnings are below the weekly lower earnings limit (£113 for 2017–18).

(c)   An individual employed by their spouse or civil partner for a non-business purpose.

(d)   People employed for a non-business purpose by a close relative in the home where they both live.

(e)   Returning and counting officers and people employed by them in connection with an election or referendum.

(f)   Certain employees of international organisations and visiting armed forces.

Special rules apply to those who go to work abroad — see **41.52** to **41.56**.

A 'home base' rule applies to aircrew and their employers operating around the EEA (see **1.3**) for determining the member state in which social security contributions are payable. The 'home base' is where crew normally start and end their periods of duty. UK NICs will only be payable by aircrew with a home base in the UK. A transitional period of up to ten years from 2012 may apply in certain circumstances.

Earnings (SSCBA 1992, ss 3, 4)

[13.3] Class 1 contributions are calculated on gross pay, which is broadly the same as pay for income tax under PAYE and includes certain benefits in kind (see **10.10**), but is before deducting employees' contributions to registered pension schemes and any charitable gifts under the payroll giving scheme. Tax on employees' earnings is calculated on the gross pay before deducting NICs. HMRC guidance needs to be studied carefully to identify other differences between pay for tax and NICs purposes, in particular CWG2, the appendix of which provides a list of other useful HMRC forms and guidance. It can be accessed online at www.gov.uk/government/publications/cwg2-further-guide-to-paye-and-national-insurance-contributions.

Expenses payments to employees count as pay except to the extent that they are for proper business expenses, for which receipts or records must be available. Reimbursement of an employee's parking expenses, for example, must be for recorded business-related journeys. Where expenses payments are exempted for tax purposes, the same treatment applies for NICs (see **10.16**), and the exemptions (see **10.15**) for incidental personal expenses and payments for directors' liability insurance also apply.

Virtually all benefits in kind that do not attract Class 1 NICs attract a liability for employers' Class 1A contributions. There is no Class 1A charge on the employee (see CHAPTER **10**, in particular **10.49**).

Class 1 contributions are not payable on benefits unless they have been made specifically chargeable, so employees earning less than £866 a week will still get a significant advantage from receiving certain benefits rather than cash pay (the saving to those earning above £866 a week in 2017–18 being 2% rather than 12%).

Pay for Class 1 NICs specifically includes benefits that are in the form of 'readily convertible assets' (see **10.31**). Readily convertible shares and share options (other than under tax-advantaged schemes) come within these provisions (see **11.3** for details). Class 1 NICs are also payable on virtually all non-cash vouchers, the exceptions being broadly those that are exempt for income tax (see **10.36**).

It is, however, important to distinguish benefits from payments by the employer for which the employee is legally responsible. The key question is who made the contract. If it is the employee, Class 1 NICs are payable (subject to deduction of any identifiable business proportion). If it is the employer, the payment is a benefit and is not liable to Class 1 NICs unless it is for one of the specifically chargeable items. For example, if an employer contracts to buy an employee a television set, or groceries, Class 1 NICs are not payable (but the employer would have a Class 1A liability). If the employee contracts to make the purchases and the bill is paid by the employer, Class 1 NICs are payable. HMRC's guidance for employers provides detailed information and careful study is recommended. See for example www.gov.uk/expenses-and-benefits-a-to-z and HMRC booklet CWG2.

Payment of a director's bills where the payment is charged to the director's account with the company is not liable to Class 1 NICs unless the account becomes overdrawn, or there is an increase in the amount by which it becomes overdrawn, and the debit is made in anticipation of an earnings payment such as fees or bonuses, see HMRC booklet CA44. See **12.16** regarding the NICs consequences of a director's account becoming overdrawn.

See **11.36** regarding employee shareholder status under which employees give up certain employment rights in return for shares in their employer's company. The first £2,000 of share value received by such employees is not subject to NICs, though the relief has been withdrawn for shares issued under new agreements from December 2016.

September 2017 Finance Bill which is expected to receive Royal Assent in November 2017 includes legislation to align the NICs and tax treatment of termination payments from 2018–19 so that employers will also have to pay NICs on the elements of termination payments that exceed £30,000 (see CHAPTER **15**). Revised social security regulations will implement the NICs change.

Contribution rates (SSCBA 1992, ss 1, 5, 8, 9)

[13.4] Employees and their employers pay Class 1 NICs based on a percentage of earnings. Payments made by employees are 'primary' contributions and employer contributions are 'secondary' contributions. Employees' primary contributions are payable at two rates, a 'main primary percentage' of 12%, applicable to earnings above the primary threshold (see below) up to the upper earnings limit of £866 a week, and an 'additional primary percentage' of 2% applies to all earnings above that level. Employers' secondary contributions are payable at 13.8% on all earnings above the secondary threshold unless the employee is aged under 21 or an apprentice aged under 25 (see below).

For 2017–18 the primary and secondary thresholds have been aligned. Employees do not pay NICs up to the primary threshold of £157 a week, but have their rights to state pensions and other contributory benefits protected by reference to a lower pay figure. They are treated as paying notional NICs between the 'lower earnings limit' of £113 a week and the primary threshold. Payments to employees at or below £113 must still be reported to HMRC. Employers do not pay NICs on pay up to the secondary threshold of £157 a week or, for those employees aged under 21 or apprentices aged under 25, up to the upper secondary threshold of £866. For these purposes the apprentice must be following an approved UK Government statutory apprenticeship framework, see www.gov.uk/government/publications/national-insurance-con tributions-for-under-25s-employer-guide.

See **13.5** for the reduced rate of employees' contributions payable by certain married women and widows.

A separate category of contributions, Class 1A, is payable annually by employers (not employees) on taxable benefits provided to employees that are not chargeable to Class 1 or Class 1B contributions — see **10.49**. Class 1B contributions are payable only by those employers who enter into a PAYE Settlement Agreement with HMRC and are payable at the same time as the tax due under that arrangement (see **10.69**). The rate for Class 1A and Class 1B contributions in 2017–18 is 13.8%.

Class 1 contributions are collected through the PAYE system (see 10.58). Class 1A contributions are paid separately to HMRC — for details, see 10.66. Voluntary Class 3 contributions may be paid by those who would otherwise not pay enough contributions to earn a full pension (see 13.13), and voluntary Class 3A contributions could be paid from 12 October 2015 to 5 April 2017 by pensioners who reached state pension age before 6 April 2016 to enable them to top up their additional state pension. Employees cease to pay contributions when they reach pensionable age (see 16.2), but employers must continue to pay secondary Class 1 contributions and Class 1A and 1B contributions (see 13.6).

There are interest and penalties for the late payment of PAYE/NICs by employers (see 9.74 and 10.68).

An employment allowance of £3,000 per year is available for businesses, charities and community amateur sports clubs to be offset against their employer Class 1 secondary NICs bill and can be claimed as part of the normal payroll process through Real Time Information (see 10.66). The allowance is not available to companies where the director is the sole employee.

Employers' NICs are deductible in arriving at their taxable profits.

Reduced rate for certain married women and widows

[13.5] Women who were married or widowed as at 6 April 1977 had the option before 12 May 1977 to choose to pay Class 1 contributions at a reduced rate. If they are still entitled to pay the reduced contributions, the certificate of election must be handed over to the employer to enable him to deduct contributions at the correct rate. The reduced rate for 2017–18, which applies once earnings exceed £157 a week is 5.85% on earnings up to £866 per week and 2% on earnings above £866 a week. If a married woman is self-employed, the election makes her exempt from paying Class 2 contributions, but not Class 4 contributions (see CHAPTER 24).

Although substantial amounts may be paid in reduced rate contributions, they do not entitle the payer to any contributory state benefits (but statutory sick pay and other statutory payments are payable where appropriate). Many married women and widows considered that they were inadequately informed about the effects of not building up a contribution record of their own, but the Government did not accept that any compensation should be paid. They cannot pay voluntary Class 3 contributions to help to qualify for the full basic retirement pension.

An election to pay reduced rate contributions is effective until it is cancelled or revoked. A woman loses the right to pay reduced rate contributions:

(a)   if she is divorced, in which case the right is lost immediately after the decree absolute, or has the marriage annulled, or

(b)   if she becomes widowed and is not entitled to widow's benefit, in which case the right is not lost until the end of the tax year in which the husband dies, or the end of the following tax year if he dies between 1 October and 5 April, or

(c)   if she pays no reduced rate Class 1 contributions and has no earnings from self-employment for two consecutive tax years.

An election can be revoked in writing at any time using form CF9 (or CF9A for widows) and the revocation will, in most instances, take effect from the beginning of the following week. If the election is revoked, the wife will start earning a pension in her own right, and she will also be entitled to claim maternity allowance, jobseeker's allowance and contribution-based employment and support allowance if appropriate. Those who are considering revoking may apply for a pension forecast (see **13.13**) to assist them in their decision. Women earning between the lower earnings limit of £113 and the primary threshold of £157 a week would benefit from revoking the election, because they would become entitled to contributory benefits even though they would not have to pay any contributions (see **13.4**). If their earnings increased to above the earnings threshold, however, they would pay 12% rather than 5.85% on the excess.

People over pensionable age

[13.6] No contributions are payable by an employee who is over pensionable age (see **16.2**), although the employer is still liable for secondary contributions where earnings exceed the secondary threshold.

Certificates of Age Exception are no longer issued so employers can confirm an employee's age using the 'Check your State Pension age' calculator on GOV.UK, retaining a screenshot of the result as proof of the employee's age.

Employee contributions

[13.7] Further rules apply to certain employees.

More than one employment

[13.8] A person who has more than one employment is liable to pay primary Class 1 NICs in respect of each job. There is, however, a prescribed annual maximum contribution.

The calculation of the maximum used to be straightforward, but now that contributions at 2% are chargeable on all earnings above the upper earnings limit (£45,000 for 2017–18), the calculation can be complex and has several stages. Detailed guidance on the calculation of the annual maximum is available in HMRC's National Insurance Manual at NIM01160.

If the contributions paid for 2017–18 exceed the maximum a refund may be claimed of the excess from NICO so long as that excess is greater than 1/15th of a Class 1 contribution at the main 12% rate on earnings at the upper earnings limit (i.e. £5.67 for 2017–18).

To avoid having to pay contributions in all employments throughout the year and being refunded any excess after the end of the year, an employee may apply to defer some of his contributions. Application for deferment can be made on form CA72A and HMRC have produced guidance notes to accompany the form. Alternatively an online service is now available. If deferment is granted the employee will remain liable to pay Class 1 NICs at the rate of 2% on all earnings above the primary threshold of £157 a week in the 'deferred' employment.

Deferment has no effect on employers' contributions, which are payable at 13.8% in each employment on the earnings above the secondary threshold. Where a person has more than one job with the same employer, earnings from those employments must be added together and contributions calculated on the total. Where a person has jobs with different employers who 'carry on business in association with each other', all earnings from 'associated' employers must be added together for the purpose of calculating contributions. These rules will not be enforced if it is not reasonably practicable to do so. See HMRC's National Insurance Manual at NIM10000 onwards for HMRC's views on these provisions, in particular NIM10009 for their interpretation of 'not reasonably practicable'.

Income from self-employment

[13.9] The position of the employee who also has income from self-employment is dealt with in CHAPTER 24.

Company directors

[13.10] Directors sometimes receive a salary under a service contract and also fees for holding the office of director. They are often paid in irregular amounts at irregular time intervals, for example a fixed monthly salary together with a bonus after the year end, once the results of the company are known. To ensure that this does not lead to manipulation of liability to pay NICs, directors in employment at the beginning of a tax year have an annual earnings period coinciding with the tax year. Those appointed during a tax year have an earnings period equal to the number of weeks from the date of appointment to the end of the tax year. No Class 1 contributions are due unless and until the director's earnings reach the annual primary threshold (£8,164 for 2017–18), or a pro rata limit for directors appointed during a tax year (using the appropriate multiple of the weekly limit). See HMRC booklet CA44.

For directors who earn regular amounts, the annual earnings period causes an unnecessary distortion in their NICs payments, but it is possible for contributions to be paid as if the special rules did not apply. The director still has an annual earnings liability, however, so that those seeking to manipulate the rules are still prevented from doing so.

All earnings paid to a director during an earnings period must be included in that earnings period (irrespective of the period to which they relate). Earnings include fees, bonuses, salary, payments made in anticipation of future earnings, and payments made to a director which were earned while he was still an employee.

If a director resigns, all payments made to him between the date of resignation and the end of the tax year that relate to his period of directorship must be linked to his other 'directorship earnings' of that tax year. If any such earnings are paid in a later tax year, they are not added to any other earnings of the year in which payment is made. Instead, they are considered independently on an annual earnings basis, and Class 1 NICs accounted for accordingly.

Many directors have payments in anticipation of future earnings, e.g. a payment on account of a bonus to be declared when the company's results are known. Liability for Class 1 contributions arises when the payments are made. The advance bonus payments are added to all other earnings of the annual earnings period. When the bonus is determined, any balance will become liable to Class 1 contributions in that tax year. A bonus is deemed to be paid whether it is placed in an account on which the director can draw or left in the company, unless exceptionally it is not placed at the director's disposal.

To the extent that a director makes drawings against a credit balance on his director's loan account, no Class 1 liability will arise as these drawings simply reduce the balance of the loan account. If the loan account has been built up from undrawn remuneration, the Class 1 liability will have arisen at the time the remuneration was credited to it. For further details of earnings in connection with the director's loan account see **12.16**.

See **12.17** regarding a director's personal liability for both his own NICs and other contributions due from the company if he has been fraudulent or negligent.

Pensions entitlement

[13.11] Payment of NICs builds up entitlement to the state pension. The main aspects of the state pension are dealt with in CHAPTER **16**.

[13.12] A single-component flat-rate state pension replaced the two-component system for individuals who reach state pension age on or after 6 April 2016. The previous state pension arrangements will continue for people who reached state pension age before that date.

The latest rules provide, broadly, that in order to get a full state pension an individual must have paid or have been credited with Class 1, 2 or 3 NICs on an amount equal to 52 times the lower earnings limit (see **13.1**) in broadly 35 'qualifying years' in working life between age 16 and pensionable age. Entitlement will be pro-rated where there are less than 35 qualifying years. A minimum number of 10 qualifying years will apply for any entitlement. There are transitional rules for those who reach pensionable age on or after 6 April 2016 and who have qualifying years attributable to tax years prior to that date. This involves comparing entitlement under the old rules and the new rules to determine the amount payable.

Under the previous rules the number of qualifying years depended on age and was different for men and women. For example, men born before 6 April 1945 usually needed 44 qualifying years. Women born before 6 April 1950 usually needed 39 qualifying years. However, men born after 5 April 1945 and women born after 5 April 1950 only needed 30 qualifying years.

For the purpose of state pension entitlement, an individual may be credited with contributions if they are not paying NICs but qualify in some other way. This includes individuals receiving certain social security benefits and those who stay at home to look after children. For a full list see www.gov.uk/natio nal-insurance-credits/eligibility.

Electing not to receive child benefit to avoid the high income child benefit charge (see **10.7**) will not affect NI credits, but HMRC advise that a child benefit claim form should still be completed for any new children to establish entitlement.

Those who stay at home to look after children or sick or elderly people used to get Home Responsibilities Protection (HRP), which reduced the number of years needed to qualify for full pension. From 6 April 2010 they get national insurance credits. If HRP had been built up before 6 April 2010, up to 22 of those years has automatically been converted into credits, see further www.g ov.uk/home-responsibilities-protection-hrp.

There are various provisions to give equality of treatment to spouses and civil partners. A spouse or civil partner could get a basic state pension based on the NICs record of the other spouse or partner, though this is not possible for those reaching state pension age after 5 April 2016. A spouse or civil partner may claim an increase for a dependent spouse or partner, although new retirees from 6 April 2010 are not entitled to this and it will be abolished completely on 5 April 2020. A person whose spouse or civil partner has died may be able to inherit additional pension from him or her. Transitional provisions under the new state pension rules applying from 6 April 2016 permit inheriting entitlement from a late spouse or civil partner who had made NI contributions in respect of tax years before the introduction of the new state pension. The pension entitlement of surviving spouses and civil partners can be com- plex. State pension guidance is available at www.gov.uk/contact-pension-serv ice. Those of pensionable age may earn a higher pension by deferring it and, for those who reached state pension age before 6 April 2016, a lump sum could be taken instead of extra pension. The lump sum option is not available for those reaching state pension age after 5 April 2016, see **16.5**.

[13.13] An individual who does not earn enough, either as an employee or in self-employment, to achieve the required level of Class 1 or 2 contributions, may pay voluntary Class 3 contributions of £14.25 per week in 2017–18 to help to qualify for the basic retirement pension and, for those under pensionable age, bereavement benefits. He can check with HMRC's NICO to see whether his contribution record is good enough to earn a full pension. Guidance notes and an application form are provided at www.gov.uk/volunt ary-national-insurance-contributions.

The general rule is that Class 3 contributions can be paid up to six years after the year to which they relate (but usually at a higher rate if payment is more than two years after the relevant tax year). Some people may buy up to six additional years of Class 3 contributions resulting in extended time limits in some earlier tax years. A person who reaches state pension age on or after 6 April 2016 may make the contributions up to 5 April 2023. HMRC normally notify people annually if their contribution record is inadequate. Guidance is provided at www.gov.uk/voluntary-national-insurance-contributions/deadlines. A pension forecast can be obtained at www.gov.uk/state-pension/what-youll-get.

[13.14] Certain married women pay reduced contributions (see **13.5**), in which case they are not entitled to contribution credits and cannot pay Class 3 contributions.

Tax points

[13.15] Note the following:

- Employees earning between £113 and £157 a week satisfy the contribution conditions for contributory social security benefits even though no contributions are payable.
- If an employee has several employments, he can get a refund of NICs in excess of the annual maximum. Refunds are not, however, available in respect of employers' contributions.
- If a wife or husband or civil partner pays maximum contributions at the 12% rate in a separate job and also does some work in the family business run by their spouse or civil partner, employers' NICs on the earnings from the family business cannot be reclaimed, so it may be more sensible to pay the spouse or civil partner less than the primary threshold of £157 a week. It should be remembered, however, that earnings of either spouse or civil partner as an *employee* of the family business must be justified if relief for tax is to be given in calculating the business profits. The national minimum wage/national living wage legislation may, however, apply (see **12.1**).
- Except for company directors, who have an annual earnings period coinciding with the tax year, or for the remainder of the tax year in which they are appointed, NICs are not calculated on a cumulative basis. If average earnings will not exceed the secondary threshold of £157, it would be beneficial to ensure that the actual earnings in any week do not do so, otherwise the employer will be liable to pay NICs for that particular week even though on a cumulative basis the threshold may not have been reached.
- If an employee has more than one job and earns more than £866 a week from one of them, he should consider applying for deferment. Even if he does not earn more than £866 a week from one job, but his *total* earnings exceed that amount, it may be better to apply for deferment rather than wait for a refund after the year end. The effect of deferment is that NICs will be payable at 2% rather than 12% on earnings above £157 a week in all jobs other than the main job.
- Dividends paid to shareholders do not attract NICs. It may be appropriate for shareholders/directors to receive dividends rather than additional remuneration (not forgetting the national minimum wage/

national living wage and personal/managed service company legislation, and the comments in **12.10** about the 'settlements' rules). It is important to ensure that dividends are properly documented so that they cannot be challenged as pay.

The NICs aspect must not be looked at in isolation. Many other factors are important, e.g. the level of remuneration for company or personal pension purposes, and the effect of a dividend policy on other shareholders. See CHAPTER **12** for illustrations.

- If a wife has been paying the reduced married woman's rate of NICs, she should watch the circumstances in which she has to revert to the full rate, for example a divorce (see **13.5**). If she underpays, even by mistake, she will probably have to make up the difference. However, no NICs at all are payable from pensionable age.

- Where a spouse/civil partner works in the business of the other spouse/partner, then even though the recipient is paid as a self-employed individual issuing invoices to the paying spouse/partner and after appropriate charging and accounting for VAT, for NICs purposes the paying spouse/partner is regarded as an employer, with Class 1 NICs being payable.

- If an individual has not satisfied the contribution conditions for a year to be classed as a qualifying year, his state pension may be affected (see **13.12**). Voluntary Class 3 contributions (see **13.13**) can be paid to maintain the contribution record.

- If an employer pays an employee's debt, it counts as pay for Class 1 NICs and for income tax. Where possible, the contract should be made by the employer. In that case, Class 1 NICs will not be payable unless the payment relates to a specifically chargeable item. The employer will be liable to Class 1A NICs.

- Records are needed to prove business use in certain areas, such as for mileage allowances to those who use their own cars (see **10.18** regarding business mileage rates), and for contributions towards an employee's telephone bill, unless, in the case of telephones, there is an agreed business proportion for tax, which will also be accepted for NICs purposes.

- Where Class 1A NICs are payable on a benefit with mixed business/private use, the employer has to pay contributions on the full amount, without any offset for the business proportion.

14

Statutory sick pay and statutory maternity etc pay

Background

[14.1] This chapter deals with the main provisions relating to statutory payments for sickness, maternity, paternity and adoption. More detailed information is available in HMRC guidance for employers, the department's Statutory Payments Manual and other published material. Various rules applying to leave periods, as distinct from paid absences, are dealt with only briefly here.

The main provisions relating to statutory sick pay (SSP) and statutory maternity, paternity, adoption and shared parental pay (SMP, SPP, SAP, ShPP) are in the Social Security Contributions and Benefits Act 1992 as amended. Much of the detail is contained in regulations.

Most employees are entitled to receive SSP from their employers for up to 28 weeks of sickness absence. Employers are, however, entitled to opt out of the SSP scheme if they pay wages or sick pay at or above the SSP rates (see **14.13**). SSP is paid at a single flat rate.

Employers are also required to pay SMP, SPP, SAP and ShPP where the relevant conditions are satisfied (although they will be able to claim reimbursement of most or all of it). SMP, SPP and SAP are paid at two rates, the higher rate being dependent on the employee's earnings and the standard rate being a fixed amount. ShPP is paid only at the standard rate. SSP, SMP, SPP, SAP and ShPP all count as pay for income tax and national insurance contributions (NICs).

For SSP payable until 5 April 2014, employers are entitled to recover SSP if and to the extent that it exceeds a stipulated monthly threshold (see **14.12**). Employers are able to recover 92% of SMP/SPP/SAP/ShPP, unless they qualify for Small Employers' Relief, in which case they can recover 100% of the SMP etc. plus a further 3% to compensate for the NICs on the SMP etc (see **14.24**).

Employers who fail to comply with the statutory requirements are liable to various penalties.

Statutory Sick Pay

Employees entitled to receive statutory sick pay

[14.2] An employee is entitled to statutory sick pay (SSP) unless he falls into one of the excluded groups (see **14.3**). Married women and widows paying reduced rate Class 1 contributions are also entitled to SSP. An employee is entitled to SSP for each job he has, so that if an individual is employed by two different employers he will be paid SSP by each employer when off work through illness. The definition of an employee is the same as that of an 'employed earner' for Class 1 NICs (see **13.2**), except that there is no age restriction for SSP (the lower age limit of 16 years old and upper age limit of 'pensionable age' (**16.2**) do not apply).

An employee that is being paid SSP is not entitled to Employment and Support Allowance or Universal Credit (**10.6**). Employees who are not entitled to SSP and those who have exhausted their SSP entitlement may claim Employment and Support Allowance or Universal Credit.

The main employer guidance can be found at www.gov.uk/employers-sick-pay.

Employees excluded from statutory sick pay

[14.3] Employees who fall into certain categories at the beginning of a 'period of incapacity for work' (see **14.6**) are not entitled to statutory sick pay (SSP). These include:

(a) Those whose average weekly earnings (usually calculated over the previous eight weeks) are below the lower earnings limit for NICs (£113 for 2017–18; see CHAPTER 13). If an employee's average weekly earnings would otherwise be too low to qualify for SSP, but would qualify if the employer included an amount for expenses or benefits subject to a PAYE settlement agreement (where Class 1B NICs are paid by the employer, see **10.69**), then the employer must recalculate the earnings including the amount on which Class 1B contributions are payable.

(b) Employees who have started or returned to work after getting Employment and Support Allowance or Universal Credit (**10.6**) and they are sick within 12 weeks of starting/returning to work. Such individuals will be entitled to benefits (as opposed to SSP).

(c) A person who has not begun work under his contract.

(d) Those who become ill while they are away from work because of a trade dispute, unless the employee can prove that he is not participating in, or directly interested in, the dispute.

(e) A woman who is pregnant or has just given birth, and becomes sick during her 'disqualifying period' (see **14.4**).

(f)   Those who have received 28 weeks' SSP and the new period of sickness 'links' to the last one.

(g)   Those who fall ill while in prison or in legal custody.

(h)   Those who are outside the UK, if their employer is not liable to pay secondary Class 1 NICs on their employees' earnings.

Agency workers and casual workers are not excluded from SSP. The basic test is that if an employer has to deduct PAYE tax and Class 1 NICs from the worker's earnings (and all the other relevant conditions are met (**14.5**)), then SSP must be paid.

An employer who cannot pay SSP because the employee is excluded is required to complete form SSP1 and give it immediately to the employee, who may be able to claim state benefits.

Pregnancy

[14.4] Statutory sick pay (SSP) cannot be paid during a disqualifying period. For those entitled to statutory maternity pay (SMP) or maternity allowance, the disqualifying period starts with the day the employee is first entitled to that payment and normally runs for 39 weeks.

For those not entitled to either of those payments and not already getting SSP, the disqualifying period runs for 18 weeks, normally starting on the earlier of the Sunday of the week in which the baby is born and the Sunday of the week the employee is first off sick with a pregnancy-related illness on or after the start of the fourth week before the baby is due. The starting date rules are sometimes slightly different if the baby is born early.

If SSP is already being paid to a pregnant woman not entitled to SMP or maternity allowance, the disqualifying period starts with the earlier of the day after the birth and the day after the first day she becomes sick with a pregnancy-related illness on or after the start of the fourth week before the baby is due.

Qualifying conditions for statutory sick pay

[14.5] For statutory sick pay (SSP) to be payable two qualifying conditions must be met:

(a)   there must be a 'period of incapacity for work'; and

(b)   there must be one or more 'qualifying days'.

Period of incapacity for work

[14.6] A period of incapacity for work (PIW) is a period of four or more consecutive days of incapacity for work, counting rest days and holidays as well as normal working days. Night shift workers falling ill during a shift are treated as working only on the day on which the shift began.

A person who is not incapable of work may be deemed to be incapable if a medical practitioner advises that he or she should not work for a precautionary reason, or he or she is a carrier of (or has been in contact with) a contagious disease.

HMRC guidance states that any changes to the statutory sick pay (SSP) scheme in the event of a pandemic alert being declared by the Government would be notified via HMRC's web pages and the Employer Helpline, and more general information would be provided via the Department for Work and Pensions' website, TV and radio.

If two PIWs are separated by 56 days or less, they are treated as one single PIW (called a linked PIW).

Example 1

An employee is incapable of work through illness from Friday 2 December 2016 to Tuesday 6 December 2016 inclusive and from Monday 23 January 2017 to Thursday 16 February 2017 inclusive. The two PIWs are separated by 47 days and are therefore treated as a linked PIW.

Tables to help employers work out whether PIWs link are included in the SSP Tables issued by HMRC.

Qualifying days

[14.7] Statutory sick pay (SSP) is payable only in respect of 'qualifying days'. These are days of the week agreed between the employer and employee and will normally be those days on which the employee is required to work. The employer and employee may, however, come to other arrangements if they wish but qualifying days cannot be defined by reference to the days when the employee is sick. There is an overriding rule that there must be at least one qualifying day each week even if the employee is not required to work during that week.

SSP is not payable for the first three qualifying days in any PIW not linked to an earlier PIW. These are 'waiting days'.

Example 2

An employee with qualifying days Monday to Friday each week, who had not been ill during the previous two months, was ill on the bracketed days in the table below and returned to work on the 31st of the month.

M	T	W	Th	F	Sa	Su
	1	2	(3)	(4)	(5)	(6)
7	8	9	10	11	12	13
14	15	16	17	18	19	20
(21)	(22)	(23)	(24)	(25)	26	(27)
(28)	(29)	(30)	31			

There are three PIWs, from the 3rd to the 6th, from the 21st to the 25th, and from the 27th to the 30th.

In the first, there are two qualifying days which count as waiting days, and no SSP is payable.

In the second, which begins not more than 56 days after the end of the first and is therefore linked with it, the 21st is the third waiting day and SSP is payable for the other four qualifying days.

The third begins not more than 56 days after the end of the second and is therefore linked with it. As there are three waiting days in the (earlier) linked PIWs, SSP is payable for each of the three qualifying days in the third PIW.

Amount of statutory sick pay

[14.8] Providing the employee's average weekly earnings are at or above the national insurance lower earnings limit (£113 for 2017–18), statutory sick pay (SSP) is payable on a daily basis at a flat weekly rate of £89.35 (from 6 April 2017).

The daily rate of SSP is the weekly rate divided by the number of qualifying days in the week (beginning with Sunday). For example, an employee who has five qualifying days in a week will receive SSP at a daily rate of £17.87 (£89.35 ÷ 5). HMRC provide a daily rates table for this purpose.

SSP will usually be paid on the employee's normal pay day. Wages paid to an employee can be offset against any SSP due for the same day. If the wages are less than the SSP due, the employer must make up the payment to the appropriate rate of SSP.

End of statutory sick pay

[14.9] Statutory sick pay (SSP) ends with whichever of the following first occurs:

(a)   the period of incapacity (PIW) ends and the employee returns to work;
(b)   the employee reaches his maximum 28 week entitlement to SSP;
(c)   the employee's linked PIW has run for three years (which could only happen in exceptional circumstances where there were a large number of very short, four-day illnesses);
(d)   the employee's contract of employment ends;
(e)   the employee is taken into legal custody;
(f)   a pregnant woman's disqualifying period begins (see **14.4**).

The maximum period for which the employer is liable to pay SSP is normally 28 weeks. Where, however, a new employee commences a PIW within eight weeks of the day when a PIW with a previous employer ended, the weeks of SSP shown on the leaver's statement provided by the previous employer (see **14.10**) are taken into account to determine the new employer's maximum SSP liability. The previous period of sickness does not, however, affect the new employer's calculations in any other way and is not treated as a linked PIW.

Where entitlement to SSP ends while the employee is still sick, the employee will be able to claim Employment and Support Allowance or Universal Credit (**10.6**). To facilitate the change-over, the employer must issue change-over form SSP1 to the employee at the beginning of the 23rd week of SSP (or, if sooner, two weeks before the employee's entitlement to SSP is due to end). If the employee's entitlement ends unexpectedly (e.g. through being taken into legal custody), the change-over form must be issued immediately. Form SSP1 must also be issued at the start of a pregnancy disqualification period.

Leaver's statements

[14.10] If an employee has a PIW which ends not more than 56 days before his employment ceases, and statutory sick pay (SSP) was payable for one week or more, a leaver's statement SSP1 (or the employer's own version of the form) must be issued if requested by the employee, showing the number of weeks SSP was payable (rounded to whole weeks, counting more than three odd days of payment as a week, and ignoring three odd days or less). The statement must be issued not later than the seventh day after the day the employee asks for it or, if that is impracticable, on the first pay day in the following tax month.

Notification and evidence for statutory sick pay

[14.11] The payment of statutory sick pay (SSP) is triggered by the employee notifying his employer that he is unfit for work. An employer can draw up his own procedure for notification subject to the following limitations:

(a)   reasonable steps must be taken to notify employees of the procedures;

(b)   where the employee is a new employee with a leaving statement from his former employer, the statement must be accepted if it is produced not later than the seventh day after his first qualifying day of sickness;

(c)   it is not legal to insist that notification:

    (i)   is made by the employee in person;

    (ii)   is made by a particular time of day;

    (iii)   is made more than once weekly for the same illness;

    (iv)   is made on a form provided by the employer or on a medical certificate; or

    (v)   is given earlier than the first qualifying day.

If no notification procedures have been drawn up, the employee should inform his employer in writing by the seventh day after his first qualifying day of absence. If an employee fails to notify within the laid-down time limits, an employer may withhold SSP until the date of notification, but late notification may be accepted if there was good cause for delay.

Having been notified by an employee of his illness, the employer must satisfy himself that the illness is genuine before paying SSP. Employers usually obtain 'self-certificates' for the first week of illness and medical notes for longer absences. The employer cannot insist on a medical certificate for the first seven days of a period of incapacity.

An employer may withhold SSP when notification is late, and he may refuse to pay SSP if he feels that the employee is not in fact sick. In both these instances the employer, if required by the employee, must provide written reasons for withholding or refusing to pay SSP. An employee who disagrees with his employer's actions has the right to appeal for an official decision.

Recovery of statutory sick pay by employer (FA 2014, s 12)

[**14.12**] For statutory sick pay (SSP) payable until 5 April 2014, employers may recover that part of the SSP paid in a tax month that exceeds 13% of their combined employer/employee NICs in that tax month (not including any Class 1A or Class 1B contributions but after deducting any contracted-out contributions rebate due.

This recovery scheme was abolished on 6 April 2014, so that from that date SSP is fully funded by employers. Recovery for earlier years will be allowable for two years from 6 April 2014. Amounts recovered in April and May 2014 for absence up to and including 5 April 2014 must be recovered using form SP32 available on the HMRC website.

Example 3

Total employer/employee NICs for October are £4,000. 13% thereof is £520. SSP would be recovered as follows:

SSP paid in month	£520 or less	£600	£1,000
SSP recovered	Nil	£80	£480

SSP is recovered from amounts due to be paid over to HMRC's Accounts Office in respect of national insurance and PAYE tax payable, and if it exceeds those amounts, the employer can either carry the excess forward or apply to the Accounts Office for a refund.

Opting out of statutory sick pay

[**14.13**] Employers may opt out of the statutory sick pay (SSP) scheme if they pay wages or sick pay above the SSP rates. They do not need to apply to do so, and may, if they wish, opt out for some but not all employees or periods of sickness. They must keep records of all dates of employee sickness lasting four or more consecutive days, and all payments of earnings or occupational sick pay.

Statutory Maternity Pay

Employees entitled to statutory maternity pay

[**14.14**] To be entitled to statutory maternity pay (SMP), an employee must satisfy the qualifying conditions (see **14.15**). Those who do not qualify for SMP may be able to claim maternity allowance from the Department for Work and Pensions instead. SMP is usually paid for 39 weeks even if the employee does not return after the baby has been born. HMRC provide detailed guidance online at www.gov.uk/employers-maternity-pay-leave/entitlement.

Married women paying reduced NICs and widows getting a state widow's benefit are entitled to SMP if they satisfy the qualifying conditions. Statutory sick pay (SSP) and SMP cannot be paid at the same time, and SSP must cease on the last day before the maternity pay period (see **14.17**) starts, even if for some reason the employee is not entitled to SMP.

Employed women are entitled to a total of 52 weeks maternity leave, comprising 26 weeks of 'ordinary maternity leave' (of which two weeks are compulsory) and 26 weeks of 'additional maternity leave'. After the 2 week compulsory maternity leave period, working mothers can choose how to split their remaining 50 weeks' leave and 37 weeks' pay with their partner. This is called shared parental leave and shared parental pay (as appropriate; see **14.23**).

Qualifying conditions for statutory maternity pay

[14.15] To qualify for statutory maternity pay (SMP) an employee must have been continuously employed (normally by the same employer) for at least 26 weeks into the 15th week (the qualifying week) before the baby is due. The employee's average weekly earnings in the eight weeks ending with the qualifying week must be not less than the lower earnings limit for NICs at the end of that week (currently £113). The employee must still be pregnant at the 11th week before the expected date of birth. There are special rules for premature births. If an employee satisfies the qualifying rules with more than one employer she can receive SMP from each employer.

If Class 1B NICs have been paid in respect of the employee, the earnings on which they are considered to have been paid must be included in calculating average weekly earnings if the employee would otherwise fail to qualify for SMP, in the same way as for statutory sick pay (see **14.3**). In that event they must also be taken into account to calculate the higher rate of SMP (see **14.18**).

As a result of a decision of the European Court of Justice, if a woman is awarded a pay rise that is backdated to cover any part of the period from the start of the eight weeks ending with the qualifying week to the end of a woman's maternity leave (either ordinary or additional leave), she may claim for her average weekly earnings to be recalculated taking into account the pay rise and for any additional SMP arising to be paid to her. Arrears of SMP are not, however, payable for any period earlier than six years before the date of the claim. Where an employee has left, the time limit for a claim is six months after her leaving date.

Employees excluded from statutory maternity pay

[14.16] An employee is not entitled to statutory maternity pay (SMP) if:

(a)   she is not employed during the qualifying week (see **14.15**);
(b)   she has not been continuously employed for 26 weeks;
(c)   the earnings rule (see **14.15**) is not satisfied;
(d)   she has not given notice at an acceptable time of the date she is stopping work;
(e)   medical evidence of her expected confinement date is not provided;
(f)   she is in legal custody at any time in the first week of her maternity pay period.

An employee who is outside the EEA (see **1.3**) is not eligible for SMP unless the employer is liable to pay Class 1 NICs (see **41.52** and **41.53**).

If an employee is not entitled to SMP at the start of the maternity pay period, she is not entitled to it at all (subject to what is said in **14.15** about backdated pay rises).

An employee who is not entitled to SMP must be given form SMP1 immediately, together with any maternity certificate she has provided. These forms will need to be produced to the Department for Work and Pensions if she claims maternity allowance.

Payment of statutory maternity pay

[14.17] Statutory maternity pay (SMP) is payable for a maximum of 39 weeks, called the maternity pay period, starting normally at the same time as the maternity leave period. The employee may work for up to ten 'keeping in touch' days without affecting her SMP (or statutory adoption pay (see **14.22**)) entitlement. She may also continue to work or start work for another employer while on maternity leave before the baby is born without affecting her entitlement. The employer will no longer be liable to pay SMP if, after the baby is born, the employee starts work for a new employer or returns to work for another employer who did not employ her in the qualifying week. SMP will also cease if the employee is taken into legal custody.

Amount of statutory maternity pay

[14.18] Statutory maternity pay (SMP) is paid at the rate of 90% of the employee's average weekly earnings for the first six weeks and then at the lower of the standard rate (£140.98 for 2017–18) and 90% of average weekly earnings for the remainder of the period.

Statutory Paternity Pay

Employees entitled to statutory paternity pay

[14.19] Statutory paternity pay is paid to the claimant for a one or two week period of leave taken around the birth/adoption of the child. Adopting couples must choose which will claim statutory adoption pay (**14.22**) and which will claim statutory paternity pay (SPP).

An employee cannot get SPP and statutory sick pay at the same time. Also, employees can't get SPP and leave if they have already taken shared parental leave (**14.23**).

In addition to SPP, claimants may be able to get statutory shared parental pay and leave; see **14.23**.

HMRC provide detailed guidance online at www.gov.uk/employers-paternity-pay-leave and www.gov.uk/shared-parental-leave-and-pay-employer-guide.

Qualifying conditions

[14.20] Statutory Paternity Pay (SPP) may be claimed by the baby's biological father, a partner/husband other than the biological father of the mother, or a female partner in a same sex couple. SPP is also payable to adoptive parents – parents having a child via a surrogacy arrangement are treated as adoptive parents.

To make a claim the claimant must have a continuous period of employment of at least 26 weeks into the 15th week before the baby is due, and must continue to work for that employer until the baby is born. For adoptions, the continuous period of employment must be at least 26 weeks by the end of the week they were matched with a child.

Payment of statutory paternity pay

[14.21] The claimant's averaged weekly earnings in the eight weeks before the 15th week before the baby is due (or, for adoptions, the eight weeks before the week the employee had been told they were matched with a child) must be at least £113. The weekly amount payable is the lower of £140.98 and 90% of average weekly earnings.

The statutory paternity pay (SPP) claimant may choose to take either one or two (consecutive) whole weeks' leave within the eight weeks after the baby's birth/adoption. For babies born more than 15 weeks before the original due date, leave may be taken within the period from the date of birth to the end of eight weeks from the Sunday of the week the baby was originally due. The employee must normally give 28 days' notice of the date he intends to take leave.

The employee must request paternity pay at least 15 weeks before the week the baby is expected using form SC3 (or the employers version). If the employee does not qualify for SPP the employer must give him a form SPP1.

Statutory Adoption Pay

[14.22] Providing the relevant conditions are satisfied, statutory adoption pay (SAP) may be claimed by male or female employees adopting a child aged up to 18. The other adoptive parent may claim statutory paternity pay (14.20). Adopting couples must choose which will claim SAP and which will claim statutory paternity pay. HMRC provide detailed guidance online at www.go v.uk/employers-adoption-pay-leave/entitlement.

The same rules broadly apply for both statutory maternity pay and SAP, adapted appropriately by reference to the time when a child is matched for adoption (i.e. the adoption agency has decided that the person is suitable to adopt that child) and when a child is placed for adoption with the adoptive parents. The SAP period must start from the date of the child's placement, or from a fixed date up to 14 days before the expected date of placement.

SAP is paid for a maximum 39-week period at the rate of 90% of the employee's average weekly earnings for the first six weeks and then at the lower of the standard rate (£140.98 for 2017–18) and 90% of average weekly earnings for the remainder of the period.

Employees must give employers notice, 28 days before the adoption pay period starts or as soon as is reasonably practicable, of the date the child is placed with them for adoption, supported by a certificate from the adoption agency confirming the date they were told that they had been matched with a child.

Employees can end their adoption pay/leave entitlement early and can choose how to split their remaining pay and leave with their partner under the shared parental pay and shared parental leave provisions (see **14.23**).

Shared Parental Pay

[14.23] Statutory shared parental pay (ShPP) is available for eligible parents (the mother and her partner) whose baby is due on or after 5 April 2015 or where a child is placed for adoption on or after the same date. ShPP is also available to employed partners of the self-employed.

To be eligible for ShPP an employee must curtail maternity pay/leave (**14.14**) or adoption pay/leave (**14.22**) so that any remaining entitlement to pay can be converted into ShPP and remaining entitlement to leave is taken as shared parental leave (SPL). Parents can choose how much of the SPL each of them will take, although SPL and ShPP must be taken between the baby's birth and first birthday (or within one year of adoption).

The weekly rate of ShPP is the lower of £140.98 and 90% of average weekly earnings (there is no higher rate for the first six week as there is for maternity pay and adoption pay even if ShPP is taken during what would have been the higher rate period).

The employee must give written notice if they want to start SPL or ShPP and must generally give at least eight weeks' notice of any leave they wish to take. The employee has a statutory right to a maximum of three separate blocks of leave, although more can be agreed.

For HMRC guidance see www.gov.uk/shared-parental-leave-and-pay-employ er-guide/overview.

Recovery of SMP, SPP, SAP and ShPP by employer

[14.24] Employers other than 'small employers' are able to recover 92% of the gross amount of SMP, SPP, SAP and ShPP paid in any month.

Small employers can recover all the SMP etc. paid, plus an extra 3% of the amount paid to compensate for the employer's Class 1 contributions on the payments. Small employers are those whose total annual employer/employee NICs (excluding Class 1A and Class 1B contributions) are £45,000 or less. The annual contributions taken into account for small employers are those for the tax year *before* that in which the SMP 'qualifying week' (see **14.15**) starts, or in adoption cases, the tax year before that in which the adoptive parents were told by the adoption agency that they had been matched with a child.

The employer recovers the amount he is entitled to via an adjustment to the remittance due to HMRC as calculated from the submitted Full Payment Submission for the previous tax month. If the employer calculates that he has insufficient money to cover all the payments he needs to make, he can apply to HMRC for an advance payment.

Employer's records

[14.25] Employer's records are particularly important, as the information required to be kept may have to be made available to HMRC. Employers may use record sheets SSP2, SMP2, SPP2 and SAP2 available from HMRC offices, if they wish. The form the records take is up to the employer, but the following must be kept:

(a)   For SSP:
- (i)   records of dates of employees' PIWs;
- (ii)   all payments of SSP made during a PIW.

(b)   For SMP, SPP, SAP and ShPP:
- (i)   records of payment dates and amount paid;
- (ii)   the date the pay period began;
- (iii)   for SMP and SAP, records of any weeks in maternity or adoption pay period when payment wasn't made, with reasons, and for SPP or ShPP records of any unpaid amounts with reasons;
- (iv)   for SMP, maternity certificates (forms MAT B1) or other medical evidence, and copies of certificates returned to employees, for example when liability has ended;
- (v)   for SPP, the declaration of family commitment (or a copy);
- (vi)   for SAP, the evidence your employee gave you from the adoption agency (or a copy).

Records must also be kept of the amounts paid, and certain details need to be included on the statutory returns for pay, tax and national insurance (see **10.65**). Records must be kept for a minimum of three years after the end of the tax year to which they relate. In addition to the records outlined above, HMRC recommends that certain other records are also retained for further reference. For details see the various HMRC guides.

15

Golden handcuffs and golden handshakes

Introduction

[15.1] A 'golden handcuff' or 'golden hello' is the popular term for a lump sum payment received on taking up an employment, and a 'golden handshake' is the term for a lump sum payment received when leaving an employment.

Lump sum payments on taking up employment (ITEPA 2003, ss 62, 225, 226)

[15.2] Where a lump sum payment is made to a prospective employee, it will be taxed as advance pay for future services unless it represents compensation for some right or asset given up on taking up the employment. It is difficult to show that a payment does represent compensation, and professional advice should be sought for payments received in this category.

Sometimes a lump sum is paid in return for agreeing to restrict conduct or activities in some way, for example agreeing not to leave to join a competitor within a certain period of time. Any such special payments are treated as pay, both for tax and for NIC purposes. If an employee makes such an agreement in return for a non-cash benefit, the value of the benefit still counts as pay for both tax and NICs.

Lump sum termination payments and benefits (ITEPA 2003, ss 62, 225, 226, 309, 393–416)

[15.3] Lump sum payments received on termination of employment are taxed depending upon the exact nature of the payment. HMRC set out a step by step process (at EIM12810) that must be followed to establish whether a payment is taxable or not, as follows:

(a)   First of all, establish whether the rules in relation to receipts from non-registered schemes and employer-financed retirement benefits schemes apply. These rules take precedence over the rules for termination payments. Guidance on unregistered schemes is at EIM15010 onwards;

(b)   If (a) above does not apply it is necessary to consider (in order) whether:

    (i)   the payments are already taxable under the normal rules for earnings from employment. A payment will be taxable as employment income if it is a payment for services rendered, i.e. it is really deferred pay. Pay in lieu of notice or compensation for loss of office are chargeable to both tax and NICs in the normal way if they are provided for in the employee's terms and conditions of employment. This may be the case even if the payment is discretionary, for example the employment contract provides for four weeks' notice to be given, or, at the employer's discretion, pay in lieu of notice. HMRC's views are set out in their Employment Income Manual at EIM12976. The September 2017 Finance Bill (which is expected to receive Royal Assent in November 2017) tightens the scope of this rule by providing that *all* payments in lieu of notice, not just contractual payments are to be taxable as earnings for 2018–19 onwards, see **15.4**;

    (ii)   the payments are for a restrictive covenant, and therefore taxable. HMRC may seek to tax them as payments made in return for a restrictive undertaking (see **15.2**), if they are paid in return for an agreement by the employee to restrict his future conduct or activities. This will not normally apply where the only undertaking by the employee is that he will not pursue an action against the employer concerning the termination of his employment (unless a specific sum was attributed to the undertaking, which would be very unusual);

    (iii)   any other income tax charge or exemption applies to the payment, for example compensation for loss of a share option on termination;

    (iv)   the payment is made in connection with termination and therefore falls within the special rules that provide an exemption for the first £30,000 (see **15.4**).

In addition to the issues detailed above, the following circumstances may give rise to further complications when making lump sum payments on a termination:

(a)   Where the employee is also a shareholder, it may be difficult to show that the payment is not a distribution, for which no deduction would be given in calculating the employer's trading profit (see CHAPTER 3).

(b)   Where the payment is made at the same time as a change in voting control, a clear distinction must be demonstrated between the payment and the share transactions if the payment is not to be regarded as part of the capital transaction.

(c)   If the employee continues with the employer in a new capacity, either as an employee or perhaps under a consultancy agreement, it becomes that much harder to show the payment was not for services rendered or to be rendered in the future.

As can be seen from these various requirements it is essential that proper documentation and board minutes are available so that the nature of payments can be demonstrated to HMRC.

Taxation of lump sum termination payments and benefits

[15.4] Provided that the payment and/or benefit is not caught as taxable earnings, a distribution or as part of a capital transaction (see 15.3), it will be taxed according to the special rules for termination payments. Under these rules (subject to what is said below at 15.5 about wholly exempt payments), the first £30,000 is exempt from income tax and only the balance is taxable. There is an unlimited NIC exemption for payments associated with the termination of employment.

Essentially to fall within these provisions, the payment must be by way of compensation because the employer has *broken* the employment contract, or be a purely ex-gratia/discretionary payment that is not part of the employer's established practice. Complete and accurate documentation will be needed to demonstrate that a payment is a discretionary/compensatory payment (and therefore potentially tax free up to £30,000) as opposed to a contractual payment in lieu of notice (and therefore taxable).

From 2018–19 onwards, provisions in the September 2017 Finance Bill (which is expected to receive Royal Assent in November 2017) aim to make the existing rules fairer and remove the incentives for employers to try and manipulate the rules. From 6 April 2018 *any* payments in lieu of notice will be subject to tax in the normal manner, as if they were earnings. This means that if, for example, an employee's contract is terminated with immediate effect, but he is paid an amount he would have received had he worked his notice, the payment will be treated as taxable earnings. This is referred to in the legislation as the 'post-employment notice pay' (PENP) and is calculated by reference to an employee's basic salary, excluding bonuses etc. Any payments in excess of the PENP will count towards the £30,000 exemption. The aim is to ensure that the exemption for the first £30,000 can only apply to 'true' termination payments. Employers will also have to pay NICs on termination payments to the extent they exceed £30,000. This aligns the employer's NIC treatment of termination payments with income tax. Employees will continue to benefit from an unlimited NIC exemption for payments associated with the termination of employment.

Example 1

An employee's contract is terminated with immediate effect, but is given a termination payment of £20,000 as compensation for loss of office and £15,000 as a non-contractual PILON. In other words a total payment of £35,000.

He has a base salary of £40,000 and a notice period of three months. For the purpose of this example it is assumed that the termination payment rules apply to the whole payment of £35,000 (i.e. no special rules etc take priority (see 15.3)).

The amount of the termination payment that is taxable/non-taxable is as follows:

Calculation in 2017–18

Taxable	Non-taxable	Explanation
£5,000		Taxable as earned income because it is in excess of the £30,000 threshold
	£30,000	Not taxable because: £20,000 is 'compensation payment' £10,000 is the balance from the non-contractual PILON

Calculation in 2018–19

The employee is contracted to a 3 month notice period. Therefore his contractual notice period pay (i.e. his PENP) is £10,000 (40,000 x 3/12). As shown below, the taxable sum will increase under the rules that are due to apply from 2018–19.

The amount of the termination payment that is taxable/non-taxable is as follows:

Taxable	Non-taxable	Tax treatment
£10,000		Taxable as earned income because is equal to PENP
	25,000	Not taxable because it is non-contractual payment in excess of PENP and less than the £30,000 threshold

Non-cash benefits are valued using the cash equivalents that apply in calculating employment income (see CHAPTER 10) unless, exceptionally, the 'money's worth' value is higher. Therefore if, for example, a house is transferred as part of the termination package and its value has increased since the employer acquired it, the money's worth value (being the higher value) will be taken into account for the purposes of the exempt £30,000. If an employee is allowed to keep a company car as part of a termination package, the market value of the car will be taken into account for the purpose of the exempt

£30,000 unless it is regarded as a reward for past services, in which case the full market value would be chargeable as pay. An alternative may be to increase the lump sum and give the employee the opportunity to buy the car at market value. If the lump sum was taxable as an unregistered retirement benefit (see **15.3**), the value of the car would similarly be taxable.

Various benefits that would normally escape tax in a continuing employment are also excluded from the taxable termination payment. Statutory redundancy payments are not taxable as earnings (see **15.3**) but are subject to the special rules for termination payments and will, therefore, use part of the £30,000 exemption.

The taxable amount is treated as income of the tax year in which it is received or (for non-cash benefits) enjoyed. This makes it easier to deal with cash amounts payable by instalments and continuing benefits. Where the continuing benefit is a beneficial loan, then unless the taxable amount is covered by the £30,000 exemption, the notional interest charged to tax is treated as interest paid by the employee, so that tax relief is given if appropriate (see **10.48**). Employers deduct tax under PAYE on cash payments (see **15.7**), and employees account for higher rate tax on such payments, and the whole of the tax on non-cash benefits, in their self-assessments.

Exemptions

[**15.5**] Some payments are completely exempt from tax, for example those on accidental death in service, in respect of disability or where the service has been predominantly abroad (foreign service relief). Where service abroad does not qualify for complete exemption, there is a proportionate reduction of the taxable amount according to the time spent abroad. Note that the Government has announced its intention to abolish foreign service relief from April 2018 (except for seafarers).

Lump sums received under registered pension schemes are exempt. They may be boosted by agreed special contributions from the employer to the fund prior to the termination of employment so long as the various limits are not exceeded (see CHAPTER **16**). In view of HMRC's position on ex-gratia payments (see **15.4**), this route provides an alternative where there is a registered pension scheme.

The £30,000 exemption applies after all other available exemptions, but it is taken into account before giving proportionate relief for foreign service that is not completely exempt.

Calculation of tax payable

[**15.6**] Tax on the chargeable amount is calculated by treating it as the top slice of taxable income (except for life policy gains (see **40.5**)), above any dividend income, and savings income see **2.5**.

Example 2

An individual's taxable income in 2017–18, after reliefs and allowances, comprises non-savings income of £22,100, dividend income of £10,000 and

£10,000 in respect of a taxable lump sum. The comparison of the tax position if the normal rules treating dividend income as the top slice of income applied with the special rules for dealing with lump sums is as follows:

	£		£	£
If no special rules applied				
Non-savings income including lump sum	32,100	@ 20%	6,420	
Dividends (part)	1,400	@ 0%	–	
Dividends (balance)	3,600	@ 0%	–	
	5,000	@ 32.5%	1,625	
	42,100			8,045
Lump sum of £10,000 treated as top slice of income				
Non-savings income other than lump sum	22,100	@ 20%	4,420	
Dividends	5,000	@ 0%	–	
	5,000	@ 7.5%	375	
	32,100			
Lump sum (part)	1,400	@ 20%	280	
Lump sum (balance)	8,600	@ 40%	3,440	
	42,100			8,515
Increase in tax through treating lump sum as top slice of income				470

The increase of £470 represents an additional 20% tax on £8,600 (the part now taxed at 40%) of the lump sum (£1,720) less 25% on £5,000 of the dividends (£1,250).

PAYE and reporting requirements

[15.7] Employers must deduct and account for income tax on the excess of chargeable termination payments over £30,000 under RTI. Currently there is no NIC liability on termination payments, but from April 2018 legislation will be introduced to partially align the NIC and tax treatment of termination payments so that employers will have to pay NIC on the elements of termination payments that exceed £30,000 (there will not be any employee's NIC payable). Employers also must deduct and account for income tax on ex-gratia sums paid on retirement or death for which approval has not yet been granted (tax being refunded as and when approval is received).

Cash payments will be shown on tax deduction sheets and forms P45 and the leaving details from it should be included in an FPS (see **10.64**). If payments are made after the employee has left, tax must be deducted under PAYE on a non-cumulative basis using the 0T tax code (i.e. on the assumption that all allowances have been used elsewhere and income is taxed at the employee's relevant tax rates, see **10.61**).

Unless the package is wholly cash, or the total value of the package including benefits is estimated not to exceed £30,000, the employer must provide details of the termination package to HMRC not later than 6 July following the end of the tax year in which the termination package was awarded (copies being provided to employees to enable them to complete their tax returns); see **10.65**. The details should cover the total value of the package, the amounts of cash and the nature of the benefits to be provided and their cash equivalents, indicating which, if any, amounts and benefits are to be provided in later years. No further report needs to be submitted unless, exceptionally, there is a subsequent variation increasing the value of the package by more than £10,000, in which case a report must be sent to HMRC by 6 July following the tax year of variation. If a report is not submitted because a package is originally estimated to have a value not exceeding £30,000, but the package is subsequently changed so that it exceeds that amount, a report and employee copy must be provided by 6 July following the tax year in which the change occurs. There are penalties for non-compliance (see CHAPTER 9).

Calculating the employer's profits (CTA 2009, ss 76–81; ITTOIA 2005, s 79)

[15.8] Expenses must be wholly and exclusively for the purposes of the trade in order that they can be deducted in arriving at taxable profits. Apart from statutory redundancy payments, which are specifically allowable, there is no special rule for termination payments, but it will usually be easier to show that they meet the 'wholly and exclusively' requirement when they are compensation rather than ex-gratia payments, and when the trade is continuing rather than when it is not (but see below regarding permanent discontinuance of a trade).

It may be particularly difficult for the employer to obtain a deduction where the payment is ex-gratia and is associated with a sale of the shares or a change in voting control, or where it is an abnormally high payment to a director with a material interest in the company.

Where a trade is permanently discontinued, it is specifically provided that an additional payment up to three times any amount paid under the statutory redundancy pay provisions is allowable as a deduction in computing the employer's profits. Any payments in excess of this amount are disallowed unless they are made to an employee on cessation under a pre-existing contractual or statutory obligation (not ex-gratia amounts).

Counselling services for redundant employees (ITEPA 2003, s 310)

[15.9] The provision of counselling services by employers for redundant employees, or payment by the employer of an employee's costs for such counselling is specifically exempt from tax for employees, and the cost is fully allowed to employers.

Expenses incurred in obtaining a lump sum payment (ITEPA 2003, s 413A)

[15.10] Some employees may incur expenses, for example fees to advisers, in obtaining a lump sum payment. These will not reduce the taxable part of the lump sum as they will not have been wholly, exclusively and necessarily incurred in the performance of the duties of the employment. Where an employer pays an employee's legal costs in obtaining a compensation payment, HMRC will not treat the payment as a taxable benefit if it is made direct to the employee's lawyer following an out of court settlement, or if it is made to the employee under a court order.

Tax points

[15.11] Note the following:

- An ex-gratia payment to a director or shareholder of a close company is especially vulnerable to HMRC attack, on either or both of the following grounds:
  (a)   it is not a deductible trading expense;
  (b)   it is a distribution of profits.
- If an ex-gratia payment by a close company is not allowed in calculating profits, HMRC may contend that each shareholder has made a proportionate transfer of value for inheritance tax. There is a specific exclusion where the payment is allowed in computing profits.
- Unless the former employee obtains new sources of income to replace his salary, the tax cost of a termination payment may be lower if the termination occurs shortly after 6 April rather than before, because all or part of the payment may fall within the basic rate band, whereas it might have attracted 40% or 45% tax if it was received in addition to a full year's salary.
- The tax reliefs for lump sum payments are only available to employees and not to those working under a contract for services, whose earnings are taxed as trading income (see **19.1**). If, exceptionally, employment income is included by agreement with HMRC in the calculation of self-employed profits, e.g. directors' fees where the directorship is held in a professional capacity and the fees are included as income of the professional practice, this in itself will not prevent a lump sum qualifying for the reliefs outlined in this chapter.

- A termination payment may affect the former employee's entitlement to social security benefits if he is then unemployed, but the employee will be entitled to unemployment credits for the period covered by the compensation payment so that his NIC record is not affected.
- In light of the changes announced to the treatment of termination payments from 6 April 2018 it may be sensible to use 2017–18 to review long established redundancy policies. Careful consideration and advice should be taken to ensure the correct tax/NI payments are made.

Part IV

Pensions

16

Occupational and state pension schemes

Background

[16.1] For those who wish to contribute to pensions other than under the state pension scheme, there are two main types of scheme — occupational (employer) schemes, and personal pension schemes to which employers may or may not contribute. Occupational pension schemes may either be 'defined benefit' schemes, i.e. final salary schemes, or 'defined contributions' schemes, i.e. money purchase schemes. Most employers will now have a workplace pension scheme following their mandatory introduction, see **16.45**. Contributions to personal pension schemes may be made by non-earners, as well as the employed and self-employed. Personal pension schemes are dealt with in CHAPTER 17.

Some employers have offered inducement payments to employees in defined benefit schemes to obtain their agreement to a reduction in benefits or a transfer to a defined contributions scheme. HMRC consider that such payments are employment income liable to tax and Class 1 NICs.

Those in defined contributions occupational schemes and personal pension schemes receive regular illustrations of what their benefits might be in present-day prices, so that people have a more realistic idea about the value of their pension funds and what options are available to them. The illustration may incorporate state pension information supplied by the Department for Work and Pensions if the pension provider and employee so wish.

State pension

[16.2] Different levels of state pension are paid depending on whether or not the individual reached retirement age before 6 April 2016. The state pension scheme for those who retired before 6 April 2016 provides a basic state pension, £122.30 a week in 2017–18, and an earnings-related 'second pension' or 'additional pension' — known as the State Second Pension (S2P). However, a single-component flat-rate of state pension, payable at a rate of of £159.55 in 2017–18, replaced the two-component system for individuals who reached state pension age on or after 6 April 2016. For guidance see www.gov.uk/new-state-pension.

Pensionable ages have been equalised for men and women, and the pensionable age for a person born after 5 April 1978 will be 68. Currently the other pension ages are as follows:

- a man born before 6 December 1953 attains pensionable age at age 65;
- a woman born before 6 April 1950 attains pensionable age at age 60;
- a woman born between 6 April 1950 and 5 December 1953 attains pensionable age on a date (between age 60 and age 65) set out in Pensions Act 1995, Sch 4;
- a person born between 6 December 1953 and 5 October 1954 attains pensionable age on a date (between ages 65 and 66) set out in Pensions Act 1995, Sch 4;
- a person born between 6 October 1954 and 5 April 1960 attains pensionable age at age 66;
- a person born between 6 April 1960 and 5 March 1961 attains pensionable age on a date (between ages 66 and 67) set out in Pensions Act 1995, Sch 4;
- a person born between 6 March 1961 and 5 April 1977 attains pensionable age at 67;
- a person born between 6 April 1977 and 5 April 1978 attains pensionable age on a date (between ages 67 and 68) set out in Pensions Act 1995, Sch 4; and
- a person born after 5 April 1978 attains pensionable age at age 68.

However, the Government has to make a periodic review of state pension age and in a report issued in July 2017 it proposed to increase the age from 67 to 68 in 2037–39, seven years earlier than is currently legislated as outlined above. This will affect people born between 6 April 1970 and 5 April 1978.

The effect of recent state pension reform is a gradual rise in the state pension age for men and women, increasing the number of years in which they will be required to pay NICs. The Government provides a state pension age calculator based on the current provisions at www.gov.uk/state-pension-age.

Tax treatment of state pensions

[16.3] State retirement and widows' pensions are taxable under the provisions of the Income Tax (Earnings and Pensions) Act 2003 (see **10.1**). The amount chargeable is the pension accruing in the tax year. Wounds and disability pensions, war widows' pensions, lump sums payable under the armed forces early departure scheme and illness or injury benefits under an armed and reserve forces compensation scheme are exempt from tax. Tax on state pensions is collected through PAYE deductions (via a coding adjustment) from earnings or other pensions (see **10.58** onwards) with any balance normally being included in the self-assessment or simple assessment (see **9.2**).

[16.4] Taxable state pensions are earned by the payment of NICs (see **13.11** and **24.1**).

Deferring state pensions

[16.5] Incentives are provided for those who defer taking their state pension. Under the previous state pension rules extra state pension could be earned at 1% for every five weeks deferral (10.4% for each year), or alternatively for a minimum deferral period of 12 months a taxable lump sum could be paid, based on the pension that would have been earned in the period of deferral plus compound interest. From April 2011 extra state pension or a lump sum cannot be built up for the days when pension credit and various other benefits are paid. Under the new rules for the flat-rate state pension payable to those who reach state pension age on or after 6 April 2016 extra state pension may be earned at 1% for every nine weeks deferral (5.78% for each year). The lump sum option is not available. Guidance is provided at www.gov.uk/deferring-s tate-pension. From 6 April 2016 a person can still choose a lump sum or periodical payment in respect of their deceased spouse's or civil partner's de-ferred 'old' state pension.

Extra state pension will be treated like any other income when calculating pension credit, housing benefit and tax credits, but the lump sum payment will not affect entitlement to pension credit or housing benefit. Taxable lump sums will be *treated* as income and taxed at the top rate applicable to the recipient's other sources of income, but will not count as part of their total income, so that entitlement to married couple's allowance (if applicable) and marginal tax rates will not be affected (see CHAPTER 2). From 6 April 2016 Scottish taxpayers will be taxed at the UK tax rates on the lump sum and not the Scottish tax rates.

Tax regime for pension schemes (FA 2004, ss 149–284 and Schs 28–36)

[16.6] The legislation covering the single scheme for all tax-privileged pension savings which commenced on 6 April 2006 is found in Finance Act 2004. Various measures have been introduced in subsequent Finance Acts, Pensions Acts and regulations which amend aspects of the scheme.

Paragraphs **16.7** to **16.43** of this chapter deal with the overall position, and the remainder covers various other pension matters. CHAPTER 17 deals with additional points relating to personal pension schemes.

[16.7] Schemes that were approved schemes before 6 April 2006 auto-matically became registered schemes on that day. Individuals may contribute to as many schemes as they wish. There were significant changes to the access members have to their pension funds in relation to money purchase (defined contributions) schemes from 6 April 2015. These mainly affect lifetime annuities and drawdown arrangements (see **16.23**).

[16.8] It used to be possible to obtain tax relief on pension contributions used to fund life assurance policies. This is not possible for occupational scheme contributions paid on or after 1 August 2007, unless the insurer received the application for the policy before 29 March 2007 and the policy was taken out before 1 August 2007. The relief for employers' contributions is not affected. For personal pension contributions the relief was withdrawn from 6 April 2007, unless the policy was taken out before 1 August 2007 and the insurer received the application before 14 December 2006 (or 13 April 2007 in some circumstances).

Key features of registered schemes (FA 2004, ss 214–238)

[16.9] Registered schemes have two key features:

- A single 'standard lifetime allowance' on the total amount of pension savings that can benefit from tax relief, which is set at £1,000,000 for 2017–18 (see **16.19**). If benefits are withdrawn in excess of the allowance, tax will be charged on the excess as indicated at **16.30**. From 2018 the allowance will rise in line with the consumer prices index.
- An annual allowance for maximum 'pension inputs', i.e. annual contributions paid to money purchase (defined contributions) schemes and/or annual increases in accrued benefits under final salary (defined benefit) schemes (calculated using a special formula). The allowance is £40,000 for 2017–18 and unused allowance can be carried forward three years. However, a tapered reduction in the allowance applies for those with an adjusted net income over £150,000, resulting in a minimum allowance of £10,000. In addition, from 6 April 2015 the allowance is reduced to £10,000 for money purchase inputs in certain circumstances, primarily where the member makes use of flexible access, and this amount cannot be increased by unused amounts from previous years (see **16.15**). September 2017 Finance Bill, which is expected to receive Royal Assent in November 2017, provides that this 'money purchase annual allowance' is reduced to £4,000 from 6 April 2017 (see **16.16**). If pension inputs exceed the annual allowance, the scheme member will pay tax at their marginal tax rate on the excess.

Taxation advantages of registered schemes

[16.10] The advantages are as follows:

(a) The employer's contributions reduce taxable business profits providing they are wholly and exclusively for the purposes of the business (see **16.13**).

(b) The employer's contributions are not treated as a taxable employee benefit, nor do they count as the employee's earnings for NICs, provided they are in respect of the employee only from 6 April 2013.

(c)   Relief for an employee's own contributions is given under the 'net pay scheme', so that the contributions reduce taxable earnings (see **16.14**). They do not, however, reduce pay for NICs.

(d)   A tax-free lump sum can be paid to the employee when benefits are taken (see **16.29**).

(e)   Provision can be made for a lump sum to be paid if an employee dies before taking benefits (see **16.37**).

(f)   The investment income and capital gains of the fund are not taxed.

Scheme investments (FA 2004, ss 174A, 185A–185I, 273ZA and Sch 29A)

[16.11] Pension providers are normally able to invest in all types of investment. Restrictions apply, however, to 'investment-regulated pension schemes', broadly those where one or more members can direct, influence or advise on the investments the scheme makes. The main examples are Self-Invested Personal Pension Schemes (SIPPS — see **17.13**) and Small Self-Administered Schemes (SSAS — see **16.51**).

The restrictions apply to investments in 'prohibited assets', namely residential property and assets such as fine wines, classic cars, art and antiques. The rules apply both to direct investment and also indirect investment where it has been used to get round the new rules (such as a SIPP holding all the shares in a company that owns residential property). The rules do not apply to genuine commercial investment, such as investment in a Real Estate Investment Trust unless the holding is 10% or more (see **32.36** onwards).

If such assets are purchased, the purchase will be subject to the unauthorised payments charge (see **16.31**), so that the member will be charged to tax at up to 55% on the value of the prohibited asset and the scheme administrator will be liable to the scheme sanction charge of 15%. If the value of the prohibited asset exceeds 25% of the value of the pension scheme's assets, the scheme may be deregistered, which would lead to a 40% tax charge on the value of the scheme's assets.

Anti-avoidance provisions

[16.12] As indicated in **16.11**, the provisions prevent tax advantages for 'investment-regulated pension schemes' of investing in residential property and assets such as fine wines, classic cars, art and antiques.

They also prevent pension funds being artificially boosted by recycling tax-free lump sums (see **16.32**).

There is anti-avoidance legislation relating to employment income provided by third parties (see **10.5**). In some circumstances pension income, purchases of annuities out of pension scheme rights after 6 April 2011, lump sums paid from certain pension schemes out of rights accruing after 6 April 2011, and transfers between certain foreign pension schemes could be taxed under these anti-avoidance provisions, if they are not taxed under other provisions.

Employer contributions (FA 2004, ss 196–201)

[16.13] In order to be deductible from profits, employers' contributions to registered schemes must be wholly and exclusively for the purposes of the trade. Where that condition is satisfied, the contributions are then normally allowed in the accounting period in which they are paid. Relief may be restricted in some circumstances where the registered scheme is linked to an unregistered 'employer-financed retirement benefits scheme' (see **16.50**).

If there is an increase of over 210% in the contributions of an accounting period compared with the previous period, and the higher amount is at least £500,000 more than 110% of the lower amount, the contributions are spread over two to four years depending on the amount of the contribution. Spreading applies to contributions made indirectly in the same way as it applies to contributions made directly by the employer.

The amount of tax relief given to employers using asset-backed pension contributions arrangements must reflect accurately the total amount of payments the employer makes to the pension scheme. There are no restrictions on any straightforward monetary pension contribution made by an employer to a registered pension scheme or on an employer's transfer of an asset to the pension scheme which is unconditional or outright so that the pension scheme has complete ownership of the asset on an irrevocable basis.

Members' contributions (FA 2004, ss 188–195A)

[16.14] There is no limit on the contributions that may be made by or on behalf of an individual, but tax relief will only be given to an individual aged under 75 who—

(a)   has earnings subject to UK tax; or
(b)   is resident in the UK at some time during the year; or
(c)   is resident in the UK at some time during the five tax years immediately preceding the tax year and at some time in the tax year when they became a member of the registered pension scheme; or
(d)   has (or his or her spouse or civil partner has) UK-taxable earnings from overseas Crown employment in the tax year.

Tax relief is available on contributions up to the higher of 100% of relevant earnings and £3,600 gross, and is further restricted by the annual allowance and lifetime allowance (see **16.9**). For employees, relevant earnings include employment income chargeable to tax, including benefits and also amounts taxable as earnings under the rules relating to lump sum termination payments (see CHAPTER **15**) and the acquisition and disposal of shares and share options (see CHAPTER **11**). Subject to transitional provisions, relief is not available for life assurance contributions (see **16.8**). Contributions may be made not only by scheme members and employers but also by anyone else on their behalf — spouse, civil partner, parents, grandparents etc. The scheme member will get tax relief on such contributions within the permitted limits. Donors would need to consider the inheritance tax implications (see CHAPTER **5**). See **16.13** in relation to employer contributions. The amount of relief on the contributions depends on the individual's marginal tax rate(s), subject to the annual allowance charge (see **16.15**). For example, someone who has sufficient earned income (after allowances) taxable at 40% will save tax on the contribution at 40%. If relevant earnings are less than £3,600, tax relief on contributions of more than 100% of relevant earnings may only be obtained if the contribution is made using the tax relief at source method, where operated by the pension scheme. See **2.41** for possible additional savings where tax credits are received.

Relief is given in various ways depending on the type of scheme. The relief at source method applies where an individual pays contributions direct to a pension scheme which operates relief at source. The contributions to the pension scheme can be treated as amounts paid after deduction of basic rate income tax. The pension scheme can then recover the tax relief at the basic rate from HMRC and add it to the pension fund. If the individual is a higher or additional rate taxpayer he will also need to make a claim for any further tax relief. If the individual pays contributions to his employer's occupational pension scheme, tax relief can be automatically given through the PAYE system. The employer deducts the contribution from gross pay before income tax is deducted on the balance and passes the contributions to the scheme administrator or other designated body. This is called the net pay arrangement and enables individuals to receive tax relief at their marginal rate of income tax. Where, unusually, the individual makes gross contributions to a registered pension scheme he can make a claim to HMRC to obtain the tax relief on the contribution. The amount of the contribution is then relieved by being deducted from total income for the tax year in which the payment is made. See also **17.9**.

Annual allowance

[16.15] The annual allowance was significantly reduced from 2011–12 onwards as a means of restricting tax relief on annual pensions inputs made by or in respect of an individual (see **16.9**), and is £40,000 in 2017–18.

From 6 April 2016 a tapered reduction in the allowance applies for those with an 'adjusted income' over £150,000. Adjusted income includes an add-back of their own and their employer's pension contributions. The allowance is reduced by £1 for every £2 that the adjusted income exceeds £150,000, to a minimum allowance of £10,000, which will apply where adjusted income is £210,000 or over. If the individual's net income (i.e. excluding pension contributions) is no more than £110,000 they will not normally be subject to the tapered annual allowance although anti-avoidance rules will apply where salary sacrifice arrangements are set up on or after 9 July 2015. Where the money purchase annual allowance applies (see **16.16**), the alternative annual allowance will be so reduced, again subject to a minimum allowance of £10,000. The carry forward of unused annual allowance (see **16.18**) will continue to be available, but the amount will be based on the unused tapered annual allowance. For HMRC guidance see www.gov.uk/guidance/pension-sc hemes-work-out-your-tapered-annual-allowance.

[16.16] Where members make use of flexible access from 6 April 2015 (see **16.26**) the annual allowance is effectively divided between money purchase inputs and defined benefit inputs, and if money purchase inputs exceed

£10,000 then that is the 'money purchase annual allowance' and the annual allowance that will apply to any defined benefit inputs will be reduced by £10,000, reducing it to £30,000 (the 'alternative annual allowance'). However, September 2017 Finance Bill, which is expected to receive Royal Assent in November 2017, provides that the money purchase annual allowance is reduced to £4,000 from 6 April 2017, meaning that the alternative annual allowance for 2017–18 will be £36,000. The money purchase annual allowance rules apply in the tax year in which the member first flexibly accesses pension rights and for subsequent years. Broadly, a member first flexibly accesses pension rights immediately before the first qualifying payment, where a flexi-access drawdown fund is first designated after 6 April 2015 (see **16.26**), but it can also occur at other times such as on the first qualifying payment where either the capped drawdown fund limits are breached or the member elects for a capped drawdown fund to become a flexi-access drawdown fund (see **16.26**), or immediately before the first payment of an uncrystallised funds pension lump sum (see **16.29**).

[16.17] Where pension inputs exceed the annual allowance, the money purchase annual allowance or the alternative annual allowance, as the case may be, an annual allowance charge arises and the scheme member should notify HMRC, normally in the tax return for the year, and he pays tax at his marginal rate on the excess. The annual allowance charge can be paid by the individual member's pension scheme out of their pension benefits if it exceeds £2,000 and provided he gives notice to the scheme administrator. In such cases a consequential adjustment is made to the individual's entitlement to benefits. The notice must be given by 31 July of the year following the end of the tax year in which the annual allowance charge arises. For example, where an individual exceeds the annual allowance in the tax year 2017–18, the notice must be given by 31 July 2019. The notice is irrevocable but can be amended.

[16.18] From 2011–12 unused annual allowance can be carried forward three years and, for these purposes, the annual allowance for 2008–09 to 2010–11 is assumed to be £50,000. Unused annual allowance is only available for carry forward where it arises during a tax year in which the individual is a member of a registered pension scheme but applies to a tax year even if the pension input amount for that year is nil. The earlier year's unused allowance is to be set off against the current year before that of the later year. The money purchase annual allowance cannot be increased by amounts brought forward, but if this applies the remaining alternative annual allowance can be increased by brought forward amounts, and any unused amount of that allowance can itself be carried forward. HMRC guidance on the allowance and the valuation of pension inputs can be found at www.gov.uk/tax-on-your-private-pension/annual-allowance.

Lifetime allowance

[16.19] Tax relief on an individual's pension savings is restricted by the lifetime allowance which is £1,000,000 for 2017–18. If benefits are withdrawn in excess of the allowance, tax will be charged on the excess as indicated at **16.30**. There are transitional provisions (see **16.34**) which provide protection from the lifetime allowance charge for those who may already have built up pension savings on the expectation that the lifetime allowance would remain at the previous higher levels that applied before 6 April 2012, 6 April 2014, and 6 April 2016. An individual protection regime provides additional protection for those affected by the reduction in the lifetime allowance from 6 April 2014 and 6 April 2016.

Retirement age and ill health

[16.20] The rules of a pension scheme determine the minimum and maximum age at which a member can take their pension benefits from the scheme. Generally, scheme rules must not allow members to be paid any pension benefits from any registered pension scheme before they reach the normal minimum pension age which is currently 55. It is proposed to be increased to 57 in 2028 and then remain ten years below state pension age thereafter, although certain public sector pension schemes do not link their normal pension age to state pension age from 2015. Early retirement may be allowed from an earlier age for those in certain occupations, such as athletes. See **16.33** for transitional provisions.

Following the Equality Act 2010, with effect from 6 April 2011 employers can no longer give employees notice to retire at age 65 or over without having to objectively justify it.

Providing the scheme rules so provide, ill-health retirement will be permitted at any age. For someone whose life expectancy is less than one year, full commutation will be possible and, where the individual is below age 75, the commuted amount below the lifetime allowance (£1,000,000 for 2017–18) will be tax-free. From 6 April 2011 such payments can also be made to individuals aged 75 or over, and from 16 September 2016 such a lump sum will be taxed as pension income at the recipient's marginal tax rate (previously subject to a scheme administrator's charge of 45%).

Drawing benefits (ITEPA 2003, ss 579CA, 636A–636C; FA 2004, ss 160–169, 218–220, Sch 28)

[16.21] Occupational schemes may offer flexible retirement, enabling employees to draw benefits while continuing to work for their employer. When benefits are drawn no payment of pension other than a scheme pension may be paid from a final salary (defined benefits) scheme. For a money purchase (defined contributions) scheme the pension payments can be a scheme pension, a lifetime annuity (see **16.28**) or a drawdown pension (see **16.23**). A person who immediately before 6 April 2011 was entitled to alternatively secured pension is treated from this date as entitled to drawdown pension. A scheme pension must be payable at least annually until the member's death or the later of the member's death and a term of ten years. If this condition is not met any payment will be an unauthorised payment (see **16.31**). No payment of pension may be paid before the member reaches the normal minimum pension age unless retirement is permitted through ill health (see **16.20**). Proposals to allow people who are already receiving income from an annuity to be able to sell that income to a third party through a secondary market have been abandoned.

See **16.29** regarding the payment of tax-free lump sums.

[16.22] From 6 April 2017, individuals may use up to £500 from their pension funds to pay for pensions advice, with no charge to tax on withdrawal. A maximum of three payments of up to £500 each are permitted, with no more than one payment in any one tax year.

[16.23] From 6 April 2015 members in money purchase defined contributions schemes have more flexible access to their pensions savings. They are able to leave their pension funds invested in a drawdown arrangement and to make withdrawals throughout their retirement. Drawdown pension can be in the form of a short-term annuity or income withdrawal. A short-term annuity, which is payable by an insurance company, provides a guaranteed income stream during the term of the annuity, which must not exceed five years. The amount payable can however decrease from year to year. Before 6 April 2015 there were two types of drawdown pension — capped (see **16.24**) and flexible (see **16.25**), and from 6 April 2015 there is also flexi-access drawdown (see **16.26**). No new capped drawdown funds or flexible drawdown funds may be set up from 6 April 2015 onwards.

[16.24] Capped drawdown that began on or before 5 April 2015 may continue, providing there have been no events since that date resulting in its conversion to flexi-access drawdown. For capped drawdown the maximum withdrawal of income that an individual may make from most drawdown funds is capped at 150% of the equivalent annuity that could have been bought with the fund value. If the member stays within the cap an existing arrangement can continue. If the cap is breached the income may still be withdrawn but the fund becomes a flexi-access drawdown fund (see below). Otherwise the member can covert it into a flexi-access drawdown at any time after 5 April 2015 by notification to the scheme administrator. Where the cap applies the maximum amount is determined at least every three years until the end of the year in which the member reaches the age of 75, after which reviews to determine the maximum capped withdrawal are carried out annually.

[16.25] Individuals who can demonstrate that they have secure pension income for life of at least £12,000 per year have unrestricted access to receive their drawdown fund as pension income — this is known as flexible drawdown and it automatically became a flexi-access drawdown fund from 6 April 2015. Any new pension savings by an individual after he has demonstrated that his secure lifetime pension income is at least £12,000 a year will be liable to the annual allowance charge (see **16.15**) on all pension input amounts.

[16.26] From 6 April 2015, unless there are pre-existing drawdown funds (see above), sums designated for drawdown go into a flexi-access drawdown fund. When new sums are designated the member may choose to take a pension commencement lump sum of an amount up to a limit of one third of the designated sums (i.e. 25% of the total assets used, see **16.29**). For example, given a pension pot of £40,000, £30,000 may be designated for flexi-access drawdown and the remaining £10,000 taken as a pension commencement lump sum, which is tax-free. Income may be taken from the flexi-access drawdown fund either through a short-term annuity (see **16.23**) or as income withdrawal of whatever amount the member chooses, whether that be a regular amount or a single lump sum or series of lump sums, all of which will be taxed in full as pension income. When money is taken from the flexi-access drawdown fund the money purchase annual allowance rules apply (see **16.15**). As the pension income itself is taxed at the member's marginal rate for the year it will be beneficial to spread withdrawals over a number of years to avoid higher tax rates. Pension providers are able to offer flexi-access drawdown even if their scheme rules would preclude it, but they are under no legal obligation to do so, and some providers have simply been giving members three options: to cash in the entire pension and thus face a tax charge at the marginal rate, swap the whole fund for a lifetime annuity income, or transfer to a rival company.

[16.27] All income withdrawals from drawdown funds are subject to tax as pension income at the member's marginal rate, but see **16.29** regarding tax-free lump sums. An individual making a withdrawal from a drawdown pension fund during a period when they are temporarily non-resident will usually be liable for UK income tax on that withdrawal for the tax year in which they become UK resident again (see **41.31** and **41.49**).

[16.28] A lifetime annuity is an alternative to a scheme pension or drawdown pension from money purchase schemes and is payable by an insurance company until the member's death or until the later of the member's death and a term certain, which for annuities beginning before 6 April 2015 must be not more than ten years. Any income paid from a lifetime annuity contract is taxable as pension income. Where the annuity may be reduced in other than prescribed circumstances, then from the date of the first payment of the annuity the money purchase annual allowance rules (see **16.15**) apply to any further pension savings.

[16.29] All schemes are able to offer a tax-free pension commencement lump sum (PCLS, see **16.26**) of up to 25% of the fund, subject to an overriding maximum of 25% of the lifetime allowance.

Normally a PCLS paid from pension savings must be taken in connection with a pension, no more than six months before the pension and must be paid from the same scheme. Where these conditions are not met the intended tax-free lump sum is an unauthorised payment and subject to various tax charges (see **16.31**).

From 6 April 2015 an uncrystallised funds pension lump sum (UFPLS) may be paid before a pension is crystallised (i.e. before it is earmarked for benefits) if certain condition are met. Generally 25% of the UFPLS is tax-free, and the remainder is treated as pension income. However, if the member is aged 75 or over and the UFPLS is more than the available lifetime allowance the tax-free amount is 25% of the available lifetime allowance.

Individuals aged 55 or over (60 before 6 April 2015) with total pension savings not exceeding £30,000 are able to take the whole amount as a lump sum if their pension provider agrees (trivial commutation lump sum). If their pension savings are in more than one pension plan, all providers must agree and all lump sums must be taken within 12 months. 25% of the lump sum is tax-free and the remainder taxed as pension income. From 16 September 2016 a trivial commutation lump sum can be paid out of both a defined benefit scheme and a money purchase scheme pension that is in payment. See **17.11** regarding payment of a lump sum where pension funds are £10,000 or less (small pots lump sum), which can apply equally to occupational pensions, though only one payment is permitted.

[16.30] The lifetime allowance must be considered at any time when there is a benefit crystallisation event. For a full list of the events see HMRC Pension Tax Manual at PTM088000. When a member becomes entitled to draw benefits from a registered pension scheme, they use up a proportion or percentage of their lifetime allowance. If the lifetime allowance changes between crystallisation events, the previous amount crystallised is adjusted to preserve the percentage of lifetime allowance used up. When the whole of the lifetime allowance has been used by one or more benefit crystallisation events, the lifetime allowance charge applies and the excess is taxed at 25% to the extent that it is used to buy a pension (the pension itself then being taxed at the member's marginal rate — see **16.26**) and at 55% where it is taken as a lump sum.

See **16.33** regarding primary and fixed protection of the lifetime allowance.

Unauthorised payments (FA 2004, ss 208–213, 239–242)

[16.31] If a registered scheme makes unauthorised payments, there is a charge of up to 55% on the scheme member, and a scheme sanction charge of 40% (usually reduced to 15%) on the scheme administrator. There is also a de-registration charge of 40% on the scheme administrator if a scheme's registration is withdrawn.

Recycling lump sums (FA 2004, Sch 29)

[16.32] There are anti-avoidance provisions to prevent pension funds being boosted by pre-planned recycling of lump sums. This applies where an individual withdraws a tax-free cash lump sum from a registered scheme and reinvests it immediately in another registered scheme, then withdraws a further tax-free cash lump sum from the second scheme. The provisions do not apply where no more than 30% of the lump sum is recycled, nor do they apply to the recycling of total lump sums received within 12 months that do not exceed 1% of the lifetime allowance (£10,000 for 2017–18). Where the provisions do apply, the lump sum(s) will be treated as an unauthorised pension payment, liable to tax at up to 55%, and the administrator of the pension scheme will be subject to a scheme sanction charge of between 15% and 40%, depending on the amount of the payment (see **16.31**).

The recycling provisions do not affect tax relief for the pension contributions, which may be claimed under the normal rules (see **16.14**).

Transitional provisions in FA 2006 — protection of lifetime allowance and retirement age

[16.33] Transitional provisions protect pre-6 April 2006 pension rights and rights to lump sums. In respect of the lifetime allowance, there are two main options:

- Primary protection applicable to the excess value over £1,500,000. The pension scheme member had to notify HMRC that there was such an excess by 5 April 2009, and each year's lifetime allowance will then be enhanced to the extent of that excess value. For example someone with funds totalling £1,800,000 at 6 April 2006 has an excess of £300,000, i.e. 20%, and their lifetime allowance for each year would be 120% of the standard amount. This protection does not extend to funds which at 6 April 2006 were surplus under the old rules. Thus if the funds of £1,800,000 were themselves £150,000 over the previously calculated permitted limit, the primary protection would only apply to £1,650,000, with the remaining £150,000 being taxed under **16.30** if withdrawn and the lifetime allowance becoming 110% of the standard amount.

- Enhanced protection available to those who ceased membership of approved schemes before 6 April 2006 and do not resume membership of any registered scheme. All benefits becoming payable after 5 April 2006 will normally be exempt from the lifetime allowance charge, providing the member notified HMRC by 5 April 2009 that enhanced protection was being claimed and thereafter all the relevant conditions are satisfied.

Separate transitional provisions apply for a member of an occupational scheme who is entitled under the pre-6 April 2006 rules to a tax-free lump sum but has not opted for primary or enhanced protection. If the member's lump sum entitlement gave an amount in excess of 25% of the lifetime allowance at 6 April 2006 (£375,000), for example because it was based on average earnings, this entitlement can be preserved, and increased in line with the lifetime limit increases stated in **16.9**. This provision only applies where all pensions payable under the scheme from 6 April 2006 become payable on the same date.

Employees who had the right to draw pensions earlier than the retirement age of 55 which applies from 6 April 2010 may have that right protected, and there is special protection for employees who are members of pre-6 April 2006 schemes with lower normal retirement ages, such as athletes. The available lifetime allowance for these protected groups will, however, be reduced.

Note that fixed and enhanced protection will be lost if the employer automatically enrols an employee into a workplace pension (see **16.45**) except for certain specific reasons (see HMRC Pension Tax Manual at PTM093400). It is provided from 6 April 2017 that employers have a discretion, rather than a duty, to enrol employees with such protection where they would be financially disadvantaged as a result.

Transitional provisions in FA 2011, FA 2013, FA 2014, and FA 2016 for reduction in lifetime allowance

[16.34] Transitional provisions, known as Fixed Protection 2012 (FP12), protect against the lifetime allowance charge from 6 April 2012 (when the lifetime allowance was reduced) for those who do not have either primary or enhanced protection (see **16.33**). An individual may give notice to HMRC that he wishes to rely on provisions which broadly treat the lifetime allowance as the greater of £1,800,000 (the lifetime allowance in 2011–12) and the standard lifetime allowance applying for the year. The provisions cease to apply however, if there is benefit accrual; an impermissible transfer; a transfer of sums or assets that is not a permitted transfer; or a new arrangement is made other than in permitted circumstances.

Similar provisions, known as Fixed Protection 2014, protect against the lifetime allowance charge from 6 April 2014 when a further reduction in the allowance applied. It is not available if primary protection, enhanced protection or FP12 apply.

In addition, Individual Protection 2014 (IP14) protects from the lifetime allowance charge from 6 April 2014. IP14 will protect any UK tax-relieved pension savings that an individual has built up at 5 April 2014 up to an overall limit of £1,500,000. It has effect from 2014–15 onwards and is in addition to Fixed Protection 2014 (FP14). Individuals are able to apply for IP14 from 6 April 2014 and applications must have been received by HMRC by 5 April 2017. It will not apply at any time when enhanced protection, FP12 or FP14 applies so will apply where fixed protection is lost.

Fixed Protection 2016 and Individual Protection 2016 protect against the lifetime allowance charge from 6 April 2016 when a further reduction in the allowance applies.

Sharing pension rights on divorce or dissolution of civil partnership

[16.35] There are provisions to enable a share in pension rights to be transferred on divorce or dissolution of civil partnership. The provisions cover all pension rights, i.e. under occupational and personal schemes (including stakeholder pensions), S2P and the flat-rate state pension applying to new pensioners from 6 April 2016. It is not compulsory for a couple to share pensions, but all schemes (whenever they were approved/registered) are regarded as including pension sharing provisions. Although the legislation overrides the provisions of existing schemes in this respect, such schemes are expected to change their rules to incorporate pension sharing as and when they make other (non-trivial) amendments. Where the pension is shared, the spouse or civil partner in a pension scheme will get reduced pension rights (a 'pension debit') and rights will be allocated to the other spouse (a 'pension credit'). The transferred pension credit rights may be held in the same scheme or transferred to another scheme. The benefits available to the ex-spouse/partner will broadly follow those available to the scheme member. The scheme member's pension debit will be taken into account in determining his entitlement under the scheme, deducted from his benefits on retirement, or on leaving pensionable service if earlier. The debit will count in the calculation of maximum benefits.

The pension flexibility rules applying from 6 April 2015 (see **16.21**) which allow the entire defined contributions pension fund to be withdrawn, could create a loophole that can override certain pension sharing agreements, known as 'earmarking' or 'attachment' orders, and such orders should therefore be reviewed to ensure that the intentions are not affected by the pension flexibility.

Provision for dependants (FA 2004, ss 167, 168 and Schs 28, 29; ITEPA 2003, ss 646B–646F; IHTA 1984, s 12; SI 2009/1989)

[16.36] Provision for dependants may be made for death both before and after taking benefits. A dependant is defined as:

(a)   a spouse or civil partner;

(b)   a former spouse or civil partner if the scheme rules so provide;

(c)   a child who is under 23;

(d)   a child over 23 who, in the scheme administrator's opinion, is dependent because of physical or mental impairment;

(e)   for pensions arising before 1 July 2008 a child over 23 who is financially dependent on the scheme member before his death, or where the financial relationship with the member at his date of death was one of mutual dependence; and

(f)   someone else who, in the scheme administrator's opinion, is dependent on the member.

A dependant's pension from a money purchase defined contributions scheme can be a scheme pension, an annuity or a drawdown pension. From a defined benefits scheme it may only be a scheme pension. This is the same as for lifetime benefits (see **16.23**).

Dependants' pensions

[16.37] A dependants' scheme pension does not have to be paid for the life of the dependant, does not have to be paid annually, and may be reduced at any time in accordance with the rules of the scheme or the terms of the annuity contract. Where a member dies after reaching age 75, the total of the dependants' scheme pension is limited to the amount of the member's pension at the date of their death. If the member died before reaching age 75 there is no restriction. The income from a dependants' scheme pension is taxed as pension income.

[16.38] An annuity payable to a dependant must be payable by an insurance company and be purchased together with the member's annuity, or after the member's death. Where the dependant is not the child of the member it must be payable until the dependant's death, or until the earlier of death or marriage/civil partnership. Where the dependant is the member's child it must be payable until the earlier of ceasing to be a dependant or dying, or until the earliest of ceasing to be a dependant, marriage/civil partnership or dying. From 6 April 2015 there is an exemption from income tax for a dependants' annuity provided various conditions are met, primarily that is paid in respect of a member of a registered pension scheme who died on or after 3 December 2014 before reaching age 75, it is purchased using drawdown funds or unused uncrystallised funds, or together with a lifetime annuity payable to the member, and broadly no payment of the annuity is made before 6 April 2015. Where the annuity is purchased using unused uncrystallised funds, entitlement must begin before the end of two years of the scheme administrator first knowing of the death, or if earlier, the day the scheme administrator could first reasonably have been expected to have known of it. This exemption also applies to a short-term annuity purchased from the dependant's drawdown or flexi-access drawdown fund.

[16.39] The rules for dependants' drawdown pensions are the same as those for lifetime benefits (see **16.23**). However, from 6 April 2015 income tax does not apply to dependants' income withdrawal in certain circumstances, primarily that the deceased member had not reached age 75, and the payment is from a dependants' flexi-access drawdown fund which does not originate from a pre–6 April 2015 dependants' drawdown pension fund which has been used to provide income withdrawal or a short-term annuity, and any designation of previously uncrystallised funds for dependants' flexi-access drawdown takes place within two years of the scheme administrator first knowing of the death, or if earlier, the day the scheme administrator could first reasonably have been expected to have known of it.

Dependants are able to continue to receive drawdown pension or flexi-access drawdown pension as authorised payments after age 23 if they reach that age on or after 16 September 2016.

[16.40] Provision may be made for an employee's pension or annuity to continue for ten years after benefits commence despite earlier death. Separate pensions for dependants can also be provided, subject to the normal limits. If the member dies before the guaranteed amount of pension has been paid, the balance can be paid as a lump sum. When a member of either a money purchase defined contributions scheme or a salary-related defined benefits scheme dies, before reaching age 75, already in receipt of a drawdown or scheme pension, from 6 April 2015 the lump sum death benefit is tax-free. If the member died age 75 or over the lump sum was charged to tax at 45% from 6 April 2015 to 5 April 2016, payable by the scheme administrator, although the tax charge is at the recipient's marginal rate of tax from 6 April 2016 provided they are not a non-qualifying person. A non-qualifying person is a person who is not an individual or is an individual in a representative capacity, other than a bare trustee. From 6 April 2015, a lifetime annuity paid after the death of a member is exempt from tax provided a member of a registered pension scheme was entitled to the annuity prior to death on or after 3 December 2014 before reaching age 75, and any payment of the annuity prior to 6 April 2015 was to the member.

When a member of a money purchase defined contributions scheme dies any uncrystallised funds can be paid to a dependant as a drawdown pension, an annuity or a scheme pension. Alternatively a lump sum death benefit can be paid. If the member was under 75 when he died this lump sum will be tax-free unless the lifetime allowance charge is payable, in which case the charge is at 55% (see **16.30**). If the member was aged 75 or over when he died there will be a tax charge at the recipient's marginal rate from 6 April 2016 in most cases (45% before 6 April 2016, see above). In addition from 6 April 2015 the charge can arise if the member dies before age 75 and the payment is not made within two years of the date the scheme administrator first knew of the death, or if earlier, the day the scheme administrator could first reasonably have been expected to have known of it. From 6 April 2015 the charge also applies in similar circumstances to a lump sum death benefit payable from a dependants' flexi-access drawdown fund.

When a member of a salary-related defined benefit scheme dies only a dependant's scheme pension or a lump sum can be paid. Where the lump sum is paid and the member had not reached 75 years of age the sum will be tax-free if within the available lifetime allowance, but from 6 April 2015 it must also be paid within two years of the date the scheme administrator first knew of the death, or if earlier, the day the scheme administrator could first reasonably have been expected to have known of it. Otherwise, or if the member had reached 75 years of age, the special lump sum death benefits charge will be payable by the scheme administrator at the recipient's marginal rate from 6 April 2016 in most cases (45% before 6 April 2016, see above).

Inheritance tax considerations

[16.41] As far as inheritance tax is concerned, there is no charge on the uncrystallised part of the fund. With effect from 6 April 2011, inheritance tax will not typically apply to drawdown pension funds remaining under a registered pension scheme, including when the individual dies after reaching the age of 75. For the avoidance of doubt following the introduction of more pension flexibility from 6 April 2015 (see **16.21**) legislation in Finance Act 2016, backdated to deaths on or after 6 April 2011, ensures that a charge to inheritance tax will not arise when a pension scheme member designates funds for drawdown but does not draw all of the funds before death.

Nominees' and successors' pensions (FA 2004, Sch 28; ITEPA 2003, ss 646B–646F)

[16.42] From 6 April 2015 death benefits can also be paid to either a nominee or a successor. In addition nominees and successors can receive payments from an annuity on the death of a member. A nominee of a member is an individual who is not a dependant (see **16.36**) that is nominated by the member or by the scheme administrator. A nominees' pension may consist of either drawdown pension (short-term annuity or income drawdown) or an annuity. Income tax does not apply to nominees' income withdrawal in certain circumstances, primarily that the deceased member had not reached age 75, the payment is from a nominees' flexi-access drawdown fund, and any designation of previously uncrystallised funds for nominees' flexi-access drawdown takes place within two years of the scheme administrator first knowing of the death, or if earlier, the day the scheme administrator could first reasonably have been expected to have known of it. However, any uncrystallised funds are measured against the deceased member's lifetime allowance (see **16.30**).

A nominees' annuity must be bought together with a lifetime annuity for a member where the member's entitlement arises on or after 6 April 2015, or it must be bought after the member's death occurring on or after 3 December 2014 with the nominee becoming entitled to the annuity on or after 6 April 2015. It must also be payable by an insurance company until the nominee's death or until the earliest of the nominee's marrying, entering into a civil partnership or dying. From 6 April 2015 it is exempt from tax in the same circumstances as a dependants' annuity (see **16.37**). This exemption also applies to a short-term annuity purchased from the nominee's flexi-access drawdown fund.

From 6 April 2015 the provisions in **16.40** relating to the payment of lump sums apply equally to nominees' flexi-access drawdown fund.

[16.43] A successor of a member is an individual that is nominated as such by a dependant, nominee or successor of the member or by the scheme administrator. The provisions for payment of a successors' pension are the same as those for a nominees' pension (see **16.42**). Income tax does not apply to successors' income withdrawal provided the deceased dependant, nominee or successor had not reached age 75, and the payment is from a successors' flexi-access drawdown fund. A successors' short-term annuity is exempt from tax if it is paid in respect of a deceased beneficiary (i.e. dependant, nominee or successor) of a deceased member of a registered pension scheme where the beneficiary died on or after 3 December 2014 before reaching age 75, and is purchased using the successor's flexi-access drawdown fund.

A successors' annuity must meet various criteria. The entitlement must arise after 5 April 2015, it must be payable by an insurance company until the successor's death or until the earliest of the successor's marrying, entering into a civil partnership or dying, it must be purchased after the death of a beneficiary (dependant, nominee or successor) occurring on or after 3 December 2014 using undrawn funds (i.e. dependant's drawdown or flexi-access drawdown fund, nominee's or successor's flexi-access drawdown fund) or sums or assets deriving therefrom. The annuity is exempt from tax when purchased from unused funds provided it is paid in respect of a member of a registered pension scheme, on the subsequent death of a beneficiary (dependant, nominee or successor) who died on or after 3 December 2014 before reaching age 75, and no payment of the annuity is made before 6 April 2015. The annuity is exempt from tax when purchased from drawdown funds if it is paid in respect of a deceased beneficiary (i.e. dependant, nominee or successor) of a deceased member of a registered pension scheme where the beneficiary died on or after 3 December 2014 before reaching age 75, and is purchased using the successor's flexi-access drawdown fund.

From 6 April 2015 the provisions in **16.40** relating to the payment of lump sums apply equally to successors' flexi-access drawdown fund.

Membership of employers' schemes

[16.44] Employees cannot be compelled to be members of their employers' schemes, and may instead (or as well) take out personal pension plans (see CHAPTER 17) or rely on the state pension scheme. See **16.45** regarding workplace pensions which all employers are now obliged to provide. Subject to various conditions, pension rights from an existing occupational scheme may be transferred to a personal pension plan and it is normally possible to transfer back from a personal pension plan to an employer's scheme if the scheme agrees or to a free-standing additional voluntary contribution scheme (FSAVCS, as to which see **16.46**). If an employer employs five or more people it may need to offer access to a registered stakeholder pension scheme (see **17.2**).

Workplace pensions

[16.45] By February 2018 all employers must provide a workplace pension scheme. It has been phased in from October 2012 depending on the size of the employer, so the smallest employers, including those who employ domestic staff such as nannies, are now being required to set up schemes. Automatic enrolment into the scheme applies to eligible jobholders, who are broadly workers between age 22 and state pension age who work in the UK and earn more than the minimum earnings threshold, which is set at £10,000 for 2017–18. Most workers who have not been automatically enrolled can choose to opt in to the scheme. If a worker asks their employer to enrol them, the employer must do so if the worker is based in the UK, is at least 16 and under 75 and is not already earning benefits in another pension scheme. Mandatory employers' contributions and tax relief will be added to employees' contributions to the schemes.

Where the employer chooses to use a money purchase (defined contributions) arrangement, the minimum contributions have been phased in to help employers and employees adjust to the additional costs gradually. The minimum contribution in the initial 'staging period' up to 5 April 2018 is 2% with a minimum of 1% coming from the employer. This will rise to 5% and 2% respectively in the year from 6 April 2018 to 5 April 2019, and to 8% and 3% respectively thereafter. The contributions are payable on employee earnings between the NICs lower and upper earnings limits, set at £5,876 and £45,000 for 2017–18.

This phasing-in of minimum contributions is not possible for defined benefit and hybrid schemes. Therefore, employers providing these types of scheme were able to delay their date for enrolling some of their employees if certain conditions were met. However, this transitional period ended on 30 September 2017.

An employee can opt out of the scheme, and, provided this is done within one month, any contributions they have made will be refunded. Employees who have opted out may rejoin the scheme and the employer must accept them back once within every 12 months, or earlier if the employer so wishes. Automatic re-enrolment by the employer will also apply, usually every three years, at which point the employee can reconsider their options.

Employers should avoid enrolling employees who have certain protections against the lifetime allowance charge (see **16.33**) as the protections will be lost if a pension contribution is made. Employers can exempt such employees from joining the scheme and this avoids the same problem arising on automatic re-enrolment in three years.

There are penalties for persistent and deliberate non-compliance, see www.th epensionsregulator.gov.uk/en/employers/what-happens-if-i-dont-comply.

See www.gov.uk/government/topics/pensions-and-ageing-society and www.the pensionsregulator.gov.uk/en/employers for more information.

Additional voluntary contributions (AVCs)

[16.46] The benefits available to an employee depend on the funds available in the employer's scheme. An employee wishing to increase his potential pension may pay additional voluntary contributions (AVCs) to the employer's scheme, or to a scheme of his choice to which only he makes contributions (free-standing AVCs). Free-standing AVCs are paid net of basic rate tax and HMRC pays the tax to the pension scheme. Relief at higher rates of tax, where appropriate, is claimed in the employee's tax return, but see **16.14** for details of restrictions on relief.

Changing employment (FA 2004, s 205)

[16.47] When an employee changes employment, then providing he has been in the pension scheme for at least two years, he may either have a preserved pension which will become payable on retirement, or a transfer payment to a new scheme (if the scheme will accept it), or to an insurance company, or to a personal pension plan. Where there is a preserved pension under a final salary defined benefits scheme, for pensionable service from 6 April 2005, it must normally be increased each year in line with the lower of the consumer prices index and 2.5%, unless the scheme rules provide for a greater amount or refer to the retail prices index.

Where a member leaves service before completing two years' qualifying service (or 30 days if it is a money purchase defined contributions scheme) and does not qualify for a statutory short service benefit the scheme is not obliged to provide the member with a benefit. In these circumstances legislation allows a refund of the member's contributions, known as a short service refund lump sum.

Tax is deducted from short service refunds at 20% on payments up to £20,000 and 50% on any excess over that amount. The refund is not, however, treated as income for tax purposes. Where employees leave after three months but within the stipulated period, they must be offered a cash transfer sum (which will include the value of employers' contributions as well as their own) to take to another occupational or personal pension scheme, or to use to buy an annuity, as an alternative to a refund of contributions.

Pension scheme surpluses (FA 2004, ss 177, 207)

[16.48] Where on an actuarial valuation, a scheme has a surplus, an 'authorised surplus payment' may be made by the scheme administrator to the sponsoring company. The administrator must deduct tax at 35% from the payment and account for it to HMRC.

Misuse of contributions by employer and scheme insolvency

[16.49] The risk for an employee of his contributions being misused is significantly reduced by a compensation scheme. Where an occupational pension scheme's funds have been misappropriated and the employer is insolvent, compensation may be payable from the Pension Protection Fund to cover 90% of the loss or to bring the fund up to 90% funding. The compensation scheme is paid for by a levy on occupational schemes.

The Pension Protection Fund also protects the pension rights of employees in final salary defined benefits schemes whose employers have become insolvent without funds having been misappropriated. Again, compensation from the Fund is partly financed by a levy on occupational schemes. The levies are based on an assessment of the risk exposure of the particular scheme and the scheme's size. The levy payments are deductible in calculating the taxable profits of the employer. If a scheme cannot be rescued, and cannot secure benefits at least equal to the compensation payable from the Pension Protection Fund, the Fund will pay compensation at broadly 100% (but with limited inflation protection) to existing pensioners, and will pay pensions at normal pension age to employees at broadly 90% of their existing accrued rights (again with limited inflation protection and with an overall cap).

Pensions Act 2008 introduced rules to enable compensation paid by the Pension Protection Fund to be shared on divorce or dissolution of a civil partnership.

Unregistered pension schemes (ITEPA 2003, ss 393–400; FA 2004, ss 245–249)

[16.50] A scheme that is not registered under the Finance Act 2004 provisions is not subject to any restrictions but is not entitled to any tax advantages. Transitional protection applies to pension rights accrued within non-registered schemes at 6 April 2006 (see **16.33**).

Before 6 April 2006, there were two types of unapproved schemes, funded schemes (FURBS) and unfunded schemes (UURBS), detailed provisions of which are in earlier editions of this book. There are transitional provisions in relation to tax-free lump sum rights at 6 April 2006.

Under Finance Act 2004, UK unregistered schemes are termed 'employer-financed retirement benefit schemes'. Under the rules for such schemes, employers will not receive tax relief for pension contributions until benefits are paid out of the fund (and employees will not be taxed on the benefit of the employers' contributions), income and gains in the fund will be taxed at the 45% trust rate, or 38.1% for dividends, and employees will be taxed on any cash or non-cash benefits from the fund at their marginal tax rates, the benefits being treated as earned income. Benefits already taxed as pension income are excluded, as are certain other 'excluded benefits', such as those paid on ill-health or disablement of an employee during service. Further benefits may be excluded by statutory instrument, and this has been done in relation to certain benefits provided to retired employees, which mirror exemptions for various minor benefits provided to employees. For example, from 6 April 2016 an exemption for trivial benefits applies in the same way as outlined for employees in **10.50**. The employers' contributions and accrued funds will not have any effect on employees' annual allowance and lifetime allowance limits.

See **10.5** regarding anti-avoidance legislation relating to employment income provided by third parties. These anti-avoidance provisions specifically apply to employer-financed retirement benefit schemes. Where the employee is taxed on any benefit from the fund under the new provisions, this amount will be excluded from the charge outlined above. In certain specified circumstances, if an employer has paid a sum of money before 6 April 2006 to an employer-financed retirement benefits scheme and an employee has been taxed in respect of this sum, then the new provisions will not apply to sums of money or assets arising or derived from this sum.

Self-administered pension schemes (SI 1991/1614; FA 2004, Sch 29A)

[16.51] A self-administered pension scheme is one where the contributions remain under the control of trustees appointed by the company, as distinct from being paid to a pensions provider such as a life assurance company. The limits on contributions and benefits are the same as for other registered schemes, but the benefits are dependent on the funds within the scheme, so to that extent they are similar to money purchase schemes. While this type of scheme gives maximum flexibility in managing a fund, the pension scheme trustees must invest in the best interests of the members in order to provide their pension benefits. It is possible to have hybrid schemes where the funds are partly managed by a pensions provider. The fund will also usually hold life assurance cover on the scheme members so that its funds are not unacceptably diminished by the payment of death in service benefits on the premature death of a member.

A small self-administered scheme — SSAS (i.e. one with less than 12 members) is dealt with under the normal rules for all registered schemes, except that the range of investments such schemes are able to make is restricted (see **16.11**).

Registration and self-assessment (FA 2004, ss 254–255B)

[16.52] Applications for scheme registration must be made online. The rules governing the registration and deregistration of pension schemes include a 'fit and proper person' test in relation to scheme administrators, for which HMRC will also take into account the fitness of an adviser, and deny registered status where a scheme has been established for purposes other than that of providing pension benefits. There are accompanying rules relating to HMRC information powers and associated appeals and penalties. HMRC can send information notices to scheme administrators to request documents and other information to help them decide whether or not to register a pension scheme. Penalties may apply for false or inaccurate information.

Scheme administrators of registered schemes must make quarterly returns online to HMRC of any tax liabilities within 45 days after the end of the quarter. The tax due is payable at that time.

Payment of pensions

[16.53] Tax on pensions under occupational schemes is dealt with under the PAYE scheme (see CHAPTER 10), with coding adjustments being made where some or all of the available allowances have been used against other income, such as state pensions. Interest that the Pensions Regulator may require an employer to pay on late paid pension contributions is paid directly to the employee's pension account and is exempt from tax.

Tax points

[16.54] Note the following:

- Contributions by employers to registered pension schemes are one of the few benefits for employees and directors that are free of both tax and NICs, so generous funding of a scheme is particularly beneficial to them. From 6 April 2013 the exemption only applies to contributions in respect of employees, and not other family members.
- A family company may be able to eliminate taxable trading profits by contributions to a registered pension scheme, and if the contributions exceed those profits, to carry the resulting loss back against the profits of the previous year (see CHAPTER 26). Some spreading forward of special contributions may be required — see **16.13**.
- For the young and highly mobile, a personal pension plan may be preferable to an employer's scheme because it can be taken from job to job, whereas there may be problems transferring a fund from one occupational scheme to another. But there is the disadvantage that when negotiating an employment contract the employee will have to agree with the employer how much the employer will contribute to his personal plan. The higher administration charges also have to be considered. Pensions Act 2014 introduced a framework to provide for a system of automatic transfers of small pension pots so that an individual's pension will follow them to their new pension scheme when they change jobs.
- An individual does not have to be an employee to become a member of an occupational registered pension fund, so that excess funds could be allocated to provide benefits for anyone in an employee's family who becomes a fund member, rather than their being charged to tax at 55% upon being withdrawn (see **16.30**). However from 6 April 2013 the rules which allow employers to pay pension contributions into their

employees' family members' pensions as part of their employees' remuneration package have been changed to remove the tax and NICs advantages from these arrangements.

- Those who retire before state pension age (see **16.2** for these changing ages for men and women) may need to pay voluntary NICs to ensure that they get a full basic pension under the state scheme (see **13.13**). But providing they are registered as unemployed and available for work, contributions will be credited (see **13.12**), and unemployed men between the women's state pension age and 65 are automatically credited with contributions without the need to be registered.

17

Personal pension schemes

Introduction (FA 2004, ss 149–284 and Schs 28–36)

[17.1] There are two types of scheme for those making pension arrangements in addition to or instead of employers' (occupational) schemes — personal pension schemes and, for arrangements made before 1 July 1988, retirement annuity contracts. Personal pension schemes incorporate stakeholder pension schemes — see **17.2**. Occupational and state pensions are dealt with in CHAPTER **16**. The separate rules for occupational, personal pension and retirement annuity schemes were replaced from 6 April 2006 by a single regime covering all tax-privileged pension schemes. The regime rules are dealt with in **16.6** to **16.43**.

The Financial Conduct Authority regulates the operation of personal pension schemes, including self-invested personal pension schemes or SIPPs (see **17.13**).

Those without earnings may pay up to £3,600 a year into a pension fund and obtain tax relief (see **17.3**). All personal pension contributions are paid net of basic rate tax, which is particularly beneficial to non-taxpayers (see **17.4**). Retirement annuity premiums may also be paid net of basic rate tax if the insurance company agrees, otherwise they continue to be paid gross. In other respects, most of the rules are the same for both types of scheme.

Personal pension schemes may allow members to direct where their funds are to be invested, subject to restrictions for 'investment-regulated pension schemes' — see **16.11**. (These are particularly relevant to SIPPs — see **17.13**). Members of personal pension schemes (including stakeholder schemes) receive regular illustrations of what their future pension might be in present-day prices, so that they have a more realistic idea about the value of their pension funds and the options open to them. The illustration may incorporate state pension information supplied by the Department of Work and Pensions if the pension provider and pension fund member so wish.

Stakeholder pensions

[17.2] A stakeholder pension is a personal pension that must meet certain standards laid down by the Government in relation to charges, flexibility and provision of information. See **16.45** regarding auto-enrolment in mandatory workplace pensions which all employers must now provide. Before their introduction, certain employers had to offer specified employees access to a stakeholder pension scheme, but this is no longer a requirement for new or returning employees. Existing stakeholder pension schemes could, however, be used by employers for auto-enrolment purposes provided the schemes meet the necessary criteria. For employees already in a stakeholder pension, the arrangements will continue until the employee stops paying contributions or leaves their employment.

Employers are not required to contribute to the scheme. If employees so wish, the employer must deduct their contributions from pay and pay them over to the scheme provider by the 19th of the following month. As with all personal pensions, contributions are paid net of basic rate tax (see **17.1**). Employers must keep detailed records of payments and must notify any changes to the scheme provider. Employers who fail to comply with the requirements of the stakeholder pension provisions are liable to fines of up to £50,000. As indicated in **17.1**, the tax treatment of stakeholder pension schemes is incorporated within the personal pension scheme provisions.

Tax relief and payment of contributions (FA 2004, ss 188–195A)

[17.3] There is no limit on the personal pension contributions that may be made by or on behalf of an individual, but tax relief on contributions (see **17.4**) will only be given to an individual aged under 75 who—

(a)   has earnings subject to UK tax; or
(b)   is resident in the UK at some time during the year; or
(c)   is resident in the UK at some time during the five tax years immediately preceding the tax year and at some time in the tax year when they became a member of the registered pension scheme; or
(d)   has (or his or her spouse or civil partner has) UK-taxable earnings from overseas Crown employment in the tax year.

The pension contributions are accumulated in a fund free of income tax and capital gains tax. Pension scheme administrators will ensure that applicants are eligible to join the scheme. Legal guardians must complete application forms for those under 18.

Personal pension contributions can be paid to a life assurance company, friendly society, bank, building society, unit trust, or personal pension scheme trust established by employers and others. Retirement annuity premiums have to be paid to an insurance company. In both cases, the retirement benefits themselves are purchased from an authorised insurance company with the fund monies at retirement, and the 'best buy' available at that time can be selected. It is also possible to have a self-invested scheme — see **17.13**.

See **16.44** regarding transferring personal pension plan funds on entering or leaving pensionable employment.

[17.4] Tax relief is available on contributions up to the higher of 100% of relevant earnings and £3,600, and is further restricted by the annual allowance (see **16.15**) and the lifetime allowance (see **16.19**). Since basic rate tax relief is deducted and retained when paying the contribution (except for some retirement annuity premiums — see **17.9**), this means that someone with no earnings can establish a pension fund of £3,600 by making a payment of £2,880 (i.e. £3,600 less 20%).

[17.5] For a self-employed person, relevant earnings means his taxable profits. For an employee, relevant earnings include not only cash pay but also the cash equivalent of benefits, as reduced by expenses allowable against those earnings, and any other amounts treated as earnings.

[17.6] A scheme may provide for personal pension contributions to be made not only in cash but by way of transfer of shares received under tax-advantaged SAYE share option schemes or share incentive plans (as to which see CHAPTER **11**). Such transfers must be made within 90 days of exercising the SAYE option or of shares being appropriated to the employee, and will be treated as contributions equal to the market value of the shares at the date of the transfer to the scheme. Tax relief will then be given on the contributions in the same way as for cash contributions.

[17.7] As indicated in **10.10**, neither employers' nor employees' NICs are payable on personal pension contributions paid by employers in respect of the employee. This means that if the employee agreed to a salary sacrifice, and the employer made a pension contribution boosted by the employer's NICs saving, the pension contribution would be higher than would result from an employee payment (see Example 1). Although the tax and NICs advantages of benefits in kind provided through salary sacrifice arrangements are largely withdrawn from 6 April 2017 (see **10.30**), HMRC confirm in their Employment Income Manual at EIM42780 that employer contributions into registered pension schemes are excluded from the changes. The potential pay must be given up before being received and the legal outcome must be that the employee is entitled to lower cash remuneration and a benefit. Other effects of reducing the employee's earnings must not be ignored.

Example 1

If a basic rate taxpayer earning £25,000 a year makes a personal pension contribution of £1,000 gross, £800 net in 2017–18, the amount of salary required to cover the contribution would be:

	£	£
Salary		1,176
Tax @ 20%	235	
NICs @ 12%	141	376
Net salary to cover contribution		800

> If he made a salary sacrifice arrangement and agreed to receive a salary of £23,824 (£25,000 – £1,176) plus a non-taxable benefit in the form of a pension contribution paid by his employer, the employer could contribute £1,176 plus the employer's NICs saving of £162 (13.8% × £1,176) giving £1,338. The employee's net pay would be £800 lower, leaving him in the same position he was before (having paid the pension contribution), but the gross pension contribution paid into the fund would increase by £338.

Funding the contributions

[17.8] With the limit for tax allowable contributions being 100% of earnings (subject to the annual and lifetime allowance), a windfall such as a legacy could be used to pay a substantial amount into the fund and thus catch up on earlier years where significant funding was not possible.

Although it is not possible for a lender to take a charge on a personal pension fund, several pension providers have arrangements under which a lender will make an appropriate loan to a taxpayer with a sufficiently large accumulated fund, or who is paying regular contributions to a fund, usually in the latter case based on a multiple of regular contributions and the age of the taxpayer. The terms of the loan are usually that interest is payable year by year but capital repayments are taken from the eventual tax-free lump sum on retirement. Whether security for the borrowing is required often depends upon the trade or profession carried on by the taxpayer.

The loan could itself be used to fund contributions to the scheme, so that a significant part of the maximum allowable contribution might be funded from a loan made at the same time from the fund itself.

Tax relief is not available on the interest paid to the lender unless the borrowing is for a qualifying purpose, such as the relief for the acquisition of a business property or a partnership share (see **2.14**), so there is no relief for interest paid on a loan used to pay pension scheme contributions.

Way in which relief is given

[17.9] As indicated in **17.1**, retirement annuity premiums may now be paid net of basic rate tax if the insurance company agrees, in which case relief is given in the same way as for personal pension contributions. Where they are paid gross, relief is given to the self-employed by deduction in the payer's self-assessment or simple assessment (see **9.2**) and to employees by a PAYE coding adjustment. The premiums are deducted from earnings in calculating the tax liability.

Personal pension contributions are paid net of basic rate tax, and the pension provider reclaims the tax from HMRC. This enables both taxpayers and non-taxpayers to get basic rate tax relief on their payments. Higher and additional rate relief must be claimed and will be given in the taxpayer's self-assessment or simple assessment, or by coding adjustment for employees. The extra higher or additional rate relief is given by extending the basic rate limit in the tax computation by the gross amount of the contribution.

See also **16.14**.

Example 2 shows the difference in treatment for personal pension contributions and retirement annuity premiums that are paid gross.

Example 2

Self-employed taxpayer has earnings of £56,500 in 2017–18. He paid a pension premium, the gross amount of which was £1,000. The treatment of the premium if it is either a retirement annuity premium paid gross or a personal pension contribution is as follows:

			Retirement annuity premium			Personal pension contribution
			£			£
Earnings			56,500			56,500
Less: Retirement annuity premium			(1,000)			
			55,500			56,500
Personal allowance			(11,500)			(11,500)
Taxable income			44,000			45,000
Tax thereon:						
Basic rate	33,500	@ 20%	6,700	34,500*	@ 20%	6,900
(balance)	10,500	@ 40%	4,200	10,500	@ 40%	4,200
	44,000			45,000		
						11,100
Less: Basic rate tax retained 1,000 @ 20%						(200)
			£10,900			£10,900

*Basic rate limit increased by personal pension contribution.

Where personal pension contributions are made in the form of shares (see **17.6**), the market value of the shares is treated as an amount net of basic rate tax, so that with basic rate tax at 20%, shares to the value of £800 would be treated as a gross contribution of £1,000.

Permissible benefits

[17.10] The pension benefits must commence not earlier than age 55 (see **16.20**), except in cases of ill health or where the occupation is one in which earlier retirement is customary, for example dancers and athletes, and the individual had the right to early retirement before 6 April 2006 protected under transitional provisions — see **16.33**.

[17.11] A taxpayer may have several different pension funds, which gives him flexibility as to when and in what manner to take benefits. See **16.21** to **16.30** for the ways in which benefits may be taken for money purchase schemes. From 6 April 2015 individuals in money purchase schemes, which includes personal pensions and retirement annuity schemes, have more flexible access to their pensions savings.

For individuals aged 55 or over funds of £10,000 or less that are held in a personal pension can be paid tax-free as a lump sum (small pots lump sum). The payment will be an authorised payment provided certain other conditions are met. The payment can be made regardless of the value of the individual's total pension savings, and in addition to another non-taxable trivial commutation lump sum (see **16.29**) payment or occupational pension scheme lump sum payment that the individual may have, or will receive. However, an individual can only receive three such tax-free small lump sum commutation payments in their lifetime.

[17.12] The position where a taxpayer with a personal pension fund dies is the same as for an employer's money purchase scheme as outlined in **16.36** to **16.43**. From 6 April 2015 certain pensions and lump sums payable on death to nominees or successors are tax-free, as are certain annuities paid to dependants, nominees or successors. The contract may provide for the death benefits to be held in trust, with the monies payable at the trustees' discretion. If paid to the personal representatives, the sum refunded will form part of the estate for inheritance tax purposes, but tax will not be payable to the extent that the estate is left to the surviving spouse or civil partner. Inheritance tax will also usually be avoided where the proceeds are held by the trustees of the fund for nominees.

Self-invested personal pension schemes (FA 2004, ss 174A, 182–185I, 273ZA and Sch 29A)

[17.13] Self-invested personal pension schemes (SIPPs) are schemes which allow members to direct where their funds are to be invested.

The original intention of the Finance Act 2004 pension provisions was that all schemes would have the same powers in relation to investments and borrowing powers. Because of the widespread promotion of SIPPs as vehicles for purchasing residential property and valuable assets, such as art and antiques, special provisions apply to 'investment-regulated pension schemes', which are those where members are able to influence the scheme's investments. Such schemes cannot invest in 'prohibited assets' (see **16.11**).

In addition to the restrictions on investments, the maximum borrowing is 50% of the total fund value, with any VAT within the cost of the property purchased being included in calculating the maximum borrowing.

SIPPs still give investors greater control over where their money is invested and how and when benefits are taken. They are, however, most likely to be beneficial for those with substantial funds. They are regulated by the Financial Conduct Authority (see **17.1**).

Payment of pensions (ITEPA 2003, s 683)

[17.14] Annuities and drawdown pensions under a personal pension plan or a retirement annuity contract are taxed through the PAYE scheme in the same way as occupational pensions (see **16.21** and **16.28**), with tax being charged at the appropriate rate and coding adjustments being made where some or all of the available allowances have been used against other income, such as state pensions (see CHAPTER 10).

Tax points

[17.15] Note the following:

- Although contributions to personal pension plans attract tax relief at the top rate, the restrictions imposed by the annual allowance (see **16.15**) make them a less tax-efficient means of providing for the future than they once were. In addition, the available pension at retirement will be determined by the investment performance of the funds into which the pension contributions are paid.
- Commission may be received on personal pension contributions. The pension contribution will be treated as the net amount paid if the commission is deducted from the contribution or a discounted premium is paid. If the contribution is paid gross and the commission received separately, tax relief will be given on the gross amount.
- Most people are entitled to pay a personal pension contribution of up to £3,600 a year whether or not they have any earnings. Basic rate tax relief is retained out of the contribution whether or not the payer is a taxpayer, provided the pension scheme operates tax at source. If contributions are paid for the payer's children (of whatever age), it must be remembered that they cannot take benefits until at earliest age 55.
- Some building societies and other lenders will allow the borrower to pay only interest during the period of a loan, with an undertaking that the loan itself will be repaid from the tax-free lump sum from a pension fund on retirement.
- Contributions to a personal pension will reduce reckonable income for working and child tax credits (see **2.41**).

Part V

Trading activities

18

Sole trader, partnership or company?

Tax and non-tax considerations

[18.1] The alternatives when a person starts in business or needs to consider a change in how to operate are to become a sole trader, to form a partnership with others or to form a limited liability company. All relevant factors need to be considered when making a decision. A sole trader is liable for the debts of the business to the full extent of his personal assets, and can in the extreme be made bankrupt. The same applies to partners, unless they have formed a limited liability partnership, which enables them to restrict their liability, broadly, to the capital contributed (see **23.33**). A company shareholder's liability is normally limited to the amount, if any, unpaid on his shares. Protection of private assets is usually one of the main reasons for trading through a company or a limited liability partnership. However, lenders, landlords and sometimes suppliers often require directors to give a personal guarantee in respect of the company's obligation, which reduces significantly the benefit of limited liability. There are also major compliance requirements for a company under the Companies Acts, including the need to produce accounts in statutory form, which must be sent promptly to Companies House. Companies which meet certain requirements do not have to have their accounts audited (see **9.24**).

Limited liability partnerships have similar reporting obligations to companies.

Micro-entities can prepare simplified accounts for financial years ending on or after 30 September 2013, provided they are filed with Companies House on or after 1 December 2013, see **9.24**. Micro-entity accounts prepared in accordance with the regulations will represent accounts prepared under generally accepted accounting practice (see **20.2**), and therefore can be submitted, along with the directors' report, to HMRC as part of a company's annual self-assessment (see **9.21**). There is no change in the requirement to keep and retain adequate business and accounting records (see **9.32**).

The general commercial and family considerations must be weighed alongside the comparative tax positions when choosing what form the business is to take. It has never been sensible to allow the tax system to dominate this important decision. There are savings to be made operating as a company, as illustrated in Example 2 at **18.8**.

Comparative tax/NICs position for the unincorporated trader and the company director

[18.2] There are so many variables to take into account in comparing the tax/NICs position for the unincorporated trader and the company director that it is impossible to draw hard and fast conclusions, and detailed calculations need to be made in every case. Simplified assumptions and comments on some of the variables are made in the illustrations which follow.

[18.3] A sole trader or partner will pay combined income tax and NICs for 2017–18 at 42% on all profits (after personal allowances) in excess of the basic rate limit of £33,500 (but see **2.5** for the differing basic rate band applying to a Scottish taxpayer's non-savings, non-dividend income) and up to the higher rate limit of £150,000, whether he leaves those profits in the business or withdraws them. The £33,500 threshold is available to each member of a married couple or civil partners working in partnership. A controlling director/shareholder of a company can decide how much profit to take in the form of remuneration or dividends (on which income tax will be paid) and how much to leave to be taxed at corporation tax rates (see **3.14**). The net of tax remuneration or dividend need not be withdrawn from the company — it can be left to credit on loan account (see **12.13**).

[18.4] Special rules apply, however, to personal service companies and managed service companies, and certain partnerships. Where the company acts as an intermediary providing the services of a director/employee to clients, and the arrangements are such that he would have been an employee of the client if he had contracted directly with the client, the intermediary company is deemed to make a salary payment on the last day of the tax year equal to the difference between the amount received from the client (less certain deductions) and the amount actually paid out as remuneration to the director/employee (see **19.4**). Personal service companies are therefore unable to allocate profits to remuneration or dividends as they see fit. Special rules also apply for managed service companies, under which any payments to those working for such a company are treated as employment income (see **19.14**).

[18.5] For those not caught by the personal service company or managed service company rules, NICs are one of the most significant factors in comparing the liabilities under the respective formats. Sole traders and partners pay much lower NICs than the combined employee/employer contributions for a company director (see CHAPTER 24). There are planned reforms of NICs for the self-employed. See **24.5** regarding the Government's intention to abolish Class 2 contributions and reform Class 4 contributions to introduce a new contributory benefit test.

In a partnership of husband and wife or civil partners both have to pay Class 4 NICs. They also both have to pay Class 2 contributions unless, in the case of a married couple, the wife elected not to do so on or before 11 May 1977 and holds a certificate of exemption (see **13.5**). Class 2 and Class 4 NICs are not an allowable deduction in arriving at business profits for tax purposes. The Class 1 NICs on remuneration paid by a company depend on the earnings (see **13.4**). If in 2017–18 remuneration is taken at £866 a week (the upper limit for employees' contributions at the 12% rate), i.e. £45,000 over the year, the combined employer's and employee's contributions would be £9,503. The employer's share (£5,083) is, however, allowable as a deduction in calculating the profits of the company which are liable to corporation tax (reducing the total figure to £8,537 because corporation tax is at 19%). The NICs cost for a sole trader with profits of £45,000 is:

Class 2 contributions 52 × £2.85	148
Class 4 contributions 9% × (45,000 – 8,164)	3,315
	£3,463

The extra NICs cost of operating through a company at that profit level would therefore be (8,537 – 3,463) = £5,074.

[18.6] The overall comparative tax position is significantly affected by whether profits are withdrawn as salary or dividends. Dividends are not subject to NICs. In addition, there is a dividend allowance of £5,000 per year and dividends within the allowance are not taxable (proposed to be reduced to £2,000 from 6 April 2018, see **2.5**). Where dividends exceed the allowance the rates applying are 7.5% on income up to the basic rate limit of £33,500, 32.5% on income above the basic rate limit up to the higher rate limit of £150,000, and 38.1% on income above the higher rate limit.

[18.7] Various other points should be borne in mind. To obtain a deduction in calculating taxable profits, earnings as a director or employee are required to be 'wholly and exclusively for the purposes of the trade', so particularly where a spouse or civil partner does not work full-time in a business, the earnings may be challenged by HMRC as excessive in calculating the taxable profit of the company. There is no such requirement for a spouse or civil partner who is an active partner in a business partnership rather than a company, albeit working less than full-time, although artificial arrangements will not work (see **23.31**).

Furthermore, HMRC have used the 'settlements' rules to challenge some commonly used tax planning measures in family companies under the rules for 'settlements'. Although outright gifts between spouses and civil partners are not normally within the settlements rules, this exception does not apply if the gift is wholly or substantially a right to income. A gift of ordinary shares from one spouse or civil partner to the other has traditionally been considered by tax advisers to be outside this exception, because ordinary shares carry other rights in addition to income rights, for example rights to a share of the assets if the company is wound up. This would obviously be particularly relevant if the couple separated. HMRC considered, however, that in some circumstances gifts of ordinary shares were caught as settlements. In July 2007 the House of Lords decided a case in favour of the taxpayers on the basis that, while there was a settlement, an exemption for outright gifts between spouses applied. The Government subsequently expressed an intention to introduce new legislation to counter 'income shifting' though it later announced it would instead keep the matter under review (see **12.10**). HMRC have recently confirmed that they will not give clearances or advice in respect of the application of the settlements legislation.

In view of the complexity of this issue anyone who is considering such tax planning measures should take professional advice. Other relevant factors are that some benefits, in particular jobseeker's allowance, are not available to the self-employed (but there are proposals to change this from 2018, see **24.5**), and the rate of inheritance tax business property relief for assets owned personally may be reduced when operating through a company (see **5.45**).

[18.8] The profit level at which the retentions after tax and NICs will be less operating through a company than as a sole trader or partner is not a static figure but one which will vary according to whether there are other sources of income, how much remuneration is paid by the company, and whether any dividends and pension contributions are paid. Example 1 shows that in 2017–18, if an individual (who is not a Scottish taxpayer, see **2.5**) with no other income is paid a salary of £45,000 by a company to leave him with taxable income equal to the basic rate threshold of £33,500, the profit level at which the tax burden using the company format equates with that of an individual trader is £67,065. (If pension contributions were being paid, this would need to be taken into account in the calculations.) The turning point would be at a lower profit level on a salary of less than £45,000 and a higher level on a salary above £45,000 (and would in any event be double for a business of husband and wife or civil partners). There could, however, be further tax liabilities on the company retentions at a later date, but these may never materialise, through changes in tax rates, exemptions, etc., and in the meantime cash will have been conserved in the company. Example 2 illustrates that the company format can be more tax-effective even at much lower profit levels if most of the profits are extracted by way of dividend. The other disadvantages of incorporation would, however, probably outweigh the tax/NICs advantage at that profit level.

Example 1

Business profits before tax and NICs are £67,065 and there are no other sources of income. A sole trader is liable to income tax on the full amount. If a company director was paid a salary of £45,000 during 2017–18 (which after the personal allowance of £11,500 leaves income of £33,500 to use the basic rate band), the comparative position is:

			Trader	Com- pany direc- tor
			£	£
Profits/ remuneration			67,065	45,000
Personal allowance			(11,500)	(11,500)
Taxable income			55,565	33,500
Tax thereon:	33,500	@ 20%	6,700	6,700
	22,065	@ 40%	8,826	
			15,526	6,700
Class 2 NICs (flat rate)			148	Employ- ee's NICs** 4,420
Class 4 NICs*			3,756	
Total personal tax and NICs			19,430	11,120
Company's tax and NICs:				
Profits				67,065
Less: Director's re- muneration				(45,000)
Company's NICs thereon				(5,083†) 5,083
Taxable profits				16,982
Tax thereon @ 19%				(3,227) 3,227
Retained profits ††				13,756
Total tax and NICs liabilities			19,430	19,430
Drawn or undrawn profits			47,635	47,635
			67,065	67,065
*	On (45,000 – 8,164) @ 9%		3,315	
	On (67,065 – 45,000) @ 2%		441	3,756
**	On (45,000 – 8,164) @ 12%			4,420
†	On (45,000 – 8,164) @ 13.8%			5,083

Each extra £1 of profit would cost the sole trader 42p in tax and NICs (until such time that his income exceeds the additional rate threshold of £150,000, in which case it would be 47p) and the company 19p (see **3.15**).

Possible further tax liabilities if company's retained profits of £13,756 (see [††]) are paid out:

If distributed as dividends, the first £5,000 would not be taxable (see **2.5**). The balance of £8,756 taxed at 32.5%	£2,845
If taxed as capital gains, 20% on £13,756 (or 10%, i.e. £1,375 if entrepreneurs' relief available — see **4.2** and **29.2**).	£2,751

Example 2

Say total profits are £26,500 and there are no other sources of income. The comparative position for a sole trader compared with a company director who is paid a salary of £12,500 and receives the balance after corporation tax as a dividend is as follows:

		Trader				*Company director*
		£				£
Profits/ remuneration		26,500				12,500
Personal allowance		(11,500)				(11,500)
Taxable income		15,000				1,000
Tax thereon:	15,000	@ 20% 3,000	1,000	@ 20%		200
Class 2 NICs (flat rate)		148		Employee's NICs		
Class 4 NICs (26,500 – 8,164 @ 9%)		1,650	(12,500 – 8,164 @ 12%)			520
Total personal tax and NICs		4,798				720
Company's tax and NICs:						
Profits					26,500	
Less: Director's remuneration					(12,500)	
Company's NICs thereon (12,500 – 8,164 @ 13.8%)					(598)	598
Taxable profits					13,402	
Tax thereon @ 19%					(2,546)	2,546
Dividend					10,856	
Tax thereon:						

£5,000 @ 0%		–
£5,856 @ 7.5%		439 439
Total tax and NICs payable	4,798	4,303
Saving through operating as company		495

Paying tax on the profits (TMA 1970, ss 59A, 59B, 59D, 59E)

[18.9] Directors' remuneration is subject to tax and NICs under the PAYE scheme (see CHAPTER 10) immediately it is paid or credited to the director's account, with corporation tax on any profits left in the company being payable nine months after the end of the accounting period.

An unincorporated business makes tax payments (including Class 4 NICs) on account half-yearly on 31 January in the tax year and 31 July following the tax year. The payments on account are based on the total income (not just the business profits) of the previous tax year, with an adjustment to the correct figure, including any tax due on capital gains, on the 31 January following the tax year. From 2015–16 Class 2 NICs are also due through the self-assessment system no later than 31 January following the tax year, though some self-employed earners do not pay through self-assessment and will be sent a bill by HMRC (see **24.2**). The extent to which the unincorporated business will be better off than the company from a cash flow point of view will depend on whether directors' remuneration has been taken (and if so, how much and when), and whether the tax payments on account are significantly less than the full amount due.

Example 3

Say accounts of a business that started in 2000 were made up for the year to 31 December 2017. The profits of that year would be part of the total income of 2017–18 and tax on that total income would be payable provisionally in two equal instalments on 31 January 2018 and 31 July 2018, based on the previous year's income. The actual tax liability on the income plus capital gains of 2017–18 would be notified by 31 January 2019 for returns filed online (see **9.13**), and a balancing payment or repayment would be made accordingly. The first provisional payment for 2018–19 would also be due on 31 January 2019, as would the 2017–18 Class 2 NICs liability. For income tax purposes, any tax on dividends is payable as part of the balancing payment when the dividends are received for the first time, but is then taken into account in arriving at payments on account for subsequent years.

If the business had been a company, tax on the profits of the year to 31 December 2017 (after paying directors' remuneration) would be due on 1 October 2018, with PAYE tax and NICs being payable broadly at the end of the month in which any remuneration was paid.

There is an additional flexibility open to unincorporated businesses. By choosing an accounting date early in the tax year, say 30 April, they may benefit from lower tax rates and higher thresholds in the year of assessment compared with those in force when most of the profits were earned (although the rates can of course go up as well as down). The possible advantage of an accounting date early in the tax year may, however, be counterbalanced by the rules for taxing profits when the business ceases. For the detailed rules on how profits are charged to tax, see CHAPTER 21.

Losses (ITA 2007, Pt 4; CTA 2010, Pt 4; TCGA 1992, s 253)

[18.10] If a new business is expected to make losses in its early years, it is essential to bear in mind the different loss reliefs available to individuals and to companies. (These are dealt with more fully in CHAPTERS 25 and 26.)

Individuals can claim generous reliefs for trading losses in a new business. Losses in any of the first four tax years of a new business may be carried back to set against *any* income of the previous three tax years, earliest first, although from 2013–14 there is a cap on tax reliefs claimed against general income, see **2.13**. The tax liability of the earlier years is recalculated accordingly to establish the tax saving. Effect is, however, given to the saving in the tax year in which the loss is incurred rather than the tax year in which the loss has been set off, so the tax saving is not boosted by a corresponding payment of interest on overpaid tax (see **9.16**). For losses in later years (or instead of a carry-back claim for opening year losses) a claim may be made to set them against the total income of the tax year in which the loss is sustained or the previous tax year (again subject to the cap in **2.13**), and tax will be discharged or repaid. The losses may have been boosted, or indeed created, by capital allowances. In some circumstances, trading losses may be set against capital gains. Unrelieved trading losses may always be carried forward to set against future trading profits of the same trade.

If a new company makes trading losses, they may only be set against any current profits of the company, such as bank interest or chargeable gains, or carried forward against the company's later *trading* profits, though September 2017 Finance Bill which is expected to receive Royal Assent in November 2017 includes legislation allowing trading losses arising from 1 April 2017 to be carried forward against total taxable profits (see **26.6**). Trading losses of an established trading company may be set against the profits from other sources, if any, in the same accounting year, then against the total profits of the previous year, with any balance being carried forward.

Funds introduced to a limited company to support losses, either as share capital or on loan, do not qualify for any immediate relief (but see **2.14** as regards relief for interest payable on any borrowing to enable the funds to be introduced). There are two relieving measures for shares and loans, but they are only available when shares are disposed of or when money lent becomes irrecoverable. The provisions are as follows:

(a)   An individual can set a capital loss on the disposal of shares that he had *subscribed for* in an unquoted trading company against any of his income in the same way as a trading loss, as an alternative to setting the capital loss against capital gains (see **38.23**). However, from 2013–14 this is also subject to the cap on reliefs against general income (see **2.13**).

(b)   The loss of money loaned to the company (or paid to cover a bank guarantee) may be deducted against the lender's capital gains (see **4.37**).

To get the first relief, the shares must be disposed of or they need to have become virtually worthless, probably because the business has failed. The second relief is also only likely to be available because the company is in financial difficulties. The distinction between the shares relief being given against income and the loan relief only against capital gains is important, because relief against income gives more flexibility and the opportunity for early relief. These two relieving measures are available both to working directors and to others providing funds to a company.

Pensions

[18.11] Self-employed persons are currently entitled to relief at the top rate of tax on contributions to a personal pension scheme, providing it is a registered scheme, subject to relevant earnings, and annual and lifetime allowance limits (see **16.9** and **16.14** for the full details).

Company directors/employees in non-pensionable employment can also take advantage of the personal pension provisions, but it is often preferable for a family company to operate its own pension scheme, and in any case by February 2018 all employers will have had to establish a workplace pension for eligible jobholders (see **16.45**). There is not normally any restriction on contributions to a registered scheme other than the consideration which must be given to relevant earnings and the annual and lifetime allowances, and the general requirement that any payment by a business must be wholly and exclusively for business purposes. In certain circumstances employers' contributions may have to be spread forward rather than all being deducted in a single accounting period. There are some special provisions where there is both a registered scheme and an unregistered employer-financed scheme. Unless these special rules apply, the company's contributions reduce the company's taxable profits when the benefits are paid. In addition, they are not charged either to tax or NICs on the employee provided that they are in respect of the employee only. The individual's contributions, if any, are allowed in calculating tax on his earnings from the company, although they are not deducted from pay in calculating employers' and employees' NICs.

For full details on pensions see CHAPTER **16** and CHAPTER **17**.

Capital gains

[18.12] Where realised chargeable gains are not covered by available reliefs, the first £11,300 of the total gains in 2017–18 is exempt from capital gains tax for individuals (£11,300 each for husband and wife and civil partners), tax being charged at the rates outlined in **4.2** (the maximum possible rate being 28%), unless entrepreneurs' relief is available to bring the rate down to 10% (see **29.2**). Companies are not entitled to any exemption and usually pay corporation tax on the full amount of their chargeable gains (see **4.7**) but, unlike individuals, companies remain entitled to an indexation allowance to compensate for inflation (see **4.22**). The rate of corporation tax on a company's gains for the year to 31 March 2018 is 19% (see **3.15**). This means that the effect of gains being realised within a company depends on the way in which the gains are passed to the shareholder. The possible effect if the gains are passed on as a dividend is shown in Example 4.

If the gains are retained within the company until the shareholder disposes of his shares or the company is liquidated, the shareholder will be liable to capital gains tax on the increase in value of his shareholding, and since the gain made by the company will have borne corporation tax when it was made this would effectively give a double tax charge. Reliefs may, however, be available at the time the shares are disposed of (see below).

Example 4

Company makes a gain of £10,000 in year to 31 March 2018, which is passed on to shareholders as a dividend.

	£
Company's capital gain	10,000
Corporation tax @ 19%	(1,900)
Leaving for cash dividend/shareholder's income	8,100
Maximum income tax @ 38.1%	(3,086)
Leaving shareholder with net cash of	5,014
Combined company and personal tax	4,986
i.e.	49.86%

Whether or not a business is incorporated, the increase in the value of its chargeable assets may lead to chargeable gains in the future, and in the case of a company there is the possibility of further personal chargeable gains where the share value is increased by profit retentions. There is no capital gains tax liability on death. Legatees effectively take over the assets of the deceased at their market value at the date of death and thus get a tax-free uplift in base cost where values of shares or personally-owned business assets have risen.

There are important reliefs which lessen the capital gains tax impact, and these reliefs are available to sole traders, partners and company shareholders.

Entrepreneurs' relief is available on a disposal of all or part of a business, or shares in a 'personal' trading company, where certain conditions are satisfied for at least a year preceding the disposal. This relief reduces the rate of capital gains tax to 10% (see **29.2**).

Holdover relief is available if gifts of certain business assets are made (see **4.32**). Gifts are generally treated as disposals at open market value, which may give rise to chargeable gains. The donor and the donee may, however, jointly claim to treat the gain as reducing the donee's cost in the event of a future disposal, and thus avoid an immediate tax charge on the donor.

Rollover relief is available to defer a capital gains tax liability where business assets are replaced. It is not available for disposals of shares, but may be claimed in relation to certain disposals of assets used by a company in which the disponer is a shareholder (see **29.16** and **29.21**).

A further relief is available under the enterprise investment scheme where gains (whether arising through the business or otherwise) are reinvested by subscribing for ordinary shares in a qualifying unquoted trading company (see **29.33**). Tax on the reinvested gains is deferred until the new shares are disposed of.

An exemption from capital gains tax on gains realised from disposals of assets applies where the gains are reinvested through the seed enterprise investment scheme (SEIS) (see **29.37**).

Social investment tax relief includes a relief from capital gains where an individual invests a sum equal to the amount of a chargeable gain in a social enterprise (see **29.55**).

See CHAPTERS **4** and **29** for discussion of these reliefs. See also CHAPTER **27** for discussion of disincorporation relief.

Inheritance tax (IHTA 1984, ss 103–114)

[18.13] There is usually no inheritance tax to pay on gifts of all or part of a business in lifetime or on death, whether it is operated by an individual or through a company. Business property relief is available at 100% on transfers of all or part of an individual's business and on transfers out of unquoted shareholdings, providing the company carries on a qualifying business and providing any lifetime gifts of such property, or qualifying replacement property, are still retained by the donee when the donor dies. The rate of inheritance tax business property relief on assets owned outside a partnership or company but used within the business is only 50% and in the case of a company the relief is only available to a controlling director. For details, see **5.45** to **5.47**.

To pass on a business gradually to other members of the family, the company format has the edge in terms of flexibility, since it is easier to transfer shares than to transfer a part of an unincorporated business.

Raising finance and attracting high calibre employees

[18.14] The enterprise investment scheme gives a qualifying company an advantage over an unincorporated business in attracting funds from outside investors. Individuals may obtain income tax relief at 30% on up to £1 million invested for (broadly) three years in shares of qualifying unquoted trading companies, and gains on disposal of the shares are exempt from tax in most cases. Similar provisions apply to investments in venture capital trusts, which are quoted companies that invest in unquoted companies. The rate of income tax relief on venture capital trust investments is also 30%.

The seed enterprise investment scheme is based on the enterprise investment scheme, but is designed to encourage investment in small, early stage companies. Individuals may obtain income tax relief at 50% on up to £100,000 invested for at least three years in shares in qualifying unquoted trading companies, and gains on disposal of the shares are exempt from tax in most cases.

Investors' relief will be available from 2019–20 for gains accruing on the disposal by individuals (excluding broadly employees and officers of the company) or trustees of ordinary shares acquired on or after 17 March 2016 in an unlisted trading company. This relief reduces the rate of capital gains tax to 10%.

The enterprise investment scheme also enables chargeable gains that are matched by equivalent investments in scheme shares to be deferred until the scheme shares are sold. The seed enterprise investment scheme provides for an exemption from capital gains tax on gains realised from disposals of assets where the gains are reinvested through the scheme and certain conditions are met. The amount of exemption is currently for half the gains invested.

Smaller, high risk companies have a further advantage over unincorporated businesses in the form of 'enterprise management incentives'. Under the enterprise management incentives (EMI) provisions, qualifying companies with fewer than 250 employees may provide employees with share options currently worth up to £250,000 per employee, up to an overall maximum of £3 million. Gains made on disposals of shares acquired through exercising EMI options on or after 6 April 2012 can also qualify for entrepreneurs' relief. For detailed provisions see CHAPTER 11 for EMI schemes and CHAPTER 29 for the other schemes.

Changing from one format to another

[18.15] It is a simple matter for an unincorporated business to change from a sole trader to a partnership or vice versa (see CHAPTER 23). Where an unincorporated business is to be incorporated, careful planning is necessary to ensure the best tax position and to minimise the disadvantages — see CHAPTER 27. A disincorporation relief applies up to 31 March 2018 to allow companies to transfer certain qualifying assets to shareholders who wish to continue the business in an unincorporated form without a charge to corporation tax arising on the transfer — details are in CHAPTER 27. However, if the company has accumulated trading losses, these cannot be transferred to the shareholders. The consequences of either paying out gains as dividends or as capital distributions in a liquidation are illustrated in CHAPTER 28.

Tax points

[18.16] Note the following:

- The tax tail should not wag the commercial dog. *All* aspects of alternative business forms should be considered.

- The loss rules for individuals, particularly the three-year carry-back of new business losses, make an unincorporated start an attractive proposition where there is heavy initial expenditure, particularly on revenue items but also on capital items which attract tax allowances. The business can later be converted to a company if appropriate. The cap on certain reliefs at **2.13** should, however, be borne in mind.

- To get income tax relief on a capital loss where shares in an unquoted trading company are disposed of, the shares must have been issued *to the disponer* by the company. Shares acquired by transfer from a previous shareholder do not qualify.

- The possible double tax charge where a company first sells chargeable assets at a profit, thus paying corporation tax on the profit and also increasing the value of its shares, can be avoided by shareholder/ directors retaining personal ownership of assets such as freeholds or leaseholds and allowing the company to use them. But inheritance tax business property relief at 50% is only available on those assets where a shareholder *controls* the company, whereas the 50% reduction is available to any partner who personally owns assets which are used by the partnership.

- Entrepreneurs' relief is available on a disposal of shares only if the company is a personal company. This means, broadly, that the disponer must have a stake of at least 5% in the company. There is no similar requirement for partners in a partnership, so that partners with very small interests may be eligible for the relief.

- Investors' relief is not generally available where either the investor or a person connected to them is an officer or employee of the company, or of a company connected with the company. See **29.13** for the exceptions.

- The differing rates of income tax and capital gains tax should be borne in mind. Income tax deductions cannot be set against capital gains. But a dividend from a company, even if payable out of a capital profit, counts as income in the hands of the shareholder, enabling available deductions to be set off and saving tax at higher rates accordingly.

19

Starting up a new small or part-time business

Is it self-employment?

[19.1] It is essential to establish at the outset whether a person is working as an employee or is self-employed. Alternatively, he may be neither employed nor self-employed but receiving sums taxable under the 'miscellaneous income' provisions (for example receiving payments for writing the occasional article, but not often enough to be regarded as an author carrying on a trade or profession). Exceptionally, the activity may not be taxable at all.

The distinction between employment and self-employment is important in deciding whether PAYE tax and employees' NICs should be deducted from payments, and employers' NICs paid; what expenses may be deducted in working out the income chargeable to tax; and whether there is a need to account for VAT. If a taxpayer operates through a personal service company the tax legislation looks through the legal structure to ensure that those in 'disguised employment' pay the same tax and NICs as someone employed directly (see **19.4**) and there are similar provisions for those working for a 'managed service company' (see **19.14**).

[19.2] One important distinction between employment and self-employment is whether a payment is made under a contract *of service* and is thus employment income subject to PAYE, or made under a contract *for services* entitling payment against an invoice or fee note, the payment being included in the self-employed accounts. However, the decision is not clear-cut. Employment status is a matter of general (not tax) law and depends on the overall circumstances rather than just the form of the contract. Indeed it was held by the Supreme Court in an important employment law case in 2011 that an employment tribunal had been entitled to disregard the terms of the written documentation and to look, instead, at the real contractual terms.

HMRC guidance on the main points to be considered can be found in their Employment Status Manual. They also have an online 'Employment Status Indicator' tool which can be used in many cases, although not for directors, agency workers and anyone providing services through an intermediary.

Factors pointing to employment are that the person needs to carry out the work personally; he has to take orders as to how, where and when to do it, and work set hours; and be paid a regular salary or wage and be paid for overtime, sickness and holidays.

Factors pointing to self-employment are that the person risks his own capital and bears any losses; he controls whether, how, when and where to do the work; provides his own equipment; is free to employ others to do the work; is required to bear the cost of correcting anything that goes wrong; and regularly works for a number of different people.

None of these factors is conclusive — indeed many of them will be irrelevant in particular cases — and all the circumstances have to be taken into account. The tax and NICs rules are not always the same, and the tax and NICs treatment is not conclusive for VAT.

The Office of Tax Simplification (OTS) prepared reports on employment status and the so-called 'gig economy' of temporary and short-term contracts for independent contractors. In addition, in a widely reported decision the Employment Tribunal found that two taxi drivers were 'employed' as 'workers' within the meaning of the Employment Rights Act 1996 despite being treated as self-employed by the company that engaged their services. In response to these developments, the Government commissioned an independent review to consider how employment practices need to change in order to keep pace with modern business models. Changes can therefore be expected in this area in the future.

HMRC provide separate guidance for contractors in the construction industry, where special rules apply — see CHAPTER **44**. There are also special rules for some taxpayers including agency workers (see below), entertainers, cleaners, individuals employed by their spouse, and individuals employed by a relative in a private dwelling house. HMRC guidance is available at www.gov.uk/gov ernment/collections/employed-or-self-employed.

Most agency workers are required to be treated as employees and there are rules to prevent the avoidance of employment taxes and obligations by disguising employment as self-employment. For the rules which ensure that the correct amount of tax and NICs is paid when UK and UK Continental Shelf workers are employed by offshore companies or engaged by or through offshore employment intermediaries, see **41.22**. Some members of limited liability partnerships are treated as employed, see **23.33**.

A person can challenge a ruling by HMRC that he is an employee, and some taxpayers have had some success, but this can be costly and time-consuming.

If a taxpayer engages a worker it is the taxpayer's responsibility to determine his or her employment status. See **10.2** regarding the re-classification of workers as employees.

Registering for tax, NICs and VAT

[19.3] Once a person has established self-employment he has responsibilities in relation to tax, NICs and possibly VAT. HMRC's leaflet SE1 — Thinking of working for yourself? — sets out the basic requirements for those who have started, or are thinking of starting, in business. The newly self-employed can also telephone a helpline on 0300 200 3500 for guidance.

A person may register for tax and NICs by telephoning the helpline or online via www.gov.uk/topic/business-tax/self-employed. There are penalties for failure to notify chargeability (see **9.60**).

HMRC provide online presentations, e-learning courses and access to tax information videos on their website (see www.gov.uk/government/collections/hmrc-webinars-email-alerts-and-videos). A new HMRC 'Small Business On-line Forum' aims to answer general tax questions and provide support with starting, running and selling a business, see www.gov.uk/government/news/new-help-for-small-businesses-launched. Help on PAYE matters for new employers is available at www.gov.uk/topic/business-tax/paye. The Government's website at www.gov.uk/ provides information and support on a wide range of topics including tax and VAT, employment, health and safety, sales and marketing, and sources of finance. See, in particular, www.gov.uk/browse/business/setting-up.

Personal service companies (ITEPA 2003, ss 48–61, 339A; ITTOIA 2005, ss 148K, 163, 164; SI 2000/727; NICA 2014, s 2; FA 2017, s 6 and Sch 1)

[19.4] Special rules known as the IR35 rules prevent people paying substantially less tax and NICs by operating through an intermediary, such as a personal service company or partnership, than they would have to pay if they were employed directly. Separate rules to counter avoidance through the use of 'managed service companies' were introduced in 2007 (see **19.14** onwards).

The personal service companies rules apply where a worker provides services under a contract between a client and an intermediary company or partnership that meets certain conditions, and the income would have been treated as employment income if the worker had contracted directly with the client. The rules apply whether the client is a business or a private individual, so that they apply to domestic workers such as nannies provided by a service company. The IR35 provisions apply to office holders for 2013–14 onwards. The existing tests to differentiate employment from self-employment outlined at **19.1** above still apply.

HMRC provide guidance at www.gov.uk/topic/business-tax/ir35 and in their Employment Status Manual. The status tests set out in the manual were, however, criticised by the judge in a judicial review of the IR35 rules, although the judge found that the rules were not a breach of the human rights legislation and European law, and following an appeal on the European issue the Court of Appeal also found that European law was not contravened. Many IR35 cases have come before the appeal commissioners and tribunals but each depended on the particular circumstances and no clear guidelines have emerged. Careful drafting of the contract is essential and professional advice is recommended.

Improvements have been made in recent years to the way in which IR35 is administered. HMRC's stated intention was to make a thorough overhaul of the administration of the provisions, focusing on—

(a)   providing greater pre-transaction certainty, including a dedicated help-line staffed by specialists;

(b)   providing greater clarity by publishing guidance on those types of cases HMRC view as outside the scope of IR35;

(c)   restricting reviews to high risk cases carried out only by specialists teams; and

(d)   promoting more effective engagement with interested parties through an IR35 Forum to monitor HMRC's new approach.

The dedicated IR35 helpline number is 0300 123 2326. As well as answering one-off queries, the helpline provides a review service, and both the helpline and the review service are independent of HMRC compliance staff, so queries regarding IR35 will not be passed on to other staff. If a taxpayer decides to use the contract review service, and HMRC conclude that the contract is outside IR35, they will provide the taxpayer with a certificate with a unique number. This certificate will be valid for three years. If HMRC subsequently open an IR35 review, on production of the number they will suspend the review while they consider all the information. They will close the review if the contract they reviewed is typical of the taxpayer's engagement terms and conditions, and the information provided is accurate.

[19.5] A company is within the IR35 provisions if the worker (alone or together with his associates) has a material interest in the company (i.e. broadly, he owns or controls more than 5% of the ordinary share capital or has rights to more than 5% of any distributions from the company), or he receives or could receive payments or benefits which are not salary but which could reasonably be taken to represent payment for services provided to clients. A partnership is within the provisions if the worker (alone or together with relatives) is entitled to 60% or more of the partnership profits, or where most of the partnership profits come from work for a single client, or where a partner's profit share is based on his income from relevant contracts.

[19.6] Unless the client is a public authority (as to which, see **19.13**), where the rules apply and the intermediary is a company, the company operates PAYE and accounts for tax and Class 1 NICs on the worker's earnings during the tax year in the normal way (see **10.58**), and pays Class 1A NICs (see **10.49**) on any benefits provided.

At the end of the year, the excess of the amount of cash and non-cash benefits that the company has received from clients for the worker's services (net of VAT and net of allowable expenses, see **19.7**, paid by the company) over the amount the company has paid to the worker as earnings plus non-cash benefits (including mileage allowance payments for use of the worker's own car and 5p per mile passenger payments if relevant — see **10.17** to **10.19**) is treated as pay on 5 April and liable to PAYE tax and Class 1 NICs accordingly. This means that the extra tax and NICs are payable by 19 April after the year-end and penalties and interest will be charged on underpayments from that date (but see **19.12** regarding an HMRC concession).

This deemed employment payment is included in the worker's year-end earnings certificate P60 and will be shown on his self-assessment return. (It is not, however, included in income for tax credits purposes.)

An employment allowance of £3,000 per year can be offset against employer Class 1 NICs (see **10.66**). For companies and businesses within IR35, the employment allowance can be claimed in relation to NICs on salary payments but not against any NICs liabilities arising from a deemed employment payment.

[19.7] When calculating the deemed employment payment, the intermediary's allowable expenses broadly comprise a flat-rate allowance of 5% of the net of VAT payment for the relevant contracts, expenses paid by the intermediary (or by the worker and reimbursed by the intermediary) that would have been allowable to an employee of the client, capital allowances that could have been claimed by the worker, employer pension contributions, and the amount of Class 1 and Class 1A employer's NICs paid by the company in respect of the worker's earnings. Allowable expenses include mileage allowances, on the same basis as if the worker had been employed direct by the client and had used his own car for the client's business (see **10.17**). However, from 6 April 2016 travel and subsistence expenses incurred on an ordinary commute from home to the client's premises are no longer allowable.

Where a salaried member of a limited liability partnership (LLP) provides services through an intermediary which is itself a member of the LLP, and that income is deemed to be the salaried member's employment income (see **23.33**), it is not included in the deemed employment payment where the IR35 rules also apply to that member.

[19.8] The excess amount arrived at is treated as inclusive of employer's Class 1 NICs, which are then deducted to arrive at the deemed employment payment.

Example 1

During 2017–18 the client pays £50,000 to the company for the worker's services. The contract is caught by the IR35 rules. The company pays the worker's salary of £18,000 through PAYE and provides taxable benefits of £2,000. It also pays pension contributions of £4,000. The deemed employment payment is:

		£	£
Total from client			50,000
Less:	5% × 50,000	2,500	
	Pension contributions	4,000	
	Employer's NICs on £20,000 (Class 1 £1,357, Class 1A £276)	1,633	(8,133)
			41,867
Less:	Salary actually paid and benefits provided		(20,000)
Excess amount			21,867
Less:	Employer's Class 1 NICs therein (13.8/113.8)		(2,652)
			£19,215

The company is deemed to pay the worker £19,215 on 5 April 2018 and must account for PAYE tax and NICs thereon by 19 April 2018.

[19.9] Similar provisions apply where the intermediary is a partnership receiving gross payment under a contract. The worker is deemed to receive employment income on 5 April, and liable to tax and NICs accordingly, and such income will be excluded from the worker's share of the partnership profits (although small amounts of employment income may be left as part of partnership profits).

[19.10] The deemed employment payment and the intermediary's NICs thereon are allowable deductions in computing the intermediary's profits of the accounting period in which the deemed payment is treated as made for corporation tax purposes or, if earlier, the accounting period in which the trade ceases. However, this relief is not available if profits are calculated on the cash basis for small businesses (see **20.4**).

[19.11] It is important to realise that later payments of salary by reference to the deemed employment payment at 5 April *cannot* be made free of tax and NICs. Actual salary payments reduce the deemed payment of the tax year in which they are *paid*. The only way to avoid double taxation on the deemed payment is to pay a dividend. The company may make a claim to regard the dividend as reduced by the deemed payment (net of tax and employee's NICs). This relief applies to dividends paid to the worker before dividends paid to anyone else, and to dividends paid in the same tax year as the deemed payment before dividends paid in later years. When the relief is claimed, the company's distributions will be reduced accordingly. The amount of the worker's dividend income would be similarly reduced. The dividend received would, however, count as income for tax credits purposes (see **2.34**).

[19.12] The time frame for paying the tax and NICs due on deemed employment payments (see **19.6**) is very short. By concession, HMRC will accept a provisional payment on account of the tax and NICs due on the deemed employment payment if the employer is unable to calculate the amount by 19 April. The provisional calculation of the deemed payment should be reported on an FPS on or before 5 April. No penalties will be charged so long as the employer files an Earlier Year Update (EYU), and pays any balance of tax and NICs due by the following 31 January, but interest will be payable. Unpaid amounts may be collected direct from the worker if the company does not pay.

The deemed employment payment is not wages for the purposes of the national minimum wage/national living wage, so that actual pay (excluding benefits other than accommodation) must be sufficient to meet the national minimum wage/national living wage requirements (see **19.22**).

HMRC's view is that the legislation preventing agency workers from avoiding employment taxes and obligations by disguising employment as self-employment will not generally apply where a worker is engaged via a personal service company.

Services provided to the public sector

[19.13] From 2017–18 the rules for engagements between an intermediary and a public authority are different. The public authority (as defined) is responsible for deciding whether the IR35 rules apply, and if so the authority has to pay to HMRC the tax and NICs on deemed direct payments (DDPs) made to the intermediary, deducting those amounts from the amount it pays to the intermediary. A deemed direct payment is a payment in money or money's worth or in the form of a benefit, reasonably taken to be for the worker's services to the public authority client. The amount of the DDP subject to tax is net of any VAT, cost of the intermediary's materials, and if agreed by the person making the payment, expenses met by the intermediary which would have been deductible had they been incurred by the worker, e.g. reimbursed expenses. The 5% flat-rate allowance which can be claimed against the deemed employment payment in non-public sector engagements cannot be deducted. A DDP is not brought into account in calculating the intermediary's profits. The rules apply to DDPs made after 5 April 2017 even if relating to services provided before that date. For HMRC guidance see www.gov.uk/guidance/off-payroll-working-in-the-public-sector-reform-of-intermediaries-legislation.

Managed service companies (ITEPA 2003, ss 61A–61J, 688A; ITTOIA 2005, ss 148K, 164A)

[19.14] Rules were introduced from 6 April 2007 to counter tax avoidance by the use of managed service companies (MSCs). Following the introduction of these provisions, MSCs appeared unlikely to be commercially viable.

The definition of MSC covers both companies and partnerships. MSCs are similar to personal service companies (as to which see **19.4** onwards), but are usually provided by an outside business that controls the administration and financial management. The personal service company rules do not apply to those within the scope of the MSC legislation. The MSC provisions apply where the business consists wholly or mainly of providing the services of an individual to another person, the individual receives most or all of the payment for his services, he receives a greater amount (net of tax and NICs) than he would have received as employment income, and an MSC provider is 'involved' with the MSC. An MSC provider is someone who is in business to promote the use of companies to provide the services of individuals. The MSC provider is involved with the MSC if it benefits financially, or influences the provision of the individual's services or the way they are paid for, or influences or controls the company's finances or activities, or undertakes to make good any tax loss.

[19.15] The MSC rules require payments for services provided through such companies that are not already treated as employment income to be treated as a deemed employment payment by the MSC. The deemed employment payment is arrived at by deducting expenses that would have been allowable, and also employers' NICs that would have been payable. Tax will not be charged if there would have been no tax liability in a direct worker/client relationship by reason of the worker being resident or domiciled abroad (see CHAPTER 41), or having had a three-year period of non-residence broadly within the three years before the tax year concerned, or the client being resident abroad, or the services being provided outside the UK. Where the worker is UK resident and provides the services in the UK, the MSC is treated as having a UK place of business whether it actually has one or not.

[19.16] If a company that is treated as making a deemed employment payment pays a dividend in the same or following tax year, it may claim to reduce the amount of the dividend for tax purposes by the deemed employment payment.

[19.17] Where HMRC consider that an amount of PAYE is due that has not been paid, they can recover it from a director, office-holder or associate of the MSC, the MSC provider, or someone who has been actively involved in providing the worker's services (excluding those providing legal or accountancy advice in their professional capacity).

[19.18] In computing its own profits, the MSC may deduct the deemed employment payment and employers' NICs thereon paid by the MSC. The deduction cannot, however, create a loss. This relief is not available to a partnership if profits are calculated on the cash basis for small businesses (see 20.4).

Computation of taxable profits

[19.19] CHAPTER 20 examines the detailed rules for calculating profits, which from 2013–14 can be calculated on the cash basis by certain unincorporated businesses. CHAPTER 22 deals with capital allowances for the purchase of equipment, etc.

A newly-established business is often run from home, perhaps using an existing car for any business travelling that is required. A claim can be made for the business proportion of car expenses, and also the business proportion of capital allowances on the value of the car at the time it was first used for business (or the purchase price if less). A deduction can also be claimed for business use of home telephone. Where the business is run from home, expenses of part of the home can be allowed against taxable profits if they are wholly and exclusively for the business, so that a proportion of, for example, the light and heat can be charged for the part of the residence used for the business, such as a study/office, surgery, workshop, etc. The business may be liable to pay business rates on that part of the property (but see **30.23**), as well as paying the council tax on the rest of the property (see **8.2**). If paid, business rates are allowable in calculating taxable profits. Where business rates are not paid, an appropriate proportion of the council tax can be treated as a business expense according to the business use of the home. Individuals in unincorporated businesses may use simplified fixed rate expenses for vehicle expenditure and business use of the home (see **20.19**).

Under self-assessment details of the business income and expenses have to be shown under specified headings in the tax return. If turnover is below £85,000 (£83,000 for 2016–17) the 'short' self-employment pages designed for more straightforward businesses may be completed in most cases. Alternatively, if other circumstances permit, the short tax return (SA200) may be completed (see **9.19**).

This does not mean that the detailed information should not be kept. Keeping records is often not a strong point for many small businesses, but under self-assessment it is vital that adequate records relating to business expenses (and indeed other tax liabilities — see **9.32**) are kept, and that, if challenged, the way in which the allowable part of mixed expenses has been calculated can be justified.

If no part of the home is used wholly and exclusively for the business, capital gains tax private residence relief (see **30.3**) will not be affected. If part of the property is so used, that part will be outside the capital gains tax owner-occupier exemption. Any gain need not be charged to tax immediately if the property is sold and the business is continued from a new residence, because a rollover relief claim may be made for the gain to be regarded as reducing the cost for capital gains tax of the business part of the new residence (see **29.16**), although it would not be necessary to make that claim if the chargeable gain was covered by the annual capital gains tax exemption (see **4.29**).

Example 2

House bought June 2001 for £60,000, sold June 2017 for £220,000.

Used to June 2011 wholly as residence then 1/6th for self-employment for remainder of period

Total gain (£220,000 – £60,000)	£160,000
Chargeable gain: Business use 1/6th for 5 years out of 15: 1/6 × 5/15 × £160,000	£8,889

The chargeable gain is covered by the 2017–18 annual exempt amount of £11,300 unless the exemption is already used against other gains.

Small amounts of trading or miscellaneous income (ITTOIA 2005, ss 783A–783AR)

[19.20] Someone who occasionally buys and sells may contend that his activities are not a trade but remain a hobby, a collector's activity or an investment, such as collecting and restoring antique furniture, sometimes selling the occasional piece at a profit. Buying and selling on eBay can in many cases be trading though HMRC's original guidance on this matter has been withdrawn. Self-assessment tax returns tell taxpayers to contact their tax office if they are unsure whether they are carrying on a business or not. If they do not do so, and HMRC subsequently enquire into their tax position, they could be faced with interest and penalties for non-disclosure.

September 2017 Finance Bill, which is expected to receive Royal Assent in November 2017, introduces a £1,000 allowance for trading income from 6 April 2017 (i.e. the basis period relating to 2017–18) and it is aimed at internet sellers and others who earn small amounts of income from occasional jobs. It applies equally to professions and vocations. The allowance is not available on income of partners or participators in a close company (see **3.29**), or where rent-a-room relief (see **30.12**) is, or could be claimed. An anti-avoidance provision also prevents an employer from trying to reclassify payments to employees as trading income to take advantage of the allowance. The restriction where rent-a-room relief could be claimed is intended to prevent individuals from using the trading allowance if they choose to deduct actual expenses in calculating the profits of any other trade, such as a bed and breakfast business within their own home.

Where the total receipts from all trades plus any miscellaneous income in the tax year are less than £1,000, the allowance is given automatically in full so that no tax is payable and the income does not have to be declared. This is, however, subject to an election which can be made on or before the first anniversary of the normal self-assessment filing date for the tax year for full relief not to be given. The most obvious situation where the election could be made is if expenses exceed receipts resulting in a loss. Care needs to be taken, particularly in early years of a new business, if receipts are below £1,000 and set up costs are high, to ensure the deadline for electing out if the automatic allowance is not missed, otherwise losses will be forfeited.

Where the total receipts from all trades plus any miscellaneous income in the tax year exceed the £1,000 allowance an election can still be made for partial relief, where the allowance is deducted from the receipts instead of the actual allowable expenses. This will clearly be beneficial if the expenses are less than the £1,000 allowance. The individual can decide how the £1,000 allowance should be split between two or more trades, or between trades and miscellaneous income.

It may be HMRC rather than the taxpayer who take the view that an activity is a hobby, particularly where there are large losses, because to accept that it is a commercial activity would open the way for loss reliefs against other income. Each case depends on the facts, with appropriate rights of appeal if HMRC do not see it in the same way as the taxpayer.

Pension provision

[19.25] Earnings from a small business can support a personal pension contribution, both in respect of the self-employed earnings and for the family employees. It does not matter that the self-employed taxpayer or family employee is also in separate pensionable employment. Tax relief can be obtained on the greater of £3,600 or the amount of earnings. Tax relief for more substantial contributions is limited by reference to annual and lifetime allowances. See CHAPTERS 16 and 17 for details.

VAT registration

[19.26] A business must register for VAT at the end of any month if turnover in the previous 12 months exceeded £85,000 (from 1 April 2017, previously £83,000). A business is required to notify HMRC and will then be registered unless it can show that turnover will not exceed £83,000 (previously £81,000) in the coming 12 months. If a business expects turnover in the next 30 days to exceed £85,000, it must register immediately. These limits must be monitored carefully because there are severe penalties for not complying with the rules. Even if turnover is below the limit a business may wish to register voluntarily in order to recover input VAT on purchases, although this will not be an advantage unless most customers are VAT-registered. There is a special VAT flat-rate scheme for small businesses. See CHAPTER 7.

National insurance contributions

[19.27] For the tax year 2017–18, a self-employed person pays Class 2 contributions of £2.85 a week, and also Class 4 contributions at 9% on profits between £8,164 and £45,000 and 2% on profits above that level. The detailed provisions are in CHAPTER 24.

There are penalties for failure to notify chargeability to tax and NICs (see 9.60). See 10.66 regarding the employment allowance of £3,000 per year which most employers can claim to offset against their Class 1 secondary NICs. The allowance is claimed as part of the normal payroll process through RTI.

Occasional earnings not treated as from self-employment

[19.28] If a person is not treated as self-employed, occasional earnings are taxed according to the amount earned in the tax year, with a deduction for justifiable expenses. The tax should be accounted for in the self-assessment along with the tax on other income. If the person is also an employee, HMRC will sometimes, for convenience, offset small amounts of occasional earnings against tax allowances when arriving at the PAYE code number.

Any losses can be set off against relevant miscellaneous income (see **2.29**), but it is unlikely that there will be any, in which case the losses are carried forward to reduce any future relevant miscellaneous income.

The £1,000 trading allowance may be available from 6 April 2017, see **19.20**.

Tax points

[19.29] Note the following:

- When a new business starts, there will be a tax liability for the tax year in which the business starts, unless the profit is covered by reliefs and allowances. If a tax return is not issued, the taxpayer must let HMRC know that he has taxable profits by 5 October following the tax year (see **9.34**), otherwise he will be liable to a penalty (see **9.60**). Unless he expects profits to be below the small profits threshold he will need to arrange to pay Class 2 NICs (see **24.4**).
- Losses incurred in the early years of a business may be set against income of the three previous tax years subject to a cap from 2013–14 (see **25.3**).
- If turnover is below £85,000 (£83,000 for 2016–17) the 'short' self-employment pages of the tax return, or the short tax return, can usually be completed — see **9.19**.
- A business should not take people on without making sure of their employment status. If a mistake is made there are only limited rights to recover underpaid tax and NICs from the worker, and interest and penalties may have to be paid as well.
- A useful test on the self-employed status is whether there is a risk of loss as well as gain, normally implying self-employment; and whether the worker has to carry out corrective work without payment.
- The rules for personal service companies bring enormous practical problems for those affected. A deemed employment payment under the IR35 rules is generally treated in the same way as actual pay, so that it counts as earnings in calculating the maximum permissible pension contributions but not in reckoning income for tax credits. On the other hand, a dividend paid out of profits represented by the deemed employment payment *is* reckoned in calculating income for tax credits.
- A business should not forget to register for VAT if appropriate. A check must be made at the end of every *month* to make sure that the annual turnover limit has not been exceeded. See **19.26** and CHAPTER 7.
- If a spouse or civil partner works in the business, then even if he or she is paid as a self-employed person issuing invoices (and charging and accounting for VAT if appropriate), for NICs purposes they are regarded as employed, and Class 1 contributions are payable (see **13.2**).

20

How are business profits calculated?

Background (ITTOIA 2005, Pt 2; CTA 2009, Pt 3)

[20.1] Taxable profits from trades, professions and vocations are broadly calculated in the same way. It is usually obvious that a trade is being carried on, but the charge on trading profits is extended beyond what would normally be regarded as trading and can cover occasional transactions and those to which an investment motive cannot be attributed, where the circumstances point to a trading intention.

Important indicators of possible trading, when there is any doubt, are the nature of the asset itself (e.g. if it is income producing, or something to get enjoyment from owning that would indicate investment rather than trading); the reason for acquiring it; how long it is owned; whether it was worked on to make it more saleable; the reason for selling; and how often such transactions were undertaken.

General rules for computing trading profits (FA 2005, ss 80–83 and Sch 4; ITTOIA 2005, ss 25, 25A, 33, 34; ITA 2007, s 997; CTA 2009, Pt 3 Chs 3–5; CTA 2010, ss 996, 1127)

[20.2] Before 6 April 2013, profits of all businesses, whether an individual trader, a partnership or a company, had to be calculated in accordance with generally accepted accounting practice (referred to here as the accruals basis) so as to give a true and fair view. While the accruals basis still applies to companies and the majority of unincorporated businesses, from 2013–14 eligible individuals carrying on a trade or profession as self-employed sole traders or in partnership with other individuals can choose to calculate taxable income using a cash basis (see **20.4**).

Where profits are calculated on the accruals basis they are then subject to adjustment as required by tax legislation, for example the prohibition of relief for items of a capital nature (see **20.11**).

Some of the rules used to calculate profits apply to both the cash basis and the accruals basis, others apply specifically to one or the other. The most important rule for expenses that broadly applies to both bases, unless otherwise stated elsewhere in this chapter, is that they must be wholly and exclusively for the purposes of the trade (see **20.5**).

Income received in non-monetary form should be brought into account when calculating taxable trading profits.

Some different rules apply for companies compared with unincorporated businesses in relation to the tax treatment of certain expenditure. The main areas are the treatment of 'loan relationships' (see **3.6** and **26.8**), intangible assets (see **20.35** to **20.41**), cleaning up contaminated or derelict land (see **20.42**), and various reliefs related to research and development (see **29.64** to **29.67**). The amount deductible from profits for tax purposes under the contaminated or derelict land and research and development provisions is greater than the amount of the expenditure, and loss-making companies may claim a cash payment in respect of the appropriate part of their unrelieved losses.

There are special 'transfer pricing' rules for businesses that are connected with one another, in particular companies in the same group, to require an arm's length price to be used on transactions between them. These are dealt with briefly in **45.30**.

See **19.20** regarding the £1,000 trading allowance available from 6 April 2017.

The Office of Tax Simplification (OTS) has published a report on simplification of the corporation tax computation. Recommendations include aligning the computation more closely with the company accounts and replacing capital allowances with a tax deduction for accounts depreciation.

Alternative finance arrangements (ITA 2007, Pt 10A; CTA 2009, ss 501–521)

[20.3] There are various finance arrangements, in particular those designed to meet the requirements of Islamic law, that do not involve paying or receiving interest but have a similar effect. The legislation broadly equates the tax treatment of such payments and receipts with the treatment of interest. They are therefore brought into account for individuals and partnerships as trading expenses or trading receipts and for companies under the loan relationships rules outlined in **3.6**.

The cash basis for small businesses (ITTOIA 2005, ss 25A, 31A–31F; SI 2017/293)

[20.4] Eligible individuals carrying on a trade, profession or vocation (referred to in this commentary as trade etc.) as self-employed sole traders or in partnership with other individuals may elect to use the cash basis to calculate the profits of the trade etc. instead of using the accruals basis (see **20.2**). To be able to make the election for a tax year, the person must not be an excluded person and the aggregate of cash basis receipts of each trade etc. carried on by them in that tax year must not exceed the relevant maximum.

In the case of partners and partnerships, the aggregate of cash basis receipts for each trade etc. carried on by an individual who controls a partnership, or a partnership controlled by an individual must not exceed the relevant maximum and the partnership or individual (as the case may be) must have also made the election. Thus partnerships with a controlling partner must add the partnership cash basis receipts to the cash basis receipts of any other businesses carried on by the controlling partner. If the resulting figure exceeds the relevant maximum amount, it will not be possible for the partnership or any of the other businesses to use the cash basis. If the resulting figure is less than or equal to the relevant maximum amount, the partnership or any of the other businesses may elect to use the cash basis. If such an election is made, the profits or losses of all the businesses, including the partnership, must be calculated using the cash basis.

The relevant maximum is the higher of £150,000 or the VAT threshold (before 2017–18, the VAT threshold), or in the case of a universal credit claimant (see **10.6**), the higher of £300,000 or twice the VAT threshold (before 2017–18, twice the VAT threshold). The threshold is proportionately reduced if the basis period is less than 12 months.

Example 1

A and B are 50/50 partners in AB partnership and the partnership cash basis receipts for year ended 5 April 2018 are £95,000. A has a separate sole trade with cash basis receipts for the same period of £50,000. B also has a separate sole trade for which cash basis receipts for the same period are £190,000. Neither claims universal credit.

The partnership can elect to calculate its profits using the cash basis, as the partnership receipts do not exceed the relevant maximum for the tax year. As there is no controlling partner, it is not necessary to take into account A's or B's receipts from their sole trades.

Since A's sole trade receipts do not exceed the relevant maximum, she can also elect to use the cash basis to calculate her profits from her trade, even if the partnership chooses not to make a cash basis election.

B's sole trade receipts mean that she is ineligible to use the cash basis.

An excluded person is a partnership in which at least one of the partners is not an individual, a limited liability partnership (see **23.33**), a Lloyd's underwriter, a person who has made a herd basis election (see **31.8**) or an averaging election (see **31.6**) for the tax year, a person who has claimed business premises renovation allowances within the previous seven years (see **32.19**), a person who has carried on mineral extraction in the basis period for the tax year (see **22.50**), and a person who, at any time before the basis period for the tax year, has claimed research and development allowances and who still owns an asset representing the expenditure (see **22.49**).

An election for the cash basis has effect for the tax year in which it is made for all trades etc. carried on by the person in that year and continues to apply until the person's circumstances change such that, broadly, their receipts exceed the higher of £300,000 or twice the VAT threshold (before 2017–18, twice the VAT threshold), they are an excluded person, or it is more appropriate for profits to be calculated under the accruals basis and the person elects to calculate their profits that way (i.e. they do not tick the cash basis box on the tax return). This could apply when their business is expanding and they want to claim more than £500 for interest on cash borrowing (see **20.17**), or they wish to claim sideways loss relief (see **25.3**). If their receipts exceed the applicable limit, they must leave the cash basis in the following year unless their receipts again drop below limit. A cash basis election may still be made again in a later tax year if the conditions are met. The legislation does not provide a specific time limit for the making of the election, and it should be made by ticking a box when the tax return is filed.

Profits of the trade etc. are calculated on the cash basis by deducting the total amount of trade expenses in the basis period for the tax year from the total amount of receipts for that basis period, subject to any adjustments required by law. Where there is a difference between the amount brought into account in respect of a transaction and the amount which would be brought in if the transaction was at arm's length, then the amount brought in must be a just and reasonable amount, although this does not apply to capital receipts (see **20.11**) or gifts to charities.

The provisions in **20.23** regarding the adjustments required on the change of basis in computing profits apply to a change to or from the cash basis.

Many of the provisions relating to expenditure allowable under the accruals basis do not apply under the cash basis, and alternative rules apply. The different rules are explained in the following relevant paragraphs. For the restrictions on loss relief which apply to cash basis businesses see CHAPTER 25. For the differing rules for capital allowances see **20.11**.

'Wholly and exclusively' (ITTOIA 2005, ss 34, 57A; CTA 2009, s 54)

[20.5] A simplified fixed rate deduction may be made for vehicle expenditure, business use of the home and private use of business premises (see **20.19**). The comments below are only relevant where the fixed rate deductions are not claimed.

A sole trader or partner cannot deduct an expense that is incurred for both business and private purposes, such as clothing bought primarily for business but also for private purposes, whether they calculate profits on the cash basis or the accruals basis. See, however, **20.17** regarding the deduction of interest on the cash basis, which may still be deducted up to a limit, even if not incurred wholly and exclusively for business purposes.

Part of a mixed expense may, however, be incurred wholly and exclusively for the purposes of the trade and thus be deductible in calculating profits, such as the business element of line rental and call charges for business telephone calls from a home telephone. The same applies to mixed business and living accommodation, where again it may be possible accurately to separate the business and private areas (see **19.19**). Where meals are taken while working away from the place of business, the cost is not generally regarded as wholly and exclusively for business, however, those who travel regularly in their work, and those who make occasional business journeys outside the normal pattern, are entitled to claim for reasonable expenses incurred. Where one or more nights need to be spent away from home, reasonable costs of overnight accommodation and subsistence are allowed.

[20.6] Sole traders or partners may have some car mileage which is wholly and exclusively for business, some which is purely for private purposes, and some may be partly both. Where expenditure is for the sole purpose of the business, any incidental private benefit would be ignored. But if trips are undertaken both for business and private purposes, strictly no claim can be made for a deduction for any part of the expenses, even though the business derives benefit from the trip. Providing the trip has a genuine business purpose, however, in practice a claim is allowed for an expenses deduction based on the time spent on business.

Example 2

A trader's recorded mileage in a 12-month period of account was as follows:

	Number of miles
Purely business journeys	5,000
Purely private journeys	4,000
Home to business	2,000
Journeys for combined business/private purposes	1,000
	7,000
	12,000

Allowable business proportion is 5/12ths. In addition, a deduction could usually be claimed for an appropriate proportion of the expenses for the mixed purpose journeys.

Alternatively the simplified fixed rate deductions for vehicle expenditure may be used, see **20.19**.

[20.7] In the case of a company, there can be no private use by the company itself. Where a company or unincorporated employer incurs expenses that benefit employees or directors, the usual treatment is that the expenses are allowed in calculating the taxable profits of the employer, but are treated as taxable earnings of the employee or director (see CHAPTER 10). Sometimes, directors' fees, wages paid or the cost of benefits provided to members of the family who do not work full-time may not be allowed in full if the payment is considered excessive in relation to the work done, because it would then not be regarded as wholly and exclusively for the business. It is also particularly important where a business employs family members that payment of wages is properly made (see **19.22**).

In the case of family and similar companies, a distinction must be drawn between company expenditure which benefits a shareholder who is a director and the payment by the company of the personal debts of the shareholder/director, for example school fees, private entertaining, or expenses of a private residence. A payment for personal debts should be treated as a payment of salary, and declared on form P11D (see **10.10**), and Class 1 NICs should be accounted for at the time of the payment. If HMRC discover that the payment has not been properly dealt with, they will normally treat the amount as a loan which the shareholder/director must repay to the company and it is then neither an allowable business expense nor taxed as a benefit on the shareholder/director. The loan has tax consequences both for the company and the director, and possible NICs consequences — see **12.13** to **12.16**.

In family companies, loans to directors and employees may sometimes be written off. For non-shareholder directors and employees, the amount written off is treated as taxable pay (see **10.48**) and is allowed as a deduction in calculating the taxable profits of the company, subject to what is said above about remuneration that is excessive for the work done. If the director or employee is a shareholder, special rules apply to prevent the company obtaining a deduction for the write-off, and to treat it as dividend income of the shareholder. See **12.15**.

[20.8] Where an employer takes out insurance against loss of profits arising from the death, accident or illness of a key employee, the premiums will usually be allowable in calculating trading profits and any policy proceeds treated as a trading receipt. If in the event of accident or illness the benefits of the policy were passed on to the employee, they would be taxed either as normal pay if the employee had a contractual right to them or as sick pay.

[20.9] Any accountancy expenses that relate to calculating the tax on profits rather than calculating the profits themselves are incurred in the capacity of taxpayer rather than trader, so they are not strictly deductible in calculating taxable profits. In practice such expenses are allowed, except where they arise as a result of an HMRC enquiry into an individual's tax affairs. Even then, they will be allowed if adjustments arising from the enquiry are made to the current year only and they do not arise through careless or deliberate behaviour.

[20.10] The costs of preparing a trader's tax return or calculating capital gains are not allowable, but if such matters are straightforward these costs are likely to be fairly low. Where a business is run through a company, and the company's accountants deal with the directors' tax returns, it is preferable for the work for the directors to be billed to them directly. If, in that event, the bill is actually paid by the company, then unless the amount has been charged to the director's loan account the company would be settling the director's personal liability and the director should be charged to tax and Class 1 NICs through the PAYE system on the amount paid. If the company has contracted with the accountant for dealing with directors' tax returns, the fees, including VAT, should be treated as a benefit in kind to the directors (as to which see CHAPTER 10). The company would be allowed a deduction for the amount paid in calculating its taxable profits, so long as the total remuneration falls within the wholly and exclusively rule.

Capital or revenue (ITTOIA 2005, ss 32A, 33, 33A, 96A, 96B, 240A–240E; CTA 2009, s 53)

[20.11] In general revenue expenditure is an allowable expense in calculating taxable profit unless specifically prohibited, such as business entertaining expenses (see **20.15**).

Where profits are calculated on the accruals basis (see **20.2**), a capital expense cannot be deducted in calculating profits, although many items of capital expenditure may attract capital allowances (see CHAPTER 22). The usual definition of a capital expense is one made 'not only once and for all, but with a view to bringing into existence an asset or an advantage for the enduring benefit of the trade'. One person's stock in trade will be another person's fixed assets. Business premises are clearly a capital item, but if a business builds and sells factories, the factories will be trading stock and the cost will be taken into account in calculating profit. Cars used by traders and employees are capital items, but cars held for sale by a motor dealer are trading stock. Normally, repair expenditure is revenue expenditure and is allowable in calculating profits, but if a trader buys a capital asset that cannot be used in the business until it is renovated, the cost of renovating it is part of the capital cost. The distinction is often hard to draw, and has led to many disputes between the taxpayer and HMRC which have had to be settled by the courts.

Similar considerations apply in deciding whether a particular item is reckonable as trading income or as a capital profit. However, where profits are (or, from 2017–18 as provided by September 2017 Finance Bill (see below), have been) calculated on the cash basis (see **20.4**) there are further considerations. Where expenditure on acquiring, creating or improving an asset has been brought into account in calculating the profit, then any proceeds from the disposal of, or grant of a right or interest in, the asset, or any damages, insurance proceeds or compensation received in respect of it must be included as a trading receipt. There are rules for dealing with the change in business use of the asset in these circumstances.

Under the cash basis, certain capital expenditure is allowable as a deduction in calculating profits. Before 2017–18 it was restricted to capital expenditure which would qualify for capital allowances, other than that on the provision of a car (but not a van or motor cycle). September 2017 Finance Bill, which is expected to receive Royal Assent in November 2017, provides that from 2017–18 capital expenditure can be deducted provided it is *not* incurred on:

(a)   the acquisition or disposal of a business or part of a business;
(b)   an asset that has a useful life of more than 20 years;

(c)   an asset not acquired or created for use on a continuing basis in the trade;

(d)   a car or land;

(e)   education or training;

(f)   an intangible asset broadly with a life of more than 20 years; or

(g)   a financial asset.

Although expenditure on fixtures generally qualifies items such as walls, ceilings, doors and windows do not.

Relief for capital expenditure on a car is given via capital allowances. Where a person enters the cash basis any unrelieved qualifying expenditure brought forward for capital allowances purposes from the previous basis period is deductible provided it would have been deductible if incurred during the current basis period. However, where the asset is not fully paid for (for example, on hire purchase), if the amount actually paid exceeds the capital allowances already claimed the excess is deductible, but if it is less than the capital allowances claimed the difference is treated as a receipt.

As indicated at 20.2, the categorisation of expenditure as capital or revenue now differs in certain respects for companies and unincorporated businesses.

Provisions for future liabilities

[20.12] Where profits are calculated on the accruals basis (see **20.2**) provisions for future liabilities are normally allowable for tax purposes, so long as they do not conflict with the tax legislation as interpreted by the courts and they follow accepted accounting practice.

The accepted accounting treatment changed following the issue by the Accounting Standards Board of the former accounting standard FRS 12, which dealt with 'Provisions, Contingent Liabilities and Contingent Assets'. The standard required a provision to be made if, at the balance sheet date, a *present* obligation exists as a result of a *past* event and a *reliable estimate* can be made of the expenditure which will probably be required to meet the obligation. FRS 12 has now been superseded by FRS 102 s 21, which is substantially the same, and FRS 12 was withdrawn for accounting periods commencing on or after 1 January 2015. HMRC's Business Income Manual has guidance on the application of FRS 102 s 21, and the International Accounting Standards equivalent IAS37 at BIM46515. With some exceptions for smaller businesses, the standard needs to be followed for tax purposes, so that appropriate tax adjustments must be made.

Any reductions of earlier provisions that have been allowed in calculating taxable profits increase the taxable profit of the period in which the adjustment is made.

Allowable and non-allowable expenses

[20.13] The principles outlined above provide a broad guide to which expenses are allowed, and points of detail relating to certain expenses are covered below. Some specific examples are listed in **20.32**, including items specifically allowed or disallowed by the tax legislation.

Payment of remuneration (ITTOIA 2005, ss 32A, 36, 37; CTA 2009, ss 1288, 1289)

[20.14] Where profits are calculated on the accruals basis (see **20.2**) directors' and employees' pay may only be taken into account as an expense of the accounting period or period of account to which it relates if it is paid during, or within nine months after the end of, the period. If the payment is provided in the accounts rather than having been paid in the accounting period, there must be sufficient evidence of the liability (e.g. a board minute) for it to be included as an expense in the accounts (see **20.12**). Otherwise, and always where profits are calculated on the cash basis (see **20.4**), it may only be deducted in the period in which it is paid.

Business entertaining (ITTOIA 2005, ss 45–47; CTA 2009, ss 1298–1300)

[20.15] The cost of business entertaining and business gifts (apart from the £50 gifts exemption noted in **20.32**) is not allowable whether profits are calculated on the accruals or the cash basis. Expenditure on entertaining staff (and their guests) is normally allowable, unless it is incidental to entertaining those with whom the employer does business, but there will be a benefits charge on employees (subject to the exception noted at **10.50**).

The VAT position is slightly different. Input VAT on business entertaining of UK customers and non-UK business contacts who are not customers is not recoverable, but where proprietors or employees act as hosts at meals with clients, etc. while away from work on business, input VAT other than that relating to the clients is recoverable (unless business entertainment was the main purpose of the trip). As far as staff entertainment is concerned, the proportion of input VAT relating to *guests* at a staff function is not recoverable, but the proportion relating to staff is recoverable. Input VAT on business entertaining of overseas customers is also recoverable, subject to any output VAT charge on the private use element (see **20.25**). For further details, including the treatment of different entertaining scenarios, see HMRC Brief 44/2010. In the same way as for income tax, there is a £50 gifts exemption (see **7.3**), and input VAT can only be reclaimed on gifts if the cost of the gift and any others given to the same recipient in the same tax year does not exceed £50.

Any unrecovered input VAT on entertaining expenditure is not allowable when calculating taxable profit.

Bad and doubtful debts (ITTOIA 2005, ss 32A, 35, 97; CTA 2009, ss 55, 94, 322–323A, 358–363A, 479, 481, 970)

[20.16] Where profits are calculated on the accruals basis (see **20.2**), but not the cash basis (see **20.4**), normal trading bad debts and specific provisions for bad debts may be deducted from profits for tax purposes. In accordance with the principles outlined in **20.12**, however, a *general* provision for bad debts cannot be allowed in calculating taxable profits. Any specific debts written off or provided for that are subsequently recovered must be included in profits for tax purposes.

A creditor may treat a debt as bad if he has released the debt as part of a statutory insolvency arrangement. The debtor in a voluntary arrangement will not have to bring into his trading profit debts that have been released in this way but debts released other than under such arrangements must be brought in as trading receipts.

For companies, bad debts that do not relate to ordinary trading transactions are dealt with under the loan relationships rules — see **26.8** to **26.9**. However, where a company is released from a trade debt, the release is also taxed under the loan relationship rules. This ensures that if the debtor and the creditor are connected there is no charge on the debtor and no tax relief for the creditor. There are provisions to impose a taxable profit on a debtor when a debt to an unconnected company is acquired at a discount by a company connected to the debtor. There is, however, an exemption from the charge for genuine corporate rescues where the debtor is in financial difficulties. A taxable profit will also be imposed on a debtor where the creditor company becomes connected with it. This now applies in all cases where previously unconnected parties to a loan relationship become connected, not just where the debt is impaired when the parties become connected. See also **12.15** regarding losses on loans to close company directors, employees and shareholders.

There is an exemption for a credit arising on releases that take place on or after 1 January 2015, where immediately before the release it is reasonable to assume that, without the release and any arrangements of which the release forms part, there would be a material risk that at some time in the next 12 months the company would be unable to pay its debts.

Interest paid (TMA 1970, ss 86–87A, 90; TA 1988, ss 826, 826A; ITTOIA 2005, ss 29, 51A, 57B; ITA 2007, Pt 8 Ch 1, Pt 15, s 809ZG; CTA 2009, Pt 5)

[20.17] Interest paid on business borrowings must be wholly and exclusively for the purposes of the business in order to be allowable as a deduction from profits on the accruals basis (see **20.2**).

Where profits are calculated on the cash basis (see **20.4**) the deduction of loan interest, including the incidental costs of obtaining loan finance, is limited to £500 for the period, but does not have to be incurred wholly and exclusively for business purposes. All cash borrowing for business purposes is covered by this provision. Payments of interest on purchases are not subject to the £500 limit, provided the purchase itself is an allowable expense, as this is not cash borrowing.

Companies pay interest in full in a wide range of circumstances. Other interest paid by companies is paid net of income tax at 20%, and the company pays over to HMRC the income tax it has deducted (see **3.23**). Interest relating to the trade is deducted from the company's trading profits. All other interest is taken into account in arriving at the profit or loss on the company's non-trading loan relationships. See **3.6** for details.

Individuals normally pay interest in full and deduct interest relating to the trade as a trading expense. Partners may obtain tax relief for interest on a loan used for lending money or introducing capital to a partnership by deducting the interest from their total income, though this is restricted under the cash basis (see **2.14** and **23.15**). See also **32.8** regarding the restriction of interest from April 2017 on loans to invest in partnerships carrying on a property business where income is generated from a dwelling. Those who introduce funds into their family company may also obtain relief by deduction from total income (see **2.14**). Note, however, that interest against total income is subject to a cap on reliefs from 2013–14 (see **2.13**).

Where interest is paid on borrowing to acquire a property that is partly private and partly business, the interest has to be split to arrive at the part that is allowable as a business expense and the part that is for the living accommodation. This will depend on the respective values of the parts of the property. Where part of the property is sometimes but not always used exclusively for business, the period of business use will also be taken into account.

Since interest on home loans does not qualify for tax relief, individuals should consider business borrowings instead, or if they are partners, borrowing money individually to lend to the firm (see **2.14**), rather than leaving undrawn profits in the business in order to boost the business capital. Capital can also be withdrawn (except to the extent that it represents asset revaluations — see **23.18**), leaving the business to obtain funding from partners' loans or from other sources. If, however, withdrawing funds leads to a proprietor's capital/current account with the business becoming overdrawn, interest on business borrowings that had enabled the drawings to be made would not be wholly and exclusively for the trade. Partners must not withdraw their capital *after* making loans to the business, because to that extent they would be regarded as merely withdrawing what was introduced, with tax relief for interest on the loans being restricted accordingly.

There are some anti-avoidance provisions affecting both individuals and companies, and professional advice is essential.

Where interest arises on overdue or overpaid tax, the treatment is different for individuals and companies. For an individual, interest paid on overdue tax is not allowed in calculating profits and interest received on overpaid tax is not taxable. For a company, interest on overdue and overpaid tax is taken into account in computing profits and losses on the company's loan relationships (see **3.6**).

September 2017 Finance Bill, which is expected to receive Royal Assent in November 2017, provides that from 1 April 2017, there is a corporate interest restriction for companies that have a net interest expense in excess of £2 million. See **3.9**.

Leasing of cars (ITTOIA 2005, ss 32A, 48–50B; CTA 2009, ss 56–58B; SI 2016/984; SI 2017/740)

[20.18] The provisions in this paragraph do not apply where profits are calculated on the cash basis (see **20.4**). Where profits are calculated on the accruals basis (see **20.2**) there is a restriction on deductible hiring costs at a flat rate of 15% for cars with CO_2 emissions of more than 130g/km (to be reduced to 110g/km for contracts entered into from 1 April 2018 for corporation tax and 6 April 2018 for income tax; 160g/km where the hire contract begins before 1 April 2013 but broadly after 31 March 2009 for corporation tax or before 6 April 2013 but broadly after 5 April 2009 for income tax). If there is a subsequent rebate of rentals, the amount brought in as a taxable receipt is reduced in the same proportion. If the rental agreement separately identifies charges for costs such as maintenance in the lease agreement, then those costs should not be included when calculating the restriction, which is only applied to the rental payment. A further restriction will apply where the sole trader or partner uses the car privately.

The restriction does not apply to motor cycles. In addition, there is no restriction on the deductible hiring costs for all cars which were first registered before 1 March 2001, regardless of their CO_2 emissions, cars registered after that date with CO_2 emissions of 130g/km / 160g/km or less (as the case may be), electric cars, and 'qualifying hire cars'. 'Qualifying hire car' for this purpose is generally a car hired under a hire-purchase agreement where there is either no option to purchase or there is an option to purchase at a maximum of 1% of the retail price, or a car leased under a long funding lease.

The restriction on the deductible hiring costs does not apply where, broadly, the car is hired by the taxpayer for a period of not more than 45 consecutive days, or where the taxpayer hires the car out to a customer for a period of more than 45 consecutive days. Further provisions detail how these periods should be calculated and what happens where two or more persons in a chain of leases are connected.

See **20.26** for the VAT position on leased cars.

Simplified fixed rate deductions (ITTOIA 2005, ss 94B–94I)

[20.19] From 2013–14 there is an option for individuals carrying on a trade, profession or vocation alone or in partnership to choose to make fixed rate deductions for vehicle expenditure, expenses relating to the business use of a home, or private use of business premises. The option is not available to partnerships where at least one partner is not an individual.

A fixed rate deduction is allowed for expenditure on acquisition, ownership, hire, leasing or use of a car, motor cycle or goods vehicle where a deduction would be allowed under normal trading income rules, or would be so allowed were it not capital expenditure. A deduction is only allowed if no other deduction is made for that expenditure, if no capital allowances have been claimed on the vehicle and, in the case of a van or motorcycle, a deduction of expenditure on acquisition has not been made in calculating profits on the cash basis (see **20.11**). Once the fixed rate has been used in relation to a particular vehicle, this method of calculation must continue to be used for as long as the vehicle remains in the business. The mileage rate does not include incidental expenses incurred in connection with a particular journey, such as tolls, congestion charges and parking fees. These will be allowable as a deduction where they are incurred solely for business purposes. The business proportion of the finance element of a hire purchase or finance lease may also be claimed as a separate deduction.

The deduction is a fixed rate per mile of business journeys and is the same as HMRC approved mileage rates as set out in **10.17**.

Kind of vehicle	Rate per business mile
Car or goods vehicle	45p for the first 10,000 miles
	25p after that
Motor cycle	24p

The deduction for use of a home for business purposes is calculated as a fixed monthly amount based on the number of hours worked wholly and exclusively on the business by the trader or an employee. The amounts are as follows:

Hours worked per month	Amount per month
25 or more	£10
51 or more	£18
101 or more	£26

The deduction covers household running costs on heat, light, power, telephone and internet, and does not prohibit a separate deduction for fixed costs such as council tax (or domestic rates in Northern Ireland), insurance and mortgage interest where an identifiable proportion can be attributed to business use. Where more than one person does work in the same home at the same time, any hour spent wholly and exclusively on that work is to be taken into account only once. Where the deduction is to be made against partnership profits the use of a partner's home qualifies in the same way as that of an individual and the work can be done by a partner or employee of the partnership. If a partnership makes a claim to use a simplified expense deduction for a partner's home, any deduction made for use of another partner's home in the same period must also be made under these provisions.

Where business premises are used partly for private purposes as a home, for example a small hotel, a fixed rate adjustment may be made in calculating profits to avoid the need to calculate the private use adjustment. The use of a partner's home qualifies in the same way as that of an individual. The non-business use adjustment is a fixed monthly amount to be deducted from the allowable expenses and based on the number of persons who occupy the premises as a home or otherwise than in the course of the trade. The amounts are as follows:

Number of occupants	Amount per month
1	£350
2	£500
3 or more	£650

The number of occupants includes children. The fixed rate includes all household goods and services, food and non-alcoholic drinks and utilities. It does not include mortgage interest, rent of the premises, council tax or rates. A reasonable apportionment of these expenses should be made based on the extent of the private occupation of the premises. See HMRC Brief 14/2013.

From 2016–17, where an individual or partnership has more than one premises which are used both for business and as a home, and makes a claim for a deduction under these provisions, then any deductions for the other premises must also be claimed under these provisions.

For further details on allowable expenses for the business use of a home where a fixed rate deduction is not claimed see **19.19**.

Finance leases of plant and machinery (FA 2006, s 81 and Schs 8, 9; ITTOIA 2005, ss 148ZA–148J; CTA 2010, Pt 21; FA 2011, s 53)

[20.20] The provisions in this paragraph do not apply where profits are calculated on the cash basis (see **20.4**). Although for accounting purposes a trader is treated as owning plant and machinery acquired under a finance lease, it is in law owned by the lessor. The tax treatment used to follow the legal position, so that the lessor was entitled to the capital allowances and the lease rental payments were a revenue expense allowable in calculating profit. This treatment still continues for leases of up to five years (or seven years in some circumstances). For longer leases (referred to as long funding leases) finalised on or after 1 April 2006 (subject to certain transitional provisions), the tax treatment is aligned with the accounting treatment. Lessors cannot claim capital allowances on the cost of the leased asset, and all the rentals received are taken into account in calculating profits. Lessees may claim capital allowances as they would have been able to if they had bought the asset, and may deduct as an expense the part of the rentals on which capital allowances are not available (effectively the finance charge).

Where there is a change on or after 1 January 2011 in the leasing accounting standard a business uses, the business will be treated for tax purposes as if the change had not taken place in most cases.

There are extensive provisions to prevent exploitation of the tax treatment and to align it more closely with the recognised accounting treatment. For a note on the position for capital allowances see **22.5**.

Goods and services for private purposes (TCGA 1992, s 161; ITTOIA 2005, ss 172A–F; CTA 2009, ss 156–161)

[20.21] The provisions in this paragraph do not apply where profits are calculated on the cash basis (see **20.4**). Goods taken from stock for private purposes are reckoned for tax purposes broadly at the amount which they would have realised if sold in the open market at the time they were appropriated. However, for capital gains tax purposes the trader can make an election to effectively roll over the gain into the cost of the asset so that no capital gain or loss arises and the trading profit is increased (or reduced) by the notional gain (or loss). Note however that September 2017 Finance Bill, which is expected to receive Royal Assent in November 2017, contains legislation to prevent the election being made where a capital loss arises in respect of appropriations made after 7 March 2017. A separate election applies where the asset is a property and the gain or loss would be ATED-related (see **4.8**), and on election that part becomes chargeable or allowable, with only any non-ATED related gain or loss being rolled over. This is subject to the same restrictions provided by September 2017 Finance Bill where a loss arises.

Services are valued at cost, so no notional profit has to be included for services provided free of charge to, say, a relative. Where business is carried on through a limited company, the directors are charged on goods and services taken for their own use under the benefits rules (see CHAPTER **10**) and the cost is allowed in calculating the company profits, unless some of the directors' total remuneration including benefits is considered not to be wholly and exclusively for the trade (see **12.9**).

Stock and work in progress — valuation (ITTOIA 2005, ss 96A, 97A, 97B, 160, 173–186, 238, 239; CTA 2009, Pt 3 Ch 11)

[20.22] Stock is valued at the lower of cost or realisable value, opening and closing stock being brought into the accounts in determining profit when profits are computed on the accruals basis (see **20.2**). Work in progress is similarly brought into account, and an appropriate addition for direct or indirect overheads must be included in its value.

It is the view of both the Consultative Committee of Accountancy Bodies and the ICAEW that the value of a proprietor's or working partner's time in an unincorporated business is not a contributory part of cost and should not be included in the value of work in progress.

The accounts should recognise unbilled revenue, albeit not within work in progress, if the work has been completed to a stage where the full anticipated amount is expected to be received. How it is described will depend upon personal preference, and how it is valued, upon the particular circumstances of the project.

Even before the introduction of the cash basis for small businesses from 2013–14 (see **20.4**), new barristers could use a cash basis and were not required to bring in work in progress for their first seven years of business. They had to include it thereafter, but they could spread the amount brought in (called the catching-up charge) over ten years, with the flexibility of increasing the amount of the charge in any of the earlier tax years, an appropriate reduction then being made in later years. These special provisions for barristers are withdrawn from 2013–14, except where profits were calculated on this basis in 2012–13, in which case they may continue to be used.

Where profits are calculated on the accruals basis (see **20.2**), when a trade ceases (other than because of the death of a sole trader), stock is valued at the price received if sold to an unconnected UK trader. Where the stock is transferred with other assets, the total price is apportioned between the assets on a just and reasonable basis. If the UK trader is connected with the vendor (e.g. through a family link, or as companies in the same group), then the stock is valued at an arm's length price. If, however, that value is greater than both the actual sale price and the cost of the stock, the two parties may make a claim to use the higher of cost and sale price instead of arm's length value. Stock that is disposed of other than by being sold to a UK trader, for example taken by a trader for his personal use, is valued at open market value.

Where a business ceases because of the death of a sole proprietor, the closing stock and work in progress is valued at the lower of cost and market value. Its acquisition value for executors or beneficiaries is, however, its market value at the date of death, both for capital gains purposes and for income tax purposes if they carry on the business.

Where profits are calculated on the cash basis (see **20.4**) the value of trading stock belonging to the trade, or the value of work in progress relating to a profession or vocation, at the time of cessation is included as a trading receipt of the business. The value is determined on a just and reasonable basis.

Change in basis of computing profits (FA 2002, ss 65–66; ITTOIA 2005, ss 25–27, 226–240; FA 2006, s 102 and Sch 15; CTA 2009, s 46, Pt 3 Ch 14)

[20.23] Where a valid basis of accounting is changed, including a change to or from the cash basis (see **20.4**), such that income is not included or expenditure is included more than once, then in calculating taxable profits the excluded income is brought in as a one-off tax charge and the double-counted expenditure is reckoned only once. Such changes might occur because of the adoption of generally accepted accounting practice or court decisions.

Where completed, unbilled work is brought into accounts for the first time, such as occurred in 2005 when UITF 40 'Revenue recognition and service contracts' was applied to professional work in progress, its value at the beginning as well as at the end of that accounting period is brought in, so that the profits of the year are stated on a consistent basis. The inclusion of the value at the start of the accounting period without a corresponding amount being included in the accounts at the immediately preceding year-end would mean that the 'uplift' would not be charged to tax but for the one-off tax charge.

The one-off charge is reckoned for income tax purposes on the *last* day of the period of account in which the change occurs, and for corporation tax purposes on the *first* day of the accounting period in which the change occurs.

The effect of reckoning an uplift within profits is spread forward in certain circumstances. Where the charge arises as a result of leaving the cash basis the adjustment may be spread over six years, with the flexibility of increasing the amount of the charge in any of the earlier tax years, an appropriate reduction then being made in later years.

The legislation does not cover a change from an invalid basis to a valid basis of accounting, for example where by reference to accepted methods of valuation, work in progress has been inadequately valued. In such cases, the tax consequences of having adopted an invalid basis have to be corrected, often with interest and penalties being incurred.

[20.24] The Financial Reporting Council has significantly changed what constitutes UK generally accepted accounting practice (GAAP). It introduced four new accounting standards between 2012 and 2014 (FRS 100, 101, 102 and 103). Accounting standards issued prior to FRS 100 were withdrawn for accounting periods commencing on or after 1 January 2015 and the new accounting standards must be used, although entities could choose to adopt the new standards for periods ending on or after 31 December 2012. The tax legislation has been revised to ensure that it applies to the accounting transition adjustments arising from the changes and the comments outlined in 20.23 regarding a possible one-off tax charge may be relevant.

The changes in accounting practice in FRS 102 will have some implications in preparing tax computations. For example, the revaluation of investment properties under the old UK GAAP was within the statement of total recognised gains and losses in the accounts but under FRS 102 such gains are recognised in the income statement (known under the old GAAP as the profit and loss account). This change will affect the tax computation as the revaluation gains will need to be deducted as they are not taxable until such time as the property is sold.

FRS 102 provides for a maximum five-year default life for the write-off of goodwill and intangibles (see **20.35**) where the entity is unable to make a reliable estimate of useful economic life. This will often result in goodwill being written off earlier than under the old UK GAAP where 20 years was often used. There was no default life within the old GAAP, but there was a prohibition on a life of more than 20 years in a small entity, and justification was required for a longer life in other entities. However, where companies have elected to claim allowances at a fixed rate of 4% (see **20.37**) a change in the rate of write-off in the accounts does not change the tax treatment. An entity can to choose to retain the goodwill treatment calculated before the date of transition to FRS 102, rather than restate it under the new standard but this may not be the most beneficial option. Note that the treatment of the relief for write-off of goodwill has changed with effect from 8 July 2015 (see **20.35**). The earlier write-off will not benefit unincorporated businesses for tax purposes as the goodwill is treated as capital and not allowed as an income tax deduction.

Another change relates to the treatment of lease incentives in the accounts of the lessee. Under old UK GAAP such incentives were recognised over the shorter of the life of the lease and the date of the next rent review. Under FRS 102 the incentive is recognised over the life of the lease.

Example 3

On 1 January 2012 A Ltd entered into a lease for £100,000 for 16 years which had a rent review after 5 years. The first 2 years are rent-free and thus the first rent payment is not actually made until the year ended 31 December 2014. A comparison of the relief under old UK GAAP (UITF 28) and FRS 102 is as follows:

Year to 31 December	Old UK GAAP	FRS 102
2012	£60,000	£87,500
2013	£60,000	£87,500
2014	£60,000	£87,500
2015	£60,000	£87,500
2016	£60,000	£87,500
2017 – 2027	£100,000 per year	£87,500 per year
Totals	£1,400,000	£1,400,000

It can be seen that under FRS 102 A Ltd receives relief for its rent payments earlier in its accounts and consequently in its tax computations. There is a transitional exemption when FRS 102 is first applied which permits entities to retain the UITF 28 treatment on leases entered into before the date of transition. As there is likely to be a tax advantage of *not* using the exemption, most entities are likely to restate the figures as if FRS 102 had always applied.

See **20.20** regarding a change in leasing accounting standard occurring on or after 1 January 2011.

Value added tax

[20.25] If a business is VAT-registered, VAT is not normally taken into account either as part of turnover or part of expenses. VAT is collected on supplies of goods and services, and any VAT that anyone has charged the business is recouped, subject to an adjustment where there is non-business use, with the balance being paid to or recovered from HMRC. Following European Court of Justice judgments, HMRC state that it is clear that the circumstances under which an individual can benefit privately from a business expense without a private use charge arising should be narrowly defined. HMRC refer to the 'necessity test' and the 'strict business purpose test'. For further details see HMRC Brief 44/2010.

Where there is non-business use, the input VAT is normally apportioned using any method which is fair and reasonable. VAT Notice 700 provides details of possible apportionment methods at para 32. Alternatively input VAT may be claimed in full and output VAT on non-business use accounted for over the economic life of the asset, although not on the purchase of land and property, boats, ships and other vessels, and aircraft. Instead on these assets input tax is restricted to the business use proportion at the time of the purchase and subsequent adjustments to the amount recoverable must be made through the capital goods scheme (see **7.28**). This input tax restriction method also applies where the non-business use is not private use, for example the use by a charity for non-commercial purposes. Where an asset on which input VAT was restricted is sold, output VAT is not charged on the non-business proportion of the sale proceeds.

[20.26] These general rules are subject to various specific provisions. VAT on business entertaining expenditure (subject to what is said in **20.15**, in particular with regard to overseas customers) and on the purchase of cars cannot be recovered from HMRC unless, in the case of cars, they are used *wholly* for business purposes, e.g. by private taxi firms, self-drive hire firms, driving schools and leasing companies. The unrecovered VAT on entertaining cannot be allowed in calculating taxable profit either, because business entertaining itself is not so allowed (subject to what is said in **20.15**). However, disallowed VAT on cars forms part of the cost for capital allowances (see **22.7**).

Where assets are acquired on lease, the VAT included in the leasing charges is normally recoverable, but if there is any private use of a leased car on which the lessor recovered the input VAT, the lessee may only recover 50% of the input VAT on the leasing charges. The balance, restricted by the actual private use proportion, would then form part of the lease charges deducted from profits. There would, however, be no 50% restriction on any input VAT relating to a charge for repairs and maintenance if the charge was made in a separate contract as mentioned in **20.18**.

For the treatment of VAT on business vehicle fuel see **7.5** to **7.7**. The VAT relating to private use of the vehicle by a sole trader or partner is disallowed along with the private expenditure itself (see **20.6**). There is no disallowance of the input VAT on car repair and maintenance expenditure, providing there is some business use (see **7.7**).

It is HMRC's view that amounts of VAT originally wrongly declared which are refunded following a repayment claim are trade receipts. See HMRC Brief 14/2009 for full details.

[20.27] If a business is not registered for VAT, any VAT suffered on business expenditure (other than on business entertaining expenses, which are disallowed, subject to what is said in **20.15**, in particular with regard to overseas customers) forms part of expenditure in calculating taxable profits. It will either qualify for capital allowances as part of the cost of a capital item or it will be an expense in arriving at the profit. The same applies where, although the business is VAT-registered, some of the supplies made are exempt from VAT (see **7.27**). The business may then not be able to recover all the input VAT from HMRC, and the non-deductible amount is taken into account as part of expenditure for income tax or corporation tax.

[20.28] If a business has joined the VAT flat-rate scheme (see **7.31**), the accounts will normally show turnover and expenses inclusive of output and input VAT. The amount of flat-rate VAT paid, calculated on the turnover inclusive of output VAT, may either be deducted from the turnover figure or treated as an expense. Under the scheme, input VAT may be recovered on capital items with a VAT-inclusive value of more than £2,000. Any such input VAT would be recovered by set-off against the flat-rate VAT payable to HMRC. It would not reduce the flat-rate VAT charged as an expense in the accounts, but would instead be deducted from the cost of the capital item. Where input VAT on capital items is not recovered, it forms part of the cost of the asset for capital allowances purposes.

National insurance contributions

[20.29] The employers' Class 1 NICs paid on employees' wages, Class 1A NICs on the provision of taxable benefits to employees and Class 1B NICs under a PAYE Settlement Agreement (see **10.69**) are allowable in calculating the taxable profit. No deduction is allowed for a sole trader's or partner's own Class 2 and Class 4 NICs.

Qualifying carers etc. (ITTOIA 2005, ss 744–747, 803–828, Sch 2 Pt 10)

[20.30] A special tax exemption is available to foster carers and shared lives carers, whose gross receipts do not exceed an individual limit. It is known as 'qualifying care relief'. Shared lives carers include adult placement carers, staying put carers and certain kinship carers who provide care for up to three people and share their home with them. A group of siblings count as one shared lives placement and where there is more than one carer in a household the placement cap of three applies to the household, not each carer. If the cap is exceeded for shared lives care, relief may still apply in respect of foster care if qualifying care receipts are also received in the year on the provision of foster care.

The exemption limit is a fixed amount of £10,000 a year, plus an additional amount of £200 a week for a child under 11 or £250 a week for an adult or a child aged 11 or older. Where the limit is exceeded, qualifying carers may either compute their profits in the normal way or they may make a written election to treat their taxable profits as being the excess over their individual limit. Such an election must be made by the first anniversary of the normal self-assessment filing date for the relevant tax year (e.g. 31 January 2020 for 2017–18).

Where qualifying carers choose to treat their profits in the normal way on the accruals basis (see **20.2**) they may claim capital allowances for capital expenditure. There are special capital allowances rules which apply to qualifying carers (see HMRC Business Income Manual BIM52775). Qualifying carers can make an election for the cash basis to apply (see **20.4**), in which case the rules throughout this chapter relating to the cash basis will apply, and any capital receipts brought into account in calculating profits (see **20.11**) will be included in qualifying care receipts for the purposes of these special rules.

Qualifying guardians and adopters are exempt from income tax on any qualifying payments they receive. Qualifying guardians are individuals who care for one or more children placed with them under a special guardianship order, or under a residence order where the individual is not the child's parent or step-parent. Kinship carers who provide care to a child who has not been placed with them under a residence order will not qualify for the exemption but can claim qualifying care relief as outlined above.

Qualifying carers are liable to Class 2 and Class 4 NICs where appropriate, although no Class 2 NICs are payable if the profits are exempt, or fall within the small profits threshold (see **24.4**). Carers may wish to pay Class 2 NICs in any event to maintain their right to various benefits, including contribution-based employment and support allowance and state pension (the amount payable for 2017–18 being only £2.85 a week). See, however, **24.5** regarding the abolition of Class 2 from April 2018. HMRC's Helpsheet HS236 deals with both the tax and NICs position for carers.

Investment managers (TCGA 1992, ss 103KA–103KH; ITA 2007, ss 809EZA–809EZH)

[20.31] Sums which arise to investment fund managers for their services for a collective investment scheme or investment trust are charged to income tax. From 6 April 2015 any 'disguised fees' (as defined) paid through structures involving partnerships are taxable as trade profits unless they are already taxed as employment or trading income. As the fees are treated as the profits of the deemed trade, not as receipts, losses or expenses cannot be set against them.

Specific rules determine from 6 April 2016 whether 'carried interest' (broadly a profit-related return) should be taxed as trading income or as chargeable gains. Previously case law had been relied upon. Broadly where an individual performs investment management services for a collective investment scheme, then any sum of carried interest arising from that fund will only be eligible for capital gains tax treatment if the fund holds investments, on average, for at least 40 months. Partial capital gains tax treatment will be available where the average holding period is between 36 months and 40 months, otherwise it will be charged to tax and NICs as trading profits. The capital gains tax the rate applying on gains from 6 April 2016 is 18% or 28% depending upon the individual's tax circumstances (see **4.2**).

Examples of allowable and non-allowable expenditure

[20.32] The following are lists of certain allowable and non-allowable expenditure. The paragraphs referred to in brackets should be consulted to determine which rules apply on the cash basis and which do not.

Allowable expenditure

Accountancy expenses (see **20.9**)

Advertising (see **20.6**)

Bad debts written off and provision for specific bad debts (see **20.16**)

Business travel (see **20.6**)

Car hire (see **20.18**)

Contributions to Flood and Coastal Erosion Risk Management (FCERM) projects, from 1 January 2015

Contributions to local enterprise organisations etc. (see **29.63**)

Cost of raising loan finance (excluding stamp duty), for example debentures (not share capital) (see **20.17**)

Cost of staff temporarily seconded to charities and educational establishments

Counselling services for redundant employees

Employer's Class 1 NICs on employees' wages, Class 1A NICs on the provision of taxable benefits to employees and Class 1B NICs under a PAYE settlement agreement (see **20.29**)

Gifts of medical supplies and equipment from a company's trading stock for humanitarian purposes

Gifts of trading stock to educational establishments, charities or registered amateur sports clubs

Interest on business borrowings (see **20.17**)

Legal expenses on debt recovery, trade disputes, defending trade rights, employees' service agreements and, by concession, renewing a short lease (i.e. 50 years or less)

Non-recoverable VAT relating to allowable expenses, for example where turnover is below VAT threshold, or VAT partial exemption applies (see **20.25**)

Premium for grant of lease for 50 years or less, but limited to the amount taxed on the landlord as extra rent (see **32.22**), spread over the term of the lease

Rent and rates of business premises

Repairs (but see **20.11** regarding renovations)

Qualifying research and development expenditure (see **29.64** to **29.67**), and certain sums paid to research and development associations

Staff wages, benefits in kind and pension scheme contributions (see **20.14**)

Non-allowable expenditure

Business entertaining expenses including the VAT thereon (subject to what is said in **20.15** regarding entertaining staff and overseas customers)

Charitable subscriptions, and charitable donations unless exceptionally the donation satisfies the wholly and exclusively rule (but see **43.16** regarding gift aid donations)

Cost of improvements, extensions, additions to premises and equipment

Depreciation (capital allowances are available on certain assets — see CHAPTER 22)

Donations to political parties

Expenses of private living accommodation (unless assessable on directors or employees as a benefit)

Fines and any legal expenses connected therewith

Gifts to customers, except gifts with a conspicuous advertisement that cost not more than £50 per person per year and are not food, drink, tobacco or gift vouchers

Illegal payments such as bribes (including payments overseas that would be illegal in the UK)

Legal expenses on forming a company, drawing up partnership agreement, acquiring assets such as leases

Payments made in response to threats, menaces, blackmail and other forms of extortion

Profit shares in the form of interest on partners' capital

Self-employed NICs (see 20.29)

Taxation (but see 20.9 regarding certain accountancy expenses and above as regards VAT)

September 2017 Finance Bill, which is expected to receive Royal Assent in November 2017, includes provisions to prevent a tax deduction for contributions on or after 6 April 2017 to a disguised remuneration scheme (see 10.5) unless the associated PAYE and NIC is paid broadly within 12 months of the end of the period for which the employer seeks a deduction in computing their taxable profits

Anti-avoidance — trading income provided through third parties (ITTOIA 2005, ss 23A–23H)

[20.33] September 2017 Finance Bill, which is expected to receive Royal Assent in November 2017, includes provisions applying from 6 April 2017 to prevent trading profits disguised as other receipts escaping the charge to tax. They apply equally to professions and vocations and to both partners and individuals. The provisions prevent arrangements involving the individual which result in a deduction from income, or exclusion of earnings, and that deduction or those earnings are used to provide a payment, loan, transfer of money's worth or other benefit to the individual or anyone connected to them. The amount of the benefit arising to the individual is treated as profits of the trade for the tax year in which the benefit arises.

> **Example 4**
>
> John is self-employed with annual business turnover in the region of £120,000 and allowable expenses £30,000. He makes his accounts up to 31 March each year. In March 2018 he enters into an arrangement such that an amount of £65,000 is paid to a third party and is purported to be an allowable deduction for his business. However, no business expense is met from this sum and an amount of £55,000 is instead lent back to him. The £10,000 balance represents the fees for the scheme.
>
> Assuming that a deduction were to be allowed for the third party payment, the amount of £55,000 lent to John would be treated as his income taxable in 2017–18. In addition, the £10,000 fees would not be deductible in computing the profits of the trade.

Loans made before 6 April 2017 and after 5 April 1999 are also treated as benefits for these purposes if they remain outstanding at 5 April 2019. However, the charge can be postponed for certain qualifying commercial loans approved by HMRC. Such loans will be quite limited because they must be a pre-9 December 2010 loan whose term cannot exceed 10 years. The charge will be postponed until the future approved repayment date and will apply only to any loan balance not repaid on that date.

Example 5

Dev has a loan of £100,000 made under arrangements which would result in it being treated as a relevant benefit, and he applies to HMRC in 2018 for approval of the loan. The loan was made on 5 April 2010 and is due to be repaid on or before 4 April 2020. The loan terms are unchanged since commencement. It meets the conditions for approval because there have been qualifying repayments and it is on commercial terms, and HMRC confirm it is qualifying. Therefore, no loan charge arises on 5 April 2019. Instead the charge is deferred until 4 April 2020 and will only apply to the extent the loan is not repaid by that date.

Non-trading income and capital profits

[20.34] Any non-trading income of sole traders and partners included in the business accounts is charged to tax under the appropriate heading rather than as part of the business profits, for example, interest as savings and investment income and rent as property income. Small amounts of rental income may be included in the trading income if they are from subletting a part of business premises that is temporarily surplus to requirements. Under self-assessment, tax on all sources of income (and capital gains) is calculated as a single figure. It is still necessary to keep different sources of income separate, however, particularly because of the treatment of losses. In the case of a partnership, non-trading income has to be shown separately from the trading profit in the partnership return, and partners show their shares of trading income and non-trading income in their personal returns (see CHAPTER 23).

A company's non-trading income is excluded in calculating the trading profit, but the company is chargeable to corporation tax on all its sources of income plus its chargeable gains (subject to the comments in **3.1** regarding certain disposals of UK residential property chargeable to capital gains tax), tax being payable by self-assessment. See CHAPTERS 3 and 9.

Capital profits of sole traders and partners are generally liable to capital gains tax (but see **20.11**), subject to any available reliefs and to the annual exempt amount (see CHAPTER 4).

Treatment for companies of intangible fixed assets (CTA 2009, Pt 8)

[20.35] From 1 April 2002 separate rules apply for companies in relation to the tax treatment of intellectual property (which includes patents, trade marks, copyrights, know-how, licences etc.) and other intangible assets (intangible assets being as defined for accounting purposes). It also applies to certain goodwill, although the treatment of other goodwill has changed from 8 July

2015 (see below). The rules generally apply to expenditure on the creation, acquisition or enhancement of intangible fixed assets on or after 1 April 2002, to abortive expenditure on the assets, and to expenditure on their preservation and maintenance. Certain intangible assets are excluded, for example rights over land, financial assets and rights in companies. Computer software treated as part of the cost of the related hardware is excluded except to the extent of any royalties payable in respect of the software. The company may *elect* to exclude capital expenditure on computer software, enabling capital allowances to be claimed instead (see **22.24**). Where a company reclassifies an asset as an intangible asset, and capital allowances had been given on it when it was treated as a tangible asset, the asset is not dealt with under the intangible assets rules despite the reclassification.

Expenditure on research and development is excluded from the rules so as to preserve the special research and development tax reliefs (see **29.64** to **29.67**). Profits from the exploitation of research and development are, however, brought into account, and in calculating gains on realisation of assets, expenditure on research and development is excluded from the allowable cost.

There are extensive anti-avoidance provisions to prevent the rules being manipulated.

It is not possible to claim relief for the annual write-down (see **20.37**) of goodwill and other customer related intangible assets acquired on or after 8 July 2015 (i.e. customer information and relationships, unregistered trade marks and signs, and licences and rights relating to any such assets). In addition, any debits (losses) arising on a realisation of such assets on or after 8 July 2015 are treated as non-trading debits and so the loss is not a trading loss. This restriction does not apply where a company acquired the goodwill or goodwill-related asset under an obligation under a contract that had become unconditional before 8 July 2015. In such situations it is possible to claim the annual write down. This change removed an advantage that was available when structuring a business acquisition as a business and asset purchase, and which is not generally available to companies who purchase the shares of the target company. See **20.41** regarding the restriction involving acquisitions of goodwill from related parties which preceded these rules.

[20.36] Gains and losses on intangible fixed assets are brought into account in calculating a company's income. There are rules similar to those for loan relationships (see **3.6**) for bringing such amounts into account. Amounts relating to a trade are brought into account in calculating trading income, amounts relating to a property in calculating property business income, and non-trading amounts are taxed as non-trading income.

Under the patent box regime which applies from 1 April 2013 companies can elect to apply a 10% rate of corporation tax to all profits attributable to qualifying patents, whether paid separately as royalties or embedded in the sales price of products. The rules were phased in over five years with 90% of the benefits available in financial year 2016, and now 100% in financial year 2017. For further details see **3.17**.

If there is a non-trading loss, the company may claim, not later than two years after the end of the accounting period, to set it against the total profits of the same period. Any loss not relieved in that way and not surrendered under the group relief provisions (see **26.16** onwards) will be carried forward to set against later non-trading profits.

[20.37] The cost of intangible fixed assets will in most cases be depreciated for tax purposes according to the amounts charged in the accounts. This will often be by way of straight line depreciation over the asset's useful life. The company may, however, make an irrevocable election, not later than two years after the end of the accounting period in which the asset was acquired or created, to claim allowances at a fixed rate of 4% per annum, which would be beneficial for assets with an indefinite life and long-life assets. Payments for the use of intangible assets, such as royalties, are also within the special rules whether they relate to assets acquired before or after 1 April 2002. Gains and losses when intangible fixed assets are disposed of are brought into account in calculating income, although companies may claim a special rollover relief where the proceeds for the assets are reinvested in new intangible fixed assets that are capitalised in the accounts. This rollover relief follows the same rules as the capital gains relief, i.e. the proceeds must be reinvested within one year before and three years after the date of disposal.

[20.38] Where a company changes its accounting policy, for example because it has changed from using UK generally accepted accounting practice to using international accounting standards, or has changed to FRS 102 (see **20.23**) an adjustment must be made where the closing and opening values of intangible assets are different, unless the company has elected to claim 4% fixed rate allowances as indicated above.

[20.39] Apart from the royalty treatment indicated above, assets acquired or created before 1 April 2002 are still subject to the previous rules. When such assets are disposed of on or after 1 April 2002, they qualify for the rollover relief referred to above. Internally generated goodwill is treated as created before 1 April 2002 if the business was carried on at any time before that date by the company or a related party, as to which see below. HMRC will challenge any arrangements to claim relief for goodwill under the corporate intangible fixed asset regime where a company has acquired a business that was carried on by a related party before commencement of the regime. They will not accept the argument that the goodwill is created through 'synergies' achieved on merging the business acquired with the existing business. Note that relief is no longer available in any case for goodwill acquired on or after 8 July 2015 (see above).

[20.40] Special provisions apply to 75% groups. Assets may be transferred from one group company to another on a no gain/no loss basis (except in certain cases relating to friendly societies, dual-resident investing companies and foreign permanent establishments), subject to a degrouping charge (as in **3.31**) if the acquiring company leaves the group within six years. The intangible fixed asset rollover relief provisions apply where one group company makes a qualifying disposal and another acquires a qualifying replacement. In addition, a degrouping charge may be reallocated to another group company, and the company chargeable in respect of the degrouping gain may claim the intangible assets rollover relief against replacement assets where appropriate.

[20.41] There are special provisions dealing with company reconstructions and also for transfers between related parties, which are normally treated as taking place at market value. The definition of related parties is complex, but is broadly as follows. Companies are related where one controls the other or the same person controls both or both companies are members of the same group. A person is related to a company if the company is a close company and the person is a participator or associate of a participator in the company or in another company that has a major interest in the company (see **3.29** regarding close companies). A company's acquisitions of intangible assets on or after 1 April 2002 from a related party will only be within the post-April 2002 provisions if the asset was within the provisions in the hands of the related party, or the related party acquired the asset on or after 1 April 2002 from an unrelated party, or the asset was created on or after 1 April 2002 by the related party or someone else. Even so, on disposal by the company, such assets no longer qualify for the capital gains rollover relief.

In relation to goodwill there was an interim restriction involving related parties which was superseded by the rules in **20.35** relating to the acquisitions of goodwill from all parties. Where a company directly or indirectly acquired goodwill and/or certain other intangible assets from an individual who is related to the company, or from a partnership, any individual partner of which is related to the company, the company is not permitted to obtain relief for any debits arising in respect of the writing down of those assets where they were acquired by the company on or after 3 December 2014 and before 8 July 2015, unless the acquisition took place under the contract which had become unconditional before that date. For acquisitions that took place before 24 March 2015 the restriction only applies to acquisitions that took place directly (as opposed to indirectly). Any loss on realisation of the asset is treated as a non-trading loss.

HMRC have identified arrangements that use partnerships or limited liability partnerships to transfer assets in ways that aim to bring the assets within the intangible fixed assets regime without an effective change of economic ownership. They therefore introduced legislation for debits and credits arising on or after 25 November 2015 which determine when the rules apply to partnerships by clarifying when they are a related party. Further rules provide when the market value rule applies on transfers between companies and partnerships taking place on or after 25 November 2015.

Tax relief for companies for cleaning up contaminated or derelict land (CTA 2009, Pt 14)

[20.42] A special relief may be claimed by companies that acquire contaminated or derelict land (excluding nuclear sites) for the purposes of a trade or property business. The relief is equal to 150% of qualifying expenditure incurred on cleaning up the contaminated land ('land remediation expenditure'). The expenditure must be additional to normal site preparation. If the deduction results in a trading or property business loss, then to the extent that the loss is not relieved against profits of the company (or where relevant, a group company), the company may claim a 'land remediation tax credit' equal to 16% of the amount of the deduction (i.e. 24% of the corresponding expenditure), or 16% of the unrelieved loss if lower. Losses available to be carried forward are reduced accordingly. The claim for the tax credit must be made in the company's tax return or an amended return. The tax credit will be paid to the company by HMRC (subject to set off against any outstanding tax liabilities). It does not count as income for tax purposes.

Creative industry tax reliefs (ITA 2007, s 115; CTA 2009, Pts 15, 15A, 15B, 15C, 15D, 15E)

[20.43] Creative industry tax reliefs are a group of corporation tax reliefs which allow certain companies to claim a larger deduction, or in some cases claim a payable tax credit, when calculating their taxable profits. There are now reliefs applying to films, television, video games, theatrical productions, orchestral concerts and museums and galleries exhibitions. The television and video games reliefs only have state aid approval until 2018 and the government will seek to extend this.

For HMRC guidance see www.gov.uk/guidance/corporation-tax-creative-industry-tax-reliefs.

Films

[20.44] There are various rules on the tax treatment of films, partly to encourage the British film industry, but mainly to block various tax avoidance practices involving films, particularly those involving film partnerships. There are film partnership anti-avoidance provisions (see **25.13**) and a provision to restrict the relief for interest available to a partner in such a partnership (see **23.15**).

For British films (as defined and certified) that commence principal photography on or after 1 January 2007, where qualifying UK expenditure is at least 10% (25% if principal photography was completed before 1 April 2014) of the production expenditure, a 'film tax relief' is available to film production companies (not to partnerships). The activities relating to each film will normally be treated as a separate trade. The relief takes the form of—

(a)   an additional deduction in computing the company's trading profits. For films, the principal photography of which was not completed before 1 April 2015, the additional deduction is 100% of the relevant qualifying expenditure; and

(b)   relief for losses. If a loss arises, and principal photography was not completed by 1 April 2015, the loss can be either:

(i)   surrendered for a tax credit at the rate of 25% of the surrender-
       able loss (being the lower of the trading loss for the period plus
       unsurrendered losses brought forward, and available qualifying
       expenditure); or
(ii)   carried forward against future income.

Where the principal photography was completed by 1 April 2015, the
additional deduction in computing the company's trading profits was 100% of
UK expenditure, or if less 80% of total qualifying expenditure for limited
budget films (i.e. where qualifying production expenditure does not exceed
£20 million). For all other films, where the qualifying expenditure exceeded
£20 million the deduction was 80% of UK expenditure, or if less 80% of the
total qualifying expenditure. The tax credit was at the rate of 25% up to the
first £20 million of the surrenderable loss, and 20% thereafter for all
productions.

The deduction or tax credit will not be given if arrangements have been entered
into specifically to obtain the deductions or credits. It is possible for a company
to elect to be treated as not qualifying as a film production company, so that
its film production activities will be taxed under the normal corporation tax
rules.

Television

[20.45] A similar corporation tax relief applies for animation and television
production (high-end television relief). The relief applies broadly to expenditure incurred on or after 1 April 2013. The provisions apply to a production
company (not in partnership) in respect of British programmes (as defined and
certified) produced to be seen on television, including the internet, which are
dramas, documentaries or animation, but not adverts, current affairs, entertainment shows, competitions, live performances or training performances.
For accounting periods beginning on or after 1 April 2015 relief applies to
children's programmes, i.e. primarily for persons under age 15, including quiz
shows, game shows and competitions if prize money does not exceed £1,000.
A programme is treated as animation if at least 51% of the total 'core
expenditure' (see below) is on animation. Where the programme is not an
animation or a children's programme it must be longer than 30 minutes with
pre- and post-production and principal photography expenditure of at least
£1 million per hour. The company's activities in relation to each relevant
programme are treated as a separate trade if the relief is claimed, and specific
rules apply in calculating the profits from that trade. Television tax relief is
available to production companies by way of additional deductions and
television tax credits where the programme is a certified British programme
intended for broadcast and at least 10% (25% where principal photography is
completed before 1 April 2015) of the 'core expenditure' (pre- and post-
production and principal photography expenditure) is UK expenditure. The
additional deduction is the amount of UK expenditure or, if less, 80% of the
total qualifying expenditure. Television tax credits at a rate of 25% may be
claimed if losses arise. It is possible for a company to elect to be treated as not
qualifying as a television production company, so that its television production
activities will be taxed under the normal corporation tax rules.

Video games

[20.46] The video games relief applies broadly to expenditure incurred on or after 1 April 2014. The provisions apply to a video games development company (not in partnership) in respect of British video games (as defined and certified) which are not produced for advertising, promotional or gambling purposes. The company's activities in relation to each video games development are treated as a separate trade if the relief is claimed and specific rules apply in calculating the profits from that trade. Video games tax relief is available to video games development companies by way of additional deductions and video game tax credits where the game is a certified British video game intended for supply and at least 25% of the expenditure on designing, producing and testing the video game is EEA (see **1.3**) expenditure. The additional deduction is the amount of EEA expenditure or, if less, 80% of the total qualifying expenditure. Any payments for subcontracting exceeding £1 million are not allowable expenditure. Video game tax credits at a rate of 25% may be claimed if losses arise. It is possible for a company to elect to be treated as not qualifying as a video games production company, so that its video games production activities will be taxed under the normal corporation tax rules.

Theatrical productions

[20.47] Relief applies for theatrical productions for accounting periods beginning on or after 1 September 2014. The provisions apply to a company (not in partnership) which is responsible for producing, running and closing a theatrical production, and which makes an effective creative, technical and artistic contribution to the production. A theatrical production is broadly a dramatic production, i.e. a play, opera, musical, or other dramatic piece which is performed live; or a ballet. There are certain exclusions such as productions which mainly advertise goods or services, or are a contest, or those involving wild animals. The company's activities in relation to each theatrical production are treated as a separate trade if the relief is claimed and specific rules apply in calculating the profits from that trade. Theatre tax relief is available to qualifying production companies by way of additional deductions and theatre tax credits where the company meets a commercial purpose condition and at least 25% of the expenditure on producing and closing the production is EEA (see **1.3**) expenditure. The additional deduction is the amount of EEA expenditure or, if less, 80% of the total qualifying expenditure. Theatre tax credits at a rate of 25% for touring productions and 20% for non-touring productions may be claimed if losses arise. For state aid purposes the total amount of any theatre tax credits for each undertaking must not exceed €50 million per year.

Production of orchestral concerts

[20.48] Relief applies for orchestral concert productions for accounting periods beginning on or after 1 April 2016. The provisions apply to a company (not in partnership) which is responsible for putting on the concert from the start of the production process to the finish, including engaging the performers.

They should be involved in decision-making, make creative, artistic and technical contributions and negotiates, contracts and pays for rights. An orchestral concert is a concert by an ensemble, group or band of mainly instrumentalists. There are certain exclusions such as productions which mainly advertise goods or services, or are a contest, or where the main purpose is to make a recording. The company's activities in relation to each concert production (or where an election is made, a series of concert productions) are treated as a separate trade if the relief is claimed and specific rules apply in calculating the profits from that trade. Orchestra tax relief is available to qualifying production companies by way of additional deductions and orchestra tax credits where the concert is a qualifying orchestral concert (or qualifying orchestral concert series if applicable) which is intended to be performed live either before the paying public or for educational purposes (or a high proportion is so intended to be in the case of a concert series) and at least 25% of the expenditure on producing the concert (or concert series) is EEA (see **1.3**) expenditure. A qualifying orchestral concert is one with at least 12 instrumentalists where only a minority of the instruments are electronically or directly amplified. The additional deduction is the amount of EEA expenditure or, if less, 80% of the total qualifying expenditure. Orchestra tax credits at a rate of 25% may be claimed if losses arise. For state aid purposes the total amount of any orchestra tax credits for each undertaking must not exceed €50 million per year.

Museum and galleries exhibitions

[20.49] September 2017 Finance Bill, which is expected to receive Royal Assent in November 2017, provides relief from 1 April 2017 for the production of museum and galleries exhibitions. The provisions apply to a company (not in partnership) which is responsible for the production of an exhibition at a venue or venues, and, in the case where an exhibition is held at just one venue, the company must also make creative, technical or artistic contributions and negotiate, contract and pay for rights. The company must be a charitable company which maintains a museum or gallery, or wholly owned by a charity or public authority which maintains such. An exhibition is a curated public display of work considered to be of scientific, historic, artistic or cultural interest and can be a touring one in certain cases, but cannot be a display in connection with a competition, one to sell, advertise or promote goods or services, one including a live performance by a person (unless incidental) or one including anything alive. The company's activities in relation to each exhibition are treated as a separate trade if the relief is claimed and specific rules apply in calculating the profits from that trade. Museum and galleries exhibitions tax relief is available to qualifying production companies by way of additional deductions and museum and galleries exhibition tax credits where the exhibition is intended to be public and at least 25% of the expenditure on producing, deinstalling and closing the exhibition is EEA (see **1.3**) expenditure. The additional deduction is the amount of EEA expenditure or, if less, 80% of the total qualifying expenditure. Museum and galleries exhibitions tax credits at a rate of 25% for touring exhibitions and 20% for non-touring exhibitions may be claimed if losses arise. The maximum amount of tax credits payable is £100,000 for a touring exhibition and £80,000 for a non-touring exhibition. In addition, for state aid purposes the total amount of any museum and galleries exhibitions tax credits for each undertaking must not exceed €50 million per year.

Profits averaging for authors and creative artists (ITTOIA 2005, ss 221–225)

[20.50] The provisions in this paragraph do not apply where profits are calculated on the cash basis (see **20.4**). Special averaging provisions are available for authors and creative artists. They used to follow the same rules as those that apply to farmers but the rules changed in 2016–17, with some of the changes applying to farmers only (see **31.6** and **31.7**). Before 2016–17 claims could be made by creative artists, either individuals or partners, to average the profits of two consecutive tax years if the profits of the lower year are less than 70% of the profits of the higher year or are nil, with marginal relief if the profits are more than 70% but less than 75%. However, where the latest of the two years is 2016–17 or a subsequent year the claim can now be made if the profits of the lower year are less than 75% of the profits of the higher year or are nil, and marginal relief is withdrawn. The time limit for averaging claims is the first anniversary of the normal self-assessment filing date for the second of the tax years, e.g. 31 January 2020 for a claim to average 2016–17 and 2017–18. The effect of the claim on Class 4 NICs needs to be taken into account. Where all or part of the higher profits were above the Class 4 upper limit, thus attracting NICs at only 2%, the averaging claim may bring profits below that limit, attracting NICs at 9% instead.

Tax points

[20.51] Note the following:

- The mixing of business and private expenditure should be avoided. Businesses should make sure they do not cloud a genuine business expense with a private element.
- Wholesalers or retailers should use their business connections to make private purchases at lower cost, rather than taking goods out of their own stock and suffering tax on a figure equivalent to the profit that would have been made if the goods had been sold to a customer.
- Since any expense for the benefit of staff is normally allowable in computing profits, it is sometimes more appropriate to provide acceptable benefits than to pay higher salaries. The employee will usually be taxable on the benefit but may prefer the tax charge to having to fund the purchase himself. As far as NICs are concerned, Class 1 NICs are payable on some benefits by both employees and employers (see CHAPTER 10). Other benefits are chargeable to Class 1A NICs, and are

payable only by employers. There is therefore an 12% NICs saving on benefits within the Class 1A category for employees paying NICs at the main rate, and a 2% saving for employees earning above the upper earnings limit of £45,000.

- If a deduction is claimed that is not commercially justifiable, interest may have to be paid on tax underpaid as a result, and possibly a penalty as well (see CHAPTER 9). This is very important when considering the 'wholly and exclusively' business element of a mixed expense, such as accommodation and motor expenses. An inaccurate claim and/or providing insufficient information to HMRC may be costly in the long run.

- Wages payments to a spouse or civil partner must not only be commercially justifiable for the participation of the spouse or partner in the business but must be properly made and the payment entered in the business records. If HMRC enquire into a tax return, they will usually challenge the charge if it has not been separately paid, but has instead been regarded as included in the amount drawn by the trader or for housekeeping, with an accounting entry being made to create the wages charge (see 19.22).

- Similar considerations apply where mature children are able genuinely to participate in the business, for example in farming, retail and wholesale trades (see 12.9).

- Wages paid after the end of an accounting period must be paid within nine months if they are to be deducted from the profits of that period calculated on the accruals basis, otherwise, and always on the cash basis, they will be deducted from profits in the period of payment (see 20.14).

- If bonuses to employees are to be paid after the end of an accounting period, they will only be allowable in calculating the profits of that accounting period on the accruals basis if there is adequate evidence before the end of the period of the obligation to pay the bonus. They will not be deductible on the cash basis if not paid in the period (see 20.14).

- Although expenses incurred by a company from which a director or employee derives a personal benefit are allowable in computing trading profit and taxed as earnings of the director or employee, this must be distinguished from using company funds to meet the private expenditure of a director/employee who is a shareholder and not treating the amount as pay. This will usually be treated as a loan from the company, which will have tax and sometimes NICs consequences both for the director and the company (see 12.16).

- Where part of the home is used for business, the trader will usually pay business rates. If not, the appropriate part of the council tax can be claimed as a business expense (see 19.19). See, however, 20.19 regarding simplified fixed rate deductions for business use of a home.

- If a trader pays congestion charges incurred by him or his employees while travelling on business in Central London (or elsewhere), they are allowable against profit. For employees who have private use of company cars, the taxable benefit covers congestion charge payments (see 10.38).

- All business records relating to tax affairs must be kept for broadly at least 5 years 10 months after the end of the tax year, although HMRC have the power to reduce the period for which records must be retained by stating this in writing. See **9.32**. Penalties of up to £3,000 per tax year apply if they are not kept. HMRC guidance is available at www.gov.uk/keeping-your-pay-tax-records.
- The value to be included for uncompleted work will always be debatable. While circumstances will differ in each business, the following is a practical way of looking at it.

Was it possible to send a bill?	'Yes'
Was a bill sent?	'No'

The full amount of the bill which could have been sent must be included in the accounts under 'debtors'.

For work in hand at an accounting date for which a bill could not properly be sent, the value should be based on the cost of the work to the business or the recoverable amount if less.

- Although there are provisions to spread tax payments forward in certain cases where there is a one-off charge to tax because of a change in accounting basis, the effect of the tax charge for one year on the payment on account for the next year reduces the benefit of the spreading.

21

How are business profits charged to tax?

Companies (TMA 1970, ss 59D, 59DA, 59E; CTA 2009, ss 5–12; FA 1998, s 117 and Sch 18)

[21.1] Although taxable business profits for individuals and companies are calculated on similar lines (see CHAPTER 20), the way company profits are taxed is much more straightforward. A company's trading profits are taxed with its other profits, such as interest, rents and chargeable gains, by reference to chargeable accounting periods (see **3.12**). A chargeable accounting period can be as short as the company wishes but cannot exceed 12 months. If a company makes up an account for say 15 months it is split into two chargeable accounting periods for tax purposes, the first of 12 months and the second of 3 months. Capital allowances (which are available on certain assets, notably plant and machinery — see CHAPTER 22) are then deducted in arriving at the trading profits. The capital allowances are not calculated for the 15-month period and divided pro rata. They are calculated for the separate periods of 12 and 3 months according to the events of those periods. Writing down allowances are proportionately reduced for accounting periods of less than 12 months.

Companies self-assess their profits and they are required to file their returns with supporting accounts and computations within 12 months after the end of the accounting period. Assessments will not normally be issued by HMRC except in cases of loss of tax due to the taxpayer's careless or deliberate actions. For details, see **9.21** to **9.23** and **9.46**.

Example 1

A company makes trading profits of £150,000 in the 15 months to 30 June 2017. The profits are charged to tax as follows:

	12 months to 31.3.2017	3 months to 30.6.2017
	£	£
12/15, 3/15	120,000	30,000
Less capital allowances (say)	(10,000)	(8,000)
	£110,000	£22,000

		£
Tax payable:		
1.4.16 – 31.3.17, £110,000 @ 20%		22,000
1.4.17 – 30.6.17, £22,000 @ 19%		£4,180

The due date for payment of corporation tax is nine months and one day after the end of the chargeable accounting period, i.e. 1 January 2018 for the 12-month account and 1 April 2018 for the three-month account in Example 1, though the return filing date is 30 June 2018 for both periods. Under corporation tax self-assessment, large companies have to pay corporation tax by quarterly instalments (see **3.25**). Interest is charged on tax paid late (see **3.27**).

Individuals (ITTOIA 2005, ss 196–220)

Basis of assessment

[21.2] The general rule is that income tax is charged on the income of the tax year. For business profits this does not mean that accounts have to be made up for the tax year itself, because businesses are free to choose their annual accounting date. Apart from special rules for the opening years and when the accounting date is changed, the taxable profits of a tax year are taken to be those of the accounting year ending in the tax year.

There is no stipulation as to the length of the first accounting period, or indeed of subsequent accounting periods. The consequences of having a first accounting period shorter or longer than 12 months are dealt with in **21.4** and the change of accounting date rules are dealt with in **21.7**. If accounts are not available at the time when the tax for the relevant tax year is due for payment, tax must be paid on an estimated basis, and interest will be charged from the original due date on any underpayment (or allowed on any overpayment) when the correct figures are known.

Capital allowances

[21.3] Capital allowances are treated as a trading expense and balancing charges as a trading receipt of the accounting period. If the accounting period is shorter or longer than 12 months, the annual writing-down allowances are reduced or increased proportionately. The detailed provisions, including those applying for periods of account exceeding 18 months, are in CHAPTER 22. Where profits are calculated on the cash basis for small businesses (see **20.4**) capital allowances are only allowed for expenditure on a car. Deductions for certain other capital expenditure are made from receipts (see **20.11**). A trader may choose to use simplified fixed rate deductions for vehicle expenditure rather than claiming capital allowances and other business expenses for the vehicle (see **20.19**).

Taxable profits in the early years

[21.4] In their first tax year, new businesses are taxed on their profit from the start date to the end of the tax year. The second year's charge is normally based on the profits of the accounting year ended in the second tax year. Part of that profit has usually already been taxed in the first year, and this is called the 'overlap profit' (see Example 2). Overlap profits can also occur on a change of accounting date. Relief for overlap profits is given when the business ceases or on a change of accounting date (see **21.5**).

Businesses that were in existence at 5 April 1994 may also have 'transitional overlap profits', which arose when the rules for taxing business profits and some other income changed from the 'previous year basis' to the current year basis. The transitional overlap profits normally cover the period between the annual accounting date in 1996–97 and 5 April 1997, that period also having been included in the taxable profits for 1997–98. For example, a pre-6 April 1994 business that makes up accounts to 30 June would have a transitional overlap period from 1 July 1996 to 5 April 1997. The detailed transitional provisions are covered in earlier editions of this book.

Example 2

Business started 1 January 2017 and made up its first accounts for 12 months to 31 December 2017, then annually to 31 December.

The taxable profits are:

2016–17	1.1.17 – 5.4.17	3/12 × 1st year's profits
2017–18	1.1.17 – 31.12.17	1st year's profits
2018–19	1.1.18 – 31.12.18	2nd year's profits
Overlap profits are:		3/12 × 1st year's profits

Where profits need to be apportioned, the apportionment may be made in days, months, or months and fractions of months providing the chosen method is used consistently. If a business makes up accounts to 31 March, the year to 31 March is treated as being equivalent to the tax year itself (unless the trader elects otherwise), so that for such a business starting on say 1 April 2017 the result of the first five days would be treated as nil, giving a nil profit for

2016–17. The profit of the first 12 months to 31 March 2018 would be taxed in 2017–18 and there would be no overlap profits and no overlap relief. Similarly, if a business changes its accounting date to 31 March, relief for all overlap profits is given at that time.

If the first accounts are made up to a date in the second tax year, but for a period of less than 12 months, the charge for the second tax year is based on the profits of the first 12 months.

Example 3

Business started 1 January 2017 and made up its first accounts for 9 months to 30 September 2017, then annually to 30 September. The taxable profits are:

2016–17	1.1.17 – 5.4.17	3/9 × 1st accounts profits
2017–18	1.1.17 – 31.12.17	Profits of 1st 9 months plus 3/12 × profits of yr to 30.9.18
2018–19	1.10.17 – 30.9.18	Profits of yr to 30.9.18
Overlap profits are:		3/9 × 1st accounts profits plus 3/12 × profits of yr to 30.9.18

If accounts are made up to a date in the second tax year, and are for 12 months or more, the charge for the second tax year is based on the profits of 12 months to the accounting date (see Example 4 and also Example 2 at **23.3** regarding the admission of a new partner).

Example 4

Business started 1 October 2016 and made up its first accounts for 15 months to 31 December 2017, then annually to 31 December.

The taxable profits are arrived at as follows:

2016–17	1.10.16 – 5.4.17	6/15 × 1st accounts profits
2017–18	1.1.17 – 31.12.17	12/15 × 1st accounts profits
2018–19	1.1.18 – 31.12.18	2nd accounts profits
Profits of 1st 15 months have therefore been used to charge tax for 18 months, so overlap profits are:		3/15 × 1st accounts profits

---

If the first accounts are made up for more than 12 months and no accounting period ends in the second tax year, the charge for the second tax year is based on the profits of the tax year itself, and the charge for the third tax year is based on 12 months to the accounting date.

Example 5

Business started 1 January 2017 and made up its first accounts for 16 months to 30 April 2018, then annually to 30 April.

The taxable profits are arrived at as follows:

2016–17	1.1.17 – 5.4.17	3/16 × 1st accounts profits
2017–18	6.4.17 – 5.4.18	12/16 × 1st accounts profits
2018–19	1.5.17 – 30.4.18	12/16 × 1st accounts profits
Profits of first 16 months have therefore been used to charge tax for 27 months, so overlap profits are:		11/16 × 1st accounts profits

Taxable profits when business ceases

[21.5] When a business ceases, it is taxed on its profits from the end of the basis period for the previous tax year to the date of cessation (unless it ceases in its second tax year, in which case it is taxed in that final year on the profits from 6 April to the date of cessation). See Example 6. Depending on the dates to which accounts are made up, there may be two accounts that together form the basis for the final taxable profit (see Example 7).

Overlap profits and overlap relief

[21.6] The effect of the rules for overlaps is that the business is taxed over its life on the profits made. There is, however, no provision for any inflation-proofing of overlap profits. A record needs to be kept not only of the amount of overlap profits but also the length of the overlapping period. If an overlapping period shows a loss, it must be recorded as an overlap of nil for the appropriate period (relief for the loss being available separately). This is important because overlap relief is given either when the business ceases, as in Examples 6 and 7, or partly or wholly at the time of an earlier change of accounting date to the extent that more than 12 months' profit would otherwise be chargeable in one year (see Examples 8 and 9 at **21.7**).

Example 6

Business started 1 January 2013 and makes up accounts annually to 31 December. It ceased on 30 June 2017. Profits after capital allowances were as follows:

		£
Year to 31 December	2013	24,000
	2014	30,000
	2015	28,000
	2016	34,000
6 months to 30 June	2017	20,000
		136,000

The profits are charged to tax as follows:

			£
2012–13	1.1.13 – 5.4.13 (3/12 × £24,000)		6,000
2013–14	1.1.13 – 31.12.13		24,000
	(Overlap profit £6,000)		
2014–15	1.1.14 – 31.12.14		30,000
2015–16	1.1.15 – 31.12.15		28,000
2016–17	1.1.16 – 31.12.16		34,000
2017–18	1.1.17 – 30.6.17	20,000	
	Less overlap profit	(6,000)	14,000
			136,000

Thus the business is taxed over its life on the profits earned.

Example 7

Facts as in Example 6 but business ceases three months earlier, on 31 March 2017, i.e. in the tax year 2016–17. The accounts for the three months ending on that date show profits of £10,000, so that the total profits are £126,000.

The taxable profits from 2012–13 to 2015–16 are the same as in Example 6, totalling £88,000. The final taxable profit for 2016–17 is as follows:

	£
1.1.16 – 31.12.16	34,000
1.1.17 – 31.3.17	10,000
	44,000
Less overlap profit	(6,000) £38,000

Total taxable profits are therefore equal to the profits earned, i.e. 88,000 + 38,000 = £126,000.

Change of accounting date

[21.7] Notice of a change of accounting date has to be given to HMRC in a tax return by 31 January following the end of the tax year of change. The fact that HMRC do not recognise a change unless notice is given means that formal accounts may be made up to an intermediate date for commercial reasons, say when a partner leaves, without the annual accounting date being altered. The rules also provide that a change of date will not be recognised if the first accounting period to the new date exceeds 18 months. This does not mean that accounts cannot be prepared for longer than 18 months, but tax has to be computed according to the old date (apportioning results as necessary) until the rules can be satisfied.

Example 8

Accounts were made up for 12 months to 30 June 2015, then for the 21 months to the new accounting date of 31 March 2017 and annually thereafter. Taxable profits will be calculated as follows:

2015–16	12 months to 30 June 2015
2016–17	12 months to 30 June 2016 (i.e. 12/21 × accounts to 31 March 2017)
2017–18	21 months to 31 March 2018 (i.e. 9/21 × accounts to 31 March 2017 and 12 months to 31 March 2018)
	Less relief for all previous overlap profits*

* The full amount of available overlap relief is given if the accounting date is changed to 31 March — see **21.4**.

Example 9

Business starts on 1 January 2017 and makes a loss in the year to 31 December 2017, profits arising thereafter. There is no taxable profit in 2016–17 or 2017–18, but the overlap period is from 1 January 2017 to 5 April 2017, i.e. (to the nearest month) three months, the overlap profit being nil. If the accounting date was later changed to 30 June, this would give a further overlap of six months. The combined overlap period would be *nine months*, with an overlap profit of nil plus a six months' proportion of the profit at the time of the later overlap.

If accounting date was subsequently changed again to, say, 30 September, 15 months' profit would be charged at that time, less a deduction for a three months' proportion of the overlap profit, but amounting to 3/9ths, not 3/6ths.

The rules for dealing with the change broadly ensure that 12 months' profit is charged in each tax year, except the first year and the last year. If accounts are made up to a date earlier in the tax year than the previous date, profits of 12 months to the new date will be charged, but this will result in overlap profits for which relief will be due later. The overlap profits and period to which they relate will be combined with any earlier overlap profits (including any transitional overlap profits on the change from previous year to current year basis) and overlap period to give a single figure for a single period. If accounts are made up to a date *later* in the tax year, more than 12 months' profits will be charged in the year of change, but a proportion of the available overlap relief will be deducted, according to how many more than 12 months' profits are being taxed. If the earlier overlap period(s) showed a loss rather than a profit, however, there would be no overlap relief due (relief for the loss having been given separately), so that the charge on more than 12 months' profit would stand. The *length* of the total overlap period is not affected by the fact that one or more earlier overlap periods showed a loss (see **21.6**). This is particularly important when calculating how much relief may be given when more than 12 months' profit would otherwise be charged in one year.

Even where losses are not involved, the overlap profit may have been seriously eroded by inflation, so that the amount deductible when more than 12 months' profits would otherwise be charged, or on cessation, may be of much less real value than the profits currently being charged to tax.

Example 10

Say a business started on 1 January 2013, making up accounts to 31 December, and the overlap profit for the three months to 5 April 2013 amounted to £6,000. If the business continued with a 31 December year end until 31 December 2021, making profits in that year of £96,000, and then made up a 9-month account to 30 September 2022, the assessment for 2022–23 would be based on the profits of 12 months to 30 September 2022, so that 3/12ths of the profits of the year to 31 December 2021, i.e. £24,000, would be taxed twice. That amount would be an additional overlap profit, which would be combined with the earlier overlap profit of £6,000, giving total overlap profits of £30,000 for six months. Overlap relief for that amount would be given either on cessation or in an earlier year to the extent that more than 12 months' profit would otherwise be taxed.

Alternatively, say that instead of making up accounts to 30 September 2022, the business made up a 14-month account to 28 February 2023, showing a profit of £112,000. The profits of the year to 31 December 2021 would be taxed in 2021–22. The profits of the 14 months to 28 February 2023 would be taxed in 2022–23, reduced by two months' overlap relief, i.e. 2/3 of £6,000 = £4,000 (although two months at the then profit rate represents profits of £16,000). The balance of the overlap relief of £2,000 would be given on cessation or when tax was again being charged for a period exceeding 12 months.

Changes of accounting date are not permitted more than once in every five years unless HMRC are satisfied that the change is for commercial reasons. In the absence of HMRC approval, the taxable profits are calculated using the previous accounting date, with the figures being apportioned on a time basis.

Pre-trading expenditure (CTA 2009, ss 61, 210, 330, 456–463; ITTOIA 2005, s 57)

[21.8] Some expenditure, for example rent, rates and interest, may be incurred before trading actually starts. So long as it is a normal trading expense and is incurred not more than seven years before the trade starts, it may be treated as an expense of the first trading period. These provisions apply to sole traders and partners and also apply to companies, except in relation to interest paid. Pre-trading interest paid by a company is brought into the calculation of the company's *non-trading* profit or loss under the loan relationship provisions at the time of payment (see **3.6**). If this results in a loss (a non-trading deficit), it is deducted from the taxable profits of that period, or carried back against loan relationship profits of the previous 12 months, or carried forward against later non-trading profits. The company may, however, make a claim, within two years after the end of the period in which the deduction was taken into account, to treat the interest as an expense of the first *trading* period instead, and it will be deducted in that period providing the trade starts within seven years after the end of the period in which the non-trading deduction was originally taken into account.

Post-cessation receipts (CTA 2009, ss 188–200, 280–286; ITTOIA 2005, ss 241–257, 349–356)

[21.9] Income may arise after a business has ceased which has not been included in the final accounts. Any such income is charged to tax separately from profits of the trade but is still treated as trading income. The chargeable amount may be reduced by any expenses, capital allowances or losses that could have been set against the income if it had been received before the business ceased. The taxable amount is treated as income of the tax year or company accounting period in which it is received. If the taxable amount is received within six years after cessation, the taxpayer or company can elect to have it treated as arising in the tax year or accounting period when trading ceased. For income tax purposes the carry-back election must be made within one year after the 31 January following the tax year in which the income was received. For corporation tax purposes the election must be made within two years of the end of the accounting period in which the income is received. In general, the amount of tax payable on the additional income will be calculated by reference to the tax position of the earlier year, but it will be treated as additional tax payable for the tax year in which the amounts were received.

Where profits are calculated on the cash basis for small businesses (see 20.4) post-cessation receipts and expenses are treated as though the business were still in the cash basis. If a trader or a company becomes non-UK resident after the cessation of the trade and the post-cessation receipts arise outside the UK, they are not chargeable to tax. Following the introduction of the statutory residence test from 2013–14 (see 41.5), strictly an individual is either resident or non-resident for the whole of a tax year. However, the tax year can be split in certain circumstances so that an individual is regarded as either resident in the UK from the day of arrival or non-UK resident from the day after departure (see 41.6). If the split-year treatment applies to an individual with post-cessation receipts he is treated as non-UK resident for the overseas part of the year. Where the trade (other than a trade of dealing in or developing UK land, see 41.64 and 41.44) is carried on wholly outside the UK, the post-cessation receipt is not chargeable to tax. For the effect of being non-UK resident see 41.36.

Post-cessation expenses (ITTOIA 2005, ss 250, 255; ITA 2007, ss 24A, 96–101, 125)

[21.10] Certain expenditure incurred by sole traders or partners in the seven years after a trade or profession has ceased that has not been provided for in the final accounts and cannot be set against any post-cessation receipts may be set against the total income and capital gains of the tax year in which it is incurred. This applies to professional indemnity premiums, the cost of remedying defective work plus any related damages and legal expenses, bad debts and debt recovery costs. For the relief to apply, a claim must be made within one year after the 31 January following the tax year in which the expenditure was incurred.

Broadly from 12 January 2012 relief is denied for payments or events arising from an arrangement whose main purpose is to obtain a tax reduction. From 2013–14 this is one of a number of reliefs against total income which is subject to a cap (see **2.13**).

Tax points

[**21.11**] Note the following:

- Choosing an accounting date early in the tax year in an unincorporated business gives more time for planning the funding of tax payments. It also means that tax is being paid each year on profits that were largely earned in the previous year, giving an obvious advantage if profits are rising. When the business ceases, however, the final tax bill may be particularly high, because the profits then being earned may be very much higher than the early overlap profits for which relief is given on cessation.
- This chapter contains examples of claims which are available to taxpayers. There is always a time limit involved, which depends on the type of claim being made. The legislation should be checked for the time limit whenever a claim is available. The general time limit under income tax self-assessment is four years after the end of the tax year where no other time limit is specified (see **25.10** and **9.15** to **9.16**).
- The time limit for notifying liability to income tax or capital gains tax if no tax return has been received is six months from the end of the tax year, e.g. by 5 October 2018 for someone who started a new business between 6 April 2017 and 5 April 2018 (see **9.34**). The taxpayer may have to complete his self-assessment on an estimated basis and amend it later, because the information may not be available in time (see the next tax point). There are penalties for late notification of liability, for late returns, and for late payments (see **9.57** to **9.79**). Interest is also charged on late payments (see **9.55** and **9.56**).
- New unincorporated businesses may often incur interest charges on underpaid tax under self-assessment, because interest runs from the 31 January online filing date for the return (or three months after the return is issued, if later) on what the tax finally turns out to be. If a business commences on say 1 January 2016 and makes up accounts to 31 December 2016, tax and Class 4 NICs were due on 31 January 2017 (i.e. the 2015–16 return filing date) on the profit from 1 January to 5 April 2016. It is unlikely that the December 2016 accounts had been completed by that date. If the tax and Class 4 NICs due were

underestimated, interest would run on the underpayment from 31 January 2017 (although the tax and NICs payment itself would not have been due until 30 days after the filing of an amendment to the return — see **9.5**).

22

Capital allowances

Introduction

[22.1] Capital expenditure cannot generally be deducted in calculating income for tax purposes, but capital allowances may be claimed instead. There is an exception where profits are calculated on the cash basis both for small businesses (see **20.4** and **20.11**) and for property businesses (see **32.6**), in which case certain capital expenditure is deducted in calculating income for tax purposes. Cash basis businesses may still claim capital allowances on a car. Certain businesses may choose to make simplified fixed rate deductions for vehicle expenditure instead of claiming capital allowances and other business motoring expenses (see **20.19**). The law on capital allowances is contained in the Capital Allowances Act 2001 as amended by subsequent legislation.

A 100% annual investment allowance is available for the first £200,000 of expenditure on plant and machinery excluding cars (see **22.26**).

The main rate of writing-down allowance for expenditure on plant and machinery is currently 18% but certain expenditure is special rate expenditure for which writing-down allowances are given at 8% (see **22.27**).

First year allowances of up to 100% are available on certain expenditure (see **22.28**).

A first-year tax credit is available where a company has incurred a loss attributable to enhanced capital allowances for expenditure on 'green' plant and machinery. The loss is surrendered in exchange for a cash payment, instead of being carried forward and set against future profits (see **22.32**).

[22.2] The most important allowances presently available are those in respect of expenditure on:

- Plant and machinery
- Patents
- Know-how
- Research and development
- Mineral extraction

These allowances are available to sole traders and partnerships (subject to the comments in **22.1** regarding cash basis businesses), and companies, except that for companies capital allowances are no longer claimed on patents and know-how acquired on or after 1 April 2002. Relief for such acquisitions is given by a deduction in computing income under the 'intangible assets' rules (see **20.35**). See also **22.24** regarding computer software.

Capital allowances at 100% are available in respect of expenditure before April 2017 on renovating business premises in designated disadvantaged areas (see **32.19**) and balancing adjustments may still arise. See **32.18** regarding the flat conversion allowances which used to be available and on which balancing adjustments may still arise.

Plant and machinery allowances are available not only to businesses but also to employees who have to provide certain plant and machinery for use in their employment (see **10.15**), and to those who let property and/or equipment, in respect of fixtures, fittings, etc. (see **22.45**). An example of qualifying expenditure on plant and machinery by an employee might be a musical instrument purchased by an employee of an orchestra.

If an asset is used partly for private purposes by sole traders or partners, or by employees claiming allowances for their own plant and machinery, allowances are given only on the business proportion (see **22.42**). There is no restriction where company assets are used privately by directors or employees, but the director/employee is taxed on the benefit obtained (see CHAPTER **10**).

Expenditure qualifying for relief (CAA 2001, ss 21–51, 57–59, 66A, 67–70YJ, 264, 532–543)

[22.3] Capital allowances are available when expenditure is incurred on a qualifying asset, even if the expenditure is funded by means of a loan or bank overdraft. Interest on such funding is generally allowed as a business expense or against total income, and not as part of the cost of the asset. However, relief is not available for interest on a loan to buy plant or machinery for partnership use if the partnership profits are calculated on the cash basis, either for small businesses (see **20.4**) or for property businesses (see **32.6**), and qualifying loan interest is one of a number of reliefs against total income which is subject to a cap from 2013–14 (see **2.13** and **2.14**). Where an asset used in a partnership belongs to one of the partners it is usually the partnership and not the partner that can claim the allowances, other than where the asset is let by the partnership or where the partnership pays for its use and the payment is deducted from partnership profits.

[22.4] When an asset is purchased under a hire-purchase agreement, the expenditure is regarded as incurred as soon as the asset comes into use, even though the asset is not strictly owned until the option-to-purchase payment is made. The hire-purchase charges are not part of the cost but are allowed as a business expense, spread appropriately over the term of the agreement.

[22.5] Where plant and machinery is acquired on a finance lease, for accounting purposes the assets are treated as owned by the lessee. With the exception of leases of less than five years (and some other longer leases), the tax treatment is aligned with the accounting treatment (see **20.20**). Lessors cannot claim capital allowances. Instead, lessees may claim the allowances as they would have been able to if they had bought the asset. Where capital allowances remain available to finance lessors, they are normally entitled only to writing-down allowances (see **22.27** for exceptions), and the allowances are restricted on a time basis according to when in the accounting period the plant and machinery was acquired. For the treatment of the lease payments see **20.20**. There are extensive anti-avoidance provisions in relation to finance leases, and to sale and leaseback or lease and leaseback transactions. These anti-avoidance provisions are not dealt with in this book.

[22.6] Subsidies or contributions from third parties must be deducted from the allowable cost of the asset. Where the qualifying expenditure on plant and machinery has been reduced by such a contribution or subsidy, the third party may claim allowances on the amount contributed, even though strictly he does not have an interest in the plant and machinery, so long as certain conditions are met. This legislation was clarified with effect from 29 May 2013 to avoid the possibility of gas and electricity distribution companies claiming tax relief for costs already paid for by business customers.

[22.7] Where VAT has been paid and cannot be recovered, for example on motor cars or, in the case of other asset purchases, because of the partial exemption rules or because the trader is not VAT-registered, it forms part of the allowable expenditure for capital allowances (see **20.26** and **20.27**). HMRC guidance is provided in Statement of Practice B1. Capital allowances computations have to be adjusted where input VAT on certain assets is later adjusted under the capital goods scheme (see **22.21**).

[22.8] If a person who leaves the cash basis, either for small businesses (see **20.4**) or for property businesses (see **32.6**), has incurred expenditure that would have been qualifying expenditure if the cash basis election had not been made, any such expenditure which has not been relieved under the cash basis will qualify for capital allowances. For the purposes of claiming the annual investment allowance or first year allowances, the expenditure is treated as being incurred in the first chargeable period for which the cash basis no longer applies. See **22.38** for the treatment of the expenditure when pooled. See **20.11** for the provisions applying where a person enters the cash basis and there is unrelieved expenditure for capital allowances purposes.

Chargeable periods (CAA 2001, s 6)

Corporation tax

[22.9] For a company, capital allowances are treated as an expense of the trade and deducted in calculating the trading profits. The chargeable period by reference to which capital allowances are given and balancing charges are made is the company's chargeable accounting period, so that where a period of account exceeds 12 months, it is split into a 12-month chargeable accounting period or periods and the remaining period, and relief for capital expenditure is first available according to the chargeable period in which the expenditure is incurred. Writing-down allowances are proportionately reduced for accounting periods of less than 12 months.

Income tax

[22.10] For individuals, capital allowances are treated as trading expenses (and balancing charges are treated as trading receipts) of the period of account. This is normally the period for which accounts are drawn up. If the period of account is longer or shorter than 12 months, writing-down allowances are increased or reduced accordingly.

If a period of account exceeds 18 months, however, capital allowances are calculated as if it was one or more periods of account of 12 months plus a period of account covering the remainder of the period. The aggregate allowances for the separate periods are then treated as a trading expense of the whole period. This prevents undue advantage being gained as a result of the long account. See Example 2 at 22.40.

See 22.1 regarding capital allowances where profits are calculated on the cash basis.

Chargeable periods for non-trading individuals

[22.11] For employees and landlords who are individuals, the chargeable period is the income tax year itself.

Date expenditure is incurred (CAA 2001, s 5)

[22.12] This is generally the date on which the obligation to pay becomes unconditional (i.e. normally the invoice date), but if any part of the payment is not due until more than four months after that date, that part of the expenditure is regarded as incurred on the due date of payment. The due date of payment is also substituted where the unconditional obligation to pay has been brought forward to obtain allowances earlier. It sometimes happens that, under large construction contracts, the purchaser becomes the owner at an earlier date than the time when the obligation to pay becomes unconditional, e.g. on presentation of an architect's certificate. Where, in those circumstances, ownership passes in one chargeable period, but the obligation becomes unconditional within the first month of the next, the expenditure is regarded as incurred in the earlier period.

Way in which capital allowances are given (CAA 2001, ss 3, 247–262, 352–353, 432, 450, 463, 478–480; ITA 2007, ss 24A, 118–120, 127A; FA 1998, Sch 18 Pt IX)

[22.13] As indicated at 22.9 and 22.10, the allowances claimed are treated as trading expenses of the period of account for sole traders and partners, and as expenses of the chargeable accounting period for trading companies, so they may form part of a loss or turn a profit into a loss. For the reliefs available for trading losses see CHAPTER 25 for individuals (i.e. sole traders and partners) and CHAPTER 26 for companies.

Allowances claimed by individual or corporate property investors are deducted as an expense in arriving at the profit of the letting business — see 32.14 onwards.

If the letting business makes a loss then an individual investor may claim to set an amount equal to the capital allowances included in the loss against any income of the same tax year or of the following tax year. However, this relief is one of a number of reliefs against general income which is subject to a cap from 2013–14 (see 2.13). The time limit for such a claim is one year from 31 January following the tax year in which the loss arises. Any loss not relieved in this way is carried forward against future income from the letting business (see 32.9). This is subject to anti-avoidance provisions which prevent relief for losses attributable to the annual investment allowance which arise in connection with certain tax avoidance arrangements (see 22.26).

A corporate investor cannot make a separate claim relating to capital allowances included in a loss on a letting business, but more generous relief for a loss on a letting business is available to a corporate investor than an individual investor (see 32.12).

Claims

[22.14] Both individuals and companies must make a specific claim for capital allowances in a tax return or amended return.

[22.15] For companies the normal time limit is two years from the end of the accounting period (see 9.23), but if HMRC enquire into the return the time limit is extended to 30 days after the time when the profits or losses of the period are finally settled (see 9.45). If the effect of a claim following an enquiry is to reduce the allowances available for a later period for which a return has been submitted, the company has 30 days from the settlement of the enquiry to make any necessary amendments to the return, failing which amendments will be made by HMRC. If HMRC make an assessment under their 'discovery' powers (see **9.46**), then providing the company had not made careless or deliberate inaccuracies, further claims may be made within one year from the end of the accounting period in which the assessment is made.

[22.16] For individuals, capital allowances are subject to the same time limits as for other entries in returns, i.e. the time limit for a capital allowances claim is the same as the time limit for filing the return (see **9.15**). Any amendment must normally be made within 12 months after the 31 January filing date for the return, although special rules apply to fixtures (see **22.45**). If HMRC enquire into the return, amendments may be made while the enquiry is in progress (see **9.41**). If HMRC make an assessment under their 'discovery' powers (see **9.46**), then providing the taxpayer had not made careless or deliberate inaccuracies, further claims may be made within one year from the end of the tax year in which the assessment is made.

[22.17] HMRC's view is that once a business has chosen to claim one type of capital allowance rather than another, that choice may not be reversed in respect of expenditure incurred in a closed year. Full details can be found in HMRC Brief 12/2009.

[22.18] A taxpayer may claim less than the full allowances available if so wished. This may enable him to make better use of other available reliefs and allowances (see Tax points at **22.52**).

Balancing allowances and charges (CAA 2001, ss 55, 56, 60–64, 70DA, 417, 418, 441–445, 457, 458, 471, 472)

[22.19] The capital allowances legislation provides that when an asset is sold, a 'balancing allowance' is given for any amount by which the sale proceeds fall short of the unrelieved expenditure on the asset. If the proceeds exceed the unrelieved expenditure, the excess is included in taxable income by means of a 'balancing charge'. If the proceeds exceed the original cost, however, the excess over cost is dealt with under the capital gains rules (see **22.46**), except for sales of know-how where special rules apply (see **22.48**).

Balancing charges may still arise on buildings in enterprise zones after April 2011 despite the withdrawal of those allowances (see **22.51**).

For plant and machinery, balancing allowances and charges are normally dealt with on a 'pool' basis for most assets (see **22.36** onwards).

Connected persons, etc. (CAA 2001, ss 61, 212A–212S, 265–268, 567–570, 573, 575; CTA 2010, ss 938–953)

[22.20] If an asset is withdrawn from a business for personal use or sold to a connected person for use other than in a business, the amount to be included as sales proceeds is usually the open market value. (The definition of 'connected person' is broadly the same as that for capital gains tax — see **4.11** — although it is slightly wider.)

On a sale of plant and machinery between connected persons, open market value is not used for the seller if the buyer's expenditure is taken into account for capital allowances (so that, for example, intra-group transfers are taken into account at the price paid).

On a sale of assets other than plant and machinery open market value is used, except that for some allowances (e.g. mineral extraction and research and development allowances), providing the sale was not made to obtain a tax advantage, a joint claim may be made by seller and buyer, within two years after the sale, for the sale to be treated as made at written-down value.

Where the transfer of an asset to a connected person takes place at the time when the business itself is transferred, the assets are treated as being sold at open market value. However, the predecessor and successor may make a joint election, within two years from the date of the transfer, for it to be treated as made at the tax written-down value, so there will be no balancing adjustment on the predecessor and the successor will take over the claims for allowances from that point. The most common example of the application of these rules is when a business is transferred to a company (see **27.3**). Such an election cannot be made for corporation tax purposes where the transferor and transferee are both carrying on a business of leasing plant and machinery.

Special rules apply where a trade is transferred from one company to another, and at some time within one year before and two years after the transfer, the same persons own three-quarters or more of the trade (see **26.24**). These rules enable the predecessor's capital allowances computations to continue. First year allowances on plant and machinery are claimed by whoever incurred the expenditure and balancing adjustments are made on the company carrying on the trade at the time of the disposal. Writing-down allowances are split on a time basis.

There are provisions to prevent tax avoidance through the transfer of an entitlement to benefit from capital allowances on plant and machinery where the tax written-down value exceeds its balance sheet value. Broadly the legislation is designed to prevent a company or group acquiring a company, or an increased share in a company, or a partnership, or a qualifying activity, for the purpose of accessing the capital allowances and claiming relief for those allowances against its existing profits. The legislation can apply in certain circumstances where the change in ownership etc. was not specifically for the purposes of accessing the allowances. It does not prevent relief being given after the change of ownership transaction, but the relief can only reduce the same profits and to the same extent that they could have been reduced before the change.

Interaction with VAT capital goods scheme (CAA 2001, ss 234–246, 345–351, 446–449, 546–551)

[22.21] Input VAT adjustments under the VAT capital goods scheme (see **7.28**) are reflected in capital allowances computations. Adjustments for VAT on computers, ships, boats and other vessels, and aircraft are made in the plant and machinery main pool or short-life asset pool in the period in which the

VAT adjustment is made. Where the original expenditure qualified for the first year allowance (FYA) or the annual investment allowance (AIA) on plant and machinery (see **22.26** and **22.28** onwards), any additional VAT liability is treated as additional expenditure qualifying for extra FYA or AIA, the extra allowance being given in the adjustment period.

Adjustments may also be required for VAT on buildings where business premises renovation allowances are claimed (see **32.19**).

Plant and machinery

What is plant and machinery? (CAA 2001, ss 21–38, 71)

[22.22] There is no overall definition of plant and machinery in the legislation, although there are certain items that are specifically stated to be within the definition, for example thermal insulation in industrial and commercial buildings.

In addition, the legislation explicitly lists certain expenditure on buildings and structures that cannot be treated as plant or machinery, and lists other items of expenditure which are not affected by the exclusions and which will in general be accepted by HMRC as plant and machinery. Most of these items derive from court decisions.

[22.23] Deciding what 'machinery' is does not pose much of a problem, but the question of what is and is not plant has come before the courts many times. The main problem lies in distinguishing the 'apparatus' *with* which a business is carried on from the 'setting' *in* which it is carried on. Items forming part of the setting do not qualify for allowances unless the business is one in which atmosphere or ambience is important, but, even so, allowances for plant are not available on expenditure on an asset which becomes part of the premises, such as shop fronts, flooring and suspended ceilings. (Although initial expenditure on a shop front is disallowed, the cost of a subsequent replacement is allowed as a revenue expense against the profit, but excluding any improvement element.) Lifts and central heating systems are treated as plant, while basic electricity and plumbing systems are not. Specific lighting to create atmosphere in a hotel and special lighting in fast food restaurants have been held to be plant. A tenant who incurs expenditure on items that become landlord's fixtures can nonetheless claim allowances — see **22.45**.

[22.24] Expenditure on computer hardware is capital expenditure on plant and machinery. Allowances will usually be claimed under the 'short-life assets' rules (see **22.41**). Unless it is developed 'in house', computer software is usually licensed for lifetime to a particular user or users rather than being purchased outright. Despite the fact that a licence to use software is an intangible asset, it is specifically provided that capital expenditure on licensed software and electronically transmitted software qualifies for plant and machinery allowances. Where computer software is treated as part of the cost of the related hardware, it is not affected by the rules for companies relating to intangible assets (see **20.35**) and it remains within the capital allowances regime. Where it is not so treated, it will be dealt with under the intangible assets provisions unless the company elects, within two years after the end of the accounting period in which the expenditure was incurred, for the capital allowances provisions to apply. Such an election is irrevocable.

If licensed software is acquired on rental, the rentals are deducted from profit over the life of the software. Where a lump sum is paid, HMRC normally take the view that the cost of software with an expected life of less than two years may be treated as a revenue expense and deducted from profit. Otherwise, subject to what is said above about the intangible assets provisions for companies, it will usually be treated as capital expenditure for which plant and machinery allowances may be claimed (and short-life asset treatment being used if appropriate — see 22.41). The treatment of in-house software is broadly similar, being either treated as capital or revenue depending on the expected period of use.

The cost of developing a website is regarded by HMRC as capital expenditure, and should qualify for allowances as computer software. Subsequent expenditure on updating the site will normally qualify as revenue expenditure, unless the whole site is completely rewritten. The cost of acquiring a domain name is incurred on an intangible asset, so capital allowances would not be available, but the expenditure would be dealt with for companies under the intangible assets rules (see 20.35).

Capital allowances on cars (CAA 2001, ss 104A, 104AA, 104E, 104F, 208A, 268A–268D; SI 2016/984)

[22.25] The capital allowances treatment for cars is based on the car's carbon dioxide (CO_2) emissions rather than cost. First year allowances are available until 31 March 2021 on cars with very low CO_2 emissions but expenditure on other cars is allocated to one of the two plant and machinery pools. Expenditure on cars with CO_2 emissions exceeding 130g/km (to be reduced to 110g/km for expenditure on or after 1 April 2018; 160g/km for expenditure before 1 April 2013 for corporation tax or 6 April 2013 for income tax) is allocated to the special rate pool (see 22.36) on which the writing-down allowance is currently 8% (see 22.27). Expenditure on cars with emissions of 130g/km or less (110g/km or less from 1 April 2018; 160g/km or less before 1 or 6 April 2013) are allocated to the main rate pool (see 22.38) on which the writing-down allowance is currently 18%. All cars registered before 1 March 2001 are also 'main rate cars', as are cars which are electrically propelled, but see 22.30 regarding first year allowances currently available on electric cars. Cars do not include motor cycles.

Cars that are used partly for private use by a sole trader or partner are allocated to a single asset pool (see 22.42) to enable the private use adjustment to be made, but the rate of writing-down allowance will still depend on the car's CO_2 emissions.

Various provisions prevent the artificial generation of balancing allowances in certain circumstances.

See **20.11** regarding the treatment of capital expenditure where profits are calculated on the cash basis. In general capital allowances are not available, except on expenditure on a car.

Allowances presently available (CAA 2001, ss 39, 45A–46, 51A–52, 55, 56, Sch A1; FA 2013, Sch 1; FA 2014, Sch 2)

[22.26] An *annual investment allowance* (AIA) of up to £200,000 applies for investment in plant and machinery for expenditure incurred on or after 1 January 2016. The AIA provides a 100% allowance for the first £200,000 of investment in plant and machinery (excluding cars but including long-life assets and integral features), irrespective of the size of the business. The allowance does not replace the existing first year allowances for specific types of expenditure (see **22.28**).

The £200,000 limit is increased or reduced where the chargeable period is more or less than a year. Qualifying expenditure in excess of the limit enters either the 'main pool' or the 'special rate' pool and is eligible for either a writing-down allowance currently at 18% or 8% (see **22.27**) or a first year allowance if appropriate (see **22.28**). There are rules to fix the maximum allowance where a chargeable period straddles the relevant date of an increase or decrease in the limit (see Example 3 in **22.40**). A claim may be limited to part of the qualifying expenditure. AIA is not available on expenditure incurred in the period in which the trade is permanently discontinued and HMRC contend that this includes a situation where a sole trader transfers his business to a limited company.

A partnership of which all the members are individuals is eligible for a single AIA of up to £200,000. A single company is also entitled to one AIA. A group of companies is entitled to only one AIA, which can be shared between the companies.

Special rules apply where two or more groups of companies are under common control. Where two or more companies are under common control but do not form a group, each company is entitled to an AIA of up to £200,000 unless:

- the companies are engaged in similar activities (determined by reference to turnover and the NACE classification system, see HMRC Capital Allowances Manual CA23090);
- the companies share the same premises at the end of the relevant chargeable period of one or both of the companies.

Further rules apply to ensure that businesses who share a single AIA do not get excessive relief where they have different chargeable periods or where the AIA limit increases or decreases.

There are anti-avoidance provisions to prevent relief against general income for a loss from a UK or overseas property business which is attributable to the AIA and arises from relevant tax avoidance arrangements. AIA is not available where obtaining it is the main benefit of the transaction.

[22.27] The allowances otherwise available for investment in plant and machinery are writing-down allowances and, in some circumstances, first year allowances (see **22.28**). There are also balancing allowances and balancing charges which arise when the business ceases or sometimes when a particular asset is disposed of.

Writing-down allowances are currently given at 18% per annum on expenditure in the main pool, on the reducing balance method. Expenditure on certain assets is 'special rate' expenditure which currently attracts writing-down allowances at 8% only (see **22.36**). A rate of 10% applies to special rate expenditure incurred wholly for the purposes of a 'ring fence' trade of companies who carry out certain oil-related activities.

For companies, the writing-down allowance is proportionately reduced in respect of accounting periods of less than 12 months. For individuals, the writing-down allowance is proportionately reduced or increased if the period of account is less than or more than 12 months, and there are special rules if it exceeds 18 months (see **22.10** and Example 2 at **22.40**).

[22.28] *First year allowances* are available in the circumstances indicated below, the allowances being instead of the first year's writing-down allowance. Any available first year allowance (FYA) may be claimed in full regardless of the length of the chargeable period. FYAs cannot be claimed for the chargeable period in which the trade is permanently discontinued. Nor can they be claimed on transactions between connected persons (as to which see **22.20**), or on plant and machinery used for other purposes before being brought into the trade or obtained as a gift, or where obtaining capital allowances is the main benefit of the transaction. Subject to what is said below, FYAs are not available for expenditure on plant and machinery for leasing or letting on hire, cars (except certain low emission cars) and taxis.

There is a wide range of assets on which FYAs are presently available, the allowance under some headings being restricted to expenditure within a specified period. The headings are as follows and the detailed rules are summarised below:

- Expenditure on energy-saving equipment* (see **22.29**)
- Expenditure on low CO_2 emissions cars* — up to 31 March 2021 (see **22.30**)
- Expenditure on natural gas/hydrogen refuelling equipment — up to 31 March 2018 (see **22.30**)
- Expenditure on environmentally beneficial plant or machinery* (see **22.31**)
- Expenditure incurred on or after 1 April 2010 and before 1 April 2018 for corporation tax and on or after 6 April 2010 and before 6 April 2018 for income tax on zero-emission goods vehicles (see **22.33**)
- Expenditure incurred by trading companies on plant and machinery for use primarily in designated assisted areas within enterprise zones where the expenditure is incurred in the eight-year period from the date the area is (or is treated as) designated (see **22.34**)
- September 2017 Finance Bill, which is expected to receive Royal Assent in November 2017, includes provision for FYAs on electric charge-point equipment (see **22.35**)

* Expenditure incurred on or after 17 April 2002 on energy-saving or environmentally beneficial plant and machinery for leasing qualifies despite the general exclusion stated above for plant and machinery for leasing, but for expenditure incurred after 31 March 2006, only if it is provided for leasing under an excluded lease of background plant and machinery for a building. Expenditure before 1 April 2013 on low CO_2 emissions cars acquired for leasing also qualifies.

[22.29] 100% FYAs are available for expenditure on new plant and machinery within stipulated categories (heat and power systems, lighting, refrigeration etc.) that have been certified as meeting energy efficiency criteria. Businesses such as energy service companies may claim the allowance on such equipment provided and operated on a client's business premises under an energy management contract if the company and the client make a joint election. The FYA for such expenditure is also available to leasing businesses, but only as outlined in **22.28**. The list of qualifying categories is regularly updated and can be found at www.gov.uk/guidance/energy-technology-list. 100% FYAs are not available for expenditure incurred on or after 1 April 2012 for corporation tax or on or after 6 April 2012 for income tax on plant and machinery to generate renewable electricity or heat where tariff payments are received under either of the renewable energy schemes introduced by the Department of Energy and Climate Change. The restriction applies from 1 or 6 April 2014 (as the case may be) for combined heat and power equipment.

[22.30] 100% FYAs may be claimed for expenditure incurred before 1 April 2021 on new electric cars and cars with low CO_2 emissions (i.e. not more than 50g/km for expenditure incurred on or after 1 April 2018; 75g/km for expenditure incurred from 1 April 2015 to 31 March 2018, 95g/km for expenditure incurred from 1 April 2013 to 31 March 2015, 110g/km for expenditure incurred from 1 April 2008 to 31 March 2013 subject to transitional rules, 120g/km before 1 April 2008). 'Car' in this case includes a taxi but does not include a motor cycle. 100% FYAs may also be claimed for expenditure incurred before 1 April 2018 on new plant and machinery for refuelling stations used to refuel vehicles with natural gas or hydrogen fuel. Expenditure incurred on low CO_2 emissions cars acquired for leasing on or after 17 April 2002 and before 1 April 2013 qualified for FYAs despite the general exclusion for plant and machinery for leasing.

[22.31] 100% FYAs are available for certain expenditure on environmentally beneficial plant and machinery (other than long-life plant and machinery). The allowances apply to expenditure on designated plant and machinery to save energy, reduce water use, or improve water quality. The qualifying technologies and products are detailed in the energy and water technology criteria lists available at www.gov.uk/government/publications/water-efficient-enhanced-capital-allowances. The list of qualifying categories is updated, usually annually, by Treasury Order. See **22.28** regarding leasing.

[22.32] With effect from 1 April 2008 it is possible for FYAs on both energy-saving plant and machinery (see **22.29**) and environmentally-beneficial plant and machinery (see **22.31**) to be converted into a repayable tax credit where they give rise to a loss. The relief applies to companies only and broadly the company may claim a first-year tax credit equal to 19% of the loss, subject to an upper limit and certain other restrictions. This relief is available until 31 March 2018.

[22.33] 100% FYAs are available on expenditure incurred on or after 1 April 2010 and before 1 April 2018 for corporation tax and on or after 6 April 2010 and before 6 April 2018 for income tax on new, unused zero-emission goods vehicles. A zero-emission goods vehicle is one which cannot under any circumstances produce CO_2 emissions when driven, and is of a design primarily suited to the conveyance of goods or burden. Certain exclusions apply. Expenditure on assets for leasing are excluded as are certain businesses, in particular, fishery, aquaculture and waste management businesses, and those considered to be in financial difficulty. Allowances are not available if another state aid has been or will be received. There is a cap of €85 million on the amount of expenditure on which connected businesses may claim the allowances over the eight-year period.

[22.34] 100% FYAs are available on expenditure incurred by trading companies on new, unused plant and machinery for use primarily in a designated assisted area within certain enterprise zones. The expenditure must be incurred in the eight-year period from the date the area is (or is treated as) designated, the area must be a designated assisted area at the time the expenditure is incurred, and the plant and machinery must not be held primarily for use in an area outside of the designated assisted area for a period of five years. Expenditure must be incurred for the purpose of, broadly, a new or expanding business carried on by the company, and must not be replacement expenditure. Certain exclusions apply. Expenditure on assets for leasing are excluded as are certain types of business, and those considered to be in financial difficulty. There is a cap of €125 million on the amount of expenditure incurred by any person on which the allowances may be claimed in respect of a single investment project over the eight-year period. A list of the enterprise zones can be found in SI 2014/3183, SI 2015/2047, and SI 2016/751.

[22.35] September 2017 Finance Bill, which is expected to receive Royal Assent in November 2017, includes provision for 100% FYAs for expenditure incurred on or after 23 November 2016 and before 1 April 2019 for corporation tax or 6 April 2019 for income tax on new, unused electric vehicle charging point equipment installed solely for the purpose of charging electric vehicles.

Pooling expenditure (CAA 2001, ss 53, 54, 57–59, 104A–C)

[22.36] Subject to certain exceptions, qualifying expenditure on plant and machinery is pooled for the purpose of calculating writing-down allowances, balancing allowances and balancing charges. There are single asset pools, class pools and the main pool. Qualifying expenditure is allocated to the main pool (see **22.38**) if it does not have to be allocated to a class pool or single asset pool (see **22.37**).

Class pools are required for:

- Special rate expenditure.

- Assets for overseas leasing (see **22.44**).

A class pool will include all expenditure on assets within the 'class' concerned.

With effect, broadly, from April 2008, 'special rate expenditure' must be allocated to a 'special rate pool' (unless it is allocated to a single asset pool — see **22.37**) for which the current rate of writing-down allowance is 8% (rather than the rate of 18% applicable to the main pool).

'Special rate expenditure' includes—

(a) Expenditure incurred on or after 1 April 2008 (corporation tax) or 6 April 2008 (income tax) on thermal insulation and integral features (as described in **22.45**);

(b) Expenditure incurred on or after 1 April 2008 (corporation tax) or 6 April 2008 (income tax) on long-life assets, and expenditure incurred before that date on long-life assets not previously allocated to a pool (see **22.43**);

(c) Expenditure incurred broadly on or after 1 April 2009 (corporation tax) or 6 April 2009 (income tax) on a car that is not a 'main rate car' (see **22.25**);

(d) Expenditure incurred on or after 1 April 2010 on gas which functions as plant in particular gas storage facilities; and

(e) Expenditure incurred on or after 1 April 2012 (corporation tax) or 6 April 2012 (income tax) on solar panels.

[22.37] *Single asset pools* are required for:

- Short life assets (at the taxpayer's option, any asset that is expected to be disposed of within nine years (five years for expenditure incurred before April 2011) — see **22.41**).
- Any asset with part private use by a sole trader or partner (see **22.42**).

A single asset pool cannot contain expenditure relating to more than one asset.

[22.38] For the main pool, the writing-down allowance currently at the rate of 18% per annum (reducing balance method) is calculated on the unrelieved expenditure brought forward from the previous period, plus expenditure in the period, but excluding expenditure on which first year allowances (FYA) have been claimed, unless the asset has been disposed of in the same period, in which case any unallowed expenditure is included, less any sales proceeds (up to, but not exceeding, the original cost — see **22.46**). If the proceeds exceed the pool balance, a balancing charge is made. Any available FYA is calculated separately and the remainder of the expenditure is then included in the pool balance carried forward (unless already included as indicated above). See Example 1.

Where a business enters the cash basis, either for small businesses (see **20.4**) or for property businesses (see **32.6**), only unrelieved qualifying expenditure in respect of a car will be brought forward from the previous period, as capital allowances may only be claimed on cars under the cash basis (see **20.11**). Where a business leaves the cash basis, the unrelieved portion of any expenditure incurred that would have been qualifying expenditure if the cash basis had not applied qualifies for capital allowances. For the purposes of pooling the expenditure, the full amount of the expenditure is added to the appropriate pool and the balance in the pool is reduced by the amount already relieved under the cash basis. For the purposes of determining any entitlement to the annual investment allowance or first year allowances the unrelieved expenditure is treated as being incurred in the first chargeable period for which the cash basis no longer applies.

Where a person incurs annual investment allowance (AIA) qualifying expenditure (see 22.26) and an AIA is made in respect of that expenditure, the expenditure is added to the pool and the balance in the pool is reduced by the amount of the AIA. This ensures that the rules on allocating disposal proceeds work correctly on a subsequent disposal of any asset on which the AIA was claimed.

There is a 'small pools' writing-down allowance, available for the main pool and the special rate pool only (i.e. not for any single asset pool). Where the pool balance is £1,000 or less the taxpayer may claim all or part of that balance as a writing-down allowance. This is a simplification measure removing the need for businesses to carry forward small balances and calculating the writing-down allowance each year.

[22.39] A balancing allowance will not arise on the main pool, except on a cessation of trade where the total sales proceeds are less than the pool balance. The same applies to long-life asset pools which applied broadly before April 2008 (see 22.43). See 22.44 for assets for overseas leasing. For single asset pools, a balancing allowance or charge is made when the asset is disposed of. If the single asset is disposed of in the period in which it is acquired for less than cost, there will be a balancing allowance on the shortfall. If it is disposed of in that period for more than cost the excess will not be brought into account for capital allowances at all and the capital profit will be dealt with under the capital gains tax legislation (the gain being exempt if the asset is a car).

[22.40] The general rules are illustrated in Example 1. See also Example 2, which illustrates the special rules mentioned in 22.10 for income tax accounting periods that exceed 18 months, and Example 3 which shows entitlement to the annual investment allowance where the chargeable period straddles the date of an increase or decrease in the limit.

Example 1

A trader has the following transactions in 'main pool' plant in the years ended 31 December 2014, 2015, 2016 and 2017, plant purchases qualifying for the FYA (see 20.28) where appropriate:

		£
May 2014	Arm's length purchase of low CO_2 emission car	10,000
June 2014	Proceeds of sales	3,000
August 2014	Purchase from associated business	5,000
October 2014	Purchase of plant and machinery for which full AIA claimed	30,000
January 2015	Proceeds of sales	7,500

| December 2015 | Arm's length purchase of main rate car | 7,000 |
| July 2017 | Arm's length purchase of zero-emission goods vehicle | 13,000 |

The main pool balance brought forward at 1 January 2014 is £8,000.

The allowances are calculated as follows:

	£	£
Year to 31 December 2014		
Pool balance brought forward		8,000
Additions not qualifying for FYA:		
Additions October 2014 for which full AIA claimed (see **22.38** regarding the requirement to add to the pool)		30,000
AIA claimed		(30,000)
August 2014 from connected person (not based on market value since dealt with as a sale in the computations of the associated business — see **22.20**)		5,000
		13,000
Less sales proceeds June 2014		(3,000)
		10,000
Writing-down allowance 18% (reduces taxable profit)		(1,800)
		8,200
Additions May 2014 qualifying for FYA	10,000	
FYA 100% (reduces taxable profit)	(10,000)	
Balance allocated to main pool		—
Pool balance carried forward		8,200
Year to 31 December 2015		
Additions December 2015 not qualifying for FYA		7,000
Less sales proceeds January 2015		(7,500)
		7,700
Writing-down allowance 18% (reduces taxable profit)		(1,386)
Pool balance carried forward		6,314
Year to 31 December 2016		
Writing-down allowance 18% (reduces taxable profit)		(1,137)
Pool balance carried forward		5,177
Year to 31 December 2017		
Writing-down allowance 18% (reduces taxable profit)		(932)
Pool balance carried forward		4,245
Addition July 2017 qualifying for FYA	13,000	

FYA 100% (reduces taxable profit)	(13,000)	
Balance allocated to main pool		—
Pool balance carried forward		£4,245

Example 2

A trader's 22-month account is made up from 1 June 2016 to 31 March 2018. Main pool balance brought forward is £100,000. The only addition was a new low CO_2 emission car qualifying for 100% FYA that cost £10,000 in March 2017. The allowances will be calculated as follows:

	£	£
Year to 31 May 2017		
Pool balance brought forward		100,000
WDA 18%		(18,000)
		82,000
10 mths to 31 March 2018		
WDA 18% x 10/12		(12,300)
		69,700
Additions qualifying for FYA	10,000	
FYA 100%	(10,000)	
Balance allocated to main pool		—
Written-down value carried forward		69,700
Total allowances for period treated as trading expense (18,000 + 12,300 + 10,000)		£40,300

Example 3

The maximum AIA entitlement of a company with a 12-month accounting period ending on 31 March 2016 is calculated as follows:

		£
1 April 2015 to 31 December 2015	9/12 x 500,000	375,000
1 January 2016 to 31 March 2016	3/12 x 200,000	50,000
		£425,000

Even though the company's maximum entitlement for the year is £425,000, there are maximum allowances which can be claimed for actual expenditure incurred in each of the periods above. The maximum allowance for expenditure actually incurred in the period 1 January 2016 to 31 March 2016 is £50,000. This does not affect the maximum AIA entitlement for the whole accounting period, just the amount incurred after 31 December 2015 which may be covered by AIA. If the company incurred no qualifying expenditure in the period 1 April 2015 to 31 December 2015, and then spent £100,000 in the period 1 January 2016 to 31 March 2016 the maximum AIA available for that part of the period would be £50,000.

Short-life assets (CAA 2001, ss 83–89)

[22.41] Some assets have a very short life and depreciate very quickly. Pooling them within the main pool would not give relief for their cost over their life span because when they are disposed of, any unrelieved expenditure remains in the pool to be written off over future years (unless the business has ceased, when a pool balancing adjustment is made — see **22.38** and **22.39**). An election may be made to have the capital allowances on specified items of plant and machinery calculated separately in single asset pools under the 'short-life assets' provisions. A balancing allowance or charge will then arise if the asset is disposed of within either four years or eight years from the end of the accounting period in which it is acquired, depending on when the asset was acquired.

For expenditure incurred before 1 April 2011 for corporation tax or 6 April 2011 for income tax, the relevant cut-off is four years, for expenditure incurred on or after those dates it is eight years. If the asset is still held at the end of that period, the tax written-down value is transferred into the main pool. Cars (including hire cars other than those hired to someone receiving mobility allowance or disability living allowance) and any assets which would not in any event have been included in the main pool of expenditure cannot be dealt with under the short-life assets rules. 'Special rate expenditure' (see **22.36**) is also excluded. Where a car hired to someone receiving mobility allowance or disability living allowance is treated as a short life asset and is still held for either four or eight years (as applicable) from the end of the accounting period in which it was acquired, the tax written-down value will be transferred to one of the two plant and machinery pools, depending on the level of CO_2 emissions (see **22.25**).

The election for this treatment is irrevocable, and must be made within two years after the end of the accounting period in which the expenditure is incurred for companies and within one year after the 31 January following the tax year in which the period of account in which the expenditure was incurred ends for individuals. HMRC have issued guidelines (Statement of Practice SP 1/86) on practical aspects of the short-life assets rules, including provisions for grouping classes of assets where individual treatment is impossible or impracticable.

Assets with part private use (CAA 2001, ss 205–208)

[22.42] Any business asset that is privately used by a sole proprietor or by a partner in a business is dealt with in a separate single asset pool. Allowances and charges for each privately-used asset are calculated in the normal way, but the available allowance or charge is restricted to the business proportion. An individual balancing adjustment is made when the asset is disposed of.

This does not apply to assets used by directors of family companies. The use of company assets for private purposes by directors or employees does not affect the company's capital allowances position, but results in a benefits charge on the director/employee (see CHAPTER 10).

Long-life plant and machinery (CAA 2001, ss 90–103; FA 2008, s 83)

[22.43] Plant and machinery first bought new with an expected working life of 25 years or more is allocated to the 'special rate pool' as a long-life asset (see 22.36). The rate of allowances is 8% on the reducing balance throughout its life. Any balance of unrelieved expenditure in the 'long-life asset pool' at 1 April 2008 for corporation tax and 6 April 2008 when the special rate pool was introduced was added to the special rate pool.

The long-life asset provisions do not apply to cars (including hire cars), taxis, motor cycles or to certain ships or railway assets bought before the end of 2010, or to assets used in a dwelling house, retail shop, showroom, hotel or office. Nor do they apply where total expenditure on such long-life assets does not exceed £100,000 a year (divided pro rata for 51% group companies, and increased or reduced proportionately for chargeable periods longer or shorter than 12 months). HMRC do not consider that modern printing equipment falls into the category of long-life assets. Most of the plant and machinery affected by these rules would have alternatively qualified for industrial buildings allowances before April 2011 and businesses could choose which allowances to claim. Those who had chosen industrial buildings allowances were denied relief for any unrelieved balance of their expenditure at April 2011 when industrial building allowances were withdrawn.

The reduced rate of writing-down allowance does not apply to second-hand assets if the pre-26 November 1996 rules applied to the vendor.

Assets for overseas leasing (CAA 2001, ss 105–126)

[22.44] Assets leased before 1 April 2006 to non-UK residents who do not use them for a UK trade are kept in a separate class pool, normally attracting writing-down allowances at 10%, balancing charges where the total sales proceeds exceed the tax written-down value of all such assets, and a balancing allowance where the tax written-down value exceeds the total proceeds in the final chargeable period (i.e. the period after which there can be no more disposal receipts). In some circumstances, no allowances at all are available.

Fixtures (CAA 2001, ss 70A–70YJ, 172–204)

[22.45] Complex rules apply in relation to plant and machinery allowances on fixtures. Those who let property can claim the allowances on expenditure incurred on fixtures and fittings, subject to what is said below, and provided they do not calculate profits on the cash basis for unincorporated property businesses (see 32.6). Where a business tenant incurs the expenditure, and the fixtures become the landlord's property in law, the tenant can nonetheless claim allowances. Where fixtures are provided by equipment lessors, the lessee (who may be the owner or tenant of the property) and the equipment lessor may elect for the equipment lessor to claim the allowances.

From (broadly) 1 April 2006, these provisions do not apply to 'long funding leases'. A long funding lease is essentially a financing transaction. Under the long funding lease provisions, the lessee is normally allowed to claim the allowances, thus equating the position with someone who borrows to buy an asset rather than leasing it (see **22.5**). Again this is subject to complex rules.

See **22.29** regarding elections by energy service companies and their clients to enable the companies to claim 100% FYAs on energy-saving plant and machinery, and also for the entitlement of equipment lessors to claim 100% FYAs on certain assets.

Allowances cannot be claimed on fixtures leased to non-taxpayers, such as charities, unless the lessor has an interest in the relevant land. Nor can they be claimed by equipment lessors or landlords on fixtures in dwelling houses. An exception was made for expenditure incurred by equipment lessors between 28 July 2000 and 31 December 2007 on boilers, radiators, heat exchangers and heating controls installed in low income homes under the Government's Affordable Warmth Programme. Where capital allowances are not available, landlords will usually be able to claim relief for replacement of domestic items (see **32.15**).

Allowances are not available on any amount in excess of the original cost of the fixtures when new and restrictions apply where there has been a capital allowances claim by a previous owner to ensure that expenditure on a fixture is written off against taxable profits only once over its economic life. The maximum amount on which the purchaser can claim allowances is the sum of the disposal value brought in by the past owner (i.e. the last person that was treated as the owner of the fixture by the fixtures legislation, which is not necessarily the person from whom the current owner purchased the fixture) and any installation costs incurred by the purchaser.

There were difficulties in applying these provisions because the legislation did not prescribe when expenditure on fixtures should be pooled, so that there was no time limit laid down to govern when a seller and purchaser should agree the part of the sale price of a property that should be attributed to the fixtures. With effect for expenditure incurred by the purchaser of qualifying fixtures on or after 1 April 2012 for corporation tax or on or after 6 April 2012 for income tax (subject to transitional provisions), the availability of capital allowances to the purchaser is conditional on the previous business expenditure on such fixtures being pooled before a subsequent transfer to another person, and the value of fixtures being formally fixed within two years of a transfer.

In most cases an apportionment of the sale price will be required to formally fix the value. This is achieved either by application to a tribunal by the past owner or current owner, or by a joint election, within two years of the sale. The time limit for election is extended where an application has been made to the tribunal but not determined or withdrawn within the two-year limit. There may be purchases by persons who are not entitled to claim capital allowances, such as charities not chargeable to tax, and such persons may miss the opportunity to make an election or apply to a tribunal to fix a value to enable a future business purchaser to claim fixture allowances. In these limited circumstances, on a future sale by the charity, the purchaser could instead obtain a written statement from the charity confirming that the apportionment is no longer able to be made, and a written statement from the past owner of the fixture of the disposal value that they brought into account on the sale to the charity. Where a previous business owner sells the former business premises with its fixtures some time after he has finalised his business cessation accounts, he may in these circumstances, within two years of cessation of ownership of the fixtures, provide a statement to the purchaser of the fixture disposal value he brought into account.

If the expenditure has not been pooled by the past owner in a chargeable period beginning on or before the date of sale (other than where he claimed a first year allowance), or if the value has not been formally fixed in cases where it should have been, the purchaser is treated as having no qualifying expenditure.

Where a claim in a return becomes incorrect, for example because of the election, the claimant must notify an amendment to the return within three months after becoming aware of that fact.

There are anti-avoidance provisions to prevent allowances on fixtures being artificially accelerated. The rate of writing-down allowance on certain 'integral features' of a building (see 22.36) is the special rate of 8%. 'Integral features' include electrical (including lighting) systems; cold water systems; space or water heating systems; powered systems of ventilation; air cooling or air purification (and any floor or ceiling comprised in such systems); lifts, escalators and moving walkways; and external solar shading.

Effect of capital allowances on capital gains tax computation (TCGA 1992, ss 41, 55)

[22.46] Capital allowances are not deducted from cost in computing a capital gain, but are taken into account in computing a capital loss. There will only be a gain if an asset is sold for more than cost, and in that event any capital allowances given will be withdrawn by the cost being taken out of the capital allowances computation and will not therefore affect the computation of the gain. There will not normally be a capital loss, since any amount by which the sale proceeds for an asset fall short of the written-down value will be taken into account in the capital allowances computation.

For plant and machinery that is moveable rather than fixed, there is no chargeable gain if it is sold for £6,000 or less. Where the proceeds exceed £6,000, the chargeable gain cannot exceed 5/3rds of the excess of the proceeds over £6,000 (see 39.4). If plant and machinery is fixed rather than moveable, gains are not exempt but they may be deferred if the item is replaced (see 29.16 onwards).

Example 4

Plant which cost a trader £50,000 in December 2010 was sold in September 2017 for £65,000. Incidental costs of sale were £1,000.

Since the plant was sold for more than cost, the capital allowances would be fully withdrawn by deducting £50,000 from the pool balance. There would be a capital gain of (£65,000 – £50,000 – £1,000 =) £14,000.

If the plant was fixed plant, the gain would be eligible for rollover relief.

If the plant was instead sold for £40,000 in September 2017, with incidental costs of sale the same at £1,000, part of the capital allowances would be withdrawn by way of a balancing charge. However, a total of £10,000 capital allowances previously given will not be withdrawn. The capital gains computation on disposal will then be:

	£	£
Proceeds	40,000	
Incidental costs of sale	(1,000)	
		39,000
Allowable expenditure		
Original cost	50,000	
Capital allowances given	(10,000)	
		40,000
Allowable loss		(£1,000)

Effectively the allowable loss is restricted to the incidental costs of sale.

See CHAPTER 4 for detailed capital gains tax provisions.

Patents (CAA 2001, ss 464–483; CTA 2009, ss 911–923; ITTOIA 2005, ss 587–599)

[22.47] Expenditure incurred in devising and patenting an invention, or an abortive attempt to do so, is allowable as a business expense and qualifies for the research and development reliefs — see **29.64** to **29.67**. Where, however, patent rights are purchased, capital allowances are available to individuals as follows. These provisions also apply to companies in respect of expenditure incurred *before* 1 April 2002. For expenditure incurred on or after that date, patents are dealt with for corporation tax under the 'Intangible assets' provisions outlined at **20.35** onwards.

The capital allowances available are writing-down allowances at 25% on the reducing balance method, with all expenditure on patent rights being pooled.

Balancing charges arise in the usual way, and a balancing allowance is given on any unallowed expenditure if the last of the rights come to an end without subsequently being revived or on the permanent discontinuance of the trade.

Although a balancing charge can never exceed the allowances given, there are specific provisions to charge a capital profit on patent rights as income rather than as a capital gain. The profit is not dealt with as part of the business profits but is charged to income or corporation tax separately over six years in equal instalments, commencing with the tax year or accounting period in which it is received, unless the taxpayer elects to have the whole sum charged in the year of receipt.

Patents allowances granted to non-traders can only be set against income from the patent rights and not against any other income.

Know-how (CAA 2001, ss 452–463; CTA 2009, ss 176–179, 908–910; ITTOIA 2005, ss 191A–195, 583–586)

[22.48] 'Know-how' is defined as any industrial information or techniques which are likely to assist in a manufacturing process, or the working of a mine, or the carrying out of agricultural, forestry or fishing operations. Revenue expenditure on creating know-how related to a trade is allowable as a business expense, and qualifies for the research and development reliefs — see **29.64** to **29.67**.

For companies, know-how is dealt with in respect of expenditure incurred on or after 1 April 2002 under the 'Intangible assets' provisions outlined at **20.35** onwards. In respect of company expenditure before that date, and expenditure by individuals, the treatment is as follows.

Capital expenditure on the acquisition of know-how for use in a trade qualifies for an annual writing-down allowance of 25% on the reducing balance method. Any additional expenditure is added to the unrelieved balance and any sale proceeds are deducted from it before calculating the writing-down allowance. If the sale proceeds exceed the tax written-down value, a balancing charge is made and this is not restricted to the allowances given, so that the balancing charge will include any excess of the proceeds over the original cost. Where there is a disposal of know-how and the trade continues, and provided the sale is not between a body of persons under common control, any disposal proceeds not brought into account for capital allowances purposes are treated as a trading receipt. This provision does not apply where profits are calculated on the cash basis for small businesses (see **20.4**).

If know-how is sold as part of a business, the payment is regarded as being for goodwill and thus dealt with under the capital gains rules, unless both seller and buyer elect within two years of the disposal for it to be treated as a sale of know-how. These provisions do not apply where profits are calculated on the cash basis for small businesses.

If the trade ceases during the writing-down period but the know-how is not sold, relief for the unallowed expenditure is given at the time of cessation by way of a balancing allowance.

Research and development (CAA 2001, ss 437–451; ITTOIA 2005, s 31C; ITA 2007, s 1006; CTA 2009, ss 1039–1142; CTA 2010, s 1138)

[22.49] Subject to any express provisions to the contrary, research and development means activities that would be treated as such in accordance with generally accepted accounting practice. Detailed guidelines can be found on the website for the Department for Business, Energy and Industrial Strategy.

Capital allowances are available at 100% on capital expenditure on research and development. The allowance need not be claimed in full. Expenditure on land and dwelling houses does not generally qualify for relief. On disposal, a balancing charge is made equal to the amount by which the disposal value (i.e. sale proceeds, compensation for destruction etc.) exceeds the allowance given, or the allowance claimed if less. If there is a capital profit it is dealt with under the capital gains rules.

If the sale takes place in the same chargeable period as that in which the expenditure is incurred, then if the proceeds are less than the expenditure the allowance is equal to the shortfall, and if the proceeds exceed the expenditure no allowance is given and the excess is dealt with under the capital gains rules.

Revenue expenditure on research and development is allowed in full as a business expense, as are certain amounts paid to research and development associations etc. Special reliefs apply to revenue expenditure on research and development by companies (see **29.64** and **29.66**).

For income tax purposes, a person who, at any time before the basis period for the tax year, has claimed research and development allowances and who still owns an asset representing the expenditure is excluded from making an election for the cash basis for small businesses (see **20.4**) for that year.

Mineral extraction (CAA 2001, ss 394–436; ITTOIA 2005, s 31C)

[22.50] Expenditure on mineral extraction qualifies for writing-down allowances on a reducing balance basis at 10% on the acquisition of a mineral asset (i.e. mineral deposits, land comprising mineral deposits, etc.), and 25% on other qualifying expenditure.

Expenditure incurred in unsuccessfully or, from 17 July 2014 successfully applying for planning permission to undertake mineral exploration and access, or to work mineral deposits, including costs of an unsuccessful appeal against refusal, qualifies for 25% relief. A mineral extraction trade is one which is chargeable to UK tax. This prevents UK taxable profits being reduced by mineral extraction allowances that are given in respect of activities where the profits are not subject to UK tax.

A balancing charge is made if sales proceeds exceed tax written-down value. A balancing allowance is given in the chargeable period when the mineral extraction trade ceases, or when particular mineral deposits cease to be worked, and in the case of pre-trading expenditure, when trading commences or exploration is abandoned before then.

A person who has carried on mineral extraction in the basis period for a tax year is excluded from making an election for the cash basis for small businesses (see 20.4) for that year.

Buildings in Enterprise Zones (CAA 2001, ss 298–313, 327–331; FA 2008, Sch 27 para 31)

[22.51] When an area was designated as an Enterprise Zone by the Secretary of State, expenditure incurred or contracted for within ten years after the creation of the zone on any buildings other than dwelling houses qualified for industrial buildings allowances at a special rate known as enterprise zone allowances or EZAs.

EZAs were withdrawn from April 2011.

Balancing allowances or charges continued to apply on the disposal of buildings on which EZAs had been claimed for chargeable periods beginning before 1 April 2011 (corporation tax) or 6 April 2011 (income tax). Despite the abolition of EZAs from April 2011, balancing charges are retained for a limited period, and a charge may still arise where a business disposes of a building within seven years of first use, even if this is in a chargeable period beginning on or after 1 April 2011 (corporation tax) or 6 April 2011 (income tax).

Tax points

[22.52] Note the following:

- HMRC guidance indicates that if a trader incurs capital expenditure in excess of the annual investment allowance (AIA) limit (see 22.26) he may allocate the 100% AIA between different types of expenditure as he sees fit. For example, he may allocate it first against expenditure on integral features that would otherwise qualify for the lower 'special rate' of, currently, 8%.
- A specific claim for capital allowances must be made by individuals, partnerships and companies, so it is important to ensure that the appropriate entries are made on the tax return.
- If claiming the maximum capital allowances on plant and machinery means wasting personal allowances, a trader can reduce his capital allowances claim, or not claim allowances at all — see 22.18. He will then get writing-down allowances on an increased amount in future years.
- Both individuals and companies can revise capital allowances claims within the period allowed for making returns or amendments to returns, but see 22.17 regarding the inability to change the choice of allowances claimed in closed years.
- Companies will benefit by not taking allowances where they want to leave profits high enough to take advantage of reliefs which are only available in the current period, such as double tax relief. The amount on

which writing-down allowances will be available in later years is increased accordingly. However, see **22.20** regarding the restriction on the transfer of entitlement to plant and machinery allowances in certain circumstances.

- Allowances available on capital expenditure incurred on commencing trading as a sole trader or in partnership may contribute to a trading loss, which may be carried back against the income of earlier years (see CHAPTER **25**).

- Whereas only a maximum 18% writing-down allowance is currently available on purchased cars (and only 8% in some cases — see **22.25**), if a car is leased instead, the whole of the leasing charge may be set against profit, subject to disallowance of any private element and the restriction on the allowable hire charge where applicable — see **20.18**.

- When a group of assets, such as goodwill, plant and machinery and trade premises are bought or sold, some will be subject to capital allowances at different rates and some will not qualify for allowances at all. It is essential that the price apportionment is realistic and is agreed with the other party at the time of purchase or sale in order to avoid complications when tax returns are submitted. See also **22.45** for the special provisions relating to fixtures.

- If there is doubt as to whether a contract for the purchase of plant or machinery is a hire-purchase contract or a leasing contract, it is advisable to check with the finance company as to the nature of the payments to them to ensure the correct treatment in accounts/tax computations.

- The option to keep short-life assets out of the plant and machinery main pool enables a trader to shorten the time over which expenditure is written off to nine years or less if the assets are sold or scrapped within that period.

- For companies, expenditure on patents and know-how from 1 April 2002 is dealt with under the 'Intangible assets' rules (see **20.35** onwards) rather than by way of capital allowances. In general the cost will be written off over the economic life of the assets, which will not normally be as generous as the capital allowances regime.

- If a trader takes over a business from someone with whom he is connected, the election to continue the predecessor's capital allowances computation has to be made within two years after the change (see **22.20**).

- Following the withdrawal of industrial buildings allowances from April 2011, a trader should make sure he maximises his allowances claims for plant and machinery within an industrial building.

23

Partnerships

Nature of partnership

[23.1] Partnership is defined in the Partnership Act 1890 as 'the relation which subsists between persons carrying on a business in common with a view of profit'. An ordinary partnership is not a separate legal entity except in Scotland. A limited liability partnership, however, is a corporate body with a separate legal personality and limits the liability of the partners for the firm's debts (see **23.33**). In the Tax Acts persons carrying on a trade in partnership are referred to collectively as a 'firm'.

Self-assessment (ITTOIA 2005, ss 846–863; TCGA 1992, s 59)

[23.2] A partnership is required to submit a partnership tax return and the individual partners must show their partnership income and gains in their personal returns (see **23.7** to **23.12**).

Partners are separately liable for their own tax on all sources of income and HMRC cannot proceed against other partners if a partner fails to pay. Partners would, however, be affected by the irresponsible conduct of their fellow partners which caused partnership profits to be understated, in that they would be liable for tax on any consequent increase in their profit shares even though the normal time limit for an HMRC challenge to their self-assessments had expired (see **9.46**).

Although partners do not have joint liability for tax on the partnership trading profits, partnership profits still have to be agreed globally, no partner being able to agree an adjustment to his share of profits independently of the others. It is only the liability for the tax that is separated.

The Government proposes to introduce legislation applying from April 2018 to provide greater clarity for partnerships over their tax affairs. This will include clarification of who should be reported as a partner on the partnership return, such as a beneficiary of a nominee or bare trust arrangement. The return will also have to show each partner's respective allocation of taxable profit, based on the firm's profit-sharing arrangements, and this will be the first point of reference for HMRC in determining the taxable profits of each partner. Where the allocation is disputed, legislation will protect the partners from being taxed on incorrect profit shares. Retrospective variation to a partnership's profit-sharing arrangements made after the period-end will not apply. See www.gov.uk/government/consultations/partnership-taxation-propo sals-to-clarify-tax-treatment.

Sharing profits and losses

[23.3] Subject to anti-avoidance provisions in relation to partnerships with a mix of individual and non-individual partners (see **23.4**), the trading profits of the accounting period, as adjusted for tax purposes, are divided between the partners according to the sharing arrangements in the period. Each partner's share of the profit is then treated as arising to him individually, and the basis period rules (see **21.2**) for opening and closing years and for overlap relief depend on when he joins and leaves the firm (see Examples 1 and 2). Again, subject to the anti-avoidance provisions for mixed member partnerships, losses are similarly shared on an accounting-period basis and treated as arising to the partners individually, loss relief claims being made accordingly.

Example 1

A, B and C, who have been in business for many years, shared profits equally in the year ended 30 November 2016. From 1 December 2016 they amended the profit-sharing ratio to 2:1:1.

The profits for tax purposes will be shared in the same way as the accounts profits, the profit of the year to 30 November 2016 (taxable in 2016–17) being shared equally and that of the year to 30 November 2017 (taxable in 2017–18) being shared 2:1:1.

Example 2

D and E commenced in partnership on 1 January 2015, making up accounts annually to 31 December and sharing profits equally. F joined them as an equal partner on 1 July 2016 and E left the partnership on 28 February 2017. Profits and their division between the partners for the first three years are as follows:

Year ended	Profits	D	E	F
	£	£	£	£
31.12.15	40,000	20,000	20,000	
31.12.16	60,000	25,000	25,000	10,000
31.12.17	90,000	42,500	5,000	42,500
Total profits for period		87,500	50,000	52,500

Assessments and overlap profits available for relief are:

	D	E	F
	£	£	£
2014–15			
1.1.15 – 5.4.15	5,000	5,000	
2015–16			
1.1.15 – 31.12.15	20,000	20,000	
Overlap profits	(5,000)	(5,000)	
2016–17			
1.1.16 – 31.12.16	25,000		
1.1.16 – 28.2.17 (25,000 + 5,000)		30,000	
Less overlap relief		(5,000)	
		25,000	
1.7.16 – 5.4.17:			
To 31.12.16	10,000		
To 5.4.17 3/12 × £42,500	10,625		20,625
2017–18			
1.1.17 – 31.12.17	42,500		42,500
Overlap profits			(10,625)

Profits assessed over 4 tax years and overlap profits relievable or available for future relief

Total assessable profits	92,500	50,000	63,125
Overlap profits	*(5,000)	—	*(10,625)
Tax adjusted accounts profits	87,500	50,000	52,500

* E receives overlap relief of £5,000 on cessation in 2016–17 as illustrated above. D will receive overlap relief of £5,000 and F will receive overlap relief of £10,625 when they leave the partnership (or on a change of accounting date).

A change in partners is not regarded as a cessation of the partnership unless none of the old partners continues after the change.

[23.4] There are rules to remove the tax advantages gained through tax-motivated profit allocations to non-individual partners (such as companies and trustees), and tax-motivated loss allocations to individual partners. The rules on profit allocation came into force on 5 December 2013 and apply for periods of account beginning on or after 6 April 2014. If a period of account straddles that date the part falling after 5 April 2014 is treated as a separate period of account and the provisions apply to that notional separate period taking account of events occurring on or after 5 December 2013. The loss allocation rules apply from 2014–15.

Part of the non-individual's (B's) profit share is to be reallocated to the individual partner (A) where either of two situations apply. The first is where an amount representing A's deferred profit is included in B's profit share. The second is where B's profit share exceeds a notional amount of profit and A has the power to enjoy all or part of B's profit share. In both cases it must be reasonable to assume that A's profit and tax thereon are lower than they would otherwise be. B's notional amount of profit is a sum equal to a return on their capital at a commercial interest rate (less any amount actually received other than as a share of profit, such as a fee) plus the arm's length value of any services they provide other than those in conjunction with another partner in the firm (less any amount actually received other than as a share of profit). A has the power to enjoy B's profits if they are connected, or A is party to arrangements a main purpose of which is to secure that B's profit share is subject to corporation tax rules rather than income tax rules, or any of several specified enjoyment conditions is met.

Where the provisions apply, the amount to be reallocated to A is either the amount of the deferred profits, or the amount attributable to A's power to enjoy but limited to the amount by which B's profit exceeds the notional amount of profit. The different computational rules for income tax and corporation tax will mean there are differences in the way that the taxable profits are calculated for A and B. Therefore, rather than simply reducing B's profit share by the amount by which A's profit share is increased, any adjustment should be made on a just and reasonable basis.

Similar rules apply where an individual (C) carries out work for a partnership and their role is similar to that which a partner would have but they are not themselves a partner, either C has the power to enjoy the profit share of a non-individual partner (D) or D's profit share includes deferred profits in relation to C, and it is reasonable to suppose that C would have been a partner in the absence of the excess profit allocation rules. If the provisions apply, then C is treated as if they were a member of the partnership and the mixed membership partnership test is then applied and C is taxed on the appropriate amount of the profits reallocated to them.

For losses made in 2014–15 and later years, no relief is available for a loss made by an individual partner (E) in a trade, profession (see CHAPTER 25), or UK or overseas property business (see CHAPTER 32) partnership where E is party to arrangements one of the main purposes of which is to ensure that losses are allocated or otherwise arise to E, or to other individuals, rather than to a non-individual (F), with a view to E obtaining loss relief. It does not matter if F is not a partner in the firm, or is unknown, or does not exist at the time, although the restriction does not apply where the partnership only consists of individuals and there are no plans or arrangements to introduce a non-individual as a partner. The restriction applies to relief for trade or property business losses and also to claims to use trading losses as relief for capital gains. If a loss arises in a period of account that begins before 6 April 2014 and ends on or after that date the loss is apportioned on a time basis between the period up to 5 April 2014 and the period from 6 April 2014, the restriction only applying to the latter part of the loss.

[23.5] There is also a mechanism for members of an Alternative Investment Fund Managers partnership to elect to allocate certain restricted profits to the partnership from 6 April 2014. Those profits are deferred remuneration which the members cannot immediately access because of requirements under an EU Directive. The legislation imposes a charge to tax on these profits at the additional rate of tax (see **2.5**) to be paid by the AIFM partnership. If the restricted profits subsequently vest in the partner who originally allocated them to the partnership, that partner will be liable to income tax on those profits in the period of vesting, but he will be able to claim a credit corresponding to the tax paid by the partnership upfront. No Class 4 NICs charge will arise until the time when the remuneration vests in the individual partner. Any subsequent payment of all or part of the forfeited profits to one or more different partners will be treated like any other distribution of partnership profits. It will not represent a taxable event and there will be no further tax liability and no entitlement to recover the tax paid on that element of the deferred remuneration.

Non-trading income

[23.6] Partnership non-trading income is shared for tax purposes according to the sharing arrangements in the accounting period. If the income is received net of tax, the partners' shares for the relevant accounting periods are then allocated to the appropriate tax year, those amounts being shown in the partnership tax return (see **23.7**) and each partner shows his income for the tax year in his personal tax return. If the income is untaxed income, it is treated as if it arose from a separate trade that commenced when the partner joined the firm and taxed according to the same periods as the trading income, so that normally the taxable amount for each partner will be his profit share in the accounting year ending in the tax year. There may be overlap relief on commencement and possibly on a change of accounting date. The overlap relief for non-trading income will be allowed to the extent that more than 12 months' income would otherwise be charged in one year as a result of a change of accounting date, and otherwise in the tax year in which a partner ceases to be a partner (even if the source of income ceased earlier). The deduction will be given against the untaxed non-trading income of the relevant tax year. If it exceeds that untaxed income it will be relieved against other income of that tax year.

Note that interest from banks and building societies is no longer taxed at source from 6 April 2016 so it will now be treated as untaxed income for these purposes. Interest arising net of tax between 6 April 2015 and 5 April 2016 had to be included in the tax return for 2015–16 (tax year basis), and that arising between 6 April 2016 and the end of the accounting year should be included in the 2016–17 return (the same period as the trading income). Dividends are specifically excluded from the definition of untaxed income, and therefore continue to be assessed on a tax year basis as taxed income even though dividend tax credits were abolished from 6 April 2016.

Self-assessment tax returns (TMA 1970, ss 12AA–12AD, 28B, Sch 1AB)

[23.7] A partnership tax return, form SA800, must be sent to HMRC each year, incorporating a statement showing the name, address and tax reference of each partner, and each partner's share of profits, losses, other income and any tax deducted. There is a short version of the partnership statement for partnerships with only trading profits and interest or alternative finance receipts from banks, building societies or other deposit takers, and a full version for partnerships with other types of income and/or capital gains. HMRC provide guidance notes with the return.

[23.8] Standardised accounts information must normally be shown in the partnership return by completing the relevant boxes. Where turnover is below £85,000 (£83,000 for 2016–17), however, only the turnover, expenses (including capital allowances) and net profit needs to be shown. If turnover is above £15 million, accounts and computations must be submitted but only certain boxes need to be completed. Otherwise, accounts need not be sent in unless HMRC ask for them, although it is advisable to submit them to make sure HMRC have full information (see **9.20**).

The return includes details of income other than from the trade and details of disposals of partnership chargeable assets. The details provided normally relate to the accounting year ended in the tax year. Details of *taxed* income (see **23.6**), partnership charges, such as an annuity to a retired partner (see **23.19**), and disposals of chargeable assets are, however, shown for the tax year itself rather than for the accounting year ended in the tax year, so that the partners will have the information they need to complete their own returns. HMRC state that apportionment of the accounts figures can be used if this gives a reasonable approximation of the figures for the tax year, otherwise the actual figures should be provided. The return will not include calculations of tax payable, because these will be in each partner's separate return. See **23.6** for how the changes to bank and building society interest from 6 April 2016 affect the tax returns.

[23.9] The partnership return must be submitted by the 31 January following the tax year if the return is filed online, i.e. by 31 January 2019 for 2017–18. However, the normal filing date for paper returns is 31 October after the end of the tax year, i.e. 31 October 2018 for the 2017–18 return. Different dates apply to partnerships with corporate partners or if the notice requiring the partnership to make the return is given after 31 July 2018. Details are given in the guidance notes.

There are automatic penalties for late returns, chargeable on the partners rather than the partnership. There is an initial automatic penalty of £100 and further penalties for continued delay (see **9.62**). The provisions for amending returns and for HMRC enquiries into them are the same as for individual returns (see **9.14** and **9.41** to **9.42**). If HMRC enquire into a partnership return, this automatically means that the enquiry extends to partners' personal returns, since the personal returns must reflect any changes to the partnership return. An enquiry into a personal return relating to non-partnership matters does not affect the other partners.

[23.10] Where there is an error or mistake in a partnership statement, an overpayment relief claim may be made no later than four years after the end of the tax year to which the claim relates. All the partners must agree to the claim for it to be made. See **9.82** and HMRC Self Assessment Claims Manual SACM12045.

[23.11] Each partner's personal return will include his share of the partnership income and charges as shown in the partnership statement, and capital gains on his share of partnership assets. Any expenses paid personally by partners and capital allowances on partners' own cars must be included in the *partnership* return (see also **22.3** regarding partnership capital allowances). They cannot be separately claimed in the personal return, where a corresponding adjustment should be made, in the partnership pages, to the partnership net profit figure with a note being made in the white space notes section.

If a partner does not agree with the profits allocated to him in the partnership statement he should enter on his personal tax return the amount he considers to be correct and advise HMRC that he has done so by making an entry in the white space notes section of the return to show the profits as allocated in the partnership statement, a deduction or addition of the disputed amount, and an explanation of why he thinks the profit allocated to him in the partnership statement is wrong. If the partner does this, then HMRC would not automatically regard the personal return as incorrect if profits, as declared by him, were a 'net' amount after deducting the disputed amount, although each case will depend on the facts. See **23.2** regarding the proposal to legislate on this matter.

[23.12] Class 4 NICs are included in a partner's personal return. The partnership pages include provision for a partner to indicate that he is excepted from contributions (see CHAPTER **24**).

[23.13] HMRC have issued forms for registering a partnership for self-assessment. Form SA400 is used for the partnership and must be completed by the nominated partner. Limited partnerships and limited liability partnerships registered with Companies House after 24 October 2010 do not need to complete the form as they will be automatically registered by Companies House. Form SA401 is to be used by new partners who are individuals to register for both self-assessment and Class 2 NICs, and must be completed by all new partners and the nominated partner. Form SA402 is for registering any new partners who are not individuals.

Work in progress and changes in accounting practice (ITTOIA 2005, ss 25–27, 227–240; FA 2006, s 102 and Sch 15)

[23.14] See 20.22 regarding work in progress. The accounting aspects of work in progress are particularly important in the interests of consistency and fairness between the parties when firms merge, often with resulting tax consequences.

This whole area is extremely complex and professional advice is essential.

Introducing funds to a partnership (ITA 2007, ss 24A, 383, 384B, 388, 398–399B, 406)

[23.15] If a partner who is neither a partner in an investment limited liability partnership (LLP — see 23.33) nor a limited partner (see 23.41) borrows to purchase a partnership share or to introduce funds to a partnership, either as capital or on loan, interest on the borrowing is allowable as a deduction from his total income at his top tax rate (see 2.14), subject to certain restrictions from 2013–14. Relief is also available to a salaried partner (see 23.39) provided he is employed in a senior capacity and acts independently in dealing with clients in a way which is indistinguishable from partners. If, however, a partner then withdraws all or part of his capital, the introduced funds will be treated as repaid up to the amount of the withdrawal, restricting or eliminating the amount on which interest relief is available whether or not any part of the personal loan has been repaid. This provision does not apply if the partner withdraws his capital *before* introducing new funds. The partnership would, however, need to be able to bridge the gap between the withdrawal of the existing funds and the introduction of the new. If the partnership profits are calculated on the cash basis, either for small businesses (see 20.4) or for property businesses (see 32.6), relief for a loan to invest in a partnership is only available where it is used for purchasing a partnership share. See 20.17 for further details on loan interest.

Relief may also be available for interest on a loan to a partner to buy plant or machinery to be owned by him for use in the partnership of which he is a member, provided that the partnership is entitled to capital allowances on the plant or machinery. Therefore, the asset must not be let by the partner to the partnership nor must any payment that would be deductible in taxing the trade be made to the partner by the partnership. Relief is not available for interest due and payable more than three years after the end of the period of account (for capital allowances purposes) in which the loan was made. Relief is also not available if the partnership calculates profits on the cash basis, either for small businesses (see **20.4**) or for property businesses (see **32.6**).

Relief on loans to invest in a partnership or to buy plant or machinery for partnership use are one of a number of reliefs against general income which are capped from 2013–14 (see **2.13**). From 6 April 2017 a restriction on deductible costs applies to interest on a loan to invest in a partnership if that partnership carries on a UK or overseas property business which generates income from a dwelling house (see **32.8**).

If borrowings are made by the partnership itself, the interest is allowed as a business expense except to the extent that the borrowing enables a partner to overdraw his personal account.

A separate anti-avoidance provision relates solely to film partnerships, affecting interest accruing on or after 10 March 2006. Relief for interest on a loan to buy into a film partnership is restricted to 40% of the interest paid where the loan is secured on an investment in another partnership in which the borrower's right to share in income is disproportionately low compared with his capital contribution to that investment partnership. The cap on reliefs in **2.13** applies after the 40% restriction. See **20.43** for the general taxation provisions relating to films.

Consultancy

[23.16] An outgoing partner may perform consultancy services for the partnership. He is taxed on the income either as employment income, if he is an employee of the partnership, or as trading or professional income, if the payments to him are in his capacity of self-employed consultant (see **19.2**). The payments are an allowable deduction in calculating the taxable profits of the partnership so long as they satisfy the 'wholly and exclusively' rule (see **20.5**).

Trading losses (ITA 2007, Pt 4)

[23.17] Chapter 25 deals with the calculation of the available loss reliefs and ways in which relief may be given. See also **23.4** regarding the tax-motivated partnership loss allocation restrictions which apply to mixed member partnerships from 2014–15. Relief for partnership trading losses may be claimed by each partner quite independently of the others. Thus one partner may decide to carry forward his share of the loss, another to set his against other income of the same tax year, another to set it against any income of the previous tax year, another to carry back against the income of the previous three tax years in the early years of his being a partner, and so on.

The carry-back loss rules for the first four years of a new trade only apply to a new partner, not to the continuing partners.

There are special anti-avoidance provisions in relation to partnership losses — see **25.12** to **25.13**. Loss relief is one of a number of reliefs against general income which are capped from 2013–14 (see **2.13**).

Partnership assets (TCGA 1992, ss 59, 286; HMRC Statements of Practice D12 (9/2015), 1/79 and 1/89)

[23.18] When partners join or leave a partnership, this usually involves a change in the persons who are entitled to share in the partnership assets. There is no capital gains tax consequence if an incoming partner introduces cash which is credited to his capital account. Nor is there normally any capital gains tax consequence when an outgoing partner withdraws his capital account. In the first instance, an incoming partner is paying in a sum which remains to his credit in his capital account, whilst in the second instance, an outgoing partner is only withdrawing what belongs to him.

Where an asset is transferred to a partnership by means of a capital contribution, the partner in question should be treated as having made a part disposal of the asset concerned equal to the fractional share that passes to the other partners. The consideration for such disposals is a proportion (based on the fractional share of the asset passing to the other partners) of either the total consideration given by the partnership for the asset, or market value of the asset if the transaction is between connected persons or not on arm's length terms.

If, however, before an outgoing partner withdraws his capital account, that capital account has been credited with a surplus on revaluation of partnership assets (e.g. premises or goodwill), his leaving the partnership crystallises a chargeable gain in respect of the excess on revaluation, and whether or not the capital is withdrawn or left on loan to the partnership, there is a charge to capital gains tax.

This charge will arise not only when a person ceases to be a partner, but whenever a partner's capital account includes a revaluation of chargeable assets and his entitlement to share in the assets is reduced. He is treated as having disposed of a proportion of the chargeable assets equivalent to the drop in his entitlement. The change will usually correspond with the change in the profit-sharing ratio, except where income and capital profits are shared differently, when the capital ratio will apply.

A payment by an incoming partner to the existing partners for a share in the chargeable assets such as goodwill or premises constitutes a disposal by the existing partners for capital gains tax, and a cost for capital gains tax to the incoming partner. The same applies where there is a payment, whether in cash or through an accounting adjustment, on a variation of profit-sharing arrangements without a change in partners. It makes no difference whether the amount is left in the partnership (by a credit to the capital account of those disposing) or is withdrawn by them, or indeed is dealt with outside the partnership itself. The test is whether a partner receives consideration for reducing his share in the partnership. Conversely, if he does not receive consideration, whilst there is still a disposal in the sense that his partnership share is less than it was, then, unless the partners have a family connection, the market value of the assets is not substituted for the purpose of calculating and charging the gain that could have been made, and thus no chargeable gain arises.

Example 3

X and Y are in partnership. Z is admitted as a partner in July 2017, sharing equally in both capital and income. He introduces £45,000 as capital which is credited to his capital account. The £45,000 is neither a capital gains tax base cost for Z nor a disposal by X and Y. The partnership assets include premises worth £180,000, which cost £63,000 when acquired in 1990.

Consider the following alternatives:

(**1**) Before Z's admission, X and Y revalue the premises up to £180,000 by crediting each of their capital accounts with £58,500.

On Z's admission they each make a chargeable gain of:

	£	
Value of premises reflected in their capital account (1/2 each)		90,000
Share of premises retained after Z's admission (1/3 each)		(60,000)
Disposal proceeds		30,000
Less cost:		
Cost was 1/2 each × £63,000	31,500	
Cost is now 1/3 each × £63,000	(21,000)	
Cost of part disposed of		(10,500)
Gain		£19,500

The £19,500 gain is the 1/3 of the increase in value of £58,500 which has been realised by the reduction in the partnership share from 3/6ths to 2/6th. The other 2/3rds which remains unrealised is not charged to tax until realisation.

The cost of Z's share in the premises is £60,000 (1/3 × £180,000), equivalent to the disposal proceeds of X and Y.

(**2**) The premises are not revalued on the admission of Z.

There is then no deemed gain by X and Y, and the cost for capital gains tax purposes for each of X and Y is 1/3 × £63,000 = £21,000. Z's cost will be £21,000.

(**3**) Z privately pays £60,000 (£30,000 each) to X and Y, for a 1/3rd share in the partnership premises.

X and Y are treated as receiving £30,000 each as in (1).

The capital gains cost for future disposals in the case of (1) and (3) is:

	X	Y	Z
	£	£	£
Original cost	31,500	31,500	—
On introduction of Z	(10,500)	(10,500)	21,000
Gains on which X and Y are assessable			39,000
	21,000	21,000	60,000

Annuities to outgoing partners (HMRC Statements of Practice D12 (9/2015) and 1/79; ITA 2007, s 900)

[23.19] An outgoing partner may be paid an annuity by the continuing partners when he retires. He will not be charged to capital gains tax on the capitalised value of the annuity so long as it is regarded as reasonable recognition for past services to the partnership. For this purpose, the average of the partner's best three years' assessable profit shares out of the last seven is calculated and the annuity is considered reasonable if it does not exceed the fraction of that average amount obtained from the following table:

Years of service	Fraction
1–5	1/60 per year
6	8/60
7	16/60
8	24/60
9	32/60
10	2/3

The paying partners can deduct their share of the annuity in calculating their taxable income. They deduct basic rate income tax when making the payment and claim relief at higher rates where appropriate by an adjustment in their personal tax returns. The annuity forms part of the recipient's taxable income. Since it is received net of basic rate tax, the recipient may have further tax to pay or tax to reclaim depending on his tax position.

An annuity paid by the continuing partners must be distinguished from a sum paid by them to an insurance company with which to purchase an annuity for the outgoing partner. The cost of such annuity counts as proceeds of the disposal of the outgoing partner's share.

Capital gains tax reliefs

Replacement of business assets (TCGA 1992, ss 152–157; HMRC Statement of Practice D12 (9/2015))

[23.20] Rollover relief for the replacement of business assets (see **29.16** onwards) is available where an asset owned personally by a partner and used in the partnership is disposed of and replaced. This is not affected by the payment of rent by the partnership. A gain realised by a partner on a reduction in his capital ratio (see **23.18**) can be rolled over into his share of the acquisition cost of a new qualifying partnership asset. The rolled-over gain will crystallise in whole or in part on a subsequent reduction in the partner's capital ratio or on his retirement from the partnership.

Entrepreneurs' relief (TCGA 1992, ss 169H–S; HMRC Statement of Practice D12 (9/2015))

[23.21] Entrepreneurs' relief for qualifying business disposals is available for certain partnership disposals. See **29.5** for further details.

Gift relief (TCGA 1992, ss 165–169G; HMRC Statement of Practice D12 (9/2015))

[23.22] Relief for gifts of business assets is available for disposals of certain partnership assets. See **4.32** for further details.

Incorporation relief (TCGA 1992, ss 162, 162A)

[23.23] Incorporation relief may be available where a partnership trade is transferred to a company. See **27.9** for further details.

Partner acquiring asset from the partnership (Statement of Practice D12 (9/2015))

[23.24] When a partner acquires an asset from the partnership, he is not regarded as disposing of his fractional share in it. The disposal of the asset is treated as being made at market value and is apportioned among all the partners. Chargeable gains attributable to partners receiving no asset are taxed at the time of the disposal. Any gain notionally accruing to a receiving partner is treated as reducing his allowable expenditure on a subsequent disposal of the asset. See **23.18** for further details on disposals of partnership assets.

Death of a partner

[23.25] Where a partner dies in service:

(a)   any gains arising on the disposal of his share in partnership assets by reason of the death are exempt from capital gains tax, like gains on any other chargeable asset held at death (see **4.44**);

(b)   the annuity dealt with in **23.19** may be paid to his spouse, civil partner or dependants.

Inheritance tax

[23.26] Inheritance tax is examined in CHAPTER 5. The amount of a deceased partner's capital account, plus his share of any increase in the value of partnership assets, qualifies for the 100% business property relief (see **5.45**) unless the surviving partners are obliged to acquire his partnership share, in which case it is regarded as an entitlement under a contract for sale and not therefore eligible for relief. Relief is not lost where there is an option, as opposed to an obligation, for the share to be acquired by the surviving partners.

The amount on which the 100% relief is available may be restricted if the partnership assets include any not required for the trade (for example excessive cash balances). The rate of business property relief for assets owned personally and used by the partnership is 50%.

Although the option to pay tax by ten annual instalments (see **5.54**) applies to the transfer of a partnership share, the instalment option is irrelevant for such transfers where the 100% relief is fully available. The instalment option is still relevant for transfers of land owned by an individual partner and used in the business, the rate of business property relief for such land being 50%. Interest is, however, charged on the full amount of tax outstanding rather than just on overdue instalments.

[23.27] A gift of an interest in a partnership, including the whole or part of the partner's capital account, will qualify for business property relief so long as it is made whilst the donor is a partner and the partnership assets all qualify for relief because of their use in the trade. A gift of the balance on the capital account after ceasing to be a partner will not qualify for business property relief since the amount will have become a partnership creditor rather than part of the business capital.

Value added tax

[23.28] HMRC need to be notified of a change of partner within 30 days, but not of a change in profit-sharing arrangements. The registration number will normally continue. A retiring partner remains liable for VAT due from the partnership until the date on which HMRC are notified of his retirement. See 23.37 regarding limited liability partnerships and CHAPTER 7 regarding VAT generally.

National insurance

[23.29] See **24.9** for the NICs position of partners generally and **23.40** regarding sleeping partners.

Stamp duty, stamp duty land tax, and land and buildings transaction tax

[23.30] There is no stamp duty on a partnership agreement, nor does stamp duty normally apply on the document effecting the division of assets when a partnership is dissolved.

The treatment of transfers of interests in a partnership for stamp duty and stamp duty land tax is dealt with in **6.21**. Stamp duty does not arise where an incoming partner merely introduces capital to his own capital or current account. See **23.35** regarding limited liability partnerships. See **6.5** and **6.17** regarding anti-avoidance provisions.

Stamp duty land tax is replaced in Scotland by land and buildings transaction tax (see **6.18**). The provisions discussed at **6.21** broadly apply, with necessary modifications to terminology etc, to transactions within the LBTT regime.

Partnerships of spouses and civil partners (ITTOIA 2005, ss 622–627)

[23.31] Many married couples or civil partners form business partnerships because of the practical and commercial advantages such a partnership can bring. The effect on their respective tax and NICs positions will be an important factor.

The NICs cost of employing a spouse or civil partner is usually greater than if the spouse/civil partner were a partner. The tax advantages of being a business partner must be weighed against a partner's legal liability, which includes the possibility of being made bankrupt if the partnership cannot pay its debts.

Taking a spouse or civil partner into a business partnership may be regarded as an appropriate way of maximising the benefit of personal reliefs and basic rate bands, but the partnership must be genuine, with the spouse's/civil partner's share being appropriate to his or her contribution to the business, otherwise there is the risk of the partnership arrangement being treated as a settlement, in which case the income would remain that of the other spouse/civil partner for tax purposes.

HMRC have contended in in the past that certain gifts between spouses were caught by the settlements legislation and were not effective for tax purposes. In July 2007 the House of Lords decided the 'Arctic Systems' case in favour of the taxpayer, a director and shareholder in a family company, on the basis that while there was a settlement an exemption for outright gifts between spouses applied. The Government subsequently consulted on proposed legislation to counter 'income shifting' but said it would instead keep the matter under review (see **12.10**). This is a difficult area and there is a good deal of uncertainty. Those who feel they may be affected should consider taking professional advice. HMRC have confirmed that they will not give clearances or advice in respect of the application of the settlements legislation.

Corporate partners (ITA 2007, s 31C; CTA 2009, ss 486A–486E, Pt 17; CTA 2010, s 357GB)

[23.32] A company may be a partner with individuals. In this case the profit share of the company for the relevant accounting period is liable to corporation tax, whilst the share applicable to the partners who are individuals is charged to income tax. There are, however, differences in the way profits are calculated for companies and individuals, so separate corporation tax and income tax calculations must be made.

See **23.4** regarding the rules to remove the tax advantages gained through tax-motivated profit allocations to non-individual partners (such as companies and trustees), and tax-motivated loss allocations from non-individual partners to individual partners.

The cash basis both for small businesses (see **20.4**) and property businesses (see **32.6**) cannot be used by partnerships where one of the partners is not an individual.

The patent box rules in **3.17** can apply to a corporate partner.

Where a money debt is owed to or by the partnership, the corporate partner computes loan relationship debits and credits on its share, and brings the result into its corporation tax computation.

There are loan relationship anti-avoidance provisions which can apply to amounts received by corporate partners. These are the disguised interest provisions which are part of numerous loan relationship anti-avoidance provisions not dealt with in this book.

Limited liability partnerships (ITA 2007, ss 31C, 107–109, 399, 1004; ITTOIA 2005, s 863; TCGA 1992, ss 59A, 156A, 169A; IHTA 1984, s 267A; FA 2003, s 65; SSCBA 1992, s 15; CTA 2009, s 1273; CTA 2010, ss 55–61; SP D12 (9/2015))

[23.33] Partners may register as a 'limited liability partnership' (LLP) under the Limited Liability Partnerships Act 2000. An LLP is a corporate entity and the liability of the partners is limited to the capital contributed, although partners in LLPs are liable in the same way as company directors for fraudulent trading and there are provisions to protect creditors. LLPs have to file annual accounts and an annual return with Companies House.

An LLP partner may be either a company or an individual. Corporate partners are liable to corporation tax on their profit shares, with individual partners being generally treated for tax and NICs purposes in the same way as partners in any other partnership. However, there is legislation which removes the presumption of self-employment for some members in order to tackle the disguising of employment relationships through LLPs. At any time when the three conditions below are met, an individual member of an LLP (M) is treated as being employed by the LLP under a contract of service instead of being a member of the partnership and his rights and duties as a member of the LLP arise under that contract of service. The income tax and NICs treatment then applying is that applying to an ordinary employee and PAYE must be operated (see **10.58**). The three conditions are:

(a) Broadly at 6 April 2014, or if later when either certain arrangements are put in place or M becomes a member of the LLP, it is reasonable to expect that at least 80% of the total amount payable by the LLP for M's services in M's capacity as a member of the LLP will be 'disguised salary';

(b) The mutual rights and duties of the members and the LLP do not give M significant influence over the affairs of the LLP; and

(c) M's contribution to the LLP is less than 25% of the disguised salary which, it is reasonable to expect, will be payable in a tax year in respect of M's performance of services for the LLP.

Salary is disguised if it is fixed, or varied without reference to the overall amount of the profits or losses of the LLP, or is not in practice affected by the overall profits or losses of the LLP.

If a salaried member of an LLP agreed before 6 April 2014 to increase their capital so that the third condition above would not apply, they had to have paid it by 5 July 2014.

The rules contain anti-avoidance provisions to counteract attempts to circumvent the salaried member provisions by means of artificial arrangements.

See **23.4** regarding the rules to remove the tax advantages gained through tax-motivated profit allocations to non-individual partners (such as companies and trustees), and tax-motivated loss allocations from non-individual partners to individual partners, which apply to LLPs.

The actions of an LLP are regarded for tax purposes as those of its members. The transfer of an existing partnership to an LLP will normally be on a tax neutral basis. The cash basis both for small businesses (see **20.4**) and property businesses (see **32.6**) cannot be used by LLPs.

If the LLP goes into formal liquidation it is treated as a company rather than a partnership for capital gains purposes. Any gains held over by partners under the business assets or gifts rollover provisions will be treated as realised by those partners at the start of the formal liquidation and will be chargeable on them accordingly.

[23.34] Certain reliefs for a trade loss incurred by a partner in an LLP cannot exceed the amount of the partner's contribution to the firm. There are anti-avoidance provisions in relation to partnership losses, which apply both to ordinary partnerships and LLPs — see **25.12** and **25.13**.

[23.35] Stamp duty or stamp duty land tax is not charged on property transferred to an LLP within one year after its incorporation if the partners' shares remain unchanged. The exemptions do not strictly apply if partners join or leave at the time the LLP is formed, but a charge can be avoided if the change takes place immediately before or after incorporation (providing evidence is available to that effect). See **6.21** for the general stamp duty/stamp duty land tax provisions for partnerships, which apply equally to LLPs.

Stamp duty land tax is replaced in Scotland by land and buildings transaction tax (see **6.18**). The provisions discussed at **6.21** broadly apply, with necessary modifications to terminology etc, to transactions within the LBTT regime.

[23.36] Inheritance tax business and agricultural property reliefs are available for shares in appropriate partnership assets (see **5.45**).

[23.37] For VAT purposes, an LLP will be registered as a separate entity. While there will be a VAT liability on the transfer of assets if an existing partnership becomes an LLP, this will be subject to the rules for transfers of going concerns (see **7.52**). The partnership's VAT number may be transferred to the LLP.

[23.38] Inactive members of an LLP who are not treated as employees under the rules in **23.33** are subject to Class 2 NICs from 6 April 2015, in the same way as sleeping partners and inactive limited partners (see **23.40**).

Miscellaneous

[23.39] A *salaried partner* must be distinguished from a partner who is allocated a salary as part of the profit-sharing arrangement. Senior employees are often described as partners in professional firms whilst retaining their salaried employee status. They remain liable to income tax as employees, receiving a salary for the duties of their employment, with NICs being payable appropriately (see **10.58**). See also **23.33** regarding the salaried member rules which can apply to LLP partners from 6 April 2014.

There is a further distinction where a partner is on a fixed share of profit, not because he is a salaried partner but his profit share being certain rather than depending on results. So long as the circumstances do not imply an employment and the rules in **23.33** do not apply, such a partner pays tax and NICs as a self-employed person.

[23.40] The profit share of a *sleeping partner* does not rank as relevant earnings and cannot, therefore, support a pension contribution higher than the £3,600 a year limit (see **17.1**). HMRC's view is that sleeping and inactive limited partners have always been liable to pay Class 2 and Class 4 NICs as self-employed earners carrying on a business (see CHAPTER **24**). They must be registered for Class 2 from 6 April 2013 and to account for Class 4 from 2013–14, as appropriate. Inactive members of an LLP who are not treated as employees under the rules in **23.33** are also subject to Class 2 NICs from 6 April 2015. Relief for losses incurred by non-active partners is restricted (see **25.13**).

[23.41] A partnership may include a *limited partner* under the Limited Partnership Act 1907, whose liability is limited to the amount of the partner's agreed capital contribution. The limited partner, who may be either an individual or a company, cannot take part in the management of the partnership, although he is not barred from taking part in a non-managerial capacity. If the profit share of a limited partner ranks as unearned income, it cannot be used to support a pension premium higher than the £3,600 per year limit (see **17.1**). Certain reliefs available to a limited partner cannot exceed the amount of the partner's contribution to the firm. There are restrictions to reliefs for trading losses against income other than trading income from the partnership (see **25.12**). See **23.40** regarding the NICs liability.

[23.42] From 6 April 2017 a private fund limited partnership structure was introduced to reduce the administrative and financial burdens that had previously affected private investment funds, such as private equity and venture capital funds, under the limited partnership rules.

[23.43] Partnership itself, and matters arising, need not be governed by *formal written agreement*. In the absence of such agreement, sometimes indeed despite it, HMRC will require other evidence of partnership, for example the name of, and operating arrangements for, bank accounts, VAT registration, names on stationery, contracts, licences, etc.

The overseas aspect of partnerships is dealt with in CHAPTER **41**.

Anti-avoidance provisions

[23.44] See **45.22** regarding the restriction of loss relief for leasing partnerships.

See **23.4** regarding the profit and loss allocation of partnerships with mixed membership.

See **23.4, 25.12** and **25.13** for restrictions on partnership losses.

See **23.33** regarding the salaried member rules which can apply to LLP partners.

See **6.5** and **6.17** regarding avoidance in relation to stamp duty and stamp duty land tax.

See **19.4** regarding the IR35 rules which prevent people paying substantially less tax and NICs by operating through an intermediary which includes a partnership.

See **20.33** regarding provisions applying from 6 April 2017 to prevent trading profits disguised as other receipts escaping the charge to tax.

See **45.12** regarding the disposal of an asset or a right to income by or through a partnership.

There are also anti-avoidance provisions designed to prevent a company from using a partnership to transfer losses and other reliefs from one company to another person where profits or losses are sold by one partner to another.

Tax points

[23.45] Note the following:

- Partnerships can elect to calculate profits on the cash basis for small businesses (see **20.4**).
- The cash basis for property businesses (see **32.6**) may apply to property partnerships without a non-individual partner, and an election may be required to prevent this basis automatically applying.
- HMRC accept that the overhead content of work in progress is likely to be minimal for professional firms of up to four partners and can normally be ignored in calculating the work in progress figure. Work in progress must, however, be distinguished from unbilled revenue (see **20.22**).
- A merger of two or more firms is strictly a cessation of each firm and the commencement of one new firm. The converse applies where one firm splits into two or more new firms. In both cases it may not be clear whether the rules for partnership changes apply. HMRC's views are explained in Statement of Practice SP 9/86. This area is one where professional advice and consultation with HMRC is essential.
- Annuities to retiring partners should be calculated within the allowable limits (see **23.19**), leaving them taxable only as income in the hands of the recipient and allowable for income tax to the payers. An inflation-linked increase to an annuity which is initially within the allowable limits does not affect the capital gains annual exempt amount.
- A pension payment by continuing partners to a retired partner, whilst assessable as income on the recipient, is not regarded by HMRC as deductible in calculating the partnership taxable profits, since it is regarded as a payment to the outgoing partner to acquire his partnership share. The annuity arrangements in the previous tax point are a more tax-efficient way of providing income to a retired partner.
- Under self-assessment, partners are responsible for paying their own tax, and the half-yearly instalments due on 31 January and 31 July are on account of a partner's total income tax liability, not just his partnership share — see **9.4**. In some circumstances it is prudent for partnerships to retain part of a partner's profit to meet the tax liability on partnership income, releasing it to HMRC as part of each partner's personal liability on the due dates.
- If there is a choice of borrowing to buy a home and borrowing to introduce funds to a partnership (other than as a limited partner or partner in an investment LLP), interest on the partnership borrowing will in general save tax at the highest rate, whereas that on the home loan will not save tax at all (but see **23.15** for certain loan interest relief restrictions from 2013–14).
- If one spouse or civil partner takes the other into a business partnership as an active partner, it should not be forgotten that the new partner has to pay Class 2 NICs. Form SA401 should be used, see **23.13**.
- A capital gain may arise where partners sell partnership assets (e.g. land and buildings) to raise funds to pay out a retiring partner. Rather than pay tax on that gain, the partners will be able to deduct it from the cost of acquisition of the outgoing partner's share of any of the remaining

business assets of the partnership that qualify for rollover relief (see **23.20**). An alternative to paying out the retiring partner's share in land and buildings might be for him to retain that share as a co-owner with his former partners. There will not have been a disposal of his share in these circumstances, since he retains what he had before, albeit it will no longer be a qualifying asset for inheritance tax business property relief (see **23.26**).

- Income and capital profit-sharing ratios need not always be the same. Established partners can retain the right to the whole of the future increase in value of partnership premises, to the exclusion of incoming partners, by excluding the incoming partners from the capital profit-sharing ratio.

Any running expenses of those premises, including interest on borrowing, remain allowable in calculating trading profit, which is divided in the income profit-sharing ratio.

24

National insurance contributions for the self-employed

Background

[24.1] HMRC are responsible for national insurance contributions (NICs) and the department's National Insurance Contributions Office (NICO) handles administration and collection of contributions. However, the Department for Work and Pensions administers state benefits including contributory benefits. The main legislation relating to NICs is found in the Social Security Contributions and Benefits Act 1992 (SSCBA 1992) and statutory instruments. See CHAPTER 13 for NICs for employees and employers.

A self-employed person over the age of 16 must, unless specifically exempted, pay both Class 2 and Class 4 contributions. Class 2 contributions are payable at a flat weekly rate and entitle the contributor to short-term contribution-based employment and support allowance, maternity allowance, widowed parent's allowance, state pension and bereavement benefits. Class 4 contributions are payable on all business profits in excess of a specified limit that are chargeable to income tax as trading income (see **2.7** and CHAPTERS **18** to **29**). They carry no entitlement to benefits of any kind. The Government does, however, intend to abolish Class 2 contributions from 2018 and reform Class 4 contributions to introduce a new contributory benefit test (see **24.5**).

National insurance credits are awarded in some circumstances in order to maintain or enhance a person's contribution or earnings record for the purpose of state benefits (see **13.12**).

Significant reforms have been made to pensions provision, both to the state pension and to workplace pensions. Although the reform to workplace pensions affects employees, there is a government scheme which employers can use to provide workplace pensions (see **16.45**) called the National Employment Savings Trust (NEST, see www.nestpensions.org.uk) and self-employed earners may join the scheme as individual members.

See **9.52** and **9.60** for interest, penalties and criminal proceedings in relation to NICs.

Class 2 contributions

Payment (SSCBA 1992, s 11; SI 2001/1004; NICA 2015, Sch 1; SI 2017/415)

[24.2] If a person becomes self-employed, he must notify HMRC (see **19.3**), and he will register for self-assessment tax returns and Class 2 contributions at the same time. New partners may register using form SA401 (see **23.13**). See **24.5** for the Government's proposal to abolish Class 2 NICs from 2018.

Arrangements must also be made to pay Class 2 NICs, unless there is no liability to pay (see **24.3** and **24.4**). The weekly rate for 2017–18 is £2.85. The amount of Class 2 NICs due is calculated based on whether profits (as determined for Class 4 NICs, see **24.6**) are at least equal to the small profits threshold (see **24.4**), and on the number of weeks of self-employment in the year. This will be determined when the individual completes their self-assessment return and paid alongside their income tax and Class 4 NICs on 31 January following the end of the tax year (i.e. no payment on account is required on 31 July, see **9.4**), though some self-employed earners do not pay through self-assessment and will be sent a bill by HMRC. For details see www.gov.uk/pay-class-2-national-insurance. Voluntary contributions may also be paid if profits are below the threshold. In addition to incurring penalties and interest, late payment of Class 2 contributions may affect entitlement to benefits, and a higher rate than the rate which applied on the due date may be payable.

People who are self-employed have to pay only one weekly Class 2 contribution no matter how many self-employed occupations they may have. HMRC may collect outstanding Class 2 by an adjustment in PAYE codes (see **10.61**), in which case it is treated as paid on the 5 April of the tax year in which it is paid.

Entertainers engaged under a contract for services should be treated as self-employed and subject to Class 2 and Class 4 NICs. Any entertainers treated for tax purposes as employees on basic principles, including those on Equity contracts, are liable to Class 1 NICs.

Exempt persons

[24.3] Class 2 contributions are payable by 'self-employed earners', which means those who are 'gainfully employed' other than as employees. The Class 2 net is wider than Class 4, because it includes a 'business', whereas Class 4 only covers a trade, profession or vocation.

The following people are not liable to pay Class 2 contributions:

(a)   persons under 16;

(b)   persons over pensionable age. See **16.2** for the age limits applying;

(c)   married women who chose on or before 11 May 1977 to pay reduced rate Class 1 contributions or to pay no Class 2 contributions (provided that this election has not been automatically revoked by divorce or possibly revoked by widowhood — see **13.5**);

(d)   someone who has profits below the small profits threshold (see **24.2**);

(e)   someone who, for a full week, is
         (i)   incapable of work, or
         (ii)   in legal custody or prison, or
         (iii)   receiving incapacity benefit, employment and support allowance or maternity allowance;

(f)   someone who, for any day in a particular week, receives carer's allowance or unemployability supplement;

(g)   volunteer development workers (who may apply to pay at a special rate); and

(h)   share fishermen (who pay at a special rate).

In the case of (e) and (f), the exemption is applicable only to the particular week concerned.

Special rules apply to those who go to work abroad — see **41.52** to **41.56**.

Small earnings

[24.4] Class 2 contributions are not payable if earnings are small, but since the amount payable is currently only £2.85 a week, then unless there are also earnings on which Class 1 contributions are paid it is probably sensible to pay Class 2 contributions voluntarily and maintain the contribution record for social security benefits, particularly the state retirement pension. The contribution record could alternatively be maintained by paying Class 3 voluntary contributions (see **13.13**), but these are at a much higher rate than Class 2, being £14.25 a week for 2017–18.

Only those with taxable profits above the small profits threshold, which is £6,025 for 2017–18, are liable to pay Class 2 NICs, but contributions may still be paid voluntarily.

Proposed abolition of Class 2 contributions

[24.5] The Government intends to abolish Class 2 contributions from April 2018 and reform Class 4 contributions to introduce a new contributory benefit test, because at present Class 4 NICs carry no entitlement to benefits of any kind. Draft legislation has been issued which provides that the majority of the self-employed will access contributory benefits (such as those listed in **24.1** which are currently due to those paying Class 2) through Class 4 NICs. Those with income below a small profits limit, which will be calculated at 52 times the lower earnings limit for the tax year (£113 for 2017–18, see **13.4**) will need to pay Class 3 NICs (see **13.13**) to access certain benefits, whilst those with profits between the small profits limit and the Class 4 lower profits limit will be treated as paying notional NICs which protect their rights to benefits. This is similar to the provision for employees, see **13.4**. Transitional arrangements will enable certain people with low profits to rely on their contribution record in the two years prior to Class 2 abolition for longer than usual when claiming contributory employment and support allowance and contribution-based jobseeker's allowance.

Class 4 contributions

Payment (SSCBA 1992, ss 15–17 and Sch 2; SI 2001/1004; SI 2017/415)

[24.6] Class 4 contributions are payable at a main percentage rate of 9% on trading income chargeable to income tax (see CHAPTER 19) which falls between specified lower and upper profit limits, and at the additional percentage rate of 2% on profits above the upper profit limit. The lower and upper profit limits for 2016–17 and 2017–18 are:

2016–17	£8,060 and £43,000
2017–18	£8,164 and £45,000

If a person has more than one self-employment, all the profits are added together when calculating the Class 4 liability.

In general, 'profits' are computed in the same way for Class 4 contributions as for income tax but certain special rules apply. For example, trading losses allowed under ITA 2007, ss 64 and 72 (see CHAPTER 25) against non-trading income and capital gains for tax purposes are set only against trading income for Class 4 NICs. Unused losses may be carried forward against future profits for calculating Class 4 contributions.

Post-cessation receipts (see **21.9**) are not liable to Class 4 as they are not taxable as trading profits.

Class 4 contributions are collected along with income tax under self-assessment, so that the half-yearly payments on account made on 31 January and 31 July include Class 4 contributions based on the previous year's figures, with any balancing adjustment shown in the tax return and payable or repayable on the following 31 January. Provision is made in returns for the taxpayer to indicate that he is exempt from Class 4 contributions (see **24.7**), in which case no contributions are shown.

See **24.2** regarding entertainers.

The Government intends to abolish Class 2 contributions from April 2018 and reform Class 4 contributions to introduce a new contributory benefit test, because at present Class 4 NICs carry no entitlement to benefits of any kind. See **24.5**.

Exempt persons

[24.7] The following people are not liable to pay Class 4 contributions:

(a)   persons under 16 at the beginning of the tax year who hold a certificate of exception;

(b)   persons over pensionable age (see **16.2**) at the beginning of the tax year;

(c)   those who are not resident in the UK for income tax purposes;

(d)   trustees and executors who are chargeable to income tax on income they receive on behalf of other people;

(e)   divers and diving supervisors working in connection with exploration and exploitation activities on the Continental shelf or in UK territorial waters;

(f)   certain self-employed earners who pay income tax on their trading income but are liable to pay Class 1 NICs on that income (see **13.2**);

(g)   persons with profits below the lower limit.

Late payment or overpayment of contributions

[24.8] The income tax rules for charging interest (see **2.30** to **2.32**) apply if Class 4 contributions are paid late and penalties for failure to notify, late payment and careless or deliberate error apply (see **9.55** onwards). The income tax provisions for interest on overpaid tax also apply where contributions are refunded.

Partnerships

[24.9] Active partners, sleeping partners, and inactive limited partners and limited liability partners (see **23.40**) are liable to both Class 2 and Class 4 contributions (unless a wife is exempt from Class 2 contributions — see **24.10**), and the Class 4 profit limits apply separately to each partner's profit share. This is subject to the provisions applying from 6 April 2014 under which members of limited liability partnerships can in certain circumstances be treated as employees and thus liable to Class 1 contributions, see **23.33**.

A partner's Class 4 contributions are entered in the partner's personal return. Where a partner carries on a further trade or trades, the profits of all such businesses are considered together when calculating his overall Class 4 liability.

Married women

[24.10] Women who were married or widowed before 6 April 1977 could elect on or before 11 May 1977 not to pay full NICs. If the election has been made, Class 1 contributions as an employee are paid at a reduced rate. Class 2 self-employed contributions do not have to be paid, however, Class 4 contributions must be paid.

The right to pay no Class 2 and reduced rate Class 1 contributions is lost in some circumstances. See **13.5**.

Self-employed and employed in the same tax year

[24.11] If a person is both self-employed and an employee, he is liable to pay Class 1, 2 and 4 contributions, and if he has more than one employment is liable to Class 1 contributions in each employment. There is, however, a maximum figure above which contributions will be refunded.

The calculation of the annual maximum can be very complicated and has up to nine stages. Detailed guidance on the calculation is available in HMRC's National Insurance Manual at NIM24150. If contributions for 2017–18 exceed the maximum, a refund of the excess may be claimed from NICO so long as the excess is greater than 1/15th of a Class 1 contribution at the main 12% rate on earnings at the upper earnings limit — i.e. £5.67 for 2017–18.

Where a person is both self-employed and an employee, payment of the correct amount of NICs should be dealt with through the self-assessment system, unless he has more than one employment and has not applied for deferment (see **13.8**). However, if a person believes he has overpaid contributions he may apply to NICO for a refund.

Tax points

[24.12] Note the following:

- HMRC should be notified of any weeks for which a Class 2 contribution is not due, for example when receiving employment and support allowance, so that an adjustment can be made.
- Trading losses set off against non-trading income for income tax purposes are carried forward against trading profits for Class 4 contributions purposes. There is a worksheet in the tax return guide to make the appropriate adjustment to the profits.
- A married woman who has elected not to pay Class 2 contributions should watch the circumstances in which contributions become payable, for example following widowhood or divorce (see **13.5**).

25

Losses of sole traders and partners

Introduction

[25.1] Losses may arise in a trade, profession or vocation carried on in the UK or abroad, or in a business of property letting. Capital losses may arise on the disposal of chargeable assets. Losses relating to rented property may normally be relieved only against rental income, and are dealt with in CHAPTER 32. Relief for losses relating to businesses controlled abroad is restricted to profits from the same source (see CHAPTER 41). Capital losses are normally set against capital gains of the same tax year, with any balance carried forward against later gains (see 4.3), although capital losses on certain unquoted shares may be set against income (see 38.23). Other aspects relating to capital losses are dealt with in context in other chapters. Company losses are dealt with in CHAPTER 26. The remainder of this chapter deals with losses of UK trades. The rules for trading losses apply equally to professions or vocations.

Calculation of losses and reliefs available

Calculation of loss (ITA 2007, s 61)

[25.2] Losses for sole traders and partners are calculated using the same basis periods as those used for calculating profits (see 21.2). So a loss of the year to 31 August 2017 would be regarded as a loss of 2017–18 in the same way as a profit of that year would be taxed in 2017–18. The loss basis period could be longer than 12 months if the accounting date has been changed (see 21.7), subject to the rules mentioned below for overlapping basis periods. Furthermore, a basis period of more than 12 months would result in the loss being increased by an appropriate proportion of available overlap relief (see Example 1).

Example 1

Trader started business on 1 July 2013, making up his accounts to 30 June annually, and made profits each year until the year to 30 June 2016. He then made up a 15-month account to 30 September 2017 showing a loss. The position is as follows:

Basis periods

2013–14	1.7.13 – 5.4.14
2014–15	1.7.13 – 30.6.14 (overlap profits 9 mths to 5.4.14)
2015–16	1.7.14 – 30.6.15
2016–17	1.7.15 – 30.6.16
2017–18	1.7.16 – 30.9.17 (loss)

Relief may be claimed for the 2017–18 loss of the 15 months to 30 September 2017, augmented by overlap relief of 3/9ths of the overlap profits (see **21.7**).

The basis period rules apply on cessation as they do in a continuing business. Any available overlap relief is taken into account in computing the result of the final accounting period. If a business that had made up accounts annually to 30 June ceased trading on 30 April 2017, making a loss in the final ten months, the loss of that ten months would be treated as a 2017–18 loss and would be increased by any available overlap relief (but see **25.9** regarding terminal loss claims). Where a loss would be taken into account in two successive tax years (for example, in the first trading period of a new business or on a change of accounting date), it is only taken into account in the first year.

Example 2

Trader starts in business on 1 August 2015 and makes a loss of £24,000 in the year to 31 July 2016 and a profit of £15,000 in the year to 31 July 2017. The assessments for 2015–16 and 2016–17 are therefore nil.

8/12ths of the loss, i.e. £16,000, is treated as the loss of 2015–16 and 4/12ths, i.e. £8,000, as the loss of 2016–17. The profit of £15,000 is assessed in 2017–18.

Loss reliefs available

[25.3] There are various ways in which relief for trading losses may be claimed by sole traders and partners — see **23.17** for general comments on partnership losses and **25.12** to **25.16** for various anti-avoidance provisions applying to sole traders and partners. In general losses, other than those arising in cash basis for small businesses (see **20.4**), may be relieved as follows:

(a) Carry forward against later profits of *same trade* (ITA 2007, s 83).

(b) Set against *general* income of tax year of loss and/or the previous tax year (ITA 2007, s 64). The claim for either year may, if the taxpayer wishes, be extended to include set-off against capital gains (ITA 2007, s 71 and TCGA 1992, s 261B).

(c) In a new trade, carry back against *general* income of previous three tax years, earliest first (ITA 2007, s 72).

(d) When a loss occurs on ceasing to trade, set against *trading* income of final tax year, then carry back against *trading* income of previous three tax years, latest first (ITA 2007, ss 89, 90).

Relief for trade losses against general income under (b) above and early trade loss relief in (c) above is commonly known as 'sideways relief'. Where a person has made an election to calculate profits, and losses, under the cash basis, relief is not available as sideways relief or capital gains relief under (b) and (c).

From 2013–14 loss relief against *general income* under ITA 2007, ss 64 and 72 is one of a number of reliefs against general income which is capped (see **2.13** and **25.6**).

Since the set-off of losses is made *before* deducting personal allowances, in many cases personal allowances will be wasted.

Capital allowances

[25.4] Capital allowances are treated as trading expenses, and therefore form part of the trading result. There is some flexibility, however, because the capital allowances claim can be reduced to whatever amount is required (see **22.18** and **22.52**). There are anti-avoidance provisions regarding losses arising in respect of first year allowances or the annual investment allowance (see **25.13**). Where profits are calculated on the cash basis capital allowances may only be claimed on a car (see **20.11**).

Loss carried forward (ITA 2007, s 83)

[25.5] The most straightforward way of obtaining relief for a loss is by carrying it forward to reduce later income of the same trade, so that in Example 1 the total available losses, including the overlap relief, would be carried forward to reduce trading profits of 2018–19 and later years. In Example 2 the total losses of £24,000 would eliminate the 2017–18 assessment of £15,000 leaving £9,000 still to carry forward. The set-off can only be made against profits of the *same* trade, so that a change in activity will cause relief to be denied. See **25.10** for time limits for claims.

There are obvious disadvantages in carrying forward a loss. The trade may cease, or its nature change, before the loss is fully relieved. There is also a considerable delay before the loss results in a cash saving by reducing or eliminating a tax liability.

Loss set against other income (ITA 2007, ss 24A, 64–70, 74E)

[25.6] Unless a cash basis for small businesses election applies for the tax year (see **20.4** and **25.3**), earlier relief may be obtained by setting off the loss against any other income of the tax year in which the loss is incurred or of the previous tax year, or, depending on the amount of the loss and the amount of other income, of both tax years. This is subject to certain anti-avoidance provisions in **25.12** to **25.16** and to the cap on reliefs against general income in **2.13** which applies from 2013–14. The limit of the cap is the greater of £50,000 or 25% of the individual's adjusted total income for the tax year but applies to the aggregate of all the reliefs listed in **2.13** taken together. Relief for trading losses made in tax years prior to 2013–14 are not subject to the cap but the cap applies where loss relief is claimed for a tax year before 2013–14 in relation to losses made in 2013–14 or later. The cap does not apply where the deduction is made from profits of the same trade or business to which the relief relates (see Example 3 below), nor does it affect relief for losses attributable to overlap relief in the final tax year or on a change of accounting date (see **21.6**), or attributable to business premises renovation allowances (see **32.19**).

If claims are to be made, and are possible, for both available years, the taxpayer must decide which claim comes first. If there are losses in successive years, and both a current year loss and a carried back loss are to be relieved in the same tax year, the earlier year's loss is set off first. If there were other sources of income, section 64 claims could be made for the 2017–18 loss in Example 1 against the income of 2017–18 and/or 2016–17, subject to the cap on relief — see Example 3. Section 64 claims could be made in Example 2 for the 2015–16 loss of £16,000 in 2015–16 and/or 2014–15, and for the 2016–17 loss of £8,000 in 2016–17 and/or 2015–16, again subject to the cap on relief. If, however, the taxpayer claimed against 2015–16 income in respect of both the 2015–16 loss and the 2016–17 loss, the 2015–16 loss would be set off first. See **25.8** regarding the claims possible in Example 2 under section 72.

Example 3

Trader has trade losses in 2017–18 of £190,000 and 2016–17 profits from the same trade of £60,000. He has other income in each year of £100,000. His relief against general income is capped at £50,000 for both 2016–17 and 2017–18, this being greater than 25% of adjusted total income.

Trader makes a claim to set £50,000 trade loss relief against his 2017–18 general income and to carry back £60,000 against 2016–17 profits from the same trade. He also claims £50,000 carried back against his general income in 2016–17. His taxable income for 2017–18 and 2016–17 will be as follows:

	£
2017–18	
Other income	100,000
Relief under ITA 2007, s 64 (capped)	(50,000)
	50,000
2016–17	
Trade income	60,000
Other income	100,000
	160,000
Relief under ITA 2007, s 64 against same trade income (uncapped*)	(60,000)

Relief under ITA 2007, s 64 (capped)	(50,000)
	£50,000

* The cap does not apply where the deduction is made from profits of the same trade or business to which the relief relates.

The unused loss of £30,000 can be carried forward.

See **25.10** for time limits for claims.

A claim under ITA 2007, s 64 cannot be made for losses incurred in 'hobby' trades as distinct from commercial activities carried on with a view to the realisation of profits, or where a cash basis for small businesses election applies (see **25.3** and **20.4**). A claim is also specifically prohibited for the sixth year of a consecutive run of farming and market gardening losses, reckoned before capital allowances (ITA 2007, s 67, see **31.5**).

Extending s 64 claim to capital gains (ITA 2007, s 71; TCGA 1992, s 261B)

[25.7] A section 64 claim (see **25.6**) may be extended to include set-off against capital gains, in either or both of the tax year of loss and the previous tax year. The claim against income of the year must be made first (personal allowances therefore being wasted, except where the transferable tax allowance or the married couple's age allowance are transferred (see **2.17** and **2.19**)) and the loss available to set against capital gains is also reduced by any other loss relief claimed, for example under section 64 in the previous year or by carry-back under section 72 in a new business (see **25.8**). Relief against capital gains is not affected by the cap on ITA 2007, s 64 loss relief against general income (see **25.6**).

The maximum amount of capital gains available to relieve the trading loss is the amount of the capital gains after deducting any capital losses of the relevant year and unrelieved capital losses brought forward from earlier years but before deducting the annual exempt amount (see **4.29**). The amount available for relief is the lower of the available loss and the available amount of capital gains. The available amount is treated as an allowable capital loss of the relevant year and is therefore set off against capital gains in *priority* to brought forward capital losses (see **4.3**). Depending on the levels of gains and losses, the claim may mean wasting all or part of the annual exempt amount, but this may still be preferable depending on the rate of capital gains tax payable (see **4.2**).

Example 4

Married trader not using the cash basis makes a loss of £50,000 in year to 31 December 2017, and claims section 64 relief for 2017–18 against his other income for that year of £10,000 (the claim not being restricted by the cap on income tax reliefs in **2.13**), and against his capital gains. His capital gains of the year (net of capital losses of the year) were £42,000 and arose on shares. There were no capital losses brought forward.

The section 64 claim against income utilises £10,000 of the loss, and wastes personal allowances (although if he is entitled to married couple's age allowance, the allowance may be transferred to his wife, as may the transferable tax allowance). The unrelieved trading loss is therefore £40,000, which is lower than the available capital gains of £42,000.

After setting off the loss of £40,000 this leaves gains of £2,000, reduced to nil by the annual exempt amount which is £11,300. Therefore, £9,300 of the annual exempt amount is wasted.

If the claim against capital gains had not been made, there would have been an unrelieved trading loss to carry forward of £40,000 and the capital gains tax payable would be:

	£
Gains	42,000
Annual exempt amount	(11,300)
Amount chargeable to tax	30,700
Tax thereon @ 10%	£3,070

The effective rate of relief on the loss of £40,000 if utilised against capital gains is therefore 8% (£3,070 ÷ £40,000). The capital gains tax rate is 10% because the trader does not have income or gains above the basic rate limit in 2017–18 and the gains were not 'upper rate gains'. It may therefore be more beneficial to carry the loss forward, when income tax relief may be at 20%. If the trader had gains above the basic rate limit, the 20% capital gains tax rate would apply. If the gain was an 'upper rate gain' the rates applying would be 18% or 28%. See **4.2** regarding the differing capital gains tax rates applying.

Where there are capital losses brought forward that already reduce gains to the exempt level, the trading loss claim would give no immediate tax saving and it would be a question of whether it would be preferable to have unrelieved trading losses carried forward or unrelieved capital losses carried forward.

New trades — carry-back of losses (ITA 2007, ss 24A, 72, 74E)

[25.8] Where a loss occurs in any of the first four tax years of a new sole trade, or of a new partner's membership of a partnership, and a cash basis for small businesses election does not apply for the tax year (see **20.4** and **25.3**), relief may be claimed against that person's general income of the three previous tax years, *earliest* first. This is subject to certain anti-avoidance provisions in **25.12** to **25.16** and to the cap on reliefs against general income in **2.13** which applies from 2013–14. See **25.6** for details of how the cap applies to loss relief against general income. A section 72 claim is a single claim and the loss must be set off to the maximum possible extent against the income of all three years. See Example 5. There is no set-off against capital gains in those previous three years. As with section 64 (see **25.6**), this carry-back claim cannot be made unless the trade is carried on commercially. There is an anti-avoidance provision which restricts relief where the trade was previously carried on by the person's spouse or civil partner. Where a loss is large enough, a section 64 claim may be preceded or followed by a section 72 claim, subject to any cap on the relief. See **25.10** for the time limit for claims.

Example 5

In Example 2 at **25.2**, the trader incurred losses of £16,000 and £8,000 respectively in his first and second tax years of trading, 2015–16 and 2016–17.

As an alternative to claiming relief under section 64 (or in addition to a section 64 claim, depending on the level of other income) relief could be claimed under section 72 as follows:

2015–16 loss of £16,000
Against total income of 2012–13, then 2013–14, then 2014–15.

2016–17 loss of £8,000
Against total income of 2013–14, then 2014–15, then 2015–16.

Any losses not relieved under either section 64 or section 72 would be carried forward under section 83 (see **25.5**).

Because of the way losses are calculated where basis periods overlap (see Example 2 at **25.2**), choosing an accounting date early in the tax year may restrict the section 72 claims available.

Example 6

New business started 1 May 2015. If there are losses in the early years and accounts are made up annually to 31 March, section 72 claims will be possible in respect of losses made in the 11 months to 31 March 2016, and the years to 31 March 2017, 2018 and 2019. If accounts are made up annually to 30 April, section 72 claims will only be possible in respect of the loss of the year to 30 April 2016 (the claim being split as to 11/12ths in 2015–16 and 1/12th in 2016–17), and the years to 30 April 2017 and 2018.

Although the tax saving from section 72 claims is *calculated* by reference to the tax position of the carry-back years, repayment interest runs from 31 January following the loss year (see **25.11**).

Loss on cessation of trade (terminal loss) (ITA 2007, ss 89, 90; CAA 2001, s 354)

[25.9] Losses towards the end of a business clearly cannot be carried forward against future profits. A claim may be made to set the loss of the last 12 months of trading (called a terminal loss) against the *trading* income (after capital allowances) of the tax year in which the business ceases, then the three tax years prior to that tax year, *latest* first. The terminal loss is calculated in two parts, splitting the last 12 months at the tax year end, i.e. at 5 April. If the *result* of either part is a profit, it is treated as nil in the calculation. Profits must, however, be taken into account in arriving at the figures for each part, as shown in Example 7. The full amount of any available overlap relief is included in the terminal loss. The tax saving flowing from carrying back the loss is calculated by reference to the tax position of the earlier years, but it is given effect in relation to the loss year, with a consequent reduction in the amount of repayment interest payable (see **25.11**).

Where there is other income, a section 64 claim (see **25.6**) may be made in addition to (or instead of) the terminal loss claim. Unlike the terminal loss calculation, a loss of the final tax year for section 64 is on an accounting period basis, as shown in Example 7. Where both claims are made, the taxpayer may choose which claim is to be dealt with first.

Example 7

Trade ceases 30 September 2016.

Previous accounts have been to 31 December, recent results up to the cessation being:

Year to 31 December 2013	Profit £17,500
Year to 31 December 2014	Profit £12,000
Year to 31 December 2015	Profit £7,200
Period to 30 September 2016	Loss £27,000

Overlap relief brought forward is £3,000.

Assessments will be (see CHAPTER **21**):

	£
2013–14 (year to 31.12.13)	17,500
2014–15 (year to 31.12.14)	12,000
2015–16 (year to 31.12.15)	7,200
2016–17 (9 months to 30.9.16)	—

Terminal loss of year to 30 September 2016:

		£	£
1.10.15 to 5.4.16			
First 3 months	Profit: 3/12 x 7,200	1,800	
Next 3 months	Loss: 3/9 x (27,000)	(9,000)	
			(7,200)
6.4.16 to 30.9.16	Loss: 6/9 x (27,000)	(18,000)	
Overlap relief (in full)		(3,000)	
			(21,000)
			(28,200)

Since there is no trading income in 2016–17, the terminal loss may be carried back and set off against trading assessments as follows:

£

2015–16		7,200
2014–15		12,000
2013–14	(balance, reducing assessment to £8,500)	9,000
		£28,200

If there had been insufficient trading income to obtain relief for the terminal loss (or as an alternative to a terminal loss claim), a section 64 claim could be made to set the 2016–17 loss against *any* income or chargeable gains of that year and/or 2015–16. The 2016–17 loss for a section 64 claim is the full £27,000 loss to 30 September 2016 plus the overlap relief of £3,000, totalling £30,000, less any terminal loss relief claimed. The cap in 25.6 may apply.

Time limits for claims

[25.10]

ITA 2007, s 64	Set off against income and gains of same tax year or previous tax year	Within one year from 31 January after the end of the tax year in which the loss occurs
ITA 2007, s 72	Set off new business losses against income for three previous tax years, taking earlier before later years	Within one year from 31 January after the end of the tax year in which the loss occurs
ITA 2007, s 83	Carry forward indefinitely against future profits of same trade	Within four years from the end of the tax year in which the loss occurs
ITA 2007, ss 89, 90	Carry-back of terminal losses	Within four years from the end of the tax year in which the business ceases

Repayment interest (TMA 1970, Sch 1B para 2; TA 1988, s 824; FA 2009, ss 102–104, Schs 54, 54A; SI 2011/701)

[25.11] A loss claim will either prevent tax being payable or cause tax already paid to be repaid. Repayment interest (see 9.55 and 9.56) runs from the date of an overpayment, but the rate of interest is significantly lower than that charged on unpaid tax (see TABLE OF RATES AND ALLOWANCES (**TRA**)). Furthermore, where a loss is carried back and set against the income of an earlier tax year, then although the tax saving is calculated by reference to the tax position of the earlier year, the adjustment is made by reducing the tax liability of the loss year (see **9.16**) and interest runs from the 31 January payment date for that year. This significantly affects the benefit of carrying back new trade losses for up to three years (see **25.8**).

Anti-avoidance provisions

Losses of limited partners and partners in limited liability partnerships (ITA 2007, ss 102–115; CTA 2009, 1273; CTA 2010, ss 55–61)

[25.12] Some partnerships have 'limited partners', whose liability for partnership debts is limited to a fixed capital contribution (see **23.41**). These limited partners may be either individuals or companies. A loss claim by such partners carrying on a trade against income other than income from the trade cannot exceed the total of the limited partner's net capital contribution plus undrawn profits to the end of that year and the amount the partner is liable to contribute on a winding up, less loss relief already given against non-trading income. This restriction applies only to trades and not to professions. The loss claims referred to are those under ITA 2007, sections 64 and 72 for individuals, and under CTA 2010, section 37 or the group relief provisions in Pt 5 for companies (see **26.4** and **26.20**). Furthermore there is an annual limit of £25,000 on the amount of trading losses for which limited partners will be able to claim relief against other income/gains. See **25.13** for provisions relating to the definition of capital contribution and recovery of excess loss relief which apply equally to limited partners and limited liability partners. There is no restriction on the right of limited partners to carry forward their unused losses against later profits from the same trade.

Similar rules apply in relation to partners in limited liability partnerships (LLPs — see **23.33** to **23.37**). Undrawn profits cannot, however, be included in a partner's subscribed capital unless such profits are unconditionally treated as part of the partner's capital. Losses unrelieved in one tax year against income other than from the trade because of the restriction are available for relief against non-trading income in subsequent years, similarly restricted by reference to the subscribed capital of the later year. Anti-avoidance provisions apply to losses of individual partners in LLPs in the first four tax years (see **25.13**), and operate for those years instead of the provisions in this section.

Loss relief for non-active partners (ITA 2007, ss 102–115, 790–795)

[25.13] There are anti-avoidance rules to prevent manipulation by individuals of the tax reliefs for partnership losses. They affect 'non-active partners', i.e. those who do not spend at least ten hours a week personally engaged in the activities of a trade whose activities are carried on on a commercial basis and with a view to realising profits. See **25.14** for similar rules for individuals.

The rules apply to losses arising in the first four tax years in which the partner carried on the trade, and do not therefore apply to professions. They prevent such partners in general partnerships and limited liability partnerships (LLPs) claiming relief for losses against non-trading income and capital gains (see **25.6** to **25.8**) to a greater extent than the amount of their capital contribution and profit share. The amount of a partner's capital contribution will exclude amounts contributed on or after 2 March 2007 where a main purpose of the contribution was to obtain tax relief for a loss against non-trading income and/or capital gains. This applies to limited partners (as to which see **25.12**) as well as general partners. Furthermore, for losses arising on or after that date, there is an annual limit of £25,000 on the amount of trading losses for which non-active partners will be able to claim relief against other income/gains (subject to an exclusion for certain film-related expenditure). The anti-avoidance provisions also impose an 'exit charge' where such partners share in large early losses in trades that acquire a licence which entails significant expenditure before any income arises, obtain relief for the losses against their other income or gains, and then dispose of their share of the benefit of the income from the licence without attracting an income tax charge.

Loss relief given against non-trading income may be recovered by an excess relief charge to the extent that the individual's capital contribution falls below the amount of loss relief claimed. This applies to limited partners (as to which see **25.12**) as well as general partners, and for limited partners the provisions are not restricted to the first four tax years in which the individual is a partner.

A separate anti-avoidance provision relates solely to film partnerships. Sideways relief (see **25.3**) can only be claimed to the extent that the loss consists of qualifying film expenditure in any tax year which broadly, is (a) one of the first four tax years in which an individual becomes a partner, (b) one in which he was a non-active partner, and (c) during which an agreement existed which guaranteed him a specified amount of income.

Loss relief for non-active traders (ITA 2007, ss 74A, 74C–D)

[25.14] There are provisions to prevent sideways relief under ITA 2007, ss 64 and 72 and capital gains relief as applied by ITA 2007, s 71 being obtained where an individual carries on a trade other than in partnership but in a 'non-active capacity'. See **25.13** for similar measures which apply to partners.

These rules apply, broadly, from 12 March 2008 and limit to £25,000 the amount of relief that can be claimed against general income or capital gains for losses arising from a trade carried on in a non-active capacity. They also provide that no relief is given where a loss arises from 'tax avoidance arrangements'.

An individual carries on a trade in a non-active capacity for this purpose if he does not spend at least ten hours a week personally engaged in the activities of a trade whose activities are carried on on a commercial basis and with a view to realising profits.

Tax-generated losses (ITA 2007, s 74ZA)

[25.15] Further anti-avoidance provisions prevent sideways relief under ITA 2007, ss 64 and 72 and capital gains relief as applied by ITA 2007, s 71 being given to a person for losses from a trade where the loss arises from tax avoidance arrangements. The legislation is specifically targeted at persons who enter into tax avoidance arrangements with a main purpose of obtaining a tax reduction by way of sideways relief. The restriction applies to losses arising as a result of such arrangements entered into on or after 21 October 2009. The loss may still be carried forward against future profits of the same trade.

Losses relating to capital allowances (ITA 2007, ss 75–79)

[25.16] Where an individual incurs expenditure on the provision of plant or machinery for leasing in the course of a trade, capital allowances on the expenditure can only be included in the loss computation for sideways relief (see 25.3) if, broadly, the trade has been carried on by the individual for a continuous period of at least six months beginning or ending in the period of loss, and the claimant devotes substantially the whole of his time to the trade throughout that period.

Sideways relief is denied where the loss arises in respect of first year allowances or annual investment allowance granted to an individual where the plant or machinery concerned was used for leasing in the course of a qualifying activity carried on by the individual and he was carrying on that activity in partnership with a company or arrangements had been or were later made for him to do so.

Such relief is also denied in respect of the allowances, broadly, where they are made in connection with relevant qualifying activities or assets and arrangements have been made where the main benefit is to reduce tax liabilities.

Losses in mixed member partnerships (ITA 2007, ss 116A, 127C)

[25.17] See 23.4 regarding the tax-motivated partnership loss allocation restrictions which apply from 2014–15.

National insurance

[25.18] Losses reduce the profit for Class 4 NICs as well as for income tax (see 24.6). If a claim is made for income tax relief for the loss against non-trading income or against capital gains, the loss can still be set against future trading income for Class 4 NICs purposes.

Where a loss claim results in Class 4 contributions being refunded, the refund attracts repayment interest.

Tax points

[25.19] Note the following:

- When considering how to claim relief for losses, the key questions are how much tax will be saved, when it will be saved and how much tax-free repayment interest will be received. The effect of changes in tax rates and allowances in the various years must be considered. See HMRC Helpsheet HS227 for guidance to traders on how to utilise their losses.

- More than one claim will frequently be possible and a trader's tax position may be different according to the order in which claims are taken into account. A trader may generally stipulate which claims take priority.

- Claiming carry-back relief under section 72, instead of current year relief under section 64, for a first year loss leaves other income of the loss year available for a possible carry-back claim under section 72 for a loss in later years.

- Loss relief against general income is restricted to those losses incurred in a demonstrably commercial trade and this may be difficult to prove. This is particularly so in the case of a new trade, so that a viable business plan is often essential to support a carry-back claim under section 72.

- A loss in the opening years carried back under section 72, in preference to a claim under section 64, must be fully relieved under section 72 before the balance of available losses can be relieved under section 64. It is not possible to carry back sufficient of the loss to relieve income of the third year back and then not to proceed against the income of the second year back and then the first. The carry-back facility must be exhausted if claimed at all, before a section 64 loss claim is made in respect of the balance remaining unrelieved.
  If there is a loss in the next year of trading this forms an entirely new claim. Relief for that loss can be claimed under section 64 in preference to section 72 but, if a section 72 claim is embarked upon first, again the carry-back facility must be exhausted in respect of that particular loss before the balance can be relieved under section 64.

- The cap on income tax reliefs from 2013–14 must be borne in mind when calculating loss relief (see **25.6** and **2.13**), as must the restrictions on loss relief from 2013–14 where the cash basis for small businesses applies (see **25.3** and **20.4**).

- There are time limits both for making claims and for amending them (see **9.15** and **25.10**). Claims do not have to be agreed by HMRC within the time limits, but HMRC may challenge the validity of the claims if they open an enquiry (see **9.42**).

26

Company losses

Introduction

[26.1] Companies may incur losses in their trades, in the course of letting property, in relation to investment income if expenses exceed the income, and in their capital transactions. In some cases the losses will relate to activities outside the UK. The overseas aspect is dealt with in CHAPTER **41**.

A company within the charge to corporation tax can have any of the following types of losses:

(a)   trading losses (see **26.3**);
(b)   property losses (see **26.7**);
(c)   non-trading loan relationship losses (see **26.8**);
(d)   non-trading losses on intangible fixed assets (see **26.10**);
(e)   miscellaneous losses; and
(f)   capital losses (see CHAPTER **4** and in context in various other chapters, including CHAPTER **3** in relation to capital losses within a group of companies and CHAPTER **45** in relation to various anti-avoidance provisions on capital losses).

A company must also consider qualifying charitable donations (**26.11**) and excess management expenses (**26.12**) which, although not actually losses, are treated in a similar way to losses.

The loss of money lent is regarded as an income loss rather than a capital loss. Such losses are dealt with in this chapter at **26.8**.

Reform of corporate loss relief rules

[26.2] The September 2017 Finance Bill, which is expected to receive Royal Assent in November 2017, introduced a complete reform of the UK tax rules governing what companies can do with carried-forward corporation tax losses from 1 April 2017. Note it is only carried forward losses that are affected by the Finance Bill changes. The rules relating to current year and carry back of losses are not directly affected.

The reforms have resulted in two sets of rules that govern the use of carried-forward losses — one for losses arising prior to 1 April 2017 and one for losses arising on or after 1 April 2017. Where an accounting period straddles 1 April 2017, it is split into two notional periods and profits and losses are allocated on a just and reasonable basis.

The new provisions make two main changes to the rules on corporation tax loss relief. They introduce:

(a)   a loss relaxation — this allows companies to use carried-forward losses arising on or after 1 April 2017 against profits from other types of income and of other companies in the group; and

(b)   a loss restriction — this imposes a limit on the amount of profits that can be relieved by carried-forward losses (incurred at any time) to 50% of group profits above £5 million (referred to in the legislation as the 'deductions allowance'). If a company is not a member of a group, the deductions allowance is £5 million. If the accounting period is less than twelve months, the amount is reduced proportionally. If a company has profits for an accounting period that do not exceed the amount of the deductions allowance, carried-forward losses may be set against those profits without restriction. Note this restriction applies to profits arising on or after 1 April 2017 regardless of when the losses were originally incurred. Where the carried-forward amounts include losses which can only be set against particular types of profits, the maximum set-off must be computed separately for trading profits and non-trading profits. The company may decide how its deductions allowance should be allocated between trading and non-trading profits.

The new rules are complex and detailed, and this chapter provides no more than an overview of the two regimes. They apply to trading losses, UK property business losses, expenses of management, non-trading loan relationship deficits and non-trading losses on intangible fixed assets.

Trading losses

[26.3] Trading losses of companies are calculated in the same way as trading profits. The losses can be used in current, preceding or future years as follows:

(a)   current year — losses can be set-off against current profits from other sources (CTA 2010, s 37(3)(*a*)), see **26.4**;

(b)   previous years — losses can be carried-back against earlier profits from all sources (CTA 2010, s 37(3)(*b*); FA 2009, s 23, Sch 6), see **26.5**;

(c)   future years — losses arising in accounting periods can be carried forward. The profits against which they can be offset differ depending upon whether the losses arise before or after 1 April 2017, see **26.6** (CTA 2010, ss 45, 45A).

Additionally, where a company is in a group, losses made in the relevant 'overlapping' period may be surrendered from one company to one or more other companies within the group, provided the necessary conditions are satisfied (see **26.16**).

Where a company (Company A) would be entitled to claim a patent box deduction (**3.17**) when calculating its trading profits, but has incurred IP losses in the relevant accounting period, it is entitled to a set-off amount equivalent to the loss. This set-off amount is firstly matched with relevant IP profits of another trade of the same company (if there is one), then against IP profits of another group company which has made a qualifying patent box claim. If there is still an excess after this, it is carried forward (in Company A) to the next accounting period for offset. This treatment applies until the set-off amount has been fully relieved.

Set-off against current profits (CTA 2010, s 37(3)(a))

[26.4] A trading loss of a company can be set against any profits of the same chargeable accounting period, thus reducing or eliminating the corporation tax bill. Profits for this purpose includes not only all sources of income (including dividends, although most will be exempt from corporation tax) but also capital gains (see **3.1**).

Claims to set off losses against current year profits are only permitted if the company carries on business on a commercial basis with a view to the realisation of profit (and see **31.5** for additional restrictions for farming companies). Claims must be made within two years after the end of the relevant accounting period, or such later period as HMRC may allow.

Carry-back against previous profits (CTA 2010, ss 37(3)(b))

[26.5] After a trading loss has been set against all profits of the current period, any balance may be carried back and set against the total profits of accounting periods falling wholly or partly within the previous 12 months (but in certain situations, this carry back is extended to three years), so long as the trade was carried on in the earlier period on a commercial basis with a view to the realisation of profit. If the loss period is less than 12 months this does not restrict the carry-back period.

The carry back is extended to three years on the cessation of trade. In such situations, the three year carry back applies to losses of accounting periods falling wholly or partly within the last 12 months of trading. Where an accounting period falls only partly within the last 12 months, the carry-back period for the part of the loss within the last 12 months is three years, the normal 12-month carry-back applying to the remainder of the loss. As far as the carry-back period is concerned, results are similarly apportioned as necessary where an accounting period falls only partly within the 12-month or three-year period.

As with the claim against current profits, the set-off in the carry-back period is not limited to trading profits and is made against profits of any description. Claims must be made within two years after the end of the relevant accounting period, or such later period as HMRC may allow.

Carry forward against future profits (CTA 2010, ss 45, 45A, 730E–730H; CTA 2010, ss 269A–269CN; F(No 2)A 2015, s 37; FA 2016, s 57)

[26.6] Any loss not relieved against current year or previous year profits (26.4, 26.5) may be carried forward for set-off. The September 2017 Finance Bill, which is expected to receive Royal Assent in November 2017, provides that the profits against which they can be offset will differ depending on whether the losses arose before or after 1 April 2017 as follows:

Losses arising pre-1 April 2017	Losses arising post-1 April 2017
Carry forward and set against future profits of the same trade. Cannot carry-forward and surrender for group relief.	Carry forward and set against total profits of a later accounting period. Can carry forward and surrender losses for group relief but subject to conditions—see **26.22**. Terminal loss relief is available where trade ceases but subject to specific anti-avoidance provision for cessation and transfer of the trade.

Where an accounting period straddles 1 April 2017, it is split into two notional periods and profits and losses are allocated on a just and reasonable basis.

It can be seen that the rules allowing offset of losses after 1 April 2017 are more flexible than the previous rules. The trade-off for this increased flexibility is a restriction on the amount of profits that can be offset against the brought forward losses. Broadly, where a company's profits exceed £5 million, only 50% of these profits are available for offset by brought forward losses (including the pre April 2017 losses). Profits under £5 million are available for offset in full. Where a company is in a group the £5 million is allocated across all group companies. This threshold is deliberately high and in practice the vast majority of businesses will not be affected.

For losses arising before 1 April 2017, there is no stated requirement that the company carries on the business on a commercial basis with a view to the realisation of profit. This is simply because the permitted set-off is only against future trading profits of that same trade. For losses arising on or after 1 April 2017 it is expressly stated that offset against future profits is only available if the company continues to trade. For both pre and post April 2017 losses, the carry forward is automatic — no claim is required. However for post April 2017 losses a claim must be made for the carried forward losses to be *offset* against subsequent profits. This must be made within two years after the end of the relevant accounting period, or such later period as HMRC may allow.

In certain situations, post 1 April 2017 losses are only available for carry forward and offset against future profits of the same trade. In practice, this restriction is most likely to apply where the trade of the company becomes small or negligible in the loss making period. These losses are carried forward automatically for offset against future trading profits. No claim is required for the offset, but a claim can be made for the offset *not* to be made. This must be made within two years after the end of the relevant accounting period, or such later period as HMRC may allow.

The offset of losses (pre or post April 2017) is without time limit on its use unless there is a change of ownership to which the anti-avoidance provisions outlined at 26.25 apply. In addition there are currently two specific anti-avoidance provisions to prevent abuse of the carry forward rules, as follows:

(a)   For accounting periods beginning on or after 18 March 2015, com-panies are prevented from converting brought forward trading losses (pre or post 1 April 2017 loses), non-trading loan relationship deficits (3.6) and management expenses into in-year deductions against profits that were created from an arrangement entered into the main purpose of which was to obtain a corporation tax advantage / CFC charge advantage and utilise the brought forward losses.

(b)   For accounting periods beginning on or after 1 April 2015 the amount of a banking company's annual taxable profit that can be offset by pre-1 April 2015 carried-forward losses is restricted by 25% (for accounting periods beginning on or after 1 April 2016) or 50% (for accounting periods beginning on or after 1 April 2015). Where a company's accounting period begins before and ends after 1 April 2015 or 1 April 2016 (as appropriate), the accounting period is split into two notional periods and profits, losses etc are apportioned. The rationale behind this restriction is to prevent banks, that had built up exception-ally large losses as a result of the financial crisis, from using these losses to eliminate tax on recovering profits.

Where both (a) and (b) could potentially apply, the rule in (b) takes precedence.

Although any carried-forward losses cannot normally be relieved after a trade ceases, where a building (in an enterprise zone) is sold after the cessation and a balancing charge is made to withdraw excess capital allowances, unrelieved trading losses may be set against that balancing charge; see 22.51.

Property losses

[26.7] A company that has incurred a loss in its UK property business for an accounting period can, in general, use that loss by offsetting it against total profits from the same accounting period or, if it not fully used up in this way, carry it forward to the next accounting period. The September 2017 Finance Bill, which is expected to receive Royal Assent in November 2017, provides that the changes to the carry forward of losses (26.2) apply to property losses from 1 April 2017. The pre and post April 2017 rules can be summarised as follows:

Losses arising pre-1 April 2017	Losses arising post-1 April 2017
Carry forward and set against total profits. Cannot carry-forward and surrender for group relief.	Carry forward against total profits, as before, but new requirement to claim as no longer automatic. Claim must be made within two years after the end of the relevant accounting period, or such later period as HMRC may allow. New requirement to claim carry forward on losses on the cessation of a UK property business that are carried forward as expenses of management of the investment business. Removal of requirement to set off carried-forward losses before other deductions from total profits. Can carry forward and surrender losses for group relief but subject to conditions—see **26.22**.

Losses from a UK furnished holiday lettings business are not included in a UK property business loss because they are treated as trading losses and special rules apply to them. For more details on property taxation see CHAPTER 32.

Loan relationship losses (CTA 2010, s 99; CTA 2009, Pt 5 Ch 16, s 574)

[26.8] Losses arising out of loan relationships (see **3.6**) for the purposes of the trade are taken into account in arriving at the trading result and relieved accordingly (see **26.3**).

For non-trading loan relationships the interest, expenses and profits and losses on disposal are aggregated. If there is an overall profit it is charged to corporation tax. If there is a loss, i.e. a 'non-trading deficit', relief for *all or part of the loss* may be claimed as follows:

(a)   by way of group relief (see **26.17**);
(b)   against any other profits (including capital gains) of the deficit period;
(c)   against any loan relationship profit of the previous 12 months.

[26.9] Any part of the deficit for which relief is not claimed under (a) to (c) above is carried forward automatically. As for trading losses, the September 2017 Finance Bill (which is expected to receive Royal Assent in November 2017) provides a more flexible loss relief regime for carried forward deficits arising on or after 1 April 2017 subject to the restriction on relief where profits exceed £5 million, see **26.2**. The pre and post April 2017 rules can be summarised as follows:

Losses arising pre-1 April 2017	Losses arising post-1 April 2017
Carry forward and set against non-trading profits. Cannot carry-forward and surrender for group relief.	Carry forward against total profits of future accounting periods. Can carry forward and surrender losses for group relief but subject to conditions—see **26.22**.

For deficits arising on or after 1 April 2017 it is necessary for a claim for offset/group relief to be made within two years of the end of the relevant accounting period.

For deficits arising before 1 April 2017 no claim is necessary for the offset — it is automatic. A claim may, however, be made for all or part of any carried forward amount not to be set against the non-trading profits of the next accounting period. This enables all or part of the carried forward deficit effectively to 'leapfrog' the period in which it would otherwise be set off which could in appropriate cases avoid loss of double tax relief in that period, such relief being available only to the extent that there are chargeable profits.

Relief may not be claimed for loans written off if the borrower and lender are 'connected persons'. A person (including another company) is connected with a company if the person holds shares, voting power or other rights that enable that person to control the company. See **12.15** for detailed notes on writing off loans to controlling shareholders.

Intangible fixed asset losses

[26.10] Gains and losses on intangible fixed assets are brought into account in calculating a company's income. There are rules similar to those for loan relationships (see **3.6**) for bringing such amounts into account. Amounts relating to a trade are brought into account in calculating trading income, amounts relating to a property in calculating property business income, and non-trading amounts are taxed as non-trading income.

If there is a non-trading loss, the company may claim, not later than two years after the end of the accounting period, to set it against the total profits of the same period. Any loss not relieved in that way and not surrendered under the group relief provisions (see **26.16** onwards) will be carried forward to set against later non-trading profits. As for trading losses, the September 2017 Finance Bill (which is expected to receive Royal Assent in November 2017) provides a more flexible loss relief regime for carried forward losses arising on or after 1 April 2017 subject to the restriction on relief where profits exceed £5 million, see **26.2**. The pre and post April 2017 rules can be summarised as follows:

Losses arising pre-1 April 2017	Losses arising post-1 April 2017
Carry forward to the next accounting period as a intangible non-trading debit of the next period and aggregate with any intangible non-trading credits. Can use any resulting non-trading loss in that next period to set off against total profits. Cannot carry-forward and surrender for group relief.	Carry forward against total profits of future accounting periods. Can carry forward and surrender losses for group relief but subject to conditions—see **26.22**.

For more details on intangible fixed assets see **20.35** onwards.

Qualifying charitable donations (CTA 2010, ss 189–217)

[26.11] Having arrived at the company's total profits (both income and capital), qualifying charitable donations are deducted to arrive at the profits chargeable to corporation tax. For details of what constitutes a qualifying charitable donation see CHAPTER **43**.

Qualifying charitable donations may be deducted not just from trading profits but from total profits, including capital gains. If, however, there are insufficient profits to cover available reliefs, both current and carried back trading losses and/or non-trading deficits take priority over qualifying charitable donations. If there are insufficient profits remaining to cover the qualifying charitable donations, they may not be carried forward for relief against later profits. They may, however, be the subject of a group relief claim (see **26.17**).

Excess management expenses

[26.12] A company with investment business can deduct the expenses of management that relate to the accounting period in question from its total profits. A company is required to make that deduction before any other deductions are made from total profits. This means that total profits are reduced by management expenses before other reliefs and losses such as current period trading losses and UK property business losses, which are also deductible from total profits. As for trading losses, the September 2017 Finance Bill (which is expected to receive Royal Assent in November 2017) provides a more flexible loss relief regime for carried forward management expenses arising on or after 1 April 2017 subject to the restriction on relief where profits exceed £5 million, see **26.2**. The pre and post April 2017 rules can be summarised as follows:

Losses arising pre-1 April 2017	Losses arising post-1 April 2017
Carry forward any excess that can-not be deducted from total in-year profits to use as a management ex-pense in next accounting period available to set against total profits. Cannot carry-forward and surrender for group relief.	Carry forward against total profits of future accounting periods. New requirement to claim carry forward. Removal of requirement to set off carried-forward expenses of man-agement before other deductions from total profits. Can carry forward and surrender losses for group relief but subject to conditions—see **26.22**.

Examples for post April 2017 loss regime

[26.13] The interaction of the loss rules that apply to pre and post April 2017 losses has created an element of complication to the loss carry forward rules. It is important to consider carefully whether to utilise pre April 2017 losses in priority to losses arising after April 2017. The increased flexibility afforded to post April 2017 losses means that the company can elect for the optimum offset. For all offsets in relation to post April 2017 losses a claim is now needed which can specify the amount of the relief (there are no automatic offsets).

The new loss relief rules are complicated and this chapter provides no more than an overview of the key changes. Example 1 below illustrates how the relation of the loss carry forward rules operate for a single company, with profits below the £5 million 'deductions allowance' threshold.

Example 1

Pre 1 April 2017 losses

B Ltd has carried on the same trade for many years. The results for the years ended 30 September 2014, 2015 and 2016 are shown below

	2014	2015	2016
	£	£	£
Trading profit/(loss)	(25,000)	10,000	5,000
Property income	3,000	1,000	2,000
Income from non-trading loan relationships	2,000	2,000	3,000
Chargeable gains	5,600	4,700	4,000

B Ltd may claim under CTA 2010, s 37 to set off the trading loss against other profits of the same accounting period. Assuming the claim is made (and that no claim is made to carry back the balance of the loss), the loss will be set off as follows:

Year ended 30 September 2014	£	Loss memorandum £
Trading loss		(25,000)
Property income	3,000	
Income from non-trading loan relationships	2,000	
Chargeable gains	5,600	
	10,600	
Deduct Trading loss	(10,600)	10,600
Taxable total profits	—	
		(14,400)

Year ended 30 September 2015		
Trading income	10,000	
Deduct Loss brought forward	(10,000)	10,000
	—	(4,400)
Property income	1,000	
Income from non-trading loan relationships	2,000	
Chargeable gains	4,700	
Taxable total profits	7,700	

Year ended 30 September 2016		
Trading income	5,000	
Deduct Loss brought forward	(4,400)	4,400
	600	
Property income	2,000	
Income from non-trading loan relationships	3,000	
Chargeable gains	4,000	
Taxable total profits	9,600	

Post 1 April 2017 losses

Z Ltd, a trading company which is not a life insurance company has the following results for the years ended 31 March 2018 and 2019

	31.3.18 £	31.3.19 £
Trading profit/(loss)	(52,000)	45,000
Income from non-trading loan relation- ships	2,000	4,000

The losses can be set off as follows

Year ended 31 March 2018

	£	Loss memoran- dum £
Trading loss		(52,000)
Income from non-trading loan relationships		2,000
		(50,000)

Year ended 31 March 2019

	£	
Trading income	45,000	
Income from non-trading loan relationships	4,000	
	49,000	
Deduct Loss brought forward		(49,000)
Carried forward trading losses		(1,000)

Example 2 illustrates the operation of the new loss relief rules where the £5 million 'deductions allowance' threshold may apply to a company that is not a member of a group.

Example 2

Single company

Stephenson Ltd, which is not a member of a group, begins to trade on 1 April 2017. It has the following results for the two years ending 31 March 2018 and 2019.

	y/e 31.3.18 £	y/e 31.3.19 £
Trading profit/(loss)	(9,000,000)	8,000,000
Property income	—	2,000,000

Taxable profits for the two years are computed as follows

	y/e 31.3.18 £	y/e 31.3.19 £
Trading profit	—	8,000,000
Property income	—	2,000,000
	—	10,000,000
Less loss brought forward from y/e 31.3.18 (restricted)*		(7,500,000)
Taxable profits	—	£2,500,000

* The restriction on the set-off of the carried-forward loss against profits for the year ending 31 March 2019 is calculated as follows:

	£
Qualifying profits	10,000,000
Less deductions allowance	(5,000,000)
Relevant profits	5,000,000
Relevant profits × 50%	2,500,000
Add deductions allowance	5,000,000
Maximum set-off	£7,500,000

Loss memorandum

	£
Loss y/e 31.3.18	9,000,000
Less relieved y/e 31.3.19	(7,500,000)
Carried forward to y/e 31.3.20	£1,500,000

Example 3 illustrates the operation of the new loss relief rules where the £5 million 'deductions allowance' threshold may apply to a company that is a member of a group. A group of companies has a single deductions allowance known as the group deductions allowance and can allocate this to any company or companies in the group as it chooses. This is done through a nominated company. The maximum amount of the allowance that is available to be shared amongst all group companies is £5 million (reduced proportionately for accounting periods of less than twelve months). The nomination must be made by all the companies in the group that are within the charge to corporation tax and must state the date the nomination takes effect, which may be before the date the nomination is made.

Example 3

Group companies

A Ltd is the ultimate parent company of B Ltd and C Ltd. All companies make up accounts to 31 March each year. The companies' results for the year ended 31 March 2019 are as follows:

		£
A Ltd	Trading profit	800,000
	Property income	185,000
	Chargeable gain	15,000
B Ltd	Trading profit	5,000,000
C Ltd	Trading profit	400,000

Non-trading loan relationships	100,000

In addition, each company has the following trading losses brought forward from the year ended 31 March 2018: A Ltd £1,000,000, B Ltd £5,000,000 and C Ltd £500,000. All of the carried-forward losses arose in the year ended 31 March 2018. A Ltd is the group's nominated company for the purpose of allocating the group deductions allowance.

If A Ltd allocates £1,000,000 of the group deductions allowance to itself and the remainder to B Ltd, the companies' taxable profits for the year ended 31 March 2019 are as follows:

	£
A Ltd	
Trading profit	800,000
Property income	185,000
Chargeable gain	15,000
	1,000,000
Deduct Loss brought forward from y/e 31.3.18	(1,000,000)
Chargeable profits	£Nil
B Ltd	
Trading profit	5,000,000
Deduct Loss brought forward from y/e 31.3.18 *	(4,500,000)
Chargeable profits	£500,000
C Ltd	
Trading profit	400,000
Non-trading loan relationships	100,000
	500,000
Deduct Loss brought forward from y/e 31.3.18 **	(250,000)
Chargeable profits	£250,000

The restriction on the set-off of the carried-forward losses against profits for the year ending 31 March 2019 is calculated as follows:

	£
A Ltd	
Qualifying profits	1,000,000
Less allocated group deductions allowance	(1,000,000)
Relevant profits	—
Relevant profits × 50%	—

Add allocated group deductions allowance	1,000,000
Maximum set-off	£1,000,000

B Ltd

Qualifying profits	5,000,000
Less allocated group deductions allowance	(4,000,000)
Relevant profits	1,000,000
Relevant profits × 50%	500,000
Add allocated group deductions allowance	4,000,000
* Maximum set-off	£4,500,000

C Ltd

Qualifying profits	500,000
Less allocated group deductions allowance	—
Relevant profits	500,000
Relevant profits × 50%	250,000
Add allocated group deductions allowance	—
** Maximum set-off	£250,000

Loss memoranda

	£
A Ltd	
Loss brought forward from y/e 31.3.18	1,000,000
Less relieved y/e 31.3.19	(1,000,000)
	—
B Ltd	
Loss brought forward from y/e 31.3.18	5,000,000
Less relieved y/e 31.3.19	(4,500,000)
Carried forward to y/e 31.3.20	£500,000

C Ltd	
Loss brought forward from y/e 31.3.18	500,000
Less relieved y/e 31.3.19	(250,000)
Carried forward to y/e 31.3.20	£250,000

Effect of carry-back of losses on tax paid

[26.14] Carry-back loss claims result in corporation tax already paid being repaid, or in tax otherwise due not having to be paid. This means that it may, where losses are carried back to periods prior to 1 April 2015 be possible to obtain loss relief at differing rates: the small profits rate, the marginal small profits rate and the main rate (see **3.15**). For losses carried back to periods commencing on or after 1 April 2015, there is only one main rate of corporation tax for all companies (bar ring-fence trades), so there will, for most companies, be no difference in the rates at which loss relief is available. Details of the various rates for earlier years are in previous editions of this book.

Interest calculations (TA 1988, ss 825, 826)

[26.15] Repayments attract interest from nine months after the end of the relevant period or, if later, from the actual date of payment of tax for that period (see **3.27**) (although the interest rate is significantly lower than the rate charged on overdue tax). The latest available interest rates are set out in the TABLE OF RATES AND ALLOWANCES (**TRA**).

For calculating interest on repayments resulting from current and carried back losses, a repayment is normally treated as relating to the *loss* period, but a repayment relating to an accounting period falling *wholly* in the 12 months before the loss period is treated as relating to that accounting period.

> **Example 4**
>
> A company has the following results up to the date it ceased to trade on 31 March 2017.
>
> | | £ | £ | £ |
> |---|---:|---:|---:|
> | **Year ended 31 March** | **2015** | **2016** | **2017** |
> | Trading profit/(loss) | 50,000 | 20,000 | (40,500) |
> | Investment income | 3,000 | 3,000 | 3,000 |
> | Chargeable gains | 4,000 | 2,500 | 2,000 |
> | Total profits | 57,000 | 25,500 | 5,000 |
> | If loss relief is claimed: | | | |
> | Profits | 57,000 | 25,500 | 5,000 |
> | Less loss | (10,000) | (25,500) | (5,000) |
> | Total profits | 47,000 | — | — |

Any tax repayment for the year to 31 March 2016 resulting from carrying the loss back 12 months will attract interest from the corporation tax payment date for that year, i.e. from 1 January 2017. The repayment for the year to 31 March 2015 will attract interest from 1 January 2018 (the payment date for corporation tax for the *loss* year to 31 March 2017).

Group relief for losses etc. (CTA 2010, ss 97–188; F(No 2)A 2015, s 35)

Group relief for current year losses

[26.16] In a group consisting of a holding company and its 75% subsidiaries, current year losses may be surrendered from one company to one or more other companies within the group, provided the necessary conditions are satisfied. This enables the company to which the loss has been surrendered to reduce its taxable profits by the surrendered amount. (Note, this 75% link for group relief purposes is defined very much more restrictively than simply 75% of ordinary share capital, to prevent companies taking advantage of the provisions by means of an artificial group relationship (CTA 2010, s 151)).

[26.17] Group relief can be claimed in respect of:

(a) trading losses;
(b) capital allowance excesses;
(c) all or part of a non-trading deficit relating to loans (see **26.8**);
(d) non-trading losses on intangible assets (see **20.36**);
(e) excess qualifying charitable donations (see **3.10**);
(f) excess qualifying contributions to grassroots sports (see **3.11**);
(g) UK property business losses (see **32.12**);
(h) excess management expenses of companies with investment business.

For (a) to (c) a company may surrender these losses without claiming other reliefs available. In other words it has an absolute choice as to how the losses are utilised. The amounts in (d) to (h) that are eligible for group relief can only be surrendered to the extent that they exceed the company's gross profits of the surrender period.

In addition, a set-off amount for a patent box deduction can be matched against IP profits of a group company to the extent that it cannot be utilised by the company initially entitled to the set-off amount (see **26.3**).

[26.18] Group relief is denied if there are arrangements in place meaning that at some point in the future one company's rights over the profits or assets of another company could change. Arrangements do not fall within this provision if they consist of conditions or requirements imposed by, or agreed with, Ministers or statutory bodies. This is to prevent these statutory public bodies being inadvertently caught by the anti-avoidance rules that restrict the flow of group relief.

Example 5

Assume that B Ltd is a 100% subsidiary of A Ltd. A Ltd made a profit of £100,000 and B Ltd a loss of £60,000.

Under the group relief provisions, it is possible to surrender the loss of £60,000 from B Ltd to A Ltd reducing A Ltd's taxable profit and its corporation tax liability.

Example 6

Assume that B Ltd is a 100% subsidiary of A Ltd. A Ltd made a loss of £100,000 and B Ltd a profit of £60,000

The group relief claim here will be a maximum of £60,000. A Ltd will have the remaining loss of £40,000 which it may be able to set off in the current year, carry back, or carry forward. Losses that are unutilised (through either group relief, carry back or current year offset) can only be carried forward in the company that originally sustained them.

The loss available to be surrendered must arise in an accounting period of the loss-making company that corresponds with that of the claimant company. Where accounts are prepared to different dates, part of a loss period will correspond with part of one accounting period of the claimant company and the remainder with part of the next accounting period. The loss available for relief and the profits against which it may be set must be apportioned as indicated below. Relief is also proportionately restricted if the parent/subsidiary relationship does not exist throughout the accounting period, usually on a time basis, but by reference to what is just and reasonable where a time basis would give an unreasonable result.

[26.19] The set-off rules are quite flexible, and broadly the loss-making company may surrender any part of its available current year loss, up to a maximum of the available total profits of the claimant company or companies for the corresponding period. The rules enable the loss to be divided among several group companies in order to obtain the maximum loss relief. A claimant company cannot, however, claim more *in total* than an amount equal to its profits of the period that overlaps with the accounting periods of surrendering companies, and a loss company cannot surrender more *in total* to fellow group companies than its loss in the overlapping period(s).

Example 7

Alpha Ltd owns all the shares in Beta Ltd; both companies make up accounts to 30 September. On 1 January 2017 Alpha Ltd acquires all the shares of Gamma Ltd which makes up its accounts to 31 March.

Beta Ltd has a trading loss for the year to 30 September 2017 and Gamma Ltd claims group relief for its accounting period ending 31 March 2017 in respect of that loss.

The period common to the accounting periods of Gamma Ltd and Beta Ltd is 1 October 2016 to 31 March 2017, but as Gamma Ltd was not a member of the

Alpha Ltd group until 1 January 2017, the overlapping accounting period will be restricted to 1 January 2017 to 31 March 2017.

Example 8

A company with a loss in the year to 30 June 2017 had two fellow group companies making up accounts to 31 December. The *total* surrender to the two companies for their year to 31 December 2016 can not exceed 6/12ths of the loss, leaving the loss of the second half of the year to be surrendered against a maximum of 6/12ths of the profits of each of the companies for the year to 31 December 2017. The profits of the claimant company available for relief are profits from all sources, including capital gains, but after deducting qualifying charitable donations.

Where a loss would otherwise be unrelieved, it might be appropriate for a profit-making company in a group to disclaim some of the allowances on its plant and machinery, to give it a higher profit against which to make a group relief claim (see **22.18** and **22.52**). The profit-making company would then have a higher pool balance carried forward on which to claim capital allowances in the future, whereas if it has insufficient current profit to cover the loss available for surrender, the surrendered loss has to be restricted.

[26.20] The group relief provisions are also available in certain circumstances to a consortium of companies that owns at least 75% of the ordinary share capital of a trading company or of a holding company with 90% trading subsidiaries, with the consortium members each owning at least 5% of that ordinary share capital. Losses in proportion to the consortium member's interest in the consortium-owned company can be surrendered both from the trading companies to the consortium companies and from the consortium companies to the trading companies.

The consortium members interest is the lower of its percentage shareholding in the company, its percentage entitlement to any profits available for distribution from the company, its percentage entitlement of any assets of the company on a winding up or the proportion of voting power that it directly owns in the consortium company.

Where a consortium company is also a member of a group, the basic premise is that group relief will take priority over consortium relief. Where a member of a consortium is also a member of a 75% group it may act as a link company. This means that any losses which are available to be surrendered to it as consortium relief may be used by the company itself, or by its fellow group members. To act as a link company the surrendering company and the claimant company must be 'UK related' (i.e. UK resident or trading in the UK through a permanent establishment).

[26.21] Group relief is restricted where an overseas entity is involved, as follows:

(a)   UK permanent establishment of a non-resident company. If the non-resident company is not resident in the EEA (**1.3**) there can be no surrender, as group relief if tax relief *may* be given in a foreign jurisdiction for any part of the loss etc. If the non-resident company is resident in the EEA losses are restricted only if they are actually (rather than potentially) relieved against the profits of a non-UK person in any period.

(b) Non-UK resident permanent establishment. There can be no surrender, as group relief if tax relief *may* be given in a foreign jurisdiction for any part of the loss etc.

(c) Non-UK resident company. Loss-making group companies resident (or with a permanent establishment) in another state in the EEA are able to surrender losses to UK group companies if they would otherwise be unrelievable. This applies only in very limited circumstances and is subject to anti-avoidance provisions to prevent abuse of the rules (see **41.59**).

Group relief for carried-forward losses (CTA 2010, Pt 5A)

[26.22] As part of the reforms to the rules on loss relief, the September 2017 Finance Bill (which is expected to receive Royal Assent in November 2017) introduced a new relief named 'group relief for carried-forward losses' which applies to groups and consortia. Companies are able to use this relief to surrender certain losses to group or consortium members for group relief. Previously, carried-forward losses could not be surrendered for group relief. This is a significant change to the previous rules, but does not apply to losses arising before 1 April 2017 (or to any qualifying charitable donations that are treated as expenses of management).

Under these new rules a company can surrender losses arising on or after 1 April 2017 that can be carried forward against a company's total profits — e.g. brought forward trading losses, property losses, management expenses and non-trading deficits.

A company cannot, however, surrender a carried-forward loss under these rules:

(a) if it has capacity to use the loss against its own profits;

(b) where it has no assets capable of producing income at the end of the period — this is to prevent groups from maintaining a dormant company to access its losses;

(c) where an investment business becomes small or negligible — this applies to carried-forward non-trading loan-relationship deficits, expenses of management or UK property business losses;

(d) where the company has changed ownership in the last five years and the losses relate to the period before the change in ownership, discussed further below;

(e) to the extent that the loss of a UK resident company is attributable to an overseas permanent establishment and relief could be claimed in the overseas territory.

The process for claiming group relief follows the process for current year group relief claims and the group and consortium conditions are the same as for current year claims.

Procedure for group relief claims (FA 1998, Sch 18 Pt VIII; SI 1999/2975)

[26.23] Companies may make, vary and withdraw group relief claims up to the latest of one year from the filing date for the claimant company's return (see **9.23**), 30 days after the completion of an HMRC enquiry into the return, 30 days after the notice of HMRC amendments to the return following an enquiry, and 30 days after the final determination of an appeal against such an amendment. Each group company makes initial claims for specified amounts of group relief and shows amounts available for group relief surrenders on its own individual corporation tax return or amended return. Claims must show the name and tax district reference number of the surrendering company and be accompanied by a copy of the surrendering company's consent. The surrendering company will send the notice of consent to its own tax district. Where a group has non-resident company members, group relief claims must identify non-resident claimant or surrendering companies and any non-resident companies through which common group or consortium membership is established. Where original claims are to be varied, the original claim must be withdrawn and replaced by a new claim. Groups dealt with mainly within one tax district may enter into simplified arrangements under which group companies may authorise one company to amend returns on behalf of all group companies in relation to making and withdrawing claims and surrenders of group relief.

From 26 March 2015, any 'loss' amounts that are in dispute with HMRC are not able to be surrendered to other group companies while the dispute is in progress; see **9.49**.

Company reconstructions without change of ownership (CTA 2010, ss 938–957)

[26.24] Where a trade is transferred from one company to another and, at some time within one year before and two years after the transfer, the same persons own three-quarters or more of the trade, the trade is treated as transferred to the successor company rather than being discontinued. This prevents the predecessor carrying trading losses back under the terminal loss rules, and enables the successor to take over the unrelieved losses of the predecessor (subject to special rules restricting the available loss where the successor does not take over all the predecessor's assets and liabilities). The successor also takes over the predecessor's capital allowances computations (see **22.20**).

See **45.16** for details of anti-avoidance provisions that apply in relation to these rules.

Company reconstructions with a change of ownership

[26.25] The group relief provisions are flexible and of great benefit to many companies. However, the rules are tightly controlled to prevent abuse of the regime (as mentioned, where appropriate, in the relevant commentary). In addition there are several specific provisions that broadly deal with the position on a change in ownership of a company. A change in ownership occurs when:

(a)   one person acquires more than half of the company's ordinary share capital;

(b)   two or more persons acquire more than half of the ordinary share capital and each of them acquires at least 5%; or

(c)   two or more persons acquire more than half of the ordinary share capital and each of them holds at least 5%, including existing holdings.

A change of ownership is disregarded though if the change occurs as a result of the insertion of an intermediate holding company below the existing parent or a new holding company is inserted at the top of a group of companies.

The most common anti-avoidance provisions dealing with ownership changes are:

(i)   Losses incurred before a change in ownership cannot be relieved under the rules that normally apply to trading losses if either:

–   within a period of three years there is both a major change in the nature or conduct of a trade carried on by a company and a change in its ownership. The September 2017 Finance Bill, which is expected to receive Royal Assent in November 2017, extends this timeframe to five years (eight years for an investment business) where both the change to the trade and the change in ownership take place on or after 1 April 2017 (CTA 2010, ss 676AA–676AL); or

–   after the scale of activities in a trade carried on by a company has become negligible and before any considerable revival, there is a change in ownership (CTA 2010, ss 673–676).

The provisions prevent losses incurred before the change of ownership being carried forward, and prevent losses in an accounting period *after* the change of ownership from being carried back to an accounting period *before* the change. HMRC Statement of Practice SP 10/91 gives their views on the meaning of a 'major change in the nature or conduct of a trade'.

(ii)   Where there is a change in ownership of a company with investment business, there are provisions to prevent the company carrying forward unrelieved management expenses, non-trading deficits on loans and derivative contracts, and non-trading losses on intangible fixed assets (CTA 2010, ss 677–691) where certain conditions are met. There are similar provisions preventing losses being carried forward on a change in ownership of a company carrying on a property business (CTA 2010, ss 704–705).

(iii)   The September 2017 Finance Bill, which is expected to receive Royal Assent in November 2017, introduces a new restriction that applies where a company changes ownership after 1 April 2017 and within five years makes a gain on an asset that was transferred to it from another group member after the change in ownership on a tax neutral basis. Where these rules apply the company is not able to carry forward post-1 April 2017 trading losses that arose before the change in ownership and set them against total profits in an accounting period after the change in ownership. For this restriction to apply, the total profits of the later accounting period must include chargeable gains or intangible credits (CTA 2010, ss 676BA–676BE).

(iv)   Group relief is not available for a part of an accounting period in which arrangements exist whereby the loss-making company could cease to be a member of the group (CTA 2010, s 154).

(v)   There are restrictions on the availability of group relief (the 'deductible amount') where there has been a change in ownership of a company. The deductible amounts that are restricted are those that, at the date of the qualifying change are highly likely to arise as deductions for an accounting period ending on or after the date of the change and the main purpose of the qualifying change in ownership is that they are deductible in the accounting period ending on or after the date of the change in ownership. This restriction also applies to claims for relief for trading losses (**45.15**) and deductible amounts where there are 'profit transfer arrangements' (i.e. arrangements which result in an increase in the total profits of the company that has been subject to the change in ownership (CTA 2010, ss 730A–730D).

See **45.17** for anti-avoidance provisions relating to capital loss buying and capital gains buying by groups.

Tax points

[26.26] Note the following:

*   The loss relaxation provisions to be introduced by the September 2017 Finance Bill are welcome but have introduced their own set of complications. There are now two sets of loss relief rules running side-by-side. Careful consideration will need to be given to decide if it would be best to try to use post-1 April 2017 losses before pre-1 April losses.

*   The £5 million restriction on loss offset is most relevant to larger businesses. Small companies that have profits which are below the annual allowance will not be affected by the restriction but will benefit from the increased flexibility. Larger companies that are subject to the loss restriction can expect to see changes to projected cashflow and profitability, with more tax expected to be paid upfront.

*   Group relief for losses is not available if there is less than a 75% link between holding and subsidiary companies.

*   If two or more companies are controlled by the same individual(s), group relief is not available. But unused trading losses are still available against the future profits of a trade if that trade is transferred from one company to another under the same control (see **26.24**).

- Anti-avoidance provisions may restrict or deny group relief. For example, an arrangement made part-way through an accounting period to sell a loss-making subsidiary will prevent group relief being claimed for the remainder of the accounting period even though the parent/subsidiary relationship exists throughout.
- Exceptional revenue expenditure, such as extraordinary repairs, or establishing or boosting a company pension scheme within permissible limits, may result in a normally profitable trade incurring a loss. When a company is planning such expenditure or considering when, or indeed whether, it should be incurred, the carry-back of losses against earlier profits, resulting in tax not having to be paid, or being repaid, is an important consideration.

27

Transfer of business to or from a limited company

Transfer of business to a limited company

[27.1] On the incorporation of a business, the assets of the business are transferred to a company which then carries on the business in succession to the former proprietor(s).

Choice of date

[27.2] When the trade of an individual or partnership is transferred to a company the trade has ceased for income tax purposes, so that the closing year rules dealt with in **21.5** apply.

Under the income tax rules, except where accounts are prepared to 31 March, there will be an amount of overlap relief (see **21.6**) to be deducted from the profits of the final trading period (unless the overlap period showed a loss). The amount to be deducted will not be affected by the choice of cessation date. The timing of the cessation still needs to be considered in the light of expected income in the years affected, for example the deduction of the overlap profit may reduce tax at higher rates, or possibly create a loss to be relieved against other income of the current tax year or carried back against earlier income. The effect of capital allowances also needs to be considered — see **27.3**.

Capital allowances (CAA 2001, ss 265–268, 567–570)

[27.3] Normally the cessation of trade would involve a balancing allowance or charge by reference to the proceeds of disposal to the company of plant and equipment on which capital allowances have been claimed.

The sole trader or partners and the company may usually, however, jointly elect within two years after the transfer date for the assets to be treated as transferred at the tax written-down value (see **22.20**) even though the justifiably higher market value is used for accounting purposes. The company gets writing-down allowances (but not first year allowances) on the price it pays or the tax written-down value as the case may be (see **22.26**).

In neither case is there a writing-down allowance or an annual investment allowance (see **22.26**) in the tax period up to cessation, consequently either increasing the written-down value carried into the company or affecting the amount of the balancing allowance or charge.

Trading stock (ITTOIA 2005, ss 173–181)

[27.4] While the legislation requires the transfer of stock to be at market value, the sole trader/partners and the company can normally elect for the greater of the cost or the price paid by the company to be used instead if that would give a lower figure. The election must be made within one year from 31 January after the end of the tax year in which the cessation occurred.

See **20.22** for the treatment of closing stock where profits are calculated on the cash basis.

Unused trading losses (ITA 2007, s 86)

[27.5] If there are unused trading losses, these cannot be carried forward to a company as such, but they may be relieved against income received by the trader or partners from the company, either in the form of directors' fees or dividends, so long as the business is exchanged for shares and the shares are still retained at the time the loss is set off. In practice, HMRC allow relief even where some of the shares have been disposed of, as long as the individual has retained shares which represent more than 80% of the consideration received for the business. Other available loss claims may be made first, e.g. under ITA 2007, s 64 against income of the year of loss or the previous year, or terminal loss relief for a loss of the last 12 months against the trading income of the previous three years, and the relief against income from the company would then be available on the balance of unrelieved losses. From 2013–14 there is a cap on loss relief against general income and a restriction on the losses available where a cash basis election applies — see CHAPTER 25 for full details.

Capital gains tax (TCGA 1992, ss 17, 18, 162, 162A, 286)

[27.6] When the transfer takes place, the general rule is that those assets chargeable to capital gains tax which have been transferred are treated as being disposed of to the company at their open market value. Current assets (stock, debtors, etc.) are not chargeable assets. Plant and equipment, even though covered by an election to transfer at the tax written-down value for capital allowances purposes, may be a chargeable asset for capital gains tax and thus treated as transferred at market value. Moveable plant and equipment is chargeable unless valued at £6,000 or less for each item (see CHAPTER 39), but it will not normally be valued at more than cost, so that capital gains tax will not usually apply, leaving the most likely assets on which a liability may arise as freehold or leasehold premises, fixed plant and machinery (but see 22.46) and goodwill.

Goodwill acquired by a company on or after 1 April 2002 is normally dealt with under the intangible assets regime. However relief for annual amortisation of goodwill is not available to a company broadly where it is acquired from any party, related or not, on or after 8 July 2015, and any loss on realisation will be a non-trading debit (see 20.35). Certain restrictions also apply to prevent abuse of the rules on an incorporation, such that where goodwill is acquired from a related party the acquisition is deemed to be at market value (see 20.41). In addition, for disposals on or after 3 December 2014 entrepreneurs' relief is not usually available on disposals of goodwill to a close company except in limited circumstances (see 29.8).

[27.7] An obvious way of avoiding the charge on premises is for the proprietor or partners to retain ownership and to allow the company to use the property either at a rent or free of charge. This also saves the stamp duty land tax that would have been incurred on the transfer (see 27.13). There is no stamp duty charge on any assets transferred to the company except marketable securities.

Whether goodwill exists and if so at what value is always arguable. It depends upon many factors, such as the type of business, its location and profitability. In HMRC's view, personal goodwill (relating to the individual's skills and personal attributes) is not capable of sale, but where the company secures the services of the sole trader or partner with a legitimate service contract, the point may be debatable. Where goodwill does attach to the business which is transferred, the only way of not reckoning its value on a transfer of the business is if the sole trader/partners continue to own it whilst licensing the company to carry on the trade, but unless this is commercially practicable, sensible and properly done, the goodwill will follow the trade in appropriate circumstances. The valuation of goodwill depends not only on the size of the profits but also on the extent to which the profits depend on the skills of the proprietor or partners, the nature of the trade and many other factors.

The capital gains tax effect of the incorporation of a business in 2017–18 is considered in Example 1.

Example 1

The net assets of a trader at the time of incorporation of his business in July 2017 were:

	£
Freehold premises at current market value	204,000
Goodwill at current market value	120,000
Plant and equipment (cost £320,000)	140,000
Net current assets other than cash	256,000
Cash and bank balances	80,000
	£800,000

The premises had been acquired for £120,000 and the trade newly commenced in 1989.

The potential chargeable gains on incorporation are:

		£
Freehold premises — market value	204,000	
Less: Cost	(120,000)	
		84,000
Goodwill — market value	120,000	
Less: Cost	Nil	
		120,000
Chargeable gains		£204,000

The gain on the premises could be avoided by the trader retaining ownership, but a gain on the goodwill would arise on the transfer of the trade, unless it was possible to retain it while licensing the company to use it.

Provided that the trader has owned the business for one year entrepreneurs' relief will be available to reduce the rate of CGT on a disposal, though not that on the goodwill — see **29.2** to **29.11** for full details of the relief. The annual CGT exempt amount of £11,300 may also be available.

[27.8] Prior to the introduction of entrepreneurs' relief there were two main alternatives for reducing or eliminating an immediate capital gains tax charge on incorporation. These alternatives still remain but the interaction of reliefs needs to be considered.

One alternative is the rollover relief provided by TCGA 1992, s 162, known as incorporation relief (see **27.9**). This requires *all* the assets (except cash) to be transferred to the company, and defers gains only to the extent that the consideration is received in the form of shares in the company. HMRC guidance is available in tax return Helpsheet HS276.

The second alternative is a combination of retaining some assets in personal ownership and making a claim under the business gift relief provisions of TCGA 1992, s 165 (outlined at **4.32** to **4.34**) to limit the gains on other chargeable assets (notably goodwill) to the amount actually received, the company then being treated as acquiring those assets at market value less the gains not chargeable on the transferor (see **27.10**). Under this alternative, any consideration received from the company for the assets that are transferred need not be in the form of shares, and a credit may be made to a loan account or cash taken instead. HMRC guidance is available in tax return Helpsheet HS295.

Another possible alternative if the company is a qualifying unquoted trading company is capital gains tax deferral relief under the enterprise investment scheme (see **27.11**).

Incorporation relief (TCGA 1992, ss 162, 162A)

[27.9] For section 162 incorporation relief (see **27.8**) to apply in Example 1, all assets other than the £80,000 cash would have to be transferred.

The chargeable gains on the disposal of the business are calculated and they are treated as reducing the capital gains tax base cost of the shares received in exchange for the business. The lower base cost for the shares will of course increase the potential capital gains tax liability on their future disposal.

The whole of the gain of £204,000 accruing on the incorporation is rolled over against the acquisition cost of the shares and no chargeable gain arises at that time. There would therefore be no 'relevant gain' for the purposes of TCGA 1992, s 169N(1) and a claim for entrepreneurs' relief would not appear to be appropriate (see HMRC Capital Gains Manual CG64136 which refers to business asset rollover relief under TCGA 1992, s 152, but which applies to a 'provision which rolls (that) gain, or a proportion of it, over against the acquisition cost of a replacement asset').

On a subsequent disposal of the shares entrepreneurs' relief (see **29.2**), enterprise investment scheme deferral relief and gift relief may be available. There is no capital gains tax if the shares are still held on death.

Example 2

In consideration of the transfer of the trade in 2017–18 in Example 1, the trader receives 700,000 shares of £1 each, fully paid, in the new company, transferring all assets except the cash of £80,000.

The base cost of the shares will be:

	£
700,000 shares (£800,000 assets – £80,000 cash)	720,000
Less gains otherwise arising on premises and goodwill	(204,000)
Cost of 700,000 shares for CGT purposes	£516,000

The difference between the £700,000 par value of the shares and the £720,000 assets value in Example 2 represents a share premium. It is almost inevitable that the par value will not correspond with the asset values since those values cannot be precisely determined before the transfer date.

If the transfer is made only partly for shares, and partly for cash or credit to a loan account, then only proportionate relief is given.

Example 3

Suppose the consideration of £720,000 in Example 2 was satisfied as to £480,000 shares and £240,000 cash. Only two-thirds of the chargeable gains of £204,000, i.e. £136,000, can be deducted from the base cost of the shares.

		Shares	Cash
Consideration		480,000	240,000
Gains	£204,000	136,000	£68,000
Cost of shares for CGT purposes		£344,000	

The chargeable gain remaining is £68,000. Provided the trader had owned the business for a year entrepreneurs' relief would be available, though there are restrictions for disposals of goodwill. See **29.2** to **29.11** for full details of the relief.

Obtaining the maximum deferral of gains under section 162 therefore requires the consideration for the shares to be locked in as share capital. If the consideration is provided through leaving money on loan account, tax will not be deferred, but the money can later be withdrawn at no personal tax cost.

The section 162 relief is given automatically without the need for a claim, although if the transferor has acquired business assets for use in another trade and wants to claim the business assets rollover relief under section 152 instead (see **29.16** onwards), that rollover relief claim takes priority over section 162. Otherwise section 162 must be applied even if gains would be covered by, say, the annual exempt amount. To avoid the problem, the appropriate part of the consideration resulting in chargeable gains equal to available exemptions could be left on loan account, so that a gain would be immediately realised, as shown in Example 3. Using the figures in that example, if £39,882 of the consideration of £720,000 was in cash, the proportionate part of the gain relating to the cash consideration would be £11,300 which is the annual exempt amount for 2017–18.

Where assets that are being transferred to the company are depreciating assets against which gains have been held over under the business assets rollover provisions (see **29.16** onwards), the disposal to the company *triggers* the deferred gains, but the deferred gains do not actually arise on the transfer, so relief for them is not available under section 162.

The taxpayer may *elect* for section 162 relief not to apply, so that gains that would otherwise have been deferred are chargeable in respect of the transfer to the company, with any later gains being chargeable when the shares are disposed of. The time limit for the election is two years from 31 January following the tax year of transfer, unless all the shares are disposed of by the end of the tax year following the tax year of transfer, in which case the time limit is one year from 31 January following the tax year of transfer. This enables taxpayers to obtain section 162 relief initially and then make the election later if appropriate. The availability of entrepreneurs' relief may affect the calculations.

> ### Example 4
>
> Say the trader in Example 1 had transferred all the assets except cash to the company in July 2017 with full s 162 relief, so that his shares had a base value of £720,000 less gains £204,000 = £516,000 as in Example 2. On 1 March 2018 he accepted an offer of £800,000 for the shares.
>
> Without the election the gain of £284,000 on disposal of the shares (£800,000 − £516,000) would have been fully chargeable, subject to the annual exempt amount if available. No entrepreneurs' relief is available as the shares have not been held for at least a year. The trader may, however, *elect* for incorporation relief not to apply, the time limit for the election being 31 January 2020. His chargeable gains for 2017–18 would then be £204,000 (as in Example 1) plus £80,000 (£800,000 − £720,000) on disposal of the shares, making £284,000 in total. The gain of £84,000 on the freehold premises (but not those on the goodwill, see **27.6**) qualifies for entrepreneurs' relief and the remaining £200,000 gain would be taxable at either 10% or 20% depending on the individual's personal tax position (because it is not an 'upper rate gain', see **4.2**). In determining which rate should apply to individuals, gains qualifying for entrepreneurs' relief are set against any unused basic rate band before non-qualifying gains. The gains could be reduced by the annual exempt amount if available.
>
> To summarise, section 162 relief on incorporation results in total chargeable gains of £284,000 (nil plus £284,000) which do not qualify for entrepreneurs' relief. If relief is disclaimed, the total gains are still £284,000 but £84,000 of the gains qualify for entrepreneurs' relief. If the trader had held the shares for at least a year and the other criteria set out in **29.2** were met, entrepreneurs' relief would have been available on the disposal of shares. In some cases it may be considered wiser to roll over the gain where possible (i.e. not elect to disapply the relief) in order to maximise the entrepreneurs' relief available on future disposals, especially where goodwill is transferred.

Where a business is owned by partners, each partner has a separate right to elect or not in relation to his partnership share.

Gifts of business assets (TCGA 1992, s 165)

[27.10] If, in Example 1, the premises were retained in personal ownership, saving capital gains tax and stamp duty land tax, this would leave the gain on the goodwill to be considered. The business gift relief enables the whole of the gain on goodwill to be deferred providing any consideration received does not exceed the capital gains tax base cost of the goodwill. In Example 1, that cost was nil, so that the full gain on the goodwill could be deferred only if nothing was charged for it. Goodwill will have a capital gains tax cost either if it was purchased or if it had a value at 31 March 1982 (see **20.35**). See **27.6** regarding the treatment of goodwill acquired on or after 8 July 2015.

The disadvantage of charging consideration only equal to the capital gains tax base cost is that the transferor is credited in the accounts of the company with that amount, not with the greater market value at the time of transfer, and that lower value will be the company's acquisition cost.

The chargeable asset could be transferred at a figure in excess of capital gains tax base cost, but less than market value, any exemptions being set off against the gains arising by reference to the transfer price. This has the advantage of more cash being received on the transfer or a higher credit to a loan account, and in either case a higher base value for the asset in company ownership. The business assets gift relief eliminates the chargeable gain on the difference between market value and the value used for the transfer.

Example 5

Say the trader in Example 1 had retained the premises in personal ownership and transferred the goodwill to the company for £50,000, claiming gift relief under s 165. As the gift relief eliminates the chargeable gain on the difference between the market value and the value used for the transfer the position would be:

	£
Trader:	
Goodwill — market value	120,000
Less: Business gift relief	(70,000)
Chargeable gain	50,000*
Company:	
Goodwill at market value	120,000
Less: Rolled over gain	(70,000)
Acquisition cost	50,000

*Entrepreneurs' relief is not available for such disposals of goodwill on or after 3 December 2014, see **29.2**.

Deferring gains under the enterprise investment scheme (EIS) (TCGA 1992, s 150C and Sch 5B)

[27.11] The disadvantage of the section 162 rollover relief is that all assets must be transferred to the company, whereas it may be preferred to retain premises in personal ownership. The disadvantage of the business gift relief is the reduced value at which the company is regarded as acquiring the gifted assets. Both disadvantages can possibly be eliminated if the company is a qualifying unquoted trading company for EIS purposes by claiming EIS deferral relief instead (see **29.33**), although the rules are extremely complex and it is not certain that the incorporation of the business can be structured in such a way as to enable the relief to be claimed. If the relief is available, an individual would only need to transfer such assets as he wished, and they would be transferred at full market value. Money need only be locked into share capital to the extent necessary to cover the gains arising on the transfer values. If the EIS option is being considered, professional advice is essential.

Value added tax (VATA 1994, s 49; SI 1995/1268, para 5; SI 1995/2518, regs 5, 6)

[27.12] On the transfer of a business to a company, VAT will not normally arise on the assets transferred and the company will take over the VAT position of the transferor as regards deductible input VAT and liability to account for output VAT (transfer of a business as a going concern, see **7.52**). This VAT-free treatment does not apply to transfers of land and buildings in respect of which the transferor has opted to charge VAT (see **32.42**), or to transfers of commercial buildings that are either unfinished or less than three years old, unless the transferee company gives written notification before the transfer that it has opted to charge VAT on future transactions in connection with the land and buildings. In that case any VAT charged by the transferor would be recovered as input VAT by the transferee, leaving HMRC in a neutral position, and VAT is not therefore chargeable on the transfer. Otherwise, VAT must be charged. A claim may be made by the trader or partners and the company for the existing VAT registration number to be transferred to the company. It is essential to contact the appropriate VAT office in good time to obtain the necessary forms and ensure that the various requirements are complied with. HMRC guidance is available in Notice 700/9 (December 2012).

Following a Tribunal decision HMRC accept that the fact that the transferor of a business retains a small reversionary interest in a transferred property does not prevent the transaction from being treated as a transfer of a going concern (TOGC) for VAT purposes. It applies to all businesses, for example where a retailer disposes of the retail business but transfers the premises by granting a lease. However, if the interest retained by the transferor represents more than 1% of the value of the part of the property over which the lease is granted, HMRC will regard that as strongly indicative that the transaction is too complex to be a TOGC — see HMRC Briefs 30/2012 and 27/2014.

HMRC also now accept that where the transferor is a tenant and he surrenders the lease, this can be a TOGC. They say this could apply where a tenant subletting premises by way of business subsequently surrenders its interest in the property together with the benefit of the subtenants, or where a retailer sells its retailing business to its landlord. In substance the landlord has acquired the tenant's business — see HMRC Brief 27/2014.

Stamp duty, stamp duty land tax, and land and buildings transaction tax

[27.13] Stamp duty applies only to instruments relating to stocks and shares and marketable securities (and also transfers of interests in partnerships to the extent of the value of any such instruments included in the partnership transfer, but this is not relevant to the incorporation of a business). Stamp duty will not therefore be payable on the transfer agreement unless and to the extent that such assets are included. Land transactions are charged to stamp duty land tax, except in Scotland they are charged to land and buildings transaction tax (LBTT). The detailed provisions are in CHAPTER 6.

On the transfer of a business, stamp duty land tax (or LBTT as the case may be) will only be payable if the business premises are transferred. In that event, then since the person transferring the business is connected with the company, stamp duty land tax or LBTT will be charged on the open market value of the premises, regardless of the transfer value (see **6.8**). The value on which stamp duty land tax or LBTT is charged includes any VAT on the transaction. However, HMRC have stated that for stamp duty land tax purposes the market value of an asset does not include VAT even if VAT is chargeable on the transfer of the asset, because market value is based on a hypothetical transaction, not on the actual transaction. Since stamp duty land tax and LBTT are self-assessed taxes, it is up to the taxpayer to calculate the amount due. If stamp duty land tax or LBTT was paid on the basis that the transfer of going concern rules applied (see **27.12**) and this turned out not to be the case, any additional stamp duty land tax or LBTT would be payable plus interest from the date of the transaction. Conversely HMRC state that there may be cases, particularly those highlighted in HMRC Brief 30/2012 (see **27.12**), where tax was charged on the grant of an interest in land when in fact the transaction qualified as the transfer of a going concern (TOGC), and no VAT was chargeable. This would have resulted in stamp duty land tax being assessed on a VAT-inclusive value rather than a VAT-exclusive one. If a business believes that it has overpaid stamp duty land tax on such a transaction, it may make a claim for overpayment relief within four years of the date of transaction — see HMRC Brief 08/2013. A similar situation may arise on the surrender of a lease, which can now also be treated as a TOGC (see **27.12**).

Inheritance tax

[27.14] There will not usually be any direct inheritance tax implications on the incorporation of a business, but three situations need watching.

The first is the effect on the availability of business property relief where partners form a company. If assets such as premises are owned within the partnership, they form part of the partnership share and 100% business property relief is available. A partner who personally owns assets such as premises used in the business is entitled to business property relief at the rate of 50%. Relief at the 50% rate for personally-owned assets is available to a shareholder only if he is a controlling shareholder, and no relief is available at all for such assets owned by minority shareholders. Shares of husband and wife or civil partners are related property and the available rate of relief is determined by their joint holdings. Where the assets are reflected in the value of the shareholdings, business property relief will apply to the value of the shares (see **5.45**).

The second situation arises where assets have been transferred using the capital gains tax provisions for gifts to the company of business assets (TCGA 1992, s 165 — see **27.10**). Gifts to a company are not potentially exempt transfers for inheritance tax. They may be covered by the 100% business property relief, but if not, the amount of the transfer of value is the amount by which the sole trader's or partner's estate has fallen in value. In measuring that fall in value, the value of the shares acquired in the company (enhanced by the ownership within the company of the gifted assets) will be taken into account. The result may be that there is no transfer of value. Alternatively, there may be an argument that there is no transfer of value because the incorporation was a commercial transaction not intended to confer gratuitous benefit (see **5.4**).

If there is a transfer of value, no tax may be payable, because of annual exemptions and the nil rate threshold. If tax is payable, the tax may be paid by instalments if the company as donee pays the tax (see **5.54**).

Thirdly, what was previously a sole trader's or partner's capital/current account which attracted business property relief will, unless converted into appropriate shares or securities, no longer qualify because it will be an ordinary debt due from the company.

See CHAPTER 5 for further information on inheritance tax.

Issuing shares to directors (ITEPA 2003, ss 421B, 421J–421L)

[27.15] On the incorporation of the business, the sole trader or partners will usually become directors, and shares in the company will be issued to them (or transferred from the formation agent if the company is bought 'off the shelf'). In most cases the issue of shares in these circumstances will not need to be reported to HMRC as being by reason of the directors' employment or prospective employment. See **11.2** for a list of reportable events. In the event that a return is required, there are penalties for failing to comply with the reporting requirements.

Care should be taken to ensure that shares are issued or transferred at market value, to avoid a potential tax liability on a benefit in kind.

National insurance

[27.16] If a sole trader or partner becomes a director and/or employee in the company, NICs on earnings from the company are payable by both the employer and the employee. The burden is significantly higher than the maximum self-employed contributions under Classes 2 and 4. See CHAPTER 18 for further details.

Business rates

[27.17] The incorporation of a business means a change of occupier for rating purposes.

See **8.10** for further information on business rates.

Transfer of business from a limited company (FA 2013, ss 58–61; TCGA 1992, ss 162B, 162C)

[27.18] There have historically been a number of businesses operating as limited companies that would prefer to operate in unincorporated form but there were a number of tax charges and administrative issues which discouraged this. Disincorporation relief removes some of the tax disadvantages.

Disincorporation relief

[27.19] Disincorporation relief applies for a period of five years from 1 April 2013 to 31 March 2018 where a company transfers its business to some or all of its shareholders, and the transfer is a qualifying business transfer. HMRC guidance can be found at www.gov.uk/guidance/corporation-tax-disincorpora tion-relief. The Office of Tax Simplification (OTS) has noted that take-up of the relief has been very low and have invited comments on the minimum improvements that would be needed for the relief to be effective or taken up before its cessation date.

Qualifying business transfer

[27.20] There is a qualifying business transfer where the following five conditions are met:

(i)   The business is transferred as a going concern.
(ii)   The business is transferred together with all of its assets, or all of its assets other than cash.
(iii)   The total market value of the qualifying assets (i.e. goodwill or interest in land not held as trading stock) included in the transfer does not exceed £100,000.
(iv)   All of the shareholders to whom the business is transferred are individuals (including partners other than members of a limited liability partnership, as to which see **23.33**).
(v)   Each of those shareholders held company shares throughout the 12 months before the transfer.

Effect of a claim

[27.21] A claim for disincorporation relief is irrevocable and must be made jointly by the company and all of the transferee shareholders within two years from the date of transfer. Where relief is claimed the goodwill and interest in land (the qualifying assets, see **27.20**) are treated as transferred at the lower of capital gains tax cost (see **4.18**) or market value, so that no corporation tax charge arises to the company on the transfer. There is an exception for goodwill created or acquired on or after 1 April 2002 (see **20.35**) and which has been written down for tax purposes. This is treated as transferred at the lower of tax-written-down value or market value. Where this post-FA 2002 goodwill is not shown on the balance sheet the transfer value is nil.

Other assets held by the company such as stock and plant and machinery are not covered by the relief. However, the elections outlined in **27.3** and **27.4** could be made if the shareholders to whom the business is transferred own 51% or more of the company's voting share capital or profits or assets on winding up of the company.

Tax points

[27.22] Note the following:

- The restriction on tax reliefs available in respect of internally-generated goodwill and customer related intangible assets on incorporations have removed one of the tax incentives to incorporate an existing business.
- Where a trader is seeking rollover relief under TCGA 1992, s 162 on the transfer of a business, he should minimise the amount locked up in share capital by not transferring cash. If the cash is needed to assist the liquidity of the company, it can always be introduced on director's loan account.
- Rollover relief on the replacement of business assets under TCGA 1992, s 152 can be claimed on premises owned personally and used in the owner's personal trading company — see **29.21**. A personal company is one in which the individual owns at least 5% of the voting rights.
- The payment of rent by the company for property owned personally by the former sole trader or partners does not affect business property relief for inheritance tax (but the size of the shareholding does).
- It is not possible to get the best of all worlds on incorporation of a business. Maximising the capital gains deferral can only be done at extra cost in terms of stamp duty land tax or LBTT (where applicable) and with the disadvantage of locking funds into share capital. Retaining premises saves stamp duty land tax or LBTT, and using gift relief on those assets that are transferred enables the funding of the company by making loans to it, but the loan account is credited with a lower figure in respect of the gifted assets and that value becomes the company's base value for capital gains. This could also significantly reduce the indexation allowance when the company disposes of the assets.
- When considering how much of the proceeds for the transfer of the business should be locked in as share capital, it should not be forgotten that funds may need to be drawn for the payment of tax relating to the former sole trade or partnership. Unless there are sufficient funds on loan account, it will not be possible to withdraw the required funds from the company without incurring a further tax liability on remuneration or dividends.

- It may be possible to reduce the problems of locking in share capital by using redeemable shares, which can be redeemed gradually as and when the company has funds and possibly using the annual capital gains tax exempt amount to avoid a tax charge on the shareholder. There are, however, anti-avoidance provisions, and also a clearance procedure, and professional advice is essential.

- If, when a sole trader or partners transfer a business to a company, shares are issued to other family members, HMRC may seek to use the settlements provisions of ITTOIA 2005, s 625 to tax the income from dividends on the former sole trader/partners rather than the share-holding family members (see **12.10**).

- The lack of writing-down allowances in the last tax period before incorporation may cost tax relief at income tax rates of 40% or 45% compared with a much lower rate of relief in the first accounting period of the company.

- It is worth considering transferring chargeable assets, such as goodwill, at their full value, with a corresponding credit to a loan account. This will increase the capital gains tax payable at the time (subject to available reliefs), but will provide a greater facility to draw off the loan account at no future personal tax cost.

- Care should be taken not to overstate the value of goodwill. To do so will risk HMRC seeking to reduce the credit to the loan account, perhaps resulting in its becoming overdrawn, leading to a liability for the company under CTA 2010, s 455 (loans to participators — see **12.14**), or the amount being regarded as a distribution of company profits. The valuation is particularly tricky, and might even be arguably nil, where it depends upon individual qualities of the former sole trader or partners.

- The private use of motor cars used in a sole trade or partnership will generally have been dealt with by excluding part of the running costs and capital allowances from the allowable business costs for tax purposes. If the cars are acquired by the company, the private use will then be reckoned under the employee benefits rules (see **10.38**). The resulting tax and NICs costs need to be considered when deciding if the cars should be transferred, or retained in personal ownership, with an appropriate business mileage claim being made. If cars previously included in the business assets up to the time of transfer are retained in personal ownership, all the assets will not have been transferred, denying section 162 rollover relief.

28

Selling the family company

Background

[28.1] There are two ways in which a business run via a family company may be sold. The shares can be sold, or the company assets can be sold and then either the company can be liquidated or kept and dividends drawn from it. The most difficult aspect of the sale negotiations is usually reconciling the interests of the vendors and the purchasers.

The vendors will often prefer to sell the shares rather than the assets to avoid the 'double' capital gains tax charge which will arise on the asset sale and then on the distribution to shareholders if the company is wound up. The purchaser may prefer to buy assets in order to be able to attract tax-efficient investment for their purchase through the enterprise investment scheme (see **29.23** to **29.36**), to claim tax allowances on purchases of equipment, plant, or capital gains rollover relief on earlier disposals, through the purchase of appropriate assets. Buying assets is sometimes more straightforward than a share purchase, with consequently lower costs. Stamp duty is charged on share transactions. Stamp duty land tax (or in Scotland, land and buildings transaction tax (LBTT)) is charged on the acquisition of land and buildings. Stamp duty land tax and LBTT rates are generally much higher (see CHAPTER 6).

It is not possible to obtain relief for the annual write down (amortisation) of goodwill and other customer related intangible assets except for acquisitions made before 8 July 2015 (or acquisitions made afterwards pursuant to an unconditional obligation entered into before then). This levels the playing field between asset purchases and share purchases as no such relief is available on share acquisitions (see **20.35**).

The vendors may intend staying in business, so that a sale of assets by a trading company, with the company then acquiring replacement assets, may give an opportunity for capital gains rollover relief. If the vendors plan to invest in another company then, providing their investment would qualify for enterprise investment scheme deferral relief (see **29.33**), all or any part of the gains on the disposal of the shares in the existing company (and any other gains they may have) may be held over to the extent that shares are subscribed for in the new company. The relief is not available where the acquisition is of shares already in existence. The gain is not deducted from the cost of the new shares and the tax payable crystallises when they are disposed of unless further relief is then available.

A capital gains tax relief is available for the disposal of shares in a trading company to a trust with specified characteristics, provided the trustees hold a defined controlling interest in the company at the end of the tax year for which the relief is claimed, and they apply the trust's property for the benefit of all the eligible employees of the company. For further details of the conditions for relief see **4.38**.

Buying a company carries certain risks that are not associated with a straightforward purchase of assets. Known and 'latent' liabilities and obligations of the company will remain as company liabilities following a sale of the shares, making it most important that extreme care is taken for commercial and taxation purposes (often referred to as due diligence). The purchaser will clearly require indemnities and warranties from the vendors, but the vendors will want to limit these as much as possible, and in any event the purchaser would have the inconvenience of trying to enforce them.

The outcome of the negotiations, including the adjustments each party agrees to in order to resolve points of difference, will depend on the future intentions of the vendor, the relative bargaining strength of each party and how keen vendor and purchaser are to conclude the transaction.

Selling shares or assets

[28.2] Part of the sale consideration may relate not to tangible assets but to the growth prospects or the entrepreneurial flair of those involved with the company, and where goodwill is a substantial factor, the valuation placed on it will be an important part of the negotiations, providing flexibility in agreeing a price. Typically also for asset purchases before 8 July 2015, it was possible to obtain relief for annual write-off (amortisation) of goodwill and other customer related intangible assets. From 8 July 2015, this is no longer available; see **20.35**.

The tax cost of selling the shares can be significantly less than that of selling the assets followed by a liquidation. See Example 1 for a straight comparison of a share sale and an assets sale based on the same values.

Example 1

Trading company was formed in 1990 and 1,000 £1 shares were issued at par. Balance sheet of company immediately prior to intended sale at the end of April 2017 was:

	£		£
Share capital	1,000	Net current assets	50,000
Accumulated profits	99,000	Premises at cost	50,000
	£100,000		£100,000

A sale is now proposed on the basis of the goodwill and premises being worth £350,000.

If the shares are sold:

	£
Assets per balance sheet	100,000
Increase in value of premises and goodwill (£350,000 – £50,000)	300,000
Sale proceeds for shares	400,000
Cost	(1,000)
Chargeable gain	£399,000
CGT @ say 20% (ignoring any set-offs and exemptions)*	£79,800

* See **4.2** for the differing capital gains tax rates which can apply depending on an individual's circumstances. If the conditions for entrepreneurs' relief (see **29.2**) are met on the sale of shares, the gain of £399,000 will be taxed at 10% giving a CGT liability of £39,900.

If assets are sold and company is liquidated:

	£	£
Assets per balance sheet		100,000
Increase in value of premises and goodwill	300,000	
Less provision for corporation tax on sale (£300,000 less, say, £71,000 for indexation to April 2017 on cost of premises)		
Gain £229,000 @ 19%**	(43,510)	256,490
Amount distributed to shareholders on liquidation (ignoring liquidation costs)		356,490
Cost of shares (no indexation allowance)		(1,000)
Chargeable gain		£355,490
CGT @ say 20% (ignoring any set-offs and exemptions)***		£71,098

** See **3.14** for corporation tax rate applying.

*** See **4.2** for the differing capital gains tax rates which can apply depending on an individual's circumstances. If the conditions for entrepreneurs' relief (see **29.2**) are met on the distribution, the gain of £355,490 will be taxed at 10% giving a CGT liability of £35,549.

Amounts received by shareholders (assuming no entrepreneurs' relief):

	Pro-ceeds	CGT	Net
	£	£	£
On sale of shares	400,000	79,800	320,200
On liquidation	356,490	71,098	285,392
Extra cost of liquidation route			£34,808

Other factors

[28.3] The disadvantages of selling assets may be mitigated if the company has trading losses. Current year trading losses (as distinct from brought-forward) are able to be set off against the gains on the assets. The use of carried forward losses, until 1 April 2017, is less attractive. Carried-forward losses arising before 1 April 2017 can only be used for offset against the trade of the company that incurred the loss, and not used by other companies in a group. Additionally, certain losses can only be set against certain types of income, for example capital losses can only be used against future capital gains.

The September 2017 Finance Bill, which is expected to receive Royal Assent in November 2017, relaxes the provisions relating to the use of carried forward losses. Carried forward losses arising on or after 1 April 2017, are able to be set against profits of different activities within a company and against profits across a group. This relaxation is however accompanied by a 'restriction' that limits the offset to 50% on profits in excess of £5 million. This is a very high threshold and in practice most companies will not be affected by the restriction.

If it is intended that the company shall continue trading in some new venture rather than be wound up, it may be possible to rollover or holdover the gains by the purchase of new assets. Alternatively, if the new trade commences before the old trade ceases, trading losses may arise in that new trade against which the gains may be set under the normal rules for set-off of trading losses.

For more details on losses see CHAPTER 26.

Goodwill (CTA 2009, Pt 8)

[28.4] Where a company buys goodwill from an unrelated party it used to be able to claim tax relief over a period on the price paid (see **20.35** to **20.41**). The relief was also available for acquisitions from related parties in certain circumstances but not where the acquisition takes place on incorporation on or after 3 December 2014 (see **20.41**). However, this annual relief for write-off of *all* goodwill has been withdrawn broadly for acquisitions on or after 8 July 2015 (see **28.1**).

Previously the purchaser in Example 1 might therefore have been reluctant to buy the shares, preferring an asset purchase so that the write-off relief on goodwill could be claimed, but as illustrated the vendor is seriously disadvantaged if the company has first to sell its assets and then distribute its available cash. This might have provided a bargaining opportunity under which the purchaser pays somewhat more for goodwill, the real cost, however, being reduced by the previously available tax relief, and whilst the vendor accepts that his company must sell assets and pay the appropriate corporation tax, his share proceeds will be higher because of the increased amount his company has received for goodwill.

The purchase of goodwill is exempt from stamp duty. See **28.11** for the stamp duty land tax position.

Payments in compensation for loss of office

[28.5] Compensation and ex-gratia payments are dealt with in detail in CHAPTER 15. There are two aspects, first whether the director/shareholder will be exempt from tax on the first £30,000 of the payment, and second whether the payment will be deductible as an expense in calculating taxable profits.

As far as the individual is concerned, in order for the £30,000 exemption to apply, the company must be able to demonstrate that any payments are wholly unassociated with a sale of the individual's shares in the company and moreover do not represent an income dividend. Ex-gratia payments may also be challenged as being benefits under an employer-financed scheme that is not a registered pension scheme (see **15.3**).

As far as the company is concerned, it must show that the payments are wholly and exclusively for the purposes of the trade, which is more difficult if the payment is ex-gratia rather than compensation for loss of office. Where the company's trade ceases following a sale of the assets, an ex-gratia or compensation payment cannot satisfy the 'wholly and exclusively' rule because there is no longer any trade. The part of the company's payment that can be set against the company's trading profits in those circumstances is limited to the amount of statutory redundancy pay to which the director is entitled plus a sum equal to three times that amount, unless the payment is made under a pre-existing contractual or statutory obligation (see **15.8**). Where a compensation or ex-gratia payment is made prior to a sale of the shares, the company's trade continuing, this restriction in calculating taxable profits will not apply.

Whether there is a sale of the shares or an assets sale followed by a liquidation, the compensation payment will reduce the value of the company's assets, and thus the amount of disposal proceeds on which the shareholder's capital gains tax liability will be calculated.

Payments into a pension scheme

[28.6] Prior to selling the shares the cash resources of the company, and thus, effectively, the eventual sale proceeds, may also be reduced by an appropriate pension scheme contribution, the benefits of which may be taken partly as a tax-free lump sum and partly as a pension. Again, the trading profits prior to the sale are reduced, with a corresponding saving in corporation tax. This is of course only acceptable if the amount of the contribution and effect on the value of the fund is within the stipulated limits. Company pension schemes are dealt with in CHAPTER **16**.

Sale of a trading subsidiary

[28.7] Where a single company is selling a trading subsidiary it may be possible for the sale to be made without a charge to corporation tax on capital gains if the 'substantial shareholding exemption' applies. See **3.34**.

For disposals on or after 1 April 2017, this exemption will apply if the vendor company's shareholding in the company which is being sold exceeds 10% and it has been owned for a continuous period of at least 12 months in the preceding six years before the date of disposal.

For disposals prior to 1 April 2017, for the exemption to apply it was necessary for the vendor company to be a trading company or member of a trading group. Also the 'look back' period was just two years — in other words it was necessary for the company being sold to have been owned for a continuous period of at least 12 months within the preceding two years.

The changes that apply from 1 April 2017 are contained in the September 2017 Finance Bill (which is expected to receive Royal Assent in November 2017). They were introduced as a part of a general package of reform to simplify the existing exemption.

Whilst this exemption relieves the selling company of the corporation tax on its gain, there is still no tax relief to the purchaser because assets have not been purchased, so there is still some inconsistency between the aims of buyer and seller.

Selling on the basis of receiving shares in the purchasing company (TCGA 1992, ss 126–139, 169Q, 279A–279D)

[28.8] Where, as consideration for the sale of their shares, the vendor shareholders receive shares in the company making the acquisition, then each vendor shareholder is normally treated as not having made a disposal of the 'old shares', but as having acquired the 'new shares' for the same amount and on the same date as the 'old shares' (known as 'paper for paper' exchanges).

Where the consideration is part shares/part cash, that part received in cash is liable to capital gains tax, whilst the 'new shares' again stand in the shoes of the old.

Example 2

Shares cost £10,000. As a result of an acquisition of the entire share capital by another company, the shareholder receives cash of £40,000 and shares in the acquiring company valued at £60,000. The capital gains position is:

	Cash £
Proceeds:	
Cash	40,000
Less cost related to cash (divided in proportion to proceeds) 40,000/100,000 x 10,000	(4,000)
Chargeable gain (subject to available exemptions)	£36,000
Cost of 'new shares' 60,000/100,000 x 10,000	£6,000

[28.9] In such paper for paper exchanges it is possible that the disposal of the original shares at the time of the exchange would result in a gain that could qualify for entrepreneurs' relief, whereas the gain on the later disposal of the new holding may not qualify, for example because the company may no longer be the individual's personal company following the exchange (see **29.3**). In such circumstances, and provided that all the relevant criteria are met, it will be possible to make an election to claim entrepreneurs' relief as if the exchange involved a disposal of the original shares, thus crystallising a gain against which entrepreneurs' relief may be claimed. The time limit for the election is one year from 31 January following the tax year in which the exchange takes place. HMRC have confirmed that where there is a share for share exchange, the 12-month ownership requirement for entrepreneurs' relief does 'in principle' include the holding period of the original shares. See **38.37** regarding entrepreneurs' relief where there is an exchange involving qualifying corporate bonds. Instead of this, and for shares newly issued on or after 17 March 2016, that have been held for three years from 6 April 2016 it may be that on a subsequent disposal the claimant will be able to claim investors' relief; see **29.12**.

Where part of the consideration depends upon future performance, say the issue of further shares or securities if a profit target is met, the value of the right to receive further shares or securities (known as an earn-out right) is normally treated as part of the disposal proceeds at the time the original shares are sold. Where the vendor is employed in the business and is to continue in employment in some capacity for a period after the sale, it must be clear that the earn-out right is not linked in any way to the future employment, otherwise the value of shares issued under the earn-out would be charged to tax and NICs as employment earnings rather than being dealt with under the capital gains rules. Where the capital gains rules apply, the value of the right is treated as a security, so that any capital gains are rolled over until the further shares or securities are sold. The taxpayer may elect for this treatment not to apply, making the value of the earn-out right itself liable to capital gains tax.

[28.10] The rollover treatment does not apply if the future consideration is to be cash. In that event, the whole of the value of the right to future consideration is liable to capital gains tax at the time of the sale, with a further liability on the difference between that value and the amount of consideration actually received, or the proceeds of selling the right. Where cash is to be received, then if the proceeds of deferred unascertainable consideration or of selling the right to receive it are less than the estimated value brought in for the right, and the disposal occurred in a tax year later than that when the original gain arose on the undeferred consideration, the taxpayer may elect for the loss to be carried back to that earlier tax year. The time limit for a carry back claim is the first anniversary of the 31 January following the tax year of the loss.

For entrepreneurs' relief purposes (see **29.2**), it may be preferable to crystallise a gain by either making the election to disapply the rollover treatment or structuring the earn-out as a cash-based transaction and claiming entrepreneurs' relief on any gain arising. Although an earn-out satisfied in the form of shares or securities could potentially qualify for entrepreneurs' relief, the company would have to qualify as the individual's personal company throughout the one year before the disposal, which means he would have to hold at least 5% of the shares in the company during the earn-out. Although note it may be possible for shares newly issued on or after 17 March 2016, that have been held for three years from 6 April 2016, that a claim for investors' relief could be made; see **29.12**.

Stamp duty, stamp duty land tax, and land and buildings transaction tax

[28.11] Where there is a sale of shares, stamp duty is normally payable by the purchaser on the consideration for the sale. Where there is a sale of assets, stamp duty is only payable on stocks, shares and marketable securities, but stamp duty land tax (or in Scotland, land and buildings transaction tax (LBTT)) is payable on land transactions and is generally at much higher rates than stamp duty (see CHAPTER 6). In some instances what is described as goodwill actually forms part of the land and is often described as inherent goodwill because it is inherent in the land. Such goodwill is included in the amount on which stamp duty land tax or LBTT is payable. Goodwill that is 'personal' goodwill does not attract stamp duty land tax or LBTT. If HMRC raise an enquiry into the stamp duty land tax return, they may well challenge the part of the consideration that has been apportioned to personal goodwill.

The value on which stamp duty land tax or LBTT is payable includes any VAT on the sale. It may not be known when a business is sold whether the VAT 'going concern' treatment will apply (see **28.12**). If VAT is excluded from the amount on which stamp duty land tax or LBTT is paid, and the 'going concern' basis proves not to be available, the appropriate amount of additional stamp duty land tax or LBTT would be payable, plus interest from the date of the sale. Conversely HMRC state there may be cases, particularly those highlighted in HMRC Brief 30/2012 (see **27.12**), where tax was charged on the grant of an interest in land when in fact the transaction qualified as the transfer of a going concern, and no VAT was chargeable. This would have resulted in stamp duty land tax being assessed on a VAT-inclusive value rather than a VAT-exclusive one. If a business believes that it has overpaid stamp duty land tax on such a transaction, it may make a claim for overpayment relief within four years of the date of transaction — see HMRC Brief 08/2013. A similar situation may arise on the surrender of a lease, which can now also be treated as a TOGC (see **27.12**)

Value added tax (VATA 1994, ss 49, 94 and Sch 9 Group 5; SI 1995/1268, para 5; SI 1995/2518)

[28.12] Where the family company is sold by means of a share sale, the sale does not attract VAT because the shares are not sold in the course of business but by an individual as an investment.

Where all or part of the business is sold as a going concern by one taxable person to another, no VAT is charged by the vendor and the purchaser has no input VAT to reclaim on the amount paid (subject to what is said at **27.12** for land and buildings). The going concern treatment only applies, however, where the assets acquired are such that they represent a business which is capable of independent operation (see **7.52**).

Where the 'going concern' concept does not apply, VAT must be charged on all taxable supplies, and any related input VAT suffered by the seller is recoverable. Taxable supplies include goodwill, trading stock, plant and machinery, and motor vehicles (except that cars on which input VAT was not recovered when they were acquired will only be chargeable to the extent, if any, that the disposal proceeds exceed original cost). Business premises on which the seller has exercised his option to tax are also included, and the seller can therefore recover any VAT relating to the costs of sale, for example on legal and professional fees. The disposal of book debts, and of business premises over three years old on which the option to tax has not been taken, is an exempt supply and does not attract VAT. For partially exempt businesses there are some complex rules as to how the sale of the business is treated.

It is important to ensure that the purchase agreement provides for the addition of VAT and that the purchase consideration is allocated over the various assets acquired. If VAT is not mentioned in the purchase agreement, the price is deemed to be VAT-inclusive.

Tax points

[28.13] Note the following:

- Because there are so many pitfalls and problems when selling or buying a family company, it is essential to get expert professional advice.
- The withdrawal of the annual relief for write-off of goodwill has removed one of the benefits of an asset sale.
- When a company ceases to trade, this denotes the end of a chargeable accounting period, and if there are current trading losses these cannot be relieved against chargeable gains arising after the cessation. However, gains are deemed to be made on the contract date, not on completion, so if the company enters into the contract for sale of the chargeable assets while it is still trading, the right to set off current trading losses against chargeable gains in that trading period will be preserved.

- Compensation for loss of office and ex-gratia payments upon cessation of employment can only be expected to escape HMRC challenge if they are genuine payments for breach of contract or reasonable ex-gratia amounts bearing in mind years of service, etc. and even so, ex-gratia payments may not qualify for the £30,000 exemption (see **28.5** and CHAPTER **15**).

- When shares are being sold in a family company with significant retained profits, HMRC may argue in some circumstances that the increased share value as a result of the retained profits represents not a capital gain but sums that could have been paid out as income, and that they are chargeable as such. Consideration should therefore be given to whether HMRC clearance should be obtained for the proposed sale. For details of HMRC clearances and approvals see www.gov.uk/seeki ng-clearance-or-approval-for-a-transaction.

- When buying the shares in a company, the purchaser should look particularly for any potential capital gains liabilities which will be inherited, such as the crystallisation after ten years of gains on depreciating business assets which have been held over because the company acquired new qualifying assets (see **29.19**), or, if the company being purchased is leaving a group, the crystallisation of gains on assets acquired by it from another group company within the previous six years (see **3.31**). Moreover, the accounts value of the company assets may be greater than the tax value because earlier gains have been deducted under the rollover relief provisions from the tax cost of the assets now held or the assets have been revalued for accounts purposes. Thus a chargeable gain may arise on the company even though the item is sold for no more than its value in the accounts. Taxation due diligence is essential.

- If a company with unused trading losses is purchased, the losses cannot be used when the company returns to profitability if the change of ownership takes place within a period of three years during which there is also a major change in the nature or conduct of the business. There is also a restriction on availability of trading losses where the company being acquired has succeeded to the trade of another company without taking over that other company's liabilities (see **26.24** and **26.25**).

- See **22.20** regarding the restriction on the set-off of certain 'acquired' capital allowances against existing profits where a company or group of companies acquires another company.

- Whether shares or assets are purchased, the purchaser will take over the predecessor company's Class 1A NICs liability for that part of the tax year before the succession. Again, taxation due diligence is essential.

- The purchase consideration may partly depend on the company's future profit performance, sometimes referred to as an 'earn-out' (see **28.9**), and when it is received it may be partly in cash and partly in the form of shares or securities in the purchasing company. The capital gains tax position is complicated and professional advisers have to look very carefully at this aspect, if possible obtaining the views of HMRC when they apply for clearance on the share sale.

- The carryback to an earlier tax year of a loss arising in relation to deferred unascertainable consideration (see **28.10**) is not limited to where the original disposal was of shares. It could equally apply to a disposal of goodwill by a sole trader or partners, where further consideration depended upon profit performance, or where the proceeds of land depended on planning consents.

- A private company may avoid the costs of putting a company into formal liquidation by distributing the assets and then having the company struck off the companies register as a defunct company. Although strictly the distribution of assets in these circumstances is an income distribution on which the shareholders would be liable for income tax, HMRC will usually agree to treat it as if it were a capital distribution in a formal liquidation (and, therefore, subject to capital gains tax, and possibly qualifying for entrepreneurs' relief — see HMRC Capital Gains Manual CG64115) providing there is a commercial objective for the dissolution as distinct from an attempt to obtain a tax advantage, that at the time of the distribution the company intends to collect (or has collected) any debts and pay off its creditors and the amount of the distribution does not exceed £25,000 in total. Care is needed where there are non-distributable reserves.

- See **27.18** to **27.21** regarding disincorporation relief which can apply in certain circumstances where a company transfers its business to some or all of its shareholders as a going concern.

29

Encouraging business investment and enterprise

Background

[29.1] This chapter deals with various schemes that encourage investment in new and expanding companies and other measures to promote business enterprise, efficiency and innovation. It gives only an outline of the provisions and professional advice is recommended.

CHAPTER **11** at **11.13** onwards deals with the enterprise management incentive share option scheme that is available to small, higher risk companies. See also **3.34** regarding the exemption for company gains on substantial shareholdings and **20.35** onwards regarding the corporation tax regime for intellectual property, goodwill and other intangible assets.

Entrepreneurs' relief (TCGA 1992, ss 169H–S; FA 2013, Sch 24 para 6)

[29.2] Entrepreneurs' relief is available for 'qualifying business disposals'. HMRC guidance can be found in Helpsheet HS275. Where the relief is available the rate of capital gains tax is reduced from the various rates which may apply (see **4.2**) to 10%. The following disposals are qualifying business disposals:

(a)   a material disposal of business assets, e.g. the disposal of all or part of a business — see **29.3** and **29.5**;

(b)   a disposal of trust business assets where there is a qualifying beneficiary of the trust — see **29.6**; and

(c)   a disposal associated with a relevant material disposal, e.g. the disposal of business assets used by a company or partnership where that disposal is associated with a disposal of shares in the company or the assets of the partnership — see **29.7**.

Where the disposal is not one of shares or securities (see **29.3**) relief under each of these three headings is restricted to the disposal of 'relevant business assets' (see **29.8**).

For disposals occurring on or after 6 April 2011, there is a lifetime limit of £10 million of gains in respect of qualifying business disposals. The lower limits applying before 6 April 2011 were—

(i)   disposals on or after 23 June 2010 but before 6 April 2011 — £5 million;

(ii)   disposals on or after 6 April 2010 but before 23 June 2010 — £2 million;

(iii)   disposals on or after 6 April 2008 but before 6 April 2010 — £1 million.

Where individuals or trustees made qualifying gains above the prevailing limit before 6 April 2011, no additional relief is allowed for the excess. But if they make further qualifying gains on or after 6 April 2011 they will be able to claim relief on up to a further £5 million of those additional gains (or up to £8 million or £9 million where the earlier £2 million or £1 million limit applied), giving relief on accumulated qualifying gains up to the current limit of £10 million.

Material disposal of business assets

[29.3] Relief is available if an individual makes a disposal of business assets and that disposal is a material disposal. A material disposal of business assets is either:

(a)   a disposal of the whole or part of a business that the individual has owned for at least a year;

(b)   a disposal of assets that were in use for the business when the business ceased, providing that the individual owned the business for at least a year up to the date of cessation and the disposal takes place within three years of that date; or

(c)   a disposal of shares or securities of a company (see below).

With regard to (c), for a period of one year up to the date of the disposal the company must be the individual's personal company (see **29.11**) and it must be either a trading company or the holding company of a trading group (as defined specifically for these purposes). The individual must be an officer or employee of the company or of another group company. Alternatively, relief is available if these conditions are met for at least a year up to the date when the company ceases to be a trading company or a member of a trading group, and the individual disposes of the shares within three years of that date. HMRC have confirmed that where there is a share for share exchange (see **28.8**) the 12-month ownership requirement does 'in principle' include the holding period of the original shares.

[29.4] For disposals on or after 6 April 2013 relief under (c) in **29.3** above also applies where the assets disposed of are relevant EMI shares, the option for the shares was granted at least a year before the date of disposal, and throughout the one-year period ending on the disposal date the company was either a trading company or the holding company of a trading group. The individual must also be an officer or employee of the company or of another group company throughout that period. Alternatively relief is available for a disposal of relevant EMI shares where the option was granted at least a year before the date when the company ceases to be a trading company or a member of a trading group (the cessation date), throughout that period the individual was an officer or employee of the company or of another group company, and the individual disposes of the shares within three years of the cessation date.

Relevant EMI shares are either shares acquired by an individual on or after 6 April 2013 as a result of exercising a qualifying EMI option within ten years of the option being granted (see **11.16**), or shares acquired as replacements for such shares as a result of certain reorganisations.

Where shares acquired during 2012–13 would be relevant EMI shares if they were acquired after 5 April 2013, the legislation treats them as relevant EMI shares provided the individual made no disposals of shares of that class in 2012–13. If shares of that class were disposed of in 2012–13, the individual could elect by 31 January 2014 to treat them as relevant EMI shares.

Where there is a qualifying reorganisation, the one-year company and employment requirements include the holding period of the original shares. There are specific rules applying where the option is a replacement option, or where the shares are acquired on the exercise of an option following a disqualifying event.

Special share identification rules apply to relevant EMI shares and the normal rules in **38.18** do not apply. Where shares of the same class are acquired on the same day and some of those shares are relevant EMI shares, the relevant EMI shares are treated as acquired separately from the other shares and as disposed of after the other shares. For disposals within the 30-day period, shares which are not relevant EMI shares are identified before those which are relevant EMI shares. Otherwise shares are identified with relevant EMI shares first on a first in/first out basis and such shares do not form part of the single pool.

[29.5] A partner in a partnership is treated for these purposes as though he is carrying on the business on his own account, so that for example a disposal of an interest in the partnership's assets is treated as a disposal of the whole of a part of the partnership's business. Each individual who is a partner in a business at any time is treated as owning the business carried on by the partnership at that time. The general effect of these provisions is that an individual's transactions in connection with becoming or being a member of a partnership can qualify for entrepreneurs' relief as they would if the individual carried on the business on his own account. Partners can therefore make claims for entrepreneurs' relief in the following circumstances—

(a)   the disposal of the whole of their interest in the partnership — by treating it as a disposal of the whole of the business;

(b)   the disposal of part of their interest in the partnership — by treating it as a disposal of part of a business;

(c)   the disposal by the partnership of the whole or part of the business — by treating the business as owned by the individual partner;

(d)   the disposal of partnership assets within the permitted period following the cessation of the partnership business — by treating the business as owned by the individual partner; or

(e)   the disposal of an asset owned by the partner personally and used in the partnership business under the associated disposal rules (see 29.7).

Disposal of trust business assets

[29.6] There is a disposal of trust business assets where the trustees dispose of settlement business assets, i.e. assets forming part of the settled property that are either shares or securities of a company or assets used (or previously used) for a business. There must be an individual who is a qualifying beneficiary (B), (i.e. an individual who has an interest in possession in either the whole of the settled property or a part of it that includes the business assets), and a further condition must be met.

The further condition in the case of a disposal of shares or securities is that, for a period of one year ending not earlier than three years before the disposal, the company is B's personal company and is either a trading company or the holding company of a trading group, and B is an officer or employee of the company or of another group company.

The further condition in the case of other assets is that the assets are used for the business carried on by B for a period of one year ending not earlier than three years before the disposal, and B ceases to carry on the business either on or within three years before the date of the disposal.

Disposal associated with material disposal

[29.7] There is a disposal associated with a relevant material disposal if:

(a)   an individual makes a material disposal of business assets (see 29.3) which is the disposal of either:

(i)   an interest in the assets of a partnership; or

(ii)   the shares or securities of a company;

(b)   the individual makes the disposal — i.e. the 'associated' disposal — as part of his withdrawal from participation in the business of the partnership or the company;

(c)   the assets disposed of are in use for the business for a period of one year up to the earlier of the date of the material disposal and the date of cessation of the business; and

(d)   where the assets are acquired on or after 13 June 2016, they have been held for a period of three years before the disposal.

For disposals on or after 18 March 2015 the disposal must be associated with a significant reduction in participation in the business. This means that in the case of (ii) above the claimant must also dispose of a minimum 5% of the shares or securities of the company carrying on the business. In the case of (i) above, he must either dispose of a minimum 5% share in the assets of the partnership carrying on the business, or alternatively he may dispose of less than a 5% share provided that he disposes of the whole of his interest and that he owned 5% or more of the assets for a continuous period of three years in the eight years preceding the disposal.

Relief is restricted where, on the associated disposal, the assets disposed of are in use for the business for only part of the period of ownership; or only part of the assets are in such use; or the individual is concerned in carrying on the business for only part of the period of such use; or the availability of the assets is dependent on the payment of rent (see **29.11**).

Relevant business assets

[29.8] Relief is restricted to the disposal of 'relevant business assets' where the disposal is not one of shares or securities. In most cases, relevant business assets include goodwill but exclude shares and securities and other assets held as investments. However, for disposals on or after 3 December 2014 goodwill is not a relevant business asset where the disposal is to a close company (see **3.29**) (or to a company which would be a close company if it were UK-resident), unless the claimant and any company or trustees connected with him, hold less than 5% of the ordinary shares, and less than 5% of the voting power, in the acquiring company. Relief will still be due where the claimant and said connected persons do have holdings of 5% or more immediately after the disposal provided they sell the entire holding to another company within 28 days, or such longer time as HMRC may allow, and, where that other company is a close company, they own less than 5% of its ordinary shares, and less than 5% of its voting power. This enables relief to be available where the transfer of the business to the company is part of arrangements to sell it to a new, independent company.

Generally, an asset is a relevant business asset if it is:

(a)   in the case of a material disposal of business assets (see **29.3**), used for the purposes of the business carried on by the individual or a partnership of which he is a member;

(b)   in the case of a disposal of trust business assets (see **29.6**), used for the purposes of the business carried on by the qualifying beneficiary or a partnership of which he is a member; or

(c)   in the case of a disposal associated with a relevant material disposal (see 29.7), used for the purposes of a business carried on by the partnership or the company.

Claims

[29.9] Entrepreneurs' relief must be claimed on or before the first anniversary of 31 January following the tax year in which the disposal is made. For example, relief must be claimed by 31 January 2020 in respect of a qualifying business disposal made on 1 September 2017. A claim relating to a disposal of trust assets is to be made jointly by the trustees and the qualifying beneficiary.

Operation of the relief

[29.10] The chargeable gain is taxed at a rate of 10%, provided that the gain together with any previous gains that benefited from entrepreneurs' relief do not exceed the lifetime limit, currently £10 million. The 10% rate only applies to gains which do not exceed the £10 million limit, any balance being taxed at the rates in **4.2** depending on the circumstances. In determining which rate should apply to individuals, gains qualifying for entrepreneurs' relief are set against any unused basic rate band before non-qualifying gains.

A chargeable gain may be deferred if the taxpayer makes a qualifying investment under the enterprise investment scheme (EIS — see **29.23**). Entrepreneurs' relief is available where gains that have been deferred under EIS prior to 6 April 2008 become chargeable because of an event occurring on or after that date (see **29.33** to **29.35**). In addition, gains which would have originally accrued on or after 3 December 2014 but which are deferred into EIS or social investment tax relief (see **29.55**) remain eligible for entrepreneurs' relief when the deferred gain becomes chargeable.

There are specific rules dealing with entrepreneurs' relief on reorganisation of share capital (see **28.9** and **38.37**), incorporation of a business (see **27.9**) and gifts of business assets (see **27.10**).

Definitions

[29.11] The legislation sets out several important definitions for the purpose of the relief, including:

A business — a trade, profession or vocation conducted on a commercial basis and with a view to the realisation of profits;

Personal company — a company in which the individual holds at least 5% of the ordinary share capital and can exercise at least 5% of the voting rights.

Rent — includes any form of consideration given for the use of the asset.

Trade — defined as in ITA 2007, s 989, i.e. 'trade' includes any venture in the nature of trade, but the commercial letting of furnished holiday accommodation is treated as a trade for the purpose of entrepreneurs' relief.

Investors' relief (TCGA 1992, ss 169VA–VR and Sch 7ZA)

[29.12] Investors' relief is available for disposals of 'qualifying shares', or an interest in such shares, in an unlisted company by an individual or trustees. Where the relief is available the rate of capital gains tax on the gain (after any allowable capital losses) is reduced from the various rates which may apply (see **4.2**) to 10%. Like entrepreneurs' relief, investors' relief is also subject to a lifetime limit of £10 million (see **29.2**). Gains exceeding the limit are charged at normal capital gains tax rates.

[29.13] Shares are qualifying shares if:

(a) they are issued on or after 17 March 2016 and *subscribed* for, solely or jointly, by the individual or trustees making the disposal ('the investor');

(b) at the time they are issued, none of the shares or securities of the company are listed on a recognised stock exchange;

(c) they are ordinary shares when issued and immediately before the disposal;

(d) the company was a trading company or the holding company of a trading group when the shares were issued and throughout the period up to disposal;

(e) neither the investor nor a connected person has been an officer or employee of the company or a connected company at any time in the period mentioned in (d) (though certain unremunerated directors and those who become an employee more than 180 days after the share issue, and had no prospect of becoming such at the date of issue, are not excluded);

(f) they are held continuously by the investor from issue to disposal; and

(g) they have been held for at least three years from 6 April 2016.

Thus the relief cannot apply until 2019–20 at the earliest.

[29.14] For the relief to apply to a disposal by trustees there must be at least one 'eligible beneficiary'. An eligible beneficiary:

(i) has an interest in possession (other than for a fixed term) in settled property that includes the holding of shares immediately before the disposal;

(ii) must have held that interest throughout the three years ending with the date of the disposal;

(iii) has not been an officer or employee of the company or a connected company (with the same exceptions as in (e) above) at any time in the three-year period; and

(iv) has elected to the trustees, by the time of the claim for relief, to be treated as an eligible beneficiary. (The election can be withdrawn within the same time limit.)

If there is more than one person with an interest in possession in the settled property in (i) above, the trustees can only claim relief in respect of the eligible beneficiary's share of the gain or, where there is more than one eligible beneficiary, on the aggregate of their shares. The lifetime limit of £10 million applies to each eligible beneficiary.

[29.15] Relief must be claimed on or before the first anniversary of 31 January following the tax year of disposal. For a disposal by trustees, the claim must be made jointly by the trustees and the eligible beneficiary or beneficiaries.

Where only some of the shares in a holding which is disposed of are qualifying shares, the gain is pro-rated accordingly and relief only applies to the gain on the qualifying shares. Qualifying shares are treated as disposed of in priority to non-qualifying shares. Where there have been previous disposals from a holding of shares, special identification rules determine what proportion of the shares subsequently disposed of are qualifying shares. There are also specific rules dealing with relief on reorganisation of share capital (see **28.9** and **38.37**). Relief is not available if the individual receives 'value' from the company within, broadly, one year before or three years after the issue of the shares. This restriction, and the definition of value, is very similar to that applying to the enterprise investment scheme relief (see **29.31**).

Rollover/holdover relief on replacement of business assets and compulsorily purchased land (TCGA 1992, ss 152–159, 175, 179B, 247)

[29.16] Where there is a chargeable gain on the disposal of a qualifying business asset and the proceeds (or deemed proceeds if the asset is given away) are matched by the acquisition of another qualifying business asset within the period commencing one year before and ending three years after the disposal, a claim may be made for the gain to be deferred. HMRC have discretion to extend the time limit. The replacement asset need not be used in the same trade where one person carries on two or more trades either successively or at the same time. For holding companies and their 75% subsidiaries, the disposal and acquisition need not be made by the same group company, but an asset acquired intra-group on a no gain/no loss basis cannot be treated as a qualifying acquisition.

Qualifying assets

[29.17] The relief applies to land and buildings, fixed plant and machinery, ships, aircraft, hovercraft, satellites, space stations and spacecraft including launch vehicles, goodwill, milk, potato and fish quotas, ewe and suckler cow premium quotas, farmers' payment entitlements under the single payment scheme (SPS) or the basic payment scheme (BPS), and Lloyd's syndicate rights. With regard to the SPS, these payment entitlements ceased in 2014 with new payment entitlements being allocated to farmers under the basic payment scheme. The milk quota system ceased to exist on 31 March 2015. The replacement asset does not have to be in the same category as the asset disposed of, providing both are qualifying assets, and the proceeds of a single disposal could be applied in acquiring several qualifying assets or vice versa.

For companies, disposals of goodwill and fish and agricultural quotas on or after 1 April 2002 and of farmers' BPS entitlements are dealt with under the intangible assets rules (see **20.35** to **20.41**) rather than the capital gains tax rules. Disposals of other qualifying assets by companies on or after 1 April 2002 cannot be rolled over against acquisitions of goodwill, quotas and BPS on or after that date.

If only part of the sale proceeds is used to acquire replacement assets within the rollover period, the remaining part of the gain is chargeable immediately, subject to entrepreneurs' relief if appropriate (see **29.2**), treating the gain as the last part of the proceeds to be used. If the claimant did not use the original asset for the purposes of the business during part of the period of ownership, the expenditure on acquisition and disposal are apportioned by reference to the period and extent of business and non-business use. Only the part of the overall gain applicable to the business use qualifies for rollover relief. For these purposes, the period of ownership excludes any period before 31 March 1982.

See **4.25** for the treatment of disposals by companies after 5 April 1988 that are affected by deferred gains on assets acquired before 31 March 1982. See CHAPTER **31** for further details in relation to farming assets. See **41.12** for the overseas aspect of rollover/holdover relief.

Rollover relief

[29.18] If the replacement asset has a predictable life of more than 60 years (e.g. freehold land or, for individuals, goodwill or farmers' basic payment entitlements), the gain may be rolled over and treated as reducing the cost of the replacement asset.

If a gain has been rolled over in this way against a replacement asset acquired before 31 March 1982, the effect of using 31 March 1982 value as the cost of such an asset is that the rolled-over gain escapes tax altogether.

Holdover relief for depreciating assets

[29.19] If the replacement is a depreciating asset with a life of 60 years or less (which in fact applies to most of the business assets qualifying for relief), the gain does not reduce the capital gains tax cost of the replacement but it is held over for a maximum of ten years. The held-over gain becomes chargeable when the replacement asset is sold or ceases to be used in a business carried on by the taxpayer, or, at latest, ten years after acquisition of the replacement asset (see Example 1). The gain will not crystallise at that point, however, if at or before that time a non-depreciating asset has been acquired against which a claim is made for the gain to be rolled over instead.

Example 1

A qualifying business asset that cost £200,000 in June 2000 was sold by a sole trader on 1 May 2017 for £300,000, giving rise to a gain of £100,000. A qualifying replacement asset (freehold land) was acquired within rollover period for:

£360,000	Full gain reinvested, therefore CGT cost of replacement reduced to £260,000. No entrepreneurs' relief is due when the whole of the gain accruing upon the disposal of the old asset is rolled over against the acquisition cost of the new asset. There is no chargeable gain at that time and therefore there is no 'relevant gain' for the purposes of TCGA 1992, s 169N(1) (see HMRC Capital Gains Manual CG64136). Entrepreneurs' relief may be available on a subsequent disposal of the replacement asset if the relevant criteria are met (see 29.2).
£290,000	£10,000 of the proceeds (and hence the gain) not reinvested, so gain of £10,000 chargeable immediately (unless other qualifying assets acquired within rollover period) but entrepreneurs' relief will be available so the gain will be taxed at 10% (see CG64136 as above). £90,000 of gain deducted from £290,000 cost of replacement, reducing CGT cost to £200,000.
£198,000	No part of gain reinvested therefore full £100,000 chargeable (at 10% because entrepreneurs' relief due) unless other qualifying assets acquired within rollover period.

If the replacement had been a depreciating asset, there would be no change in the gains immediately chargeable. The CGT cost of the replacement asset would, however, not be reduced. Instead that part of the gain that was reinvested would be deferred for up to ten years (see above).

Both rolled-over and held-over gains escape tax completely on the tax-payer's death.

Claims

[29.20] Rollover/holdover relief claims must give full details of assets disposed of and acquired, including dates and amounts (and where two group companies are involved, they must make a joint claim). For companies, the time limit for the original rollover or holdover claim is four years from the end of the accounting period to which the claim relates. The time limit for individuals is four years from the end of the tax year to which the claim relates. The claim will normally be sent in with the tax return. There is a form for individuals to make the claim in HMRC Helpsheet HS290.

Where the replacement asset(s) have not been acquired by the due date for the return, a provisional claim may be made with the return for the tax year or company accounting period in which the disposal took place, and the relief is then given as for an actual claim. The provisional claim will be superseded by an actual claim, or will be withdrawn, or will cease to have effect:

(a)   for an individual, three years from 31 January following the tax year of disposal (e.g. for a disposal in 2016–17 provisional relief would no longer apply after 31 January 2021), or

(b)   for a company, on the fourth anniversary of the last day of the accounting period of disposal.

All necessary adjustments will then be made, including interest on underpaid tax from the date the tax would have been payable if no provisional claim had been made. Where a holdover claim is being replaced by a rollover claim as a result of the later acquisition of a non-depreciating asset (which could in fact be up to 13 years after the disposal giving rise to the gain that had been held over), it is thought that the claim to switch from holdover to rollover relief would need to be sent in with the return for the year in which the non-depreciating asset was acquired.

The strict rules for rollover relief are relaxed by various HMRC concessions, notably D16 and D22–D25. There are anti-avoidance provisions to counter abuse of the concessions (see **4.39**).

Personally owned assets and investment property

[29.21] Rollover relief is also available where an asset owned personally and used in the owner's trading or professional partnership or personal trading company is disposed of and replaced. A 'personal trading company' is one in which the individual owns 5% or more of the voting rights. The receipt of rent from the partnership or trading company does not affect the availability of the relief. HMRC consider that both assets should be used for the purposes of the trade of the same personal company.

Apart from that exception, rollover relief is only available on investment property in two instances. If the property is the subject of compulsory purchase (or compulsory acquisition by a lessee), the relief is available provided that the replacement is not a capital gains tax exempt dwelling house — see **32.34**. Companies in a 75% group can claim this relief if one company makes a disposal under a compulsory purchase order and another acquires the replacement. The relief is also available on property let as furnished holiday accommodation (see **32.30**).

[29.22] There are several anti-avoidance provisions designed to prevent a person rolling over a gain into an asset which would not itself give rise to a chargeable gain on disposal because of the residence status of the person concerned. From 6 April 2015, relief for replacement of business assets on a non-resident CGT disposal (see **41.50**) may only be claimed where the new assets are interests in UK land which consist of or include a dwelling immediately after they are acquired.

Enterprise investment scheme

Income tax relief (ITA 2007, Pt 5)

[29.23] Income tax relief currently at 30% is given where a 'qualifying investor' subscribes for shares in a company, and both the shares and the company meet several requirements. The relief is subject to detailed anti-avoidance provisions. HMRC guidance on the enterprise investment scheme (EIS) is available at www.gov.uk/guidance/venture-capital-schemes-apply-for-the-enterprise-investment-scheme. Subject to any future legislation, it is proposed that the relief will cease on 6 April 2025.

The subscription must normally be wholly in cash and be fully paid up at the time of issue. The shares must be issued to raise money for a qualifying business activity (see below) and, for shares issued on or after 22 April 2009, it must all be so used within two years of the date of issue of the shares, or commencement of the trade if later. In addition, for shares issued on or after 18 November 2015 the money raised must be used for the growth and development of the company (or subsidiary company), and not for funding a takeover or buyout of an existing trade.

The are detailed rules about the requirements to be met by the investors, the issuing company and the shares issued, and these are summarised below.

[29.24] A 'qualifying investor' is one who is not 'connected' with the company in a specified period. This rule mainly excludes someone who is or has been an employee or director, or who controls more than 30% of the company's capital (excluding loan capital for shares issued after 5 April 2012) or voting power (the rights of associates being counted), or is able to secure that the company's affairs are conducted in accordance with his wishes. Someone who was not connected with the company before the shares were issued may, however, become a paid director without affecting his entitlement to relief. Non-resident investors are eligible but should bear in mind that EIS reliefs are reliefs against UK tax. In addition, for shares issued on or after 18 November 2015, investors must be independent from the company at the time of its first share issue. Therefore, if an individual subscribes for shares in a company in which he already holds shares, the new shares will not be eligible for EIS unless the existing shares are from an investment in the company under either EIS, the seed enterprise investment scheme (see **29.37**), or social investment tax relief (see **29.55**), or the shares are founders' shares.

[29.25] The shares must be new ordinary shares that are not redeemable for at least three years, but which, for those issued from 6 April 2012, may carry certain preferential rights to dividends. The arrangements surrounding the issue of shares must not provide for a 'pre-arranged exit', though September 2017 Finance Bill, which is expected to receive Royal Assent in November 2017, provides that this does not prevent the company from issuing shares after 4 December 2016 which carry a right to a future conversion into shares of another class within that company; there must be no disqualifying arrangements which result in investment in companies which would otherwise be unlikely to exist in the first place, or would be unlikely to carry on the proposed activities; the shares must be issued for genuine commercial reasons and not as part of a tax avoidance scheme; and there is an exclusion for shares linked to certain loans.

[29.26] For shares issued after 5 April 2012 the annual amount raised by an issuing company through risk capital schemes, including the EIS and any other investment which constitutes a state aid, must not exceed £5 million. In addition, for shares issued on or after 18 November 2015 there is a limit on the amount of risk finance investment at the issue date of £12 million (£20 million for knowledge-intensive companies), and this can be extended for a further three years in some cases. The issuing company must be an unquoted company (shares on the Alternative Investment Market and the PLUS Markets, with the exception of PLUS-listed, being regarded as unquoted), have a permanent establishment in the UK, and must be neither a subsidiary of, nor under the control of, another company. Relief is not available if it is reasonable to assume that the company would be treated as an 'enterprise in difficulty' for the purposes of the European Commission's Rescuing and Restructuring Guidelines.

For shares issued after 5 April 2012 the total gross assets of the company (and, where relevant, other companies in the same group) must not exceed £15 million immediately before the issue of the shares, nor £16 million immediately afterwards. The issuing company (or, where, relevant, the group) must have fewer than 250 full-time equivalent employees (500 for knowledge-intensive companies for shares issued on or after 18 November 2015).

Any subsidiary of the qualifying company must be its 'qualifying subsidiary', i.e. broadly a 51% subsidiary, and any 'property managing subsidiary' must be a 'qualifying 90% subsidiary'.

[29.27] The issuing company must exist wholly for the purpose of carrying on one or more qualifying trades or be the parent company of a group whose business does not consist wholly or substantially in carrying on 'non-qualifying' activities. A qualifying business activity must be carried on by either the issuing company or a qualifying 90% subsidiary, and is defined as (a) carrying on, or preparing to carry on, a qualifying trade (see below), or (b) carrying on research and development meeting certain conditions.

A qualifying trade is a trade that is conducted on a commercial basis and with a view to the realisation of profits and does not at any time in a specified period consist wholly or substantially in carrying on excluded activities. Dealing in land or shares, banking, insurance, leasing, providing legal or accountancy services, property development and farming are among the many excluded activities (ITA 2007, ss 192–199).

Various amendments have been made in recent years to what constitutes a qualifying business activity. In particular, for shares issued after 5 April 2012 money used to buy shares or stock in a company is not a qualifying business activity, and for shares issued after 5 April 2016 all energy generation activities are excluded.

For shares issued on or after 18 November 2015 there is an age limit on the business activities of companies issuing shares under EIS. A company's first EIS investment must be within seven years of making its first commercial sale (ten years if a knowledge-intensive company) unless certain other conditions are met.

HMRC state that relief will not be available for film and TV co-productions because the trade of the company will be carried on by a person other than that company or a 90% subsidiary. They also consider that relief is not available where the activity is carried on by the company in partnership or by a limited liability partnership of which the company is a member (see **23.33**), see HMRC Brief 77/2009 for full details.

[29.28] HMRC's Small Company Enterprise Centre operates an 'advance assurance scheme' that allows a company to submit its plans before the shares are issued and seek advice on whether the proposed issue is likely to qualify for

EIS relief, and this process was updated from 6 April 2015 to exclude certain companies, see www.gov.uk/government/publications/enterprise-investment-scheme-and-venture-capital-trusts-new-procedures. The application can be made on Form EIS/SEIS(AA). The Enterprise Investment Scheme Association (EISA), whose members are accountants, lawyers and professional firms advising EIS companies and investors, may also be able to give general advice.

HMRC are in the process of creating a digital submission and claims process for venture capital schemes. It is initially available by invitation only for unrepresented companies seeking to obtain an advance assurance for a proposed investment under EIS, SEIS or from a VCT. Companies should be able to submit a compliance statement online by late 2017 and eventually agents will be able to submit applications on behalf of clients.

Claims

[29.29] Claims for relief cannot be made until a certificate has been received from the company, issued on the authority of an HMRC officer, stating that the relevant conditions have been satisfied. Providing the certificates are received in time, claims may be included in tax returns, or amendments to returns. Otherwise claims are made on the form incorporated in the certificate from the company, and this form must also be submitted, even if a claim is made in a return, if the shares were issued in a previous year, and/or if the claim is for capital gains deferral relief. The overall time limit for claiming the relief is five years from the 31 January following the tax year in which the shares are issued. If any of the requirements for a 'qualifying individual' are breached during a 'relevant period' — broadly three years after the issue of the shares, the relief will be withdrawn (see **29.31**).

Amount of relief

[29.30] From 6 April 2012 the maximum amount on which an individual can claim income tax relief in a tax year is £1 million.

This annual limit is available to each spouse or civil partner. Relief is given in the tax year in which the shares are subscribed for, but the amount subscribed can be carried back for relief in the previous tax year, subject to the overriding investment limit for any year. Although the tax saving from the carry-back claim is calculated by reference to the tax position of the earlier year, it reduces the tax liability of the tax year in which the shares are subscribed for, so that any interest on overpaid tax will run only from 31 January after the end of that tax year — see **9.16**. The claim for carry-back must be made at the same time as the claim for relief.

Income tax relief is given at 30% of the qualifying amount in calculating the individual's income tax liability for the year. The tax saved cannot, however, exceed the tax payable on the investor's income. Investors may restrict a claim in respect of a single issue of shares in order to obtain income tax relief on only some of the shares.

Withdrawal of relief

[29.31] The shares must be held for a minimum of (broadly) three years (other than disposals to the investor's spouse or civil partner, or when the investor dies), otherwise the relief is withdrawn completely if the disposal is not at arm's length, and the tax saving is lost on the amount received for an arm's length bargain.

Relief is also withdrawn if the individual receives value from the company within, broadly, one year before or three years after the issue of the shares. 'Value' is exhaustively defined and includes the repayment of loans that had been made to the company before the shares were issued, the provision of benefits, and purchase of assets for less than market value. It does not, however, include dividends that do not exceed a normal return on the loans made ꓸꓸꓸ ꓸ receipts of insignificant value are ignored. The repayment of unless the repayment is' ꓵꓸꓸꓸ were issued does not constitute value received acquisition of the shares. ꓸꓸꓸction with any arrangements for the

An amount received in respect of an option to sell EIS shares will cause the loss of an appropriate amount of relief, but an arrangement to sell them (say to the controlling shareholders) after the qualifying period will not.

Relief is withdrawn at the original EIS rate at which it was given — i.e. 20% before 6 April 2011, 30% thereafter. Where relief is to be withdrawn, HMRC will issue an assessment outside the self-assessment system. The due date for payment of any income tax charged, and therefore the start date for interest, in such an assessment is in line with the general date for income tax, i.e. 31 January following the tax year for which the assessment is made.

Capital gains tax reliefs

CGT exemption (TCGA 1992, ss 150A, 150B)

[29.32] There is no charge to capital gains tax if shares for which EIS income tax relief has been given are disposed of at a profit after a retention period of (broadly) three years, although deferred gains may become chargeable under the deferral relief provisions outlined below. There is no exemption for disposals within the retention period (and EIS income tax relief will be withdrawn as indicated above). Gains may, however, be deferred if reinvested in new EIS shares (see **29.33**). If the disposal results in a loss, relief is available for the loss whether the disposal is within or outside the retention period, but in calculating a loss, the allowable cost is reduced by the EIS income tax relief that has not been withdrawn (see Example 2). A loss can be relieved either against chargeable gains (including deferred gains triggered by the disposal), or against income (under the provisions outlined at **38.23**).

Example 2

	£
Cost of shares acquired under EIS	10,000
Income tax relief at 30%	(3,000)
Net cost of investment	7,000
Disposed of six years later for	6,500
Cost net of EIS relief	(7,000(
Loss available for relief	(£500)

The normal capital gains tax identification and pooling rules (see **38.18**) do not apply to EIS shares. Where shares have been acquired at diff... where disposals are identified with shares acquired earlier ranked first with shares shares were acquired on the same day, disposal capital gains deferral relief (see to which neither EIS income tax reli... **29.33** to **29.35**) nor SEIS relief (see **29.37**) is attributable, then with shares to which SEIS relief is attributable, then with shares to which deferral relief but not income tax relief is attributable, then with shares to which income tax relief but not deferral relief is attributable, and finally shares to which both reliefs are attributable.

CGT deferral relief (TCGA 1992, ss 150C, 150D, 169U and Schs 5B, 5BA)

[29.33] A claim may be made for all or any part of a chargeable gain on the disposal of *any* asset (or a gain arising on a chargeable event under the EIS, see **29.32**, or venture capital trust provisions, see **29.44**) to be deferred to the extent that it is matched by a qualifying subscription for EIS shares within one year before and three years after the disposal. HMRC may extend these time limits in some circumstances.

There are several conditions and anti-avoidance rules attached to deferral relief, and professional advice is recommended before proceeding with an investment. The relief is only available if the investor is resident in the UK. The subscription for the shares must be wholly in cash, the issue must not be part of arrangements to avoid tax, and the shares must be issued to raise money for a qualifying business activity. The money raised must be used for that purpose within two years. Relief is not available where there are guaranteed exit etc. arrangements. For shares issued after 5 April 2012 the annual amount raised by an issuing company through risk capital schemes including the EIS must not exceed £5 million.

Gains may be deferred whether or not income tax relief was available on the EIS shares. For disposals on or after 23 June 2010 and before 4 December 2014 an individual could choose between claiming entrepreneurs' relief and paying tax on the gain at 10%, or deferring the gain under the EIS rules and paying tax later when the gain comes into charge at the appropriate rate (see **4.2**). However, gains which would have originally accrued on or after 3 December 2014 but which are deferred into EIS remain eligible for entrepreneurs' relief when the deferred gain becomes chargeable (see **29.10**).

[29.34] The deferred gain (as distinct from the gain on the EIS shares, which is dealt with at **29.32**) becomes chargeable on any of a number of specified events occurring within a certain period (normally three years). These events include disposal of the shares (other than to a spouse or civil partner living with the investor during the tax year); the investor becoming non-resident; and the shares ceasing to be eligible shares (for example, where the company ceases to be a qualifying company). The deferred gain is not triggered if the investor (or a spouse or civil partner to whom the shares have been transferred) dies. Where the gain is triggered, it may be further deferred by another EIS investment if the conditions are satisfied.

> **Example 3**
>
> In May 2017 an investor buys shares in a qualifying EIS company from an existing shareholder for £40,000. On 1 January 2018 he subscribes £90,000 for further shares, so that his total investment in the tax year is £130,000.
>
> He will get 30% income tax relief on the £90,000 subscribed for new shares. No relief is available for the purchased shares.
>
> Gains realised up to three years before (or 12 months after) an EIS subscription can be deferred into the EIS shares. Therefore gains of up to £90,000 can be so deferred if they are realised between 1 January 2015 (i.e. three years before the subscription) and 1 January 2019 (i.e. 12 months after the subscription).

[29.35] Where a charge to capital gains tax in respect of all or part of a gain arising to an investor before 6 April 2008 has been deferred and all or part of it comes into charge on the occasion of a 'chargeable event' on or after 6 April 2008, entrepreneurs' relief (see **29.2**) may be claimed at the time of the 'first relevant chargeable event' in respect of the whole of the deferred gain that attaches to the shares held by the investor immediately before that event. The gain attached to any shares transferred to a spouse or civil partner, and not held by the investor at the time of that event will not be eligible for the relief. The entrepreneurs' relief can only be claimed in respect of the deferred gain if the 'relevant disposal' (broadly the disposal on which the original gain arose) would have been a 'material disposal of business assets' if entrepreneurs' relief were in force at the time of that disposal (for further details see HMRC Capital Gains Manual CG64170, and CG64171 which gives an example).

Withdrawal of investment after relevant period

[29.36] Potential investors may see a disadvantage in their being locked in as minority shareholders. The company may, however, build up reserves by retaining profits, and use the reserves to purchase its own shares after three years, using the rules described in **29.58**. The rules regarding 'pre-arranged exits' (see **29.25**) and a possible trap where value is received by other investors must be borne in mind.

Seed Enterprise Investment Scheme (ITA 2007, Pt 5A; TCGA 1992, ss 150E–150G and Sch 5BB)

[29.37] Investment relief is available through the Seed Enterprise Investment Scheme (SEIS), which is similar to the Enterprise Investment Scheme (EIS — see **29.23**) in many of its scheme rules. However, SEIS is focused on smaller, early stage companies carrying on, or preparing to carry on, a new business in a qualifying trade. HMRC guidance on the SEIS is available at and www.go v.uk/topic/business-tax/investment-schemeswww.gov.uk/guidance/venture-cap ital-schemes-apply-to-use-the-seed-enterprise-investment-scheme.

SEIS is available to companies which, together with any subsidiaries, have less than 25 full-time equivalent employees and assets of no more than £200,000. Any trade carried on by a company at the date of issue of the shares must be less than two years old (whether or not the trade was begun by the company, or another person and then transferred). The amount of all SEIS investment together with any other de minimis state aid received by the company in a three-year period must not exceed £150,000. If the relevant issue of shares takes the total over £150,000, then the excess will not qualify for relief.

[29.38] A qualifying investor is entitled to income tax relief for his investment within certain limits (see **29.42**), and a capital gains tax reinvestment relief is available for investments into SEIS (see **29.43**). In addition, there is no charge to capital gains tax if shares on which SEIS income tax relief has been given are disposed of at a profit after a retention period of three years. A 'qualifying investor' is one with no control over the issuing company or a subsidiary, and no more than a 30% interest in the share capital, voting power or assets on winding up of those companies in the period from incorporation of the issuing company to three years after the date of issue of the shares (the rights of associates being counted). He must not be an employee of the issuing company or a subsidiary during the three-year period from the date of issue of the shares. Directors are not excluded, provided they do not have a substantial interest, but an associate of the investor cannot be an employee in the specified period. There are exclusions for linked loans, related investment and tax avoidance arrangements. A subsidiary is broadly a 51% subsidiary for these purposes.

[29.39] The subscription must normally be wholly in cash and be fully paid up at the time of issue. In this regard, HMRC advise companies and investors to ensure that any shares on which it is intended SEIS relief will be claimed are not issued during the company registration process but are issued only at a later date when the company is able to receive payment for them. The shares must be new ordinary shares that are not redeemable for at least three years, but which may carry certain preferential rights to dividends. They must be issued to raise money for a qualifying business activity carried on, or to be carried on, by the company or by a qualifying 90% subsidiary and all that money must be spent on that activity within three years of the date of issue of the shares. The arrangements surrounding the issue of shares must not provide for a 'pre-arranged exit', though September 2017 Finance Bill, which is expected to receive Royal Assent in November 2017, provides that this does not prevent the company from issuing shares after 4 December 2016 which carry a right to a future conversion into shares of another class within that company; there must be no disqualifying arrangements which result in investment in companies which would otherwise be unlikely to exist in the first place, or would be unlikely to carry on the proposed activities; and the shares must be issued for genuine commercial reasons and not as part of a tax avoidance scheme.

[29.40] The company must be a qualifying company in relation to the shares. Broadly it must exist wholly for the purposes of carrying on one or more qualifying business activities or be the parent company of a group whose business does not consist wholly or substantially in carrying on 'non-qualifying' activities. The issuing company or a qualifying 90% subsidiary must carry on the qualifying business activity, which is defined broadly as (a) carrying on, or preparing to carry on, a relevant new qualifying trade, or (b) carrying on research and development meeting certain conditions. The issuing company must have a permanent establishment in the UK and relief will not be available if it is reasonable to assume that the company would be an 'enterprise in difficulty' for the purposes of the European Commission's Rescuing and Restructuring guidelines.

The activities which are excluded from being a qualifying trade, and the definition of qualifying trade are the same as those for EIS (see **29.26** and **29.27**). The issuing company must be unquoted (shares on the Alternative Investment Market and the PLUS Markets, with the exception of PLUS-listed, being regarded as unquoted) and it must not be under the control of another company. However, for shares issued on or after 6 April 2013 the 'on-the-shelf period' is not taken into account for determining whether a company is under the control of another. This period is one in which the issuing company has not issued any shares other than subscriber shares and has not begun to carry on or make preparations to carry on any trade or business. This means that companies established in the first instance by corporate formation agents before being sold on to their ultimate owners will not inadvertently be disqualified from taking advantage of SEIS. The issuing company or any 90% subsidiary cannot be a member of a partnership and neither the issuing company nor any 51% subsidiary may have previously raised money under either EIS or venture capital trust (VCT — see **29.44**) schemes.

[29.41] HMRC's Small Company Enterprise Centre operates an 'advance assurance scheme' that allows a company to submit its plans before the shares are issued and seek advice on whether the proposed issue is likely to qualify for SEIS reliefs. The company must be incorporated but does not have to be registered for corporation tax to be able to apply for advance assurance. The application can be made on Form EIS/SEIS(AA).

See **29.28** regarding the new digital submission and claims process being created for venture capital schemes.

Income tax relief

[29.42] Income tax relief at 50% is given to a qualifying investor on the amount he subscribes for shares, subject to an overall investment limit per tax year of £100,000. All or part of an investment made in one year may be treated as made in the previous year, subject to the overall limit for that year. The rules for claiming relief and the way in which the relief is given are broadly the same as outlined for EIS in **29.29** to **29.30**, except a compliance statement must not be made by the company, and therefore relief cannot be claimed by investors, until the new qualifying trade has been carried on for at least four months or at least 70% of the money raised has been spent. As is the case for EIS, the shares must be held for a minimum of three years (other than disposals to the investor's spouse or civil partner, or when the investor dies), otherwise the relief is withdrawn completely if the disposal is not at arm's length, and the tax saving is lost on the amount received for an arm's length bargain. Relief is also withdrawn if the individual receives value from the company within the period from incorporation to three years after the issue of the shares. 'Value' for these purposes is as defined for EIS (see **29.31**). Assessments will be raised in the same way as for EIS to effect the withdrawal of the relief.

Capital gains tax reliefs

[29.43] There is no charge to capital gains tax if shares on which SEIS income tax relief has been given are disposed of at a profit after a retention period of three years. If the disposal results in a loss, relief is available for the loss whether the disposal is within or outside the retention period, but in calculating a loss, the allowable cost is reduced by the SEIS income tax relief that has not been withdrawn. A loss can be relieved either against chargeable gains, or against income (under the provisions outlined at **38.23**).

> **Example 4**
>
> In January 2018 B invested £50,000 in SEIS shares and claimed SEIS income tax relief of £25,000. In May 2021 he sells the shares for £20,000 making a loss of £30,000. If the income tax relief is not withdrawn he will have an allowable loss of £5,000.

The normal capital gains tax identification and pooling rules (see **38.18**) do not apply to SEIS shares. Where shares have been acquired at different times, disposals are identified with shares acquired earlier rather than later. Where shares were acquired on the same day, disposals are identified first with shares to which no SEIS income tax relief is attributable, then with shares to which SEIS income tax relief but not SEIS reinvestment relief (see below) is attributable, and finally shares to which both reliefs are attributable.

Individuals may claim capital gains reinvestment relief where they realise capital gains on disposals of assets and in the same tax year make investments that qualify for, and they claim, SEIS income tax relief. From 2013–14 the relief applies to half the qualifying reinvested amount. An investor could thus make a maximum tax-free gain of £50,000 where the conditions are met. If the investor subscribes for shares eligible for SEIS income tax relief that are issued in 2017–18, he may make a carry-back claim as if a specified part of that issue had instead been issued in 2016–17. The reinvestment relief then also has effect as if that part had been issued on a day in 2016–17 and consequently matched with gains on disposals made in 2016–17. Note that the whole of the proceeds need not be reinvested for relief to be available. The exemption is restricted where the amount subscribed for SEIS shares exceeds the maximum £100,000 on which income tax relief may be claimed. The formula used is—

SA/TSA x £100,000

where SA is the SEIS expenditure and TSA is the total amount subscribed for shares issued in the relevant year in respect of which the investor is eligible for and claims SEIS relief for that year.

Example 5

In 2017–18 an investor makes a gain of £120,000. He subscribes for £40,000 SEIS shares on 1 August 2017. He subscribes for a further £110,000 of shares on 1 February 2018. He claims full SEIS income tax relief in respect of both share issues. The SEIS reinvestment relief is restricted to—

Subscription 1 August 2017   £40,000/150,000 x 100,000 = £26,667
Subscription 1 February 2018   £110,000/150,000 x 100,000 = £73,333

Total reinvestment relief is £100,000 on which relief is available at 50% and so the gain is reduced to £70,000.

The time limit for claims is the same as for the income tax relief but the investor can make the SEIS reinvestment claim before the SEIS income tax relief claim. If the income tax relief is reduced or withdrawn (see **29.42**), the reinvestment relief is reduced or withdrawn in the same proportion and a capital gain will arise. Unlike EIS there is no stipulation in the legislation that becoming non-resident triggers a gain.

Venture capital trusts (ITA 2007, Pt 6; TCGA 1992, ss 100, 151A, 151B and Sch 5C; ITTOIA 2005, ss 709–712)

[29.44] Those who wish to support new and expanding companies but are unwilling to invest directly in unquoted shares may obtain tax relief for investment through venture capital trusts (VCTs) that is similar in many respects to that available under the EIS (see **29.23**). HMRC guidance on VCTs is available at www.gov.uk/topic/business-tax/investment-schemes. Subject to any future legislation, it is proposed that the relief will cease on 6 April 2025.

Individual investors aged 18 or over can acquire shares in a VCT in order to be entitled to two income tax reliefs and relief from capital gains tax as set out below. From 17 July 2014 the subscription can be made on the individual's behalf by a nominee, and where this occurs, HMRC are able to identify the beneficial owner.

VCTs are quoted companies holding at least 70% of their 'investments' (known as 'qualifying holdings') in shares or securities they have subscribed for in qualifying unquoted companies with a permanent establishment in the UK. Shares listed on the Alternative Investment Market and the PLUS

Markets, with the exception of PLUS-listed, are regarded as unquoted. Disposals of shares held for at least six months will not be taken into account for the six months after disposal when considering the 70% rule. At least 70% of such holdings must be in 'eligible' shares (broadly ordinary non-redeemable shares which may carry certain preferential rights to dividends but no right to the company's assets in a winding up), and no single holding may be more than 15% of total investments. Furthermore, loans or securities that are guaranteed are excluded and at least 10% of the total investment in any company must be ordinary, non-preferential shares. Shares are excluded if it is reasonable to assume that the company would be treated as an 'enterprise in difficulty' for the purposes of the European Commission's Rescue and Restructuring Guidelines. For investments made on or after 18 November 2015 a VCT's investment in a company must be within seven years of the company making its first commercial sale (ten years if a knowledge-intensive company) unless certain other conditions are met.

[29.45] VCTs are exempt from tax on their capital gains. There are anti-avoidance provisions to prevent the exemption being exploited by means of intra-group transfers, or by transferring a company's business to a VCT or to a company that later becomes a VCT.

There are regulations that enable VCTs to retain their tax approval when they merge (see in particular **29.49**) and also treat VCTs as being approved while they are being wound up. Investors do not therefore lose their tax reliefs in these circumstances.

[29.46] All of the money invested in a company by the VCT must be used for the purposes of the company's trade within two years. The VCT must not retain more than 15% of its income from shares and securities and must satisfy the gross assets test (see below).

The issuing (investee) company must meet the same trading requirement as an EIS set out at **29.27** and the main exclusions from the definition of qualifying trading company are the same as for the EIS. The total gross assets of the issuing company (and, where relevant, other companies in the same group) must not exceed £15 million immediately before the VCT acquired the holding, or £16 million immediately afterwards.

[29.47] The issuing company (or, where relevant, the group) must have fewer than 250 full-time equivalent employees (500 for knowledge-intensive companies for shares issued on or after 18 November 2015), and the annual amount raised by an issuing company through risk capital schemes (including any which constitute a state aid), including VCTs, must not exceed £5 million. In addition, for shares issued on or after 18 November 2015 there is a limit on the amount of risk finance investment at the issue date of £12 million (£20 million for knowledge-intensive companies), and this can be extended for a further three years in some cases. The VCT cannot make an investment in the investee company which will result in the total annual investment in that investee company through risk capital schemes by any company exceeding £5 million (with the same £12 million or £20 million limit applying at the issue date for shares issued on or after 18 November 2015). VCTs cannot invest more than £1 million in any single company where, broadly, that company is a member of a partnership or joint venture which carries on the qualifying trade. For investments made on or after 18 November 2015, a VCT is prevented from investing in a company that goes on to use the money to acquire an existing trade, or part of a trade.

[29.48] See 29.28 regarding the advance assurance scheme that operates for EIS and which was updated from 6 April 2015 to exclude certain companies. For VCTs there is a risk that investments made in such companies may count as non-qualifying holdings.

Income tax reliefs

[29.49] When new ordinary shares are *subscribed for*, income tax relief may be claimed on up to £200,000 of the amount subscribed each tax year. The rate of relief is 30%. Claims may be made in tax returns. The tax saved cannot exceed the tax payable on the investor's income.

There is an exclusion from relief if a linked loan is made to the individual or an associate. For shares issued on or after 6 April 2014 there is a restriction in relief in certain circumstances where the individual receives consideration for a sale of shares which is linked to the subscription for shares. It will not apply to subscriptions for shares where the monies being subscribed represent dividends which the individual has elected to reinvest. Where shares are acquired from a spouse or civil partner, the acquiring spouse/civil partner is treated as if he or she had subscribed for the shares.

The relief will be withdrawn to the extent that any of the shares are disposed of (other than to the holder's spouse or civil partner, or after the holder's death) within five years. If the disposal is at arm's length relief is withdrawn in the proportion that the consideration received on disposal bears to the amount subscribed. A disposal not at arm's length results in the withdrawal of relief that was obtained for the shares disposed of.

The relief will also be withdrawn if the VCT loses its qualifying status within the five-year period. This will apply if the company returns share capital to investors on or after 6 April 2014 and within three years of the end of the accounting period in which the VCT issued the shares, although it will not apply to payments made to redeem or repurchase shares, or to payments which are distributions of assets on a winding up of the company. It will also not apply if two or more VCTs merge and the new share issue corresponds to old shares in the merging VCTs issued before 6 April 2014. Where relief is to be withdrawn, HMRC will issue an assessment outside the self-assessment system, tax being payable within 30 days after the assessment is issued. For assessments made on or after 6 April 2014, the assessment must be made within six years after the end of the tax year.

Dividends from ordinary shares in VCTs are exempt from tax to the extent that not more than £200,000 in total of shares in VCTs are *acquired* each year, whether the shares were acquired by subscription or by purchase from another shareholder.

The reliefs are not available if avoiding tax is a main purpose of acquiring the shares.

Capital gains tax position

CGT exemption

[29.50] Gains arising on the disposal of VCT shares that were acquired by subscription or purchase up to the £200,000 limit in any year are exempt from capital gains tax (and any losses are not allowable). There is no minimum period for which the shares must be held. Disposals are matched with acquisitions according to the rules outlined in **29.52**. Where gains are chargeable, they may be deferred if reinvested in new EIS shares (see **29.33**).

> **Example 6**
>
> Say the facts were the same as in Example 3, except that the purchase of and subscription for shares related to a VCT instead of an EIS company.
>
> The position regarding the income tax relief would be the same. In addition, dividends on both the shares bought for £40,000 and the £90,000 of shares subscribed for would be exempt from income tax. The CGT exemption would apply to the same amount if the shares were disposed of.
>
> It would not, however, be possible to defer capital gains by reference to the investment in the VCT shares (see **29.51**).

CGT deferral relief

[29.51] Deferral relief is not available for gains reinvested in VCT shares issued on or after 6 April 2004. This relief enabled all or any part of gains on the disposal of *any* assets by someone resident or ordinarily resident in the UK to be deferred to the extent that they were reinvested, within one year before or one year after the disposal, in VCT shares on which income tax relief was given and which (where relevant) were still held at the time of the disposal.

Despite the withdrawal of deferral relief, the *deferred* gains (not the gains on the VCT shares themselves) may still become chargeable if the VCT shares are disposed of (other than to a spouse or civil partner), or the VCT loses its approval, or the income tax relief is otherwise withdrawn. The deferred gain is not triggered by the death of the investor (or spouse/civil partner to whom the shares have been transferred). Where deferred gains are triggered, they may again be deferred if further reinvested in new EIS shares (see **29.34**) if the conditions are satisfied. The same provisions regarding entrepreneurs' relief apply as for EIS shares as illustrated in **29.35**, except that the gain deferred would have arisen before 6 April 2004 when the VCT deferral relief was withdrawn.

CGT rules for matching disposals with acquisitions

[29.52] Any disposals of shares in a VCT are identified first with shares acquired before the trust became a VCT. To decide whether other disposals relate to shares acquired in excess of the £200,000 limit in any year (£100,000 for shares acquired before 6 April 2004), disposals are identified with shares acquired earlier rather than those acquired later. Where shares are acquired on the same day, shares acquired in excess of the £200,000 (or £100,000) limit are treated as disposed of before qualifying shares. Any shares not identified with other shares under these rules qualify for the VCT capital gains exemption on disposal, and they are not subject to the normal capital gains tax rules in 38.18 for matching disposals with acquisitions.

Corporate venturing scheme (FA 2000, s 63 and Sch 15)

[29.53] The corporate venturing scheme was available to companies in respect of qualifying shares issued on or after 1 April 2000 and before 1 April 2010. The main rules of the scheme can be found in earlier editions of this book.

Despite the withdrawal of the relief, capital gains may still arise, and previously deferred gains may come back into charge, when the investing company disposes of the qualifying shares.

Community investment tax relief (ITA 2007, ss 333–382; CTA 2010, ss 218–269)

[29.54] Investments made by individuals and companies in a community development finance institution (CDFI) qualify for community investment tax relief (CITR) of 5% per annum of the amount of the investment for a period of five years, so that the total relief is 25%. For an individual, the five-year period commences in the tax year in which the investment is made. For a company the relief applies to the accounting period in which the investment is made and the accounting periods in which the next four anniversaries of the investment date fall. The relief is set against the amount of tax payable. For investments from 1 April 2013 for companies and 6 April 2013 for individuals, the unused balance of the 5% relief can be carried forward and used in a later year as long as some part of the investment still remains within the CDFI. Carry forward will not, however, be permitted beyond the five-year investment period. From 1 April 2013 there is a limit on the amounts of relief a company can obtain in any three-year period — the amount of CITR and any de minimis aid from other sources must not exceed €200,000.

The aim of the relief is to encourage private investment in businesses and social enterprises in disadvantaged communities (referred to as Enterprise Areas) via accredited CDFIs. Investments may be by way of loans or subscription for shares or securities, and CDFIs will supply investors with a tax relief certificate. Claims for relief cannot be made earlier than the end of the tax year or company accounting period in which the investment is made. In the case of loans, the amount of the investment is calculated in each of the five years following the investment date according to the average balance in that year (or, for the third, fourth and fifth years, the average capital balance for the period of six months starting 18 months after the investment date if less).

As with all such schemes, there are detailed conditions that must be complied with, and if the CDFI loses its accreditation in the five years after the investment date, investors will lose the right to claim further relief. The relief will be restricted, or in some circumstances withdrawn completely, if the investor disposes of all or part of the investment or receives value within the five years after the investment date.

For HMRC guidance see www.gov.uk/government/publications/community-i nvestment-tax-relief-citr.

Social investment tax relief (TCGA 1992, ss 255A–255E, Sch 8B; ITA 2007, Pt 5B)

[29.55] Social investment tax relief (SITR) is designed to support social enterprises seeking external finance by offering income and capital gains tax reliefs to individual investors who invest in new shares or new qualifying debt investments in those social enterprises. HMRC guidance is available at www.g ov.uk/topic/business-tax/investment-schemes and www.gov.uk/guidance/ventu re-capital-schemes-apply-to-use-social-investment-tax-relief.

A social enterprise is broadly a community investment company, a community benefit society that is not a charity, a charity, or an accredited social impact contractor (broadly a company limited by shares that has entered into a social impact contract as defined and that is accredited by the Cabinet Office). It must be unquoted at the investment date (broadly the date of issue of the shares or debentures), continue to be a social enterprise until three years after that date, and must not, in that period, control, either alone or with any connected person, a company other than a qualifying subsidiary, or be under the control of another company, or be under the control of another company and any person connected with that company without being a 51% subsidiary. Any subsidiary must be a 'qualifying subsidiary', i.e. broadly a 51% subsidiary, and any 'property-managing subsidiary' must be a '90% social subsidiary' (i.e. a 90% subsidiary which is also a social enterprise). The social enterprise or each 90% social subsidiary must not be a member of a partnership in the three years following the investment date. The social enterprise, or where relevant the group of which it is the parent company, must have less than 500 full-time equivalent employees at the time of investment (though September 2017 Finance Bill, which is expected to receive Royal Assent in November 2017, reduces this to 250 employees for investments made after 5 April 2017), and the total gross assets of the social enterprise (and, where relevant, other companies in the same group) must not exceed £15 million immediately before the investment date, nor £16 million immediately afterwards. The original provisions provide that in the three-year period from the investment date the amount of the investments made in the social enterprise multiplied by the sum of the highest rate of capital gains tax plus the highest rate of social investment income tax relief applying in that period must not exceed €200,000, reduced by any other de minimis aid received from other sources.

Example 7

Social Enterprise Ltd has previously received €50,000 of qualifying investments and had also received a grant of €20,000 which constituted de minimis aid. During the previous three years the highest rate of capital gains tax has been 28% and the highest rate of social investment income tax relief has been 30%.

Social Enterprise Ltd can therefore raise

$$\left(\frac{€200,000 - €20,000}{28\% + 30\%}\right) - €50,000 = €260,344$$

under social investment tax relief.

However, September 2017 Finance Bill provides that for investments made after 5 April 2017 the investment limit is increased to £1.5 million if the social enterprise receives a relevant investment within seven years of its first commercial sale. For investments outside the seven-year period the original limit above will continue to apply unless the relevant investment is a further relevant investment, the first one having been made in the seven-year period and used for a relevant activity.

A social enterprise can still raise money from further investments, but any investments beyond the above limits will not qualify for SITR. If the investment is not made in euros, the amount of the investment should be converted into euros at an appropriate spot rate of exchange at the date the investment was made.

The shares must be subscribed for wholly in cash and be fully paid up at the time of issue and the full amount of the advance covered by debentures must have been made wholly in cash by the investment date. HMRC advise social enterprises to ensure that any investments on which it is intended to claim relief are not issued during the social enterprise registration process but are issued only at a later date when the social enterprise has set up a bank account and is able to receive payment for them, otherwise relief may be denied. The shares must be ordinary shares which do not carry any rights to a fixed return or any rights to the social enterprise's assets in the event of a winding up which rank above the debts of, or other shares in, the social enterprise. A debt investment must be in the form of a debenture which must not carry any charge over assets and must not offer more than a commercial rate of return. The debt must also be subordinated to all other debts of the social enterprise and must rank equally with shares that do not rank above any other shares so far as the law allows.

An investor, or his associate, cannot be an employee, partner, remunerated director, or trustee of the social enterprise or of certain other bodies with relationships with the enterprise, in the period beginning on the incorporation of the social enterprise, or if later 12 months before the investment date, and ending three years after the investment date. The investor or associate cannot have control of the social enterprise or a 51% subsidiary and cannot have, or be entitled to acquire, more than a 30% interest in the share capital, loan capital or voting power of those companies in that same period. September 2017 Finance Bill provides that for investments made after 5 April 2017 the investor, at the time of the investment, must not hold other shares or debentures in the enterprise or its subsidiaries, other than risk finance investments or permitted subscriber shares. There are rules preventing pre-arranged exits, risk-avoidance protection, collusion with a non-qualifying investor, and linked-loans and one of the main purposes of the investment must not be tax avoidance. September 2017 Finance Bill provides that for investments made after 5 April 2017 there must be no disqualifying arrangements — broadly those entered into for the main purpose of ensuring relief is available under SITR, EIS, SEIS, VCTs or share loss relief where the money raised is paid to a person party to the arrangements. The Finance Bill also provides from the same date that relief will not available if it is reasonable to assume that the social enterprise would be treated as an 'enterprise in difficulty' for the purposes of the European Commission's Rescuing and Restructuring Guidelines. Relief is denied to any investor who directly or indirectly owned the trade before it came to be owned by the social enterprise, or who alone or together with others controlled the company which carried on that particular trade.

If the social enterprise is not a charity or an accredited social impact contractor then it, or the group of which it is parent, must carry on a business which does not at any time in the three years from the investment date consist wholly or substantially in carrying on 'excluded' activities (see below) and it must not to any extent carry on non-trade activities. A charity is treated as fulfilling this condition and a social impact contractor will already have entered into a trading contract by the time it seeks accreditation, and it must exist only for that purpose. The social enterprise will not cease to meet this requirement if it, or any of its subsidiaries, go into receivership or administration for genuine commercial reasons. For social enterprises other than an accredited social impact contractor, the money raised (other than insignificant amounts) must be employed within 28 months of the investment date for the purposes of a qualifying trade carried on by the social enterprise or a 90% social subsidiary, or for the purposes of preparing to carry on such a trade which must commence within two years of the investment date. Buying shares or stock in a body is not employing money for these purposes, and September 2017 Finance Bill provides that for investments made after 5 April 2017, nor is the repayment of a loan. The trade must be carried on for at least four months unless the social enterprise is wound up, dissolved, or put into administration or receivership for genuine commercial reasons within that four-month period. A qualifying trade is a trade that is conducted on a commercial basis and with a view to the realisation of profits and does not at any time within three years of the investment date consist wholly or substantially in carrying on excluded activities. Dealing in land or shares, banking, insurance, leasing and property development are among the many excluded activities (ITA 2007, ss 257MQ–257MT). September 2017 Finance Bill added nursing homes and residential care homes to the list of excluded activities, but the Government aims to introduce an accreditation system for these activities in the future. For an accredited social impact contractor the money raised must be employed with 24 months in the carrying out of the social impact contract concerned.

HMRC's Small Company Enterprise Centre operates an 'advance assurance scheme' that allows a social enterprise to submit its plans and seek advice on whether a proposed investment will qualify for SITR.

Income tax relief

[29.56] The investor can claim income tax relief at 30% of the amount invested on or after 6 April 2014 and before 6 April 2019 (though September 2017 Finance Bill, which is expected to receive Royal Assent in November 2017, extends this date to 6 April 2021), on a maximum annual investment of £1 million and may invest in more than one social enterprise. All or part of an investment made in one year may be treated as made in the previous year, subject to the overall relief limit for that year. No relief may be carried back to a year before 2014–15. The investment can be made by a nominee. Investors must have a UK tax liability against which to set the relief but they need not be UK-resident (see, however, the rules for capital gains holdover relief in **29.57**). Relief is not available on any investment in respect of which the investor has obtained relief under EIS (see **29.23**), SEIS (see **29.37**) or the CITR (see **29.54**) scheme. As is the case for EIS and SEIS, the social holding asset must be held for three years (other than disposals to the investor's spouse or civil partner, or when the investor dies), otherwise the relief is withdrawn completely if the disposal is not at arm's length, and the tax saving is lost on the amount received for an arm's length bargain (see **29.31**). Relief is also withdrawn if the investor receives value from the company within three years of the investment date. 'Value' for these purposes is similar, but not identical, to that defined for EIS (see **29.31**). Relief may also be withdrawn if various conditions are breached within the period for which they apply. Assessments will be raised in the same way as for EIS to effect the withdrawal of the relief.

The claim for relief may not be made earlier than the end of the period of four months for which the trade must have been carried on (other than where the social enterprise is an accredited social impact contractor for which this trading provision does not apply), and not later than the fifth anniversary of the self-assessment filing date for the tax year in which the investment is made. The investor must receive a compliance certificate from the company before making the claim.

Capital gains tax relief

[29.57] There are two capital gains tax reliefs available. There is a holdover relief for gains reinvested in social enterprises, and a disposal relief where the investment is subsequently disposed of after a minimum period. Holdover relief is available where an individual investor has a chargeable gain, he acquires one or more social holding assets, he is entitled to the social investment income tax relief on the consideration paid for the assets under ITA 2007, Pt 5B, and the following conditions are also met:

(a)   The gain accrues on or after 6 April 2014 and before 6 April 2019 (though note that this date can be extended by regulations, and September 2017 Finance Bill, which is expected to receive Royal Assent in November 2017, extends the date for the income tax relief to 6 April 2021) either on the disposal of any asset, or under the entrepreneurs' relief provisions (but only to the extent that the deemed gain would not be chargeable to capital gains tax at the 10% rate), or when a chargeable event occurs on the disposal of the social holding because either the asset is cancelled, extinguished, redeemed or repaid, or any of the conditions for eligibility for the income tax relief fail to be met.

(b)   The investor must be UK-resident when the gain accrues and when the social holding is acquired, and must be acting on his or her own behalf in making the investment, and not as a partner, trustee or personal representative.

(c)   The social holding is acquired in the period of one year before or three years after the day that the gain accrues.

Gains realised on or after 3 December 2014 which are eligible for entrepreneurs' relief, but which are instead deferred into investments which qualify for social investment tax relief, will remain eligible for entrepreneurs' relief when the gain is realised (see **29.10**).

There is an upper limit of £1 million on the gains which may be relieved under these provisions by the investor in any tax year. It is not necessary that the social investment income tax relief is claimed in order for holdover relief to be available. The relief can also be used to continue to defer a gain which accrues on the occurrence of certain chargeable events if the asset is replaced by a second social holding issued by the same enterprise, even if no cash is given for the second holding. There are provisions to prevent relief where relief has already been obtained under EIS deferral (see **29.33**) or SEIS reinvestment relief (see **29.43**).

The claim may not be made earlier than the end of the period of four months for which the trade must have been carried on (other than where the social enterprise is an accredited social impact contractor for which this trading provision does not apply), and not later than the fifth anniversary of the self-assessment filing date for the tax year in which the investment is made. The investor must receive a compliance certificate from the company before making the claim.

A gain equal to the amount held over will be brought back into charge on any of a number of specified events occurring. These events are a disposal of all or part of the asset other than to a spouse or civil partner; a disposal of all or part of the asset by a person who acquired it from their spouse or civil partner, other than a disposal back to the investor; all or part of the asset is cancelled, extinguished, redeemed or repaid; or any of the conditions for eligibility for the income tax relief fail to be met. A gain does not accrue if the investor (or spouse or civil partner to whom the asset has been transferred) dies. Unlike EIS there is no stipulation in the legislation that becoming non-resident triggers a gain.

Where some assets of the same class, for example shares, are retained after a chargeable event there are specific rules for identifying the assets disposed of. The assets disposed of are identified with assets of the same class on a first-in, first-out basis, taking acquisitions on a daily basis. Where assets of the same class were acquired on the same day they are treated as disposed of in the following order. Firstly assets to which neither this holdover relief nor the social investment income tax relief is attributable, secondly assets to which this holdover relief but not the social investment income tax relief is attributable, thirdly assets to which the social investment income tax relief but not this holdover relief is attributable, and finally assets to which both this holdover relief and the social investment income tax relief are attributable. The capital gains tax identification rules in **38.18** do not apply to assets to which holdover relief but not income tax relief is attributable.

Where there would be a loss on the disposal of an asset to which social investment income tax relief is attributable the consideration for the asset is treated as reduced by the amount of the income tax relief, thus reducing or eliminating the loss or creating a gain. Where an asset to which social investment income tax relief is attributable is disposed of three years or more after acquisition, any gain accruing on the disposal is not a chargeable gain. However, if the disposal creates a loss it will be an allowable loss. Although it is not a requirement of the scheme to make a claim for income tax relief, if no such claim is made, then any subsequent disposal of the investment will not be exempt from capital gains tax.

Purchase by company of its own shares (CTA 2010, ss 1033–1048)

[29.58] Where an unquoted trading company or the unquoted holding company of a trading group buys back its own shares (or redeems them or makes a payment for them in a reduction of capital) in order to benefit a trade, the transaction is not treated as a distribution, and thus liable to income tax in the hands of the vending shareholder, but as a disposal on which the vending shareholder is liable to capital gains tax. This does not apply if there is an arrangement the main purpose of which is to get undistributed profits into the hands of the shareholders without incurring the tax liabilities on a distribution.

The main requirements are that the shareholder must be UK-resident, he must normally have owned the shares for at least five years, and he must either dispose of his entire holding or the holding must be 'substantially reduced'.

A company may apply to HMRC for a clearance that the proposed purchase will not be treated as a distribution.

Any legal costs and other expenditure incurred by a company in purchasing its own shares are not allowable against the company's profits.

Where the purchase of its own shares by a company is *not* covered by the above provisions, the purchase is treated as a distribution on which income tax is payable.

It used to be common, where capital gains tax reliefs were not available, for a purchase of own shares to be deliberately structured so as to breach the conditions for capital gains tax treatment because the effective tax rate on net dividend distributions for higher rate taxpayers was much lower. However, the position is likely to be different now that the tax rate on dividend distributions can be as high as 38.1% (see **2.26**), there is a maximum capital gains tax rate of 28% (see **4.2**) and entrepreneurs' relief (see **29.2**) may be available to reduce the rate to only 10%. Comparative calculations are therefore advisable.

Buy back from trustees (ITA 2007, s 482)

[29.59] There is a special treatment for shareholders who are trustees if a company makes distributions in the form of payments on the redemption, repayment or repurchase of its own shares, or on the purchase of rights to buy its own shares. The trustees are taxed on such distributions at the dividend trust rate (currently 38.1%, see **42.28**). This does not apply where trust income is treated as belonging to the settlor, or where the trust is a unit trust, charitable trust, or pension trust.

Management buyouts

[29.60] The provisions enabling a company to purchase its own shares could assist a management buyout team to acquire the company for which they work, in that only shares remaining after those bought in by the company need then be acquired by them.

If only part of a trade is to be acquired, the existing company could transfer the requisite assets into a subsidiary company using the reconstruction provisions of CTA 2010, Pt 22 (see **26.24**), the buyout team then buying the shares in the subsidiary.

Alternatively, if the buyout team form an entirely new company and purchase assets from their employing company, capital allowances will be available where appropriate and the new company may be able to raise some of the funds it needs through the enterprise investment scheme, or by attracting investments from venture capital trusts (see **29.44**).

Demergers (CTA 2010, ss 1073–1099; TCGA 1992, s 192)

[29.61] The aim of the demerger legislation is to remove various tax obstacles to demergers, so that businesses grouped inefficiently under a single company umbrella may be run more dynamically and effectively by being allowed to pursue their separate ways under independent management. The detailed provisions are very complex, the following being an outline.

A company is not treated as having made a distribution for corporation tax purposes (and the members are not treated as having received income) where the company transfers to its members the shares of a 75% subsidiary, or transfers a trade to a new company in exchange for that new company issuing shares to some or all of the transferor company's shareholders.

In order for these provisions to apply, all the companies must be UK-resident trading companies, the transfer must be made to benefit some or all of the trading activities, and the transfer must not be made for tax avoidance reasons.

A qualifying distribution by the holding company of shares in subsidiaries to its members is also not treated as a capital distribution for capital gains tax purposes, and the capital gains charge when a company leaves a group on assets acquired within the previous six years from other group companies (see **3.31**) does not apply.

There are detailed anti-avoidance provisions, and there is also provision to apply for HMRC clearance of proposed transactions.

Enterprise zones

[29.62] The Government is encouraging investment in enterprise zones to stimulate business growth, with first-year capital allowances being made available to trading companies which invest in new plant and machinery for use primarily in a designated assisted area within certain enterprise zones (see **22.34**). Businesses starting up or relocating to an enterprise zone within certain defined periods depending on the zone will qualify for relief from business rates. Relief is available on up to 100% of the business rates for five years, up to a maximum of £275,000.

Contributions to local enterprise organisations etc. (ITTOIA 2005, ss 82–86; CTA 2009, ss 82–86)

[29.63] Businesses may claim a deduction from their profits for contributions they make to local enterprise organisations and urban regeneration companies. The legislation defines local enterprise organisations but some of them have been subsequently replaced by other bodies. They currently include local enterprise agencies, the Education and Skills Funding Agency (ESFA) and Scottish local enterprise companies (LECs).

Local enterprise agencies are bodies approved by the Secretary of State that promote local industrial and commercial activity and enterprise, particularly in forming and developing small businesses. The ESFA is mainly concerned with government education and training programmes. LECs are private companies working under contracts entered into with Scottish Enterprise or Highlands and Islands Enterprise and their role covers economic development and environmental functions as well as training.

Revenue expenditure on research and development (CTA 2010, s 1138; FA 1998, Sch 18 Pt 9A; FA 2004, s 53; ITTOIA 2005, ss 87, 88; SI 2004/712; CTA 2009, s 87, Pt 3 Ch 6A and Pt 13)

[29.64] Tax relief is available for revenue expenditure on research and development (R&D) related to the trade. R&D is defined as activities falling to be treated as research and development in accordance with generally accepted accounting practice, but the definition is modified by Treasury regulations.

The way the relief is given depends on whether the companies are small/medium-sized or large (see **29.65** and **29.66**). Claims must be made in the company's tax return. Capital expenditure on research and development qualifies for 100% capital allowances (see **22.49**).

Companies that treat R&D for accounts purposes as part of the cost of an intangible asset rather than as revenue expenditure may nonetheless still claim R&D tax reliefs.

There are provisions to deny relief for R&D expenditure where the company is not a going concern, and to limit the 'total R&D aid' in respect of a research and development project to €7.5 million.

It is not a requirement that any intellectual property deriving from R&D expenditure by a small/medium-sized company be vested in the company. For expenditure incurred on or after 1 April 2015, where a company sells or otherwise transfers ownership of the products of its R&D activity as part of its ordinary business then the cost of materials that go to make up those products is excluded from expenditure qualifying for relief.

Expenditure by small and medium-sized companies (CTA 2009, Pt 13)

[29.65] From 1 April 2015 small and medium-sized companies as defined can claim R&D tax relief for 230% of their qualifying revenue expenditure on research and development. Relief at 230% of the expenditure gives companies a tax saving equal to 46% of the R&D expenditure.

Companies carrying on R&D before they start to trade may treat the R&D relief as a trading loss. Where a company has an unrelieved trading loss (excluding brought forward or carried back losses), it may surrender the R&D tax relief (or the unrelieved loss if lower) in exchange for a tax credit equal to 14.5% of the surrendered amount. The tax credit will be paid to the company, or used to discharge outstanding corporation tax liabilities.

Small and medium-sized companies are broadly defined as those with fewer than 500 employees, having a turnover of not more than €100 million and/or assets of not more than €86 million.

Small and medium-sized companies that do subcontract R&D work for large companies, or who have certain subsidised in-house R&D expenditure, may claim relief in respect of their expenditure on such work as indicated in **29.66**, in addition to the relief outlined above for other R&D expenditure.

Companies with an annual turnover of no more than £2 million and less than 50 employees which have not previously made a claim for R&D relief may apply for HMRC's Advance Assurance. This means that for the first three accounting periods of claiming the relief, HMRC will allow the claim without further enquiries. For details see www.gov.uk/guidance/research-and-develop ment-tax-relief-advance-assurance.

Expenditure by large companies etc —research and development expenditure credit (CTA 2009, Pt 3 Ch 6A)

[29.66] With effect from 1 April 2016 the R&D relief available to large companies, and SMEs that either do subcontract R&D work for large companies or that have certain subsidised in-house R&D expenditure, is an above the line R&D expenditure credit (RDEC) of 11% of their qualifying expenditure (or 49% for a 'ring fence' trade relating to certain oil-related activities). The credit is fully payable, net of tax, to companies with no corporation tax liability.

Universities and charities are unable to claim the credit on expenditure incurred on or after 1 August 2015.

Expenditure on vaccines research

[29.67] Before 1 April 2017 large companies (see **29.66**) could claim an extra 40% relief for their qualifying expenditure on research and development related to vaccines and medicines for TB and malaria, HIV and AIDS. The relief was also available for contributions to charities, universities and scientific research organisations for funding independent research related to a trade carried on by the company.

Tax points

[29.68] Note the following:

- The detailed conditions and anti-avoidance rules in relation to most of the provisions dealt with in this chapter are too extensive to deal with in detail, but should be looked at carefully by interested companies and investors.
- Although individuals investing under EIS, SEIS or SITR will be issued with compliance certificates, each individual must make a specific claim for tax relief within the time limits indicated at **29.29** and **29.56**.
- When gains are reinvested by subscribing within the appropriate limits for EIS shares, 30% income tax relief can be obtained on the shares and any capital gains tax liability deferred. Although deferral is not the same as an exemption, further deferral may be possible when the deferred gains are triggered. The gains may eventually become chargeable if they are triggered before death.
- Although gains deferred under the EIS provisions may become chargeable as indicated above, gains on the disposal of the shares themselves up to the relevant holding limits are exempt, providing that they were subscribed for and held for the three-year period.
- EIS income tax relief is not available to individuals connected with the company, but the connected persons rules do not apply to the EIS deferral relief enabling a deferment of tax on capital gains up to the amount invested.
- SEIS income tax relief is available to certain former employees and to directors provided they do not have a substantial interest in the company.
- Although a company will not be able to issue SEIS shares if it has previously raised funds under either the EIS or VCT schemes, it can raise EIS or VCT monies after a SEIS investment.

- Shares in companies on the Alternative Investment Market (AIM) and the PLUS Markets, with the exception of PLUS-listed, are treated as unquoted, so EIS relief is available providing the company is a qualifying company. The limit on the company's assets of £15 million immediately before the issue of the shares and £16 million immediately afterwards will, however, exclude many of these companies.
- HMRC will not usually give a clearance under the demerger provisions where companies in the same ownership are first merged and then demerged so that each company ends up in the ownership of independent people.
- Several specialist R&D tax credit units have been set up around the country to deal with all R&D tax credit claims except those dealt with by the Large Business Service. See HMRC Corporate Intangibles Research & Development Manual CIRD80350 for details.

Part VI

Land and buildings

30

The family home

Background

[30.1] There are various tax aspects to consider in relation to the family home. Apart from inheritance tax considerations, the most important are the capital gains tax aspects, but consideration also needs to be given to the income tax position when rental income is received for the property (see **30.12**) or it is used for employment or business (**30.23** to **30.24**). The relevant provisions in relation to council tax and business rates must also be borne in mind — see **30.16**. Stamp duty land tax is an increasingly important factor. See **6.9** for the rates of stamp duty land tax on residential property. This is replaced in Scotland by land and buildings transaction tax (LBTT, see **6.18**). Relief may be available for purchasers of more than one dwelling from the same vendor.

A package of three taxes that affect UK residential properties held by certain non-natural persons (broadly companies, partnerships with company members and collective investment schemes) which currently applies to such properties valued at over £500,000 could possibly have effect in relation to a family home. The three taxes, which are covered in other chapters, are:

(i) stamp duty land tax at 15% on acquisition of a residential property (see **6.9**).
(ii) an annual tax on enveloped dwellings (see **32.48**).
(iii) capital gains tax at 28% on any gain on disposal of the property (see **4.8**).

From 6 April 2015 capital gains tax may also be charged on gains realised on disposals of UK residential property by non-residents (see **41.50**).

The main capital gains tax provisions relating to the family home are dealt with in this chapter. See also **33.16** for the capital gains tax provisions in relation to the family home on separation or divorce, or dissolution of a civil partnership, and **33.20** for points in relation to cohabiting couples.

Older people may be considering raising money from their homes by some sort of equity release plan. These are dealt with in **34.9**.

As far as inheritance tax is concerned, the large increases in property values that have taken place over recent years, coupled with the minimal increases in the inheritance tax nil rate band, have left many people with significant inheritance tax problems in relation to the family home. However, for deaths on or after 6 April 2017 a 'residence nil rate band' (RNRB) will be applied to the taxable value of the estate in the same way that the nil rate band is applied (see **5.24**) except that it will only be available to be used against the value of residential property included in the death estate which passes to direct descendants. The RNRB will initially be £100,000, increasing to £175,000 by 2020–21. There will be a tapered withdrawal of the band for estates valued at more than £2 million. In certain circumstances the RNRB will be available where an individual has downsized or has ceased to own a residence on or after 8 July 2015 and other assets are passed on death to direct descendants. For HMRC guidance see www.gov.uk/guidance/inheritance-tax-residence-nil-rate-band and www.gov.uk/guidance/how-downsizing-selling-or-gifting-a-home-af fects-the-additional-inheritance-tax-threshold.

Leaseholders' rights

[30.2] As a result of the Commonhold and Leasehold Reform Act 2002, those acquiring property in new developments are able to buy the freehold of their individual flats and become members of a 'commonhold association' that is responsible for the management and upkeep of the common parts of the property. Commonhold land is registered with the Land Registry. Leaseholders of existing developments may convert to commonhold if all leaseholders agree.

Leaseholders are able to acquire the freehold of their flats through a nominee purchaser or through an RTE (Right to Enfranchisement) company. In the latter case, the rate of stamp duty land tax on the consideration for the acquisition of the freeholds is arrived at by dividing the total amount payable by the number of flats and the rate on that fractional amount is applied to the total consideration. Whether or not the leaseholders form an RTE, they may take over the management of the common parts of the development through an RTM (Right to Manage) company.

For those participating in commonhold associations or RTM/RTE companies, various tax points need to be borne in mind, particularly where some tenants buy and some do not. Someone has to be responsible for dealing with the tax on any income, such as interest on the maintenance fund, and there are also capital gains tax considerations. Professional advice is essential.

Capital gains tax private residence relief (TCGA 1992, ss 4–4BB, 222–226D)

[30.3] The basic capital gains tax treatment on the disposal of a main residence is that any gain is exempt from capital gains tax providing the property has been the only or main residence throughout the period of ownership, or throughout that period except for all or any part of the last 18 months (36 months for certain people moving into a care home, see **30.6**). This is subject to various provisions to cover situations such as non-qualifying tax years (see **30.4**), other periods of absence (see **30.6**), owning two or more residences (see **30.17**), using part of the property for business (see **30.23**) or letting (see **30.13**) and so on, which are dealt with later in the chapter.

The word 'residence' is not defined by the legislation for this purpose and there is plenty of case law on the subject of whether or not a property is a taxpayer's residence. HMRC focus on the quality, and not length, of occupation. Recent cases illustrate that intention when moving in can be more important.

See **4.2** for the capital gains tax rates applying to 'upper rate gains' which include gains on residential property which do not qualify for private residence relief.

Non-qualifying tax year (TCGA 1992, ss 222B, 222C)

[30.4] For disposals on or after 6 April 2015 a property, wherever situated, is treated as not being occupied as a residence for tax years when neither the taxpayer nor their spouse or civil partner is tax-resident (as defined) in the territory in which the property is situated, and they do not stay overnight at the property at least 90 times during the year (prorated if only part of the tax year falls into the period of ownership). The effect of this provision is that the property can neither be exempt as the individual's factual only or main residence, nor as their main residence by nomination (see **30.17**) for a non-qualifying tax year. Any gain attributable to non-qualifying tax years is chargeable to capital gains tax when the property is sold, at which date the owner may be resident or non-resident in the UK. In the latter case the charge will be under the non-resident CGT regime (see **41.50**). The exemptions for non-occupation (see **30.6**) and job-related accommodation (see **30.21**) can still apply for a non-qualifying tax year.

Buying and not moving in immediately

[30.5] If the owner does not move into the house immediately HMRC will, by concession D49, allow them to treat any non-occupation in the first 12 months as covered by the owner occupier capital gains exemption if they do not move in because they are having the property built, or are altering or redecorating the property, or because they remain in their old home while they are selling it.

HMRC may extend the 12-month period to up to a maximum of 24 months if there are good reasons that are outside the owner's control. See also **30.17** regarding second homes and **30.21** regarding job-related accommodation.

Empty property may be liable to council tax, but newly built or structurally altered property is not subject to the tax for up to six months after the work is substantially completed, and there is no charge on property that is empty and unfurnished for up to six months (see **8.3**).

Periods of absence (TCGA 1992, ss 223, 223A, 225E)

[30.6] Provided that a house has at some time been an individual's only or main residence, the last 18 months of ownership are always exempt in calculating capital gains tax, whether he is living there or not. The period is 36 months for disposals by disabled persons and long-term residents of care homes who do not own the whole or part of another dwelling on which they may claim private residence relief at the time of the disposal, or disposals by the spouse or civil partner of such a person where neither of them have any other such interest in a private residence. A long-term resident of a care home is an individual who is resident there and has been, or can reasonably be expected to be, resident there for at least three months. This extension to 36 months applies to trustees of a settlement where the individual occupying the property meets the conditions.

Other periods of absence also qualify for exemption provided that the house was the individual's only or main residence at some time *before* the period of absence, and that *after* the period of absence there is either a time when the house was his only or main residence, or in a case in (b) to (d) below, he was prevented from resuming residence in the house because the terms of his employment required him to live elsewhere. (This latter rule also applies to a spouse or civil partner living with the individual who was prevented from resuming residence.)

These qualifying periods of absence are any or all of the following:

(a)   three years for any reason whatsoever (not necessarily a consecutive period of three years);

(b)   any period of absence abroad in an employment *all* the duties of which were performed abroad (this applies to a spouse or civil partner who lives with the individual);

(c)   up to four years (whether in a single period or not) where self-employment or the duties of a UK employment require an individual to live elsewhere; and

(d)   up to four years where the individual lives with a spouse or civil partner to whom (c) above applies for that period.

If these periods are exceeded, only the excess is counted as a period of non-residence. There can thus be long periods of absence without losing any part of the capital gains tax exemption.

...u in calculating the ...ortion of residence/deemed ...snip after 30 March 1982. The ...s of ownership still applies, however, no ...or residence was before or after 31 March 1982.

...e whole or part of the gain on the residence is a non-resident ...the period of ownership does not include any period before 6 April ...15, unless the individual has made an election for the retrospective basis of computation to apply (see **41.50**). In order to determine whether any of the permitted periods of absence above apply in relation to such a residence, the rule that it must have been occupied as the only or main residence at some time before the period of absence is determined ignoring times before 6 April 2015. However, pre-6 April 2015 periods can be used to satisfy the requirement if the individual so elects.

[30.8] If the individual occupies rented property during his absence, then although the tenancy may have no capital value, the property he is occupying would even so strictly 'qualify for relief' as his dwelling (see **30.17**). In those circumstances HMRC will accept a main residence election for his own property, so that the rules for qualifying periods of absence can apply. By HMRC concession D21, where in these circumstances he did not know at the appropriate time that an election was required, HMRC will accept an out of time election providing he makes it promptly as soon as he becomes aware, the election then taking effect from the time the tenancy was acquired.

[30.9] If an individual acquires an interest in a property from his/her spouse or civil partner when they are living together (including an acquisition as legatee when the spouse or civil partner dies), the individual's period of ownership is treated as starting when his/her spouse or civil partner acquired the property, and the individual's tax position would take into account any part of that period when the spouse or civil partner was not resident in the property.

[30.10] There are no special council tax provisions about permitted absences, other than the exemptions listed at **8.3** and the discount for a property that is no-one's only or main home (see **8.5**).

Dwelling occupied under a trust or by a dependent relative (TCGA 1992, ss 225, 226, 226A, 226B)

[30.11] The private residence exemption may be claimed by trustees when they dispose of a property occupied by someone entitled to occupy it under the terms of the trust. The beneficiary is treated as if they were occupying the property as the owner for the purposes of determining any exemptions for circumstances and length of occupation. It is also the beneficiary's circumstances which are taken into account for the purposes of deciding whether there is a non-qualifying tax year (see **30.4**). Anti-avoidance provisions deny the relief for such disposals where the calculation of the gain would take into account holdover relief for gifts (see **4.32**) on an earlier disposal, unless the earlier claim is revoked. Where the earlier disposal on which gifts relief was given was before 10 December 2003, the private residence relief in respect of the period from that date (and the exemption for the last 18 months of ownership will not include any post-10 December 2003 period). See **33.16** for the use of the trust exemption where couples get divorced.

If an individual disposes of a property owned by him on 5 April 1988 that was occupied rent-free by a dependent relative on that date, and the relative continued to live there rent-free until up to 18 months before the time the individual disposes of the property, any gain arising on the disposal is exempt from capital gains tax. Payment of council tax by the relative does not affect the exemption.

The capital gains tax exemption ceases if there is a change of occupant after 5 April 1988 even if the new occupant is also a dependent relative, but any period from 31 March 1982 which did qualify for the exemption reduces the chargeable period when calculating any chargeable gain.

In view of the fact that 'dependent relative' is defined as an individual's own or his/her spouse's (but not civil partner's) widowed, separated or (broadly) divorced mother, or any other relative of the husband or wife unable to look after themselves because of old age or infirmity, this exemption will now rarely apply.

If the home is let (TCGA 1992, ss 4–4BB, 223(4); ITTOIA 2005, ss 784–802)

Income tax

[30.12] A 'rent-a-room' relief is available for owner-occupiers and tenants who let furnished rooms in their only or main residence. The relief is available both where the rent comes under the property business rules (see **32.3**) and where substantial services are also provided, for example guest houses and bed and breakfast businesses, so that the rent is charged as trading income (see CHAPTER 21). If part of the property is let unfurnished in the same year, however, the relief cannot be claimed. Letting of rooms as office accommodation does not qualifying for the relief.

No tax is payable if the gross rents for the tax year (or for trades, the accounting year ended in the tax year), before deducting expenses, do not exceed £7,500. If more than one person is entitled to rent in the same period, then the limit for each individual is one half of the basic amount — £3,750 each. HMRC state that this applies irrespective of the number of individuals who are eligible for the relief and thus total relief given on the property could exceed £7,500 where there are more than two such individuals (see HMRC Property Income Manual PIM4010). The rent taken into account for the relief is the payment for the accommodation plus payments for related goods and services.

An election can be made for the relief not to apply for a particular year, for example if the expenses exceed the rent and a claim for a loss is made. The time limit for the election is one year from 31 January following the end of the relevant tax year (or longer at HMRC's discretion, see HMRC Property Income Manual PIM4050). The election may be withdrawn within the same time limit. If the rent exceeds £7,500, there is a choice to pay tax either on the excess over £7,500, or on the rent less expenses under the normal rules described below. If the individual wants to pay on the excess over £7,500 he must make an election to do so, and that basis will then apply until the election is withdrawn. The time limit for such an election is the same as that for electing for the relief not to apply at all.

Profits can be calculated under the cash basis, either for small businesses (see **20.4**) or for property businesses (see **32.6**), as the case may be.

Where 'rent-a-room' relief is, or could be, claimed the trading allowance (see **19.20**) and the property allowance (see **32.5**) are not available.

If the 'rent-a-room' relief does not apply, then unless the letting amounts to a trade (see above), the letting income is chargeable to income tax along with other letting income, if any, after setting off appropriate expenses (see **32.7**). It is normally treated as property income, but if the letting qualifies as furnished holiday accommodation (which would be unusual — see **30.15** and **32.25**), the income is treated as trading income except for loss relief purposes.

Capital gains tax

[30.13] As far as the capital gains tax exemption is concerned, the last 18 months of ownership of the home always count as a period of residence (see **30.6**), so moving out and letting the property during that time will not affect the exemption.

If the owner continues to live in the property while letting part of it, the capital gains tax exemption is not affected if the letting takes the form of boarders who effectively live as part of the family. It has been confirmed that letting under the rent-a-room scheme would not normally affect the availability of the exemption. Where, however, the letting extends beyond this, or the whole property is let, other than during the last 18 months of ownership or during another allowable absence period (see **30.6**), the appropriate fraction of the gain on disposal is chargeable but there is an exemption of the smaller of £40,000 and an amount equal to the exempt gain on the owner-occupied part.

Example 1

The gain on the sale of a dwelling in 2017–18 is £80,000. The agreed proportion applicable to the let part is £48,000, the exempt gain being £32,000.

The £48,000 gain on the let part is reduced by the lower of—

(a)   £40,000 and
(b)   an amount equal to the exempt gain, i.e. £32,000.

Therefore a further £32,000 is exempt and £16,000 is chargeable. The gain will be reduced by the annual exempt amount (£11,300 for 2017–18) if not already used. As this is an 'upper rate gain' the capital gains tax rates applying will be 18% or 28% depending on the individual's tax circumstances (see **4.2**).

Where a married couple, civil partners, or any other joint owners jointly let part of the home, each is entitled to the residential lettings exemption of up to £40,000.

The exemption is not available if the let part of the property is effectively a separate dwelling, such as a self-contained flat with its own access. However, where part of the home is let, without substantial structural alterations, it will qualify, even if it has separate facilities.

[30.14] The courts have held that the residential lettings exemption was available to the owners of a small private hotel who occupied the whole of the property during the winter months, with one or two guests, but lived in an annexe during the summer. The exemption can be claimed only if the property qualifies as the capital gains tax exempt residence for at least part of the period of ownership, so it cannot be claimed on a property which, although he lives in it sometimes, has never been an individual's only or main residence for capital gains tax purposes. Subject to that, it can be claimed where all of the property has been let for part of the period of ownership, or part of the property has been let for all or part of the period of ownership.

[30.15] The position of furnished holiday lettings is not clear. See **32.25** onwards regarding tax reliefs for such lettings. Gains on such property are specifically eligible for rollover relief when the property is sold and replaced (see **29.16** to **29.21**), but providing the rules outlined above are complied with, it would seem that if the property is the qualifying main residence the residential lettings exemption could apply instead. Where a chargeable gain has been rolled over under TCGA 1992, s 152 or s 153 into the cost of furnished holiday accommodation and a gain on which private residence relief applies accrues on the disposal of that accommodation, that relief will be restricted to the part of the chargeable gain which exceeds the amount of the gain rolled over (see HMRC Capital Gains Manual CG61452). To continue to get the other benefits of the furnished holiday lettings provisions, the rules for such lettings would have to be complied with (in particular ensuring that neither the owner nor anyone else normally occupied the accommodation for a continuous period of more than 31 days — see **32.28**).

Council tax and business rates

[30.16] If the let part of the property is self-contained living accommodation that counts as a separate dwelling, the tenants are liable to pay the council tax. For any period when it is not anyone's only or main home, for example when it is untenanted, the owner is liable to pay up to 90% of the council tax (subject to certain exemptions, for example unfurnished property for up to six months — see **8.3** and **8.5**).

If the let part of the home is not self-contained, the owner is liable to pay the council tax, but will usually include an appropriate amount in the rent to cover the proportion applicable to the tenants. If the owner does not live in the property while it is let, the council tax will be paid by tenants who occupy it as their main home, except for multi-occupied property such as bedsits, where the owner will remain liable. If the let part is let as short-term living accommodation, and is therefore no-one's only or main home, the owner will pay up to 90% of the council tax unless the property is available for short-term letting for 140 days or more in a year (for example self-catering holiday accommodation), in which case he will pay business rates instead (see **31.27**). If bed and breakfast facilities are offered in the owner's home, he is not liable to business rates providing he does not offer accommodation for more than six people, lives in the house at the same time and the house is still mainly used as his home. If part of the home is let for business purposes rather than as living accommodation, business rates are payable on that part.

A deduction of an appropriate part of the council tax, or the business rates, paid on let property may be made from the rent in arriving at taxable letting income (see **32.7**).

Council tax and business rates are discussed fully in CHAPTER **8**. Differing rules may apply in Wales, Scotland and Northern Ireland.

More than one home (TCGA 1992, ss 222(5), (6), 222A)

Capital gains tax and income tax

[30.17] An individual may notify HMRC within two years after acquiring a second home which of the two is to be the exempt home for capital gains tax. If he had bought a second home but did not move in immediately because of work being done etc. — see **30.5** — the two-year period would not start until the second home became available for use. The nominated property may be in the UK or abroad (see **30.19**). Only a property used as a home qualifies for the exemption, however, and an individual cannot nominate a property he has never lived in. After nominating the exempt property, in most cases he may later notify a change of choice from a specified date (but see **30.18** regarding nominations in relation to non-resident CGT disposals), which cannot be earlier than two years before the date of the later notification. If no notification is made, and a dispute between the individual and HMRC arises, the main residence will be decided as a question of fact. Provided that both houses have been a qualifying main residence for capital gains tax at some time, the last 18 months of ownership of both will in any event be counted as owner-occupied in calculating the exempt gain. An election is not required where the individual has a residence that he owns and a second residence that he neither owns nor leases (e.g. accommodation with relatives, or a hotel room). A property occupied as a tenant would, however, need to be taken into account even if the occupation rights have no capital value (see **30.8**).

The ability to change the election as to which of two homes is the main residence may be helpful where an individual has owned two homes for many years, one of which has never been his qualifying main residence, and he sells that property at a gain.

Example 2

A taxpayer has owned and occupied two homes, Westcote and Eastcote, for many years and made a valid election for Westcote to be his main residence. He

---

sells Eastcote at a substantial gain in December 2017 and on 10 January 2018 notifies HMRC that Eastcote is to be treated as his main residence from 11 January 2016. On 17 January 2018 he notifies HMRC that Westcote is to be his main residence from 18 January 2016. The elections enable him to obtain the exemption for the last 18 months' ownership of Eastcote, at the expense of having one chargeable week in respect of Westcote.

A married couple or civil partners living together can only have one qualifying residence and where there are two or more residences owned jointly, or each owns one or more residences, the notice as to which is the main residence needs to be given by both. Where both spouses own a residence when they marry, or civil partners each own a house before registering their civil partnership, a new two-year period starts for notifying which is the main residence. A new two-year period does not start if on marriage/registration one spouse or civil partner already owns more than one residence and the other owns no property. If a couple jointly own more than one property before and after marriage or registration, a new two-year period still begins, because the election after marriage or registration must be a joint election.

Where such a nomination (a section 222 nomination) has been made, it does not cease to be effective at any time simply because at that time another residence is treated as not being occupied as a residence for tax year because it is a non-qualifying tax year (see **30.4**).

[30.18] With effect from 6 April 2015, there is a separate, more restricted nomination (a section 222A nomination), available where a taxpayer disposes of a residence which is the subject of a non-resident CGT disposal (see **41.50**). Whilst a section 222A nomination can generally vary a previously made section 222 nomination, it cannot vary a previous nomination for a residence which has already been disposed of. In addition, a section 222A nomination cannot subsequently be varied, either under section 222A or section 222. It must be made in the NRCGT return (see **9.31**).

[30.19] If a second home is abroad, then although it may be nominated as a main home, and a reduction possibly obtained in the UK tax liability as shown in Example 2, the taxation position in the overseas country would also need to be considered.

Council tax

[30.20] For council tax, an individual pays up to 90% of the tax on a property which is no-one's only or main home (see **8.5**). The question of which of two or more homes is the only or main home for council tax is a question of fact, decided in the first place by the local authority, but an appeal may be made against their decision. In some circumstances, one of the properties might be the main home of one spouse or civil partner and the other property the main home of the other, in which case the resident partner would be liable to pay the council tax at each property, with a 25% single resident reduction if the property was not also the main residence of anyone else over 18. This could apply, for example, if a wife lived at a house in the country and her husband at a house in town, going to the other house at weekends, etc.

However, the length of time spent at the property would not necessarily be the deciding factor and all relevant circumstances would be taken into account. If the second home was a holiday property available for short-term letting for 140 days or more in a year, it would be liable to business rates rather than the council tax.

If the second home is a caravan, it will not usually be liable to council tax. The owner of the site where the caravan is kept will pay business rates, which will be included in his charge to caravan owners. Touring caravans kept at home when not touring are not subject to council tax.

Differing rules may apply in Wales, Scotland and Northern Ireland (see CHAPTER 8).

Job-related accommodation (TCGA 1992, s 222(8), (8A)–(8D), (9))

[30.21] If an employee lives in accommodation related to employment, for example as a hotel manager or minister of religion, or a trader lives in accommodation related to self-employment, for example as the tenant of licensed premises, that individual may buy a property that is to be the future home. The property qualifies for capital gains tax exemption, even though they do not live there.

If the property is let, a deduction is allowed from the letting income of interest incurred wholly and exclusively for the purposes of the property business.

Unless the property is someone's only or main home (for example if let long-term), a discount of up to 50% of the council tax will be due (see 8.5).

Moving home (ITEPA 2003, ss 271–289; TCGA 1992, s 223)

[30.22] Owning two houses at the same time is usually covered for capital gains tax purposes by the exemption of the last 18 months of ownership.

An individual may need to take out a bridging loan when he moves house. Employees are charged to tax on the benefit of certain low rate or interest-free loans from their employers (see 10.48). This includes bridging loans, but specific rules apply to removal and relocation expenses and employees are not taxed on qualifying expenses paid by their employers up to a limit of £8,000 (see 10.22). If the £8,000 limit has not been fully used, any balance is available to cover an equivalent amount of the notional interest chargeable to tax on a low rate or interest-free bridging loan from the employer providing the relevant conditions are met.

See 10.23 for the tax treatment if an employee sells his home to his employer or to a relocation company.

See **6.9** regarding the 3% 'additional residential property rate' applying to purchases of additional residential properties, which can apply where a person's first residence has not been sold on the day of completion of the new purchase.

Part use for business purposes (TCGA 1992, s 224; ITTOIA 2005, s 94H)

[30.23] Interest on that part of any borrowing attributable to the use of part of the home exclusively for business is allowed as a business expense. Unincorporated businesses can claim simplified fixed rate deductions for the business use of home (see **20.19**). That paragraph also provides details of similar fixed rate adjustments which can be used to calculate private use of business premises, such as a guest house. See also **19.19** for allowable expenses when an individual runs a business from home and does not claim the fixed rate deduction.

Business rates will be paid on the business part of the property (allowable against profits for tax). Where part of the property is used for both business and domestic purposes, and the business use does not prevent the continued domestic use, such as a study where the individual does some work and the children do their homework, business rates are not payable, and a deduction may be claimed against profit for the appropriate proportion of the council tax.

As far as capital gains tax is concerned, the private residence exemption is not available on any part of a property that is used *exclusively* for business purposes. Where a replacement property is acquired that is similarly used partly for business, rollover relief may be available to defer the gain (see **29.16** to **29.21**) and see also **30.13** to **30.15** for letting businesses. The capital gains tax exemption is not affected if no part of the home is *exclusively* used for business purposes.

Where a person cares for an adult under a local authority placement scheme (see **20.30**), their contract with the local authority may require them to set aside one or more rooms exclusively for the use of the adult in care. For disposals on or after 9 December 2009 the private residence exemption will not be prevented from being available on that part of the property.

Effect of home expenses claim against employment income on capital gains tax relief (ITEPA 2003, ss 316A, 336; TCGA 1992, s 158(1)(c); SP 5/86)

[30.24] If it is necessary for an employee to work at home, an income tax deduction may be claimed for the appropriate proportion of certain costs. If an employee regularly works at home under homeworking arrangements, reasonable payments by the employer to cover additional household expenses are exempt from income tax (see **10.15**). The treatment of expenses for income tax does not affect the capital gains tax exemption unless a substantial part of the home is *exclusively* used for the purposes of employment. Where there is such exclusive use, a 'just and reasonable' proportion of the gain is chargeable. A claim for rollover relief (see **29.16** to **29.21**) is then possible where the employer does not make any payment or give other consideration for his use of the property nor otherwise occupy it under a lease or tenancy, thus making it an investment property. Alternatively, any gain might be wholly or partly covered by the capital gains tax annual exempt amount (£11,300 in 2017–18).

Selling to make a profit, including selling off part of the garden (TCGA 1992, ss 222, 224(3))

[30.25] The capital gains tax exemption for the main residence does not apply if the property was acquired with the intention of reselling at a profit and, if after acquiring a property, expenditure is incurred wholly or partly to make a gain on sale, an appropriate part of the gain will not be exempt. HMRC have stated, however, that expenditure to get planning permission does not affect the exemption.

The capital gains tax exemption covers grounds not exceeding half a hectare (approximately 1¼ acres), or such larger area as is appropriate to the size and character of the house. If some of the land is sold, perhaps for building plots, the sale is covered by the exemption so long as the land was enjoyed as part of the garden and grounds and is sold before the house and immediately surrounding grounds.

In exceptional circumstances, HMRC may assert that selling part of the garden, or frequent buying and selling of properties (particularly when accompanied by substantial work on them while owned), amounts to a trade, resulting not only in the loss of the capital gains tax exemption but also in the taxation of the profits as trading income.

Death of home owner

[30.26] When the home owner dies, the capital gains tax and inheritance tax aspects need to be considered. There is no capital gains tax charge on death, but gains may arise during the period of administration. See **42.5** for the capital gains tax position of the personal representatives (including whether the private residence exemption is available) and the beneficiaries. The treatment of the home for inheritance tax depends on the terms of the will, as amended by any subsequent variation. For inheritance tax planning in relation to the family home see **35.7** to **35.10**. For details of a 'residence nil rate band' applying for deaths on or after 6 April 2017 see **30.1**.

Tax points

[30.27] Note the following:

- Since tax relief cannot be claimed for interest on home loans, consideration should be given to reducing the home loan and instead borrowing for other tax allowable purposes on which relief at the top tax rate may be available. This is subject to a cap on reliefs against general income, and a restriction on loan interest relief where the cash basis for small businesses is used; see **2.14** and **20.17**.

- If a second home is acquired, careful consideration should be given to which is the main residence for council tax purposes and which is to be treated as the capital gains tax exempt residence, remembering that the last 18 months of ownership of a house which at some time has been a main residence for capital gains tax can in any event be counted as years of owner-occupation in the capital gains tax calculation.

- Where a property has been nominated as the exempt residence for capital gains tax, a change to a different property can be notified and the election can be backdated for two years, and then a further change back to the original property can be notified if wished, provided the election is not under section 222A (see **30.18**). However, if an election is not made within the permitted two-year period from the date of acquiring a second home, the right to make it is lost and the question of the main residence will be decided as a matter of fact.

- An employee living in job-related accommodation should tell HMRC about the acquisition of a dwelling for his own occupation, thus avoiding any doubt that he regards it as his main residence for capital gains tax.

- When considering the business proportion of mixed premises for the purpose of claiming relief for expenses, the possibility of capital gains tax when the premises are sold should be borne in mind.

- To qualify for 'rent-a-room' relief (see **30.12**), the owner needs to live in the property at the same time as the tenant for at least part of the relevant tax year. The relief can still be claimed for that tax year even if the owner has left the property. However, if the owner does not live in the property at all while it is tenanted, rent-a-room relief is not available.

- If the owner takes in a lodger under the 'rent-a-room' provisions, he should make sure he tells his contents insurer. Even so, he will probably be covered for theft only if it is by breaking and entering. He should also check with his mortgage lender that he is not contravening the terms of the loan.

- The maximum £40,000 capital gains tax exemption where the family home has been let (£40,000 each if jointly let by husband and wife or by civil partners or other joint owners) applies where it is wholly let for residential occupation for part of the period of ownership, or partly let for residential occupation at some time during the period of ownership. Because of the residential requirement, it could not exempt a gain that was chargeable because part of the accommodation was used by the family company for trading purposes.

- Where a house has separate buildings to accommodate staff, they may count for the capital gains tax exemption if they are 'closely adjacent' to the main property, but not if they are so far away that the house and buildings cannot really be regarded as a single dwelling.

- If an individual undertakes a barn conversion for his own occupation, he can reclaim the VAT on the building materials (see form VAT431C).
- Each member of a married couple or civil partnership has a separate capital gains tax annual exempt amount. Joint ownership of a second home might therefore reduce the capital gains tax on an eventual sale.
- If the owner is selling off part of the garden, he should make sure it is sold before the house and immediately adjoining land.
- If a house sale falls through and the prospective buyer forfeits his deposit, this is treated in the same way as an abandoned option (see **4.46**), so the person who forfeited the deposit cannot claim relief for a capital loss. The seller is taxable on the amount received, reduced by the annual exempt amount if available. Private residence relief does not apply.
- If, following the owner's death, the home is to be sold by the personal representatives, there may be a significant increase in value before the sale takes place, and personal representatives may not qualify for the private residence exemption. See **42.5**.
- If the owner has converted part of the home into a self-contained flat for letting, he will be liable to pay up to 90% of the council tax on it if it is untenanted, except for the first six months if it is unfurnished.
- A bed and breakfast provider will not pay business rates providing he does not offer accommodation for more than six people, still lives there as well and the property's main use is still as his home, and because of the 'rent-a-room' relief there will be no income tax to pay if the gross income does not exceed £7,500 in a tax year.

31

A country life: farms and woodlands

Farming and market gardening profits

Introduction

[31.1] The profits of farmers and market gardeners are generally calculated in the same way as those of other businesses, but because of the particular characteristics of farming, various special rules apply, some of which are mentioned below. Proper professional advice on the agreement of tax liabilities is recommended. Farming typically generates a modest income and the availability of tax credits (see **2.34**) should not be overlooked.

It is common in farming for members of the family to be employed on the farm. As with all businesses, expenses must be incurred 'wholly and exclusively for the purposes of the trade'. The High Court found that a farmer's wages to his young children were pocket money and were therefore neither allowable as an expense in calculating farm trading profits nor to be treated as the children's income to enable their personal allowances to be used. The fact that the children were below legal employment age was taken into account, although it was not conclusive. See **12.9** on paying family members.

Stock valuations and grants

[31.2] HMRC guidance on farming stock valuations can be found in Helpsheet HS232. Their view of the treatment to be followed if a change in the basis of valuation is made is in HMRC Business Income Manual BIM33199.

The valuation of cattle bred on the farm can be included at 60% of market value, and likewise that of home-reared sheep and pigs at 75% of market value, but no reduction is permissible for mature bought-in animals.

There are many different grants and subsidies available to farmers. The general tax treatment is that where the amounts are to meet particular costs, they should be set against those costs (and the costs net of such amounts would then be included, where appropriate, in stock valuations). Where they are to subsidise the sale proceeds of a particular crop they should be recognised as income when the crop is sold.

Amounts received by sugar beet growers for the sale of all or part of their contract tonnage entitlement are taken into account in calculating trading profits. For companies, agricultural quotas are dealt with under the intangible assets rules (see **31.18**).

Basic Payment Scheme

[31.3] Following the negotiation of a new Common Agricultural Policy by the EU the basic payment scheme (BPS) replaced the single payment scheme (SPS) in 2015. Guidance is available at www.gov.uk/government/collections/basic-payment-scheme.

Each part of the UK has different basic payment scheme arrangements and this guide broadly covers England only. To qualify for BPS the claimant must be an 'active farmer', have at least five hectares of 'eligible' land at their disposal on 15 May in the scheme year, and have at least five BPS entitlements.

An active farmer is generally one who carries out a qualifying agricultural activity (as defined). A farmer who received €5,000 or less for the previous scheme year for BPS will also automatically qualify as an active farmer. If a farmer did not claim for BPS in the previous year, the Rural Payments Agency will work out whether they reach the €5,000 threshold. In addition, farmers may still qualify for BPS even if they operate one of the non-agricultural activities, if one of three criteria are met: either their annual payments for BPS are at least 5% of their total non-agricultural receipts in the most recent financial year; or their total agricultural receipts are at least 40% of their total receipts in the most recent financial year; or they have at least 36 hectares of eligible land. Under the BPS scheme the farmer needs to comply with EU standards in relation to public, animal and plant health, environmental and animal welfare on all his agricultural land.

Eligible land is arable land, permanent grassland and permanent crops, and the land must be eligible for the scheme both at the time of application and throughout the calendar year. Land parcels with solar panels on them will not be eligible for the BPS. An active farmer without any previous SPS entitlements can obtain BPS entitlements by transferring them (i.e. leasing in or purchasing them) from someone else, or he might also be able to apply for new BPS entitlements from a national reserve set up by DEFRA.

For those who continue to farm, albeit possibly on only part of their land, or cease production only temporarily, the basic payment is part of the trading income. If the farming trade ceases, but the other conditions for receiving the payment are satisfied, it will be taxed as non-trading miscellaneous income unless another trade is commenced on the land. In that event, any losses in the farming trade would not be allowable against the profits of the new trade.

HMRC stated that the disposal of an entitlement to receive a single farm payment would normally be a chargeable disposal for capital gains tax, and the treatment of the basic payment is most likely to be the same. Entitlements under the BPS for those who continue farming are qualifying non-wasting assets for capital gains tax rollover relief (see **29.17**). Where the land and BPS entitlement are sold together, the proceeds are split between the two assets and the capital gains position computed separately for each asset. For corporation tax the entitlements come within the intangible assets rules (see **20.35** to **20.41**).

For inheritance tax purposes, the basic payment entitlement does not qualify for agricultural property relief. The land itself may still qualify as agricultural land depending on the circumstances. Alternatively it may qualify for business property relief if it is an asset of a trading business. The basic payment entitlement may similarly qualify as a business asset if it is transferred as part of a trading business. The fact that the basic payment entitlement is a separate asset from the farmland should be remembered when wills are being drawn up or amended.

For value added tax, the basic payment itself is outside the scope of VAT. The VAT treatment on sale of basic payment entitlement will depend on the circumstances. The 'transfer of a going concern' treatment (see **7.52**) will apply where appropriate.

Farming as a single trade (ITTOIA 2005, ss 9, 859; CTA 2009, s 36)

[31.4] All farming carried on by one farmer is treated as a single trade, so that several holdings are treated as a single business and a move from one farm to another is not treated as the cessation of one business and the commencement of another. The single trade treatment applies whether the farmer is a sole trader, a partnership or a company, but farming carried on by a partnership is treated as a trade separate from any farming carried on by individual partners.

Loss relief (ITA 2007, Pt 4; CTA 2010, Pt 4)

[31.5] The usual reliefs for losses are available to farming businesses and the usual restriction applies to prevent losses being set against other income if the business is not operated on a commercial basis (see CHAPTER 25 and CHAPTER 26). In addition, a loss in the sixth tax year or sixth accounting period of a consecutive run of farming and market gardening losses (calculated before capital allowances) can only be relieved against later profits of the same trade, unless (very broadly) it can be shown that the taxpayer's farming or market gardening activities are such as would justify a reasonable expectation of profits in the future. If losses are required to be carried forward, any related capital allowances are similarly treated. Once one year shows a profit, another six-year period then applies to later losses.

Income tax relief for losses against general income is one of a number of reliefs subject to a cap from 2013–14 (see **2.13**).

Averaging (TMA 1970, Sch 1B para 3; ITTOIA 2005, ss 221–225)

[31.6] Averaging enables farmers to lessen the effect of high tax rates on a successful year when preceded or followed by a bad year or years. The profits of an individual farmer or market gardener, or of a farming or market gardening partnership, can be averaged over either two or five tax years where the latest of the two or five year period is 2016–17 or a subsequent year. The two-year rule applies where the profit of one year is less than 75% of the profit of the other year or nil.

The five-year rule applies where—

(a) either A or B is less than 75% of the other, A being the average of the relevant profits of the first four tax years to which the claim relates, and B being the relevant profits of the last of the tax years to which the claim relates; or

(b) the relevant profits of one or more (but not all) of the five tax years to which the claim relates are nil.

Where profits are calculated on the cash basis for small businesses (see **20.4**) an averaging election cannot be made. The two-year averaging rules, but not the five-year ones, also apply to authors and creative writers (see **20.50**).

If profits are averaged, the adjusted profits are then used as the profits on which further averaging claims are based. Losses are counted as nil profits in the averaging calculation, with relief for the loss being available separately.

Averaging claims are not made by partnerships. The individual partners may make separate claims on their profit shares if they wish. The time limit for an averaging claim is one year from 31 January following the end of the last tax year to which the claim relates, claims being made in the tax return or an amendment to it. Averaging may not be claimed by farming companies nor in relation to any profits charged to tax as property income (see CHAPTER **32**). An averaging claim cannot be made in the tax year in which a sole trader or partner starts or ceases to trade.

The tax and Class 4 NICs payable under the various alternatives need to be calculated, taking into account, if appropriate, the possibility of not claiming plant and machinery capital allowances or claiming a reduced amount (in which case the written-down value carried forward to attract writing-down allowances in later years would be increased).

[31.7] The adjustment to the tax and Class 4 NICs of an earlier year resulting from a farmer's averaging claim is *calculated* by reference to the position of the earlier year, but the adjustment is made in relation to the *later* year. If the adjustment is an increase, it is added to the tax and Class 4 NICs payable for the later year. If it is a decrease, it is treated as a payment on account for that year. If the adjustment and payments on account for the later year exceed the tax and Class 4 NICs due on the averaged profit for that year, the excess amount will be repaid (or offset if other tax is due or will become due shortly). Interest on overpaid or underpaid tax and Class 4 NICs relating to the adjustment for the earlier year, where relevant, runs from 31 January following the later year (see **9.16**).

Averaging does not affect the payments on account for the earlier year, which are still based on the previous year's tax and Class 4 NICs, subject to any claim to reduce them to the amount payable on the unaveraged profits. Payments on account for the later year will initially be based on the unaveraged profits of the earlier year. Once the liability for the later year can be accurately ascertained, based on the averaged profits, a claim can be made to reduce payments on account if appropriate.

The change to the assessable profit of the later year affects the payments on account for the *next following* year. The increase or decrease in the later year's tax and Class 4 NICs as a result of the averaging adjustment for the earlier year does not, however, enter into the figure for the later year on which payments on account for the next following year are based. Example 1 illustrates the position for a two-year averaging claim.

Example 1

A Welsh farmer's profits after capital allowances are as follows:

Year ended 31 December		£
2015	Profit	45,000
2016	Loss	(7,000)
2017	Profit	53,000

The farmer is a single man with no other sources of income. The relevant tax rates and allowances are:

	Basic rate limit £	Personal allowance £	Income limit for 40% tax £
2015–16	31,785	10,600	42,385
2016–17	32,000	11,000	43,000
2017–18	33,500	11,500	45,000

Class 4 NICs are payable as follows:

	Profits between	Chargeable at 9%
2015–16	£8,060 to £42,385	£34,325
2016–17	£8,060 to £43,000	£34,940
2017–18	£8,164 to £45,000	£36,836

In addition, Class 4 NICs are payable at 2% on profits in excess of the upper limit.

Assessable profits may variously be as follows:

	No averaging £	Averaging 2015–16 and 2016–17 only £	All three years averaged in separate claims £
2015–16	45,000	22,500	22,500
2016–17	—*	22,500*	37,750*
2017–18	53,000	53,000	37,750

* Loss of £7,000 available for relief

The loss of the year to 31 December 2016 is treated as a loss of 2016–17, for which relief may be claimed under ITA 2007, s 64 in 2016–17 or 2015–16. Alternatively it may be carried forward under ITA 2007, s 83 and set off in 2017–18. (Losses are dealt with in CHAPTER 25.)

With no averaging, but claiming relief for the loss of £7,000 in 2015–16 to save some tax at 40% in that year, 40% tax would be payable on £8,000 in 2017–18, and the personal allowance and basic rate band of 2016–17 would be wasted.

If 2015–16 and 2016–17 are averaged, and the loss is carried forward to 2017–18, reducing the taxable profit of that year to £46,000, the 2016–17 personal allowance would be utilised, and the 40% tax of 2015–16 would be eliminated, and only £1,000 would be chargeable at 40% in 2017–18. The 2016–17 averaged figure of £22,500 would be used to calculate the payments on account for 2017–18.

If 2015–16 and 2016–17 are averaged, and then 2016–17 and 2017–18 are averaged, and loss relief is carried forward to 2017–18, no 40% tax would be payable in any year, the 2016–17 personal allowance is utilised and the profits chargeable to the higher Class 4 NICs rate of 9% in 2017–18 are reduced. Following the first claim, the total tax and Class 4 NICs payable in respect of 2016–17 can be ascertained, comprising a reduction in tax payable for 2015–16 and increase for 2016–17. A claim can then be made to reduce the 2016–17 payments on account (which were originally based on the £45,000 profit for 2015–16) to the amount payable on the averaged 2016–17 figure of £22,500 less the reduction for 2015–16. The 2016–17 averaged figure of £22,500 would be used in arriving at payments on account for 2017–18. This would not alter following the second claim, the increase in tax payable for 2016–17 being treated as extra tax due for 2017–18. This extra tax would not, however, be taken into account in calculating payments on account for 2018–19, which would be based on the 2017–18 averaged figure of £37,750.

The third alternative eliminates all 40% tax and utilises the 2016–17 personal allowance. Even though it moves more profit into 2016–17, giving a higher Class 4 liability for that year, it also reduces the profit in 2017–18 chargeable to Class 4 at the higher rate of 9%, and thus gives the greatest overall saving.

HMRC guidance can be found in Helpsheet HS224.

Herd basis (ITTOIA 2005, ss 25A, 30, 31F, 111–129; CTA 2009, ss 50, 109–127)

[31.8] Farm animals and other livestock are normally treated as trading stock, except where profits are calculated on the cash basis for small businesses (see **20.4**). A production herd may, however, effectively be treated as a capital asset if an election is made for the herd basis, although the election cannot be made where profits are calculated on the cash basis. The election is irrevocable. In addition to being available to individuals, companies and partnerships the herd basis is available where animals are held on a shared basis, for instance in share farming. HMRC guidance is available in the Business Income Manual at BIM55501–55640 and in Helpsheet HS224. A production herd is a group of living animals or other livestock kept for obtaining products such as milk, wool, etc. or their young.

For companies, the time limit for making the election is two years from the end of the first accounting period in which the herd is kept. The time limit for individuals and partnerships is one year from the 31 January following the tax year in which the first 'relevant period of account' ends. The first relevant period of account is the first period of account in which the farmer keeps a production herd of the class to which the election relates. If a farmer (other than a partnership) started to carry on the trade in that tax year, the time limit is extended by a year.

> **Example 2**
>
> A production herd is acquired in May 2017 by an established business that makes up its accounts to 31 December.
>
> The time limit for a claim by individuals and partners is 31 January 2020.
>
> The limit would remain the same if the year to 31 December 2017 was the first year of business for a sole trader, because the account ends in the second tax year. If accounts had been made up to 5 April and the year to 5 April 2018 had been the first accounting year of a sole trader, then the relevant account would end in the first tax year of trading, i.e. 2017–18, and the time limit would be 31 January 2021.

A change in the partners in a farming partnership requires a new herd basis election to be made even where the farming business has owned the herd for several years. There are, however, anti-avoidance provisions to prevent the change being used solely or mainly for the purposes of obtaining a benefit resulting from the right to make a herd basis election or flowing from the election. A herd basis election is not affected when a partnership becomes a limited liability partnership (see **23.33**).

Under self-assessment, partnerships make a single election for the herd basis, even though partners are assessed separately. HMRC have stated that they will not require farmers to make a separate written election where it is clear from material submitted that the herd basis has been applied.

The effect of the election is that the initial purchase of the herd and any subsequent purchases that increase the herd attract no tax relief, but a renewals basis applies where animals are replaced, so that the cost of the replacement is charged as an expense and the sale proceeds are brought in as a trading receipt. Where there is a minor disposal without replacement ('minor' usually meaning less than 20% of the herd), profits on the disposal are also brought in as a trading receipt. If the whole or a substantial part of the herd is sold and not replaced, no part of the proceeds is charged as income, because it represents the sale of a capital asset, and capital gains tax does not arise since the animals are wasting assets on which capital allowances are not available and are therefore exempt (see **4.12**).

Compensation for compulsory slaughter (ITTOIA 2005, ss 31F, 225ZA–ZG; CTA 2009, ss 127A–G)

[31.9] Where compensation is paid for compulsorily slaughtered stock to which the herd basis does not apply, the compensation may be left out of account in the year of receipt and brought in over the next three years in equal instalments. This treatment of the compensation is not available where profits are calculated on the cash basis for small businesses (see **20.4**).

Farm plant and machinery

[31.10] Capital allowances on farm plant and machinery are generally available in the usual way (see CHAPTER 22 for a summary of the rules), subject to the restriction of their availability where profits are calculated on the cash basis for small businesses (see **22.1**). Expenditure should be carefully analysed to make sure that plant and machinery is properly treated as such, rather than being treated as part of an agricultural building which does not qualify for capital allowances.

HMRC Brief 3/2010 on capital allowances in the pig industry provides examples of plant and machinery which can qualify for capital allowances (including outdoor items, fixtures in buildings and structures, non-fixtures other than cars, and cars themselves) and outlines the rules relating to buildings and structures, revenue expenditure and double allowances. For fixtures generally see **22.45**.

Value added tax

[31.11] For VAT purposes, most of a farm's outputs are zero-rated, but there may also be standard-rated outputs, such as sales of equipment, shooting rights, holiday accommodation, and exempt outputs such as rents for residential caravan sites, possibly leading to partial exemption restrictions. Many farmers have diversified into non-farming activities, and special care needs to be taken in relation to the VAT position. HMRC have paid particular attention to shooting businesses and have found widespread VAT irregularities. The usual input VAT restrictions for entertaining, private use, etc. apply (see CHAPTER 7). For the treatment of land and buildings and of the farmhouse, see **31.14** and **31.16**.

Flat-rate farmers (VATA 1994, s 54; SI 1992/3221; SI 1995/2518, regs 202–211)

[31.12] Farmers may opt to become 'flat-rate farmers' for VAT purposes, regardless of their turnover, providing they satisfy HMRC that the total flat-rate compensation they will be entitled to in the year after they join the scheme will not exceed the input VAT they could have claimed by £3,000 or more and the value of non-farming activities does not exceed the VAT registration threshold (see **7.8**). They do not need to register for VAT and therefore make no VAT returns, but they add a fixed flat-rate compensation percentage of 4% to their sale prices when they sell to VAT-registered businesses, which they keep to offset the input VAT they have suffered. The VAT-registered businesses are able to reclaim on their VAT returns the compensation amount charged to them. Farmers below the VAT registration threshold need not become flat-rate farmers unless they wish to. A flat-rate farmer whose non-farming turnover goes over the registration threshold must leave the scheme and register for VAT.

Agricultural landlords (ITA 2007, ss 24A, 118, 120, 127B; CAA 2001, ss 361–393; ITTOIA 2005, ss 9–11; CTA 2009, ss 36–38; CTA 2010, ss 62–67)

[31.13] Income from letting agricultural land is taxed in the same way as for any investment property (see CHAPTER 32).

For individuals, all rental income is charged as the profits of a property business. If expenses exceed income, and provided the profits of the property business are not calculated under the cash basis (see **32.6**), the landlord may claim to set the loss against his total income of the same tax year and/or the following tax year, to the extent that the loss consists of capital allowances (see **31.10**) and/or maintenance, repairs, insurance or management expenses (but not loan interest) relating to agricultural land that is managed as one estate. Note, however, that this is one of a number of reliefs against general income which is subject to a cap from 2013–14 (see **2.13**). Any part of the loss remaining unrelieved is carried forward to set against later rental income. Relief is denied where the agricultural expenses deducted in calculating the loss arise as a result of tax avoidance arrangements, unless there was an unconditional obligation in a contract made before 13 March 2012. See HMRC Helpsheet HS251 for guidance.

Companies are subject to broadly the same rules as individuals, although the treatment of losses is not the same. Companies may set property business losses against their total profits of the same accounting period, or alternatively surrender the losses by way of group relief, any unrelieved balance being carried forward to set against the *total* profits of succeeding periods, provided, for losses arising on or after 1 April 2017, a claim is made (see **26.7**). Post-1 April 2017 losses may also be surrendered for group relief in certain circumstances (see **26.22**). For further details on property business losses in general, see CHAPTER 32.

The occupation of land for farming purposes (such as growing crops and raising farm livestock) is treated as a trade. This will apply where an owner receives income from short-term grazing lets, providing the owner's activities in growing the grass, fertilising, etc., and general upkeep and maintenance of the land, can be regarded as farming. In that event, the land will qualify as a business asset on which rollover relief for capital gains tax is available if it is sold and the proceeds reinvested in a qualifying replacement asset within one year before and three years after the sale (see **29.16** onwards).

Although gifts relief for capital gains tax normally applies only to business assets or to gifts that are immediately chargeable to inheritance tax (see **4.31** to **4.34**), it applies to agricultural property held as an investment providing the conditions for inheritance tax agricultural property relief are satisfied (see **5.48**).

Value added tax (VATA 1994, Sch 8 Group 5, Sch 9 Group 1 and Sch 10; FA 2009, s 79)

[31.14] Grants of long or short leases of agricultural land and buildings, and rents received therefrom, are exempt from VAT, but the landlord has the option to charge VAT. Written notice must be given to HMRC within 30 days. VAT is then charged from the day the landlord exercises his option, or any later date he specifies. If the landlord is not already VAT-registered, he will have to become registered. If the option is taken, it can be revoked within a six-month 'cooling off' period from the time it takes effect, or more than 20 years after it takes effect (or it revokes automatically, where six years have lapsed since anyone had a relevant interest in the property, see **32.42**). Where a landlord has interests in several different estates, an election can be made for specific discrete areas (such as one farm). The landlord may increase existing rents by the VAT charged if the lease allows VAT to be added or is silent as to VAT. If not, the rent has to be treated as VAT-inclusive.

Following the exercise of the option, VAT must be charged not only on rents and lease premiums, but also on any sale proceeds as and when any of the land and buildings are sold (subject to what is said in **32.42**). An apportionment will be made in each case, however, to exclude any private dwelling/charitable element. Making the election enables the landlord to recover any VAT he suffers, for example on the acquisition of the property, or on repairs, and the farmer tenants will usually be VAT-registered and will therefore be able to recover the VAT charged.

Provisions prevent the exercise or revocation of the option to tax or a change in the VAT rate from qualifying as a change of rent for the purposes of the Agricultural Holdings Act so the parties to a lease are not prevented from referring the rent to arbitration.

Small agricultural holdings

[31.15] The profits of a commercial smallholding are taxed as trading profits, but if losses arise, HMRC may contend that the trade is not conducted on a commercial basis with a view to profit, so that the losses may only be carried forward against future income from the smallholding and not set against any other income. This is quite separate from their right to disallow farming losses from the sixth year onwards (see **31.5**).

The smallholder may seek voluntary VAT registration even though his taxable supplies are less than £85,000 per year (the VAT registration threshold from 1 April 2017, see **7.8**), because he will then be able to reclaim input VAT on his expenditure and he will have no liability on his supplies, which are zero-rated. HMRC are required to register anyone making taxable supplies who seeks voluntary registration. The smallholder may alternatively join the flat-rate scheme for farmers (see **31.12**).

The farmhouse (TCGA 1992, ss 222–224; IHTA 1984, s 115(2); ITTOIA 2005, s 94H–94I)

[31.16] In arriving at the farm profits, an appropriate part of the establishment charges of the farmhouse is allowed, based on the extent to which the farmhouse is used for business. See **20.19** for details of simplified fixed rate deductions which can be made for the business use of a home. Alternatively it may be the case that there is private use of business premises in respect of the farmhouse, particularly if it used as a guest house, and **20.19** also details the fixed rate adjustment which may be made to expenses for the private element.

HMRC adopt a similar 'business proportion' approach in relation to the recovery of input VAT on farmhouse expenses such as light and heat. They may, however, allow a sole proprietor or partner working full-time to recover 70% of the input VAT on repair and maintenance costs where certain conditions are met, under an agreement reached with the NFU. Where farming is not a full-time business, the allowable percentage will need to be agreed with HMRC.

The business expenses deduction will not jeopardise the capital gains tax private residence exemption (see **30.3**) provided that no part of the farmhouse has been used exclusively for business purposes. Where part is so used and a chargeable gain arises, rollover relief may be claimed if the farmhouse is replaced (see **29.16** onwards). The capital gains tax exemption usually extends to grounds up to half a hectare, but for a farmhouse a larger area may be allowed because of the situation and character of the farmhouse and immediately surrounding grounds. The capital gains tax exemptions and reliefs are dealt with in CHAPTER **4**.

Agricultural property relief for inheritance tax (see **5.48**) is available on the farmhouse providing the owner also owns the agricultural land, the farmhouse is 'of a character appropriate to the property', and occupation of the farmhouse is ancillary to that of the agricultural land. These conditions are often considered by HMRC not to be satisfied and case law has given support to HMRC's views. They will investigate in detail exactly what the occupier of the residence was doing in the way of agricultural activity in the relevant period, to determine whether the residence could properly be called a 'farmhouse' for these purposes, paying particular attention to cases where the farmer had retired and let his land on grazing agreements. The latest view of the courts is that cottages, farm buildings and farmhouses must be of a character appropriate to agricultural land or pasture in the same *occupation*, but that it is not required that they should be in the same *ownership* as the agricultural land or pasture in order to qualify for agricultural relief. Even if it is available, the relief is given on the 'agricultural value' of the property only, not the open market value. Where there is part business use of the farmhouse, for example for bed and breakfast, business property relief will apply on the business proportion.

Agricultural property relief is available on qualifying property in other EEA states (see **1.3**).

Land let by partners to farming partnership, or by directors to farming company (TCGA 1992, ss 152–158)

[31.17] Where land is owned personally by a partner or director, and let to the farming business, any rent paid is allowed as an expense of the business and treated as property income in the partner's or director's hands. If interest is paid on a loan to buy the land it may be deducted in arriving at the net property income (see CHAPTER 32).

Capital gains tax rollover relief may sometimes be claimed if the land is disposed of and the proceeds used to acquire a qualifying asset within one year before and three years after the sale. Charging rent as indicated above does not affect this relief. See **29.16** onwards.

Capital gains tax (TCGA 1992, ss 155, 169H–169S, 249)

[31.18] Various capital gains tax aspects are dealt with elsewhere in this chapter. As far as rollover relief for replacement of business assets is concerned, some categories of qualifying asset specifically relate to farming, namely agricultural quotas (see **29.17**). For companies, agricultural quotas acquired on or after 1 April 2002 come within the intangible assets provisions and are dealt with in calculating income rather than under the capital gains rules (see **20.35** onwards). The following provisions now apply only for individuals.

Quota is treated as a separate asset from land, and where nothing was paid for the quota there is no allowable cost to set against the gain on disposal. HMRC regard quotas as being non-depreciating assets for rollover relief. Where quota and land is transferred in a single transaction, values have to be apportioned on a just and reasonable basis. See also **31.1**.

Where a tenant receives statutory compensation following a notice to quit, or for improvements at the end of the tenancy, the compensation is not liable to capital gains tax.

Although all farming carried on by one farmer is treated as a single trade, for entrepreneurs' relief purposes (see **29.2**) the relief will be allowed, provided all the other qualifying conditions are met, if a farmer ceases one type of farming business in its entirety and then starts another.

Farming companies are not qualifying companies for enterprise investment scheme and seed enterprise investment scheme relief. For social investment tax relief there is a similar restriction for companies involved in production of agricultural products. See CHAPTER 29.

Inheritance tax (IHTA 1984, ss 115–124C)

[31.19] When agricultural property is transferred, inheritance tax agricultural property relief is given on the agricultural value, and where the property is also business property, business property relief is given on the non-agricultural value. The detailed rules for each relief are in CHAPTER 5. Farmland that is managed in an environmentally beneficial way under the Countryside Stewardship Scheme will usually qualify for agricultural property relief providing the land was occupied for agricultural purposes at the time it was brought within the Scheme. Agricultural property relief is not, however, available on farmland converted to woodland used for the production of commercial timber, but the special provisions for woodlands may apply (see **31.25**).

The rate of relief for some tenanted agricultural property used to be 50%, as against 100% for owner-occupied land, but relief at the 100% rate is now available for all qualifying tenanted property where the letting commenced on or after 1 September 1995, including successions to tenancies following the death of the previous tenant on or after that date (see **5.48**). The grant of the tenancy itself is specifically exempt from inheritance tax so long as it is made for full consideration. Although tenanted property normally has to be owned for seven years to qualify for agricultural property relief (see **5.48**), the period is only two years where the tenant is a partnership in which the donor is a partner or a company controlled by the donor.

The relief applies to lifetime transfers which are not potentially exempt, or which, having been so, become chargeable because the donor dies within seven years, and to transfers on death. The relief is only available in calculating the tax or additional tax payable as a result of the donor's death within seven years if the donee still owns the property (or qualifying replacement property) when the donor dies, or if earlier, when the donee dies.

Where relief at the time of the transfer is at 100%, there will be neither a chargeable transfer nor a potentially exempt transfer at that time, but the transfer will be counted at death if the donor does not survive the seven-year period (see **5.47**).

The 100% rate of agricultural property relief discourages lifetime gifts, because a lifetime gift will attract capital gains tax (although payment can be deferred by claiming gifts relief — see **4.32**), whereas on death there is a capital gains tax-free uplift in asset values. There is, of course, no certainty that the present favourable regime will continue.

Agricultural property relief applies to qualifying property in other EEA states (see **1.3**).

Stamp duty land tax, and land and buildings transaction tax

[31.20] Stamp duty land tax is payable on the sale of farm land and buildings. This is replaced in Scotland by land and buildings transaction tax (LBTT, see **6.18**). It is not usually payable on a gift, but if, say, mortgaged farmland was transferred from a farmer to a family farming partnership, or from one family partnership to another, and the transferee took over liability for the mortgage, the amount of the mortgage would be subject to stamp duty land tax or LBTT unless it fell within the nil rate band (see **6.9**).

Woodlands and short rotation coppice

[31.21] The tax treatment of woodlands is dealt with below. See **31.26** for short rotation coppice which is treated as farming, rather than under the woodlands provisions.

Income and corporation tax (ITTOIA 2005, s 11; CTA 2009, s 37)

[31.22] There is no income or corporation tax charge on profits from the commercial occupation of woodlands in the UK, so relief for losses incurred and interest paid in the initial planting period cannot be claimed, but as and when profits arise they are not taxed. Payments under the Farm Woodland Premium Scheme, which are made for 10 or 15 years depending on the type of woodland, are taxable as farming income, even if paid to someone who does not carry on a farming business. Most woodland grants, on the other hand, are not taxable. The Farm Woodland Premium Scheme is closed to new applicants but existing agreements will continue until the contracted expiry date.

Capital gains tax (TCGA 1992, ss 158, 250)

[31.23] There is no charge to capital gains tax on trees that are standing or felled. Proceeds of sale of timber are therefore not charged to tax at all. The land is, however, a chargeable asset for capital gains purposes. It is therefore important on acquisition and disposal to establish the different values applicable to the timber and the land.

For commercially run woodlands, gains on sale of the land may be deferred by rolling them over against the cost of replacement assets where the land sale proceeds are reinvested in qualifying business assets within one year before and three years after the sale (see **29.16** onwards). If a gain is made on a disposal by way of gift, it will not qualify for gifts relief (see **4.31**) unless the woodlands operation is a trade. Entrepreneurs' relief would also not be available unless there was a 'qualifying business disposal' (see **29.2**).

Where woodlands are owned by a company, the land is a qualifying asset for rollover relief as far as the company is concerned, but an individual shareholder will not get rollover relief when he sells his shares and reinvests the proceeds (unless he qualifies for enterprise investment scheme relief — see

29.33). He will not be entitled to gifts relief (see **4.32** to **4.34**) or entrepreneurs' relief (see **29.2**) in respect of the shares unless the company is a trading company and the other conditions for relief are satisfied.

Value added tax (VATA 1994, Sch 1 para 9)

[31.24] A commercially run woodland is within the scope of VAT, the supply or granting of any right to fell and remove standing timber being standard-rated. It is possible to register for VAT before making taxable supplies, the intention to make taxable supplies being sufficient for registration purposes even though they will not be made for some years (see **7.8**). Having registered, input VAT on goods and services in connection with the woodlands operation can be recovered.

Inheritance tax (IHTA 1984, ss 125–130)

[31.25] Where an estate on death includes growing timber, an election may be made to leave the timber (but not the land on which it stands) out of account in valuing the estate at death. The election must be made within two years after the date of death and is only available if the deceased either had been beneficially entitled to the land throughout the previous five years or had become entitled to it without consideration (for example by gift or inheritance). Commercially managed woodlands will usually qualify for 100% business property relief, in which case the election would not be made — see below.

The election cannot be made if the occupation of the woodlands is subsidiary to the occupation of agricultural land, but agricultural property relief would be given if the necessary conditions were fulfilled, except that agricultural property relief will not be available on any part of the land that has been converted to woodland used for the production of commercial timber.

Following the election, when the timber is later disposed of by sale or gift, there will be a charge to inheritance tax on the sale price or, if the disposal is for less than full consideration, the market value, less allowable expenses in both cases. Allowable expenses are the costs of sale and expenses of replanting within three years after disposal, or such longer time as HMRC allow.

The net disposal proceeds or market value are treated as value transferred at the date of death, forming the top slice of the property passing on death, but using the scale and rates current at the time of disposal to find a notional liability on the estate first excluding and then including the timber proceeds, the tax on the timber proceeds being the difference between the two. The tax is due six months after the end of the month in which the disposal takes place, with interest on overdue tax payable from that date. The person entitled to the sale proceeds is liable for the tax. Where there are no proceeds because the disposal is by way of gift, the donee is liable for the tax, which may be paid by instalments over ten years.

The relief applies to qualifying woodlands in other EEA states (see **1.3**).

A lifetime gift of woodlands not qualifying for business property relief either attracts inheritance tax or is a potentially exempt transfer (see CHAPTER 5). Where the disposal is one on which tax is payable following its being left out of account on an earlier death, the value transferred by the lifetime transfer is reduced by the tax charge arising out of the previous death.

If the person who inherits woodlands on which an election has been made dies before the timber is disposed of, no inheritance tax charge can arise in respect of the first death. Furthermore, a new election may then be made on the second death.

Where woodlands are managed on a commercial basis, despite there being no income tax charge, they qualify for 100% business property relief so long as they have been owned for two years (see **5.45**). Where tax is payable, it may be paid by instalments in the case of a death transfer where the value has not been left out of account and where a lifetime transfer is not potentially exempt and the *donee* pays the tax (see **5.54**). If an election is made to leave the timber out of account on a death, business property relief is given on the net sale proceeds when it is disposed of, but only at 50% rather than 100%. This will be relevant where the election has already been made, but clearly no new elections will be made where the 100% business property relief is available.

Short rotation coppice (ITA 2007, s 996; CTA 2010, s 1125)

[31.26] Short rotation coppice, which is a way of producing a renewable fuel for 'green' biomass-fed power stations from willow or poplar cuttings, is regarded as farming for income tax, corporation tax and capital gains tax, and as agricultural land for inheritance tax.

HMRC consider that the initial cultivation costs of the short rotation coppice are capital expenditure, the net amount of which (after deducting any grants offset against the expenditure) may be used to roll over gains on disposals of other business assets. The expenditure (net of both grants and any rolled-over gains) will be allowable in calculating gains when the land is disposed of, providing the coppice stools are still on the land at that time.

Subsequent expenditure after the initial cultivation will be revenue expenditure.

Council tax and business rates

[31.27] Agricultural land and buildings are generally exempt from business rates, although riding stables, farm shops and self-catering holiday cottages which are available for short-term letting for 140 days or more in a year are all usually subject to business rates. Any buildings or parts of buildings that are for domestic rather than agricultural use attract up to 90% of the council tax if the building or part is no-one's only or main home (see **8.5**). If it is someone's only or main home, the residents are liable to pay council tax. The valuation takes into account the restricted market for the property because of the agricultural use. Where farms diversify into non-agricultural activities, business rates are payable.

In small rural communities, sole post offices and/or village food shops (other than confectionery shops or catering businesses) with rateable values up to £8,500, sole pubs or petrol stations with rateable values up to £12,500, and farm shops etc. on what was previously agricultural land and buildings have previously been entitled to 50% mandatory rural business rates relief, with councils having the power to increase the relief to 100%. From 1 April 2017 the Government expects 100% relief to be given by all councils, in advance of regulations making the increase mandatory. Councils may also grant relief to other rural businesses important to the community that have rateable values up to £16,500. Following the 2017 revaluation of business rates (see **8.10**), businesses that no longer qualify for rural rate relief will be subject to a cap on the amount by which their rate bills can rise, which is broadly £50 a month from 1 April 2017 to 31 March 2018.

Tax points

[31.28] Note the following:

- A smallholding may show consistent losses, and it is unlikely that these can be relieved against other income. A smallholding that amounts to a trade may prejudice the capital gains tax private residence exemption, and it may be worthwhile making a note in the annual tax return that the working of the holding is not by way of trade but only for the maintenance of the holding and that no profits arise.
- Where a smallholding or market garden is clearly a trade, it should be ensured if possible that no part of the dwelling house is used exclusively for business, to avoid any possible loss of the capital gains tax private residence exemption (see **30.23**).
- If losses are being made and there is a danger of falling foul of the six-year rule (see **31.5**), repairs or other expenses could perhaps be delayed for a year in order to show a small profit. The six-year cycle will then start again.
- Owning agricultural land personally and renting it to his partnership or company will not stop an individual getting capital gains tax rollover relief (see **29.16** onwards) if the land is sold and replaced. Rollover relief is not available to other agricultural landlords.
- Capital gains tax gifts relief *is* available to agricultural landlords if the conditions are satisfied (see **4.32** to **4.34**).
- Entrepreneurs' relief may be available if there is a 'qualifying business disposal' (see **29.2**).
- A farmer's averaging claim affects income for two or more years, but the claim has no effect on the dates on which tax is due for payment (see **31.6**).
- If ownership of the farm is transferred to the family, but the transferor still lives in the farmhouse, the farmhouse will no longer qualify for inheritance tax agricultural property relief as it will not have been occupied for the required period for the purposes of agriculture. The transferor needs to be a partner with a share, albeit small, in the farm to remain entitled to the relief.

- Farmers and landowners involved in game shooting should look at the income tax and VAT implications very carefully. HMRC have targeted the shooting industry because they considered there was evidence of non-compliance and misunderstanding.
- A number of specialist organisations advise on an investment in woodlands, not only from the taxation point of view but also on the question of cash grants through the Forestry Commission, and on estate management.

32

Investing in land and buildings

Introduction

[32.1] This chapter deals with both commercial and private investment properties in the UK. The detailed treatment of let agricultural buildings is covered in **31.13**. Companies may claim relief equal to 150% of qualifying expenditure on cleaning up contaminated and derelict land that has been acquired for the purposes of a trade or property business (see **20.42**).

Rental income is charged under the heading of property income, either of a UK property business or an overseas property business as the case may be (see **2.7** for individuals and **3.4** for companies), but see **32.25** for the treatment of property businesses that are, or include, the commercial letting of furnished holiday accommodation. The treatment of UK property let by those who live abroad and of property abroad let by UK residents is dealt with in **41.29** and **41.43**. Where the 'split year' rule (see **41.6**) applies to an individual carrying on an overseas property business, only the profits of the UK part of the year are taxable in the UK. See also **10.32** regarding the exemption from a benefit in kind for living accommodation in certain circumstances where holiday homes outside the UK are bought through the taxpayer's own company.

Landlords of multiple properties will frequently hold service charges and sinking funds on trust. Income from such trust funds held by any UK landlord is taxable at income tax rates and not the trust rate (see CHAPTER **2**). See **6.13** for special stamp duty land tax provisions for Registered Social Landlords.

September 2017 Finance Bill, which is expected to receive Royal Assent in November 2017, introduces changes to the taxation of property from 6 April 2017 — a £1,000 allowance for property income (see **32.5**) and a cash basis for unincorporated property businesses (see **32.6**).

Income from land and buildings

[32.2] Income from UK land and buildings is usually charged to tax as property income, except for income from furnished holiday lettings, which is treated as trading income for the purpose of certain reliefs (see **32.25** onwards). The distinction between trading income and property income is important to individuals in relation to pension contributions, although those without earnings may get tax relief on personal pension contributions up to £3,600 a year (see **16.14** and **17.4**). The distinction between trading and property income is also important for capital gains tax purposes because an investment property does not qualify for capital gains tax rollover relief (see **29.16** onwards) when it is replaced (unless it is compulsorily purchased — see **32.34**). Gifts relief (see **4.31**) will not usually be available either. See also **29.2** regarding entrepreneurs' relief on qualifying business disposals, which would not include a disposal of an investment property.

Non-resident companies may be liable to corporation tax on the entire profits arising from dealing in or developing UK land, and similarly non-resident persons may be liable to income tax. See **41.64** and **41.44**.

As far as inheritance tax is concerned, business property relief is not available where the business consists of making or holding investments, which includes land which is let (see **5.45**). The relief has been denied in Court cases even where the owners played a very active role in the letting, management and maintenance of their properties, and one decision in favour of the taxpayer in a case concerning a caravan site was overruled in the High Court. From 6 April 2017 non-domiciled individuals are chargeable to inheritance tax on UK residential property held indirectly by them (see **5.2**). See **32.31** regarding furnished holiday lettings. Agricultural property relief is available to landlords of let agricultural property (see **31.19**).

Income tax on rents is usually paid as part of the half-yearly payments on account on 31 January in the tax year and 31 July following, with a balancing adjustment on the next 31 January (see **9.4**). Companies pay corporation tax on all their profits under self-assessment, the due date normally being nine months after the end of the accounting period, except for certain large companies who are required to pay their tax by instalments (see **3.24**).

The tax treatment of individuals is dealt with from **32.3** to **32.11** and that of companies at **32.12** and **32.13**. The capital allowances provisions for both individuals and companies are dealt with at **32.14** to **32.19**. The treatment of furnished holiday lettings, which applies both to individuals and companies, is dealt with at **32.25** to **32.33**. The treatment of lease premiums, which is again broadly the same for individuals and companies, is dealt with at **32.20** to **32.24**.

Tax treatment of individuals (ITA 2007, ss 399A–B, 836, 837; CAA 2001, ss 15, 16, 35; ITTOIA 2005, ss 272A–B, 274A–C, 263–275)

[32.3] Special rules apply where furnished rooms are let in an individual's own home, and in some circumstances the letting may amount to a trade. This is dealt with in **30.12** to **30.16**. Profits from the provision of accommodation in hotels or guest houses are wholly trading income and are not property income. With these exceptions, all income from UK property (including the right to use a fixed caravan or permanently moored houseboat) is treated as the profits of a UK property business, whether there is just one letting or a number of lettings, whether the property is let furnished or unfurnished, and no matter whether repairs are the responsibility of the landlord or the tenant (although income from qualifying furnished holiday lettings is kept separate and the provisions outlined at **32.25** to **32.33** apply).

[32.4] Where there are joint owners of a let property, in some cases the letting may form part of a partnership business. More usually each joint owner's share is treated as their personal property business income. HMRC state in their Property Income Manual at PIM1030 that for joint owners other than spouses or civil partners, although normally shares of rental income are equal to the respective shares of ownership of the property, the joint owners may agree to share the income differently. Their taxable share would be the share actually agreed. It would be sensible to have written evidence of any such arrangements. Splitting income differently from capital shares is generally not possible for spouses or civil partners, but see the comments about furnished holiday lettings in **33.6**.

Small amounts of property income (ITTOIA 2005, ss 783B–783BQ)

[32.5] September 2017 Finance Bill, which is expected to receive Royal Assent in November 2017, introduces a £1,000 allowance for property income from 6 April 2017 and it is aimed at those who receive small amounts of property income from ad hoc lettings during the year. The allowance is not available on income of partners or participators in a close company (see **3.29**), on income from property Authorised Investment Funds or Real Estate Investment Trusts (see **32.36**), where rent-a-room relief (see **30.12**) is, or could be, claimed (see **19.20** for an explanation of this restriction), or where a tax reduction is claimed for non-deductible finance costs (see below). An anti-avoidance provision also prevents an employer from trying to reclassify payments to employees as property income to take advantage of the allowance.

Where the total receipts from all property businesses in the tax year are less than £1,000, the allowance is given automatically in full so that no tax is payable and the income does not have to be declared. This is, however, subject to an election which can be made on or before the first anniversary of the normal self-assessment filing date for the tax year for full relief not to be given. The most obvious situation where the election could be made is if expenses exceed receipts resulting in a loss, and the deadline must not be missed otherwise losses will be forfeited.

Where the total receipts from all property businesses in the tax year exceed the £1,000 allowance an election can still be made for partial relief, where the allowance is deducted from the receipts instead of the actual allowable expenses. This will clearly be beneficial if the expenses are less than the £1,000 allowance.

Calculation of property income (ITTOIA 2005, ss 268–275)

Cash basis for unincorporated property businesses

[32.6] The property income charged to tax is that of the tax year from 6 April to 5 April, but different rules apply to partnerships — see **23.6**. September 2017 Finance Bill, which is expected to receive Royal Assent in November 2017, introduces a cash basis of calculation from 2017–18 for most unincorporated property businesses with receipts of up to £150,000, reduced proportionately if the business is not carried on for the whole of the tax year. Certain business must continue to use generally accepted accounting practice (GAAP) as in previous years (see non-cash basis in **32.7**), and others can elect to do so. Those businesses which must continue to use GAAP are companies, limited liability partnerships, partnerships with at least one non-individual partner, trustees, and businesses where a business premises renovation allowance balancing adjustment (see **32.19**) would be due in the year if the profits were calculated under GAAP. The election must be made on or before the first anniversary of the normal self-assessment filing date for the tax year.

The £150,000 threshold and decision on whether to make the election apply to each property business, so a person with multiple property businesses could apply differing bases to each business. If spouses or civil partners are joint owners of let property, and they have not made a declaration of unequal beneficial interests (see **33.6**) they cannot calculate their profits on differing bases. Other joint owners are able to use different bases of calculation, so one may use the default cash basis whilst the other may elect to use GAAP.

Under the cash basis the receipts are brought into account at the time they are received, and expenses at the time they are paid, subject to any adjustments required by law. A number of the general accounting rules for working out trading profits still apply in the same way that they apply to rental profits calculated using GAAP and allowable revenue expenditure will be very similar (see **32.7**), but the treatment of capital expenditure and receipts is aligned with that relating to the cash basis for small businesses (see **20.11**) and capital allowances are only available on a car.

On leaving the cash basis the same spreading rules in **20.23** apply.

Relief for loans costs is proportionately reduced where the total amount outstanding on property loans is greater than the value of the properties involved in the property business. Where the loan relates to residential property the further restrictions outlined in **32.8** apply.

The relief for replacement of domestic items outlined in **32.15** can apply when the cash basis is used.

Non-cash basis property businesses

[32.7] The income charged to tax is that of the tax year from 6 April to 5 April, but different rules apply to partnerships — see **23.6**. Where profits are not calculated under the cash basis for unincorporated property businesses (see **32.6**), the general accounting rules for working out trading profits apply, but the cash basis rules for small businesses (see **20.4**) cannot be used. Allowable expenses are broadly those that are of a revenue rather than a capital nature (but see **32.14** regarding capital allowances) and are wholly and exclusively for the purpose of the lettings, so that appropriate adjustments must be made where there is part private use of the let property (see **20.5**).

Allowable expenses include business rates or council tax if appropriate (see **32.46**), rent payable to a superior landlord, insurance and management expenses, including advertising for tenants, and maintenance, repairs and redecorations. Allowable expenditure will include that incurred before letting commences, in the same way as for pre-trading expenditure (see **21.8**). This does not, however, include repairs to newly acquired property that were necessary before the property could be brought into use, which form part of the capital cost of the property. Improvement expenditure on, for example, building extensions or installing central heating, is not allowable in calculating income, although it is counted as part of the cost for capital gains tax purposes. Replacing single glazing with double glazing is, however, accepted as repair expenditure. See the HMRC Property Income Manual at PIM2020 for detailed information on what HMRC accept as allowable repair expenditure.

See **32.34** for the treatment of a payment for dilapidations by an outgoing tenant.

In calculating the taxable rent, adjustments are made for rent and expenses in arrear or in advance. Where total gross rents do not exceed £15,000 a year, HMRC have historically accepted profit calculations on the basis of amounts received and paid, with no adjustments for amounts in arrear or in advance, providing this cash basis is used consistently and does not give a materially different result from the statutory method. This is unlikely to be relevant from 2017–18 when the statutory cash basis for property businesses applies.

Because rental income is calculated in the same way as trading profits, it is possible for a landlord to increase the amount borrowed on the let property (the total borrowing not, however, exceeding the original cost of the property) and to withdraw some of the capital he originally invested.

Where capital allowances are available, they are calculated in the same way as for trades and are deducted as an expense (see **32.17**).

Where total property income before expenses is below £85,000 a year (£83,000 for 2016–17), only total figures of rent, expenses and net income need to be included on the tax return. See HMRC Worksheet SA105 Notes.

Finance cost deductions

[32.8] Finance costs including fees and interest payable on loans to buy land or property, or to fund repairs, improvements or alterations, including interest payable to a non-resident lender, are allowed in calculating profits, subject to the 'wholly and exclusively' rule. From 6 April 2017 restrictions on income tax relief for finance costs on 'dwelling-related' loans are being phased in over a four-year period to eventually allow tax relief at the basic rate only. The restriction does not apply to companies, commercial property or furnished holiday lettings, nor does it apply to loans for property development trades, or loans secured on a let dwelling house which are applied for the purposes of a trade. Where the amount borrowed for the purpose of the property business is only partly used for generating income from a dwelling it is apportioned on a just and reasonable basis. The costs to be restricted are loan interest, or any economical equivalent such as disguised interest or alternative finance arrangements, plus incidental costs of obtaining the loan finance.

The restriction is applied by initially restricting the amount allowable as a deduction in calculating the profits of the property business as follows—

Tax year	% of costs of dwelling-related loan allowable as a deduction	Non-deductible costs
2017–18	75%	25%
2018–19	50%	50%
2019–20	25%	75%
2020–21	0%	100%

A tax reduction is then applied in calculating the individual's income tax liability essentially equivalent to a basic rate tax deduction for the non-deductible costs. So in 2017–18, 75% of the finance costs will be deductible in full against profits and thus relievable at the taxpayer's marginal tax rate, and the remaining 25% will be relievable at the basic rate of tax only by means of a tax reduction. In 2020–21 all the costs will be relievable at the basic rate only. However, the relief cannot exceed the property income profits for the year at the basic rate, or if lower, the adjusted total income for year at the basic rate (this would apply where the profits are partly covered by the personal allowance). Any excess costs which cannot be relieved in a tax year are carried forward and used to calculate the tax reduction in future years, even if the loan has been repaid. HMRC guidance and examples can be found at www.gov.uk/guidance/changes-to-tax-relief-for-residential-landlords-how-its-worked-out-including-case-studies.

The restriction on deductible costs also applies to interest on a loan to invest in a partnership if that partnership carries on a UK or overseas property business which generates income from a dwelling house. Where a trustee receives property income to which beneficiaries are entitled, the individual beneficiaries will be eligible for the basic rate tax reduction, but the trustees will obtain the reduction where costs have been restricted in calculating their accumulated or discretionary income.

Treatment of losses (ITA 2007, ss 24A, 117–127A)

[32.9] The reliefs in respect of trading losses (see CHAPTER 26) do not apply to losses of a property business. If losses arise, they are normally carried forward to set against later rental income. Relief is, however, available against other income of the same and/or the following tax year in respect of excess capital allowances (see **22.13**) and certain agricultural expenses, although subject to restrictions in some circumstances, and does not apply if the profits of the property business are calculated on the cash basis (see **32.6**). It can be restricted from 13 March 2012 where anti-avoidance arrangements apply, see **31.13**. The relief against general income is also one of a number of reliefs against general income which is subject to a cap, see **2.13**. With the exception of the provisions covered here, relief against general income is not available for property business losses.

HMRC have stated that losses from a UK property business can be set against profits from a UK furnished holiday lettings business, and similarly losses from an overseas property business can be set against profits from an EEA furnished holiday lettings business (see **32.27**).

Anti-avoidance provisions prevent individuals within the charge to income tax obtaining relief for tax-generated losses attributable to the annual investment allowance (see **22.26**) against general income. The legislation is specifically targeted at persons who enter into tax avoidance arrangements on or after 24 March 2010 with a main purpose of obtaining a tax reduction by way of property loss relief attributable to the annual investment allowance.

Post-cessation receipts and expenses (ITTOIA 2005, ss 349–356; ITA 2007, ss 24A, 98A, 125)

[32.10] Post-cessation receipts and expenses can arise for property income in the same way as they do for trading income (see **21.9** and **21.10**) and are taxable or relievable as outlined in those paragraphs. Broadly from 12 January 2012 relief is denied for expenses payments or events arising from an arrangement whose main purpose is to obtain a tax reduction. The relief for post-cessation expenses is one of a number of reliefs against general income which is subject to a cap, see **2.13**. Where the property business that ceases calculated profits under the cash basis (see **32.6**) post-cessation receipts are only recognised if they would be recognised under the cash basis.

National insurance contributions

[32.11] Property letting will rarely be regarded as self-employment for NICs purposes, although if the extent of the landlord's involvement in managing the lettings and looking after the properties is substantial and extends beyond those generally associated with being a landlord (which might be particularly relevant for furnished holiday lettings — see **32.25** to **32.33**), it is possible that the activities will constitute a business, in which case Class 2 NICs will be payable (see **24.2**). HMRC give guidance in their National Insurance Manual at NIM23800. Class 4 NICs are only payable where income is taxed as trading income. Although rents are *treated* as being from a business in calculating property income, this is not the same as saying that a business actually exists, and it does not alter the NICs position, even for furnished holiday lettings which are treated as a trade for many other purposes.

Tax treatment of companies (CTA 2009, Pt 4; CTA 2010, ss 62–67)

[32.12] All rental income of companies is treated as the profits of a property business. See **32.34** for the treatment of a payment for dilapidations by an outgoing tenant and **32.13** for the treatment of loan interest. Capital allowances are deducted as expenses in arriving at the rental profit or loss as for income tax (see **32.17**). If a loss arises, then providing the business is conducted on a commercial basis, the loss may be set against the total profits of the same accounting period, or surrendered by way of group relief (see **26.17**). Any unrelieved loss is carried forward to set against future *total* profits, though September 2017 Finance Bill, which is expected to receive Royal Assent in November 2017, provides that the carry-forward of losses arising post-1 April 2017 must be claimed (see **26.7**), and that such losses may also be surrendered for group relief in certain circumstances (see **26.22**). The treatment of losses in a furnished holiday lettings business is different (see **32.29**). The post-cessation receipts provisions apply to companies, but the post-cessation expenses provisions do not (see **32.10**).

Relief for interest

[32.13] Interest on company borrowings is dealt with under the 'loan relationships' rules outlined at **3.6**. Interest relating to furnished holiday lettings (see **32.27**) is deducted from the income from those lettings, since expenses may be deducted as if such lettings were a trade. All other interest relating to let property is taken into account in arriving at the overall non-trading surplus or deficit on loans. If there is a deficit, relief is available as indicated at **26.8**.

Capital allowances and other expenditure (CAA 2001, ss 13B, 15, 16, 35, 172–204, 219; ITTOIA 2005, ss 308A–308C; ITA 2007, Pt 11A; CTA 2009, ss 248A–248C; CTA 2010, Pt 21)

[32.14] Capital allowances are not available on plant and machinery let for use in a dwelling house, except for furnished holiday lettings (see **32.25** to **32.33**), and, in the case of non-cash basis property businesses (see **32.7**), subject to the exception outlined at **22.45** for fixtures. For non-cash basis businesses where the let property is not a dwelling, allowances are available not only on plant and machinery in the let buildings but also on plant and machinery for the maintenance, repair or management of premises. Cash basis businesses (see **32.6**) can claim capital allowances on a car only. The allowances are calculated in the same way as for trades — see CHAPTER 22. With regard to expenditure on fixtures, the expenditure may be incurred either by the landlord or by the tenant, or the items may be leased from an equipment lessor. There are special provisions to deal with the various possibilities (see **22.45**). See also the provisions at **22.5** relating to finance leases and at **22.43** relating to long-life plant and machinery.

[32.15] Although there is no relief for plant and machinery in dwelling houses as indicated above, from 1 April 2016 for corporation tax and 6 April 2016 for income tax a deduction from profits is allowed for capital expenditure incurred on replacing furnishings, appliances (including white goods) and kitchenware provided for the use by the tenant. Relief is not available for fixtures. Where the new item is substantially the same as the old item, the deduction is equal to the expenditure incurred on the new item. Where the new item is not substantially the same the deduction is limited to the amount which would have been incurred if it *were* substantially the same. In addition a deduction is permitted for incidental capital costs of disposing of the old item or acquiring the replacement. If the item is part-exchanged the value of the old item is treated as being included in the expenditure incurred on the new item and the deduction is reduced by that amount. The deduction applies for both cash basis and non-cash basis property businesses (see **32.6** and **32.7**) but is not available for furnished holiday lettings or if rent-a-room relief is claimed.

HMRC state that the replacement of a kitchen in an unfurnished property is treated as a repair (see BIM46911).

[32.16] From April 2011, where an asset is used in rotation between different types of property business whilst the owner retains ownership, he is treated as having incurred notional capital expenditure on different plant and machinery in the first property business on the day after ceasing to use it in the second property business. The amount of deemed qualifying expenditure is the market value of the plant or machinery on the cessation date or the amount of the original expenditure if lower.

[32.17] Capital allowances are deducted as an expense and are thus taken into account in arriving at the letting profit or loss. See **22.13** for the relief available to individuals for excess allowances. No separate relief for excess allowances is available to companies (see **32.12**).

Conversion of parts of business premises into flats (CAA 2001, ss 393A–393W; FA 2012, Sch 39)

[32.18] Capital allowances were available for expenditure by property owners and occupiers on the renovation or conversion of empty or underused space above qualifying shops and other commercial premises to provide residential flats for short-term letting. The allowances are abolished for expenditure incurred on or after 1 April 2013 (corporation tax) or 6 April 2013 (income tax) and the entitlement to claim writing down allowances on any residue of qualifying expenditure is withdrawn from the same dates. However, balancing adjustments may still be relevant. A balancing charge or balancing allowance is made if there is a balancing event (sale, long lease, flat ceasing to be available for letting etc.) within seven years from the time the flat is available for letting, and this will still apply despite the repeal of the allowances. There is no clawback of allowances if a sale, lease etc. occurs after that time. Further detail are available in earlier editions of the book.

Business premises renovation allowance (CAA 2001, ss 186A, 360A–360Z4; ITTOIA 2005, s 31C; ITA 2007, s 24A; SI 2007/945; SI 2014/1687)

[32.19] A business premises renovation allowance is available in respect of expenditure incurred between 11 April 2007 and 1 April 2017 (corporation tax) and 6 April 2017 (income tax). The allowances are subject to EU state aid controls and anyone claiming any other state aids cannot also claim business premises renovation allowances. The allowances are available to both individuals and companies. The provisions of the scheme are outlined below.

Under the scheme, 100% capital allowances are available for the costs (capped at €20 million from 11 April 2012) of renovating or converting qualifying business properties that have remained empty for at least a year in designated disadvantaged areas known as Assisted Areas into qualifying business premises. Qualifying business premises are those used for the purposes of a qualifying trade, profession or vocation or as offices. Various trades are excluded including fisheries, shipbuilding, transport, energy generation and distribution, and those carried on by a business considered to be in financial difficulty.

Expenditure incurred on or after 1 April 2014 (corporation tax) or 6 April 2014 (income tax) must be incurred on either building works; architectural or design services; surveying or engineering services; planning applications; or statutory fees or permissions; or any additional associated but unspecified activities (such as project management services), provided they do not exceed 5% of the total expenditure on building works, architectural or design services, and surveying or engineering services. Expenditure incurred on or after those 2014 dates on any works, services etc. not completed within 36 months of the date the expenditure was incurred is not allowable, and is treated as never having been incurred, unless the works etc. are completed at some later date in which case the expenditure is treated as having been incurred at that later date.

The 100% initial allowance need not be taken in full. Where the full allowance is not taken, writing down allowances of 25% per annum on the reducing balance basis will be available on the unclaimed residue of expenditure (again being reduced to whatever amount is required).

Balancing allowances or charges will be made where there is a 'balancing event', e.g. the building is sold, let on a long lease, demolished or destroyed, or ceases to be a qualifying building, or the person who incurred the qualifying expenditure dies. No balancing adjustments will be made if the balancing event occurs more than five years (seven years for expenditure incurred before 1 April 2014 (corporation tax) or 6 April 2014 (income tax)) from when the premises were first brought back into use or made suitable and available for letting. Unclaimed allowances cannot be transferred to a subsequent purchaser. However, where a property that has qualified for business premises renovation allowance is sold, the new owner can claim capital allowances on fixtures but only to the extent that the original expenditure was not relieved under these provisions.

A person carrying on a trade, profession or vocation who has claimed business premises renovation allowances within the previous seven years is excluded from being able to make a cash basis election for small businesses (see **20.4**) for that tax year. The cash basis for property businesses cannot be used where a business premises renovation allowance balancing adjustment would be due in the year if the profits were calculated on the non-cash basis (see **32.6**). The cap on certain income tax reliefs (see **2.13**) does not apply to the extent that relief is attributable to business premises renovation allowances.

Where a premium is payable (TCGA 1992, Sch 8; ITTOIA 2005, ss 60–65, 99–103, 277–283, 287–295, Sch 2 para 28; CTA 2009, ss 62–67, 96–100, 217–223)

[32.20] A premium is a sum paid on the creation of an interest in a property. Premiums may be payable by an incoming tenant to an outgoing tenant when a lease is assigned. They may also be paid by a tenant to a landlord when a lease or sublease is granted. A third type of payment is a payment by a landlord to induce a potential tenant to take out a lease — usually called a reverse premium.

A distinction is made between a premium paid for the grant of a lease and a capital sum paid on the sale of a lease. A sale (or assignment) of a lease is usually a capital gains tax matter. For example, a payment to an outgoing tenant from an incoming tenant is dealt with under the capital gains tax rules.

Premium paid to landlord on grant of lease or sublease

[32.21] The treatment of premiums paid to landlords on the grant of a lease or sublease depends on the length of the lease. If a lease is granted for more than 50 years, it is treated as a part disposal for capital gains tax purposes (see **4.27** and **4.28**). The cost of the part disposed of is the proportion of the total cost that the premium paid bears to the sum of the premium paid and the reversionary value of the property.

Example 1

Individual buys a freehold property for £200,000 in May 2017 and grants a 60 year lease of the property for £250,000 in December 2017. The value of the freehold reversion is £40,000. The capital gain is calculated as follows:

	£
Premium received	250,000
Less: $\text{Cost } £200,000 \times \dfrac{250,000}{250,000 + 40,000}$	(172,414)

Capital gain	£77,586

The gain will be reduced by the capital gains tax annual exempt amount if not otherwise used (see **4.29**).

There are both capital and income aspects on the grant of a lease of 50 years duration or less (known as a short lease), in that the premium is partly treated as income and partly as disposal proceeds for capital gains tax. The income portion is treated as additional rent and is the amount of the premium less 2% for each complete year of the lease except the first. The amount by which the premium is reduced is treated as the proceeds of a part disposal for capital gains, the cost of the part disposed of being the proportion of the total cost that the capital portion of the premium bears to the full premium plus the value of the freehold reversion. See Example 2.

The income portion of a premium on a short lease is wholly charged in the year the lease is granted, although the lease may run for anything up to 50 years. The cash basis for property businesses (see **32.6**) cannot be applied to income from premiums.

Since the income part of the premium is treated as additional rent, any expenses of the letting can be relieved against it. The premium might in fact have been charged to recover some extraordinary expenses, perhaps necessitated by a previous defaulting tenant.

[32.22] Where a premium on the grant of a short lease is paid by a business tenant, he may deduct the income portion (i.e. after the 2% deduction) as a business expense, but spread over the term of the lease rather than in a single sum (see Example 2), provided he does not calculate his profits on the cash basis for small businesses (see **20.4**). A similar deduction may be claimed by a tenant who sublets, his deduction being against rental income and depending on the length of the sublease. No deduction is available if he calculates his rental profits on the cash basis for property businesses (see **32.6**). Any deductions allowed in calculating income are not allowed in calculating the capital gain if the lease is disposed of.

[32.23] Any expenditure on the acquisition of a lease is treated for capital gains purposes as wasting away during the last 50 years (or shorter period for which the lease was granted) and only the depreciated cost (using a special table in TCGA 1992, Sch 8) may be used. If a lease is held for its full term, no allowable loss may be claimed for the unrelieved expenditure on acquisition, so that any expenditure for which relief has not been given in calculating income will not have been allowed for tax at all.

Example 2

Individual charges a premium of £80,000 on granting a lease for 21 years commencing 20 June 2017. The cost of the freehold was £150,000 in 1996. The value of the freehold reversion after the grant of the lease was £240,000.

The amount treated as additional rent for 2017–18 is:

	£
Premium	80,000

Less Treated as part disposal for capital gains (21 – 1) = 20 years at 2% = 40%	(32,000)
Amount treated as additional rent	£48,000

The chargeable gain is:

Capital proportion of premium	32,000
Less Allowable proportion of cost	

$$£150,000 \times \frac{32,000}{80,000 + 240,000} \qquad (15,000)$$

$$£17,000$$

If the tenant was a business tenant, he could claim a deduction in calculating taxable profits for £48,000 spread over 21 years, i.e. £2,286 per annum, in addition to the deduction for the rent paid.

If he subsequently assigned the lease within the 21 years, the allowable cost for capital gains would be arrived at by reducing the premium paid of £80,000 by the total annual deductions allowed to the date of assignment as a business expense, and depreciating the reduced amount according to the table in TCGA 1992, Sch 8.

Payments from landlord to tenant — reverse premiums

[**32.24**] Where a landlord pays a sum to induce a potential tenant to take a lease (a reverse premium) then, unless the payment reduces expenditure qualifying for capital allowances, it is treated as income for income tax or corporation tax in the hands of the tenant (either trading income or letting income as the case may be). The tax charge is generally spread over the period in which the premium is recognised in the tenant's accounts, although HMRC are not always obliged to accept the spread of the receipt adopted in the accounts, see HMRC Business Income Manual BIM41125. The tax charge does not apply where the premises are to be the tenant's main residence or to sale and leaseback arrangements.

As far as the landlord is concerned, the reverse premium paid will be a capital payment, which will normally be regarded as enhancement expenditure in computing a capital gain on disposal of the property. It will not be deductible from the rental income. A reverse premium paid by a builder or developer, on the other hand, will normally be an income payment allowed as a deduction from trading profits.

For VAT, HMRC accept that the majority of such payments will be outside the scope of VAT.

Furnished holiday lettings (TCGA 1992, ss 241–241A; CAA 2001, ss 13B, 17–17B, 249–250A; ITTOIA 2005, ss 20, 322–328B; ITA 2007, ss 127, 127ZA; CTA 2009, ss 43, 264–269A; CTA 2010, ss 65–67A)

[32.25] As indicated in 32.2, the furnished holiday lettings provisions apply to both individuals and companies, although clearly many of the provisions dealt with in this section are applicable only to individuals.

[32.26] As with other furnished lettings, the 'rent-a-room' relief exempting gross rent of up to £7,500 may be available to individuals who let rooms in their homes (see **30.12**) and this may be more beneficial than the furnished holiday lettings treatment described below. Note, however, that because 'rent-a-room' relief is only available on an individual's only or main residence HMRC state that they will look critically at any claim for holiday homes.

[32.27] Income from qualifying furnished holiday lettings is broadly treated as trading income although it remains chargeable as property income. See **32.6** regarding the cash basis that applies to most unincorporated property income businesses from 2017–18. Before 2009, furnished holiday lettings (FHL) elsewhere in the EEA (see **1.3**) other than the UK did not qualify for this treatment. However, the Government was advised that this may not be compliant with European Law and HMRC accepted the treatment as applying to FHL elsewhere in the EEA. Finance Act 2011 introduced changes to the FHL legislation which put the extension of the relief to EEA properties on a statutory footing.

Qualifying criteria

[32.28] To qualify, the accommodation must be let on a commercial basis. HMRC look at this aspect very carefully, and will often ask for business plans and accounts to support the contention that the letting is a business venture. Many HMRC enquiries have been raised in this connection, particularly relating to the letting of holiday caravans (see below).

The accommodation must be available to the public as holiday accommodation for at least 210 days in the relevant period, and actually let as such for at least 105 of those days. HMRC do not consider the property to be available for letting while the taxpayer is in occupation, but relief may still be available if the taxpayer moves out during the holiday season and returns afterwards (see HMRC Property Income Manual PIM4112). The relevant period is a period of 12 months which is usually the tax year or accounting period. However, if the accommodation was not let by the person or company as furnished accommodation in the previous tax year or accounting period, then the relevant period starts on the first day in the tax year or accounting period on which it is so let. Where the letting ceases, the relevant period is the 12 months ending on the last day the property is let as furnished accommodation.

The 105 days test may be satisfied by averaging periods of occupation of any or all of the holiday accommodation let furnished by the same person, but the election has to be made separately for properties in the UK and properties in the EEA. An averaging election must be made within two years of the end of the first accounting period in which the letting condition is not met for corporation tax or within one year of 31 January following the end of the first tax year in which the letting condition is not met for income tax. Alternatively a period of grace is available. If the property qualifies as FHL accommodation in one accounting period or tax year but then does not qualify in the next, or next two, accounting periods or tax years only because it does not meet the letting condition of 105 days, an election can be made to treat the property as qualifying. The election must be made within two years of the end of the first accounting period in which the letting condition is not met for corporation tax and within one year of 31 January following the end of the first tax year in which the letting condition is not met for income tax.

Accommodation is not normally regarded as holiday accommodation for any period during which it is let in the same occupation for a continuous period of more than 31 days. Any such periods of longer term occupation must in any event not exceed 155 days in the relevant period. Where only part of the let accommodation is holiday accommodation, apportionments are made on a just and reasonable basis. Where there is part private use of the property, the normal rules for restricting allowable expenditure apply (see **20.5**). In these circumstances, great care must be taken to ensure that the letting can be shown to be commercial, rather than producing income merely to offset costs.

Income tax and corporation tax treatment

[32.29] Income from a furnished holiday lettings business (either in the UK or in the EEA) has to be computed separately from other property business income (either in the UK or overseas respectively) for the purposes of capital allowances, loss relief and relevant earnings for pension contributions. If interest is paid on a loan to purchase or improve the property, it is allowed as a trading expense (restricted if necessary by any private use proportion). Capital allowances (see CHAPTER 22) on plant and machinery, such as furniture and kitchen equipment, may be claimed, and the income qualifies as relevant earnings for personal pension purposes (although non-earners may get tax relief in any event on personal pension contributions of up to £3,600 a year — see CHAPTER 17). The trade loss reliefs outlined in CHAPTER 25 and CHAPTER 26 are not available. Losses from an FHL business can only be carried forward and set against income from the same UK or EEA FHL business. They cannot be set against any other property business profits. The treatment of post-1 April 2017 losses outlined in **32.12** does not apply.

Income tax is payable under the self-assessment provisions (see **2.30** and **3.24**). Except for instalment paying companies (see **3.25**), corporation tax is payable nine months after the end of the accounting period. Despite the trading treatment, individuals do not have to pay Class 4 NICs, because Class 4 contributions only apply where profits are actually charged as trading income. Class 2 NICs would, however, usually be payable unless already paid by reference to other self-employment or the landlord's activities in managing the properties were insufficient to be regarded as carrying on a business (see **24.3**).

Capital gains tax treatment

[32.30] FHL property is eligible for capital gains rollover relief either when it is itself replaced, or as a qualifying purchase against which gains on other assets may be set, and for business gifts relief (see **4.34** and **29.16**). Entrepreneurs' relief may also be available if there is a qualifying business disposal (see **29.2**). If the property has been the main residence for capital gains tax, it may be possible to claim the residential lettings exemption (see **30.13**). Capital gains relief for loans to traders (see **4.37**) and exemptions for disposals by companies with substantial shareholdings (see **3.34**) may also apply.

Inheritance tax treatment

[32.31] As far as inheritance tax is concerned, property used for holiday lettings does not qualify for agricultural property relief and it is unlikely to qualify for business property relief. The Upper Tribunal have upheld HMRC's view (see HMRC's Inheritance Tax Manual at IHTM25278) that the letting of a bungalow as holiday accommodation was 'mainly that of holding the property as an investment', and this did not qualify for business property relief. HMRC do, however, concede that in some cases the level of additional services provided may be so high that the activity can be considered as non-investment, and each case will be treated on its own facts.

Caravans

[32.32] The letting of holiday caravans is, depending on the scale, either treated as a trade or as a furnished letting. In the latter case, the income may be treated as trading income from furnished holiday accommodation if the conditions are satisfied. Long-term lets would accordingly not qualify. Caravans occupying holiday sites are treated as plant and machinery qualifying for capital allowances, even if they are on hard standings and not required to be moved.

Where activities connected with the operation of a caravan site amount to a trade, or a part of a trade, then the receipts and expenses of letting caravans or pitches for caravans may be dealt with in calculating the profits of that trade, rather than a separate property business (see CHAPTER 20). The treatment is optional, but will usually be beneficial. In practice, operators of caravan sites commonly provide a trading element, such as a café or site shop. However, if the trading requirement is met for only part of a tax year, then the optional trading treatment for letting receipts and expenses is confined to that part of the tax year.

Even where caravan sites are accepted as trading businesses, inheritance tax business property relief has usually been denied because the rent from caravan pitches was regarded as being from holding investments. The Court of Appeal has held, however, that business property relief was available for a caravan park with a wide range of activities, of which the pitch letting was only one. The HMRC guidance in IHTM25278 referred to in **32.31** does also apply to caravan sites, however.

Council tax and business rates

[32.33] For the treatment of furnished property, including holiday property and caravans, in relation to council tax and business rates, see **32.46**.

Capital gains on sale of investment properties (TCGA 1992, ss 243–248; HMRC Statement of Practice SP 13/93)

[32.34] See **41.50** for the capital gains tax charge which applies from 6 April 2015 on gains realised on disposals of UK residential property by non-residents.

Aside from the non-resident CGT charge, the usual capital gains tax principles apply to investment properties (see CHAPTER **4**), including the relief dealt with in **30.13** to **30.15** where part of the property is owner-occupied, and that dealt with in **32.30** where the property is let as furnished holiday accommodation. Apart from those instances, there is generally no rollover relief on disposal and replacement of investment properties although where the disposal is occasioned by compulsory purchase, there is no tax charge if the proceeds are reinvested in another property, provided that the reinvestment is made within the period beginning one year before and ending three years after the disposal (see **29.16** to **29.21**). The replacement property cannot, however, be the investor's capital gains tax exempt dwelling house (see **30.3**) at any time within six years after its acquisition. From 6 April 2015, rollover relief for replacement of business assets on a non-resident CGT disposal (see **41.50**) may be claimed but only where the new assets are interests in UK land which consist of or include a dwelling immediately after they are acquired.

As an alternative to rollover relief where part of a holding of land is compulsorily purchased, small proceeds (not defined but taken in practice to mean not exceeding 5% of the value of the holding) may be treated as reducing the capital gains tax cost of the holding rather than being charged as a part disposal. Compulsory purchase includes not only purchase by an authority but also purchase of the freehold by a tenant exercising his right to buy.

If a lease is surrendered and replaced by a new lease on similar terms except as to duration and rent payable, by HMRC concession D39 the surrender is not treated as a disposal for capital gains tax so long as a capital sum is not received by the lessee and certain other conditions are met. When the extended lease is disposed of, it will be treated as acquired when the original lease was acquired. There are anti-avoidance provisions to prevent people escaping tax by abuse of this concession — see **4.39**.

Where at the end of a lease a tenant makes a payment to a landlord in respect of dilapidations, a decision needs to be made as to whether the amount received by the landlord is a capital or income receipt. If the landlord sells the property, the receipt will probably be regarded as compensation for a breach of the terms of the lease and will be treated as additional proceeds. If on the other hand the landlord carries out the repairs, or relets at a reduced rental, the amount received will probably be treated as reducing the cost of repairs for tax purposes in the first instance and treated as letting income in the second instance.

Differing capital gains tax rates apply to gains depending upon the type of gain and 'upper rate gains' include gains on residential property (see **4.2**).

See **31.13** for the availability of capital gains tax gifts relief for agricultural landlords.

HMRC have two separate schemes relating to valuations for large property portfolios. The first applies to taxpayers who dispose of 30 or more interests in land in one tax year or company accounting period. HMRC use a sampling process in order to avoid, if possible, the need to agree individual valuations for all the properties disposed of. The second relates to pre-disposal valuations. Companies or groups with a property portfolio including either 30 or more properties held since 31 March 1982 or properties held since that date with a current aggregate value higher than £20 million may ask HMRC to agree 31 March 1982 values for all relevant property. For notes on these schemes see HMRC's Tax Bulletin 67 of October 2003 and HMRC Capital Gains Manual CG74082.

Property dealing, etc.

[32.35] The income from letting is assessed as income of a property business. Any surplus on disposal of a property may be liable to income tax or corporation tax or as a trading transaction, instead of as a chargeable gain. Whether or not a trade may be inferred is dealt with in CHAPTER 20, but the letting, whilst not conclusive, will at least indicate an investment motive and be influential in the surplus being treated as a capital gain. Non-resident companies may be liable to corporation tax on the entire profits arising from dealing in or developing UK land, and similarly non-resident persons may be liable to income tax. See **41.64** and **41.44**

Real Estate Investment Trusts (CTA 2010, Pt 12; SI 2014/518)

[32.36] A Real Estate Investment Trust (REIT) is a limited company or group that invests mainly in property and distributes at least 90% of its rental business profits to investors, although, with effect for accounting periods beginning on or after 17 July 2013, an investing REIT must distribute 100% of any property income distribution it receives from investing in another REIT to its investors. The REIT tax regime shifts the burden of taxation from the company to the investors, and enables investors to obtain returns broadly similar to those they would have obtained by direct investment. Companies and groups are able to elect to join the REIT regime. See HMRC Guidance on Real Estate Investment Trusts Manual.

[**32.37**] The qualifying rental income of REITs and their capital gains on investment properties are exempt from corporation tax. Any distributions made out of such tax-exempt property income or capital gains are generally treated as UK property income and tax is deducted at the basic rate from distributions to most types of shareholder and accounted for to HMRC. The £1,000 property allowance (see **32.5**) is not available against such property income. This is subject to an exemption for property income distributions made to a REIT investor (see below). Other income and gains of the REIT are taxed at the main rate of corporation tax, and dividends paid out of such profits are treated like any other dividends. A company with tied premises can treat the rental income from those premises as part of the property rental business. REITs can issue stock dividends in lieu of cash dividends in meeting the requirement to distribute 90% of their rental business profits. The investors will be taxed on the stock dividends in the same way as on cash dividends. A tax penalty will be imposed if a distribution is paid to a corporate shareholder that holds 10% or more of the distribution, share capital or voting rights in the REIT.

[**32.38**] The main requirements for a company to qualify as a REIT are that the company must be UK-resident and, for accounting periods beginning on or after 17 July 2012 (but subject to a relaxation in the first three years for new REITs), its shares must be admitted to trading on a recognised stock exchange and either listed or traded on a recognised stock exchange. Previously its shares had to be listed on a recognised stock exchange and the change allows REITs to be listed on trading platforms such as AIM, PLUS and their foreign equivalents.

The company cannot be a close company (broadly as outlined in **3.29** but subject to a slightly wider definition), although it will not be considered close if it is close only because one of its shareholders is a limited partnership that is also a collective investment scheme and, furthermore, for notices specifying entry to the regime on or after 17 July 2012, and for existing REITS in relation to accounting periods beginning on or after that date, shareholdings of certain institutional investors (as defined) will not, on their own, make a company close for the purposes of the regime. For accounting periods beginning on or after 1 April 2014 REITs are included in the definition of institutional investor meaning that REITs can invest in other REITs and not violate the non-close company rule. For notices specifying entry to the regime on or after 17 July 2012, the close company condition does not have to be met for the first three years of a new REIT.

At least 75% of its income must be rental income and for accounting periods beginning on or after 17 July 2013, the sum of cash and any relevant UK REIT shares (broadly shares held by a REIT in another REIT) relating to the residual business plus the value of investment property must be at least 75% of the total assets of the business. The property letting business must be ring-fenced and must involve at least three properties, with no single property representing more than 40% of the value of the portfolio. A tax charge may be made if the amount of debt financing of the business exceeds a specified level.

A property income distribution that a UK REIT receives from another UK REIT in which it invests is treated as part of the investing REIT's tax exempt property rental business for accounting periods beginning on or after 17 July 2013. A property income distribution for these purposes is treated as separate from other property rental business profits.

[32.39] A company may give notice that it wishes to leave the REIT regime, and HMRC may give notice that the company must leave if it has repeatedly failed to meet the conditions or been involved in tax avoidance. Certain breaches will trigger automatic termination. Anti-avoidance provisions prevent exploitation of the rules where businesses restructure to gain the benefits of the regime.

Value added tax (VATA 1994, Sch 4, Sch 7A, Sch 8 Group 5, Sch 9 Group 1 and Sch 10; FA 2007, s 99; SI 2008/1146; SI 2009/1966; SI 2010/485)

[32.40] The VAT position on land and buildings is very complex and the legislation very tortuous, and what follows is a brief summary only.

Sales of commercial buildings that are either new or less than three years old are standard-rated. Sales or leases for more than 21 years of new residential properties (including dwellings created by the conversion of non-residential property) and new buildings occupied by charities for charitable purposes are zero-rated. A single dwelling formed from more than one building can be zero-rated provided the buildings are constructed under a single project and single planning consent. HMRC accept that a person acquiring a completed residential or charitable building as part of a transfer of a going concern (see 7.52) inherits 'person constructing' (or 'person converting') status and is capable of making a zero-rated first major interest grant in that building or part of it provided certain conditions are met. See HMRC Brief 27/2014 for full details. Land and buildings are subject to the capital goods scheme (see 7.28 and below) and input tax incurred on the construction of the building and wholly attributed to the zero-rated long lease will have to be adjusted should a subsequent exempt disposal be made of the building. The sale of renovated houses that have been empty for ten years or more is zero-rated.

Otherwise, unless the vendor has exercised his option to charge VAT (see 32.42), all sales of buildings that are more than three years old are exempt, and grants of long or short leases (other than those mentioned above) are also exempt, except for holiday accommodation (see 32.43). Rents received are exempt unless the landlord has opted to charge VAT.

Most landlords letting domestic property are exempt from VAT. Any VAT on their expenditure therefore forms part of their costs, and must be taken into account in fixing their rents. Landlords letting commercial property are in the same position, unless they opt to charge VAT (see 32.42). If the expenditure is revenue expenditure, such as repairs, the unrecovered VAT may be claimed as part of the expense in calculating the rental profit (see 20.27). If it is capital expenditure, such as on property conversion, reconstruction, extension, improvement, etc., no deduction can be claimed in calculating the rental profit, but the unrecovered VAT will form part of the cost for capital gains tax purposes when the property is disposed of.

The reduced rate of VAT of 5% applies on the installation of energy saving materials in residential accommodation, and on central heating systems etc. if funded by government grants (see **7.23**).

Where there is non-business use of commercial land and buildings input tax is restricted to the business use proportion (see **20.25**) at the time of the purchase of the asset and subsequent adjustments to the amount recoverable must be made through the capital goods scheme (see **7.28**).

Following a Tribunal decision HMRC accept that the fact that the transferor of a business retains a small reversionary interest in a transferred property does not prevent the transaction from being treated as a transfer of a going concern (TOGC) for VAT purposes (see **7.52**). It applies to all businesses, for example where a retailer disposes of the retail business but transfers the premises by granting a lease. However, if the interest retained by the transferor represents more than 1% of the value of the part of the property over which the lease is granted, HMRC will regard that as strongly indicative that the transaction is too complex to be a TOGC — see HMRC Briefs 30/2012 and 27/2014 (see **27.12** and **27.13**).

HMRC also accept that where the transferor is a tenant and he surrenders the lease, this can be a TOGC. They say this could apply where a tenant subletting premises by way of business subsequently surrenders its interest in the property together with the benefit of the subtenants, or where a retailer sells its retailing business to its landlord. In substance the landlord has acquired the tenant's business — see HMRC Brief 27/2014 (see **27.12**).

Residential conversions, renovations and alterations

[32.41] VAT is charged at the reduced rate of 5% on the supply of services and building materials for the conversion of non-residential property into dwellings, conversion of residential property into a different number of dwellings, conversion of residential or non-residential property into a multiple occupancy dwelling (e.g. bed-sit accommodation), conversion of non-residential property or one or more residential properties into a care home, children's home, hospice etc. (where the services are supplied to the person who intends to use the property for that purpose), the conversion of a care home etc. into a multiple occupancy dwelling, and the renovation or alteration of dwellings, multiple occupancy properties and care homes etc. that have been empty for two years or more. A single dwelling formed from more than one building can be reduce-rated provided the buildings are converted under a single project and single planning consent. Constructing a garage, or turning a building into a garage, as part of a renovation also qualifies for the reduced rate. Where someone buys a house that has been empty for two years or more and lives in it while it is being renovated, the 5% rate will still apply to the building work providing it is completed within one year from the date the property was purchased. The reduced rate also applies to the installation of certain mobility aids in the homes of elderly people.

Option to charge VAT

[32.42] The provisions of VATA 1994, Sch 10 dealing with the option to tax supplies in relation to land and buildings are set out in SI 2008/1146. An option to tax can be revoked (a) in the six-month cooling-off period, subject to certain conditions; (b) automatically, where six years have lapsed since anyone had a relevant interest in the property; and (c) where more than 20 years have lapsed since the option first had effect. There are anti-avoidance provisions to prevent the application of the option to tax by land developers in certain circumstances. However, the option to tax will not be disapplied where a development financier or a person connected to the development financier occupies 10% or less of any building included in the grant. Further, it will not be disapplied where a grantor or a person connected to the grantor occupies 2% or less of any building included in the grant.

Guidance is available in an updated VAT Notice 742A, VAT Information Sheet 14/09 and HMRC Brief 51/2009.

Holiday accommodation, etc.

[32.43] If turnover is above the VAT registration limit (currently £85,000), the provision of short-term holiday accommodation in hotels, inns, boarding houses, etc. is charged to VAT at the standard rate (but see **32.44** for off-season letting for more than 28 days). If holiday accommodation, including time share accommodation, that is less than three years old is sold or leased, then both the initial charges and any periodic charges, such as ground rent and service charges, are also standard-rated. If the property is over three years old, the initial charges are exempt from VAT but periodic charges are still standard-rated.

The standard rate applies to charges for pitching tents and to seasonal pitch charges for caravans (charges for non-seasonal pitches being exempt). If the pitch charges to the caravan owners include water and sewerage services and the landlord can ascertain how much is provided to the caravans as distinct from the rest of the site (shops, swimming pools, etc.), this can be apportioned between the caravans and shown separately on the bills, and VAT need not then be charged on those services. Similarly, separately metered supplies of gas and electricity are charged at the reduced rate of 5%. The VAT on any part of the pitch charge that represents business rates on the individual caravans follows the same VAT liability as the rental of the caravan pitch and is therefore standard-rated for seasonal pitches. VAT is also charged on any business rates element that relates to the rest of the site.

The sale of building plots for holiday accommodation is standard-rated.

[32.44] For guests who stay longer than 28 days in a hotel, boarding house etc., a reduced VAT charge is made from the 29th day, by excluding the 'accommodation' element from the amount on which VAT is payable. This has previously applied only where the tenant paid the charges. HMRC accept, however, that it applies where hotels etc. contract with a local authority or other organisation to supply accommodation, for example to homeless people.

Where holiday accommodation is let as residential accommodation for more than 28 days in the off-season (providing the accommodation is in a 'seasonal' area), the whole of the letting (including the first 28 days) may be treated as exempt.

Stamp duty land tax, and land and buildings transaction tax

[32.45] See CHAPTER 6 for the general stamp duty land tax provisions. Stamp duty land tax is replaced in Scotland by land and buildings transaction tax (LBTT, see **6.18**). Subject to the following provisions, no stamp duty land tax is payable if residential property is purchased for £125,000 or less, or if non-residential property is purchased for £150,000 or less. For LBTT the thresholds are £145,000 and £150,000 respectively.

See **6.11** regarding the relief available for purchasers of more than one dwelling from the same vendor. See **6.10** for the stamp duty land tax provisions in relation to leases. Residential leases are generally exempt from LBTT with the exception of certain long leases which are qualifying leases (see www.rev enue.scot/land-buildings-transaction-tax/guidance/lbtt-legislation-guidance/ex emptions-reliefs/lbtt3002/lbtt3005).

Any stamp duty land tax or LBTT paid forms part of the cost for capital gains tax purposes on a subsequent disposal.

Where VAT is included in the cost of property, stamp duty land tax or LBTT is charged on the VAT-inclusive amount. See **6.15** for the position relating to the option to charge VAT.

Certain transfers of land and buildings involving Registered Social Landlords are exempt (see **6.13** and **6.18**).

See **27.13** regarding the transfer of property rental businesses as going concerns and the effect on stamp duty land tax.

Council tax and business rates

[32.46] The detailed council tax and business rates provisions are in CHAPTER 8, which outlines the exemptions and discounts available.

When considering liability to council tax and/or business rates, each self-contained unit is looked at separately. Where there is mixed business and domestic use, business rates are payable as well as the council tax, even if there is no separate business part of the property, unless the business use does not materially detract from the domestic use. Any charges that fall on a landlord are allowable in calculating tax liabilities according to the normal expenses rules (see CHAPTER 20).

Let property that is domestic property and is not someone's only or main home is liable to a council tax charge of up to 90%, unless any other discount or exemption applies (see CHAPTER 8). Where let property is someone's only or main home, that person is liable to pay the council tax and there are no council tax or rates implications for the landlord, unless the property is multi-occupied property, such as bedsits, with rent paid separately for different parts of the property, in which case the council tax is payable by the landlord.

Non-domestic property, such as commercial property, boarding houses, etc., is liable to business rates. Staff accommodation, however, is domestic property. If the owner lives there as well, he is liable to pay the council tax. If he does not live there, the staff are liable to council tax if it is their only or main home. If the domestic accommodation was no-one's only or main home, the owner would be liable to pay up to 90% of the council tax. In the case of self-catering holiday accommodation, business rates are usually payable if it is available for short-term letting for 140 days or more in a year. Bed and breakfast accommodation is not subject to business rating providing it is not offered for more than six people, the provider lives there at the same time and the bed and breakfast activity is only a subsidiary use of the home. Where holiday property is not business-rated, the council tax charge of up to 90% is payable on any self-contained accommodation that is not someone's only or main home.

If someone lives in a caravan as his or her only or main home, he or she pays the council tax. For other caravans, the site owner pays business rates on the caravans and pitches, passing on the charge to the caravan owner in the site rents.

Differing rules may apply in Wales, Scotland and Northern Ireland (see CHAPTER 8).

Time shares

[32.47] Owners of time shares need to consider the taxation aspects of receiving income from it, or of making a capital gain on the sale of it.

The nature of the rights acquired depends on the particular agreement, but most time share agreements do not give any rights of ownership over the property itself, but merely a right to occupy it at a certain time.

If the time share is let, the individual will be liable to tax on the rental income less expenses. Where time share property is abroad, income is charged as overseas property income (see **41.15** and **41.29**). Many people will not have any time share income, but will sometimes exchange time shares. If this is done on a temporary basis, there are no tax implications, but a long-term arrangement could be treated as a part disposal for capital gains tax.

When a time share is sold, the individual is liable to capital gains tax on the gain. If the time share has less than 50 years to run, a depreciated cost must be used (on a straight line basis — see **4.28**).

Time share property in the UK is usually subject to business rates. The owner of time share property charges VAT on the selling price for the time share if it is less than three years old and on any service charges made, including business rates. If the property is over three years old, the sale proceeds for the time share, but not the service charges, are exempt from VAT.

HMRC's view is that in most cases the timeshare agreement will be a form of personal contract which constitutes a licence to occupy land and is not a chargeable interest for stamp duty land tax purposes, see HMRC Stamp Duty Land Tax Manual SDLTM10022. Exceptionally where the agreement provides for exclusive and complete occupation of an individual unit of land or property for a defined period it may constitute a lease, the grant or assignment of which is chargeable to stamp duty land tax.

Annual tax on enveloped dwellings (FA 2013, ss 94–174, Schs 33–35; SI 2016/1244)

[32.48] There is a package of three taxes that affect UK residential properties held by certain non-natural persons (broadly companies, partnerships with company members, and collective investment schemes) which currently applies to such properties valued at over £500,000. The package was originally designed to disincentivise the ownership of high value property in structures that would permit indirect ownership or enjoyment of the property to be transferred in a way that would not be chargeable to stamp duty land tax. Two of the three taxes are covered in other chapters:

(i)   stamp duty land tax at 15% on acquisition of the property (see **6.9**).
(ii)   capital gains tax at 28% on any gain on disposal of the property (see **4.8**).

The third tax is the annual tax on enveloped dwellings (ATED) which took effect from 1 April 2013. There are a number of reliefs from ATED. Such reliefs apply, in particular, to property rental businesses, property developers and property traders. There are also exemptions for charities, public and national bodies and dwellings conditionally exempt from inheritance tax. Some of these reliefs operate in tandem, where possible, with similar reliefs from the 15% rate of stamp duty land tax, so that broadly if the 15% rate is applied then the property will also be within ATED.

There are various provisions on what constitutes an interest in a dwelling and the meaning of dwelling for these purposes. HMRC guidance on ATED is at www.gov.uk/government/publications/annual-tax-on-enveloped-dwellings-tec hnical-guidance. The interests of certain connected persons must also be taken into account.

ATED chargeable periods are the 12 months from 1 April to 31 March. The tax is currently charged for a chargeable period if, on any day within that period, a company, partnership or collective investment scheme is entitled to the interest in a single-dwelling that has a taxable value of more than £500,000. For 2017–18, where the charge applies from the first day of a chargeable period, the amount of tax chargeable for that period is:

Taxable value of the interest on the relevant day	Annual chargeable amount
£500,001 to £1,000,000	£3,500
£1,000,001 to £2,000,000	£7,050

£2,000,001 to £5,000,000	£23,550
£5,000,001 to £10,000,000	£54,950
£10,000,001 to £20,000,000	£110,100
More than £20,000,000	£220,350

The 'taxable value' is market value on the last previous valuation date. The first valuation date for ATED is 1 April 2012 and there is then a valuation date on 1 April every five years subsequently, so 1 April 2017 was the next date. Other valuation dates can apply in certain circumstances, broadly where a person acquires or part-disposes of an interest for which the consideration is £40,000 or more. The 'relevant day' is the first day of the chargeable period in which the charge applies. An application form is available on the HMRC website enabling taxpayers to apply for a pre-return banding check to determine which ATED band a property falls into.

If the charge does not apply from the first day of the chargeable period, then a fraction of the annual charge is payable based on the number of days from the day the charge first applies in the chargeable period to the end of that period. An interim relief may be claimed *before* the end of the chargeable period if that period contains one or more days on which the charge does not apply because:

(a)   it is a relievable day, broadly a day on which the interest is, or is being used for qualifying purposes by, one the following:
        (i)   property rental businesses;
        (ii)   dwellings opened to the public;
        (iii)   property developers;
        (iv)   property traders;
        (v)   financial institutions acquiring dwellings;
        (vi)   regulated home reversion plans;
        (vii)   occupation by certain employees etc;
        (viii)   farmhouses;
        (ix)   providers of social housing.
(b)   it is a day, after the first one in the chargeable period in which the person first became chargeable, on which the person is not chargeable; or
(c)   the taxable value has decreased, possibly on a part-disposal.

Interim relief must be claimed in a return or amendment to a return. Where a relief is claimed in relation to a dwelling that reduces the ATED liability to nil, it is possible to use a simplified 'Relief Declaration Return'. For details of returns and payment of tax, see **9.30**.

See **5.2** regarding the inheritance tax charge from April 2017 for non-domiciled individuals on UK residential property held indirectly by them. The Government states that the change may incentivise some non-domiciles to transfer their UK residential properties from overseas vehicles into simpler structures outside the scope of ATED charges.

Tax points

[32.49] Note the following:

- It is only the interest element of the repayments on a 'buy to let' mortgage, or any other loan relating to let property, that is an allowable deduction in calculating rental profit. See **32.8** regarding the reduction in tax relief from 6 April 2017 on 'dwelling-related' loans.
- If interest paid cannot be relieved against rents, individuals cannot set it against a capital gain on disposal of the property but investment companies can — see **32.13** and **26.8**.
- Management expenses are allowed as a lettings expense. This covers a landlord's expenses of travelling to his properties solely for the purposes of property management. The expenses are not allowable if the travelling is for mixed business/private purposes but a deduction may be allowed if any personal benefit is only incidental.
- To benefit from the furnished holiday lettings treatment, an individual must demonstrate the commercial viability of the lettings and show that all the various conditions are satisfied.
- The fact that property is being let does not of itself prevent an income tax charge instead of a chargeable gain on a profit on disposal if a trading motive in buying and selling the property can be proved. There are various possibilities for reducing or deferring tax liabilities, but it is important to establish which tax applies so that the proceeds can be invested in an appropriate purchase (see CHAPTER **29**).
- The VAT provisions relating to property letting, including holiday letting, are extremely complex. HMRC provide various booklets relating to different circumstances.
- If property let for residential use is empty for a period of time, it is still liable for council tax, subject to any available discounts and exemptions (see **32.46**).
- Bed and breakfast providers can escape business rates if they offer the facility as a subsidiary use of their own homes for not more than six people. Otherwise, business rates are payable.
- See **20.19** for details of fixed rate adjustments which may be made to expenses in calculating the profits of a *trade* to account for the private use of premises used mainly for a business, such as a guest house.
- If a rental property has increased in value, this may enable the owner to take out a further loan and get tax relief for the interest against the letting income, providing the total of the original and further borrowing does not exceed the original cost of the property. This would enable the release of some of the capital.
- For loans to buy property for letting abroad, income tax relief is available on the interest.
- Under self-assessment, individuals are required to keep the records relating to their property income for at least 5 years 10 months after the end of the tax year (see **9.32**). Penalties of up to £3,000 per tax year apply if individuals do not comply. The self-assessment provisions for companies similarly require records to be kept for six years, with the same penalty for failing to do so of up to £3,000 per accounting period.

Part VII

Tax and the family

33

Family matters

Introduction

[33.1] The members of a married couple or a civil partnership are taxed separately. Same-sex couples who register as civil partners have the same rights and responsibilities under tax law as married couples, in relation to both beneficial provisions and anti-avoidance provisions. They also receive the same treatment for social security benefits such as pensions and tax credits (see **2.34** onwards). Close blood relatives are not permitted to register a civil partnership.

Some provisions apply equally to married couples, civil partners and cohabiting couples (see **33.20**). See also **10.7** regarding the high income child benefit charge on a taxpayer who is entitled to child benefit (or whose partner is entitled to child benefit) and whose adjusted net income exceeds £50,000 in a tax year. Partners for these purposes are a married couple or those in a civil partnership who are not separated under a court order or in circumstances likely to become permanent, and a couple who are not married or in a civil partnership but who are living together as if they were so.

Married couples and civil partners

[33.2] The incomes of married couples and civil partners are taxed separately. Each spouse or partner is entitled to a personal allowance, and married couple's allowance is available where one spouse or partner was born before 6 April 1935 (i.e. attained the age of 65 before 6 April 2000). The detailed provisions on married couple's allowance are discussed at **2.19**.

A transferable tax allowance is available but couples entitled to claim the married couple's allowance are not entitled to elect for the transferable tax allowance (see **2.17**).

The capital gains of married couples and civil partners are also taxed separately, each spouse or partner being entitled to the annual exempt amount, currently £11,300 (see **4.29**). Losses of one spouse or civil partner may not be set against gains of the other.

Transfers of assets between spouses or civil partners who are living together are not chargeable to capital gains tax, the acquiring spouse or civil partner taking over the other's acquisition cost. However, this has no relevance to assets acquired on the death of a spouse or civil partner, which are treated as acquired at probate value (see **42.5**).

The capital gains tax rules enable couples to plan in advance and make appropriate transfers one to the other before negotiating disposals to third parties, so that, for example, one does not have gains in excess of the annual exempt amount while the other has unrelieved losses. Such transfers must, however, be outright gifts (see **33.4**). If capital losses are brought forward from before the introduction of independent taxation of husband and wife on 6 April 1990, the losses of each spouse must be separately identified so that they are set only against that person's gains.

Despite the fact that married couples and civil partners are treated independently for tax purposes, they are required to make a joint claim for tax credits and the claim is based on their joint income. The same requirement applies to couples, including same-sex couples, who are living together as husband and wife or civil partners. Tax credits are examined at **2.34** to **2.41**.

For inheritance tax purposes, each spouse or civil partner is taxed separately and has a separate entitlement to exemptions and a separate nil rate band (see **5.2**). Transfers between the two in lifetime and on death are exempt unless one of them is not domiciled in the UK, in which case the transfers on or after 6 April 2013 to the non-domiciled spouse or civil partner are exempt up to the nil rate band (currently £325,000, see **5.24**) less the amount of any previous transfers covered by the same exemption (see **5.11**). For transfers before 6 April 2013, the limit was £55,000. Where a surviving spouse or civil partner dies after 8 October 2007 any part of the nil rate band unused on the death of the first spouse or civil partner to die may be added to the survivor's own nil rate band, see **35.4**. For deaths on or after 6 April 2017 a 'residence nil rate band' will apply, to be used against the value of residential property (or certain substituted assets) included in the death estate which passes to direct descendants (see **5.24**).

Stamp duty/stamp duty land tax/land and buildings transaction tax (see CHAPTER **6**) is not normally charged on the value of assets transferred between spouses or civil partners, but see **33.6** regarding mortgaged property.

See **36.17** regarding the additional ISA investment permitted after the death of a spouse or civil partner.

Using available allowances and basic rate

[33.3] Some people on lower incomes need to make sure that they make the best use of their allowances and the basic rate of tax. The 0% starting rate for savings is not available to most taxpayers on modest incomes but the savings allowance and dividend allowance which apply from 6 April 2016 provide a 0% tax rate for some savings and dividends (see **2.5**).

Transferring property to a spouse or civil partner (ITA 2007, ss 836, 837; ITTOIA 2005, s 626)

[33.4] In order for spouses and civil partners to take best advantage of being taxed separately, it may be sensible for property to be transferred from one spouse or partner to the other. Any such transfers are fully effective for tax purposes providing the transfer is an outright gift of the property with no question of the transferring spouse/partner controlling it or deriving a benefit from it; that the gift carries a right to the whole of the income from the property; and that the gift is not effectively just a right to income.

HMRC have contended that certain gifts between spouses were caught by the settlements legislation and were not effective for tax purposes because one or more of these provisos did not apply. In July 2007 the House of Lords decided the 'Arctic Systems' case in favour of the taxpayers on the basis that while there was a settlement, the exemption for outright gifts between spouses did apply. The Government had intended to make changes to the legislation to counter 'income shifting' and consulted on the matter but instead decided to keep the matter under review. See **12.10** for further comments.

It is not possible to transfer a right to income while retaining a right to the capital (but see **33.5** regarding jointly owned property). The rules do not prevent the spouse or civil partner who gave the property getting it back at some stage in the future as a gift, or on the death of the other spouse or partner, providing there were no 'strings' attached to the initial transfer. Where property is transferred into the joint names of spouses or civil partners and they own it under the normal 'joint tenants' provisions, HMRC do not regard this as breaching the 'outright gift' rules, even though the property goes automatically to the survivor when one dies (see **33.5**).

Such transfers will be beneficial where a spouse or civil partner would otherwise waste their personal allowance (but see **2.17** regarding the transferable tax allowance), or where one spouse or partner would be paying tax at higher rates while the other did not fully use the basic rate band. Evidence of transfers in the proper legal form must be kept.

Stamp duty/stamp duty land tax/land and buildings transaction tax (see CHAPTER 6) is not charged on gifts (except possibly in relation to mortgaged property — see **33.6**).

Where spouses or civil partners are living together and one acquires the other's interest in the family home in lifetime or on death, the joint period of ownership is taken into account for the purpose of the capital gains private residence exemption (see **30.9**).

Jointly owned property

[33.5] Spouses or civil partners normally own joint property as 'joint tenants', which means that each has equal rights over the property and when one dies, it goes automatically to the other. The joint tenancy can, however, be severed, and replaced by a 'tenancy in common', in which the share of each is separate, and may be unequal, and may be disposed of in lifetime or on death as the spouse or partner wishes. If this is done, proper documentary evidence of what has been done must be kept. Severing the joint tenancy may be particularly relevant if couples separate. Otherwise one's share of the property would automatically go to the other in the event of their death.

[33.6] Where property is held in joint names, it is generally treated as being owned equally for income tax purposes unless it is actually owned in some different proportion *and* a declaration is made to that effect. Such a declaration can be made only if the beneficial interests in the property correspond with the interests in the income. It takes effect from the date it is made, providing notice of the declaration is given to HMRC on Form 17 within 60 days of the declaration. It is not possible to make a declaration about partnership income, income from furnished holiday lettings, or dividends on shares in close companies (which would include most family companies, see **3.29**). Evidence of beneficial interest must be provided with the form. Form 17 only covers the assets listed on it. Any new assets must be covered by a separate form.

HMRC state in their Property Income Manual at PIM4105 that income from furnished holiday lettings should be split in the way that the parties agree. This approach may be more generous than the law allows and could result in the income falling within the settlements legislation (see **12.10**) as the income received is wholly or substantially a right to income. To avoid this possibility it may be better to split the income either by the underlying beneficial ownership of the property or by reference to the actual work done in letting the property, provided there is evidence to support the latter.

The tax treatment of joint ownership may be useful to overcome one practical difficulty of maximising the benefits of being taxed separately — that the richer spouse or partner may be unwilling to make a significant transfer to the other. The reluctant spouse or partner could transfer an asset (other than family company shares) into joint ownership as tenants in common, retaining 95% ownership and giving the other spouse or partner a 5% share; if no declaration of the actual shares is notified to HMRC, the general rule applies and the income is treated as being shared equally.

This treatment applies to transfers of any sort of property other than family company shares — land and buildings (other than furnished holiday accommodation), non-close company shares, bank accounts, etc. When joint bank and building society accounts are opened, a declaration is normally made that they are in joint beneficial ownership. The ownership can be changed to tenants in common later, but this must be done formally, for example by deed. To provide against the bank or building society still acting on the basis of the original declaration, and thus treating the account as belonging to the survivor when one dies, the personal representatives need to be left clear instructions so that they can deal properly with the estate. Another point that needs to be watched is in relation to mortgaged property. If the spouse or partner to whom the property is transferred takes over responsibility for the mortgage, the mortgage debt is treated as consideration for the transfer and is liable to stamp duty land tax unless covered by the £125,000 limit (see **6.9**). This will not apply if the spouse or partner who is transferring the property undertakes to pay the mortgage. (See also **33.16** regarding separation, divorce and dissolution.)

[33.7] Regardless of the way income is treated for income tax purposes, it is the underlying beneficial ownership of assets that determines the capital gains tax treatment. Again, it is essential to have evidence of the proportions in which property is held.

[33.8] For inheritance tax purposes, there are special 'related property' rules which require transfers of assets owned by spouses or civil partners to be valued as part of their combined value (see **5.36**). This applies in particular to unquoted shares and freehold or leasehold property. There are also 'associated operations' rules to link a series of transactions as a single transaction (see **5.43**). The combined effect of these two sets of provisions prevents spouses or civil partners obtaining an undue advantage by using the exemption for transfers from one to the other to route a transfer to their children or other family members via the other spouse or partner.

Children

Child tax credit

[33.9] Child tax credit is a means tested social security benefit paid to the main carer. Working tax credit, including a childcare element, may also be payable. These are being phased out and replaced by universal credit, see **2.34** to **2.41**.

Children's income (ITTOIA 2005, s 629; SI 2011/1780)

[33.10] Children's income is theirs in their own right, no matter how young they are, and they are entitled to the full personal allowance. For a child under 18 and unmarried, this does not apply to income that comes directly or indirectly from a parent (including income from ISAs for 16- and 17-year olds, but excluding income from a junior ISA (see **36.25**)), which is treated as the parent's own income with the exceptions (a) to (g) below. A child who is in a civil partnership is not regarded as 'unmarried'.

(a) Each parent can give each child sums of money from the total of which the child receives no more than £100 gross income per annum (say interest on bank and building society deposits). If the income exceeds the limit, the whole amount and not just the excess over £100 will be taxed on the parent.

(b) The National Savings 'children's bonds' for under 16-year olds can be given in addition because the return on such bonds is tax-exempt.

(c)   A parent may pay premiums (maximum £270 per annum) on a qualifying friendly society policy for a child under 18 (see **40.15**).

(d)   A parent may pay personal pension contributions of up to £3,600 a year on behalf of a child under 18. Such contributions are paid net of basic rate tax, which is retained whether or not the child is a taxpayer (see CHAPTER **17**). The pension fund is, of course, not available to the child until he/she reaches the qualifying age for personal pensions.

(e)   Parents may contribute towards the permitted £4,128 a year to a Child Trust Fund account for their children, in addition to any gifts under (a) above (see **33.11**).

(f)   Income from an 'accumulation and maintenance' settlement established by a parent for his children is not treated as his income in certain circumstances (see **42.37**).

(g)   A lone parent may establish a trust for a child under 18 under the provisions relating to trusts with a vulnerable beneficiary (see **42.43** to **42.48**), the income from which is not treated as the parent's in specified circumstances.

Gifts within (a) to (e) above are not taken into account as far as inheritance tax is concerned providing they are regular gifts out of income (see **5.9**).

The above rules do not affect gifts to children over 18, but the inheritance tax provisions need to be borne in mind for children of any age. There would be no inheritance tax effect if any gifts were covered by the regular gifts, family maintenance, small gifts or annual inheritance tax exemptions (see **5.3**). Otherwise the gifts would be reckonable for inheritance tax, either (i) as potentially exempt transfers which would not attract inheritance tax unless the parent died within seven years or (ii) being immediately reckonable in the case of (f) above.

Doubts were expressed as to whether gifts by parents or grandparents to children under 18 might be brought within the revised inheritance tax provisions for trusts that have applied since 22 March 2006. HMRC confirmed that whether a child is under or over 18, outright gifts will be potentially exempt transfers and thus not subject to inheritance tax unless the parent/grandparent dies within seven years.

Many parents help to fund their children through higher education. Although student maintenance loans are available, means testing according to the parents' or student's income (including income arising from parental gifts) may reduce available loans. Where parents buy property for the use of a student child, they will be treated as any other landlord if they retain ownership (see CHAPTER **32**). If the property was given to the child, the inheritance tax effect would need to be considered, but if other students shared the property the child might be able to claim rent-a-room relief for income tax (see **30.12**) and so long as it remained the child's main residence the property would be exempt from capital gains tax on disposal (see **30.3**).

Child Trust Funds (CTFA 2004)

[33.11] Child Trust Funds used to be available for eligible children born before 3 January 2011.

Income and capital gains from Child Trust Fund (CTF) investments are exempt from tax (interest being paid gross) and do not affect tax credits. No relief is given for any capital losses. Guidance is available at www.gov.uk/child-trust-funds.

Vouchers for specified amounts of money were provided by the Government and had to be invested in a CTF account in the beneficial ownership of the child, but the parent could choose the account provider. Where vouchers were not used to open an account within 12 months, and also for children in care, accounts were opened by HMRC.

Although government payments have stopped, additional contributions may continue to be made to CTFs by family, friends and others, up to an annual limit of £4,128 in 2017–18. The limit of £100 income from funds provided by a parent referred to in **33.10** does not apply to CTF accounts.

When a child reaches 16 they are responsible for managing their own CTF account if they so elect, although from 6 April 2015 another person who has authority may manage the account. No withdrawals may normally be made until the child is 18 (at which stage the child is treated as acquiring the fund at market value), and only the child will be entitled to make such withdrawals. Access to the CTF account will, however, be available for children under 18 because they are terminally ill and on a child's death.

Various penalties may be imposed, including a penalty of up to £300 for fraudulently withdrawing funds from a CTF, and a penalty of up to £3,000 in the case of fraud or negligence by account providers.

When a CTF matures, which will be from 2020 onwards, it will be possible to rollover the CTF into an ISA, see **36.16** onwards. From 6 April 2015 it is also possible to transfer a CTF account into a Junior ISA account (see below) and the transfer will not count against the Junior ISA subscription limit for the relevant year.

Junior ISAs

[**33.12**] See 36.25 regarding Junior ISAs.

Death of a spouse or civil partner

[**33.13**] Where a spouse or civil partner was born before 6 April 1935, married couple's allowance is available as indicated in **2.19**. For those married before 5 December 2005 the allowance is given to the husband. For couples marrying and civil partners registering on or after 5 December 2005 the allowance is given to the spouse with the higher income. In either case, the other spouse/partner can claim half of a specified part of the allowance (half of £3,260 for 2017–18) or the whole of the specified amount by agreement.

In the tax year of the claimant's death, the surviving spouse or civil partner can receive the benefit of any of the allowance which has not been used against the claimant's tax liability up to the date of death. This might be particularly relevant where the claimant died early in the tax year. The executors must notify HMRC that the surplus married couple's allowance is being transferred to the survivor. Similarly, in the year in which the claimant's spouse or civil partner dies, then if the deceased spouse or partner had insufficient income in the tax year of death to cover the full amount of married couple's allowance to which he or she was entitled, the unused amount can be transferred back to the other spouse or partner, providing the deceased's personal representatives notify HMRC accordingly. The income of a surviving spouse or civil partner will include any he or she is entitled to from the assets in the deceased's estate.

See **2.17** regarding treatment of the transferable tax allowance in the tax year that the transferee dies.

See **30.9** for the capital gains position when a surviving spouse or partner acquires the other's interest in the family home.

Someone who is under state pension age (see **16.2**) when their spouse or civil partner dies, or whose late spouse or civil partner was not entitled to the state retirement pension, received a tax-free bereavement payment of £2,000 from the Department for Work and Pensions (DWP) for deaths before 6 April 2017, providing the late spouse or partner satisfied the contribution conditions or the death was caused by the spouse's or partner's job. Widowed parent's allowance or bereavement allowance may also be available to widows, widowers and surviving civil partners for deaths before 6 April 2017. These benefits are taxable, apart from additions to the widowed parent's allowance for dependent children (see **10.6**). For deaths after 5 April 2017 the bereavement payment, bereavement allowance and widowed parent's allowance are replaced by bereavement support payments which are exempt from tax. A one-off funeral payment may be available to those on low incomes. A widow who remarries before age 60 may be worse off in terms of her state retirement pension. See the section on bereavement benefits at www.gov.uk/browse/benefits/bereavement for further details.

HMRC has set up a dedicated bereavement service for PAYE and self-assessment taxpayers, see www.gov.uk/after-a-death.

See **36.17** regarding the additional ISA investment permitted after the death of a spouse or civil partner, and the draft regulations which provide for ISAs to retain their tax-advantaged status following the death of the account holder.

Separation and divorce or dissolution

[33.14] Where a same-sex couple have registered as a civil partnership, the Civil Partnership Act 2004 makes provision for the partnership to be dissolved or for the partners to have a legal separation. The tax treatment therefore follows that of married couples who divorce or separate.

For the treatment of the married couple's allowance for those born before 6 April 1935 in the year of separation or reconciliation see **2.19**.

The tax position of divorced couples or civil partners whose partnership has been dissolved is broadly the same as that of separated couples. There are some provisions, for example the rules for employee benefits and close company associates, that apply up to divorce or dissolution (but not thereafter) even though the couple are not living together.

Protection against the loss of maintenance on the death of a spouse or civil partner can be obtained by one spouse or partner taking out a policy on his/her own life in trust for the other, or by one spouse or partner taking out a policy on the other's life. There will be no tax relief on the premium.

Maintenance payments (ITA 2007, ss 453–455)

[33.15] Tax relief for maintenance payments is only available where one spouse or civil partner was born before 6 April 1935 (see **34.4** for details). The relief is given at 10% of the lower of (a) the total of qualifying maintenance payments (as defined) falling due in the tax year, and (b) a specified part of the married couple's allowance (£3,260 for 2017–18). All maintenance payments received are free of tax.

The family home (TCGA 1992, ss 222, 223, 225B, 248E; FA 1985, s 83; FA 2003, Sch 3; SI 1987/516)

[33.16] For capital gains tax, when a married couple or civil partners separate, the family home will cease to be the main residence of the spouse or partner who leaves it. His or her share of any calculated gain on a subsequent sale will therefore be chargeable to the extent that it relates to the period of non-residence, subject to any available exemptions or reliefs. The last 18 months of ownership always count as a period of residence, even if a new qualifying residence has been acquired (see **30.3**). If the property is disposed of more than 18 months after a spouse or partner leaves it, part of the calculated gain will be chargeable, but only in the proportion that the excess period over 18 months bears to the total period of ownership since 31 March 1982. Even then the chargeable gain may be covered by the annual exempt amount, currently £11,300. Relief is available for absences of more than 18 months following separation or divorce or dissolution of a civil partnership, but only where the property is eventually transferred to the spouse or partner remaining in it as part of the financial settlement, and an election for a new qualifying residence has not been made by the spouse or partner moving out in the meantime.

If a property in joint ownership is divided into separate and identifiable homes, each of which is exclusively occupied, each owner is entitled to private residence exemption only in respect of his share of the gain arising on the part occupied by him. However, in certain circumstances, the joint owners may exchange their interests so as to acquire sole ownership of the part each occupies without incurring a charge to capital gains tax. The provision provides a form of rollover relief on certain disposals of joint interests in private residences. The provisions may be relevant in some circumstances where a couple who own two residences, each living in only one of them, exchange their interests so that each owns only one property, but the detailed provisions need to be looked at carefully.

The private residence exemption can be preserved on divorce or dissolution if a court order known as a Mesher order is made, under which the sale of the home is postponed, with a spouse or civil partner and children remaining in occupation until a specified event, such as the children reaching a specified age or ceasing full-time education. This is treated as a trust, and occupation of the property by a trust beneficiary qualifies for the private residence exemption (see **30.11**). On the sale of the home by the trustees when the trust ends, the proceeds will not be liable to capital gains tax. The rules for trusts introduced in Finance Act 2006 have, however, affected the inheritance tax position (see CHAPTER **42**). The inheritance tax exemptions for transfers not intended to confer a gratuitous benefit and transfers for family maintenance (see **5.3**) should avoid any inheritance tax charge on the creation of the Mesher trust, but the exit and possibly ten-year charges would apply (see **42.31**).

If property is transferred from one spouse or civil partner to the other on break-up of a marriage or civil partnership, neither stamp duty nor stamp duty land tax (or in Scotland land and buildings transaction tax, see CHAPTER **6**) is payable on property of any description, even if the acquiring spouse or civil partner takes over a mortgage.

Other chargeable assets

[33.17] The special capital gains tax rule (see **4.6**) for transfers between spouses or civil partners only applies in a tax year when the couple are married or civil partners and living together at some time during the year. For transfers in later tax years, capital gains tax is chargeable in the normal way, and this must be remembered when considering a matrimonial or civil partners' settlement following separation. If qualifying business assets are transferred from one to the other after separation but before the divorce or dissolution, gains need not be charged to tax at that time if the couple jointly claim the 'business gifts relief' (see **4.32**), under which the recipient takes over the other's original cost for the purpose of calculating the tax payable on an eventual disposal. Where, following divorce or dissolution, assets are transferred under a court order (even a 'consent' order ratifying an agreement made by the couple), HMRC accept that business gifts relief is available for appropriate assets.

Inheritance tax (IHTA 1984, s 18)

[33.18] The inheritance tax exemption for transfers to a spouse or civil partner is not lost on separation but continues until the time of divorce or dissolution. Even then there is an exemption for transfers to former spouses or civil partners for the maintenance of themselves and the children. See CHAPTER **5**.

Pension schemes

[33.19] See 16.35 for the provisions enabling pension rights to be shared on divorce or dissolution.

Cohabiting couples

[33.20] The following relates to couples, including same-sex couples, who are living together as husband and wife or civil partners but who are neither married nor registered as civil partners.

As far as child tax credits and working tax credits are concerned, the rules for cohabitees are the same as those for married couples or civil partners, and claims must be made jointly taking into account the incomes of both partners (see **2.34** to **2.41**).

Where the home is in the name of only one of the cohabitees, but they regard it as their joint property and want the survivor to have the property when one of them dies, it is important to ensure that the other cohabitee's rights in relation to the home are safeguarded. This may be done by the property owner making a declaration that the property is held in trust for them both as joint tenants in equal beneficial shares. The lifetime declaration of trust would not be reckoned for inheritance tax to the extent that both parties had contributed, directly or indirectly, to the cost. If a transfer of value remained, it would be potentially exempt and (subject to the transferor not retaining any benefit in respect of the share transferred — see **5.41**) would only become chargeable if the property owner died within seven years. The declaration would ensure that once the seven years had elapsed, the property owner's estate for inheritance tax would only include the market value of a one-half share, which would be discounted because the cohabitee would still occupy the property. If such a declaration was not made, then even if both parties contribute to the cost and upkeep, HMRC may treat the whole property as part of the owner's estate at death. The exemption from inheritance tax for property passing from one spouse or registered civil partner to the other does not apply to cohabitees, so that an unwelcome charge to tax will arise when the inheritance tax threshold is exceeded.

See **10.7** for the position for cohabiting couples in relation to the high income child benefit charge.

Council tax

[33.21] Couples who are cohabiting but are neither married nor registered as civil partners are jointly liable for payment of council tax in the same way as married couples or civil partners. For all couples, the joint liability only applies for any part of the year when they are living together, and would not apply after separation, divorce or dissolution. A partner is not liable unless the authority has issued a bill to him or her.

Tax points

[33.22] Note the following:

- HMRC require a married couple or registered civil partners to send in a separate Form 17 (notification of unequal shares — see **33.6**) for any new jointly owned assets. This needs to be borne in mind if they have a joint share portfolio, where there may be frequent changes.
- Proper evidence is required if the ownership of bank and building society accounts is changed so that they are held as tenants in common rather than joint tenants.
- Although the capital gains tax private residence exemption applies only to a qualifying main residence, if a married couple or civil partners own a second home jointly they will each be entitled to the annual exempt amount when they sell it (unless used against other gains). See also **30.17** regarding changing a qualifying main residence.
- In a bona fide business partnership of husband and wife or registered civil partners, where both play a significant role in the business, profits can be shared so as to maximise the benefit of being taxed separately. However, the risk of such arrangements being challenged under the 'settlements' rules needs to be borne in mind (see **23.31**).
- If joint wealth is substantial, inheritance tax may be saved by re-arranging the ownership of assets between spouses or civil partners. See CHAPTER 35 for details.
- Social security regulations for cohabiting couples are different from those relating to tax. They should be researched before making financial arrangements between the couple, and for children.
- As far as the high income child benefit charge is concerned, the rules for cohabitees are the same as those for married couples or civil partners (see **10.7**).

34

Especially for the senior citizen

Introduction

[34.1] This chapter deals with various aspects of the tax system that are of particular interest to older people. HMRC guidance is available at www.gov.uk/tax-national-insurance-after-state-pension-age.

Personal reliefs (ITA 2007, ss 33–58)

Personal allowance

[34.2] For details of the personal allowance available see **2.15**.

An individual who is not liable to income tax above the basic rate is able to transfer £1,150 of their personal allowance to their spouse or civil partner, provided the transferee is also not liable to income tax above the basic rate. Married couples or civil partnerships entitled to claim the married couple's allowance will not be entitled to make a transfer (see **2.17**).

Married couple's allowance

[34.3] Married couple's allowance is available only where one or both of a married couple or civil partnership was born before 6 April 1935. For full details see **2.19**. The allowance is reduced where income exceeds a certain limit (see **2.20**) though there is a minimum amount.

Separation and divorce or dissolution (ITA 2007, ss 453, 454)

[34.4] When couples separate, get divorced, or dissolve a civil partnership, relief for maintenance payments is available if either or both were born before 6 April 1935.

The relief may be claimed when a marriage or civil partnership is dissolved, in respect of payments made by one of the couple to the other for the other's maintenance. It may also be claimed by one of a separated couple (whether or not they have been married or civil partners) who makes payments to the other for the maintenance of a child of the family under 21 (or a child who has been so treated, other than a child boarded out with the family by a public authority or voluntary organisation). The payments may be made under a court order or written agreement governed by UK (or EU state) law. The claimant is entitled to reduce his/her tax bill by a maintenance relief of 10% of £3,260 in 2017–18 (or 10% of the maintenance paid if less).

The full relief is available in the year of separation, as well as the married couple's allowance (as to which see **34.3**). Payments due after a former spouse remarries or former civil partner registers with another partner do not qualify for relief. Maintenance relief is available to qualifying nationals of the EEA (see **1.3**) who are resident in the UK and to qualifying UK nationals paying maintenance by order or written agreement of an EEA country. The relief is given by an adjustment to PAYE codings or in the payer's self-assessment or simple assessment (see **9.2**).

All maintenance received is free of tax.

For further discussion of separation and divorce or dissolution see CHAPTER **33**.

Pensions and state benefits

[34.5] State pensions are taxable but tax is not deducted under the PAYE system, so an increase in state pension results in a larger deduction of tax under PAYE from an occupational or personal pension. The state pension increase takes up another slice of tax allowances, reducing the amount available to set against occupational or personal pension. People with small occupational pensions may find that they do not get the full benefit of their allowances and may need to claim a refund (see Example 6 at **2.33**). See **16.2** for details of entitlement to state pension and CHAPTER **16** for further points about pensions generally, in particular **16.5** about deferring or suspending the state pension.

Where allowances (in particular married couple's allowance) are restricted to 10%, estimates of income are used to adjust the PAYE code (see **10.61**) so as to charge the correct amount of tax. Variations in income will lead to under- or overpayments and a taxpayer should let the tax office know if his income varies substantially, though RTI (see **10.58**) does enable HMRC to amend tax codes to reflect certain in-year changes.

Some state benefits are taxable and others are not (see list in **10.6**), so care needs to be taken where there is a choice. See **13.12** for details of the inherited additional state pension entitlement of a surviving spouse or civil partner, and **33.13** for the bereavement benefits that may be available to widows, widowers and surviving civil partners. For general points on state benefits, see CHAPTER **13**.

Home provided for a dependent relative or trust beneficiary

[34.6] See **30.11** for the capital gains exemption available where there is a disposal of a property provided rent-free to a dependent relative who had occupied the property from 5 April 1988 until up to 18 months before the date of disposal, and for the capital gains exemption available to trustees where the occupier is entitled to occupy property as a beneficiary of a trust.

Purchased life annuities

[34.7] A purchased life annuity is an annual sum received for life, in exchange for a capital payment. Part of the annuity is regarded as a return of capital and thus escapes tax; tax is deducted from the income element at 20% (see **2.25**). The older the individual, the greater the tax-free capital element of the annuity. The capital required to buy the annuity is sacrificed, and this loss of capital must be weighed against the greater income arising. The loss of capital may be considered worthwhile to enable an improvement in the standard of living, particularly if there are no dependants or others to whom to leave capital. However, it is important to have regard to annuity rates and to get proper professional advice before making this sort of arrangement. See also **36.15** and **40.3**.

Payments for long-term care (ITTOIA 2005, ss 725, 726)

[34.8] Payments made under an 'immediate needs annuity' (which is a special form of life annuity) to a care provider or local authority are exempt from tax. The exemption applies where the annuity is provided to fund long-term care for someone who is unable to live independently because of physical or mental infirmity.

Making the most of the dwelling house

[34.9] The home is often the most significant asset, yet it can be the biggest liability because it has to be maintained, and in most cases it does not produce income.

If an individual decides to let part of his home, he will not have to pay income tax on the rent unless it exceeds £7,500 — the 'rent-a-room scheme', see **30.12**. This form of letting should not cause any loss of the capital gains tax private residence exemption (see CHAPTER 30) when the property is sold. Taking in boarders who live as part of the family also does not affect the capital gains tax exemption.

There are numerous schemes, known as equity release schemes, to enable homeowners to realise capital from their property. Some of the schemes are outlined below. Proper financial advice is essential and it must also be ensured that the scheme gives security of income and does not put the home at risk.

[34.10] Sometimes the money to purchase a life annuity (see **34.7**) is raised by a loan secured on an individual's home (a home income plan). If the loan was taken out before 9 March 1999 (or a written offer of the loan had been made before that date), the individual is still entitled to relief on the interest on the first £30,000 of the loan. Relief may be given under the MIRAS scheme despite the general MIRAS relief having been withdrawn. The rate of relief is 23%. The entitlement to relief for the interest payable continues even if the individual remortgages, or moves to another property or into a nursing home. The interest paid clearly reduces the extra income from the annuity and careful calculations are necessary to see if the result is a meaningful increase in spending money. Another possibility is an arrangement whereby no interest is paid on the loan during lifetime and the compensating interest payable to the lender on death is fixed in advance.

[34.11] A further possibility is a home reversion scheme, under which all or part of the house is sold to the reversion company for much less than its value (the discount usually being at least 50%) in return for the right to live in it until death. Some schemes give a lower initial sum but give a share in future increases in value of the property. The initial cash sum does not attract capital gains tax but shares of future increases in value may be liable. The investment of the initial capital sum gives extra spendable income.

[34.12] Yet another possibility is a shared appreciation mortgage, where an individual gets an interest-free mortgage equal to a percentage of the value of the property in return for giving up a substantial part of any increase in value of the property when he either sells it or dies. Unlike some earlier home income plans, there is no risk of losing the home if property values fall, because if there is no increase only the amount of the mortgage is repaid.

[34.13] Certain types of equity release scheme are subject to regulation by the Financial Conduct Authority. This includes home reversion plans from 6 April 2007. The Government has stated that there will not be a tax charge under the pre-owned assets provisions (see **5.42**) for bona fide equity release schemes involving the disposal of all or part of the taxpayer's interest in the property. This also applies to non-arm's length part sales (for example within a family) effected before 7 March 2005 if they were on arm's length terms, and to later similar part sales made for a consideration other than money or readily realisable assets.

Helping the family

[34.14] An individual may be in a position to give financial help to his family rather than requiring help from them. The following gifts may be made without inheritance tax consequences:

(a)   habitual gifts out of income that leave enough income to maintain the usual standard of living (see **5.9**);

(b)   gifts of not more than £250 per donee in each tax year (see **5.7**);

(c)   the first £3,000 of total gifts in each tax year, plus any unused part of the £3,000 exemption for the previous tax year (see **5.10**). This exemption applies to gifts on an 'earliest first' basis, so if an individual gave away nothing last year and gives £5,000 in May and £5,000 in June, the May gift is exempt and £1,000 of the June gift is exempt.

Even if the gift is not exempt, there is still no immediate inheritance tax to pay since lifetime gifts (other than to most trusts) are only brought into account for inheritance tax if the donor does not survive the gift by seven years. In the meantime they are 'potentially exempt transfers' (see **5.26**). If the donor does not survive the seven-year period, there is still no question of inheritance tax being payable if the gift is within the nil rate band for inheritance tax, currently £325,000. This nil rate band is used against gifts in the seven years before death in the order in which they are made. When the cumulative lifetime gifts exceed the nil rate band, the excess is chargeable, but the tax is reduced on a sliding scale if the donor has survived the gift by more than three years (see **5.32**). The tax is payable by the donee. All non-exempt gifts within the seven years before death affect how much of the nil rate band is left to reduce the chargeable estate at death.

Spouses and civil partners are treated separately for inheritance tax, each being entitled to the available exemptions and the nil rate band (see **5.2**).

Tax position on death

[34.15] On death, an individual's wealth and the chargeable transfers made in the previous seven years determine whether any, and if so how much, inheritance tax is payable (see CHAPTER 5). There is no inheritance tax on assets passing to a spouse or civil partner. There is no liability to capital gains tax on any increase in the value of assets up to the date of death, and those who acquire the assets are treated as having done so at their market value at the date of death. Further details on the position at death are in CHAPTERS 33 and 35.

If capital gains have been made in that part of the tax year before death, they are chargeable if they exceed the annual exempt amount, currently £11,300. Any capital losses in the tax year of death may be carried back to set against gains on which tax has been paid in the three previous tax years, latest first, and, in that event, tax will be repayable to the estate. Interest on the repayment runs from the payment date for the tax year of death (see **9.16**).

As far as income tax is concerned, the income to the date of death is charged to tax in the usual way, and a full personal allowance is available. For married couples and civil partners, if one (or both) was born before 6 April 1935, married couple's allowance is still available, and there are provisions for each spouse or partner to claim part of the allowance (see **2.19**). The treatment of the married couple's allowance in the tax year in which either the main claimant or the spouse or civil partner dies is dealt with in **33.13**. See **2.17** regarding treatment of the transferable tax allowance in the tax year that the transferee dies.

Council tax

[34.16] Property is exempt from council tax if it is left unoccupied while the owner is a long-term hospital patient, or is being looked after in a residential care home, or is living elsewhere to receive care (see **8.3**). The owner may qualify for a one-band reduction for council tax if the home has special features because he or another resident is disabled (see **8.6**). Other discounts may be available (see **8.5**).

People on low incomes may be entitled to help from council tax support schemes (see **8.7**).

Tax points

[34.17] Note the following:

- The structure of tax rates, even for those on modest incomes, can be very confusing. The 0% starting rate for savings is complicated and will not be available to most taxpayers, but the savings allowance and dividend allowance which apply from 6 April 2016 provide a 0% tax rate for some savings and dividends (see **2.5**).

- HMRC estimate that there are a large number of pensioners who do not claim either the transferable tax allowance or the tax repayments to which they are entitled.

- In reckoning income for married couple's allowance, any investment bond withdrawals over the 5% limit have to be taken into account even though there is no tax to pay on that excess at the higher rate (see **40.6**). Conversely, the gross amount of a properly recorded donation to a charity reduces income when calculating whether the allowance is to be restricted. The same applies to a personal pension contribution.

- There is no point in increasing available income now if this jeopardises capital and causes worry and uncertainty for the future.

- Since lifetime transfers (other than those into most trusts) are potentially exempt from inheritance tax and do not have to be reported, it is most important to keep accurate records of gifts out of income and capital so that there can be no doubt about dates and amounts of gifts. Personal representatives are responsible for dealing with the inheritance tax position of lifetime transfers and carefully kept records are essential for the avoidance of doubt.

- If, because of disability, an individual has to provide, adapt or extend a bathroom, washroom or lavatory in his private residence, the cost is not liable to VAT. There is, however, no income tax relief on the cost or on money borrowed to finance the work.
- If an individual's spouse or civil partner does not have enough income to cover his/her personal allowance for income tax, the transferable tax allowance may apply (see 2.17). Alternatively, the individual should consider transferring some assets to the spouse or partner if this is practicable, so that the income from them will then be his/hers and not the individual's (see 33.4).
- If it is not appropriate to transfer assets from one spouse or civil partner to the other, placing them in joint ownership but in unequal shares will still have the effect of the income being split equally even if the ownership share of one spouse or partner far exceeds that of the other (see 33.6). This does not, however, apply to dividends on shares in family companies.
- If an individual makes a lifetime gift not covered by the annual exemptions, it is essential that the donee is aware that he is responsible for the payment of any inheritance tax on it if the individual dies within the next seven years.

35

Making a will and estate planning

Intestate death

[35.1] If a person dies intestate, that is without making a will, the law divides the estate in a particular way. For married couples and registered civil partners, the spouse or civil partner automatically acquires the family home and any other assets such as bank accounts owned as joint tenants (see **35.6**). The intestacy rules apply only to the remainder of the estate. If, on the other hand, the house and other assets were owned either in the sole name of the person who died or jointly with his spouse or civil partner as tenants in common (see **35.6**), the deceased's share would form part of his estate and would be subject to the intestacy rules.

The intestacy rules currently applicable in England and Wales are set out in **35.2**. A spouse or civil partner will not inherit under these rules unless he/she survives the deceased spouse or partner by at least 28 days.

Current intestacy rules (ITPA 2014)

[35.2] The intestacy rules were simplified for deaths occurring on or after 1 October 2014. Where there is a surviving spouse or civil partner they apply as follows.

Where there is a surviving spouse or civil partner

If there are no children, or their issue*, the residuary estate is held in trust for the surviving spouse or civil partner absolutely.

If there are children, or their issue:

(a) the surviving spouse or civil partner takes the personal chattels absolutely;

(b) the surviving spouse or civil partner gets a fixed net sum (currently £250,000), free of death duties and costs; and

(c) the residuary estate is held one half, in trust for the surviving spouse or civil partner absolutely, and the other half, on statutory trusts for the issue of the intestate.

Where there is no surviving spouse or civil partner

If there are children, or their issue*, they take the whole estate absolutely.

If there are no children or their issue*, the whole estate goes to surviving relatives in the following order of precedence, each category taking the whole estate to the exclusion of any later category:

(a) Parents
(b) Brothers and sisters (or their issue*)
(c) Half brothers and sisters (or their issue*)
(d) Grandparents
(e) Uncles and aunts (or their issue*)
(f) Parents' half brothers and sisters (or their issue*)

If there are none of these relatives, the estate goes to the Crown.

* 'Issue' means children and their children, grandchildren, great grandchildren etc., each such person being entitled to an appropriate proportion of the deceased parent's share.

The share of anyone under 18 is held on trust to age 18.

Chattels are defined as tangible movable property, other than money, property used at the date of death solely or mainly for business purposes, or property held solely as an investment.

Making a will: tax considerations

General considerations

[35.3] In making the best arrangements from a taxation point of view, it must not be forgotten that the prime objective is to ensure that those left behind are properly provided for in a sensible, practical and acceptable way. There are important tax implications, which it can be expensive to ignore, but they should not be allowed to override the main aim.

It should be borne in mind that wills need to be regularly reviewed to ensure that they remain appropriate. In particular, the effect of marriage or civil partnership, separation, divorce or dissolution, or changes in the legislation, need to be borne in mind. A will is generally revoked by marriage or registration of civil partnership. It is not revoked on divorce or dissolution, although bequests to the former spouse or civil partner would no longer apply, nor any appointment of the former spouse or civil partner as executor. Separation has no effect on a will. If the family home is held as joint tenants, the joint tenancy will not be affected by either separation or divorce/dissolution, so it will usually be appropriate for separating couples to sever the joint tenancy in order to ensure that if one dies before the couple's affairs are settled, the property does not automatically go to the other (see **35.6**).

Inheritance tax: spouses and civil partners (IHTA 1984, ss 8A, 18; TCGA 1992, s 58)

[35.4] Gifts between spouses or civil partners are exempt from inheritance tax for both lifetime and death transfers (unless the donee is not deemed to be domiciled in the UK, in which case gifts are exempt up to a limit of £325,000 (the current nil rate band; see **5.11**). Transfers between spouses or civil partners in a tax year when they are living together are also exempt from capital gains tax, and there is no stamp duty or stamp duty land tax on gifts.

Spouses/civil partners are each entitled to the inheritance tax nil rate band, currently £325,000. Where a surviving spouse or civil partner dies, a claim may be made for any part of the nil rate band unused on the death of the first spouse or civil partner to die to be added to the survivor's own nil rate band on his or her death (**5.24**). HMRC guidance can be found at www.gov.uk/guidance/inheritance-tax-transfer-of-threshold.

The proportion of the first nil rate band to be transferred is calculated by reference to the amount of the nil rate band in force at the time of the survivor's death. In many cases it will now be beneficial, therefore, to arrange for assets to pass to the surviving spouse/civil partner rather than arranging for a chargeable transfer to utilise some of the nil rate band on the first death.

Example 1

H died on 1 May 2012 leaving £81,250 to his sister and the remaining estate to his wife W, when the inheritance tax nil rate band was £325,000. The unused proportion of his nil rate band was 75%.

If W dies on 1 November 2017, when the nil rate band is still £325,000, and a claim is made for the transfer of H's unused nil rate band, W's nil rate band will become £325,000 + (75% × £325,000) = £568,750.

Unused residence nil rate band (RNRB; see **5.24**) can also be transferred between spouses/civil partners. RNRB can be transferred to a surviving spouse/civil partner who dies on or after 6 April 2017. Where the first death has occurred before 6 April 2017, the survivor's RNRB is increased by 100% of whatever the value of the RNRB is at the time of the second death, provided that the value of the estate of the first to die did not exceed £2 million.

The claim is made on form IHT216. Since it may be necessary for claimants to ascertain the unused nil rate band in relation to a death that occurred many years ago, HMRC have published tables showing the nil rate band in force over the years, going back to 1914, for inheritance tax and its predecessors, capital transfer tax and estate duty. The normal time limit for the claim is two years after the end of the month in which the surviving spouse/partner died, although this can be extended at HMRC's discretion.

A will can be drafted to ensure that a spouse/partner enjoys the income but the assets themselves are eventually to go to others, for example children by a previous marriage/civil partnership. This is normally achieved by a will declaring a trust providing for precisely that. The spouse/partner exemption for inheritance tax will still apply so long as the terms of the trust are appropriately drawn. Professional advice is essential.

Where the nil rate band is used by each spouse/partner it may be better on the first death to leave the excess over the nil rate threshold to the surviving spouse/partner so that tax would be paid later rather than earlier, with the survivor being able to make further tax-exempt lifetime gifts. For income tax, it is tax-efficient for each spouse/civil partner to have sufficient capital to produce enough income to use the personal allowance and basic rate bands.

Use of discretionary trusts

[35.5] It is possible, in order to use up the nil rate band, to leave £325,000 or other appropriate amount to a trust where the trustees have a discretion as to what they do with the income and capital, leaving, for example, a spouse/partner as one of the beneficiaries. The supporting capital is thus not transferred to the survivor directly to swell his/her estate for tax purposes on eventual death, but any unexpected need may be made good by the trustees exercising their discretion to pay amounts to him/her. Where land is involved, stamp duty land tax may be payable in connection with nil rate band discretionary trusts. See HMRC's stamp duty land tax manual at SDLTM04045 for detailed comments.

A discretionary trust is also useful where there is some uncertainty at the time of making the will as to who should benefit. A transfer of the capital to one or more individuals by the trustees within two years after death (but not within the first three months of that two years) is treated for inheritance tax purposes as having been made by will, and has the same effect. Capital gains tax may, however, be payable (see **35.17**).

Discretionary trusts are dealt with in more detail at **42.27** to **42.36** within the mainstream inheritance tax rules for trusts. The use of trusts in tax planning is a complicated area, and professional advice is essential, particularly in assessing the suitability of discretionary trusts following reforms to the use of the nil rate band discussed at **35.4**.

Jointly owned assets

[35.6] There are two ways in which assets may be held jointly — as joint tenants or as tenants in common. If an asset is held jointly with someone else as a joint tenant, it passes to the other joint tenant(s) through operation of the law by survivorship (i.e. outside the terms of any will) on death. With a tenancy in common, each has a separate share which can be disposed of in lifetime or on death as the person wishes. Spouses and civil partners are normally presumed to own assets as joint tenants, and other people are presumed to own them as tenants in common, although this normal presumption can be varied. It must, however, be done in the proper legal manner appropriate to the asset.

The appropriate share in a jointly held asset still forms part of a person's estate for inheritance tax whether the asset is held on a joint tenancy or as tenants in common, but where assets are held jointly by spouses or civil partners, any assets passing to the other are covered in any event by the spouse/civil partner exemption. In the case of a joint bank or building society account, holding as joint tenants has the advantage in that when a spouse or civil partner dies, all that is needed to enable the survivor take over sole ownership of the account is production of the death certificate. There is no need to wait for grant of probate or administration. But a joint account has other tax implications, particularly in relation to income tax, since the shares of income accruing to each spouse or civil partner may not give the best income tax position.

The family home

[35.7] Although most taxation aspects relating to the family home are dealt with in CHAPTER 30, there are various points which are of particular importance when making a will, albeit the taxation considerations should never be allowed to get in the way of the security and comfort in body and mind of the surviving spouse/civil partner or other dependants.

Whatever is done will have an impact not only on inheritance tax but also on capital gains tax, income tax and stamp duty land tax, so it is essential that no aspect is considered in isolation. The possibility that the spouse/civil partner or dependant who would normally occupy the property might need to go into care should not be forgotten, bearing in mind that the house value might have to be realised to pay fees which might otherwise be subsidised by the authorities if the spouse/civil partner or dependants did not have an entitlement to occupy the house or receive the sale proceeds.

[35.8] Where the will provides that the home is left to a surviving spouse or civil partner outright, or that he/she is entitled to occupy it for life, then on the death of the survivor, the value of the home at that time will be reckonable for inheritance tax, but no capital gains tax will be payable on the increase in value to that time. The value on the survivor's death will be the capital gains tax cost for a future disposal.

The uplift in value for capital gains tax will also apply where the house is left absolutely or in trust for a dependant, but the exemption for inheritance tax on the first death will not apply.

[35.9] A spouse or civil partner who inherits the house and is considering giving it away must not fall foul of the clear rule that he/she must not retain a benefit after doing so if the value is not to be reckoned for inheritance tax at his/her death. This could be avoided by the survivor paying a commercial rent to the donee upon which the donee would pay income tax (but perhaps in the process reducing any income surplus of the survivor which would otherwise increase his or her wealth on eventual death). The gift would drop out of the inheritance tax reckoning after seven years.

If, having given away the property, instead of paying rent the survivor paid a market rate lump sum for the right to occupy the property for life, the value of the survivor's estate for inheritance tax would deplete at once by the purchase price of the lease for life, with the gift of the property dropping out of the reckoning after seven years.

A variation on this theme might be the next generation purchasing the house at full market value from the survivor with a commercial loan, the interest being funded by the full market rent received from the survivor and income tax only being paid on the net surplus. This would provide cash to the former house owner who could either use it to produce income or to make capital gifts, the value of the house in the meantime increasing in the hands of the next generation.

But none of the arrangements in the previous three paragraphs would protect the increasing value of the home from capital gains tax, since the property at the time of death of the survivor would neither be owned by him/her nor occupied under the terms of a trust.

[35.10] Mention has been made in 35.5 of the use of a discretionary trust with the survivor being a beneficiary under the trust. Such an arrangement may well be unnecessary now that the surviving spouse or civil partner may benefit from the unused nil rate band on the first death (see **35.4**).

So far as existing arrangements are concerned, where the family home is included in the trust and the survivor allowed to occupy it there is a risk that HMRC might argue that the occupation amounts to a life interest in possession, with the value of the house being reckonable for inheritance tax on the survivor's death as well as having been included earlier in the reckoning for inheritance tax. If instead, the survivor is not a beneficiary under the discretionary trust, he could purchase it from the trustees, thus having the comfort and security of ownership, with the capital gains tax uplift applying at his/her death. If he had insufficient resources for the purchase, the trustees could allow the purchase price to remain on loan from them. This would effectively leave the present value of the house out of the estate of the survivor (i.e. the amount of the loan for the purchase would be a debt deductible in calculating the value of the survivor's estate), but the wealth of the survivor would still include the market value of the house itself. This might, however, attract capital gains tax private residence relief on a subsequent sale by the survivor and there would be no capital gains tax on the increase in value if the property was held until death.

A number of more sophisticated arrangements might be considered, but with these and indeed the others outlined in this section, a word of caution is necessary in that what might be attractive for one purpose is often not so for another, with savings on the one hand sometimes being eroded by costs on the other, and HMRC also being able to challenge arrangements which might be considered to be artificial. Professional advice is essential.

Leaving to charity

[35.11] Bequeaths to charity reduce the reckonable value of an estate for inheritance tax purposes. In addition, if 10% or more of the net value of a person's estate is left to a qualifying charity (i.e. one recognised as such by HMRC) the tax due may be paid at a reduced rate of 36% (as opposed to 40%). For details see 5.30.

Legacies and their effect on the spouse/civil partner exemption

[35.12] Unless a will states otherwise, legacies are payable out of the residue of an estate, after inheritance tax has been paid, reducing the amount available to the person entitled to the balance of the estate — called the residuary legatee. The legacies are not themselves reduced by inheritance tax unless the will specifically says so. It follows that the amount available to a residuary legatee is often less than is apparent at first sight.

If the residuary legatee is the surviving spouse or civil partner, this has an effect on the tax payable because the exempt part of the estate (which goes to the spouse/civil partner) is first reduced by the tax.

Example 2

A has made no transfers in the seven years before his death in 2017–18. He leaves an estate of £445,000 as follows:

£86,250 to each of his four children = £345,000

Residue to his wife

The IHT position on A's death is as follows:

	Gross	Tax	Net
	£	£	£
Net legacies up to the nil rate threshold	325,000		325,000
Balance grossed up at 100/60	33,333	13,333	20,000
	358,333	13,333	345,000

The estate will accordingly be divided as follows:

	£
Gross estate	445,000
Legacies to children	(345,000)
IHT payable out of residue	(13,333)
Remainder to widow, covered by spouse exemption	£86,667

Out of a gross estate of £445,000, A's children receive legacies totalling £345,000, leaving an apparent residue of £100,000 for the widow. She does not, however, get £100,000, but only that amount less the tax on the rest of the estate. This is calculated by working out the tax on a figure sufficient to leave the

---

legacies intact, called grossing-up. The tax amounts to £13,333 as shown above, leaving the widow with £86,667. If the will had provided that the children should pay the tax on their legacies, the widow would have received £100,000 and the total tax payable by the legatees on £345,000 would have been £8,000 (40% of the £20,000 excess over £325,000). The children could have provided for this liability by insuring their father's life, using the proceeds of the policy to pay the tax on the legacy.

Deaths in quick succession (IHTA 1984, s 141)

[35.13] Where at the time of death a person's estate has been increased by a lifetime or death gift made to him within the previous five years, the tax charge on the second transfer is reduced by quick succession relief. Although the relief is deducted from the tax payable on the second transfer, it is calculated as a percentage of the tax paid on the earlier transfer (see CHAPTER 5).

Quick succession relief is therefore not relevant in the case of assets received from a spouse or civil partner by gift, in lifetime or by bequest on death, or where they have been acquired otherwise than from a spouse or civil partner in lifetime but no tax has been paid by reference to that transfer. While not losing sight of the overriding principle of family provision, there are cases where it is clearly not sensible to increase a person's estate by lifetime gifts or bequests on death, if they have adequate resources already. Thus it will often be more tax-efficient to leave to grandchildren instead of to children. This gives the added advantage that the income arising is then that of the grandchildren in their own right, on which they will not have to pay tax if it is covered by their available income tax allowances.

Simultaneous deaths and survivorship clauses (IHTA 1984, s 92)

[35.14] Where two closely related people die at the same time, or in circumstances in which it is impossible to decide who died first, neither estate has to be increased by any entitlement from the other in calculating the inheritance tax payable. This is not so if it is clear who died first. It is therefore often advisable to include a survivorship clause in a will making a bequest conditional on the beneficiary outliving the deceased by a given period, and this is effective for inheritance tax providing the period does not exceed six months. This is particularly useful to spouses or civil partners who wish to leave their estates to each other to make sure that there is adequate provision for the survivor's lifetime. If the wills include an appropriate survivorship clause then, if they both die within six months, the estate of the first will not pass to the second, inheritance tax being payable at each death on the value of the separate estates. This will often attract less tax than if no tax was paid on the first death (because of the spouse/civil partner exemption), but tax was calculated on the combined estates for the second, with the survivor having had little or no benefit from the assets in the meantime. The assets in each estate and the extent to which the inheritance tax nil rate band is available need to be taken into account.

A 28-day spouse/civil partnership survivorship period is also prescribed under the intestacy rules (see **35.1**).

Variations and disclaimers etc (IHTA 1984, ss 17, 142–144, 218A; TCGA 1992, s 62)

[35.15] It is possible for those entitled to a deceased's estate (either under a will, on an intestacy or otherwise) to vary the way in which it is distributed, or to disclaim their entitlement, provided that they do so within two years after the death. The variation or disclaimer then takes effect as if it had applied at the date of death and inheritance tax is charged as if the revised distribution had operated at death. For variations (but not disclaimers) this applies only if the variation contains a statement by those making it, and by the personal representatives if additional tax is payable, that they intend the variation to have that effect. Where additional tax is payable, then within six months after the date of the variation the personal representatives must notify the amount of additional tax to HMRC and send a copy of the variation. Court consent is needed for a variation that adversely affects the shares of beneficiaries under 18. If an original beneficiary has died, his personal representatives can act in his place but there may be restrictions on what they are able to vary.

Such a variation or disclaimer can also be effective for capital gains tax purposes (subject to what is said below about trusts) providing, in the case of a variation, the document specifies that it is to apply for capital gains tax. The ultimate beneficiary then takes the asset at the market value at the date of death, so that any increase in value since death is not charged to capital gains tax until the beneficiary disposes of the asset. The original entitlement under the will, while the estate is in administration, is itself a right (a chose in action), and but for the specific application of the variation to capital gains tax, the variation might itself be regarded as a disposal of that right, causing a liability to capital gains tax.

As far as income derived from the assets is concerned, the personal representatives will have paid income tax on it at the trust rate (see **42.4**), but the income is regarded as having been received not by the person who actually receives it following the variation but by the original beneficiary, and any tax due in excess of the amount paid on the income up to the date of variation or disclaimer will be calculated by reference to the original beneficiary's tax rates. It may be appropriate for the person actually receiving the income to agree to pay any income tax at excess rates. Where a variation includes the setting up of a trust, those whose entitlement (but for the variation) goes into the trust are regarded as settlors of the trust fund for income tax and capital gains tax. This means that, for example, parents whose share is given up in favour of infant children will still be taxed on the income so long as the children are under 18 and unmarried (or not in a civil partnership), and trustees' capital gains may be treated as the original beneficiary's gains if that person is a beneficiary under the trust.

[35.16] A deed of variation or disclaimer could be used to advantage where, for example, an estate has been left to the surviving spouse/civil partner without the deceased's nil rate band having been used. If the survivor is already adequately provided for, part of the estate could be diverted to, say, the children. It could also be useful where, for example, children have sufficient assets of their own and would prefer legacies to go to their own children, subject to what is said above about trusts.

Where quoted shares fall in value within the 12 months after death and are sold, cancelled, or dealings are suspended within that period, the lower value may be substituted in calculating tax on the death estate (see 5.35). The reference to cancellation is apparently intended mainly to apply to liquidations, but it may be that the liquidation is not completed within the 12-month period, so that the relief cannot be claimed. One way of avoiding the tax liability on the higher death value of the shares would be to use a deed of variation to re-direct the shares to an exempt beneficiary, such as a spouse or civil partner, so that there would be no tax payable on that higher value.

Deeds of variation and disclaimer can be used to lessen the overall tax burden on death, but it is necessary for all concerned to consent to the arrangement, and they should usually be regarded as something in reserve rather than a substitute for appropriate planning.

[35.17] Two other ways of building flexibility into a will are worth consideration. It is possible for someone making a will to leave a 'letter of wishes' asking the personal representatives to give effect to the requests in the letter. This is particularly useful for dealing with chattels and personal effects, and is treated for inheritance tax purposes as if it had been part of the will. The letter of wishes is not, however, binding upon the personal representatives. The other useful provision is the ability to create a discretionary trust by will, out of which the trustees can make distributions within two years after the death, which are again treated as having been made by the will, providing they are not made within the first three months after the death. This can, however, have capital gains consequences if the assets have grown in value since the date of death and the gift relief normally available for transfers out of discretionary trusts does not apply because inheritance tax is not reckonable on the distribution. It is possible for the capital gains charge to be avoided if the trustees appoint assets out of the trust to beneficiaries *before* the personal representatives transfer the assets to them. Where the assets are redirected in a settlement, the deceased is regarded as the settlor for capital gains tax and income tax purposes. This is a complex area and professional advice is essential.

Court orders (IHTA 1984, s 146)

[35.18] Where the court considers that the terms of a will or the intestacy rules do not make reasonable financial provision for certain people, such as a spouse or civil partner, former spouse or civil partner who has not remarried or registered a new civil partnership, child, or cohabitee, they may make an appropriate order, for example for the payment of a lump sum or maintenance. Such orders take effect as if they had applied at the date of death and override the provisions of the will or intestacy rules.

Insurance

[35.19] Life insurance may often be useful in planning for inheritance tax. It is not always possible to reconcile making adequate provision for the family with reducing the tax liability, and insurance may then be used to cover the anticipated liability.

If the proceeds of life insurance belong to an estate, they will attract inheritance tax. Furthermore, they will not be available until the grant of probate or administration is obtained. If, however, a policy on the deceased's life is arranged and funded by someone with an insurable interest, say his children, the funds will not belong to the deceased's estate and hence will not be liable to inheritance tax. Funds will also not be taxable in the deceased's estate if he takes out a policy himself and pays the premiums, with the proceeds in trust for someone else, again say his children. In that event each premium payment is a separate gift, but the deceased will usually be able to show that it was normal expenditure out of income, and thus exempt from inheritance tax, or, if not, covered by the annual exemption of £3,000 for transfers out of capital. Further details are at 40.11.

Tax points

[35.20] Note the following:

- The regime allowing a surviving spouse or civil partner to utilise any of the inheritance tax nil rate band remaining unused on the first death means that a good deal of routine tax planning is no longer necessary, but changing legislation as well as family circumstances make it important to review wills and potential tax liabilities regularly.
- If an entire estate is left to a spouse or civil partner, he/she can make lifetime transfers out of the combined wealth to an extent which he/she sees as sensible depending on the family circumstances from time to time. Those transfers may be completely exempt if they are covered by annual or marriage/civil partner exemptions, or potentially exempt, becoming completely exempt if the spouse or civil partner survives for seven years after making them (and where they exceed the nil rate threshold any tax arising would be subject to tapering relief on survival for three years). It is not possible for the deceased to ensure that his

spouse or civil partner will carry out his wishes, since if his estate is left to him/her unconditionally, he or she is free to decide what to do with it. See above regarding transferability of the nil rate band.

- Where tax at death cannot be avoided, consider covering the liability through life insurance, the policy being written so that the proceeds belong to those who will have to bear the tax.

- A further advantage of paying regular premiums on an insurance policy which provides a lump sum outside an estate is that the estate does not grow by the unspent income, thus effectively saving the further 40% inheritance tax which would arise on unspent accumulated income.

- If a person is apprehensive about leaving outright bequests to certain people, but still wants them to benefit, an amount could be left in trust for them to receive the income it produces, and in certain circumstances, the capital. This may provide the comfort of knowing that, for example, an adult child, whilst able to benefit immediately from the income, does not have an outright capital sum until a later stage when he/she is better able to manage it. The inheritance tax consequences depend on the circumstances.

- Since all gifts to a spouse or civil partner are exempt from inheritance tax, it may be more tax effective to leave agricultural and/or business property to someone else to avoid wasting agricultural and business property relief. Again, the transferability of the nil rate band should be borne in mind and in any event the tax position should not override family and commercial considerations.

- Where inheritance tax business property and agricultural property reliefs are at the rate of 100%, deferring gifts of such property until death avoids any charge to capital gains tax and also any problems of the inheritance tax relief being withdrawn at death because the donee has disposed of the property. But today's reliefs may not be available tomorrow, and a person may still prefer to make lifetime gifts now, deferring any capital gains tax under the gift relief provisions (see **4.31**).

- Wealth left to the next generation is liable to inheritance tax on a person's death (although see **5.24** for details of the 'additional' IHT nil rate band for a main residence left to the next generation), whereas it is not liable if left to a spouse or civil partner. However, if the next generation inherits at the death of the first rather than the second, inheritance tax is avoided on any increase in value between the first death and that of the spouse/civil partner.

- If shares are held through a nominee holding with a broker, the broker has the legal right to sell them before probate is granted. The broker may be willing to do this at the executors' request in order to raise sufficient funds for the executors to pay the inheritance tax due without borrowing. See also **42.2** for provisions enabling personal representatives to arrange for banks etc. holding the deceased's funds to pay inheritance tax direct to HMRC.

- It will make the executors' task far easier if an up-to-date schedule of investments, mortgages, pensions etc is kept, with the will, showing where all the relevant documents are kept. Any potentially exempt gifts for inheritance tax (see CHAPTER 5) should also be recorded.

- Although those entitled to the deceased's estate have the right to vary the way it is to be distributed, it is sometimes useful for a will to contain authority for a deed of variation, since this may help the beneficiaries to accept that they would not be acting against the deceased's wishes.
- When varying the provisions of a will or intestacy, it is important to remember that the variation must not be in consideration of something outside the estate being received instead by the individual whose entitlement decreases.
- For cohabiting couples, it should be remembered that the spouse/civil partner exemptions for inheritance tax and capital gains tax do not apply to them. It should be established whether joint assets are held under a joint tenancy or a tenancy in common. Careful thought and action is necessary to deal with each of those problems.
- A direct bequest to grandchildren is better than a bequest to their parent who then disclaims it in their favour since, while there is no effect on the inheritance tax payable on death, in the latter case the variation would be regarded as a parental settlement for income tax and capital gains tax purposes if the children were under 18 and unmarried or not in a civil partnership. The parent would be charged on the income where the child's total income from parental gifts exceeded £100, and on chargeable gains on disposal of the assets.
- For further post-death planning points see CHAPTER 42, which deals with the administration of a deceased's estate.

Part VIII

Choosing investments

36

Tax on investments

Introduction

[36.1] This chapter outlines the tax position on the main forms of investment available to the majority of taxpayers. More detailed information is given in CHAPTER 37 on investing in banks and building societies and in CHAPTER 38 on stocks and shares. The following investments are not dealt with in this chapter but are covered in the chapters indicated:

(a) shares in unquoted trading companies through the enterprise investment scheme or the seed enterprise investment scheme (CHAPTER 29);

(b) investments in qualifying social enterprises (CHAPTER 29);

(c) single premium life insurance policies — investment bonds and guaranteed income bonds (CHAPTER 40);

(d) chattels and valuables (CHAPTER 39).

The information given on each type of investment details the effect of taxation on income and capital growth. It is not intended to give advice on the investments themselves, nor is it offered as guidance on investment strategy, which should be obtained from appropriate sources.

There are various alternative finance arrangements, in particular those designed to meet the requirements of Islamic law, that do not involve paying or receiving interest but have a similar effect. The tax treatment of such payments and receipts is equated with the treatment of interest.

If investments are made through an authorised investment adviser, and a loss is suffered as a result of bad advice, poor investment management or the adviser going out of business, it is possible to claim compensation under the

Financial Services Compensation Scheme (FSCS, see **37.1**). Further information is provided at www.fscs.org.uk. Any interest included in the compensation
payment made to individuals by the FSCS when a financial institution defaults
is to be taxed in the same way as if it were paid by the financial institution
which defaulted.

Tax on investment income (ITTOIA 2005, Pt 4; ITA 2007, Pt 15; FA 2017, ss 4, 11 and Sch 5)

Investment income: general

[36.2] Most investment income (dividend and interest income) is paid free of
tax.

If the investment income is dividend income it is received gross and the income
is taxed as follows:

(a)   there is a 'dividend nil rate' which applies to dividends within the
£5,000 'dividend allowance'. This allowance is available to basic,
higher and additional rate taxpayers. The dividend allowance is not a
deduction in arriving at total income or taxable income so is perhaps
better thought of as a dividend nil rate band. Note that the September
2017 Finance Bill, which is expected to receive Royal Assent in
November 2017, includes legislation to reduce the dividend nil rate to
£2,000 from 2018–19 onwards;

(b)   where dividends exceed the dividend allowance the rates applying are
7.5% (called the dividend ordinary rate) on income up to the basic rate
limit, 32.5% (the dividend upper rate) on income above the basic rate
limit up to the higher rate limit, and 38.1% (the dividend additional
rate) on income above the higher rate limit — see **2.22** to **2.26**.

See **36.12** for further points on dividends.

If the investment income is interest income it also received gross and is taxed
as follows:

(a)   there is a 'savings nil rate' applies to an individual's savings income
which is within their 'savings allowance'. The savings allowance is
£1,000 per year for basic rate taxpayers and £500 for higher rate
taxpayers. It is not available to additional rate taxpayers. The savings
allowance is not a deduction in arriving at total income or taxable
income so is perhaps better thought of as a savings nil rate band;

(b)   where savings income exceeds the savings allowance it may fall within
the 0% 'starting rate for savings' band, which applies to savings income
other than dividends up to a 'starting rate limit' of £5,000. Note though
that for the purposes of this rate, savings income is treated as the top
slice of income (below only dividend income, and subject to certain
exceptions) so would probably only be beneficial to those with very
little forms of other income.

See **2.5** onwards for details.

Tax on investment income is included in the half-yearly payments on account on 31 January in the tax year and 31 July following for continuing sources (unless covered by the de minimis limits), with any balance being part of the overall balancing payment due on 31 January following the tax year. An employee or pensioner with small amounts of untaxed interest may have the tax collected through PAYE coding.

From 6 April 2017 interest distributions from open-ended investment companies, authorised unit trusts, investment trust companies and interest on peer-to-peer loans are paid gross. This brings these types of savings income into line with the treatment of interest paid on bank and building society accounts detailed above.

Investment income: disguised interest

[36.3] There is also an income tax charge on disguised interest. It applies to an 'arrangement' that produces (in any way), for the person who is party to it, a return which is 'economically equivalent to interest'. This includes anything done in relation to the arrangement from which a return will be produced, such as disposing of an instrument before maturity, or a person otherwise ceasing to be party to the arrangement. This charge (under ITTOIA 2005, s 381A) applies only where the return is not taxed under any other income tax provision. The full amount of the return that actually arises is taxed in the tax year. Listed shares are excluded from these rules if they were issued before 6 April 2013, or were issued after that date and do not provide an interest-like return on issue.

Investment income: companies

[36.4] For companies, most forms of interest income and dividend income received is received gross; see **36.2**. Where tax is deducted from income, the company still has to pay corporation tax on the income, but gets a credit against the tax payable for the income tax deducted. See also **36.9** for interest on government stocks

Investing in building societies and banks

[36.5] The majority of investors in building societies and banks invest in normal interest-bearing accounts. The interest on such accounts is received gross. For detailed commentary on the tax treatment of bank and building society accounts other than ISAs, see CHAPTER 37.

National Savings and Investments

[36.6] National Savings and Investments (NS&I) is a government agency, with the Post Office acting as a distributor for its products. NS&I offers various savings accounts (see **37.5**) and a range of other investments backed by the Treasury. See also www.nsandi.com. The current products offered are:

(a) Premium bonds. Any person over 16 can buy premium bonds and an adult can buy them for a child under 16. The minimum purchase is £100, and the current maximum holding is £50,000. They do not carry interest, but once a bond has been held for a clear calendar month it is included in a regular monthly draw for prizes of various amounts. All prizes are free of income tax and capital gains tax and the bond itself can be cashed in at face value at any time. This gives the holder the chance to win a tax-free prize, but at the cost of any income or protection of the real value of the capital.

(b) Guaranteed growth bonds. These are on sale until April 2018 and offer a guaranteed growth over a fixed three year period. The minimum holding is £100 and the maximum £3,000 per person. Withdrawals made before the end of the term are subject to a penalty equal to 90 days' interest on the amount withdrawn. A minimum amount of £100 must remain in the bond at all time to keep the bond open. At the end of the fixed term the bond can be cashed in with no penalty.

(c) Direct saver accounts. These offer a convenient saving account. Money can be paid in or taken out with no notice and no penalties. Anyone aged 16 or over can open an account, either individually or jointly with someone else. The minimum holding per person is £1 and the maximum is £2 million. The interest is paid gross and is taxable in the usual manner **2.5**.

(d) A direct access ISA. This is open to anyone who is eligible to subscribe to an ISA under the current rules; see **36.16**. There is no minimum subscription limit just a maximum in accordance with the current ISA rules.

(e) Guaranteed income bonds. These offer a guaranteed monthly income and normally a choice of investment terms of one, three or five years. Interest is paid to a bank or building society account. The minimum holding is £500 and the maximum £1 million, for either an individual or joint holding. Withdrawals made before the end of the term are subject to a penalty equal to 90 days' interest on the amount withdrawn. The interest is paid gross and is taxable in the usual manner **2.5**.

(f) Children's bonds. Children's bonds can be bought for children under 16. The minimum investment is £25 and the maximum holding per child is £3,000 in each issue. The investment term is five years at a time, and the bonds earn a fixed rate of interest guaranteed for each five-year period. They mature on reaching the first five-year anniversary on or after the child's 16th birthday and no further returns are earned after that time. The bonds may be cashed in early but are subject to a penalty equal to 90 days' interest on the amount withdrawn. All returns are exempt from tax, and parents may provide the funds without affecting their own tax liability.

(g) Investment account. These offer a convenient saving account. Money can be paid in or taken out with no notice and no penalties. Anyone aged 16 or over can open an account, either individually or jointly with someone else. The minimum holding per person is £20 and the maximum is £1 million. The interest is paid gross and is taxable in the usual manner **2.5**.

The Treasury have published guidance on the Government's new Help-to-Save Scheme, which is intended to help people on low incomes to save. Help-to-save savings accounts will be provided by NS&I and are expected to be available by April 2018. The Treasury guidance sets out how such accounts will operate and provides worked examples of when account holders will be entitled to tax-free bonuses. See www.gov.uk/government/uploads/system/uploads/attach ment_data/file/576030/Help_to_Save_policy_design_note_2016.pdf.

Broadly, the Help-to-Save Scheme allows qualifying individuals to save a maximum of £50 a month for four years. Withdrawals can be made at any time, but it is not possible to make deposits in excess of the monthly £50 limit, for example to make up for prior withdrawals or unused deposits in previous months.

The deposits will be topped up by a total Government bonus of up to £1,200, which is tax free. The first bonus will be calculated two years after the account has been opened. This will be will be 50% of the highest overall balance achieved within the first 24 calendar months of the account. The second bonus payment will usually be made after four years, when the account reaches maturity. This second bonus will be calculated at 50% of any additional highest balance built up in years three and four of the account.

Local authority stock, bonds and loans

[36.7] Some local authority stocks are listed on the Stock Exchange and interest on the stocks is paid gross to individuals. Interest paid by local authorities to companies is also paid gross (see 3.23).

Local authority stocks, bonds and loans that are transferable are subject to the accrued income provisions described at 36.11. They are also within the definition of 'qualifying corporate bonds' and are exempt from capital gains tax. See 38.6.

Income, gains and losses relating to a company's holdings of local authority stocks, etc. are taken into account in calculating the company's income, and disposals are not within the capital gains regime (see 3.6 and 38.5).

Gilt-edged securities (ITA 2007, ss 890–897; TCGA 1992, s 115)

[36.8] Gilt-edged securities represent borrowings by the British Government, and they vary considerably in terms of interest. Some are issued on an index-linked basis so that the interest paid while the stock is held and the capital payment when it is redeemed are dependent on increases in the retail prices index. Interest is paid gross on *all* gilt-edged securities acquired on or after 6 April 1998, unless application is made for net payment. See 36.2 for the way in which tax is accounted for. Special rules apply to companies (see 36.9).

Gilt-edged securities are exempt from capital gains tax. Some securities have a redemption date upon which the par value, or index-linked value as the case may be, is paid to the holder, so if they are bought below par there will be a guaranteed capital gain at a given date. The gain on non-index-linked securities is fixed in money terms whereas on index-linked securities it is fixed in real terms. In the meantime, the value of the securities fluctuate with market conditions, so that there may be opportunities to make tax-free capital gains before the redemption date. If, however, losses are made they are not allowable for set-off against chargeable gains.

Gilt-edged securities can be useful as a means of providing for future known commitments, such as school fees, and for those that are inclined to overspend, the securities are not so conveniently accessible as a bank or building society account.

Looked at on a pure money return basis, however, a purchase for capital growth may sometimes be no better for a higher rate taxpayer than an investment producing a greater income with no growth prospects. It depends upon the rates of interest being paid from time to time, and the price at which gilt-edged securities can be purchased.

For individuals (but not companies), interest on gilt-edged securities is subject to the accrued income scheme (see **36.11**).

[36.9] For companies, capital gains on gilt-edged securities are not exempt from corporation tax (with one exception (see **38.5**)) and both the income from the securities and profits and losses on disposal of them are taken into account in calculating a company's income. In the case of indexed gilt-edged securities held other than for trade purposes, the index increase in each year is not taxed as part of the company's profits at that time, and tax is chargeable on disposal only on the increase in capital value excluding the index increase over the period. Other indexed securities are normally treated in the same way as other loan stock.

Companies receive interest on gilt-edged securities in full, accounting for the tax along with the tax on their other profits.

Company loan stock

[36.10] Company loan stock is normally within the definition of 'qualifying corporate bonds' and exempt from capital gains tax in the same way as government stocks, although for companies holding such stock, their gains and losses are brought into account when calculating the company's income (see **38.5**). Most company loan stock is a less attractive investment than government stocks for the individual taxpayer because it may not be so readily marketable, there is a greater degree of risk and brokers' commission charges are higher. For individuals, trustees and personal representatives, the 'accrued income' rules for reckoning interest on a day-to-day basis apply (see **36.11**). Company loan stocks may be held in an Individual Savings Account (ISA), see **36.16**.

Accrued income scheme (ITA 2007, Pt 12)

[36.11] The accrued income scheme applies to interest-bearing marketable securities such as government stocks and to most local authority and company loan stock. It also applies to building society permanent interest bearing shares (see **37.4**). It does not apply to ordinary or preference shares in a company, units in unit trusts, bank deposits or securities within the 'discounted securities' provisions at **38.35**.

The accrued income scheme does not apply to companies because they are already taxed on accrued interest under the 'loan relationships' rules (see **3.6**). Nor does it apply to an individual if the nominal value of all accrued income scheme securities held does not exceed £5,000 at any time either in the tax year in which the next interest payment on the securities falls due or in the previous tax year.

Where the scheme applies, interest received is included in income according to the amount accrued on a day to day basis, so that selling just before an interest date does not enable income tax to be avoided on the interest by effectively receiving it as part of the sales proceeds. If securities are sold before they go 'ex dividend', the vendor is taxed on the accrued interest to the settlement date and the buyer's taxable income is correspondingly reduced. If securities are sold ex dividend (so that the vendor gets the full interest at the payment date), the vendor's taxable income is reduced and the buyer's increased by the interest applicable to the period between the settlement date and the interest payment date. The accrued income adjustments are made in the tax year in which the next interest payment date falls, the savings income being charged at the taxpayer's marginal rate.

Example 1

If securities were bought or sold in February 2017, on which interest is paid in June and December, the two tax years to look at are 2017–18 (in which the June interest date falls) and 2016–17 (the previous year). If the interest had been payable in March and September the two tax years to look at would have been 2016–17 (the interest date year) and 2015–16.

Where a sale is through a bank or stockbroker, the accrued interest is shown on the contract note.

The accrued income scheme applies not only to sales but also to any other transfers, except that it does not apply on death.

Accrued income charges and reliefs must be shown in the investor's tax return. Most securities covered by the accrued income scheme are exempt from capital gains tax (see **38.6**).

Example 2

An individual investor who is a 40% rate taxpayer sells £10,000 12% stock (on which interest is payable half-yearly on 9 June and 9 December) to a buyer who is a basic rate taxpayer. Stock goes ex dividend on 1 June 2017.

If sold for settlement on 25 May 2017 (i.e. sold cum dividend)

Buyer receives the full 6 months' interest on 9 June 2017, but effectively 'bought' part of this within his purchase price. The interest accrued from 10 December 2016 to 25 May 2017 is:

$$£1,200 \times \frac{167}{365} = £549.04$$

Seller's taxable income is increased (by an accrued income charge) and buyer's taxable income reduced (by accrued income relief) of £549.04.

If sold for settlement on 1 June 2017 (i.e. sold ex dividend)

Seller receives the full 6 months' interest on 9 June 2017, but effectively 'bought' part of this by receiving reduced sale proceeds. The interest from 2 June 2017 to 9 June 2017 when he did not own the stock amounts to:

$$£1,200 \times \frac{8}{365} = £26.30$$

Seller's taxable income is reduced (by accrued income relief) and buyer's taxable income increased (by an accrued income charge) of £26.30.

The accrued income adjustments are made in the tax year in which the next interest payment date falls, 2017–18 in this example, and are recorded in the tax returns for that year. In the first instance (sale for settlement 25 May 2017), the seller will pay tax at 40% on the accrued income charge of £549.04 and the buyer will save tax at 20% on that amount. In the second instance (sale on 1 June 2017), the seller will save tax at 40% on the amount of £26.30 by which his income is reduced and the buyer will pay tax at 20% on that amount.

Ordinary shares in listed companies

[36.12] Ordinary shares are 'risk capital' and investors have to be prepared to accept the risk element in return for seeking rising income and capital appreciation. Although listed shares are readily marketable, the price can fluctuate considerably and the capital is not readily accessible.

Dividends are payable gross. There is a 'dividend nil rate' which applies to dividends within the £5,000 'dividend allowance'. Where dividends exceed the dividend allowance the rates applying are 7.5% (called the dividend ordinary rate) on income up to the basic rate limit, 32.5% (the dividend upper rate) on income above the basic rate limit up to the higher rate limit, and 38.1% (the dividend additional rate) on income above the higher rate limit. Note that the September 2017 Finance Bill, which is expected to receive Royal Assent in November 2017, includes legislation to reduce the dividend nil rate to £2,000 from 2018–19 onwards. For details see **2.22** to **2.26**.

Dividends are included in income as they arise and are not subject to the 'accrued income' provisions that apply to government, local authority and company loan stocks.

Investment in ordinary shares can be free of income tax and capital gains tax if the investment is through an ISA (see **36.16** onwards).

The detailed treatment of shares, and further information on company loan stock and government stocks, is in CHAPTER **38**.

Certified SAYE savings arrangements

[36.13] These HMRC-approved schemes enable an employer company to grant to employees and directors an option to acquire shares in the company in the future at today's price, the shares eventually being paid for out of the proceeds of a linked Save as you Earn (SAYE) scheme. For details of such schemes see **11.10**.

The employee does not get tax relief for the SAYE contributions, but bonuses (within specified limits) and interest paid under the scheme are tax free. When the shares acquired under the SAYE arrangement are eventually sold, the resulting gain or loss will be subject to capital gains tax, with the base cost of the shares being the actual price (as opposed to the market value) paid for the shares by the participant.

Unit and investment trusts and venture capital trusts

[36.14] The tax treatment of investments in unit and investment trusts is dealt with at **38.27** to **38.34**. Venture capital trusts are dealt with at **29.44**.

Purchased life annuities

[36.15] If a lump sum is paid to a life insurance company to get a fixed annual sum in return, the annual sum is partly regarded as a non-taxable return of capital, thus giving a comparatively high after-tax income. However, it must be remembered that capital has been spent to purchase the annual income, which reduces the amount of capital in the death estate.

Purchased life annuities are therefore often acquired in conjunction with life insurance policies, part of the annual income being used to fund the life insurance premium so that at the end of the annuity period the life insurance policy proceeds can replace the purchase price of the annuity. There are numerous variations on this sort of arrangement (see CHAPTER **40**).

Individual Savings Accounts (ITTOIA 2005, ss 694–701; SI 1998/1870; SI 2017/186; SI 2016/977)

[36.16] Individual Savings Accounts (ISAs) are free of income tax and capital gains tax; they provide a tax-free 'wrapper' for investments and are available to individuals aged 18 or over who are resident in the UK. Cash ISAs are available to those aged 16 or over (see **36.19**). In addition, a Junior ISA is available for certain UK resident children under 18 (see **36.25**).

Joint accounts are not permitted. There is no statutory minimum period for which the accounts must be held and there is no lifetime limit on the amount invested.

ISA subscription limits

[36.17] It is possible to invest up to £20,000 (2017–18) annually into an ISA.

Following the death of a spouse or civil partner the surviving spouse/civil partner is able to invest a further amount equal to the value of the deceased saver's ISAs; this investment is additional to the surviving spouse/civil partners own annual ISA allowance.

There is no statutory minimum subscription, although interest rates on the cash element may vary according to the amount invested. Investors that become non-resident, may retain the tax-exempt benefits of existing ISAs but no further investments may be made.

The ISA tax exemption ceases on the death of the investor, so that tax will be deducted from any interest received during the administration period (see **42.4**). However, draft regulations have been laid to provide for ISAs to retain their tax-advantaged status following the death of the account holder. This will mean that income and gains from ISA investments received by the personal representatives of a deceased account holder, or by a beneficiary to whom the ISA is distributed, will be exempt from income tax and capital gains tax during the administration of the deceased's estate.

ISA subscription types

[36.18] There are three main types of ISA – cash ISAs (**36.19**), stocks and shares ISAs (**36.21**), innovative finance ISAs (**36.22**) and, from 6 April 2017, lifetime ISAs (**36.23**). It is possible to have a single ISA for all categories or separate ISAs for each one if desired.

Cash ISA

[36.19] Cash ISAs are simply savings accounts where the interest is never taxed. Any interest earned does not count towards the personal savings allowance (**2.5**) so for higher-rate taxpayers or savers who have used up the personal savings allowance, there are big tax advantages of saving in a cash ISA. It is generally only possible to subscribe to one cash account in any one year, although it is possible to subscribe to a Junior ISA (**36.25**) at the same time.

Individuals age 16 or over can subscribe for a cash ISA. If a parent gives money to his/her children to invest in an ISA, then unless the income arising from all capital provided by the parent is within the £100 limit, the income is treated as that of the parent until the child reaches age 18 and it must be reported on the parent's tax return (see **33.10**). It is possible for Junior ISA account holders to open cash ISAs from the age of 16, and Junior ISA contributions do not impact upon adult ISA subscription limits.

[36.20] From 1 December 2015, a specialist form of cash ISA is available to help first time buyers. The Help to Buy ISA is available from 1 December 2015 to 30 November 2019. After 30 November 2019 the Help to Buy ISA will not be available to new savers, but it will be possible to keep saving into those opened before that date.

Under the Help to Buy ISA each person is able to save up to £200 a month into their account. The Government will then top this amount up by 25%. So, for people who manage to save the maximum each month, the Government will be topping up the account with £50 for every £200 saved. The Government bonus will be capped at a total of £3,000 on £12,000 of savings. First time buyers will then receive the Government bonus at the time of completion of the purchase of their first home. It can be put toward homes that are worth a maximum of £450,000 in London and £250,000 in all other areas of the UK. The bonus must be claimed by 1 December 2030. During the 2017–18 tax year, those who already have a Help to Buy ISA are able to transfer the savings they have built up into the Lifetime ISA (36.23) and still save an additional £4,000.

Opening a Help to Buy ISA is in most ways, identical to opening a regular ISA under the existing cash ISA rules. Saving into a Help to Buy ISA is also very similar to saving into any other cash ISA account (for example, interest received on the account is tax free). There are, however, some additional rules in that the Help to Buy ISA has a monthly maximum saving limit of £200 and an opportunity to deposit an additional £1,000 when the account is first opened.

It is not possible for an account holder to subscribe to a Help to Buy ISA with one provider, and another cash ISA with a different provider. Some providers may permit contributions to another of their cash ISAs at the same time, subject to the overall annual ISA investment limit not being breached. Help to Buy ISA accounts are limited to one per person rather than one per home — so those buying together can both receive a bonus.

Stocks and shares ISA

[36.21] It is possible to use the ISA allowance for investing in stocks and shares. It is possible here to invest in funds (shares or bonds from various companies pooled into one investment), bonds (basically a loan to a company or a government), and shares in individual companies.

Where ISA investments are in shares, there may be no significant tax benefits for many taxpayers, since the capital gains tax exemption will often not be relevant and there will be no tax relief for any capital losses.

The shares held in a stocks and shares ISA are kept separate from the investor's other holdings for the purpose of the capital gains rules for matching disposals with acquisitions. If the investor withdraws his investments, their base cost for capital gains tax is the market value at the date of withdrawal.

Shares received from savings-related share option schemes and approved share incentive plans (see CHAPTER 11) may be transferred within 90 days into the stocks and shares ISA free of capital gains tax, so long as, together with any other investments, they are within the annual subscription limit. There is no facility to transfer shares acquired under a public offer or following demutualisation of a building society or insurer into an ISA.

Innovative finance ISA

[36.22] From 6 April 2016 an innovative finance ISA account is available. This extends the ISA tax advantages to investment through peer to peer lending platforms that have received full authorisation from the FCA, and ISA manager approval from HMRC. Also included are certain debentures, debt securities and bonds issued as transferable securities by companies and charities (including those offered via a crowdfunding platform).

Lifetime ISA

[36.23] From 6 April 2017 individuals aged between 18 and 39 are able to open a new Lifetime ISA. A lifetime ISA is designed to help a person buy their first home, or save for retirement. Up to £4,000 cash can be contributed each year and a 25% bonus from the Government is paid at the end of the year. Contributions can be made until reaching the age of 50. The bonus is similarly payable each year until savers reach the age of 50. Contributions can be made to one Lifetime ISA in each tax year, as well as a cash ISA, a stocks and shares ISA, and an Innovative Finance ISA, within the overall ISA limit of £20,000.

A Lifetime ISA can be funded by transfers from other ISAs in accordance with normal rules. Funds, including the Government bonus, can be used to buy a first home at any time from 12 months after opening the account, and can be withdrawn from age 60 for use in retirement. The limit for property purchased using Lifetime ISA funds is set at £450,000 and applies nationally. Savers can continue to open a Help to Buy ISA until November 2019 and can also choose to open a Lifetime ISA, but will only be able to use the Government bonus from one of their accounts to buy their first home. During the 2017–18 tax year, those who already have a Help to Buy ISA are able to transfer the savings they have built up into the Lifetime ISA and still save an additional £4,000. HMRC guidance is available at www.gov.uk/government/news/lifetime-isas-available-from-6-april-2017.

Withdrawals

[36.24] ISA account holders (excluding Junior ISA account holders(36.20)) are able to withdraw money from their ISAs and pay it back in again during the same tax year without the second transaction counting towards the ISA subscription limit for that year.

Example 3

Assume an individual deposited £5,940 in a cash ISA in 2017–18 (on 15 May), and unexpectedly needed to withdraw £2,000, leaving only £3,940 invested. He will still be able to reinvest a further £16,060 (£20,000–£3,940) in the 2017–18 tax year.

Junior ISAs: Children under 18 with no child trust fund (SI 2004/1450; SI 2017/185)

[36.25] A Junior ISA is available for UK resident children under 18 who do not have a Child Trust Fund account (33.11) or to those who wish to transfer a Child Trust Fund account to a Junior ISA. Junior ISAs have many features in common with existing ISA. There is an overall annual contribution limit of £4,128 for 2017–18.

There are no rules on how contributions have to be allocated between cash and stocks and shares, and it is possible to transfer funds from one type of Junior ISA to another. Having a Junior ISA does not affect an individual's entitlement to adult ISAs. It is possible for Junior ISA account holders to open adult cash ISAs from the age of 16 (36.25), and Junior ISA contributions do not impact upon adult ISA subscription limits.

At the age of 18, the Junior ISA by default becomes a normal adult ISA. Withdrawals from Junior ISAs are not permitted by account holders until the child reaches 18, except in cases of terminal illness or death. The normal settlement rules treating income as that of the parent (33.10) do not apply in the case of junior ISAs.

Withdrawals

For Junior ISAs there are restrictions on withdrawals made throughout the tax year. If any part of the amount invested in a year is withdrawn, that part of the limit for the year is not then available for further investment.

> **Example 4**
>
> If an individual deposited £1,940 in a junior cash ISA in 2017–18 (on 15 May), and unexpectedly needed to withdraw £1,000, the funds cannot subsequently be replaced in that tax year. As the limit for investment is £4,128 for 2017–18, a further £2,188 (4,128 minus 1,940) can be paid in.

Administration

[36.26] If tax relief on an ISA is found to have been wrongly given, HMRC may make a direct assessment on either the account manager or the investor to recover the relief. In limited circumstances, and with the approval of HMRC, invalid ISAs may be 'repaired' rather than being closed, although any tax relief up to the date of the repair will still be forfeited.

The Government's aim with ISAs is to encourage more people to save but equities are not normally considered suitable for those who do not have a firm underlying core of low risk investments. Non-taxpayers cannot benefit from a tax-free account, and basic rate taxpayers may find any other benefits being eroded by the account charges.

Tax points

[36.27] Note the following:

- A cash ISA can be invested in accounts with building societies and banks, including National Savings and supermarket bank accounts.
- Cash ISA interest doesn't count towards the personal savings allowance (PSA). So for higher-rate taxpayers or savers who have used up the PSA, there are big tax advantages of saving in a cash ISA.
- A small investor can benefit from a wide range of investments through a unit or investment trust. The trust is exempt from tax on its gains. The investor pays tax on income and gains in the normal way, unless the investment is through an ISA. See **38.27** to **38.34**.
- If an investor has children under 16, it is possible to invest the maximum £3,000 in *each issue* of children's bonds. See **36.6**.

37

Investing in banks and building societies

Investing in building societies and banks (ITA 2007, ss 564A–564Y; 850–873; FA 2009, s 45; SI 2011/22)

[37.1] Investing in building societies and banks is generally regarded as a low risk investment and additional protection is available under the Financial Services Compensation Scheme. The compensation limit for protected deposits is £85,000 per person for claims against firms declared in default. Detailed guidance is available at www.fscs.org.uk.

The compensation scheme does not cover investments in building society permanent interest bearing shares (see **37.4**). Nor does it cover investments in offshore banks and building societies in the Channel Islands and Isle of Man, although some UK banks and building societies may offer their own protection for those who save with their offshore subsidiaries.

There are various alternative finance arrangements, particularly to meet the requirements of Islamic law, under which interest is not received but the arrangements have a similar effect (see **2.10**). Receipts that equate economically with interest are taxed on the same basis as interest.

Building societies and banks, including the National Savings Bank, may be required to notify HMRC how much interest has been paid to customers under the HMRC data gathering powers; see **9.37**.

Interest counts as income for tax purposes according to the date when it is credited to the recipient's account. It is not apportioned over the period when it accrues. Whether tax has been deducted by the payer or not the recipient may have to pay some more tax or claim some back, depending on his tax position.

Balances in dormant bank and building society accounts can be transferred to a reclaim fund to be used for social or environmental purposes. Any interest credited to a dormant bank or building society account on transfer to the reclaim fund and any interest credited whilst the funds are held in the reclaim fund is only treated as paid for the purposes of income tax and tax reporting requirements if a customer reclaims his money and the balance is then repaid. Such transfers are treated as involving no disposal for capital gains tax purposes (see **4.17**).

Receiving bank and building society interest (ITA 2007, ss 850–873)

[37.2] Interest paid by banks, building societies and some other institutions to individuals is paid gross. Any tax due on savings income will be settled directly with HMRC either via an adjustment in the PAYE code, or reported directly on a tax return.

There is a 0% 'starting rate for savings', which applies to savings income other than dividends. It applies to income, up to a 'starting rate limit' of £5,000, that is savings income. In addition to this there is a 'savings nil rate' which applies to an individual's savings income which is within their 'savings allowance'. The savings allowance is £1,000 per year for basic rate taxpayers and £500 for higher rate taxpayers. It is not available to additional rate taxpayers. See **2.5**.

Savings already in tax-free accounts like ISAs (**36.16**) and some National Savings and Investments accounts (**36.6**) don't count towards the savings allowance.

Income tax is not deducted from bank and building society interest paid to companies (see **3.6**) and charities (see **43.3**). Nor is tax deducted from interest on building society permanent interest-bearing shares (PIBS, see **37.4**), because they are within the definition of quoted Eurobonds (see **3.23**).

Building societies: conversion to banks, takeovers, mergers (FA 1988, Sch 12; TCGA 1992, s 217)

[37.3] Building societies are able to convert to companies under the Building Societies Act 1986. If they do, they are subject to normal company and bank legislation. Possible adverse consequences of conversion for building society members are prevented by specific rules which provide that members are not liable to capital gains tax on rights to acquire shares in the company in priority to other subscribers, or at a discount, or on rights to acquire shares free of charge; these provisions apply whether the rights are obtained directly or through trustees. As and when the shares are disposed of, there will be a capital gain equal to the excess of the proceeds over the amount (if any) paid for the shares which may be covered by the annual capital gains tax exemption if not already used.

Similar rules apply when a building society is taken over by a company rather than being converted.

Where a cash payment is received on a conversion or takeover, the payments are not chargeable to income tax. Cash payments to *deposit* account holders are also exempt from capital gains tax (since such an account represents a loan, i.e. a simple debt, gains on which are exempt (see **4.16**)). Presumably cash payments to borrowers are also exempt, since they do not derive from an asset. Cash payments to share account holders are not exempt but in many cases the amounts concerned will be covered by the capital gains tax annual exempt amount so that calculations will not be necessary. If taxpayers are unable to make the necessary calculations for their tax returns, HMRC will, if asked, use their computer programme to produce the figures.

As far as building society *mergers* are concerned, HMRC's view is that any payments on the merger (whether paid in cash or credited to an account) are chargeable to income tax. Such payments would be treated in the same way as other income from the building society and taxpayers need to make appropriate entries on their tax returns.

Building society permanent interest bearing shares (ITA 2007, ss 619, 850–873; CTA 2009, s 302; TCGA 1992, s 117)

[37.4] Building societies may issue a special type of share — permanent interest bearing shares (PIBS). These shares are acquired through and listed on the Stock Exchange and are freely transferable, dealing charges being incurred on buying and selling. If the building society fails, investors are not entitled to compensation. PIBS are irredeemable, so proceeds received on sale will depend on prevailing interest rates and the soundness of the building society. Interest on PIBS is paid gross.

For non-corporate shareholders PIBS are within the definition of qualifying corporate bonds (see **38.6**) and are exempt from capital gains tax, so that no allowable losses may be created. They are also within the accrued income scheme (see **36.11**), so that adjustments for accrued interest are made when they are transferred.

For companies, the accrued income scheme does not apply. Dividends, interest and capital gains on the PIBS are dealt with under the loan relationships rules (see **3.6**).

Where PIBS are issued to existing members in priority to other people the right to buy them does not result in a capital gains tax charge.

National Savings Accounts

[37.5] National Savings & Investments (NS&I) offer a direct savings account and an investment account. They also offer accounts that are eligible for the cash component of ISAs (see **36.16** onwards).

The direct savings account can be managed online or by phone. The minimum balance is £1 and the maximum is £2 million (£4 million for joint accounts). Interest is calculated daily on balances of £1 and over and is credited to the account once a year after close of business on 31 March. Withdrawals can be made at any time without giving notice or paying a penalty. The money is simply transferred to the account holder's nominated bank account.

The investment account is an easy access passbook savings account which pays interest on 1 January annually at varying rates depending on the amount invested. The minimum balance is £20 and the maximum is £1 million. No notice is required for withdrawals.

For both these accounts, although the interest is liable to tax, it is paid gross, which gives a cash flow advantage compared with investing in other banks or building societies if interest must be paid net (i.e. the investor is not entitled to register to receive interest gross).

In addition to their savings accounts, NS&I have a wide range of other investments. These are dealt with in **36.6**.

Tax points

[37.6] Note the following:

- When filling in a tax return, it is necessary to include interest received on current bank accounts, as well as interest on savings accounts.
- A cash windfall received on a building society takeover/conversion, is liable to capital gains tax (although the gain may well be covered by the capital gains tax annual exempt amount). A cash windfall on a building society *merger* is liable to income tax in the usual manner.
- An investor in a building society ISA, is a member of the building society and will thus qualify if there is an offer of free shares on the conversion of the building society to a company.

38

Investing in stocks and shares

Background

[38.1] The term 'quoted securities' has in general been replaced in the tax legislation by 'listed securities'. For EEA countries (**1.3**), listed securities means securities listed by a competent authority and admitted to trading on a recognised stock exchange. For other countries it means securities admitted to trading by a recognised stock exchange. AIM securities are unlisted.

Many of the provisions in the capital gains legislation deal with stocks and shares acquired many years ago, in respect of which the old terminology may still apply. For simplicity, the terms 'quoted' and 'unquoted' have been retained in this chapter.

The principal securities that may be acquired when investing through the Stock Exchange are company shares or loan stock, gilt-edged securities, local authority loan stock and building society permanent interest bearing shares (see **37.4**). Other investments may include unquoted company stocks and shares and unquoted local authority loans (see **36.7**).

The treatment of foreign stocks and shares is dealt with at **41.32** (with 'foreign' meaning that the issuing company is not resident in the UK).

There are various special provisions relating to trading on the Stock Exchange by broker/dealers, including provisions for stock lending and manufactured payments. Where shares are held as trading assets (either by dealers or others such as banks), dividends and other distributions received, and also manufactured payments treated as received, are treated as trading profits (and manufactured payments made are deducted as trading expenses).

Stamp duty is payable on most transactions in stocks and shares, usually at 0.5%, but higher rates apply in some circumstances. The relevant provisions are outlined in CHAPTER **6**.

Tax treatment of income from stocks and shares

Dividends (CTA 2010, s 1109; ITA 2007, ss 6–21)

[38.2] Dividends paid by companies on their shares represent a distribution of profits to the members. Dividends are received gross, there is a 'dividend nil rate' which applies to dividends within the £5,000 'dividend allowance' and dividends in excess of this amount are taxed at 7.5%, 32.5% or 38.1% depending upon the recipient's marginal rate. Note that the September 2017 Finance Bill, which is expected to receive Royal Assent in November 2017, includes legislation to reduce the dividend nil rate to £2,000 from 2018–19 onwards. For more details see **2.22** onwards.

Scrip options (CTA 2010, s 1049; ITTOIA 2005, ss 410–414)

[38.3] Where scrip shares are taken up by an individual, instead of a cash dividend from a UK resident company (a scrip dividend or stock dividend), the cash dividend forgone is treated as income, unless it is different from the market value of the shares by 15% or more. In that event the deemed income is the market value of the shares on the first day of dealing. The recipient is treated as receiving a dividend and taxed on dividend income in the usual manner (**38.2**).

If scrip dividend options are taken up by personal representatives, the income is treated as income of the estate.

Where scrip dividend options are taken up by trustees of discretionary trusts (except trusts in which the settlor retains an interest — see below), they are liable to the 38.1% dividend trust rate (**42.28**). The capital gains tax effect is dealt with at **38.21**.

Where scrip dividends are issued to a company, or to a trust in which the settlor retains an interest, they are not treated as income, and have a capital gains base cost of nil. This also applies to scrip dividends issued to a life interest trust unless the scrip dividend is income of the life beneficiary under trust law. If the trustees take the view that the scrip dividend belongs to the life tenant, the shares are effectively treated as acquired directly by the life tenant outside the trust's holding of shares (except in Scotland, where the rules are different — see HMRC Statement of Practice SP 4/94), and the life tenant is treated as having notional income in the same way as if he had acquired the shares directly.

Some companies have dividend reinvestment plans (DRIPs), under which shareholders use their dividends to acquire shares bought on the market by the company on their behalf. There is, however, a cost to the shareholder because part of the dividend is used to cover the cost of brokers' fees and stamp duty. The dividend is taxable as income, with the cash forgone representing the cost of the new shares.

Interest (ITA 2007, ss 6–21, 847–986; FA 2017, s 11, Sch 5)

[38.4] Interest is paid gross (i.e. tax is not deducted) in the following situations:

(a)   interest paid by companies and local authorities if it is on quoted stocks or is paid to another company, local authority or a pension fund (see **3.23** for details);

(b)   interest on gilt-edged securities unless the holder applies to receive it net;

(c)   interest paid by banks and building societies (see **36.2**); and

(d)   from 6 April 2017 interest distributions from open-ended investment companies, authorised unit trusts, investment trust companies and interest on peer-to-peer loans.

The situations covered above mean that in practice most interest payments will now be paid gross.

Where tax is deducted, those liable at a rate other than 20% will either have further tax to pay or be entitled to a refund. See **36.2** for the way tax is collected and **36.11** for the special accrued income scheme provisions that may apply to individuals in relation to interest-bearing securities. The treatment of interest received by companies is dealt with at **3.6**.

There are some special provisions for discounted securities held by personal investors (see **38.35**).

Capital gains treatment of stocks (TCGA 1992, ss 104–106A, 108, 115–117 and Sch 9; CTA 2009, Sch 2 para 69)

Companies

[38.5] A company's gains and losses on the disposal of most loan stock are brought into account in calculating the company's income under the 'loan relationships' rules outlined at **3.6**. This does not apply to disposals of 5½% Treasury Stock 2008–12, which is outside the loan relationships rules and is exempt under the capital gains rules, so that there can be neither a chargeable gain nor an allowable loss. Nor do the loan relationships rules apply to certain non-trading increases and decreases in the value of derivatives, which are dealt with under the capital gains rules.

As far as loan stock is concerned, the distinction between qualifying and non-qualifying corporate bonds for individuals (see **38.6**) does not apply to a company's holdings, and the definition of a qualifying corporate bond for companies is *any* asset that represents a loan relationship (as to which see **3.6**). See **38.38** for the treatment in takeovers where shares are exchanged for corporate bonds or vice versa.

Individuals

[38.6] As far as individuals, personal representatives and trustees are concerned gilt-edged securities and qualifying corporate bonds are exempt from capital gains tax, so that there are neither chargeable gains nor allowable losses when they are disposed of (subject to some special rules for losses on qualifying corporate bonds (see **38.40**)).

Qualifying corporate bonds are quoted or unquoted non-convertible sterling loan stock purchased or issued on commercial terms. Building society permanent interest bearing shares (see **37.4**) are also within the definition of qualifying corporate bonds for individuals (but not for companies). Profits and losses on certain securities issued at a deep discount are dealt with under the income tax rather than the capital gains provisions (see **38.35**). Index-linked securities that are outside the deeply discounted securities provisions (i.e. those that are linked to the value of a share index) are also outside the definition of qualifying corporate bond and are thus chargeable to capital gains tax.

The capital gains exemption for qualifying corporate bonds cannot be used to avoid income tax by selling just before an interest date, because of the accrued income provisions (see **36.11**). There are special provisions for company reorganisations to ensure that the appropriate exemption is given on loan stock converted into shares or vice versa (see **38.36**).

Disposals of interest bearing stocks that are not gilt-edged securities or qualifying corporate bonds are subject to capital gains tax (unless they are deeply discounted securities within the charge to income tax). The same matching rules apply as for shares (**38.18**) unless the stock falls within the definition of a relevant security (which in practice catches most stock); being stock which falls within the accrued income scheme (**36.11**), qualifying corporate bonds and certain securities which are interests in a non-reporting fund.

Capital gains treatment of shares (TCGA 1992, ss 35, 53–55, 104–110 and Sch 2)

[38.7] The rules governing the capital gains tax implications of share disposals have been changed so frequently that this area has become one of the most complicated in the tax legislation and we now have the situation where there are two separate sets of rules running side by side (one for corporate shareholders (see **38.8**) and one for shareholders other than companies (see **38.17**)). It is not possible for this book to deal with all the complexities of share disposals, and the rules discussed below cover the tax treatment of such disposals in the current tax year.

It must be remembered that the provisions outlined below may well not affect individuals with modest holdings. If a person does not regularly buy and sell, he may acquire shares in a company by a single purchase and sell them by a single sale, so unless there have been rights issues, takeovers, etc., the calculation merely requires a comparison of the cost with the sale proceeds. If any gains arising are below the capital gains annual exempt amount (£11,300 for 2017–18) it may not be necessary to show calculations of gains in a tax return. If, however, the transaction produced a loss, calculations would have to be shown in order to claim loss relief.

Example 1

Shareholder acquired 2,000 shares in A plc in June 2008 for £8,000 (including acquisition costs) and sold them in May 2017. He had no other capital transactions in 2017–18.

If he sold them for £10,500 (net of selling costs), the gain would be exempt as it falls within the 2017–18 annual exempt amount of £11,300.

If he sold them for £6,500 (net of selling costs), there would have been an allowable loss of £1,500.

Disposals by corporate shareholders

[38.8] The rules detailed at **38.9** to **38.16** apply to disposals by companies where gains/losses are not otherwise exempt under the substantial shareholding exemption (**3.34**).

Disposals are matched with acquisitions in the following order (subject to the special rules that apply for scrip and rights shares (see **38.19**)):

(a)   Acquisitions on the same day as the disposal.
(b)   Acquisitions within the previous nine days (and no indexation allowance is available on the disposal).
(c)   The post-1982 pool (**38.9**).
(d)   The pre-1982 pool (**38.11**).
(e)   Pre-6 April 1965 acquisitions that are not included in the pre-1982 pool, latest first (**38.13**).
(f)   Acquisitions after disposal, earliest first.

Where partly paid shares are acquired, the instalments of the purchase price qualify for any available indexation allowance from the date the shares are issued, unless they are paid more than 12 months later, in which case they qualify from the date they are paid.

Shares acquired on or after April 1982

[38.9] Rules were introduced from 1 April 1985 (6 April 1985 for taxpayers other than companies), to treat each holding of quoted or unquoted shares of the same company and class acquired on or after 1 April 1982 (6 April 1982 for taxpayers other than companies) as a single asset. This asset is called a 'section 104 holding' in the legislation, but it is referred to in this chapter as a post-1982 pool. (Shares acquired by an employee that are subject to disposal restrictions are treated as being of a different class from any other shares held). Post-1982 pools grow with acquisitions and are depleted by disposals.

Indexation

[38.10] Indexation allowance on post-1982 pools is worked out from the month in which the expenditure was incurred. The holdings are maintained at both an unindexed value and an indexed value, and the indexed value is uplifted by further indexation every time an event occurs that alters the value of a holding (such as a purchase or a sale, but not a bonus issue (**38.19**)). Unlike other indexation allowance calculations, the indexation adjustment on the post-1982 pool should strictly not be rounded to three decimal places. If the index has fallen since the previous event, no adjustment is made to the indexed value. The post-1982 pool rules were introduced on 1 April 1985 (6 April 1985 for taxpayers other than companies) and an opening figure for the indexed value was required at that date, working out indexation allowance on each acquisition from 1 April 1982 (6 April 1982) onwards. (If the calculation was delayed until the time of the first event affecting the value of the holding, it would not significantly affect the figures).

For individuals, personal representatives and trustees, no further shares are added to post-1982 pools after 5 April 1998 (except for scrip issues and rights shares (see **38.19**)) and each acquisition of shares after that date is treated as a separate, free-standing acquisition. Acquisitions continue to increase post-1982 pools for company shareholders.

Example 2

A corporate investor acquired 5,000 shares in AB plc in May 2009 for £7,500 and a further 2,000 shares in December 2012 for £4,000. All the shares were sold in February 2017 for £28,000. The retail price index for the various dates are as follows:

May 2009 — 212.8
December 2012 — 246.8
February 2017 — 268.4

The capital gains computation is:

AB plc post-1982 share pool

	Number of shares	Unindexed value £	Indexed value £
May 2009 Bought	5,000	7,500	7,500
Dec 2012 Indexation on £7,500 from May 2009			
$\dfrac{246.8 - 212.8}{212.8}$			1,198
December 2012 Bought	2,000	4,000	4,000
	7,000	11,500	12,698

February 2017 Indexation on
£12,698 from Dec 2012

$$\frac{268.4 - 246.8}{246.8}$$

			1,111
			13,809
Sold	(7,000)	(11,500)	(13,809)
Amounts c/fwd	—	—	—

CGT computation for February 2017 disposal:

	£
Proceeds	28,000
Indexed cost	(13,809)
Chargeable gain	£14,191

It is important to remember that indexation cannot increase or create a loss so if, in this example, the disposal proceeds were say £13,000 then the indexation will simply reduce the gain to nil.

Shares acquired before April 1982

[38.11] When calculating the gain/loss on disposals of shares held on 1 April 1982 (6 April 1982 for taxpayers other than companies) different calculations will have to be made depending upon whether a general rebasing election has been made (see **4.23**).

Where a rebasing election has been made all shares of the same class in the same company held on 1 April 1982 (6 April 1982 for taxpayers other than companies), including any acquired before 6 April 1965, are treated as acquired at their 31 March 1982 market value and are regarded as a single asset. Any such holding is called a '1982 holding' in the legislation, but it is referred to in this chapter as a pre-1982 pool. Any gain/loss on a subsequent disposal is calculated using this March 1982 value as the base cost.

If the rebasing election has not been made, then unless some of the shares in the company concerned were acquired before 6 April 1965, the single asset treatment still applies but when calculating a gain/loss on disposal two calculations are performed. The gain/loss is calculated using firstly the March 1982 value as base cost and secondly the actual cost as the base cost, with the lower gain/ larger loss being taken for capital gains tax purposes. If one calculation shows a loss and the other a gain, the transaction is treated as giving rise to neither a gain nor a loss. In both calculations, the indexation allowance is based on the *higher* of the cost and 31 March 1982 value. If some of the shares were acquired before 6 April 1965, then they must be kept separate from the pre-1982 pool. This does not apply to *quoted* shares if an election had been made (under provisions introduced in 1968) to treat them as acquired at their market value on 6 April 1965, in which case they are included in the pre-1982 pool at that value. The treatment of unpooled pre-6 April 1965 acquisitions is dealt with at **38.13** to **38.16**.

Where 31 March 1982 valuations of unquoted holdings are needed by several shareholders, HMRC Shares and Assets Valuation department will open negotiations with the shareholders or their advisers before being asked by a tax office, providing all shareholders with similar holdings will accept the value agreed.

Indexation

[38.12] For pre-1982 pools of shares the indexation allowance is calculated by taking the increase in the retail prices index between March 1982 and the month of disposal. Where a rebasing election has been made to treat all assets acquired before 31 March 1982 as being acquired at their market value on that date, the indexation allowance is based on that 31 March 1982 value. Where the election has not been made, the indexation calculation is based on the higher of the value of the shares at 31 March 1982 and their cost or, for shares held at 6 April 1965, their 6 April 1965 market value when using that value to calculate the gain or loss (see **38.13**). Where the rebasing election has been made, the pre-1982 pool can be maintained at both unindexed and indexed values in the same way as the post-1982 pool, although this is not provided for in the legislation. This can still be done even if there is no rebasing election, but figures would be required both for indexed cost and indexed 31 March 1982 value, basing indexation allowance in both cases on the higher of those two figures, but not so as to create or increase a loss.

Example 3

Quoted shares in CD plc are acquired by a company as follows:

	Number	Cost (£)
Between 6.4.65 and 5.4.82 (pre-1982 pool)	5,000	35,000
31.5.08 (post-1982 pool)	6,000	66,000

Sales	Number	Consideration (£)
16.2.17	10,000	300,000

Market value was £3 per share at 6 April 1965 and £8 per share at 31 March 1982. No election had been made to include shares acquired before 6 April 1965 in the pre-1982 pool nor a rebasing election to treat all assets acquired before 31 March 1982 as being acquired at 31 March 1982 value.

	£	Gain £
Sale of 10,000 on 16.2.17:		
Proceeds for sale out of post-1982 pool 6,000/10,000 × £300,000	180,000	
Indexed cost (see Example 4)	(82,302)	97,698

Sale of 4,000 shares in pre-1982 pool:

Gain (see Example 5) | 11,904

Giving total chargeable gains on CD plc shares of | £109,602

Example 4

CD plc post-1982 pool	Number of shares	Unindexed value	Indexed value
		£	£
Bought: 31.5.08	6,000	66,000	66,000
Indexation from May 2008 to February 2017 (0.247)			16,302
			82,302
Sale: 16.2.17	(6,000)	(66,000)	(82,302)
	—	—	—

Example 5

CD plc pre-1982 pool
5,000 shares cost £35,000, value at 31.3.82 £8
each = £40,000

	£	£
Sale proceeds: 4,000/10,000 × £300,000	120,000	120,000
Cost: 4,000/5,000 × £35,000	(28,000)	
31.3.82 value: 4,000 × £8		(32,000)
Indexation allowance of 2.379 on 31.3.82 value	(76,128)	(76,128)
	15,872 or	11, 872
Lower gain		£11,872

Shares held on 6 April 1965 (TCGA 1992, Sch 2, Parts I and III)

[38.13] If a rebasing election has been made to treat all assets acquired before 31 March 1982 as acquired at their market value on that day, gains and losses are computed on that basis for both quoted and unquoted shares. Where the rebasing election has not been made, the procedure is as follows.

Unquoted securities

[38.14] For unquoted securities, the legislation requires two computations to be made, as follows.

(a)   Firstly:

(i)   Calculate the gain or loss over the whole period of ownership.

(ii) Adjust for the available indexation allowance based either on cost or 31 March 1982 value, whichever is higher (but not so as to create or increase a loss), then calculate the proportion of the resulting gain or loss that relates to the period after 5 April 1965 (but ignoring any period of ownership before 6 April 1945).

(iii) As an alternative to the result in (ii), the taxpayer may make an irrevocable election to have the result computed by reference to the value of the asset on 6 April 1965, with indexation allowance based on the higher of 6 April 1965 value and 31 March 1982 value (but the indexation allowance cannot create or increase a loss). If this calculation would give a loss instead of a gain, the transaction is deemed to give neither gain nor loss. The election cannot give a greater loss than the amount by which the cost exceeds the sale proceeds.

(Losses will not usually arise under either calculation because the costs of many years ago are being compared with current sale proceeds).

(b) Secondly, calculate the gain or loss as if the shares had been bought on 31 March 1982 at their market value on that date. The available indexation allowance is based on the higher of 31 March 1982 value and either cost or 6 April 1965 value according to which was used to give the result in the first computation (but not so as to create or increase a loss).

If both computations show a loss, the lower loss is taken, and if both show a gain, the lower gain is taken. See Example 6. If one computation shows a gain and the other a loss, the result is treated as neither gain nor loss. If, however, the first computation has already resulted in no gain, no loss, that result is taken and the 31 March 1982 value calculation is not made. Where a gain arises it will be obvious in many cases that the lower gain will result from using the 31 March 1982 calculation, without making the alternative calculation. As far as losses are concerned, there can only be an allowable loss if the sale proceeds are below both the cost and the 31 March 1982 value.

Example 6

1,500 unquoted shares were acquired by a corporate investor on 6 October 1962 for £2 per share.

Market value considered to be £2.50 per share at 6 April 1965 and £8 per share at 31 March 1982. No rebasing election had been made to treat all assets acquired before 31 March 1982 as being acquired at 31 March 1982 value.

The shares were sold on 6 April 2017 for £50 per share.

RPI from March 1982 to April 2017 is 2.406

First computation				
Using time apportionment			Using 6 April 1965 market value	
	£			£
Sale 1,500 shares @ £50	75,000	Sale		75,000
Cost 6.10.62 @ £2	(3,000)	6.4.65 MV		
		1,500 @ £2.50		(3,750)
Indexation allowance (2.406 x March 82 value of £12,000)	(28,872)			(28,872)
Overall gain	43,128			
Proportion after 6.4.65				
$\dfrac{6.4.65 - 6.4.17}{6.10.62 - 6.4.17} = \dfrac{52}{54.5}$				
Gain	41,149			42,378
Lower gain is				£41,149
Second computation				£
Sale 1,500 shares @ £50				75,000
31.3.82 value @ £8				(12,000)
Indexation allowance				(28,872)
Gain				£34,128

Both computations produce a gain, so the lower gain of £34,128 is taken.

Quoted securities

[38.15] For quoted securities, unless a rebasing election has been made, or the shares on hand at 6 April 1965 are included at their value at that date in the pre-1982 pool (see **38.11**), two computations are also made. The procedure is similar to that for unquoted securities, except that time apportionment does not apply. In the first computation, the sale proceeds are compared with both the cost and the 6 April 1965 value and the lower gain or lower loss is taken. If one method shows a gain and the other a loss, the computation is treated as giving rise to neither gain nor loss. The available indexation allowance is deducted in each case (based on the higher of the cost/6 April 1965 value and 31 March 1982 value) but not so as to create or increase a loss. The second computation treats the shares as acquired at 31 March 1982 value (but the available indexation allowance is nonetheless based on cost/6 April 1965 value if it exceeds 31 March 1982 value). The lower gain or lower loss produced by the two computations is then taken. If one computation shows a loss and the other a gain, the result is neither a gain nor a loss. If the first computation has already given a no gain/no loss result, then the second computation is not made. As with unquoted securities, it will often be obvious that the lower gain will result from the 31 March 1982 calculation. Allowable losses will not arise except to the extent that the proceeds are less than the lowest of the cost, 6 April 1965 value and 31 March 1982 value.

Effect of the above rules

[38.16] The examples show that where a taxpayer has acquired shares at various times before and after 31 March 1982 the rules may require several calculations to be made. If the rebasing election has been made, the position is simpler because there are only two share 'pools' for any class of shares in any company, one covering all acquisitions up to 5 April 1982 (the pre-1982 pool) and the other all later acquisitions (the post-1982 pool). Even so, complications arise through scrip and rights issues, takeovers, etc. The calculations can be simplified by using the publications that detail 31 March values and other relevant information.

Disposals by individuals, personal representatives and trustees

[38.17] Finance Act 2008 greatly simplified the rules for share disposals by individuals, personal representative and trustees. For disposals after 5 April 2008 by such shareholders automatic rebasing to 31 March 1982 applies and there is no indexation allowance. The current applicable rates for share disposals are:

(a)   for individuals, gains are taxed at a flat rate of 10% (or 20% for gains that exceed the basic rate band); see **4.2**;

(b)   for personal representatives and trustees, gains are taxed at a flat rate of 20%.

Furthermore, the simpler identification rules set out below have removed much of the complexity associated with capital gains tax computations for companies.

[38.18] Disposals by individuals, personal representatives and trustees are matched with acquisitions in the following order:

(a)   Acquisitions on the same day as the disposal.

(b)   Acquisitions within 30 days after the disposal.

(c)   Assets in the (enlarged) 'section 104 holding'. This is the holding mentioned in **38.9** (and described elsewhere in this chapter as a post-1982 pool) as enlarged, where appropriate, to include shares acquired at any time before the date of the disposal. The allowable cost for this holding is the market value of such shares held at 31 March 1982 plus the cost of shares acquired since that date. Indexation allowance must be excluded because it was abolished for disposals after 5 April 2008. Where part of this holding is sold, a proportion of the allowable cost is deducted from the proceeds.

For the purpose of the matching rules, all the shares acquired on the same day are treated as having been acquired by a single transaction, with scrip and rights issue shares being treated as acquired when the original shares were acquired (see **38.19**). Different rules do however apply for approved employee share scheme shares (**11.32**), employee shareholder shares for, broadly, arrangements entered into before 1 December 2016 (**11.36**), relevant EMI shares (**29.3**), EIS shares (**29.32**), VCT shares (**29.52**), SEIS shares (**29.43**), employee ownership trust shares (**4.38**) and for assets disposed of out of a holding of fungible assets, such as shares (**29.55**).

Example 7

Investor (a basic rate taxpayer) acquired 2,000 shares in AB plc in 1981 for £4,000. Their market value at 31 March 1982 was £4,500. He acquired 3,000 shares for £9,000 in 1999 and 5,000 shares for £16,500 in 2004. He sold 5,000 shares for £28,000 in October 2017. There is a single pool (the enlarged 'section 104 holding') of 10,000 shares with an acquisition value of £30,000. Having sold 50% of the shares, he is entitled to set £15,000 of that value against the proceeds, giving a gain of £13,000. No indexation is available, so assuming that the annual exempt amount of £11,300 is available, CGT is payable at 10% on £1,700 = £170.

The 30-day rule in (b) prevents 'bed and breakfast' transactions, where shares are sold and bought back on the following day in order either to use the capital gains exemption or to produce losses to reduce chargeable gains. The rules do not prevent a spouse or civil partner repurchasing the shares on the market, providing the spouse or civil partner is the beneficial owner of the shares bought. Alternatively, a similar effect could be achieved by acquiring shares in a company in the same business sector.

The above matching rules apply not only to shares but also to non-exempt interest bearing stocks that are not 'relevant securities' (see **38.6**). For relevant securities a disposal is matched in the following order:

(i)   Acquisitions of relevant securities within 30 days after the disposal;
(ii)   Acquisitions made at any time on a last in/first out basis.

Scrip and rights issues (TCGA 1992, ss 57, 122, 123, 126–132)

Corporate shareholders

[38.19] A scrip issue/bonus issue of shares to a corporate shareholder is treated as acquired at the same time as the shares out of which they arise. Where the original shares were in the post-1982 pool (**38.9**) it is not necessary to increase the indexed value of the pool to the date of the bonus issue — the number of shares in the pool is simply increased.

A rights issue is also treated as being acquired at the same time as the shares out of which they arise. Where the original shares were in the post-1982 pool, the number of shares, amount paid for them and indexation (to the date of the rights issue) is added to the pool. Where the original holding is in the pre-1982 pool (and earlier acquisitions) indexation is only available on the rights issue shares from the date of issue.

If rights are sold nil paid, the proceeds are treated as a part disposal of the holding, unless they are 'small', in which case they are deducted from the cost instead. Proceeds may be treated as 'small' if they are either not more than 5% of the value of the holding or they amount to £3,000 or less. The taxpayer may use the normal part disposal treatment if he wishes. (The value of the holding is arrived at by taking the ex-rights value of the existing shares plus the proceeds for the rights shares sold. If not all the rights shares were sold, those retained would also be valued at nil-paid price in this calculation.)

Example 8

A corporate taxpayer acquired 2,000 shares in EF plc on 23 February 2008 for £2,000. On 10 December 2009 there was a scrip issue of 1 for 2. On 19 April 2017 there was a rights issue of 1 for 6 at £2 per share. The ex-rights value of the shares was £3.00, giving a value of £9,000 for 3,000 shares.

EF plc post-1982 pool
If rights are taken up:

	Shares	Unindexed value £	Indexed value £
23.2.08	2,000	2,000	2,000
10.12.09 Scrip	1,000		
	3,000		
19.4.17 Rights	500		
Indexed February 2008 to April 2017 (0.280)			560
Rights cost		1,000	1,000
Pool values carried forward	3,500	3,000	3,560

If rights are sold nil paid for £1 per share = £500, which is 'small' being less than £3,000, even though more than 5% of (£9,000 + £500 =) £475:

	Shares	Unindexed value £	Indexed value £
Pool values bought forward	3,500	3,000	3,560
Less: Rights shares	(500)	(1,000)	(1,000)
Rights proceeds		(500)	(500)
Pool values carried forward	3,000	1,500	2,060

Example 9

In addition to the post-1982 pool in Example 8, the taxpayer had acquired 3,000 shares for £1,500 on 11 April 1979. These shares comprise the pre-1982 pool. The 31 March 1982 value of the shares was 75p per share. Rebasing election not made.

EF plc pre-1982 pool
If rights are taken up:

	Shares	Unin- dexed cost £	In- dexed cost £	Unin- dexed 31.3.82 value £	In- dexed 31.3.82 value £
At 31.3.82	3,000	1,500	1,500	2,250	2,250
10.12.09 Scrip	1,500				
	4,500				
19.4.17 Rights	750				
Indexn. March 1982 to Apr 2017 (2.406 × £2,250)			5,413		5,413
Rights cost		1,500	1,500	1,500	1,500
Pool values carried forward	5,250	3,000	8,413	3,750	9,163

If rights are sold nil paid for £1 per share:

	Shares	Unin- dexed cost £	In- dexed cost £	Unin- dexed 31.3.82 value £	In- dexed 31.3.82 value £
Pool values bought forward	5,250	3,000	8,413	3,750	9,163
Less: Rights shares	(750)	(1,500)	(1,500)	(1,500)	(1,500)
19.4.17 rights proceeds			(750)	(750)	(750)	(750)
Pool values carried forward	4,500	750	6,163	1,500	6,913

Although Examples 8 and 9 show small proceeds on a sale of rights being deducted from the value of the holding, if treating them as a part disposal would produce a gain covered by other capital losses, the part disposal treatment would be better. The part of the cost of the holding that is taken into account against the cash proceeds is arrived at in the same way as for cash on a takeover (see **38.36**).

Individual, personal representative or trustee shareholders

[38.20] For individual, personal representative or trustee shareholders, the rules detailed above for corporate shareholders apply equally, but within the greatly simplified regime that applies to such shareholders. Consequently any scrip/bonus or rights issue shares will enter the enlarged 'section 104 holding' and be taxed accordingly on a subsequent disposal.

Scrip dividend options (TCGA 1992, s 142)

[38.21] If individuals, personal representatives or trustees of discretionary trusts take scrip shares (stock dividends) instead of a dividend, the capital gains tax cost is the amount treated as their income (see 38.3). Scrip shares issued in lieu of dividends are treated as free-standing acquisitions.

Where scrip shares in lieu of a dividend are issued to a company, they are treated in the same way as ordinary scrip shares, i.e. there is no deemed cost and the shares are treated as acquired when the original shares were acquired.

The same applies if the recipient is a life interest trust unless the trustees treat the shares as income of the life tenant (see 38.3). Where trustees adopt that treatment, the scrip shares do not go into the trust's holding at all, and are regarded as belonging to the life tenant directly, so that the life tenant is treated in the same way as other individuals, even if the shares are held by the trustees (except in Scotland, where the treatment is different).

Reliefs

Shares of negligible value (TCGA 1992, s 24)

[38.22] Where shares (or any other assets) have become of negligible value, it is possible to establish an allowable loss by claiming for them to be treated as if they had actually been disposed of either on the date of the claim or at a stipulated time within the two tax years before the tax year in which the claim is made, providing the shares were of negligible value on the chosen date. Details of quoted shares that are regarded as being of negligible value, and the date from which that applies, are published by HMRC. In the case of unquoted shares, the fact that the shares are of negligible value has specifically to be agreed with HMRC. Even though shares are on HMRC's list, it is not necessary to make a negligible value claim. If a claim has not been made before a time at which the shares cease to exist (e.g. if the company has been dissolved), they are treated as disposed of at that time and a normal loss claim, rather than a negligible value claim, may then be made. See also HMRC Helpsheet 286.

Relief against income for losses on shares in qualifying trading companies (ITA 2007, ss 24A, 131–151; CTA 2010, ss 68–90)

[38.23] Where an individual disposes of shares at a loss (including SEIS shares, see 29.43), or the shares become valueless, the loss is normally relievable, like any other capital loss, against gains on other assets. However, relief may be claimed instead against any other *income* of the tax year of loss or of the previous tax year if the shares disposed of are ordinary shares or stock:

(a)   in a 'qualifying trading company' for which the individual subscribed. HMRC accept that this also includes subscriptions by nominees and joint owners (HMRC Brief 41/2010). Where some shares were acquired other than by subscription, there are rules to identify which shares have been disposed of; or

(b)   which would have qualified for EIS income tax relief (see 29.23), although the relief is not restricted to EIS shares. This includes subscriptions that are made by a nominee on behalf of the individual, or subscriptions made on behalf of joint owners.

A qualifying trading company is essentially a company that has, throughout the six years before the sale, been an unquoted trading company or the parent of such a trading group and its gross assets before and after the sale do not exceed £7 million and £8 million respectively. Note if a company has ceased to trade prior to sale, the relief is still available provided the cessation is not more than three years before the date of sale and in the three year period the company has not been an investment company or carried out non-trading activities. The claim to set off such losses takes priority over any claim for relief for trading losses. Claims must be made within one year from 31 January following the tax year of loss (e.g. by 31 January 2020 for a 2017–18 loss).

Where an investment company realises a loss on a disposal of ordinary unquoted shares in a qualifying trading company it may claim relief for the loss by setting it against its income (as opposed to its chargeable gains) of the same or preceding year provided the company making the disposal is an investment company on the date of the disposal and either:

(i)   has been an investment company for a continuous period of six years ending on that date; or

(ii)   has been an investment company for a shorter continuous period ending on that date, and must not have been, before the beginning of that period, a 'trading company' or an 'excluded company'.

A claim for this relief must be submitted within two years of the end of the accounting period in which the loss arose.

Share loss relief on non-EIS/SEIS shares is one of a number of reliefs against general income which is subject to a cap (see 2.13).

Disposal by gift (TCGA 1992, ss 67, 165)

[38.24] Where shares or securities are disposed of by gift, the proceeds are regarded as being their open market value. If a gain arises, the donor and donee may make a joint election for the donee to adopt the donor's base cost for capital gains tax purposes. This election is only available if the gift is made by an individual or trustees and comprises shares or securities in an unquoted trading company, or in a quoted trading company in which the donor owns 5% of the shares, or the gift is immediately chargeable to inheritance tax, or would be if it were not covered by the donor's annual inheritance tax exemption and/or inheritance tax nil rate band (see **4.31** to **4.34**).

If a loss arises on a gift to or other transaction with a connected person — which broadly means close family of the donor and of his spouse or civil partner, trustees of family trusts and companies controlled by the donor — the loss is not allowed against gains generally but only against a gain on a subsequent transaction with the same person. This does not apply to gifts between spouses or civil partners, which are treated as made at neither a gain nor a loss (see **4.6**).

Entrepreneurs' relief (TCGA 1992, ss 169H–169S; FA 2013, Sch 24 para 6)

[38.25] Entrepreneurs' relief is available for 'qualifying business disposals' taking place after 5 April 2008. Where the relief is available the rate of capital gains tax is reduced to 10%. A person's qualifying gains for entrepreneurs' relief is subject to a lifetime cap of £10 million. See further **29.2**.

Investors' relief (TCGA 1992, ss 169VA–169VR)

[38.26] For shares that were newly issued on or after 17 March 2016 'investors' relief' is available. This relief applies a 10% rate of capital gains tax to gains accruing on the disposal of ordinary shares in an unlisted trading company held by individuals, that were newly issued to the claimant and acquired for new consideration on or after 17 March 2016, and have been held for a period of at least three years starting from 6 April 2016. A person's qualifying gains for investors' relief will be subject to a lifetime cap of £10 million. See further **29.12**.

Investment funds/trusts and savings schemes

Authorised investment funds (CTA 2010, ss 612–620; CTA 2009, ss 487–497; ITA 2007, ss 504, 941–943: TCGA 1992, ss 99–99AA, 100; FA 1995, s 152; F(No 2)A 2005, ss 17, 18; SI 2006/964; FA 2017, s 11, Sch 5)

[38.27] Authorised investment funds (AIFs) consist of open-ended investment companies (OEICs) and authorised unit trusts (AUT). An OEIC is a company in which the shares may be continuously created or redeemed, depending on investor demand. An AUT is a professionally managed fund which enables an investor to obtain a wide spread of investments. There are various types of funds to suit particular circumstances, for example some aimed at capital growth and some at maximising income. Both OEICs and AUTs are treated essentially the same way for taxation purposes.

AIFs pay corporation tax at 20% on their taxable income (essentially interest income as they do not pay tax on dividends) and they are exempt from tax on capital gains (subject to various anti-avoidance provisions). Relief for management expenses is given against profits chargeable to corporation tax. Distributions to unit holders may be dividend distributions or interest distributions. An AIF can only pay interest distributions where its interest-bearing investments comprise more than 60% of the total market value of the trust fund.

Where certain conditions are met, an AIF can elect to be treated as a tax elected fund (TEF). This essentially means that there will be no corporation tax levied on its taxable income provided such income is distributed to its shareholders. This is achieved by the TEF receiving a deduction, for tax purposes, equal to the amount of interest distributions made.

[38.28] The tax treatment of individual investors is broadly similar to the position had they invested directly:

(a)   dividend distributions are received gross. There is a 'dividend nil rate' which applies to dividends within the £5,000 'dividend allowance' and dividends in excess of this amount are taxed at 7.5%, 32.5% or 38.1% depending upon the recipient's marginal rate. Note that the September 2017 Finance Bill, which is expected to receive Royal Assent in November 2017, includes legislation to reduce the dividend nil rate to £2,000 from 2018–19 onwards. For more details see **2.22** onwards;

(b)   from 6 April 2017 interest distributions from OEICs, AUTs and investment trust companies are paid gross. Prior to 6 April 2017, interest distributions were paid net of 20% tax. This brings the treatment of these types of savings income into line with that of interest paid on bank and building society accounts from 6 April 2016; see **2.5**).

An individual investor's gains are similarly taxed as if the funds had been invested directly, except that gains on sales of gilt units are taxable, whereas gains on gilts themselves are not. 'Equalisation' payments received on the acquisition of new units are not taxed as income. They reduce the cost of an individual's units for capital gains tax.

[38.29] Dividend distributions paid to companies from the AIF are not liable to corporation tax, unless part of the AIFs income is not dividend income, in which case an equivalent part of the dividend distribution from the AIF is treated as interest received by the company. Any such amount is brought into account along with interest distributions as part of the company's income chargeable to corporation tax. The income tax suffered at source (prior to 6 April 2016) is deducted from the tax payable by the company, but if the investor company is claiming an income tax repayment, the repayment cannot exceed the company's proportion of the AIFs corporation tax liability on the gross income. The trustees are required to state their net liability to corporation tax on the distribution statement sent to the company and this is usually expressed as an amount per unit held so that the company can calculate the maximum income tax available for repayment. Gains and losses on disposals of a company's unit trust investments also form part of the corporation tax profit or loss (see **3.6**). Anti-avoidance provisions apply to prevent abuse of these provisions.

Investment trusts (CTA 2010, ss 1158–1165; ITA 2007, ss 276–277; TCGA 1992, s 100; FA 2009, s 45; SI 2011/2999)

Definition of an investment trust

[38.30] Investment trusts are actually companies and not trusts, and investors buy shares in them in the usual way. Some trusts with a limited life are split level trusts, i.e. they have income shares that receive most of the trust's income and a fixed capital sum on liquidation, and capital shares that receive little or no income but get most of the capital surplus (if any) on a liquidation.

A company can be approved by HMRC as an 'investment trust' if:

(a) it meets the following conditions laid down in statute:
  (i) all, or substantially all, of its business consists of investing in shares, land or other assets with the aim of spreading investment risk and giving the members of the company the benefit of the results of the management of the funds;
  (ii) its shares are admitted to trading on a regulated market; and
  (iii) it is not a venture capital trust or a UK REIT; and
(b) it meets the following conditions laid down in regulations:
  (i) the company is not close;
  (ii) the company (unless it falls within one of the exceptions, see (1), (2) below) meets the income distribution requirement — i.e. it must not retain more than 15% of its income for the accounting period and it must distribute income before the filing date for its tax return for that period.
  A company does not have to satisfy the income distribution condition if:
  (1) the amount that the investment trust would be otherwise required to distribute is less than £30,000; or
  (2) because of a legal restriction (e.g. company law requirement) the investment trust is required to retain more than 15% of its income and it either does not retain any more than it is legally required to do, or the amount of the excess retained plus the amount actually distributed does not exceed £30,000.

Tax treatment

[38.31] Investment trusts are exempt from tax on their capital gains if they are approved investment trusts (approval has to be given every year by HMRC) but the gains may only be reinvested and cannot be distributed as dividends. There are anti-avoidance provisions to prevent the exemption being exploited either by transferring a company's business to a company that is, or later becomes, an investment trust, or by transferring assets intra-group to a company that is, or later becomes, an investment trust. The Treasury has the power to make regulations concerning the treatment of specified transactions of investment trusts for the purposes of the Corporation Tax Acts (i.e. whether they form trading transactions or not).

Investment trusts are normally charged to corporation tax in the normal way, which puts them at a disadvantage as against unit trusts. However an investment trust can opt to receive a deduction, for tax purposes, for the interest distributions made to its shareholders. This enables it to invest in interest producing assets tax efficiently and moves the point of taxation for income received from the investment trust to the shareholder with the result that shareholders face broadly the same tax treatment as they would have had they owned the interest bearing assets directly. The income and gains of UK Real Estate Investment Trusts are exempt from tax in certain circumstances (see **32.36**).

Investment schemes

[38.32] Individuals may invest in qualifying unquoted trading companies through one or more of a number of investments schemes. These schemes are aimed at promoting investment and enterprise. For details see CHAPTER **29**.

Savings schemes

[38.33] Unit trusts, open-ended investment companies and investment trusts operate monthly savings schemes, which give the investor the advantage of 'pound cost averaging', i.e. fluctuations in prices are evened out because overall investors get more units/shares when the price is low and fewer when it is high.

Individual savings accounts

[38.34] Investors can invest up to £20,000 from 6 April 2017 in unit and investment trusts and open-ended investment companies through the stocks and shares component of ISAs. For details of ISAs generally see **36.16** onwards.

Deeply discounted securities (ITTOIA 2005, ss 427–460; ITA 2007, s 24A)

[38.35] The provisions for deeply discounted securities outlined below do not apply to companies, because a company's gains and losses are dealt with under the 'loan relationships' rules (see **3.6**).

Special rules apply to all securities issued at a discount to private investors. The accrued income scheme (see **36.11**) does not apply to securities within these provisions. Securities are deeply discounted securities where their issue price is lower than the redemption price by more than 0.5% per year between issue and redemption, or, if that period exceeds 30 years, by more than 15%. The provisions do not cover shares, gilt-edged securities (except for gilt strips, for which there are special rules), indexed securities that are linked to the value of a share index, life assurance policies and capital redemption policies.

There is no capital gains tax charge on deeply discounted securities, and investors are charged to income tax in the tax year of disposal or redemption on the profit made. For securities acquired before 27 March 2003 the expenses of acquisition and disposal incurred before 6 April 2015, may be deducted. If a loss arises on securities acquired before that date, a claim may be made by the first anniversary of 31 January following the relevant tax year to set the loss against the total income of that tax year. Trustees may only set losses against income from discounted securities of the tax year of loss or, if that is insufficient, of a later tax year. When someone dies, they are treated as disposing of the securities to the personal representatives at market value at the date of death, income tax being chargeable accordingly. Transfers from personal representatives to legatees are treated as made at market value at the date of the transfer, with income tax being charged on the estate on the difference between the value at death and the value at the date of the transfer.

Relief for losses on deeply discounted securities is one of a number of reliefs against general income which is subject to a cap (see **2.13**).

Takeovers, mergers and reconstructions (TCGA 1992, ss 57, 116, 126–131, 135, 136, 138A and Sch 5AA)

Share and cash consideration

[38.36] An exchange of new shares for old does not normally involve a chargeable gain, instead the new shares are treated as standing in the shoes of the old, both as regards acquisition date and cost. This often happens when one company (whether or not its shares are quoted on the Stock Exchange) acquires another (either quoted or unquoted) by issuing its own shares to the holders of the shares in the company which is being taken over (known as 'paper for paper' exchanges).

Where both cash and new shares are received, a partial disposal arises, in the proportion that the cash itself bears to the market value of the securities acquired in exchange.

Part of a takeover package may take the form of shares or securities to be issued at some future date, the number of such shares or securities depending for example on future profits (known as an earn-out right). For the treatment of such transactions, including the treatment where the future consideration is to be in cash, see **28.8** to **28.10**.

> **Example 10**
>
> X Ltd owns 10,000 shares in a company, A, which cost £6,000 in September 1987. The shares do not qualify for the substantial shareholding exemption.
>
> Company A is taken over by company B on 6 March 2017.

Scenario (a)

12,000 shares in company B, valued at £30,000, are received in exchange for the 10,000 shares in company A.

No chargeable gain arises on the £24,000 excess value of the company B shares over the cost of the company A shares.

Instead the 12,000 shares in company B are regarded as having the same £6,000 base value as the 10,000 company A shares which they replace.

Scenario (b)

12,000 shares in company B, valued at £24,000, together with £6,000 in cash are received in exchange for the 10,000 shares in company A, the shares in company A having an indexed cost of (say) £16,750. The cash represents 20% of the total consideration and the shares 80%.

The 12,000 shares in company B have base values as follows:

Unindexed value 80% × £6,000	£4,800
Indexed value 80% × £16,750	£13,400

The indexed cost to set off against the £6,000 cash received for the part disposal is 20% × £16,750 = £3,350 reducing the gain to £2,650.

If X had been an individual, the treatment would have been the same, except that indexation allowance would not be available and the gain would have been taxed at a flat rate (of either 10% or 20%, depending upon his personal tax position (see 4.2)).

Corporate bonds

Qualifying corporate bonds

[38.37] As indicated at **38.6**, qualifying corporate bonds are not chargeable assets for capital gains tax, and can create neither a chargeable gain nor allowable loss (subject to the special rules at **38.40**). Sometimes on a takeover or reorganisation qualifying corporate bonds may be exchanged for shares or vice versa. When qualifying corporate bonds are exchanged for shares the shares are treated as acquired at their market value at the date of the exchange. If shares are exchanged for qualifying corporate bonds, the gain or loss on the shares at the date of the exchange is calculated and 'frozen' until the qualifying corporate bonds are disposed of, when the frozen gain or loss crystallises. No gain or loss can be established on the bonds themselves (with the exception stated at **38.40**). In some cases, this could mean that a gain is chargeable even if the qualifying corporate bonds have become virtually worthless. One solution may be to give them to a charity. The frozen gain on the shares would not then be charged, nor would the charity have any tax liability when it disposed of the bonds. A frozen gain escapes being charged to tax if the taxpayer dies. If a frozen gain arises on shares held by personal representatives, however, it is charged when the loan stock is disposed of by the personal representatives, or when disposed of by a legatee following the transfer of the stock to him by the personal representatives.

Where a frozen gain would otherwise become chargeable, it may be deferred if an equivalent investment is made by subscribing for unquoted shares under the enterprise investment scheme provisions (**29.33**) the seed enterprise investment scheme (**29.37**) or, the social investment tax relief scheme (**29.57**). Where shares are exchanged partly for cash and partly for qualifying corporate bonds, the EIS/SEIS/SITR relief may be claimed on the gain on the cash element.

It is possible that when shares are exchanged for qualifying corporate bonds, a gain on the disposal of the shares could have qualified for entrepreneurs' relief (see **29.2** to **29.11**). An election can therefore be made for the gain not to be deferred but instead brought into charge at that time and entrepreneurs' relief claimed (see further **29.10**). If no election is made and the gain is deferred it is unlikely that the frozen gain will qualify for entrepreneurs' relief when it crystallises. Where gains were deferred on an exchange of shares for qualifying corporate bonds before 6 April 2008, when the frozen gain comes into charge entrepreneurs' relief can be claimed on the first disposal of qualifying corporate bonds after that date.

[38.38] For corporate investors, all loan stock is included within the definition of a 'qualifying corporate bond' (see **38.6**). Where a company receives shares in exchange for corporate bonds, the gain or loss on the bond is taken into account in computing the company's income under the 'loan relationships' rules (see **3.6**). If a company receives corporate bonds in exchange for shares, the 'frozen gain or loss' treatment outlined above applies, with the frozen gain or loss on the shares being brought in as a *capital* gain or loss when the bonds are disposed of. (Any gain or loss on the disposal of the bonds themselves will be brought into account under the 'loan relationships' rules).

Non-qualifying corporate bonds

[38.39] If, on a takeover, shares are exchanged for non-qualifying corporate bonds, the bonds stand in the shoes of the shares as regards date and cost of acquisition, with a later disposal of the bond giving a capital gain or loss at that time.

Losses on qualifying corporate bonds (TCGA 1992, ss 254, 255)

[38.40] Since qualifying corporate bonds are exempt from capital gains tax, no allowable loss can arise under the normal rules. For qualifying corporate bonds issued before 17 March 1998, relief for losses may be claimed according to the rules outlined at **4.37** if the claimant made the loan to a UK resident trader. Someone to whom the bond has been assigned cannot claim the relief. A claim may also be made when the value of such a loan has become negligible (see **4.36**). The relief for losses outlined above does not apply to individuals for bonds issued on or after 17 March 1998. Nor does it apply to companies, because a company's gains and losses are dealt with under the 'loan relationships' rules (see **3.6**).

See **38.37** and **38.38** for the treatment of losses on qualifying corporate bonds acquired on a takeover and **38.39** for the treatment of non-qualifying corporate bonds.

Tax points

[38.41] Note the following:

- It is not possible to sell shares and buy them back the next day (bed and breakfast) to use the annual capital gains exemption (currently £11,300), although a person's spouse or civil partner could repurchase them on the open market.
- Investment managers frequently prepare capital gains reports for clients at the tax year end. Care needs to be taken with the 30-day rule for matching disposals with acquisitions where disposals take place shortly before the end of the tax year.
- For a small investor, unit and investment trusts can be a useful way of getting the benefit of a wide spread of investments, with the added advantage of expert management. Such trusts are exempt from tax on their capital gains. capital gains tax is due in the usual way on the disposal of the investment in the trust. The investment is particularly tax-efficient when made through an ISA, although the tax exemption has sometimes been more than offset by falling investment values.
- Investing regular amounts on a monthly basis into a unit or investment trust evens out the ups and downs of share prices.
- When an ISA investor dies, his personal representatives should notify the ISA manager promptly, because the tax exemption ceases at the date of the investor's death. The Treasury is empowered, via regulations to be effective at some point after 15 September 2016, to provide for ISAs to retain their tax-advantaged status following the death of the account holder (see **36.17**).
- If shares are given away, they are regarded as disposed of for market value, but tax does not have to be paid at that time if they qualify for gift relief and a claim is made for the relief to apply (see **4.32**).
- It is possible to avoid a frozen gain crystallising on qualifying corporate bonds that were acquired on a takeover, etc. and have since become valueless by giving them to a charity (see **38.37**).
- If shares have become virtually worthless, it may be advantageous to make a negligible value claim as soon as they have been included on HMRC's list (see **38.22**). But if, for example, making the claim immediately would reduce gains and cause annual exemption to be wasted, it is possible to defer the claim to a later year, but not later than that in which the shares cease to exist.
- If there is some control over the time of payment of a dividend, as with a family or other small company, watch that the date of payment does not aggravate an already high taxable income where the income of the major shareholders varies from year to year.

- If not more than £5,000 nominal value of gilt-edged securities or other securities are held to which the accrued income scheme applies, remember that the accrued interest is neither charged to nor relieved from income tax (see **36.11**). The securities will usually be exempt from capital gains tax (see **38.6**). If they are not, the accrued interest is taken into account for capital gains tax in arriving at the cost or proceeds as the case may be.

- If more than £5,000 nominal value of accrued income scheme securities are held, it will be necessary to consider what adjustment is required on a disposal of any of them. Details must be shown on a tax return. If dealings are through a bank or stockbroker, the amount of accrued interest will be shown on the contract note. Accrued income charges or reliefs are taken into account in the tax year in which the next interest payment is made on the stock.

- Since spouses and civil partners are each entitled to an annual capital gains tax exemption, currently £11,300, it may be appropriate to split share portfolios so that each may take advantage of it. Transfers between spouses or civil partners are not chargeable disposals. If shares are held jointly in unequal proportions, watch the provisions about notifying HMRC for income tax purposes (see **33.6**).

39

Chattels and valuables

What are chattels? (TCGA 1992, ss 21, 262, 263, 269; AEA 1925, s 55; ITPA 2014, s 3)

General definition

[39.1] Chattels are defined generally as tangible movable property, for example coins (**39.2**), furniture, jewellery, works of art, motor vehicles. For IHT purposes, for the intestacy rules (**35.2**), the term is defined generally and includes tangible movable property, other than money, property used at the date of death solely or mainly for business purposes, or property held solely as an investment.

Coins

[39.2] Although coins come within the definition of a chattel, sterling currency is specifically exempt from capital gains tax, as are deposits or withdrawals to or from foreign currency bank accounts (**4.14**).

Coins that do not fall within these exemptions are chargeable to capital gains tax in the normal way. Demonetised coins (which include pre-1837 sovereigns) fall within the definition of a chattel and, if they have a predictable life of more than 50 years, which obviously applies to collectors' items, the wasting asset exemption for chattels does not apply but the £6,000 exemption is available, (see **39.4**).

Collectors' coins are normally liable to VAT at the standard rate, whether they are legal tender or not, unless they are dealt with under the special scheme for antiques and collectors' pieces or under the global accounting scheme for second-hand goods (see **7.30**). Subject to certain special rules, coins that are 'investment gold' as defined are exempt from VAT and are not eligible to be sold under the second-hand schemes.

Income tax

[39.3] When investing in valuable objects, the appreciation in value does not generally attract income tax (see below regarding capital gains tax), but on the other hand there is no tax relief for expenses of ownership such as insurance or charges for safe custody.

A succession of profitable sales may suggest to HMRC that chattels and valuables are being held for trading purposes rather than investment, particularly where the scale and frequency of the sales, or the way in which they are carried out, or the need for supplementary work between purchase and sale, suggest a trading motive. Indeed, even a single purchase and sale has on occasion been held to be a trading transaction. However, an important indicator of trading is the lack of significant long term investment value or pride of ownership.

Capital gains tax on sales of chattels (TCGA 1992, ss 44–47B, 262)

[39.4] The capital gains tax treatment of a chattel depends on the nature of the chattel, and sometimes on its value, as follows:

(a)   The following chattels are exempt:
   (i)   sterling currency, foreign currency (see **4.14**) and motor cars are completely exempt. This does not however apply to one-seater cars; these are exempt as wasting assets unless they have been used in a business;
   (ii)   chattels with a predictable life of 50 years or less (called wasting assets), are totally exempt from capital gains tax. This includes plant or machinery where capital allowances cannot be claimed provided they have been used in the seller's own business. The exemption does not apply however, if the wasting assets are used in a business and capital allowances have been, or could have been, claimed on them, in which case the capital gains tax computation is as detailed at **22.46**. Eligible individuals that have opted into the cash basis (**20.4**) will not realise chargeable gains or losses on the disposal of wasting assets because the proceeds are liable to income tax;

(b)   Chattels that do not fall within (*a*) will potentially be chargeable but may be eligible for chattels relief. This relief provides that a gain on such chattels is exempt if the sale consideration is £6,000 or less. If there are joint owners, such as husband and wife or civil partners, each has a separate £6,000 limit to compare with their share of the sale proceeds. Where the proceeds exceed £6,000, the chargeable gain cannot exceed 5/3rds of the excess proceeds over £6,000. If the chattel is sold at a loss for less than £6,000, it is treated as sold for £6,000 to calculate the allowable loss. This means that there can only be an allowable loss if the chattel cost more than £6,000, and if it is a business chattel there will not be an allowable loss in any event (see below).

Example 1

	£
An antique collector's sale proceeds for an antique dresser in June 2017 are	7,200
Cost was	(4,570)
Chargeable gain	£2,630
But limited to 5/3 × (7,200 − 6,000)	£2,000

The gain will be eliminated completely if the annual exempt amount of £11,300 has not been used against other gains.

No allowable loss could arise on the dresser, no matter what the sale proceeds, because proceeds of less than £6,000 are treated as £6,000 to calculate a loss.

Example 2

A painting that had cost a collector £11,000 in January 1997 was sold for £8,000 in June 2017. The allowable loss is £3,000. If the painting had been sold for £4,000, it would be treated as sold for £6,000, giving an allowable loss of £5,000 rather than £7,000.

Chargeable chattels comprising a set or collection are treated as separate assets unless they are sold to the same or connected persons (see **4.11**), in which case the sales are added together for the purposes of the £6,000 exemption. Chattels form a set if they are essentially similar and complementary and their value, taken together, is higher than if they were considered separately. Where the set is sold over a period spanning more than one tax year, the gain is calculated on the total sale proceeds but it is then apportioned between the different tax years according to the respective amounts of sale proceeds in each tax year. Splitting up a set and selling it to different unconnected people would usually not be sensible because it would substantially reduce its value. See **39.5** for chargeable chattels given away by a series of transactions with connected persons.

As far as business chattels are concerned, capital allowances are taken into account in computing income liable to income tax or corporation tax. If the chattel is sold for more than cost, the capital allowances will be withdrawn by means of a balancing charge, so that they will not affect the computation of a capital gain. Where a business chattel is sold for less than cost, the capital allowances computation will automatically give relief for the loss on sale in arriving at taxable income, so there will be no allowable loss for capital gains tax purposes.

For HMRC comments on the treatment of wines and spirits and pairs of shotguns, see HMRC RI 208, and RI 214 respectively.

Gifts of chattels

Capital gains implications

[39.5] A gift of a chargeable chattel is treated as a disposal at open market value at the date of the gift. In order to arrive at an estimated valuation, some evidence of the transaction in the form of correspondence, etc. is advisable. If the value is below the £6,000 exempt level, no tax charge will arise, but the market value at the time of the gift counts as the cost of the asset to the donee when calculating his capital gains tax position on a subsequent disposal.

There are provisions similar to the rules for sets of articles in **39.4** where chargeable assets are given away or otherwise disposed of by a series of transactions with connected persons within a period of six years, and they are worth more together than separately. These provisions apply not only to chattels but also to any other assets, particularly unquoted shares and land and buildings. See **4.31** for details.

If the value of the gifted chattel exceeds the £6,000 exempt level and there is a chargeable gain, tax may not even so be payable because the gain, together with other gains, may be covered by the annual exemption (£11,300 for 2017–18). For gifts of business assets, certain other gifts for public benefit, etc. and gifts into and out of certain trusts, it is possible for donor and donee to claim gift relief (see **4.31** to **4.34**). A tax reduction (against income tax, capital gains tax or corporation tax) may be available on gifts of chattels that qualify for pre-eminent gifts relief (**2.21**).

Inheritance tax implications

[39.6] For inheritance tax purposes, a gift of a chattel may fall within one of the many exemptions (see **5.3** to **5.22**). If it is not, it will either be a potentially exempt transfer, or a chargeable transfer in the case of transfers to a company or some trusts. If the donor does not survive the gift by seven years, the potential exemption will be lost and the value at the time of the gift will be taken into account in calculating the inheritance tax payable at death. The person who received the gift will be primarily responsible for the inheritance tax triggered by the death within seven years, including any additional inheritance tax payable on a lifetime chargeable transfer because the death rate applies rather than the lifetime rate originally used. HMRC have the right to look to the estate of the donor if necessary. There will not be any potential liability if the value of the gift was within the nil rate band, but, if there is a potential liability it may be worth insuring against by a term assurance policy on the life of the donor in favour of the donee.

Tax points

[39.7] Note the following:

* HMRC have the power to require auctioneers to provide details of all chattel sales exceeding £6,000.

- Details of chattel acquisitions are frequently required at a later date, perhaps for capital gains tax purposes or to demonstrate that funds for some other investment or business enterprise were available from their sale. Evidence can be provided by purchase invoices that identify the object, and/or by having substantial items included specifically on a household contents insurance policy when they are acquired.

- A profit on the sale of a vintage or classic car is exempt from capital gains tax (unless it is 'unsuitable to be used as a private vehicle') provided it is not bought and sold with the aim of making a profit (in which case it is likely that the transaction will be viewed as a trading transaction and liable to income tax (or corporation tax)).

- 'Machinery' is always regarded as a wasting asset and is therefore exempt from capital gains tax unless it is used in a business. A private individual will therefore not pay tax on a gain on a valuable antique machine, such as a clock. The same would apply to a gain by a private individual on a vintage or classic vehicle not covered by the cars exemption.

- It is important to be aware of the trading trap if regularly buying and selling chattels and valuables.

40

Sensible use of life insurance

Qualifying policies (TA 1988, ss 266, 267 and Sch 15; ITTOIA 2005, s 497)

Definition of qualifying policy

[40.1] The key difference between a qualifying and non-qualifying policy is that gains on the former are generally free of tax (**40.2**).

The definition of a 'qualifying policy' is complex, but broadly:

(i)   the policy must be on the individual's own life or the life of his spouse or civil partner;

(ii)   it must secure a capital sum payable either on death or earlier disability or not earlier than ten years after the policy is taken out;

(iii)   the premiums must be reasonably even and paid at yearly or shorter intervals;

(iv)   any requirements relating to the amount of the sum insured and sometimes the surrender value must be met; and

(v)   for qualifying policies issued on or after 6 April 2013, the amount of premiums payable into the policy must be no more than £3,600 in any 12 month period. Transitional rules apply for policies issued from 21 March 2012 to 5 April 2013 inclusive. Policies issued in this period are restricted so that full relief is available in relation to premiums payable in the transitional period, but the £3,600 annual limit will apply to premiums payable thereafter. Policies issued before 21 March 2012 will only be affected by this annual limit where there is a relevant substitution, variation or exercise of an existing option within the policy on or after 21 March 2012.

The offer of a free gift on taking out a policy could breach the 'qualifying policy' rules, but gifts costing up to £30 are ignored.

Capital gains tax treatment of qualifying policies (ITTOIA 2005, ss 465, 498–514; TCGA 1992, s 10A; FA 2013, s 218 and Sch 45)

[40.2] When a qualifying policy matures (provided it has not been varied etc in the meantime), the policy proceeds are tax-free, unless the policy is surrendered etc. early.

Where a qualifying policy is varied, surrendered or assigned less than ten years after the policy is taken out (or, for endowment policies, before the expiry of three-quarters of the term if that amounts to less than ten years), any profit arising is charged to tax at the excess of higher rate tax over the basic rate of 20% to the extent that the profit falls within the taxpayer's higher rate income tax band (but top-slicing relief is available (see **40.8**)).

Details of gains must be shown on the tax return, as for non-qualifying policies.

A variation which acknowledges the exclusion of an exceptional risk of critical illness or disability, with a consequent effect upon the future premium or the sum insured, does not cause a policy to lose its qualifying status.

The provisions charging gains on qualifying and non-qualifying policies do not apply to someone who was not resident in the UK when the gain arose. Gains arising to a UK resident individual in the overseas part of a split year (**41.6**) are treated as arising to a non-UK resident. If the individual is only temporarily non-resident (**41.49**) when the gains arise, a charge will arise in the year of return. See **40.11** for the position for policies held in trust.

Purchased life annuities (ITTOIA 2005, ss 422–426, 717–726)

[40.3] A qualifying policy is sometimes useful to higher rate taxpayers in conjunction with a purchased life annuity (see **36.15**).

Only part of the purchased annuity is liable to income tax, with tax being deducted at the basic rate of 20%, and further tax payable or repayable depending on the annuitant's tax position. The remainder of the annuity is regarded as a return of capital.

Instead of making a conventional investment and losing a substantial part of the income in tax, a higher rate taxpayer could purchase a life annuity and use the net income arising to fund a qualifying life policy, the profits on maturity of the policy being tax-free. Whilst the reduction in tax rates has reduced the advantages of this form of investment, it can still be attractive in some circumstances, but specialist advice is essential.

For an older taxpayer, a variation is available under which only part of the net annual sum from the annuity is used to pay the premiums on a qualifying policy to replace the initial cost of the annuity, the remainder being retained as spendable income.

Anti-avoidance provisions apply to prevent life insurance companies manipulating the purchased life annuity rules to obtain an excessive deduction against their profits in respect of annuities taken out by financial traders.

Non-qualifying policies

Definition of a non-qualifying policy

[40.4] A policy that does not fall within the definition of a qualifying policy is termed a 'non-qualifying' policy. A non-qualifying policy usually takes the form of a single premium investment bond. When invested by the life insurance company, the single premium should ideally grow more rapidly than an equivalent amount in the hands of a higher rate taxpayer reinvesting net income from a conventional investment. Guaranteed income bonds are another form of single premium life policy.

Non-qualifying policies do not have the capital gains advantages that qualifying policies have. Gains realised on the surrender (full or part) of a qualifying policy that fall within the policyholder's higher or additional rate band will be subject to tax. The gains are chargeable to income tax at the excess of higher/additional rate tax over the basic rate of 20% subject to certain special provisions which are outlined below.

Capital gains tax treatment of non-qualifying policies (ITTOIA 2005, ss 461–546)

[40.5] A taxable life policy gain arising on a full or part surrender is treated as part of the total income of an individual in the year in which the chargeable event occurred, with a non-repayable deemed tax payment of 20%.

For individuals that are not higher rate taxpayers, no further tax is due. Where a gain pushes a taxpayer into the higher rate band, top slicing relief is available to lessen the impact of the tax charge. Although savings income is treated as the top slice of income for all other purposes (except for calculating tax on payments covered by the 'golden handshake rules' (see **15.6**)), life policy gains (including any gains chargeable on qualifying policies) are added in last of all in order to calculate any tax liability.

An astute investor will usually want to switch investments from time to time, say from equities to properties, then to gilts and so on. For a small administration charge, a life insurance company will allow investors to switch the investments underlying the bond, and the switch has no adverse tax effect.

To give added flexibility in the timing of bond surrenders, it is possible to take out a number of smaller bonds, so that they need not all be cashed in the same tax year. Not only can the original investment be cashed in over a number of years but the amount liable to tax in any year is itself top-sliced (see **40.8**) in arriving at the tax payable. This type of arrangement may be used as an alternative to a purchased life annuity in order to pay the premiums on a qualifying policy, and also to pay large items of anticipated recurrent expenditure such as school fees.

5% allowance

[40.6] It is possible to make withdrawals of not more than a cumulative 5% per annum of the initial investment in each policy year (ending on the anniversary of the policy) without attracting a tax liability at that time, such withdrawals being treated as partial surrenders which are only taken into account in calculating the final profit on the bond when it is cashed in.

The 5% is a cumulative figure and amounts unused in any year swell the tax-free withdrawal available in a later year, which could be useful for some particularly heavy item of future expenditure. If more than the permitted 5% figure is withdrawn, the excess is charged to tax, but only if, taking into account the excess, and also the top-slicing rules in **40.8**, taxable income exceeds the basic rate limit.

> *Example 1*
>
> A policyholder invests £100,000 in a policy on 16 April 2017 and withdraws £6,000 on 17 December 2017, by way of a part surrender, then a gain of £1,000 (the excess of the withdrawal over the 5% tax allowance) would arise at the next policy anniversary (i.e. 15 April 2018). This gain is chargeable to tax.

In certain situations, the operation of this 5% rule can result in disproportionate gains being charged to tax. Therefore the September 2017 Finance Bill (which is expected to receive Royal Assent in November 2017) allows affected taxpayers to apply to HMRC for such gains to be recalculated on a just and reasonable basis. Any such application must be made within four years of the end of the tax year in which the gain arose.

> *Example 2*
>
> If the policyholder in Example 1 above had withdrawn £75,000 on 17 December 2017 the gain arising on 15 April 2018 would have been £70,000. Such a gain is likely to be disproportionate to the underlying economic gain. Indeed, it would arise even if the policy was not in profit.
>
> Therefore, from the date of Royal Assent to the September 2017 Finance Bill, the policyholder is able to apply to HMRC to have the gain recalculated on a just and reasonable basis.

Bear in mind though that if the excess occurs in a year when, after adding in the excess, taxable income does not exceed the basic rate limit, no charge will arise. The same applies when the bond is finally cashed in, because if this can be arranged in a year when income, even with the addition of the appropriate 'slice' of the bond profit, does not attract the higher rate, no tax is normally payable. Thus it may be possible to surrender in a year when income is low, for example, because of business losses or following retirement. Rather than surrendering the bond, it is possible to defer any tax liability by extending the period of the policy and thus its maturity.

Calculation of tax due on life policy gains

Calculation of gain (ITTOIA 2005, ss 461–546)

[40.7] The amount of gain, when a policy comes to an end, or on a part surrender/assignment that exceeds the 5% limit (40.6), is calculated by deducting the total amount of premiums paid into the policy plus gains that have previously arisen under the policy (earlier gains) from the total value of any benefits received over the whole life of the policy.

For new policies taken out on or after 21 March 2012 (and certain pre-existing policies) a deduction for earlier gains is only allowed to the extent that those earlier gains are attributable to a person chargeable to tax on gains under this regime and that interdependent policies (under which the value of benefits paid from one policy is dependent on premiums paid into another policy) will be treated as a single policy.

The gain is reduced in the following circumstances:

(a)   following the introduction of the premium limit (40.1), certain gains realised on policies issued after 21 March 2012 and before 5 April 2013 that are varied after 5 April 2013 may be reduced so that effectively the chargeable gain is limited to that part relating to premiums payable after the variation;

(b)   for policies issued on or after 6 April 2013, gains are reduced where the person liable to income tax on the gains has not been UK resident for all/part of the year. For policies issued before 6 April 2013, gains are reduced where the gain is realised on life insurance policies issued by a foreign insurer and the policyholder has not been resident in the UK for part of the life of the policy up to the time of the chargeable event. In other words, from 6 April 2013, reductions are available for policies issued by UK and overseas insurers and the reduction is calculated by reference to the residence history of the person liable to tax on the policy, as opposed to the legal owner of the policy.

Anti-avoidance provisions apply where premiums totalling more than £100,000 have been invested over a specified period in short to medium-term policies. The amount of premiums allowable in calculating the gain is reduced by commission that has been rebated or reinvested.

Gains must be shown on the tax return. The insurance company should provide the taxpayer with the relevant details. They are also required to inform HMRC if the chargeable event is the sale of the policy or if the aggregate gains in a tax year exceed half the basic rate income threshold. HMRC provide a comprehensive tax calculation guide, which deals with the tax on the life insurance gains.

If the bond is cashed in on death, any mortality element of the profit as distinct from the surplus on the underlying investments is not taxable, and since the income of the year of death will usually not cover a full tax year, even on the taxable portion there may be little tax liability at the higher rate.

There is no relief if there is a loss when the bond is cashed in, but if any deficiency on the bond in the tax year in which that event occurs exceeds the cumulative 5% tax-free withdrawals from the bond, a higher rate taxpayer may deduct the excess from his income of that tax year in calculating the amount of extra tax payable on income above the basic rate threshold. The relief is given at the taxpayer's marginal rate. For policies taken out or varied on or after 3 March 2004, relief for a deficiency is only available where the earlier taxable withdrawals formed part of the taxable income of the bond-holder. This is to counter avoidance schemes where earlier gains were made by a different person, such as a spouse. No loss relief can be claimed when an offshore life insurance policy is cashed in. Anti-avoidance provisions apply to 'personal portfolio bonds'. These are aimed particularly at offshore bonds, but they also apply to UK bonds. For details see **45.29**.

The provisions charging gains on qualifying and non-qualifying policies do not apply to someone who was not resident in the UK when the gain arose. Gains arising to a UK resident individual in the overseas part of a split year (**41.6**) are treated as arising to a non-UK resident. If the individual is only temporarily non-resident (**41.49**) when the gains arise, a charge will arise in the year of return. See **40.11** for the position for policies held in trust.

Top-slicing relief for chargeable events (ITTOIA 2005, ss 465B, 535–538)

[40.8] In the tax year when a chargeable event arises on a qualifying or non-qualifying policy (for example when a bond is cashed in) top-slicing relief is available to lessen the impact of the charge to income tax at the higher rate or additional rate (there is no top-slicing relief if the taxpayer is only a basic rate taxpayer). The surplus on the policy is divided by the number of complete policy years (ending on the anniversary of the policy) that the policy has been held. For policies issued (broadly) on or after 6 April 2013, if the gain is reduced through non-UK residence (see **40.7**), the number of complete policy years is reduced by the number of complete years consisting wholly of days on non-UK residence in the relevant period.

The amount arrived at is treated as the top slice of income to ascertain the tax rate, which is then applied to the full profit. The amount chargeable is the excess of higher rate tax over the basic rate of 20%. The longer the policy has been held the smaller the annual equivalent on which the tax charge is based.

It might be possible to avoid paying higher rate tax on the bond profit by taking steps to reduce taxable income. Note, however, that a gift aid donation to charity does *not* reduce taxable income for top-slicing purposes.

Top-slicing relief is only available when paying tax above basic rate. Chargeable event gains arising during a period of temporary non-residence (**41.49**) are treated as income of the individual for the year of return.

Second-hand life policies

[40.9] When a life policy is assigned, the assignee may have an income tax liability as in 40.5 to 40.8 if the policy proceeds exceed the premiums paid. In addition, an assignee who receives a policy as a gift is subject to the capital gains rules if *someone else* has previously purchased the policy. (There is an exception for consideration paid by one spouse or civil partner to the other, or paid in connection with a divorce or dissolution of civil partnership, or on an intra-group transfer). The assignee will be deemed under the normal capital gains rules to have acquired the policy at open market value. Furthermore, the loss allowable for capital gains tax cannot be greater than the loss actually incurred by comparing the assignee's proceeds and cost. The assignee might still have an income tax liability on the difference between the amount of the premiums paid by the original policy holder to the insurance company and the assignee's disposal proceeds.

Transferring shares in life policies (ITTOIA 2005, ss 498–514)

[40.10] Where a life policy is changed from joint to single names or vice versa, such as in marriage or divorce settlements, or forming or dissolving civil partnerships, no tax is payable if a share in a policy is transferred for no consideration, nor do the chargeable events rules apply to assignments between spouses or civil partners living together or to the transfer of rights under a court order as part of a divorce/dissolution settlement.

Trust policies

[40.11] Where a life policy matures on the death of the person who took it out, and that person remained the beneficial owner, the policy proceeds are included in his estate for inheritance tax.

Where, under a lifetime trust created before 22 March 2006, someone is entitled as of right to the trust income (i.e. he has an interest in possession), the trust fund itself is regarded as belonging to that person for inheritance tax purposes (see **42.23**).

If, therefore, an individual has taken out such a policy on his own life in trust for, say, his children, the policy is treated as belonging to them, and, when the proceeds are received by the trustees, there is no inheritance tax charge because the children have held an interest in the trust fund throughout, which now comprises cash instead of a life policy. Nor is there any inheritance tax when the trustees pay the cash to the children, because the trust fund, embracing whatever was within it for the time being, was always regarded as belonging to them (the interest in possession).

> *Example 3*
>
> In 2004 a taxpayer took out a qualifying policy on his own life assuring £100,000 on his death and paid the first annual premium of £5,000. The policy was gifted

to trustees for the benefit of his son, but the taxpayer continues to pay the annual premiums of £5,000 out of his income. The effect is that (a) the gift of the annual premiums is covered by the IHT exemption for gifts out of income, and (b) the son will receive the eventual proceeds when the taxpayer dies without any tax charge whatsoever.

In the case of a married couple or civil partnership a policy will often have been written so that the proceeds do not arise until the second death. This enabled the survivor to take the whole of the deceased's estate at the first death without inheritance tax (because of the surviving spouse/civil partner exemption), with the liability to inheritance tax on the second death being covered by the policy proceeds in the hands of the policy beneficiaries.

This useful way of providing for an anticipated inheritance tax liability by putting funds in the hands of those who will inherit the estate has fallen foul of Finance Act 2006 changes relating to trusts, since interest in possession trusts created in lifetime on or after 22 March 2006 are not excluded from the mainstream inheritance tax rules unless they provide for the future disability of the settlor. Hence any new arrangements would be within the mainstream inheritance tax rules, albeit with the policy proceeds still outside the estate of the deceased (because he never had an interest in the policy). HMRC indicated that straightforward policies in place at 22 March 2006 should not be affected, despite premiums to maintain the policy having been paid after that date. Insurance companies are always considering the consequences of changing legislation and how they might adapt their products to provide sensible inheritance tax protection. Whatever future changes are made, the principle of providing a lump sum outside the estate by means of suitable life cover enabled by affordable premiums within normal expenditure or the annual £3,000 exemption still holds good (see CHAPTER 42 for current trust rules).

The rules for charging income tax on gains on non-qualifying policies outlined at **40.5** apply to life policies held in trust, but they are taxed on the settlor if he is UK resident. If the settlor is either dead or non-resident when the gain is made or the gain arises in the overseas part of a split year (**41.6**), but there are UK resident trustees, the gains are taxed on the trustees. If the trustees are non-resident, UK beneficiaries are taxed as and when they receive benefits from the trust funds under the anti-avoidance rules re transferring assets abroad (as to which see **45.27**).

Where a life policy is held in a bare trust for a minor, HMRC take the view that minors who have an absolute entitlement to trust income and capital have unimpaired beneficial ownership of the life insurance policies held under a bare trust. Therefore the beneficiaries, rather than the settlor, are taxable on any gains arising. However, where the child's parents are settlors of the bare trust, the parents may still be taxable on the gains under the settlements legislation (see **42.15**).

Specially adapted trust policies

[40.12] There are several tailor-made insurance products which are aimed at mitigating inheritance tax liabilities whilst giving financial comfort in the meantime. These are very specialised areas requiring advice in each case from appropriately qualified advisers, with the insurance companies themselves providing helpful explanatory literature and guidance. Here again the provisions of Finance Act 2006 caused insurance companies to reconsider what they were able to offer. Reference to their literature and expert views is essential in considering appropriate ways forward.

Endowment mortgages

[40.13] Endowment mortgages are a combination of a loan on which interest is paid, plus a qualifying life insurance policy which is intended to pay off the loan when it matures, although there have been very many instances recently where the policy proceeds have proved woefully inadequate. No capital repayments are made to the lender, so the interest cost never falls because of capital repaid. The profit element in the policy when it matures is not liable to tax.

If the mortgage is reduced because capital becomes available, or is repaid early, usually on change of residence, it is worth considering whether the existing insurance policy should be retained usually because to cash in the policy would have an adverse effect on its value. If the existing policy were surrendered and a new policy taken out to cover the whole borrowing, no life insurance relief would be available on the premiums and the comparative cost would be higher because of the individual's increased age.

If the early surrender causes the rules for qualifying policies to be breached, tax may be payable (see **40.2**).

Any compensation received because a qualifying policy is held to have been mis-sold is not liable to income tax or capital gains tax, although any interest element included in such a compensation package is normally taxable as savings income under general principles.

Pension mortgages

[40.14] Some lenders will grant mortgages or loans with no capital repayments, but with an undertaking that the borrowing will eventually be repaid out of the capital sum received from a pension fund (see CHAPTERS **16** and **17**), the borrowing in the meantime being covered by appropriate life insurance. The lender cannot take a legal charge on the pension fund, but the borrower can give an undertaking to use the lump sum from the fund to discharge the loan.

The effect is that tax relief at the borrower's various marginal rates while building up his pension fund is obtained on the capital repayment since the fund used to make the repayment has resulted from pension contributions upon which the tax relief has been obtained at the time of payment. Unless these arrangements are part of an overall plan to provide adequately for retirement, it must be remembered that part of the money that was intended to finance retirement will be used to pay off a mortgage.

Friendly societies (FA 2012, ss 150–179)

[40.15] Whereas the profits of other life insurance companies are taxable, the profits of friendly societies arising from life or endowment business are generally exempt from income tax and corporation tax. The exemption applies where the premiums in respect of the policies issued by the friendly society, generally assuring up to about £2,500 over a ten-year term, do not exceed £270 a year, or the annuities which they grant do not exceed £156 a year.

Policies taken out by children under 18 qualify for the exemption and payment of the premiums by a parent does not contravene the income tax rules about parental gifts (see 33.10); there is therefore no tax charge on the parent.

The society's tax exemption gives an added advantage to a qualifying policy with a registered friendly society, although the restrictions on premiums and annuities limit the scope accordingly and as with all life assurance products the society's operating charges may significantly reduce the benefit of the tax exemption.

Friendly societies are able to offer their insurance policies within the stocks and shares component of ISAs (see 36.16 onwards).

Where, on or after 17 July 2007, a friendly society transfers its business to a life insurance company, any of its policies that are tax-exempt will retain their exempt status, providing there is no increase in premiums. The life insurance company will not, however, be able to issue any new tax-exempt policies.

Demutualisation

[40.16] If an insurance company demutualises, and as a result investors receive either free shares or cash or a mixture of the two, the tax treatment depends on the circumstances. There will usually be no immediate tax consequences on the issue of free shares, which will have a nil cost. Cash payments to compensate members for loss of membership rights are not treated as 'unauthorised payments' under the pension regime that came into effect on 6 April 2006. Cash payments are, however, chargeable to capital gains tax. Gains may be covered by the annual exemption (currently £11,300) if it is not used elsewhere.

See HMRC's Tax Bulletin 34 of April 1998, where it is stated that building society windfall payments made to joint holders are treated as received equally, with the gain being divided between the joint holders (even though such payments were made only to the first-named holder). Presumably the same treatment will apply to any other insurance windfall payments.

Group policies (ITTOIA 2005, ss 480–483)

[40.17] It is sometimes commercially sensible and convenient to insure a group of lives within one policy, e.g. a number of borrowers. Gains on such policies which provide only death benefits are generally exempt from a tax charge.

Gains on policies held by charitable and non-charitable trusts

[40.18] Gains on life policies held by charitable trusts are treated as the trustees' gains, liable to tax at the basic rate of 20%. Gains accruing to non-charitable trusts are taxed on the trustees if no other person is liable, and sums lent to trustees by or at the direction of the insurer are deemed to be part surrenders equal to the amount of the loan.

Compensation scheme

[40.19] If an insurance company goes out of business, compensation may be payable under the terms of the Financial Services Compensation Scheme (FSCS). Guidance is available at www.fscs.org.uk. HM Treasury have authority to make regulations in connection with how taxes apply after an intervention by the FSCS in relation to insurance contracts.

Tax points

[40.20] Note the following:

- While there is no tax relief on premiums on life insurance policies taken out after 13 March 1984, trustees of a pension fund may take out life cover on the lives of the beneficiaries so as to produce sufficient liquidity within the fund as to enable lump sum benefits to be paid upon death in service (see **16.37**).
- A policy on an individual's own life forms part of his estate unless the benefits are payable direct to others. Proceeds falling within the estate will increase inheritance tax payable, and moreover will not be available until a grant of probate or administration has been obtained. A policy on an individual's life for the benefit of someone else will escape tax in the individual's estate if the arrangements are outside Finance Act 2006 mainstream inheritance tax rules for trusts. The policy monies will be available to the beneficiary on production of the death certificate and appropriate claim form.
- A wide range of methods of investing through life insurance and purchased annuities is on offer by the various life insurance companies who are constantly reviewing their products to ensure continued tax efficiency. An arrangement can often be tailored to specific requirements. Specialist advice is essential.
- A single premium bond can be a simple and convenient way of investing without the need for any complex records such as those required when investing on the Stock Exchange.

- Bonds are also a convenient way to get into and out of the property market by choice of appropriate funds, and it is possible to give away one of a series of property fund supported bonds much more easily than giving land itself, with no inheritance tax charge if the gift is covered by exemptions, or if the donor survives for seven years after making the gift.

- Many people with endowment mortgages may be considering surrendering their policies because of concerns as to whether sufficient will be realised to pay off the mortgage. The tax consequences need to be taken into account if the surrender is within ten years (or within three-quarters of the term if less). Care also needs to be taken with selling the policy on the open market, because the same tax consequences will occur if the sale is within that period.

- There is no magic way of paying school fees. Sensible use of the types of life insurance contracts mentioned in this chapter will help, but early planning is essential, and contracts should be taken out soon after the child is born.

- An insurance company may rebate commission to investors, net it off against the premium, or invest it on the investors' behalf. The rebated commission does not count as income for tax purposes. See **40.5**, however, for anti-avoidance provisions in relation to rebated or reinvested commission.

Part IX

Miscellaneous

41

The overseas element

Overview

[41.1] Today's global business environment presents many challenges for personal and business taxpayers wishing to manage their tax affairs effectively, making use of available reliefs and avoiding 'double taxation'. At the same time, governments are keen to protect against loss of revenue through tax evasion and avoidance.

The treatment of the overseas aspects of the tax affairs of individuals and companies is complex, and this chapter gives no more than a brief overview of the various provisions.

Professional advice is likely to be essential for UK resident individuals who are eligible for the 'remittance basis' of taxation for foreign income and gains. The remittance basis provisions are lengthy and complex, and a very brief summary is provided at **41.16, 41.17**.

From 6 April 2013 a statutory residence test (**41.5**) was introduced, replacing the former rules which were based largely on HMRC guidance and court decisions. The test is designed to give taxpayers greater certainty and clarity as to whether or not they are UK-resident for tax purposes and therefore whether or not they are subject to UK income tax and capital gains tax. Again the provisions are complex and in many situations professional advice will be needed, although HMRC do provide useful guidance on their website.

This chapter focuses on the tax position of individuals but matters relevant to companies (see **41.57**) and trusts (see **41.85**) are outlined briefly.

HMRC's have published Statement of Practice SP 1/11 which describes the UK's practice in relation to methods for reducing or preventing double taxation.

Persons affected

[41.2] There are two main aspects to the overseas element — the tax treatment of UK-resident individuals and companies with income or assets abroad, and the tax treatment of non-resident (or non-UK domiciled) individuals and non-resident companies with income or assets in the UK. The overseas element also affects the taxation of trusts, see **41.85** to **41.88**.

The tax liability determined under domestic tax law may be affected by double taxation relief, so the relevant double tax agreement needs to be looked at to see if the tax treatment is varied under the provisions of the UK's agreement with the country concerned. Double taxation agreements normally provide for the profits of a trade to be taxed only in the country of the taxpayer's residence, unless there is a 'permanent establishment' (defined, broadly, as a fixed place of business or an agency) in the other country. In relation to electronic commerce, HMRC's view is that websites and servers do not of themselves constitute permanent establishments.

Determination of liability

[41.3] An individual's liability to UK tax depends on whether he is resident and domiciled in the UK. A statutory residence test (**41.5**) applies to determine residence. A company's tax liability also depends on its residence (**41.57**).

HMRC have the power to obtain relevant tax information from taxpayers and third parties in order to counter tax evasion, and for such information to be exchanged with tax authorities from jurisdictions with which the UK has made a double taxation agreement or a tax information exchange agreement. EU member states provide mutual assistance in collecting taxes, and one state may require another to take proceedings to recover taxes owed to its tax authority. An EU Savings Directive requires paying agents to report details of savings income payments made to certain non-residents. See also CHAPTER 45 regarding anti-avoidance provisions.

Administration

[41.4] If a person leaves the UK permanently or indefinitely they are asked to complete form P85 (Leaving the United Kingdom), available at www.hmrc.gov.uk/cnr/p85.pdf. This applies both to UK citizens leaving the UK and non-UK citizens leaving the UK after completing a work assignment here.

UK resident individuals: determination and effect of residence

Residence: 2013–14 onwards (FA 2013, s 218 and Sch 45)

[41.5] The statutory residence test was introduced by Finance Act 2013 and applies for 2013–14 onwards. Note though that transitional rules may apply such that the pre 2013–14 residence rules (41.7) apply until 2015–16. Broadly, these transitional rules will affect individuals that were not ordinarily resident at the end of 2012–13 where that year was the first, second or third year of residence.

The tests to determine residency are complex and professional advice is advisable. HMRC guidance can be found at www.hmrc.gov.uk/international/residence.htm. In particular detailed guidance on the statutory residence test can be found at www.gov.uk/government/publications/rdr3-statutory-residence-test-srt.

The first part of the test is an 'automatic overseas test'. The automatic overseas test sets out factors which, if they are met, prove that a taxpayer is conclusively non-resident. If the individual is not conclusively non-resident, it is then necessary to consider the automatic residence test, which sets out factors which prove someone is definitely UK-resident. If neither the automatic overseas or residence test are met, it is still necessary to establish whether a person has 'significant ties' with the UK such that they can be considered UK resident.

Automatic overseas test

An individual is automatically non-UK resident if he meets one of the following conditions during the relevant tax year:

(a)   he spends fewer than 16 days in the UK in that year, does not die during the year, and was resident for one or more of the three tax years immediately preceding that year;

(b)   he spends fewer than 46 days in the UK in that year and was resident for none of the three tax years immediately preceding that year;

(c)   he works, on average, 35 hours a week overseas for that year without a significant break from work, has fewer than 31 UK work days in that year, and spends fewer than 91 days in the UK in that year. A UK work day is a day in which more than three hours' work in the UK is done;

(d)   he dies during the year and spends fewer than 46 days in the UK in that year, and either he was non-resident for the two tax years immediately preceding the tax year in which he dies or was non-resident for the tax year immediately preceding that tax year and the tax year before that was a split year (41.6);

(e)   he dies during a tax year, having already been non-resident under (c) above for the two preceding tax years (or for the year preceding the current tax year, with the year before that qualifying for Case 1 split year treatment (41.6)), and he meets test (c) as modified to reflect the fact that he has died during the tax year.

Automatic residence test

An individual will meet the automatic residence test if none of the automatic overseas tests ((a)–(e) above) are met and he:

(i)   spends at least 183 days in the UK; or

(ii)   has a home in the UK during all or part of the year, spends at least 30 days (not necessarily consecutively) in this home in a year and during any 91-day period (of which at least 30 days must be in the relevant tax year) he has no overseas home or if he has an overseas home he spends less than 30 days there in the tax year. If the individual has more than one home in the UK, this test must be applied to each of those homes individually; or

(iii)   works 'full time' in the UK. To satisfy this test more than 75% of the individual's working days in a 365-day period must be UK work days. A UK work day is a day in which more than three hours' work in the UK is done; or

(iv)   dies in the relevant tax year, having been resident in the UK for the past three years by virtue of meeting one of conditions (i)–(iii) above, the year before his death not being a split year (**41.6**) and when he died he had a home in the UK.

Significant ties test

If an individual meets none of the automatic UK residence tests and none of the automatic overseas tests, he will still be resident if he has sufficient UK ties. There are five UK ties that must be considered:

•   a family tie — a spouse, civil partner, co-habitee or child under 18 years of age that is UK resident;

•   an accommodation tie — a place to live in the UK and that place is available to the individual for a continuous period of 91 days or more during the tax year;

•   a work tie — more than three hours' work a day in the UK on at least 40 different days in the tax year;

•   a 90-day tie — spends more than 90 days in the UK in either or both of the two tax years immediately preceding the year in question; and

•   a country tie — the country the individual is in at midnight for the greatest number of days in the year in question is the UK.

If an individual was resident in the UK for one or more of the three tax years preceding the tax year in question, he will have sufficient UK ties in accordance with the following table:

Days spent in UK in relevant tax year	Number of ties that are sufficient
More than 15 but not more than 45	At least 4
More than 45 but not more than 90	At least 3
More than 90 but not more than 120	At least 2
More than 120	At least 1

If an individual was UK resident in the UK for none of the three tax years preceding the tax year in question, he will have sufficient UK ties in accordance with the following table:

Days spent in UK in relevant tax year	Number of ties that are sufficient
More than 45 but not more than 90	All 4
More than 90 but not more than 120	At least 3
More than 120	At least 2

These rules are modified slightly if an individual dies during the tax year in question.

For all of the above tests, a UK day means UK presence at midnight, with the exception of UK in-transit days where the individual leaves the UK on the following day and does not engage in activities substantially unrelated to their passage through the UK. The facts in each case will be important, as HMRC will consider whether the individual enjoyed the benefit of being in the UK (for example, going to the theatre would not be acceptable). Doing any work at all, including reviewing emails, is unrelated to an individual's passage through the UK and will result in a day spent in the UK.

Split year treatment: 2013–14 onwards

[41.6] Although strictly an individual is either resident or non-resident for the whole of a tax year, the tax year can be split (so that an individual is regarded as either resident in the UK from the day of arrival or non-UK resident from the day after departure) if their circumstances fall within any of Cases 1 to 8. Cases 1 to 3 deal, broadly, with individuals going abroad. Cases 4 to 8 deal, broadly, with individuals coming to either work or live in the UK.

Case 1

An individual will fall within Case 1 for a tax year if they were UK resident for the previous tax year, are non-resident for the following tax year because they meet the third automatic overseas test (see **41.5**), work on average 35 hours a week overseas (without a significant break) and keep days in the UK within permitted limits over a period to the end of the year.

Case 2

An individual will fall within Case 2 for a tax year if they were UK resident for the previous tax year, are non-resident for the following tax year and have a partner who falls within Case 1 for the relevant year or the previous tax year and the individual has left the UK to join his/her partner so they can continue to live together while the partner is working overseas. After their departure the taxpayer must either have no UK home or, if they have homes in both the UK and overseas, must spend the greater part of the time living in the overseas home.

Case 3

An individual will fall within Case 3 for a tax year if they were UK resident for the previous tax year, are non-resident for the following tax year, and at the start of the tax year had at least one home in the UK but at some point in that year they cease to have any UK home and this continues until the end of that year.

Case 4

An individual will fall within Case 4 if he was non-resident for the previous tax year and, at the start of the tax year, he did not have his only home in the UK, but during the year he did and he then continues to have his only home in the UK for the rest of the tax year.

Case 5

An individual will fall within Case 5 if they were non-resident for the previous tax year and are coming to work in the UK in circumstances such that they meet the third automatic UK residency test (see **41.5**).

Case 6

An individual will fall within Case 6 if they were non-resident for the previous tax year because they met the third automatic non-UK residency test (see **41.5**), are UK resident for the following tax year (whether or not it is a split year) and satisfy the overseas work criteria for a period from the beginning of the year. The overseas work criteria require the taxpayer to have worked an average of 35 hours a week overseas (without a significant break) and to have kept days in the UK within permitted limits over a period to the end of the year.

Case 7

An individual will fall within Case 7 if they were non-resident for the previous tax year, are UK resident for the following tax year (whether or not it is a split year) and have a partner whose circumstances fall within Case 6 for the previous tax year or the relevant year and the taxpayer moves to the UK so that the taxpayer and partner can continue to live together. In addition, for the part of the year before the deemed arrival date, the taxpayer must either have no UK home or, if they have homes in both the UK and overseas, must spend the greater part of the time living in the overseas home.

Case 8

An individual will fall within Case 8 if they were non-resident for the previous tax year, are UK resident for the following tax year (whether or not it is a split year) and from the point at which the taxpayer starts to have a home in the UK, they continue to do so for the rest of the tax year and all of the following tax year.

Residence: pre 2013–14 (ITA 2007, ss 829–833; TCGA 1992, s 9)

[41.7] The provisions in this paragraph and **41.8** to **41.9** generally apply for tax years before 2012–13. Note though that transitional rules may apply such that these rules apply until 2015–16. Broadly, these transitional rules will affect individuals that were not ordinarily resident at the end of 2012–13 where that year was the first, second or third year of residence. Further, if it is necessary to determine for the tax year 2013–14 or any subsequent year whether a tax year before 2013–14 was a split year, the pre April 2013 rules will apply.

Residence usually requires physical presence in a country. An individual will always be regarded as resident in the UK if he is physically present here for 183 days or more in the tax year. The residence status of a spouse or partner is determined separately. An individual can be resident in more than one country for tax purposes.

Ordinary residence is taken to be broadly equivalent to habitual residence. HMRC consider that the word 'ordinary' indicates that residence in the UK is 'typical and not casual'. It is therefore possible to be regarded as remaining resident and ordinarily resident in the UK despite a temporary absence abroad, or it is possible to be resident but not ordinarily resident here.

Strictly an individual is either resident or non-resident for the whole of a tax year, but by HMRC concession A11 a tax year may be split for income tax purposes into resident and non-resident periods as indicated in **41.8**. (HMRC have however specifically stated that this split year treatment does not apply from 2011–12 onwards when computing liability to UK tax in respect of flexible drawdown pensions (**16.21**) which arise during a part of the year in which a UK resident individual would otherwise be treated as not being 'resident' due to this concession). There is also a similar concession for capital gains tax, see **41.48**.

In the event of a dispute regarding residence status it is possible to request a review by an HMRC officer other than the one who made the decision, or ask for an independent appeal tribunal to hear an appeal (see **1.6**).

An individual is treated as spending a day in the UK, in calculating days spent here to determine residence status, if he is present here at midnight at the end of that day. This is subject to an exception for passengers in transit between two places outside the UK.

Leaving the UK: pre 2013–14

[41.8] Although strictly an individual is either resident or non-resident for the whole of a tax year, by virtue of concession A11, the tax year can be split (so that an individual is regarded as not resident and not ordinarily resident in the UK from the day after departure) if an individual leaves the UK for:

(a)   full-time service under a contract of employment abroad and both the absence from the UK and the employment itself span a complete tax year; or

(b)   permanent residence abroad. HMRC must be notified if leaving the UK 'permanently or indefinitely'. Their guidance says 'By leaving the UK "permanently" we mean that you are leaving the country to live abroad and will not return here to live. By leaving "indefinitely" we mean that you are leaving to live abroad for a long time (at least three years) but you acknowledge that you might eventually return to live here.'

In both situations, return visits to the UK must amount to less than 183 days in any tax year and average less than 91 days a tax year.

HMRC consider that links with the UK that continue after leaving the country may mean that an individual remains resident or ordinarily resident here. Residence may be affected by several factors, including the reason for leaving the UK, the visits made to the UK after departure, and connections that are kept in the UK, e.g. 'family, property, business and social connections'. Evidence will usually be required by HMRC to demonstrate non-residence.

If an individual accompanies a spouse or civil partner who goes abroad to work full-time (but does not work full-time himself), his liability for the tax years in which he leaves and returns is based on the time spent in the UK in each year, in the same way as for the employed spouse or civil partner, providing the absence spans a complete tax year and subject to the same rules for intervening UK visits (concession A78).

Arriving in the UK: pre 2013–14

[41.9] Although strictly an individual is either resident or non-resident for the whole of a tax year, by virtue of concession A11, the tax year can be split (so that an individual is regarded as resident in the UK from the day of arrival) where an individual comes to live in the UK permanently or to stay for at least two years. This treatment might be revised if circumstances change and the UK stay is in fact short-term.

In all other situations HMRC will regard individuals as either 'short-term visitors' or 'longer-term visitors', depending on the circumstances. A short-term visitor is someone who is not going to remain in the UK for an 'extended period' and will visit for limited periods in one or more tax years. A longer-term visitor is someone who has not come to the UK permanently, but has come here indefinitely or for an 'extended period' which might cover several tax years. Such visitors will fall to be treated as resident in the UK if they are physically present here for 183 days or more in the tax year and will be regarded as resident in the UK from the beginning of the relevant tax year.

Domicile (ITA 2007, s 835BA)

[41.10] Domicile is relevant only if an individual has non-UK income or gains. It is not the same as nationality, and unlike residence for tax purposes it is possible to have only one domicile at any one time. An individual's domicile is usually the country in which he has his permanent home. A domicile of origin is acquired at birth, and under UK law this is normally the father's domicile (or the mother's domicile where the parents are not married).

An individual will be UK domiciled for income tax and capital gains tax purposes if:

(a)   he was born in the UK (i.e. domicile of origin);

(b)   from 6 April 2017, he had been resident in the UK for at least 15 out of the past 20 tax years immediately preceding the year of transfer; or

(c)   from 6 April 2017, he returns to the UK to become UK resident, having had a UK domicile at birth but later emigrated and acquired a foreign domicile.

An individual will be UK domiciled for inheritance tax purposes if:

(i)   he was UK domiciled within the three years immediately preceding the transfer;

(ii)   from 6 April 2017, he was resident in the UK for at least 15 out of the past 20 tax years immediately preceding the relevant year *and* at least one of the four tax years ending with the relevant year. Prior to 6 April 2017, the requirement was that he was resident in the UK for at least 17 out of the past 20 years ending with the relevant year; or

(iii)   from 6 April 2017, he returns to the UK to become UK resident, having had a UK domicile at birth but later emigrated and acquired a foreign domicile.

The domicile tests introduced from 6 April 2017 above are commonly referred to as the deemed domicile tests and were legislated for in the September 2017 Finance Bill, which is expected to receive Royal Assent in November 2017. These changes mean that from 6 April 2017, the domicile rules for income tax, capital gains tax and inheritance tax are broadly aligned.

It is worth noting that for IHT purposes an individual will only need to leave the UK and remain non-UK resident for four consecutive UK tax years to lose their deemed UK domicile for IHT purpose.

It is possible to acquire a new domicile of choice. This necessitates positive action, e.g. settling in a different country and making a will under the law of the new country. A high standard of proof is required to establish a change of domicile. This is a difficult area where professional advice is recommended. Domicile has no relevance for companies except in very limited circumstances.

Effect of residence and domicile

Income tax

[41.11] UK resident individuals are charged to income tax, broadly, on their worldwide income, subject to certain deductions (e.g. a foreign earnings deduction for seafarers) and special rules for individuals who are not domiciled in the UK.

UK resident individuals are normally charged on the full amount of foreign income arising abroad, whether it is brought into the UK or not (the 'arising basis'). However, if an individual is resident in the UK, but not domiciled here, he may choose to be taxed either on the arising basis (see **41.15**) or on the 'remittance basis' (see **41.16**), which taxes UK income as it arises but taxes foreign income only as it is brought into the UK. The remittance basis must be claimed, except in some circumstances.

Capital gains tax

[41.12] Different rules apply for capital gains tax, as follows:

(a)   individuals who are resident in the UK and have a UK domicile — liable to capital gains tax on gains arising anywhere in the world; or

(b)   individuals who are resident in the UK but have a domicile elsewhere —
        may be taxed either on the arising basis or on the remittance basis,
        which taxes UK gains as they arise but taxes foreign gains only as they
        are brought into the UK (see **41.16**).

If a year is a split year (**41.6** or **41.8** prior to 2013–14), gains accruing during
the overseas part of the year are not chargeable to capital gains tax unless the
non-resident CGT rules outlined at **41.50** apply or, on a later return to the UK,
liability is established under the temporary non-residence rules outlined at
41.49 or the gains are realised through a UK branch or agency carried on by
the non-resident.

Inheritance tax

[41.13] Residence has no bearing on inheritance tax (except in relation to the
extended meaning of 'domicile', see **5.2**). Inheritance tax applies to worldwide
property if an individual is domiciled in the UK and to UK property only if an
individual is domiciled elsewhere. Holdings in authorised unit trusts and
open-ended investment companies (see **38.27** to **38.29**) are, however, not liable
to inheritance tax for people who are not domiciled in the UK. In addition, the
switching of UK assets in a trust settled by a non-UK domiciled individual, to
investments in open-ended investment companies and authorised unit trusts, is
exempt from inheritance tax.

Owning property abroad may lead to problems on death because foreign
probate may be required before the assets can be dealt with by the executors.
For jointly held assets this will normally occur only on the second death,
because the ownership normally passes by survivorship to the other joint
owner. The costs involved should be borne in mind when considering investing
abroad.

VAT

[41.14] As far as VAT is concerned, when returning from a non-EU country,
it is possible to bring personal possessions into the UK free of VAT and
Customs duty providing the individual has been abroad for at least a year, paid
VAT or duty on the items abroad and has owned and used them for at least six
months prior to returning to the UK. When returning from an EU country,
VAT will have been paid abroad when purchasing the possessions, except for
new motor vehicles, ships, aircraft, etc., on which UK VAT must be paid on
returning to the UK.

UK resident individuals: basis of charge for foreign income and gains (ITTOIA 2005, ss 574–689, 829–845; ITA 2007, ss 809A–809Z7; TCGA 1992, s 12; FA 2013, s 218 and Sch 45)

Arising basis

[41.15] Income and gains accruing to UK residents are taxed on the arising basis (i.e. taxed on the full amount of foreign income arising abroad, whether it is brought into the UK or not) where an individual is not eligible for, or does not claim, the remittance basis outlined at **41.16**. In general, where income arises to a UK resident in the overseas part of a split year (**41.6** or **41.8** prior to 2013–14) it is treated as arising to a non-UK resident.

Where the arising basis applies, tax on foreign income (other than the profits of a foreign business) is charged on the income arising in the current tax year. Where a business is carried on wholly abroad, tax is charged according to the same rules as for UK businesses, i.e. generally on the profits of the accounting period ending in the tax year.

Income that is locked into a foreign country is treated as not arising until it can be brought to the UK (but as and when it can be extracted, it is taxable at that time whether or not it is in fact brought to the UK).

See **41.21** for the treatment of certain specific sources of income.

Remittance basis

[41.16] If an individual is resident in the UK but is not domiciled here, income and gains arising abroad may be taxed on the remittance basis rather than the arising basis — in other words the income and gains arising abroad are charged to tax if and when they are remitted to the UK. It is possible to also make an election to obtain relief for foreign losses in certain situations.

The remittance basis applies automatically in some cases, but in other situations it must be claimed. The remittance basis applies automatically (to otherwise eligible individuals) if:

(a)   their unremitted foreign income and gains are less than £2,000 in a tax year; or

(b)   they have no UK income or gains (other than taxed investment income of £100 or less), do not remit any foreign income or gains to the UK, and are either under 18 or have been UK resident in not more than six of the previous nine tax years. In these circumstances such individuals also retain entitlement to personal allowances and the capital gains tax annual exemption. (This rule ensures that an individual does not have to complete a self-assessment return only so that they may claim the remittance basis and then have no tax to pay.) As a consequence of the introduction of the savings allowance and the savings nil rate, from 6 April 2016 there is no longer a requirement for banks, building societies and some other institutions to deduct tax from the interest and other returns they make on certain savings income (see **2.9**). This means that such income no longer falls within the definition of 'taxed investment income' and consequently, from 6 April 2016, individuals who receive such income may no longer be eligible for automatic application of the remittance basis.

The remittance basis must be claimed in all other cases and if it is not claimed the individual will be liable to UK tax on the arising basis. Individuals are able to opt in and out of the remittance basis from year to year, and choosing the arising basis in one year does not preclude claiming the remittance basis in a future year.

If an individual is taxed on the remittance basis but is temporarily non-resident (**41.49**) foreign income and gains remitted to the UK during the period of non-residence are treated as being remitted to the UK in the period of return. If an individual is taxed on the remittance basis but the year is a split year (**41.6**), any gains are taxed according to which part (overseas part or UK part) in which they arise. Therefore, foreign gains arising to a remittance basis user in the overseas part of a split year of residence and remitted in the UK part of the year are not charged to tax. There are complex rules to decide whether or not income or other sums are being remitted.

If a claim for the remittance basis is made, a 'remittance basis charge' or RBC (an annual tax charge) will need to be paid. The charge levied depends upon how long the claimant has been resident in the UK, as follows:

(a)   £30,000 if the claimant has been UK resident in at least seven of the previous nine tax years;

(b)   £60,000 if the claimant has been UK resident in at least 12 of the previous 14 tax years.

Prior to 6 April 2017, there was also an additional charge of £90,000 if the claimant had been resident in at least 17 of the previous 20 tax years. This charge was repealed from 6 April 2017 by the September 2017 Finance Bill, which is expected to receive Royal Assent in November 2017. The reason for the repeal was simply that it was no longer needed on the grounds that, from 6 April 2017, individuals who have been UK resident for 15 of the previous 20 tax years will be deemed to be UK domiciled and therefore not eligible to claim the remittance basis of taxation.

If a claim is made for the remittance basis for a tax year, and the individual has at least £2,000 of unremitted foreign income and gains, it is not possible to use the income tax personal allowance, married couple's allowance, blind person's allowance, or the capital gains tax annual exemption. This rule is subject to an exception for certain 'dual residents' of the UK and a number of specified countries that have particular provisions in their double tax agreements.

Individuals are required to nominate an amount of their foreign income or gains for each tax year in which they are liable to pay the annual RBC. The RBC is then collected by taxing this nominated amount on an arising basis for the relevant year. (The amount of nominated income or gains should give rise to a tax charge of £30,000 or £60,000 as appropriate on the arising basis of taxation). When this income is actually remitted to the UK, no further tax charge will apply.

If an individual nominates an amount of income and gains which produce a charge of less than £30,000 or £60,000 (for example because they do not wish to disclose details of their unremitted income or gains to HMRC), they are treated as if they had nominated enough income to give rise to a £30,000 or £60,000 annual charge.

If foreign income is used to make a payment on account to HMRC (**9.4**) the foreign income is not treated as remitted to the UK if:

(i)   the tax year for which the payment on account is made (year 2) is one in which the individual is not liable to pay the RBC and it follows one where the individual was liable to pay the RBC; and

(ii)   an amount equal to the lower of the RBC charge and the foreign income used to make the payment on account is taken offshore by 15 March following the end of year 2, or such later date as may be agreed with HMRC, on the making of a claim.

Exceptions to the remittance basis

[41.17] There are a number of exemptions/reliefs available such that the remittance basis of taxation will not apply in certain circumstances, as summarised below. For HMRC guidance see www.gov.uk/government/public ations/residence-domicile-and-remittance-basis-rules-uk-tax-liability.

Exempt property relief (ITA 2007, ss 809X–809Z10)

[41.18] This relief permits an individual to bring property purchased out of unremitted foreign income and gains to the UK without being taxed on the remittance of those income and gains and applies where the property is:

(a)   a work of art, collectors' item or antique brought to the UK for the purposes of public display at an approved establishment;

(b)   an item of clothing, footwear, jewellery or watch for personal use;

(c)   brought to the UK for the purposes of repair or restoration;

(d)   imported into the UK temporarily for a period of no more than 275 days; or

(e)   worth less than £1,000.

When such property is subsequently sold in the UK, the remitted income and gains remain exempt from taxation under the remittance basis and any gain realised is treated as a foreign chargeable gain provided certain conditions are met, including the following:

(i)   the sale is to an independent third party;

(ii)   the entire sale proceeds are paid to the seller by the first anniversary of the 5 January following the tax year in which the sale takes place (whether they are paid in a series of instalments or in a single instalment); and

(iii)   the entire sale proceeds are either taken offshore or used to make a qualifying investment (i.e. buy newly issued shares in a private limited company or make a loan to a such a company and do not, as a result, receive any related benefit) within 45 days of the sale proceeds being paid to the seller. If payment is in instalments, within 45 days of the day on which each instalment is released.

If conditions (i)–(iii) are not met when the property is sold, it is treated as remitted to the UK at the time of sale. Similarly if the property ceases to be exempt because conditions (a)–(d) cease to apply, it will be treated as remitted to the UK at the time the condition no longer applies.

Compensation payments made for exempt property which has been lost, stolen or destroyed will not be treated as a remittance to the UK provided the payment is taken offshore or used to make a qualifying investment.

Notice can be given to HMRC in writing for this provision not to apply. The notice must be given on or before the first anniversary of the 31 January following the tax year in which the sale takes place, and by this date, is irrevocable.

Business investment relief (ITA 2007, ss 809VA–809VO; SI 2012/1898)

[41.19] Foreign income and gains which are brought to the UK are not taxed under the remittance basis if they are used for making a qualifying investment within the 'business investment relief' regime. An investment is qualifying if it is a share subscription or loan to an unlisted company, or one listed on exchange regulated markets, which carries out trading activities on a commercial basis or undertakes the development or letting of commercial property. The September 2017 Finance Bill (which is expected to receive Royal Assent in November 2017) extends these provisions from 6 April 2017 to permit business investment relief to be claimed by an investor on the acquisition of existing shares in a company.

There are specific anti-avoidance provisions to ensure the investment is made on proper commercial terms, including the requirement that the investment does not provide any related benefit.

Where a potentially chargeable event occurs (e.g. the company subsequently breaches the qualifying conditions, the investor disposes of the investment etc.), the affected income and gains are treated as having been remitted and are taxed accordingly. There is however a 45 or 90-day period of grace (depending upon the exact nature of the potentially chargeable event) before the charge applies. If, during this time, the relevant income or gains are taken offshore or re-invested in a qualifying investment the exemption from the remittance basis of taxation remains. This 45 or 90-day period of grace is extended where a potentially chargeable event occurs and the investor is not able to dispose of a holding of shares, either because the investment is subject to a lock-up agreement related to the listing of a company on a recognised stock exchange or because of a statutory or regulatory barrier.

Double taxation relief (ITA 2007, ss 29, 1026; TCGA 1992, s 277; TIOPA 2010, ss 2–145)

[41.20] Where the same income and gains are liable to tax in more than one country, relief from double taxation is given either under the provisions of a double tax agreement with the country concerned or unilaterally. The relief is calculated separately for each source of income or capital gains. There are anti-avoidance provisions to prevent manipulation of the double taxation rules, but they should not affect the majority of double tax relief claimants.

Where there is a double tax agreement, it may provide for certain foreign income and gains to be wholly exempt from UK tax. If not, UK tax is charged, but a claim may be made for a credit to be given against the UK tax for the lower of the overseas tax liability and the UK tax liability. Alternatively, a claim may be made to simply treat the foreign tax suffered as a deductible expense. As credit relief cannot exceed the amount of UK tax suffered on the foreign income it is generally only beneficial to make a claim to expense foreign tax, in a loss making situation. See **41.62** for an example.

UK paying and collecting agents do not deduct UK tax from foreign interest and dividends (see **41.32**). Taxpayers must therefore pay any amount by which the UK tax exceeds the foreign tax. If the foreign tax exceeds the UK tax, the double tax relief will be restricted to the amount of the UK tax.

As stated in **41.32**, UK taxpayers will sometimes receive interest in full from overseas paying agents in the EU and certain other countries. Alternatively, a special withholding tax may be deducted. In that event double tax relief may be claimed. The withholding tax will not be deducted if the UK taxpayer authorises the foreign paying agent to report information about the payments made or provides him with a certificate from HMRC.

Additional double tax relief is given for overlap profits arising when a business starts and on changes of accounting date, and the additional relief is recovered as and when overlap relief is given.

If the amount of foreign tax payable is later adjusted, the amount of double tax relief claimed is similarly adjusted. If an adjustment to foreign tax results in too much relief having been claimed, HMRC must be notified within one year after the adjustment.

Where credit is claimed for foreign tax and a payment is made either to the claimant or a connected person, the foreign tax relief will be restricted to the net amount.

UK resident individuals: specific sources of income/gains (ITEPA 2003, ss 573–576; ITTOIA 2005, s 402)

[41.21] Specific sources of income are subject to special rules. In particular employment income (see **41.22**), trading profits (see **41.28**), property income (**41.29** but see **32.47** regarding time shares), savings and investment income (**41.30**), pension income (**41.31**) and other miscellaneous items (**41.32**).

UK residents with earnings from employment abroad (ITEPA 2003, ss 15–41E, 44–47, 378–385; SI 1978/6189; SI 2003/2682; NICA 2014, s 12; NICA 2015, s 6)

[41.22] Non-residents escape UK tax on all overseas earnings. UK residents are liable to tax on earnings from employment both in the UK and abroad unless they are seafarers (see 41.26). Special rules apply to non-domiciled individuals becoming UK resident (41.23), artificially dividing the duties of a single employment into a UK and an overseas contract (41.24) and earnings attributable to the overseas part of a split year (41.25).

Offshore agencies

Anti-avoidance provisions apply when UK workers (and UK Continental Shelf workers) are employed by offshore companies or engaged by or through offshore employment intermediaries, as follows:

(a) if a worker is employed by or through an offshore intermediary: Where there is a UK agency in the contractual chain, the UK agency is responsible for operating PAYE and NICs. Where there is no UK agency in the contractual chain, the client the employed person works for is responsible for operating PAYE and NICs;

(b) if a person is employed on the UK Continental Shelf in the oil and gas industry by or through an offshore intermediary. In this situation, an associate company of the offshore employer is first made responsible for operating PAYE and NICs. If there is no onshore associate company then the licensee is made responsible for operating PAYE and NICs. If the offshore employer is correctly meeting all PAYE and NICs obligations on behalf of the licensee, then HMRC will issue a certificate exempting the licensee from their PAYE and NICs obligations. As long as this certificate is in force, the licensee cannot be pursued for any PAYE or NICs obligations.

If a company does not comply with the above requirements, the debt can be recovered from a person who was a director of the company at the relevant time. Anti-avoidance provisions apply to prevent third parties setting up structures to avoid NIC under these provisions which focus on the intention of the parties and the reduction (if any) in NIC payable. Penalties may apply to employment intermediaries for failure to comply with any record keeping requirements in certain situations; see 9.39. HMRC guidance can be found in their guidance note, 'NICs guidance for offshore employers in North Sea oil and gas industry' issued 9 September 2014.

For details of agency workers and PAYE generally see 10.2.

Non-residents becoming UK resident

[41.23] Individuals who come to the UK and become UK resident are able to benefit from a statutory 'overseas workday relief'. The relief is restricted to non-UK domiciles and is available for the tax year that they become UK resident and the following two tax years if they work partly in the UK and partly overseas. On the making of a claim, the overseas earnings are treated as foreign earnings and only taxed when they are remitted (**41.16**) to the UK. Overseas workday relief does not apply to an individual who is not resident in the UK. If an individual is non-UK resident, their overseas earnings are not taxable in the UK, even if they are remitted. If the tax year for which overseas workday relief is claimed is a split year (**41.6** or **41.8** prior to 2013–14) the relief will only apply to foreign earnings which relate to the UK part of the year.

Artificial use of dual contracts by non-domiciles

[41.24] UK resident non-domiciles are taxed on income that arises in respect of overseas employments according to the 'arising' basis if that income passes a series of tests to establish whether or not there has been an artificial separation of UK and overseas employments. The rules apply, broadly, by taking certain overseas earnings, income relating to employment-related securities and securities options and employment income provided through third parties, out of the scope of the remittance basis for UK resident non-domiciles where:

(a)   an individual has both a UK employment and one or more 'relevant' (i.e. foreign) employments;

(b)   the UK employer and the relevant employer are 'associated' with each other;

(c)   the UK employment and the relevant employment are 'related'; and

(d)   the foreign tax rate that applies to income in respect of a relevant employment, calculated in accordance with the amount of foreign tax credit relief which would be allowed against income tax if the income were not taxed on the remittance basis, is less than 65% of the UK's additional rate of tax (currently 45%).

The above provisions do not apply to overseas income that falls within the three-year period for overseas workday relief (**41.23**). HMRC guidance can be found at www.hmrc.gov.uk/international/dualcontracts.pdf.

Earnings during a split year

[41.25] From 6 April 2013, earnings of an individual who is UK resident that is attributable to the overseas part of a split year (**41.6**) are not charged to tax unless the earnings relate to duties performed in the UK or to overseas Crown employment that is subject to UK tax. Attribution of earnings between the two parts of the year is done on a just and reasonable basis.

Prior to 6 April 2013, if an individual's employment abroad was full time and both his absence from the UK and the employment abroad spanned a complete tax year, he could be treated by concession (see the conditions in **41.8**) as non-resident from the day after departure and as a new resident on return. Note that it was not the length of the absence but whether it spanned a tax year that was important. Therefore if, for example, an individual was working away from 1 April 2011 to 30 April 2012, a period of 13 months spanning a complete tax year, he would be non-resident for that period. However if he was working away from 1 July 2011 to 31 December 2012, a period of 18 months that does not span a complete tax year, he would remain UK resident throughout.

Seafarers (ITEPA 2003, ss 378–385)

[41.26] Seafarers are entitled to a deduction of 100% in respect of earnings abroad during a qualifying period of at least 365 days. This deduction is available to UK residents and EU and EEA resident seafarers. For details see EIM33011.

A qualifying period is one consisting either wholly of days of absence or of days of absence, linked by UK visits, where those visits do not exceed 183 consecutive days and also do not in total exceed one-half of the days in the period. A day counts as a day of absence if the individual is absent at the end of it, i.e. midnight.

If a seafarer who satisfies the 365-day qualifying period rules has both overseas earnings and UK earnings the 100% deduction is limited to a reasonable proportion of the earnings, having regard to the nature of the duties, and the time devoted to them, in the UK and overseas.

Duties performed on a ship that is engaged on a voyage beginning or ending outside the UK (but excluding any part of it beginning and ending in the UK), or engaged on a part beginning or ending outside the UK of any other voyage, are treated as performed outside the UK.

The 100% deduction also applies to earnings in a period of paid leave at the end of the employment, but if the paid leave is spent in the UK it cannot be counted as part of the 365-day qualifying period.

The 100% deduction is given where possible through the PAYE system, but where this is not possible the relief due is taken into account in the employee's self-assessment. It is claimed in the additional information pages and claimants are required to name the ships on which they have worked.

Travelling and board and lodging expenses (ITEPA 2003, ss 341, 342, 370, 371, 376)

[41.27] For an employee resident in the UK, the costs of travelling from and to the UK when taking up and ceasing an employment wholly abroad, and the costs of travelling between a UK employment and a foreign employment and between foreign employments, are allowed as a deduction from earnings. The costs of any number of outward and return journeys whilst serving abroad are also allowed so long as the expense is met by the employer (thus offsetting the tax charge on the employee in respect of the employer's expenditure). If the employer pays or reimburses the employee's board and lodging costs for an employment wholly abroad, the amount paid or reimbursed is also offset by an equivalent expenses allowance, but no deduction is given for board and lodging payments that an employee bears himself.

If an absence lasts for 60 days or more (not necessarily in one tax year) an employee can claim a deduction for the travelling expenses of two outward and two return journeys per person in any tax year for his or her spouse or civil partner and children (under 18 at the start of the journey) to visit him or her, but only where the travelling expenses are paid or reimbursed by the employer (so that the deduction offsets the benefits charge on the expenditure) and not where the employee bears them personally.

A round sum expenses allowance cannot be treated as payment or reimbursement of expenses by an employer, so care must be taken that the expenses are paid in a way that entitles the employee to an equivalent deduction.

Earned income from self-employment abroad (ITA 2007, s 95; ITTOIA 2005, ss 17, 92–94, 849–858; FA 2013, s 218 and Sch 45)

[41.28] Where a business is carried on wholly abroad, the expenses of travelling to and from it are allowed in computing profits. A deduction is also allowed for board and lodging expenses at any place where the trade is carried on and, where the trader's absence spans 60 days or more, for not more than two visits in any tax year by a spouse or civil partner and children (under 18 at the start of the journey). Expenses of travelling between an overseas business and another business carried on wholly or partly abroad are similarly allowable.

If a sole trader is resident in the UK, it would be highly unlikely for him to be able to show that his business was carried on *wholly* abroad. The main instance would be where he was only technically resident in the UK and normally lived and carried on the business abroad. If, exceptionally, that was the case, it would not make any difference to the calculation of his profits. If the business made a loss, however, the loss could be relieved only against the profits from the same or any other foreign business, and against foreign pensions and, if the trader was not domiciled in the UK, any employment earnings from a foreign employer.

As far as partners are concerned, the profit shares of UK resident partners include both UK profits and profits earned abroad. For a foreign-controlled partnership, this does not apply to a UK resident partner who is not domiciled in the UK. Such a partner is charged on the full amount of his share of UK profits, and on the part of his share of foreign profits that is remitted to the UK. (Non-resident partners are taxed on their shares of UK profits (see **41.40**)).

When someone carries on business wholly or partly abroad and there is a change of residence, he is treated as ceasing one business and starting another. This does not prevent the carry-forward of any losses before the change if they cannot otherwise be relieved. There is a change of residence if the individual becomes or ceases to be UK resident or if the tax year is a split year (**41.6** or **41.8** prior to 2013–14).

Class 4 NICs are not payable where the trader is non-resident in the UK (see **24.7**).

Income from overseas property (ITA 2007, ss 117–124; ITTOIA 2005, ss 265, 269, 328A, 328B, 465B; FA 2013, s 218 and Sch 45)

[41.29] If investment property is purchased abroad, the foreign rental income is calculated in a similar way to UK rental income (see CHAPTER 32). Profits and losses for all foreign let properties are aggregated, any overall profit being treated as the profits of an 'overseas property business'. The profit or loss for properties in different countries needs to be calculated separately, however, in order to calculate the amount of double tax relief available (see **41.20**). Allowable expenses include interest on borrowings to buy or improve the foreign property. If there is an overall loss, the rules at **32.9** apply, so that the loss is normally carried forward to set against the total foreign letting profits of later years.

Income from an overseas furnished holiday lettings business in the EEA has to be computed separately for the purposes of capital allowances, loss relief and relevant earnings for pension contributions. Property that forms a furnished holiday lettings business (in the UK or the EEA) is treated as trading income. For further details see **32.29**.

If an individual is UK resident but not UK domiciled and the remittance basis applies (see **41.16**), then the rental income will be chargeable only when it is remitted to the UK. If an individual is carrying on an overseas property business, in the case of a split year (**41.6** or **41.8** prior to 2013–14), tax is charged only on profits of the business that arise in the UK part of the year. Apportionment of profit between the two parts of the year is done on a just and reasonable basis.

Saving and investment income (ITTOIA 2005, ss 401C, 408A, 413A, 689A)

[41.30] Foreign savings income is taxed at the same rates as UK savings income (see **2.5**). Savings and investment income which arises to a UK resident individual in the overseas part of a split year (**41.6** or **41.8** prior to 2013–14) is treated as arising to a non-UK resident.

Special rules apply to UK distributions (including stock dividends) from a close company to a participator if:

(a)   they arose during a period of temporary non-residence (**41.49**) in a year for which the individual was UK resident; and

(b)   the UK charge was limited by the terms of a double taxation treaty.

Such dividends are taxed further in the year of return. The additional tax is calculated such that the overall tax paid is the amount that would have been paid if the individual had not been temporarily non-resident. Similar rules apply to distributions from a non-resident company which would be close if it were UK resident.

Pension income (ITEPA 2003, ss 394A, 572–579D, 642; TIOPA 2010, s 130A; FA 2017, s 3 and Sch 9)

[41.31] Foreign pensions are subject to UK tax. From 6 April 2017, 100% of foreign pension income is charged to tax. Prior to 6 April 2017, only 90% of such income arising was charged to tax . In the case of a split year (**41.6** or **41.8** prior to 2013–14), the taxable foreign pension income for the year is that arising in the UK part of the year. Certain foreign pensions are exempt from income tax, for example, pensions or annuities paid to victims of Nazi persecution; see HMRC Help Sheet HS310.

Where an individual is temporarily resident outside the UK (41.49), the following provisions apply:

(a)   a withdrawal from a drawdown pension fund (see 16.21) made during a tax year in which an individual is temporarily non-resident, is taxed as pension income in the year of return to the UK where the pension funds have received UK tax relief;

(b)   lump sums paid under certain pension schemes to an individual who is temporarily non-resident are treated as if they had been received in the period of return if, ignoring any relevant double tax treaty, they would have been taxed otherwise.

Anti-avoidance legislation ensures that where a UK resident receives a pension or lump sum from savings transferred to a pension scheme established outside the UK, the terms of a tax treaty will not be able to prevent a UK tax charge where the transfer was entered into in order to avoid tax. If any tax is payable in the other country on the foreign pension or lump sum, tax credit relief is allowed in the UK. Without these rules it was possible for a UK resident to transfer pension savings to a country which did not tax a pension or lump sum paid to a UK resident, and therefore receive their pension or lump sum entirely tax free from that country.

Further details on the current pensions regime generally can be found at CHAPTER 16. HMRC guidance can be found at www.gov.uk/topic/business-ta x/pension-scheme-administration/latest.

Other sources of foreign income (TMA 1970, s 17; ITA 2007, ss 6–21)

[41.32] Other sources of foreign income apart from business profits and rents are taxed as outlined at 41.15.

As for UK bank and building society accounts (from 6 April 2016), offshore bank and building society accounts do not have tax deducted at source from the interest. However, for those required to make half-yearly payments on account (9.4), the payments are based on the amount of tax paid directly for the previous tax year, so an amount is included for continuing sources of untaxed interest.

Interest on foreign gilt-edged securities, is received through a UK paying or collecting agent, such as a bank. UK tax is not deducted from such income, so the full amounts received will be charged to UK tax, subject to any claim for double tax relief (see 41.20). Under arrangements with the EU and various other countries, individuals may also receive interest in full from overseas paying agents. Alternatively a special withholding tax may be deducted. The gross amount is chargeable to UK tax, subject to any claim for double tax relief (see 41.20).

Foreign fixed interest stocks are subject to the accrued income scheme (see 36.11), unless the recipient is only liable to tax on income remitted to the UK (see 41.16). The special rules for scrip dividends (see 38.3) do not apply to scrip dividends from non-UK resident companies. There are anti-avoidance provisions to counter the rolling-up of income in an offshore fund with the intention of realising it in a capital form. The provisions are dealt with briefly at **45.26**.

Banks, building societies and other paying and collecting agents are required to provide information to HMRC on interest paid to investors, including investors who are not resident in the UK. HMRC exchange information on savings income on a reciprocal basis with other countries. HMRC recently used their powers to obtain information from major UK banks about offshore accounts. As a result of the large volume of information received, HMRC run a number of campaigns to make a disclosure of previously undeclared UK tax liabilities. For details see **9.87** onwards.

Offshore assets

[41.33] As part of the introduction of the deemed domicile rules (**41.10**), a one off capital gains tax rebasing relief was introduced by the September 2017 Finance Bill (which is expected to receive Royal Assent in November 2017). This applies to gains realised on the disposal of offshore assets where an individual becomes deemed UK domiciled under the 15 out of 20 year rule in 2017/18 and he was a was a non-UK domiciled remittance basis user prior to 2017/18. It does not apply to individuals returning to the UK with an existing UK domicile of origin.

When calculating the gain or loss accruing on the disposal of such offshore assets the acquisition cost of the asset(s) will be automatically rebased to its value at 5 April 2017 provided that during the person's ownership the asset was not situated in the UK in the period 16 March 2016 to 5 April 2017, and the person remains deemed domiciled under the 15 out of 20 year rule at all times until disposal.

It is possible to make an election for this automatic rebasing not to apply. Such an election must be made within four years after the end of the year of disposal. Once made, the election is irrevocable.

Assets which qualify for rollover relief

[41.34] A person who is resident in the UK can roll over a gain arising on a disposal of assets which qualify for rollover relief on replacement of business assets (see **29.16**) against the acquisition of new qualifying assets situated either in the UK or overseas. HMRC will not seek to deny relief if the person has ceased to be resident in the UK when the new assets are acquired, so long as the various conditions for the relief are met (see HMRC's Capital Gains Manual at CG60270). If the replacement assets are sold in a tax year when the individual is not resident in the UK (and not carrying on a business in the UK through a branch or agency) there will be no UK tax on the rolled over gains (unless on a later return to the UK liability is established under the temporary residence rules outlined at **41.49**). There may, however be liability in the new country of residence.

Assets eligible for gift relief

[41.35] If an individual becomes not resident within six years after receiving a gift on which capital gains tax was deferred under the gift relief provisions, the deferred gain is chargeable to tax (see **4.33**). Becoming non-resident within a specified period also triggers gains deferred under the enterprise investment scheme (see **29.33**), although for gains deferred under the social investment tax relief (**29.55**) there is no stipulation that becoming non-resident triggers a gain.

Non-UK resident individuals: basis of charge (ITA 2007, ss 33–58, 811–814)

Chargeable income

[41.36] Non-residents are liable to income tax only on income that arises in the UK, unless it is specifically exempted etc. They are not liable to UK tax on income arising outside the UK.

Non-residents are exempt from UK tax on UK gilt-edged securities (see **41.45**) and may be exempt on other sources of income under a double tax agreement. Tax is not usually deducted from bank and building society interest (see **41.45**), or from social security benefits (see **41.41**), although such income is not actually exempt from tax. If other income is from property, tax may have been deducted at the basic rate (see **41.43**). Any amount of tax treated as paid in respect of dividend income is not repayable but the recipient may be entitled to credit relief in their country of residence (see **41.46**). In all cases, the treatment of income and gains may be varied by the provisions of a double tax treaty (see **41.38**).

Calculation of liability

[41.37] Certain classes of non-resident are eligible to claim UK personal allowances. These include EEA nationals, residents of the Isle of Man or the Channel Islands, those who have previously resided in the UK but are resident abroad for the health reasons, Crown employees (and their bereaved spouses or partners) and those in the service of a territory under the protection of the British Crown or in the service of a missionary society. Additionally, a claim for allowances may be provided for by the terms of a double tax agreement. Where allowances are available, they are given in full against the UK income.

The *maximum* tax payable by a non-resident is the sum of the following:

(a) the tax, if any, deducted from 'disregarded income' (i.e. interest, dividends, pensions, social security benefits etc);
(b) amounts representing income tax that is treated as paid in respect of that income (this includes the 7.5% tax treated as paid in respect of dividend income);
(c) the tax on any other taxable income (i.e. excluding the disregarded income), calculated as if personal allowances were not available.

If a claim is made for personal allowances, all non-exempt income is taken into account. This may limit or eliminate the benefit of making a claim.

Example 1

In 2017–18 a non-resident British national who is a single person, born on 6 April 1946, has untaxed income from UK banks and building societies amounting to £2,000 and a state pension of £10,000. No UK tax is payable, since the maximum tax on such income is the tax, if any, deducted from it.

If the non-resident also had rental income of £2,400, from which tax of £480 was deducted, his maximum liability would be tax on that income as if it were his only UK income. He could not benefit from a claim for personal allowance, because his untaxed income of £12,000 would have to be taken into account in such a claim and that income exceeds the personal allowance of £11,500.

If in addition to the rental income of £2,400 the only untaxed income had been the pension of £10,000 the position would be:

	£
Total income	12,400
Personal allowance	(11,500)
	900
Tax at 20%	180
Tax deducted at source	480
Tax repayable	300

Special rules apply to UK distributions from a close company to a participator if:

(a)   they arose during a period of temporary non-residence (**41.49**) in a year for which the individual was non-resident; and

(b)   the UK charge was limited by the terms of a double taxation treaty.

Such dividends are taxed further in the year of return. The additional tax is calculated such that the overall tax paid is the amount that would have been paid if the individual had not been temporarily non-resident.

Foreign nationals assigned to the UK who have paid too much tax can claim a refund from HMRC on form R38 (Expat).

Those completing tax returns must show any non-exempt income and whether tax is payable or not, otherwise the return will be incomplete. (The UK tax liability of someone who is non-resident for only *part* of a tax year is calculated by reference to *all* taxable income of the year and the treatment indicated above does not apply.)

If an individual is in the UK long enough to be classed as resident, he will be liable to income tax on foreign as well as UK sources of income although the remittance basis (see **41.16**) may apply. It might be appropriate to invest abroad and leave the income there. An alternative for those of foreign domicile who are resident in the UK is an ISA (see **36.16** onwards).

Double tax relief (ITTOIA 2005, ss 397–401)

[41.38] Income or gains may be exempt from UK tax under a double tax agreement.

As far as earned income is concerned, many treaties provide that someone working in the UK on a short-term basis will be taxed only in their own country. HMRC broadly operate a '60 day' rule in this connection (see HMRC PAYE online manual PAYE82000 for detailed comments).

Sometimes a double tax agreement may provide for income that is not exempt from UK tax to be charged at a reduced rate, for example, interest may be taxed at only 10%. Non-residents in receipt of dividend income are treated as having paid income tax at source at the dividend ordinary rate (7.5%, from 6 April 2016 and 10% prior to 6 April 2016). The amount so treated as paid is not repayable, but the recipient may be entitled to credit relief in their country of residence (see **41.46**). In all cases, the treatment of income and gains may be varied by the provisions of a double tax treaty.

Non-UK resident individuals: specific sources of income

Income from employment (ITEPA 2003, ss 20–41, 373–375)

[41.39] The treatment of a non-resident's UK earnings depends on the length of his visit. Where he does not remain long enough to be classed as resident he is nonetheless liable to UK tax on UK earnings (although sometimes he may be exempt under the provisions of a double tax treaty (see **41.38**)). UK personal allowances are available only to certain non-residents (see **41.36**).

Expenses of travel and of visits by spouses or civil partners and children are allowed if they are paid or reimbursed by the employer (thus offsetting the benefits charge) in the same way as described at **41.27** for a UK resident working abroad. This only applies, however, where the employee was either not resident in the UK in either of the two tax years before the tax year of his arrival in the UK, or was not in the UK at any time during the two years immediately preceding his arrival. Where this condition is satisfied, the expenses are allowed for a period of five years beginning with the date of arrival in the UK to perform the duties of the employment.

A non-UK resident individual, who remains in the UK long enough to be classified as resident in the UK, is liable to tax on UK earnings as they arise, but he may be able to claim the remittance basis in respect of foreign income (see **41.23**). It is important for visitors to keep records (for example, separate bank accounts for capital and for different sources of income) to enable them to demonstrate whether or not remittances out of foreign earnings have taken place.

Employers may make special PAYE arrangements for foreign national employees (known as tax equalisation arrangements) under which the employers meet all or part of the employees' tax. Details are in HMRC Help Sheet HS212. See also HMRC's Tax Bulletin 81 (February 2006) regarding tax equalised employees and Tax Bulletin 50 (December 2000) on benefits and expenses provided to employees sent on secondment by overseas employers.

Income from a UK business

[41.40] Non-residents who carry on business in the UK either on their own or in partnership are charged to tax on the UK business profits in the same way as UK residents. In the case of a split year (**41.6** or **41.8** prior to 2013–14), for the overseas part of the year the individual/partner is deemed to be non-UK resident. Tax due on the profits is dealt with under the self-assessment rules and is paid by the non-resident or, where the business is carried on through a UK branch or agency, by a UK representative.

State pensions, other pensions and state benefits

[41.41] Non-residents receive state pensions and other relevant social security benefits in full, and tax is not charged on them (but see **41.36** in relation to tax repayment claims). As far as occupational and personal pensions paid to non-residents are concerned, such pensions are chargeable to UK tax unless (as will usually be the case) they are exempt under a double taxation agreement. Tax is deducted from such pensions under PAYE where the payer has been instructed to do so by the tax office. In this event, the code number may take personal allowances into account.

Non-resident performers (ITTOIA 2005, ss 13, 14; ITA 2007, ss 965–970; CTA 2009, s 1309; SI 1987/530; FA 2013, ss 8, 9; FA 2014, ss 47, 48; SI 2016/771; SI 2017/614)

[41.42] Basic rate tax may be deducted by the payer from the UK earnings of non-resident entertainers, sportsmen and sportswomen. Royalty payments received from the sale of records are excluded (as they are already exempt under many double taxation agreements).

Tax does not need to be deducted however:

(a)   where the person making the payment does not expect to pay more than a total of the current year personal allowance to the individual in question during that tax year;

(b)   where the payments are to accredited competitors in the UEFA Champions League Final 2017, London Anniversary Games, the Glasgow Commonwealth Games, the Glasgow Grand Prix, the 2016 London Anniversary Games and the 2017 World Athletics and Paralympics Championships (as such competitors are exempt from income tax (**2.2**)). To meet the non-residence condition, an accredited competitor must be non-UK resident for the tax year in which the Games activity is performed or, where that year is a split year as regards the competitor, the Games activity must be performed in the overseas part of that split year; or

(c)   where the payment is made in respect of classical music artists included on the HMRC list; see www.gov.uk/government/publications/simplifie d-tax-system-for-classical-music-payees-for-non-uk-resident-performer s/payees-for-non-uk-resident-classical-music-performers.

Where tax is deducted, HMRC may agree a rate below the basic rate. The tax deducted is set against the final tax liability for the year, or repaid to the extent that it exceeds that liability. The rules are administered by HMRC's Foreign Entertainers Unit and guidance is provided in Help Sheet HS303.

Rental income of non-resident landlords (ITA 2007, ss 971, 972; SI 1995/2902)

[41.43] Where UK property is let, the rental income from all let properties is treated as being from a single property business, as outlined in CHAPTER 32. There are, however, special regulations dealing with the taxation of rental income of non-resident landlords. The reference to a non-resident landlord is not in fact accurate, because the legislation refers to someone whose 'usual place of abode' is outside the UK, the aim being to make it easier to collect tax from someone who is usually abroad. HMRC's interpretation is to regard an individual as having a usual place of abode outside the UK if he is away for more than six months. Companies will not be so treated if they are UK resident for tax purposes. References to non-residents in the remainder of this section should be read accordingly.

A UK agent handling let property for a non-resident landlord, or the tenant where there is no such agent, must notify HMRC's Centre for Non-Residents (CNR). The agent or tenant must then deduct basic rate tax from the property income (net of allowable expenses paid by the agent or tenant and net of VAT on the rent where this has been charged), and pay it over to HMRC within 30 days after the end of each calendar quarter. The agent or tenant must give the non-resident an annual certificate showing the tax deducted by 5 July following the tax year and must also send in a return to HMRC by the same date. These provisions apply whether the non-resident landlord is an individual, trustee or a company, except that they do not apply to the rental income of a UK permanent establishment of a non-resident company (see **41.67**).

Tax does not have to be deducted at source if the agent or tenant receives written notice to that effect from CNR. Tenants paying rent of, broadly, £100 a week or less do not have to deduct tax unless told to do so by CNR. The non-resident landlord is required to pay any excess of tax due over the tax deducted at source (or claim a refund) to HMRC (**9.2** onwards), so that unless the tax paid directly to HMRC for the previous tax year was below the de minimis thresholds, payments on account should be made on 31 January in the tax year and 31 July following, with the balance due at the same time as the tax return on 31 January following the end of the tax year.

A landlord may apply to CNR to receive his rental income in full providing his UK tax affairs are up to date, or he has never had any UK tax obligations, or he does not expect to be liable to UK tax. He must undertake to complete tax returns if required and pay any tax due on time. Unless covered by the de minimis thresholds, the non-resident landlord will be required to make payments on account in the same way as landlords who receive taxed rent (see above). CNR have stated that they will not normally issue self-assessment returns to non-resident individual landlords who have no net tax liability, although returns may still be sent occasionally to ensure that the tax position remains the same.

Profits from UK land (ITTOIA 2005, ss 6–6B; ITA 2007, ss 517A-517U; FA 2016, ss 78, 79)

[41.44] The September 2017 Finance Bill (which is expected to receive Royal Assent in November 2017) provides that non-resident persons that deal in or develop land in the UK are liable to income tax on the profits of that trade for amounts recognised in a period of account beginning on or after 8 March 2017. Where an accounting period straddles 8 March 2017, a notional period starts on 8 March 2017. This liability was originally legislated for by Finance Act 2016, but had applied only to amounts recognised on disposals made on or after 5 July 2016. The widening of the scope ensures that amounts are brought into charge even when the relevant contract was entered into many months before the property is transferred and the profit recognised.

The taxable profits are computed broadly in the same manner as for UK resident persons. Anti-avoidance provisions apply from 16 March 2016 to counteract arrangements that aim to avoid these rules. Equivalent provisions apply for corporation tax purposes; see **41.64**.

Interest, securities and investment income

[41.45] Non-residents are exempt from tax on UK income from gilt-edged securities, interest on which is paid gross. Interest on quoted Eurobonds (i.e. interest-bearing stock exchange listed securities issued by a company) is paid gross. UK bank and building society interest is also paid without deduction of tax. For ISAs (see **36.16** onwards) the tax exemption on the investment is not lost on becoming non-resident but it is not possible to contribute further or take out another ISA.

As far as bank accounts are concerned, if UK bank and building society accounts are replaced with foreign accounts, the interest will be free of UK tax while non-resident, and will not be taken into account in calculating relief under a non-resident's personal allowances claim. Closing foreign accounts before a return to the UK will prevent any of the foreign interest being subject to UK tax. If offshore roll-up funds (see **45.26**) have been invested in there is no UK tax if they are disposed of before UK residence is resumed. See **45.29** for the anti-avoidance provisions in relation to personal portfolio bonds.

Dividend income

[41.46] Despite the changes to dividend taxation from 6 April 2016, there is no practical impact on dividends paid to non-residents. Non-residents in receipt of dividend income are treated as having paid income tax at source at the dividend ordinary rate (7.5%, from 6 April 2016). The amount so treated as paid is not repayable, but credit relief may still be available in the individual's country of residence (see **41.45**).

Patent royalties

[41.47] Tax is normally deducted at the basic rate from patent royalties paid to overseas companies and individuals. A paying company may, however, pay royalties gross, or deduct tax at a reduced rate according to the terms of the double tax agreement, if it believes the recipient to be entitled to double tax relief (see **41.38**). The company will have to pay the tax shortfall, plus interest and possibly penalties, if its belief turns out to be incorrect.

Capital gains tax (TCGA 1992, ss 10, 10A, 14B–14F, 86A; FA 2015, s 76)

[41.48] As a general rule an individual is not liable to capital gains tax if he is not resident in the UK and if the year is a split year (**41.6**), gains accruing during the overseas part of the year are not chargeable to capital gains tax. This general rule is however subject to a number of exceptions:

(a)   non-residents carrying on a business in the UK through a branch or agency are liable to capital gains tax on gains arising on assets used in the business or by the branch or agency;

(b)   individuals that have been temporarily non-resident are liable to tax on gains realised on the disposal of assets owned before they left the UK (**41.49**);

(c)   non-residents that realise a gain, on or after 6 April 2015, on the disposal of UK residential property are liable to tax on the gain arising on or after 6 April 2015 (**41.50**).

The liability in (c) takes precedence over the temporary non-residence rule, meaning that the temporary non-residence rules only apply to gains which are not of UK residential property. Special rules apply to the capital gains tax position on a private residence when absent abroad (see **30.6**).

Temporary non-residence

[41.49] Individuals are treated as temporarily non-resident if, for any part of at least four of the previous seven tax years prior to departure, they were solely UK resident (either fully, or as part of a split year (**41.6**) and they cease to have sole UK residency for a period of five years or less.

All such gains in the tax year of departure are chargeable in that year. Gains on such assets arising while abroad are charged in the tax year in which the individual becomes UK resident again. Losses are allowed on the same basis as gains are taxed. If an individual has an interest in a non-resident trust, he will also be taxed on his return on gains during his absence that would have been taxed on him as settlor had he not been non-resident (see **41.87**). Gains on assets acquired while the individual is resident abroad that are realised in the years between the tax year of departure and the tax year of return are exempt (subject to certain anti-avoidance provisions).

In certain circumstances, temporary non-residents who resume UK residence will not be deemed UK domiciled under the 15 out of 20 year test (**41.10**). They will therefore not be subject to CGT on the disposal of their foreign assets during their period of non-residence if a claim for the remittance basis is made.

Non-resident CGT on UK residential property

[41.50] From 6 April 2015 non-UK residents disposing of UK residential property are subject to non-resident CGT. The non-resident capital gains tax (non-resident CGT) potentially applies not only to non-resident individuals, but also to non-resident personal representatives, trustees, certain companies or funds. The charge does not apply in certain cases, in particular, it does not apply:

(a)   to a diversely-held company, which is any company that is not a closely-held company. A closely-held company is broadly the same as a close company (**3.29**) except that directors who are not participators are not taken into account when considering control;

(b)   to a unit trust scheme, or open-ended investment company (or non-UK equivalent) which is widely-marketed throughout the period from the date the scheme acquired the interest in land which is the subject of the non-resident CGT disposal to the date of disposal, or if shorter, throughout the period of five years before the date of disposal;

(c)   where the gain is already chargeable as a gain of a permanent establishment trading in the UK (**41.67**), a gain of a branch or agency trading in the UK (see **41.2**), or under the ATED regime (**32.48**); or

(d)   to gains that are liable to corporation tax or income tax as profits arising from dealing in or developing UK land; see **41.64, 41.44**.

For the exclusion to apply under (a) or (b), an appropriate claim has to be made.

The non-resident CGT applies to qualifying individuals, personal representatives, trustees, companies or funds if:

(i)   that person is non-resident in the UK broadly in the tax year that the gain accrues, or, in the case of a company or fund, at the time the gain accrues; and

(ii)   the disposal is of UK residential property that is used or intended to be used as a dwelling (excluding certain types of residential property such as care or nursing homes, purpose built student accommodation, hospitals, hospices, military accommodation, prisons etc).

The rates of tax which apply are 18% and 28% for unincorporated persons and 20% for corporates. The reduced CGT rates applying from 6 April 2016 (**4.2**) do not apply to non-resident CGT gains. The gains and losses themselves are calculated under the normal rules applicable to those types of persons, for example, non-resident companies can benefit from indexation allowance whereas non-resident individuals cannot. The annual exempt amount is

.c usual manner, to reduce the amount of the
.ve provided an online non-resident CGT calculator
...ce/capital-gains-tax-for-non-residents-calculating-taxab

.c gain arising on or after 6 April 2015 is chargeable. The default
...nod to calculate the gain that is potentially chargeable is referred to as the
'rebasing method'. This involves a calculation of the gain as if the vendor had
acquired the property at market value on 5 April 2015. The resultant gain is
then apportioned from 6 April 2015 to the date of disposal so that only days
during which the land consists of or includes a dwelling are chargeable as an
NRCGT gain. An irrevocable election can be made for the gain to be simply
time-apportioned over the whole period of ownership to calculate the post-
5 April 2015 gain, or alternatively for the whole of the gain/loss (not just the
post-5 April 2015 proportion) to be chargeable/allowable. The latter election
is of use when a loss is made. Special computational rules apply where the
property disposed of is also within the ATED regime which ensure that the
non-resident CGT only applies to any proportion of the gain that does not fall
within the ATED charge.

Tax is charged on the gain (the NRCGT gain) after deduction of any losses on
disposals of UK residential property interests of the tax year concerned, and
any such losses brought forward from previous years. If, under these calculations, a loss accrues (a NRCGT loss), it cannot be carried back with the
exception of those which may be carried back following death (see 42.3).
NRCGT losses are effectively ring-fenced for use against NRCGT gains in the
same tax year, although unused NRCGT losses are available for carry forward
to set against NRCGT gains in later years. Where a previously non-resident
person becomes UK resident any brought forward NRCGT losses can be
utilised in the same way as any other brought forward allowable capital losses
and set-off in the most tax efficient way against general chargeable gains. In a
split year, NRCGT losses from the overseas part of the year can be set against
general chargeable gains in the UK part of the year.

An election can be made by a group of companies (the non-resident CGT
group) to pool NRCGT gains and losses. All members of the group which are
qualifying members must make the election.

Alongside these rules, changes have been made to the main residence election
for the principal private residence (PPR) relief provisions to ensure the person
has to be UK resident for the property to be a main residence or spend a
minimum number of nights at the property in the tax year (see 30.4). To
prevent further abuse, it is also provided that roll-over relief is not available on
NRCGT gains unless the new asset is a 'qualifying residential property interest'
on acquisition. Furthermore amendments have been made to the rules governing gift relief for business assets and assets subject to an immediate
inheritance tax charge to ensure that relief is still available where UK
residential property is gifted to a non-resident in certain circumstances and
that any held-over gain on the gift of a business asset does not crystallise on the
emigration of the donee, so long as it would be subject to the non-resident
CGT rules; see 4.35.

For details of the non-resident return filing requirements see 9.31.

National insurance contributions and social security

[41.51] The detailed national insurance and social security provisions are complex, so whether leaving or coming to the UK, it is advisable to contact HMRC and the Department for Work and Pensions (DWP) to establish the liability to make NICs and the overall benefits position. Contact details for HMRC's centre for non-residents, and the DWP's international pensions centre, are provided in leaflet NI38 (www.hmrc.gov.uk/pdfs/nico/ni38.pdf).

For details of the anti-avoidance provisions that apply when UK and UK Continental Shelf workers are employed by offshore companies or engaged by or through offshore employment intermediaries see **41.22**.

Leaving the UK

[41.52] If an individual leaves the UK his liability to pay national insurance contributions (NICs) will normally cease unless he works abroad for an employer who has a place of business in the UK, in which case Class 1 NICs continue for the first 52 weeks. Where there is no liability to pay Class 1 NICs, it may be to an individual's advantage to pay Class 3 voluntary NICs. Alternatively if an individual is employed or self-employed abroad, it is possible to maintain a contributions record for certain benefits by paying the lower Class 2 NICs, providing certain conditions are satisfied, although note that Class 2 NICs are to be abolished from April 2018 (see **24.5**). See HMRC's leaflet NI38 for details.

Employment abroad

[41.53] If an individual is working temporarily abroad, or moving from one foreign location to another, he may be required to continue to pay Class 1 NICs for as long as there is an intention to remain UK resident. The position is different if an individual goes to a country with which the UK has a reciprocal social security agreement, when home country liability may sometimes continue for several years. The position is also different if an individual goes to a country in the European Union (or Switzerland, Iceland, Liechtenstein or Norway), in which case there will usually be liability in the country of employment from the outset, except for a short-term visit of up to 24 months. During the short term visits an individual will remain liable in the UK. See also www.hmrc.gov.uk/nic/work/new-rules.htm.

If a person normally works in more than one EEA country, he will be liable in his state of residence, provided he performs a substantial part of his duties in that state. (This rule applies even if he has multiple employments and the employers are in different member states). If he does not perform a substantial amount of his work in his state of residence, then he will be liable in the state that his employer resides.

A 'home base' rule applies to aircrew and their employers operating around the EEA for determining the member state in which social security contributions are payable. For details see **13.2**.

Employers should ensure that where UK liability continues, they account for the appropriate amount of NICs on all relevant pay and benefits.

Self-employment abroad

[41.54] If an individual leaves the UK and is self-employed abroad, there is not normally a *requirement* to pay Class 2 NICs but there may be an *entitlement* to pay them in some circumstances to maintain contribution records. Note that Class 2 NICs are to be abolished from April 2018.

Again, the position is subject to variation for workers in the EEA or in a country with which the UK has a reciprocal social security agreement. A self-employed person who is not resident in the UK in a tax year is not liable to pay Class 4 NICs. Class 4 contributions do not apply where a trader is not UK resident.

Arrival in the UK

[41.55] Visitors to the UK and new permanent residents who are employees are normally not liable to pay Class 1 NICs for the first 12 months. This does not apply to those coming from an EEA country or a country with which the UK has a reciprocal social security agreement, who will either be liable to UK NICs from the outset or remain liable under their home country's rules. Where an employee is liable, the employer is liable to pay employer's secondary NICs. This applies to all overseas employers, subject to special rules for EEA countries and countries with which the UK has a reciprocal social security agreement.

People coming to the UK who are self-employed are only *required* to pay Class 2 NICs if they are resident in the UK, or have been resident in the UK for 26 or more weeks out of the last 52. They are *entitled* to pay Class 2 NICs if they are *present* in the UK for the relevant contribution week. Note that Class 2 NICs are to be abolished from April 2018.

Again, the general rules are varied for EEA countries and countries with which the UK has a reciprocal social security agreement. Class 4 NICs are payable where relevant unless the person is not resident in the UK for the tax year concerned.

State pension

[41.56] As far as the state pension is concerned, if an individual emigrates, he is normally entitled to a pension based on contributions made, but it is frozen at the rate payable when leaving the UK or when first becoming entitled to the pension, if later. This may be varied by the provisions of reciprocal social security agreements. Again, the position needs to be checked with the DWP's pensions service.

UK resident companies: determination and effect of residence (CTA 2009, ss 5, 13–32)

[41.57] Under UK tax law, any company that is incorporated in the UK is treated as being UK resident no matter where it is managed and controlled. Companies incorporated abroad are regarded as UK resident if they are managed and controlled here. Where, however, a company is treated as non-resident under the terms of a double tax treaty, this overrides these rules and the company is regarded as not being UK resident.

A company that is UK resident is liable to corporation tax on all 'profits', i.e. income and chargeable gains, wherever they arise. Further, for accounting periods commencing on or after 1 January 2016, a UK-resident ultimate parent entity of a multinational enterprise with a consolidated group turnover of EUR 750 million or more is required to make an annual country-by-country report to HMRC.

A company may have more than one country of residence. Anti-avoidance provisions apply to dual resident investment companies (see **45.24**).HMRC provide guidance on company residence in their International Manual.

UK resident companies: basis of charge (CTA 2009, ss 18A–18S, 931A–931W; CTA 2010, ss 66, 67, 107–128, 1141; TIOPA 2010, ss 18–104)

Overseas property income

[41.58] A company's income from letting of overseas property is treated as the profits of an 'overseas property business' and computed in broadly the same way as for UK lettings, but with the profit or loss computed separately for properties in different countries in order to calculate the amount of any available double tax relief (see **41.62**). Interest on any borrowing to acquire foreign property is deducted under the 'loan relationships' rules in the same way as for UK property (see **32.13**). Providing the lettings are on a commercial basis, any losses arising may be carried forward to set against later profits from the overseas property business.

Overseas permanent establishments/subsidiaries

Overseas permanent establishment

[41.59] The losses of a foreign 'permanent establishment' (broadly, a fixed place of business) of a UK resident company are not available for surrender to other UK group companies under the group relief provisions to the extent that the loss could be relieved for foreign tax purposes in the country in which it arose. There is a similar restriction for losses of a UK permanent establishment of an overseas company although this rule is relaxed somewhat for losses of a UK permanent establishment of an EEA resident company in that losses are able to be surrendered if they are not actually relieved elsewhere (rather than, as before, if they could potentially be relieved elsewhere).

It is possible to elect that profits (apart from profits arising from dealing in or developing UK land; see **41.64**) of a foreign permanent establishments of a UK company are exempt from UK tax. If such an election is made, losses also will be excluded. Once an election is made, the exemption applies from the start of the next accounting period.

Special rules apply to the calculation of branch profits (see **41.67**), which may alter the amount of double taxation relief available.

Overseas subsidiary

[41.60] Where business is carried on through a foreign subsidiary, the UK company's liability will arise only on amounts received from the subsidiary by way of interest or, in some cases, dividends. However the majority of foreign dividends received by UK companies are not taxable, provided they fall into an exempt class and anti-avoidance provisions do not apply.

A non-UK resident company that is resident or carrying on a trade in another state in the EEA may surrender losses to UK group companies if the losses would otherwise be unrelievable either in the country in which they were incurred or any other country. The amount of loss available for surrender must be recomputed according to UK tax principles. Loss relief will not be available where there are arrangements the main purpose (or one of the main purposes) of which is to obtain UK tax relief.

Controlled foreign companies and dual resident companies

[41.61] The controlled foreign company legislation provides that in certain circumstances tax is charged on a UK company in respect of profits of a foreign company, and are outlined very briefly at **45.25**.

There are also anti-avoidance provisions in relation to dual resident companies, which are outlined at **45.24**. Companies are required to declare amounts taxable under the controlled foreign companies rules in their tax returns.

Double tax relief (TIOPA 2010, ss 2–134)

[41.62] Double tax relief is available in respect of the foreign tax suffered on both income and gains. Normally, only direct foreign taxes are taken into account for double tax relief but if a UK company receives dividends from a foreign company in which it owns 10% or more of the voting power, underlying taxes on the profits out of which the dividends are paid are taken into account as well. In this case the amount included in UK profits is the dividend plus both the direct and underlying foreign taxes. However the majority of foreign dividends received by UK companies are not taxable, provided they fall into an exempt class and anti-avoidance provisions do not apply. Double tax relief is also available both for direct and underlying foreign tax suffered by UK permanent establishments of non-resident companies, other than tax paid in the taxpayer company's home state.

Double tax relief is given either unilaterally or under the provisions of a double tax agreement. For unilateral relief, companies can (as can individuals (see **41.20**)) choose whether to claim credit relief against their UK tax liability, or simply treat the foreign tax suffered as a deductible expense. As credit relief cannot exceed the amount of UK tax suffered on the foreign income it is generally only beneficial to make a claim to expense foreign tax, in a loss making situation.

Example 2

For the accounting period ended 31 March 2018, A Ltd had taxable trading income of £3m. During that accounting period it also had overseas income of £50,000, with £10,000 foreign tax suffered.

Assuming A Ltd claims credit relief, its tax computation will be as follows—

	£
Trading income	3,000,000
Overseas income	50,000
Total profits chargeable to tax	3,050,000

The total UK corporation tax will be—

	£
UK corporation tax @ 19%	579,500
Less: Foreign tax	(10,000)
Total UK tax due	569,500

Example 3

Assume the facts are as for Example 2 above, but during the accounting period A Ltd had in fact made a £100,000 loss. If a claim is made to expense the foreign tax, A Ltd's tax position is—

	UK trading	Foreign income
	£	£
Profit/(loss)	(100,000)	50,000
Less: Foreign tax		(10,000)
Assessable income	Nil	40,000

The trading losses then can be relieved in the usual manner (see **3.13**).

The relief on overseas income cannot exceed the UK corporation tax payable on the overseas income, after all deductions (other than advance corporation tax set off under the provisions of the shadow ACT system). It is, however, provided that in deciding how much corporation tax is attributable to the overseas income, any available deductions may broadly be set against any source of profits in the most beneficial way (although not so as to turn profits into a loss for which loss relief is claimed). The main point to bear in mind on interest relating to the trade is that it should be set against UK trading profits in priority to foreign trading profits. As far as non-trading interest is concerned, if there is a non-trading deficit for which relief is claimed against total profits (see **26.8**), the deficit must be set against the same profits for both loss relief and double tax relief. Any non-trading deficit brought forward (see **26.9**) must be regarded for double tax relief as reducing non-trading profits.

Double tax relief in respect of foreign tax paid on chargeable gains is limited to the UK corporation tax payable thereon.

If double tax relief is restricted because it exceeds the UK tax it is wasted and cannot be carried forward or back. However, unrelieved foreign tax on permanent establishment profits and, where applicable, foreign dividends may be carried back to the previous three years or carried forward indefinitely for offset against tax on income from the same source (providing, in the case of underlying tax, that the required 10% interest continues to be held). Unrelieved foreign tax may also be surrendered within a group of companies (including group companies that are dual-resident).

If the amount of foreign tax payable is later adjusted, the amount of double tax relief claimed is similarly adjusted. If an adjustment to foreign tax results in too much relief having been claimed, HMRC must be notified within one year after the adjustment.

Where credit is claimed for foreign tax and a payment is made either to the claimant, a connected person (or another person as a consequence of a scheme that has been entered into), the foreign tax relief will be restricted to the net amount.

There are various anti-avoidance provisions that restrict the amount of relief available for underlying tax, and also prevent financial traders getting excessive relief for foreign tax paid on overseas interest. All traders with foreign profits must take expenses into account on a just and reasonable basis, and there is a general anti-avoidance provision relating to 'prescribed schemes and arrangements designed to increase relief'.

Non-resident companies: basis of charge (TCGA 1992, ss 25, 171; ITA 2007, ss 815, 816; CTA 2009, ss 5, 19–32; CTA 2010, s 968; FA 2015, s 37 and Sch 7)

[41.63] It is common practice for non-resident companies to operate in the UK via a permanent establishment, or a subsidiary (see **41.67–41.69**). However in certain circumstances, non-resident companies may be liable to corporation tax, income tax or capital gains tax even though they do not have a UK presence (see **41.64–41.66**).

Corporation tax (CTA 2010, ss 5–5B, 3560A-3560T: FA 2016, ss 76, 77, 80)

[41.64] The September 2017 Finance Bill (which is expected to receive Royal Assent in November 2017) provides that non-resident companies that deal in or develop land in the UK are liable to corporation tax on the profits of that trade for amounts recognised in a period of account beginning on or after 8 March 2017. Where an accounting period straddles 8 March 2017, a notional period starts on 8 March 2017. This liability was originally legislated for by Finance Act 2016, but had applied only to amounts recognised on disposals made on or after 5 July 2016. The widening of the scope ensures that amounts are brought into charge even when the relevant contract was entered into many months before the property is transferred and the profit recognised.

The taxable profits are computed broadly in the same manner as for UK resident companies. Anti-avoidance provisions apply from 16 March 2016 to counteract arrangements that aim to avoid these rules. In certain situations relief for pre-trading expenditure may be available where a company that was previously trading in the UK through a permanent establishment now falls within these rules.

Equivalent provisions apply for income tax purposes; see **41.44**.

Income tax

[41.65] A non-resident company is liable to income tax if it is not trading in the UK through a permanent establishment, but has income arising in the UK. Any profits that fall to be taxed under **41.61** are excluded from this charge.

Capital gains

[41.66] Non-resident companies may be liable to UK capital gains tax as follows:

(a) on a disposal of a UK dwelling that is owned by non-resident 'non-natural persons' (i.e. companies and certain collective investment schemes) and is subject to the annual tax on enveloped dwellings (ATED) charge. This charge also applies to such disposals by UK resident companies etc and is discussed at **4.8**;

(b) on a disposal of UK residential property on or after 6 April 2015, that is owned by a non-resident closely-held company — special computational rules apply where the property disposed of is also within the ATED regime which ensure that the non-resident CGT only applies to any proportion of the gain that does not fall within the ATED charge; see **41.50**.

UK permanent establishment/subsidiaries

UK permanent establishment (ITTOIA 2005, s 577A; FA 2016, s 42)

[41.67] A non-resident company is chargeable to corporation tax only if it carries on a trade in the UK through a permanent establishment (broadly, a fixed place of business) in the UK. The company is liable to tax on profits, wherever they arise, that are attributable to the permanent establishment, with the exclusion of profits arising from dealing in or developing UK land; see **41.64**. From, broadly, 28 June 2016 payments in respect of royalties or other intellectual property made by a non-resident in respect of a trade carried out in the UK through a permanent establishment by that person are treated as arising from a UK source and therefore fall within the deduction of income tax at source provisions; see **3.23**.

A permanent establishment is treated as having the amount of equity and other capital it would need if it were operating as a separate company. This restricts the amount of interest that may be deducted in calculating taxable profits. The permanent establishment is responsible for dealing with the UK tax liabilities on the company's profits. The rules relating to non-resident landlords at **41.43** do not apply. The company is liable to income tax on any UK sources of income not connected with the permanent establishment in the same way as companies not operating through a permanent establishment (see below).

If the UK trade ceases, or the assets are removed from the UK, the company is treated as if it had disposed of the assets, and gains are charged to tax accordingly (see CHAPTER **4**). If, however, the permanent establishment is converted into a UK subsidiary, the assets are transferred from the parent to the subsidiary on a no gain/no loss basis. The subsidiary may also take over stock at cost, and be treated for losses and capital allowances as if there had been no change.

[41.68] If a non-resident company does not trade in the UK through a permanent establishment, it is not liable to corporation tax but is liable to income tax (at the basic rate) on UK sources of income, e.g. on rental income from UK property, subject to an overriding limit where certain disregarded company income is received. The charging provisions for rental income are the same as those for individuals (see **41.43**). A gain on the disposal of such a let property would not be charged to tax (unless the property was disposed of on or after 6 April 2015 and fell within the non-resident CGT regime; see **41.50**). For companies liable to income tax, interest paid is dealt with under the income tax rules rather than the loan relationships rules.

UK subsidiary (CTA 2010, s 1109)

[41.69] A UK resident subsidiary of a foreign company is liable to corporation tax in the same way as any other resident company. Where this results in double taxation on the overseas parent, relief should be available to the parent either unilaterally or from the relevant double tax treaty. See **41.70** re group relief for losses.

Groups of companies (CTA 2010, ss 107–128, 973–980)

[41.70] A UK permanent establishment of an overseas company or an overseas company carrying on a trade of dealing in or developing UK land (see 41.64) may claim group relief against its UK profits in respect of losses surrendered by UK resident subsidiary companies of the overseas parent, and may surrender its losses as group relief to such companies, providing the losses relate to UK activities and are not relievable in the overseas country. From 1 April 2013, this rule is relaxed somewhat for losses of a UK permanent establishment of an EEA resident company. From this date, losses are able to be surrendered if they are not actually relieved elsewhere (rather than, as before, if they could potentially be relieved elsewhere).

Tax payable by a non-resident company within a group that remains unpaid for six months after the due date may be recovered from another company within the same group.

Non resident companies: cessation of residence (TMA 1970, Sch 3ZB; TCGA 1992, ss 185, 187, 187A)

[41.71] If a foreign-registered company that is resident in the UK ceases to be so resident, it is charged to tax as if it had disposed of all its assets at that time, unless they are retained in a UK permanent establishment. The tax charge is postponed if the company is a 75% subsidiary of a UK resident company and the two companies so elect within two years. The parent company is then charged to tax on the net gains on the deemed disposal as and when the subsidiary disposes of the assets, or ceases to be a subsidiary.

If gains are not deferred as above, it is possible for the company to elect for an exit charge payment plan such that any tax due in the UK is payable in instalments. These plans are available to companies incorporated in the EEA, including UK companies, which transfer their business and their place of residence for tax purposes to another member state. Deferred tax payments will be subject to interest under the usual rules. An exit charge payment plan may include provision for HMRC to take security for the deferred payments where they consider that there would otherwise be a serious risk to the collection of tax. This security would generally take the form of a bank guarantee.

ATED-related gains

[41.72] Where the deemed disposal under these provisions generates an ATED-related gain chargeable to capital gains tax (or an ATED-related loss), see 4.8, the gain is not charged immediately (and a loss is not immediately available for set off). Instead the ATED-related gain or loss is treated as coming into charge (or being allowable) at a later time when the company disposes of the asset.

Transfer pricing (TIOPA 2010, ss 146–230)

[41.73] The transfer pricing provisions require non-arm's length transactions (including interest on 'excessive' debt finance) between associated persons to be adjusted for tax purposes to the normal arm's length price. These provisions apply not only where one of the companies is non-resident but also where both are UK resident. There are, however, exemptions for most small and medium-sized companies. The transfer pricing provisions are covered briefly in **45.30**.

Computations relating to foreign exchange matters (see **41.81**) are in any event made using arm's length principles and are outside the transfer pricing rules. Taxpayers may make 'advance pricing arrangements' with the tax authorities that their transfer pricing arrangements are acceptable to those authorities. Such agreements are mainly made by multinational companies.

European Union

[41.74] The EU is playing an increasing part in the taxation of member states, and its directives and regulations must be taken into account in UK tax legislation (even in the current climate of uncertainty as to the future of the UK within the EU). The EU's executive body, the European Commission, provides information on the EU tax policy and strategy at http://ec.europa.eu/taxation_customs/index_en.htm and proposals for future EU-wide taxation rules, ultimately with the aim of promoting better co-ordination of direct tax systems in EU states. Clearly some of the suggested changes would take a considerable time both to devise and implement, and indeed may never come to fruition.

European Economic Interest Groupings (ITA 2007, s 842; CTA 2010, s 990)

[41.75] A European Economic Interest Grouping (EEIG) is a form of business entity that may be set up by enterprises of states in the EEA (i.e. the European Union plus Iceland, Liechtenstein and Norway) for activities such as packing, processing, marketing or research.

The EEIG's profits are taxable and losses allowable only in the hands of the members. The EEIG cannot be formed to make profits for itself. Any trade carried on by the members is treated as carried on in partnership, with the normal rules of income tax, corporation tax and capital gains tax applying.

The 'fiscal transparency' of the EEIG does not apply to provisions other than those charging tax on income and gains, so that an EEIG registered in the UK is required to collect and account for tax on interest, etc. and under PAYE.

European Company

[41.76] Companies operating in more than one EU member state may form a 'European Company' (Societas Europaea — SE) or a European Co-operative (Societas Co-operative Europaea — SCE). Various provisions in the UK tax legislation have been amended to incorporate references to SEs and SCEs.

Such companies may effect a merger, under which the SE or SCE could be within or outside the charge to UK corporation tax. The UK legislation has already been amended to ensure that various UK tax provisions that could have an effect on the merger, i.e. those relating to capital gains, intangible assets, loan relationships, derivative contracts, capital allowances and stamp taxes, will operate broadly on a tax neutral basis, with any further amendments to be included in regulations. There are anti-avoidance provisions to ensure that the merger is for bona fide commercial reasons and not as part of a tax avoidance scheme. Advance clearance may be obtained that this condition is met.

Interest and royalty payments (ITTOIA 2005, ss 757–767; ITA 2007, Pt 15)

[41.77] Companies may pay interest and royalties without deducting tax where the payments are made to an associated company in another EU state. Companies are associated where one directly owns 25% of the capital or voting rights in the other or a third company directly owns 25% of both. Such payments from a UK company to an EU associate are exempt from tax. For interest, but not for royalties, the paying company must apply for an exemption notice from HMRC. Certain EU countries will be allowed to continue to apply a withholding tax to such payments for a transitional period.

Anti-avoidance provisions apply for payments made on or after 17 March 2016. These impose a withholding tax where a payment of a royalty is made to a non-resident connected person as part of arrangements the purpose of which is to obtain a tax advantage by virtue of a provision of a double tax agreement.

Transfer of a trade (TCGA 1992, ss 140–140D)

[41.78] A claim can be made for the transfer of a UK business to be made on a no gain/no loss basis if the transfer is to an EU resident company in exchange for shares or securities issued by the transferee company and provided certain conditions are satisfied.

There are similar provisions to permit a claim to be made to defer a capital gains charge on the transfer of a non-UK business to a company resident overseas. The deferred gain is brought back into charge on either a subsequent disposal by the UK company of any of the securities in the overseas company (by treating the disposal as a separate chargeable transaction) or the disposal by the overseas company of any of the assets transferred, within six years of the transfer. Alternatively, if the transfer is of a non-UK business to a company resident in another EU state it is possible instead to claim a tax credit for any tax that would have arisen were it not for the mergers directive.

Value added tax

[41.79] The VAT treatment of transactions between European Union countries is outlined at 7.37. If a trader suffers VAT in another EU state on goods or services bought and used there (say while participating in a trade fair), it cannot be treated as input VAT in the UK, but it may be recoverable from the other EU state. Details are in HMRC Notice 723.

Single currency; the euro (FA 1998, s 163; SI 1998/3177)

[41.80] Businesses may pay their taxes and national insurance contributions in euros, although liabilities will still be calculated in sterling and under- or overpayments may arise because of exchange rate fluctuations before payments are actually credited by the tax authorities. There is legislation to prevent unintended tax consequences arising as a result of the adoption of the euro by other EU states.

Foreign currency (CTA 2010, ss 5–13, 1127 and Sch 2 paras 11–15; CTA 2009, s 328; SI 2013/1815)

[41.81] Both trading and non-trading companies use the currency of their accounts (or branch financial statements) to calculate their taxable profits and determine their exchange gains and losses, so long as the use of that currency follows generally accepted accounting practice. Generally accepted accounting practice means either UK generally accepted accounting practice (GAAP) or, where appropriate, generally accepted accounting practice in accordance with international accounting standards (IAS). There are provisions to prevent groups of companies gaining a tax advantage through one company using UK GAAP and the other using IAS.

UK resident companies

[41.82] The basic rule is that a UK resident company is required to compute its profits and losses in sterling. If the company's functional currency is non-sterling, the relevant income or loss is translated into sterling using an appropriate exchange rate.

Any losses carried forward are carried forward in the company's functional currency. When the loss is relieved against taxable profits of a future period, the loss is translated to sterling as follows:

(a) where the company's functional currency for the future period is the same as that for the period in which the loss arose, the loss that is relieved is translated into sterling at the same exchange rate as the profits they are offsetting;

(b) where the company's functional currency for the future period is different from the period in which the loss arose, the loss that is relieved is translated into the company's functional currency for the later period using the spot rate of exchange at the start of the first accounting period for which it began to prepare its accounts in the new functional currency. The loss is then translated into sterling at the same exchange rate as the profits they are offsetting.

This rule is relaxed somewhat when a company, with a non-sterling functional currency, disposes of shares, ships, aircraft and interests in shares. In such circumstances, gains and losses are computed in the functional currency and converted to sterling using the spot rate on the day of the disposal.

For the treatment of profits and losses arising from exchange rate fluctuations see **41.84**.

UK resident investment companies

[41.83] Where a UK resident investment company prepares its accounts in a non-sterling currency it can either identify sterling as its functional currency or it can elect for a designated currency to be used for tax purposes. Such an election is valid only to the extent that the designated currency reflects the assets and liabilities held by the company or where the designated currency is the same as the ultimate parent company of the group to which the company belongs.

This provision means that UK resident investment companies can elect for a designated currency to be used for tax purposes, other than the functional currency used in the accounts. Such elections can be made (or revoked) by notice in writing to HMRC at any time on or after 9 December 2010.

This rule is relaxed somewhat when a company, with a non-sterling designated currency, disposes of shares, ships, aircraft and interests in shares. In such circumstances, gains and losses are computed in the designated currency and converted to sterling using the spot rate on the day of the disposal.

For the treatment of profits and losses arising from exchange rate fluctuations see **41.84**.

Foreign exchange

[41.84] The treatment of profits and losses arising from exchange rate fluctuations is broadly as follows. Foreign exchange gains and losses on monetary assets and liabilities (such as cash, bank deposits and debts), and on forward contracts to buy or sell currency, are taxed as income or allowed as deductions as they accrue. Exchange differences on monetary items are taken into account as they accrue. Unrealised gains above certain limits on long-term capital items may be partly deferred. Exchange differences on borrowing that 'matches' a non-monetary asset are deferred until the asset is disposed of, and then dealt with under the capital gains tax rules. See HMRC's Statement of Practice SP 2/02 for the detailed provisions.

There are anti-avoidance provisions to prevent companies from sheltering an exchange gain from tax whilst still obtaining relief for an exchange loss. Additionally, specific provisions ensure that when a UK resident investment company changes its functional currency (**41.83**) any foreign exchange gains or losses that arise with respect to loan relationships or derivative contracts in the first period of account under the new currency are not brought into account. This therefore means that investment companies cannot generate tax deductible foreign exchange losses by changing their functional currency.

Gains and losses on certain financial instruments for managing currency risk are also taken into account in calculating income profits and losses.

As far as VAT is concerned, HMRC consider that, in general, forex transactions are supplies for VAT purposes if the registered person adopts a spread position (a difference between a bid price and a sell price from which a person would expect to derive a profit) over a period of time when buying and selling currency. In relation to such supplies, the consideration would be the net result of all forex transactions over a period and would be VAT exempt (see HMRC Brief 05/2007).

Trusts (ITA 2007, ss 474–476; TCGA 1992, ss 2, 10A, 13(10), 68–73, 79A–98A and Schs 5, 5A)

[41.85] Trustees are treated, both for income tax and capital gains tax, as a single person unless the context otherwise requires. That notional person is treated as resident in the UK if either (a) all the trustees are UK resident or (b) at least one trustee is UK resident (at least one trustee being non-UK resident) and the settlor was resident or domiciled in the UK either when he made the settlement or, for settlements created on death, immediately before his death. If an individual is a trustee of a settlement only in the overseas part of a split year (**41.6** or **41.8** prior to 2013–14) then he is treated as not resident for that year. Anti-avoidance provisions prevent trustees exploiting the residence terms of double taxation agreements to reduce or eliminate a capital gains tax charge (see **45.34**).

Trustees are not directly chargeable to UK income tax for a tax year throughout which they are non-resident. Income from a UK source is paid to them under deduction of tax.

Non-resident trusts are dealt with by HMRC's Centre for Non-Residents. Special provisions apply to reduce or eliminate the tax advantages of offshore trusts as indicated in **41.86** to **41.88**. See **40.11** in relation to the income tax charge on gains on offshore life policies held in trust and **45.34** for brief notes on other anti-avoidance provisions.

Exit charge when trust becomes non-resident

[41.86] Where a trust becomes non-resident, all the trust assets (except any that remain within the scope of UK tax, for example assets that continue to be used in a UK trade) are treated as disposed of and reacquired at market value, and gains are charged to capital gains tax. Further, if the trustee elects, no gain or loss will accrue at the time of becoming non-resident, if the gain at that time would be a chargeable NRCGT gain (**41.50**). On a subsequent disposal, the NRCGT gain or loss that would have accrued on the deemed disposal will accrue at the time of the subsequent disposal, in addition to any gain or loss which actually accrues.

Rollover relief on replacement of business assets (see **29.16** to **29.21**) cannot be claimed if the new assets are acquired after the trust becomes non-resident and are outside the UK tax charge. These provisions also apply to dual resident trusts that are exempt from UK tax on gains because of a double tax treaty.

The acquisition cost of a beneficiary's interest in an emigrating trust for capital gains tax is normally uplifted to the market value at the time of the trust's emigration. This uplift is, however, prevented by anti-avoidance provisions where the trust has a stockpile of gains that have not been attributed to beneficiaries.

Charge on settlor (TCGA 1992 s 86; ITTOIA 2005, s 624; ITA 2007, ss 721–724)

[41.87] Where gains are made by a non-resident trust (or a dual resident trust outside the UK capital gains charge), the settlor may be taxed on the gains if the settlor has an interest in the trust in the tax year in which the gains arise, and in that year he is UK domiciled and UK resident or, prior to 2013–14, ordinarily resident at some time during the year.

The gains can be reduced by the settlor's unused personal capital losses for the current year and earlier years. Any chargeable gains are treated as forming the highest part of the gains on which the settlor is chargeable for that year. The settlor has the right to recover from the trustees any tax charged on him.

A settlor is treated as having an interest in a trust if his or her spouse or civil partner, or his or her children or their spouses or civil partners have an interest, or an interest is held by a company controlled by the settlor and/or those persons. The settlor is also treated as having an interest in a trust in which grandchildren have an interest, if the trust was set up on or after 17 March 1998, or it was set up before that date but became non-resident, or funds were added, or grandchildren became beneficiaries, thereafter.

Where a settlor who is resident in the UK settles property on a non-resident trust and has power to enjoy income therefrom, either immediately or in the future, that income is broadly deemed to be the settlor's income. Certain exemptions may apply and there are provisions to prevent double charging.

The September 2017 Finance Bill (which is expected to receive Royal Assent in November 2017) provides that there will be no charge on the settlor if the settlor of a non-UK trust becomes deemed domiciled under the 15 out of 20 year rule (**41.10**) on or after 6 April 2017. Any gains of the trust will not be attributed to the UK resident settlor when he becomes deemed domiciled in the UK provided he makes no direct or indirect additions to the trust. Such trusts are referred to as 'protected trusts'. Capital gains will instead be matched with capital payments received by UK resident beneficiaries.

Charge on beneficiaries (TCGA 1992, ss 87–87H, 91)

[41.88] Where gains are not charged on a settlor as indicated above, UK beneficiaries are charged to capital gains tax on their share of the gains of a non-resident trust if they receive capital payments from the trust when they are resident in the UK.

The tax on a capital payment to a beneficiary is increased by a supplementary charge if gains are not distributed to the beneficiaries in the tax year in which they are made or the following year. The charge runs from 1 December in the tax year following that in which the trustees' gains arose to 30 November in the tax year after that in which the gain is distributed to the beneficiary. The charge is at an annual rate of 10% of the tax on the capital payment, for a maximum of six years.

Gains realised by beneficiaries on *disposal* of their interests in a non-resident trust are taxable if the trust is, or has at any time been, an offshore trust.

In arriving at the gains to be attributed to beneficiaries under these provisions, the beneficiaries' own losses cannot be set against the trustees' gains.

Income from a non-resident trust attributable to a beneficiary resident in the UK is chargeable as miscellaneous income. Credit will be available for any tax suffered by the trustees.

Various schemes have been devised to avoid the tax charge on the beneficiaries and specific anti-avoidance legislation has been introduced to counteract them. See **45.34** for brief details.

Tax points

[41.89] Note the following:

- Taxpayers, other than short-term visitors to the UK, who are eligible for the remittance basis may be able to claim the benefit of that basis only if they pay an additional tax charge of £30,000 or £60,000 (depending upon their period of UK residency — see **41.16**). They need to consider carefully the pros and cons of making the claim.
- An employee whose work is wholly carried out abroad, should try to arrange for the employer to meet the cost of overseas board and lodging, so that the taxable benefit can then be offset by an expenses claim; otherwise the employee will get no tax relief on it.
- If UK property is let out it is not necessary to be *non-resident* to be within the rules requiring tax to be deducted from the rents. The rules apply if the landlord's 'usual place of abode' is abroad (see **41.43**).
- An individual who is resident and domiciled in the UK, has to pay tax on all income wherever in the world it arises. It is not possible to escape income tax by investing in offshore roll-up funds (see **45.26**).
- Many people invest in offshore bank and building society accounts to get the benefit of receiving gross income (although tax is still payable unless covered by reliefs and allowances). Much of the cash flow benefit is lost for those making half-yearly payments on account under

self-assessment. There are also problems in the event of death, because of the possible need to take out probate of the will abroad. These points need to be borne in mind when considering whether the investment is worthwhile.

• Individuals that are taxed on income or gains remitted to the UK, might consider keeping funds abroad separate where possible, supported by detailed records, so that it can be demonstrated, where appropriate, that remittances do not represent either income or chargeable gains.

42

Trusts and estates

Background

[42.1] A trust, or settlement, arises when someone transfers assets to trustees who hold them and the income from them for the benefit of one or more persons.

A trust can be created in lifetime, or on death by a will or under the intestacy rules where a person does not leave a will (sometimes referred to as a statutory trust). See CHAPTER 35, which also deals generally with planning points relating to a deceased's estate.

The overseas aspect of trusts is dealt with at **41.85** to **41.88**. See also **40.11** regarding gains on offshore life policies held in trust.

There are a number of anti-avoidance provisions that specifically relate to trusts. The rules for gains on disposal of a private residence occupied under the terms of a trust are dealt with in **30.11**. The 'pre-owned assets' income tax charge on benefits received by those who continue to enjoy a benefit from property they have disposed of, including the disposal of property to a trust, is dealt with briefly in **5.42**. See **29.59** for the special tax provisions where trustees receive a distribution arising out of the purchase by a company of its own shares and **45.34** for other trust anti-avoidance provisions.

HMRC guidance is available at www.gov.uk/topic/personal-tax/trusts. The Tell Us Once service allows the reporting of a death to most Government organisations in one go, and will notify HMRC to deal with the deceased's personal tax affairs but not his business tax affairs, for which HMRC must be contacted separately.

The HMRC Trusts Registration Service was launched in July 2017 and provides a single online route for trusts and complex estates (as defined) to comply with their registration obligations. All trusts with a UK tax consequence will need to be registered and trustees must ensure and confirm the Trust Register is accurate and up to date. Trusts that have already registered with HMRC must sign up to the register, as must estates that have already registered and are still being administered, but not trusts and estates that have closed.

The tax law and practice relating to estates and trusts is complex and was made more so by Finance Act 2006. It is essential to seek appropriate professional advice.

Administration of an estate

[42.2] Where a trust is created on death, the personal representatives must first complete the administration of the estate. They need to deal with the deceased's tax position for the year of death (and earlier years if returns have not been submitted) and also their own tax position as personal representatives until the administration of the estate is completed. Personal representatives can use form 64-8 to authorise an agent to deal with some individual tax affairs for the estate (see **9.6**). The normal time limit for enquiring into a tax return is 12 months after the date on which the return is filed (see **9.41**). To minimise delays in winding up estates and trusts, and distributing estate or trust property, HMRC will, on request, issue tax returns before the end of the tax year of death, or of winding up an estate or trust, and will give early confirmation if they do not intend to enquire into the return. See **9.53** regarding limits in relation to HMRC enquiries into the tax position of a deceased taxpayer.

The personal representatives will not usually be able to settle the deceased's tax liabilities until probate is obtained, and the inheritance tax due must be paid before probate is granted (see **5.52**). Under an agreement between HMRC and the British Bankers' and Building Societies' Associations, participating institutions accept instructions from personal representatives to transfer sums standing to the credit of the deceased direct to HMRC in payment of inheritance tax before the issue of the grant. This is of considerable practical help where the personal representatives do not have ready access to other funds outside the estate, such as the proceeds of an insurance policy on the life of the deceased which do not belong to the estate. The deceased's tax office should be asked to arrange for the HMRC Accounts Office not to issue any further self-assessment statements pending probate being obtained, since they can often cause needless distress to the family. Interest on tax falling due after death will not start to run until 30 days after the grant of probate.

The administration period during which the personal representatives deal with the collection of assets and payment of liabilities and the distribution of the estate may last some months or even years if the estate is complex.

[42.3] Personal representatives deal with the estate of a deceased either under the terms of the will, according to the rules of intestacy where there is no will, or under a deed varying the will or entitlement in the intestacy. (For the way an intestate person's estate is distributed see **35.1**.) Income tax is payable on the income of the deceased up to the date of death, with a full year's allowances, any unused married couple's allowance of the deceased spouse or civil partner being transferable to the other if the personal representatives notify HMRC (see **33.13**). If the deceased had chargeable gains in excess of the annual exempt amount in the tax year of his death, capital gains tax is payable but there is no capital gains tax on the increase in the value of assets held at death. If there are capital losses in the year of death, they may be carried back to set against gains of the three previous tax years, latest first (ignoring any gains already covered by the annual exempt amount), and tax will be repaid accordingly (but interest on the repayment will run from the payment date for the tax year of death — see **9.16**). The capital losses carried back cannot be set against gains treated as accruing to a beneficiary of a non-UK resident settlement (see **41.88**), or against NRCGT gains (see **41.50**) but any NRCGT losses which cannot be deducted from NRCGT gains in the year of death may be carried back and set against NRCGT gains of the three preceding tax years.

Inheritance tax is payable if transfers of wealth by the deceased in the seven years before death which were either then chargeable or potentially exempt, together with the amount chargeable at death, exceed the nil rate band (currently £325,000). See **35.4** regarding the transfer of any unused part of the inheritance tax nil rate band, on the death of the first spouse or civil partner to die, to the survivor. See **5.24** regarding the 'residence nil rate band' which applies to deaths on or after 6 April 2017.

See **9.25** to **9.29** for further details, including the provisions under which an inheritance tax account does not have to be submitted for small estates. Assets to which a surviving spouse or civil partner becomes entitled either absolutely, or to enjoy the income with the assets being predestined for others upon the death of the survivor, are not chargeable to inheritance tax at that time, but will be included in the survivor's estate for inheritance tax upon his or her death or earlier lifetime transfer. The value of business and agricultural property can be eliminated from the calculation of inheritance tax in some circumstances. The way in which the tax is calculated is dealt with in CHAPTER 5.

Personal representatives need to be aware that HMRC take a harsh view in relation to provisional figures included without proper enquiry in calculating inheritance tax for the purpose of obtaining probate, even though those calculations can be revised later and any additional tax paid via a 'corrective' account. Before including such figures, personal representatives are required to make 'the fullest enquiries that are reasonably practicable in the circumstances' and HMRC have in the past unsuccessfully sought to exact a penalty despite the fact that accurate figures were submitted long before the due date for payment of inheritance tax. The due date is often meaningless in any case because of the need to pay the inheritance tax before obtaining probate. HMRC pay close attention to the values included for inheritance tax in respect of household and personal goods and may open an enquiry to satisfy themselves that all of the goods have been included and that they have been valued on the correct 'market value' basis.

Where the deceased's residential property is rebanded after death for council tax purposes, any refund arising from an earlier overpayment will be subject to inheritance tax, although the value of the refund may be reduced by 50%.

Where property is transferred to those entitled under a will or intestacy, neither stamp duty nor stamp duty land tax (or in Scotland land and buildings transaction tax (LBTT, see CHAPTER 6)) is payable. Nor is stamp duty land tax or LBTT payable when personal representatives dispose of a deceased's home to a property trader.

Income during the administration period (ITA 2007, ss 11, 14, 403–405; ITTOIA 2005, ss 649–682A; CTA 2009, ss 934–967)

[42.4] Personal representatives are liable to income tax at 7.5% on dividend income and at the basic rate on other income. Personal representatives are not taxed at higher rates, nor can they claim personal allowances, or the savings allowance or dividend allowance applying to individuals (see **2.5**). If the deceased held individual savings accounts (ISAs), the tax exemption ceases at the date of death, so that the basic rate of 20% will be charged on any subsequent interest. However draft regulations provide for ISAs to retain their tax-advantaged status following the death of the account holder (see **36.17**). Where the personal representatives have borrowed to pay any inheritance tax which they are liable to pay on the delivery of the account, preparatory to obtaining a grant of probate, interest payable for up to one year from the date of the loan may be deducted from the estate income of the tax year of payment. If the interest exceeds the estate income of that tax year, it may be carried back against estate income of preceding tax years, and any remaining amount may be carried forward against future estate income. Note that the cap on certain reliefs against general income (see **2.13**) does *not* apply to this interest.

The income during the administration period will be distributed to the beneficiaries entitled to it either because they are entitled absolutely to the assets or because, while the assets remain in trust, they are entitled to the income. Any payments to a beneficiary on account of income during the administration period are net of the 'applicable rate' of tax, i.e. the dividend ordinary rate of 7.5% or the basic rate of 20% according to the income they represent. The gross equivalent is included in taxable income in the tax year when it is received by the beneficiary from the personal representatives. Payments to beneficiaries are treated as being made first out of brought-forward and current income charged at the basic rate, then dividends taxed at the dividend ordinary rate. Dividend income includes normal dividends, scrip dividends, loans written off by close companies and bonus issues of redeemable shares or securities. The total income will first have been apportioned between beneficiaries on a just and reasonable basis, the personal representatives being required to provide a certificate showing the types of income and the tax deducted.

The rate of tax treated as deducted from payments to beneficiaries is not necessarily the same as that borne by the personal representatives, since the relevant rate is the applicable rate in force at the time of the payment to the beneficiaries, rather than the rate in force when the income was received. When the administration period is completed and the final amount of income due to each beneficiary ascertained, the beneficiary is treated as having received the balance due to him in the tax year in which the administration is completed (or, for someone with a life entitlement whose interest ceased earlier, say because of his death, in the tax year when the interest ceased). The amount due to each beneficiary is grossed up at the relevant rate in force at the time according to the income it represents. Where dividends are received in the estate before 6 April 2016 (the date from which dividend tax credits were abolished) and the income is paid to the beneficiary after that date the beneficiaries will receive a non-payable tax credit of 7.5%, i.e. the applicable tax rate for 2016–17.

Capital gains during the administration period (TCGA 1992, ss 3(7), 4–4BB, 62, 225A)

[42.5] No capital gains tax arises on the transfer to legatees of assets comprising specific legacies, the legatees acquiring them at market value at the date of death. Assets that pass to the personal representatives (out of which they pay debts due and distribute the residue of the estate) are also acquired by them at market value at the date of death. Any gains arising on a disposal of assets by the personal representatives are calculated by reference to the sales proceeds less the value at death. The personal representatives are entitled in their own right to the annual exempt amount, currently £11,300, against any gains on their disposals in the tax year of death and the next two tax years, but not thereafter. Gains accruing on or after 6 April 2016 in excess of the exempt amount are taxed at either 20% or 28% depending on the type of gain (see **4.2**). If any losses arise, they may only be set against gains of the personal representatives and cannot be transferred to beneficiaries.

If the private residence is to be sold by the personal representatives, a chargeable gain may arise between death and sale. The private residence exemption (see **30.3**) is available following a claim by the personal representatives where the property has been used immediately before and after death as the main residence of individuals who are entitled to at least 75% of the net sale proceeds either absolutely or for life. It is the circumstances of the individual entitled to occupy the house which are taken into account when deciding whether there is a non-qualifying tax year for these purposes (see **30.4**). Where the private residence exemption is not available it might be appropriate for personal representatives to consider a transfer of the property to beneficiaries if they have any unused capital gains annual exempt amount or any unused basic rate limit available, so that some or all of the gain is exempt or charged at 18% (see **4.2**) rather than the 28% rate applicable to the personal representatives on such gains above the annual exempt amount. A transfer might also be effective if the personal representatives have used their annual exempt amount but the beneficiaries have not.

Personal representatives do not qualify for gift holdover relief, but trustees do (see **4.32**). Where the residue of the estate is left on trust, the personal representatives should ensure that assets on which gift holdover is available and is appropriate to be claimed have been formally appropriated by the personal representatives to the trustees (which will usually but not necessarily be themselves, but then acting in a different capacity) before being allocated to those entitled under the trust.

End of administration period

[42.6] The administration period ends either when the whole estate is finally distributed if no trust has been created, or when the residue of the estate after payment of debts and legacies is transferred to a trust fund. There is no chargeable gain on personal representatives when they transfer assets to beneficiaries or trustees, the assets transferred being regarded as acquired by the beneficiaries or trustees at market value at the date of death or the cost to the personal representatives if acquired later.

Types of trust

[42.7] Apart from a bare trust, which effectively means that someone holds an asset as nominee for another (see **42.15**), trusts broadly come within the following categories for taxation purposes:

(a)   Trusts in which before 22 March 2006 one or more individuals were entitled under a lifetime settlement or by will or intestacy to the income (called the 'interest in possession'), with the capital being predestined elsewhere at a future point, and the trustees sometimes having overriding powers. The person entitled to the interest is called the life tenant (see **42.16**).

(b)   As in (a) but either:
(i)   the present life interest came to an end by death or otherwise before 6 October 2008, with a new life tenant then being entitled to the interest in possession, or
(ii)   the present life interest comes to an end on or after 6 October 2008 on the death of the life tenant and a surviving spouse or civil partner then becomes entitled to an interest in possession.
An interest arising under (i) or (ii) is called a 'transitional serial interest'.

(c)   Trusts in which from 22 March 2006, one or more individuals are entitled under a will or intestacy to the income, with the capital being predestined to go to one or more individuals or to remain in an appropriate trust at a future point — called an immediate post-death interest.

(d)   Accumulation and maintenance trusts (see **42.37** to **42.42**). Before 22 March 2006 these trusts received favourable inheritance tax treatment where they provided for children of a common grandparent to have income used for their benefit or accumulated, with a child being entitled to his or her share at age 25. It was sufficient for the child's entitlement at that age to be the right to his or her share of the income whilst the capital remained in trust.

New accumulation and maintenance trusts from 22 March 2006 only fall within the special provisions for such trusts if they are established for bereaved minors either on an intestacy, under the will of a deceased parent or under the Criminal Injuries Compensation Scheme, or the Victims of Overseas Terrorism Compensation Scheme. The requirement for beneficiaries to have a common grandparent no longer applies. Under the new provisions, the beneficiary must be entitled to his or her share of the capital at age 18 in order for inheritance tax not to be chargeable. Where the child has a right only to income at that age, but has an entitlement to his or her share of the capital by age 25, special inheritance tax provisions apply.

For trusts in existence at 22 March 2006, the terms could be changed by 5 April 2008 to bring them within the new rules. If such changes were not made, the trusts now come within the 'mainstream' inheritance tax rules (as to which see (g)).

(e)   Trusts for a vulnerable beneficiary, i.e. a disabled person or a child under 18, one or both of whose parents have died (see **42.43** to **42.47**).

(f)   Self-settlements under which from 22 March 2006 an individual with a condition expected to lead to disability can settle assets on himself/herself for lifetime (see **42.47**).

(g)   Trusts within the 'mainstream' inheritance tax rules for trusts (see **42.27** to **42.36**). Before 22 March 2006 these rules were generally known as the rules for discretionary trusts, i.e. trusts where the trustees had a discretion as to what they did with the income and capital. Finance Act 2006 gave the rules the label 'mainstream' and extended their coverage so that they apply in all cases except those listed in (a) to (f) above.

Prior to Finance Act 2006, on the death of a life tenant entitled to the income under (a) above, the capital supporting that interest was included in his estate at death for inheritance tax. This still applies where that life tenant, or one with a transitional serial interest under (b) above, dies (see Example 2 in **42.23**). It also applies on the death of the life tenant under (c). In all of these cases the value of the assets for capital gains tax purposes is increased to the value at the date of death, without any capital gains tax being payable.

For trusts under (d) and (g) above, the value of the capital within a trust fund will not be reckoned for inheritance tax at the death of a beneficiary, and neither will the value of the trust assets be uplifted to the value at a death in calculating the capital gains tax payable on a later disposal by the trustees.

For trusts falling within (g) above, there is a charge to inheritance tax every ten years (called a 'periodic charge'), based on the value of the trust funds at that point, together with a further charge when capital is distributed to beneficiaries (called an 'exit charge') (see **42.31**). There is no capital gains tax effect at the ten-year anniversary. There is a disposal by the trustees for capital gains tax purposes when they distribute assets to beneficiaries, but holdover relief may be available (see **4.32**).

There is no inheritance tax ten-year or exit charge on an accumulation and maintenance trust in (d) provided the capital is required to be distributed to beneficiaries at age 18. Where that is not so, there will be an exit charge, the calculation of which is restricted by reference to the years after age 18 (see **42.42**). There will be a disposal for capital gains tax where the trustees distribute assets to beneficiaries, but holdover relief (see **4.32**) is available.

Trusts for vulnerable beneficiaries and qualifying self-settlements (see (e) and (f) above) are broadly dealt with as if the assets and income belong to the beneficiary, and the trust assets will be included in the beneficiary's estate at death.

There are several other types of trust where the inheritance tax ten-year or exit charges do not apply. These types of trust are often referred to as favoured trusts and include those in (d) created post-22 March 2006, (e) and (f) above. The other favoured trusts are:

(A) Protective trusts. Property is held in such trusts for the benefit of the beneficiary until he does, or attempts to do, or suffers any act or thing whereby he would be deprived of the right to receive the income, or any event happens which would deprive him of that right, for example, bankruptcy.

(B) Employee trusts. Such trusts are ones which either indefinitely, or until the end of a defined period, do not permit any of the settled property to be applied otherwise than for the benefit of certain employees and their relatives (see **42.49**). Newspaper trusts are employee trusts set up specifically for employees of newspaper publishing or holding companies.

(C) Registered pensions schemes (see CHAPTER **16**).

(D) Charitable trusts (see CHAPTER **43**).

(E) Miscellaneous other trusts including political and heritage trusts, and trade or professional compensation funds.

Further details on each type of trust in (a) to (g), including the income tax position, are given in the remainder of this chapter. Employee trusts and employee-ownership trusts are also covered in more detail in see **42.49**.

Powers over trusts (IHTA 1984, ss 47A, 55A, 272)

[42.8] Trusts may include a general power for the settlor to dispose of trust property as he sees fit. Powers over trusts are normally not treated as part of a person's property for inheritance tax purposes. This is subject to anti-avoidance rules where such powers are purchased.

Trusts in which the settlor retains an interest — income tax and capital gains tax position (ITTOIA 2005, ss 619–648; TCGA 1992, Schs 4A–4C; FA 2000, s 44)

[42.9] A settlor who is an individual remains liable for income tax on the trust income if he or his spouse or civil partner retains a present or future right to the income or assets of the trust, or where the settlement transfers income but not capital (see **12.10**, **18.7** and **23.31** for detailed comments). 'Spouse or civil partner' does not include a future, former, separated or deceased spouse or civil partner.

Even though a settlement is of capital in which the settlor does not retain an interest, if income of the settlement is paid to or for the benefit of an unmarried child of the settlor who is under 18, it is treated as the settlor's income, subject to the exceptions at **33.10** (see also **42.15** and **42.38**).

The income tax liability on the settlor does not apply to the extent that the trustees give the income to charity, or a charity is entitled to the income under the trust, or where the settlor is not an individual. The settlor is entitled to recover the tax paid by him from the trustees, or from the person who received the income. The net effect where such a recovery is made is that the trustees or beneficiary of the settlement effectively pay the tax on the income but at the settlor's highest tax rate. If the settlor obtains a repayment of tax on the trust income because his liability is lower than the tax funded by the trustees, he must pay the amount of that repayment to the trustees.

[42.10] As far as capital gains tax is concerned, see **42.14** regarding the denial of gift holdover relief on transfers to a settlor-interested trust.

[42.11] Where a beneficiary disposes of an interest in a trust in which the settlor has an interest (or had an interest at any time in the two previous tax years), there is a deemed disposal and reacquisition by the trustees at market value. The trustees are charged to tax on the deemed disposal although they are entitled to recover it from the person who made the disposal of the interest, whether that is the settlor or any other person. Gift holdover relief is not available. See **45.34** for anti-avoidance provisions to counter a tax avoidance device known as the 'flip flop'.

Tax liability on setting up a trust (IHTA 1984, ss 3A, 13, 13A, 28, 28A, 200; TCGA 1992, ss 165, 169B–169G, 260; ITA 2007, s 508)

Inheritance tax

[42.12] The appropriate amount of inheritance tax is charged on a deceased's estate before property is transferred to a trust created by his will or on intestacy (see **5.28**).

The only lifetime transfers to trusts which do not come within the mainstream rules for inheritance tax (see **42.27**) are those for the disabled and by the settlor for himself to provide for his future disability (see **42.47**). Otherwise the settlor is liable to inheritance tax on the property transferred to the trust at one-half of the full scale rate (see **5.24** and **5.27**), except to the extent that the transfer is within the nil rate band. The transfer has to be grossed up if the settlor also pays the inheritance tax (see **5.27**). If the settlor dies within the next seven years, tax on the lifetime transfer is recalculated using the full rate and scale applicable at the date of death less a credit up to the amount of any tax already charged in lifetime (see **5.31** to **5.32**).

Employee trusts are generally set up by close companies by dispositions which are not transfers of value provided certain criteria are met. Individuals can also make transfers of shares and securities to such trusts but the transfers are exempt provided certain conditions are met (see **5.18, 5.19**).

Capital gains tax

[42.13] As indicated in 42.6, no capital gains tax arises when property is transferred to trustees by personal representatives.

When assets are placed into trust in lifetime, they are treated as disposed of at market value for capital gains tax, but where the mainstream inheritance tax rules for trusts apply, the gains may be held over under the gift holdover relief provisions (see **4.32** to **4.34**).

Where gift holdover relief has been claimed, the effect is to increase the chargeable gain when the donee disposes of the asset.

[42.14] Gift holdover relief is not available on disposals to a trust in which either a settlor (who need not be the transferor) has an interest or there are arrangements under which a settlor will acquire an interest (although this rule is relaxed for gifts to maintenance funds for historic buildings where the trustees have (or could have) made an election that the income of the fund or the expenditure on maintenance shall be treated as income of the trust, rather than the settlor (**5.17**)).

Gift relief is also denied in respect of a gain on a disposal to a trust if the expenditure allowable in calculating the gain is reduced by gift relief on an earlier disposal, and immediately after the disposal the transferor has an interest in the trust, or there are arrangements under which he will acquire an interest. Where gift relief is not available, the transferor will be entitled to the annual exempt amount.

Where a disposal is made to a trust that is not initially a settlor-interested trust, any gift relief on the disposal is clawed back if the settlor acquires an interest within six years after the disposal.

Bare trusts (ITTOIA 2005, ss 629–631)

[42.15] A bare trust is one in which the beneficiary has an absolute right to the assets and income, but the trustees are the legal owners and hold the property effectively as nominee. The transfer to the bare trust is a potentially exempt transfer for inheritance tax (see **5.26**), becoming completely exempt if the donor survives the seven-year period.

A bare trust could simply be a bank or building society account in the settlor's name as trustee for the beneficiary, and in that event the trust income would not be depleted by administration expenses.

The tax position of the trust depends on the beneficiary's circumstances rather than those of the donor or the trustee, so that the trust income is included with that of the beneficiary in calculating how much of the beneficiary's income tax allowances and basic rate band are available (see 2.5). Likewise the question of whether any capital gains tax reliefs and exemptions are available on the disposal of chargeable assets depends upon the circumstances of the beneficiary (see CHAPTER 4). Beneficiaries must show their income and gains from a bare trust in their own tax returns and trustees are not required to complete returns. HMRC have, however, stated that the trustees may, if they wish, send in a return of income (but not capital gains). This will not affect the liability of the beneficiaries to send returns of both income and gains. Any tax deducted at source will be refunded if covered by reliefs and allowances.

The income tax treatment described above applies to bare trusts created before 9 March 1999 even if such a trust was made by a parent in favour of a child (and the parent could be the trustee), providing the income is not actually paid to or for the benefit of the child while the child is unmarried and under 18. If it is, the income would then be treated as the parent's under the provisions at 42.9. The child cannot be prevented from having the property put into his own legal ownership at age 18.

For bare trusts created by parents on or after 9 March 1999 in favour of their children under 18, and for income on funds added to existing trusts on or after that date, income is taxed as that of the parent, unless covered by the £100 limit dealt with at 33.10. Bare trusts created by a parent's will are still effective to treat income as that of the beneficiary, and also bare trusts created by other relatives, although it is not possible to make a reciprocal arrangement for someone to create a trust for his relative's children and for the relative to do the same for his children.

Bare trusts created by parents are effective for capital gains purposes, so that it is possible to use such trusts to acquire investments for children that produce capital growth rather than income. Where capital gains are made, a bare trust is not affected by the rules in 42.18 regarding the reduced annual exempt amount for trustees, and the full exemption (currently £11,300) will apply if the beneficiary has not used it elsewhere.

Trusts with an interest in possession

Income tax (ITA 2007, ss 6–21, 484–487; CTA 2010, s 611)

[42.16] Where there is an interest in possession, one or more beneficiaries has a right to the trust income.

The trustees are charged to tax on dividend income at the dividend ordinary rate of 7.5% (see 2.26) and on other income at the basic rate (see 2.5). Trustees are not liable to tax at higher rates. Income is calculated in the same way as for an individual. There are, however, no deductions for personal allowances, or for the savings allowance or dividend allowance applying to individuals (see **2.5**). There is no relief in calculating the tax payable by the trustees for expenses of managing the trust, which are therefore paid out of the after-tax income. Expenses are treated as paid out of savings income in priority to non-savings income and out of dividend income before other savings income.

The income beneficiaries are personally liable to income tax on that income less the trust expenses, whether they draw the income or it remains in the trust fund as an amount owed to the beneficiary (except where the settlor has retained an interest and the tax is payable by him — see **42.9**). The beneficiaries are entitled to a credit for the tax paid by the trustees on that part of the trust income that has not been used to pay trust expenses. Individual beneficiaries are entitled to the savings allowance and dividend allowance (see **2.5**) to set against dividends and savings income they receive from the trust.

Example 1

Trust's income in 2017–18 comprises rents of £3,195 gross, £2,556 net after 20% tax of £639. The trust expenses are £156. The beneficiary will receive (2,556 − 156 =) £2,400, which is equivalent to gross income of £3,000. If he is a basic rate taxpayer he will have no further liability and will retain the £2,400. If he is not liable to tax he will reclaim tax of (3,000 @ 20% =) £600. If he is a higher rate payer he will have an additional liability of 20% of £3,000, i.e. £600, and if he is an additional rate taxpayer he will have an additional liability of 25% of £3,000, i.e. £750.

If instead the trust's net income comprised rents of £1,597 gross, £1,278 net after 20% tax of £319, and cash dividends of £1,382, i.e. £1,278 net after 7.5% tax of £104, the trust expenses of £156 would reduce the dividend income to £1,122, with a resulting credit for tax of £91 (i.e. £1,213 gross). The beneficiary would still receive £2,400, but the gross income would be (1,597 + 1,213 =) £2,810. A basic rate taxpayer would retain the £2,400. A non-taxpaying beneficiary would be able to reclaim the £319 tax on rents and the £91 tax on dividends. A higher rate payer would have to pay 20% (40–20%) of £1,597 = £319 plus 25% (32.5–7.5%) of £1,213 = £303, resulting in total extra tax of £622. An additional rate taxpayer would have to pay 25% (45–20%) of £1,597 = £399 plus 30.6% (38.1–7.5%) of £1,213 = £371 resulting in total extra tax of £770.

The need to pay expenses out of the taxed income of the trust may be minimised if specific income is paid direct to the beneficiary, for example, by a mandate to a building society to pay interest direct, with a consequent saving in administration expenses. This will improve the position of a beneficiary who is entitled to a tax repayment, but for a higher rate or additional rate taxpayer it will deny relief on the trust expenses at the excess of the higher rate or additional rate over that paid by the trustees.

Capital gains tax (TCGA 1992, ss 4–4BB, 71–74, 79A, 165 and Schs 1, 7)

[42.17] The only interest in possession trusts created in lifetime after 21 March 2006 which are not subject to the mainstream inheritance tax rules are a trust for a disabled person and a trust in favour of the settlor to provide for his future disability (see **42.47**). For such a self-settlement, if the settlor transfers chargeable assets to the trust, he is liable to capital gains tax. The gift holdover relief is not available since he retains an interest in the trust (see **42.14**). Anti-avoidance provisions apply to counter a tax avoidance device known as the 'flip flop', which aimed to reduce or eliminate the tax on disposals from a trust. These are outlined at **45.34**.

[42.18] Trust gains are reduced by an annual exempt amount (£5,650 for 2017–18) and the remaining gains are taxed at either 20% or 28% depending on the type of gain (see **4.2**). Where there are a number of trusts created by the same settlor, the annual exempt amount of £5,650 is divided equally between them, subject to a minimum exemption of £1,130 for each trust. Trusts for the disabled qualify for the full annual exempt amount of £11,300, reduced where the same settlor has created several disabled trusts, with a minimum exemption for each disabled trust of £1,130.

Where losses arise on disposals by the trustees, they cannot be set against any gains made by the trustees on assets that had been transferred to the trust if the transferor or someone connected with him had bought an interest in the trust and had claimed gift holdover relief on the transferred assets (see **45.34**).

[42.19] When a beneficiary becomes absolutely entitled to trust property following the death of the person entitled to the income, the trustees are regarded as disposing of the property to the beneficiary at its then market value, but no capital gains tax liability arises. Any increase in value up to that time escapes capital gains tax (and any losses are not allowable). Where the capital gains tax cost of the property had been reduced by gift holdover relief (see **4.32** to **4.34**), there is a chargeable gain equal to the held-over amount. If the property is still qualifying business property for gift holdover relief, a further claim to defer the tax liability may be made by the trustees and beneficiary, so that the gain will be treated as reducing the acquisition cost of the beneficiary.

Broadly gift relief applies to settled property if the trustees make a non-arm's length disposal of a specified business asset and a claim is made by the trustees and the transferee, or the trustees alone where they are also the transferee. The specified assets are:

(a)   an asset, or interest in an asset, used for the purposes of a trade, profession or vocation carried on by the trustees, or by a beneficiary who had an interest in possession in the settled property immediately before the disposal; or

(b)   shares or securities of a trading company, or of a holding company of a trading group, where either the shares are unlisted or the trustees held at least 25% of the voting rights at the time of the disposal.

[42.20] When a life interest terminates other than on death, for example because a widow remarries, but the property remains in trust, there is neither a chargeable gain nor any change in the base value of the property for future capital gains tax disposals by the trustees.

When, however, a beneficiary becomes absolutely entitled to trust property other than on the death of the person entitled to the income, this is regarded as a disposal at market value at that date, and capital gains tax is payable on the increase in value. The same provisions for deferring the gain apply as stated above if the property still qualifies for business gift holdover relief. Where the deemed market value disposal to the beneficiary results in an allowable loss that the trustees cannot use against gains arising at the time of the transfer or earlier in the same tax year, the loss is treated as made by the beneficiary who has become absolutely entitled to the asset, but the beneficiary can use the loss only to reduce a gain on the disposal of the asset, or in the case of land, an asset derived from the land, thus restricting his chargeable gain to that which would have arisen had he adopted the base value of the trustees as his own.

[42.21] If, when a life interest ends, the property goes back to the settlor, the trustees are only chargeable to tax to the extent that gains have been held over, and even then, the special rules for assets acquired before 31 March 1982 (see 4.25) may apply. The settlor is treated as acquiring the property at its cost (and as having held it on 31 March 1982 if it was settled before that date, enabling him to use 31 March 1982 value to compute a gain if appropriate).

[42.22] If a beneficiary under a trust transfers his interest to someone else, this is not normally treated as a chargeable disposal for capital gains tax, whether he is transferring a life interest or a reversionary interest (i.e. the right to the capital of the trust when those with life interests die or give up their interests). There is a chargeable disposal if the beneficiary had bought the interest from someone else, or had acquired it by gift from someone who had bought it.

See **42.11** for the position where a beneficiary sells an interest in a settlement in which the settlor has an interest (or has had an interest at any time in the two previous tax years). See also **41.88** for disposals of an interest in an overseas trust.

Inheritance tax (IHTA 1984, Pt III)

[42.23] Someone who became entitled to the income for the time being from a trust fund established before 22 March 2006, or became so entitled on or after that date and the interest is a transitional serial interest (see **42.7** at (b)), or an immediate post-death interest (see **42.7** at (c)), or a disabled person's interest (see **42.47**), is regarded for inheritance tax purposes as entitled to the underlying capital, so that he is treated as making a chargeable transfer of that capital on his death. This also applies to an interest in possession to which a person domiciled in the UK becomes beneficially entitled after 8 December 2009 by virtue of a disposition which was prevented from being a transfer of value by the commercial transactions exception. This is to prevent the avoidance of inheritance tax on assets transferred into a trust where the individual purchases an interest that had not been subject to UK inheritance tax when the property was originally transferred into it. Although any tax on such chargeable transfers outlined here is calculated by reference to the income beneficiary's chargeable position, it has to be paid by the trustees. The fact that trust funds are treated as belonging to the beneficiary entitled to the income in these circumstances prevents wealth being protected from inheritance tax through the use of these particular interest in possession trusts. It may also result in inheritance tax being paid on the income beneficiary's own estate whereas his estate would have been below the nil band if the trust funds had not been included.

Example 2

A taxpayer died on 30 September 2017, having made no transfers in lifetime other than a potentially exempt transfer of £226,000 after annual exemptions of £6,000 in June 2015. At his death, his own assets less liabilities (called his free estate) were valued at £100,000. He had also been entitled for many years to the income from trust funds, the value of which were £50,000 and to which his daughter became absolutely entitled. He was a widower, his estate being left to his son.

The inheritance tax payable on his death is:

		Gross	Tax
		£	£
Lifetime transfer*		226,000	—
Free estate at death	100,000		
Trust funds at death	50,000	150,000	20,400**
		£376,000	£20,400

** (376,000 – 325,000) = £51,000 @ 40% = £20,400

The tax is payable as follows:

From free estate (payable by personal representatives)	$\dfrac{100,000}{150,000} \times £20,400$	13,600
From trust funds (payable by trustees)	$\dfrac{50,000}{150,000} \times £20,400$	6,800
		£20,400

If the trust fund had not counted as part of the chargeable estate, the amount reckonable for inheritance tax on the estate would have been (326,000 – 325,000) = £1,000 @ 40%, i.e. £400.

*Although potentially exempt in lifetime, the transfer must be taken into account at death because the taxpayer died within seven years after making it (see 5.31).

Where there are successive inheritance tax charges on the trust property within five years, the tax payable on the later transfer may be reduced by quick succession relief (see **5.50**).

[42.24] Where the individual entitled to a life interest gives it up in favour of another individual or a disabled trust, or the life tenant changes under the rules for a transitional serial interest (see **42.7** at (a)), this will be a potentially exempt transfer in so far as that individual is concerned. This will also apply where someone with an immediate post-death interest (see **42.7** at (c)) gives it up in favour of a bereaved minor's trust (see **42.7** at (d)). Otherwise, the transfer of the interest will be regarded as an immediately chargeable lifetime transfer by the former life tenant, and will fall within the mainstream inheritance tax rules.

[42.25] Prior to Finance Act 2006 the creation of a trust fund in which someone was entitled to the income was a potentially exempt transfer for inheritance tax, and only attracted tax if the settlor died within seven years. This provided the settlor with an efficient means of tax planning, since the individual entitled to the income could not access the capital. This is not possible for lifetime settlements from 22 March 2006 (except for settlements for a disabled person — see **42.47**), because the settlement comes within the mainstream inheritance tax rules, so that the transfer of funds itself will be a chargeable transfer attracting inheritance tax at the lifetime rate of 20% (rising to 40% if death occurs within seven years) and the charges every subsequent ten years and on distribution of the capital to the beneficiary apply. It follows that the capital value of such a settlement is no longer included alongside the free estate of the income beneficiary as illustrated in Example 2.

[42.26] For a pre-22 March 2006 interest in possession settlement (including one with a transitional serial interest), or a disabled person's settlement, inheritance tax is not chargeable if the settled property reverts to the settlor, or if his/her spouse or civil partner (or surviving spouse/civil partner if the settlor had died less than two years earlier) becomes beneficially entitled to the property and is UK-domiciled. The value of the capital supporting the life interest is also excluded from the reckoning on a life tenant's death if the interest is an immediate post-death interest (see **42.7** at (c)), the settlor died less than two years earlier than the life tenant and the settlor's spouse or civil partner then takes the assets.

However, where one party to a couple succeeds to a life interest to which their spouse or civil partner was previously entitled during the latter's lifetime and that interest is not a transitional serial interest (see **42.7**), the settled property will then come within the mainstream inheritance tax rules (see **42.31**).

Subject to certain exceptions, the capital supporting a life interest will not be reckoned as a chargeable transfer upon the cessation of the life interest in possession if the person entitled to the life interest then becomes entitled to the capital itself.

Where an individual transfers property into a trust in which they or their spouse or civil partner retains a future interest (a reversionary interest), or where the individual purchases such a reversionary interest, there will be an inheritance tax charge when the interest comes to an end and they become entitled to the property or if they gift the reversionary interest. It applies to reversionary interests in relevant property to which the individual becomes entitled after 8 December 2009 (and does not therefore apply to certain interests in possession such as a disabled person's interest).

Tax rules for trusts within the mainstream inheritance tax regime

[42.27] What are now referred to as the 'mainstream' inheritance tax rules for trusts previously applied only where the trustees had discretionary power over the distribution of income and appointment of capital. From 22 March 2006 the provisions were extended to all trusts except qualifying interest in possession trusts, qualifying accumulation and maintenance trusts and trusts for the disabled (see 42.7).

Income tax (ITA 2007, ss 479–503; CTA 2010, s 611)

[42.28] Even though many life interest trusts are now within the mainstream inheritance tax rules, the income tax treatment of such trusts remains as stated in 42.16. For trusts in which the trustees have discretionary power over the distribution of income and no-one is entitled to it as of right, income tax is currently chargeable at 45% (known as the trust rate) on income other than dividend income. Dividend income is charged at the dividend trust rate of 38.1%.

The first £1,000 of the trust's income (known as the 'standard rate' band) is not, however, taxable at these special rates but is taxable instead at the basic rate of 20%, or the dividend ordinary rate of 7.5%. Although this enables trusts with a small amount of income to avoid a tax liability at the 45% or 38.1% rate, the 45% rate would still apply to any distribution of the income (see 42.29 and Example 3). In arriving at the amount chargeable at the 45% or 38.1% rate, trustees are entitled to deduct their expenses. Expenses are set first against dividend income then against other income, so that the part of the trust's income used to pay expenses will bear tax at 7.5% if it is dividend income, or the basic rate if it is other income. If the trust has any exempt income, either because the trustees are not resident or are treated as being non-resident under a double tax treaty, the allowable expenses are proportionately restricted. The trustees are not chargeable if the income is treated as the settlor's income (see 42.9), and the settlor remains liable. However, in that event the settlor may recover from them (or from beneficiaries who receive the income) the tax he pays. The net effect where such a recovery is made is that the trustees or beneficiary of the settlement effectively pay the tax on the income but at the settlor's highest tax rate.

[42.29] Any income paid to beneficiaries (other than any that is treated as the settlor's income) is net of 45% tax, the beneficiary being entitled to an income tax repayment to the extent that the income is covered by available personal allowances or chargeable at less than 45%. As the beneficiary is treated as receiving taxed trust income rather than dividend or savings income he is not entitled to set the savings allowance or dividend allowance (see **2.5**) against the trust income.

Even though the trustees are charged to tax at 38.1% (or, where appropriate, the dividend ordinary rate of 7.5%) on dividend income, the rate of tax regarded as deducted from payments to beneficiaries is still 45%, and non-taxpaying beneficiaries will still be able to recover that tax. The trustees tax pool keeps track of the income tax the trustees pay. When the trustees pay income to beneficiaries, the amount in the tax pool is reduced by the value of the 45% tax credit for each payment. If the tax credit on payments to beneficiaries cannot be covered by the amount of tax in the tax pool, the trustees must pay the difference. A shortfall can arise, for example, where some of the income falls into the basic rate band and is taxed at the lower rates. However, if there is any balance at the end of a tax year, it is carried forward to the next tax year and can be offset against payments then. For further administrative details of the pool see **42.50**.

Example 3

The following example ignores the effect of trust expenses and assumes that the trust has other income that has utilised the £1,000 'standard rate band' (see **42.28**) and has no pool of unused tax.

Dividend of £200 was received by a discretionary trust in 2017–18 and distributed to the beneficiaries. The tax position is as follows:

	£
Tax payable by trustees on trust income of 200 @ 38.1%	76
Leaving net income of (200 – 76) = £124	
Distribution to beneficiaries equal to cash dividend	200
Tax at 45%	90
Net payment to beneficiaries	£110
Further tax to be accounted for by trustees (90 – 76)	£14

Net payment to beneficiaries of £110 plus further tax payable of £14 = net trust income of £124.

Non-taxpaying beneficiaries could recover the tax of £90, so that their income would be £200.

Capital gains tax (TCGA 1992, ss 4, 165, 260, Schs 1, 7)

[42.30] The settlor is chargeable to capital gains tax on any gains on chargeable assets transferred to the trust, but gains may instead be treated as reducing the trustees' acquisition cost under the gift holdover relief provisions (see **4.32** to **4.34**). The holdover relief is not restricted to business and other qualifying assets, the reasoning being that there is an immediate reckoning for inheritance tax (see **42.31**). The settlor cannot, however, claim gift holdover relief if he retains an interest in the trust (see **42.14**).

Gains on disposals of chargeable assets by the trustees are calculated in the normal way. The trustees are entitled to an annual exempt amount of £5,650 for 2017–18 (or proportionate part thereof where there are associated trusts — see **42.18**) and the rate of tax on any remaining gains is either 20% or 28% depending on the type of gain (see **4.2**).

When a beneficiary becomes absolutely entitled to any chargeable assets of the trust, the trustees are treated as disposing of the assets at market value at that date for capital gains tax purposes (subject to the special rules for assets acquired before 31 March 1982, see **4.25**), but if a gain arises the trustees and beneficiary may jointly elect for gift holdover relief, the gains treated as reducing the beneficiary's acquisition cost for capital gains tax, unless the distribution from the trust takes place within three months after its creation or within three months after a ten-year anniversary for inheritance tax (see **42.31**). If the distribution takes place within such a three-month period, gift relief will still be available if the assets are qualifying business assets (see **4.32**). It may not be possible to defer capital gains tax where a distribution is made out of a discretionary will trust as described in **35.17**. See **42.39** regarding accumulation and maintenance trusts.

Inheritance tax (IHTA 1984, Pt III)

[42.31] A trust within the mainstream inheritance tax rules has its own threshold for inheritance tax, with tax being charged every ten years by reference to the value of the trust funds (called a 'periodic charge' on 'relevant property'), and also upon distribution of capital sums to beneficiaries (called an 'exit charge'). The rate of tax is 30% of the 20% scale rate, giving a maximum of 6% on the amount chargeable, although the 'effective rate' may be less than 6% after the nil rate threshold has been taken into account (see Examples 4 to 6). In the case of the exit charge this rate is multiplied by the number of complete quarters that have elapsed in the ten-year period up to the day before the exit charge to give a discounted rate. In the case of a ten-year charge on property which has not been relevant property for the whole of the ten-year period, the rate is reduced for each complete quarter which elapsed *before* the property became relevant property. The rules apply to trusts set up in lifetime or on death.

For tax charges arising on or after 18 November 2015 there is no longer a requirement to include non-relevant property in the initial transfer value to determine the rate of tax.

For tax charges arising on or after 6 April 2014 income in the trust which remains undistributed for more than five years at the date of the ten-year anniversary is treated as part of the trust capital when calculating the ten-year anniversary charge. However, to avoid the need for trustees to keep very detailed records, tax is charged on the ten-year anniversary at the full rate (maximum 6% but see comments above regarding the 'effective rate') on any such undistributed income without any proportionate reduction to reflect the shorter period during which the income has been retained.

A useful way of utilising the inheritance tax threshold at death by means of a discretionary trust is illustrated at **35.5**.

Gifts into a lifetime trust within the mainstream inheritance tax rules are not potentially exempt, so that if the nil rate threshold of the settlor is exceeded, inheritance tax is payable at the 20% lifetime rate, increased to the full 40% rate if the settlor dies within seven years.

Business and agricultural property reliefs are available where the trust assets include qualifying property.

For reporting requirements for periodic and exit charges, see **9.28**.

[42.32] If an exit charge arises within the first ten years, the inheritance tax payable is calculated by reference to the chargeable transfers of the settlor before he settled the funds, and the initial value of the trust funds.

Example 4

A settlor, having made a transfer of £55,000 four years earlier that was a chargeable transfer rather than being potentially exempt, settled £300,000 on discretionary trusts on 1 October 1998, personally paying the inheritance tax so that the trustees received the full £300,000.

If the trustees distributed £100,000 to a beneficiary on 10 June 2003 (which is 18 complete quarters after trust commenced), the inheritance tax payable (assuming that the tax was payable out of the £100,000 so that no grossing up (see 5.27) was necessary) would be:

	£
Previous chargeable transfer of settlor	55,000
Initial value of trust fund	300,000
	355,000
Trust's nil rate threshold (2003–04 scale)	(255,000)
	£100,000
Inheritance tax at 20% lifetime rate	£20,000

Representing an effective tax rate of: $\dfrac{20,000}{300,000} =$ 6.67%

Of which 30% (the rate applicable to discretionary trusts) = 2%

£100,000 @ 2%	2,000

Inheritance tax payable out of the £100,000 distribution is

$$2,000 \times \frac{18}{40} *$$

£900

*18 complete quarters have elapsed in the ten-year period from the commencement of the trust to the day before the date of exit charge

[**42.33**] The charge at the first ten-year anniversary is found by reference to the settlor's chargeable transfers before he settled the funds, plus the distributions liable to exit charges in the first ten years and the value of the fund at the ten-year anniversary.

Example 5

Say that at 30 September 2008 the value of the trust fund in Example 4 was £500,000. The tax payable by the trustees is calculated as follows:

	£
Previous chargeable transfer of settlor	55,000
Distributions in the first ten years	100,000
Value of fund at ten-year anniversary	500,000
	655,000
Nil rate threshold 2008–09	(312,000)
	£343,000
Inheritance tax at 20% lifetime rate	£68,600

Representing an effective tax rate on fund of:

$$\frac{68,600}{500,000} = 13.72\%$$

Of which 30% (the rate applicable to discretionary trusts) = 4.116%

Giving tax payable on the £500,000 trust fund of £20,580

[**42.34**] Following a ten-year charge, exit charges in the next ten years are based on the effective rate at the last ten-year anniversary, that rate, however, being recalculated by reference to the nil rate threshold at the date of the distribution.

Example 6

Say the trustees at Example 5 made a distribution of £100,000 to a beneficiary on 8 April 2017, at which time the nil rate threshold was £325,000.

Rate applicable on distribution is:

Ten-year total as in Example 5	655,000
Nil rate threshold	(325,000)
	£330,000
Inheritance tax at 20% lifetime rate	£66,000

Representing an effective tax rate of:

$$\frac{66,000}{500,000} = 13.2\%$$

Of which 30% (the rate applicable to discretionary trusts) =   3.96%

£100,000 @ 3.96%   3,960

Inheritance tax payable out of the £100,000 distribution is

$$3,960 \times \frac{34}{40}*$$

£3,366

*34 complete quarters have elapsed in the ten-year period from the last ten-year charge to the day before the date of exit charge.

[42.35] Where a discretionary trust is created at death in order to utilise but not exceed the then nil rate threshold, a distribution within the first ten years will not attract any inheritance tax.

Example 7

	£
Initial value of settled fund at death on 31 August 2017	325,000
Trustees' nil rate threshold at time of distribution will not be less than	325,000
Amount on which rate on distribution will calculated	—

So rate on distributions in the first ten years is 0%.

The ten-year charge will apply to the value of the fund at 31 August 2027, and exit charges on distributions in the ten years after that will be based on the rate at the ten-year anniversary, as reduced by the quarterly discount (see 42.31).

[42.36] Another use of a discretionary trust created by a will is to leave the estate on discretionary trusts, with the trustees being aware of (but not bound by) the preferred wishes of the testator as to its distribution. Distributions within two years after death are regarded as under the will. This includes distributions to a trust for a bereaved minor (see **42.47**), an accumulation and maintenance trust within the 18–25 years of age rules (see **42.42**) and an immediate post-death interest (see **42.7** at (c)). The distributions must not be made within the three months after death but must be made before there is an interest in possession in the property.

Accumulation and maintenance trusts

[42.37] These are a special sort of discretionary trust giving flexibility to a parent or grandparent in providing funds for the benefit of children. The position of such trusts was changed from 22 March 2006 as indicated in **42.7**. Further details of the tax position are given below.

Income tax (ITA 2007, ss 479–483; ITTOIA 2005, ss 629, 631)

[42.38] The rule that a parent remains chargeable to income tax on income from funds settled on his own unmarried children under age 18 (see **33.10**) does not apply where the capital and income are held on qualifying accumulation and maintenance trusts for the benefit of the children, except to the extent that any income is paid to or for the benefit of the child (for example for education or maintenance). Payments of capital to or for the benefit of the child are also treated as income to the extent that the trust has any undistributed income. Any such income or capital payments are treated as the parent's income and taxed on him (unless, together with any other income from the parent, they do not exceed £100 in any tax year).

Since the trust is a discretionary trust, the trustees pay income tax at 38.1% on dividend income and 45% on other income accumulated within the fund (see **42.28**). When the accumulated income is transferred when the child reaches the appropriate age, it does so as capital and thus does not attract any further income tax at that time.

Capital gains tax (TCGA 1992, ss 4, 165, 260, Schs 1, 7)

[42.39] Gifts from 22 March 2006 into an accumulation and maintenance trust do not qualify as potentially exempt transfers for inheritance tax, so that capital gains gift holdover relief (see **4.32**) is available to the settlor at that point.

Gains made by the trustees are calculated in the normal way, with an annual exempt amount of £5,650 being available (or proportionate part thereof where there are associated trusts — see **42.18**) and the rate of tax on any remaining gains is either 20% or 28% depending on the type of gain (see **4.2**). When a distribution from a trust is reckonable for inheritance tax (see **42.40**), gains may be held over and treated as reducing a beneficiary's capital gains tax cost.

Inheritance tax (IHTA 1984, ss 66, 69, 70, 71, 71A–71H; FA 2006, Sch 20)

[42.40] As indicated in 42.7 at (d), accumulation and maintenance trusts are within the mainstream inheritance tax rules for trusts if created in lifetime from 22 March 2006. Trusts in existence at that date came within the mainstream rules from 6 April 2008 unless by then they had changed their constitution so that beneficiaries have an absolute entitlement to their share of the assets at age 18. For both pre- and post-22 March 2006 trusts, however, the mainstream rules are modified for 'age 18 to 25 trusts' as indicated in **42.42**.

Many settlors/trustees may have decided to accept the new regime rather than take what they regard as unacceptable risks within their planning for the family. For trusts existing at 22 March 2006 that did not make the necessary changes to their constitution, there was no immediate inheritance tax effect. The first ten-year charge will apply on the first ten-year anniversary after 5 April 2008, time apportioned as explained in **42.31** and illustrated in Example 8.

Example 8

An accumulation and maintenance trust set up on 29 September 1997 does not modify its constitution to come within the new rules. The first ten-year charge after 5 April 2008 is on 29 September 2017. The tax payable will be reduced for each complete quarter from 29 September 2007 to 5 April 2008 (i.e. the period when the property was not relevant property — 2 complete quarters), and hence only 38/40ths of the ten-year charge applies.

In calculating any subsequent exit charges (see **42.34**) within ten years after the first post-5 April 2008 anniversary, the calculation of the effective rate will take into account a full ten years, and not just the number of quarters since 5 April 2008.

[42.41] Trusts that comply with the rules of the new regime receive favourable treatment for inheritance tax. During the period until the beneficiary becomes absolutely entitled to the capital at age 18, the trust income must either be accumulated or used for the beneficiary's benefit. There is no ten-yearly charge on the trust funds and no exit charges when a distribution is made to a beneficiary or when a beneficiary becomes absolutely entitled to the trust property or to the income from it. The transfer of property from the settlement to the beneficiaries is thus free of tax in these circumstances.

[42.42] Special treatment is available where there is an income entitlement at age 18 but a capital entitlement does not arise until age 25. These rules apply to trusts created both before and after 22 March 2006. The provisions are relevant where the settlors/trustees wish to retain the capital within the trust until the beneficiary reaches age 25 but are prepared for the beneficiary to have the right to income at age 18. For such trusts, the inheritance tax exit charge will apply at age 25 when the beneficiary becomes entitled to the capital, but the charge will be based on only 7/10ths of the normal calculation (representing the seven years from 18 to 25). In view of the charge to inheritance tax, capital gains tax holdover relief (see **42.39**) will be available.

Example 9

On 1 February 2006 taxpayer transferred £300,000 into an accumulation and maintenance trust for his three children aged 8, 10 and 13, each being entitled to an equal share of the capital or to the income arising from it upon attaining age 25 but the trustees being able to make advances of capital in the meantime. He had not made any gifts in the previous three years.

The inheritance tax position is:

Settlor

1.2.06	Gift to accumulation and maintenance trust			300,000
	Annual exemption	2005–06	3,000	
		2004–05	3,000	(6,000)
	Potentially exempt transfer			£294,000

Accumulation and maintenance trust

There would have been a ten-year charge at the tenth anniversary on 1 February 2016 (calculated pro rata from 6 April 2008 — see Example 8), an exit charge on capital advances and a final charge on distribution, unless the entitlement of each beneficiary is changed before 6 April 2008 to an absolute entitlement in his/her share of the assets at age 18. There would be no inheritance tax charges on any of these occasions if that modification is made.

Had the transfer into trust been a year later, on 1 February 2007, it would not have been potentially exempt, inheritance tax of £1,800 (£294,000 – £285,000 = £9,000 @ 20%) being payable. The mainstream inheritance tax rules for trusts would apply, with none of the advantages of an accumulation and maintenance trust being available.

Trusts with a vulnerable beneficiary

Income tax and capital gains tax (TCGA 1992, s 72, Sch 1A; FA 2005, ss 23–45 and Sch 1)

[42.43] Income tax and capital gains tax provisions were introduced with effect from 6 April 2004 for trusts with a vulnerable beneficiary, i.e. a disabled person (as specifically defined in FA 2005, Sch 1A) or a 'relevant minor' (which means someone under 18 one or both of whose parents have died). An election for vulnerable beneficiary trust treatment must be made by the trustees and (strangely) the vulnerable person, no later than 12 months after 31 January following the tax year for which the treatment is to take effect (i.e. no later than 31 January 2020 for 2017–18). The election is irrevocable, but it ceases to have an effect if the beneficiary is no longer a vulnerable person or the trust fails to qualify or comes to an end. Claims for the special tax treatment must be made each year.

[42.44] In order to qualify, a trust for a disabled person must provide that during the disabled person's lifetime (or, for protective trusts, the period for which the property is held on trust for him), or until the termination of the trust if earlier, neither trust property nor income may be applied for the benefit of anyone other than the disabled person. A trust for a relevant minor must either be a statutory trust arising on intestacy, or a trust established under the will of a deceased parent or under the Criminal Injuries Compensation Scheme, or the Victims of Overseas Terrorism Compensation Scheme. For non-statutory trusts, the relevant minor must become absolutely entitled to the property at age 18, and until that time neither trust property nor income may be applied for the benefit of anyone other than the relevant minor. However, with effect from 2013–14, the trusts are not prevented from being qualifying trusts if there are powers which enable the trustees to apply a small amount of capital or income for the benefit of persons other than the vulnerable person. The amount is the lower of £3,000 or 3% of the trust fund each tax year.

[42.45] The broad effect of vulnerable person trust treatment is that the income tax and capital gains tax charged on the trustees is the amount that would have been charged had the trust's income and gains accrued directly to the beneficiary. There are special provisions where a beneficiary is non-resident (see CHAPTER 41).

[42.46] On the death of a beneficiary of a vulnerable beneficiary trust there is a deemed disposal and re-acquisition at market value of the settled property by the trustees, but there is no charge to capital gains tax.

Inheritance tax (IHTA 1984, ss 71A–71G, 89, 89A–89C)

[42.47] The term 'vulnerable beneficiary' is not used in the inheritance tax legislation, and trusts for disabled persons and for bereaved minors are dealt with separately.

A trust for a disabled person does not come within the mainstream inheritance tax rules for trusts, so that there will be no ten-year or exit charges, the disabled individual effectively being treated as one who owns the assets. The definition of disabled person for this purpose includes the settlor of a self-settlement made because the settlor has a condition expected to lead to a disability.

Also excluded from the mainstream inheritance tax rules for trusts are those established under the Criminal Injuries Compensation Scheme, or the Victims of Overseas Terrorism Compensation Scheme, for a bereaved minor and where a fund is held in trust for a bereaved minor under the will of a deceased parent or the intestacy rules. In these cases the minor becomes entitled to the capital at age 18 but the special treatment for age 18 to 25 trusts is also applicable (see **42.42**).

Where the trust has been established on death, inheritance tax will have been paid before arriving at the available fund. For transfers in lifetime the value transferred will be a potentially exempt transfer.

[42.48] Where a self-settlement is made on or after 22 March 2006 otherwise than as indicated in **42.47**, the mainstream inheritance tax rules for trusts apply, with the transfer of funds into the settlement being a chargeable transfer and the ten-year and exit charges applying. This is so even though the settlor has simply predestined the funds upon a later event (for example death or remarriage) and retained the income in the meantime. (Self-settlements created before 22 March 2006 come within the rules for interest in possession trusts and 'transitional serial interests' — see **42.7** at (a) and (b).)

Employee trusts (IHTA 1984, ss 72, 75, 75A, 86)

[42.49] The inheritance tax definition of an employee trust is one which either indefinitely, or until the end of a defined period, does not permit any of the settled property to be applied otherwise than for the benefit of:

(a) persons employed in a particular trade or profession; or
(b) employees, or office holders, of a body carrying on a trade, profession or undertaking; or
(c) spouses, civil partners, relatives or dependants or partners of (a) or (b) above.

For the settled property to qualify under (a) or (b), either all or most of the employees or office holders must be included as beneficiaries, or the trust must be an approved profit sharing scheme or a tax-advantaged share incentive plan.

In addition, from 6 April 2014, the relief applies to employee trusts which hold ordinary shares in a trading company (or parent company of a trading group), and broadly the trust is for the benefit of all eligible employees on the same terms, and the trustees control the company (commonly known as employee-ownership trusts). Trustees will have control if they hold a majority of the company's shares, are entitled to the majority of profits available for distribution and are entitled to a majority of assets available for distribution on a winding up (see further **4.38**). Where there are beneficiaries falling within (a), (b) or (c) above, the trusts are not disqualified by reason only that they also permit settled property to be applied for charitable purposes.

There is no exit charge (see **42.31**) when shares in a company which is already held in trust become held in an employee trust to which the above provisions apply. Property in the trust is not subject to the ten-year or exit charges. However, a tax charge can arise when the property ceases to qualify under the above conditions (although not where the settled property ceases to be within the employee ownership requirement because either the trading requirement or the controlling interest requirement are no longer met), or where certain payments or dispositions are made out of the trust. The rate of charge varies depending on how long the property has been in the trust.

For the inheritance tax treatment of transfers into employee trusts see **5.18**, **5.19**.

Trusts and estates — self-assessment

[42.50] Trustees and personal representatives are subject to the normal self-assessment rules in relation to their tax liabilities (see CHAPTER 9). They are required to make payments on account half-yearly on 31 January and 31 July, based on the previous year's net income tax (unless covered by the de minimis thresholds — see **9.4**), and a balancing payment, including any capital gains tax, on the following 31 January (the due date for submission of the online tax return).

However, HMRC have confirmed that for 2016–17 and 2017–18 they will not require notification from trustees or personal representatives where the only source of income is savings interest and the tax liability is below £100.

There is a special tax return (SA900) for trusts and estates. The format of the return broadly follows that for individuals, with supplementary pages for various types of income and gains and a tax calculation working sheet. Only some supplementary pages are sent with returns. Others need to be requested from HMRC. Trust returns require certain additional information to be provided, such as details of capital added to a settlement, capital payments to minor children of the settlor, discretionary payments to beneficiaries, and changes in personal representatives and trustees.

Details of the trustees tax pool (see **42.29**) are included in the tax calculation working sheet. HMRC also provide a calculator at www.hmrc.gov.uk/tools/t rusts/calculator.htm. Any tax paid directly in respect of the dividend trust rate or the trust rate enters into the calculation of the half-yearly payments on account for the following year.

See **42.1** regarding the HMRC Trusts Registration Service.

Position of infants

[42.51] Where income is paid to beneficiaries (and is not treated as a parent's income), it is after deduction of tax at 7.5% if it relates to dividends, and at the basic rate for other income, except for discretionary trusts where the rate on all income other than dividend income is 45% (see **42.28**). If the beneficiaries are infants, a repayment of tax is often due because of their personal allowances. The parent or guardian can make the repayment claim, or it may be made by the beneficiary himself in respect of the previous four years on his reaching age 18.

Married couples and registered civil partners

[42.52] The spouse/civil partner exemption for inheritance tax applies where a capital sum is put into trust for the benefit of the survivor under a *will or intestacy*, so long as the capital goes absolutely on the death of the survivor to one or more individuals or to an appropriate trust (see 35.4). The spouse/civil partner exemption is otherwise denied.

See 5.11 regarding appointments from a trust within three months of the date of death on or after 10 December 2014.

The trust will come within the rules for an immediate post-death interest (see 42.7 at (c)), with the income being included within that of the surviving spouse or civil partner for income tax purposes (as the life tenant in possession) and the capital value being reckonable for inheritance tax on his/her death together with the free estate (see Example 2 at 42.23).

The spouse/civil partner exemption does not apply where a capital sum is put into trust for a spouse or civil partner during *lifetime*. In this event, the mainstream inheritance tax rules for trusts apply (see 42.31 to 42.36), with inheritance tax being payable at the lifetime rate (see 5.27) when the assets are placed into trust, rising to the death rate (see 5.24) if death occurs within the next seven years, and the ten-year and exit charges also applying. The same applies where a settlor settles assets on himself/herself for life with the surviving spouse or civil partner taking an absolute or life interest on the settlor's death unless the self-settlement comes within the rules for providing for future disability (see 42.47). For pre-22 March 2006 trusts these rules are subject to the provisions for 'transitional serial interests' (see 42.7 at (b)).

In the case of lifetime settlements, the income will be taxed on the settlor during his lifetime, with there being no holdover relief for capital gains tax when the assets are placed into trust (see 42.14).

Stamp duty, stamp duty land tax, and land and buildings transaction tax (FA 2003, ss 49, 105 and Schs 3, 16; LBTT(S)A 2013)

[42.53] Stamp duty applies only to transactions relating to shares and securities (see 6.2). For stamp duty land tax purposes, the acts of bare trustees are treated as those of the person who is absolutely entitled as against the trustees. For trustees other than bare trustees, the stamp duty land tax provisions apply to acquisitions of land and buildings by the trustees as if they had acquired the whole interest in the property, including the beneficial interest. Stamp duty land tax is not payable where land and buildings are transferred to a beneficiary. If trustees receive consideration for exercising a power of appointment or a discretion in relation to a land transaction, the consideration is treated as chargeable consideration for stamp duty land tax. In some circumstances, stamp duty land tax may be payable in connection with nil rate band discretionary trusts. (See HMRC's Stamp Duty Land Tax Manual at SDLTM04045 for HMRC's detailed comments.)

Stamp duty land tax is replaced in Scotland by land and buildings transaction tax (see **6.18**) and broadly the same reliefs apply.

Tax points

[42.54] Note the following:

- Personal representatives have to include in their inheritance tax account details of earlier transfers affecting the inheritance tax liability. Providing they have done everything possible to trace potentially exempt transfers made by the deceased in the seven years before his death and disclose them to HMRC, then once they have received a certificate of discharge and distributed the estate, they will not usually be asked to pay the tax if untraced transfers subsequently come to light.
- Where a person entitled to trust income has unused personal allowances, it is better to arrange for income to be paid direct to him, because the income will not then be depleted by trust expenses, and he will get a higher income tax repayment where tax has been deducted.
- Since inheritance tax is less where the value transferred is lower, it is usually beneficial to transfer assets that are growing in value earlier rather than later. Even if the donor dies within seven years the benefit of transferring assets when their value was lower is retained.
- Assets transferred into or out of a trust may qualify for capital gains gift holdover relief (see **4.32** to **4.34**) unless the settlor has an interest in the trust (see **42.14**).
- Where assets are put into a trust, the trustees may pay the inheritance tax rather than the settlor. If they do, and dependent upon the type of asset, the tax may be payable by instalments (see **5.54**). The requirement to treat the amount settled as its gross equivalent when calculating the tax is also avoided (see **5.27**).
- If, since before 22 March 2006, an individual has been the beneficiary of an interest in possession trust and does not need all the income, he could disclaim his entitlement to the income on an appropriate amount of capital which could be released early to the individual eventually entitled to it. Part of the disclaimed amount would be covered by inheritance tax annual exemptions if not otherwise used and the balance would be treated as a potentially exempt transfer, so there would be no immediate tax charge. If the potentially exempt transfer was within his nil rate band, no tax would be payable even if he died within seven years (although in that event the nil rate band available on death would be correspondingly reduced). If the potentially exempt transfer was above the nil rate band, tax would be payable by the donee if the donor did not survive the seven-year period, but it would be reduced if the donor had survived for more than three years (see **5.32**).
- For capital gains tax purposes, those entitled to the assets in a deceased's estate acquire them at market value at the date of death. If assets have fallen in value since death, losses made by the personal representatives on disposal cannot be used by the beneficiaries. If, on

the other hand, the assets themselves, rather than cash proceeds from their sale, are transferred to beneficiaries, losses on disposal by the beneficiaries will be their own allowable losses for capital gains purposes.

- To obtain the spouse/civil partner exemption on death, assets must be left absolutely to the survivor or in trust for him/her to have the income for life with one or more individuals or an appropriate trust taking the capital on the death of the life tenant or earlier.

- A lifetime settlement in favour of one's spouse/civil partner is a chargeable transfer for inheritance tax. For a gift to be potentially exempt, the assets must be given outright.

- Where the settlor, spouse or civil partner retains an interest in a settlement, holdover relief for capital gains tax is not available despite the transfer of the asset being immediately reckonable for inheritance tax.

- In the case of an accumulation and maintenance settlement set up before 22 March 2006, the exemption of the trust from the exit charges applicable to discretionary trusts will only apply if the trust was modified before 6 April 2008 so that each beneficiary is entitled to his/her share of the capital at age 18.

  The ten-year charge (but not the exit charge) can be avoided if the right to income applies at age 18, with the absolute entitlement to capital applying at age 25.

- The inheritance tax ten-year charge will apply to a trust established after 21 March 2006 which holds a lifetime insurance policy for the purpose of paying inheritance tax on the death of the settlor. The principles of valuation of the policy and the available inheritance tax threshold will usually eliminate any tax payable. But since the policy proceeds will not be available until the death of the settlor a means will have to be found of paying any inheritance tax that does become due in the meantime.

- For additional tax points on trusts, see CHAPTER 35.

43

Charities and charitable trusts

Definition of a charity (FA 2010, s 30 and Sch 6)

[43.1] An organisation is eligible for UK charity tax reliefs if:

(a)   it is established for charitable purposes only;

(b)   it is located in the UK or a member state of the EU or a specified country (Norway, Liechtenstein and Iceland are so specified);

(c)   it meets the registration condition (i.e. where the organisation is required under the law of its home country to be registered with a charity regulator similar to the Charity Commission for England and Wales, it must be so registered); and

(d)   all persons in the organisation having control and management responsibilities are 'fit and proper' persons (this phrase not being further defined, but guidance is provided by HMRC at www.gov.uk/governm ent/publications/charity-tax-relief-model-declaration).

In order to register a charity (which can now be done online), it is necessary to satisfy the Charity Commissioners in England and Wales, the Office of the Scottish Charity Regulator in Scotland or the Charity Commission for Northern Ireland in Northern Ireland, that the purposes or objects of the organisation are of 'charitable purpose', and not only must the purpose be one of those listed but must be for the public benefit. All new charities must meet this requirement and some existing charities will be asked to show how they meet the requirement. Charities will not be registered if their annual income does not exceed £5,000. Charities and CASCs can register to take over the compliance history of a predecessor following a merger. This must be done by the earlier of 90 days from the date when the new charity or CASC began to carry on the activities of the old body, or 60 days before the new body makes its first gift aid claim.

A charity may be a limited company with a separate legal existence independent of its members, or an unincorporated association which has no separate status so that assets must be held on its behalf by trustees.

Guidance is available at www.charity-commission.gov.uk for England and Wales, and www.oscr.org.uk for Scotland.

How the tax system operates for charities

[43.2] Detailed guidance on how the tax system operates for charities is provided at www.gov.uk/topic/running-charity/money-accounts. Guidance on 'reasonable and prudent' tax planning, within trustees' fiduciary duty to act in the best interests of the charity is also provided at www.gov.uk/government/publications/charity-tax-reliefs-guidance-on-charity-commission-policy.

The tax status of charities is outlined below. HMRC issue returns only to a sample of charities each year. If a charity that does not receive a return has a tax liability, it is under the usual obligation to notify HMRC (9.3).

Income tax and corporation tax (ITA 2007, ss 518–564; CTA 2010, ss 466–517)

[43.3] Investment and rental income is exempt from income tax if it is the income of a charitable trust, or it is required (for example, by law or trust deed) to be applied to charitable purposes only.

Profits of a trade carried on by a charitable trust are exempt if the profits are applied solely for the purposes of the trust and the trade is a 'charitable trade'. Broadly, a trade is a charitable trade if it is conducted in the course of carrying out a primary purpose of the trust, or the work is mainly done by beneficiaries.

Where a trade is conducted only partly for a primary purpose of the charity, or is conducted partly but not mainly by beneficiaries of the charity, the parts of the trade that are and are not carried on for a primary purpose, or the parts that are and are not carried on by beneficiaries, are treated as two separate trades, with income and expenses being apportioned appropriately. This avoids the loss of tax relief that might otherwise occur. Smaller charities whose profits are not otherwise exempt from income tax are exempt from tax on trading income used solely for charitable purposes if it is less than the lower of £50,000 and 25% of the charity's income, or in any event if it is less than £5,000 (the amounts of £50,000 and £5,000 being reduced pro rata for accounting periods of less than 12 months). This may remove the need in some cases for charities to have a trading subsidiary (as to which see 43.30), although charities must still consider their position under charity law. The profits of a charity's fundraising events such as bazaars, jumble sales, etc., are exempt providing the events would be covered by the VAT exemption (see 43.6) and the profits are used for charitable purposes. There are corresponding exemptions for charitable companies in respect of income applied to charitable purposes only.

Interest on money deposited with a bank or building society by a charity is paid gross.

Charities are allowed to submit 'in year' income tax repayment claims in advance of filing a tax return (to claim, for example, income tax on gift aid payments, royalties etc).

See **40.18** for the provisions relating to life policies held by charitable trusts.

Capital gains tax (TCGA 1992, ss 256–256D)

[43.4] A charity is not liable to capital gains tax, or corporation tax on chargeable gains, on gains applied for charitable purposes.

Value added tax (VATA 1994, Sch 8 Groups 4, 12 and 15)

[43.5] The general tax exemption for charities does not extend to VAT, and the detailed provisions need to be looked at carefully to ensure that the rules are complied with.

Various leaflets are available from HMRC on the subject of charities and guidance on VAT and charities is available online at www.gov.uk/vat-charitie s/overview. Further guidance on charities generally is available at www.gov.u k/running-charity/money-accounts.

Fundraising

[43.6] Income from one-off fundraising events, including admission charges, is normally exempt. Exemption is also available in respect of a series of events, providing not more than 15 events of the same kind are held in any one location in any year. (Small events do not count towards the limit providing aggregate takings for such events do not exceed £1,000 a week). Where income is exempt, there is a corresponding restriction in the recovery of VAT on purchases and expenses for the event. Except for fund-raising events, admission charges are normally standard-rated. Where a charity supplies goods or services consistently below cost for the relief of distressed persons, for example, meals on wheels, such supplies are not regarded as being made in the course of business and hence are not liable to VAT. Sales of donated goods to the general public at charity shops etc. and donated goods sold only to disabled people or people receiving means tested benefits are zero-rated. Sales of bought-in goods are standard rated. VAT Leaflet 701/1 explains in detail the VAT treatment of charity challenge events.

Admission (VATA 1994, s 33A)

[43.7] Membership subscriptions to 'bodies with aims of a political, religious, patriotic, philosophical or philanthropic nature' are exempt from VAT if the necessary conditions are satisfied. Exemption does not apply where free admission is provided in return for the subscription. Where the members receive publications as part of their subscriptions, the relevant part of the subscription is treated as zero-rated, enabling the bodies to recover an appropriate part of their input VAT.

Certain national museums and galleries who offer free admission are able to claim a refund of the VAT they incur in connection with the provision of the free admission.

Supplies by a charity

[43.8] Where a charity makes taxable supplies it must register for VAT, subject to the normal rules relating to exempt supplies and taxable turnover (see CHAPTER 7). Where funds raised by donation are used to fund business activities, any input VAT on fundraisers' fees may be recovered. Where funds are used for both business and non-business activities, or for making taxable and exempt supplies, the VAT will need to be apportioned under the partial exemption rules.

If a charity has a number of branches which are virtually autonomous, each branch having control over its own financial and other affairs, each branch is regarded as a separate entity for VAT purposes and is required to register only if its taxable supplies exceed the VAT threshold of £85,000 (£83,000 before 1 April 2017).

Supplies of nursery and crèche facilities by charities are not treated as business activities for VAT in specified circumstances — see HMRC Brief 02/2005 for details.

Supplies to a charity

[43.9] Certain supplies to charities may be zero-rated in specified circumstances, such as media advertising, building work (see below), motor vehicles, mechanical products and equipment supplied to those who provide care for the handicapped, aids for disabled people, medicinal products, and bathrooms provided for disabled people in day centres and other charity premises. The 5% reduced rate applies to the provision by charities of advice or information connected with or intended to promote the welfare of elderly or disabled people or children.

Palliative care charities, air ambulance charities, search and rescue charities and medical courier charities are able to claim refunds of the VAT they pay on goods and services which they purchase for their non-business activities.

Buildings

[43.10] As far as buildings are concerned, zero-rating does not apply to new buildings bought by charities or to services provided in the construction of buildings for charities, unless the charity uses the building solely for charitable purposes (which means otherwise than in the course of a business), or as a village hall, or to provide social or recreational facilities for a local community. Any other use strictly falls foul of these provisions (for example, allowing someone to rent a room for a children's party), but, by concession, HMRC are prepared to disregard use of a building for a non-charitable purpose where such use is less than 5% of total use.

If zero-rating applies to a building, but within ten years of completion there is an increase in non-charitable use, a grant of a lease or sale to a third party who will not be using it for charitable purposes, VAT is chargeable. The amount chargeable is based on the VAT which would have been incurred on acquisition (had the supply not been zero-rated), the proportion of the building that is affected by the change in use and the number of complete months that the building has been used solely for a qualifying purpose prior to the change in use.

Even if zero-rating applies, it does not apply to the services of architects and surveyors, which are standard-rated.

In relation to repair and maintenance work the UK has a special grant scheme (the Listed Places of Worship Grant Scheme) enabling churches to receive grants to cover all VAT incurred on the repair and maintenance of listed places of worship, including works to pipe organs, turret clocks, bells and bell ropes. Professional services directly related to eligible building work such as architect fees are also eligible. The UK also has a Memorials Grant Scheme which provides grants to charities and faith groups for the VAT incurred in building and maintaining memorials. Further details of the schemes may be found at w ww.lpwscheme.org.uk and www.memorialgrant.org.uk respectively.

When buildings are rented, landlords have the option to charge VAT on rents except for buildings or parts of buildings used for charitable purposes (but the exception does not cover the charity's offices). The landlord is entitled to add VAT to existing rents unless the agreement specifically prevents him from doing so. In that event, the rent would have to be treated as VAT inclusive until such time as the landlord has a right under the agreement to increase it.

Stamp duty, stamp duty land tax and land and buildings transaction tax (FA 1982, s 129; FA 2003, s 68 and Sch 8; LBTT(S)A 2013, Sch 13)

[43.11] No stamp duty is payable on documents transferring assets to charities. Exemption also applies to the stamp duty land tax transactions and (in Scotland) the land and buildings transaction tax transactions of charities, providing the land is to be held for qualifying charitable purposes and is not being acquired for tax avoidance reasons. This also applies to acquisitions by trusts and unit trusts where all the beneficiaries or unit holders are charities.

The relief must be claimed in a SDLT/LBTT return or amendment to a return, and it will be withdrawn if within three years the purchaser ceases to be a charity or the land is used other than for charitable purposes. If a charity retains a gift of land, buildings or shares it will be exempt from any stamp taxes/LBTT.

Where a charity purchases property jointly, as tenants in common, with a non-charity purchaser, partial relief from SDLT/LBTT is available on the charity's share of the property.

National insurance

[43.12] Charities receive no special treatment. Employers' national insurance is dealt with in CHAPTER 13.

Business rates

[43.13] There is both mandatory and discretionary relief from business rates on premises occupied by a registered charity and used for charitable purposes; see **8.15**.

Restriction of charity tax reliefs (ITA 2007, ss 518–564; CTA 2010, ss 492–517)

[43.14] A charity's tax relief may be restricted if it uses its funds for non-charitable purposes, or makes payments to overseas bodies without taking reasonable steps to ensure that they are used for charitable purposes, or makes certain loans or investments for tax avoidance rather than for the benefit of the charity. In such situations, the amount of income and gains eligible for tax relief is reduced by an amount equal to the amount of any non-charitable expenditure.

Where a charity receives a grant from another charity, the grant is chargeable to tax unless it is used for charitable purposes.

Any claim that a payment overseas qualifies for relief as charitable expenditure must be supported by evidence sufficient to satisfy HMRC that the charity's trustees took reasonable steps to ensure the money would be spent charitably. In practice this will mean that charities will be required to maintain records of how charitable funds are spent overseas and be able to produce evidence of charitable works undertaken. The level of record keeping required will depend upon the circumstances relating to the expenditure. For example, it may not be possible for a charity providing aid during an emergency to maintain the same level of record keeping as for routine overseas expenditure.

Giving to charity: individuals

Tainted donations (ITA 2007, ss 809ZH–809ZR)

[43.15] Tax relief available to the donor on a gift to a charity will be denied if the donation is a 'tainted donation'. The tax reliefs concerned are detailed in the legislation and include relief on gifts made under the gift aid regime (43.14–43.22), payroll giving (43.23), and gifts by companies (43.27–43.30).

Three conditions, A, B and C, must be met for a donation to be a tainted charity donation, as follows:

(a)   Condition A — a donation and arrangements entered into between the donor and another party in respect of the donation are connected to each other;

(b)   Condition B — the main purpose, or one of the main purposes of the arrangement, is for the donor (or someone connected to the donor) to receive a financial advantage directly or indirectly from the charity; and

(c)   Condition C — the donation is not from 'qualifying charity-owned companies' or 'relevant housing providers' (although note the exclusion for donations from qualifying charity owned companies does not apply where a person who stands to obtain a financial advantage from the arrangement was previously in control of the charity owned company at the relevant time). This condition means that wholly-owned trading companies of charities, which generally donate their profits to their parent charity each year, and relevant housing providers that often donate to linked charities within a housing group will not be caught by this rule.

Where the donation would have been a qualifying donation under the gift aid scheme (see **43.16**), an income tax charge will arise on the repayment of tax due to the charity. The donor, a connected person or any other advantaged person is liable for this tax. No charge will arise on the charity unless, exceptionally, it was party to and fully aware of the arrangements. There are no thresholds for these rules; it is based instead on a 'purpose test'.

Example 1

A conservation charity offers donors who make donations of £5,000 or more a special membership package called gold membership, which entitles the member to a benefits package consisting of an opportunity to attend an event at which an 'expert' will talk about conservation issues, plus 12-monthly newsletters and a charity branded mug.

The donation of £5,000 and the receipt of a benefits package as a result may be arrangements caught by Condition A. It is then necessary to consider the relevant facts of each donation. If the circumstances suggest the donation would have been made without the benefits package, Condition A will not apply. However, if the donation was made in order to obtain the benefits package, Condition A of the legislation would apply — it would then be necessary to consider if the donor receives a financial advantage from the arrangement (Condition B). The legislation gives examples of circumstances in which a financial advantage can arise; however a financial advantage is ignored if it falls within the gift aid benefit limits.

In this example, it is extremely likely that the value of the financial advantage will fall within those limits (as the packages are normally designed with the gift aid benefit limits in mind). If, of course, the sort of expert advice received as part of the benefits package could not be received by a person without making a donation of £5,000 the donation would not be a tax relievable donation in the first place and merely a payment for services from the conservation charity.

Gift aid donations by individuals

Money gifts (ITA 2007, ss 413–430; ITTOIA 2005, s 627; SI 2013/938)

[43.16] Tax relief at the payer's top tax rate is available for money given to charities under the gift aid scheme. The scheme covers both single donations and a series of donations, including covenanted payments. There is no minimum limit for gift aid payments, although charities may stipulate their own minimum limit for donations to be brought within the scheme. Gift aid relief is available not only to UK residents but also to non-residents who are liable to pay sufficient UK tax to cover the basic rate on the grossed up amount of the donation (e.g. £20 UK tax for a cash donation of £80). Tax returns contain notes about gift aid. A claim may be made in the return for relief to be given in the tax year to which the return relates for gift aid payments made between 6 April following that tax year and the date the return is submitted (see **43.19**).

To qualify for gift aid relief donors, or from 6 April 2017, intermediaries representing the donor are required to make a declaration. The declaration may cover any number of donations already made or to be made. The declaration need not be written, and may be made by telephone or over the internet, providing the donor's name and address is obtained. Where a donation is given by oral declaration, the charity must maintain detailed auditable records. Detailed HMRC guidance on gift aid declarations is at www.gov.uk/gift-aid-declarations-claiming-tax-back-on-donations. Intermediaries are not required to receive a Gift Aid declaration for each individual charity a donor gives to through them. This also eases the process for donors giving to multiple charities via a single intermediary.

[43.17] HMRC have a special process enabling charities to reclaim tax on gift aid donations without completing a tax return and charities are able to make repayment claims online; see HMRC guidance at https://www.gov.uk/claim-gift-aid/how-to-claim.

In addition charities (and community amateur sports clubs) that receive small donations of £20 or less are able to apply for a gift aid style repayment of 25 pence for every pound collected in the UK without the need to obtain gift aid declarations for those donations. This is known as the gift aid small donations scheme (GASDS); see www.gov.uk/guidance/claiming-a-top-up-payment-on-small-charitable-donations for HMRC guidance. The total amount of small donations on which the repayment can be claimed is, in most situations, capped at £8,000 per year, per charity. However where a charity has more than one community building they are permitted to claim for a further £8,000 of small donations collected in each community building. In order to qualify for this repayment, the payments must be in cash or, from 6 April 2017, contactless payment. In addition, for gifts on or after 6 April 2017, the charity will need to have claimed gift aid in the same tax year as they wish to claim a GASDS repayment and have not incurred a penalty on a gift aid or GASDS claim in the current or preceding year. For gifts made prior to 6 April 2017 there was an additional requirement that the charity had to be recognised by HMRC for gift aid purposes for at least two years.

In view of the fact that tax relief on gift aid donations is given at the payer's top rate of tax, a higher rate taxpayer may be persuaded to increase his donation, thus making a larger contribution to the charity.

Example 2

A taxpayer who is liable to 40% tax makes a cash gift to charity of £1,000. The tax position is:

	£	£
Cash gift	1,000	1,000

Basic rate tax treated as deducted (20/80)	250	250
Amount received by charity	1,250	1,250
Tax saved at 40%		500
Net cost to donor		750

If the donor was prepared to contribute £1,000 out of his after-tax income, he could increase the cash gift to £1,334, as follows:

	£	£
Cash gift	1,334	1,334
Basic rate tax treated as deducted (20/80)	333	333
Amount received by charity	1,667	1,667
Tax saved at 40%		667
Net cost to donor		1,000

Thus the charity would receive extra income of £417 (£1,667 – £1,250) at an extra net cost to the donor of £250.

The tax saving to a higher rate taxpayer may be even higher where the donations are paid out of dividends (see Example 4).

[43.18] Donations are treated as being net of basic rate tax, but in order to retain the tax relief, donors must be liable to pay an equivalent amount of income tax (including tax at rates below the basic rate) and capital gains tax. In order to put this into effect, donations are not deducted from income in calculating the tax position for the year. Instead the basic rate threshold is increased by the gross amount of the donations.

Where the amount of income tax and capital gains tax chargeable after deducting personal allowances does not cover the tax deducted from the donation, the personal allowances are restricted accordingly. If despite the restriction of personal allowances there is still insufficient tax payable, the donor is liable to pay tax equal to the shortfall. In calculating the shortfall the amount of tax taken into account is before deducting the 10% relief on married couple's age allowance. Any unused married couple's allowance is available to transfer to the spouse or civil partner. HMRC have the right to issue an assessment to collect the tax due. They may not do so if the amount involved is small but where a tax repayment is being claimed, the repayment is restricted to cover the amount due because of the charitable payment.

Example 3

In 2017–18 an unmarried taxpayer has income as shown below and makes charitable donations of £800 net, £1,000 gross.

	£
Interest	16,910
Dividends	2,000

		£		£
				18,910
Personal allowance				(11,500)
Taxable income				7,410

		£		£
Tax thereon:	Interest covered by the savings allowance (2.5)	1,000	@ 0%	—
		4,410	@ 20%	882
	Dividends covered by the dividend allowance (2.5)	2,000	@ 0%	—
		7,410		882

Since the tax chargeable exceeds the £200 retained out of the donations, the taxpayer is entitled to keep that amount.

Example 4

In 2017–18 an unmarried taxpayer has income as shown below and makes charitable donations of £2,400 net, £3,000 gross.

	£
Earnings	33,335
Interest	5,000
Dividends	10,000
	48,335
Personal allowance	(11,500)
Taxable income	36,835

		£		£
Tax thereon:	Earnings	21,835	@ 20%	4,367
	Interest covered by the savings allowance (2.5)	500	@0%	—
	Interest	4,500	@ 20%	900
	Dividends (part)	5,000	@ 0%	—
		4,665	@ 7.5%	349
		36,500*		
	Dividends (balance)	335	@ 32.5%	108

36,835	5,724

* Basic rate band extended by £3,000 because of charitable donation.

The extension of the basic rate band has saved tax of £750 (£3,000 @ 25% (32.5% – 7.5%) because an extra £3,000 of dividend income is now below the basic rate threshold). The net cost of the gift is therefore £2,250 (£3,000 – £750).

Carry back election for gift aid payments (ITA 2007, ss 426–427)

[43.19] A taxpayer may treat a gift aid donation as made in the previous tax year provided, broadly, that the grossed up amounts of donations made in that year, when added to donations carried back, do not exceed chargeable income and gains. The claim must be made on or before the date the tax return for the previous year is sent in and not later than 31 January in the tax year in which the gift was made. Provision is made in tax returns for the claim to be made (see **43.16**). The relief for the carried back amount will reduce the tax payable for the previous year and the normal treatment of backdated claims in **9.16** will not apply.

Exclusions

[43.20] If individuals give goods to charities the gifts do not qualify for gift aid (although see **43.22** re gifts of stocks, shares etc). The charity may, however, sell the goods on behalf of the donor, who may then donate the proceeds to the charity. The conditions for relief in these circumstances are set out in HMRC's guidance notes. The charity will normally obtain a gift aid declaration in advance, which will not, however, relate directly to the goods that are being sold. The individual must have the opportunity of changing his mind about the donation when the charity notifies him that the goods have been sold.

[43.21] Donations do not qualify for relief if the donor receives a benefit from the gift, unless the benefits come within stipulated limits, i.e. 25% of a gift up to £100, £25 for a gift between £100 and £1,000, and 5% of a gift in excess of £1,000. In addition to these limits, the total value of benefits received by a donor from the same charity in one tax year may not exceed £2,500. An unrestricted right of admission for at least a year to charity premises in return for a donation is not treated as a benefit for these purposes. For shorter periods or single visits, there is no benefit providing the cost to the donor is at least 10% higher than the amount charged to other members of the public. If any additional benefits are provided, they must fall within the benefits limits stated above.

Shares, securities and real property (ITA 2007, ss 431–445)

[43.22] In addition to cash gifts, relief is available against income for gifts to charities of shares and securities that are listed on a recognised stock exchange or dealt in on any designated UK market (AIM shares thus being included), units in unit trusts, shares in open-ended investment companies and interests in offshore funds. Relief is also available for gifts of UK land and buildings.

In general, the amount of the relief is the market value of the gifted assets (the net benefit received by the charity), plus any incidental costs of making the gift. However this is restricted to the donors acquisition cost where the:

(a) qualifying investment gifted to the charity (or anything from which the investment derives) was acquired within four years of the date of disposal; and

(b) main purpose(s) of acquiring the qualifying investment was to dispose of it to a charity and claim the tax relief.

The relief for the gift is given to individuals by deducting the value of the gifted assets from income, rather than extending the basic rate band. If the donor receives a benefit from the gift, the amount deductible from income is reduced accordingly.

If the charity retains the gift of land, buildings or shares it will be exempt from any stamp taxes.

Payroll deduction scheme (ITEPA 2003, ss 713–715; CTA 2009, ss 72, 1236)

[43.23] Employees can authorise participating employers to deduct a stipulated amount from their earnings before tax, for passing on to charities chosen by the employee, through HMRC approved charity agencies with which the employer has made an arrangement. The employee thus receives full tax relief for the contributions made. There is no limit on the amount that may be deducted under the scheme. The charity agencies are required to pass on the donations to the relevant charities within 35 days of receiving them. Voluntary payments to the agency by the employer to cover running costs are allowed in calculating the employer's taxable profits.

Gifts made under payroll giving are exempt from tax in the hands of the charity only to the extent the income is spent on charitable purposes (this aligns the treatment of donation income under payroll giving with the treatment of other donation income).

Inheritance tax (IHTA 1984, ss 23, 58, 70, 76)

[43.24] All gifts to charity are exempt for inheritance tax purposes whether made in lifetime, on death or at the discretion of trustees. Where the charity is a discretionary trust, inheritance tax is not payable by the trustees unless property leaving the trust is used for a non-charitable purpose. A reduced rate of inheritance tax applies where 10% or more of a deceased's net estate (after deducting inheritance tax exemptions, reliefs and the nil rate band) is left to a charity or registered community amateur sports club (5.30).

Pre-eminent gift relief (FA 2012, s 49 and Sch 14)

[43.25] Gifts (via the relevant government minister) can be made by individuals or companies, of objects which are of pre-eminent national, scientific, historic, artistic, architectural or scenic interest. These gifts are then loaned or given by the minister to appropriate institutions, including certain charities for safe-keeping and to provide public access. The donor receives a tax reduction as a fixed percentage of the object's agreed value — 30% for individuals and 20% for companies. For further details see **2.21**.

Giving to charities: companies

Tainted donations (CTA 2010, ss 939A–939I)

[43.26] The provisions detailed at **43.15** apply equally (with obvious necessary modifications to terminology etc.) to charitable donations by companies.

Gift aid donations by companies

Money gifts (CTA 2010, ss 189–202C)

[43.27] The gift aid provisions enable companies to obtain tax relief when they make payments to a charity or a CASC (subject to anti-avoidance provisions aimed at discouraging abuse of companies owned or controlled by CASCs). As for individuals, payments under the gift aid provisions by companies include covenanted payments. Companies are not required to deduct tax from any of their charitable payments and the full amount of the payment is deducted from the profits of the company in calculating corporation tax payable for the accounting period in which the payment was made. (See **43.30** for the special provisions for payments by a company owned by a charity).

The same provisions apply as for individuals (see **43.21**) where a company receives a benefit from the gift, including the allowability of benefits within stipulated limits. Additional restrictions apply to prevent the company receiving a repayment of the gift or either the company or a connected person receiving benefits in excess of stipulated limits. See **43.28** for the treatment of gifts in kind.

The after-tax cost to the company depends on the company's tax position. The cost may indeed be 100% if the company has no taxable profits, because in that case loss relief cannot be claimed for charitable payments (except within a group of companies by way of group relief).

Shares, securities and real property (TCGA 1992, ss 257, 257A; CAA 2001, s 63; CTA 2009, s 105; CTA 2010, ss 203–217)

[43.28] If businesses make gifts of their stock or plant and machinery to charities, they do not have to bring amounts into account as trading receipts or disposal proceeds for capital allowances.

Relief is available against income for gifts to charities of shares and securities that are listed on a recognised stock exchange or dealt in on any designated UK market (AIM shares thus being included), units in unit trusts, shares in open-ended investment companies and interests in offshore funds. Relief is also available for gifts of UK land and buildings.

In general, the amount of the relief is the market value of the gifted assets (the net benefit received by the charity), plus any incidental costs of making the gift. However this is restricted to the donors acquisition cost where the:

(a)   qualifying investment gifted to the charity (or anything from which the investment derives) was acquired within four years of the date of disposal; and

(b)   main purpose(s) of acquiring the qualifying investment was to dispose of it to a charity and claim the tax relief.

The relief for the gift is given by deducting it as a qualifying donation to charity. If the donor receives a benefit from the gift, the amount deductible from income is reduced accordingly.

Gifts in kind to charities are exempt for capital gains purposes (unless the gift is a 'tainted donation' (**43.15**)), so neither a chargeable gain nor allowable loss will arise. If the charity retains a gift of land, buildings or shares it will be exempt from any stamp taxes.

Pre-eminent gift relief (FA 2012, s 49 and Sch 14)

[43.29] The provisions detailed at 43.25 apply equally to companies, with obvious necessary modifications where necessary.

Companies owned by charities (CTA 2010, s 199)

[43.30] Many charities have fund-raising subsidiaries that gift their entire profits to the charity under the gift aid provisions. Moreover, a company which makes a gift aid payment may claim to have it treated as made in an earlier accounting period that ended in the nine months preceding the gift aid payment. This removes any need for the trading company to estimate its profit before making a payment in respect of a particular period. Any donation payment made by a subsidiary company to its parent charity which exceeds the subsidiary's profits available for distribution is unlawful under the Companies Act 2006. No tax deduction will be given for unlawful distributions for accounting periods commencing on or after 1 April 2015. For HMRC guidance see www.gov.uk/government/publications/charities-detailed-guidance-notes.

Employees seconded to charities etc. (ITTOIA 2005, s 70; CTA 2009, ss 70, 1235)

[43.31] The salaries of employees temporarily seconded to charities, local education authorities or other approved educational bodies may be deducted as a business expense even though, because of the secondment, the salaries are not paid wholly and exclusively for the purposes of the trade.

Intermediary charities

[43.32] Individuals and companies may want to give regularly to several charities, but may not want to commit themselves to any one of them. As well as making one-off payments under the gift aid provisions (see **43.16, 43.27**), there are two ways of achieving this and still retaining the tax advantages. The simplest way is to make payments to an intermediary organisation such as the Charities Aid Foundation. It is possible to tell the organisation which particular charities are to benefit. The organisation will, if requested, make annual payments to the chosen charities by standing order. Alternatively, and especially where the size of the donation is more significant, it is possible for individuals or companies to set up their own intermediary charity. A simple charitable trust can be set up relatively easily although it is essential to have proper professional advice. Additionally, for small amounts, the payroll deduction scheme (**43.23**) may enable the recipient charity to be varied.

Community amateur sports clubs (CTA 2010, ss 658–671)

[43.33] Some sports clubs may be able to satisfy the tests for charitable status. For those who do not, or who do not wish to apply to be charities, they may be able to register with HMRC as community amateur sports clubs (CASCs), which will entitle them to various tax exemptions and reliefs. Registration is available to non-profit making amateur sports clubs that are open to the whole community and provide facilities for, and promote participation in, one or more eligible sports.

CASCs are exempt from:

(a)   corporation tax on all interest and gift aid income;
(b)   corporation tax on trading income (before expenses) of up to £50,000;
(c)   corporation tax on property income (before expenses) of up to £30,000; and
(d)   capital gains on the disposal of assets.

Donations from individuals or a business to a CASC qualify for tax relief under the gift aid provisions (see **43.16**). There are anti-avoidance provisions aimed at discouraging abuse of companies owned or controlled by CASCs. The relief for business gifts of stock or plant and machinery applies (see **43.28**) and the capital gains exemption for gifts in kind to charities and the inheritance tax exemption for gifts to charities also apply (see **43.28** and **43.24**). CASCs are entitled to 80% mandatory relief from business rates.

As for charities, CASCs are allowed to submit 'in year' income tax repayment claims in advance of filing a tax return (to claim, for example, income tax on gift aid payments, royalties etc).

HMRC guidance on CASCs can be found at www.gov.uk/government/public ations/community-amateur-sports-clubs-detailed-guidance-notes.

Tax points

[43.34] Note the following:

- If a donor sets up his own charitable trust, the trustees must not profit from their position or allow their duties and responsibilities to conflict with their personal interests. It is possible, however, to appoint a professional trustee, such as a solicitor or accountant, and an appropriate charging clause in the trust deed will enable his fees to be paid.
- Although gift aid donations may be evidenced by a simple declaration (possibly made by telephone or online), the donor must be a taxpayer to be able to retain tax relief on the donation. If an oral donation is made, the charity must keep detailed records to enable HMRC to check that the conditions for relief have been satisfied. Charities receiving regular amounts in cash (for example church collections) must have a system that demonstrates that the donations have been received.
- For the paying company to get relief from corporation tax for an accounting period on a charitable payment, the payment must be made in that accounting period, except for charity-owned companies, who can obtain relief for payments made up to nine months after the end of the accounting period.
- 'Charity affinity cards', i.e. credit cards on which some of the money spent goes to a charity, will not cause the charity to have a tax liability if the money is channelled through a trading subsidiary that donates its income to the charity. For VAT purposes, HMRC will usually treat at least 20% of the charity's initial payment from the card provider as being liable to VAT as income from promotional activities, with the remaining 80% or less, plus all subsequent payments based on turnover, not attracting VAT.

44

Contractors and subcontractors in the construction industry

Employed or self-employed?

[44.1] Although this chapter deals with the special scheme for contractors and subcontractors in the construction industry, the scheme has no relevance where the worker concerned should in fact be classified as an employee. The IR35 provisions requiring personal service companies to account for tax and national insurance contributions (NICs) on deemed pay if an employee would have been treated as employed by a client of the company had he contracted directly with the client (see **19.4**) also need to be taken into account. Where the IR35 rules apply, the tax and NICs on the deemed payment are due in the same year, under the RTI provisions (**10.58**).

Where the construction industry scheme applies, subcontractors may have suffered tax which is not repayable until accounts have been submitted. It may also be necessary to consider whether payments to a participator in a managed service company are to be treated as employment income (see **19.14**).

The decision as to whether someone is employed or self-employed is often difficult to make (see **19.1**), particularly in the construction industry, but the consequences of getting it wrong can be extremely serious. HMRC's factsheet CIS349 'Are your workers employed or self-employed? — advice for contractors' outlines the factors to be taken into account, and HMRC provide an employment status indicator tool at www.gov.uk/guidance/check-employment -status-for-tax which they consider can be used in 'all but the most complex cases' (see **19.2**). However, it is only an 'indicator' and the accompanying HMRC notes state that it will not give a definitive or legally binding opinion.

In the event of reclassification, the worker's self-employed business will cease in the tax year of reclassification. See **10.2** for the treatment of construction industry employees supplied by agencies.

If contractors are found not to be complying with the PAYE regulations for those who should properly be treated as employees, they will have to account to HMRC for the amount of the unpaid tax and NICs.

The consequences of reclassification are far-reaching and potentially extremely costly for contractors, not only in relation to tax but also in relation to employment law and health and safety law.

Contractors' monthly returns (see **44.6**) include a declaration that the employment status of each worker has been considered and that payments have not been made under contracts of employment.

Construction industry scheme (FA 2004, ss 57–77 and Schs 11, 12; SI 2005/2045)

Current construction industry scheme

[44.2] The current construction industry scheme broadly requires subcontractors to register either to receive payments from contractors gross or net of 20% tax. If contractors make payments to unregistered subcontractors they must deduct 30% tax at source.

Any tax withheld by the contractor must be paid over to HMRC and it counts as advance payment towards the sub-contractors tax and National Insurance bill.

This scheme is aimed at reducing the regulatory burden on construction businesses, improving compliance with tax obligations and helping construction businesses to get the employment status of their workers right.

Registration of contractors

[44.3] New contractors must register with HMRC before taking on their first subcontractor.

A 'contractor' has a wider meaning than just a construction company and covers many other businesses involved in construction work. Gangleaders who organise labour for construction work are included. Non-construction businesses are also included if they spend on average more than £1 million a year over a three-year period on construction-related work. Private householders and smaller non-construction businesses are excluded. Construction work includes repairs, decorating and demolition. Work outside the UK is not included, but the scheme applies to UK construction work even if the subcontractors and/or contractors are non-resident, and even if payment is made abroad.

Registration of subcontractors

[44.4] Subcontractors need to register with HMRC. Those seeking registration must contact HMRC and if they are not already paying tax or NICs they will need to take specified identification documents to a local HMRC office.

There are two types of registration, registration for gross payment and registration for payment under deduction of tax at 20% (see **44.5**). HMRC may cancel the registration at any time if the qualifying conditions no longer apply or the rules have been breached. The subcontractor has a right of appeal against HMRC's decision. If a subcontractor does not register, the contractor is required to deduct 30% tax at source from payments made to the contractor.

Payment of subcontractors

[44.5] Contractors must obtain basic identification details from subcontractors (e.g. name, taxpayer reference number and national insurance number) and must verify the status of their subcontractors with HMRC. From 6 April 2017 onwards verification by contractors can *only* be done online using the free HMRC CIS online service, or commercial CIS software. Before 6 April 2017 2017 it was possible for verification to be either by telephone or online. This must be done before any payments are made. Contractors may assume that the subcontractor's status remains unchanged unless HMRC notify them to the contrary.

Registered subcontractors can either be registered for:

(a)   payments to be made gross. To be registered for such payments subcontractors must comply with detailed conditions. The business must operate in the UK and be run 'to a substantial extent' through a bank account. They must have complied promptly with certain tax obligations for the previous year and meet the following turnover limits:

   (i)   £30,000 for sole-traders;
   (ii)   £30,000 for each partner in a partnership, or at least £100,000 for the whole partnership;
   (iii) £30,000 for each director of a company, or at least £100,000 for the whole company;
   (iv)   £30,000 for each individual that controls the company, if five people or fewer control the company;

(b)   payments to be made net of 20% tax deducted at source.

Contractors may pay unregistered subcontractors, but tax must be deducted from payments at 30%.

Administration

[44.6] Where contractors deduct tax from payments to either registered or unregistered subcontractors, they must supply them with statements showing the gross amount and the tax deducted. Deductions under the scheme are normally paid over to the HMRC Accounts Office each month. Payments may instead be made quarterly if contractors expect their average payments of amounts due under the PAYE system and subcontractor deductions to be less than £1,500 a month. Interest is charged on underpayments as for PAYE (see 9.56), and penalties will apply if the tax is not paid by a specified date (see 9.74).

[44.7] Contractors must submit monthly returns (form CIS300), even if they make payments quarterly, and must provide details of recipients and payments made, together with a 'status declaration' confirming that 'employment status' has been considered (see 44.1). The return must be delivered electronically. Contractors do not need to file a nil return when they have not paid subcontractors in a tax month. Penalties will apply if a return is not submitted; see 9.64.

Real Time Information for PAYE (10.58) has not changed the CIS process. Employers must continue to complete and file CIS300 returns due under the existing CIS arrangements. But, where a limited company acting as a subcontractor has suffered CIS deductions, they report these amounts to HMRC on an 'employer payment submission' (EPS) and subtract these from the amount of PAYE due to be paid to HMRC.

> **Example 1**
>
> A limited company has deducted PAYE tax and NI of £4,500. CIS tax deducted from payments it has received is £350. Net PAYE payment due to HMRC by the company is £4,150. If the EPS is not submitted showing CIS tax of £350 suffered, HMRC will issue demands for £350.

Where the business also has a PAYE scheme HMRC will know the amount of the tax due under CIS from the CIS300 return. HMRC will also know, from the full payment submission (FPS) and EPS submitted, the amount of tax and NIC withheld from any employees that is due to be paid by the 19th (or 22nd for electronic payments) following the end of the tax month. HMRC will add these amounts together and chase any underpayments. Late submissions of RTI returns does not lead automatically to the loss of gross payment status for a business.

Tax position of non-corporate subcontractors

[44.8] The subcontractor's earnings are brought into the self-employed accounts of the subcontractor, and the amount deducted becomes a payment on account of the tax and Class 4 NICs due. The deduction by the contractor does not absolve the subcontractor from preparing accounts and submitting returns, and if his liability is greater than the amount deducted there is the possibility of interest and penalties if he has not complied with time limits for submission of returns and payment of tax and NICs.

Where tax and Class 4 NICs have been overpaid, a repayment may be claimed in the subcontractor's tax return. For subcontractors who make up accounts to a date earlier than 5 April, repayment claims may be made before the end of the tax year, but before making a repayment HMRC will ensure that the subcontractor's tax affairs are up to date and that all tax and Class 4 NICs due for earlier years has been paid.

Tax position of corporate subcontractors

[44.9] Tax deducted under the subcontractors' scheme from payments to companies is set off against amounts due to be paid by the company to HMRC in respect of PAYE, NICs etc. and, where the subcontractor itself uses further subcontractors, subcontractors' scheme deductions.

If a CIS repayment claim is made, HMRC aim to process it within 25 working days from the date of receipt where the information sent matches the information held by HMRC. In the event of a discrepancy, repayment of the amount matched or verified may be made while HMRC investigate the discrepancy. Repayments will be made by BACS transfer if full bank details are provided. HMRC may set a company's CIS repayment against corporation tax or VAT liabilities in certain situations.

Tax points

[44.10] Note the following:

- Where tax is deducted from the full labour content of a payment to a subcontractor, an overpayment will normally arise because of the expenses of the trade and because individuals will normally have personal allowances available (but, on the other hand, Class 4 NICs will increase the liability).
- The definition of operations covered by the scheme is wide. It is important to check the legislation to see if the contractors' operations are included. If the scheme is not applied when it should have been, all the tax that should have been deducted from payments to subcontractors plus interest may be due. If the workers should have been treated as employees, the position is even worse (see below).
- New businesses need to be able to satisfy turnover requirements in the previous 12 months in order to obtain registration for gross payment. In the meantime, tax will be deducted at 20%. If the new business's own subcontractors are registered for gross payment, those gross payments will have to be made out of net payments received.
- Contractors should be very careful to ensure that the terms under which workers operate bring them within the self-employed category if they are to treat them as subcontractors.
- If workers are wrongly classified, the contractor could be held liable for the PAYE tax that should have been deducted, plus employers' and employees' NICs, and possibly penalties as well. Where a subcontractor company is caught by the IR35 personal service company rules, it is the subcontractor company rather than the contractor who suffers the burden of employer's PAYE and NICs.
- See also **19.14** for the special rules which treat payments to participators in managed service companies as employment income.

45

Main anti-avoidance provisions

Background

[45.1] HMRC's ability to counter what they regard as unacceptable tax avoidance has been strengthened by various court decisions and the rules requiring the disclosure to HMRC of tax avoidance schemes meeting certain criteria (see **45.2**). In addition there is a general anti-abuse rule or GAAR (for all taxes) which applies, broadly, for any tax arrangements entered into on or after 17 July 2013 (see **45.5**). Most double taxation agreements with other countries contain a provision allowing for the exchange of information between the taxation authorities of the countries concerned and many countries have tax information exchange agreements (TIEAs) which are bilateral agreements under which territories agree to co-operate in tax matters through exchange of information.

Schemes that include steps inserted purely for tax avoidance may well prove unsuccessful, although bona fide commercial arrangements will usually be effective provided that they do not breach any of the specific provisions.

It is important to bear in mind that tax avoidance is legal and tax evasion is illegal. HMRC have issued guidance to taxpayers on tax avoidance and what can happen if they enter a tax avoidance scheme, see www.gov.uk/guidance/tax-avoidance-an-introduction.

Anti-avoidance rules are necessarily complex, and what follows is only a brief outline of some of the more common rules. It should not be regarded as an exhaustive list of anti-avoidance measures. Much of the legislation granting reliefs has anti-avoidance measures within it. Examples include the rules relating to demergers; companies purchasing their own shares; the enterprise investment scheme; capital allowances and relief for trading losses.

Much of the present legislation is intended to prevent income being converted into a capital gain, and this is likely to become of greater significance now that gains are taxed at a flat rate, ranging from 10% to 28% (see **4.2**), significantly lower than the current 45% higher rate of income tax.

As well as measures affecting direct taxes, there are numerous anti-avoidance provisions relating to VAT. Examples include provisions relating to multinational groups of companies, transfers of businesses as going concerns, business splitting, charity reliefs, the option to charge VAT on buildings, the treatment of staff hire, the margin scheme for second-hand goods, cash accounting, the treatment of credit vouchers, the capital goods scheme and rules to counter exploitation by commercial sports clubs of the exemption for non-profit making organisations.

Disclosure of tax avoidance schemes

Income tax, corporation tax, capital gains tax, national insurance, stamp taxes, inheritance tax and ATED (TMA 1970, s 98C; SSAA 1992, s 132A; FA 2004, ss 306–319)

[45.2] 'Promoters' who market certain tax avoidance schemes and arrangements are required to make a disclosure of information about them to HMRC. The types of schemes and arrangements that come within these provisions include:

(a)   (from August 2006) any income tax, corporation tax, or capital gains tax scheme, where the main benefit expected under the scheme is a tax advantage and the arrangement bears one or more 'hallmarks';

(b)   (from May 2007) national insurance saving schemes, where the main benefit is the obtaining of a NIC advantage and the scheme bears one or more 'hallmarks';

(c)   (from August 2005) schemes intended to avoid stamp duty land tax on UK property transactions, where the schemes are made available or implemented on or after 1 August 2005 (SI 2005/1868). They apply to commercial property with an aggregate market value of £5 million or more, residential property with a market value of at least £1 million and mixed commercial and residential property where either the residential property is worth at least £1 million or the value of all the property is at least £5 million;

(d)   (from 6 April 2011) certain inheritance tax arrangements involving transfers of property into trust (SI 2011/170). Broadly, disclosure of schemes or arrangements will have to be made where property held by an individual is transferred during his or her lifetime and is, at some point as part of the scheme or arrangement, settled on relevant property trusts, and the inheritance tax entry charge, which would otherwise apply when property is transferred into trust, is avoided, reduced or deferred;

(e) (from 4 November 2013) transactions which enable or might be expected to enable any person to obtain a tax advantage in relation to the annual tax on enveloped dwellings charge (**32.48**). The duty to disclose arises when the ownership condition is no longer met, the value of the property falls below the relevant threshold (£500,000 from 1 April 2016) or the taxable value of the property is reduced with a result that the ATED charge is lower. Certain transactions, e.g. ones on commercial terms, transfers between group companies etc, are excluded (SI 2013/2571).

For HMRC guidance see www.gov.uk/government/publications/disclosure-of-tax-avoidance-schemes-guidance.

A 'promoter' is anyone who provides taxation services in the course of a trade if he has responsibility for designing such schemes, or markets or promotes schemes designed by someone else. It also includes a person who 'makes a firm approach' to another person 'with a view to' making the scheme available for implementation. The person approached can therefore either be a user or a scheme introducer (an 'introducer' is defined as a person who makes a marketing contact with another in relation to a scheme). The provisions do not apply to legal advisers in relation to anything covered by legal professional privilege (unless the clients have waived privilege, allowing the promoter to make the disclosure).

The scheme promoter must make the disclosure to HMRC within five business days of a 'firm approach' being made. Where a person has disclosed a proposal or arrangement that provides a tax advantage, HMRC may require that person to provide additional documents or more information about the proposal or arrangement. HMRC may ask the tribunal for an order requiring the information or documents to be provided if they have reasonable grounds for suspecting that it will not be provided. From 26 March 2015 persons are able to voluntarily provide information or documents to HMRC which they suspect may assist HMRC.

HMRC register all such schemes and give each a reference number, which promoters must provide to their clients together with information specified in regulations. Clients are then under a duty to pass on this information to anyone else they might reasonably be expected to know is likely to benefit or be a party to the arrangements. In addition, for scheme reference numbers notified by HMRC on or after 26 March 2015, where an employer receives a tax advantage relating to an employee's employment, the employer must provide the prescribed information to the employee, and notify HMRC accordingly.

Promoters who issue reference numbers to clients must also provide a quarterly return of these client names, addresses, UTR or NI numbers (i.e. a client list) to HMRC and, for reference numbers issued on or after 26 March 2015 must notify HMRC of changes to the scheme name or promoters name/address. Further, where HMRC suspects that the client is not the user of the scheme, they may require the promoter to produce further information about users of the scheme and other parties involved in the selling and execution of the scheme. Failure to provide information under these powers will make the promoter or the promoter's client, as appropriate, liable to a penalty not exceeding £5,000.

Taxpayers have to provide details of schemes themselves where they have purchased the scheme from an offshore promoter who has not made a disclosure, where the promoter is protected from disclosure by legal professional privilege or where the scheme was devised in-house. The time limit for taxpayers to provide such details to HMRC is five days (extended to 30 days where the scheme was devised in-house), after the first transaction forming part of the arrangements. Neither individuals nor businesses that are small or medium-sized enterprises, however, have to disclose in-house schemes. A 'small or medium-sized' enterprise for this purpose is as defined by the European Union, i.e. a business that has fewer than 500 employees, with a turnover of less than €100 million and/or balance sheet total of less than €86 million.

Taxpayers using the schemes will usually only be required to include the reference number of the scheme on their tax returns (except where they are required to disclose as indicated above).

There are penalties for failure to disclose a scheme, or to provide a client with a reference number.

The disclosure requirements have necessitated notification of a number of avoidance schemes, which has resulted in anti-avoidance legislation in subsequent Finance Acts.

VAT (VATA 1994, s 58A and Sch 11A; SI 2004/1933)

[45.3] Businesses that use certain VAT avoidance schemes must disclose their use to HMRC. There is a statutory register of VAT avoidance schemes, each of which has a reference number. There are 'designated schemes' (i.e. schemes which the Treasury designate by order) and 'notifiable schemes' (i.e. schemes which are designated or hallmarked and have a tax avoidance motive).

Businesses must notify HMRC of the schemes, unless their VAT exclusive value of supplies is less than £600,000 (in relation to a designated scheme) or £10 million (in relation to a hallmarked scheme).

Notification must be made within 30 days from the last day for submission of the relevant return, or within 30 days after the date of a relevant claim for a refund of output VAT or increase of allowable input VAT. Penalties are imposed for failure to notify use of a scheme.

High risk promoters (FA 2014, ss 234–283, Schs 34–36; SI 2015/130)

[45.4] From 17 July 2014 certain 'high risk' promoters may be issued with a conduct notice for a period of up to two years if they have triggered a threshold condition in the previous three years or, with effect from 26 March 2015, if another person in business as a promoter is treated as triggering the threshold condition by virtue of being associated with the promoter as a body corporate or a partnership. This legislation is designed to improve the transparency of certain promoters with HMRC with appropriate sanctions if the promoter does not want to comply voluntarily under the DOTAS regime (**45.2**).

A promoter, for the purposes of these rules, is more widely drawn than under the DOTAS regime in that it is not restricted to providers of tax or banking services. A person is a promoter in respect of a relevant proposal if, at any time, the person is responsible for the design of the proposed arrangements and makes a 'firm approach' to someone with a view to making the proposal available for implementation. Companies that provide tax services only to other group companies and advisers who do not provide tax advice in relation to an avoidance scheme are specifically excluded from these provisions.

There are 11 general threshold conditions detailed in the legislation that apply to a promoter:

(a)   the promoter has had information published about himself as deliberate tax defaulter;

(b)   the promoter has been named in a report for a breach of the Code of Practice on Taxation for Banks;

(c)   the promoter has received a conduct notice as a dishonest tax agent;

(d)   the promoter has failed to disclose a tax avoidance scheme or to provide details of clients to HMRC (even if he had a reasonable excuse);

(e)   the promoter has been charged with a specified tax offence;

(f)   the majority of a sub-panel of the GAAR Advisory Panel has given an opinion that entering into one of the promoter's tax avoidance schemes is not a reasonable course of action;

(g)   the promoter has been found guilty of misconduct by a professional body;

(h)   a regulatory authority has imposed a sanction on the promoter;

(i)   the promoter has failed to comply with an information notice issued by HMRC;

(j)   the promoter has required a client to keep details of a tax avoidance scheme confidential from HMRC or to contribute to a fighting fund;

(k)   the promoter has continued to market or make available a tax avoidance scheme after being given a notice to stop following a judicial ruling.

Where conditions (a), (c), (e)–(k) are met by a person who controls a company, the company is treated as having met the threshold condition. A partnership is treated as a person for the purpose of these provisions and the rules are applied, with necessary modifications, to encompass partnerships as promoters.

In addition, from 15 September 2016, if HMRC is aware that a promoter continues to promote a series of avoidance schemes that do not work, they must consider whether to issue a conduct notice.

Breach of any conduct notice that may be issued may lead to the promoter being monitored by HMRC. The monitored promoter will have a right of appeal against the monitoring notice. A monitored promoter will be subject to specific information powers and penalties for non-compliance of up to £1 million. In addition HMRC will have the power to name the monitored promoter and require it to inform its intermediaries and clients. The naming details will include information on why the conduct notice was breached. A higher standard for the defences of reasonable excuse and reasonable care will apply to the monitored promoter. Intermediaries who continue to act for a monitored promoter are subject to the same information powers and penalties. Clients of a monitored promoter will be supplied by the monitored promoter with a reference number that they have to report to HMRC so that they can be identified and compliance action by HMRC accurately targeted. Clients of a monitored prompter are also subject to an extended assessing period of 20 years if any tax is lost because they fail to pass on the reference number and a penalty.

For HMRC guidance see www.gov.uk/government/publications/promoters-of -tax-avoidance-schemes-guidance.

General anti-abuse rule (GAAR) (FA 2013, ss 206–215 and Sch 43; NICA 2014, s 10)

[45.5] The GAAR provides for the counteraction of tax advantages arising from arrangements that are abusive. It applies, from 17 July 2013, to income tax, corporation tax (including amounts chargeable/treated as corporation tax), capital gains tax, petroleum revenue tax, inheritance tax, and stamp duty land tax. It also applies to the annual tax on enveloped dwellings (**32.48**), national insurance contributions (from 13 March 2014) and the diverted profits tax (from 1 April 2015; **3.33**).

The GAAR is another element of HMRC's approach to tackling tax avoidance and is not intended to replace or supersede targeted anti-avoidance rules or any obligations under DOTAS.

If HMRC wish to make adjustments under the GAAR, they must follow detailed procedural requirements and in any proceedings before a court or tribunal in connection with the GAAR, the burden of proof lies with HMRC (not the taxpayer). As part of the hearing a sub-panel of three members will consider the matter and may invite the taxpayer or the designated officer (or both) to supply further information before making their decision. Only after the Advisory Panel has issued its opinion to both parties can the designated officer issue a final notice to the taxpayer on whether tax advantages are to be counteracted and, if necessary, what adjustments are required to give effect to the counteraction. The panel's opinions are not binding on HMRC or the taxpayer and the normal rights of appeal will apply to any adjustments made by HMRC. For arrangements entered into on or after 15 September 2016, a penalty of up to 60% of the counteracted tax may be charged.

HMRC's guidance on the GAAR can be found at www.gov.uk/government/pu blications/tax-avoidance-general-anti-abuse-rules and details of the framework within which the GAAR Advisory Panel will operate can be found at www.gov.uk/government/groups/general-anti-abuse-rule-advisory-panel.

Scottish GAAR

[45.6] The Scottish general anti-avoidance rule (GAAR) is designed to combat unacceptable avoidance. It is wider than the UK GAAR in that it targets tax advantages arising from artificial tax avoidance arrangements, rather than focussing on the counteraction of tax advantages arising from arrangements that are abusive. Revenue Scotland have the power to counteract such a tax advantage by adjusting the tax liability of a taxpayer who would otherwise benefit from it, and they may make any adjustments that they consider to be just and reasonable. Such adjustments may be made in respect of the tax for which a tax advantage has been gained, or in respect of any other devolved tax. The Scottish GAAR has effect in relation to any tax avoidance arrangement entered into on or after 1 April 2015 and applies only to devolved taxes (i.e. Land and Buildings Transaction Tax (**6.18**) and Scottish Landfill Tax). The Scottish GAAR does not apply to the Scottish rate of income tax (**2.4**) which is subject to the UK GAAR.

Penalties for enablers

[45.7] The September 2017 Finance Bill, which is expected to receive Royal Assent in November 2017, introduced a new penalty for any person who enables the use of abusive tax avoidance arrangements, which are later defeated. The penalties will apply to advice provided or actions taken on or after the date of Royal Assent to the September 2017 Finance Bill.

Enablers are those who design, market or otherwise facilitate the tax avoidance. The legislation is widely drafted to cover everyone in the supply chain who benefits from the arrangements. Arrangements are defeated if they are defeated either in the courts, the tribunal or by agreement between HMRC and the relevant parties.

The penalty charged will be equal to the amount of consideration received or receivable by an enabler for their role in enabling the tax avoidance arrangements which were defeated. Where an enabler has enabled more than one person to implement the same proposal for arrangements, further rules will apply to determine when the penalties will be charged.

Serial tax avoiders (FA 2016, s 159 and Sch 18)

[45.8] Finance Act 2016 introduced tax avoidance rules that target 'serial tax avoiders'. These rules are set to come into force on 6 April 2017, but tax schemes entered into before then will be relevant. HMRC guidance can be found at www.gov.uk/guidance/serial-tax-avoidance.

In broad terms, the rules provide a series of escalations starting with a warning if the taxpayer has participated in a defeated scheme, followed by a penalty if a further scheme fails while the taxpayer is on a warning, with the penalty increasing if more arrangements fail. If the taxpayer suffers three defeats while on a warning their name can be published. For tax schemes that seek to abuse tax reliefs, HMRC can deny further claims until the warning period has expired. If a taxpayer entered into a tax scheme before 6 April 2017 it will, if defeated, count for the purposes of the regime unless the taxpayer disclosed full details of the arrangements to HMRC. Any defeat before 6 April 2017 is disregarded as long as the arrangement was entered into before 15 September 2016. It will be essential for any taxpayer who is at risk of a tax scheme failing after 5 April 2017 to ensure that HMRC has been provided with full details of the scheme or that it has been notified of the intention to do so. Arrangements entered into after 5 April 2017 will always count if defeated and arrangements entered into before 6 April 2017 will count only if not disclosed to HMRC before that date or within such further time as HMRC agrees.

Large business sanctions (FA 2016, s 161 and Sch 19)

[45.9] From 15 September 2016 a special measures regime applies. This is aimed at tackling the small number of large businesses that engage in aggressive tax planning, or refuse to engage with HMRC in an open and collaborative manner. A large business is, broadly, a UK group, company or partnership with a turnover of more than £200 million and/or a balance sheet total of more than £2 billion. The legislation allows a designated HMRC officer to issue a warning notice to a business that has persistently engaged in uncooperative behaviour contributing to two or more significant unresolved tax issues (where the amount in dispute is in excess of £2 million), and there is a reasonable likelihood of further uncooperative behaviour contributing to significant tax issues in the future. The business then has 12 months to make representations, but if, at the end of the 12 month period, the business has not 'improved' HMRC are able to issue a special measures notice, which renders the business liable to potential sanctions, such as removing the defence of 'reasonable care' for the purpose of penalties in respect of inaccurate returns. HMRC have also indicated that administrative sanctions could include the removal of access to non-statutory clearances.

Transactions in securities (ITA 2007, ss 682–713; CTA 2010, ss 731–751)

[45.10] Where in consequence of a transaction in securities a person has obtained a tax advantage, then unless he shows that the transaction was for bona fide commercial reasons or in the course of making or managing investments, and that none of the transactions had as their main object, or one of their main objects, the realising of a tax advantage, that tax advantage may be nullified.

These provisions have been used particularly where elaborate schemes have been devised with the aim of extracting the undistributed profits of companies in a capital form. In view of the far reaching implications there is an appropriate clearance procedure which it is wise to follow wherever shares are being sold in closely controlled companies with significant distributable reserves.

The provisions do not apply until HMRC serve a notice specifying the adjustment to be made, and taxpayers are not required to deal with the liability in their self-assessment returns, nor are HMRC bound by the self-assessment enquiry time limits. See HMRC Tax Bulletin 46 (April 2000).

Avoidance relating to financial products

[45.11] Schemes relating to financial products are routinely notified under the disclosure provisions outlined in **45.2** and are usually blocked by legislation. A few of these rules are outlined below, but in general this type of anti-avoidance legislation is beyond the scope of this book and professional advice should be sought in such situations.

Transfer of an income stream (CTA 2010, ss 752–757B, 779A–779B; ITA 2007, ss 809AZA–809AZG, 809AAZA–809AAZB, 809DZA–809DZB)

[45.12] There is a general principle, set out in statute, that consideration received for the sale or transfer of an income stream is subject to tax in the transferor's hands in the same way that the income itself would have been (so there is no possibility of converting income into capital). These provisions only apply where certain conditions are met. Similar provisions also apply for income tax purposes, which essentially mirror the corporation tax rules with a few minor exceptions simply to cater for the different structure of income tax.

Further, a charge to tax on income is imposed where, in consequence of an arrangement, there is a disposal of an asset or a right to income by or through a partnership from a member of the partnership or a connected person to another member, and one of the main purposes of one or more steps taken in effecting the disposal is the obtaining of a tax advantage in relation to the charge to income tax or the charge to corporation tax on income. This includes both part disposals and in substance disposals such as may be effected by a change of partnership profit sharing ratios. The transferor will be charged to tax on the consideration given, or the deemed market value if the consideration is much less but will not apply if the transferor and transferee are relatives.

Finance agreements (CTA 2010, ss 758–776)

[45.13] Specific provisions counter cases where:

(a)   a taxpayer sells the right to income receipts for a predetermined period in return for a lump sum payment which is treated as a capital receipt for the purposes of corporation tax on chargeable gains, or where the taxpayer is within the charge to income tax or capital gains tax; and

(b)   the transaction is, in economic substance, a financing transaction and this is how the transaction is accounted for in the taxpayer's accounts.

In such cases, subject to certain exceptions, the transfer of the asset is disregarded in computing the taxpayer's taxable income and the taxpayer is able to obtain tax relief for the financing charge which it reflects in its accounts in respect of the transaction, provided that its accounting treatment is in accordance with generally accepted accounting practice.

Manufactured payments (CTA 2010, ss 814A–814D; ITA 2007, ss 614ZA–614ZD)

[45.14] There are provisions to prevent the rules relating to manufactured payments in respect of UK securities (which are largely relevant to companies trading in the financial markets) being used by individuals to generate tax-deductible manufactured payments coupled with non-taxable receipts.

There are also provisions preventing the purchase and sale of securities being used to create tax allowable trading losses or to enable tax-exempt persons to claim repayments.

These provisions are complex, and have been the subject of a number of avoidance schemes. For manufactured interest or dividends made on or after 1 January 2014, the following rules apply:

(a) Manufactured interest: The current treatment of manufactured interest is not changed. This regime provides that where the recipient is a company, the manufactured interest is treated as a trading credit or a non-trading credit in accordance with the loan relationship provisions, as if it was real interest. Where the recipient is a person other than a company, the manufactured interest is treated as if it was real interest, i.e. it is assessed as savings and investment income;

(b) Manufactured dividends: When they are received by a financial trader, they will be taxed as trade receipts, and when they are paid by a financial trader they will generally be allowed as a trade deduction. In other circumstances, the receipt of a manufactured dividend will not be taxable and the payment of a manufactured dividend will not be allowable as a deduction.

Change in ownership of a company etc

Trading losses (CTA 2010, ss 673–676, 724, 730A–730D, 944)

Change in ownership

[45.15] Trading losses may not be carried forward where within a period of three years there is both a change in ownership of a company and a major change in the nature or conduct of its trade. The rules also apply where ownership changes after activities have sunk to a low level and before any significant revival. Similar provisions apply to prevent trading losses of an accounting period ending *after* the change of ownership being carried back to an accounting period beginning *before* the change. The September 2017

Finance Bill, which is expected to receive Royal Assent in November 2017, extends the timeframe to five years (eight years for an investment business) where both the change to the trade and the change in ownership take place on or after 1 April 2017. Statement of Practice SP 10/91 sets out HMRC's interpretation of a 'major change in the nature or conduct of a trade'. See **26.25**.

There are also restrictions on the deductibility of certain trading losses where there has been a change in ownership of a company. The losses that are restricted are those that, at the date of the qualifying change, are highly likely to arise as deductions for an accounting period ending on or after the date of the change and the main purpose of the qualifying change in ownership is that they are deductible in the accounting period ending on or after the date of the change in ownership. This restriction also applies to claims for group relief (**26.25**) and deductible amounts where there are 'profit transfer arrangements' (i.e. arrangements which result in an increase in the total profits of the company that has been subject to the change in ownership). Restricted deductible amounts include trading profits (other than expenditure qualifying for research and development allowances) and non-trading loan relationship, derivative contract or intangible fixed asset debits etc.

Hive downs

[45.16] Where a trade is transferred between companies in common ownership (a 'hive down') losses can be carried forward against subsequent profits of the successor company as if the predecessor had carried on the trade. Any restriction on trading losses on a change in ownership (**45.15**) will apply whether the hive down occurred before or after the change in ownership of the company. In other words there will be a look back to the nature and conduct of the company from which the trade was initially transferred to the company that eventually carries on the trade to see if there has been a major change in the nature or conduct of its trade.

Capital loss buying and capital gains buying

[45.17] There are detailed and complex provisions to prevent groups of companies avoiding tax on capital gains by acquiring a company with capital losses and using the intra-group no gain/no loss rules to transfer assets to the purchased company before disposing of them outside the group.

Loss buying/gain buying (TCGA 1992, ss 16A, 184A–184F)

[45.18] The provisions broadly operate where there is a change of ownership of a company that, amongst other things, occurs in connection with arrangements to secure a tax advantage. The rules provide that unused losses brought forward at the time the company joins the group (or later losses realised on the disposal of assets owned by the company before the change in ownership) cannot be offset against gains realised by the company after the change in ownership.

There are parallel provisions to prevent the reverse procedure, i.e. acquiring a company with realised gains in order to utilise unrealised group losses. Capital gains (realised or unrealised) on assets held by a company before a change in ownership cannot (once realised) be offset against a capital loss accruing to the company where, amongst other things, the change of ownership occurs in connection with arrangements to secure a tax advantage.

Other restriction on pre-entry losses (TCGA 1992, s 177A and Sch 7A)

[45.19] Where the loss buying provisions do not apply (generally where there is no tax avoidance motive, e.g. on a takeover or merger) there are separate provisions to prevent a company buying another company in order to use its capital losses. Broadly, these rules restrict the use of losses in the company that has changed ownership. Realised, unused capital losses brought forward at the time the company joins the group, may be used against gains arising on assets used in the same *business* that the company conducted before joining the group. Losses that are realised after the company joins the group are not restricted at all — they can be set off against corporate capital gains in the usual manner.

Where an asset has been appropriated to trading stock and there has been an election to 'roll-over' a loss which is not ATED-related (**20.21**), then if the company becomes a member of a group of companies before the asset is sold in the course of the trade the effects of the election will be reversed. The cost of the asset as trading stock will be its market value at the time it was appropriated (without any 'roll-over') and the loss which is not ATED-related will be allowable at the time of the appropriation, but will be subject to restriction under TCGA 1992, Sch 7A. Note however that the September 2017 Finance Bill, which is expected to receive Royal Assent in November 2017, contains legislation to prevent the election being made where a capital loss arises in respect of appropriations made on or after 8 March 2017.

Schemes to avoid corporation tax liabilities (CTA 2010, ss 710–715)

[45.20] There are provisions to counteract schemes under which a company's trading assets are transferred to another group company prior to the sale of the first company and the new owners strip the company of the remaining cash assets, leaving the company unable to pay its corporation tax. Corporation tax liabilities arising before the sale of a company may in prescribed circumstances be collected from the previous owners. The provisions also apply to corporation tax liabilities arising after the sale if it could reasonably have been inferred at the time of the sale that they were unlikely to be met.

Pre-sale distributions etc. (CTA 2010, ss 157–182; TCGA 1992, ss 31–33, 170)

[45.21] There are provisions to prevent companies reducing or eliminating capital gains by reducing the value of a subsidiary before its sale. Where unrealised gains are distributed by a subsidiary to its parent company as group income prior to the sale of the subsidiary, the parent company is treated as if it had received additional consideration of an equivalent amount. The provisions also cover the transfer of a subsidiary to a non-resident company in the group prior to its onward sale, where the subsidiary leaves the group within six years after being transferred to the non-resident company.

There are also provisions to prevent companies retaining a subsidiary within a group for capital gains purposes by means of issuing special types of shares, while selling commercial control of the company.

Change in ownership of, or change in interest in, plant or machinery leasing business (CTA 2010, ss 382–436)

[45.22] Legislation targets changes in the economic ownership of a plant or machinery leasing business carried on by a company on its own or in partnership. It applies to both simple sales of shares in a leasing company and changes in partnership sharing arrangements, in addition to any other route by which the economic ownership of a business could be changed. Furthermore it also applies when a company joins the tonnage tax regime.

The legislation aims to prevent an unacceptable permanent deferral of tax. It had previously been possible for a leasing company to generate losses in the early years of a long leasing contract as a consequence of the availability of capital allowances, such losses being available for group relief. In the later years of the lease the capital allowances would be reduced and the company would become profitable. If the leasing company was sold in the interim to a loss-making company or group, the leasing company's profits would be covered by the new owner's losses. Thus, an acceptable temporary deferral of tax became an unacceptable permanent deferral of tax.

The legislation acts by bringing into charge an amount of income which is calculated by reference to the difference between the commercial position of the company and the tax position. The charge is calculated by comparing the sum of the balance sheet values of the net investments in the leases and the plant and machinery with the tax written down value of the plant and machinery. Consequently the tax benefit derived by the leasing company from the capital allowances is recovered.

Shell companies (CTA 2010, ss 705A–705G)

[45.23] For a change in ownership of a shell company there are restrictions on the availability of non-trading debits, non-trading loan relationship deficits and non-trading losses on intangible fixed assets. A shell company is simply defined as a company that is not trading, does not have investment business and is not carrying on a UK property business.

On the change of ownership, the accounting period in which the change of ownership occurs (AP) is split into two notional accounting periods. The first notional accounting period (AP1) ending with the date of change and the second (AP2) covering the balance of the period. The profits or losses of the accounting period of the change are apportioned to periods AP1 and AP2 and any losses occurring in AP1 cannot be set against profits arising after that date.

Overseas issues

Dual resident investment companies (CTA 2010, s 109; TCGA 1992, ss 171, 175)

[45.24] Where an investment company is resident both in the UK and in another country, that company cannot surrender losses etc. under the group relief provisions (see **3.31**). Such companies are also unable to take advantage of the various capital allowances provisions that would normally prevent transfers to them being treated as being at open market value.

For capital gains purposes, assets may not be transferred intra-group on a no gain/no loss basis if the transferee is a dual resident investment company. Nor may business asset rollover relief be claimed within a group in respect of assets acquired by a dual resident investment company.

Controlled foreign companies (TIOPA 2010, ss 371AA–371VJ; ITA 2007, s 725; SI 1998/3081)

[45.25] A UK resident company is charged to tax in respect of the profits of a foreign company in certain circumstances under the Controlled Foreign companies (CFC) rules.

A CFC charge is imposed provided that none of the statutory exemptions apply to completely exempt the CFC charge. The exemptions are wide ranging and include the following:

(a) the temporary period of exemption — essentially this allows a foreign trading subsidiary to be exempt from the CFC regime for the first 12 months;

(b) the excluded territories exemption — a CFC is exempt if it is resident and carries on business in an excluded territory (which are specified in regulations (SI 2012/3024)) and the total of its relevant income does not exceed 10% of the its accounting profits or £50,000 (if greater);

(c) the low profits exemption — a CFC is exempt if it has accounting profits (or total taxable profits) of no more than £50,000 or total taxable profits of no more than £500,000 (of which no more than £50,000 represents non-trading income);

(d) the low profit margin exemption — a CFC is exempt if its accounting profits are no more than 10% of its relevant operating expenditure; and

(e) the tax exemption — a CFC is exempt if the local tax amount is at least 75% of the corresponding UK tax.

If none of the above exemptions apply, it is then necessary to look at the CFC profits to determine which profits are potentially liable. Profits will only be liable if they pass through one of the 'gateways' and are not otherwise excluded by any of the entry conditions, safe harbours or exemptions. Such profits will be apportioned to the UK and taxed on any UK resident company with a 25% assessable interest in the CFC. The CFC charge will be reduced by a credit for any foreign tax attributable to the apportioned profits and (for accounting periods commencing before 8 July 2015) by the offset of relevant UK reliefs. For accounting periods commencing on or after 8 July 2015, UK companies are not able to set UK losses and expenses against a CFC charge.

This regime does initially appear to be relatively simple to operate and indeed as a result of the entry conditions, exemptions etc, in practice only a small proportion of companies are likely to be affected by the CFC rules.

Offshore funds (TIOPA 2010, ss 354–363A; SI 2009/3001)

[45.26] Regulations provide that realisation of an interest in an offshore fund investment is charged to tax as income rather than chargeable gains, unless certain conditions are met. Under the regulations, funds are recognised as either reporting funds or non-reporting funds. Reporting funds must comply with strict guidelines laid down in the regulations in order to qualify as such.

Broadly, UK resident investors in reporting funds will be taxable on their share of the funds' reported income each year, regardless of whether it is distributed to them, and any gain or loss on disposal will be treated as a capital gain or loss. Annual payments made to a participant in an offshore fund are not qualifying annual payments for the purposes of the requirement to deduct tax (3.23) if the person making the payment has reasonable grounds for believing that the participant is not resident in the UK.

UK investors in non-reporting funds remain chargeable to income tax or corporation tax on any distributions made to them. Alternatively if the fund is transparent for income purposes they will be chargeable to tax on the underlying investments. Untaxed accumulated income and gains in a non-reporting fund are treated as offshore income on realisation. A disposal of an interest in a non-reporting fund will give rise to a gain chargeable to income tax (an offshore income gain).

Transfer of assets abroad (ITA 2007, ss 714–751)

[45.27] The purpose of the transfer of assets provisions is to prevent an individual who is resident in the UK avoiding UK tax by transferring income-producing property abroad in circumstances which enable him to benefit from the property either immediately or in the future, such as a transfer to trustees of a foreign settlement made by him, of which he is a beneficiary. The provisions also impose a charge when benefits go not to the transferor but to someone else, such as his children or grandchildren. The provisions apply to life policies held in trust in certain circumstances (see 40.11). There is however an exemption from this charge for 'genuine transactions' where EU treaty freedoms are engaged.

Enablers of offshore tax evasion (FA 2016, s 162 and Sch 20; SI 2016/1249)

[45.28] From 1 January 2017, there are civil penalties for deliberate enablers of offshore tax evasion, or other non-compliance. The penalties apply when a person has deliberately enabled someone else to:

(a)   commit offences such as the fraudulent evasion of income tax etc; or

(b)   become liable to civil penalties for matters relating to errors in returns (**9.58**), a failure to notify (**9.60**), a failure to make a return (**9.61**) or penalties in relation to relevant offshore asset moves (**9.80**).

The penalty is a financial penalty which varies according to the nature of the offence. This is coupled with increased public naming of tax evaders.

Personal portfolio bonds (ITTOIA 2005, ss 515–526)

[45.29] Special provisions apply to 'personal portfolio bonds', which are insurance policies where the policyholder or his adviser may select and vary the underlying investments. Such bonds are within the 'chargeable events' provisions for life insurance policies. Although particularly aimed at offshore bonds, the provisions also catch UK bonds. The effect of the rules is that there is an annual income tax charge on the bonds for each policy year other than the last year. The annual charge is 15% of a deemed gain that is equal to the total of the premiums paid and the total deemed gains from previous years, net of any taxable amounts withdrawn in earlier years. The gains are charged in the same way as other gains on insurance bonds (see **40.6**), i.e. on the excess, if any, of higher rate tax over the basic rate of 20%, but top slicing relief is not available. The total amount of gains taxed under the yearly provisions is deducted from any gain arising when the policy terminates. If gains arising during the life of a policy are reversed when the policy comes to an end, a compensating deduction will be made from taxable income.

Most bonds taken out before 17 March 1998 are excluded from the provisions, and policyholders who were not UK resident on 17 March 1998 will have at least 12 months after becoming resident to change the terms of the policy so that they also are excluded.

Transfer pricing (TIOPA 2010, ss 146–217)

[45.30] Where any sales take place between persons connected with each other, including partnerships and companies, at a price other than open market value, the sale price of one and purchase price of the other must be adjusted to the open market value for tax purposes. Similarly, adjustments may be required in relation to interest on 'excessive' debt finance.

The rules are designed to bring about the result that would have occurred had arm's length pricing been employed, by increasing the taxable profit of one of the parties to the transaction and providing for the other party to claim a compensating adjustment to its profit if it is a UK taxpayer. Anti-avoidance provisions apply, to prevent individuals from claiming a compensating adjustment where the other party to the transaction is a company. These aim to target the use by some partnerships and individuals of the transfer pricing rules to extract income from their businesses, paying tax at the corporation tax rate rather than at the income tax higher rate.

The transfer pricing rules apply to transactions between UK parties, as well as transactions between UK and overseas parties. There are exemptions for most small and medium-sized companies. Any transfer pricing adjustments must be made in the self-assessment tax returns. The normal penalties for careless or deliberate actions apply.

Documentation must be maintained to support any transfer prices. Guidance was published by the OECD in September 2014 for the countries participating in the OECD/G20 Base Erosion and Profit Shifting (BEPS) Project; the 'Guidance on Transfer Pricing Documentation and Country-by-Country Reporting'. Based on this, the UK has implemented the country-by-country reporting recommendations for multinational enterprises with a consolidated group revenue of €750 million or more.

Transfers between dealing and non-dealing companies

[45.31] Transfers of assets between dealing companies and associated non-dealing companies are covered by the transfer pricing scheme.

Special rules apply where a dealing company makes a payment etc to an associated non-dealing company which is tax deductible for the dealing company but not taxable for the non-dealing company. In such situations the non-dealing company is deemed to receive income of an amount equal to the deduction allowed to the dealing company.

Sale and lease-back

Land (CTA 2010, ss 838, 849–862)

[45.32] Where land is sold and leased back, the deduction allowed for rent is limited to a commercial rent. A sale at an excessive price (subject to capital gains tax) cannot therefore be compensated by an excessive rent payment allowable in calculating taxable income.

Further, if a short lease (less than 50 years) is sold and leased back for 15 years or less, part of the sale price is treated as income, that part being $(16 - n)/15$ where n is the term of the new lease.

Assets other than land (CTA 2010, ss 865, 870–886)

[45.33] If assets other than land are sold and leased back similar rules will apply to those that apply for the sale and leaseback of land. Furthermore, if a deduction has been received in relation to a lease of an asset other than land and a capital sum is received by the lessee in respect of his interest in the lease, then the lower of the deduction obtained and the capital sum received will be charged as income.

Avoidance using trusts (TCGA 1992, ss 71, 76B, 79A, 83A, 85A and Schs 4B, 4C; FA 1986, ss 102, 102ZA and Sch 20)

[45.34] There are provisions to prevent artificial schemes under which capital losses generated within trusts are sold to purchasers to reduce their capital gains on other assets. A loss on an asset transferred to a trust beneficiary may be used only against gains on the disposal of the same asset (or in the case of land, an asset derived from the land). Further anti-avoidance provisions apply to a variation of the above schemes. Losses arising on disposals by trustees cannot be set against any gains made by the trustees on assets that have been transferred to the trust if the transferor or someone connected with him had bought an interest in the trust and had claimed gift holdover relief on the transferred assets.

Where the trustees of any trust (except a UK trust) in which the settlor does not have an interest, borrow money and advance it to another trust, the trustees are deemed to dispose of the trust assets and reacquire them at market value, and no claim for gift holdover relief may be made, thus crystallising the chargeable gains in the first trust.

There are rules to ensure that UK beneficiaries of offshore trusts cannot escape capital gains tax on capital payments. Anti-avoidance provisions apply to prevent trustees who are within the charge to UK capital gains tax at some time in a tax year avoiding that tax by realising gains at a time when they are resident in a country with which the UK has a double tax agreement, and thus taxable on the gain in that country (but with little or no liability arising on the gain). The gain will be chargeable to UK tax, with the usual double taxation relief available.

Inheritance tax anti-avoidance provisions prevent married couples and civil partners using trusts to get round the rules in **5.41** about retaining benefits from a gift.

Other anti-avoidance provisions relating to trusts are mentioned in CHAPTERS **41** and **42**.

Other measures

[45.35] There are also measures to counter avoidance in the following circumstances.

- Companies leaving a group and taking out a chargeable asset acquired intra-group on a no gain/no loss basis within the previous six years (TCGA 1992, ss 179–181).
- Group companies seeking to avoid tax by channelling disposals of assets through tax-exempt bodies such as venture capital trusts and friendly societies (TCGA 1992, s 171).
- Claiming group relief for losses when arrangements exist where a company may leave the group (CTA 2010, ss 154–156).

- Companies avoiding tax through the use of tax arbitrage (i.e. exploiting differences between or within national tax codes) (TIOPA 2010, ss 231–259). From 1 January 2017, these rules are replaced by the 'hybrid mismatch arrangement' rules which will put an end to multiple deductions for a single expense and for deductions in one country without corresponding taxation in another (TIOPA 2010, ss 259A–259NF).
- Transfers of plant and machinery between associated persons in order to obtain capital allowances (CAA 2001, s 215).
- Losses arising from depreciatory transactions, e.g. dividend-stripping (TCGA 1992, ss 176, 177).
- Value passing out of shares, which could have been avoided by a controlling shareholder (TCGA 1992, ss 29–31A).
- Individuals realising capital gains abroad through a non-resident close company, unless the gains arise from assets used in genuine business activities (TCGA 1992, s 13).
- Transferring relief for partnership losses which would otherwise relate to a partner who is a company (CTA 2010, ss 958–962).
- Annual payments for non-taxable consideration (ITA 2007, ss 843, 898–905).
- Transfer of chargeable assets on which holdover relief for capital gains tax is obtained into dual resident trusts (TCGA 1992, s 169).

Also in cases involving tax avoidance arrangements, a prohibitive rule has priority over a permissive rule when determining if a deduction is allowable from profits of a trade or property business (ITTOIA 2005, ss 31, 274; CTA 2009, ss 51, 214).

A binding anti-abuse clause has been added to the EU parent-subsidiary directive (2011/96/EU) to prevent tax avoidance by corporate groups. The clause will prevent member states from granting the benefits of the directive to non-genuine arrangements such as those designed to obtain a tax advantage without reflecting economic reality.

Subject index

H